W9-BJP-037

GROLIER

ENCYCLOPEDIA
OF KNOWLEDGE

Grolier Incorporated
Danbury, Connecticut

ISBN 0-7172-5300-7 (complete set)
ISBN 0-7172-5316-3 (volume 16)

Printed and manufactured in the United States of America.

This publication is an abridged version of the *Academic American Encyclopedia.*

referendum and initiative Referendum and initiative are related forms of direct legislative democracy that were used in ancient Greece and are practiced in various modern countries, especially Switzerland. Referendum is the referring of a bill or political question to the direct vote of the electorate. It may be an obligatory or optional supplement to the usual procedures of legislative passage.

Initiative is the proposal of a law or constitutional amendment proposed by a specified percentage of voter signatures on a popular petition. There are two types of initiative: direct and indirect. In the former, a proposed law is placed directly on the ballot for the approval of the state's voters; in the latter, a proposal is first sent to the state legislature. If the proposal is not enacted by the legislature, it is then placed on the ballot for consideration by the electorate. A referendum by petition provides an opportunity for voters to veto a legislative enactment. In states with this referendum procedure, a legislative bill takes effect only after a certain period of time during which the bill may be suspended by a voter petition. The bill is then submitted to a referendum.

Parts of Switzerland have used the referendum since the 1500s. Countries that now use types of referenda include Australia, France, Ireland, Italy, Sweden, and some new nations in Africa and Asia.

In the United States the use of referendum and initiative grew out of the movement for progressive reform at the beginning of the 20th century. Although referendum and initiative do not exist in all states (37 states had provisions for referenda in 1988, and only 21 provided for initiative), in many they are important instruments for expressing public opinion and implementing policy. California, where initiative and referendum are widely used, presented its voters in 1988 with 29 statewide propositions. The state's 1978 proposal on property tax, Proposition 13, is one example of the procedure, as is the controversial 1988 initiative, reducing rates on automobile and casualty insurance. Voters in nearly every state are given the opportunity to vote on bond issues and amendments to state constitutions in this matter.

refinery See PETROLEUM INDUSTRY

refining, metal Refining is a process through which oxides, gases, and other impurities are removed from a metal. This process is generally the final step in the production of metals from ores (see METALLURGY).

reflection Whenever light strikes the surface of any material substance, part of the light is turned back from the surface. This is called reflection. The remainder of the light is transmitted into the material. If the surface is rough or matted, the reflected light goes off in all different directions. This is called diffuse reflection. An example is the paper on which this printing appears. Diffuse reflection of light renders nonluminous objects visible. If the surface is very smooth, however, the reflected light goes in a definite direction determined by the direction of the incident light (see OPTICS). This phenomenon is known as regular, or specular, reflection.

The term *reflectance* is used to denote the fraction of light energy that is reflected by a material. Metals generally have high values of reflectance, silver being the best reflector with a reflectance of about 96%. The reflectance of a clean glass surface is about 6%. Light is reflected from a plane surface at an angle equal to the angle made by the incoming (incident) light. The angles of incidence and reflection are customarily measured as the angles made by the light rays and the normal, a line drawn perpendicular to the surface at the point of incidence. Thus, the law of reflection states that the angle of incidence equals the angle of reflection.

If the surface is not plane but curved, it may still be considered to be made up of many very small, elementary plane surfaces. The path of any light ray striking a curved surface can still be determined from the law of reflection. This law is the basis for computing the image-forming characteristics of curved MIRRORS.

reflex The reflex, an involuntary act that represents the lowest level of nervous response to natural stimuli, underlies all animal behavior. This pattern of neuronal activity, which may or may not involve conscious thought, is conducted by three components of the NERVOUS SYSTEM—a sensory system, a neuronal center of integration, and a motor system—that are simple enough to ensure accurate, quick transmittal of impulses in response to stimuli.

The sensory system consists of afferent nerve cells (neurons)—which relay sensory information to the central nervous system—and receptor cells. Receptor cells, located for the most part in the skin, eyes, tongue, nose, inner ear, muscles, and joints, convert the energy of a stimulus—usually chemical, mechanical, light, or heat energy—into electrochemical nerve impulses. In turn, the impulses are carried over specific pathways of the nervous system to the nerve centers located in the spinal cord, the medulla, the hypothalamus, and the cerebellum. A particular nerve center integrates sensory input from various afferent fibers as well as from other nerve centers. Finally, nerve centers discharge impulses as motor responses to muscles, organs, and glands. The motor output involves efferent neurons known as motor neurons.

The synapse, a functional connection between neurons, is the site at which integration or modification of reflex activity occurs. The transmission across synapses is mediated by a neurotransmitter, a chemical released from a nerve ending that has received an impulse. The neurotransmitter diffuses across the synaptic cleft between the neurons and activates receptors that either enhance or inhibit impulse transmission.

The intensity and pattern of stimuli largely shape the strength and type of reflex. Increasing intensity and frequency of impulses to a nerve center will reach a threshold, at which point the response is triggered. Increments

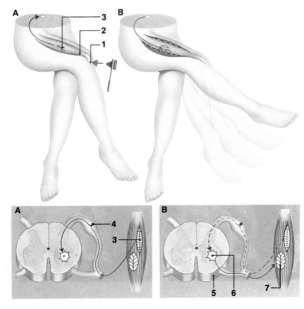

A reflex action is the involuntary response of a muscle or gland to a sensory stimulus. Once initiated, the reflex travels from the stimulated body part to the spinal cord and back again, along an arc made of connected neurons. A neuron is a nerve cell with long extensions, or axons, that branch out from a central cell body. In the first part of a typical reflex sequence (A), a light hammer tap on the patellar tendon, below the kneecap (1), stretches the quadriceps muscle (2) of the thigh. This action stimulates receptor cells called muscle spindles (3), which translate the pressure of the tap into an electrochemical message. A sensory neuron (4) conveys the message from the receptor cells to the spinal cord. In the second part of the reflex sequence (B), the spinal cord (5), having received the electrochemical message, immediately passes it on to a motor neuron (6), which conveys the message to nerve terminals, called endplates (7), in the quadriceps muscle, causing the muscle to contract. The entire sequence, from hammer tap to knee jerk, is accomplished in a fraction of a second. Such purely spinal reflexes as the tendon tap involve no action by the brain; their only contact with the central nervous system is in the spinal cord. Other examples of spinal reflexes are sneezing, coughing, yawning, and blinking. Reflex actions work so quickly that they are completed before the conscious mind has registered the stimulus.

immediately from the object precedes the sensation of pain.

The medulla oblongata, part of the brain stem, contains nerve centers for cardiovascular and respiratory reflexes. For instance, an increase in blood pressure activates special receptors in the carotid sinus and the aortic arch, which are large arterial blood vessels; impulses signaling the increase in pressure are carried by nerves to the medulla oblongata. The reflex response from this center slows down the heart rate, which returns blood pressure to normal.

A number of respiratory reflexes are controlled by spinal and brain stem nerve centers. These reflexes include coughing and gagging, as well as involuntary regulation of carbon dioxide and oxygen levels in circulating blood. Related reflexes are vomiting, yawning, sneezing, and hiccuping.

Important reflex nerve centers related to posture, balance, and eye position also are located in the brain stem. Receptors for these reflexes are found in the vestibule of the inner ear. These reflexes serve two functions: to stabilize the position of the head and provide information about angular and linear acceleration of the head, and to maintain visual image by stabilizing the eyes during head movement.

Reflex nerve centers of the midbrain involve movement of the eyeballs, constriction of the pupils in response to light, and adjustment of the lenses in order to focus on objects.

Conditioned Reflexes

Reflexes that may be modified by learning are called conditioned reflexes. Model systems include one outlined by Edward L. THORNDIKE (1895) and another by Ivan P. PAVLOV (1906). Thorndike found that animals modify their behavior if a reward is imminent, that is, learning occurs faster if the correct performance is rewarded. Pavlov found that dogs could be trained to salivate in response to an inappropriate stimulus (a bell ring) if the bell was previously associated with the appropriate stimulus (the presence of food).

of the impulse after that threshold has been attained, however, do not elicit a corresponding increase in the reflex response. For this to happen, more motor units must be activated.

Types of Reflexes

Vertebrate postural reflexes involve primarily the spinal cord, the most familiar being the monosynaptic stretch, or knee jerk. When the kneecap tendon is tapped the muscle is stretched and the muscle spindles in the thigh muscle are excited. Because this reflex response involves sensory neurons that directly synapse with motor neurons in the spinal cord, transmission time is brief, and the thigh muscle quickly contracts, extending the leg.

The flexor withdrawal reflex, a spinal reflex, results in the withdrawal of a limb from the stimulus. If a person touches a hot object, for example, the reflex to withdraw

Reform Acts   The Reform Acts were a series of British legislative measures (1832, 1867, 1884–85) that broadened the parliamentary franchise. Electoral reform had been urged in the 1780s by William PITT the Younger as well as Charles James Fox, but the reaction against the French Revolution created a more conservative political climate. By the late 1820s the movement for reform was again strong, and the Whig government of the 2d Earl GREY enacted the first Reform Bill in 1832.

The first Reform Act eliminated many "rotten boroughs" (depopulated constituencies) and "pocket boroughs" (constituencies controlled by the crown and other landowners), transferring their representation to such previously unrepresented large cities as Birmingham and Manchester and to the more populous counties. The vote was extended to males who occupied premises valued at

£10 annually, bringing the middle class into the political arena. Although the act expanded the franchise by 50 percent, still, only 1 out of 30 persons could vote, and the landowning class remained dominant.

Popular agitation spurred by John BRIGHT and others led to a further extension of the franchise in 1867. After the failure of the Liberals under Lord John Russell (later 1st Earl RUSSELL) to win passage of their Reform Bill, the Conservative Benjamin DISRAELI succeeded with more radical proposals. The act of 1867 extended the vote to most homeowners and renters and thus enfranchised many urban laborers. The final Reform Acts, which were passed in 1884 and 1885 under the Liberal government of William GLADSTONE, gave the vote to most agricultural workers.

The secret ballot (1872) and the Corrupt and Illegal Practices Act (1883) were other important 19th-century measures of electoral reform. The Representation of the People Acts of 1918 and 1928 extended the vote to women; the act of 1949 eliminated plural voting; and the 1969 act lowered the voting age from 21 to 18.

—

Reformation [ref-ur-may'-shuhn] The Reformation of the 16th century was a movement within Western Christendom to purge the church of medieval abuses and to restore the doctrines and practices that the reformers believed conformed with the Bible and the New Testament model of the church. This led to a breach between the ROMAN CATHOLIC CHURCH and the reformers whose beliefs and practices came to be called PROTESTANTISM.

Causes

Precursors of the Reformation proper included the movements founded by John WYCLIFFE (the LOLLARDS) and John HUSS (the HUSSITES) during the 14th and 15th centuries. These reform groups, however, were localized (in England and Bohemia) and were largely suppressed.

The cultural RENAISSANCE that occurred during the preceding century and a half was a necessary preliminary to the Reformation, because it raised the level of education, reemphasized the ancient classics, contributed to thought and learning, and offered HUMANISM and rhetoric as an alternative to SCHOLASTICISM. Especially through its emphasis on the biblical languages and close attention to the literary texts, the Renaissance made possible the biblical exegesis that led to Martin LUTHER's doctrinal reinterpretation. Moreover, Christian humanists such as Desiderius ERASMUS criticized ecclesiastical abuses and promoted the study of both the Bible and the church fathers. The invention of printing by Johann Gutenberg provided a powerful instrument for the spread of learning and Reformation ideas.

That grave ills were spreading through the church was already evident at the Fourth LATERAN COUNCIL in 1215, at which Pope INNOCENT III called for reform. The papacy itself was weakened by its move from Rome to Avignon

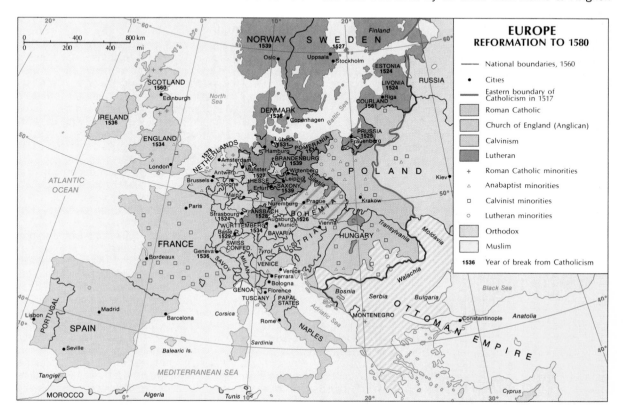

EUROPE
REFORMATION TO 1580

— National boundaries, 1560
• Cities
— Eastern boundary of Catholicism in 1517
Roman Catholic
Church of England (Anglican)
Calvinism
Lutheran
+ Roman Catholic minorities
△ Anabaptist minorities
□ Calvinist minorities
○ Lutheran minorities
Orthodox
Muslim
1536 Year of break from Catholicism

(1309–77), by the Great SCHISM of the papacy, which lasted four decades thereafter, and by the doctrine that supreme authority in the church belonged to general councils (CONCILIARISM). The Renaissance popes were notoriously worldly. Abuses such as simony, nepotism, and financial excesses increased. The church was riddled with venality and immorality. The sale of INDULGENCES was a particularly unfortunate practice because it impinged upon true spiritual repentance and improvement of life. At the same time, a genuine upsurge of popular religiosity manifested itself and increased the disparity between the people's expectations and the church's ability to satisfy spiritual needs. Some turned to mysticism and inward religion, but the great mass of people were restless and dissatisfied.

A significant political change occurred during the later Middle Ages as well. The HOLY ROMAN EMPIRE, which had lost cohesion partly as a result of its struggle with the papacy in the INVESTITURE CONTROVERSY, was weakened by the growth of virtually independent territorial princedoms and free imperial cities. Economically, the rise of commerce and the shift to a moneyed economy had the effect of creating a stronger middle class in a more urban society. The church met financial difficulty during this time because it had become involved in the manorial economy, possessed landed wealth, and had trouble meeting its many obligations.

Development

Luther. The Reformation began in Germany on Oct. 31, 1517, when Martin Luther, an Augustinian university professor at Wittenberg, posted 95 theses inviting debate over the legitimacy of the sale of indulgences. The papacy viewed this as a gesture of rebellion and proceeded to take steps against Luther as a heretic. He was excommunicated in 1521, but in April of that year at the Diet at Worms he stood before Holy Roman Emperor CHARLES V and the German princes and refused to recant unless proven wrong by the Bible or by clear reason. He believed that salvation was a free gift to persons through the forgiveness of sins by God's grace alone and received by them through faith in Christ.

The German friar and scholar Martin Luther precipitated the Protestant Reformation when he nailed his 95 Theses to the door of the Wittenberg Church in 1517.

Luther was protected by FREDERICK III, elector of Saxony, and other German princes—partly out of intellectual and religious conviction, partly out of the desire to seize church property, and partly to assert independence of imperial control. In 1530 many princes and cities signed the AUGSBURG CONFESSION presented at the Diet of Augsburg as an expression of the evangelical faith. After years of conflict the settlement reached in the Peace of Augsburg (1555) provided that each German prince would determine the religious affiliation (Roman Catholic or Lutheran) of the territory he ruled. LUTHERANISM also became the established religion of Denmark, Sweden, Norway, and Finland. Apart from the role of the princes, however, the Reformation spread rapidly as a popular movement. It penetrated Poland, Bohemia, Moravia, Hungary, and Transylvania.

Zwingli. The Reformation in Switzerland initially developed in Zurich under the leadership of the priest Ulrich ZWINGLI, who arrived at an evangelical understanding of Christianity from his study of the Bible and from contacts with Lutherans. On Jan. 1, 1519, he began a 6-year series of sermons on the New Testament that moved the city council and the people of Zurich toward reform. He called for the abolition of the Mass (and its replacement by a symbolic Lord's Supper), independence from episcopal control, and a reform of the city-state in which both priests and Christian magistrates would conform to the will of God. His influence spread to other Swiss cantons such as Basel, Saint Gall, and Bern.

Calvin. Through Lutheran tracts and merchant missionaries, the evangelical movement spread to France, where it won many converts, among whom was John CALVIN. In 1536, Calvin went to Geneva. In his *Ordinances* of 1541, he gave a new organization to the church consisting of pastors, doctors, elders, and deacons. His *Institutes of the Christian Religion* (1536) had great influence in France, Scotland (where John KNOX carried the Calvinist reformation), and among the PURITANS in England. Geneva became the center of a great missionary enterprise that reached into France, where the HUGUENOTS became so powerful that a synod met in Paris in 1559 to organize a nationwide church of some 2,000 reformed congregations. As a result of the French Wars of Religion (see RELIGION, WARS OF), the Huguenot party was checked and the French monarchy kept the kingdom Catholic. (See also CALVINISM; PRESBYTERIANISM; REFORMED CHURCHES.)

England. Although England had a religious reform movement influenced by Lutheran ideas, the English Reformation occurred as a direct result of King HENRY VIII's efforts to divorce his first wife, CATHERINE OF ARAGON. The formal break with the papacy was masterminded by Thomas CROMWELL, the king's chief minister. Under Cromwell's direction Parliament passed the Act in Restraint of Appeals (to Rome; 1533), followed by the Act of Supremacy (1534) fully defining the royal headship over the church. As archbishop of Canterbury, Thomas CRANMER annulled Henry's marriage to Catherine, allowing the king to marry Anne BOLEYN. Although Henry himself wished to make no doctrinal changes, Cromwell and Cranmer authorized the translation of the Bible into English, and Cranmer was largely responsible for the Book of Common Prayer, adopted under Henry's successor, Edward VI. The gains that Protestantism made under Edward (r. 1547–53) were lost under his Catholic sister Mary I (r. 1553–58). The religious settlement (1559) under Elizabeth I, however, guaranteed the Anglican establishment. (See also England, Church of).

The Radicals. The radicals consisted of a great variety of sectarian groups known as Anabaptists because of their common opposition to infant baptism. The Anabaptist leader Thomas Münzer played a leading role in the Peasants' War (1524–26), which was suppressed with the support of Luther. In Münster, radical Anabaptists established (1533) a short-lived theocracy in which property was held communally. This too was harshly suppressed. The radicals also encompassed evangelical humanists and spiritualists who developed highly individualistic religious philosophies.

Reformed Church in America

The Reformed Church in America is a Protestant denomination with roots in Dutch Calvinism. By 1628, Dutch settlers had established a church in New Amsterdam (now New York City). This and other American churches were directed from Amsterdam until the 18th century when, under the influence of revivalist Theodore Jacob Frelinghuysen (1691–1747), an American body was formed (1748). Difficulties between this group and others loyal to the Dutch body were eventually resolved (1771) through the efforts of John Henry Livingston (1746–1825), an influential leader at Queens College (now Rutgers University), New Brunswick, N.J., which had been founded by the Dutch Reformed. The Reformed Protestant Dutch Church adopted a new constitution in 1792; in 1867 it changed its name to the Reformed Church in America.

The denomination's doctrinal standards are the Belgic Confession (1561), the Heidelberg Catechism (1563), and the canons of the Synod of Dort (1619). Its organization is essentially Presbyterian. It is somewhat closer to mainline Protestant bodies than is a sister denomination of Dutch Calvinists, the Christian Reformed Church.

Reformed churches

The Reformed churches, which originally used this designation to distinguish themselves from the "unreformed" Roman Catholic church, are those denominations of Protestants which are Calvinistic in theology and usually Presbyterian in church organization (see Calvinism; Presbyterianism). They trace their origin to the reforming work in Zurich of Ulrich Zwingli and in Geneva of John Calvin. The Reformed perspective spread rapidly to Germany, France (see Huguenots), Holland, Hungary, Bohemia, and elsewhere on the Continent. In the British Isles its principles shaped the Church of Scotland (see Scotland, Church of) and influenced the Church of England, especially through Puritanism. The Presbyterians are the largest Reformed bodies in America. Since 1877 a World Alliance of Reformed Churches has provided a forum for discussion.

refraction

When a beam of light enters a medium in which its velocity is different from that in its original medium, the path of the beam changes. This bending of the beam, called refraction, is characteristic of all waves—sound, radio, and mechanical. Most experience with refraction, however, is with light. The principles of refraction find application in a variety of common optical devices, such as eyeglasses, microscopes, cameras, and binoculars.

Snell's Law. The basic law of refraction, first proposed in 1621 by the Dutch scientist Willebrord Snell, relates the magnitude of refraction to the velocity of light in the two media (equivalent to the index of refraction). If i is the angle the incident beam makes with the normal (in optics, all such angles are measured from the normal, a line perpendicular to the surface), and r the angle of the refracted beam, then $\sin i / \sin r = n_r/n_i$, where n_r is the index of refraction of the medium containing the refracted beam and n_i the index of refraction of the medium with the incident beam. Thus, light entering a denser medium, from air into glass, for example, is bent toward the normal; on entering a less dense medium, light is bent away from the normal. If light goes through a substance with parallel surfaces, such as a window, the beam that emerges will be parallel to its incident beam but laterally displaced, or shifted.

Total Internal Reflection. Suppose a beam of light passes from glass to air. Air has a lower index of refraction, so the emerging beam is bent away from the normal. As the angle of incidence is increased, the beam in air moves farther from the normal until it makes a 90° angle with the normal and grazes the surface. The angle of incidence when this occurs is known as the critical angle. Increasing the angle of incidence still further results in no light penetrating the glass-air boundary; instead, all the light is reflected back into the glass. This is known as total internal reflection, an effective way of reflecting light without using a mirror. (One disadvantage of mirrors is that they have two reflecting surfaces, resulting in a faint "ghost," or double image.) Total reflecting prisms are used in fine cameras, binoculars, and other optical instruments to change the direction of light. Light may be "transported" by transparent fibers and by glass or plastic rods; whether straight or curved, the light stays inside them because of successive internal reflections.

Photorefraction. It has long been known that the passage of light through some materials can slightly alter their refractive properties. In the late 20th century scientists began to investigate certain substances, such as barium titanate and various polymers, whose refractive properties are in fact markedly changed by light. In these substances the passage of light (or an electric field) redistributes the electrical charges within their molecular structures, sometimes in less than one trillionth of a second, thereby affecting their indexes of refraction. These so-called photorefractive substances are giving rise to a new field, photorefractive nonlinear optics. It may prove of great use in laser and computer technology, optical communications, and holography.

refractory materials Refractory materials, or refractories, are materials that do not break down under great heat, have low thermal conductivity, and can withstand rapid changes in temperature. Most refractories are classified as acid, basic, or neutral according to their chemical reactions at high temperatures.

Ordinary refractories are usually made from fireclays, naturally occurring clays containing aluminas and silicas. Fireclay is often formed into firebrick, which is used to line FURNACES, boilers, CHIMNEYS, and other structures that are operated at high temperatures. Refractories made from magnesite or dolomite offer greater heat resistance and are used in smelters, open-hearth furnaces, and cement KILNS. Other refractories are made from chrome ore, cement, zircon, silicon carbide, and graphite. In addition to brick (see BRICK AND BRICKLAYING), items made from refractories include crucibles, electric insulators, kilns, and rocket nose cones.

refrigeration Refrigeration is the cooling of a space or its content to a lower value than that of the surrounding space or of the ambient atmosphere. Until the advent of modern technology, natural ice was the only means of refrigeration. Ice acts as an efficient refrigerant because the temperature of melting ice remains at 0° C (32° F) until it is entirely melted. It absorbs heat from warmer surroundings, thereby cooling them while not itself becoming warmer until completely melted. Since the time of the Greeks and Romans, snow and ice were harvested in winter and stored in insulated pits for later use. Ice was a valuable cargo for 19th-century clipper ships, but it was difficult and expensive to ship. The demand for ice created a strong impetus for inventors to develop artificial cooling methods.

Development of Artificial Refrigeration

A volatile liquid absorbs heat when it evaporates and can therefore be used to cool its surroundings. Moreover, the temperature at which evaporation occurs can be controlled by varying the pressure on the liquid. Jacob Perkins, an American engineer living in London, patented (1834) the first practical ice-making machine, a volatile-liquid refrigerator using a compressor that operated in a closed cycle and conserved the fluid for reuse.

The first successful refrigeration machine in the United States was developed in 1844 by John Gorrie. His device did not use a volatile liquid but operated by the principle that air gets hot when compressed and cools when it expands.

Another type of refrigeration unit, the absorption-type machine, was developed by Ferdinand Carré in France between 1850 and 1859. Such devices, which can operate exclusively by burning natural gas or other fuel, were commonly used prior to the widespread availability of electricity.

By 1860 the basic concepts underlying modern-day refrigeration had been developed, and the continuing problem to the present day has been mainly to develop

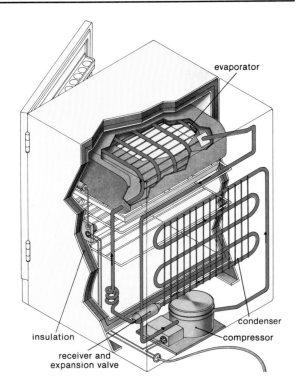

The refrigeration cycle alternately evaporates and condenses a refrigerant such as Freon-12. Liquid refrigerant stored at high pressure in the receiver is released through an expansion valve into the evaporator coils inside the refrigerator. With the pressure reduced, the refrigerant evaporates and absorbs heat from the interior. A compressor circulates the vaporized refrigerant to the exterior condenser coils, where it is condensed by pressure. Heat from the inside of the refrigerator is lost to the environment there. The cooled liquid then returns to the receiver.

and produce more efficient machines and better refrigerants and to adapt each to the refrigeration requirements of many new applications.

An early aspect of the fledgling refrigeration industry was ice manufacture, and refrigeration was soon introduced into cold-storage facilities, breweries, and the railway and shipping industries. Starting in the early 1900s, air conditioning for comfort and for industrial use became significant.

With the widespread dissemination of mechanical refrigeration in homes, the development of a frozen-food industry became possible. Industrial uses of refrigeration are greatest in the areas of food storage and distribution. The chemical industry also uses refrigeration in enormous amounts. Refrigeration at temperatures below −150° C (−240° F) is a special field called CRYOGENICS.

Refrigerants

A satisfactory refrigerant for a vapor-compression machine should be a stable, incombustible, nontoxic, and nonirritating chemical that vaporizes and condenses at pressures and temperatures appropriate for its application. Unsatisfactory materials such as ethyl alcohol and sulfur dioxide were at first used. Ammonia, although irritating and somewhat toxic, represented a great improvement when it came into use after 1850. It is still widely used in industrial refrigeration. In 1930 researchers found that by positioning chlorine and fluorine atoms in hydrocarbon compounds they could make safe refrigerants. These halogenated hydrocarbons, or halocarbons, were developed under the trademark Freon. Since then other similar refrigerants have been produced. A search for new refrigerants is again under way, however, because chlorine atoms released by halocarbons have harmful environmental effects, damaging the atmosphere's OZONE LAYER.

The Refrigeration Process

Refrigeration takes place when heat flows to a receiver colder than its surroundings. In the vapor-compression system the heat receiver is called an evaporator. Liquid refrigerant boils in it at a controlled temperature, absorbing heat to create the desired cooling. If the refrigerant is, for example, ammonia compressed to 290.9 kPa (42.2 psi) pressure, it will boil at $-10°$ C ($14°$ F) and absorb heat from any surrounding material at a higher temperature. The warmed vapor from the evaporator is then compressed and pumped outside the refrigerated space. When the pressure is raised to 1350 kPa (195.8 psi), ammonia condenses at $35°$ C ($95°$ F) and cooling water or air carries away the excess heat. The liquid refrigerant then enters an expansion valve that causes the pressure to drop, and the cycle repeats itself. Two basic pressures exist: a low one that sets the desired refrigerating temperature, and a high one that sets a condensation temperature sufficiently high to dissipate heat. Most modern systems are of this vapor-compression type. Each system is tightly sealed; if no leakage occurs the refrigerant serves for the life of the unit.

Absorption refrigeration is largely limited to large air-conditioning units. Because the evaporator temperatures of these units usually are about $5°$ C ($41°$ F) to $12°$ C ($54°$ F), water can be used as a refrigerant, boiling under high vacuum conditions. A concentrated solution of lithium bromide is sprayed in an absorber vessel, where it absorbs water that boils off in the evaporator. The diluted solution is pumped into a vessel called the generator, where the absorbed water is boiled off. The solution then returns to the absorber to pick up another charge of water vapor.

▬

refugee   Refugees are persons who have fled their country or been expelled from it and who cannot or will not return because they fear persecution. A refugee is not quite the same as a displaced person; the latter term denotes someone displaced from his or her home as a result of war or disaster. In many cases, however, the distinction is hard to make.

Although refugees have existed throughout human history—the Spanish Jews in the 15th century, for example—the problem has assumed increasing importance in the 20th century. It is estimated that more than 40 mil-

lion people have been uprooted since the outbreak of World War II. In 1991 there were more than 15 million refugees worldwide.

The majority of World War II refugees were Europeans; they included a large number of Jews who had escaped from German-occupied territories and other persons who had fled from advancing Soviet armies. In the postwar period the refugee problem has been most acute in Africa, the Middle East, Asia, and Central America. The dislocations were largely the result of ethnic and political strife, much of it attending the establishment of new governments and independent countries. In the Middle East the formation of the state of Israel and subsequent Arab-Israeli Wars led to the wholesale exodus of Palestinian Arabs.

In Asia, after the establishment of a Communist government in China in 1949, about 2 million refugees settled on Taiwan and others escaped to Hong Kong. The partition of the Indian subcontinent in 1947 resulted in what amounted to a population exchange between Hindu India and Muslim Pakistan. Indochina has also been the scene of population upheavals, with 2 million Vietnamese and Cambodians fleeing their countries. Other groups of refugees have included about 203,000 Hungarians who fled Hungary in the wake of the 1956 revolution, about 850,000 Cubans who emigrated to the United States following the revolution in 1958, between 2.5 and 3 million Afghans who fled to Pakistan after the Soviet invasion of 1979, and many thousands of people who fled war-torn El Salvador.

In 1921 the League of Nations appointed Fridtjof NANSEN high commissioner for refugee work. Nansen's primary concerns were the large numbers of stateless Armenians and Greeks who had fled Turkey and the approximately 1.5 million Russians who had left their country after the 1917 revolution. Other international agencies established to work with refugees have included the United Nations Relief and Rehabilitation Administration (1943–47) and the International Refugee Organization (1947–51). In 1951 the UN High Commission for Refugees was established.

The U.S. Refugee Act of 1980 provided for uniform admission of refugees. In practice, however, the U.S. RIGHT OF ASYLUM policy has favored refugees from Communist regimes.

▬

Refugees, Office of the United Nations High Commissioner for   After the International Refugee Organization (IRO) was abolished in 1951, the Office of the United Nations High Commissioner for Refugees (UNHCR) was established to carry on with providing legal and political aid to refugees. The primary responsibilities of the UNHCR include helping to return refugees to their homelands or to resettle them abroad, ensuring legal rights regarding employment and social benefits, and providing identity and travel documents. In promoting its goal, the UNHCR requires that governments accept refugees for at least a period of asylum. The UNHCR office was awarded the Nobel Peace Prize in 1954 and again in 1981.

Regan, Donald Thomas   Donald Thomas Regan, b. Cambridge, Mass., Dec. 21, 1918, served as U.S. secretary of the treasury under Ronald Reagan from 1981 to 1985, when he became the president's chief of staff. He previously spent 35 years with the brokerage firm Merrill Lynch and Company, rising through the ranks to the position of chairman. In Washington he earned a reputation as a Reagan loyalist with stronger executive than political skills. Criticized for White House "chaos" in reacting to the IRAN-CONTRA AFFAIR, Regan resigned in February 1987.

Regency   The last nine years (1811–20) of the reign of GEORGE III of Great Britain (r. 1760–1820) are known as the Regency. During this time, the king's son, the prince of Wales (later GEORGE IV), acted as regent because of his father's insanity. The period gave its name to a style of architecture and furniture design synthesizing the neo-classical and the exotic. In this era of considerable social and moral permissiveness, literary and artistic romanticism reached its climax.

During the Regency, the successful conclusion of the NAPOLEONIC WARS was followed by economic recession and the rise of early working-class movements. Ultraconservative Toryism, however, reigned supreme, and such movements were suppressed with force and legislation. The major events of the period included the WAR OF 1812 with the United States, the Congress of Vienna (1814–15; see VIENNA, CONGRESS OF), passage of the CORN LAW of 1815, and the Peterloo Massacre (1819) of workers in Manchester.

The Royal Pavilion at Brighton, a seaside villa remodeled (1815–23) by John Nash for the Prince Regent, exhibits the orientalizing style that became popular during the early 1800s.

regeneration   The term *regeneration* describes a variety of biological repair processes ranging from the continuous replacement of dying cells on the surface of a human cornea, for instance, to the growth of a new head on an earthworm whose previous head has been amputated. The ability to replace lost cells through mitosis (cell division) of those remaining cells is primary to all living systems. For example, a wound in the epithelial covering of most animals is quickly closed and the missing tissues are soon restored. Within 48 hours after removal of 68% of a rat's liver, the remaining 32% will double in mass. These are examples of regeneration after injury; in most living things there is also a continuous replacement of many cell types that have short lives.

The capacity to reconstruct body appendages is much less widespread than the ability to compensate for lost tissues; the complex anatomy of appendages requires more elaborate regeneration-control mechanisms. This type of regeneration is dramatically illustrated in worms such as planaria and coelenterates such as the hydra, which can each grow a new head after losing the old one. Among the vertebrates, lizards, frog tadpoles, and salamanders are the best regenerators of appendages. All three can regenerate a tail, but only frog tadpoles and salamanders can produce new limbs.

The restoration of lost appendages best exemplifies the meaning of the term *regeneration*. In animals with an organized nervous system, that system is usually indispensable for regeneration to occur. If the nerves of supply are severed, salamanders can no longer replace an amputated limb. Removal of the spinal cord in the region of amputation renders salamanders and lizards unable to produce a new tail. Usually worms will not regenerate a head if the nerve cord is missing.

One of the mechanisms guiding regeneration may involve inhibitory substances. A tubularia, an organism similar to a hydra, has a head with tentacles attached to a stem containing a central cavity. If both ends of the stem are amputated, a head will usually form only on the end toward the original head. If, however, the stem is constricted with a string so that the central cavity is obliterated, a head will form on both ends. As the head develops on one end, inhibitory material normally passes to the other end and prevents head formation there. Constriction prevents the passage of this material, and thus a head forms on both ends.

In amphibians, normal limb tissues seem to revert (dedifferentiate) to an embryonic type of cell in the region of amputation. These cells accumulate and produce a bump called the blastema. The lost structures are formed by cell division and differentiation of the blastema. Blastemas also occur in fish, annelids, arthropods, and planaria. In some cases, cells in the amphibian regenerate become something other than what they were previously. For example, if limb bones are removed and the limb is amputated, the regenerated portion will contain a bone. The bone must have come from cells that were not bone prior to amputation. This observation is extremely important because it shows that cells are not irreversibly restricted to a particular line of development.

A wound epidermis is indispensable for limb regeneration. If a salamander limb is amputated and a flap of whole skin is grafted over the amputation surface, regen-

If cut in two, both sections of a Hydra *polyp will regenerate. The top half will grow a new foot, the bottom half, a new head.*

Certain lizards break off their tails to escape from predators. The tail regenerates, but the original vertebrae are replaced by cartilage.

A single arm severed or torn from certain starfishes will regenerate a central body and new arms, producing an entire new individual.

eration will not occur. It appears that the dermis intervening between the epidermis and the other stump tissues blocks regeneration. In animals that cannot regenerate, the dermis reappears prematurely. The wound epidermis promotes mitosis and somehow causes the distal accumulation of blastema cells. Human children below the age of about 11 have regenerated lost fingertips if the wounds are not prematurely covered.

Tumors seem to be rare in appendages capable of regeneration. In fact, injection of carcinogens into salamander limbs produces extra limbs rather than tumors. Some scientists think that regeneration-controlling mechanisms can prevent carcinogen-activated cells from becoming tumorous and can guide them instead into structures compatible with life.

Regensburg [ray'-gens-boork] Regensburg (English: Ratisbon) is a Bavarian city in southeastern Germany, at the confluence of the Danube and Regen rivers. Its population is 123,821 (1987 est.). Regensburg's location—at the point where the Danube narrows—promotes the city's transshipment industry, port, and railroad yards. Electronics, chemicals, textiles, cement, leather goods, ships, beer, and sausages are among the chief products of the city. Several regional governmental agencies and the seat of a Roman Catholic bishopric are located there. Regensburg University was founded in 1962.

Regensburg escaped severe damage during World War II. Many medieval buildings thus remain, including the Cathedral of Saint Peter (1275–1524), a famous stone bridge across the Danube (1135–46), and the Romanesque Saint Emmeram's Church, which was remodeled in the 18th century.

The site of the city was an early Roman camp (1st century AD) that was chosen (530) by the dukes of Bavaria as their seat until they were deposed by Charlemagne. Regensburg experienced great prosperity during the 12th and 13th centuries. Frequently a locus for diplomatic conferences, the city became the seat of the Imperial Diet of the Holy Roman Empire from 1663 to 1806. After the Napoleonic invasion, Regensburg was returned (1810) to Bavaria. It became part of the German Empire in 1871.

regent A regent governs during the absence, minority, or incapacity of a monarch. This position can be assumed by an individual or by a council, and the appointment may be made by the reigning monarch or by a governing body. Historically, periods of regency, especially when a minor heir was involved, were times of tension between those attempting to preserve centralized power for the crown and those—usually the nobility—seeking to augment their own power. In British history, the most famous regency was that assumed by the future George IV for his father, George III, in 1811.

Reger, Max [ray'-gur] Max Reger, German composer, organist, and pianist, b. Mar. 19, 1873, d. May 11,

1916, was a controversial figure who was welcomed by some as a successor to Brahms and dismissed by others as a pedantic technician.

Exceedingly prolific, Reger disdained program music and wrote nothing for the stage, but he left no other genre untouched. The pervading chromaticism of his music and the arbitrary modulations decried by his detractors are less in evidence in his numerous songs: these works, together with a few orchestral, chamber, keyboard, and choral compositions, comprise his contribution to the current repertoire.

reggae [reg'-ay] Reggae is a Jamaican musical style based on American soul music but with inverted rhythms and prominent bass lines. Rooted in Kingston's slums, reggae is the expression of Jamaica's poorest blacks. The themes of reggae lyrics include Rastafarianism, political protest, and the "rudie" (hooligan hero). The film *The Harder They Come* (1973) brought the style to the United States. With the exception of a few bands and composers, the style has lost much of its old vitality.

Reggio di Calabria [red'-joh dee kah-lah'-bree-ah] Reggio di Calabria is a port city in the Calabria region of southern Italy, situated on the eastern shore of the Strait of Messina, which divides the mainland from Sicily. The population is 178,666 (1988 est.). Reggio is a seaport, tourist resort, and industrial center. A ferry operates across the strait to Messina, Sicily.

Greek colonists founded the city in the 8th century BC, and it was conquered by Rome in the 3d century BC. Alaric the Visigoth overran the city in AD 410, and during the following centuries it was captured and ruled successively by the Byzantines, Arabs, and Normans. During the 12th century the city became part of the kingdom of Sicily. Reggio was completely rebuilt after a devastating earthquake occurred in 1908.

regiment In traditional military organization the regiment was the basic combat component of a nation's army. All three combat groups—infantry, cavalry, and artillery—were organized into regiments. Commanded by a colonel, the regiment consisted of battalions and service and administrative units. The term, which comes from the Latin *regimen* ("rule"), was first used in the 16th century to refer to French cavalry troops. In the early 19th century Napoleon I created larger components than the regiment; they were (in ascending order) the brigade, the division, the corps, and the army. Other nations soon followed the French practice, and the regiment lost its status as an independent component. By the early 20th century 3 infantry regiments of about 3,000 soldiers each typically constituted an infantry division. Today most nations have reorganized their armies into battle groups, combat arms, and other such modern configurations.

Regina [ruh-jy'-nuh] Regina, a city of 175,064 (1986), is the capital and second largest city of Saskatchewan, Canada. Located in the south central part of the province on Wascana Creek, Regina is the distribution center for the surrounding agricultural region. The city is the headquarters for the Saskatchewan Wheat Pool, the world's largest grain cooperative. Petroleum and natural-gas refining are also important to the local economy. Steel and wood products as well as automobiles, chemicals, cement, and fertilizers are manufactured there. The provincial government facilities and many of the city's cultural buildings are located in the parklike Wascana Center, built around artificial Wascana Lake.

Founded in 1882 and named Pile of Bones, the city was later renamed Regina to honor Queen Victoria. It was capital of the Northwest Territories from 1882 until 1905, when it became capital of the new province of Saskatchewan.

Regiomontanus [ree-jee-oh-mahn'-tay-nuhs] The German astronomer Regiomontanus (originally named Johann Müller), b. June 6, 1436, d. July 8?, 1476, played an important role in the revival of Renaissance astronomy. He was a student (graduated 1452) and later colleague (1457–61) of Georg von Peurbach at the University of Vienna and completed (c.1461–63) Peurbach's translation (pub. 1496) of Ptolemy's *Almagest*. His reflection that Ptolemy's lunar theory required the apparent diameter of the Moon to vary in length much more than is actually observed caught Copernicus's attention. Regiomontanus also wrote an important work on trigonometry, published in 1533.

regulation, government see GOVERNMENT REGULATION

Regulators The Regulator movements in North and South Carolina were the products of sectional and economic conflict on the eve of the American Revolution. Both movements were tied more closely to local discontent than they were to any widespread dissatisfaction with British rule. In fact, many of the Regulators later sided with the crown against the colonial ruling class that led the independence movement.

The conflict in North Carolina came to a head about 1768, when small farmers in the backcountry protested against the inequitable and inefficient system of local government prevailing in their area. Conflict between the Regulators and Gov. William Tryon continued for several years, culminating in the defeat of the farmers at the Battle of Alamance on May 16, 1771. One of their leaders was executed on the battlefield, and six Regulators were hanged for treason following a court-martial.

The Regulators in South Carolina were also backcountry farmers. Upset by banditry and Indian attacks about which their local government did little, they formed associations in 1767; they refused to pay taxes and took vigilante action to impose their own form of law and order. In 1769, South Carolina set up a court system for the backcountry and conditions stabilized there.

Regulus, Marcus Atilius [reg'-ue-luhs] Marcus Atilius Regulus, d. c.250 BC, was a Roman general and statesman. As consul (267 BC) he captured Brundisium (now Brindisi). Again consul (256 BC) during the First PUNIC WAR, he defeated the Carthaginian army and navy. Regulus's demands for unconditional surrender backfired, however, and in 255 he was defeated by Carthage. Sent on parole to Rome to negotiate peace terms and an exchange of prisoners, he supposedly convinced the Romans to reject the Carthaginian terms and returned voluntarily to Carthage, where he died in prison, possibly tortured to death.

rehabilitation medicine Rehabilitation medicine is a medical speciality that deals with the diagnosis and treatment of neuromuscular-musculoskeletal disorders and the restoration of the physically disabled to their highest possible levels of physical, psychological, social, vocational, and economic functions. The object of rehabilitation medicine is to eliminate or alleviate the disability or retrain the physically disabled to live as normal and productive a life as can be done within the limits of the impairment.

Services of Rehabilitation Medicine. Modern rehabilitation medicine has developed primarily since World War II as an extension of physical medicine; both branches have merged as the speciality of physical medicine and rehabilitation, the specialist often being referred to as a physiatrist.

The number of physically disabled has increased, and public attitudes toward these people have radically changed, as reflected in the establishment of state and federal programs of vocational rehabilitation and other legislation recognizing the needs of the disabled. As a result, the speciality of rehabilitation medicine has expanded rapidly, and demands for its services have increased. Comprehensive rehabilitation therefore has been provided best by a multidisciplinary team of paramedical professionals, including physical therapists, occupational therapists, psychologists, rehabilitation nurses, social workers, speech pathologists, vocational counselors, teachers, recreational therapists, home economists, home planning consultants, orthotist-prosthetists, rehabilitation engineers, driver educators, and dietitians. All of these specialists work closely with the patient and the patient's family under the direction of the physiatrist.

The practice of rehabilitation medicine ranges from short-term management of various musculoskeletal ailments and pain syndromes to the long-term and complicated management of severe disabilities resulting from spinal-cord injuries, spina bifida, brain injuries, strokes, cerebral palsy, multiple sclerosis, muscular dystrophy, polyneuritis, amputations, arthritis, and major bone fractures, to mention a few. Minor disorders are treated by the primary physician and a small team of rehabilitation professionals employed by most hospitals and health-care facilities. The more complicated problems, however, are best managed in larger rehabilitation centers, which provide a wide range of services.

Recent Developments. The "whole-person concept" of rehabilitation medicine is being utilized in the management of disabilities other than neuromuscular or musculoskeletal in origin, such as those resulting from heart and lung diseases, cancer, and mental disorders. There is an increasing demand for electrodiagnostic procedures for assessing nerve and muscle impairment, such as nerve-conduction studies and electromyography. The quality of life for the physically disabled is being improved through the application of bioengineering, which has provided such items as improved artificial limbs and braces; equipment for training, work, and recreation; nursing supplies; modified vehicles; and aids for mobility and driving.

Rehnquist, William [ren'-kwist] William Hubbs Rehnquist, b. Milwaukee, Wis., Oct. 1, 1924, was appointed to the U.S. Supreme Court by President Nixon in 1971; in 1986, President Reagan appointed him the 16th chief justice of the United States, succeeding Warren Burger, who retired. After graduating from Stanford Law School, Rehnquist served (1952–53) as law clerk to Supreme Court Justice Robert H. Jackson. He then established a private law practice in Phoenix, Ariz. Identified with the conservative wing of the Republican party, he was an assistant attorney general (1969–71) in the Nixon administration. Often standing in dissent on the Court, Rehnquist has taken strong positions generally on the side of law and order and against labor and civil rights advocates. His opinions have also reflected a flexible interpretation of the separation of church and state.

Rehoboam, King of Israel [ree-uh-boh'-uhm] Son and heir of King SOLOMON, Rehoboam was the last king of a united Israel and the first king of the southern Kingdom of JUDAH. His reluctance to temper his father's despotic rule precipitated (920 BC) the revolt of the ten northern tribes, which was followed by persistent warfare between the northern Kingdom of ISRAEL, united under JEROBOAM, and Judah.

Reich, Steve [rysh] The composer Steve Reich, b. New York City, Oct. 3, 1936, is closely identified with the concept of minimalism. Minimalist music uses the smallest possible amount of material to produce works that may evolve over long periods of time. In Reich's "phase music," instruments or voices begin together and gradually go out of phase. Chord progressions in his pieces shift gradually, one note at a time, within simple repeated patterns. The unfolding of this process in time is also known as "process music." Characteristic pieces by Reich are

Come Out (1966; spoken-word tape loops) and *New York Counterpoint* (1985; 11 clarinets, 10 of which are taped).

Reich, Wilhelm [ryk] The Austrian psychoanalyst Wilhelm Reich, b. Mar. 24, 1897, d. Nov. 3, 1957, was perhaps the boldest figure in the history of modern psychiatry. He became a psychoanalyst in 1920. Reich's most controversial psychiatric concept was that of orgastic potency—the full surrender of the organism to the emotions of love and the sensations of pleasure during the sexual embrace—as the basis of mental health.

Reich delineated the "character-muscular armor" as the main internal obstacle to healthy psychological functioning. The character armor consists of defensive character traits, such as arrogance or apprehensiveness, that developed in childhood to ward off painful feelings. The muscular armor refers to chronic muscular spasms that represent the bodily expression of characterological rigidities. Thus a stubborn, "stiff-necked" person might literally have a stiff neck.

Between 1927 and 1933 in Vienna and Berlin and under the aegis of leftist political parties, Reich brought sex education and counseling to large numbers of people in a way that connected emotional issues with social concerns. In the 1940s and 1950s in the United States, Reich investigated orgone energy, an energy that, he asserted, functioned as the life energy. Reich invented the orgone energy accumulator, which he believed had therapeutic properties. When he defied an injunction against selling this device, many of his publications were burned, and he was sentenced to a federal penitentiary, where he died.

Reichstag [ryks'-tahk] The Reichstag was originally the parliament of the Holy Roman Empire, which was dissolved in 1806. The modern Reichstag, the German national legislature, first met in 1871, following the establishment of the unified German Empire under Otto von BISMARCK. Its powers were broadened during the WEIMAR REPUBLIC (1918–33). On Feb. 27, 1933, soon after Adolf HITLER became chancellor, the Reichstag building was destroyed by fire. Alleging that the fire was part of a Communist plot, the government immediately suspended civil rights and suppressed the opposition. In the elections of Mar. 5, 1933, Hitler's National Socialists fell short of the absolute majority they sought. Nevertheless, on Mar. 23, 1933, the new Reichstag, by more than the requisite two-thirds majority, voted Hitler the dictatorial powers he demanded, thereby relinquishing its authority.

Reid, Whitelaw A noted journalist and diplomat, Whitelaw Reid, b. Xenia, Ohio, Oct. 27, 1837, d. Dec. 15, 1912, is best remembered for his brilliant eyewitness accounts of major Civil War battles. Reid established a reputation in journalism during the Civil War as war correspondent (1862–64) for the *Cincinnati Gazette*. He later

joined the staff of the *New York Tribune,* and in 1872 he became its editor and publisher. Reid's diplomatic career included three years as U.S. minister to France (1889–92) and tenure as the ambassador to the Court of Saint James (1905–12).

Reign of Terror   see FRENCH REVOLUTION

Reimarus, Hermann Samuel [ry-mah'-rus] A German theologian and philosopher of the ENLIGHTENMENT, Hermann Samuel Reimarus, b. Dec. 22, 1694, d. Mar. 1, 1768, was a follower of Christian WOLFF in his philosophy; in theology Reimarus was an adherent of DEISM. He was one of the founders in Germany of the higher criticism—the attempt to examine the Bible from a purely scholarly point of view. Among his contentions was the claim that the accounts of the resurrection and miracles were the product of conscious fraud on the part of the Apostles.

Reims [reemz or rans] Reims (also Rheims) is a city in northeastern France on the Vesle River and the Aisne-Marne Canal, about 134 km (83 mi) northeast of Paris. It has a population of 194,656 (1982). Reims is the center of a major wine-growing region (especially champagne). The city has been known for its textiles since the Middle Ages. Other important industries include the manufacture of chemicals, electrical and automotive equipment, bicycles, and food products. The city has port facilities on the Aisne-Marne Canal. The University of Reims was established in 1961.

Reims, named for the Remi, a Gallic tribe, was one of the principal urban centers of Gaul during Roman times. Later it was the coronation place of most of the French kings. The city suffered severe destruction during World War I when German forces captured and pillaged Reims for 10 days. The German army then occupied the heights overlooking the city for 4 years, and periodic bombing damaged or destroyed many of the buildings, including Rheims Cathedral (built 1211–1311), one of the greatest monuments of GOTHIC ART AND ARCHITECTURE. Destruction also took place during World War II. The Germans surrendered unconditionally to the Allies on May 7, 1945, in a hall of the Collège Modèrne in Reims, which had served as headquarters of the Allied command.

Reims Cathedral   see GOTHIC ART AND ARCHITECTURE

reindeer The reindeer of northern Europe and Asia and the caribou of North America were formerly considered different species. They are now classified as one, *Rangifer tarandus,* but the common names are still used to distinguish the two groups. Reindeer originally inhabited the tundra and northern woodlands of Eurasia, but it is believed that no truly wild reindeer still exist; all free-living reindeer are thought to be feral, that is, descended from escaped domestic stock. Reindeer husbandry is still

Reindeer, a deer of Arctic regions, migrate in herds across great distances between summer and winter grounds. The herds are usually followed by wolf packs, their primary enemies.

practiced by the Lapps, Yakuts, and Tungus in northern Scandinavia and Siberia. Reindeer have been introduced into Alaska, Newfoundland, and other parts of North America with various degrees of success; caribou also occur across the Bering Strait in eastern Siberia. Reindeer are generally smaller than caribou, the larger males reaching 1.2 m (4 ft) high at the shoulder and 115 kg (250 lb) in weight. They (and caribou) are the only deer in which the females bear antlers. The antlers are long and slender, and the branching points, or tines, usually assume a broad shape. The mating season extends from August to early November. Gestation is about 8 months, and usually a single young is born.

Reinhardt, Ad [ryn'-hahrt] The painter and art theoretician Ad Reinhardt, b. Adolf Frederick Reinhardt in Buffalo, N.Y., Dec. 24, 1913, d. Aug. 30, 1967, is known for the extremely abstract paintings of his later career, particularly the "black paintings" of the 1960s. At Columbia University in New York City, Reinhardt studied art history; later, he taught at Brooklyn College (from 1947 until his death). His early works, which belong to the formative years of ABSTRACT EXPRESSIONISM, are composed of small rectilinear shapes painted in bright, contrasting colors. During the 1950s his canvases became increasingly monochromatic and symmetrical.

Reinhardt, Max Max Reinhardt, originally named Max Goldmann, b. Sept. 9, 1873, d. Oct. 31, 1943, was an Austrian stage director and producer who established himself as one of the most eclectic leaders of the modern experimental theater. In his early career he headed several experimental theaters in Berlin before becoming director of the noted Deutsches Theater in 1905. Two of Reinhardt's most dazzling productions, *The Oresteia* (1919)

and *Danton's Death* (1920), were performed before audiences of thousands in Berlin's massive Grosses Schauspielhaus. In 1920 he founded the Salzburg Festival, for which he staged *Everyman*. When the Nazis came to power, Reinhardt continued his career in New York and Hollywood; his notable productions for the American stage include *A Midsummer Night's Dream* (1934), *Six Characters in Search of an Author* (1940), and *Rosalinda* (1942).

relapsing fever Relapsing fever is an INFECTIOUS DISEASE caused by a bacterial spirochete of the genus *Borrelia* and transmitted by human body lice or by ticks. The type spread by lice occurs under conditions of poor hygiene and famine. The type spread by ticks is transmitted to humans from such rodents as chipmunks and squirrels as well as from armadillos, opossums, and other small mammals. Symptoms manifest themselves after an incubation period of about 7 days and include a sudden onset of chills, followed by high fever, headache, muscle pain, cough, sore throat, and eye pain, all of which last from 3 to 6 days. The fever falls and then returns after about a week; relapses may continue 2 to 10 more times. Treatment includes the administration of tetracycline or chloramphenicol.

relativity Albert Einstein's theory of relativity is viewed as one of the greatest achievements in theoretical physics. It introduced to science the concept of "relativity"—the notion that there is no absolute motion in the universe, only relative motion—thus superseding the 200-year-old theory of mechanics of Isaac Newton. Einstein showed that we reside not in the flat, Euclidean space and uniform, absolute time of everyday experience, but in another environment: curved space-time. The theory played a role in advances in physics that led to the nuclear era, with its potential for benefit as well as for destruction, and that made possible an understanding of the microworld of elementary particles and their interactions. It has also revolutionized our view of COSMOLOGY, with its predictions of apparently bizarre astronomical phenomena such as the BIG BANG, NEUTRON STARS, BLACK HOLES, and gravitational waves (see GRAVITATION).

Scope of Relativity

The theory of relativity is a single, all-encompassing theory of space-time, gravitation, and mechanics. It is popularly viewed, however, as having two separate, independent theoretical parts—special relativity and general relativity. One reason for this division is that Einstein presented special relativity in 1905, while general relativity was not published in its final form until 1916. Another reason is the very different realms of applicability of the two parts of the theory: special relativity in the world of microscopic physics, general relativity in the world of astrophysics and cosmology.

A third reason is that physicists accepted and understood special relativity by the early 1920s. It quickly became a working tool for theorists and experimentalists in the then-burgeoning fields of atomic and nuclear physics and quantum mechanics. This rapid acceptance was not, however, the case for general relativity. The theory did not appear to have as much direct connection with experiment as the special theory; most of its applications were on astronomical scales, and it was apparently limited to adding miniscule corrections to the predictions of Newtonian gravitation theory; its cosmological impact would not be felt for another decade. In addition, the mathematics of the theory were thought to be extraordinarily difficult to comprehend. The British astronomer Sir Arthur Eddington, one of the first to fully understand the theory in detail, was once asked if it were true that only three people in the world understood general relativity. He is said to have replied, "Who is the third?"

This situation persisted for almost 40 years. General relativity was considered a respectable subject not for physicists, but for pure mathematicians and philosophers. Around 1960, however, a remarkable resurgence of interest in general relativity began that has made it an important and serious branch of physics and astronomy. (By 1977, Eddington's remark was recalled at a conference on general relativity attended by more than 800 researchers in the subject.) This growth has its roots, first, beginning around 1960, in the application of new mathematical techniques to the study of general relativity that significantly streamlined calculations and that allowed the physically significant concepts to be isolated from the mathematical complexity, and second, in the discovery of exotic astronomical phenomena in which general relativity could play an important role, including quasars (1963), the 3-kelvin microwave background radiation (1965), pulsars (1967), and the possible discovery of black holes (1971). In addition, the rapid technological advances since the 1960s have given experimenters new high-precision tools to test whether general relativity was the correct theory of gravitation.

The distinction between special relativity and the curved space-time of general relativity is largely a matter of degree. Special relativity is actually an approximation to curved space-time that is valid in sufficiently small regions of space-time, much as the overall surface of an apple is curved even though a small region of the surface is approximately flat. Special relativity thus may be used whenever the scale of the phenomena being studied is small compared to the scale on which space-time curvature (gravitation) begins to be noticed. For most applications in atomic or nuclear physics, this approximation is so accurate that relativity can be assumed to be exact; in other words, gravity is assumed to be completely absent. From this point of view, special relativity and all its consequences may be "derived" from a single simple postulate. In the presence of gravity, however, the approximate nature of special relativity may manifest itself, so the principle of equivalence is invoked to determine how matter responds to curved space-time. Finally, to learn the extent that space-time is curved by the presence of matter, general relativity is applied.

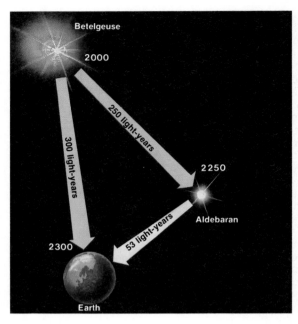

If Betelgeuse, a star in the constellation Orion, were to explode, and the explosion were noted on Earth in the year 2300, then, knowing that Betelgeuse lies 300 light-years distant, the event could be postdated as having occurred in the year 2000, Earth time. Similar dates could be assigned for the notice of that explosion elsewhere, as on the star Aldebaran. These would be simply Earth dates, however; the notion of absolute time must be abandoned in relativity because objects move in different inertial frames relative to one another.

Special Relativity

The two basic concepts of special relativity are the inertial frame and the principle of relativity. An inertial frame of reference is any region, such as a freely falling laboratory (see FREE FALL), in which all objects move in straight lines with uniform velocity. This region is free from gravitation and is called a Galilean system. The principle of relativity postulates that the result of any physical experiment performed inside a laboratory in an inertial frame is independent of the uniform velocity of the frame. In other words, the laws of physics must have the same form in every inertial frame. A corollary is that the speed of light must be the same in any inertial frame (because a speed-of-light measurement is a physical experiment) regardless of the speed of its source or that of the observer. Essentially all the laws and consequences of special relativity can be derived from these concepts.

The first important consequence is the relativity of simultaneity. Because any operational definition of simultaneous events at different locations involves the sending of light signals between them, then two events that are simultaneous in one inertial frame may not be simultaneous when viewed from a frame moving relative to the first. This conclusion helped abolish the Newtonian concept of an absolute, universal time.

Another consequence of relativity is that the transformation law, which permits the change from the coordinates of one inertial frame to another moving with velocity v relative to the first, is no longer the Galilean transformation dependent only on the velocity and time. It becomes the Lorentz transformation, which takes into account the ratio of the velocity to the speed of light (c). This transformation law was derived in 1895 by Hendrik A. Lorentz as a result of his work on electromagnetism and the theory of electrons. Einstein demonstrated that the law was a fundamental property of space-time. One effect predicted by the Lorentz transformation is the FITZGERALD-LORENTZ CONTRACTION, an apparent shortening by a factor $\sqrt{1 - v^2/c^2}$ of the length of a moving rod compared to an identical rod at rest. This effect was first proposed by George F. Fitzgerald in 1892 as a way to explain the failure of the 1887 MICHELSON-MORLEY EXPERIMENT to detect any dependence of the velocity of light on the Earth's motion through the so-called ETHER, the medium through which light was thought to propagate. Einstein pointed out that the principle of relativity made the ether concept superfluous, since the Michelson-Morley result could be accounted for using any inertial frame.

Another effect of special relativity is the apparent lengthening of time intervals measured by a moving clock

The Michelson-Morley experiment (A) was designed to detect the ether medium once thought to carry light waves. A light beam (1), split by a mirror (2), followed separate light paths (3, 4) and recombined (5), forming interference bands (6). If ether were present, light should take longer to make the round trip in the direction (7) of Earth's motion than at right angles to it. No time difference was observed, indicating no ether. Newton's laws of motion (B) predict that a shell fired with a velocity v from a tank moving at a speed V should have a velocity $V+v$ relative to an outside observer. Einstein showed that the relative velocity should be $(v+V) \div (1+vV/c^2)$, where c is the velocity of light. Thus (C), if a shell is fired at $\frac{1}{2}c$ on a planet orbiting at $\frac{1}{2}c$, an outside observer will see the shell moving at 0.8 c.

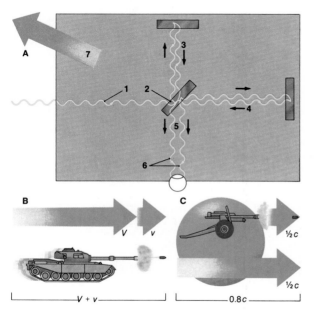

by a factor $1/\sqrt{1 - v^2/c^2}$ compared to a clock at rest. This "time dilation" has been confirmed to high precision by numerous laboratory experiments, including one in 1966 in which unstable muons (μ-mesons) moving at velocities of $0.997c$ were found to live longer than muons at rest by exactly the correct factor of 12.

The law of composition of two velocities, given by $v_3 = v_1 + v_2$ in classical Newtonian mechanics, is now given by $v_3 = (v_1 + v_2) / (1 + v_1 v_2/c^2)$. Therefore no combination of velocities, each less than c, can ever produce a velocity in excess of c; furthermore, if one of the velocities is c, the combined velocity v_3 is automatically c, consistent with the postulate that the speed of light is the same in every inertial frame.

One consequence of modifying the Galilean-invariant mechanics of Newton to make it Lorentz-invariant is that the momentum of a particle of rest mass m is no longer mv, but $mv/\sqrt{1 - v^2/c^2}$, which means that the particle's mass increases as it moves faster. This relativistic increase of inertia prevents particles from being accelerated up to and beyond the speed of light and has been observed countless times in high-energy particle accelerators. Einstein also showed that what was energy in one inertial frame could be mass in another; therefore both are manifestations of the same entity and are related by the famous equation $E = mc^2$.

In some ways the most important consequences and confirmations of special relativity arise when it is merged with quantum mechanics, leading to many predictions in agreement with experiments, such as elementary particle spin, atomic fine structure, antimatter, and so on.

The mathematical foundations of special relativity were explored in 1908 by the German mathematician Hermann Minkowski, who developed the concept of a "four-dimensional space-time continuum," in which time is treated the same as the three spatial dimensions—the fourth dimension of Minkowski space-time.

The Principle of Equivalence and Space-Time Curvature

The exact Minkowski space-time of special relativity is incompatible with the existence of gravity. A frame chosen to be inertial for a particle far from the Earth where the gravitational field is negligible will not be inertial for a particle near the Earth. An approximate compatibility between the two, however, can be achieved through a remarkable property of gravitation called the weak equivalence principle (WEP): all modest-sized bodies fall in a given external gravitational field with the same acceleration regardless of their mass, composition, or structure. The principle's validity has been checked experimentally by Galileo, Newton, and Friedrich Bessel, and in the early 20th century by Baron Roland von Eötvös (after whom such experiments are named). If an observer were to ride in an elevator falling freely in a gravitational field, then all bodies inside the elevator, because they are falling at the same rate, would consequently move uniformly in straight lines as if gravity had vanished. Conversely, in an accelerated elevator in free space, bodies would fall with the same acceleration (because of their inertia), just as if there were a gravitational field.

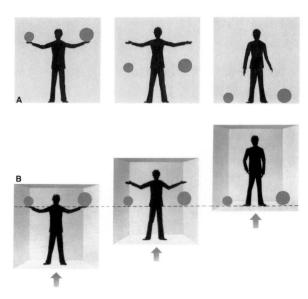

The behavior of two balls in Earth's inertial frame (A) and in that of an accelerating elevator in free space (B)—even if the balls differ in mass—is an example of Einstein's equivalence principle in special relativity. The balls in the elevator "drop" with the same uniform acceleration, just as if they dropped in Earth's gravitational field.

Einstein's great insight was to postulate that this "vanishing" of gravity in free-fall applied not only to mechanical motion but to all the laws of physics, such as electromagnetism. In any freely falling frame, therefore, the laws of physics should (at least locally) take on their special relativistic forms. This postulate is called the Einstein equivalence principle (EEP). One consequence is the gravitational redshift, a shift in frequency f for a light ray that climbs through a height h in a gravitational field, given by $\Delta f/f = gh/c^2$ where g is the gravitational acceleration. (If the light ray descends, it is blueshifted.) Equivalently, this effect can be viewed as a relative shift in the rates of identical clocks at two heights. A second consequence of EEP is that space-time must be curved.

Any theory of gravity that fulfills EEP is called a "metric" theory (from the geo*metric*al, curved-space-time view of gravity). Because the equivalence principle is a crucial foundation for this view, it has been well tested. Versions of the Eötvös experiment performed in Princeton in 1964 and in Moscow in 1971 verified EEP to 1 part in 10^{12}. Gravitational redshift measurements using gamma rays climbing a tower on the Harvard University campus (1965), using light emitted from the surface of the Sun (1965), and using atomic clocks flown in aircraft and rockets (1976) have verified that effect to precisions of better than 1 percent.

General Relativity

The principle of equivalence and its experimental confirmation reveal that space-time is curved by the presence of matter, but they do not indicate how much space-time

curvature matter actually produces. To determine this curvature requires a specific metric theory of gravity, such as general relativity, which provides a set of equations that allow computation of the space-time curvature from a given distribution of matter. These are called field equations. Einstein's aim was to find the simplest field equations that could be constructed in terms of the space-time curvature and that would have the matter distribution as source. The result was a set of 10 equations. This is not, however, the only possible metric theory. In 1960, C. H. Brans and Robert Dicke developed a metric theory (see GRAVITATION) that proposed, in addition to field equations for curvature, equations for an additional gravitational field whose role was to mediate and augment the way in which matter generated curvature. Between 1960 and 1976 it became a serious competitor to general relativity. Many other metric theories have also been invented since 1916.

An important issue, therefore, is whether general relativity is indeed the correct theory of gravity. The only way to answer this question is by means of experiment. In the past scientists customarily spoke of the three classical tests proposed by Einstein: gravitational redshift, light deflection, and the perihelion shift of Mercury. The redshift, however, is a test of the equivalence principle, not of general relativity itself, and two new important tests have been discovered since Einstein's time: the time-delay by I. I. Shapiro in 1964, and the Nordtvedt effect by K. Nordtvedt, Jr., in 1968.

The confirmation of the deflection of starlight by the Sun by the solar eclipse expedition of 1919 was one of the triumphant moments for general relativity and brought Einstein worldwide fame. This method has been supplanted by measurements of the deflection of radio waves from distant quasars using radio-telescope interferometers, which can operate in broad daylight. Between

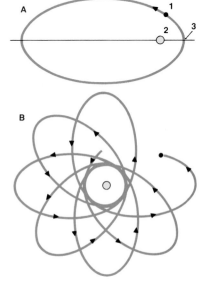

(A) Mercury (1) moves around the Sun (2) in an elliptical orbit. The planet's perihelion (3)—the point closest to the Sun—also moves about the Sun, or precesses, so that Mercury follows a rosette-shaped orbital path (B). The gravitational pull of other planets accounts for nearly all of the precession, except for a small residual amount. This remaining amount is accounted for by Einstein's general theory of gravitation, which considers that part of the precession results from warping of space by the Sun's enormous mass.

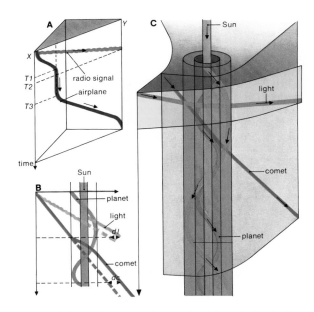

The concept of space-time requires time as a fourth dimension in order to specify location—because relative motion affects both space and time. An object's path in space-time is called a world line, and a graph of a world line uses two space coordinates and time as a third. (A) In an airplane's flight from X to Y, the slope of its world line increases as its speed decreases, becoming vertical when the plane makes a fueling stop (times T1 to T3). A radio signal starting from X arrives at Y at time T2. In relativity theory, acceleration of an object as it passes near a massive body is viewed as a local distortion in space-time. (B) A comet passing the Sun is deflected (dc) in space-time, as is a ray of light (dl); a planet, slower, oscillates between extreme positions. (C) Space-time around the Sun is distorted differently for objects moving at different speeds, but each object, in its own version of space, appears to travel in a path of constant velocity.

have confirmed this agreement to about half of 1 percent.

The Nordtvedt effect is one that does not occur in general relativity but is predicted by many alternative metric theories of gravity, including the Brans-Dicke theory. If the Nordtvedt effect were to occur, then the Earth and Moon would be attracted by the Sun with slightly different accelerations, resulting in a small perturbation in the lunar orbit that could be detected by lunar laser ranging. In data taken between 1969 and 1976, no such perturbation was detected.

A number of secondary tests of more subtle gravitational effects have also been performed during the last decade. General relativity has passed every one, while many of its competitors have failed. Tests of gravitational radiation and inertial frame-dragging are now being devised. One experiment would involve placing spinning objects in Earth orbit and measuring expected relativistic effects.

Cosmology

One of the first astronomical applications of general relativity was in the area of cosmology. The theory predicts that the universe could be expanding from an initially condensed state, a process known as the big bang. Despite many challenges (including the popularity during the 1950s of the steady-state theory), the big bang is now accepted as the standard model of the universe.

1969 and 1975, 12 such measurements ultimately yielded agreement, to 1 percent, with the predicted deflection of general relativity.

The time-delay effect is a small delay in the return of a light signal sent through the curved space-time near the Sun to a planet or spacecraft on the far side of the Sun and back to Earth. For a ray that grazes the solar surface, the delay amounts to 200 millionths of a second. Since 1964, a systematic program of radar ranging to the planets Mercury and Venus, to the spacecraft *Mariners 6, 7,* and *9,* and to the *Viking* orbiters and landers on Mars has been able to confirm this prediction to better than half of 1 percent.

Another of the early successes of general relativity was its ability to account for the puzzle of Mercury's orbit. After the perturbing effects of the other planets on Mercury's orbit were taken into account, an unexplained shift remained in the direction of its perihelion (point of closest approach to the Sun) of 43 seconds of arc per century; the shift had confounded astronomers of the late 19th century. General relativity explained it as a natural effect of the motion of Mercury in the curved space-time around the Sun. Recent radar measurements of Mercury's motion

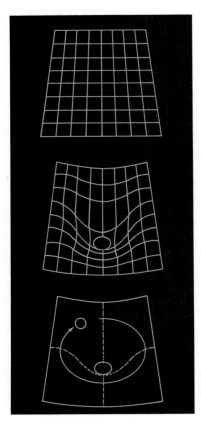

The curvature of space-time by the presence of matter is illustrated in this sequence of diagrams. Space is represented here as a flat rubber sheet that is covered with a grid of lines. A weight placed on the sheet depresses it and distorts the grid. In a similar manner the presence of a massive object, such as a star, distorts space-time. The area around the mass is now curved. Because the area of space-time around the star's mass is curved, a nearby mass, such as a planet, is held in orbit, like a bicycle on a banked racetrack, or else it falls in toward the star.

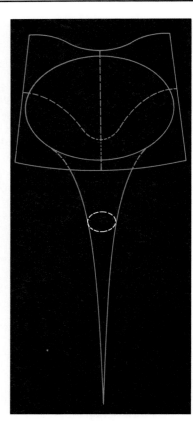

The preceding diagram is carried a drastic step further to show what happens near a black hole—a mass so great that it has collapsed inward upon itself. It has, in effect, gone out of existence, except for the extreme distortion of its neighborhood. A passing object that is pulled in toward the black hole cannot escape once it passes the event horizon or Schwarzschild radius (small broken circle). Evidence is growing for the existence of black holes, predicted by general relativity.

Another important application of general relativity is to the theory of neutron stars, bodies that have been so compressed by gravitational forces that their density is comparable to that within the atomic nucleus, and their composition is primarily neutrons. One of the most exotic predictions of general relativity is the black hole, for which there is some evidence. A prediction of general relativity that has not yet been verified is GRAVITATIONAL WAVES.

See also: WORLD LINE.

Relay   Relay was an early experiment by NASA in the field of active-repeater COMMUNICATIONS SATELLITES. The two Relay satellites were designed to receive and retransmit a variety of television, telephone, and radio signals between the United States, Europe, Japan, and South America. *Relay 1* was launched from Cape Canaveral by a Delta rocket on Dec. 13, 1962, and entered an orbit with an apogee of 7,422 km (4,612 mi) and a perigee of 1,318 km (819 mi) at an angle of 47.5° to the equator, with a period of 186 minutes. *Relay 2* was similarly launched on Jan. 21, 1964. Its orbit was 7,412 km (4,606 mi) by 2,088 km (1,298 mi) at an angle of 46° to the equator and with a period of 195 minutes. Both satellites continued to perform satisfactorily until they were

shut off: *Relay 1* in February 1965, and *Relay 2* in September 1965.

relay   A relay is essentially an electrically controlled switch (see SWITCH, ELECTRIC) that is used to open or close an electric circuit. The switch can be actuated by various means. Electromechanical operation is the most common and will be emphasized below, but other types of actuation are possible. An electromechanical device produces mechanical motion when it is energized by an electric current. A SOLENOID is such a device, and solenoids are often used in relays.

A standard type of relay consists of a coil with an enclosed, fixed iron core and a nearby movable armature. When the coil is energized, the armature is attracted to it; the resulting motion is then used to open or close the relay circuit. Such a relay requires a power of several watts for proper operation. The appearance of transistorized switching systems, which operate at powers of a few tenths of a watt, necessitated the design of relays that could function at these lower powers. The reed relay not only solved this problem but was also much smaller. It consists of two flat magnetic strips enclosed in a sealed capsule filled with an inert gas to prevent corrosion. The capsule is situated inside a coil; when the coil is energized, an electromagnetic field is created, causing the two contact strips, which are normally separated, to attract each other, make contact, and close the circuit. When the coil is deenergized, the field vanishes and the strips, because of their spring action, return to their normal separation. Reed relays are common in telephone switching equipment.

Many types of relays have been designed for various applications. They are used in COMPUTERS, IGNITION SYSTEMS, circuit breakers, electric bells, telegraph systems, and electrical and electronic equipment.

religion   Religions are complex systems of beliefs, practices, and attitudes by which people relate their lives to supernatural beings or principles. The major religious traditions still widespread are PRIMITIVE RELIGION; the Western tradition of JUDAISM, CHRISTIANITY, and ISLAM; and the Eastern tradition of JAINISM, HINDUISM, and BUDDHISM.

Characteristics of Religion

Keeping in mind the dangers of general characterizations, what are the distinctive features of religion? Several concepts may be isolated that, even though not necessary or sufficient conditions if taken separately, may jointly be considered "symptomatic" of religions.

The Holy. Religious belief or experience is usually expressed in terms of the holy or the sacred. The holy is generally in opposition to the everyday and profane and carries with it a sense of supreme value and ultimate reality. The holy may be understood as a personal GOD, as a whole realm of gods and spirits, as a diffuse power, as an impersonal order, or in some other way. Although the holy may ultimately be nothing but the social order, a projection of the human mind, or some sort of illusion, it is nevertheless experienced in religion as an initiating power, coming to human life and touching it from beyond itself.

Religions frequently claim to have their origin in REVELATIONS, that is, in distinctive experiences of the holy coming into human life. Such revelations may take the form of visions (MOSES in the desert), inner voices (MUHAMMAD outside Mecca), or events (Israel's exodus from Egypt; the divine wind, or *kamikaze*, which destroyed the invading Mongol fleet off Japan; the death and RESURRECTION of JESUS CHRIST). Revelations may be similar to ordinary religious experience, but they have a creative originating power from which can flow an entire religious tradition.

Response. Response to the holy may take the form of participation in and acquiescence to the customs and rituals of a religious community or of a commitment of faith. Faith is not merely belief but an attitude of persons in which they commit themselves to the holy and acknowledge its claim upon them. In a deeply religious person, faith commitment tends to shape all of that person's life and character.

Beliefs. As religious traditions develop, they generate systems of belief with respect to both practice and doctrine. These systems serve to situate the members of the religious tradition in the world around them and to make

The reading of the Torah is a fundamental part of Jewish liturgical services. The Torah, or the first five books of the Bible, presents a system of moral and religious conduct and is revered as the divine revelation received by Moses on Mount Sinai.

Some Buddhist monks live solely on offerings from the laity, for possession of property is forbidden. Buddhism, one of the world's major religions, teaches that one of the paths to salvation is renunciation of all material goods.

intelligible this world in relation to the holy. In early or primitive traditions this practice and doctrine usually find expression in bodies of myth (see MYTHOLOGY) or in ritual law. In those traditions which develop an extensive literate class, THEOLOGY often comes to supplant myth as the vehicle for refining and elaborating belief. The more this happens, the more the belief system has to be evaluated. The importance attached to right belief ("orthodoxy") has varied from religion to religion and from period to period. It has loomed large in Christianity, as for example in the great Christological and Trinitarian controversies from the 3d century onward.

Rituals and Liturgy. Religious traditions almost invariably involve ritual and liturgical forms as well as systems of belief. These may take the form of SACRIFICE or SACRAMENT, passage rites (see PASSAGE, RITES OF), or invocations of God or the gods. The most important cultic acts are in most cases those performed by the entire community or a significant portion of it, although in many traditions private devotional forms such as prayer, fasting, and pilgrimage are also practiced. A distinction is often made between religion and magic in this context. In magic, attempts are made to manipulate divine forces through human acts. In truly cultic acts such as prayer and sacrifice, the prevailing attitude is one of awe, worship, and thanksgiving.

Participation in communal rituals marks a person as a member of the community, as being inside and integral to the community that is articulated in the system of beliefs. That in many traditions the disfavor of the community is

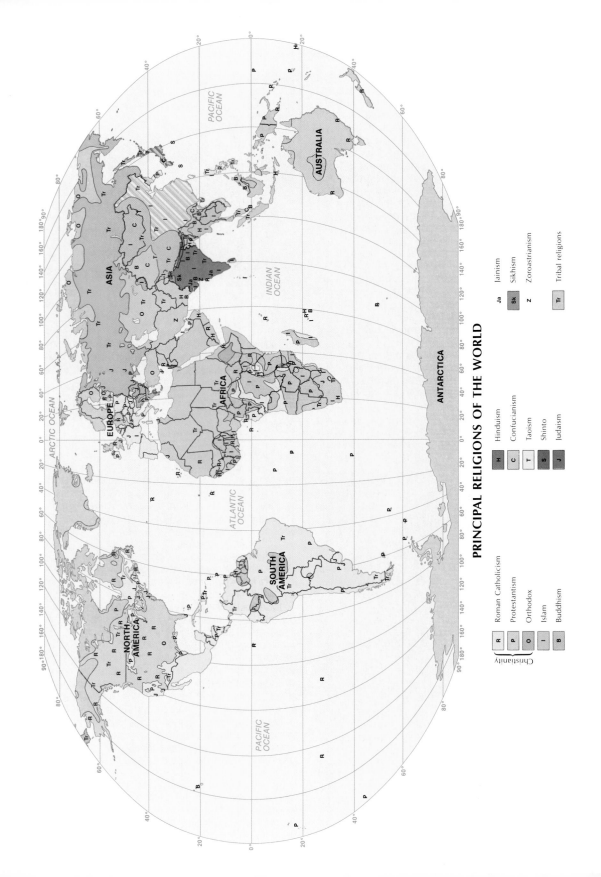

PRINCIPAL RELIGIONS OF THE WORLD

Christianity

R	Roman Catholicism
P	Protestantism
O	Orthodox
I	Islam
B	Buddhism

H	Hinduism
C	Confucianism
T	Taoism
S	Shinto
J	Judaism

Ja	Jainism
Sk	Sikhism
Z	Zoroastrianism
Tr	Tribal religions

expressed in its barring a person from the important cultic acts is not surprising because these acts insure the proper standing of the individual and community in relation to the holy.

Ethical Codes. Connected with beliefs is yet another aspect of religion, the possession of an ethical code incumbent upon the members of the community. This is particularly evident in highly structured societies such as India, where the CASTE system is an integral part of traditional Hinduism. MARDUK in ancient Babylon and Yahweh in ancient Israel were believed to be the authors of the laws of those nations, thus giving these laws the weight and prestige of holiness. The PROPHETS of Israel were social critics who claimed that righteous acts rather than cultic acts are the true expression of religion. As religions develop they come to place increasing stress on the ethical, and sometimes religion is almost totally absorbed into morality, with only a sense of the holiness of moral demands and a profound respect for them remaining.

Community. Although religious solitaries exist, most religion has a social aspect that leads its adherents to form a community, which may be more or less tightly organized. In earlier times the religious community could scarcely be distinguished from the community at large; all professed the same faith, and the ruler was both a political and a religious leader. In the course of time, however, religious and civil societies have become distinct and may even come into conflict. In modern secular states—the United States, for example—a plurality of religious communities coexist peacefully within a single political entity. Each religious community, whether in a pluralistic or homogeneous society, has its own organized structure. A common though by no means universal feature of these religious organizations is a priesthood (see PRIEST) charged with teaching and transmitting the faith and performing liturgical acts.

Forms of Religious Experience

The complex phenomenon described above constitutes what may be called the religious experience of humankind. In different religions and in different individuals, one or more of the characteristics mentioned may predominate, whereas others may be weak or almost nonexistent. This difference explains why religion is best treated as a polymorphous concept and why it is better to see religions as linked by variable family likenesses than by some constant but elusive essence.

Basic Forms. Even though many varieties of religious experience exist, they seem to occur in two basic forms. In the first, the sense of the holy is conjoined markedly with an awareness of human finitude. This conjunction is expressed in Friedrich SCHLEIERMACHER's characterization of religion as a "feeling of absolute dependence"; it might be called the negative approach to religious experience. The awareness of the holy is set against the foil of finitude, sinfulness, and meaninglessness. At an earlier stage in his career, however, Schleiermacher defined religion differently—as the "sense and taste for the Infinite." Here the awareness of the holy is conjoined with the human experience of transcendence, of going beyond every state of existence to a fuller existence that lures on the human being. This method may be called the affirmative approach.

Although one approach or another may dominate, both belong to the full range of religious experience. Both find their place in Rudolf OTTO's classic, *The Idea of the Holy* (1917; Eng. trans., 1923), as a person's encounter with the *mysterium tremendum et fascinans. Mysterium* points to the otherness of the holy; *tremendum* to its overwhelmingness in relation to human finitude; and *fascinans* to the lure that draws individuals out of and beyond themselves. Otto's work has been regarded as a masterly achievement in the phenomenology of religious experience.

Validity of Religious Experience. The question about the validity of religious experience must also be raised. Do religious people or worshiping communities encounter a holy reality that is outside of themselves and other than anything purely natural? Schleiermacher believed that the capacity for religious experience is universal in human beings. He therefore claimed that it could be accepted as self-authenticating and could take the place of the traditional proofs offered for the existence of God. Few people today would concede Schleiermacher's claim. Not only might they deny having the kinds of experiences he described, they might also suggest quite different interpretations for them. Many traditional revelations, which seemed to be miracles in a prescientific age, might now be judged as natural events or coincidences. Inner voices and private visions might be explained psychologically as subconscious mental processes. From Ludwig FEUERBACH to Sigmund FREUD, belief in God has been explained as a projection of the human mind; Karl MARX and other social analysts have seen religious belief as the product of socioeconomic forces. Each of these naturalistic explanations of religious belief has drawn attention to some element that enters into the religious complex, but it may be questioned whether such theories account exhaustively for the phenomenon of religion. The question about the validity of religious experience must ultimately be dealt with by returning to rational arguments for and against theism or, more broadly, for and against the existence of some holy reality, despite Schleiermacher's arguments to the contrary.

▬

Religion, Wars of The Wars of Religion were religious and political civil wars fought in France intermittently from 1562 to 1598, at a time when French Calvinists (HUGUENOTS) formed a strong and often aggressive minority. The wars were led by rival aristocratic factions during the rule of two weak monarchs, Charles IX (r. 1560–74) and HENRY III (r. 1574–89). From 1562 to 1576, the Huguenots, led at first by Louis I de Condé (see CONDÉ family) and Gaspard de COLIGNY, were supported only by external Protestant armies in their conflict with the Catholic crown. After 1572, when several thousand Huguenots were killed in the SAINT BARTHOLOMEW'S DAY MASSACRE, a third party of moderate Catholics, known as the Politiques, emerged under the family of Montmorency.

An ultra-Catholic party called the Holy League, led by the house of GUISE, was formed in 1576. When the Bourbon Protestant leader, Henry of Navarre (later HENRY IV), became heir to the throne in 1584, the league grew more militant, and it procured the assassination of Henry III in 1589. Henry IV (r. 1589–1610) eventually defeated the league, and in 1598 the Huguenots received a more stable form of toleration under the Edict of Nantes (see NANTES, EDICT OF).

During the period of the Wars of Religion, the French crown began to depend on ennobled lawyer-administrators, who held their offices almost as private property and alienated the warrior aristocracy. As the wars continued, however, the emergence of urban and peasant protest movements caused the higher orders to draw together and look to the crown for protection. The French social structure became less flexible, and the monarchy was able to initiate the system of absolutism that governed France for the next two centuries.

religious broadcasting   Religious broadcasting in the United States dates back to the earliest days of radio; the first radio broadcast, on Christmas Eve 1906, was religious in content. Regularly scheduled religious broadcasting began with the establishment of continuous programming in 1920. When television superseded radio in the 1950s, Roman Catholic bishop Fulton J. SHEEN, with his program "Life Is Worth Living," was among the medium's first superstars. Typical religious programming of the 1940s and '50s, however, was of the public-service variety. Broadcasting stations distributed free air time to religious groups—usually on Sunday morning—dividing it between Protestants, Catholics, and Jews.

The big networks had a close relationship with the liberal "mainline" Protestant denominations represented by the National Council of Churches. Protestant fundamentalist and evangelical groups, which did not belong to the council, were effectively locked out of national broadcasting and also found it difficult to buy time on local stations. In 1960, however, the Federal Communications Commission ruled that stations might sell time for religious programs and still count it as part of the public-service broadcasting that was required of them. Evangelical groups then became major purchasers of air time, and by the mid-1970s they dominated religious broadcasting.

The "electronic church" ministry of popular television evangelists such as Oral ROBERTS, Jim Bakker, Jerry FALWELL, M. G. "Pat" ROBERTSON, and Jimmy Swaggart has been widely criticized on a number of counts. TV evangelists support themselves by appealing to their audiences for donations, often offering premiums to respondents. Mainline church leaders claim that such "commercializing" cheapens religion. Others have charged that radio and TV preachers lure people from local pews with superior pulpit oratory, and that viewers then cease to contribute to local churches, giving their dollars to religious broadcasters instead. In 1984, however, the Gallup Organization released a study showing that regular consumers of religious broadcasting actually tend to be more in-volved in local congregations than nonviewers, and that their financial contributions to local churches are greater.

In 1987 scandal rocked the world of TV evangelism as Jim Bakker and his wife, Tammy Faye, were forced off the air amid charges of financial irregularities, drug abuse, and sexual misconduct; a year later Jimmy Swaggart was defrocked by the Assemblies of God after revelations that he had had contacts with prostitutes. In 1989, Bakker was convicted of fraud and sentenced to 45 years in prison.

Advocacy of conservative political causes by TV evangelists such as Falwell, founder of the MORAL MAJORITY, and Robertson, who was a candidate for the Republican presidential nomination in 1988, has also caused criticism.

religious cults   The term *cult* is popularly applied to groups characterized by some kind of faddish devotion to a person or practice that is significantly apart from the cultural mainstream.

Cults and Other Forms of Religious Organization. The most commonly used classification of religious organizations is as churches or sects.

Church refers to a religious organization claiming a monopoly on knowledge of the sacred, having a highly structured or formalized dogma and hierarchy, but also being flexible about membership requirements as the organization attempts to minister to the secular society of which it is a part. Sects, on the other hand, are protests against church attempts to accommodate to secular society. A sect views itself as a defender of doctrinal purity, protesting what it interprets as ecclesiastical laxity and excesses. As protectors of the true faith, sects tend to withdraw from the mainstream of worldly activities, to stress strict behavior codes, and to demand proof of commitment.

Cults have some of the same characteristics as sects, but they do not usually view themselves as rebelling against

More than 900 members of the California-based People's Temple, a cult led by the Rev. Jim Jones, died (1978) in a mass murder-suicide at the Temple's commune in Jonestown, Guyana.

The Hare Krishna sect, a cult based on Hindu religious beliefs, is one of the largest contemporary Hindu movements outside India. Over the last two decades the cult has flourished, especially in the United States, where there has been renewed interest in Eastern religion and philosophy.

established churches. Actually, the practices of cults are often considered to enrich the life of the parent church of which they may be a part. Cults do not ordinarily stress doctrinal issues or theological argument and refinement as much as they emphasize the individual's experience of a more personal and intense relationship with the divine. Most of these groups are ephemeral, seldom lasting beyond a single generation.

MYSTICISM is frequently a strong element in cult groups. Religious orders such as the FRANCISCANS began as cults built around the presence of a charismatic leader who emphasized a life-style dedicated to attaining high levels of spirituality. MORMONISM began as a cult, became a sect, and eventually evolved into a church. All the great world religions followed this same pattern of development as they accumulated members and formalized hierarchy and dogma.

Contemporary Cults. Cults are as old as recorded history, but contemporary interest in cults became amplified during the late 1960s and early 1970s as numbers of educated middle-class youths abandoned traditional religions and embraced beliefs and practices that were either culturally unprecedented (Eastern religions) or seemed to be throwbacks to an earlier era (Fundamentalist Christianity). During this period young people were increasingly found living in various types of religious communes and engaging in unconventional behavior, such as speaking in tongues (glossolalia), faith healing, meditating, and following leaders that conventional society tended to look upon with suspicion and distaste. Interest in cults turned to a combination of fascination and revulsion upon the mass suicide of the Jones cult in November 1978 (see JONESTOWN).

Some cults have a flexible, functional leadership, such as many groups in the CHARISMATIC MOVEMENT emanating from the mainline Christian religions, and others have mentors who control and orchestrate cult events, such as the Reverend Sun Myung MOON, leader of the Unification Church. Some Hindu gurus, such as Bhagwan Shree Rajneesh of the Rajneeshee sect, have been believed by their followers to be living embodiments of God. The com-

mon denominator of all the modern cults is an emphasis on community—as well as on direct experience of the divine. In a cult, participants often find a level of social support and acceptance that rivals what may be found in a nuclear family. Cult activity, which is often esoteric and defined as direct contact with the divine, generates a sense of belonging to something profound and of being a somebody. The modern cult gives adherents a sense of meaning in a world that has failed to provide them these things.

religious freedom   see FREEDOM OF RELIGION

---

religious orders   In the Christian tradition, religious orders are associations of men or women who seek to lead a life of prayer and pious practices and who are devoted often to some specific form of service. Members usually bind themselves publicly, or sometimes privately, by vows of poverty, chastity, and obedience to lead a dedicated life.

In the Roman Catholic church these associations are of several types. The religious orders, narrowly defined, include monastic orders (of which the largest is the BENEDICTINES), mendicant orders or friars (such as the FRANCISCANS or the DOMINICANS), and canons regular (priests living in a community attached to a specific church). All of these make solemn vows and say office in choir. In general they all have their origin in the Middle Ages. Clerks regular are societies of priests who make vows and are joined together for the purpose of priestly ministry; the JESUITS are a well-known example. Societies in which priests, brothers, or sisters, bound by vows, live in community to perform certain kinds of services are called religious congregations and include, among others, the Passionists, Redemptorists, and Vincentians. Religious institutes such as the Christian Brothers are usually composed of unordained persons who take vows and devote themselves to such tasks as teaching. Members of secular institutes are generally laypersons who do not live in community or wear a particular kind of garb but who make promises of poverty, chastity, and obedience and live an ordinary life within conventional circumstances. Roman Catholic orders of nuns or sisters, generally smaller but more numerous than those of their male counterparts, are devoted primarily to teaching. Some communities are enclosed—the monks or nuns rarely leaving their monastery or convent—and devoted to the contemplative life.

In the Eastern church, where MONASTICISM had its beginnings, religious orders are not differentiated as they are in the West, and most Eastern Orthodox religious are monastics.

Following the Reformation, monasticism disappeared in Protestant countries, but the influence of the OXFORD MOVEMENT in the 19th century brought about the reestablishment of religious orders among Anglicans (Episcopalians).

---

reliquary [rel'-uh-kwair-ee]   A reliquary is a receptacle, usually richly decorated and made of precious materials, for the safekeeping or exhibition of a relic, an object venerated for its association with a holy person, often a martyr. Relics are often credited with curative or miraculous powers and are associated with various religions throughout the world. The cult of holy relics in the Christian church began around the 7th century AD, and reliquaries were numerous by the 10th century. The Crusades were a stimulus to the traffic in relics, many being brought back to Europe by the Crusaders for presentation to monasteries and cathedrals, where they became the goals of pilgrimages.

Reliquaries took many forms: caskets, miniature church buildings such as the Eltenberg Reliquary (c.1170; Victoria and Albert Museum, London), and figural works—for example, the reliquary bust of Charlemagne (1215; Aachen Cathedral). Related to these are "anatomical" reliquaries in the form of the contained relic, such as those for the arm of Saint Magnus and the leg of Saint Theodore (both 11th century; Saint Mark's Basilica, Venice). A flat, rectangular form called *staurotheke* was devised during the 11th century to contain relics of the True Cross (the one on which Christ was crucified). Small reliquaries were also made to wear as amulets. The SAINTE-CHAPELLE in Paris was built (1248) in the form of a reliquary to house the Crown of Thorns.

—

rem   Rem, an acronym for roentgen equivalent man, is a special unit used to measure the absorption of ionizing radiation by human soft tissue (see RADIATION INJURY). One rem is equal to one RAD, a dosage unit, multiplied by a factor that depends on the type of radiation and its relative biological effectiveness (RBE). In SI units (see UNITS, PHYSICAL) the equivalent unit, the sievert, equals 100 rem.

—

Remarque, Erich Maria [ruh-mahrk']   Erich Maria Remarque, b. Erich Paul Remark in Osnabrück, Germany, June 22, 1898, d. Sept. 25, 1970, became world famous following the publication of his first novel, ALL QUIET ON THE WESTERN FRONT (1929; Eng. trans., 1929), one

Erich Maria Remarque is best remembered as the author of one of the most highly regarded novels dealing with World War I, All Quiet on the Western Front *(1929).*

of the most influential works of the 20th century. Remarque drew on his experiences as a young soldier in World War I for the book, whose title contrasts ironically with the naturalistically described horrors of a "quiet" day on the front. A sequel, *The Road Back* (1931; Eng. trans., 1931), and *Three Comrades* (1938; Eng. trans., 1937) had more limited success. With his books banned (1933) by the Nazis and his citizenship abrogated (1938), Remarque emigrated (1939) to the United States. Later novels, dealing mostly with war or exile, include *Spark of Life* (1952; Eng. trans., 1951), *The Black Obelisk* (1956; Eng. trans., 1957), and *The Night in Lisbon* (1963; Eng. trans., 1964). Only *Arc de Triomphe* (1946; Eng. trans., 1946) achieved widespread success.

—

Rembrandt [rem'-brant]   The Dutch artist Rembrandt Harmenszoon van Rijn, b. July 15?, 1606, d. Oct. 4, 1669, was one of the greatest masters of European art. His paintings, drawings, and etchings have been admired and avidly collected since the 17th century. They express a range of emotions and moods that convey Rembrandt's sensitivity to humanity and to nature. Above all, his works reveal a profound understanding of complex psychological interactions.

During his early career Rembrandt made many studies of peasants, the elderly, and members of his family in paintings, prints, and drawings. He also produced a number of self-portraits. In a series of etchings dating from the late 1620s, he experimented with different expressions and with CHIAROSCURO, or contrasting light and shadow effects, to determine how it could enhance the drama of a composition. In the *Presentation in the Temple* (1631; Mauritshuis, The Hague), Rembrandt's chiaroscuro effect focuses attention on the main figure group by shrouding the surrounding space in darkness.

Rembrandt apparently moved to Amsterdam about 1632 because of the opportunities available there in PORTRAITURE. In his first major portrait commission, *The Anatomy Lesson of Dr. Tulp* (1632; Mauritshuis), he used strong chiaroscuro accents and expressive poses to transform a staid group portrait into an animated gathering. This facility with group portraits greatly enhanced Rembrandt's reputation, and for the remainder of the decade he was at the height of his fame.

The culmination of Rembrandt's popular success as an artist was his largest work, *Night Watch* (1642; originally *Militia Company of Captain Frans Banning Cocq*; Rijksmuseum, Amsterdam). The drama and excitement of this painting, which depicts figures apparently readying themselves for a procession, provides yet another example of Rembrandt's ability to transform a traditional group portrait into a dramatic event.

The 1640s were a period of transition for Rembrandt. The exuberance of his earlier works gave way to more restrained treatment, especially after his wife, Saskia, died (1642) shortly following the birth of Titus (d. 1668), Rembrandt's only surviving son. Rembrandt turned his attention to such quiet and reflective scenes

(Above) *Rembrandt, whose ability to dramatize facial expression is unrivaled, painted several portraits of himself. In this* Self Portrait *(1658), done in his 52nd year, he is transfixed by anxious introspection. (Kunsthistorisches Museum, Vienna.)* (Left) *Commissioned to paint a philosopher, Rembrandt executed* Aristotle Contemplating the Bust of Homer *(1653). Aristotle, dressed as a man of Rembrandt's time, is surrounded by darkness but bathed in light that seems to emanate from the poet's image. (Metropolitan Museum of Art, New York City.)*

as that depicted in his etching called *The Hundred Guilder Print* (mid-1640s), which represents Christ as a warm and understanding teacher preaching to the poor and infirm.

Rembrandt's paintings of the 1650s and 1660s gained in power and conviction through his ability to focus on the essential elements of the pictorial subject. One of the most impressive of his mature paintings is *Jacob Blessing the Sons of Joseph* (1656; Gemäldegalerie, Kassel). Leonardo da Vinci's *Last Supper,* known to Rembrandt through a 16th-century print, was the compositional basis for a number of his paintings, including the *Syndics* (1661–62; Rijksmuseum) and his *Conspiracy of Julius Civilis* (1661 or 1662; Nationalmuseum, Stockholm).

Although Rembrandt was not a fashionable artist during his later years and had many financial difficulties, including a declaration of insolvency (1656), the myths surrounding his isolation from Dutch society are ill-founded, as he continued to receive important commissions until his death.

Remembrance of Things Past see PROUST, MARCEL

Remington, Frederic An American artist who recorded the rapidly disappearing Wild West, Frederic Sackrider Remington, b. Canton, N.Y., Oct. 1 or 4, 1861, d. Dec. 26, 1909, first made his reputation as an illustrator and painter. In 1881 he began wandering around the western United States, working for a time as a cowboy. He later followed the campaigns of the U.S. cavalry. His first commission for *Harper's Weekly* illustrated an incident that occurred in the last great Indian war led by Geronimo. No matter how exciting the scenes, Remington's literal definition of the blue-jacketed pony soldiers and Indians and the naturalistic relation of form and space save his work from sensationalism. In 1895 he began to model his cowboys, Indians, and troopers in clay. Such sculptures as his bronze *Bronco Buster* (1895; one version in New-York Historical Society, New York City) contain all the details characteristic of his paintings.

During the Spanish-American War, Remington worked as an artist and correspondent in Cuba, supplying illustrations for periodicals. The Old West, however, remained his favorite subject. *Comin' through the Rye* (1902; Metropolitan Museum of Art, New York City) presents four uproarious cowboys riding out on ponies whose hooves

Trooper of the Plains *(1868), a small bronze sculpture by Frederic Remington, displays this 19th-century artist's fascination with the American pioneer. (The Thomas Gilcrease Inst. of American History & Art, Tulsa, OK.)*

barely touch the ground. The group rejects such traditional sculptural principles as the expression of weight and support and suspended action in favor of levitation and directed movement.

Remonstrants

Remonstrants [rem-ahn'-struhnts]   The name Remonstrants was given to the followers of the Dutch Protestant reformer Jacobus Arminius (1560–1609; see ARMINIANISM), who in 1610 drew up a document known as the Remonstrance. This document, after asserting the primacy of Scripture over creeds, set forth a revision of CALVINISM: Christ died for all, not only for the elect; divine GRACE is not irresistible; Christians can fall from grace, through free will, and be lost. These affirmations constituted a rejection of the most extreme Calvinist interpretation of PREDESTINATION.

The Remonstrants were condemned by the Dutch Reformed Church at the Synod of Dort (1618–19). Fourteen years of persecution followed, during which their services were forbidden and their clergy silenced or exiled. Among the refugees arose a Remonstrant Reformed Brotherhood, which, after the ban was lifted in 1623, became the Remonstrant Reformed Church Community. It continued as a small free church after 1795, when full toleration was established.

remora

remora [rem'-uh-ruh]   Remoras are about nine species of long-bodied fishes, ranging from approximately 15 cm to 1 m (6 in to 3.3 ft) in length, that spend much of their lives attached to sharks, whales, and other large marine bodies. Attachment is by means of an oval disk on the top of the head. The disk is a modification of the spiny first dorsal fin, with the spines split in two and spread downward to form about 11 to 24 movable cross-ridges that

divide the disk into many small, shallow chambers. To attach to an object, the remora presses the disk against it, sealing the chambers; the cross-ridges are then raised, forming a partial vacuum that holds the fish securely. Remoras are commonly thought to attach to feed on leftover scraps of their hosts' meals or on their external parasites, but instead it appears likely that the remoras have primarily evolved an almost energy-free method of travel. Remoras, constituting the family Echeneididae, are found worldwide in warm seas.

remote control   SEE AUTOMATION; FEEDBACK; SERVOMECHANISM

remote sensing

remote sensing   Remote sensing is the science of detecting and measuring or analyzing a substance or object from a distance.

There are two broad classes of remote sensors: active and passive. Active remote sensors—for example, radar—transmit some form of energy such as an electromagnetic pulse and detect the energy reflected or otherwise returned from the subject. Passive remote sensors, such as cameras, depend on emissions or reflections of energy from natural sources.

Applications. The first uses of remote sensing were primarily military, but environmental and energy-related applications are now the most promising. Some of these include: hydrological applications, such as precipitation measurement, monitoring snow depth and ice cover, flood control, hydroelectric generation, and water transport management; agricultural applications, such as monitoring crop types, acreage, stage of growth, soil moisture, blights or infestations, and expected yields; and forestry applications, such as monitoring types of trees, stage of growth, and lightning and fires.

Meteorological applications encompass monitoring severe storms, detecting and measuring precipitation, monitoring clouds and their movement, measuring winds and turbulence, and monitoring insolation (the daily influx of

Remote-sensing equipment is often carried in aircraft to gather and record data about the Earth's surface and atmosphere. Types shown include nonimaging electromagnetic systems (1); microwave radar systems (2); photographic optical systems (3); television systems (4); systems for measuring gamma radiation (5); systems for sampling air (6); and systems for measuring the magnetic field (7).

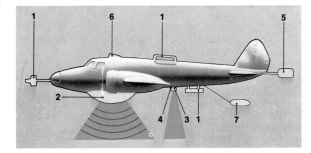

solar energy). Ecological and pollution applications consist of biological monitoring, thermal pollution (waste-heat) monitoring, and air- and water-pollution monitoring. Geographic and geologic applications include land-use and terrain mapping, geological mapping, and detection of mineral deposits. Oceanographic applications encompass monitoring of waves, currents, temperature, salinity, turbidity, and other parameters and phenomena. Other diverse applications include air-traffic control, probing other planets and deep space, and law enforcement.

Principles and Instrumentation. Most active and passive remote sensors employ a detecting or sensing system that scans or surveils the subject, a recording system that stores the information received, and an analysis or display system. Sometimes a combined analysis and display system is operated concurrently with the sensing system in order to aid in data gathering and to provide some preliminary information. In that case recordings are made and later analyzed in the typical manner. The displays are two-dimensional, usually composed of many scan lines from the sensor similar to aerial photographs or television pictures.

The term *signature* is applied in remote sensing to any identifying feature that appears in the analysis or display process through which a desired subject can be positively identified against what may be a complex background or surroundings. For example, it may be necessary to identify a particular mineral, crop blight, or type of air or water pollution. Signature, as applied to imagery, usually refers to visual characteristics that identify the subject and separate it from other similar objects. However, other types of signatures may be much more complex, requiring spectral analysis or other techniques.

Remote sensors may be surface-based, stationary or mobile, on land or sea; airborne in aircraft, helicopters, or balloons; or carried aboard spacecraft, such as satellites, a space shuttle, or a space station. These various bases are usually referred to as sensor platforms. The resolution, or detail with which a remote sensor can monitor a subject, generally depends on the distance from the sensor platform to the subject, and/or the wavelength used. Remote sensors that employ the shortest wavelengths (highest frequencies) usually provide the best resolution of the subject.

▬

Renaissance [ren'-uh-sahns] The term Renaissance, describing the period of European history from the early 14th to the late 16th century, is derived from the French word for rebirth, and originally referred to the revival of the values and artistic styles of classical antiquity during that period, especially in Italy. To Giovanni BOCCACCIO in the 14th century, the concept applied to contemporary Italian efforts to imitate the poetic style of the ancient Romans. In 1550 the art historian Giorgio VASARI used the word *rinascita* (rebirth) to describe the return to the ancient Roman manner of painting by GIOTTO DI BONDONE about the beginning of the 14th century.

It was only later that the word *Renaissance* acquired a broader meaning. Voltaire in the 18th century classified the Renaissance in Italy as one of the great ages of hu-

This painting is probably a likeness of Petrarch, a primary force in the development of the humanism characteristic of Renaissance thought. Petrarch inaugurated the age in which the intellectual focus shifted from theology to the development and experience of the individual.

man cultural achievement. In the 19th century, Jules Michelet and Jakob BURCKHARDT popularized the idea of the Renaissance as a distinct historical period heralding the modern age, characterized by the rise of the individual, scientific inquiry and geographical exploration, and the growth of secular values. In the 20th century the term was broadened to include other revivals of classical culture, such as the Carolingian Renaissance of the 9th century or the Renaissance of the 12th century. Emphasis on medieval renaissances tended to undermine a belief in the unique and distinctive qualities of the Italian Renaissance, and some historians of science, technology, and economy even denied the validity of the term. Today the concept of the Renaissance is firmly secured as a cultural and intellectual movement; most scholars would agree that there is a distinctive Renaissance style in music, literature, and the arts.

The Renaissance as a Historical Period. The new age began in Padua and other urban communes of northern Italy in the 14th century, where lawyers and notaries imitated ancient Latin style and studied Roman archaeology. The key figure in this study of the classical heritage was PETRARCH, who spent most of his life attempting to understand ancient culture and captured the enthusiasm of popes, princes, and emperors who wanted to learn more of Italy's past. Petrarch's success stirred countless others to follow literary careers hoping for positions in government and high society. In the next generations, students of Latin rhetoric and the classics, later known as humanists, became chancellors of Venice and Florence, secretaries at the papal court, and tutors and orators in the despotic courts of northern Italy. Renaissance HUMANISM became the major intellectual movement of the period, and its achievements became permanent.

By the 15th century intensive study of the Greek as well as Latin classics, ancient art and archaeology, and classical history, had given Renaissance scholars a more sophisticated view of antiquity. The ancient past was now viewed as past, to be admired and imitated, but not to be revived.

Desiderius Erasmus, seen in a portrait by Hans Holbein the Younger, is considered the greatest classicist of the northern Renaissance. (Louvre, Paris.)

The culture of Renaissance Italy was distinguished by many highly competitive and advanced urban areas. Unlike England and France, Italy possessed no dominating capital city, but developed a number of centers for regional states: Milan for Lombardy, Rome for the Papal States, Florence and Siena for Tuscany, and Venice for northeastern Italy. Smaller centers of Renaissance culture developed around the brilliant court life at Ferrara, Mantua, and Urbino. The chief patrons of Renaissance art and literature were the merchant classes of Florence and Venice, which created in the Renaissance palace their own distinctive home and workplace, fitted for both business and rearing and nurture of the next generation of urban rulers. The later Renaissance was marked by a growth of bureaucracy, an increase in state authority in the areas of justice and taxation, and the creation of larger regional states. During the interval of relative peace from the mid-15th century until the French invasions of 1494, Italy experienced a great flowering of culture, especially in Florence and Tuscany under the MEDICI. The brilliant period of artistic achievement continued into the 16th century—the age of LEONARDO DA VINCI, RAPHAEL, TITIAN, and MICHELANGELO—but as Italy began to fall under foreign domination, the focus gradually shifted to other parts of Europe.

During the 15th century, students from many European nations had come to Italy to study the classics, philosophy, and the remains of antiquity, eventually spreading the Renaissance north of the Alps. Italian literature and art, even Italian clothing and furniture designs were imitated in France, Spain, England, the Netherlands, and Germany, but as Renaissance values came to the north, they were transformed. Northern humanists such as Desiderius ERASMUS of the Netherlands and John Colet (*c.*1467–1519) of England planted the first seeds of the Reformation when they endeavored to discover the original intent and meaning of the New Testament by applying to it the critical historical methods developed in Italy. The northern humanists created a flexible, colloquial Latin style so that their writings would have a broad appeal. Through their efforts, knowledge of classical mythology, ancient history, and Greek and Latin literary forms became widespread and was soon absorbed into the vernacular literature.

Philosophy, Science, and Social Thought. No single philosophy or ideology dominated the intellectual life of the Renaissance. Early humanists had stressed a flexible approach to the problems of society and the active life in service of one's fellow human beings. In the second half of the 15th century, Renaissance thinkers such as Marsilio FICINO at the Platonic Academy in Florence turned to more metaphysical speculation. Though favored by the humanists, Plato did not replace Aristotle as the dominant philosopher in the universities. Rather there was an effort at philosophical syncretism, to combine apparently conflicting philosophies, and find common ground for agreement about the truth as did Giovanni PICO DELLA MIRANDOLA in his *Oration on the Dignity of Man* (1486). Renaissance science consisted mainly of the study of medicine, physics, and mathematics, depending on ancient masters, such as Galen, Aristotle, and Euclid. Experimental science in anatomy and alchemy led to discoveries both within and outside university settings.

Under the veneer of magnificent works of art and the refined court life described in Baldassare CASTIGLIONE's *Book of the Courtier*, the Renaissance had a darker side. Warfare was common, and death by pestilence and violence was frequent. Interest in the occult, magic, and astrology was widespread, and the officially sanctioned persecution for witchcraft began during the Renaissance period. Many intellectuals felt a profound pessimism about the evils and corruptions of society as seen in the often savage humanist critiques of Poggio Bracciolini (1380–1459) and Desiderius Erasmus. Sir Thomas MORE, in his *Utopia*, prescribed the radical solution of a classless, communal society, bereft of Christianity and guided by the dictates of natural reason. The greatest Renaissance thinker, Nicolò MACHIAVELLI, in his *Prince* and *Discourses*, constructed a realistic science of human nature aiming at the reform of Italian society and the creation of a secure civil life. Machiavelli's republican principles informed by a pragmatic view of power politics and the necessity of violent change were the most original contribution of the Renaissance to the modern world.

Influence. The Renaissance lives on in established canons of taste and literature and in a distinctive Renaissance style in art, music, and architecture, the last often revived. It also provided the model of many-sided achievement of the creative genius, the "universal man," exemplified by Leonardo da Vinci or Leon Battista ALBERTI. Finally, the Renaissance spawned the great creative vernacular literature of the late 16th century: the earthy fantasies of RABELAIS, the worldly essays of MONTAIGNE, the probing analysis of the human condition in the plays of William SHAKESPEARE and in the work of Miguel de CERVANTES.

Renaissance art and architecture The term *Renaissance,* adopted from the French equivalent of the

Italian word *rinascita,* meaning literally "rebirth," describes the radical and comprehensive changes that took place in European culture during the 15th and 16th centuries. Italian scholars and critics of this period proclaimed that their age had progressed beyond the barbarism of the past and had found its inspiration, and its closest parallel, in the civilizations of ancient Greece and Rome.

The Renaissance in Italy

The "rebirth" of art in Italy was connected with the rediscovery of ancient philosophy, literature, and science. Secular themes became increasingly important to artists, and with the revived interest in antiquity came a new repertoire of subjects drawn from Greek and Roman history and mythology. The emergence of the artist as a creator, rather than a mere artisan, was both a result and a prime cause of the development of Renaissance art. As the social role of the artist changed, so did attitudes toward art. Art was valued not merely as a vehicle for religious and social didacticism, but as a mode of personal expression to be judged on aesthetic grounds.

Although the evolution of Italian Renaissance art was a continuous process, it is traditionally divided into three major phases: Early, High, and Late Renaissance. Some scholars date the beginning of the Italian Renaissance from the appearance of GIOTTO DI BONDONE in the early 14th century; others regard his prodigious achievements in naturalistic art as an isolated phenomenon. According to the second view, the consistent development of Renaissance style began only with the generation of artists active in Florence at the beginning of the 15th century.

The Early Renaissance. The principal members of the first generation of Renaissance artists—DONATELLO in sculpture, Filippo BRUNELLESCHI in architecture, and MASACCIO in painting—shared many important characteristics. Early Renaissance artists sought to create art forms consistent with the appearance of the natural world and with their experience of human personality and behavior. The challenge of accurate representation as it concerned the mass, weight, and movement of sculptural form, or the pictorial considerations of measurable space and the effects of light and color, was addressed in the spirit of intense and methodical inquiry.

Although these artists were keenly observant of natural phenomena, they made an effort to go beyond straightforward transcription of nature, to instill the work of art with ideal, intangible qualities, endowing it with a beauty and significance greater and more permanent than that actually found in nature. These characteristics—the rendering of ideal forms rather than literal appearance and the concept of the physical world as the vehicle or imperfect em-

(Left) *Donatello's bronze* David *(c.1430–32), the first nude statue in the round to be made since ancient times, embodies the revitalized classicism that infused Italian art during the Early Renaissance. (Bargello, Florence.)*

(Below) *Florence Cathedral, also known as Santa Maria del Fiore and as the Duomo, was begun by Arnolfo di Cambio in 1295 and, after innumerable enlargements and delays, completed in 1462. In 1420, Filippo Brunelleschi, the first great architect and engineer of the Early Renaissance, began the vast dome.*

bodiment of monumental spiritual beauty—were to remain fundamental to the nature and development of Italian Renaissance art.

The term *Early Renaissance* characterizes virtually all the art of the 15th century. Florence, the cradle of Renaissance artistic thought, remained one of the undisputed centers of innovation. About 1450 a new generation of artists that included such masters as Pollaiuolo (see POLLAIUOLO family) and Sandro BOTTICELLI came to the fore in Florence. Other Italian cities—Milan, Urbino, Ferrara, Venice, Padua, Naples—became powerful rivals in the spreading wave of change. Leon Battista ALBERTI's work in Rimini and Mantua represented the most progressive architecture of the new HUMANISM; Andrea MANTEGNA's paintings in Padua displayed a personal formulation of linear perspective, antiquarianism, and realistic technique; and Giovanni Bellini's (see BELLINI family) poetic classicism exemplified the growing strength of the Venetian school.

By the late 15th century the novelty of the first explosive advances of Renaissance style had given way to a general acceptance of such basic notions as proportion,

(Above) *In* The Virgin and Child with Saint Anne *(begun c. 1501), Leonardo da Vinci exhibits all of the High Renaissance achievements in technique and approach. The solidly modeled figures, bathed in serene light, are silhouetted against a spectral mountain landscape. (Louvre, Paris.)*

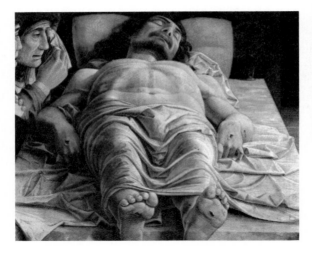

(Above) *In* The Dead Christ *(c. 1480), Andrea Mantegna transforms an exercise in foreshortening into an unforgettable expression of grief and suffering. (Brera, Milan.)*

(Right) Venus and Mars, *painted (c. 1480) by Sandro Botticelli, is imbued with the same fervor as his religious works. (National Gallery, London.)*

contraposto (twisted pose), and linear perspective; consequently many artists sought means of personal expression within this relatively well-established repertoire of style and technique. Early Renaissance painting seems to fall short of thoroughly convincing figural representation, however, and its expression of human emotion is stylized rather than real.

The High Renaissance. The art of the High Renaissance sought a general, unified effect of pictorial representation or architectural composition. The High Renaissance style endured for only a brief period (c.1495–1520) and was created by a few artists of genius, among them LEONARDO DA VINCI, Donato BRAMANTE, MICHELANGELO, RAPHAEL, and TITIAN. Leonardo da Vinci's unfinished *Adoration of the Magi* (1481; Uffizi Gallery, Florence) is regarded as a landmark of unified pictorial composition, later realized fully in his fresco *The Last Supper* (1495–97; Santa Maria delle Grazie, Milan). Michelangelo's talents are exemplified by the tomb of Julius II (c.1510–15), San Pietro in Vincoli, Rome; the Medici Chapel (1519–34), Florence; the SISTINE CHAPEL ceiling (1508–12) and *Last Judgment* (1536–41), Rome; and the cupola of SAINT PETER'S BASILICA (begun 1546)—works that represent major and inimitable accomplishments in the separate fields of sculpture, painting, and architecture. Raphael, a man of very different temperament, evoked, in paintings of Madonnas and in frescoes, not overwhelming forces but sublime harmony and lyric, graceful beauty.

The Late Renaissance. A major watershed in the development of Italian Renaissance art was the sack of Rome in 1527, which temporarily ended the city's role as a source of patronage and compelled artists to travel to other centers in Italy, France, and Spain. Even before the death of Raphael, in 1520, anticlassical tendencies had begun to manifest themselves in Roman art. Some early exponents of MANNERISM, including Jacopo Carucci PONTORMO, PARMIGIANINO, and ROSSO FIORENTINO, contributed to the development of a style that reached its most extreme expression in the work of Giorgio VASARI and Giovanni da BOLOGNA. Mannerism was an aesthetic move-

Raphael's tender Madonna of the Chair *(1513–14) is perhaps the most intimate of his many versions of the subject. Intended for private devotion, the painting is in the tondo (circular) form fashionable in the High Renaissance. (Pitti Palace, Florence.)*

ment that valued highly refined grace and elegance—the beautiful *maniera*, or style, from which Mannerism takes its name. Although the fundamental characteristics of Late Renaissance style were shared by many artists, this period, dominated by Mannerism, was marked by artistic individuality—a quality demonstrated to its fullest extent by the late works of Michelangelo.

The Renaissance in the North

The Netherlands. Fifteenth-century northern artists did not intensively cultivate classical sources, nor did they show the predilection for abstract and theoretical systems of representation that characterized Italian art. Nonetheless, the radical transformation of northern artistic traditions that took place during the 15th and 16th centuries can be appropriately described as a Renaissance.

Jan van EYCK, the supreme master of the Netherlandish school, is recognized as having been the first to exploit the full potential of the new medium of oil painting. In his masterwork, the *Ghent Altarpiece* (1432; Church of Saint Bavo, Ghent), and in portraits such as the wedding portrait of Giovanni Arnolfini and his wife (1534; National Gallery, London), this technique is used with refinement to render minute detail, delicate textures, and the luminous effects of light.

The enigmatic Master of Flémalle (see CAMPIN, Robert) made an equally important contribution to the vivid, miniaturizing realism of Netherlandish painting. In his two most famous works, the Dijon *Nativity* (c.1420; Musée des Beaux-Arts, Dijon) and the *Merode Altarpiece*

The Tempietto, built in 1502 by the High Renaissance architect Donato Bramante, stands in the courtyard of Rome's San Pietro in Montorio over the traditional site of Saint Peter's crucifixion.

Michelangelo's marble Pietà *was commissioned in 1497 and completed by 1500, when the great High Renaissance master was in his mid-20s. The figures are carved with extreme delicacy, and the entire surface is highly polished, in the Early Renaissance sculptural tradition that Michelangelo had learned in Florence. (Saint Peter's Basilica, Vatican city.)*

(*c.*1426; The Cloisters, New York City), the Master of Flémalle, like van Eyck, combined his direct, fresh observation of nature with elaborate symbolic structures within his religious scenes.

Rogier van der WEYDEN, famous for portraits and altarpieces such as the *Descent from the Cross* (1439–43; Prado, Madrid), worked in a more idealistic vein, instilling his compositions with unprecedented monumentality and emotional intensity. Van der Weyden exercised a dominant influence on many later figures including Dirk BOUTS, Hans MEMLING, and Gerard DAVID.

The greatest painter of the late 15th century, Hugo van der GOES, was active in Ghent and Bruges. His *Portinari Altarpiece* (1474–76; Uffizi Gallery, Florence), depicting the Nativity, is a work of crucial importance because it was executed for the Florentine church of San Egidio and introduced many Italian artists to the earthy and lively realism of Netherlandish oil-painting technique.

Germany. German art of the 15th century was dominated by many local, independent schools. Largely based on the Gothic International Style, German art received important influences from the Netherlands that intensified as the century progressed. In Basel the painter Konrad WITZ created a severe and impressive style indebted to van Eyck; the painter-engraver Martin SCHONGAUER emerged, through his graphic work, as an incredibly refined draftsman, eventually to serve as a model for Albrecht DÜRER.

The Renaissance in Germany is dominated by the great genius of Dürer, both a painter and an engraver. His astonishing and unequaled performances in woodcut and engraving permanently transformed the graphic arts and greatly enhanced their potential (see ENGRAVING).

The art of Dürer's contemporary Mathias GRÜNEWALD, most fully represented by the multipaneled *Isenheim Altarpiece* (1515; Musée d'Unterlinden, Colmar, France), is by contrast filled with high-pitched expressive power conveyed through agonized human forms and brilliant, piercing color schemes. The visionary and irrational aspects of Grünewald's art, rooted in the medieval world, were to repeat themselves many times in the subsequent development of German art.

The DANUBE SCHOOL—whose principal members, Lucas CRANACH the Elder, Albrecht ALTDORFER, and Wolf Huber, reflected an extraordinary awakening of interest in landscape painting—was a loose grouping of masters who shared a common sympathy for miniaturizing anticlassical tendencies derived from late Gothic art.

Hans HOLBEIN the Younger, originally a member of the Augsburg school, later practiced in Basel, and finally in England as court painter to Henry VIII, developing in the process a psychologically penetrating style of portraiture.

The Descent from the Cross *(1439–43), the central panel of a lost altarpiece, is perhaps Rogier van der Weyden's most impressive achievement. (Prado, Madrid.)*

France. In the 15th century the art of France, like that of Germany, came increasingly under the influence of the Netherlandish school. The painter Jean FOUQUET and the anonymous master responsible for the celebrated *Villeneauve Pietà* (*c.*1460; Louvre, Paris) were also aware of contemporary Italian art. By introducing elements of clarity and stability in their work, they achieved a unique combination of formal weight and factual and portraitlike design.

At the beginning of the 16th century Italian styles became extremely popular in France because artists such as

Leonardo da Vinci, Benvenuto CELLINI, Francesco PRIMATICCIO, Rosso Fiorentino, and Niccolò dell'Abbate (c.1512–71) were employed there by Francis I. Features of Italian Renaissance style were adopted at first by French artists in a rather superficial manner, producing such hybrid structures as the Château de Blois (1515–20), which incorporates Italian decorative architectural elements with the medieval-style architecture.

Architecture burgeoned with the construction of the massive and luxurious Château de Chambord and Château de FONTAINEBLEAU. The court workshop established at the Château de Fontainebleau became an important center, known as the school of Fontainebleau (see FONTAINEBLEAU, SCHOOL OF), that in its exaggerated elegance and complex fantasies combining sculpture, painting, and architecture, represented a high point in the development of Mannerism.

The Château de Fontainebleau, one of the largest palaces in France, was begun by Francis I in 1528. In the Fountain Court, seen here across the Carp Pond, the inner left wing and the Gallery of Francis I at its back are parts of the original Renaissance palace.

One of the most brilliant paintings of the German Renaissance is The Resurrection *from the* Isenheim Altarpiece *(1515) by Matthias Grünewald. (Musée d'Unterlinden, Colmar, France.)*

By the mid-16th century a number of highly talented French masters made their appearance, among them the painter Francois Clouet (see CLOUET family), who developed a highly polished and sensuous style of court portraiture, and the architect Philibert DELORME, who reasserted a classical style based on measure and proportion.

See also: FLEMISH ART AND ARCHITECTURE; FRENCH ART AND ARCHITECTURE; GERMAN ART AND ARCHITECTURE; ITALIAN ART AND architecture.

Renaissance music The Renaissance is characterized musically by a style of predominantly vocal POLYPHONY that prevailed roughly from 1420 to 1600. Until about 1500, however, this style had only a slight relationship to Renaissance humanism; rather, it was differentiated from the late medieval style that preceded it by such purely musical features as its greater melodic and rhythmic integration, enlarged range and texture, and subjection to harmonic principles of order. After 1500 this integrated style developed into distinct vocal and instrumental idioms, and vocal music, under the influence of humanism, became increasingly devoted to the expression of texts. This development weakened the dominance of polyphony, which some musicians considered inimical to expression. By 1600 harmony had come to dominate polyphony, musical coherence was sometimes subordinated to expression, and instrumental music was liberated from the forms and styles of vocal music. At that point Renaissance musical style was eclipsed by a new style—the baroque.

Practitioners of the new polyphonic style in the 15th century included Guillaume DUFAY, JOSQUIN DES PREZ, Jacob OBRECHT, and Jean d'OKEGHEM. They cultivated the forms of the CHANSON, MASS, and MOTET. The style reached its peak in the 16th century, in the works of William

BYRD, Roland de LASSUS, Giovanni Pierluigi da PALESTRINA, and Tomás Luis de VICTORIA. Orlando GIBBONS and Thomas TALLIS reflected the simpler style of Protestant music. Humanism in secular music gave rise to the MADRIGALS of Carlo GESUALDO and Claudio MONTEVERDI, the lute songs of John DOWLAND, the harpsichord music of John BULL, the instrumental ensemble music of the GABRIELI family, and the eventual replacement of polyphony with FIGURED BASS accompaniments.

Renan, Ernest [ruh-nahn']   Ernest Renan, b. Feb. 28, 1823, d. Oct. 2, 1892, was a French scholar whose *Life of Jesus* (1863; Eng. trans., 1864) generated enormous controversy because it portrayed Jesus in purely human terms. Renan began training for the priesthood but lost his faith and took up independent biblical studies. He wrote *Life of Jesus* while traveling in Palestine on an archaeological expedition. After its publication he lost his position as professor of Hebrew at the Collège de France, although he was restored to the post in 1870 and was elected to the Académie Française in 1878.

Renault, Mary [ruh-nawlt']   The English writer Mary Renault, pseudonym of Mary Challans, b. Sept. 4, 1905, d. Dec. 13, 1983, was known for her fictional re-creations of the ancient Greek world. Based on careful research and enlivened by credible characters and often exciting narratives, her historical novels achieved a rare authenticity. Among the best were *The Last of the Wine* (1956), set in the Athens of Plato and Socrates; *The King Must Die* (1958), an evocation of the legend of Theseus; and her trilogy on Alexander the Great—*The Persian Boy* (1972), *The Nature of Alexander* (1980), and *Funeral Games* (1981).

René of Anjou, King of Naples [ruh-nay' ahn-zhoo']   King of Naples (1435–42), René of Anjou, b. Jan. 6, 1409, d. July 10, 1480, occupies a place in both the political and the literary history of his time. René inherited (1434) from his brother Louis III of Anjou the French lands of Provence and Anjou, as well as a claim to the throne of Naples (see NAPLES, KINGDOM OF). In 1435 on the death of Joan II of Naples he became titular king but was driven out (1442) by a rival claimant, ALFONSO V of Aragon. He then turned his attention to his interests in France. He fought (1449–50) alongside CHARLES VII of France against the English in Normandy and in 1466 accepted the title king of Aragon from the Catalans rebelling against John II of Aragon. He was the author of two romances in prose and verse.

Renfrew [ren'-froo]   Renfrew is a former county in southwestern Scotland along the firth of Clyde, situated on fertile, undulating lowlands west of Glasgow. Paisley and Renfrew are the principal urban centers. One of the most heavily industrialized areas of Scotland, Renfrew produces

ships, automobiles, and heavy machinery; livestock raising, dairy farming, and the cultivation of potatoes, wheat, and oats supplement industry. After the Romans left the region during the early 5th century, Renfrew became part of the kingdom of Strathclyde. Renfrew was made a separate county of the Scottish kingdom in 1404, at which time the title baron of Renfrew was conferred on the oldest son of the Scottish monarch. During the reorganization of Scotland's local government in 1975, Renfrew was incorporated into the administrative region of STRATHCLYDE.

Reni, Guido [ray'-nee]   The Italian painter and engraver Guido Reni, b. Nov. 4, 1575, d. Aug. 18, 1642, was a leading master of the classical baroque style. Born in Bologna, Reni was originally trained by the Flemish Mannerist painter Denis Calvaert, but joined the Carracci family workshop about 1595. Reni went (c.1600) to Rome as an independent master. His early works show the influence of Caravaggio in color, composition, and lighting, as in the *Crucifixion of Saint Peter* (c.1604; Pinacoteca Vaticana, Rome). Thereafter, he was drawn to the art of classical antiquity and that of Raphael. One of his most famous works, the *Aurora* ceiling fresco (1613–14; Casino Rospigliosi, Rome), combines these influences, which also inspired the *Deeds of Hercules* series (1617–21; Louvre, Paris) and the *Apollo Flaying Marsyas* (c.1625; Musée des Augustins, Toulouse). He was the dominant artist in Bologna from 1614.

Rennes [ren]   Rennes is a city in Brittany, northwestern France, located about 300 km (190 mi) southwest of Paris. The population is 234,000 (1982). Long a regional center rich in customs and historical monuments, Rennes is an agricultural market and industrial center producing railroad and farm equipment and automobiles. Historic landmarks include the Jardin du Thabor and the 17th-century Palais de Justice. The University of Rennes is there.

The principal town of the Celtic Redones tribe, Rennes was subsequently taken by the Romans and by the 10th century had emerged as the capital of Brittany. The city was almost completely destroyed by fire in 1720 and suffered heavy bombing during World War II.

Reno [ree'-noh]   Reno, on the Truckee River in western Nevada, is the seat of Washoe County. It has a population of 133,850 (1990). A famous resort city, Reno is popular for its crisp climate, magnificent scenery, recreation in the Sierra Nevada, and its casinos and night entertainment. Reno's industries process potatoes and livestock and manufacture lumber products, chemicals, and mining machinery. Because of Nevada's Free Port Law, Reno is an important warehousing and distribution center. It is the location of the University of Nevada (1864), especially noted for the Mackay School of Mines Museum and the Desert Research Institute. The city is also the headquarters for the Toiyabe National Forest.

The site was settled in 1858 by pioneers en route to

California via the Donner Pass. Arrival of the Central Pacific Railroad in 1868 ensured the town's development. First called Lake's Crossing, the town was renamed for the Union general Jesse Lee Reno, a Civil War hero.

Renoir, Jean [ren-wahr']   One of the greatest and best-loved of all French filmmakers, Jean Renoir, b. Sept. 15, 1894, d. Feb. 13, 1979, the second son of the impressionist painter Auguste Renoir, exercised a major influence on French cinema for almost 50 years. From his beginnings in the silent era, aspects of his mature film style were apparent: a love of nature, rejection of class values, and a mixture of joy and sorrow.

During the 1930s Renoir was at the top of his form in two celebrations of anarchy, *La Chienne* (The Bitch, 1931) and *Boudu sauvé des eaux* (Boudu Saved from Drowning, 1932). A new social concern appeared in *Toni* (1935), *Le Crime de Monsieur Lange* (1936), and especially *La Vie est à nous* (People of France, 1936), made for the French Communist party during the heyday of the Popular Front. Renoir's reputation, however, rests mainly on *A Day in the Country* (1936, completed 1946), based on a bittersweet de Maupassant story; a free adaptation of Gorki's *The Lower Depths* (1936); and the widely acclaimed *Grand Illusion* (1937). Two very different masterpieces written and directed by Renoir, the tightly structured *The Human Beast* (1938) and the largely improvised *Rules of the Game* (1939)—which perfectly captured the mood of France before its collapse in 1940—crowned this prolific period.

Even the best of his films made in the United States, such as *The Southerner* (1945) and *The Diary of a Chambermaid* (1946), lack the excitement of his prewar work. He found a new approach in India, where he made his first color film, *The River* (1950), before returning to Europe to make the colorful and relaxed films of his maturity: *The Golden Coach* (1952), *French Can Can* (1954), and *Paris Does Strange Things* (1956). Always an innovator, Renoir used television techniques in the 1959 filming of *Le Testament du Docteur Cordelier* and *Picnic on the Grass*.

Renoir, Pierre Auguste   The French painter Pierre Auguste Renoir, b. Limoges, France, Feb. 25, 1841, d. Dec. 17, 1919, was one of the founders of IMPRESSIONISM. Within the impressionist group his work stands out as the most traditional in outlook and technique, as well as the most sensual.

By the time (1869) that he, Claude Monet, and Alfred Sisley worked together outdoors at La Grenouillère, on the Seine, Renoir had developed a delicate touch and vibrant brushwork that were distinctly his own. In the early 1870s, Renoir and his friends joined with other avant-garde artists to form a loose-knit artistic circle now known as the impressionist movement. He participated in the first impressionist exhibition (1874) and throughout the 1870s remained committed to impressionist ideals. Re-

Pierre Auguste Renoir's The Luncheon of the Boating-Party *(1881) displays the qualities of French impressionism to their best advantage: intense color and brightly lit open-air subjects painted directly from nature. Festive social events were a favored subject for Renoir. (Phillips Collection, Washington, D.C.)*

noir, however, continued to produce paintings of a more traditional sort, including portraits and scenes of leisure enjoyment, such as *Le Moulin de la Galette* (1876; Musée d'Orsay, Paris). In his portraits and society paintings, Renoir masterfully rendered the shimmering interplay of light and color on surfaces, the prime goal of impressionism, but he also retained an underlying sensuality.

Renoir's growing dissatisfaction with the formal restrictions of pure impressionism intensified during a visit (1881–82) to Algiers and Italy. In response, he made his figures larger and placed them closer to the picture-plane, with a setting treated like a simple backdrop. This friezelike treatment, best exemplified in his *Dance at Bougival* (1883; Museum of Fine Arts, Boston), led to his so-called "harsh manner" of the mid-1880s, in which he purified his contours and used frozen, static poses. Beginning in the 1890s, Renoir concentrated almost exclusively on the female figure, using warmer flesh tones, more exotic colors, and a tapestried treatment of landscape. After 1913 he also executed sculpture with the aid of an Italian assistant.

Rensselaer Polytechnic Institute [ren'-suh-leer] Established in 1824 and the oldest engineering school in the United States, Rensselaer Polytechnic Institute is a private coeducational college in Troy, N.Y. The courses of study, leading to bachelor's, master's, and doctorate degrees, emphasize science and technology. The institute has cooperative engineering programs with many colleges and six-year medical and law programs with Albany Medical College and Albany Law School, both in Albany, N.Y.

rent control   Rent control is a legal restriction on rents that landlords can charge tenants. Its initial purpose was to stabilize rents and to curtail unnecessary evictions. Initiated in the United States during World War I, rent control was a temporary wartime response to rises in the cost of living and to housing shortages caused by the allocation of building materials and labor to defense industries. In 1921 the Supreme Court, in *Block* v. *Hirsch* and *Brown Holding Co.* v. *Feldman*, upheld the constitutionality of rent control. After the war, controls were extended in order to aid tenants, because, in many cities, the demand for residential housing far exceeded the supply.

During World War II rent control was instituted on a broader scale by the federal government with the enactment of the Emergency Price Controls Act of 1942. With the Housing and Rent Act of 1947, the termination of federal controls—allowing local municipalities to extend rent control—was begun, and in *Woods* v. *Miller* (1948) the Supreme Court ruled that the continuation of rent control by state and local statutes was constitutional. In the late 1980s there were about 940,000 rent-stabilized units in New York City buildings constructed from 1947 to 1974 and those built after 1974 with city tax abatements. Other cities and states have enacted similar rent-control legislation to prevent inordinate increases in rent while providing owners with reasonable increments.

Renwick, James [ren'-wik]   The architect James Renwick, b. New York City, Nov. 18, 1818, d. June 23, 1895, is best known as the designer of New York City's SAINT PATRICK'S CATHEDRAL (begun 1858; dedicated 1879), a major monument of the American GOTHIC REVIVAL.

Grace Church in New York City was his first important commission and one of his most admired buildings. Completed in 1846, this English Gothic edifice led to other important church commissions, including that for Saint Patrick's. Renwick's penchant for architectural styles with strongly romantic overtones was influenced by the writings of the English architect Augustus Pugin and his followers, known as the Ecclesiologists. In Washington, D.C., Renwick's picturesque composition of the original Smithsonian Institution, familiarly called "The Castle" (1844–55), in a Norman Romanesque style stands out among the neoclassical buildings. His other important buildings include the first Corcoran Gallery (1859; Washington, D.C.), now named the Renwick Gallery, and the Main Hall at Vassar College (1860; Poughkeepsie, N.Y.).

Saint Patrick's Cathedral (1858–88), New York City, a Gothic Revival structure designed by James Renwick, fuses elements of continental and English Gothic styles.

reparations   *Reparations* is the term for money or other compensation that a defeated country pays to the victors or to individuals who have suffered in war. The word came into use after World War I. Germany was forced to pay reparations under the Versailles Treaty (see PARIS PEACE CONFERENCE), which blamed Germany for starting World War I and held it responsible for the resulting damage. Germans protested that the amount set by the interallied Reparations Commission in 1921, 132 billion gold marks, was unrealistically high and could not be paid. The United States waived most of its reparations claims.

When Germany defaulted on its reparations payments, France and Belgium moved (1923) troops into the Ruhr district in western Germany to force payment. The occupation ended (1924) after an international commission headed by American Charles G. DAWES formulated the Dawes Plan, which lowered German payments to one billion gold marks annually for five years and 2.5 billion thereafter. This schedule was replaced (1929) by the Young Plan, named after another American, Owen D. YOUNG, which lowered payments again. All payments ceased with the economic crisis of the 1930s.

After World War II reparations were imposed on Germany, Japan, and the other defeated powers, and the USSR enforced some claims against Germany. Victims of Nazi persecution, including the state of Israel, received about $2 billion from West Germany, but other reparation payments were modest.

—

repertory theater   The permanent, professional, nonprofit stage organizations outside New York City, known as repertory, regional, and resident theater, have profoundly altered the presentation of drama in the United States since the mid-20th century. Prior to their emergence, Broadway was the dominant center for the production both of classics and of new plays that touring companies or commercial "stock" entrepreneurs later distributed across the country. Today Broadway is dependent upon resident theaters for some of its best productions. Several factors—particularly economic depression and such rival entertainment media as movies, radio, and television—eroded the old Broadway monopoly.

The earliest rebels included the still-active Cleveland Play House (begun in 1916), the Hedgerow Theater in Moylan, Pa., and the Barter Theater in Abingdon, Va. The experimental theater launched (1947) by Margo JONES in Dallas, Tex., however, proved the most important seminal effort in the genesis of regional theater. Other early troupes were the Mummers Theater, founded in 1949 in Oklahoma City, Okla., and one of the most important and prestigious companies of all, the Arena Stage, started in 1950 by Zelda Fichandler in Washington, D.C.

The Ford and Rockefeller foundations contributed to the theater's greatest expansion when in the late 1950s they extended their philanthropic activities to the performing arts. By 1965 regional theater was employing more Actors Equity union members than Broadway itself. Some groups failed, but other companies, such as the Guthrie Theater in Minneapolis, Minn., the Mark Taper Forum in Los Angeles, the Trinity Square in Providence, R.I., the American Conservatory Theater in San Francisco, and the Long Wharf in New Haven, Conn., have provided high-quality leadership.

—

Repin, Ilya Yefimovich [rep'-in]   The leading Russian realist painter of the 19th century, Ilya Yefimovich Repin, b. Aug. 5 (N.S.), 1844, d. Sept. 29, 1930, belonged to the group known as the Peredvizhniki (Wanderers), who frequently addressed political and social issues in their art. His first major work was *The Volga Boatmen* (1870–73; State Russian Museum, Leningrad); he later achieved great popularity with his colorful historical canvases and large-scale genre paintings. *They Did Not Expect Him* (c.1884; Tretyakov Gallery, Moscow) depicts the return of an emaciated political exile to his startled family. Repin also produced portraits of his friend Leo Tolstoi and the composer-conductor Anton Rubinstein. He died in Kuokkala, Finland (now USSR), which was renamed Repino in his honor.

—

representation   Representation, in politics, is the process by which one person stands or acts for a large number of individuals in formulating the policies and operations of a GOVERNMENT. A monarch, a diplomat, or even a flag may represent. Modern representative government, however, is typically characterized by an elected LEGISLATURE. Legislative representation is usually based on numbers of or territorial groupings of the general population. Electoral districts may correspond to existing political subdivisions (for example, preexisting states, counties, cities, cantons, and so on) or may be specially drawn, usually on the basis of population. For example, U.S. senators are elected at large from each state, whereas members of the House of Representatives represent congressional districts, whose boundaries are altered as population shifts. Some countries have used PROPORTIONAL REPRESENTATION, a system in which representatives are apportioned among political parties in proportion to the number of votes each party receives. Various other methods of representation exist; for example, the fascist governments of Italy, Germany, and Spain used corporative representation based on such economic groupings as farmers, trade unions, and business interests.

Origins of Representatives. Both institutionally and conceptually, representation largely originated during the Middle Ages. Ancient Greece had no concept of representation. Although political practices included selecting some officials by lot and sending delegates abroad, DEMOCRACY in the Greek city-states was direct rather than representative, with all citizens entitled to meet and act on each political issue personally. Rome used some political representatives and developed legal agency, but the Latin verb *repraesentare* meant only artistic representing, or literally making present an absent thing. Medieval monarchs consulted with feudal and church lords; later they sometimes summoned knights and burgesses (townsmen) to meet with them in council. This practice was initially a duty, not a right, and the function of the representatives was advisory. Nevertheless, such councils became increasingly powerful as periodic financial crises forced monarchs to summon representatives of lower estates to ask for more financial support. As these councils became more institutionalized, representative legislatures evolved, began to challenge monarchial power, and came to be regarded as representing the whole realm. During the 17th century, individual members came to be called representatives, and representation came to be considered a matter of right. During the 18th century, representation became a particularly explosive issue. The inadequacy of their representation in the British Parliament was a major complaint of the American colonists, and "No taxation without representation" became a rallying cry for the American Revolution. During the 19th and 20th centuries, representation was further institutionalized and democratized; executives were made responsible to elected legislature; POLITICAL PARTIES developed; SUFFRAGE was gradually extended; and various electoral systems were tried. Today the idea of representation is so widely accepted that every government in the world claims to be completely representative of those it governs.

Theories of Representation. A number of controversies arise in the theory of representation. First, there is dispute over what representation is or means. Thomas HOBBES defined representation as acting in the name of another, who has authorized the action, so that the representative's act is ascribed to and binds the represented. When people authorize a sovereign in the SOCIAL CONTRACT, they make the sovereign their unlimited representative; whatever the sovereign does is authorized and binds them. Some modern theories of representative democracy stress the diametrically opposite view: a representative is someone ultimately held to account by the represented. Representation is defined not by initial authorization, as in Hobbes, but by final accountability. The representative has special obligations, and the represented, special rights and powers. For still other theorists, representation is "standing for" or "acting for" something or someone absent. Representatives may stand for others by resemblance so that the legislature is regarded as a miniature of the nation (for instance, in proportional representation), or the individual representative, as typical of his constituency. Representation may mean standing for others as a symbol (see FASCISM); here no resemblance is required. Finally, seen as "acting for" others, representation is not a merely passive "standing for" and goes beyond merely formal authorization or accountability: it is a substantive kind of activity.

A second controversy in the theory of representation concerns this substantive activity. It may be called the "mandate-independence controversy," usually formulated as a dichotomous choice: should a representative do what the constituents want or what the representative thinks best? Mandate theorists stress the representative's obligations to the constituents, arguing that the representative really represents them only if the representative's actions reflect their opinions and wishes. Independence theorists, such as Edmund BURKE, stress the representative's role in a national legislature and the representative's obligation to the public good; they say that the representative is not representing if he or she merely acts as a mechanical transmitter of decisions others have made.

A third controversy concerns the value and the very possibility of genuine representation. Jean Jacques ROUSSEAU argued that so-called representative institutions only substitute the will of a few for that of the whole community, with no likelihood that the two might coincide. He concluded that voters are free only at the moment of elections; as soon as they are represented, they are once more subject to an alien will. Since the 17th century, representation has been advocated on the grounds that a modern nation is too densely populated to govern itself directly. This view has repeatedly been challenged along Rousseauian or populist lines; that participation in self-government is intrinsically, not just instrumentally, valuable; that only a politically involved and active people is free; and that representative institutions have come to discourage active citizenship.

repression   see DEFENSE MECHANISMS

▬

reproduction   Asexual or sexual reproduction is the mechanism by which cellular life perpetuates itself. In asexual reproduction, new individuals are produced by simple division of nonreproductive cells; by budding from a parent system; by formation of spores, which germinate directly into a new individual; or by other means. Asexual generations are identical, because a single parent transmits its exact set of genes to each descendant (see CLONING). In sexual reproduction, new generations arise after fusion between nuclei or cells from different parental lineages, producing genetic variety. Cells that fuse are usually sex cells, called gametes, such as SPERM and EGGS (ova). The sex cells pair to form a zygote, such as a fertilized egg, which begins the new generation.

Each kind of reproductive mechanism provides some evolutionary advantages. Asexual systems are prolific and quickly colonize new habitats. Sexual species are variable, so that at least a few out of many genetic types often can adapt to new and sometimes abruptly changing living conditions, thus providing more chance for continuation of the population.

Gametes

The two major events in a sexual cycle are gamete formation and gamete fusion. There are male and female sexes in most animals and plants, but there may be more than two sexes or mating types in various protozoans, algae, and fungi. Each sex produces one kind of gamete, and fusion occurs between different types of gametes. In mammals, production, maturation, and release of gametes are regulated by hormones.

Gametes usually fuse only with gametes of the opposite type. In some protozoans, algae, and fungi, they may resemble ordinary growing (vegetative) cells, but most animals and the land plants produce specialized, large, nonmotile eggs and smaller, motile sperm. Sperm reach the egg by swimming or by muscular propulsion from female structures after insemination, or they may be taken to the egg during pollen-tube growth within female structures of seed-bearing plants.

Bacteria

Bacteria, as well as protozoans, generally reproduce asexually by a process called binary fission, in which the cell simply divides into two. Cell conjugation can occur in the colon bacillus, *Escherichia coli*, during which some genetic material is exchanged between two individuals. No new individual is formed, but conjugation introduces genetic variation that is passed on to the next generation during binary fission.

Algae and Fungi

Algae and fungi display quite varied reproductive patterns, including life cycles in which there is a predominant haploid (having one set of chromosomes) phase, or a predominant diploid (having two sets of chromosomes) phase, or an alternation between haploid and diploid phases (see ALTERNATION OF GENERATIONS), among others. Different species of the unicellular green alga *Chlamydomonas* may produce similar or dissimilar gametes, but the zygote is the only diploid stage. The zygote undergoes a reduction division (meiosis) almost immediately, producing haploid vegetative cells that later may behave as gametes. Among the branched, filamentous green alga *Cladophora*, there are species that produce both haploid and diploid plants of similar appearance. The diploid plant produces haploid, motile vegetative cells by meiosis, and these develop into haploid plants capable of producing gametes. Gamete fusion then leads to new diploid plants of another cycle. *Oedogonium* is another filamentous green alga, but it produces separate and dissimilar haploid male and female plants. Sperm from a dwarf male plant will fertilize eggs from the larger female plant to produce the diploid zygotes. Zygote meiosis leads to new haploid plants of the next generation. There is a predominant diploid phase in the life cycle of the brown alga *Laminaria*, a marine kelp. The large diploid plant is a sporophyte in which spores are produced by meiosis; these develop into small, haploid male and female gamete-producing plants, or gametophytes, which produce sperm and eggs, respectively. The fertilized egg develops into the large, familiar seaweed plant. Such an alternation of sporophyte and gametophyte phases in a life cycle is typical of mosses, ferns, and seed-bearing plants but is unusual among algae.

Among fungi, reproductive patterns generally are of a different nature than among algae. In sac fungi (class Ascomycetes), ascospores are produced by meiosis; these germinate to become the mass of filaments forming the mycelium, or fungal body. Gamete-producing structures develop along the filaments, and after a complex series of events there is nuclear fusion that leads to diploid cells. Meiosis occurs in these cells, producing ascospores, and the cycle begins again. In mushrooms (class Basidiomycetes), haploid basidiospores germinate to produce a mycelium consisting of uninucleate haploid cells. Cell fusion occurs between filaments from individuals of different mating types, producing binucleate cells, which form the mushroom. On the surface of "gills" on the underside of the mushroom cap, terminal cells expand to become specialized bodies called basidia. Paired nuclei fuse within the basidium to form diploid nuclei, which then undergo meiosis to form haploid basidiospores.

Plants

Among the land plants there has been an evolutionary trend toward decreasing size of the gametophyte and increasing size of the sporophyte, as well as complete dependence of the gametophyte on the sporophyte plant.

In mosses the well-known plant is the gametophyte, and the small sporophyte grows from the zygote retained within the gametophyte, so that the sporophyte is dependent on the gametophyte for food and water. Meiosis occurs in sporophyte cells, producing spores that germinate into gametophytes. Sperm and eggs are produced within the leafy, green gametophytes.

Fern gametophytes are tiny, independent, green plants in which eggs and sperm are produced. Sperm require water in order to swim to the egg, where fertilization occurs. The fertilized egg develops into the large, familiar fern sporophyte. Spores are produced by meiosis on the underside of the fern leaf; these spores germinate and become gametophytes.

In gymnosperms and angiosperms the prominent sporophyte produces two kinds of spores, each kind developing into an inconspicuous male or female gametophyte. The male gametophyte consists of two cells surrounded by protective cells of the pollen grain. Pollen is carried to the female sporophyte containing one or more female gametophytes that have developed from large spores; the egg is produced within the female gametophyte. Sperm do not require water for delivery to the egg, because germination of the pollen grain on receptive sporophyte structures leads to growth of the pollen tube; the pollen tube then carries the sperm down to the egg within the microscopic, protected gametophyte.

The fertilized egg develops into an embryo that remains in the protected confines of the female sporophyte. Certain maternal tissues develop into the layers of seed coat around the embryo, and stored foods are also present around the embryo. Naked seeds are released by gymnosperms, but in angiosperms the seeds are enclosed by a fruit formed from sporophyte tissues of the flower. Seeds and the embryonic plants within are dispersed by various means (for example, wind, water, and insects) to different environments. Some of these environments prove suitable for seed germination and the eventual development of a new sporophyte plant.

Animals

The predominant sexual mode in animals is separate male and female individuals. Some invertebrate species are hermaphroditic, consisting of individuals having both ovaries and testes, and self-fertilization can occur. Cross-fertilization generally takes place between mating pairs such that each releases sperm, which fertilize the partner's eggs.

Most fishes and amphibians release sperm and eggs directly into the water, where fertilization occurs and embryo development begins. Vertebrate land animals (reptiles, birds, and mammals) usually experience internal fertilization. Males deposit sperm within the female reproductive tract during cloacal contact or by insertion of a penis into the vagina or other reproductive duct.

Evolutionary modifications for life on land also involve increased protection for the egg and developing embryo. The egg is retained after fertilization, and the embryo develops to a certain stage within the mother's body. In land vertebrates, special embryonic membranes separate the embryo from its maternal surroundings. The embryo is nourished by foods stored in the yolk sac or other structures, and it continues to grow in warm and safe conditions. Embryonic development continues for a time after the egg is laid, until the foods are gone. In most mammals the embryo can develop for a longer term within its mother, because nutrients and oxygen are provided from the mother's bloodstream to the embryo through the placenta. In birds and mammals there is continued parental care after hatching or birth.

Except for humans, mammals are reproductively active only when they are capable of breeding. This interval, called estrus in the female, is the time when the female ovulates and the male is prepared and able to inseminate her. Most animals engage in courtship displays, produce vocalizations, or secrete chemical attractants that signal sexual and reproductive readiness.

There is no particular correlation in human beings between sexual activity and the optimum time for conception and pregnancy. Sexually mature women ovulate once per monthly cycle throughout the year—unless they are pregnant—until menopause, when these menstrual cycles cease. Sexually mature men produce sperm every day and can inseminate the female and initiate pregnancy anytime a viable egg is present. Menstruation indicates that conception has not occurred. Human females are unique in having a menstrual cycle instead of an estrous cycle.

reproductive system, human
Male and female human reproductive systems develop from a similar set of embryological structures, and many structural and functional parallels exist. Individual differences occur in the shape and structure of genitals, but without interfering with reproductive or sexual function. Also, the sexual anatomy of a young child differs from that of a mature adult, and, in turn, adult sexual anatomy alters in the later years of life.

Male Reproductive System

The male reproductive system basically is designed to produce and transport sperm cells. At the same time, the male genitals play an obvious role in sexual behavior, because reproduction cannot take place unless sperm cells are deposited in the female reproductive system. The major organs of the male reproductive system are the testes (testicles), the prostate, the seminal vesicles, the vas deferens, the epididymis, and the penis.

Testes. The testes, which are contained in a pouch of skin called the scrotum, are located outside of the body because they require a lower temperature than the rest of the body in order to accomplish one of their main functions: the production of sperm cells (spermatogenesis). Each of the two testes are suspended from the body and held in place by a spermatic cord; the skin of the scrotum contains numerous sweat glands that assist in the cooling process.

Spermatogenesis. Within the scrotum, each testis is contained by a thick protective capsule, within which is a network of tightly coiled tubes called the seminiferous tubules. Spermatogenesis takes place within the seminiferous tubules. Sperm production fully occurs usually by the age of 16, even though it can begin before a boy reaches puberty. The male continues to produce sperm throughout his life but with a marked slowing of the process in the later years. A man often is able to father children when he is into his seventies or eighties, but the peak of his fertility is typically earlier in the life cycle. The testes also produce the male hormones, or androgens, in large cells called the interstitial cells of Leydig. Like the production of sperm, the manufacture and secretion of these hormones begins about the time of puberty and continues throughout life. The hormones circulate throughout the body, affecting various organs.

Pathway of the Sperm. Sperm produced in the seminiferous tubules move through the testes into another system of coiled ducts called the epididymis. The sperm remain here and continue to mature for about 2 weeks and then pass into a duct called the vas deferens. The male sterilization procedure, or vasectomy, involves cutting the vas deferens so that the sperm cannot travel from the testes to the penis.

Seminal Fluids. Before the sperm cells reach the penis, they travel through the seminal vesicles and the prostate and Cowper's glands. The major function of these internal organs is to produce fluids that will provide the sperm with a nourishing and balanced environment. Only a very small proportion of the male ejaculate is made up of sperm cells; the remainder consists of the seminal fluids secreted by these internal organs. Thus a male who undergoes vasectomy will continue to ejaculate about the same volume of fluid as a fertile male. Seminal fluids are not absolutely necessary for a man to be fertile, but these fluids allow the sperm to live longer within the vagina's acidic environment.

The Penis. In the final phase of their journey, the sperm cells pass through the urethral duct, which runs through the center of the penis. The penis contains a large number of arteries, veins, and small blood vessels as well as erectile tissue, the last of which consists of three hollow, spongelike cylinders of tissue. When a male has an erection, these spongy tissues fill with blood and become firm. Unlike that of a number of other mammals—for instance, the whale—no bones are located within the human penis. Erection is caused solely by the relaxation of the blood vessels within the penis. Thus when a man is under emotional or physical stress, he may experience some difficulty achieving a firm erection because the blood vessels may not relax sufficiently.

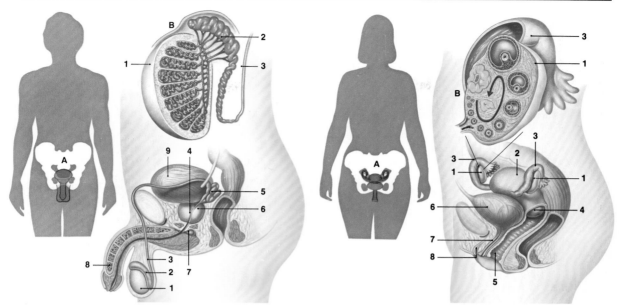

The male reproductive system (A) is designed to produce spermatozoa and to transmit them into the female reproductive system, where one of them may fertilize an egg. Sperm and eggs are both gamete cells, containing chromosomes, that join together to create new life. Millions of sperm are produced each day in the testicles (1). Because the temperatue within the body is too high to permit sperm production, the testicles hang just outside the pelvic area in a pouch of skin called the scrotum. Mature sperm are stored in the epididymis (2). A cross section of a testicle (B) shows a system of conical lobules, each of which contains one or more coiled tubules in which sperm are made. Channels lead from the lobules to the epididymis and from there to the vas deferens, or sperm ducts (3). During sexual stimulation, sperm pass through the vas deferens into the urethra (4), where they mix with fluids from the seminal vesicles (5), prostate gland (6), and Cowper's gland (7) to form semen. Simultaneously, spongelike structures in the penis (8) become filled with blood, causing it to elongate and become erect. If stimulation continues, the muscles of the penis contract rhythmically, expelling the semen. The penis and urethra also function as parts of the urinary system, eliminating urine from the bladder (9). The bladder's entrance to the urethra is closed when sexual stimulation occurs.

The female reproductive system (A) functions on a continuous cycle of preparation for childbearing. Each month a mature egg (ovum) is released by one of the ovaries (1). The cross section of an ovary (B) shows, counterclockwise, the changes in an egg follicle as it develops (bottom), rises toward the surface (right), releases the mature egg (top), becomes an estrogen-producing "yellow body" (left), and disappears, leaving a temporary white scar (center). The ovum is transmitted to the uterus (2) through the oviducts, or Fallopian tubes (3), a journey that takes approximately 3 days. The uterus, also known as the womb, is a hollow, muscular organ about the size of a fist. Its lower end, the cervix (4), protrudes into the vagina (5), which is the sheath of soft skin that receives the penis during intercourse. During the first half of the ovulatory cycle, the inner lining of the uterus is enriched with blood and glandular fluids. If the egg is not fertilized in the oviduct by a male sperm cell, this lining is shed in a process called menstruation. If fertilization does occur, the egg attaches itself to the uterine lining and begins the 9-month period of growth that will culminate in the birth of a child. The bladder (6) and urethra (7) function separately from the female reproductive system. In front of the urethral opening is the clitoris (8), a sensory organ that fills with blood and rhythmically contracts during sexual stimulation.

Female Reproductive System

The female reproductive organs are designed for conception, pregnancy, and childbirth. Like that of the male, female anatomy includes both internal and external sexual organs. The internal organs are more closely related to reproductive function, and the external organs tend to be related to sexual function.

Function. The two ovaries, located to the right and the left of the uterus, to which they are connected by the fallopian tubes, produce eggs, or ova. During each menstrual cycle one of the ovaries matures and releases an egg cell (see MENSTRUATION). At birth a female infant already has in her ovaries all the egg cells that will be released during her life. These eggs, however, do not mature until the time of puberty, when the menstrual cycle begins. This process continues until MENOPAUSE, when the men-

strual cycle ceases.

The second major function of the ovaries is the production of the female hormones estrogen and progesterone. Like the male, the female produces hormones that circulate throughout the body and serve to keep the sexual system ready for reproduction. Unlike the male, however, the female secretes varying amounts of different hormones in a distinct, monthly cycle. During the first half of the cycle, hormones cause a single egg cell to mature; at midcycle, ovulation, or the release of the egg cell from the ovary, takes place. Also during the first half of the cycle, the lining of the uterus (endometrium) prepares to receive and nourish a fertilized egg. If fertilization and pregnancy have not occurred, hormone levels tend to decrease, the uterine lining is shed, and the cycle begins anew. The pattern of ovarian hormone release is regulated by the pituitary gland, which is located in the brain.

When fertilization occurs (A), a sperm cell fuses with an egg cell. As the two merge, the acrosome—a caplike vesicle in the head of the sperm—releases enzymes (orange) that enable the sperm to penetrate the egg. After the sperm nucleus enters the egg, a fertilization membrane forms (B), which prevents other sperm from entering. The sperm nuclei then migrate toward the egg nucleus; the two nuclei fuse; and the chromosomes align prior to cell division.

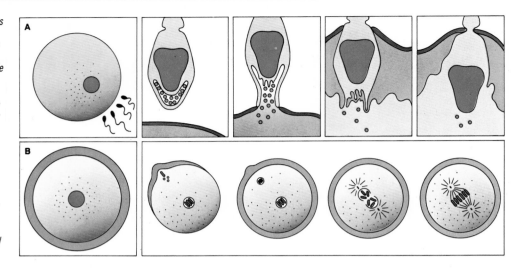

Ovulation. In the adult female each of the two ovaries is about the size and shape of an unshelled almond. During ovulation the egg cell breaks through or ruptures the wall of the ovary, at which time a small amount of bleeding may occur. Within the ovary are a number of compartments called follicles, which contain egg cells at various stages of development. After the egg cell is released, the follicle, referred to in this instance as the corpus luteum, remains within the ovary and continues to secrete hormones. If no pregnancy develops, the corpus luteum shrinks and disappears by the next menstrual cycle; if pregnancy does occur, the corpus luteum continues to secrete hormones for about 6 months.

Pathway of the Egg. After the mature egg is released from the ovary, it must travel a short distance to the entrance of the fallopian, or uterine, tube, which moves the egg from the ovary to the uterus and, at the same time, secretes substances that nourish the egg. If fertilization—the meeting of egg and sperm—is to occur, it must take place within the fallopian tube. Generally, the egg takes about 3 days to make the short journey from ovary to uterus; however, fertilization can take place only within the first 24 hours of this passage.

The Uterus. The uterus, or womb, is about the size and shape of an inverted pear in women who have never borne children. During pregnancy this muscular container increases enormously in size and weight. After childbirth the uterus tends to remain slightly larger in size but retains the same shape. The bulk of the uterus is a network of dense muscular fibers interlaced in all directions; the contractions of childbirth begin when these muscles work to move the fetus toward the vagina.

At the bottom of the uterus is the cervix, a passageway between the uterus and vagina. It is normally very small and, at times, is blocked entirely by mucus that is secreted by the cervical glands. During birth, however, it opens wide enough to allow for passage of the fetus.

The Vagina. The vagina is normally small, with little internal space: in the resting state, its walls touch one another. The muscles of the vagina expand greatly during intercourse or childbirth, after which they return to their normal size. The vagina also contains a rich network of blood vessels; when a woman is sexually aroused this network fills with blood in much the same way that the male's penis becomes erect due to increased blood flow. In turn, the pressure of this blood causes the mucous lining of the vagina to secrete drops of fluid; this lubrication response is a primary sign of female sexual arousal.

Female external sexual anatomy consists of the labia majora, labia minora, and clitoris. The labia majora, or outer lips, are two folds of skin that normally enclose the external genitals. The labia minora, or inner lips, are two smaller skin folds containing a rich network of blood vessels. They are normally pinkish in color but may show a variety of color changes when a woman is sexually stimulated.

The Clitoris. According to sex researchers William Masters and Virginia Johnson, the clitoris is a unique organ in human anatomy, having as its major purpose the sensation of sexual pleasure. The clitoris, like the penis, to which it is homologous, is made up of erectile tissue—that is, when a woman is sexually stimulated, the clitoris fills with blood and becomes firm. Normally, the clitoral body is covered by a fold of skin called the clitoral hood.

See also: BIRTH CONTROL; DEVELOPMENT, HUMAN; FERTILITY, HUMAN; SEX; SEX HORMONES; SEXUAL DEVELOPMENT; SEXUAL INTERCOURSE.

---

reptile Reptiles are vertebrate, or backboned, animals constituting the class Reptilia and are characterized by a combination of features, none of which alone could separate all reptiles from all other animals. Among these characteristics are (1) cold-bloodedness; (2) the presence of lungs; (3) direct development, without larval forms; (4) a dry skin with scales but not feathers or hair; (5) an amniote egg; (6) internal fertilization; (7) a three- or four-

Of the living orders of reptiles, two arose earlier than the Age of Reptiles, when dinosaurs were dominant. Tuataras, of the order Rhynchocephalia, are found only on New Zealand islands, whereas the equally ancient turtles, order Chelonia, occur nearly worldwide; shown is the chicken turtle. The order Crocodilia emerged along with the dinosaurs; shown is the East Indian saltwater crocodile. Snakes and lizards, order Squamata, are today the most numerous reptile species; shown are the black-necked spitting cobra; land iguana; and white-bellied worm lizard.

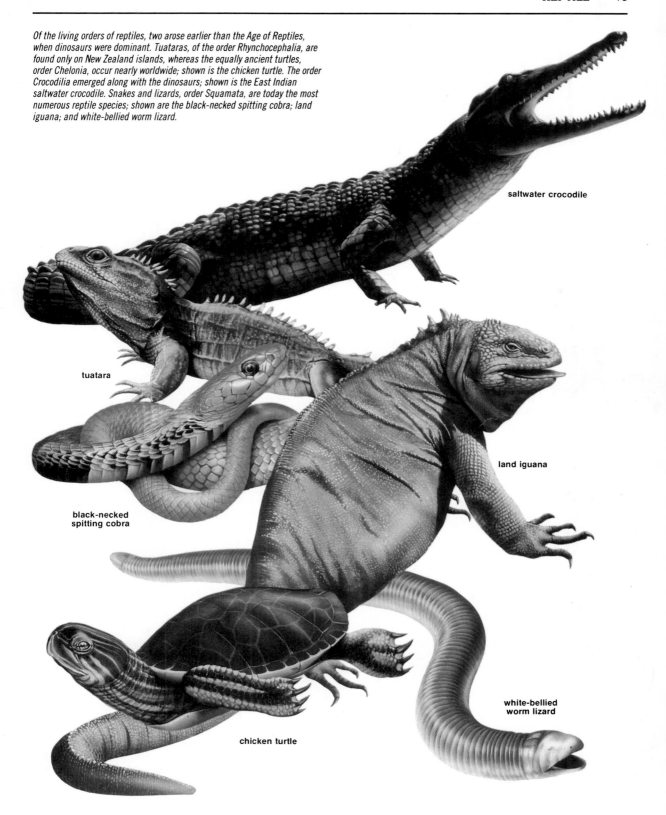

saltwater crocodile

tuatara

black-necked
spitting cobra

land iguana

chicken turtle

white-bellied
worm lizard

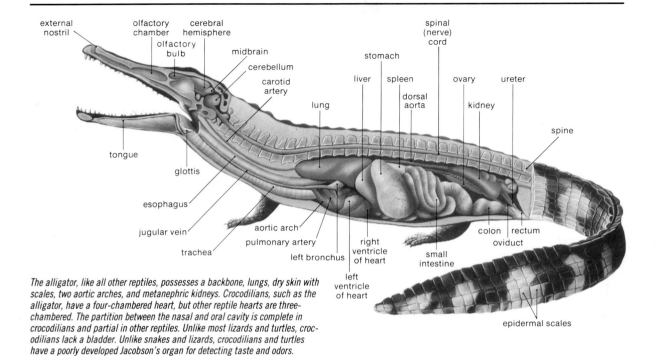

external nostril
olfactory chamber
cerebral hemisphere
olfactory bulb
midbrain
cerebellum
carotid artery
tongue
glottis
esophagus
jugular vein
trachea
aortic arch
pulmonary artery
left bronchus
lung
stomach
spinal (nerve) cord
liver
spleen
dorsal aorta
ovary
ureter
kidney
spine
colon
rectum
oviduct
small intestine
right ventricle of heart
left ventricle of heart
epidermal scales

The alligator, like all other reptiles, possesses a backbone, lungs, dry skin with scales, two aortic arches, and metanephric kidneys. Crocodilians, such as the alligator, have a four-chambered heart, but other reptile hearts are three-chambered. The partition between the nasal and oral cavity is complete in crocodilians and partial in other reptiles. Unlike most lizards and turtles, crocodilians lack a bladder. Unlike snakes and lizards, crocodilians and turtles have a poorly developed Jacobson's organ for detecting taste and odors.

chambered heart; (8) two aortic arches (blood vessels) carrying blood from the heart to the body; (9) a metanephric kidney; (10) twelve pairs of head (cranial) nerves; and (11) skeletal features such as (a) limbs with usually five clawed fingers or toes, (b) at least two spinal bones (sacral vertebrae) associated with the pelvis, (c) a single ball-and-socket connection (condyle) at the head-neck joint, and (d) an incomplete or complete partition (the secondary palate) along the roof of the mouth, separating the food and air passageways so that breathing can continue while food is being chewed.

These and other traditional defining characteristics of reptiles have been subject to considerable modification in recent times. The extinct flying reptiles, called PTEROSAURS or pterodactyls, are now thought to have been warm-blooded and covered with hair; and the DINOSAURS are also now considered by many authorities to have been warm-blooded. The earliest known bird, ARCHAEOPTERYX, is now regarded by many to have been a small dinosaur, despite its covering of feathers; and the extinct ancestors of the mammals, the therapsids, or mammallike reptiles, are also believed to have been warm-blooded and haired. Proposals have been made to reclassify the pterosaurs, dinosaurs, and certain other groups out of the class Reptilia into one or more classes of their own.

Cold-bloodedness. Reptiles are cold-blooded; that is, they lack the ability to regulate their metabolic heat (heat derived from the oxidation, or "burning," of food and from other processes) for the production of sustained body warmth and a constant body temperature. Cold-bloodedness, however, does not mean that a reptile is necessarily cold. A LIZARD basking in the sun may have a higher body temperature than a mammal. Because cold-bloodedness is a misleading term, biologists employ two others instead, describing reptiles as poikilothermic and ectothermic. *Poikilothermy* refers to the condition in which body temperature varies with the temperature of the environment; it is contrasted with homeothermy, a characteristic of birds and mammals, in which body temperature remains essentially the same through a wide range of environmental temperatures. *Ectothermy* refers to the condition in which an animal depends on an external source, such as the Sun, rather than its own metabolism, for body warmth. Birds and mammals, which use their internal metabolic heat for body warmth, are referred to as endothermic.

Respiration. All reptiles have lungs. In SNAKES, presumably as an adaptation to their long, thin bodies, the left lung is reduced in size or lacking. Although lungs are the primary means of respiration in all reptiles and the only means of respiration in most reptiles, some species can also utilize other parts of the body. In aquatic TURTLES, for example, the mucous membranes lining the inside of the mouth can extract oxygen from the water; some snakes, including SEA SNAKES, as well as the softshelled turtle, genus *Trionyx*, can use their skin for respiration when submerged.

Skin and Scales. Part of the ability of the early reptiles to invade dry land was the development of a dry skin that acted as a barrier to moisture and greatly reduced the loss of body water. The reptile skin, like that of other vertebrate animals, has two main parts: an outer epidermis and an underlying dermis. The epidermis produces horny (like fingernails) scales on its upper surface. The scales increase the skin's resistance to water, further reducing moisture loss; some scales may be modified for specialized functions, such as protective spines. Reptile scales may be small and overlapping, as in many lizards, or large and adjoining, as in turtles, where they are commonly called scutes. Some reptiles also have bony plates or nodules formed and lying within the dermis. Called dermal scales or osteoderms, these are similar in origin to fish scales. When present in lizards and crocodilians (see CROCODILE), the dermal scales are separated from one another. In turtles they are fused together to form a bony shell beneath the epidermal scales.

In lizards and snakes the scales do not increase in size as the animal grows; consequently, the old scales must be periodically shed and replaced by a new set of somewhat larger scales. Shedding may also occur when the outer layer becomes worn or when much food is consumed, as well as for causes not yet fully understood. In the shedding, or molting, process, also called ecdysis, the older upper layer of the epidermis with its attached scales loosens and breaks away from a newer layer that has developed beneath it. In turtles and crocodilians the large scutes are not molted but are retained and are enlarged and thickened by additional layers of keratin from beneath; the uppermost layers of the scutes, however, may be lost through wear or other factors.

The Amniote Egg. A necessary part of the invasion of dry-land environments by the early reptiles was the development of an egg that could be laid out of water without drying up and that could "breathe" air rather than water. This egg, the amniote egg, is so named because it contains a membrane called the amnion. The amniote egg is found not only in reptiles but also in birds and (ancestral) mammals.

Reptiles produce an amniote egg, rich in yolk and enclosed in a shell, that is adapted to development on land. The developing embryo is connected to the main food supply, the yolk, which is enclosed in a yolk sac. A fluid-filled sac, the amnion, surrounds the embryo and keeps it from drying out. Another sac, the allantois, stores the embryo's wastes and permits gas exchange through the shell. The chorion surrounds both the amnion and allantois. In crocodilians and turtles the egg white, or albumen, functions as a water reserve.

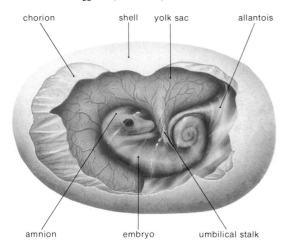

chorion   shell   yolk sac   allantois

amnion   embryo   umbilical stalk

The amniote egg is enclosed in a protective shell, which is either flexible and leathery or rigid and calcareous. Within the shell is the fertilized egg cell lying on top of a large mass of yolk. The yolk is surrounded by a membrane (the yolk sac) and provides nourishment for the developing embryo. As the fertilized egg cell divides and redivides, and the embryo begins to form and grow, a folded membranous tissue grows up around the embryo, enclosing it in a double-walled sac. The outer wall of the sac is called the chorion; the inner wall, the amnion. The embryo is surrounded by fluid held within the amnion.

Another sac, the allantois, projects from the embryo's lower digestive tract and acts as a bladder to receive the embryo's waste products. The allantois becomes quite large, expanding out until its wall joins that of the chorion to form the chorioallantoic membrane, which is pressed up against the inside of the shell. In addition to serving as a bladder, the allantois acts as a sort of "lung," allowing oxygen and carbon dioxide to pass to and from the embryo through the slightly porous (permeable) egg shell.

Internal Fertilization. Because the egg cell reaches the outside environment surrounded by the shell of the egg, it is necessary that it be fertilized before it leaves the female's body; thus in all reptiles fertilization is internal, with the male depositing sperm within the female's genital tract. In snakes and lizards the male organ, called the hemipenes, is actually a pair of structures, with one of the pair, or hemipenis, situated internally on each side of the male's vent. Each hemipenis, which itself may be forked, is a functional structure: either one may be protruded from the vent and used in mating, the choice usually depending on the placement of the male's mate. In turtles and crocodilians there is a single penis, which serves only for the transmission of sperm and not also for the elimination of excretory products, as in mammals. In the lizardlike TUATARA, *Sphenodon,* the male lacks a copulatory organ, and mating is accomplished by the pressing together of the male's and female's cloacae, as in most birds.

The Heart. Except for crocodilians, which have a four-chambered heart, all reptiles have a three-chambered heart consisting of two atria and one ventricle. The chamber called the right atrium receives deoxygenated, or "spent," blood returning from the body tissues. It passes this blood into the ventricle, from where it is pumped to the lungs for oxygenation. The oxygenated blood from the lungs returns to the left atrium and once again enters the same ventricle, from which it is pumped to the body tissues.

Even in the three-chambered heart, however, there is little mixing of oxygenated and deoxygenated blood. This has been achieved by the development within the ventricle of interconnected "subchambers" within which a sequence of changes in blood pressure takes place.

Metanephric Kidney. Adult amphibians have an opisthonephric kidney, that is, one that developed from the main mass of kidney-forming tissue in the embryo; the collecting tubules are connected to a drainage tube called the archinephric, or Wolffian, duct. In contrast, the metanephric kidney of adult reptiles (and birds and mammals) arises from the rearmost part of the embryonic kidney-forming tissue. The collecting tubules of this kidney connect to a "newly evolved" drainage tube, the ureter. The Wolffian duct is partly involved in the transmission of sperm in male reptiles but is vestigial in females. The reptilian ureter empties into the cloaca, a chamber leading to the outside and into which empty the excretory products of the kidneys, the waste products of the intestines, and the reproductive products of the testes and ovaries.

Skull. The reptilian skull ranges from the reduced, loosely joined, or kinetic, skull of snakes to the large, solid skull of crocodilians. On each side of the skull behind the eye sockets there may be one or two openings formed at the junctions of certain bones. The openings are believed to be an adaptation for more-efficient functioning of the jaw muscles, possibly by allowing them to bulge outward when the jaws are closed. Because the positions of the openings, as determined by the bones surrounding them, were considered critical in the classification of reptiles, skull types were designated by the row, or arch, of bones beneath each opening rather than by the openings themselves. The Greek root *apse,* meaning "arch," was used in the naming of the skull types. A reptile skull without any temporal openings, and hence without arches, was termed *anapsid* (*an,* "without"; *apsid,* "arches"). Anapsid skulls are characteristic of the extinct, primitive cotylosaurs and of the living turtles.

When openings are present, their positions are best described in relation to the two skull bones extending from behind each eye socket to the rear of the head: the postorbital and squasmosal bones. In the skull type called *euryapsid* there is a single opening high on each side of the head situated in the upper part of the junction between the postorbital and squamosal bones, which form the opening's lower border, or arch. In the skull type *parapsid* there is also a single opening high on each side of the head, but it is located above the postorbital and squamosal bones; its lower border, or arch, is formed by the supratemporal and postfrontal bones. A euryapsid-type skull was present in the extinct plesiosaurs, a parapsid-type skull in the extinct icthyosaurs.

A skull with a single low opening on each side of the head, situated in the lower part of the junction between the postorbital and squamosal bones and bordered below by parts of the squamosal, quadratojugal, and jugal bones, is termed *synapsid.* The extinct mammallike reptiles, order Therapsida, from which the mammals evolved, had synapsid skulls.

If a reptile skull has two openings, one high and one low, on each side of the head, situated in both the upper and lower parts of the junction between the postorbital and squamosal bones, it is classified as *diapsid.* Diapsid skulls are characteristic of dinosaurs and of the living crocodilians. Modern lizards and snakes also have diapsid skulls, but in the lizards the arch of the lower opening has been lost during evolution, leaving only the single upper opening and its arch. In snakes both the lower and upper arches have been lost, leaving no openings and very little bone.

Sense Organs. Vision is the most commonly employed reptilian sense for the detection of objects in the environment. The most notable exceptions to this are the blind snakes, which burrow through the ground and have only vestigial eyes. Some turtles and lizards that are active by day—and perhaps some snakes as well—definitely are able to see colors rather than simply shades of gray. Snakes and some lizards are noted for their unblinking stares, having apparently lost the ability to shut their eyes.

A so-called "third eye," or parietal body, is present in the upper skull of some lizards and in the tuatara. It has a cornea, lens, and retina and is able to respond to differences in light and dark, but it cannot distinguish shapes. The parietal body is involved in the control of certain secretions and in certain adaptive behaviors.

The ear structure in most reptiles consists of an eardrum, which lies close to or near the surface of the skin (there is no external ear); a small bone, called the columella or stapes, which conducts the vibrations of the eardrum through the middle ear; and the inner ear, which receives the vibrations being transmitted by the columella. Turtles have well-developed ear structures but usually give little evidence of hearing ability. Certain TORTOISES (land turtles), however, appear sensitive to low sounds of about 100 Hz.

Snakes lack both the eardrum and the middle-ear cavity but retain the columella, which is positioned against the lower part of the skull at the jaw hinge (the quadrate bone). Lacking eardrums, a snake cannot "hear" airborne sounds in the usual sense. Experiments have shown, however, that the snake's inner ear does respond to low-frequency airborne sounds, or pressure vibrations, possibly by transmission of the vibrations through the skull bones. A snake can readily detect earthborne sounds, or vibrations.

The Jacobson's, or the vomeronasal, organ is a specialized chemical detector located in the roof of the reptilian mouth. It is present in rudimentary form in turtles and crocodilians but is highly developed in snakes and lizards. The rapid in-and-out flicking of a snake's tongue is to pick up tiny chemical particles, which adhere or dissolve in the moisture on the tongue and are then conveyed back to the two openings of the Jacobson's organ for identification. PIT VIPERS also possess organs that are highly sensitive to heat.

Origin and Evolution. The first known reptiles appeared during the Pennsylvanian Period (or upper Carboniferous), about 300 million years ago. The oldest of these, *Hylonomus,* was about 70 cm (27 in) long and lizardlike in shape. The reptiles evolved from AMPHIBIANS known as anthracosaurs, which were part of the labyrinthodont group (amphibians with highly complex patterns in the surface of the teeth). The reptiles probably evolved during the Mississippian Period (or lower Carboniferous), about 40 million years earlier.

The reptiles expanded during the Permian, the last period of the Paleozoic Era, but it was during the following Mesozoic Era, from about 225 million to 65 million years ago, that they came to dominate not only the land but also the sea and air. During this era, known as "the age of reptiles," they radiated out into many diverse forms and occupied a wide array of ecological niches. The dinosaur group, if still regarded as reptiles, included the largest land animals that ever lived. The age of reptiles came to a close at the end of the Cretaceous, the last period of the Mesozoic Era. The undetermined reasons for this decline have been the subject of intensive study for many years (see EXTINCTION).

Classification and Types. The class Reptilia (living and extinct reptiles) is divided into 6 to 12 subclasses by different authorities. A number of these subclasses are completely extinct. The subclasses contain about 24 orders, but only 4 of these are still represented by living animals. The living reptiles comprise the turtles (about 250 species), the lizards (about 3,000 species), the tuatara (one species), the amphisbaenians, or WORM LIZARDS (about 40 species, usually included with the lizards), the snakes (about 2,700 species), and the crocodilians (about 21 species). Of these, the reticulated PYTHON, *Python reticulatus,* is the longest reptile on record, reaching 10 m (33 ft) in length. The heaviest living reptile is the leatherback turtle, *Dermochelys coriacea,* which has attained 725 kg (1,600 lb) in weight. The smallest reptile is possibly the dwarf gecko, *Sphaerodactylus elegans,* which reaches only about 34 mm (1.3 in) in length.

The following is a brief, acceptable classification of the living reptiles, class Reptilia:

> Subclass Anapsida
>   Order Chelonia (turtles)
>   Suborder Cryptodira
>   Suborder Pleurodira
> Subclass Lepidosauria
>   Order Rhynchocephalia (tuatara)
>   Order Squamata
>   Suborder Amphisbaenia (worm lizards)
>   Suborder Sauria (lizards)
>   Suborder Serpentes (snakes)
> Subclass Archosauria
>   Order Crocodylia (crocodilians)

Repton, Humphry [rep'-tuhn]   Humphry Repton, b. May 2, 1752, d. Mar. 24, 1818, succeeded the distinguished Capability Brown to become the most prominent English landscape gardener of his day. The aim of the landscape gardener, according to Repton, should be to articulate and reinforce the natural beauty of the landscape, avoiding both the extremes of cultivated artificiality and excessive ruggedness. Believing that the successful practice of his art required a knowledge of architecture, he collaborated (*c.*1792–99) with the architect John Nash.

republic   A republic is a form of GOVERNMENT in which SOVEREIGNTY rests in those people entitled to elect, either directly or indirectly, representatives who hold office for limited periods of time. In a republic the head of state is a nonhereditary officer most often called the president. The president may also be the actual chief executive, or such power may reside with a prime minister or premier.

A republic may or may not be a democracy, depending on voting qualifications, the degree of suffrage, and the presence of real electoral alternatives. Some political systems are democratic but are not republics because they have a hereditary head of state, as, for example, Great Britain.

Republic, The   The major work of the Greek philosopher PLATO, *The Republic* (*c.*370 BC) advances many of Plato's principal ideas, notably those concerned with government and justice. Composed as a debate between Socrates and five other speakers, *The Republic* is best known for its description of the ideal state (based on Sparta), which Plato argues should be ruled by philosopher-kings. The principles of justice that govern the state correspond to those which rule the individual, and the philosopher is best suited to govern because he perceives this natural harmony. An important section, the allegory of the cave (book 7), presents Plato's concept of the ideal Forms. The cave is the world of illusion and ignorance; only the philosopher has ventured beyond the shadows of the cave to perceive the ideal models of justice.

Republican party   The Republican party is one of the two major political parties in the United States, the other being the Democratic party. From the time it ran its first presidential candidate, John C. FRÉMONT, in 1856, until 1988, Republican presidents were in the White House for 80 years, and another, George BUSH, was inaugurated in 1989. Generally speaking, the Republican party is the more conservative of the two major parties, taking political stances generally in favor of free enterprise, fiscal responsibility, and laissez-faire, and against the welfare state.

The Founding of the Party. The origins of the party grew

The first national convention of the Republican party (1856) selected John C. Frémont as its presidential candidate and William Dayton as his running mate.

JN⁰ C. FREMONT.   W⁰ L. DAYTON.
THE CHAMPIONS OF FREEDOM.

out of the sectional conflicts regarding the expansion of slavery into the new Western territories. The stimulus for political realignment was provided by the passage of the Kansas-Nebraska Act of 1854. That law repealed earlier compromises that had excluded slavery from the territories. The passage of this act served as the unifying agent for abolitionists and split the Democrats and the Whig party. "Anti-Nebraska" protest meetings spread rapidly through the country. Two such meetings were held in Ripon, Wis., on Feb. 28 and Mar. 20, 1854, and were attended by a group of abolitionist Free Soilers, Democrats, and Whigs. They decided to call themselves Republicans—because they professed to be political descendants of Thomas Jefferson's Democratic-Republican party. The name was formally adopted by a state convention held in Jackson, Mich., on July 6, 1854.

The new party was a success from the beginning. In the 1854 congressional elections 44 Republicans were elected as a part of the anti-Nebraskan majority in the House of Representatives, and several Republicans were elected to the Senate. In 1856, at the first Republican national convention, Sen. John C. Frémont was nominated for the presidency but was defeated by Democrat James Buchanan. In 1858, however, the Republicans won control of the House of Representatives for the first time. One Republican who failed that year was Abraham LINCOLN, defeated in his bid for a U.S. Senate seat by Stephen A. Douglas.

Lincoln, the Civil War, and Reconstruction. At the second Republican national convention, in 1860, a hard-fought contest resulted in the presidential nomination of Abraham Lincoln. The Republican platform specifically pledged not to extend slavery. Lincoln was opposed by three major candidates—Douglas (Northern Democrat), John Cabell Breckinridge (Southern Democrat), and John Bell (Constitutional Union party). Lincoln collected almost half a million votes more than Douglas, his nearest competitor, but he won the election with only 39.8 percent of the popular vote.

Shortly thereafter, the Civil War began. Reverses on the battlefield, disaffection over the draft and taxes, and the failures of army leadership brought Lincoln and the Republicans into the 1864 election with small hope for victory. Party leaders saw the need to broaden the base of the party, and accordingly, they adopted the name National Union party. Andrew JOHNSON of Tennessee, a "War" Democrat, was nominated as Lincoln's running mate. Significant military victories intervened before election day and contributed to Lincoln's overwhelming reelection. After Lincoln's assassination the Radical Republicans, led by Sen. Charles SUMNER and Rep. Thaddeus STEVENS, fought President Johnson's moderate RECONSTRUCTION policies. Ultimately, relations between Johnson and Congress deteriorated, culminating in impeachment of the president; he was acquitted by a single vote.

The Republican Era. The defeat of the South left the Republican party in the ascendancy. With the election of Ulysses S. GRANT, the Republicans began a period of national dominance. Between 1860 and 1932 the Demo-

The battered GOP elephant in Thomas Nast's cartoon symbolizes the damage sustained by the Republican party in the hotly disputed victory of its candidate, Rutherford B. Hayes, over Democrat Samuel Tilden in the 1876 presidential election.

crats controlled the White House for only 16 years. Grant's administration became riddled with scandal and corruption. Grant was not personally involved, however, and was renominated in 1872. A split among the Republicans ensued: the more liberal elements, opposed to the harshness of the Radical Republicans on the Reconstruction issue and the scandals of the administration, broke away and took the name LIBERAL REPUBLICAN PARTY. They, along with a faction of the Democratic party, nominated Horace GREELEY for president. Despite this opposition, Grant was reelected by a substantial margin. A continuation of the scandals along with the panic of 1873 caused the Republicans to lose control of the Congress in 1874. The Republicans did, however, emerge from that election with a new party symbol, the elephant, after it first appeared in a newspaper cartoon by Thomas NAST.

In 1876 the Republicans nominated a virtual unknown, Rutherford B. HAYES of Ohio. The Democratic candidate, Samuel J. TILDEN of New York, received the greatest number of popular votes, but widespread charges of electoral irregularities led to the appointment of a congressional electoral commission to review the results and decide who should receive disputed votes in four states. The commission, controlled by Republicans, granted all the votes to Hayes, thereby giving him the election by an electoral-college margin of 185 to 184.

Hayes ended Reconstruction and reformed the civil service. He did not seek a second term, and James A. GARFIELD was nominated as the Republican candidate in 1880. Chester A. ARTHUR of New York was nominated for vice-president. After winning a close election, Garfield was assassinated and Arthur became president. Arthur astonished many with his success in getting passed the Pendleton Act, creating a civil service based on the merit system. He was, however, the only president denied renomination by his party's convention. James G. BLAINE of Maine received the nomination instead and faced Democrat Grover Cleveland of New York in the 1884 election. Cleveland defeated Blaine by a narrow margin.

In 1888 the Republicans chose Benjamin HARRISON of

Indiana as their nominee. Campaigning strongly in favor of the protective tariff, Harrison defeated Cleveland by an electoral vote of 233 to 168, although he received 100,000 fewer popular votes. For the first time in years the Republicans also captured both houses of Congress. The Republicans passed the SHERMAN ANTI-TRUST ACT, admitted several new states to the Union, and passed the highly protective McKinley Tariff Act. President Harrison was renominated in 1892 but lost the election to Grover Cleveland. This defeat was the worst the Republicans had suffered since the party's birth.

In 1896, William MCKINLEY of Ohio became the Republican candidate and went on to beat William Jennings BRYAN by a substantial margin. McKinley received support from the industrial Northeast and the business community. Bryan received his votes from agricultural areas, the South, the West, and from the laboring man. These alliances presaged those that were ultimately to shape the political coalitions of the first half of the 20th century. The Republicans had committed themselves to conservative economics—a stance that they consistently retained thereafter.

McKinley's first term was dominated by the 10-week-long SPANISH-AMERICAN WAR (1898) and the subsequent acquisition of Guam, Puerto Rico, the Philippines, and the annexation of Hawaii. These events increasingly thrust the United States into world politics. With Gov. Theodore ROOSEVELT of New York as his vice-presidential running mate, McKinley again defeated William Jennings Bryan but was assassinated in 1901. Theodore Roosevelt was sworn in as president, inaugurating a remarkable era in American political history.

Theodore Roosevelt and Progressivism. Under Theodore Roosevelt the country saw reforms in economic, political, and social life. Republicans took the lead in conservation efforts and began implementing Roosevelt's trust-busting ideas. Roosevelt's overwhelming reelection in 1904 inaugurated a new era of regulatory legislation (see GOVERNMENT REGULATION) and conservation measures. He chose not to run in 1908 and urged the party to nominate William Howard TAFT of Ohio.

Taft defeated Bryan, who was running for the third time; Taft's style, however, and his conservatism alienated the liberals within the Republican party. Those liberals, led by Robert M. LA FOLLETTE of Wisconsin, organized (1911) the National Progressive Republican League as a means of wresting party control from the conservatives. At the Chicago convention in 1912, Roosevelt challenged Taft for the nomination. Failing to win, Roosevelt bolted the party and ran as the PROGRESSIVE PARTY candidate. Thus split, the Republicans decisively lost the presidency to Woodrow Wilson.

In 1916 the Republicans nominated Supreme Court Justice Charles Evans HUGHES, but Wilson's domestic record, his personal popularity, and his pledge to keep the United States out of the war in Europe were obstacles too great for Hughes to overcome. Despite Wilson's promises, the United States was drawn into World War I, and party politics gave way to bipartisan prosecution of the war. At the end of the war, however, Republicans prevent-

Youthful, charismatic Theodore Roosevelt was selected as William McKinley's running mate in 1900 by Republican party leaders who hoped that the activist governor of New York would be relegated to obscurity by the vice-presidency. Elevated to the chief executive's office by McKinley's assassination in 1901, Roosevelt dominated the Republican party and national politics for the next decade.

ed the United States from joining the League of Nations by rejecting ratification of the Versailles Treaty.

The Republican ticket of Warren G. HARDING and Calvin COOLIDGE won the 1920 election by a landslide. Harding's administration was plagued by scandals (see TEAPOT DOME), which were inherited by Coolidge after Harding's death in 1923. Nominated in his own right in 1924, Coolidge was reelected by a large margin. In 1928, Coolidge declined to run again, and the Republicans turned to Herbert HOOVER of California. Hoover won by an unprecedented landslide against Alfred E. SMITH. Republicans also won control of both houses of Congress, but a rapidly escalating worldwide economic depression brought Hoover and his party to their knees. Although the Hoover administration took steps to stop the decline of the economy, its remedies were generally thought to be ineffectual and too late. Hoover was renominated in 1932

Calvin Coolidge (left) accompanies president-elect Herbert Hoover before the latter's inauguration in 1929. Hoover, a former cabinet member, had become the Republican presidential nominee after the incumbent Coolidge had surprised the country by announcing that he would not run for reelection.

Arms raised in the victory sign, President Dwight D. Eisenhower accepts the Republican party's presidential renomination in 1956 as Vice-President Richard M. Nixon looks on. The Eisenhower-Nixon ticket won a second term in another landslide election.

in the depths of the Depression of the 1930s, but Franklin D. Roosevelt defeated him in one of the great landslide victories in U.S. history. The 70-year era of Republicanism was at an end. One of Roosevelt's major accomplishments was wooing the black vote away from the Republicans.

The Republicans in the Minority: 1932–52. The Republicans were unable to find a candidate who could match Roosevelt's popular appeal. Alf LANDON and Wendell L. WILLKIE failed in 1936 and 1940, respectively. Mostly isolationist before World War II, the Republicans backed the war effort, a stance that was to lead to support—enunciated by Sen. Arthur H. VANDENBERG—for bipartisan foreign policy after the war. The 1944 elections came at a critical time in the midst of World War II, and New York governor Thomas E. DEWEY became the fourth Republican candidate to be overwhelmed by Roosevelt. In 1948, Dewey again was the Republican nominee, this time against Roosevelt's successor, Harry S. Truman. Truman defeated Dewey in a great upset.

The Eisenhower Era. In 1952 the Republican national convention nominated Gen. Dwight D. EISENHOWER to head its ticket. He went on to win a landslide victory, carrying 39 states. Eisenhower's running mate was California senator Richard M. NIXON. The 1956 ticket of Eisenhower and Nixon won another decisive victory, due in part to Eisenhower's moderate course in foreign policy, his successful ending of the Korean War, and his great personal popularity. Democratic control of both houses, however, won in 1954, was continued.

In 1960, Vice-President Nixon won an easy victory for nomination but lost the election to John F. Kennedy of Massachusetts by the smallest popular margin in the 20th century—a difference of only about 113,000 votes out of more than 68 million cast. At the 1964 Republican convention, Sen. Barry M. GOLDWATER of Arizona won the presidential nomination and began an attempt to convert the party into an ideologically pure conservative party. His landslide defeat by Lyndon B. Johnson, however, left the party organization in shambles.

The Nixon-Ford Years. In 1968, Richard Nixon reappeared to win the party's nomination and selected Maryland governor Spiro T. AGNEW as his running mate. Nixon went on to win the election over Democrat Hubert H. Humphrey.

President Nixon's first term was marked by many successes, including improved relations with China, a more cooperative relationship with the USSR, an improved economy, and what appeared to be significant steps toward peace in Vietnam. In 1972 the Democrats nominated a prominent antiwar senator, George S. McGovern of South Dakota. Nixon was reelected by an enormous popular-vote margin. Even so, the Democrats continued to control both houses of the Congress. The campaign, however, carried the seeds of the political destruction of Richard Nixon. A burglary of the Democratic National Committee headquarters in the WATERGATE office complex during the campaign led to revelations of widespread civil and criminal misconduct within the campaign organization, the administration, and the White House; impeachment hearings were held, and eventually Nixon resigned in 1974. An earlier scandal involved Vice-President Agnew, who was forced to resign in 1973 after being convicted of income-tax evasion.

Nixon was succeeded by Vice-President Gerald R. FORD of Michigan, who had been appointed to the office after the resignation of Agnew. After a difficult primary contest against conservative Ronald REAGAN of California, Ford lost the 1976 election to Democrat Jimmy Carter.

The Reagan Administrations. In 1980, Reagan easily won the party's presidential nomination and went on to gain a landslide victory over Carter. At the same time the Republicans took control of the U.S. Senate for the first time in 25 years. This Republican resurgence, however, was only partially confirmed in the 1984 elections. Although in his reelection bid Reagan routed Walter F. MONDALE, the Republicans lost two Senate seats, while

President Ronald Reagan, in a press conference on Nov. 19, 1986, defended his authorization of secret arms sales to Iran. It was subsequently revealed that some of the profits from the arms sales had been diverted to Nicaraguan rebels.

retaining a majority. Democrats continued to control the House; the Republicans won back only about half of the 26 seats that they had lost in 1982. The pattern of Republican presidential triumphs and Democratic gains in Congress continued in 1986 and in the election of 1988, when Vice-President George BUSH won the presidency by a solid margin, but both the House and Senate maintained their Democratic majorities.

requiem [rek'-wee-uhm]   The Latin term *requiem* for the Roman Catholic Mass for the dead comes from the opening words of the service, *Requiem aeternam dona eis* (Grant them eternal rest). Originally set to plainchant, the requiem has existed in polyphonic settings at least since the 15th century. Its musical sections normally consist of Introit: *Requiem aeternam*; *Kyrie* (Lord, have mercy); Gradual: *Requiem aeternam*; Tract: *Absolve Domine* (Absolve, O Lord); Sequence: *Dies irae* (Day of wrath); Offertory: *Domine Jesu Christe*; *Sanctus*; *Agnus Dei* (Lamb of God); Communion: *Lux aeterna* (Light eternal shine upon them). In some early requiems, the texts for the Gradual and Tract differ from those listed, whereas most later settings, such as Verdi's, conclude with the *Libera me, Domine* (Deliver me, O Lord) from the Absolution, which begins the burial service. An overall historical view of the extant settings reveals instances of divergence despite the fixed forms of the liturgical Mass.

Reserve Officers Training Corps   The Reserve Officers Training Corps (ROTC) system trains high school and college students to serve as officers in the U.S. armed forces. Established in 1916, the ROTC has roots in a much older citizen-soldier tradition embodied in the U.S. Constitution. The nation's founders opposed large standing armies and preferred to vest the country's security in a MILITIA system. The training of officers for the armed forces became primarily the responsibility of the civilian higher-education system. The antecedents of ROTC are found in such colleges as Norwich University, founded in 1819, by a former acting superintendent at West Point, as the American Literary, Scientific, and Military Academy.

Military training was institutionalized by the Morrill Act (1862), which in creating the land-grant colleges required that they provide a block of instruction on military tactics. In 1888 additional institutions were approved to receive federal assistance for military training.

In 1916 the National Defense Act created the ROTC to develop a reserve of trained officers, available for service in national emergencies, with senior units based in colleges and universities and junior units based in high schools and approved academies. The program was expanded with the additions of the Naval ROTC (NROTC) in 1926 and the Air Force ROTC (AFROTC) in 1946. Today the ROTC program is the primary source of officers for all of the armed forces.

Programs conducted separately by the U.S. Army, Navy, and Air Force offer a wide variety of opportunities.

These include flight training, summer training on military installations and ships, and classroom training in leadership and management, communication skills, and the theory, history, and dynamics of military affairs. Full 4-year scholarships are available in all programs, and scholarship recipients accept a commitment to serve on active duty.

reservoir   see DAM; HYDROELECTRIC POWER; WATER SUPPLY

resin   Resins are natural or synthetic compounds that can form thin, continuous films, enabling them to be molded into solid objects or spun into thread. They have broad, diverse chemical composition and various applications. Many resins are thick, viscous fluids, and others are hard, brittle, noncrystalline solids. At the molecular level, they are characterized by large numbers of relatively simple repeating units called monomers, which when combined form polymers. Few resins are directly soluble in water, accounting for their use in areas where water resistance is paramount.

Natural Resins. The term *resin* once referred only to naturally available compounds, for example, rosin, copal, dammar, amber, and mastic. All of these are derived from vegetable sources and are collected as exudates from living trees and plants. Lac, used in SHELLAC, is a clear, yellow or orange resin secreted from a scalelike insect. Other natural resins, such as myrrh and aloe, are used in perfumes, incense, and medicines.

Synthetic Resins. In the 20th century the chemical industry experienced a dramatic growth in both technology and volumes produced. CELLULOSE, nitrated heavily during World War I to produce smokeless gunpowder, was modified to provide a film-forming resin. Although extremely flammable, it offered exceptional qualities, such as high gloss, durability, and fast drying in inks, paints, and wood coatings. Cellulose acetate, another modification, was the basis for the fiber rayon. Alkyd resins, the backbone of modern solvent-based paints and other varied products, were widely commercialized.

Demands for synthetic RUBBER during World War II led to the development of styrene butadiene resins and latexes. Vinyl and acrylic resins, largely limited to military use, were later made available for general use. These resins offered unsurpassed stability and durability under most adverse climatic conditions and eventually totally supplanted other grades as paint binders and in exterior plastic displays, automobile coatings, and food packaging applications.

Numerous other chemical varieties have proliferated in recent years. Such resins as polystyrene, vinyl toluene, phenolics, epoxies, urethanes, polyethylene, and polyamides (nylon) are available. They all offer specific qualities as films, PLASTICS, or coatings.

resistance, electrical   Electrical resistance is a property of an electrical circuit that opposes the flow of current. In circuits where the current (*I*) and voltage (*V*) are related by a simple proportionality constant, as in OHM'S LAW, $V = RI$, the proportionality constant R is the resistance of the circuit. Resistance is analogous to friction in hydraulic or mechanical systems and causes energy dissipation in the form of heat. A physical device that displays these properties is called a RESISTOR. The power (P) dissipated in a resistor is given by $P = VI = (RI)I = RI^2$ Watts (Joule's law).

The unit of resistance is the ohm (1 ohm = 1 volt/ampere) and is usually denoted by the Greek omega, Ω. The resistance of metals usually increases with temperature while that of semiconductors decreases. At very low temperatures, the resistance of some elements or alloys falls to zero (see SUPERCONDUCTIVITY).

Because electric charges give up energy in passing through a resistor, there is a voltage drop in the positive current direction, which establishes the usual sign convention. Ohm's law is sometimes written as $I = GV$, where $G = 1/R$ and is called the conductance and is measured in mhos (inverse ohms).

resistivity The resistivity of a material is a measure of its ability to conduct current as a result of an applied electric potential or voltage. Resistivity and conductivity are complementary concepts. Resistivity is an inherent property of a substance, unrelated to its shape or size as is resistance. Its units of measure are ohm-meters. The resistivity of common materials varies over a tremendous range (more than a factor of 10^{20}) and in most (but not all) materials increases with temperature. A material with zero resistivity is called a superconductor. SUPERCONDUCTIVITY occurs in certain metals and alloys (for example, niobium-tin) at very low temperatures, usually below 20 K.

resistor A resistor is an electrical component designed to oppose the flow of current in a circuit (see CIRCUIT, ELECTRIC) and to convert electrical energy into heat energy. In electronic circuits, resistors are introduced to limit current to a safe value, to drop voltage to some required value, to divide up voltage, or to discharge energy, as from a CAPACITOR.

Resistors may be described in terms of their resistance (see RESISTANCE, ELECTRICAL) (in ohms), their ability to dissipate heat (in watts), their functional makeup (fixed or variable), their construction, or the percentage tolerance of their resistive value. Fixed-carbon-composition resistors are available from 2 ohms to 30 million ohms, in power ratings from 0.1 to 2 watts. Power-type resistors, consisting of an alloy ribbon wrapped around a ceramic support, can dissipate hundreds of watts. A film-type resistor, in which a film of carbon or metal is deposited on an insulating cylinder, has high-frequency and high-voltage uses. Variable resistors have a sliding contact for varying the resistance. Low-powered types called potentiometers are used for volume controls in radios and amplifiers; high-powered types called RHEOSTATS may be used, for example, in light-dimming switches. (See THERMISTOR.)

Resnais, Alain [re-nay'] Known for his innovative literary approach to film, Alain Resnais, b. June 3, 1922, became one of the leading directors of French NEW WAVE cinema when it emerged in the late 1950s. Before his feature debut Resnais had spent 11 years making documentary films, including the celebrated *Night and Fog* (1955), an unforgettable description of the Nazi extermination-camp system.

Most of Resnais's full-length films were made in collaboration with a novelist or playwright of note—early collaborators include Marguerite Duras on *Hiroshima, Mon Amour* (1959), Alain Robbe-Grillet on *Last Year at Marienbad* (1961), and Jorge Semprun on *La Guerre est finie* (1966)—yet each film is characterized by Resnais's own distinctive exploration of time and memory, and by a totally novel structure. After a long break from filmmaking in the early 1970s, Resnais returned with two exquisitely shot films, *Stavisky* (1974) and *Providence* (1977). *Mon Oncle d'Amerique* (1980), a sophisticated mixture of fiction and fact, natural science, philosophy, and comedy, won the New York Critics Circle Award for the year's best foreign film. His more recent films have met with less success.

resonance (chemistry) In chemistry, resonance is a concept of molecular bonding in which the structure of a molecule can be represented by two or more different structures that differ only in the position of electrons. An example is sulfur dioxide, SO_2, shown as an electron-dot formula:

$$:\ddot{O}: \; :\ddot{S}: \; :\ddot{O}: \;\; \leftrightarrow \;\; :\ddot{O}: \; :\ddot{S}: \; :\ddot{O}:$$

The two-headed arrow is conventionally used to indicate resonant structures. The term is an unfortunate one because it creates the erroneous impression that a pair of electrons is sometimes a part of one bond and sometimes the other, or that the molecule resonates (flips back and forth) between the two structures. Sulfur dioxide and other resonant molecules have only one structure, which is not representable by the simplified methods of writing structures according to the octet rule.

In addition to explaining molecular structure, the concept of resonance is important because resonant molecules are more stable than predicted; that is, they are less reactive because more energy is required to break resonant chemical bonds than nonresonant bonds.

resonance (physics) Resonance usually refers to the large absorption of energy and the resultant large amplitude of motion that occurs when a vibrating system is driven by an external force at its natural frequency of vibration. The principles of resonance are at work when a person pushes a child in a swing; the greatest effect will be achieved for the least effort if the force is applied at the natural frequency of the swing and in phase with the motion. In molecular, atomic, nuclear, and subnuclear systems, the concept of resonance is of considerable importance. The reason lies in the quantum-mechanical nature of these systems. Their energy can change only in discrete steps; only certain amounts of energy, and therefore only certain frequencies of radiation, are absorbed. Some subnuclear particles are so elusive that their existence is known only through a resonant absorption of energy.

Respighi, Ottorino [rays-peeg'-ee]   Ottorino Respighi, b. July 9, 1879, d. Apr. 18, 1936, was Italy's most important postromantic composer. Unusually versatile, he wrote in diverse forms and styles; his love of medieval and Renaissance music inspired original scores and arrangements of delicacy and subtlety that contrast with the large-scale orchestral works at which he excelled. His most famous works are the tone poems *The Fountains of Rome* (1917), *The Pines of Rome* (1924), and *Roman Festivals* (1929). Also popular are his three sets entitled *Ancient Airs and Dances* (1917, 1924, 1932) and the suite *The Birds* (1927).

respiration, cellular   see METABOLISM

respirator   The respirator is a mechanical device used to ventilate the lungs of patients who cannot readily breathe by themselves. The "iron lung"—the first operative respirator—consisted of a long, metal cylinder in which a patient was placed, covering the body except for the head. The machine created external, positive pressure to help expand the lungs. The more recently designed portable, lightweight respirator device is generally attached to a surgically incised opening in a patient's trachea and pushes air into the lungs. Once the pressure is released the lungs relax, pushing the air back out.

respiratory system   An aerobic organism must abstract oxygen from environmental air or water in order to support its life functions. The process of obtaining oxygen (O_2) and releasing the cellular waste product, carbon dioxide (CO_2), into the environment is known as respiration. A tiny unicellular organism can obtain oxygen and dispose of carbon dioxide by means of passive diffusion through its cell membrane. Multicellular organisms, however, have had to evolve specialized respiratory systems for supplying O_2 to their tissues and removing excess CO_2.

The simplest invertebrates, such as sponges and flatworms, rely on gas exchange across the body surface to meet respiratory needs. Invertebrates having more-complex body structures, such as the earthworm, have not only gas exchange across the body surface but also a simple circulatory system, which carries oxygenated blood to deeper regions of the body. Arthropods such as insects have a network of tracheal tubes that open at the body surface and connect with inner tissues. Gas exchange in echinoderms such as starfish occurs across the surface of the tube feet. Many invertebrates have gills, ranging from

a single layer of cells protruding from the body surface to stacked layers of highly vascular tissue. Book lungs of spiders consist of internal, leaflike plates of tissue; air enters through abdominal openings and circulates through these plates.

Skin, Gills, and Lungs

All successfully evolved respiratory systems have certain common characteristics. First, they have a large, thin, and highly vascular respiratory membrane that allows efficient gas diffusion to occur between the blood and the external medium. Second, the CIRCULATORY SYSTEM is capable of carrying sufficient oxygen to, and carbon dioxide from, the body tissues. Third, they have the ability to replenish the oxygen that is in immediate contact with the respiratory surface.

Within these constraints, three types of vertebrate respiratory systems have evolved: gills, LUNGS, and specialized areas of skin. Gills are located in the back of the mouth; water passes through the mouth, past the gills, and out via gill slits. Gas exchange occurs in the secondary lamellae of the gills. Lungs are connected to bronchial tubes that in turn connect to the trachea, leading to oral and nasal passages; gas exchange takes place in terminal air sacs (alveoli) within the lungs. In amphibians and some fishes, specialized areas of skin function as a respiratory membrane.

Blood and Oxygen Transport. The blood flowing through a respiratory organ is able to load sufficient oxygen and deliver it to body tissues. It then loads carbon dioxide and carries it back to the respiratory organ. Blood transports oxygen by means of hemoglobin, a substance present in all vertebrate blood except for some Antarctic fishes. Hemoglobin contains ionized iron molecules to which oxygen temporarily bonds during transport to the tissues. The carbon dioxide produced in the tissues during metabolism is carried away primarily in the form of bicarbonate ions (HCO_3^-), which are soluble in the blood plasma.

Respiratory Pump. Oxygen is continually replenished and carbon dioxide discarded at the interface between the air or water and the blood by the action of a respiratory pump. This provides fresh air or water to the respiratory membrane, which is the process of inspiration, and expels water or air that is low in oxygen and high in carbon dioxide, the process of expiration. This cyclical process is known as ventilation. During the repetitions of this cycle, the quantity of inspired air or water that passes across the membrane in one minute is called the minute volume and is the product of the number of breaths in a minute (respiratory rate) and the amount of air or water that passes through with each breath (tidal volume). Alterations in respiratory rate and tidal volume, or both, adjust gas exchange in order to accommodate an animal's changing metabolic needs.

Fishes

Most fishes employ a double pumping system that provides an almost uninterrupted flow of water into the mouth and across the gills. During inspiration the floor of the mouth cavity depresses, forming a negative pressure that causes water to flow into the mouth. The gill flaps close, and the postgill cavity expands, causing an even greater negative pressure on the postgill side. This creates a pressure gradient that permits water to flow across the lamellae. The mouth floor then rises, causing a more positive pressure in the mouth cavity, which maintains the pressure gradient and water flow. When pressure in the postgill chamber exceeds that of the ambient water, the gill flaps open and stale water is expelled. Many fishes, such as a catfish making an overland migration, also respire through their skin.

Amphibians

Amphibians utilize skin, lungs, and, in some forms, such as tadpoles and salamanders, gills. The system that predominates depends on a species' environment. The frog depends on a positive-pressure pump to inflate its lungs. The floor of the mouth depresses, and air is suctioned through the nostrils. The nostrils close and the mouth floor rises, causing air to flow into and inflate the lungs. Expiration is by means of passive elastic recoil of the lungs.

Reptiles

Reptiles depend primarily on lung respiration. Complex airways consist of a distinct trachea and bronchi. The respiratory pump is powered by suction that is created by lowering the pressure in the lungs to below that of the atmosphere. This is accomplished by muscular expansion of the rib cage and the thoracic cavity. The respiratory cycle has three phases: inspiration, apnea, and expiration. During inspiration the rib cage expands and the glottis

Lungs are the basic respiratory organs of air-breathing vertebrates. Diagrams of a frog (A), rabbit (B), and duck (C) represent various respiratory cycles; cross sections of their lungs (D) illustrate the structure of the respiratory surface in an amphibian, mammal, and bird. A frog's lungs are relatively simple, with a modest surface area of about 100 cm^2 (15.5 in^2); by comparison, the gas-exchange surface of a pair of human lungs is about 70 m^2 (750 ft^2).The frog depends on a positive pressure mechanism for ventilation. The floor of the mouth is lowered (A1), drawing air through the nostrils and into the mouth cavity. The previously inflated lungs then expel (A2) oxygen-poor air past the mouth cavity (with minimal mixing) and out through the nostrils. The nostrils close as the floor of the mouth contracts (A3), creating a positive pressure that pumps the "fresh" air into the lungs. The airway between the mouth cavity and lungs closes (A4), retaining air in the lungs, and the nostrils open; the cycle can then repeat. Mammalian lungs have a complex structure, with a large alveolar surface for gas exchange. Contraction of inspiratory muscles (B1) causes the diaphragm and rib cage to expand the chest cavity; the resulting negative pressure (suction) draws air through the nostrils, filling the lungs. When the muscles relax (B2), the diaphragm and rib cage cause air to be pushed out of the lungs. This inhalation-exhalation cycle repeats (B3–4). A paired set of air sacs characterizes a bird's respiratory system; the relatively inelastic lungs, which contain a system of air capillaries for gas exchange, constitute only 9 to 17 percent of the total respiratory air space. Contraction of inspiratory muscles expands the chest and abdominal cavities; the reduced pressure draws fresh air into the posterior air sacs (C1) and stale air from the lungs into the anterior sacs (C3). When expiratory muscles contract, fresh air is expelled from the posterior sacs (C2) through the lungs; stale air is expelled from the anterior sacs (C4) through the nostrils.

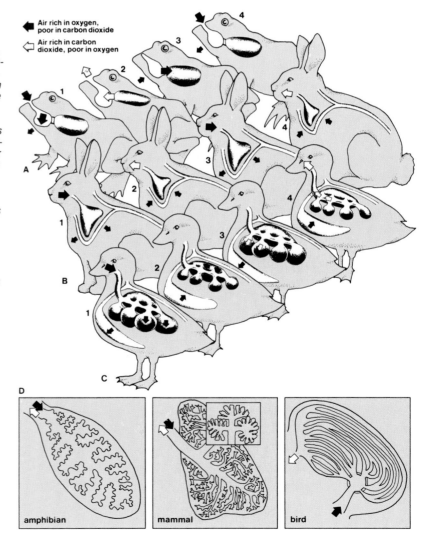

Air rich in oxygen, poor in carbon dioxide

Air rich in carbon dioxide, poor in oxygen

amphibian

mammal

bird

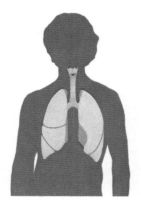

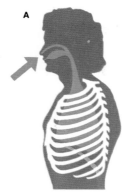

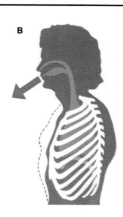

(Left) *In the human respiratory system, the lungs are two cone-shaped structures in the chest cavity. Inhaled air passes through the trachea, or windpipe, and infiltrates the lungs by branching tubes that terminate in alveoli, or tiny air sacs. The alveoli are surrounded by capillaries, or minute blood vessels, and the blood picks up oxygen from the inhaled air and releases its waste carbon dioxide, which is then exhaled.* (Right) *The breathing process is made possible by the diaphragm, a muscle (shown in orange) under the lungs. During inhalation* (A) *the diaphragm and rib cage expand the chest cavity; during exhalation* (B) *the diaphragm and the muscles of the rib cage relax, allowing the release of air.*

opens, lowering the pressure in both the abdomen and the lungs in comparison to that of the ambient air. This causes air to flow into the lungs. During apnea, in which no respiratory movement occurs, the glottis closes and the respiratory muscles relax. Expiration is usually by passive elastic recoil of the lungs.

Mammals

Mammals have a highly developed respiratory system, containing a trachea, bronchi, and extensive branchings (bronchioles) that terminate at the alveoli. Inflation of the lungs is accomplished by contraction of inspiratory muscles, which, by enlarging the thoracic cavity, reduce the lung pressure and allow air to flow into them. The major muscle used during inspiration is the diaphragm, which separates the abdominal and thoracic cavities. Quiet expiration occurs passively by means of the elastic recoil of the respiratory muscles and lungs. If rapid expiration is required, expiratory muscles must come into play.

Birds

The respiratory system of birds is adapted to a high metabolic rate, the high energy demands of flying, and the need for sufficient oxygen at high altitudes. The system consists of two lungs and an extensive, paired series of air sacs that fill much of the chest and abdominal cavities and are connected to auxiliary air spaces, located in the bones.

The bird's trachea, which splits into two primary bronchi, carries fresh air through the lungs and delivers it to the two abdominal air sacs. Secondary bronchi direct air to the other air sacs. Air is then transported by tertiary bronchi that penetrate the lung tissue and terminate in air capillaries, a dense network of minute air channels that are the site of gas exchange. Stale air flows from the lungs to the anterior air sacs and is expelled through the trachea. Fresh air courses through the air capillaries during both inspiration and expiration. During inspiration inspiratory muscles enlarge the thoracic-abdominal cavity, decreasing the pressure in all the air sacs. Fresh air flows into all the air sacs except the anterior sacs. Some air then enters the lungs, while stale air in the lungs flows into the anterior sacs. Expiration is accomplished by ex-

piratory muscles, which increase pressure in the thoracic-abdominal cavity. Stale air is expelled into the environment, and fresh air from the air sacs is pushed into the lungs by way of the posterior air sacs. The entire process is facilitated by the action of the diaphragm, which in birds is a thin membrane of connective tissue instead of a sheet of muscle. It is connected to muscles that are attached to the body wall. Contraction of these muscles causes the diaphragm to flatten. The avian diaphragm diminishes the lung volume during inspiration and expands it during expiration.

In a bird during flight, inspiration occurs on the upstroke and expiration on the downstroke. The downward stroke of the wings compresses the rib cage, expelling the stale air from the anterior air sacs out through the trachea.

---

respiratory-system disorders Respiratory diseases affect the RESPIRATORY SYSTEM, which in humans includes the nose, mouth, throat, larynx, trachea, bronchial tubes, and lungs. These diseases may be acute or chronic.

Infections

Viruses. Infections are the most common cause of respiratory diseases and may be produced by viruses, bacteria, fungi, protozoans, and microorganisms that are species of *Mycoplasma, Legionella*, and *Rickettsia*. Viruses are highly communicable from person to person and cause the common head cold (RHINITIS) and chest cold (tracheobronchitis; see COLD, COMMON). Other viruses cause INFLUENZA, PNEUMONIA, and other illnesses, such as measles, polio, and chicken pox, that may be associated with respiratory-tract complications.

Bacteria. A large number of bacteria, the most common being species of *Streptococcus, Staphylococcus*, and *Hemophilus*, may infect any part of the respiratory system, causing such diseases as BRONCHITIS, SINUSITIS, STREP THROAT, TONSILLITIS, WHOOPING COUGH, pharyngitis, and pneumonia. A bacillus, *Mycobacterium tuberculosis*, causes TUBERCULOSIS, and other *mycobacteria* cause diseases with almost identical symptoms. The latter live in soil and water and are not transmitted from person to person as is the tuberculosis bacillus.

Fungi. Pathogenic fungi can infect the lungs and cause pneumonialike FUNGUS DISEASES such as COCCIDIOIDOMYCOSIS, HISTOPLASMOSIS, and blastomycosis. Fungi, which live primarily in the soil and are inhaled into the lungs, are not transmissible from person to person.

Protozoa and Worms. Paragonimiasis, caused by a flatworm known as the lung fluke, is prevalent in the Orient. The hydatid disease, or echinococcosis, caused by a tapeworm, is prevalent in Australia, New Zealand, and Argentina. A protozoan, *Pneumocystis carinii*, causes pneumonia in children and has become the most common cause of pneumonia in adults who suffer from acquired immune deficiency syndrome (see AIDS).

Mycoplasmas, Legionellas, and Rickettsiae. *Mycoplasma pneumoniae* is a tiny bacterialike organism that causes sinusitis, pharyngitis, bronchitis, and mycoplasmal pneumonia. Infection is spread by close and frequent contact. Another form of pneumonia, LEGIONNAIRES' DISEASE, is caused by the tiny bacterium *Legionella pneumophila*. It is usually acquired from contaminated water in air-conditioning systems. RICKETTSIAE are very small microorganisms having some characteristics common to both bacteria and viruses. They cause Q FEVER, ROCKY MOUNTAIN SPOTTED FEVER, TYPHUS, and other diseases, most of which may have respiratory-tract involvement. Infection is spread by fleas, lice, ticks, or mites.

Chronic Obstructive Pulmonary Diseases

These conditions are also among the most common respiratory disorders. Characterized by narrowing of the bronchi (air passages) of the lungs, they include ASTHMA, EMPHYSEMA, and CHRONIC BRONCHITIS. The bronchial narrowing obstructs the flow of air in and out of the lungs. In asthma the size of the airways is reduced by spasm of the muscles in the bronchial walls. Emphysema and chronic bronchitis are nearly always the result of long-term cigarette SMOKING, which causes swelling of the membrane lining the air passages. In emphysema actual destruction of lung tissue results in the formation of cystlike spaces in the lungs. Air is trapped in these structures during respiration and becomes useless.

Allergies

Allergies produce hay fever, asthma, and certain forms of pneumonia. The individual suffering from these conditions has become oversensitive to contact with particular substances such as plant pollen and various types of organic dusts or chemicals. When these agents are inhaled, the body overreacts, producing the symptoms of the specific illness. Allergic pneumonia includes such disorders as farmer's lung, caused by exposure to bacteria in moldy hay; air-conditioner or heating-system disease, caused by exposure to bacteria-contaminated mist from humidifiers (see DISEASE, OCCUPATIONAL); and other forms (see ALLERGY).

Pneumoconioses

Diseases due to inhalation of nonallergenic inorganic dusts are classified as pneumoconioses: silica causes silicosis; coal dust causes BLACK LUNG, or coal worker's pneumoconiosis; ASBESTOS fibers cause asbestosis; and beryllium causes berylliosis. These dusts injure the tissues of the lungs and often result in pulmonary fibrosis (scar formation) with resulting impairment of lung function and progressive disability.

Pleurisy

Pleurisy is an inflammation of the pleural membranes, which surround the lungs and line the chest cavity. It can develop as a result of pneumonia, rheumatic fever, or such chronic obstructive lung disorders as a tumor.

Tumors

Benign Tumors. TUMORS can be divided into two groups, benign (noncancerous) and malignant (cancerous). Benign tumors do not spread to other parts of the body, but they may cause damage by local growth and pressure on other structures, producing serious complications such as airway obstruction and bleeding. In addition, they may undergo malignant transformation.

Cancer. The most common form of malignant tumor of the respiratory tract is lung CANCER. Lung cancer has been attributed to cigarette smoking and to environmental pollution: exposure to materials such as asbestos, chromium, and radioactive substances increases the probability of its development. The main cancer types are carcinomas, lymphomas, and sarcomas. Bronchial carcinomas arise from the trachea or bronchi, and alveolar cell carcinomas arise from lung tissue. Lymphomas arise in the lymph nodes related to the lungs and other body tissues. Sarcomas may originate in the lungs or in some other structure such as bone.

Drug-Induced Pulmonary Diseases

Various drugs can cause either pulmonary fibrosis or edema (fluid in the lung). Such drugs include heroin, methadone, Darvon, and drugs used in the treatment of cancer (methotrexate and bleomycin), leukemia (busulfan), and infection (nitrofurantoin).

Structural Disorders

Structural changes in the lungs or pleurae result from a variety of causes, including pneumothorax and bronchiectasis. Pneumothorax is a condition characterized by collapse of the lung due to rupture of the membrane covering the lung and subsequent escape of air into the space between the lung and the chest wall. Pneumothorax may result from penetrating injury to the lung or as a complication of other diseases.

Bronchiectasis is the abnormal dilation of one or more bronchi, usually resulting from weakening of the bronchial wall by infection. This condition may follow pneumonia, whooping cough, or tuberculosis, or may be hereditary.

Pleural effusion, or fluid on the lung, is the accumulation of fluid in the pleural space; it can result as a complication of heart failure, pneumonia, lung cancer, tuberculosis, pulmonary infarction, and many other conditions. Atelectasis is a form of collapse of the lung due to occlusion of a bronchus by a tumor, a foreign body such as a peanut, or thick mucus.

Generalized Diseases

A vast number of disorders, although not primarily respiratory, produce major or minor pulmonary manifestations. For instance, sarcoidosis, a tuberculosislike disease characterized by tumorous collections of cells, can involve the lungs. Blood clots originating in the veins or heart can break loose and travel to the lungs, creating a PULMONARY EMBOLISM by obstructing the lung arteries. This causes damage or death of the tissue supplied by the obstructed vessel. Heart failure may cause fluid to collect in the lungs, leading to shortness of breath (dyspnea) on exertion and attacks of breathlessness at night. Kidney failure may also be associated with collection of fluid and with other changes in the lung, referred to as uremic pneumonia. Other diseases that may be associated with pulmonary lesions are the autoimmune disorders that cause a person's immune defenses to attack the person's own body; these diseases include lupus erythematosis, periarteritis, systemic sclerosis (scleroderma), and rheumatoid arthritis.

Children's Diseases

CYSTIC FIBROSIS is a hereditary disease of children and young adults affecting the secretion of the glands that produce mucus, sweat, saliva, and digestive juices. The secretions become viscous, and an abnormally large amount of salt is present in the sweat. The disease affects the glands throughout the body, but pulmonary complications are very common.

Whooping cough caused by a bacteria, *Bordetella pertussis*, is a children's disease characterized by a high-pitched whooping sound accompanying frequent coughing.

Respiratory distress syndrome (RDS), or HYALINE MEMBRANE DISEASE, occurs in newborn infants. It is an indication of incomplete development of the lungs; the infant suffers from difficulty in breathing and deficient transfer of oxygen into the blood. A similar condition in adults, called ARDS (adult respiratory distress syndrome), has many causes, including severe infection, trauma, and the aspiration of stomach contents into the lungs.

▬

Reston [res'-tuhn]   Reston (1990 pop., 48,556), a suburb of Washington, D.C., in northern Virginia, is a NEW TOWN—a planned community with its own commercial, industrial, and residential areas. Gulf Reston, Inc., financed the project from 1967 until 1978, when the Mobil Oil Corporation purchased about half the land and continued to develop it.

▬

Reston, James Barrett   The American journalist James Barrett Reston, b. Scotland, Nov. 3, 1909, has covered numerous major events during a long and distinguished career—among them the Yalta Conference, the Robert Oppenheimer case, and the death of Stalin. He became known for his liberal views and for his influence on public opinion. Reston began his career with the *Springfield* (Ohio) *Daily News* (1932–33) and then became a reporter for the Associated Press (1934–39). He

James Reston's career with the New York Times spans five decades, during which he has served as a war correspondent, bureau chief, executive editor, and vice-president. Reston retired as a regular Times columnist in 1987 but continued to write occasionally as "senior columnist."

Photo Jill Krementz © 1974

achieved prominence with his fervently patriotic book *Prelude to Victory* (1942) and as London correspondent (1939–41) for the *New York Times*. In 1941 he joined the paper's Washington bureau and subsequently was chief Washington correspondent (1953–64), associate editor (1964–68), executive editor (1968–69), and vice-president (1969–74). From 1974 to 1987 he wrote the Washington political column. Reston's numerous awards and honors include Pulitzer Prizes for national reporting in 1945 and 1957.

▬

Restoration   In English history, *Restoration* refers to the period after the fall (1660) of the republican Commonwealth and Protectorate, when the monarchy was restored in the person of CHARLES II. Early in 1660 the Convention Parliament invited Charles to return from exile on condition that he grant an amnesty to his former enemies (excepting those responsible for the execution of his father, Charles I) and guarantee religious toleration. Having met these conditions in the Declaration of Breda, Charles landed in England on May 25, 1660. The promise of religious toleration was broken when the royalist Cavalier Parliament adopted the CLARENDON CODE (1661–65).

In French history, *Restoration* means the period (1814–30) of the restored Bourbon monarchy, after the overthrow of Napoleon I.

▬

Restoration drama   The reopening of London theaters by Charles II in 1660 began the 40-year period of Restoration drama, noted for such theatrical innovations as movable scenery, opera, and the introduction of actresses, and especially for its satiric comedy and bombastic tragedy. Although criticized for its libertinism and narrow social focus, at its best Restoration comedy intelligently explores the social and sexual gamesmanship of fashionable society, whether as comic spectacle, as in the plays of Aphra BEHN, Sir George ETHEREGE, and George FARQUHAR; as questionings of personal and social morality, as in the plays of William CONGREVE and Thomas OTWAY; or as evidence of moral self-betrayal by hypocrisy and lust—an aspect of the drama of William WYCHERLEY. Restoration tragedy, however, is generally undistinguished. John DRYDEN championed the heroic, or rhymed, couplet as a tragic form early in his career but later abandoned it.

---

resurrection   The concept of resurrection from the dead is found in several religions, although it is associated particularly with Christianity because of the central belief in the resurrection of Jesus Christ. Hope of a resurrection may have entered Judaism from Persian sources, although the idea has deeper roots in Old Testament Yahwism and the concept of God's covenant with Israel. The resurrection life was variously conceived, but the type of hope that passed into early Christian thought centered on the transformation of human life from the dead into a transcendental mode of existence.

After the EASTER experiences, earliest Christianity expressed its faith in what had happened to Jesus as resurrection in the transcendental sense. This concept is sharply distinguished from resuscitation, or a return to this-worldly existence, as narrated in the raisings of Lazarus and others attributed to Jesus. Saint Paul conceived the resurrection of Jesus as the first instance of an apocalyptic-like resurrection (1 Cor. 15:20, 23); as a result of Christ's resurrection, all believers may hope for resurrection at the SECOND COMING OF CHRIST. Paul indicates that the resurrection body will be new and "spiritual" (1 Cor. 15:35–54).

See also: IMMORTALITY; JUDGMENT, LAST.

---

retailing   Retailing is the selling of finished goods and services to the consumer for personal or family consumption. It includes store retailing (for example, DEPARTMENT STORES and SUPERMARKETS), nonstore retailing (for example, door-to-door sales, vending machines, and the MAIL-ORDER BUSINESS), and service retailing (for example, HOTELS and such personal services as dry cleaners). Approximately one out of eight employed persons in the United States works in retailing.

Small, privately owned retail businesses may be either independent or franchised. Franchising, in which the retailer pays to adopt the name and sell the product of the firm selling the franchise, has grown in the United States in recent years, whereas the independents have declined. Franchisees and small independents account for about one-half of all retail sales in the United States and Canada, mainly in nonstore and service retailing and in selected store operations. In most other countries small independent merchants are more prevalent.

Department stores command large sales volumes by providing a wide variety of nonfood merchandise while offering extensive customer service. Their importance grew steadily from their inception during the mid-19th century until about 1930, when a decline set in that lasted until they more effectively met the challenge of chain stores and discount houses. Today department stores account for more than one-tenth of retail sales in the United States and Canada.

Supermarkets are large self-service food stores that dominate today's grocery-store business. They began as no-frills operations and first flourished in response to the economic pressures of the 1930s. The spread of household refrigeration enhanced their attraction by reducing the need for frequent purchases. Supermarkets now devote increased attention to nonfood merchandise, such as toys, hardware, and clothing.

Chain stores are groups of stores with similar characteristics and merchandise operating under central ownership. By buying in quantity and underselling their competitors, they expanded so successfully in the 1920s and '30s that many people feared the demise of the independent retailer. Attempts to limit chain stores in the United States included the Robinson-Patman Act (1936), pricing laws, and license fees. Today chains account for more than one-third of all retail sales.

Shopping centers are planned clusters of complementary stores. Originally developed for the suburbs, today they are also found in urban areas. Shopping centers emerged as an important retail development after World War II, with the growth of the suburbs, increased use of the automobile, and traffic congestion in downtown areas. After years of phenomenal growth, their future development is expected to be moderate because of saturated markets, slower population growth, and tighter legal restrictions.

Mail-order retailers solicit purchases and accept orders by telephone or mail. Developed in the late 19th century to offer greater merchandise assortments at reasonable prices to rural customers, mail order is now used by urban retailers to supplement their regular sales.

See also: MARKETING; WHOLESALING.

retardation, mental   see MENTAL RETARDATION

retarded, education of the   see SPECIAL EDUCATION

---

retrovirus   A retrovirus is a VIRUS that reproduces itself in a manner distinct from that of most other viruses. The core of any virus is a single molecule of nucleic acid, either DNA or RNA. When a virus invades a cell, this genetic material is usually replicated in its original form. A number of RNA viruses, however, make a copy of their genetic material in the form of DNA instead. In order to do so, they must be able to produce a particular enzyme that can construct a DNA molecule using an RNA template. This enzyme, called RNA-directed DNA polymerase, is also called reverse transcriptase because it reverses the normal cellular process of transcription (see GENETIC CODE). An RNA virus whose life cycle involves the process of reverse transcription is called a retrovirus. The DNA molecules produced by this process are then inserted into the genetic material of the host cell, where they are replicated as DNA along with the DNA of the host's chromosomes; they are thereby distributed to all daughter cells during subsequent cell divisions. At some later time, in one or more of these daughter cells, the virus then produces RNA copies of its genetic material. These become covered with protein coats and leave the cell to repeat the life cycle.

Retroviruses have gained wide attention because they can cause severe diseases in organisms. If a retrovirus contains an ONCOGENE within its nucleic acid, the infected cell will be transformed into a CANCER cell. Retroviruses without oncogenes can also cause cancer, however, by inserting themselves into the host-cell DNA near certain genes that then become abnormally activated and make the cell malignant.

Several related retroviruses, named human T-cell lymphotropic viruses (HTLV), are involved in various diseases that affect the T-type of lymphocyte (see BLOOD; IMMUNITY). One of these, HTLV-I, causes adult T-cell LEUKEMIA. A second, HTLV-II, is associated with a T-cell variant of hairy-cell leukemia. A third, once labeled HTLV-III, destroys T-cells rather than causing them to become cancerous. Now linked to acquired immune deficiency syndrome (see AIDS), it has been renamed human immunodeficiency virus (HIV). Another form of the virus, HIV-2, has also been found.

Walter Reuther was a prominent U.S. labor leader from the 1930s until his death. As president of the United Auto Workers (UAW) and the Congress of Industrial Organizations (CIO), Reuther was instrumental in the 1955 merger of the American Federation of Labor (AFL) and the CIO.

Return of the Native, The   Thomas HARDY's novel *The Return of the Native* (1878) achieves the intensity of classical Greek tragedy in its depiction of a pitiable human struggle against relentless fate. The author's somber view of human existence is expressed both in the superb opening description of Egdon Heath and in the tragic lives of Clym Yeobright, the returned native of the heath, his cousin Thomasin, Damon Wildeve, and Eustacia Vye. Nature is shown to be both beautiful and morally indifferent, and humankind is depicted as responsible to a great degree for its own tragedy.

Réunion [ray-oon-yohn']   Réunion, an overseas department of France since 1946, is an island in the western Indian Ocean located about 645 km (400 mi) east of Madagascar. The island covers an area of 2,512 km² (970 mi²) and has a population of 600,000 (1990 est.). Saint-Denis is the capital.

A narrow coastal plain gives way inland to high plateaus and mountains. The cultivation of sugar, tourism, and the distillation of rum are important to the island's economy.

Discovered by Portuguese explorers, Réunion was claimed in 1642 by the French, who established a permanent settlement in 1665. It was a French colony until 1946.

Reuther, Walter P. [roo'-thur]   Walter Philip Reuther, b. Wheeling, W.Va., Sept. 1, 1907, d. May 9, 1970, was president of the United Auto Workers (UAW) from 1946 until his death, president of the Congress of Industrial Organizations (CIO) from 1952 to 1955, and vice-president of the AFL-CIO between 1955 and 1968. Reuther started factory work at the age of 16 and quickly became involved in union affairs. Prominent in the sit-down

strikes of the late 1930s that accompanied the establishment of the UAW, Reuther won many benefits for his membership, including annual wage increases based on productivity, cost-of-living raises, and health and pension benefits. As president of the CIO, he helped to plan its merger with the American Federation of Labor (AFL) in 1955.

revelation   Revelation, in the religious sense, is an insight into divine reality usually claimed by the founder or original adherents of a religion. Revelations may take various forms. They may be visions, inner voices, or a combination of these (for example, Moses' experience at the burning bush, or Muhammad's revelations, which he said were like the ringing of a bell that later resolved itself into words). In the Judeo-Christian tradition, especially, revelations may be historical events that are understood to yield an interpretation of history as a whole (for example, Israel's deliverance from Egypt, and the death and resurrection of Jesus Christ).

The Eastern religions stress the manifestation of the divine in all nature ("general revelation"). This concept is also present in Judaism, Christianity, and Islam, but these religions focus on particular revelations. Muslims believe that the Koran was dictated verbatim to Muhammad. Judaism and Christianity also hold that their holy book, the Bible, was divinely inspired, although most modern theologians interpret its propositions as deriving from, rather than constituting, revelation (the content of the latter being understood as a fundamental experience of the divine rather than as a series of verbal statements). Among Christians, Protestants believe that the Bible, with latitude of interpretation, is the sole source of revelation, whereas Roman Catholics and Orthodox find the authority of revelation in apostolic traditions as well.

Revelation, Book of   The Book of Revelation is the last book of the New Testament of the Bible. Its title comes from the first verse of the text, "the revelation of Jesus Christ ... to his servant John." The book is also called The Apocalypse, and it is the only piece of New Testament writing cast almost entirely in the apocalyptic mode (see APOCALYPTIC LITERATURE). Irenaeus states that Revelation was written during the reign of the Roman emperor Domitian, probably about AD 95. Tradition asserts that the apostle Saint JOHN wrote Revelation during his exile on Patmos. Some scholars do not accept this attribution because of the stylistic differences between Revelation and the other works attributed to John—the Gospel and Epistles.

After a prologue, the book comprises two main parts. The first (chapters 2–3) contains letters to the seven churches of Asia, warning them against false teachers and offering encouragement. The second (chapters 4–22) consists of a series of visions, replete with allegories, numbers, and other symbols, and a strong eschatological message. These features are characteristic of the apocalyptic writing then in vogue.

Interpretation of the Book of Revelation has been a source of much controversy. Some have held that it had a message only for the 1st-century world. Others maintain that the book is a prophecy to be fulfilled totally in the future (see MILLENARIANISM). Undoubtedly, John spoke to the situation of his day. The letters to the seven churches indicate a situation of crisis, probably brought on by Roman persecutions of the Christians. From his understanding of the revelation of God for his day, he painted a vision of God's final triumph over evil that has sustained many Christians in later eras.

Revels, Hiram R. [rev'-ulz]   Hiram Rhoades Revels, b. Fayetteville, N.C., Sept. 1, 1822, d. Jan. 16, 1901, became the first African American to serve in the U.S. Senate. The child of free black–Indian parents, he was educated in a seminary in Ohio and at Knox College in Il-

Hiram Revels, the first black U.S. senator, appears (far left) *with the black representatives in the 41st and 42d Congresses:* (from the left) *Benjamin S. Turner, Robert C. De Large, Josiah T. Walls, Jefferson F. Long, Joseph H. Rainey, and Robert B. Elliott.*

linois and was ordained (1845) a minister in the African Methodist Episcopal church. When the Civil War began Revels recruited blacks for the Union army and enlisted as chaplain of a black regiment. A Republican senator from Mississippi in 1870–71, he filled the seat once held by Jefferson Davis. Revels advocated the restoration of civil and political rights to former Confederates. On leaving the Senate he became president of Alcorn Agricultural and Mechanical College in Mississippi.

revenue sharing   Revenue sharing is a program in which the federal government shares a set percentage of federal tax collections with local and state or provincial governments. The advocates of these plans emphasize two advantages: federal governments are more effective tax collectors than are smaller governmental units, and local communities can best decide the allocation of federal moneys. Control of resources is a central issue in the Canadian and U.S. revenue-sharing debates.

In the United States the Nixon administration urged revenue sharing as a way to slow the growth of the federal bureaucracy and return important federal programs to localities. In 1972, Congress approved revenue sharing. This federal aid program provided no-strings-attached subsidies to more than 39,000 municipalities, townships, and counties. Because personal income was considered in allocating revenue-sharing funds, poor areas received more on a per-capita basis than did wealthy ones. The program remained controversial—in part because some moneys went to communities with no demonstrable need. In 1981, President Reagan announced his intention to eliminate revenue sharing; it ended on Sept. 30, 1986, after disbursing about $85 billion over 14 years.

Revere, Paul [ruh-veer']   An American patriot and silversmith, Paul Revere, b. Boston, Jan. 1, 1735, d. May 10, 1818, became a legendary hero at the start of the American Revolution, when he rode from Charlestown to Lexington, Mass., on the night of Apr. 18, 1775, to warn the populace of approaching British troops. An official courier for the Massachusetts Committee of Correspondence, he arrived in Lexington shortly before another rider, William DAWES, and warned John HANCOCK and Samuel ADAMS to escape. Revere then started for Concord accompanied by Dawes and Samuel Prescott but was halted by a British patrol. Only Prescott reached Concord. Revere's exploit was celebrated in Henry Wadsworth Longfellow's famous but generally inaccurate poem, "Paul Revere's Ride" (1863).

A leader of the SONS OF LIBERTY, Revere had earlier been involved in numerous patriot activities including the BOSTON TEA PARTY (1773). In 1779 he participated in the Penobscot expedition in Maine; although Revere was accused of cowardice, a court-martial two years later cleared him.

Revere is remembered as much as an artisan as he is as a patriot. His anti-British engravings of episodes such property of a system that may be changed by processes in the system and also by interactions of the system with its external environment. It may be thought of as a measurement of randomness, or disorder. According to the second law, the change in entropy because of processes in the system must be either positive or zero. For reversible processes the change in entropy is zero, and for irreversible processes it is always positive. Thus an irreversible process always leads to an increase in entropy, or amount of disorder. The system may be restored to its original state only by energy from outside the system. An example of a process that increases disorder is the shuffling of a deck of cards.

Many general results for irreversible processes may be proved in thermodynamics. For instance, engines that use heat energy to do work may use irreversible or (approximately) reversible processes. Those which use irreversible processes do less work for the same amount of energy than those which use reversible processes.

Time Reversal. For a so-called microscopic system, such as an atomic or subatomic system consisting of a small number of components, a more useful definition of reversibility is that a process is reversible if the time-reversed process, which would occur if time could run backwards, may also occur in the system. This type of reversibility is called TIME REVERSAL INVARIANCE. It holds for processes such as collisions of idealized billiard balls, where reversing time corresponds to reversing velocities so that the balls retrace their paths. Collisions of molecules and atoms appear to be time reversal invariant, so the fundamental laws governing the KINETIC THEORY OF MATTER are reversible in this sense. At the level of elementary particles, all but one class of interactions appear to be time reversal invariant. The exception involves weak interactions of neutral kaons (K-mesons).

Paul Revere, a Boston silversmith and patriot, appears in a portrait (1768) by John Singleton Copley. Revere is remembered for riding across the Massachusetts countryside on the night of Apr. 18, 1775, to warn American patriots of a British advance on Lexington. (Boston Museum of Fine Arts.)

as the Boston Massacre were effective propaganda. He cast musket balls and cannon during the war and designed and printed the first Continental currency. After the war he became one of New England's leading silversmiths and a pioneer in the production of copper plating in America.

reversible and irreversible processes All events or processes in nature may be considered reversible or irreversible according to whether the original state may be restored. The distinction between the two kinds of processes is vital to the understanding of THERMODYNAMICS, and the general properties of such processes have useful applications in physics, chemistry, biology, and engineering.

Reversibility. Precise definitions of reversible and irreversible processes depend on the type of system in which the process occurs. For a so-called macroscopic system, such as a machine or a collection of a large number of independent components of the type studied in thermodynamics, a process is considered reversible or irreversible depending on whether or not it is possible to return the system to its initial state by a slight (infinitesimal) change in the external conditions acting on the system. This condition for reversibility is very stringent; essentially all processes involving macroscopic systems are irreversible, and the concept of a reversible process in those systems is an abstract idealization.

Entropy. An alternative definition of reversible and irreversible processes uses the concept of ENTROPY and the second law of thermodynamics. Entropy is a quantitative

revivalism Revivalism is a predominantly North American Protestant phenomenon in which itinerant preachers exhort their hearers to accept forgiveness of personal sin through faith in Jesus Christ and to commit themselves to spiritual self-discipline and religious exercises such as prayer, Bible reading, and church support.

Revivalism in America has been in reaction to a perceived overemphasis by the major denominations on ritual, cultural accommodation, and doctrinal or ideological correctness at the expense of personal religious experience. Four specific periods of intense religious revival were the GREAT AWAKENING (c.1720–70), in which Jonathan Edwards and George Whitefield played major roles; the Second Great Awakening and its aftermath (c.1787–1860); the period of Dwight L. MOODY, the Holiness Movement, and the reaction to liberalism (c.1870–1926); and the renewal of mass evangelism in the 1950s, characterized by Billy GRAHAM.

revolution A political revolution involves fundamental changes in the structure of a society, its basic beliefs, and individual behavior. During the 20th century impor-

The storming of the Bastille by the Paris mob on July 14, 1789, marked the beginning of popular participation in the French Revolution. Parisians played a key role in the Revolution until the establishment (1795) of the Directory. The Revolution overthrew the absolutist monarchy and rigid social hierarchy of the ancien regime and eventually transferred power to the middle classes.

tant revolutions have occurred in Russia (see RUSSIAN REVOLUTIONS OF 1917), China, Vietnam, and Cuba. Earlier revolutions include those in Puritan England (see ENGLISH CIVIL WAR), the AMERICAN REVOLUTION, and the FRENCH REVOLUTION.

Revolutionary Goals. Revolutionaries seek to achieve extensive changes in the social and political system. In place of the old order, with its emphasis on status and privilege, for instance, they may seek a society that values social equality and individual achievement. In particular, revolutionaries may support greater equality of economic conditions. They may encourage equal social interaction among young and old, men and women, and members of different social classes. Revolutionaries also strive for basic structural changes. They aim to redistribute land, achieve rapid industrialization, secure economic independence from foreign powers, increase educational facilities, and improve health services. Revolutionaries in many cases also hope to create a new person in a new society. The values they seek in the new revolutionary citizen include austerity, discipline, hard work, altruism, and a concern for the political order that transcends self-interest and group privileges. Revolutionaries try to instill such values and attitudes through mass political education.

How Revolutions Occur. Revolutionaries must begin by gaining control of the government. In order to win support, they must convince at least some groups in the country that change is both possible and desirable; their arguments about this goal comprise a systematic set of beliefs, or IDEOLOGY. In addition, revolutionary leaders need an organization—a political party, a guerrilla band, an army, or a movement—to mobilize human and material resources. By bringing together those who support the revolutionary cause and scattering the supporters of the old regime, these organizations help destroy the established political order. In this connection, most revolutionaries are prepared to use coercion and violence to counter the physical force of leaders opposed to fundamental change.

The revolutions of the 20th century have occurred in societies dominated by rigid, repressive regimes that were facing disintegration. The most notable examples have been Russia in 1917, China and Vietnam after World War II, and Cuba during the late 1950s. In most instances war, demands for modernization, and internal conflicts cause institutional breakdowns. The established elites lose confidence in their abilities and rights to govern. Revolutionary leaders such as Vladimir Ilich LENIN and Leon TROTSKY in Russia, MAO ZEDONG and ZOU ENLAI in China, HO CHI MINH in Vietnam, and Fidel CASTRO in Cuba have voiced programs that seem to promise a deliverance from the grievances felt by disaffected groups. In every successful revolutionary takeover, the leaders of the revo-

Vladimir Ilich Lenin addresses a crowd of soldiers soon after the Russian Revolution of November 1917. The Bolsheviks found much of their support among the Russian armed forces.

Fidel Castro, who seized control of Cuba in January 1959 after a 2-year guerrilla campaign, sought to transform Cuba into a socialist state along Marxist-Leninist lines.

lution manage to encourage defections from the police and army defending the old regime. After gaining political power, they organize a strong political party, army, and secret police to carry out their aims and maintain themselves in power.

Consequences of Revolution. Even when revolutionaries succeed in seizing political power and keeping it for a long period, they do not necessarily realize their long-term goals. The Marxist-Leninist revolutionaries of the 20th century were relatively successful in developing strong political institutions, particularly in the USSR, China, Vietnam, and Cuba (see COMMUNISM). They were able to centralize political power and expand resources through programs of industrialization, education, and health care. In each instance a powerful political party controlled and organized society. Revolutionary attempts to create a new citizen, however, were for the most part unsuccessful. Although there were advances in industry and education, the attitudes and behavior patterns characteristic of the old society remained. Party leaders acquired privileges not available to the masses. Corruption was, in many instances, still widespread. Private enterprise was replaced by a rigid, centralized bureaucracy. Finally, despite the revolutionary rhetoric, equality of economic opportunity was not matched by equality in economic condition, social status, or access to political power. This inability of the Marxist-Leninist revolutionaries to achieve many of their basic goals inevitably led to the collapse of communism in Eastern Europe and elsewhere.

Revolutions of 1848 During 1848 a series of revolutions broke out in rapid succession across Europe. The most general causes were the economic depression and crop failures of the preceding three years coupled with the political frustration felt by liberal middle-class and nationalistic groups.

The first outbreak occurred on Feb. 22 in Paris, driving LOUIS PHILIPPE from his throne and bringing in a provisional government dedicated to a democratic franchise and "national workshops" to reduce unemployment. The election of a French national assembly, however, brought

to Paris provincial deputies who opposed the workshops. The result was a working-class uprising in June that was crushed with frightful bloodshed. The national assembly, dominated by the middle class, went on to establish the Second Republic with a democratically elected legislature and executive. In December Louis Napoléon (see NAPOLEON III) was elected president.

In Vienna, capital of the Austrian Empire, the news from Paris inspired popular demonstrations that drove the conservative minister Klemens von METTERNICH from office. A sequence of German liberal reform ministries followed, but the other nationalities within the Austrian Empire wished to control their own affairs. On March 5, Hungary gained autonomy; in turn the Croats organized to seek freedom from Hungary. In Italy a Venetian republic was proclaimed, and a revolution in Milan (March 18–22) was promptly supported by a new liberal regime in Sardinia-Piedmont. But the tide soon turned.

In June, Czech leader František PALACKÝ organized a Pan-Slav Congress in Prague to demand equality with the Germans. Austrian forces crushed this rebellion and regained control in Milan. Then a constituent assembly convened in Vienna to draft a constitution for the empire, but in October it was driven from Vienna by a working-class rebellion. In December the young FRANCIS JOSEPH succeeded FERDINAND I as emperor of Austria and imposed a severely centralized administration. On Apr. 13, 1849, the Hungarians, under Lajos KOSSUTH, declared their independence. Prime Minister Felix Schwarzenberg called in a Russian army, and in August the Hungarians surrendered. That summer a Roman republic created by Giuseppe MAZZINI and Giuseppe GARIBALDI collapsed, and Austrian forces recaptured Venice.

In Germany a bloody confrontation in Berlin (March 15–21) forced the Prussian king FREDERICK WILLIAM IV to summon a constitutional assembly, an example followed in other German states. Above all, however, the liberals hoped to create a unified German empire, and to this end the FRANKFURT PARLIAMENT was elected and convened (May 18). It adopted a bill of rights and a moderately democratic form of government, and in March 1849 offered the crown of a constitutional Germany to the king of Prussia. He declined, and without Prussia the work of the parliament came to nothing. Meanwhile, in Prussia itself the king dissolved the constituent assembly and imposed his own constitution, which favored the wealthy classes but gave Prussia a measure of parliamentary government.

Despite a few lasting gains, the Revolutions of 1848 resulted in severe defeats for liberal nationalists seeking democratic reform.

revolver A revolver is a FIREARM in which ammunition is fed to the firing mechanism by a revolving barrel. The weapon may be a pistol, a shoulder gun, or a machine gun, but most early models were pistols. Consequently, a revolver is generally assumed to be a particular type of repeating pistol.

Handguns working on the revolver principle first appeared in 16th-century Europe. The difficulty with early

The main parts of a revolver are indicated in this cutaway view of a Smith and Wesson .38-caliber model. They include the main spring (1), trigger springs (2), cylinder stop (3), trigger guard (4), lever (5), trigger (6), hammer (7), bullet in chamber (8), ratchet (9), revolving cylinder (10), barrel (11), rifling (12), and sight (13). The firing sequence begins when the trigger is squeezed, forcing back the hammer and compressing the main spring (A). Rotating the cylinder brings a bullet into position (B). The final pull on the trigger releases the spring; the hammer drops forward and strikes a charge contained in the cartridge. The charge ignites (C), firing the bullet down the barrel.

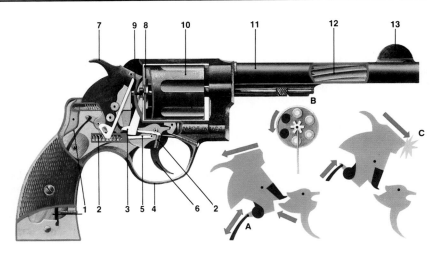

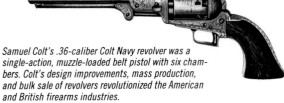

Samuel Colt's .36-caliber Colt Navy revolver was a single-action, muzzle-loaded belt pistol with six chambers. Colt's design improvements, mass production, and bulk sale of revolvers revolutionized the American and British firearms industries.

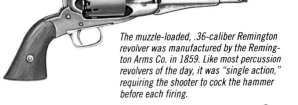

The muzzle-loaded, .36-caliber Remington revolver was manufactured by the Remington Arms Co. in 1859. Like most percussion revolvers of the day, it was "single action," requiring the shooter to cock the hammer before each firing.

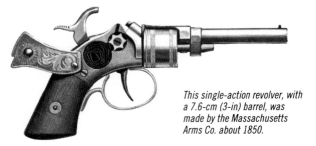

This single-action revolver, with a 7.6-cm (3-in) barrel, was made by the Massachusetts Arms Co. about 1850.

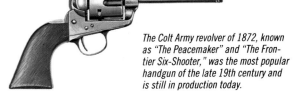

The Colt Army revolver of 1872, known as "The Peacemaker" and "The Frontier Six-Shooter," was the most popular handgun of the late 19th century and is still in production today.

The Darling pepperbox pistol had six barrels. It was awarded (1832) the first U.S. patent for an automatic rotating barrel.

cover, was judged to be the best of its time. Not until the invention of the copper percussion cap (1815) could a reliable revolver be developed, and during the 19th century the first "pepperbox" revolvers (so called because their clusters of barrels resembled pepper shakers) made their debut. But pepperboxes were heavy and cumbersome; they also had an unfortunate tendency to act as a Roman candle: when one cap fired, it ignited the rest. And because the barrels were smoothbore, their accuracy was poor.

In 1836 the American inventor Samuel Colt began manufacturing a simple cocking mechanism that has since formed the basis of almost every modern revolver. As the hammer cocking the trigger was pulled back, the cylinder rotated and locked in position. Colt's first models were fitted with percussion ignition. The Colt's light trigger pull was popular because it permitted accurate shooting, and rapid fire was accomplished by "fanning" (holding the trigger back while slapping the hammer).

Revolvers have a high rate of fire, but reloading is

models was igniting the propellant, because matchlocks and flintlocks did not work well unless they were upright. The flintlock designed in 1818 by the American gunsmith Elisha Collier, which incorporated a clockwork mechanism to rotate the cylinder and a self-priming pan slow. The revolver principle is employed in the modern Vulcan aircraft gun, which has a cyclic rate of fire of 600 rounds per minute.

Rexroth, Kenneth

Rexroth, Kenneth [reks'-rawth]   In the early 1950s, American poet, critic, and painter Kenneth Rexroth, b. South Bend, Ind., Dec. 22, 1905, d. June 6, 1982, helped found the San Francisco Poetry Center with Allen Ginsberg and Lawrence Ferlinghetti. Rexroth made a crucial link between the modernism of Ezra Pound and William Carlos Williams and the more rambunctious experiments of the beat-generation poets, among whom he was often counted.

Largely self-educated, Rexroth worked at many jobs and described his bohemian life in *An Autobiographical Novel* (1966). Devoted to Oriental poetry, he published excellent translations in *One Hundred Poems from the Japanese* (1955) and other collections. His own poems combine a delicate imagism with strong social concerns and were published in such collections as *The Phoenix and the Tortoise* (1944), *In Defense of Earth* (1956), and *New Poems* (1974).

Reye's syndrome

Reye's syndrome [rys]   Reye's syndrome is a rare, often serious, and sometimes fatal disease of children. It typically occurs after a viral infection such as influenza or chicken pox. Because the administration of salicylates such as aspirin to children with these diseases has been strongly associated with onset of Reye's syndrome, people are warned against the practice. Onset is sudden and is marked by high fever, headache, vomiting, and disturbances of the central nervous system, sometimes followed by convulsions, coma, permanent brain damage, or death. The disease is named for an Australian pathologist, R. D. K. Reye, who first described it in 1963.

Reykjavik

Reykjavik [rayk'-yah-veek]   Reykjavik is the capital and largest city of Iceland, situated on Faxa Bay on the southwest coast. The population is 96,708 (1989 est.). A transportation center with road and air connections, Reykjavik is also the main industrial and commercial city of Iceland. Industries include food and fish processing, metalworking, textile manufacturing, and shipbuilding. It is also a fishing port. This modern-looking city is heated by water obtained from nearby hot springs. It has a university (1911), a school of music (1930), a national library (1818), a national museum (1863), and a national theater. Landmarks include the parliament building, the cathedral, and the library.

Founded by Ingólfur Arnarson in 874, Reykjavik began as a small fishing village inhabited mostly by Danish settlers. A charter was granted in 1786, and the city became an episcopal see of the established Lutheran church in 1796. Since 1843, Reykjavik has been the seat of Iceland's parliament, the Althing, which has been in existence for more than 1,000 years. Reykjavik was made the capital of Iceland in 1918.

Reymont, Władysław Stanisław

Reymont, Władysław Stanisław [ray'-mohnt, vlahd-is'-lahf stahn-ees'-lahf]   The Polish novelist Władysław Stanisław Reymont, b. May 7, 1867, d. Dec. 5, 1925, received the Nobel Prize for literature in 1924. His epic novel, *The Peasants* (1904–09; Eng. trans., 1924–25), in four volumes, documents the life and rituals of a small peasant village. The novel celebrates nature and the peasants, who are seen as elemental, close to the earth and the animals they tend. In this world, Christian and pagan themes contend, poetry and brutality coexist. Reymont frequently uses dramatic contrasts, such as a death during a wedding or a seduction during a High Mass. His prose, impressionistic and sometimes operatic, includes dialect and fairy-tale stylization. In *The Peasants* and other works, such as *The Promised Land* (1899; Eng. trans., 1927), the author describes human misery and social injustice and obliquely suggests the need for political change.

Reynard the Fox

Reynard the Fox [ray'-nahrd]   A series of loosely connected beast fables in verse that became popular in medieval Europe, *Reynard the Fox* appears in French, Flemish, and German literature. The fables usually concern the struggle between the sly Reynard and the powerful wolf Isengrim. The story may be regarded as an allegory of social conflict, and by the 15th century it had assumed the didactic purpose of satirizing political power struggles. Versions include the French *Le Roman de Renart* (c.1175), William Caxton's English translation of the Flemish (1481), and T. J. Arnold's adaptation (1860) of Goethe's *Reinecke Fuchs*.

Reynolds, Sir Joshua

Reynolds, Sir Joshua   Joshua Reynolds, b. July 16, 1723, d. Feb. 23, 1792, was the leading English portrait painter of the 18th century and the author of the classic *Discourses* on the principles of art.

In the 1750s he executed several portraits that brought him into prominence in London society, and soon he was inundated with commissions from fashionable and literary patrons. With impeccable social and artistic credentials, Reynolds was chosen (1768) as first president of the newly formed Royal Academy and began (1769) to deliver the series of addresses that would eventually (1778) be compiled in the *Discourses*. His exaltation of the so-called grand style of the Renaissance and baroque painters set the aesthetic standard of the day. His position as the supreme arbiter of English painting style was cemented further by his appointment (1784) as Painter-in-Ordinary to the king.

Reynolds's output was enormous, and his impact on contemporary artistic taste was strengthened by the number of replicas of his work produced with the aid of assistants. His ability to bring his sitters to life is manifested in his portrait *Samuel Johnson* (1772; Tate Gallery, London). An equal facility with women's portraits is apparent in his characterization of renowned society beauty *Nelly O'Brien* (1762–63; Wallace Collection, London).

Sir Joshua Reynolds's portrait Nelly O'Brien *(1762–63), like other early works evokes the sitter's character in a direct and sympathetic manner. (Wallace Collection, London.)*

The pictorial effects of the grand manner he espoused so ardently are most apparent in the "quotations" that dignify many of Reynolds's portraits. His *Sarah Siddons as the Tragic Muse* (1784; Huntington Art Gallery, San Marino, Calif.), for example, employs a gesture borrowed from Michelangelo's *Isaiah* in the Sistine Chapel. Homage to the great masters of the 16th and 17th centuries is also apparent in the baroque lighting effects he used so frequently. In *Self-Portrait* (1780; Royal Academy of Art, London), Reynolds acknowledged his debt to past artists by formulating a composition inspired by Rembrandt and by placing a bust of Michelangelo within the picture.

Reynolds, Osborne   Osborne Reynolds, b. Aug. 23, 1842, d. Feb. 21, 1912, was an English scientist whose classical papers on fluid dynamics remain basic today to turbine operation, lubrication, fluid flow and streamlining, cavitation, and even tidal motion as it affects shores and estuaries. In both hydrodynamics and aerodynamics the Reynolds number is a dimensionless ratio related to the velocity at which smooth flow shifts to turbulent, as is the Reynolds stress to the drag between adjacent layers in counterflow. These quantities are particularly useful in experimental studies.

Reza Shah Pahlavi [ree'-zah shah pah'-luh-vee]   Reza Shah Pahlavi, b. Mar. 16, 1878, d. July 26, 1944, shah of Iran (1925–41), created the modern Iranian state and founded the Pahlavi dynasty. An army officer, he helped organize a nationalist coup in 1921; in 1923 he became prime minister. He deposed the weak Qajar dynasty two years later and assumed the imperial crown. He stamped out tribal independence; forced the British and Soviet governments to give up their privileges in Iran; adopted a secular legal code; appropriated ecclesiastical income; built schools, roads, hospitals, and the Trans-Iranian Railroad; and promoted the emancipation of women. When British and Soviet forces occupied Iran to ensure their supply lines in World War II, Reza Shah abdicated in favor of his son, MUHAMMAD REZA SHAH PAHLAVI.

Rh factor   The Rh factor is an ANTIGEN whose name is derived from the rhesus monkey, on whose red BLOOD cells it was first discovered. Later found in humans, the Rh factor, along with other blood antigens, must be taken into account in blood transfusions. Blood from an Rh-positive donor will cause an Rh-negative recipient to produce antibodies against the Rh factor. The antibodies will cause a hemolytic transfusion reaction if the recipient again receives Rh-positive blood. The hemolytic reaction destroys the donated cells.

Erythroblastosis fetalis, or Rh hemolytic disease of the newborn, occurs if a pregnant woman is Rh-negative and her fetus is Rh-positive. The disease develops if fetal Rh factor enters the mother's circulatory system through a breach in the placenta, usually late in the pregnancy or during delivery. The mother's immune system treats the fetal Rh factor as a foreign protein and produces antibodies against it. The antibodies can pass through an intact placenta into the fetal circulation (usually in a later pregnancy) and cause a potentially fatal anemia. The life of an affected infant may be saved through a nearly complete transfusion of Rh-negative blood at birth. The injection of the mother with a special vaccine within 72 hours of the birth of each child prevents the antibody formation in most cases.

Rhea [ree'-uh]   In Greek mythology Rhea was one of the TITANS, the daughter of URANUS and his mother GAEA, whose position as goddess of the Earth she assumed. Rhea is also known as the "mother of the gods" because she and her brother CRONUS were the parents of the original gods of Olympus: HESTIA, DEMETER, HERA, HADES, POSEIDON, and ZEUS. Cronus tried to swallow all of his children as potential usurpers, but the brood was rescued by the trickery of Rhea, Gaea, and eventually Zeus, whom the goddesses had rescued beforehand. Rhea was identified with the Anatolian goddess CYBELE, and her worship spread across Greece and eventually to Rome.

rhea   Rheas, or pampas ostriches, are two species of large flightless birds in the family Rheidae, order Struthioniformes. The common rhea, *Rhea americana*, lives on pampas of southern Brazil and central Argentina, where it is hunted for sport and food by gauchos (cowboys) with bolas (leather slings weighted with stones). It reaches 1.7 m (5.6 ft) in height and 25 kg (55 lb) in weight. Males fight for a harem. Six or more females may lay 12 to 18 eggs in one nest before the male drives them away, incubates the eggs for 6 weeks, and shepherds the young for another 6 weeks. The rhea's diet consists primarily of vegetables but also includes insects and small animals. The slightly smaller Darwin's rhea, *Pterocnemia pennata*, occupies Andean foothills from Peru to Patagonia.

The common, or greater, rhea is the largest New World bird. Although flightless, the rhea runs as fast as a horse can gallop.

Syngman Rhee, a Korean nationalist, was elected as the first president of the Republic of (South) Korea in 1948. Although Rhee commanded the loyalty of his nation during the Korean War and the years of recovery, his rule became despotic and he was deposed in 1960.

1960. A staunch anti-Communist, he worked vainly for the toppling of the Communist North Korean government during the KOREAN WAR. Rhee was forced to resign in the midst of the April 1960 student uprising against his increasingly despotic rule.

rhenium [ree'-nee-uhm]   Rhenium is a metallic chemical element and one of the TRANSITION ELEMENTS. Its symbol is Re, its atomic number is 75, and its atomic weight is 186.2. Two isotopes exist in nature: ^{185}Re is stable, and ^{187}Re is radioactive. Rhenium is found in gadolinite, molybdenite, columbite, rare-earth minerals, and some sulfide ores. It was discovered by Walter Noddack, Ida Tacke, and O. C. Berg in 1925. Rhenium alloys are used in electron tubes, as semiconductors, and in thermocouples. The metal's usefulness is limited because of its expense.

rheostat [ree'-uh-stat]   A rheostat, like a potentiometer, is a variable RESISTOR usually used to control the flow of electricity (current) through an electric circuit. A rheostat is commonly in the form of a tightly wound coil of wire over which a contact may be moved. The resistance of the device is determined by the length of coil through which the current must pass before entering the contact. A plate of resistant material—such as graphite—or a conducting liquid may be used as the resistive element instead of the coil. A light-dimming switch is a typical application of a rheostat.

Rhee, Syngman [ree, sing'-muhn]   Syngman Rhee, b. Apr. 26, 1875, d. July 19, 1965, led the Korean movement for independence from Japan and was the first president (1948–60) of the Republic of Korea (South Korea). After attending a U.S. mission school in Seoul, Rhee joined (1896) the Independence Club, advocating progressive reform and opposing foreign domination. Beginning in 1898 he was imprisoned for 6 years; he then went to the United States, where he received (1910) a doctorate from Princeton University. Having converted to Christianity, he returned to Korea as a YMCA worker shortly before Japan annexed his country in 1910. Opposed to Japanese rule, he was forced to flee to the United States in 1912. There Rhee was elected (1919) president of the Korean provisional government in exile. Following World War II he returned to the U.S.-controlled area of Korea and in 1948 became the first president of South Korea. He was reelected in 1952, 1956, and

rhesus monkey [ree'-suhs]   The rhesus monkey, *Macaca mulatta*, of the family Cercopithecidae, is more properly called a macaque, as are the other members of the genus *Macaca*. Native to southeastern Asia, rhesus monkeys are found in forests, on rocky hillsides, and in temples and villages. They live in troops averaging about 18 and typically consisting of 4 adult males, 8 adult fe-

The rhesus monkey was used extensively in biological research until its export was banned by India, formerly the principal supplier. The rhesus was used in the development of the Salk poliomyelitis vaccine and was the first monkey carried into the stratosphere by rocket.

males, and their young. Rhesus monkeys range in length from about 46 to 63 cm (18 to 25 in), plus a furry tail about half as long as the head and body; they weigh from 4.5 to about 10 kg (10 to 22 lb). Their silky coats are dull yellowish brown in color. The monkeys were extensively used in medical research—a use that seriously depleted the rhesus population. The Rh factor, a protein substance in red blood cells, was discovered in and named for the *Rh*esus in 1940.

rhetoric and oratory

As defined by Aristotle, rhetoric is that branch of discourse which concerns persuasion. In Aristotle's time rhetoric was considered one of the two primary forms of expression—the other being poetry. The word is derived from the Greek *rhetor*, meaning "speaker in the assembly," and in ancient times rhetoric was concerned with the practice of oratory.

The art of rhetoric is said to have originated with Corax of Syracuse and his pupil Tisias in Greece during the first quarter of the 5th century BC in response to the citizens' need for help in pleading their own cases in court for the restoration of their property. Aristotle's *Rhetoric* (*c.*330 BC), the oldest extant complete text on the subject, contains most of the concepts and principles that informed education in rhetoric and oratory for the next 2,000 years.

Aristotle's Classifications. Aristotle defined three kinds of persuasive oratory: forensic or judicial, the oratory of the courtroom, which is intended to prove the justice or injustice of a past action; deliberative, the oratory of the public forum, which is intended to move an audience to—or restrain an audience from—an action; and epideictic, the oratory of ceremony, which is intended to display sentiments appropriate for such occasions as funerals, in-

augurations, and dedications. Aristotle then identified three means of persuasion: the appeal to reason (*logos*), the appeal to emotion (*pathos*), and the appeal of the speaker's character (*ethos*).

Under the influence of Aristotle's teachings, the study of rhetoric came to be divided into five parts: invention, the process of finding arguments for the speech; arrangement, the process of organizing the speech; style, the process of putting into words what has been discovered and arranged; memory, the techniques for memorizing the speech for oral presentation; and delivery, the techniques for managing voice and gesture in the act of presenting the speech.

Later Developments. The Romans Cicero and Quintilian greatly expanded Aristotle's account of rhetoric. They also insisted that to be successful the orator must acquire a broad liberal education. In the medieval period rhetoric was extended to sermons and letter writing. During the Renaissance, when rhetoric became the dominant discipline in the English grammar schools and universities, rhetoricians concentrated more on written prose and on such literary forms as drama and poetry than on speechmaking. The long tradition of classical rhetoric begun by Aristotle is generally regarded as having ended with the publication of the rhetoric texts of George Campbell (1776), Hugh Blair (1783), and Richard Whately (1828).

Rhett, Robert Barnwell

[ret]   Robert Barnwell Rhett, b. Beaufort, S.C., Dec. 21, 1800, d. Sept. 14, 1876, an American secessionist, was an early and unremitting proponent of an independent South. A state-rights Democrat and disciple of John C. CALHOUN beginning in the 1820s, he was a U.S. representative (1837–49) and senator (1850–52). Convinced that the Democratic party would not protect Southern interests, he formed (1850) a secessionist movement in South Carolina. During the U.S. Civil War he used the *Charleston Mercury*, edited by his son, to denounce any tendency toward compromise on the part of the Confederate leadership and to attack the policies of President Jefferson Davis.

rheumatic fever

Rheumatic fever is an acute fever, generally of childhood, in which inflammation of the joints (arthritis) is often the most prominent symptom (hence the name) but which may leave the heart seriously damaged. It is a sequel to a *Streptococcus* bacterial infection of the throat, usually occurring 10 to 14 days earlier, although only a small percentage of persons with streptoccocal infection develop this complication. High fever of sudden onset is accompanied by arthritis, skin nodules, and rashes. Involuntary movements termed chorea may occur in conjunction with rheumatic fever. In some patients arthritis affects one joint after another, with the overlying skin becoming red and every movement causing pain; in others, however, the joint pain may be mild and thus regarded as "growing pains." In most cases the heart tissues become inflamed (carditis), and permanent damage to the heart valves and muscles may result.

Treatment for rheumatic fever includes rest in bed and therapy with aspirin or steroids. After recovery patients with carditis are particularly susceptible to further attacks of rheumatic fever, which tend to cause progressive damage to the heart and especially deformity of the heart valves. Such subsequent attacks can be minimized by efforts to prevent the streptococcal infection that precedes and leads to rheumatic fever. Regular doses of antimicrobial drugs, such as penicillin, given throughout the childhood years or longer are effective in preventing recurrent attacks.

rheumatism *Rheumatism* is a nonspecific term for several diseases that cause inflammation or degeneration of joints, muscles, ligaments, tendons, and bursae. Rheumatic deseases include rheumatoid ARTHRITIS and other degenerative diseases of the joints; BURSITIS; fibrositis; gout; lumbago; myositis; rheumatic fever; sciatica; and spondylitis.

Palindromic rheumatism is a disease that causes frequent and irregular attacks of joint pain, especially in the fingers, but leaves no permanent damage to the joints. Psychogenic rheumatism is common in women between the ages of 40 and 70, although men also contract this disease. Symptoms include complaints of pain in various parts of the musculoskeletal system that cannot be substantiated medically. This condition can be alleviated by psychotherapy.

One of the common forms of rheumatism is rheumatoid arthritis, a disease of unknown cause that affects 1 to 3 percent of the population. This disease is characterized by joint deformities and impaired mobility as a consequence of chronic inflammation and thickening of the synovial membranes, which surround joints. As the disease progresses it produces ulceration of cartilage in the joints. The onset of rheumatoid arthritis usually occurs between ages 35 and 40 but can occur at any age. The disease typically follows a course of spontaneous remissions and exacerbations, and in about 10 to 20 percent of patients the remission is permanent.

Rhine, J. B. [ryn] A pioneer of PARAPSYCHOLOGY, Joseph Banks Rhine, b. Juniata County, Pa., Sept. 29, 1895, d. Feb. 20, 1980, founded (1935) the Duke University Parapsychology Laboratory together with William McDougall. Rhine's statistical studies of extrasensory perception were fundamental to the development of parapsychology as a field for quantitative research. Rhine founded the *Journal of Parapsychology* in 1937.

Rhine River The Rhine, the longest river in western Europe, flows across Switzerland, Germany, and the Netherlands to the North Sea. Its watershed covers about 252,000 km² (97,300 mi²). The Vorderrhein and Hinterrhein rivers, which rise on the Saint Gotthard massif in the Alps, join at Tamins to form the Rhine. The river then flows northeast about 100 km (60 mi) between the

mountains to Lake Constance (see CONSTANCE, LAKE).

At Basel the Rhine's course turns northward and for about 320 km (200 mi) flows across a plain lying between the Vosges mountains and the BLACK FOREST. For much of this distance it follows the boundary between France and Germany. HORST AND GRABEN topography dominates this segment of the Rhine valley, where the major port cities of Strasbourg, Karlsruhe, Mannheim, and Mainz are located. The Rhine is joined by the MAIN RIVER at Mainz and the Neckar River at Mannheim.

Below Mainz the Rhine enters its gorge tract, one of the most scenic parts of its valley. The steep slopes are crowned with ruined castles, and the valley walls are terraced for growing wine grapes. Within this tract the Rhine is joined from the west by the MOSELLE RIVER at Koblenz.

The river leaves the gorge at Remagen, and the riverbed widens and forms meanders across the plain of northwest Germany, passing Cologne, Düsseldorf, and Duisburg before entering the Netherlands. There it divides into three main streams: the Waal, the Lek, and the Ijssel, the last of which drains into the IJSSELMEER. The

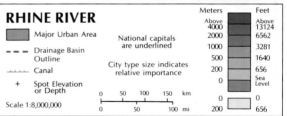

RHINE RIVER

	Meters	Feet
Major Urban Area	Above 4000	Above 13124
	2000	6562
Drainage Basin Outline	1000	3281
	500	1640
Canal	200	656
	0	Sea Level
+ Spot Elevation or Depth	0	0
	200	656

National capitals are underlined

City type size indicates relative importance

Scale 1:8,000,000

0 50 100 150 km

0 50 100 mi

Waal and the Lek further divide to form the delta of the Rhine. Rotterdam lies on the Lek, 45 km (28 mi) from the sea. The Hook of Holland is located at the mouth of an artificial cut known as the New Waterway, which connects Rotterdam to the sea.

The upper Rhine is fed primarily by the melting snow of the Alps. Farther downstream the dominant source of water is the heavy rains in winter.

Following extensive work on the river's bed, the Rhine became the most easily navigated and most-used river in Europe. Its middle course was straightened, its gorge section was deepened, and its lower course was protected by levees.

The Rhine is linked by canal with the Ruhr industrial region and with northern Germany; the Moselle provides access to France. The great volume of commerce carried on the river has made Rotterdam the foremost port in Western Europe.

Rhineland [ryn'-land] The Rhineland—that part of Germany lying west of the Rhine River—consists of several regions: the Upper Rhine Valley, the Palatinate Upland, the Saar Basin, the Western Rhine Valley, the Lower Rhine Plain, and the Lower Rhine Bay, and the Lower Rhine Plain. The major cities are COLOGNE, BONN, and AACHEN. The name *Rhineland* also refers to the demilitarized zone established by the Allies after World War I, which included an area east of the Rhine.

rhinitis [ry-ny'-tuhs] Rhinitis is an inflammation of the nasal mucous membrane, usually caused by the common cold virus, as well as by irritants and ALLERGY to pollens and other agents. Chronic rhinitis may occur in disorders such as syphilis and leishmaniasis that are characterized by destruction of soft tissue and cartilage. Most cold viruses are members of a group called rhinoviruses, hence the name *rhinitis*. Rhinitis is the major symptom that occurs when the nose is the primary site of infection during a cold, although a cold can also settle in the pharynx, larynx, and chest. The main symptoms of rhinitis are sneezing, burning sensations, discharge of mucus, and obstruction resulting from swelling of nasal membranes. The infection can spread to other parts of the respiratory system and to the sinuses and middle ear. The symptoms of rhinitis caused by a cold usually disappear in about a week.

rhinoceros The once-numerous rhinoceros family, Rhinocerotidae, in the order Perissodactyla, now contains only five living species. All are threatened with extinction, some imminently. The three species of Asiatic rhinos include the Indian rhino, *Rhinoceros unicornis*; the nearly extinct Javan rhino, *R. sondaicus*; and the Sumatran rhino, *Dicerorhinus sumatrensis*. The two species of African rhinos are the black rhino, *Diceros bicornis*, and the white rhino, *Ceratotherium simum*.

Rhinoceroses are large mammals with large heads, small eyes, one or two horns on the snout, and three toes

The Indian rhinoceros appears to have an armored hide, which is actually loose folds of skin.

on each foot. They range from 2 to 4.2 m (6.5 to 14 ft) long, from 1 to 2 m (40 to 80 in) high at the shoulder, and from 1 to more than 3 tons in weight. All but the Sumatran rhino are virtually hairless except for the tip of the tail and a fringe on the ears. The Sumatran rhino is covered with a fairly dense coat of hair and is related to the extinct long-coated woolly rhino, *Coelodonta antiquitatis*, of Ice-Age Europe. The Indian and Javan rhinos are one-horned; the other three species are two-horned.

The rhino's horn is composed of keratin, as is the cow's horn, but unlike the cow's horn it is of a fused, fibrous construction and solid throughout, with no hollow for a core of bone. The fibers represent greatly modified hairs. The horn is attached to the skin and is supported by a raised, roughened area on the skull. Because many Asians, particularly the Chinese, believe that the rhino horn has aphrodisiac properties, the horns are widely sought after, and this demand accounts for much of the illegal killing of rhinos.

The square-lipped African white rhinoceros has a symbiotic relationship with oxpecker birds, which clean the rhino of ticks and make a warning cry if danger is near.

The Indian rhino, native to northeastern India, is now found only in a few protected areas. The Javan rhino, once distributed across southeastern Asia into the East Indies, today survives only in a small preserve on the island of Java. The Sumatran rhino is now confined to a few widely scattered areas in southeastern Asia and in the East Indies.

Rhizopoda [ry-zah'-puh-duh] Rhizopoda, or Sarcodina, is a class of PROTOZOA containing the amoeboid protozoans—those which move about and capture food by means of pseudopodia—and including the common *Amoeba proteus* and *Entamoeba histolytica*, the organism that causes amoebic DYSENTERY. The AMOEBA is a naked mass of PROTOPLASM, but also included in the Rhizopoda are several groups of protozoans that secrete hard shells, or tests, around themselves. An arcella, for example, lays down a chitinous test; a FORAMINIFER deposits a shell of calcium carbonate; and a RADIOLARIAN secretes an outer shell usually containing siliceous substances. The shells of radiolarians and foraminifers have formed vast deposits in the Earth's crust, and the shells of the foraminifer *Globigerina* form a thick ooze covering vast areas of the ocean floor.

Rhode Island Rhode Island, one of the 13 original colonies and the smallest in area of the 50 states, is bounded on the north and east by Massachusetts, on the south by Rhode Island Sound, and on the west by Connecticut. The state is almost cut in two parts by NARRAGANSETT BAY, which penetrates 45 km (28 mi) to the state capital of Providence. Within the bay are 36 islands; Block Island lies 16 km (10 mi) offshore.

The official name, the State of Rhode Island and Providence Plantations, refers to early settlements on Aquidneck Island (later known as Rhode Island) and the Proprietors' Company for Providence Plantations on the mainland. Rhode Island was the first colony to declare its independence from Great Britain and was a pioneer industrial state in the new nation. With increased competition from larger states with broader resource bases, Rhode Island has been forced to search for different paths leading to economic prosperity.

Land and Resources

Rhode Island's two physiographic regions are the eastern lowlands and the western uplands. The eastern lowland, including the bay shores and islands, is gently rolling. Within Narragansett Bay the largest islands are Conanicut, Dutch, Prudence, and Rhode Island. The second region, the western upland, occupies the western half of the mainland. It has steep slopes and rocky outcrops and encompasses about 20 hills exceeding 180 m (590 ft) in elevation.

Soils. The highest upland area has deep, poorly drained soils, whereas the largest portion of the mainland is covered by deep, well-drained podzols. Sandy and gravelly soils are found near Narragansett Bay and in scattered valley locations.

Providence, the largest city of Rhode Island, is located on the Providence River at the head of Narragansett Bay. Providence was founded in 1636 by Roger Williams, a religious dissident who had been exiled from Massachusetts.

Drainage. The northern half of the state drains into Narragansett Bay via the Blackstone, Pawtuxet, Seekonk, and Woonasquatucket rivers. The Pawcatuck drains much of the south.

Climate. Rhode Island's average annual temperature is 10° C (50° F). The coldest months are January and February, with mean temperatures of –2° C (29° F); July, the hottest month, has a mean temperature of 23° C (73° F). The annual precipitation averages 1,016 mm (40 in).

Vegetation and Animal Life. About 60% of Rhode Island's land area is wooded. Hemlock, white pine, birch, maple, and several varieties of oak are common. Many mammal and bird species can be found within the state. Block Island, on the Atlantic flyway, is known for its diverse bird population. A wide variety of freshwater fish and amphibians inhabit inland waters in addition to the many finfish and shellfish found offshore.

Resources. Water is Rhode Island's major resource. Rivers furnished power for early mills and continue to supply water for homes and factories today. The largest mineral deposits are those of sand and gravel. Limestone is profitably mined.

Environmental Protection. Public and private groups are working to overcome environmental problems brought about by Rhode Island's dense population and long industrialization. Water pollution and flooding problems are the foremost concerns of this ocean-oriented state. The fragile environments of marsh and wetland areas are protected by law.

People

The smallest of the 50 states has the second highest

RHODE ISLAND

Land: Area: 3,140 km^2 (1,212 mi^2); rank: 50th. Capital and largest city: Providence (1990 pop., 160,728). Counties: 5. Elevations: highest—247 m (812 ft), at Jerimoth Hill; lowest—sea level, at the Atlantic coast.

People: Population (1990): 1,005,984; rank: 43d; density: 320 persons per km^2 (830 per mi^2). Distribution (1988 est.): 92.6% metropolitan, 7.4% nonmetropolitan. Average annual change (1980–90): +0.6%.

Government (1991): Governor: Bruce Sundlun, Democrat. U.S. Congress: Senate—1 Democrat, 1 Republican; House—1 Democrat, 1 Republican. Electoral college votes: 4. State legislature: 50 senators, 100 representatives.

Economy: State personal income (1988): $16.8 billion; rank: 42d. Median family income (1979): $19,448; rank: 28th. Agriculture: income (1988)—$78 million. Fishing: value (1988)—$69 million. Forestry: sawtimber volume (1987)—916 million board feet. Mining: value (1987)—$19 million. Manufacturing: value added (1987)—$4.9 billion. Services: value (1987)—$4 billion.

Miscellany: Statehood: May 29, 1790; the 13th state. Nicknames: Ocean State and Little Rhody; tree: red maple; motto: Hope; song: "Rhode Island."

Violet

Rhode Island Red

---

population density in the nation. In 1990 the 7 Rhode Island cities with more than 25,000 residents accounted for 52% of its total population. CRANSTON, PAWTUCKET, PROVIDENCE, East Providence, and WARWICK had more than 50,000 people. After declining by 0.3% during the 1970s, Rhode Island's population increased by 6.2% during the period from 1980 to 1990.

The 1990 census enumeration counted 38,861 blacks, or 3.9% of the state's population. Most of the recent immigrants are Hispanics. Although the early populations were overwhelmingly Protestant, Roman Catholics now constitute the largest single religious denomination.

Education. Public education dates from the Henry Barnard School Law of 1845. Today the state board of regents for education and its subboards have policymaking power over all public schools.

The State University of Rhode Island (1892) in Kingston and Rhode Island College (1854) in Providence are state-supported institutions. Eight private degree-granting schools also operate within the state, including BROWN UNIVERSITY, Bryant College (1863), and Rhode Island School of Design (1877).

Cultural Activities and Historic Sites. In NEWPORT, Touro Synagogue (1763), the oldest synagogue building in the United States, has been designated a national historic site. Of the state's many buildings dating from colonial times, a number have been named national historic structures. The AMERICA'S CUP competition was held in Newport from 1930 to 1983, the most famous of many yachting races held there. Among the state's theatrical companies, the Trinity Square Repertory Company in Providence is the most famous.

Recreation. Many of Rhode Island's recreational opportunities are associated with its coastline, where boating, sailing, and fishing dominate. Inland, freshwater swimming and fishing from stocked streams are popular.

Communications. Rhode Island is served by 7 daily and 3 Sunday newspapers. Broadcasting facilities include 22 radio stations and 2 television stations.

Economic Activity

About 60% of all Rhode Island workers are engaged in nonmanufacturing activities, particularly insurance, printing and publishing, wholesale and retail trade, education, and government. Growing tourism has provided opportunities for many service jobs.

Agriculture, Forestry, and Fishing

Agriculture has steadily declined in importance, although specialty crops and produce for nearby urban markets are still grown. Dairy products, livestock, and poultry account for 43% of the total. Potatoes are the major field crop.

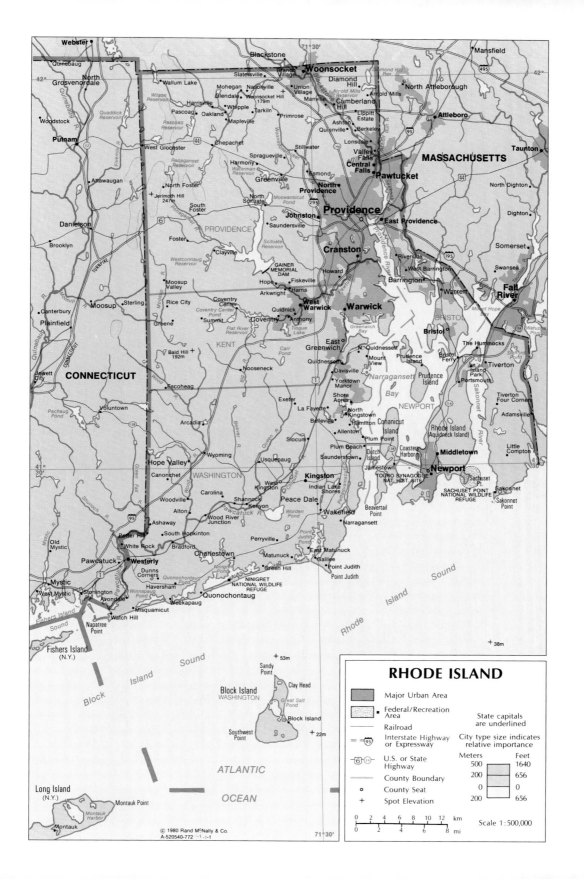

RHODE ISLAND

Webster • | Mansfield •
Quinebaug
Blackstone
North
Grosvenordale
42° Wallum Lake
Woonsocket
Slatersville Branch Diamond Hill Res.
Village
North Attleborough •
Diamond
Hill
Slatersville
Mohegan Nasonville Union Arnold Mills
Village Reservoir
Glendale Woonsocket Hill Manville Arnold Mills
Harrisville 179m Cumberland Attleboro •
Pascoag Whipple Tarkiln Hill Lippitt
Oakland Estate
Quaddick Mapleville Ashton
Reservoir Primrose Quinnville Berkeley
Woodstock • Pascoag Lonsdale
Reservoir Taunton •
Stillwater
West Glocester Valley
Putnam Falls North Dighton
Chepachet Spragueville Central
Wilson Falls
Reservoir Esmond Pawtucket MASSACHUSETTS
Greenville North Dighton •
Altawaugan • Watatman Harmony Providence
Reservoir North Providence Dighton •
Ponaganset North Scituate Moswansicut
Reservoir Foster Pond
North Providence Somerset •
Jerimoth Hill Johnston East Providence
Danielson • 247m South Saundersville
Foster PROVIDENCE
Foster Cranston Riverside Swansea •
Brooklyn • Clayville West Barrington
Scituate Howard Barrington Fall
Reservoir GAINER Warren River
Westconnaug MEMORIAL Fiskeville
Reservoir DAM Hope BRISTOL Mount Hope
Moosup Harris Bay
Valley Arkwright West Bristol
Rice City Warwick Warwick
Moosup Coventry Quidnick Bristol
Sterling Center Anthony Ferry The Hummocks
Canterbury • Greene Summit Tiogue BristolBristol
Plainfield • Flat River Lake Ferry
Reservoir East
Greenwich N. Quidnessett Island
CONNECTICUT KENT Carr Mount Park
Pond Quidnessett View Prudence Portsmouth
Bald Hill Island
192m Davisville Prudence Tiverton
Jewett Nooseneck Yorktown Island Four Corners
City Manor NEWPORT Adamsville •
Escoheag Shore Rhode Island
Acres North (Aquidneck Island)
Exeter Kingston Little
Voluntown La Fayette Hamilton Conanicut Compton
Belleville Island Coasters
Arcadia Allenton Harbor Middletown
Plum Point
WASHINGTON Slocum Dutch Newport
Plum Beach Island
Hope Valley Saunderstown Jamestown
Canonchet Usquepaug Kingston TOURO SYNAGOGUE Sachuset
NAT. HIST. SITE Pt.
West Indian Lake Beavertail SACHUSET POINT
Kingston Shores Point NATIONAL WILDLIFE Sakonnet
Carolina Shannock REFUGE
Woodville Kenyon Peace Dale Sakonnet
Alton Wakefield Point
Ashaway Wood River
Pedler Hill Junction Narragansett
White Rock Perryville
Bradford East Matunuck
Pawcatuck Westerly Charlestown Matunuck Galilee
Dunns Green Hill Point Judith
Mystic Corners Point Judith
West Mystic Haversham Quonochontaug NINIGRET
Stonington Winnapaug NATIONAL WILDLIFE
Avondale Pond REFUGE
Watch Hill Weekapaug
Misquamicut
Napatree Watch Hill
Point
38m
Fishers Island
(N.Y.)
Long Island Sound
53m
Sandy
Point Rhode
Block Island Clay Head Island
Sound
Block WASHINGTON Sound
Island Great Salt
Pond
Block Island

Long Island Southwest 22m
(N.Y.) Point
Montauk Point ATLANTIC
Montauk OCEAN
Harbor

© 1980 Rand McNally & Co.
A-520540-772 -1 -1 -1-1

RHODE ISLAND

	Major Urban Area
	Federal/Recreation Area
	Railroad
	Interstate Highway or Expressway
	U.S. or State Highway
	County Boundary
○	County Seat
+	Spot Elevation

State capitals are underlined

City type size indicates relative importance

Meters	Feet
500	1640
200	656
0	0
200	656

Scale 1:500,000

km 0 2 4 6 8 10 12
mi 0 2 4 6 8

Much of the state's forestland is low-value growth, but oak and white pine are of commercial value. Unlike other New England areas, the state's fishing industry is prospering. Industrial fish rank first in weight of total catch, but a wide variety of table fish and shellfish are also caught.

Manufacturing. Rhode Island was among the first industrial states in the nation. Ships were its earliest products, but they have fallen in economic importance. The leading industries manufacture jewelry and silverware, textiles, machinery, fabricated metals, rubber, and plastics.

Tourism. Once the playground of the rich, Newport has many mansions open to visitors. Increased investments have resulted in expanded accommodations and enlarged boating facilities. Camping and recreational areas have been developed inland.

Transportation. Interstate 95, linking New York and Boston, traverses Rhode Island and is an essential route for the state's industries and residents. The Newport Bridge (1969) replaced the last major ferry link in the lower bay. The main line of the Amtrak system is reached by independent feeder lines. Providence's deepwater port accommodates supertankers. The state operates seven airports.

Energy. Although Rhode Island produces little of its power, electrical power is available through participation in the New England Power Grid. Rhode Island is dependent on imported fuels. Offshore drilling for petroleum has been initiated.

Government and Politics

The state constitution was adopted in 1842. The governor and four elected state officers—lieutenant governor, secretary of state, attorney general, and general treasurer—serve 2-year terms. The General Assembly consists of the 100-member House of Representatives and the 50-member Senate. The state's 5 counties serve only as judicial districts under the chief justice of the State Supreme Court. Superior, district, and family courts hold sessions in several locations. The state's municipalities consist of 8 cities and 31 towns.

From the Civil War period until the 1920s, Rhode Island favored the Republican party in U.S. presidential elections. Since that time, however, the Democrats have won a good share of electoral victories.

History

At the time of the first white settlement in Rhode Island four Indian tribes lived in the area: the NARRAGANSETT, WAMPANOAG, Niantic, and Nipmuck. In 1511, Miguel Corte Real, a Portuguese navigator, is believed to have sailed along Rhode Island's coast. Narragansett Bay was explored by Giovanni da Verrazano in 1524, and at the beginning of the 17th century Dutch traders—including Adriaen Block—sailed through the offshore waters.

Colonial Period. In 1636 the first permanent white settlement was founded by Roger WILLIAMS at present-day East Providence. In 1638 he and 12 other settlers on the mainland formed the Proprietors' Company for Providence Plantations. In that same year William CODDINGTON and John Clarke obtained an Indian deed to Aquidneck Island in Narragansett Bay and settled the northern end of the island at present-day Portsmouth. Because of a 1639 dispute between Coddington and Hutchinson, the former moved south and established Newport. In 1644, Aquidneck was renamed Rhode Island. Williams returned from England that same year with a charter for the colony

Many of Newport's opulent mansions, which front the Atlantic coast of Aquidneck Island, were built during the late 19th century, when the region became fashionable as a summer resort. Several mansions are maintained as museums and are opened to the public.

that united the three settlements into "The Incorporation of Providence Plantations in the Narragansett Bay in New England." The colony's first legislative session was held in May 1647, at which time the Warwick colony of Samuel GORTON was included with the larger incorporation. In 1663 a royal charter recognizing Rhode Island's religious freedom and self-government was granted by the English king CHARLES II; the document remained in effect until the state constitution was drawn up in 1842.

Rhode Islanders maintained good relations with the Indians, but they were forced to flee to Newport when colonists in Connecticut and Massachusetts instigated KING PHILIP'S WAR (1675–76).

The maritime era arrived when surplus agricultural products enabled farmers to take to the seas. Large plantations on Rhode Island and in the southern part of the mainland grew corn and processed wool, meat, and cheese for export. Foreign trade developed with the West Indies, the ports of Europe, and the Pacific via South America or Africa. Maritime activities included privateering against the enemies of Britain, slave trading, and whaling. Disputes with Britain over trade and British determination to collect taxes resulted in the assignment of a fleet of armed revenue ships to Narragansett Bay. Increased hostility and violence resulted.

On May 4, 1776, Rhode Island became the first colony to declare independence, and Rhode Islanders fought in every Revolutionary War battle. Gen. Nathanael GREENE of Coventry, R.I., was second in command to George Washington. Newport was occupied by the British from December 1776 to October 1779. Rhode Island was the last of the 13 colonies to ratify (1790) the constitution, a delay brought about by its citizens' apprehensions at yielding power to the federal government.

The Era of Manufacturing. The factory system in America was introduced when Samuel SLATER and Moses Brown established (1793) the first cotton textile mill in Pawtucket. The skills developed in colonial forges were used in making machinery. The gold-plating technique of Nehemiah Dodge (1794) and the establishment (1831) of a silver factory by Jabez Gorham were milestones in jewelry-silverware production. As foreign commerce decreased in the 1840s, rubber manufacture began. By 1890 the Providence area had become the largest producer of woolen goods in the United States. Many villages developed around the textile mills, which were located at waterpower sites. The tide of immigrants supplied the necessary laborers for the factories. Whaling, once an important part of Rhode Island's economy, declined after the mid-19th century.

Beginning in the 1920s the textile industry began to move to the South, lured by cheaper labor and modern equipment. Local prosperity increased, however, with the development of defense-related industries during the two world wars. From World War II until its closing in 1973, the Naval Air Station at Quonset Point remained the largest civilian employer in the state. Electrical machinery, fabricated metals, and plastics manufacturing have strengthened the postwar economy. Today, increasing numbers of Rhode Islanders work in the fields of insurance, printing and publishing, wholesale and retail trade, and government. The expanding tourist industry provides jobs in a variety of service positions.

Rhodes   Rhodes (Greek: Ródhos), the largest island of the Greek Dodecanese group, lies in the Aegean Sea off the southwestern coast of Turkey. The total area is 1,404 km² (542 mi²), and the population is 87,831 (1981). The city of Rhodes is the capital. A mountain range extending the length of the island reaches a height of 1,215 m (3,986 ft) in Mount Atláviros. Agriculture is the economic mainstay. Sponges are taken from offshore waters. Tourism is an important supplement to the economy. The city of Rhodes, the site of the ancient Colossus of Rhodes (one of the SEVEN WONDERS OF THE WORLD), has many medieval buildings erected by the Knights HOSPITALERS. Important ancient remains are at Ialysos, Kamiros, and Lindos.

Occupied in Minoan times, Rhodes was invaded (*c.*1000 BC) by the Dorians. The cities of Ialysos, Kamiros, and Lindos became major commercial centers. They founded colonies in the western Mediterranean (including Gela on Sicily). Dominated by Persia from the late 6th century BC, the Rhodian cities joined (*c.*470) Athens in the DELIAN LEAGUE but aligned with Sparta in the Peloponnesian War. During the war the city of Rhodes was founded as the capital of the Rhodian federation. It became a leading commercial and cultural center, retaining its preeminence into the Roman period.

In 1310 the island was granted to the Knights Hospitalers, who ruled until expelled by the Ottoman Turks in 1522. From 1912 to 1947, Rhodes was occupied by the Italians.

Rhodes, Cecil John   A British imperialist and statesman, Cecil John Rhodes, b. July 5, 1853, d. Mar. 26, 1902, helped establish British rule in southern Africa. Rhodes went to southern Africa in 1870. Between

Cecil Rhodes, British entrepreneur and statesman, amassed a fortune in diamonds and gold in South Africa during the late 19th century. He died in 1902 and left funds for the scholarship program in his name at Oxford University.

1871 and 1888 he became a rich man, forming the De Beers Mining Company and eventually controlling 90 percent of the world's diamond production.

In 1890 he took office as prime minister of Cape Colony, resolving to work for a policy guaranteeing both the British and the Afrikaners equality under the British flag. Rhodes meanwhile used his influence and wealth to create a new British foothold north of the Transvaal, to reduce Afrikaner political influence in southern Africa, and to promote the dream of a British empire from the "Cape to Cairo." In 1889 he received from the British government a charter setting up the British South Africa Company, a commercial concern with vast administrative powers. The company occupied Mashonaland in 1890 and defeated the powerful kingdom of the Ndebele in 1893. By the end of the century Rhodes's company controlled a huge area, including Southern Rhodesia (now Zimbabwe) and Northern Rhodesia (now Zambia), which were named for him.

In 1896, Rhodes's premiership was brought to an end by the Jameson Raid (see JAMESON, SIR LEANDER STARR), which unsuccessfully sought to topple the Afrikaner government of Paul KRUGER in the Transvaal. Rhodes, however, continued to exercise vast power in the affairs of the two Rhodesias. He bequeathed part of his fortune to found the Rhodes scholarships at Oxford.

Rhodes scholarships   Rhodes scholarships are awards established by the will (1899) of Cecil Rhodes to bring to Oxford University young men from the British Commonwealth and the United States. They were first awarded in 1903. Rhodes hoped to establish close ties among an Anglo-Saxon elite to "secure the peace of the world." The scholarships, which are for graduate work and cover tuition and living expenses for two years, may be extended for a third. They are now also open to women and are awarded by competition. About 71 scholarships are awarded annually.

Rhodesia   see ZIMBABWE

rhodium [roh'-dee-uhm]   Rhodium is a hard, white metallic chemical element of the platinum group of TRANSITION ELEMENTS. Its symbol is Rh, its atomic number is 45, and its atomic weight is 102.906. Rhodium was discovered in 1803 by William H. Wollaston. It is used primarily as an alloying agent for platinum and iridium; these alloys have greater mechanical strength and ability to withstand higher temperatures than do the pure metals.

rhododendron [roh-duh-den'-druhn]   *Rhododendron* is the generic and common name of approximately 600 species of flowering shrubs and trees, usually evergreen, in the heath family, Ericaceae. Approximately 10,000 named varieties are listed in the International Register, and about 2,000 of these are available. Azaleas are also included in the genus *Rhododendron,* but they are gener-

The royal rhododendron has pink, freckled flowers that bloom in spring. Its leaves turn a variety of colors in fall. Some species of rhododendron grow up to 12 m (40 ft) tall.

ally excluded from the "true rhododendrons." The name *rhododendron* comes from the Greek and means "red tree." The plant's large, beautiful blooms appear in the spring in a variety of colors including red, lilac purple, white, light rose, apple-blossom pink, rosy lilac, and deep rose. The flowers are usually produced in trusses. Rhododendrons range from 12-m (40-ft) flowering trees to matlike ground covers.

rhodonite [roh'-duh-nyt]   The manganese, iron, and calcium SILICATE MINERAL rhodonite [$(Mn,Fe,Ca)SiO_3$] is valued not only as a rose red ornamental stone but also as a major ore of manganese in India. Usually associated with rhodochrosite and other manganese minerals, it forms large, rounded, tabular crystals (triclinic system).

rhombohedral system   see HEXAGONAL SYSTEM

Rhône River [rohn]   The Rhône River, one of Europe's longest rivers, rises in Switzerland, flows southward through eastern France, and empties into the Mediterranean Sea after a course of about 800 km (500 mi). Its source is the Rhône glacier in the Swiss Alps at an altitude of about 1,830 m (6,000 ft). For about 160 km (100 mi) it flows through deep Alpine valleys before entering Lake Geneva. The city of Geneva lies at the river's outflow from the lake. Flowing into France, the Rhône is joined at Lyon by the SAÔNE, its principal tributary. It then turns southward between the Alps and the Massif Central. It empties into the Mediterranean by a large delta. In addition to the Saône, important tributaries include the Arve, Ardèche, Isère, and Durance. The Rhône is fed chiefly by the melting snows of the Alps.

The Rhône is turbulent and has been little used for navigation. In recent years, however, its course from Lyon to the sea has been improved by the construction of dams to regulate flow and generate hydroelectric power. The river is paralleled by heavily used roads and railroads from Lyon to the delta. The chief cities on its banks are Lyon, Vienne, Valence, Avignon, and Arles. The delta has no ports; a canal links the lower river with Marseille 40 km (25 mi) to the east.

rhubarb   Rhubarb, *Rheum rhabarbarum,* is a perennial herb and one of the few vegetables cultivated for the leaf stalks, or petioles. The broad, leafy portions and the roots contain poisonous substances, including oxalic acid, and should not be eaten. Rhubarb is a member of the buckwheat family, Polygonaceae, and is believed to be native to the region of Turkey. A number of closely related plants, including *R. officinale,* are also called rhubarbs and are raised as garden foliage plants or for their roots, which are the source of pharmaceutical compounds sometimes used as laxatives. Several of the docks, or sorrels, in the genus *Rumex* of the same family but with edible leaves are also often called rhubarbs.

Rhubarb is best adapted to cool climates and is usually grown from crown and roots rather than from seed. The plants should be located where small children do not have access to the poisonous parts.

The rhubarb plant produces reddish stalks used in pies and sauces. The roots and large leaves are poisonous. Rhubarb, which probably originated in Asia, grows best in cool climates.

rhyme   see VERSIFICATION

rhyolite   [ry'-uh-lyt]   Rhyolite is a light-colored, fine-grained volcanic rock (see IGNEOUS ROCK) with a very high (more than 70%) silica content. It often contains phenocrysts of quartz and feldspar in a glassy matrix. Iron and magnesium minerals are rare or absent. Similar to the coarser-grained granites in mineralogy and chemistry, rhyolite tends to be very viscous because of its high silica content, and on eruption it generally forms steep-sided domes and plugs. Gas-rich rhyolite, however, erupts violently to form welded tuffs, or ignimbrites, and may spread out over great distances.

Rhys, Jean   [rees]   A highly acclaimed British novelist of the 1920s and '30s who had fallen into obscurity, Jean Rhys, b. Aug. 24, 1894, d. May 14, 1979, was recognized afresh in the 1970s as much for her enduring modernity as for the feminist implications of her work. Her unrelentingly pessimistic early novels all deal with vulnerable, middle-class women cast adrift in large cities both by circumstances and by the men they have failed to keep. Rhys describes their precarious psychological state with rigorous objectivity and an admirably spare style in *Quartet* (1928), *After Leaving Mr. MacKenzie* (1931), *Voyage in the Dark* (1934), and *Good Morning, Midnight* (1939). After World War II, Rhys published *Wide Sargasso Sea* (1966), about the first, mad wife of Mr. Rochester, hero of Charlotte Brontë's *Jane Eyre,* and two collections of short stories, *Tigers Are Better Looking* (1968) and *Sleep It Off, Lady* (1976).

rhythm   Rhythm is the temporal element of music, the pattern of musical notes with regard to their duration and accentuation. (In a broader sense, rhythm is not restricted to music: speech, certain machines, and many natural processes may be described as rhythmic.) In most Western music rhythm occurs within a framework of regular pulsation, or METER; all time values are multiples or fractions of a metrical unit. (In *isometric* music, prevalent from the 17th to the 19th century and associated with the classical dance, the units are grouped in measures of equal length, with the first beat of each measure accented; in *multimetric* music, prevalent during the Middle Ages and the Renaissance and revived during the 20th century, the measures are unequal and the accents, consequently, irregular.) Meter is not, however, a prerequisite of rhythm: much non-Western music and some early European folk music is essentially *ametric.*

rhythm and blues   The term *rhythm and blues* (R & B) began as a music industry designation for records by black musicians for black audiences. Beginning as a replacement for the industry term *race records,* it eventually came to denote the styles of music created by black, urban musicians since the 1940s.

In the late 1940s, when many jazz musicians began to play the rhythmically complex style known as BEBOP, black dancers turned to big bands playing a blues-derived, saxophone-dominated music with a heavy beat. It was louder, larger-scaled, and less subtle than the older blues and jazz styles, and it was soon supplemented by

B. B. King, the "king of the Blues," is one of the most influential contemporary blues artists. During the 1960s, as rock musicians developed a style derivative of King's, he became a major force in the popularization of rhythm and blues.

other styles: small sax-and-piano "jump bands" using boogie-woogie rhythms; country-blues bands featuring electric guitars and harmonicas; and black teenage vocal groups.

ROCK MUSIC, in its beginnings a white-produced music, borrowed the form, the beat, and the sound of rhythm and blues. While many black R & B performers became rock musicians, many others expanded their R & B styles. In the mid-1950s, Ray CHARLES and James BROWN combined the emotional, vocally complex style derived from GOSPEL MUSIC with R & B, creating what came to be known as SOUL MUSIC. R & B, recorded with strings and adolescent lyrics by such groups as the Supremes, became "uptown" or MOTOWN R & B. Aretha FRANKLIN sang in an R & B style that was closer to blues roots. In the 1970s, musical modes like SALSA were added, producing new complexities of rhythm and instrumentation. Much of the disco music of the 1970s was formularized R & B. Modified by rock sound and production values, the style continued into the 1980s, performed by Smokey Robinson, L. L. Kool J., Dionne Warwick, and many others.

Riabouchinska, Tatiana [ree-ah-boo-chin'-skah] Tatiana Riabouchinska, b. Moscow, May 23 (N.S.), 1917, was known as one of the "baby ballerinas" of the 1930s, along with Irina Baronova and Tamara Toumanova. Trained in Paris by the émigré ballerina Mathilde Kshessinska, Riabouchinska made her debut at the age of 15 in the *Chauve-Souris* revue. In 1932 she was chosen by choreographer George Balanchine for Col. W. de Basil's Ballet Russe de Monte Carlo. She remained with that company for a decade, creating roles in numerous ballets by Balanchine, Leonid Massine, and David Lichine, whom she married in 1943.

Ribaut, Jean [ree-boh'] Jean Ribaut, b. c.1520, d. Oct. 12, 1565, French navigator and colonizer, founded a Huguenot colony in North America in 1562. Sent by Admiral Gaspard de COLIGNY, he explored the northern

Florida coast and then established a settlement called Charlesfort at the present Port Royal, S.C. Ribaut returned to France in July 1562. He was unable to bring back assistance because of the religious war in France, and the colonists abandoned Charlesfort. In 1565, Ribaut sailed with reinforcements for the Huguenot colony of Fort Caroline that had been established a year earlier on Florida's Saint John's River by René Goulaine de LAUDONNIÈRE. After arriving there he sailed south to attack Pedro MENÉNDEZ DE AVILÉS, sent by the Spanish to drive the French from Florida. But Menéndez's forces, moving by land, destroyed Fort Caroline. They then killed Ribaut and his men, who had been shipwrecked.

Ribbentrop, Joachim von [rib'-en-trohp, yoh'-ah-keem fuhn] Joachim von Ribbentrop, b. Apr. 30, 1893, d. Oct. 16, 1946, was German foreign minister (1938–45) under the National Socialist (Nazi) regime. He joined the Nazi party in 1932 and became Adolf Hitler's leading foreign-policy advisor in 1933, serving as ambassador (1936–38) to Great Britain before becoming foreign minister. An ardently loyal follower of Hitler, he implemented major Nazi foreign policy initiatives, including the Anglo-German naval agreement (1935) and the NAZI-SOVIET PACT (1939). His influence declined during World War II. Found guilty of war crimes at the NUREMBERG TRIALS after the war, he was hanged.

Ribera, Jusepe de [ree-bay'-rah] The Spanish painter and etcher Jusepe (or José) de Ribera, baptized

Jusepe de Ribera's The Clubfooted Boy *(1652) demonstrates the affinity of the Spanish baroque for the striking naturalism of Caravaggio. Like Diego Velázquez, Ribera combined this characteristic with a peculiarly Spanish mysticism, giving the deformed peasant boy an air of tragicomic dignity and pathos. (Louvre, Paris.)*

Feb. 17, 1591, d. Sept. 2, 1652, combined the mysticism and religious intensity of his native country with the naturalism of Caravaggio. During his lifetime his popularity was immense, and his influence persisted long after his death.

Ribera's tenebrist works, constructed with dense pigment, mainly in strong earth colors, were in the tradition of Caravaggio, as were his single-figure compositions, usually in half or three-quarter length, against a dark background. Ribera, however, retained a distinctive Spanish sensuality in all his work. An example is *The Sense of Touch* (c.1615; Norton Simon Museum of Art, Pasadena, Calif.). *The Martyrdom of Saint Bartholomew* (1639; Prado, Madrid) shows the more even illumination, lighter colors, and more vigorous, looser brushstrokes characteristic of his later style, which placed less emphasis on mass and volume. The works of his later years—such as the sensitive and graceful *Holy Family with Saint Catherine* (1648; Metropolitan Museum of Art, New York City)—tend to be calmer and more radiant than his earlier paintings.

His pictures made Ribera an important influence in Spanish art, although he spent most of his life in Naples, where he acquired the nickname "Lo Spagnoletto" ("the little Spaniard"). His accomplished etchings, mostly done in the 1620s and of which only 16 can be attributed to him with certainty, also played a part in spreading his fame.

ribosome [ry'-buh-sohm] Ribosomes, which are bead-like cellular organelles, are the site of protein synthesis in all cells. Ribosomes of prokaryotic organisms are dispersed throughout the cytoplasm. They can be dissociated into a large and a small subunit, each of which can be further broken down into proteins and ribonucleic acid (RNA) molecules. Eukaryotic ribosomes are also found in the cytoplasm—either free or bound to the endoplasmic reticulum—as well as in the nucleus, mitochondria, and chloroplasts. Although larger in size, they resemble prokaryotic ribosomes in structural organization and properties. During protein synthesis, many ribosomes simultaneously attach to a single messenger-RNA molecule and translate the information of the genetic code into amino acids, which are used to build specific proteins.

See also: CELL; GENETIC CODE.

Ricardo, David [ri-kahr'-doh] David Ricardo, b. Apr. 19, 1772, d. Sept. 11, 1823, was a leader of the British classical school of economists. Like Adam Smith before him, Ricardo believed in limiting state intervention in economic life. His early publication *An Essay on the Influence of a Low Price of Corn on the Profits of Stock* (1815) argued against high tariffs on grain imports, and his theory of comparative advantage showed how the unimpeded flow of commodities among nations could be of mutual benefit to all parties (see FREE TRADE).

The Ricardian world, however, was not particularly harmonious, nor was its outlook very optimistic. Ricardo shared the population doctrine of his friend Thomas Robert MALTHUS and believed that population pressure would tend to keep wages near the subsistence level. Further, he saw the future progress of society as marked by conflicts among economic classes. His "labor theory of value," which held that commodities exchange in proportion to the labor embodied in their production, had great impact on Karl MARX, although it was later discredited by Western economists.

Noted for his theoretical rigor, Ricardo actually was a practicing economist only briefly. He came to it late from a business career and died at the age of 51, a scant 13 years after his first publication. He was successful on the stock exchange and, in the last years of his life, served in Parliament.

Ricci, Matteo An Italian Jesuit missionary and scientist, Matteo Ricci, b. Oct. 6, 1552, d. May 11, 1610, was a founder of the Christian church in China and an originator of cultural and scientific interchange between Europe and China. In 1582, Ricci joined another Jesuit, Michele Ruggieri, in Macao, and from there they entered China. Together they made a radical break with traditional missionary methods. In order to reach the cultured society of China, the missionaries confronted this educated elite on its own level by demonstrating comparable scholarship, culture, and talent. Their goal was to convert China as an entire culture.

Ricci's major contributions were not only his method of evangelization but also his numerous works, written in Chinese, on scientific, apologetic, catechetical, literary, and mathematical topics. His method of adapting Chinese ceremonies to the performance of Christian rites caused a prolonged controversy in the Roman Catholic church and was finally condemned by the pope in 1704 and 1715. Modern missionary methods have vindicated Ricci's foresight.

rice Since ancient times, rice has been the most commonly used food grain for a majority of the people of the world. A member of the grass family, Gramineae, rice, *Oryza sativa*, can be grown successfully under climatic conditions ranging from tropical to temperate. Properly cultivated, rice produces higher yields than any other grain with the exception of corn; and although the total area planted in rice is far smaller than that devoted to wheat—the world total is about one-third less—the rice crop feeds a far greater proportion of the world's population.

Cultivation and Harvesting. Rice plants require a steady supply of water, and therefore, fields are often flooded by irrigation or planted during periods of excessive rainfall. Rice is planted with drills on dry land; on wet land, the seed is broadcast by hand and sometimes by airplane. Much rice is grown in nurseries, and the young plants are transplanted by hand into swampy soil. Rice fields are kept flooded until just before harvest. Water control retards weed growth, but chemical controls are also often necessary.

Rice plants start from a single shoot and then develop many tillers and pointed, flat leaves; the plants grow from 0.6 to 1.8 m (2 to 6 ft) tall. The plant is commonly self-pollinating. The kernel, with its rough outer hull, consists of bran or aleurone layers, germ, and endosperm.

More than 7,000 botanically different rice varieties have been identified. They are classified as short, medium, or long kerneled. Long-grain rice is often preferred over short or medium grains because it has less tendency to stick together when cooked. Rice varieties are also classified according to how early they mature, an important property because the harvest must be handled during dry weather. When rice is harvested the kernels contain about 20% moisture, and the crop cannot be processed or stored safely until the moisture content is reduced to approximately 12%. In large operations rice is taken directly from the combine to dryers, where moisture is reduced gradually to avoid cracking, which would make processing more difficult. When dry, the rice can be taken to the mill or stored in warehouses.

Throughout much of the world rice is harvested by hand, using knives or sickles. The stalks are cut, tied in bundles, and left in the sun to dry. All sorts of means are used to thresh the grain, ranging from using the weight of animals or tractors to threshing with various types of machines. On large farms rice is harvested by self-propelled combines. Whole kernels of rice are desirable; therefore, threshing with a minimum of breakage is necessary. Small rice producers sell their paddy (the unhulled, or brown, rice) before storage becomes necessary.

Where Rice Is Grown. China, India, Indonesia, Bangladesh, Thailand, Vietnam, and Japan are the leading rice-growing countries. In the United States the leading states in rice production are Arkansas, Texas, California, Louisiana, Mississippi, and Missouri. A separate genus, WILD RICE (*Zizania aquatica*), is native to North America and is not cultivated.

Rice Breeding. During the past quarter-century, rice-breeding programs have been initiated in several countries. Resistance to diseases and insects was the major objective of the earlier research, but hybrid programs

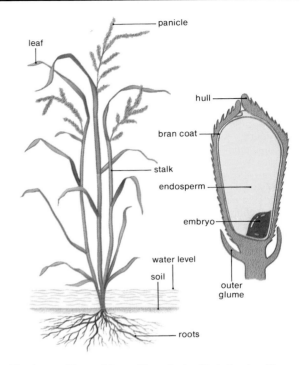

Rice is one of the world's most important cultivated grains. The kernel (right) consists of a hull and a bran coat—both of which are removed in polishing "white" rice—and the endosperm and embryo, which constitute the edible portion.

have dominated recently. High-yielding dwarf plants that can withstand water depths and that respond to fertilizers have been developed. Improved grain quality and higher protein levels have been added objectives of new programs designed to improve nutrition. New varieties can, under good cultural conditions such as soil fertility and water control, increase yields as much as 100% compared with conventional varieties.

The process of rice cultivation has changed little since its earliest production, centuries ago. Rice seedlings are grown in nurseries (A) and transplanted to irrigated paddies (B) after 25–50 days. The plants must be carefully weeded despite their covering of 5–10 cm (2–4 in) of water (C). High-yield strains require the use of fertilizers and insecticidal sprays. Rice is commonly harvested using simple instruments, tied in bundles to dry, and threshed when moisture has been reduced to approximately 20% (D).

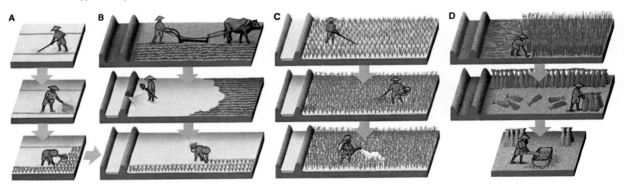

The proximate analysis of rough rice is: protein, 7–11%; starch, 62–66%; lipids, 1–2½%; and minerals, 4½–6%. The protein content of rice is lower than that of wheat and other major cereal grains, although the new strains are somewhat higher in protein content. The whole (unhulled) rice kernel contains vitamins, thiamine, niacin, and riboflavin.

Uses. Rice is usually eaten as milled whole grain. Parboiling rice before it is milled—a centuries-old technique—is now a potential industrial procedure. Parboiled rice can be stored for long periods because cooking hardens the kernel, sterilizes, and controls moisture content. Quick-cooking rice is made by procedures that produce porosity of the kernel, permitting rapid water penetration and thus shortening cooking time. Cooked rice can be flaked or puffed for breakfast food and is used in prepared baby foods. Rice flour, prepared from broken grain, is used in the baking and confectionery industries. Rice flour does not contain gluten and therefore cannot be used for baking bread. Flour from waxy-type rice has wider application as a thickening agent because of its more glutinous starch.

Rice bran, rich in lipids that can be refined into a high-grade edible oil, has long been a standard ingredient of livestock feed. Laundry starch and a powder used for cosmetics are made from rice starch. Rice hulls are used as polishing material, as cattle feed, and as fertilizer and can also be converted to furfural, an industrial solvent. Fermented beverages are also produced from rice (see SAKE).

Because the milling process removes vitamins, an enriched rice, coated with vitamins and mineral supplements, is available. As much as 20% of paddy is hull, 13% bran, and 3% polishings, all products that are removed when rice is milled. Unmilled, or brown, rice retains the outer bran layer and much of the nutrient value of whole rice.

Rice, Elmer   Elmer Rice, b. Leopold Reizenstein, New York City, Sept. 28, 1892, d. May 8, 1967, was a lawyer turned dramatist who began his writing career with the courtroom drama *On Trial* (1914). Rice is best remembered for *The Adding Machine* (1923), an experimental play about mechanization, and *Street Scene* (1929), which depicts New York tenement life. His later dramas focus on the depression years and fascism. *The Living Theatre* (1959) is a collection of his essays.

Rice, Grantland   Henry Grantland Rice, b. Murfreesboro, Tenn., Nov. 1, 1880, d. July 13, 1954, was considered the dean of sportswriters in the United States. Rice entertained fans for nearly 50 years with his colorful turn of phrase ("Four Horsemen," "Galloping Ghost," "Manassa Mauler"), accurate judgment, and high moral standards ("It's not whether you won or lost but how you played the game"). His widely syndicated column was called "The Spotlight." His autobiography was titled *The Tumult and the Shouting: My Life in Sport* (1954).

Rice University   Established in 1891 and adopting the full name of its founder, William Marsh Rice, in 1960, Rice University is a private coeducational institution in Houston, Tex. It offers a full range of undergraduate and graduate degree programs.

Rich, Adrienne   The work of the American poet and feminist Adrienne Cecile Rich, b. Baltimore, Md., May 6, 1929, has evolved from the formal elegance of *A Change of World* (1951) to engagement of the issues of oppression and feminism in *Diving into the Wreck* (1973; National Book Award) and *A Wild Patience Has Taken Me This Far: Poems 1978–81* (1981). She began to describe women's sensibilities in *The Diamond Cutter and Other Poems* (1955) and *Snapshots of a Daughter-in-law: Poems, 1954–62* (1963). Also an essayist and polemicist, Rich describes motherhood with candor in the prose study *Of Woman Born: Motherhood as Experience and Institution* (1976).

Adrienne Rich, a feminist poet and author, received the 1974 National Book Award for her collection of poems *Diving into the Wreck (1973).* Her poetry, precise and elegant, has evolved into a continuing chronicle of her spiritual and political growth.

Photo Jill Krementz © 1974

Richard, Gabriel   [ree-shahr']   Gabriel Richard, b. Oct. 15, 1767, d. Sept. 13, 1832, a French Roman Catholic priest, made many contributions to early Michigan society. In the United States he was initially assigned to Illinois Territory and, in 1798, was transferred to Detroit, where he established a seminary and other schools. He published the *Michigan Essay or Impartial Observer*, the first paper in Michigan, and helped to found (1817) the University of Michigan, where he served as vice-president, professor, and trustee. In 1823, Richard was elected to Congress.

Richard, Maurice   Joseph Henri Maurice "Rocket" Richard, b. Montreal, Aug. 4, 1921, was an aggressive professional ice hockey player and the first National Hockey League (NHL) player to score 50 goals in a season (1944–45). Richard, who played his entire career with the Montreal Canadiens, was an extremely fast skater—hence his nickname. He played right wing, and for years was the offensive backbone of the Canadiens. In his 18-season career (1942–60) he scored 544 goals; he was selected for 8 all-star teams, led the NHL in goal scoring 5 times, and won (1947) the MVP award once. Richard was elected to the Hockey Hall of Fame in 1961.

Richard II (play)

Richard II (play) With *The Tragedy of King Richard II* (written *c*.1595), William SHAKESPEARE began a history tetralogy that continues in *Henry IV,* Parts 1 and 2, and *Henry V*. Richard II exiles Henry Bolingbroke and confiscates his lands to finance his war in Ireland. Bolingbroke returns and, with the Percy family's aid, forces Richard to abdicate and proclaims himself Henry IV. After instigating Richard's murder, Henry expresses remorse and vows a pilgrimage to expiate his crime. The play constitutes an eloquent dramatic debate on the nature of kingship.

Richard III (play)

Richard III (play) *The Tragedy of King Richard III* (written *c*.1592), one of William SHAKESPEARE's most popular history plays, owes its success to the portrait of the villainous Richard, duke of Gloucester. On the death of his brother Edward IV, Richard usurps the crown by murdering Edward's two sons, the so-called "Princes in the Tower." These and his other crimes are avenged by Henry, duke of Richmond, who kills Richard at the Battle of Bosworth Field and becomes Henry VII, the first Tudor king. Richard's hunchbacked body matches the perversion of his mind, but his disarming frankness and comic ingenuity compensate for the play's relative crudity.

Richard I, King of England

Richard I, King of England Richard I, the Lion-Hearted, b. Sept. 8, 1157, d. Apr. 6, 1199, king of England (1189–99), was the third son of HENRY II and ELEANOR OF AQUITAINE. Renowned as a Crusader and gallant knight, Richard neglected his kingdom, and spent all but six months of his reign outside England campaigning or in captivity. Battle leader of the Third CRUSADE, Richard was shipwrecked near Venice on his return in 1192 and imprisoned by Duke Leopold of Austria. Leopold turned Richard over to Holy Roman Emperor HENRY VI, who released him in February 1194 only after a huge ransom had been pledged.

For the English, probably the most significant event of the crusade was Richard's assent to the Treaty of Messina (1191) with PHILIP II of France, an ally early in the Crusade; by that treaty the English king formally acknowledged his continental holdings as Philip's fief. Philip later used his position as overlord of the English king for his French dominions to justify his attack against Richard's brother and successor, King JOHN. Richard spent the last five years of his reign warring with Philip. Although he was later romanticized by Sir Walter Scott and others,

Richard I, king of England, earned the title "Coeur de Lion," or "Lion Heart," for his boldness in combat. He used his kingdom as a source of money to finance his overseas expeditions, including the Third Crusade, returning from which he was captured and held for ransom by the Holy Roman emperor.

Richard did little more than contribute to the financial exhaustion of his realm through the expenses of the Crusade and other wars, the king's ransom, and subsidies to his continental allies.

Richard II, King of England

Richard II, King of England Richard II, b. Jan. 6, 1367, d. February 1400, king of England (1377–99), son of EDWARD, THE BLACK PRINCE, succeeded his grandfather EDWARD III. Precocious, clever, and ruthless, Richard had exalted notions of royal power but proved unable to implement them. Richard's uncle, JOHN OF GAUNT, duke of Lancaster, was effective ruler of England during the young king's minority. When an oppressive poll tax sparked the PEASANTS' REVOLT in 1381, Richard himself negotiated a truce with the rebels. After the death (1385) of his mother, Joan of Kent, he began to take control.

Richard offended much of the English populace with

Richard II, last of the Angevin kings of England, was 10 years old at his coronation and 14 when he outwitted the rebellious peasants led by Wat Tyler. A reckless and ineffectual ruler, Richard was deposed by his cousin Henry Bolingbroke, who began the Lancastrian line of kings.

his high-handed style of government, lack of interest in the French war (see HUNDRED YEARS' WAR), and reliance on a few young friends, especially Robert de Vere, earl of Oxford, and Michael de la Pole, earl of Suffolk, the chancellor. After Gaunt left for Spain in 1386, Suffolk was impeached in Parliament and a council was imposed on the king, despite Richard's charges of treason. The Merciless Parliament of 1388 met under the threat of rebellion by the king's five leading opponents, known as the Lords Appellant—the king's uncle, the duke of Gloucester; Gaunt's son, Henry Bolingbroke; the earl of Arundel; the earl of Warwick; and the earl of Nottingham (later duke of Norfolk)—who forced the exile or execution of several royal favorites.

Determined to exact revenge, Richard gradually built up a royalist faction. In 1397, Gloucester was murdered and Warwick and Arundel were condemned in Parliament. In 1398, Richard exiled Bolingbroke, who, taking advantage of the king's temporary absence in Ireland, invaded England the following year. Richard quickly returned but was forced to abdicate and died in prison, perhaps murdered. Soon after, Bolingbroke became HENRY IV.

Richard III, King of England   Richard III, b. Oct. 2, 1452, d. Aug. 22, 1485, king of England (1483–85), the last ruler of the House of York (see YORK dynasty), seized power during the final years of the Wars of the ROSES. He was the youngest son of Richard, duke of York. After his eldest brother, EDWARD IV, deposed the Lancastrian monarch HENRY VI and became king in 1461, Richard was made duke of Gloucester. In March 1471, Richard's troops played a decisive role in English victories against the Lancastrians at Barnet and Tewkesbury. Two months later Henry VI and his son were murdered, an act in which Richard is believed to have participated.

On the succession of the boy king EDWARD V in April 1483, Richard established himself as protector in London, supported by William, Lord Hastings, and Henry Stafford, 2d duke of Buckingham. In the ensuing struggle

Richard III was the last English king of the House of York. Although he was an effective administrator, his ruthlessness in securing the throne and in eliminating potential opposition brought large-scale revolt. After a brief reign (1483–85) Richard was killed in battle by the future Henry VII.

for power, many of Richard's opponents—and his one-time ally, Hastings—were executed, and Edward was declared illegitimate. Richard was crowned on July 26. His position as king was weakened by his lack of a son; by reports, probably true, that he was responsible for the murders of Edward and his brother in August; and by the disaffection of supporters, including Buckingham, who rebelled in October 1483. After the successful invasion of Henry Tudor in August 1485, Richard was killed at Bosworth Field and Henry was crowned HENRY VII. A controversial figure, Richard was portrayed as a villain by writers under the Tudor monarchs, most notably by William Shakespeare in his play *Richard III.*

Richards, Bob   Robert E. Richards, b. Champaign, Ill., Feb. 20, 1926, was a champion pole vaulter. Although he divided his time between athletics and the ministry, in 1948 he won a bronze medal in the 1948 Olympic Games. After winning (1951) the Sullivan Award, Richards went on to win the Olympic gold medal in the pole vault in 1952 and again in 1956. He won or tied for the national Amateur Athletic Union (AAU) outdoor title 9 times (1948–52, 1954–57) and the indoor title 8 times (1948, 1950–52, 1954–57).

Richards, I. A.   The English literary critic Ivor Armstrong Richards, b. Feb. 26, 1893, d. Sept. 7, 1979, laid the groundwork for the later development of the NEW CRITICISM in America. Richards's important books include his study of semantics, *The Meaning of Meaning* (with C. K. Ogden, 1923); *Principles of Literary Criticism* (1924), an exploration of the connections between art and science; and the influential *Practical Criticism* (1929). His research into the functions of language led him to work with the much-publicized learning system called Basic English. Among his collections of poetry are *Goodbye Earth and Other Poems* (1958) and *Beyond* (1974).

Richards, Sir William Buell   Sir William Buell Richards, b. Brockville, Ontario, May 2, 1815, d. Jan. 26, 1889, was the first chief justice of the Canadian Supreme Court (1875–79). In 1851 he was appointed attorney general for Upper Canada (Ontario), a post that he held until 1853 when he was appointed to the Court of Common Pleas. In 1868 he became chief justice of the Queen's Bench in Ontario.

Richardson, Elliot L.   Elliot Lee Richardson, b. Boston, July 20, 1920, has held a number of top governmental and diplomatic posts, including three cabinet positions during the administration of President Richard Nixon: secretary of health, education and welfare (1970–72), secretary of defense (1972–73), and attorney general (1973). Under President Gerald Ford, he served as ambassador to Great Britain (1975–76) and as secretary of commerce (1976–77).

Richardson received a law degree from Harvard University after a distinguished army career during World War II. He was appointed (1959) U.S. attorney for Massachusetts and served (1965–67) as lieutenant governor of Massachusetts. A moderate Republican, Richardson became well known for having resigned as attorney general after refusing to fire Archibald Cox, the special prosecutor during the WATERGATE scandal.

Richardson, Henry Hobson   The American architect Henry Hobson Richardson, b. Saint James Parish, La., Sept. 29, 1838, d. Apr. 27, 1886, became the most innovative and influential designer in his field during the latter part of the 19th century.

Richardson's early designs in the United States include Grace Church (1867; West Medford, Mass.), derived from English Victorian models with pyramidal massing and the use of rough-faced granite, and his own house (1868; Staten Island, N.Y.), which combines high-pitched French mansard roofs with the fussy, shedlike forms of 19th-century American wood construction. Such conflicting tendencies are more marked in the State Asylum for the Insane (1871–81; Buffalo, N.Y.).

In later projects Richardson introduced the massive and simple masonry architecture, inspired by the Romanesque, for which he is famous, for example, Trinity Church (consecrated 1877; Boston), his most elegant religious structure, and Harvard University's rectangular Sever Hall (1878; Cambridge, Mass.). All of Richardson's buildings tend to avoid the extremes of picturesqueness then popular. Although many of his designs were based on European sources, they are thoroughly American in materials and character.

The Marshall Field Wholesale Store (1885–87), in Chicago, designed by Henry Hobson Richardson, exhibits the rhythmic and textural variation and the massive proportions typical of Richardson's style. The structure was demolished in 1930.

Richardson's last buildings achieve a monumentality unequaled in American architecture. In the huge Marshall Field Wholesale Store (1885–87; Chicago), his demolished masterpiece, Richardson emphasized the structure's blocklike function in the urban environment.

Richardson, Sir Ralph   The English actor Ralph David Richardson, b. Dec. 19, 1902, d. Oct. 10, 1983, was one of the best-loved actors of the English-speaking stage. He also appeared in many films. During the 1930s he acted in many Old Vic and Sadler's Wells productions with Laurence Olivier, and the two were appointed directors of the Old Vic in 1944. That same year he played the title role in *Peer Gynt*, which became one of his most memorable performances, along with that of Falstaff in *Henry IV*. As willing to perform in cameo roles as in major ones, Richardson invested the most ordinary characters with qualities that he drew from his own somewhat eccentric and mischievous nature. He appeared on Broadway with John Gielgud in *Home* (1970) and in Harold Pinter's *No Man's Land* (1975).

Richardson, Samuel   Samuel Richardson, b. July 31, 1689, d. July 4, 1761, often described as the first major English novelist, exercised a profound influence on the development of the NOVEL. Born to a "Family of middling Note," he was apprenticed (1706) to a London printer. Early in life he acquired a passion for writing letters, which he composed on his own and others' behalf. At the age of 50, well established as a printer, he was asked by two London booksellers to write a series of letters that might be used as models. *Letters Written to and for Particular Friends* (1751) contained a letter from a pious father to his daughter who, as the servant in a wealthy man's house, defends her virtue against a libidinous master.

From this correspondence grew Richardson's first epistolary novel, *Pamela; or, Virtue Rewarded* (1740). Both acclaimed and reviled, the book led to a host of imitations and burlesques, among them *Shamela* and *Joseph*

Samuel Richardson, an 18th-century English novelist, secured an enthusiastic following with Pamela; or Virtue Rewarded (1740). Richardson's protagonists are regarded as the first realistic, emotionally complex characters in the English novel.

Andrews (1742), which launched Henry Fielding on his career as a novelist. In 1747–48 appeared the enormously long and powerful *Clarissa; or The History of a Young Lady*, arguably the greatest fictional work of the 18th century. Also written as a series of letters, allowing shifting perspectives and minute analysis of psychological traits, the novel tells the tragic story of the contest between the saintly Clarissa and the libertine Lovelace, who obsessively pursues her into madness and death. Its chief characters became types, constantly referred to in the writings of the age. Richardson's final novel, *The History of Sir Charles Grandison*, was published in 1753–54. Whereas *Clarissa* had presented an exemplary woman, this novel tries to provide the ideal man, a corrective to the seductive Lovelace who, the author feared, was all too attractive to the reader. After publishing his last novel, Richardson worked as a printer, enjoyed the attentions of literary women, and continued writing letters.

Richardson, Tony   Film director Tony Richardson, b. Jan. 5, 1928, has been a key figure in the development of the modern British cinema and theater. Richardson directed the first production of John Osborne's *Look Back in Anger* (1956) and later made a film of the play (1959). He has since worked primarily as a film director, producing *Saturday Night and Sunday Morning* (1960) and directing the film version of Henry Fielding's *Tom Jones* (1963). His many memorable films include *The Entertainer* (1960), *A Taste of Honey* (1961), *The Loneliness of the Long Distance Runner* (1962), *The Charge of the Light Brigade* (1968), and *Joseph Andrews* (1977).

Richelieu, Armand Jean du Plessis, Cardinal et Duc de [ree-shel-yu'] Armand Jean du Plessis, Cardinal Richelieu, b. Sept. 9, 1585, d. Dec. 4, 1642, ruled France as the principal minister of Louis XIII from 1624 to 1642, helping to establish the basis of royal absolutism in France and of French preeminence in Europe. The regent and queen mother, Marie de Médicis, made Richelieu secretary of state for foreign affairs in 1616. Expelled from office when King Louis XIII overthrew (1617) his mother's authority, Richelieu then mediated the continuing disputes between Marie and her son, gaining a cardinalate in 1622 and becoming chief of the royal council in 1624. His title was changed to first minister in 1628.

Richelieu's policy was to develop the absolute authority of the crown and to crush the independent power of the Huguenots (French Protestants) while thwarting the European hegemony of the Spanish and Austrian Habsburgs by allying France with Protestant states in the Thirty Years' War. Although he took pains to justify his actions, for Richelieu the interests of the state overrode religion, ordinary morality, and constitutional procedures. As a result he alienated the devout Catholic party, the nobility, and the judicial hierarchy. Several noble conspiracies were raised against him, all of which he frustrated. Among the lower classes heavy taxation to support war caused an endemic state of revolt in the provinces. To control local privilege and disorder, Richelieu employed commissioners sent by the royal council, known as intendants. He also took an interest in literary and theological matters and founded the Académie Française in 1635.

In the Thirty Years' War the cardinal supported the Dutch, the Danes, and the Swedes in the struggle against the Habsburgs. After the defeat of his Swedish and Protestant German allies, he declared war against Spain in 1635. In 1640, Richelieu backed anti-Spanish revolts in Catalonia and Portugal. His actions led to a sharp decline of Spanish power.

Richler, Mordecai [rich'-lur] The characteristic subject of the Canadian novelist Mordecai Richler, b. Montreal, Jan. 27, 1931, is Jewish life in the working-class districts of Montreal. Duddy Kravitz, the determined young schemer of *The Apprenticeship of Duddy Kravitz* (1959; film, 1974), Richler's most popular novel, lives in the Saint Urbain Street area of Montreal, where Richler himself was brought up. *Saint Urbain's Horseman* (1971) is a complex meditation on the problems of being Jewish in contemporary society. Other works by Richler include the collection of essays *Notes on an Endangered Species* (1974) and the novels *Joshua Then and Now* (1980) and *Solomon Gursky Was Here* (1989).

Richmond [rich'-muhnd] Richmond is the capital and one of the largest cities of Virginia. Located in the eastern part of the state on the James River near the Atlantic Ocean, it is the seat of Henrico County and has a population of 203,056 (1990). The Richmond-Petersburg metropolitan area has a population of 865,640. With its deepwater port, extensive rail facilities, and dense highway network, Richmond is a regional distribution, commercial, and finance center. Tobacco processing and chemical manufacturing are among its diversified industries. The city's historic sites include Saint John's Church (1741), where Patrick Henry made his "Liberty or Death" speech; the state capitol (1785), designed by Thomas Jefferson; the Confederate White House; and nearby Richmond National Battlefield Park (1944). U.S. presidents John Tyler and James Monroe and Confederate president Jefferson Davis are buried in the city's Hollywood Cemetery. Richmond is the home of several educational institutions, including the University of Richmond (1830) and Virginia Commonwealth University (1838).

The area was first explored in 1607 by members of the Jamestown colony. Permanently settled in 1637 by Thomas Stegg, who established a trading post, Richmond was laid out in 1737 by Maj. William Mayo and was named for Richmond on Thames, England. It was made state capital in 1779, replacing Williamsburg. It was attacked by the British in 1781. Major Civil War battles raged around Richmond, which replaced (1861) Montgomery, Ala., as capital of the Confederacy. Gen. Ulysses S. Grant took the city on Apr. 3, 1865, after much of it was burned.

Richter, Hans   A painter who was drawn to kinetic abstraction, Hans Richter, b. Berlin, Apr. 16, 1888, d. Feb. 1, 1976, is best known for his contributions to avant-garde cinema. In 1918—having been associated with De Stijl, constructivism, and Dadaism—Richter and the Swedish painter Viking Eggeling began producing abstractions on scrolls, which led them to conceive the idea of the first abstract motion picture, *Rhythmus 21* (1921). Richter immigrated to the United States in 1941, becoming a professor at City College in New York City. Working with Marcel Duchamp, Max Ernst, Fernand Léger, and Alexander Calder, he explored the fantasies of a group of psychiatric patients in the film *Dreams That Money Can Buy* (1944–47).

Richter, Johann Paul Friedrich   The German writer Johann Paul Friedrich Richter, b. Mar. 21, 1763, d. Nov. 14, 1825, helped establish the 19th-century German novel as a literary form. Richter signed his works using the pen name Jean Paul. An admirer of Jean Jacques Rousseau, he achieved literary recognition with *The Invisible Lodge* (1793; Eng. trans., 1833). Richter's major work, *Titan* (1800–03; Eng. trans., 1862), is a four-volume novel that idealizes the life of the poor and contrasts the dreamer with the man of action. His other works include satirical essays and treatises on education and poetic theory.

Richter, Sviatoslav   [svee-ah'-toh-slahf]   The Soviet pianist Sviatoslav Teofilovich Richter, b. Mar. 20 (N.S.), 1915, is one of the great keyboard virtuosos in the romantic tradition. He was trained principally in Odessa, and made his official debut in 1935. In 1937 he enrolled in the Moscow Conservatory, studying with H. Neuhaus until 1947. He was awarded the Stalin Prize in 1949 and subsequently was declared "People's Artist of the USSR." His U.S. debut (1960) brought him great renown and was followed by similar triumphs in Western Europe.

Richter scale   The Richter scale, named for the American seismologist Charles Richter (1900–85), is used to measure the magnitude of an EARTHQUAKE. Magnitude is a measure of an earthquake's size, but rather than being a direct measure of the intensity of ground shaking, it is a reflection of the strength of the seismic sound waves emitted by the earthquake, phenomena that can be detected at great distances from the earthquake's epicenter. Because an earthquake's magnitude can be determined solely from routine measurements made with SEISMOMETERS (instruments used to detect seismic waves), magnitude has become an important measurement commonly made on seismograms, the graphic record of earthquake events.

The Richter scale is logarithmic. This means that a factor-of-ten difference in actual earthquake energy corresponds to a difference of one whole number on the scale.

Earthquakes having magnitudes in excess of 6.0 are considered dangerous. The most powerful earthquake recorded in North America, the Alaska quake of 1964, reached 8.5 on the Richter scale; the quake that struck the western coast of Mexico and devastated Mexico City in 1985 registered 8.1.

Manfred Richthofen, a World War I German fighter pilot, became known as the Red Baron. After 2 years of combat flying, Richthofen was killed when his famous red triplane was shot down in 1918.

Richthofen, Manfred, Freiherr von   [rikt'-hoh-fen]   Manfred Richthofen, b. May 2, 1892, d. Apr. 21, 1918, was a German flying ace in World War I who became famous as the Red Baron because he flew a red Fokker triplane. A fighter pilot from 1916, he was credited with shooting down 80 Allied planes in dogfights. He died when he was shot down.

Rickenbacker, Eddie   [rik'-en-bak-ur]   Captain Edward Vernon Rickenbacker, b. Columbus, Ohio, Oct. 8,

Eddie Rickenbacker was the most decorated American combat pilot of World War I. He was later president of Eastern Airlines, which he developed into one of the nation's major passenger carriers.

1890, d. July 23, 1973, was an American flying ace in World War I and later an airline executive. After an early career as an automobile racer, Rickenbacker volunteered in the army flying service during World War I. He was accepted as a fighter pilot in March 1918 and shot down 22 enemy planes and 4 balloons, making him the top U.S. flying ace. Reentering the aviation field after unsuccessfully running an automobile company, he eventually became president (1938–53) and chairman of the board (1954–63) of Eastern Airlines.

rickets   Rickets, a childhood disease of the bone, results from a diet deficient in vitamin D and inadequate exposure to sunlight. Lack of vitamin D interferes with the proper mineralization of bone and causes bone softness. This leads to such deformities as extreme bowlegs and spinal curvature, as well as general body tenderness. It has been estimated that at the turn of the 20th century about 90 percent of the children who died before the age of 4 years in northern European cities had rickets. Improved nutrition, however, has made the disease rare in North America and Europe (see NUTRITIONAL-DEFICIENCY DISEASES).

rickettsia [rik-et'-see-uh]   Rickettsiae are a group of small, often disease-causing, rod-shaped bacteria of two genera, *Rickettsia* and *Coxiella*, in the family Rickettsiaceae. They have typical bacterial cell walls and membranes and the biochemical means for protein synthesis and enzymatic activities. They differ from other bacteria in that they are obligate intracellular parasites dependent on a host, usually a bloodsucking insect, for part of their life processes. Like viruses, rickettsiae cannot be cultivated outside a living host; in laboratories, they are usually cultivated in fertile chicken eggs or appropriate tissue cultures and are maintained in this manner.

The life cycle of the majority of rickettsiae involves an insect as the vector (carrier) and an animal as the alternate host. The infection of humans is not essential for maintaining the cycle. Rickettsiae, however, can cause many serious human diseases that are usually transmitted by the bite of various animals: epidemic TYPHUS by the body louse; tsutsugamushi fever (scrub typhus) by the mite; and ROCKY MOUNTAIN SPOTTED FEVER by the tick. The exception is Q FEVER, which humans contract by drinking infected milk from cattle or by inhaling dust containing infected material. All rickettsial diseases respond to drug treatment with chloramphenicol and tetracyclines.

Rickey, Branch   Wesley Branch Rickey, b. Stockdale, Ohio, Dec. 20, 1881, d. Dec. 9, 1965, was one of baseball's foremost executives. His own playing career was undistinguished. In 1917 he became president of the St. Louis Cardinals organization, and 3 years later he initiated the baseball farm system. His innovation produced the talented ball players who later won five pennants for the Cardinals. Rickey became general manager (1942–50) of the Brooklyn Dodgers and built them into a championship team. He broke the color barrier in baseball by signing (1947) Jackie ROBINSON. Rickey later served (1950–55) as general manager of the Pittsburgh Pirates. He was voted into the Baseball Hall of Fame in 1967.

Rickover, Hyman [rik'-oh-vur]   An admiral in the U.S. Navy, Hyman George Rickover, b. Russia, Jan. 27 (N.S.), 1900, d. July 8, 1986, was a leader in the development of nuclear propulsion for submarines and other naval ships. During World War II he was head of the electrical section of the navy's Bureau of Ships. Rickover became convinced of the feasibility of nuclear-powered naval vessels, and in 1947 he was put in charge of the navy's nuclear-power program and appointed head of the Atomic Energy Commission's naval reactor branch. He directed the planning and construction of the world's first nuclear-powered submarine, the U.S.S. NAUTILUS, launched in 1954. A critic of the U.S. educational system, Rickover wrote *Education and Freedom* (1959) and *American Education: A National Failure* (1963).

RICO Act   The U.S. Congress in 1970 passed the Racketeer-Influenced and Corrupt Organizations (RICO) Act to fight ORGANIZED CRIME. The sweeping law permits seizure of assets illegally gained or used at the time of indictment—before conviction—and calls for triple damages if private plaintiffs can prove that defendants engaged in a "pattern of racketeering activity." Much used during the 1980s in criminal and civil cases unrelated to organized-crime activity—notably in securities fraud and other WHITE-COLLAR CRIME—RICO and its assets-seizure provision raised questions for civil libertarians about violations of DUE PROCESS.

riddle   A riddle is a question or a statement of a problem worded so that it has a double, or hidden, meaning. Riddles are of ancient origin. Oracles and soothsayers often couched predictions in riddle form, believing that knowledge was a precious commodity not to be freely given to those of inferior intellect. Aristotle saw riddles as metaphorical statements of the symbolic meaning of natural phenomena. Riddles occur in the Bible and the Koran and form a central part of Zen Buddhism (see KOAN). A famous riddle of Greek mythology was the one asked by the Sphinx of Thebes (see OEDIPUS).

Ride, Sally   Sally Kirsten Ride, b. Encino, Calif., May 26, 1951, the first woman U.S. astronaut and third woman in space, received a Ph.D. in physics from Stanford University in 1977 and was selected as an astronaut in 1978. She flew on SPACE SHUTTLE missions on June 18–24, 1983, and Oct. 5–13, 1984. In 1986, Ride served on the presidential commission that investigated the

Shuttle *Challenger* disaster. Ride left NASA in 1987 to join the Stanford University Center for International Security and Arms Control. In 1989 she joined the staff of the University of California (San Diego) and became head of its California Space Institute.

Ridgway, Matthew B. Matthew Bunker Ridgway, b. Fort Monroe, Va., Mar. 3, 1895, a U.S. commander in World War II, became commander of the United Nations forces during the KOREAN WAR. A 1917 West Point graduate, Ridgway was named commander of the 82d Airborne Division in March 1942 and then planned and led the first important airborne attack in American military history in the assault on Sicily (July 1943). In June 1944 he jumped with his troops into Normandy and later led the 18th Airborne Corps in Europe in the closing months of World War II.

Ridgway assumed command of the U.S. Eighth Army in December 1950 and halted the Chinese Communist invasion of South Korea. Becoming a full general and succeeding Douglas MacArthur as U.N. commander in April 1951, he drove the enemy out of most of South Korea and penetrated into North Korea. Ridgway was named NATO supreme commander in Europe in 1952 and U.S. Army chief of staff a year later. He retired in 1955.

riding Riding and the equestrian arts comprise the techniques used to control a horse in its direction, gait, and speed; the knowledge of equine equipment (known as tack) and how it functions; and the ability to train and groom a horse. Riding styles, as well as apparel and tack, were developed out of specific historical requirements that were then modified to suit contemporary sporting needs.

Whatever the riding style, riders communicate to their horses by means of aids, or cues. Leg, hand (by means of reins), body weight, and voice are the natural aids, while whip and spurs are the so-called artificial aids. After learning to mount, dismount, and attain proper body position, the novice rider must undertake to coordinate the aids, an important step in becoming proficient. To make the transition from the halt to the walk, for example, the rider squeezes his or her lower legs against the horse's sides at the girth to generate forward impetus while simultaneously relaxing the hands to allow the horse to begin moving. If necessary, a call or gentle application of crop (whip) or spurs will reinforce the command.

Various styles of riding require different techniques, as well as specialized tack and apparel. Basic to each style is the "seat," or the rider's position in the saddle.

English-style riding is characterized by relatively lightweight, flat saddles. Posting to the trot, a continuous up-and-down body movement, is common to this style.

Hunter-seat riding takes its name from the sport of fox hunting. Until the end of the 19th century, fox hunters leaned backward when jumping. The introduction of the forward seat, however, shifted the rider's weight to a point

Jessica Ransehousen and her mount canter about an earthen enclosure. The canter—along with the walk, trot, and gallop—is one of the natural gaits assumed by pleasure horses. For a brief moment, all four legs are raised off the ground.

over the horse's center of gravity, in front of the saddle. The result was greater safety and control. In hunter-seat equitation the rider's upper body inclines forward at the trot and canter and especially over fences. Hands follow the horse's head and neck motion, particularly when jumping. Short stirrups enable the rider to clear the saddle, which has a slightly elevated cantle, or rear, designed to facilitate the proper jumping position.

In HORSE SHOWS, hunter-seat events include equitation classes; hunter classes, in which horses are judged on style, pace, and manners; and jumper classes, in which they are scored on their ability to clear high fences. Most of the horses so used are Thoroughbreds. Training a hunter or jumper begins by teaching the animal to negotiate low obstacles athletically and responsively; the heights and widths of fences are increased gradually.

Saddle-Horse breeds and types originally provided comfortable mounts on which Southern plantation owners inspected their land. In saddle-seat riding the rider's legs are extended farther down than in hunter-seat riding and are not held against the horse's sides; hands are held high and somewhat apart; and the upper body is maintained at the vertical in all gaits. Thin, flat saddles interfere as little as possible with Saddle Horses' rapid, elevated leg movements; double bridles, with both snaffle and curb bits, afford maximum control.

Cattle roping and other such ranch chores required cowboys to have secure yet maneuverable seats. In stock-seat riding the rider sits erect with legs extending almost straight down. Both reins are held in one hand above the high pommel, or saddle horn, of the heavy Western stock saddle. Western-trained horses are taught to neck rein (change direction in response to pressure on their necks) and to make sliding, rapid halts at the touch of the long-shanked curb bits. Stock-seat riding is seen primarily at rodeos.

In dressage (a French word for "systematic training") competition, horses and riders are scored on how well they perform prescribed tests of patterns that vary in difficulty according to proficiency and experience. More advanced levels call for collection and extension (shortening and lengthening stride) and lateral movements. Dressage saddles are similar to saddle-seat tack, although with slightly more padding.

Ridley, Nicholas

Ridley, Nicholas [rid'-lee] Nicholas Ridley, b. c.1500, d. Oct. 16, 1555, was an English reformer and bishop who was martyred under Queen Mary I. Following studies at Cambridge and in France, he returned (1530) to Cambridge as a fellow of Pembroke College. Ridley served as chaplain to Archbishop Thomas Cranmer, whom he later helped compile (1549) the Book of Common Prayer; as bishop of Rochester; and from 1550 as bishop of London. Deprived of his see under the Catholic Queen Mary, he was convicted of heresy and burned at the stake in Oxford with Hugh LATIMER.

ridley turtle

ridley turtle Two species of sea turtles in the family Cheloniidae are called ridley turtles. Both may attain a length of about 700 mm (27.5 in) and commonly weigh between 30 and 36 kg (65 and 80 lb). The Indo-Pacific ridley, *Lepidochelys olivacea,* occurs in parts of the Indian, the Pacific, and possibly the Atlantic oceans. It is almost uniformly olive colored and has at least six or seven large scales (pleural scutes) on each side of the midline of the upper shell (carapace). This turtle is mainly vegetarian. Populations of this overexploited species are becoming seriously depleted. The Atlantic ridley, *L. kempi,* the smallest of the Atlantic sea turtles and an endangered species, is found from the Gulf of Mexico northward along the Atlantic coast to Massachusetts. It has a gray coloration and only five pleural scutes on each side of the carapace. Its main nesting site is a beach in Tamaulipas, Mexico.

The Indo-Pacific ridley, a sea turtle, has been exploited for leather and oil in such areas as the Pacific coast of Mexico.

Riefenstahl, Leni

Riefenstahl, Leni [ree'-fen-shtahl] Adolf Hitler's favorite film director, Leni Riefenstahl, b. Berlin, Aug. 22, 1902, achieved an international reputation on the basis of two extraordinary documentaries. Her first film, the mystical *Blue Light* (1932), excited Hitler's imagination, and following her short documentary of the Nazi party's 1933 Nuremberg rally, *Victory of Faith* (1934), he commissioned her to give feature-length treatment to the same event in 1934. The result, *Triumph of the Will* (1935), was an impressive spectacle of Germany's adherence to Hitler and a masterpiece of romanticized propaganda. Equally famous, and far less controversial, was her coverage of the 1936 Olympic Games in Berlin, the four-hour epic *Olympia* (1938). Blacklisting by the Allies (1945–52) and postwar ostracism ended Riefenstahl's career as a filmmaker. She was subsequently acclaimed for *The Last of the Nuba* (1974), a superb volume of photographs of Nuba tribal life in southern Sudan, and for *Vanishing Africa* (1982).

Riel, Louis

Riel, Louis [ree-el'] Louis Riel, b. Saint Boniface (now in Manitoba), Oct. 23, 1844, d. Nov. 16, 1885, Canadian rebel, led the métis—persons of mixed French and Indian background—in western Canada. Of métis origin, he began but did not complete studies for the priesthood in Montreal. Returning to the RED RIVER SETTLEMENT, where he had been born, he assumed (1869) leadership of the métis there who feared that their land rights and other interests were jeopardized by the transfer of HUDSON'S BAY COMPANY territories to Canada. Riel was chosen president of a provisional government, and he and his representatives negotiated the admission of the settlement (1870) into the Canadian Confederation as the province of Manitoba. Riel fled when Canadian troops suppressed his government.

Called to Saskatchewan in 1884 to lead métis and whites in protests against Canada's western policies, Riel at first employed peaceful methods, but he soon (1885) set up a rebel government with the backing of the métis and Indians. On the defeat of his forces, he was captured and executed for high treason despite evidence of insanity. His execution intensified latent ethnic animosity in Canada.

Riemann, Georg Friedrich Bernhard

Riemann, Georg Friedrich Bernhard [ree'-mahn] Georg Friedrich Bernhard Riemann, b. Sept. 17, 1826, d. July 20, 1866, was one of the most influential 19th-century German mathematicians. He developed the subjects of partial differential equations, complex variable theory, differential geometry, and analytic number theory and laid the foundations for modern topology. Some of his work on the foundations of geometry was incorporated into Albert Einstein's relativistic theory of gravitation.

Riemenschneider, Tilman

Riemenschneider, Tilman [ree'-men-shny'-dur] Tilman Riemenschneider, c.1460–1531, was perhaps the greatest German sculptor of the late Gothic period. His major works were either stone tombs or large wooden altarpieces. The delicately carved *Altarpiece of Mary Magdalen* for the parish church of Münnerstadt (1490–92; now dispersed), based largely on engravings by Martin Schongauer, was his earliest masterpiece. His finest later works include the *Altar of the Holy Blood* in the Jakobskirche at Rothenburg (1501–05) and the *Altar of the Virgin* in the Herrgottskirche at Creglingen (*c.*1505–10). The architectural structures of these works are characteristically late Gothic in their extravagance and complexity, but the compositions of the individual scenes are remarkable for their balance and restraint.

Riemenschneider's tombs are among the most important monuments of their kind. The outstanding examples are the monuments of Prince Bishop Rudolf von Scherenberg in the Cathedral of Würzburg (1496–99); of Marshal Konrad von Schaumberg in the Marienkapelle at Würzburg (*c.*1499–1502); and of Emperor Henry II and his wife, Kunigunde, in the Cathedral of Bamberg (1499–1513).

Rienzo, Cola di [ree-ent'-soh] Cola di Rienzo (or Rienzi), b. 1313, d. Oct. 8, 1354, Roman demagogue and revolutionary, tried to restore the Roman republic with himself at its head. A notary, he became (1344) the representative in Rome of Pope Clement VI, who was in Avignon, and in 1347 he proclaimed himself tribune. He briefly won the support of the Roman people by lowering taxes but was soon forced into exile. After imprisonment in Prague and Avignon, Rienzo returned to Rome in 1354 as envoy of Pope Innocent VI. Popular discontent with his oppressive government led to a revolt during which Rienzo was killed.

Riesman, David, Jr. [rees'-muhn] David Riesman, Jr., b. Philadelphia, Sept. 22, 1909, collaborated with Nathan Glazer and Reuel Denney on *The Lonely Crowd: A Study of the Changing American Character* (1950). Riesman made the famous distinction between "tradition-directed," "inner-directed," and "other-directed" societies; the first type uses tradition, the second a person's internal values, and the third other people's expectations to develop conformity in its members.

Rif [reef] The Rif is a mountain range in northwestern Africa, which extends 270 km (180 mi) from Tangier along the Mediterranean coast of Morocco. It is a rugged region of difficult access inhabited by BERBERS. Of its many minerals, only iron ore is mined on a large scale. The highest peak is Tidiquin (2,455 m/8,054 ft).

rifle A rifle is a small FIREARM that is braced against the shoulder when it is discharged. Its name is derived from the rifling, the shallow spiral grooves within the barrel that impart a spin to the bullet in order to give it greater accuracy. The term *rifle* may therefore be applied to any gun with a rifled barrel.

Rifled barrels were made and fitted to muzzle-loading muskets as early as the 15th century. As early as 1732, German-American gunsmiths produced the forerunners of the accurate, long-barreled Kentucky rifle, which took its name from its use by Kentucky sharpshooters in the Battle of New Orleans (1815).

The conversion from muzzle-loading smoothbore muskets to muzzle-loading rifles of the Kentucky type was the first stage in progression toward the modern rifle. The

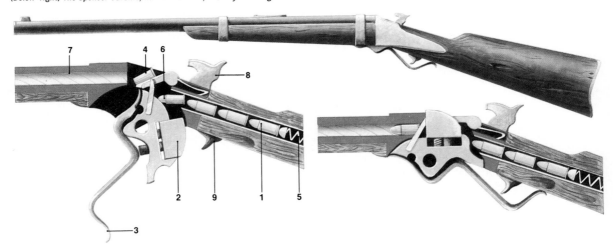

The Spencer Carbine (top) *uses the action of a lever to load and eject cartridges; its operation is seen in the cutaway drawing* (below left). *Cartridges are stored in a tubular magazine* (1) *in the butt of the gun, where they are held in place by the breech block* (2). *Depressing the lever* (3) *ejects the spent cartridge* (4) *and, by lowering the breech block, allows the spring* (5) *to push a fresh cartridge into the breech* (6). *Raising the lever brings the breech block into contact with the fresh cartridge, pushes it into the barrel* (7), *and closes the breech. The gun is fired by cocking the hammer* (8) *and then pulling the trigger* (9). (Below right) *The Spencer Carbine, hammer cocked, is ready for firing.*

The German 7.92-mm (0.31-in) Mauser (top) is a typical bolt-action rifle; the cutaway drawing (above left) illustrates its operation. The Mauser is loaded by inserting a five-round clip of ammunition (1) into a magazine (2) containing a spring (3). The cartridges are held in place by the bolt mechanism (4)—a metal cylinder containing the firing pin (5)—which is moved back and forth over the magazine using the bolt handle (6). When the bolt mechanism is retracted, the spring pushes a cartridge into the breech (7); when pushed forward, the bolt mechanism slides a cartridge into the firing chamber (8), closes the breech, and cocks the rifle. (Above right) The loaded Mauser is ready for firing.

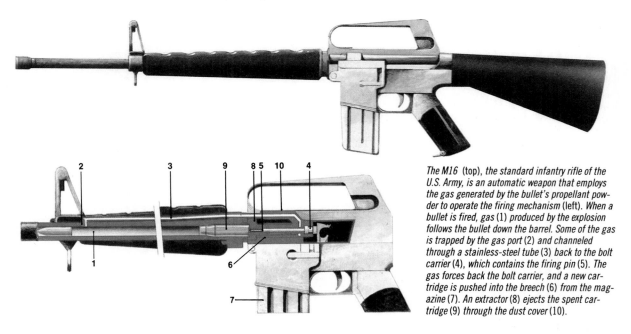

The M16 (top), the standard infantry rifle of the U.S. Army, is an automatic weapon that employs the gas generated by the bullet's propellant powder to operate the firing mechanism (left). When a bullet is fired, gas (1) produced by the explosion follows the bullet down the barrel. Some of the gas is trapped by the gas port (2) and channeled through a stainless-steel tube (3) back to the bolt carrier (4), which contains the firing pin (5). The gas forces back the bolt carrier, and a new cartridge is pushed into the breech (6) from the magazine (7). An extractor (8) ejects the spent cartridge (9) through the dust cover (10).

next development was the breech-loading rifle, loaded at the rear of the barrel, which was first issued in quantity in 1819.

The next development, the magazine rifle, came in response to a military demand for increased firepower. Such weapons had magazines that stored several rounds of ammunition and had a means of transferring the rounds to the firing chamber. A reduction in the caliber size and better propellants permitted a smaller charge to be used and consequently reduced the size and weight of the ammunition. Improvements in manufacturing techniques also facilitated the production of interchangeable components.

The bolt-action magazine rifle was perfected by about 1890, and within 10 years the armies of all the major nations were equipped with a version of it.

Since its introduction the magazine rifle has undergone little design change. Minor refinements have been made, better ammunition has been developed, and smokeless powder has replaced black powder. The only concessions to modernity have been in the simplification of the sights, reductions in barrel and overall length, and the adaptation of designs suitable for mass-production techniques.

The final stage in the development of the rifle—automatic rifles—came recently. After many imperfect attempts during the interwar years new designs of semiautomatic and fully automatic rifles were tested in several countries, but by 1939 only the United States and the USSR had issued self-loading weapons to their troops. The U.S. M1 Garand rifle, despite its failings, was the outstanding weapon of its class in the early years of World

War II. The design of automatic rifles has probably now reached its zenith in such weapons as the Soviet AKM (Kalashnikov), the U.S. M16, the Swiss SG510, and the various U.S.-made Stoner and Armalite guns.

Rift Valley fever   see VIRUS

rift valleys

Rift valleys are characteristically long, nearly linear valleys with steep, straight valley walls and often flat bottoms. They are formed by faulting along one or both valley walls; the floor of the valley is downdropped relative to the surrounding regions in response to extension of the crust. Rift-valley development is often considered to mark the site of the initial rifting apart of a continent prior to its separation by seafloor spreading, but not all rift valleys result in complete continental separation. The floor of the Gulf of Suez, for example, is a rift valley forming where Arabia is moving apart from Africa; seafloor spreading has not yet commenced, however, because the floor of the gulf is entirely continental. If the process continues, magma will eventually be injected into the center of the rift, forming new seafloor and marking the inception of seafloor spreading and the formation of a new ocean basin, as in the RED SEA. Alternatively, extension may cease, leaving a fully continental rift valley as a scar.

When active extension is taking place, rift valleys are sites of earthquake activity and, if extension is sufficient, volcanic activity. The most spectacular rift valleys are those of the East African Rift System, a series of rift valleys extending more than 4,000 km (2,500 mi) through eastern Africa from Ethiopia to Mozambique. This rift system is the site of active volcanism and seismic activity, and although it has been active for the past 50 million years, it is still a continental rift.

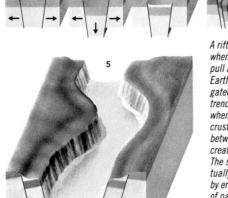

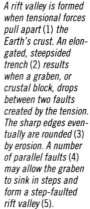

A rift valley is formed when tensional forces pull apart (1) the Earth's crust. An elongated, steepsided trench (2) results when a graben, or crustal block, drops between two faults created by the tension. The sharp edges eventually are rounded (3) by erosion. A number of parallel faults (4) may allow the graben to sink in steps and form a step-faulted rift valley (5).

Other active rift valleys include the one that marks the axis of the MID-OCEANIC RIDGE, the DEAD SEA rift, and the Baikal rift in central USSR. *Graben* (see HORST AND GRABEN) is a term sometimes used synonymously with rift valley.

Riga

[ree'-guh]   Riga, the capital of Latvia, in the USSR, is situated along the Western Dvina River near its mouth on the Gulf of Riga of the Baltic Sea. The city's population is 915,000 (1989), making it the largest city in the Baltic republics.

Riga consists of an old medieval city center, with narrow, winding streets and distinctive Gothic architecture, and a newer section with a grid street plan and modern buildings. An attractive seacoast of sand dunes to the west of the city has given rise to one of the USSR's leading beach resorts, the city of Jurmala (1987 est. pop., 65,000).

Riga is a major Soviet seaport and manufacturing center, specializing in telephone equipment, radios, electrical equipment, transport equipment (electric railcars and streetcars), and machine tools. The port carries on an active commercial cargo trade with Western Europe and serves as the base for an Atlantic deep-sea fishing fleet. As the cultural center of Latvia, the city is the seat of Latvian University (1919) and of the Latvian Academy of Sciences.

Founded in 1201 by the Teutonic Knights, Riga developed as a trading center between Russia and the Baltic Sea. It was a member of the Hanseatic League. It passed to Russia in 1721 and became one of that country's major seaports; manufacturing began in the later 19th century. Riga was the capital of independent Latvia from 1918 to 1940.

right of asylum

The right of asylum is the right to receive sanctuary or refuge in a foreign state, granted by that state to an individual who has been forced to flee his or her native country. The right most often pertains to political refugees, who are prevented from returning to their own countries because of a "well-founded fear of being persecuted for reasons of race, religion, nationality, or political opinion"—to quote from the United Nations Convention of 1951, which first established a definition of these refugees and outlined their rights in their country of asylum.

For many centuries, fugitives from the law, war, or private disputes could often find asylum in churches (see SANCTUARY). It has always been the prerogative of a state, however, to choose whether or not to grant asylum to a refugee. Diplomatic asylum, based on EXTRATERRITORIALITY—that is, the principle that a nation's embassies and consulates are an extension of its territory—has sometimes been granted to political fugitives.

After World War II, many thousands of European refugees were allowed to settle in the United States. From 1952, however, with the passage of the restrictive McCarren-Walter Immigration Act, the U.S. recognized as political refugees only those who had fled from Communist countries. Even though the law was liberalized in 1980, the U.S. Immigration and Naturalization Service rarely grants the status of "political" refugee, labeling many of those who would claim it as "economic" refugees who seek a more comfortable life rather than political asylum.

right to bear arms The right to bear arms is stated in the 2d Amendment to the U.S. Constitution: "A well regulated militia being necessary to the security of a free State, the right of the people to keep and bear arms shall not be infringed." Opponents of gun-control laws cite the 2d Amendment as authority to declare all such laws unconstitutional. The Supreme Court, however, has consistently ruled that the 2d Amendment protects only the states' rights to maintain a MILITIA and does not apply to the private ownership of guns.

right-handedness see HANDEDNESS

right-to-life movement see ABORTION

right of search The right of search, in international law, permits a country at war to stop and search vessels on the high seas to prevent CONTRABAND of war from reaching the enemy. The right extends to private vessels from neutral countries. It is often used in conjunction with a BLOCKADE of the enemy's ports. During the Napoleonic Wars, British warships seized the cargoes of U.S. merchant ships trading with France and sometimes impressed American sailors into the Royal Navy. The United States, insisting on its neutral right (see NEUTRALITY) to trade with any nation, argued that the only contraband of war subject to seizure was munitions. The British replied that almost any product could aid the French war effort. This wrangle over neutral rights poisoned Anglo-American relations and was a precipitating factor of the WAR OF 1812. Today the British position prevails (except for impressment), and nations at war have a wide leeway in defining contraband.

right-to-work laws Right-to-work laws are state laws that prohibit union-management agreements requiring a worker to join a union in order to obtain or hold a job. Most of these laws prohibit the CLOSED SHOP, in which employers hire only union members; the UNION SHOP, in which workers must join the union within a certain period of time after being hired; and agreements that require workers to maintain union membership in order to keep their jobs.

The "right to work" was originally a socialist slogan, formulated (1808) by Charles FOURIER, that became associated with trade unionism. It was a guaranteed right in the constitutions of many Communist countries.

In the United States the phrase has become associated with management's efforts to put a brake on the growth of union membership. Aid was given to right-to-work advocates by the Taft-Hartley Act (1947; see LABOR-

MANAGEMENT RELATIONS ACT), which banned the closed shop. It did permit the union shop under certain conditions but allowed state laws to take precedence.

Riis, Jacob August [rees] A journalist, photographer, and reformer, Jacob August Riis, b. May 3, 1849, d. May 26, 1914, publicized the plight of immigrants in New York City slum tenements. Born in Denmark, he moved to the United States at the age of 21, drifted into newspaper work, and worked as a police reporter for the *New York Tribune*. His photographs, articles, and books focused on the squalid living conditions of the city's poor and spurred legislation to improve those conditions. Among his books, *How the Other Half Lives* (1890) was most effective in this regard. Also celebrated is Riis's autobiography, *The Making of an American* (1901; repr. 1983). After retiring from newspaper work, Riis continued to campaign for improvements in urban living, such as better housing, parks, and playgrounds.

Jacob Riis's 1890s portrait of the Talmud School on Hester Street starkly records the poverty of immigrants to New York's Lower East Side. (Museum of the City of New York.)

Rijeka [ree-ek'-ah] Rijeka, or Fiume, is a major port and naval base of Yugoslavia. The population is 166,400 (1987 est.). Rijeka is located in the republic of Croatia on the Kvarner Gulf of the Adriatic Sea, about 60 km (40 mi) southeast of Trieste. The Julian Alps separate the city from the interior. Fishing, building and repairing ships, petroleum refining, and the production of machinery, paper, and leather goods are the mainstays of the economy. Among the city's ancient landmarks are a Roman arch (1st century AD) and a 17th-century cathedral.

A fishing settlement before the Christian era, Rijeka was occupied by the Romans and named Tarsatica. Slavs settled the area during the 6th–7th century. In 1471 the city fell to Austria. Rijeka gained importance as a free port early in the 18th century, but its main growth came after Hungary took control in 1779. The city was held by Austria-Hungary for most of the 19th century. At the end of World War I, Rijeka was disputed between Italy and Yugoslavia, and in September 1919 the Italian nationalist poet Gabriele D'ANNUNZIO led an Italian free corps in seizing the city. He withdrew after the Treaty of Rapallo (1920) established Rijeka as a free port. In 1924, Rijeka was incorporated into Mussolini's Italy. Taken by the Yugoslavs in 1945, the city became part of Yugoslavia in 1947.

Riley, James Whitcomb   The American author James Whitcomb Riley, b. Greenfield, Ind., Oct. 7, 1849, d. July 22, 1916, was a Hoosier poet whose book *The Old Swimmin' Hole and 'Leven More Poems* (1883) made him one of the highest-paid poets of his time. His popularity had much to do with his humorous use of dialect and his sentimental celebration of the homely virtues. "Little Orphan Annie" and "When the Frost Is on the Punkin" are two of his best-known poems.

Rilke, Rainer Maria [ril'-ke, ry'-nur]   The most influential German poet of the 20th century, Rainer Maria Rilke, b. Prague, Dec. 4, 1875, d. Dec. 29, 1926, produced a body of verse characterized by a succession of new beginnings, a result of his continuous struggle to define the task of the poet and to find the value of life.

After abandoning his university education, Rilke met (1897) Lou Andreas-Salomé, who remained influential in the poet's life even after she ceased being his mistress. Rilke traveled widely—to Munich, Berlin, Italy, Russia—and moved to Paris in 1902. During World War I he served briefly in the Austrian militia. From 1919 until his death from blood poisoning and leukemia he lived mainly in Switzerland.

Rilke's early poetry cultivated the themes and aesthetic poses of fin de siècle romanticism. The hymnic *Book of Hours* (1905; Eng. trans., 1941) is his best-known work from this period. *New Poems* (2 vols., 1907–08; Eng.

Rainer Maria Rilke was one of the foremost German poets of his time and one of the most influential of the 20th century. His search for objective lyric expression and mystical vision was manifested in works that convey a sense of sublime tragedy. Rilke expounded his theories of life and art in Letters to a Young Poet *(1929).*

trans., 1964) bears the imprint of his friendship with the sculptor Rodin, from whom he sought to learn how to conquer his subjectivity so that he could create continuously, without depending on inspiration. The term *Ding-Gedicht* ("thing-poem"), associated with these meticulously crafted poems, describes the re-creation of the essence of external objects.

In Rilke's protoexistentialist novel *The Notebook of Malte Laurids Brigge* (1910; Eng. trans., 1930), the young protagonist, a poor Danish poet in Paris, tries unsuccessfully to turn his wretchedness into beatitude. The longing for transcendence is also a theme of the celebrated *Duino Elegies* (1911–22; Eng. trans., 1930, 1939), in which the poet pits the highest possible order of intensity against his tragic sense of life's brevity. With these and *Sonnets to Orpheus* (1923; Eng. trans., 1936), Rilke arrived at a mystical sense of the unity of life and death, proclaiming his monistic cosmology in bold, mythopoeic, expressive metaphors. *Late Poems* (1934; Eng. trans., 1938) and *Letters to a Young Poet* (1929; Engl. trans., 1954) are important posthumous collections.

Rimbaud, Arthur [ram-boh']   Arthur Rimbaud, b. Oct. 20, 1854, d. Nov. 10, 1891, the precocious boy-poet of French symbolism, wrote some of the most remarkable poetry and prose of the 19th century. He has been identified as one of the creators of free verse because of the rhythmic experiments in his prose poems *Illuminations* (1886; Eng. trans., 1957). His *Sonnet of the Vowels* (1871; Eng. trans., 1966), in which each vowel is assigned a color, helped popularize synesthesia—the description of one sense experience in terms of another. The hallucinatory images in *The Drunken Boat* (1871; Eng. trans., 1952) and his urging, in *Letter from the Seer* (1871; Eng. trans., 1966), that poets become seers by undergoing a derangement of the senses reveal him as a precursor of surrealism. Following his own dictum, Rimbaud lived an inordinately intense, tortured existence that he described in *A Season in Hell* (1873; Eng. trans., 1939). His homosexual relationship with Paul VERLAINE formed part of his spiritual disillusionment. Soon after it ended in 1873, Rimbaud abandoned his writing; he had not yet attained the age of 20. In another dramatic transformation he became a trader and gunrunner in Africa; 18 years later he died in Marseille following the amputation of his tumor-ridden right leg.

Rime of the Ancient Mariner, The   Written by Samuel Taylor COLERIDGE and first published in The LYRICAL BALLADS (1798), *The Rime of the Ancient Mariner* is a narrative poem that uses the narrative and prosodic technique of old ballads. It was planned with William WORDSWORTH, who contributed several lines and ideas. The narrator of the tale is an ancient mariner who commits a motiveless crime by killing a friendly albatross. Thereafter he is pursued relentlessly. Only after he repents do supernatural powers carry his ship back home; but ever afterward he must do further penance by teaching others the lesson he has learned: to love and revere all things that God has made and loves.

Rimini [ree'-mee-nee]   Rimini is a port city in the Emilia-Romagna region of north central Italy. The city is situated at the foot of the Apennines on the Adriatic coast. The population is 114,600 (1987 est.). The city serves as an agricultural market, railroad junction, tourist resort, and industrial center for shipbuilding, railroad repairs, brick and tile making, and flour milling. Fishing is also important. Rimini's Roman remains include the Arch of Augustus and a bridge built by Tiberius. Other landmarks are the 15th-century Malatesta Castle, the Malatesta Temple (designed by Leon Battista Alberti in the 15th century), and several medieval and Renaissance churches.

Founded by Umbrians, the city came under the control of Rome in 268 BC. It was a free commune in the Middle Ages but was ruled by the Malatesta family from 1239 to 1509, at which time it was annexed by the PAPAL STATES. The city joined Italy at unification in 1860. Rimini suffered severe Allied bombing in World War II.

Rimmer, William [rim'-ur]   The American visionary sculptor William Rimmer, b. Liverpool, England, Feb. 20, 1816, d. Aug. 20, 1879, learned stone carving as a boy. He held various jobs until, as a self-taught doctor, he began (1855) to practice medicine, subsequently earning his medical degree. The violent anguish of his *Falling Gladiator* (1861; bronze replica in the Boston Museum of Fine Arts) is expressed in the figure's powerful musculature.

Rimsky-Korsakov, Nikolai Andreyevich [rim'-skee-kohr'-suh-kawf]   Nikolai Andreyevich Rimsky-Korsakov, b. Tikhvin, Novgorod province, Russia, Mar. 18 (N.S.), 1844, d. June 21 (N.S.), 1908, is best known for his operas and orchestral works. Both parents, cultured members of the nobility, were amateur musicians. Music was Rimsky's avocation when in 1856 he entered the Imperial Naval Academy. In 1861 he joined the group of amateur composers taught by Balakirev, whom the critic Stasov, their intellectual mentor, would dub "the mighty handful"—Balakirev, Borodin, Cui, Mussorgsky, and Rimsky. The Five (or "mighty five") vaunted their amateurism and aggressively launched their nationalist music against the professional establishment (primarily Anton Rubinstein). Rimsky's general strategy appeared in his symphonic sketch *Sadko* (1867), in which folkloric elements are couched in coloristic harmony and orchestration. In 1871 he resigned his commission and accepted a teaching post at the Saint Petersburg Conservatory. Already a recognized composer, he had to teach himself the traditional musical disciplines and techniques before he could teach his students. An unfortunate academicism then tinctured his music, disappearing only in the 1880s with the appearance of such works as the opera *The Snow Maiden* (1882) and *Scheherazade* (1888), a symphonic suite. A master orchestrator, he undertook the controver-

Nikolai Rimsky-Korsakov was a great Russian composer of the late 19th century. He challenged the musical tastes of his time by adopting elements of folk music in such works as The Snow Maiden *(1882).* Scheherazade *(1888) evokes an Oriental atmosphere.*

sial task of editing the works of his deceased friends Mussorgsky and Borodin. Eleven of Rimsky's 15 operas appeared between 1895 and 1907, beginning with *Christmas Eve* (1895) and ending with *The Golden Cockerel* (1907).

The folk music of Russia's Caucasus and Trans-Caucasus peoples permeates Rimsky's music. Asymmetrical rhythms are also derived from this source, foreshadowing the radical experiments of Stravinsky, his most famous student.

Rinfret, Thibaudeau [rin'-fret]   Thibaudeau Rinfret, b. Montreal, June 22, 1879, d. July 25, 1962, a graduate of McGill University Law School, served as chief justice of the Canadian Supreme Court from 1944 to 1954. His knowledge of both English common law and the Napoleonic Code enabled him to reconcile differences between the two systems to the mutual benefit of English- and French-speaking Canadians.

Ring of Fire   *Ring of Fire* is the popular name for a narrow zone of active volcanoes that nearly encircles the Pacific Ocean basin. It is composed of a series of island arcs (see PLATE TECTONICS), some of which are connected and some isolated. Its northern section is the ALEUTIAN ISLANDS, extending from the Gulf of Alaska to Kamchatka. From Kamchatka, an arc continues southwest through the KURIL ISLANDS and JAPAN. From there the Ring of Fire splits into the RYUKYU and BONIN islands, which meet again in the Philippines. It then extends easterly in a complex series of arcs to Tonga and from there, south to New Zealand. The eastern margin is composed of the Andean arc (see ANDES), extending from southern Chile to central Mexico, and of the CASCADE RANGE in the northwestern United States.

Ring of the Nibelung, The   see WAGNER, RICHARD

Ringling (family) see CIRCUS

ringtail monkey   see CAPUCHIN

ringworm   Ringworm is a skin infection characterized by circular or ringed lesions whose infectious agent is a fungus. The most common sites of infection are the scalp and the groin. Scalp ringworm, occurring almost exclusively in children, is highly contagious and sometimes epidemic. Ringworm of the groin is also often called "jock itch." (See also FUNGUS DISEASES.)

Rio de Janeiro [ree'-oh day zhah-nay'-roh]   Rio de Janeiro, until 1960 the capital of Brazil, is a major port, the country's second largest city, and capital of the state of Rio de Janeiro. The city proper has a population of 5,603,388 (1985), and the metropolitan area has 10,063,110 residents. Located in southeastern Brazil, the city is bounded on the east by the Bay of Guanabara, on the south by an Atlantic coastline with many beautiful beaches, and on the west and north by forested mountains. The inhabitants of this cosmopolitan city, located in one of the world's most beautiful settings, are called Cariocas.

Contemporary City. Recreation and tourism are among the leading sources of income. Sugarloaf Mountain rises 395 m (1,296 ft) at the entrance to the Bay of Guanabara, and a 40-m (131-ft) statue of Christ the Redeemer, sculptured in 1931, stands on Mount Corcovado (704 m/2,310 ft). In addition to the beaches, a major tourist attraction is Carnival, a colorful celebration held just prior to Lent.

Rio de Janeiro is a major financial center and a focal point for business and domestic commerce. The outstanding harbor has long made the city an important port. Industries include food and tobacco processing; garment, shoe, glass, tire, chemical, and pharmaceutical manufacturing; publishing and printing; and shipbuilding and repairing.

Among Rio's 200 churches, the most noteworthy is the Candelaria (begun 1755), now serving as the cathedral. Other landmarks include the National Museum of Art, the Municipal Theater, and the National Library (1810). Maracaña Stadium (capacity: 200,000) is the world's largest. The Federal University of Rio de Janeiro (1920) is located there. Most buildings in Rio, a city with broad avenues, skyscrapers, and beautiful squares, were built during the 20th century. Three world-famous architects, Oscar NIEMEYER, Affonso Reidy, and Lúcio COSTA, designed many of Rio's buildings.

History. According to tradition, Guanabara Bay was discovered by the Portuguese Gonçalo Coelho, who entered it on Jan. 1, 1502, and, thinking that it was a river, named it Rio de Janeiro ("river of January"). The first settlers were French Huguenots, who settled there from 1555 to 1567, when the Portuguese forced them out.

Rio de Janeiro, a major port and one of South America's largest cities, is situated along Guanabara Bay in southeastern Brazil. The city was the nation's capital from 1763 to 1960.

Growth followed the discovery of gold in the nearby state of Minas Gerais in 1698. Rio was selected as the only port through which the gold could be exported. In 1763, Rio became the seat of the governor general of Brazil, and by the end of the 18th century it was the largest city in the colony.

The Portuguese court, fleeing from the invading French armies of Napoleon I, established its residence in Rio in 1808 and remained until 1821, making the city the capital of the Portuguese empire. When Brazil declared its independence in 1822, Rio became the capital.

In 1960 the seat of the federal government was moved to the newly built city of Brasília, and the former federal district that included Rio became the state of Guanabara. On Mar. 15, 1975, Rio was made the capital of the new state of Rio de Janeiro, which incorporates the former states of Rio de Janeiro and Guanabara.

Río de la Plata [ree'-oh day lah plah'-tah]   The Río de la Plata is the estuary formed by the confluence of the PARANÁ RIVER and URUGUAY RIVER in southeastern South America. About 275 km (170 mi) long and 225 km (140 mi) wide at the mouth, the Río de la Plata covers an area of 35,000 km^2 (13,500 mi^2). The shores—Uruguay to the north and Argentina to the south and west—are densely populated. Because of 57 million m^3 (2,000 million ft^3) of silt deposited each year, the estuary must be dredged frequently. The principal ports are Buenos Aires in Argentina and Montevideo in Uruguay. Although probably entered by the Portuguese in 1501, the estuary is known to have been discovered by the Spaniard Juan Díaz de Solís in c.1515.

Rio Grande [ree'-oh grand]   The Rio Grande, rising in the Rocky Mountains of western Colorado, is the fifth longest river of North America. From an elevation of more than 3,660 m (12,000 ft), it flows generally southeast through the high valleys of Colorado and New Mexico to Texas, where it follows the border between that state and Mexico. It empties into the Gulf of Mexico at Brownsville, Tex. The Rio Grande is about 3,025 km (1,880 mi) long and drains about 445,000 km^2 (172,000 mi^2). Major tributaries are the Pecos, Devils, Chama, and Puerco rivers in the United States and the Salado, San Juan, and Conchos in Mexico.

Much of the drainage area is arid and barren, suitable only for grazing, but large irrigated sections produce grains, vegetables, cotton, and citrus fruits. Irrigation projects provide flood control as well as hydroelectric power. Tourism and mining of petroleum, gas, coal, silver, gypsum, and potash are also economically important. The Rio Grande is not navigable for commerce. Major cities along its course are Albuquerque, Brownsville, and El Paso in the United States and Ciudad Juárez, Matamoros, Nuevo Laredo, and Reinosa in Mexico.

The river was explored by the Spanish in the early 1500s, and mining and settlement began in the late 16th century.

Riopelle, Jean Paul [ree-oh-pel']   Jean Paul Riopelle, b. Montreal, 1923, is the first Canadian painter to have established an international reputation. In 1947 he settled permanently in Paris, where he participated in the surrealist movement. During the 1950s he moved toward pure abstraction, creating mosaic patterns of brilliant color applied with a palette knife, as in his triptych *Pavane* (1954; National Gallery of Canada, Ottawa). Riopelle employs a variety of media, from colored ink and gouache to pastel and watercolor. In 1962 he was awarded the coveted UNESCO prize at the Venice Biennale.

riot   A riot is a violent offense against public order by three or more assembled persons. Legally it is a misdemeanor, punishable by fine or imprisonment; inciting to riot carries the same penalty. A 1715 English statute, the Riot Act, provided that 12 or more assembled persons who disturbed the peace and refused to disperse when read the Riot Act were guilty of a felony.

Rip Van Winkle   The central character of a short story by Washington IRVING, first published in *The Sketch Book of Geoffrey Crayon, Gent.* (1819), Rip Van Winkle was a ne'er-do-well in a village in the Hudson River Valley who slept for 20 years. Chased from home by his shrewish wife, Rip drank from a keg belonging to a band of little men who were playing ninepins. The brew caused his long sleep, and Rip awoke to find that his wife was dead, that no one in the village recognized him, and that he had slept through the American Revolution.

Ripley, George [rip'-lee]   The religious thinker, writer, and philosopher George Ripley, b. Greenfield, Mass., Oct. 3, 1802, d. July 4, 1880, began his career as a Unitarian minister but resigned from the ministry in 1841 because he wished to apply the principles of transcendentalism to society and considered Unitarianism too conservative. With Ralph Waldo Emerson and Margaret Fuller he cofounded the *Dial*, a transcendental publication. Ripley established BROOK FARM, an experimental cooperative community, and was its president from 1841 to 1847. There he edited *The Harbinger*, an influential journal of social reform. A popular book reviewer for the New York *Tribune* from 1849 to 1880, Ripley produced and edited the *New American Cyclopedia* (1858–63) with Charles A. Dana.

Risorgimento [ree-sohr-jee-men'-toh]   The Italian Risorgimento (resurgence) was the liberal, nationalist movement for unification (1796–1870). Its origins lay in a nationalistic reaction against the invasion and occupation of Italy by Napoléon Bonaparte (later NAPOLEON I), and it culminated with the annexation of Rome in 1870.

The Risorgimento was interrupted by many internal conflicts. With the majority of Italians remaining on the sidelines through most of the struggle, Italy was unified in large measure by an opportunistic intellectual elite and with considerable foreign assistance, especially from NAPOLEON III's France.

In 1815 the Congress of Vienna (see VIENNA, CONGRESS OF) restored the old European order. Prince METTERNICH's Austria regained Lombardy, annexed Venetia, and indirectly dominated most of the rest of the Italian peninsula.

Members of the Carbonari, a nationalist society active in Italy during the early 19th century, hold a clandestine meeting. Uprisings organized by the Carbonari in 1820 and 1821 stimulated the larger movement for Italian unification called the Risorgimento.

The pope recovered the Papal States, and the Kingdom of Naples and Sicily reverted to the Bourbons. Only the Kingdom of Sardinia-Piedmont (see SARDINIA, KINGDOM OF) was free of foreign control, but its ruling SAVOY dynasty, despite a reputation as a military power, did not become interested in unification until 1848.

The first Risorgimento movement was sparked by the Carbonari, a secret organization that fomented unsuccessful popular uprisings in the 1820s. More important was Giuseppe MAZZINI's republican Young Italy movement, founded in 1831, which called for liberation through grass-roots revolts. Mazzini's influence peaked during the REVOLUTIONS OF 1848.

Mazzini's republicanism frightened the more moderate Italian leaders. Vincenzo Gioberti's Catholic neo-Guelph group hoped to enlist the papacy in the national cause, but PIUS IX repudiated the Risorgimento in 1848. More significantly, the conte di CAVOUR, prime minister of Sardinia-Piedmont (1852–59, 1860–61), took steps to unite Italy as a liberal parliamentary monarchy under the house of Savoy. Cavour skillfully enlisted the support of Napoleon III in a joint war against Austria in 1859, thereby acquiring Lombardy. The next year Romagna, Parma, Modena, and Tuscany voted for union with Sardinia-Piedmont. In exchange for recognizing this arrangement, France received Savoy and Nice.

In 1860, Giuseppe GARIBALDI conquered Sicily and Naples with his Red Shirts. The Kingdom of Italy, headed by Sardinian king VICTOR EMMANUEL II, was proclaimed in March 1861 after Sardinia absorbed Umbria and the Marches and the Two Sicilies chose union with Sardinia. Venetia was acquired as a result of Italy's alliance with Prussia in the SEVEN WEEKS' WAR (1866). Rome, which was seized in 1870, soon became the capital of Italy.

Ritchie (family) [rich'-ee]

The Ritchie family of Kentucky has long been known for its huge repertoire of folk songs, many of them dating from before the family's immigration to America in 1768. They were a primary source for musicologists John and Alan Lomax (see LOMAX family), who recorded them for the Archives of American Folk Song in the 1930s. Jean Ritchie, b. Viper, Ky., Dec. 8, 1922, is a prolific writer, singer, and expert dulcimer player.

rites of passage   see PASSAGE, RITES OF

Ritschl, Albrecht [rich'-ul]

German theologian Albrecht Ritschl, b. Mar. 25, 1822, d. Mar. 20, 1889, influenced a generation of Protestant theologians. His early work followed the Tübingen school of New Testament interpretation, but by the mid-1850s he rejected the view that placed the Apostles and Saint Paul in antithesis. His most influential work was *The Christian Doctrine of Justification and Reconciliation* (3 vols., 1870–74; Eng. trans., 1872–1900).

Ritschl stressed that religious knowledge comes not from reason but from faith, in the form of value judgments. He emphasized the church as the community of faith that has received the gospel and for which Christ died. Individuals experience forgiveness and redemption personally—but in the church, not in individual mystical experience. He also placed a strong ethical emphasis on the Kingdom of God as the goal and result of the moral reformation of human beings.

Ritsos, Yannis [reet'-saws]

Yannis Ritsos, b. May 1, 1909, d. Nov. 12, 1990, was one of the most celebrated poets of modern Greece. His popular poems *Epitaphios* (1936) and *Romiosini* (1958) were set to music by Mikis Theodorakis. His work was associated with left-wing political movements, and he was twice imprisoned (1948–52, 1967) by right-wing governments. *Romiosini* is a tribute to the Greek resistance fighters of World War II.

Rittenhouse, David [rit'-en-hows]

The American astronomer and mathematician David Rittenhouse, b. Paper Mill Run, near Germantown, Pa., Apr. 8, 1732, d. June 26, 1796, made finely crafted clocks and mathematical instruments, including two large orreries that were recognized for their beauty and precision. He built what may have been the first American-made telescope. He served as treasurer (1777–89) of Pennsylvania and as the first director (1792–95) of the U.S. Mint. Rittenhouse was president of the American Philosophical Society from 1791 until his death.

river and stream

Rivers convey the excess waters of the land areas that they drain to larger bodies of water or

In mountain regions slopes often fit together to form drainage areas bounded by ridges, or divides (red dots), which separate different stream systems. Melted snow or rainwater initially flows down the slopes in sheets and along small channels, or rills (1). A number of rills meet at the bases of converging slopes and form a larger and deeper channel, or gully (2), which eventually widens into a stream channel. When a stream reaches the main valley floor (3), its velocity decreases and its load is deposited in the form of an alluvial fan (4).

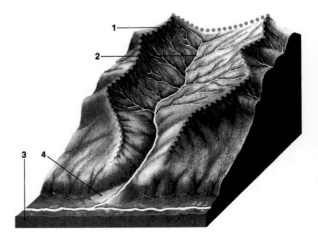

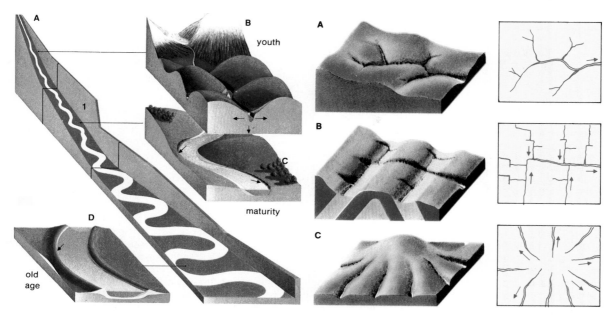

A longitudinal profile of a river (A) reveals its changing width and bed slope from source to mouth, which results from erosion of the original land surface (1) and from deposition of debris. Cross-profiles illustrate three erosion stages. (B) Vertical erosion in the steep-sloped upper section results in a V-shaped youthful valley. (C) Lateral erosion during the maturity stage leads to shallow valleys and gentle slopes. (D) During the old stage, lateral erosion and stream debris deposition eventually reduce the valley floor to an almost flat plain.

The direction in which rivers flow depends on the nature and structure of the underlying rock layers. In an area of uniform rock erosion a branching, treelike drainage pattern results (A) in which all tributaries flow toward the main stream. In regions with alternating weak and strong rock strata, tributary streams form along bands of easily eroded rock, resulting in a trellislike flow pattern (B). The slope of an area also affects the stream pattern. Thus rivers flow down all sides of a dome, or uplifted area, in a radial flow pattern (C).

directly to the oceans. Collectively, they represent the world's WATER RESOURCES, as they carry virtually all the water that is available for human management and use.

The four great civilizations of early human history developed in close dependence on rivers and the fertile, easily worked soils of their floodplains: the Sumerians on the TIGRIS and EUPHRATES rivers in Iraq, the Harrapans on the INDUS in Pakistan, the Chinese on the HUANG HE ("Yellow River") and the CHANG JIANG in central China, and the Egyptians on the NILE RIVER in Egypt. Rivers and their valleys have continued to play important roles in the course of history.

In addition to providing direct sources of water for domestic, agricultural, and industrial uses, rivers produce energy directly through hydropower generation (see HYDROELECTRIC POWER); they also provide the cooling water for many fossil- and nuclear-fueled power plants. They serve as transportation routes, as carriers and natural "treatment plants" for human wastes, and as habitats for fish and wildlife.

River Discharge and Watersheds

On a global basis, the significance of rivers as a water resource lies not in the amount of water they contain at a given time (only about 0.14% of the Earth's liquid fresh water and about 0.01% of all water), but in their average discharge, which is the total volume carried in a given

time period. Worldwide, this amounts to about 39,000 km^3 per year, or, expressed differently, 28 trillion gallons per day. The flow of the Amazon is about five times greater than that of the second largest river, the Congo, and amounts to more than 17% of the world's total river flow.

The area of land that contributes water to a river network upstream of a given point on a river is called the drainage basin, or watershed, of the river at that point. Such an area is generally defined on the basis of topography, by tracing drainage divides—ridge lines that separate the area contributing to one river network from that contributing to another—on a topographic map. In a given region, the average volume of discharge at a given point on a river is directly proportional to the area of the drainage basin above that point.

Water can enter the river network by falling directly onto a water surface, by traveling as overland flow from the surface of the drainage basin, or by moving as subsurface flow beneath the basin. About one-third of the discharge of the world's rivers comes from subsurface flow, which is of critical importance in maintaining streamflow between periods of rain and snowmelt. Virtually all of the remaining two-thirds comes from overland flow. In arid regions and urbanized areas, almost the entire drainage basin may contribute to this flow, whereas in humid regions generally only the low areas adjacent to stream channels supply it. In these areas, the GROUNDWA-

TABLE 1: TEN LARGEST RIVERS OF THE WORLD

River	Country	Average Discharge m³/sec	ft³/sec
Amazon	Brazil	180,000	6,350,000
Congo	Zaire	40,000	1,400,000
Chang Jiang	China	34,000	1,200,000
Paraná	Argentina	22,000	777,000
Orinoco	Venezuela	20,000	706,000
Brahmaputra	Tibet, India, Bangladesh	20,000	706,000
Ganges	India	19,000	670,000
Yenisei	USSR	19,000	670,000
Mississippi	USA	18,300	645,000
Lena	USSR	15,500	547,000

TABLE 2: TEN LONGEST RIVERS OF THE WORLD

River	Location of Mouth	Approximate Length km	mi
Nile	Mediterranean Sea	6,650	4,150
Amazon	Atlantic Ocean	6,450	4,000
Chang Jiang	East China Sea	5,950	3,700
Huang He	Yellow Sea	4,850	3,000
Congo	Atlantic Ocean	4,650	2,900
Missouri	Mississippi River	4,350	2,700
Lena	Laptev Sea	4,250	2,650
Niger	Gulf of Guinea	4,200	2,600
Yenisei	Arctic Ocean	4,100	2,550
Mississippi	Gulf of Mexico	3,800	2,350

TER level is typically close to the ground surface and rises due to infiltrating rain or snowmelt. When it reaches the surface, no further infiltration can take place, and subsequent rain or snowmelt on these areas runs off quickly to the stream as overland flow. In the remainder of the drainage basin, particularly if it is forested, the soil is so permeable, and the groundwater so far beneath the surface that virtually all the precipitation infiltrates.

River Channels

In general, a river shapes its own channel. Most of the time, however, streamflow is considerably less than the discharge required to fill the channel, and it only occasionally exceeds the channel's capacity. This general disparity between streamflow and channel capacity arises because the channel size is determined by flows that are large enough to overflow the banks and cause major erosion. These occur relatively frequently (every 2 to 3 years).

When the rate at which water is delivered to a channel changes, the river will adjust its discharge by changing its velocity, its depth, and its width. The greatest change is usually in depth, because of both scouring of the channel bottom and adjustment of the level of the water surface. The second largest adjustment to a change in discharge is in velocity, and the smallest is in width. As one proceeds downstream in a river network, however, the increase in discharge almost always accompanying the increase in drainage area is accommodated mostly by an increase in width, with a smaller rate of increase in depth. Thus rivers become relatively as well as absolutely wider as one proceeds downstream. Average velocity also usually increases downstream in a river system, but at a slow rate. Exceptions to the downstream increase in discharge that characterizes most stream networks occur in arid regions. Channels there remain dry for most of the year. During rainstorms runoff is rapid, sometimes causing flash floods. As the water proceeds along the previously dry channel, it gradually infiltrates, causing discharge to decrease downstream.

The slope of a river channel decreases between its source and its mouth, and the longitudinal profile of a well-established stream is thus a smooth curve, concave upward. The slope also changes with time, in response to changes in the river's discharge, sediment load, and baselevel (the level at which it enters a large body of standing water, such as an ocean). During a flood, for example, a river has a high velocity and is capable of carrying more sediment than normal. It therefore cuts down into the river bottom, picking up more sediment and decreasing its slope until its velocity matches its sediment load. When the flood ends and the discharge returns to normal, the river rids itself of the excess sediment by redepositing it in the channel, building up its slope until velocity and sediment load are once more in balance. The river thus constantly tends toward the ideal of a graded stream—one in which slope and velocity are perfectly adjusted to carry the sediment load. Because baselevel, discharge, and sediment load are all highly variable, this process is never complete.

River channels display a variety of patterns when viewed from the air or on a map. Braided streams consist of a network of interconnected channels, with numerous bars and islands between. Generally streams with relatively steep slopes, they carry a considerable load of sand or gravel or both. Meanders (see MEANDER, RIVER) are series of rather regularly spaced symmetrical bends that tend to appear in streams with low slopes and channels made of silt and clay.

See also: ICE, RIVER AND LAKE; LANDFORM EVOLUTION; RIVER DELTA; WATERFALL.

---

river blindness   River blindness, or onchocerciasis, is an infection of the skin by a threadlike worm, *Onchocerca volvulus*. It is one of the FILARIASIS diseases, a group of infections caused by various roundworms that are spread by a genus of blackflies, *Simulium*, which thrive near fast-running rivers. Prevalent in parts of Africa, Central America, and South America, it is characterized by skin irritation, skin nodules, and eye damage. The adult worms, which lie within the skin nodules, mate and produce larval forms called microfilariae, which invade the surrounding tissues and cause inflammation. Their metabolic products can cause hypersensitivity in eye parts and may lead to blindness. The World Health Organization (WHO) approximates that in some tropical African villages more than 15 percent of the adults have been so blinded.

Treatment of river blindness consists of surgically removing as many nodules as possible. The drug ivermectin, introduced in 1981, has only mild side effects, and one or two doses a year provide protection.

river delta

river delta Much of the detritus produced by continental erosion is carried away as sediment by rivers (see RIVER AND STREAM) and is subsequently deposited either in lakes or in oceans. These deposits may accumulate to form deltas. The term *delta* (from the Greek letter Δ) was first used (*c*.450 BC) by the Greek historian Herodotus in referring to the triangular landform built of alluvial deposits at the mouth of the Nile River.

Most large deltas form in relatively quiet bodies of water characterized by weak coastal currents, low tidal range, and low wave energy. Conversely, strong coastal currents and high wave energy on exposed coasts disperse sediment and militate against delta formation. Small deltas found in quiet freshwater lakes are generally simple in structure and lobate in shape. They are layered horizontally near the shore and farther out along the lake bottom; rapid deposition of the river's bed load caused by the abrupt halting of its current produces inclined layers along the delta's sloping face.

Large deltas formed in the ocean are complex from both a process and a structural point of view. Depending on the density of the sediment-laden river water, the river flow may spread over the ocean water, disperse through it, or slide down the face of the delta as a density underflow. Continued sedimentation results in the building of a low-lying delta plain fringed seaward by a shallow marine platform. Branching distributary channels, bordered by partly submerged levees, may cross the delta surface, and swamps and marshes may cover it. Growth of a bar at the mouth of a main distributary channel has been suggested as one of the main causes of the branching of a river. During floods the bar acts as an obstruction; floodwaters are thus diverted to form another channel. The classic delta formed in this way has a "birds-foot" pattern of distributaries.

Rivera, Diego

Rivera, Diego [ree-vay'-rah] Diego Rivera, b. Dec. 8, 1886, d. Nov. 24, 1957, was the most prominent painter of the modern Mexican mural movement. Rivera executed some cubist works but soon discarded European avant-garde aesthetics in favor of an approach that reflected his view of the struggle between social classes. By the time he returned (1921) to Mexico, he was committed to a new popular art movement based on large mural works depicting contemporary Mexican life.

In his early mural projects, such as those at the National Preparatory School (1922) and the Ministry of Education Building (1923–28) in Mexico City, he concentrated on social and political themes expressed in bold, dramatic forms. After a visit (1927–28) to Russia, where his Marxist views were reinforced, he painted more ideologically oriented and realistically rendered murals, as at the National Palace (1929–55) and at Cuernavaca's Palace of Cortés (1929–30). His growing reputation led to

A fresco from the Ministry of Education Building in Mexico City, painted (1923–28) by Diego Rivera, depicts industrial workers showing support for Marx's Communist Manifesto.

A river discharging into a quiet sea deposits a load of sediment at its mouth (A). The deposits eventually build up above sea level, extend the shoreline, and form a delta through which the river cuts radially branching channels, or distributaries (B). Deltas vary in shape. The Nile Delta (1) has a broadly curving, triangular-shaped shoreline, whereas the Mississippi Delta (2) has long, fingerlike land areas projecting out into the water along its distributaries.

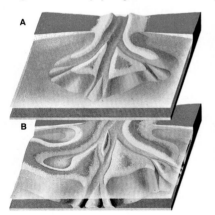
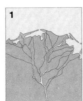

invitations to paint frescoes at the San Francisco Stock Exchange (1931), the Detroit Institute of Art (1932), and Rockefeller Center (1933) in New York City—although the last-named work was destroyed by its sponsors because it contained a portrait of Lenin.

Rivera's murals are rich in archaeological detail and painted in a sharply outlined, linear style. Most of them have clear, three-dimensional figures in a shallow space, although a deep spatial extension of landscape appears at the top of some works. Rivera also executed many easel paintings and portraits and designed and built his Mexico City house, the Anahuacalli, which is now a museum housing the extensive collection of pre-Columbian art that he left to the Mexican people.

Rivera, Fructuoso   Fructuoso Rivera, b. *c.*1785, d. Jan. 13, 1854, was a Uruguayan independence leader and president (1830–34, 1839–42) of Uruguay. One of the Thirty-three Immortals, the revolutionary group that won Uruguay's independence from Brazil, Rivera became the first president with the support of Juan Antonio LAVALLEJA, the leader of the Immortals. Rivera supported Manuel Oribe as his successor in 1834, but the two soon split. Rivera's faction, the Colorados (reds), forced Oribe and the Blancos (whites) out of office in 1838. In the ensuing civil war (1840–51), Oribe, backed by Juan Manuel de ROSAS of Argentina, drove Rivera into exile. Rivera returned in 1853 to help direct the provisional government of Uruguay.

Rivers, Larry   The well-known painter and draftsman Larry Rivers, b. New York City, Aug. 17, 1923, began his career as a jazz saxophonist. The strongest influence on his early work was the action painting that dominated New York painting in the late 1940s and early 1950s, particularly the work of Willem de Kooning. Rivers adapted action painting, mainly an abstract style, to the representation of several types of subject matter—intimate portraits (*Double Portrait of Birdie,* 1955), historical themes (*Washington Crossing the Delaware,* 1953), and the everyday details of urban life, including late-model cars, bank notes, clothes, and cigarette packages. Although much of his imagery anticipates pop art, Rivers's highly distinctive draftsmanship has its roots in the expressionism of New York art in the immediate post–World War II era.

Riverside   Riverside, the seat of Riverside County in southern California, lies beside the Santa Ana River 85 km (53 mi) east of Los Angeles. The population is 226,505 (1990). The city is the hub of a large citrus-fruit and vegetable-growing region. Aircraft parts, paints, and air conditioners are manufactured in Riverside. The University of California at Riverside (1961) is located there. Originally part of the Rancho Jurupa, the town was laid out in 1870 and was first known as Jurupa.

Riviera [riv-ee-air'-uh]   The Riviera is the strip of Mediterranean coast generally considered to extend from Cannes, France, to La Spezia, Italy. In France the limestone Maritime Alps descend abruptly to the sea to create the dazzling white cliffs and beaches of the CÔTE D'AZUR between Cannes and Menton. In Italy, where the Maritime Alps are joined by the limestone Ligurian Apennines, the Riviera is divided at Genoa into the Riviera di Ponente (west) and the Riviera di Levante (east). The Corniches, a network of roads on three levels between Nice and Menton, provide transportation between the coastal communities. The interior hills of PROVENCE to the north provide magnificent scenery and protect the French Riviera from the mistral, a cold wind that sweeps down the Rhône Valley.

The picturesque French Riviera town of Saint-Tropez is located along a sheltered Mediterranean bay, making it a popular harbor for both fishing and pleasure vessels. Overlooking the town, which is a fashionable summer resort, is the Massif des Maures.

Because of its picturesque scenery, mild, sunny climate, and subtropical vegetation, the Riviera is one of Europe's primary centers for tourism. The principal resorts of the western section include Saint-Raphaël, Saint-Tropez, and Fréjus. The Côte d'Azur has an almost continuous line of resorts—CANNES, Antibes, NICE, MONTE CARLO (Monaco), and Menton. The Italian Riviera features SAN REMO, Alassio, Santa Margherita, Rapallo, and LA SPEZIA. Grasse, northwest of Cannes, remains a center of the perfume industry. Nice is the regional center of the French Riviera; GENOA is the chief port of the industrial Po River valley of northern Italy.

Riyadh [ree-ahd'] Riyadh, the royal capital and largest city of Saudi Arabia, is located in the east central part of the Arabian Peninsula about 390 km (240 mi) from the Persian Gulf. Riyadh has a population of 1,308,000 (1981 est.). Riyadh is also the nation's commercial and transportation center. Petroleum refining and cement manufacturing are the major industries. Riyadh University (now King Saud University) was founded in 1957.

Riyadh was a center of Wahhabism and the capital of the powerful Saud family from the early 19th century. The city was under the power of the rival Rashids from 1891 until 1902, when the Sauds regained control. In 1932, when the unified Kingdom of Saudi Arabia was proclaimed, Riyadh became the capital.

RNA see GENE

roach see COCKROACH

Roach, Max Drummer, composer, and teacher Maxwell Lemuel Roach, b. Elizabeth City, N.C., Jan. 19, 1924, is a leading figure in modern jazz. Roach was drummer in Charlie Parker's quintet in the 1940s and played with all the seminal figures of the BEBOP movement, developing a drum style—the use of cymbals to create a sustained, legato rhythmic backup—that jazz drummers have since almost universally adopted. He led his own small group in the 1970s, experimenting with unconventional percussion instruments. As a teacher, Roach has developed courses in jazz and jazz history.

roadrunner The roadrunner, *Geococcyx californianus,* a large ground bird native to arid scrublands of the southwestern United States and Mexico, belongs to the cuckoo family, Cuculidae. It measures about 58 cm (23 in) and has brown plumage streaked with white above and on the throat, and white plumage below. It also has a bushy crest; blue and red eye rings; long, spindly legs; and a long tail.

The roadrunner seldom flies, preferring to depend on its swiftness afoot to reach safety when surprised. It preys on small snakes as well as on insects, lizards, and, occasionally, the young of ground-nesting birds.

The roadrunner is a fast-running ground bird native to the southwestern United States and northern Mexico. Also called the chaparral cock, it can attain speeds up to 40 km/h (15 mph).

roads and highways A road or highway is an overland route between two points. A road is generally a narrow route in a rural area; a street is an urban route; and a highway is a wide road that can carry more traffic at higher speeds. In the United States, a major highway—a multilane divided roadway with limited entrances and exits—is called an expressway, a freeway (if it has no tolls), or a turnpike (if it has tolls). Other names are used elsewhere: motorway (Great Britain), autobahn (Germany), and autostrada (Italy).

History

Perhaps as early as 3000 BC, the civilizations of Egypt, Mesopotamia, and the Indus Valley developed roads, first for pack animals and then for wheeled vehicles. The Persians, beginning from the 6th century BC, linked up existing highways, and in the 3d century BC the Qin dynasty in China established a countrywide network of roads.

Roman Empire. The greatest road builders of the ancient world were the Romans. As they developed from a city-state by conquering other small states, they built roads into the conquered regions to help consolidate their gains (see ROMAN ROADS). By the time of Hannibal's invasion, the Roman road system was well established in central and southern Italy.

A POSTAL SERVICE was organized for transmitting government messages, and the service was soon used for private letters as well. Most road users traveled on horseback or on foot; high officials and the wealthy used carriages (see COACH AND CARRIAGE). Posting stations where horses could be changed and attended to were placed about every 16 km (10 mi) along the roads for government use;

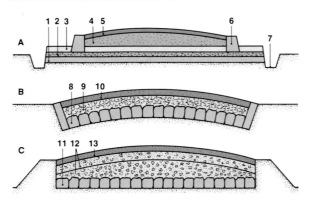

Roman roads (A) *consisted of a footing* (1) *of compacted earth, a base of stones* (2), *a concrete layer* (3), *filling material* (4), *and the road surface* (5). *They often had retaining stones* (6) *and drainage ditches* (7). *Roads built by Pierre Tresaguet* (B) *used a cambered layer of heavy stone* (8) *followed by a base course of large stones* (9) *and the road surface* (10). *Roads designed by Thomas Telford* (C) *called for a layer of flat, heavy stones* (11) *laid over level earth, followed by two cambered layers of small stones* (12) *and a gravel surface* (13).

there were also inns (see HOTEL) for private travelers.

The barbarian tribes, which broke into the Western empire from the 4th century AD onward and finally destroyed it, were not concerned with centralized power; they tended to avoid the Roman roads, which gradually decayed.

Middle Ages. As national states began to form in Europe, major routes became necessary to provide for the itinerant royal courts to move about. Pilgrimages to sacred shrines accelerated the development of international trade and made the roads busier than they had been since the collapse of the Roman Empire.

Great Britain. The development of centralized government was not accompanied by centralized responsibility for road maintenance. In England the responsibility originally lay with the parishes.

Next came the era of the turnpike trusts. A number of people would join together to obtain parliamentary powers under which they would take over a length of road for 21 years or build a new one and pay for its maintenance by collecting tolls. Road engineering, however, was still rudimentary, and many trusts did not know how to preserve the roads.

Real and lasting improvement came through the work of three engineers. John Metcalf (1717–1810) worked mainly in the north of England and, despite the fact that he was blind from the age of 6, devised a method of car-

rying roads across marshy ground on rafts of ling or heather tied in bundles. John Loudon McAdam (1756–1836), a Scot, became a commissioner for highways. He devoted himself to studying methods of road improvement and, after settling in Bristol, became famous for his success in building roads capable of carrying relatively high-speed wheeled traffic. Macadamized, or macadam, roads were almost standard in Britain until the onset of the motor age. The rubber tires of high-speed automobiles tended to loosen the stone surface. This problem led to a search for better road surfaces, such as asphalt (see TAR, PITCH, AND ASPHALT). Thomas Telford (1757–1834) was another Scot who gained worldwide fame as an engineer. His method was to make the roads strong enough to take the maximum likely weight of traffic.

France. To the strongly centralized government of 18th-century France must be given the credit of making the first determined effort to evolve an adequately funded national system of roads. A department of bridges and roads (Corps des Ponts et Chaussées) was set up in 1716, and specifications were laid down for various types of road. Road engineering was recognized as a profession, largely because of the achievements of Pierre Tresaguet, who became inspector general of roads in 1775. He used layers of stones decreasing in size toward the top, making each layer slightly cambered (curved from side to side, higher in the middle, and sloping downward toward both edges) for better drainage. Napoleon had French road engineers make great improvements in the roads in many parts of western Europe regardless of the cost. The new roads over the SIMPLON PASS and Mont Cenis Pass were outstanding examples.

United States. The coming of the first TRANSCONTINENTAL RAILROAD in the 1860s reduced the importance of the trails, until the development of the internal-combustion engine and automobile gave roads renewed importance. The British general Edward BRADDOCK in 1755 built a road out from Cumberland, Md. (the Cumberland Road) to assist in his march on the French at Fort Duquesne.

In 1811 the federal government contracted for the construction of the NATIONAL ROAD, virtually a reconstruction and extension of the Cumberland Road. William White Niles, a member of the New York Zoological Society, persuaded the city in 1907 to buy sufficient land along the Bronx River to stop pollution of its water, and, as a part of the scheme, the four-lane Bronx River Parkway was constructed with limited access and no crossings on the road level. This small beginning led to the widespread system of scenic parkways.

In developing the complete highway, American engineers learned that the attainment of high speeds could

A cross section of an American highway demonstrates dramatic improvements in modern road construction. Laid over a footing (1) of compacted earth, the base course (2) is composed of sand, gravel, and minerals, to which asphalt is added. The road surface (3) is formed of asphaltic concrete, a mixture of sandstone, sand, gravel, and asphalt.

not be the sole consideration. A road designed to avoid monotony for the driver is a contribution to safety (see SAFETY, AUTOMOTIVE). One difficulty facing all highway planners is how to connect highways with central cities without destroying part of the city itself. Tunnels and viaducts both have environmental drawbacks, and cloverleaf junctions consume large amounts of land.

A National System of Interstate and Defense Highways was proposed in 1944. Under the Federal Aid Highway Act (1956), the Federal Highway Trust Fund was established. Supported by certain federal taxes, it contributes 90% of the cost for roads in the INTERSTATE HIGHWAY SYSTEM, comprising thousands of kilometers of highways.

Canada. In Canada, even though roads are a provincial responsibility, the government of the Dominion paid much of the cost of the TRANS-CANADA HIGHWAY, a 7,820-km (4,859-mi) stretch of highway constructed in 1950–62, and has contributed to the Alaska Highway (originally built in 1942 for U.S. military purposes).

International. The first advances were made by the Italian and German dictatorships, mainly for military reasons. Mussolini encouraged private firms to construct the autostrada; the first one opened in 1924. Hitler grasped the value of an adequate road network, and in 1933, Fritz Todd was appointed inspector general of roads with orders to build 4,023 km (2,500 mi) of autobahnen. By 1942 he had constructed 2,108 km (1,310 mi) of roadway.

Britain set out to build special motor roads (motorways) in 1956 and opened its first in 1959, linking London and Birmingham.

Organizations seeking to improve roads exist in most developed countries. The International Road Federation, which has offices in Washington, D.C., and Geneva, promotes the building of intercontinental highways or the improvement and linking of existing roads. Perhaps the most well-known highway project is the PAN AMERICAN HIGHWAY system, which, when complete, will link the capitals of all the American nations.

Road Construction

France is generally credited with the first successful laying of pavements of asphalt mastic in the early 19th century. In the middle of the century both France and England used compressed rock asphalt for city streets, and in the United States, bitumen (a natural asphalt) was used. The rapid growth of motoring in the early 20th century encouraged the use of asphalt because it produced a dustproof surface.

An asset to the modern highway engineer has been the development of aerial photography, which greatly assists the preliminary ground surveys for new roads and the planning of routes on the map (see SURVEYING). The expensive stage of earth moving must be kept to the minimum, and in areas where a road necessarily has an undulating course, the aim is to balance the cut (the excavations) against the fill (the embankments; see EARTH-MOVING MACHINERY).

The process of road construction starts with the loosening of the topsoil by a scraper; next, a bulldozer pushes the loosened earth to one side, so that the line of the road is clear. At this point the road is discernible from the air, even though it is nowhere near its final form. Excavations may have to be made, embankments constructed, and sharp curves straightened out. Once the road has its predetermined line and gradients, excavation can begin for the foundations, which must be capable of bearing the expected weight of traffic on the road. Since the mid-century it has become possible in some situations to stabilize the subsoil itself rather than create a foundation of crushed rocks or concrete.

(Below) The construction of modern roads requires the use of many highly specialized machines. A foundation of sand and crushed rock is first laid down on a roadbed that has been scraped and leveled. Concrete is then poured by a spreader, running on tracks that also act as side supports, and compacted by vibrator.

(Above) The increasing use of automobiles in large urban areas has led to complex highway-interchange systems, such as that seen in an aerial photograph of downtown Chicago. Interchanges are generally located at main crossroads and connect city streets to major highways by means of curved sloping roads, or ramps.

Above the foundation, or stabilized soil, is laid a base course, usually of concrete, and then the top surface, or pavement, of asphalt or concrete. A machine then roughens the surface and checks that the camber is proper for good drainage.

Roanoke [roh'-uh-nohk]   Roanoke (1990 pop., 96,397) is a city in Virginia between the Blue Ridge and Allegheny mountains. Situated on both the Sky Line Drive and the Blue Ridge Parkway, Roanoke is the area's commercial, industrial, and transportation center. Electrical equipment, furniture, apparel, and chemicals are manufactured there. Roanoke is headquarters for Jefferson National Forest, and the Booker T. Washington National Monument is located 32 km (20 mi) southeast of the city. Settled about 1740, Roanoke flourished as a transportation center for the region's coal mines after 1882, when the Shenandoah Valley Railroad connected with the Norfolk and Western Railroad.

Roanoke Colony   Roanoke Colony was an English settlement established on Roanoke Island, off modern North Carolina, in the 1580s. In 1584, Sir Walter RALEIGH, authorized to colonize in North America, sent out two ships, which landed on Roanoke. In 1585–86 a group led by Sir Richard GRENVILLE made an abortive attempt at settlement. Raleigh then dispatched three ships and 117 people (including women and children) to Roanoke in 1587. Their leader, John White, sailed back to England for supplies, but when he returned in 1590 the settlers had vanished without trace. Their fate remains a mystery.

Rob Roy   Rob Roy, actually Robert MacGregor, b. 1671, d. Dec. 28, 1734, was a Highland freebooter known as the Scottish Robin Hood. Nominally a cattle dealer, he became a cattle thief who sold his neighbors protection against other rustlers. When the protection business failed, Rob Roy was accused of fraud and declared an outlaw. After his principal creditor, James Graham, 1st duke of Montrose, seized his lands, Rob Roy warred with the duke until 1722, when Rob Roy was forced to surrender. Later imprisoned, he was finally pardoned in 1727. His memory has been perpetuated and romanticized by Sir Walter Scott in the novel *Rob Roy* (1818).

Robbe-Grillet, Alain [rohb-gree-ay']   The French author Alain Robbe-Grillet, b. Aug. 18, 1922, pioneered in the development of the "new novel," a form of fiction he explained in his influential *Toward a New Novel: Essays on Fiction* (1964; Eng. trans., 1964). Beginning with his first work, *The Erasers* (1953; Eng. trans., 1964), Robbe-Grillet has consistently produced novels that avoid conventional renditions of plot and character but focus on an "objective" world, composed of visual images and of objects that seem to exist without reference to anything beyond themselves. His novels include *The Voyeur* (1955; Eng. trans., 1958), *In the Labyrinth* (1959; Eng. trans., 1960), *Topology of a Phantom City* (1976; Eng. trans., 1977), and *Djinn* (1981; Eng. trans., 1982). In the screenplays for such films as *Last Year in Marienbad* (1961) he attempts to visualize his fictional techniques.

robbery   Robbery, in law, is LARCENY with force. It involves the unlawful and forcible taking of property or money from another against that person's will by using violence or intimidation. Robbery is generally regarded as a FELONY offense that is punishable by a term in a federal or state prison. If the assailant threatens the victim with a weapon, the assailant is liable to prosecution for the more serious offense of armed robbery.

Robbins, Harold   Although his novels are consistently derided by critics as sensationalist and slipshod, writer Harold Robbins, b. New York City, May 21, 1916, is among the most widely read authors of modern times. Since his first novel, *Never Love a Stranger* (1948), he has written a string of successes, including *The Carpetbaggers* (1961; film, 1963), *The Adventurers* (1966; film, 1969), *The Betsy* (1971; film, 1977), *Spellbinder* (1982), and *Descent from Xanadu* (1984).

Robbins, Jerome   Jerome Robbins, b. New York City, Oct. 11, 1918, is America's most distinguished native-born choreographer of ballet and musical theater. Robbins performed as a dancer in Broadway shows (1938–40) and with American Ballet Theatre (ABT; 1940–44). His initial choreography demonstrated his interest in theatrical ballets and technically complex "show" dancing: the ballet *Fancy Free* (1944) and the musical *On the Town* (1944), an elaboration of that ballet, were the first of many collaborations with composer Leonard Bernstein.

Jerome Robbins is one of the most acclaimed and versatile American choreographers of the 20th century. Robbins integrates distinctly American themes and music into his classical and modern works. West Side Story *(1957), which Robbins choreographed for both Broadway and Hollywood, is one of his most popular works.*

From 1949 to 1959, Robbins was associate artistic director of NEW YORK CITY BALLET (NYCB) and created such noted ballets as *Afternoon of a Faun* (1953), *The Cage* (1951), and *The Concert* (1956). At the same time, he choreographed several musicals, including *The King and I* (1951), *Peter Pan* (1954), and *Gypsy* (1959), the last two of which he also directed. For *West Side Story* (1957), Robbins was director-choreographer and created a new form of musical, integrating dancing with the narrative action. He repeated his dual activities with the musical *Fiddler on the Roof* (1964).

Robbins returned to NYCB as ballet master in 1969, and from 1983 until 1990 he was co–ballet master in chief. Significant later works are the ballets *Goldberg Variations* (1971), *The Four Seasons* (1979), *Glass Pieces* (1983), *In Memory of...* (1985), and *Ives, Songs* (1988). *Jerome Robbins' Broadway*, a retrospective of Robbins's musical theater pieces, was produced in 1989.

Robert the Bruce, crowned king of Scotland as Robert I in 1306, restored his country's freedom from English rule by his victory in the Battle of Bannockburn in 1314. Robert's legendary determination and courage have made his name a byword for Scottish nationalism.

Robert, Hubert [roh-bair']   The French landscape architect and painter Hubert Robert, b. May 22, 1733, d. Apr. 15, 1808, was particularly noted for his romantic paintings of ancient Roman ruins. Typical of these elegant, stylized views are the *Pont du Gard* (1787; Louvre, Paris) and *The Terrace* (1794; Baltimore Museum of Art). Robert's work became enormously fashionable. He and his better-known contemporary Jean Honoré Fragonard borrowed much from each other's styles. Robert was a member of the Académie Royale and one of the first curators at the Louvre. As a landscape architect he helped to design the gardens at the Petit Trianon (1778), installing grottoes and ruins much like those in his paintings.

Robert Guiscard [gees-kahr']   Robert Guiscard, b. c.1015, d. July 17, 1085, son of Tancred of Hauteville, was the leading NORMAN conqueror of southern Italy. In 1046 he joined his three brothers and other Norman adventurers who were aiding the Lombard princes in their rebellion against the Byzantine Empire. Robert, however, soon set out to conquer Calabria and Apulia on his own and in 1059 was recognized by Pope Nicholas II as duke of Calabria, Apulia, and Sicily. Aided by his brother Roger, who took (1061–91) Sicily from its Muslim rulers, Robert conquered Calabria (1060), Bari (1071), and Palermo (1072). Robert helped deposed Byzantine Emperor Michael VII regain his crown in 1082. His plans to usurp Michael's throne were interrupted when he was summoned (1083) by Pope GREGORY VII to expel Holy Roman Emperor HENRY IV from Rome. Guiscard died after returning to the Byzantine campaign.

Robert I, King of Scotland (Robert the Bruce)   Robert I, known as Robert the Bruce, b. July 11, 1274, d. June 7, 1329, king of Scotland, restored Scottish independence from England. In 1292, Bruce's grandfather lost his claim to the Scottish throne to John de BALIOL in a succession suit decided by English King EDWARD I. Dur-

ing the next decade Bruce, then 8th earl of Carrick, switched his allegiance back and forth between Edward and the independence of Scotland.

After the execution (1305) of Sir William WALLACE, a national hero, Bruce, not fully trusted by either side, murdered his old enemy John Comyn. This act committed him to the Scottish patriots, because Comyn had inherited Baliol's claim to the throne and was supported by Edward. On Mar. 27, 1306, Bruce was crowned at Scone. Following major setbacks in 1306–07, he rallied and began systematically winning back his kingdom from the English. On June 24, 1314, at the Battle of Bannockburn, Bruce defeated EDWARD II, who had succeeded Edward I in 1307. This great victory established independence for Scotland and confirmed Bruce's claim to the throne. Robert I spent the remainder of his life fighting the English in Ireland and along the Scottish borders. In 1328, England formally recognized Scottish independence. Robert was succeeded by his son, David II.

Roberts, Frederick Sleigh, 1st Earl Roberts of Kandahar   A British field marshal, Frederick Sleigh Roberts, b. Sept. 30, 1832, d. Nov. 14, 1914, was the last commander in chief of the British army. He helped suppress the INDIAN MUTINY (1857–58) and distinguished himself in the Second Afghan War (1878–80), defeating the Afghan army near Kandahar. He was commander in chief in India (1885–93). Roberts became a field marshal in 1895, and from December 1899 to November 1900 he was commander in chief in the SOUTH AFRICAN WAR, defeating the Boer forces in several key battles. In 1901 he was made an earl and became commander in chief of the British army, serving until 1904, when that post was abolished.

Roberts, Oral   Granville Oral Roberts, b. Ada, Okla., Jan. 24, 1918, is one of America's leading evangelists and faith healers. In the 1930s and '40s, Roberts was pastor of several Pentecostal Holiness churches; in 1947 he began traveling extensively as a healing evangelist. He founded the Oral Roberts Evangelistic Association in 1948 and Oral Roberts University in Tulsa, Okla., in 1963. After 1968, Roberts preached mainly on television and was associated with the United Methodist church.

Roberts, Owen J.   Owen Josephus Roberts, b. Philadelphia, May 2, 1875, d. May 17, 1955, was an associate justice of the U.S. Supreme Court from 1930 to 1945. Appointed to the court by President Herbert Hoover, Roberts at first opposed the New Deal measures of Hoover's successor, Franklin D. Roosevelt, but became a New Deal supporter in the late 1930s. In 1942 he headed an investigation that blamed the U.S. military for being unprepared when the Japanese attacked Pearl Harbor.

Robert's Rules of Order   see PARLIAMENTARY PROCEDURE

Robertson, James   The American pioneer James Robertson, b. Brunswick County, Va., June 28, 1742, d. Sept. 1, 1814, was the founder and a leader of frontier settlements in present-day Tennessee. In 1771 he established the Watauga Colony on the Doe River in eastern Tennessee and helped organize a government under the Watauga Association. He also founded a community at the site of Nashville in 1780, headed the settlers' government, and led the region's defense against the Spanish-backed Creek Indians during the late 1780s.

Robertson, Oscar   Hall of Fame member Oscar Robertson, b. Charlotte, Tenn., Nov. 24, 1938, played basketball as a 3-time All-American at the University of Cincinnati (1958–60) before winning an Olympic gold medal (1960) and starring in the National Basketball Association for 14 seasons (Cincinnati Royals, 1960–70; Milwaukee Bucks, 1970–74). He was the NBA's Rookie of the Year in 1961 and its Most Valuable Player in 1964. During his career Robertson, a 6-ft 5-in (1-m 95-cm) guard nicknamed the "Big O," scored 26,710 points (25.7 per game) and had 7,804 rebounds (7.5 per game), 7,694 foul shots, and 9,887 assists, the NBA record until surpassed by Magic Johnson in 1990–91. He was a first-team All-NBA selection 9 times. In the 1961–62 season, Robertson averaged 30.8 points, 12.5 rebounds, and 11.4 assists per game—the only time in league history that a player achieved double figures in all three categories.

Robertson, Pat   Marion Gordon "Pat" Robertson, b. Lexington, Va., Mar. 22, 1930, is a U.S. Baptist minister, religious broadcaster, and political figure. The son of U.S. senator A. Willis Robertson (1887–1971), he is the founder (1960) of the Christian Broadcasting Network

and from 1968 to 1986 was the host of "The 700 Club," a conservative television talk show. He resumed the talk show in 1988, after he had campaigned unsuccessfully for the Republican presidential nomination.

Robeson, Paul   [rohb'-suhn]   The son of a former slave, American black actor and bass-baritone Paul Robeson, b. Princeton, N.J., Apr. 9, 1898, d. Jan. 23, 1976, was one of the most distinguished Americans of the 20th century. After graduating with Phi Beta Kappa honors from Rutgers University, where he twice received All-American football honors, he attended Columbia Law School and practiced law briefly before turning to the theater.

Robeson's performances in Eugene O'Neill's plays during the early 1920s established him as a brilliant actor, and for two decades he was hailed as one of the greatest bass-baritones in the world. In the course of his many travels abroad, he learned numerous foreign languages and was greatly lionized. He played the title role in the 1943 Broadway production of *Othello*, which ran a record 296 performances. His acting in that play earned him, in 1944, the Academy of Arts and Letters' Gold Medal for best diction in the American theater and the Donaldson Award for best actor.

Robeson championed the cause of the oppressed throughout his life, insisting that as an artist he had no choice but to do so. A trip to the Soviet Union early in his career had made him a lifelong friend of the USSR, which in 1952 awarded him the Stalin Peace Prize. Following World War II, when he took an uncompromising stand against segregation and lynching in the United States and advocated friendship with the Soviet Union, a long, intense campaign was mounted against him. Thereafter he was unable to earn a living as an artist in the United States and was also denied a passport. Finally in 1958 he was allowed to leave the country for Great Britain. He returned in 1963 in ill health and spent the last 13 years of his life in self-imposed seclusion.

Paul Robeson became a controversial figure during the 1950s when his outspoken stance on civil rights and admiration for Soviet Communism culminated in the revocation of his passport. As a singer, Robeson is best known for his rendition of "Ole Man River" in Show-boat (play, 1928; film, 1936).

Robespierre, Maximilien   [roh-bes-pee-air']   Maximilien Marie Isidore Robespierre, b. Arras, France, May

Maximilien Robespierre, a leader of the French Revolution, believed that those who govern must possess absolute moral virtue. Convinced of his own rectitude, he came to regard all opposition as endangering the community and thus justified the use of Terror.

6, 1758, d. July 28, 1794, is regarded by many historians as the most significant figure in the FRENCH REVOLUTION. A small man with a weak voice, fiercely concerned with first principles, he only gradually won recognition in the National Assembly (1789–91). Although later labeled an atrocious tyrant, he then advocated humanitarian reforms such as the abolition of capital punishment. An uncompromising democrat, he opposed the restriction of the franchise because he believed that goodness and good sense were to be found only in the common people. After King Louis XVI fled in 1791, Robespierre showed superb political skill; eschewing both premature republicanism and conservative reaction, he re-created the fragmented JACOBIN Society. There, excluded from the Legislative Assembly (1791–92) by his own decree against reelections, he continued to speak out. He condemned the frenzy for war with Austria.

Justified by events when the French army suffered reverses in the war and concluding that the king and the GIRONDISTS were betraying the Revolution, Robespierre promoted the republican revolution of Aug. 10, 1792; in September he was named a deputy for Paris to the National Convention. Although relentlessly attacked as a potential dictator, he justified the September Massacres of imprisoned nobles and clergy as inevitable and demanded the execution of the king as a political necessity. Believing unanimity to be imperative, he prompted the proscription of the Girondists in June 1793.

Robespierre's election to the Committee of Public Safety in July 1793 heralded a new era of repression; after September he became the principal spokesman for Terror. Believing that ruthless revolutionary government is legitimate when the community is endangered, he eliminated the factions of Jacques René HÉBERT and Georges Jacques DANTON in 1794, centralized political justice in Paris, and by the notorious Law of 22 Prairial expedited the work of the revolutionary tribunal. He also sought to promote social unity by accepting price controls and inaugurating the cult of the Supreme Being to check attacks on Christianity and to stimulate patriotic virtue. When French military victories

made this regime seem superfluous, Robespierre was overthrown. Arrested on July 27 (9 Thermidor), 1794, he attempted suicide but was guillotined.

robin   Robin is the common name for a number of songbirds, notably the American robin, *Turdus migratorius*, and the European robin, *Erithacus rubecula*, in the thrush family, Turdidae. American colonists named the medium-sized (25 cm/10 in), slate-backed, russet-breasted bird they found abundant in their new land for the much smaller (14 cm/5 in), friendly robin so popular in Europe, which has a brown back and orange breast. Depending on the severity of the local winter, the robin is either a resident or a migrant. Several other thrushes and some Old World flycatchers (family Muscicapidae) also are called robins.

The American robin commonly eats earthworms and insects. It ranges from Guatemala to the tree line in Alaska.

Robin Hood   Robin Hood is a legendary hero of medieval England who stole from the rich to give to the poor, thus showing his love for the common people. He is the subject of nearly 40 English and Scottish ballads and numerous tales, plays, and films. Robin Hood and his band, including Little John, Maid Marian, and Friar Tuck, are supposed to have lived in Sherwood Forest near Nottingham. Although constantly at odds with the sheriff of Nottingham, Robin was always loyal to the king—sometimes identified as Edward IV (15th century), sometimes as Richard I (12th century). Several film versions of the legend have been made, most notably *The Adventures of Robin Hood* (1938), starring Errol Flynn.

Robinson, Brooks   The Hall of Fame baseball player Brooks Calbert Robinson, b. Little Rock, Ark., May 18, 1937, is considered the greatest defensive 3d baseman in major league history. Playing (1958–77) for the Baltimore Orioles, Robinson had a .971 lifetime fielding average and won a record 16 consecutive Gold Gloves (1960–75). He appeared in 18 straight All Star games and was the American League's MVP in 1964.

Robinson, Charles   Charles Robinson, b. Hardwick, Mass., July 18, 1818,·d. Aug. 17, 1894, was a U.S. politician. He went to Kansas in 1854 as an agent of the New England EMIGRANT AID COMPANY, formed to assist free-soil partisans in Kansas. He helped lead the FREE-SOIL PARTY and was elected (1856) governor of Kansas under the free-state constitution adopted by a convention at Topeka. Because he ignored laws passed by the proslavery territorial legislature, members of the proslavery party arrested him on charges of treason and usurpation of office. Acquitted by a federal grand jury, Robinson was reelected (1859) under Kansas's new Wyandotte constitution. He assumed office in 1861, when Kansas was admitted to the Union, serving until 1863.

Robinson, Eddie   Grambling State University football coach Edward Gay Robinson, b. Baker, La., Feb. 13, 1919, has won more games than anyone else in collegiate history, breaking Bear BRYANT's record in 1985. Robinson began at Grambling in 1941 and has coached over 200 eventual professional players—more than anyone else—in accumulating, through 1990, a record of 367 wins, 127 losses, and 15 ties.

Robinson, Edward G.   Edward G. Robinson, stage name of Emanuel Goldenberg, b. Romania, Dec. 12, 1893, d. Jan. 26, 1973, became one of the major figures of Hollywood films of the 1930s. Short and dynamic, with a distinctive voice, he specialized in gangster parts but later proved equally adept at comedy or in benevolent character roles. His most important films include *Little Caesar* (1930), *Dr. Ehrlich's Magic Bullet* (1940), *Double Indemnity* and *The Woman in the Window* (both 1944), and *Key Largo* (1948).

Robinson, Edwin Arlington   Edwin Arlington Robinson, b. Head Tide, Maine, Dec. 22, 1869, d. Apr. 6, 1935, was a major American poet who is admired for his moving poetic vision and for his superb mastery of verse forms. Robinson grew up in Gardiner, Maine, which he immortalized in his poetry as Tilbury Town. His early short poems, such as "Richard Cory" and "Miniver Cheevy," about unhappy and disappointed individuals, remain the most widely read portion of his work. Character studies modeled on townspeople and members of Robinson's own family, these verses display his gift for ironic detachment and his shrewd awareness of the hidden aspects of human nature.

Although Robinson would eventually receive three Pulitzer Prizes for his poetry, he remained virtually destitute for many years of his career. In 1905, President Theodore Roosevelt, an early admirer of Robinson's work, secured him a clerkship in the New York Custom House. Wider recognition came with the publication of *The Town down the River* (1910). Thereafter, Robinson was able to support himself on his writings and to spend most of his summers in the company of other artists at the MacDowell Colony in Peterborough, N.H. "The Man against the Sky," published in 1916, is typical of his later poetry in its somber outlook and transcendental overtones. Other later works of importance include *Merlin* (1917), the first of three Arthurian tales dealing with the modern world, and the narratives *Amaranth* (1934) and *King Jasper* (1935). Robinson also wrote several plays.

Robinson, Frank   Baseball Hall of Fame outfielder Frank Robinson, b. Beaumont, Tex., Aug. 31, 1935, is noted not only for his outstanding playing career but also for becoming the first black manager in the major leagues (Cleveland Indians, 1975–77; San Francisco Giants, 1981–84; Baltimore Orioles, 1988–91). Robinson joined the National League's Cincinnati Reds in 1956 and was Rookie of the Year. Five years later he was named NL Most Valuable Player (MVP). In 1966, after being traded to the Baltimore Orioles, he won the Triple Crown—leading the American League in batting (.316), home runs (49), and runs batted in (122)—and was voted that league's MVP, the only man ever to be MVP in both leagues. Robinson hit 586 career home runs, 4th on the all-time list behind Henry Aaron, Babe Ruth, and Willie Mays.

Robinson, Henry Peach   The English photographer Henry Peach Robinson, b. July 9, 1830, d. Feb. 21, 1901, was a pioneering exponent of pictorialist photography. He crystallized 19th-century photographic aesthetics through his prolific writings and the publication of his photographs, which resemble the large narrative paintings popular in the Victorian era. In his influential *Pictorial Ef-*

The work of British photographer Henry Peach Robinson, such as Fading Away *(1858), emulated the sentimental genre paintings popular during the mid-19th century.*

fect in *Photography* (1869), he applied the academic rules governing composition in painting to the newer medium, advocating contrived artificial compositions in photography. To produce prints like his famous *Fading Away* (1858), for example, he combined as many as five negatives.

Robinson, Jackie   The American Jack Roosevelt Robinson, b. Cairo, Ga., Jan. 31, 1919, d. Oct. 24, 1972, major 'league baseball's first black player in modern times, was one of the game's most aggressive competitors. Robinson joined the Brooklyn Dodgers of the National League in 1947 at the age of 28 and helped lead the team to 6 World Series appearances in 10 years. A versatile athlete, he also starred in football and track while in college at the University of California in Los Angeles. While playing with the Kansas City Monarchs of the Negro National League he was signed to a major league baseball contract by Branch Rickey and assigned (1946) to the Dodgers' Montreal farm team of the International League. Robinson was brought to Brooklyn the next year, where he hit .297, scored 125 runs, and led the league in stolen bases (29) as the Dodgers won their first pennant since 1941. He was named Rookie of the Year. Primarily a second baseman, he also played at third and first base and in the outfield. In 1949 he was named the league's Most Valuable Player, leading the league in batting (.342) and stolen bases (37), scoring 122 runs, batting in 124 runs, and amassing 203 hits. Robinson was an outstanding fielder as well. He was elected to the Baseball Hall of Fame in 1962.

Jackie Robinson, an American baseball player, became the first black athlete to play in the major leagues when he debuted (1947) with the Brooklyn Dodgers. Robinson played for 10 seasons (1947–56) with the Dodgers, winning the Most Valuable Player award in 1949 and leading the team to the world championship in 1955.

Robinson, John   John Robinson, b. *c.*1576, d. Mar. 1, 1625, was the pastor in Leiden of the PILGRIMS before they sailed to America on the *Mayflower*. About 1607 he

joined a Separatist congregation at Scrooby, Nottinghamshire, whose members believed that it was the duty of serious Christians to separate from the Anglican church and form exclusive churches where true faith and strict morals would be characteristic of all members.

Within a year the unpopular dissenters fled to Holland and organized (1609) a church at Leiden with Robinson as their pastor. When some of his flock wanted to leave Holland, Robinson supported their plans to relocate in the New World, but he died in Leiden before he could join them.

Robinson, Lennox   A leading figure in the IRISH LITERARY RENAISSANCE, Lennox Robinson, b. Oct. 4, 1886, d. Oct. 14, 1958, was manager and later director of Dublin's ABBEY THEATRE. Robinson's anthologies of Irish verse fostered new interest in Irish poetry. His own writings include the play *The Lost Leader* (1918) and the autobiographical *Curtain Up* (1942).

Robinson, Sugar Ray   Walker Smith, Jr., b. Detroit, May 3, 1921, d. Apr. 12, 1989, was an American professional boxer whom many boxing experts consider to have been the best pugilist of modern times. He acquired his ring-name when he borrowed the birth certificate of a friend named Ray Robinson so he could fight while he was yet below the minimum age. Sugar Ray won his first world title in the welterweight class on Dec. 20, 1946, when he defeated Tommy Bell. He then went on to win the middleweight title five times. The first time was on Feb. 14, 1951, when he knocked out Jake LaMotta. He soon lost the title to Randy Turpin but regained it 2 months later. Robinson failed in an attempt to wrest the light-heavyweight title from Joey Maxim in 1952; he then announced his retirement. Robinson returned, however, in 1955 and recaptured the middleweight title from Carl

Sugar Ray Robinson was the first professional fighter to win the championship of a single weight division five times. After capturing the welterweight title in 1946, Robinson moved into the middleweight class, first winning its title in 1951. Although he lost that title in the ring three times and relinquished it once, Robinson was able to regain the crown four times before retiring in 1965.

"Bobo" Olson. He lost the title to Gene Fullmer (Jan. 2, 1957) but retrieved it by beating Fullmer on May 1, 1957. Robinson again lost the title, this time to Carmen Basilio on Sept. 23, 1957, but won it back Mar. 25, 1958. He lost the title for good to Paul Pender on Jan. 22, 1960. Robinson possessed balance, quickness, and devastating combination punches. In 202 professional fights he posted 109 knockouts, won 66 decisions on points, had 6 draws, lost 18 decisions, was knocked out once, and had 2 no contests.

Robinson Crusoe   Daniel DEFOE's famous novel, fully titled *The Life and Strange Surprising Adventures of Robinson Crusoe of York, Mariner* (1719), was suggested by the actual experiences of Alexander Selkirk, a marooned sailor. Robinson Crusoe, a young Englishman, disregards his father's advice and runs off to sea to seek his fortune. After various adventures, he suffers a shipwreck and is cast ashore on a deserted island. There he spends many years alone, creating a home for himself in a new environment. Eventually he acquires a companion, an Indian whom he rescues from cannibals and names Friday. After encounters with pirates and mutineers, Crusoe and Friday manage to escape from the island.

Robinson-Patman Act   The Robinson-Patman Act, passed in 1936 to protect small businesses against discriminatory practices that favor large chain stores, supplemented the Clayton Anti-Trust Act of 1914. The Robinson-Patman Act prohibits a businessperson from discriminating in price between purchasers of commodities of equal grade and quality if this results in less competition or in monopoly. The act was cosponsored by Sen. Joseph T. Robinson and Rep. Wright Patman.

robot   A robot may be defined as a completely self-controlled device consisting of electronic, electrical, or mechanical units; more generally, it is a machine devised to function in place of a living agent. The word *robot* comes from a story and play produced in 1921 called *R.U.R.* (for Rossum's Universal Robots), by Karel Ĉapek. In Czech the word *robot* means "worker," but the English translation (1923) retained the original term.

Most robots sit alongside assembly lines and perform such tasks as welding, painting, and inspection. Japan is both the leading maker and user of robots, with a majority of them employed on automobile assembly lines. In general, such robots do not have the ability to learn new tasks; instead they perform carefully orchestrated procedures, guided by a computer program (see AUTOMATION).

Robots have ventured into other areas. In medicine, a robotic arm equipped with surgical tools has assisted doctors in a delicate brain operation; in the field of COMPUTER-AIDED DESIGN AND COMPUTER-AIDED MANUFACTURING (CAD/CAM), robotic structures have been used to manufacture such things as integrated circuits and solid models.

Roca, Julio A.   [roh'-kah]   Julio Argentino Roca, b. July 17, 1843, d. Oct. 19, 1914, was an Argentine general and statesman who was twice president of Argentina (1880–86, 1898–1904). As President Nicolás Avellaneda's minister of war, Roca drove (1878–79) the Patagonian Indians south, opening vast areas of the Pampas for colonization. During Roca's first term as president, the Argentine economy expanded rapidly, but inflation, graft, and corruption were persistent problems. During his second administration, Roca stabilized the currency and settled boundary disputes with Chile and Brazil. After leaving office, he continued to dominate Argentine politics.

Rocard, Michel   [roh-kahr']   Michel Rocard, b. Aug. 23, 1930, served as prime minister of France from 1988 to 1991. Rocard entered politics as leader of the small Unified Socialist Party in 1967, joining the mainstream Socialists led by François Mitterrand in 1974; he was minister of agriculture from 1983 to 1985. After the 1988 elections Mitterrand as president chose Rocard, a "free market socialist," to head France's new left-center government. Rocard was replaced by the Socialist Edith Cresson.

Rochambeau, Jean Baptiste Donatien de Vimeur, Comte de   [roh-shahm-boh', doh-nah-see-an' duh vee-mur']   The comte de Rochambeau, b. July 1, 1725, d. May 12, 1807, was a career general who, during the American Revolution, commanded the French forces that helped defeat the British army in the YORKTOWN CAMPAIGN. As a young officer, Rochambeau served ably in the War of the Austrian Succession (1740–48) and Seven Years' War (1756–63).

Dispatched by King Louis XVI to help the American revolutionists, he landed in Newport, R.I., with about 5,500 troops in 1780 but remained inactive for a year because the French fleet was blockaded off Narragansett Bay. In 1781 he persuaded George Washington to join forces with the troops of the marquis de LAFAYETTE and the fleet of the comte de GRASSE to trap Gen. Charles CORNWALLIS at Yorktown.

In the early months of the French Revolution, Rochambeau commanded France's northern army; he was made marshal of France in 1791.

Roche, Kevin   [rohch]   The architect Kevin Roche, b. Dublin, June 14, 1922, is a leading designer for business and industry in the United States. His structures, with their elegant, taut glass skins, resemble mammoth, shimmering greenhouses or crystal palaces—for example, the Power Center for the Performing Arts, University of Michigan, Ann Arbor (1965–71); One United Nations Plaza in New York City (1969–76); and Union Carbide Headquarters, Danbury, Conn. (1980). Roche was profoundly influenced by Eero SAARINEN, whose firm he joined in 1950. After Saarinen's death in 1961, Roche and John Dinkeloo completed the existing Saarinen projects; in 1966 the firm became Kevin Roche, John Dinkeloo, and Associates. Its work has shown, primarily, a vastness of scale that makes each project look like a first model of the original idea—as in the Ford Foundation, New York City (1963–68), or the Knights of Columbus, New Haven, Conn. (1965–69). Some of the projects show an ingenious progression of scale within a single building.

Roche's limit [rohsh]   The French mathematician Édouard Roche (1820–83) calculated that if a satellite were to approach a planet within a certain distance, called the Roche limit, then the tidal forces exerted by the planet would overcome the gravitational forces holding the satellite together, and the satellite would disintegrate. For a satellite having the same average density as the planet, the critical distance is 2.44 times the radius of the planet. The rings of Jupiter, Saturn, and Uranus lie entirely within the Roche limit for each planet and may be the remains of a satellite. This reasoning takes no account of the cohesiveness of the material of the satellite and does not apply to artificial satellites.

Rochester (New York)   Rochester, the seat of Monroe County, N.Y., is a city and port on the Genesee River and Lake Ontario. The city's population is 231,636 (1990); that of the metropolitan area is 1,002,410. Once the home of photography pioneer George Eastman, abolitionist Frederick Douglass, and women's rights leader Susan B. Anthony, Rochester is a major industrial city, a cultural and educational center, and a port of entry on the St. Lawrence Seaway. Since the late 19th century, medical instruments, optical equipment, and photographic industries have been the mainstays of the Rochester economy, along with office machinery, clothing, shoes, and foods.

Rochester's many educational institutions include the University of Rochester (1850), with its prestigious EASTMAN SCHOOL OF MUSIC, and the Rochester Institute of Technology (1829). Cultural facilities include the Rochester Museum and Science Center, the International Museum of Photography, and the Rochester Philharmonic Orchestra.

Rochester's first white settler was Ebenezer Allen. His land was purchased by Col. Nathaniel Rochester and two partners, and their settlement was incorporated as the village of Rochesterville in 1817. The village grew quickly, with the construction of the Erie Canal (1822) improving transportation for the local farmers and for an active flour industry. Rochester's role as Flour City ended with the country's westward expansion and the coming of the railroad, but a flourishing nursery industry took its place. Modern industrial development began in the second half of the 19th century.

rock   Rock is the solid substance that forms the Earth's crust. Most geologists exclude SOIL from this category and further restrict the term to materials formed by natural processes.

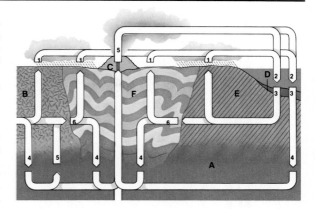

Igneous, sedimentary, and metamorphic rocks gradually and continuously change into one another. Cooling of molten magma (A) forms intrusive igneous rocks (B) below the Earth's surface and extrusive igneous rocks (C) above the surface. Surface rocks eventually erode (1) into particles, which are washed into the seas and deposited (2) as sediment (D). Compaction and cementation (3) of accumulated sediment form sedimentary rocks (E). Accumulation of more sediment forces these rocks into the hot plastic mantle, where they melt (4), mix with other materials, rise, and solidify again (5). Combined heat and pressure (6) may change igneous and sedimentary rocks into metamorphic rocks (F).

Rocks are classified as igneous, sedimentary, or metamorphic according to how they formed. Those which solidified from molten or partly molten material are called IGNEOUS ROCKS. SEDIMENTARY ROCKS form by the accumulation of sediment, mineral particles that have either settled from a state of suspension in air or water or have been precipitated from a state of solution. METAMORPHIC ROCKS are those which have undergone marked transformation, in response to heat, pressure, or chemical alteration.

The molten material (MAGMA) from which all igneous rocks form may issue as LAVA from volcanoes; such rock is said to be extrusive. Intrusive igneous rocks are those which form from consolidation of magma underground.

Sedimentary rocks are said to be clastic if they consist of particles of older rock (gravel, for example), chemical if precipitated from solution (rock salt, for example), or organic if formed from the remains or secretions of plants or animals (coal, for example). Particles of lava exploded into the air during volcanic eruption may settle to the ground and form deposits of volcanic ash. Such rocks are called pyroclastics.

See also: PETROLOGY.

rock music   Rock music emerged during the mid-1950s to become the major popular musical form of young audiences in the United States and Western Europe. Its stylistic scope is too broad to be encompassed by any single definition; the only feature common to all rock music is a heavy emphasis on the beat.

Rock 'n' Roll, 1950–62. The primary source of rock 'n' roll was RHYTHM AND BLUES, an idiom popular among black audiences that combined elements of urban BLUES (in the structure, vocal style, and use of amplified guitar), GOSPEL

Chuck Berry displays his flamboyant technique during a typically energetic performance. Berry became one of the formative figures of rock 'n' roll, recording such classics of the genre as "Maybelline" (1955) and "Johnny B. Goode" (1958). Berry's powerfully rhythmic blues style greatly influenced the British groups who revitalized rock 'n' roll during the 1960s.

(Right) Elvis Presley shocked conservative audiences and delighted youthful fans with the uninhibited hip gyrations that became a hallmark of his early performances. Presley emerged as the dominant male vocalist of the early years of rock 'n' roll, blending rhythm and blues, gospel, and country and western music.

MUSIC (in the piano accompaniments and vocal harmonizing), and JAZZ (in the saxophone solos). Rhythm and blues began to gain a wider audience during the late 1940s, and in 1951 the disc jockey Alan Freed, who played an important role in attracting white teenagers to the music, substituted the term "rock 'n' roll," previously used as a sexual reference in lyrics. Major record producers issued "covers" of rhythm and blues songs—competing, "sanitized" versions recorded by white artists. Covers brought new stylistic influences to rock 'n' roll (white COUNTRY AND WESTERN and popular music). Bill Haley's "Rock Around the Clock" (1955) was the first important breakthrough for white rock 'n' roll. What appealed to the postwar white audience was rock 'n' roll's driving dance rhythms, its direct, adolescent-level message, and its suggestion of youthful rebellion.

Rock 'n' roll's first superstar was Elvis PRESLEY. With his country-and-western background, Presley led the way for other "rockabilly" (rock plus hillbilly) artists; with his spasmodic hip gyrations, he introduced a sexual suggestiveness that outraged conservative adults; with his legions of teenage fans, he became the archetype of the rock star as cultural hero.

Other popular figures also made significant contributions to the style: Chuck BERRY nourished the music's roots, Jerry Lee Lewis expanded its country branch, and Little Richard provided frantic showmanship. By the late 1950s, however, a malaise had set in; the music had become formula-ridden, sentimental, and often—as in love-death ballads like "Teen Angel"—distinctly maudlin.

Rock, 1963–69. The renewal of rock 'n' roll came from the unlikely locale of Liverpool, England. Here, The BEATLES made their start in 1960, at first imitating American styles and then weaving from the various strands of American rock 'n' roll an individual style marked—in both music and lyrics—by wit, poetry, and a sense of fun. Their successes came quickly during 1963 and '64. From

1965 to 1969 they introduced new sonorities, textures, forms, rhythms, melodic designs, and lyric conceptions, and were at the forefront of a revolutionary epoch in popular music. Rock 'n' roll had evolved into an expression of greater sophistication, complexity, and breadth. It had become a new idiom: rock.

Other English groups also came into prominence around 1964. The ROLLING STONES, the most prominent and durable of these groups, presented yet another image of rock—one of anger, alienation, and sensuality.

Other trends of the 1960s included the merging of rhythm and blues with black gospel styles to create SOUL MUSIC, and the beginnings of jazz-rock, as originally synthesized by the band Blood, Sweat and Tears. The folk-rock style, first suggested by Bob DYLAN at the 1965 Newport Folk Festival, brought to folk music a hard beat and amplification, and to rock a new poetic sensibility

The Beatles, a phenomenally successful English quartet from Liverpool, became the major innovative force in rock 'n' roll during the 1960s.

An estimated 500,000 people attended the Woodstock Festival, held Aug. 15–17, 1969, near Bethel, N.Y. This musical celebration, featuring some of the most famous rock and folk musicians of the 1960s, was the most publicized counterculture event of the decade.

and social consciousness.

The "California sound" was not a uniform style but a term that reflected that state's rise as a center of rock activity and experimentation. In the early 1960s, California was the scene of "surfing music" (popularized by the BEACH BOYS), but over the course of the decade the music reflected the trends of hippies (the Mamas and the Papas), student protest (Country Joe and the Fish), and the drug culture. Widespread popularity of hallucinogenic drugs (particularly LSD, or "acid") produced psychedelic "acid rock," whose apostles included JEFFERSON AIRPLANE and the GRATEFUL DEAD.

Rock's first major effort in musical theater was the hippie revue *Hair* (1967), a spectacularly successful pageant celebrating youth, love, and drugs. Closely following were such rock-opera successes as *Tommy* and *Jesus Christ Superstar*.

Led Zeppelin, one of the most successful "heavy metal" rock groups, featured the powerful voice of Robert Plant and the instrumentation of Jimmy Page, John Paul Jones, and John Bonham.

By the end of the 1960s, the rock 'n' roll instrumentation of saxophone, piano, amplified guitar, and drums had been replaced by rock's several amplified guitars, drums, and electronic technology. To the standard patterns of 12-bar blues and 32-bar song form were added extended, unique forms, sometimes encompassing the entire side of a long-playing record. Descriptive group names (Crew Cuts, Everly Brothers, Beach Boys) were replaced by nondescriptive, enigmatic names (The WHO, Jefferson Airplane, Big Brother and the Holding Company). Finally, the formerly separate roles of performer and composer were merged in a single artist. As demonstrated by the WOODSTOCK FESTIVAL in August 1969, rock music was by this time an intrinsic element in the life of American youth and a powerful articulation of their moods, hopes, and fears.

Rock, 1970–79. Rock continued to develop by blending with other established idioms, as in folk-rock and country-rock, the rock contribution invariably being a heavy beat and electronic technology. REGGAE, which emerged from Jamaica around 1972, is an integration of rock, soul, calypso, and other Latin rhythms. Jazz-rock fusion, or simply fusion, was a meeting between rock instrumentalists, attracted to the broad creative opportunities and musicianship of jazz, and jazz musicians, attracted to rock's electronics and commercial potential.

Other styles, more clearly based on rock precedents, ranged from the benign bubble-gum rock of the Osmond Brothers, directed toward the youngest popular-music fans, to the intentionally vile punk rock, which punctuated its strident denunciations with vulgarity. Heavy-metal rock aimed for the hallucinogenic effect of acid rock, using the hypnotic power of repetitiveness, loud volume, and electronic distortion. Glitter rock was more a theatrical approach than a musical style; it offered glittering costumes and bizarre, sometimes androgynous, exhibitions (Alice Cooper, David Bowie, Kiss). New-wave rock appeared late in the 1970s, preaching a return to a more basic metric emphasis and a greater lyricism.

Most rock music of the period was intended almost solely for listening, not for dancing. The inevitable reaction was disco, a music first and foremost for dancing. With its thumping regularity of accented beats divided into minibeats, disco was decried by hardline rock fans as mechanical, commercial, and unlyrical. Nevertheless, its following increased and, after the BEE GEES composed and recorded their disco-beat soundtrack for the film *Saturday Night Fever* (1977), disco became for a while a major sector of rock music.

The Eclectic 1980s. Rock music, by the mid-1980s, had presented no clear-cut new musical direction. Videotapes, depicting televised concerts or acted-out versions of rock songs, proved to be a powerful tool for introducing new groups. With their emphasis on the visual, however, they encouraged the use of bizarre, grotesque "stories" and staging, while the music remained secondary. Videos contributed to the immense popularity of such glittery, androgynous performers as Michael JACKSON and Prince. Bruce SPRINGSTEEN, whose "populist" explorations of the American experience in the 1970s earned him a wide following, achieved superstar status in the mid-1980s.

At the same time, there was a nostalgic return to older, simpler rock and prerock idioms. British musician Elvis Costello's songs harked back to rhythm-and-blues and country-western styles, and Los Angeles–based Los Lobos fused rock music with traditional Mexican music.

Artists such as Paul Simon (formerly of SIMON AND GARFUNKEL) and David Byrne (of the TALKING HEADS), "borrowed" from styles outside rock music, particularly from African music. Conversely, almost every country in the world has begun to develop indigenous forms of rock music.

The scope and significance of rock remains without precedent in the history of popular music. Beginning as a minority expression on the fringe of American society, it developed into a distinct counterculture during the 1960s, and a decade later had become a dominant cultural force.

rock salt   see SALT (sodium chloride)

John D. Rockefeller took the first step toward establishing his industrial empire during the 1860s, when he and his partners founded the business that became Standard Oil.

Rockefeller (family)   American industrialist and philanthropist **John Davison Rockefeller**, b. Richford, N.Y., July 8, 1839, d. May 23, 1937, began his career in Cleveland, Ohio, before the Civil War. In 1863 he and his partners formed an oil business that eventually absorbed many Cleveland refineries and expanded into Pennsylvania oil fields to become the world's largest refining concern. Rockefeller founded (1870) the Standard Oil Company of Ohio; the Standard Oil Trust, which he formed in order to avoid state controls, was dissolved (1892) by the Ohio Supreme Court. The division of his operations into 18 companies—later to include more than 30 corporations—under the umbrella of Standard Oil of New Jersey (1899) helped him to accumulate a personal fortune of more than $1 billion. In 1911 this venture, however, was interpreted by the U.S. Supreme Court as "a monopoly in restraint of trade" and thus illegal according to the Sherman Anti-Trust Act; Standard Oil was broken up into 39 separate companies. Rockefeller retired the same year but expanded his efforts in philanthropy, which claimed about one-half of his vast fortune. He created such institutions as the Rockefeller Foundation, the General Education Board, and the Rockefeller Institute for Medical Research; founded the University of Chicago; and presented many gifts to colleges and churches. His son, **John D. Rockefeller, Jr.**, b. Cleveland, Jan. 29, 1874, d. May 11, 1960, continued and expanded his father's philanthropic interests. John D., Jr., invested in new enterprises such as Rockefeller Center and also donated the land on which the United Nations headquarters were built. **John D. Rockefeller III**, b. New York City, Mar. 21, 1906, d. July 10, 1978, operated family businesses and philanthropies. The second son, **Nelson**, is covered in a separate article below. **Laurance**, b. New York City, May 26, 1910, a third son, is a conservationist. A fourth son, **Winthrop**, b. New York City, May 1, 1912, d. Feb. 22, 1973, was governor of Arkansas (1966–70). **David**, b.

New York City, June 12, 1915, headed New York's Chase Manhattan Bank (1961–81). Among more than 20 present-day Rockefeller offspring, the most prominent, **John (Jay) D. Rockefeller IV**, b. New York City, June 18, 1937, was elected governor of West Virginia in 1976 and reelected in 1980. In 1984 he was elected to the U.S. Senate.

Rockefeller, Nelson A.   Nelson Aldrich Rockefeller, b. Bar Harbor, Maine, July 8, 1908, d. Jan. 26, 1979, served (1959–73) as Republican governor of New York for four terms and was appointed vice-president (1974–77) by President Gerald R. Ford under the provisions of the 25th Amendment. A grandson of the industrialist John D. Rockefeller, Nelson Rockefeller was graduated (1930) from Dartmouth College and worked in family

Nelson A. Rockefeller, U.S. public official, served as vice-president (1974–77) under Gerald Ford and as governor (1959–73) of New York, where his administration was notable for programs in education and social welfare and increased taxes. He was one of the heirs to the dynasty begun by his grandfather, John D. Rockefeller, during the late 19th century.

enterprises until his appointment by President Franklin D. Roosevelt as coordinator (1940–44) of inter-American affairs. He then became assistant secretary of state (1944–45) for Latin American affairs, head (1950–51) of the International Development Advisory Board, undersecretary of health, education, and welfare (1953–54), and special assistant (1954–55) to President Dwight D. Eisenhower. In 1958, Rockefeller defeated W. Averell Harriman in the New York gubernatorial race. As governor he greatly increased the size and scope of the state government. He ran unsuccessfully for the Republican nomination for president in 1960, 1964, and 1968, and in 1973 he resigned as governor.

Rockefeller Center

In the official, corporate sense, the designation *Rockefeller Center* refers to a group of 21 office buildings and a theater under single ownership (since 1989 the Mitsubishi Estate Co. of Japan) that are distributed over an area of midtown Manhattan fronting on Fifth and Sixth avenues between 48th and 52d streets. According to historical usage and the popular view, however, the term applies only to the original 14 buildings standing entirely between Fifth and Sixth avenues and constructed between 1931 and 1939 under the financial sponsorship of John D. Rockefeller, Jr.

The 14 buildings of the 1939 group, designed by a consortium of architects, are arranged in what might be called a rectilinear pinwheel form. The anchor and central focus of this plan is the 70-story RCA (Radio Corporation of America) Building. The smaller buildings, of which 3 are skyscrapers in their own right, are sited so that their long horizontal axes lie either parallel to that of the RCA or at right angles thereto. All the office towers and other structures are steel-framed, and the high, narrow, slablike form of the RCA Building had to be specially braced because of its vulnerability to wind loads. In addition to office space, Rockefeller Center includes broadcasting studios, restaurants, shops, Radio City Music Hall, an ice-skating rink, a network of underground streets and walkways, and numerous murals, statuary, and sculptural decoration.

Rockefeller Foundation

The Rockefeller Foundation, a private foundation with a mandate "to promote the well-being of mankind throughout the world," was founded in 1913 by John D. Rockefeller. In addition to making grants to individuals and institutions, it operates its own programs and maintains a field staff of specialists in agriculture, health, and the social sciences to work where needed around the world. It currently supports programs covering agricultural science, equal opportunity, international relations, population and health, and the arts and humanities.

Rocket

The *Rocket* was the early English LOCOMOTIVE, built by George and Robert STEPHENSON, that won the Rainhill trials, a competition sponsored by the Liverpool &

Manchester Railway in 1829. By winning, the *Rocket* proved its reliability and convinced the railway of the practicality of steam motive power. The *Rocket* had a multitube boiler and an efficient method of exhausting the steam and creating a draft in the firebox. It completed the trials with an average speed of 24 km/h (15 mph) and a maximum of 47 km/h (29 mph).

rockets and missiles

A rocket, in its conventional form, is an internal combustion engine that needs no outside air to operate. It carries both fuel and oxidizer, which are burned together in a combustion chamber and produce hot gases that are discharged through a nozzle. Inside the combustion chamber the burning gases exert pressure in all directions. If the chamber were sealed, all these pressures would be balanced and the rocket would not move. The gases are allowed to escape at high speed through the nozzle, however, causing an imbalance in the chamber. Because the pressure exerted on the rocket in the forward direction is much greater than in the backward direction, the rocket shoots forward. It obeys Newton's third law of motion: for every action there is an equal and opposite reaction. In the rocket the escaping exhaust gases are the action, and the forward pressure, or thrust, is the reaction.

Because a rocket carries its own fuel and oxidizer, and because Newton's law is valid everywhere, the rocket can operate both within the Earth's atmosphere and in the vacuum of space. Rockets can thus be used to launch artificial satellites (see SATELLITE, ARTIFICIAL), probes, or manned spacecraft for SPACE EXPLORATION, or to power a variety of short- or long-range missiles for military purposes.

Although since World War II almost all of the costly research and development in rocketry has been accomplished by governments, in the early 1980s U.S. business began to investigate the profit potential in operating private launch facilities for satellite-carrying rockets, many of which could be bought from the military's outmoded rocket stocks.

Early History

The first rockets were probably made in China. When Mongol hordes besieged the town of Kaifengfu in AD 1232, the townsfolk repulsed them with "arrows of flying

A Chinese warrior ignites the fuse of an early military rocket, to which a long stick was attached for stability in flight. The use of gunpowder-propelled rockets probably originated in China in the 13th century.

fire." In the Middle East, and Europe, the art of rocketry appeared soon afterward. In 1242 the English Franciscan monk Roger Bacon produced a secret formula for gunpowder to achieve the faster rates of burning that would make rockets more practicable.

The British first encountered rocket warfare in India, to which the secret of rocket manufacture had probably been brought during the 17th century by Arab traders. The first examples of the Indian rockets reached England about 1770, but only in 1804 did William Congreve take up the challenge and produce an 11-kg (24-lb) rocket with a range of about 1,800 m (6,000 ft). Congreve rockets were first used in battle during the Napoleonic Wars on the night of Oct. 8, 1806.

By 1844, William Hale, an Englishman, had invented spin-stabilized rockets, which eliminated the cumbersome guide sticks. These rockets were set into rotation by deflecting the exhaust through offset nozzles drilled in the baseplate, and, later, by restricting the expanding exhaust gases on one side of the nozzles by the use of semicircular vanes.

Development of Modern Rocketry

Rocketry had to wait half a century before further big advances were made, and these were of a theoretical nature.

Pioneers. A Russian schoolteacher, Konstantin E. TSI-OLKOVSKY, established in 1883 that a rocket would work in the vacuum of space; in 1903 he published his first treatise on space travel, advocating the use of liquid propellants. Tsiolkovsky also advocated staged rockets, gyroscopes, and stabilizing rockets, but a long road still had to be traveled before rockets could be applied so ambitiously. Robert H. GODDARD, the founder of U.S. rocketry, had invented a bazooka-type solid-fuel rocket during World War I and in 1919 published *A Method of Reaching Extreme Altitudes*. Two years later he began the experiments with liquid fuels that Tsiolkovsky had never attempted. On Mar. 16, 1926, at Auburn, Mass., Goddard became the first to launch a liquid-propellant rocket. Fueled by gasoline and liquid oxygen, it rose to a height of 12.5 m (41 ft), reached a top speed of 100 km/h (60 mph), and landed 56 m (184 ft) from the launch stand. Although few people recognized it as such at the time, it was a turning point in history. Meanwhile, in Germany, Hermann OBERTH had published, in 1923, *Die Rakete zu den Planetenräumen* (The Rocket into Planetary Space). Like Goddard, he favored liquid fuels because they were more energetic and controllable. Inspired by Oberth's enthusiasm, German rocket enthusiasts in July 1927 founded the Verein für Raumschiffahrt (VfR, or Society for Space Travel). Its members included Willy Ley, Johannes Winkler, Hermann Oberth, Max Valier, Walter Hohmann, Guido von Pirquet, Klaus Riedel, Kurt Hein-

Hermann Oberth (foreground) and Wernher von Braun (fourth from left) pose before models of rockets that they helped to develop. These German scientists came to work for the United States after World War II and contributed greatly to the American space program.

(Right) American technicians ready a captured German V-2 rocket for launching at the U.S. Army Missile Range in White Sands, N. Mex. The V-2, a liquid-fueled rocket used as a ballistic missile, measured 14 m (46 ft) in height and had an effective range of 322 km (200 mi).

Robert Goddard (left), who conducted the first successful launch of a liquid-fueled rocket, works with assistants at his laboratory in Roswell, N. Mex.

ish, and Rudolf Nebel, all of whom passionately desired to improve the performance of the often-erratic liquid-fueled rockets. On Feb. 21, 1931, Winkler became the second person to launch a liquid-fuel rocket. The entire VfR built a series of small test models known as Mirak and Repulsor.

In 1933, the same year in which Adolf Hitler came to power, a special section of the Army Weapons Department was established at the army proving grounds at Kummersdorf with Captain (later General) Walter Dornberger at its head. The young Wernher VON BRAUN, an early member of the VfR, was placed in charge of rocket development while he was still studying for his doctoral degree, and work began on a series of experimental liquid-fuel rockets. Within a few years highly improved rockets were being fired in secret by von Braun's small team at the North Sea island of Borkum, near Emden. In December 1934 two A-2 rockets, called Max and Moritz, ascended approximately 2.5 km (1.5 mi).

In April 1937 a major rocket research station was completed near the village of Peenemünde on the Baltic coast. Former VfR stalwarts Klaus Riedel, Hans Hueter, Kurt Heinish, and Helmut Zoike were now able to resume their work in rocketry alongside von Braun. At Peenemünde the large A-4 rocket was developed as an artillery weapon. This rocket was later used to bombard London, Antwerp, and other targets in 1944–45. The German High Command called it the V-2 (for Weapon of Vengeance No. 2; see V-2). The first such weapon, the V-1 (see V-1), had been the Fieseler Fi 103 flying bomb, a small, pilotless aircraft powered by a simple pulse-jet engine, and it was also directed against London and southeastern England. After the war the V-2 was used as a SOUNDING ROCKET for upper-atmosphere research; other sounding rockets such as Viking and AEROBEE were built using the same technology.

The Soviets, too, had not been idle. On Aug. 17, 1933, a group of Soviet researchers led by Mikhail K. Tikhonravov launched the GIRD 09 rocket, which flew to a height of about 400 m (1,310 ft). Its builders included a young man, Sergei P. Korolev, who many years later would develop the rocket that launched *Sputnik 1*, the world's first artificial satellite. A more conventional Soviet rocket, the GIRD X, designed by Friedrich A. Tsander, was powered by gasoline and liquid oxygen. On Nov. 25, 1933, it soared nearly 4,900 m (16,000 ft).

Military Missiles

From these beginnings grew the immense challenge of the postwar era; as tension developed between the USSR and the Western Allies, the demand for weapons of even greater power increased. In little more than a decade missiles that at best could carry chemical explosives a few hundred kilometers were superseded by multistage ballistic missiles capable of lobbing thermonuclear warheads into the heart of another continent. These gave rise to the ANTIBALLISTIC MISSILE and also focused attention on the merits of short-range tactical missiles. Any long- or short-range missile equipped with a GUIDANCE AND CONTROL SYSTEM is called a guided missile.

Ballistic missiles that are launched from land include the intercontinental ballistic missile (ICBM), with a range exceeding 8,000 km (5,000 mi); the intermediate-range ballistic missile (IRBM), with a range between 2,500 and 8,000 km (1,500 and 5,000 mi); the medium-range ballistic missile (MRBM), with a range between 800 and 2,500 km (500 and 1,500 mi); and the short-range ballistic missile (SRBM), with a range up to 800 km (500 mi).

ICBM development was spurred in 1954 by the development of the hydrogen bomb and by reductions in the dimensions of atomic bombs, which made possible the design of warheads that could be carried by missiles. The first ICBMs successfully launched in the United States were the ATLAS (1958), the TITAN (1959), and the MINUTEMAN I (1961). These were followed by Minuteman II (1965) and Minuteman III (1970), which together with the Titan make up the land-based U.S. strategic nuclear force. Development of the MX MISSILE, a 10-warhead ICBM, began in 1979.

The United States began to develop the submarine-

(Left) *A U.S. Minuteman ICBM is poised for launching in its protective silo. Most recent versions of this three-stage, solid-fuel missile have a range of 13,000 km (8,000 mi). The Minuteman missiles, along with Trident submarines and B-52 bombers, constitute the U.S. strategic nuclear force. (Below) Surface-to-Air Missiles (SAMs) are important in modern warfare for their ability to intercept supersonic aircract.*

launched ballistic missile (SLBM) in 1954, the same year that the first nuclear submarine, the *Nautilus*, was launched. Since that time the POLARIS, POSEIDON and TRIDENT missiles have been built for submarines. The military significance of the SLBMs lies in their near-invulnerability when the submarines carrying them are submerged (see NUCLEAR STRATEGY).

A system for the use of multiple warheads on a single missile first became operational in 1964. At the end of 1967 the multiple independently targeted reentry vehicle (MIRV) concept was originated, whereby multiple warheads are independently targeted near the end of the bal-

Soviet and U.S. programs to develop modern rockets, both for military and civilian purposes, owe much to the V-2 ballistic missile developed by Germany during World War II. Testing of captured V-2s directed scientists in their early efforts to construct a launch vehicle. The first artificial satellite, Sputnik 1, was launched into orbit on Oct. 4, 1957, by a Soviet A rocket. The United States soon responded, and its second satellite, Vanguard 1, was boosted by a Vanguard rocket, which had a lift-off thrust of 12,250 kg (27,000 lb). Research continued with the Jupiter C, developed to test nose-cone materials for reentry into the Earth's atmosphere. The Juno II, modified from a Jupiter IRBM, served as a satellite booster. The Soviet Union boosted the first manned capsule, bearing Yuri Gagarin, into orbit on Apr. 12, 1961, with an A-1 rocket, a modification of that used in the Sputnik launch. On May 5, 1961, the United States successfully accomplished a nonorbital manned spaceflight, utilizing a Redstone booster to lift Alan Shepard's Mercury capsule. The Delta was used to place Pioneer, Intelsat, TIROS, and Telstar satellites in orbit. The first U.S. manned orbital spacecraft, bearing John Glenn, was launched using an Atlas rocket on Feb. 20, 1962. Using an A-2 booster, the Soviet Union launched Voskhod 1, the first three-man capsule, into orbit on Oct. 12, 1964. The Titan II, a converted ICBM generating 193,500 kg (430,000 lb) of lift-off thrust, boosted the Gemini capsules into orbit. The addition of two solid-fuel tanks gave its successor, the Titan III, a lift-off thrust of 1,000,000 kg (2,400,000 lb). The Soviet Union embarked on its Soyuz manned space program during the late 1960s and early 1970s using an uprated A-2 rocket that can place up to 7,500 kg (16,500 lb) into low Earth orbit.

V-2   Soviet A   Vanguard   Jupiter C   Juno II

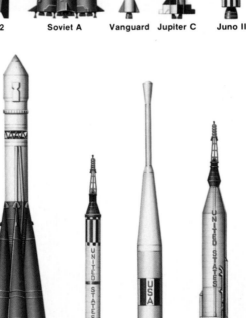

Soviet A-1   Redstone   Delta   Atlas   Soviet A-2   Titan II   Titan III   Soviet A-2 (uprated)

The need to loft larger, heavier payloads led U.S. aerospace engineers to develop the Saturn 1B, which was used for several Apollo missions and Skylab crew launchings. Larger still, the Saturn V, which became operational in 1967, developed 3,442,500 kg (7,650,000 lb) of lift-off thrust. This rocket boosted the Apollo 11 spacecraft on its historic voyage to the Moon. The Soviet Union upgraded the size and power of its rockets in 1965 with the development of the D-1 rocket, which, in various configurations, has been used in the Proton, Zond, Luna, and Salyut programs. The U.S. Space Shuttle, a reusable vehicle that became operational in the early 1980s, reduces the excessive cost of spaceflight. The shuttle is boosted by two reusable solid-fuel rockets attached to a detachable fuel tank.

listic missile flight (see MIRV MISSILE). A further refinement was the installation of a homing system in the MIRV warhead for navigation and target recognition. A maneuvering reentry vehicle (MARV), utilizing radar scanning devices and a computerized guidance system, has been developed to deliver multiple nuclear warheads with pinpoint accuracy.

Tactical missiles are intended for battlefield use rather than against distant targets. They include surface-to-surface missiles, surface-to-air missiles (SAMs), air-to-surface missiles, and air-to-air missiles. Surface-to-surface missiles were first used on a large scale in World War II and were still being developed during the 1960s. SURFACE-TO-AIR MISSILES, used primarily against enemy aircraft and rockets, have been developed since World War II as have air-to-surface rockets such as the American SIDEWINDER.

The CRUISE MISSILE is more accurately classified as an unmanned airplane rather than a rocket, because it is propelled by a jet engine and travels over a flat, nonballistic path.

Saturn IB

Saturn V

Soviet D-1

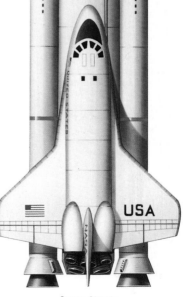

Space Shuttle

Space Rockets

Many of the rockets that opened the space age were straightforward adaptations of ballistic missiles to which upper stages were added to give the higher speeds necessary to achieve Earth orbit or to project payloads on lunar and interplanetary missions. In addition, the National Aeronautics and Space Administration (NASA) developed or contracted for new launch vehicles, including the Delta, SCOUT, and SATURN rockets.

With the growth of space exploration and its commercial applications, a number of countries have developed their own launch capability. The ARIANE, of the EUROPEAN SPACE AGENCY, became a leader in the 1980s in the international competition for launching satellites; other such rockets include France's Diamant and Japan's H-1. (In 1990, Japan launched an unmanned rocket to the Moon.) Private firms such as Space Services, Inc., of the United States and OTRAG of Germany are also developing their own rocket fleets—for example, Space Service's Conestoga booster for small payloads. The concept of employing reusable rockets instead of expendables such

as the above was explored in the early 1980s by the U.S. SPACE SHUTTLE program, with its recoverable solid-propellant boosters and craft. The craft demonstrated its abilities in satellite launch and repair, but even before the 1986 *Challenger* disaster the concept of reusable rockets—as designed thus far—had been found far less economical in fact than that of expendables. Nevertheless, West Germany, France, Great Britain, the Soviet Union, and Japan were all pursuing shuttle-type plans in addition to their other programs.

Principles of Rocket Propulsion

A rocket propulsion system produces a force, known as the thrust, that acts (according to Newton's third law) in the direction exactly opposite to the flow of ejected propellants. According to Newton's second law, this thrust force is equal to the rate of change of momentum of the ejected matter, which depends on both the rate at which the propellants are burned in the engine and the effective exhaust velocity at which the resulting gases are expelled. The effective exhaust velocity for chemical propellants is usually between 1,500 and 4,500 m/sec (4,900 and

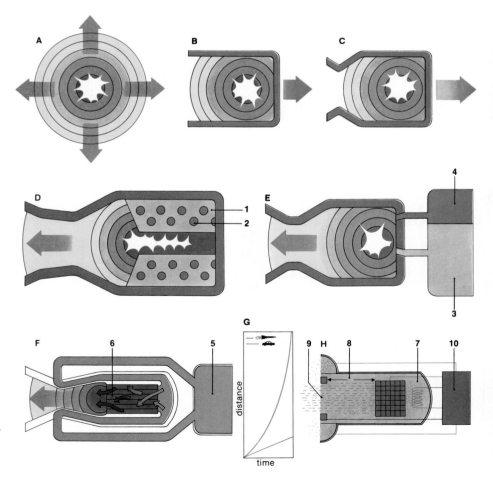

The force of an explosion in an unrestricted space (A) is evenly distributed. Should that explosion occur in a semienclosed chamber (B), its force escapes through the one possible exit, providing an equal and opposite reaction that impels it in the opposite direction. The chamber of a rocket engine (C) is designed to maximize thrust as its fuel undergoes a sustained explosion. In the solid-propellant rocket (D), fuel (1) and oxidant (2) are packed together in the combustion chamber. In the liquid-propellant rocket (E), fuel (3) and oxidant (4) are pumped into the chamber, where they are burned. The nuclear rocket (F) is fueled by liquid hydrogen (5), which is vaporized, rather than burned, in its reactor (6). The outwardly expanding gases thus created provide its propulsive force. Rockets accelerate constantly while their engines are in operation (G). An ion rocket (H), because of its extended period of operation, could therefore possibly approach the speed of light. A propellant such as cesium or mercury, is ionized in a vaporizer (7) and accelerated through an electrostatic field (8)—both powered by a nuclear reactor (10)—before exiting (9), providing the rocket's propulsive force.

14,700 ft/sec). Its value increases with the square root of the combustion temperature (hotter flames are better) and inversely as the square root of the average molecular weight of the exhaust gas (low-molecular-weight elements such as hydrogen are best).

The Saturn space-launch vehicle has a takeoff thrust of about 3.45 million kg (7.6 million lb) and consumes about 12,700 kg (28,600 lb) of propellant per second at an effective exhaust velocity of 2,600 m/sec (8,600 ft/sec) for about 2½ minutes. In contrast, a small attitude-control rocket engine may produce only 0.045 kg (0.1 lb) of thrust with a very small propellant flow for short, pulsed durations of 0.02 to 0.2 seconds.

The impulse, or total impulse, of a rocket is the product of thrust and the effective firing duration. A typical shoulder-launched short-range rocket may have an average thrust of 300 kg (660 lb) for an effective duration of 0.2 seconds, giving a total impulse of 60 kg-sec (132 lb-sec). In contrast, the Saturn rocket has a total impulse of 510 million kg-sec (1,140 million lb-sec).

Specific impulse is the amount of thrust derived from each pound of propellant in one second of engine operation. It is equal to the exhaust velocity (in ft/sec) divided by the acceleration of gravity (32.2 ft/sec^2). Specific impulse is the common measure of propellant and propulsion-system performance, and is somewhat analogous to the reciprocal of the specific fuel consumption used with conventional automobile or aircraft engines. The larger the value of this specific impulse, the better a rocket's performance. Improving specific impulse by using propellants of higher energy means that more thrust will be obtained for each pound of propellant consumed. Specific impulse is often expressed in terms of the number of seconds for which 1 pound mass of propellant will produce a thrust of 1 pound force.

The most important parameter affecting the ultimate maximum flight velocity is a rocket's mass ratio, the relationship between a rocket vehicle and the amount of propellant it can carry. The mass ratio is obtained by dividing the total mass at lift-off by the total mass remaining after the propellants have burned. In general a high mass ratio

means that a maximum amount of propellant is pushing a minimum amount of inert vehicle mass, resulting in a high vehicle velocity. High values of specific impulse (high-energy propellants and low-molecular-weight exhaust gases) and mass ratio are necessary for difficult missions.

Rocket Propulsion Systems

Rocket propulsion systems can be classified according to their energy source (chemical combustion, nuclear, solar), the types of vehicles they are used on (missiles, spacecraft, sounding rockets), the amount of thrust produced, or the type of propellant.

Liquid-Propellant Rockets. A liquid-propellant rocket engine system consists of one or more thrust chambers, one or more vehicle tanks that contain the propellants, a feed mechanism to force the liquids into the thrust chamber, a power source to furnish the energy required by the feed mechanism, suitable valves and piping to transfer the liquids, a structure to transmit the thrust forces, and control devices to start and regulate propellant flow rates.

The thrust chamber, consisting of an injector, a combustion chamber, and a nozzle, is the device where the liquid propellants are metered, injected, atomized, mixed, and burned to form hot, gaseous reaction products, which in turn are accelerated and ejected at a high velocity to impart thrust. The injector is usually an intricate assembly of pipes and accurately oriented injection holes that introduce the propellants into the combustion chamber, atomizing and mixing them in such a way as to create a relatively uniform mixture of fuel and oxidizer in droplets that will readily evaporate and burn in the combustion chamber. The chamber may be cooled by circulating one of the propellants (usually the fuel) through cooling jackets or passages. Heat may also be absorbed by ablative materials, ceramics, or special metals. Alternatively, certain special high-temperature materials, such as molybdenum metal, can be used to radiate away excess heat. The exhaust nozzle allows the hot gas to expand and accelerate to supersonic velocities. A convergent-divergent nozzle with smooth internal contours is commonly used. In some applications the nozzle axis is

CHARACTERISTICS OF ROCKET PROPULSION SYSTEMS

Engine Type	Specific Impulse (sec)	Duration of Operation	Typical Working Fluid	Status of Technology
Chemical: liquid bipropellant	200 to 460	Seconds to minutes	Liquid oxygen and hydrogen	In production
Chemical: liquid monopropellant	150 to 235	Seconds to minutes	Hydrazine	In production
Chemical: solid propellant	180 to 300	Seconds to minutes	Nitroglycerin in nitrocellulose, or powdered metal and oxidizer	In production
Nuclear fission	300 to 1,100	Seconds to minutes	Hydrogen	Development stopped
Electrothermal: arc heating	300 to 2,000	Days	Hydrogen	Development essentially stopped
Electromagnetic: magnetoplasma	300 to 15,000	Weeks	Hydrogen	Several have flown
Electrostatic: ion	1,000 to 25,000	Months	Cesium	Several have flown
Solar heating	300 to 700	Days	Hydrogen	Not yet developed

moved (by hinging or gimballing the thrust chamber, or sometimes the complete engine) so as to steer the vehicle by changing the direction of the thrust vector.

Two principal types of feed systems are used for liquid-propellant rocket engines: those which use pumps for moving the propellants from their tanks to the thrust chamber (this type is usually found in high-thrust booster applications), and those which use high-pressure gas for expelling or displacing the propellants from their tanks (usually used in spacecraft attitude-control and maneuvering applications). Because liquid propellants float in the zero-gravity environment of space, special devices are necessary to ensure that the outlet pipe will always be filled with liquid.

For low-thrust attitude-control applications, rocket engines are usually mounted in pairs at the perimeter of a spacecraft; two thrust chambers pointing in opposite directions are fired simultaneously to give a true turning moment to the vehicle. A minimum of 12 thrust chambers is needed to allow rotational control in each of two directions about three perpendicular axes. For precise angular position control in space, only a small impulse need be applied at one time; position-control rockets typically operate for pulsed durations of from 20 to 100 milliseconds.

Solid-Propellant Rockets. Solid-propellant rocket engines, commonly called rocket motors, come in many different types and sizes. The solid propellant to be burned is contained within the combustion chamber, or case. The propellant charge is called the grain and contains the chemical elements for complete burning. Once ignited, it usually burns smoothly on all of its exposed surfaces.

By changing the design of the internal exposed grain surfaces, it is possible to vary the amount of propellant exposed and thus the amount of propellant that will burn. The burning rate of the solid propellant—usually between 0.3 and 3.3 cm/sec (0.1 and 1.3 in/sec) in a direction perpendicular to the burning surface—depends on the propellant ingredients. The rate increases with chamber pressure (which in turn is determined by the nozzle design and the grain configuration) and the ambient temperature of the propellant grain prior to ignition.

The objective of a good design is to pack as much solid propellant as possible into a given chamber volume. The ideal unit is an end-burning grain, where the grain burns in cigarettelike fashion from one end to the other. This grain type has been used in past jet-assisted takeoff rockets for aircraft. For higher thrust and shorter duration a more complex initial internal surface is chosen, such as a two-dimensional internal star grain (used in air-launched missiles).

Nuclear and Electric Rockets. The nuclear rocket generates its power not by chemical combustion, but by heating a propellant such as hydrogen in a fission reactor and expelling that propellant at a high velocity. In this way, exhaust velocities twice those of the best chemical rockets can be reached. Although extensive efforts have been directed toward nuclear-fission-reactor rocket propulsion, notably the now-abandoned NERVA project in the United States, none of the different concepts and approaches has as yet been selected for a practical propulsion system, and prospects for developing one in the future do not look promising.

Among the ideas for electric propulsion, there exist three basic types: electrothermal, electrostatic, and electromagnetic. In an electrothermal system the propellant is heated or vaporized by electric resistance heaters or electric arcs, and the heated gas is expanded through a nozzle as in a chemical rocket. The electrostatic system achieves acceleration through the interaction of electrostatic fields on charged propellant particles such as ions or small, charged liquid droplets or colloidal particles. Rockets that make use of ions such as cesium or mercury are known as ion rockets. The electromagnetic system achieves acceleration through the interaction of electric and magnetic fields on a propellant plasma, which is a high-temperature, electrically neutral gas that contains electrons, ions, and neutral molecular species.

All types of electric propulsion depend on a relatively large, heavy, high-output, vehicle-borne power source—usually employing solar radiation, chemical, or nuclear energy—and heavy power conversion and conditioning equipment to transform the power into the proper voltage and frequency. The weight of the electrical generating or conversion equipment, even when solar energy is employed, can become excessive, particularly if the efficiency in converting electricity to thrust is low.

Electric propulsion systems can be used for changing the orbits or overcoming perturbations of artificial satellites, for correcting spaceflight trajectories, for space-vehicle attitude control, and for achieving interplanetary transfers or solar-system escape. A small number of electrical propulsion systems have been flown in spacecraft. Electromagnetic thrusters operated successfully for about five years in a communications satellite launched in 1968, producing a total of about 12 million pulses. Electrostatic and electromagnetic propulsion systems give very good performance. They have high values of specific impulse but are limited to a very low thrust (0.45 g to 0.9 kg/0.001 to 2.0 lb) and a very low vehicle acceleration.

Future Trends. Certain types of novel rocket engines are currently being developed. Several of the rocket propulsion units for the space shuttle vehicle have required new technology: the reuse capability and automatic self-check features of the liquid-propellant main engine have not been built into prior rocket engines, and the specific impulse of this engine is slightly better than that of any previous hydrogen-oxygen rocket.

It is unlikely that further major performance improvements can be achieved with conventional chemical propellants. For certain deep-space flight missions, electrical rockets have good potential, but the number of these built will probably be small. Several other advanced and imaginative concepts have been and are being studied, but none has yet shown sufficient promise to warrant intensive development. These concepts include laser beams that interact with propellant in a spacecraft, solar sails, the photon rocket, fusion nuclear rockets, and metastable chemical propellants. While these ideas are speculative and will require major new inventions, they enhance the prospect of high-speed, long-distance space travel.

Rockford [rahk'-furd]   Rockford is a city straddling the Rock River in northern Illinois near the Wisconsin border. The seat of Winnebago County and the state's second largest city, it has a population of 139,426 (1990). It is an important commercial and industrial city and a leading producer of machine tools, fasteners, supplies, and furniture. Much of Rockford's present population is of Swedish descent, and a Scandinavian Midsummer Festival is held annually. Rockford was founded in 1834 and originally named Midway for a stagecoach stop between Chicago and Galena. The earliest settlers were from New England, but in 1852, Swedish immigrants began arriving, establishing a thriving furniture industry.

Rockingham, Charles Watson-Wentworth, 2d Marquess of [rahk'-ing-uhm]   Charles Watson-Wentworth, 2d marquess of Rockingham, b. May 13, 1730, was prime minister of Great Britain from July 1765 to July 1766 and from March 1782 until his death on July 1, 1782. He and his followers in Parliament, dubbed Rockingham Whigs, advocated a conciliatory policy toward the North American colonists. During his first ministry Rockingham secured repeal of the STAMP ACT of 1765 but passed (1766) the only slightly less objectionable Declaratory Act, asserting Parliament's right to legislate for—and tax—the colonies. After George III replaced him with William PITT the Elder, Rockingham spent 16 years as opposition leader. A poor orator, he relied on Edmund BURKE to press the case against the war (1775–83) with the American rebels. During his brief second ministry Rockingham opened peace negotiations with the Americans.

Rockne, Knute [rahk'-nee, noot]   Knute Kenneth Rockne, b. Voss, Norway, Mar. 4, 1888, d. Mar. 31, 1931, was an American college football player and coach at the University of Notre Dame, South Bend, Ind. Although he is remembered primarily as a coach, he made his biggest impact on the sport as a player. In 1913, as a receiver, he and quarterback Gus Dorais made the forward pass an offensive weapon. As a coach (1918–30), Rockne tallied 105 wins, 12 losses, and 5 ties, an 89.7 percent winning average, the best record of any college coach. His inspirational half-time speeches have become part of the Rockne legend. Rockne died in a plane crash shortly after his 43d birthday. He was elected to the College Football Hall of Fame in 1951.

Rockwell, Norman   Norman Rockwell, b. New York City, Feb. 3, 1894, d. Nov. 8, 1978, was America's most famous and popular illustrator. His name became synonymous with his colorful, realistically detailed, and frequently humorous views of Middle America. As Rockwell's reputation grew, his range extended to include the major events and personalities of the period. He did many of his major illustrations for the *Saturday Evening Post*, whose more than 300 covers by Rockwell became its trademark.

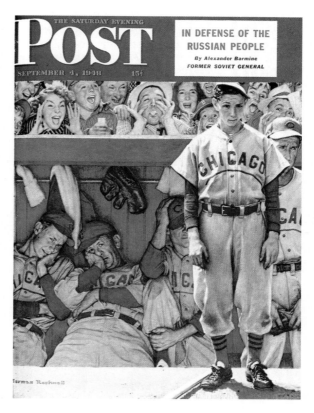

The Dugout, *an oil painting by the American illustrator Norman Rockwell done for the Sept. 4, 1948, cover of the* Saturday Evening Post, *captures the spirit and flavor of American life. (The Brooklyn Museum, New York City.)*

His best-known work was the series the *Four Freedoms*, which were reproduced as posters during World War II. In addition, Rockwell did numerous illustrations for the Boy Scouts of America, including the official Scout calendar (1926–76), and contributed work to such periodicals as *Boys' Life, Life,* and *Look*. Since his death Rockwell's paintings, many of them originals for magazine covers, have become highly prized. His autobiography, *My Adventures as an Illustrator*, was published in 1960.

Rocky Mountain spotted fever   Rocky Mountain spotted fever, or tick fever, is a severe rickettsial infection transmitted to humans by tick bites. It occurs throughout the Rocky Mountain region, the eastern seaboard of the United States from Delaware to Florida, and Central and South America.
      Initial symptoms—headache; high fever; chills; painful bones, joints, and muscles; and growing weakness—appear 2 to 14 days after contact with infected ticks. During the first few days of sickness, a generalized skin rash develops and in severe cases becomes hemorrhagic, reflecting damage to the circulatory system. Central-ner-

vous-system effects, appearing after about a week of fever, range from agitation and insomnia to delirium and coma. The fever usually disappears after about 2 weeks, but full recovery may require several weeks or months in untreated individuals. Individuals treated late in their illness or not at all may suffer brain or heart damage. Treatment with antibiotics is effective if started early.

Rocky Mountains   The Rocky Mountains, the major mountain system of North America, are part of the great cordillera extending through the western regions of both North and South America. They extend for about 4,890 km (3,000 mi) in a north-south orientation from northern Alberta, Canada, to central New Mexico. The width of this region varies from 120 to 645 km (75 to 400 mi). Elevation varies from approximately 1,525 m (5,000 ft) to 4,399 m (14,432 ft) at Mount Elbert, Colo. The Rockies received their name from explorers during the early 19th century because of the mountains' rugged topography.

Topography and Geology. The Rockies are high, rugged, young mountains. The present landscape is the product of regional uplift during the late Cretaceous Period (100 million–65 million years ago) and subsequent etching by weathering and erosion. These mountains may be divided into four provinces: the southern Rockies, Wyoming Basin, middle Rockies, and northern Rockies.

The major mountain groups making up the southern Rockies are the Elk, Front, Gore, Jemez, Laramie, Park, Sangre de Cristo, and Sawatch ranges and the San Juan and Wet mountains. The southern Rockies extend from western New Mexico up through west central Colorado and into southern Wyoming. These ranges are the highest of the Rockies; Mount ELBERT (4,399 m/14,432 ft) in the Sawatch Range of Colorado is the entire system's highest peak.

The Wyoming Basin, with topography similar to that of the GREAT PLAINS, is located mostly in southwestern Wyoming and northwestern Colorado. Mountains are buried beneath the relatively flat terrain, probably representing severe erosion and filling of intermontane basins.

The middle Rockies divide into eastern and western segments. The eastern part includes the Beartooth, Bighorn, Laramie, and Wind River mountains, in western Wyoming. The western part of the middle Rockies includes the TETON, WASATCH, Gros Ventre, Owl Creed, Snake, and Vinta ranges in northern Utah, southwestern Wyoming, and southeastern Idaho.

The northern Rockies are located in Canada (in British Columbia and western Alberta) and in the United States (in northwestern Montana and the northern tip of Idaho). The Canadian part of the northern Rockies, usually called the Canadian Rockies, includes the Cariboo and Selkirk mountains; the Bitterroot, Clearwater, and Salmon River mountains lie mostly south of the border, in the United States.

Glaciation during the Pleistocene Epoch (2.5 million–70,000 years ago) played a major role in producing the present Rocky Mountain landscape. The peaks of all provinces illustrate classic examples of glacial erosion and deposition features. In addition, steep hillslopes, intense thunderstorms accompanied by copious precipitation, and recently exploitive activities of clear-cut lumbering and livestock overgrazing have subjected the geologic structures to intense soil erosion.

Environment. In most of the Rockies five vegetation zones are often recognized. At elevations below 1,645 m (5,400 ft), plains with associated grasses are common. On the foothills (elevations to 2,135 m/7,000 ft), sagebrush, juniper, and piñon grow. Montane vegetation—ponderosa pine, Douglas fir, lodgepole pine, and aspen—prevails up to 2,750 m (9,000 ft). In the subalpine zone (to 3,500 m/11,500 ft), englemann spruce, lodgepole pine, and aspen grow. Above 3,500 m (11,500 ft) alpine flowers and grasses are found. Soils range from desert types to poorly developed, rocky soils at higher elevations and on steep slopes. Fauna includes Rocky Mountain goats; bighorn sheep; black, brown, and grizzly bear; coyotes; lynx; and wolverines.

The CONTINENTAL DIVIDE winds through the Rockies, bifurcating drainage; to the east of the divide rivers flow to the Gulf of Mexico, and the rivers of the western slopes drain toward the Pacific Ocean. The Colorado, Columbia, Green, Salmon, San Juan, and Snake rivers flow west-

Rugged Ypsilon Mountain (center) reaches 4,116 m (13,504 ft) in the Mummy Range, a spur of the Front Range of the Rockies. These lofty peaks are located in the northeastern corner of Rocky Mountain National Park, in Colorado.

ward; the Arkansas, Missouri, North and South Platte, and Yellowstone rivers flow eastward. Runoff and meltwater from the snow-covered peaks supplying these rivers and lakes provide the water supply for one-quarter of the United States.

Economic and Cultural Geography. Economic development centers on mining, forestry, agriculture, recreation, and the service industries that support the other economic activity. A wide variety of metallic minerals is found in the Rockies, including significant deposits of copper, gold, lead, molybdenum, silver, tungsten, and zinc. The Wyoming basin and several smaller areas contain significant reserves of coal, natural gas, oil shale, and petroleum. Forestry is a major industry in the Rocky Mountain region. Agriculture includes dry-land and irrigated farming, plus livestock grazing. The scenic splendor and recreational opportunities draw hundreds of thousands of tourists to the Rockies annually. National parks, forests, resorts, and vacation ranches attract an international clientele. The Rockies are sparsely populated; probably less than a million permanent residents live there.

rococo music [roh-koh'-koh]   The musical manifestations of the rococo style (early and mid-18th century) developed most conspicuously in France and Germany but differed markedly according to the artistic predilections of those two countries.

The *style galant* (gallant style) was the French musical reaction to the formality and complex counterpoint of the baroque era; it emphasized highly ornamented melody in short, regular phrases supported by simple harmonies. It appeared typically in the smaller forms, emphasizing charm and grace rather than serious expression. The leading composers were François Couperin (see COUPERIN family) and Jean Philippe RAMEAU.

The *empfindsamer Stil* (sensitive style) was the German reaction to the baroque style. Instead of the lavish ornament of the *style galant*, the Germans cultivated shifting moods in which every phrase was laden with expressive feeling. Works by C. P. E. BACH, Johann Stamitz (see STAMITZ family), J. J. Quantz (1697–1773), and Christian Cannabich (1731–98) are typical.

rococo style   The term *rococo style,* or *the rococo,* refers to a style of decoration current in Europe, particularly France, during the 18th century. It applies both to interior decoration and to ornaments. By extension it may also be applied to some sculpture, paintings, furniture, and architectural details. Rococo is derived from the French word *rocaille,* originally meaning the bits of rocky decoration sometimes found in 16th-century architectural schemes. It was first used in its modern sense around 1800, at about the same time as baroque, and, like baroque, was initially a pejorative term (see BAROQUE ART AND ARCHITECTURE).

The earliest rococo forms appeared around 1700 at Versailles (see VERSAILLES, PALACE OF) and its surrounding *châteaux* as a reaction against the oppressive formality of

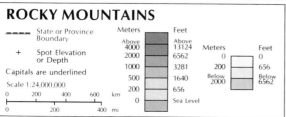

ROCKY MOUNTAINS

- - - -   State or Province
        Boundary

+   Spot Elevation
    or Depth

Capitals are underlined

Scale 1:24,000,000

| 0 | 200 | 400 | 600 | km |
| 0 | | 200 | | 400 | mi |

Meters		Feet	
Above 4000		Above 13124	
2000		6562	
1000		3281	
500		1640	
200		656	
0		Sea Level	

Meters	Feet
0	0
200	656
Below 2000	Below 6562

(Right) *Jean Honoré Fragonard's* The Swing *(c.1767) epitomizes the frivolous and erotic "gallant scenes" at which he excelled. Influenced by the luxurious work of Boucher, Fragonard descended to sentimentality in his later works in this genre. (Wallace Collection, London.)*

(Above) *The Abbey Church of Ottobeuren (1748–67), completed by Johann Michael Fischer, typifies south German church rococo. This style, retaining some elements of baroque, features a profusion of polychromatic decorative elements.* (Right) *The Amalienburg (1734–40), a hunting lodge in the park of Nymphenburg Palace, was designed by François Cuvilliés, one of the earliest and most inventive exponents of French rococo in Bavaria.*

Regency (1715–23) and the long reign of Louis XV (1723–74) may be seen in such Parisian interiors as the *Galerie dorée* at the Hôtel de Toulouse (1718–19), the Hôtel de Lassay (late 1720s), and the Hôtel de Soubise (1736–39).

The essence of rococo interior decoration is twofold; first, the forms are almost flat instead of being, as in baroque schemes, in high relief; second, architectural and sculptural features are eliminated so that the designer is confronted with a smooth surface. In a typical rococo decorative scheme, series of tall wooden panels (including the doors), decorated with brilliantly inventive carved and gilded motifs in low relief, are arranged around the room. After 1720 the panels were usually painted ivory white. Decorative objects abound, such as wall brackets, candlesticks, and table ornaments, the master designer of which was Juste Aurèle MEISSONNIER. The overall effect is glittering and lively, a fitting background to 18th-century aristocratic social life.

In rococo painting, the powerful rhythms, dark colors, and heroic subjects characteristic of baroque painting gave way to quick, delicate movements, pale colors, and subjects illustrating the varieties of love: romantic love, as in Antoine WATTEAU's *Pilgrimage to Cythera* (1717; Louvre, Paris); erotic love, as in François BOUCHER's *Cupid a Captive* (1754; Wallace Collection, London); or mother love, as in Jean Baptiste CHARDIN's *The Morning Toilet* (c.1740; Nationalmuseum, Stockholm). Sculpture was equally lively and unheroic, but its most typical manifestation was portrait busts, the outstanding quality of which was realism, as is evident in Jean Baptiste LEMOYNE's *Réaumur* (1751; Louvre).

During the second quarter of the century the rococo style spread from France to other countries, and above all to Germany, where it took a more fanciful and wayward turn, with greater emphasis on forms derived from nature.

French classical-baroque in those buildings. In 1701 a suite of rooms at Versailles, including the king's bedroom, was redecorated in a new, lighter, and more graceful style by the royal designer, Pierre Lepautre (1648–1716). Versailles remained the creative center of the rococo until Louis XIV's death, in 1715, after which the initiative passed to Paris. Successive waves of the style during the

The supreme example of German rococo style is François CUVILLIÉS's Hall of Mirrors in his Amalienburg Pavilion (1734–40), a hunting lodge in the park of NYMPHENBURG PALACE, near Munich. Germany also produced an indigenous form of rococo, a style evolved out of, rather than in reaction against, the baroque. Its most beautiful manifestation is the interior of the pilgrimage church of Die Wies (1745–54) in southern Bavaria.

Germany's other great contribution to the rococo style was the rediscovery (1709–10) of the Chinese art of porcelain manufacture (see POTTERY AND PORCELAIN) at Meissen, near Dresden. Meissen ware achieved enormous popularity. Small porcelain figures such as those made by Franz Anton Bustelli (1723–63) at Nymphenburg are perhaps the quintessence of the rococo, fusing all its qualities into a single miniature art.

The rococo style began to decline in the 1760s, denounced by critics who condemned it as tasteless, frivolous, and symbolic of a corrupt society. Within 20 years it was supplanted, together with the baroque, by NEOCLASSICISM.

Rodchenko, Aleksandr Mikhailovich [rawt'-chink-uh] Alexander Mikhailovich Rodchenko, b. Nov. 23 (N.S.), 1891, d. Sept. 3, 1956, was the founder of Russian nonobjectivism, a style related to suprematism but less pure in color and texture. He began his career under the influence of Kasimir Malevich. At an exhibition in 1919, Rodchenko showed *Black on Black* (1918; Tretyakov Gallery, Moscow), painted in reaction to Malevich's *White on White* (1918; Museum of Modern Art, New York City). In 1919, with the constructivist Vladimir Tatlin, Rodchenko made three-dimensional constructions in wood, metal, and cardboard. Soon after, he turned to more practical arts to serve the USSR.

rodent Rodents are mammals of the order Rodentia and are characterized by an upper and lower pair of front teeth (incisors) specialized for gnawing. Most rodents are small, enabling them to occupy habitats that could not support larger mammals. Rodents are found in nearly every terrestrial habitat. Some, such as the house mouse, genus *Mus,* and house rat, *Rattus,* have been accidentally transported by humans to all parts of the world; others, such as the muskrat, *Ondatra,* and nutria, *Myocastor,* have been deliberately released in new areas to provide a source of fur.

Rodents are of considerable value to humans. Some, such as the muskrat, nutria, and beaver, *Castor,* are important fur animals; others, such as the squirrels, *Sciurus,* of North America, the hutias, *Capromys,* of Cuba, and the pacas, *Cuniculus,* of Central and South America, are used as human food. Rodents are also beneficial in destroying large quantities of insects and weeds, and many of the significant achievements in biological research were made possible only through the use of laboratory rats and mice. Several rodents, including the golden hamster, *Mesocricetus,* and the guinea pig, *Cavia,*

make fine pets. Rodents are herbivorous or omnivorous, omnivorous rodents adding insects and other small organisms to their plant diet. Because of their usually large numbers and the consequent effects of these numbers on food sources, as well as because they are all preyed upon by other animals, rodents are a vital element in the ecology of most regions.

Rodents also have detrimental aspects, one of the most critical being the transmission of disease. Rat-borne plague, for example, has caused innumerable human deaths (and the deaths of the rats as well) throughout the centuries and has inexorably affected human history. Rodents also cause serious economic damage by feeding on crops and stored foods.

Characteristics. The number of rodent species is estimated at between 1,700 and 5,000; the more modern classifications tend toward the lower number. These species are grouped into roughly 100 to more than 350 genera and into 34 or 35 families, including 8 extinct families. Rodents range in size from the North and Central American pygmy mice, *Baiomys,* which range from 50 to 80 mm (2 to 3 in) long, plus a 35- to 55-mm (1.4- to 2.2-in) tail, and weigh about 7 g (¼ oz); to the Central and South American capybara, *Hydrochoerus,* which may reach 1.3 m (4 ft) long, plus a very short tail, 53 cm (21 in) high at the shoulder, and more than 50 kg (110 lb) in weight. The extinct North American beaver, *Castoroides,* which lived during the Pleistocene Epoch, about a million years ago, was 2.3 m (7.5 ft) long, including the tail, and about the height of a small bear. Most rodents are the familiar mouse or squirrel types, but some, such as the Eurasian mole rats, *Spalax,* resemble moles, and the South American maras, *Dolichotis,* suggest nonhopping rabbits. Most rodents are fully haired, except possibly for the tail, with some, such as the chinchilla, *Chinchilla,* having especially thick coats, whereas the East African naked mole rat, *Heterocephalus,* is practically hairless. Some rodents, such as the beaver, have webbed hind feet or are otherwise modified for swimming; the North and Central American flying squirrels, *Glaucomys,* have a flap of skin along each side of the body between the front and hind legs and use these flaps for gliding through the air.

Internally, all rodents are similar. The upper and lower jaws each have a pair of ever-growing incisor teeth. The front face of each incisor consists of hard enamel, but the rest of the tooth is of softer dentin; this results in differential wear, always leaving a sharp cutting edge on the tooth. There are no other incisors or a canine tooth, and the first and (in the lower jaw) the second premolars are also lacking, leaving a gap between the incisors and the cheek teeth. The cheek teeth (premolars and molars) may be short (low-crowned) and rooted, or tall (high-crowned) and ever growing. The front teeth and the cheek teeth are offset in relation to each other, so that when the upper and lower incisors are together in gnawing, the cheek teeth do not meet and wear uselessly, and vice versa. The skull depression (glenoid fossa) at the rear of the skull that acts as a socket for the rearward-projecting hinge (articular condyle) of the lower jaw is shallow and elon-

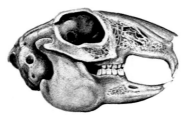

Jaws of rodents have continuously growing chisellike incisors, adapted for gnawing, in the front and cheek teeth on each side for grinding vegetation.

gated from front to rear, permitting the lower jaw to move back and forth as well as from side to side.

In rodents the masseter muscle—which runs from the skull to the lower jaw and in many mammals serves in the closing of the jaws—is principally involved in moving the lower jaw back and forth and from side to side. The masseter muscle on each side of the head is divided into three parts; the outermost part is essentially similar in all rodents, but the remaining two parts, referred to as outer and inner (or deeper), vary in their attachments on the lower jaw and skull.

Reproduction. Rodents are generally nocturnal and are usually social animals; some, however, are solitary. Breeding cycles vary considerably. Females have a duplex type of uterus, in which the two uteri remain separated but are joined to a single vagina. Males commonly have a penis bone (os penis, or baculum). Gestation varies from about 16 days in the golden hamster to 4½ months in the capybara. Litter size varies from 1 to more than 18. Usually only the female raises the young, but in the pygmy mice, for example, the male parent also contributes to their care. Reproductive age may be attained at 60 days or earlier, as in the Eurasian steppe lemming, *Lagurus,* and reproductive life may continue into old age, but most rodents are short-lived, rarely surviving naturally beyond 2 to 3 years. Old World porcupines, *Hystrix* and *Acanthion,* however, may live more than 20 years.

Evolution. The earliest-known rodent, *Paramys,* lived in North America from the late Paleocene Epoch to the middle Eocene, about 56 million to 45 million years ago. It was unquestionably a rodent and not a transitional form, and no definite information exists as to its origins. It is believed, however, that the rodents evolved from early insectivores, as did the primates, and that the ancestors of the rodents and of the primates were themselves closely related.

rodeo A rodeo is a festival consisting of a set of competitive sports based on the traditional working skills of cowhands—riding and roping cattle and horses. *Rodeo* is a Spanish word that denotes a gathering place of cattle— literally, a roundup. Most major rodeos are held under the auspices of the Professional Rodeo Cowboys Association (PRCA), founded in 1945. Among the most important are the Frontier Days Celebration in Cheyenne, Wyo., the Roundup in Pendleton, Oreg., the California Rodeo in Salinas, Calif., the Stampede in Calgary, Alberta, Canada, and the National Finals Rodeo in Las Vegas, Nev.

The first rodeo with an admission charge for spectators was held in Prescott, Ariz., in 1888. Then, as now, the rodeo consisted of five standard events—bareback bronc-riding, saddle bronc-riding, bull-riding, calf-roping, and steer-wrestling, sometimes called bull-dogging.

In bareback bronc-riding, an untamed horse, called a bronco, tries to buck the rider off its back. Using only one hand, the rider tries to hold on to a special rigging for a specified time period of 8 to 10 seconds. If the rider falls, or if his or her free hand touches any part of his or her own body or that of the horse, the rider is disqualified. Saddle bronc-riding is similar to bareback riding, except that a special lightweight saddle is used and the rider holds on to a single piece of rope. Again, the free hand must not be used. Bull-riding, because of the ferocity of the Brahma bull, is the most dangerous event in the rodeo. The rider holds on to a bull-rope that circles the trunk of the bull and, using just one hand, must stay on for a 10-second period. In all three events the spirit and strength of the animals are factors in the judging.

Calf-roping and steer-wrestling are events in which the contestant tries to accomplish a set of maneuvers in the shortest possible time. In calf-roping, a calf is released into the arena through a chute and the cowhand, mounted on horseback, pursues. The rider must throw the lariat, or rope, over the calf's neck, dismount, throw the calf to the ground, and tie its feet while the horse keeps the rope taut. In steer-wrestling, a steer is released from the chute, and the mounted cowhand rides alongside it and then leaps from the saddle, grabbing the steer by the horns in midflight. By digging in with the heels, the cowhand first must halt the steer and then flip it over onto its back as quickly as possible.

A somewhat new event is team roping, in which two cowhands working together rope a steer.

A contestant attempts to keep his seat for a full 10 seconds during the bull-riding competition of the Calgary Exhibition and Stampede, the oldest and one of the most celebrated rodeos of the Canadian west.

Rodgers (family) The Rodgers were a family of distinguished American naval officers. **John Rodgers**, b. near Havre de Grace, Md., 1773, d. Aug. 1, 1838, helped capture the French frigate *Insurgente* in 1799 and was promoted to captain that year. In 1805, Rodgers imposed a peace treaty on Tripoli, ending the TRIPOLITAN WAR. As commanding officer of the frigate *President*, he engaged the British warship *Little Belt* on May 16, 1811, an act contributing to the onset of the War of 1812. After peace was restored he served until 1837 as president of the Board of Navy Commissioners (the ranking commissioned post in the navy), except for the years 1824–27, when he was commander of the Mediterranean squadron.

His son, **John Rodgers**, b. near Havre de Grace, Md., Aug. 8, 1812, d. May 5, 1882, served in the navy during the U.S. Civil War and led the punitive Rodgers-Low expedition to Korea in 1871. He headed the first Naval Advisory Board, which in 1881 laid the foundations for creation of a revamped navy of steam-driven, steel-hulled warships. Numerous other military officers bore the Rodgers surname.

Rodgers, Richard   Richard Rodgers, b. Hammels Station, N.Y., June 28, 1902, d. Dec. 30, 1979, was the American musical theater's most successful and influential composer. His work with the lyricist Lorenz HART between 1925 and 1942 produced a series of innovative works, including *A Connecticut Yankee* (1927), *On Your Toes* (1936), and *Pal Joey* (1940). After Hart's death, Rodgers began an equally successful collaboration with Oscar HAMMERSTEIN II, a 16-year partnership that began with *Oklahoma!* in 1943. The Rodgers-Hart shows were unique amalgams of story and music. The Rodgers-Hammerstein collaboration in effect created a new form, the American music-drama, and produced such notable works as *Carousel* (1945), *South Pacific* (1948), and *The King and I* (1951). After Hammerstein's death in 1960, Rodgers wrote his own lyrics for the musical *No Strings* (1962) and worked with the lyricist Stephen SONDHEIM on *Do I Hear a Waltz?* (1965).

Rodin, Auguste [roh-dan']   One of the greatest and most prolific sculptors of the 19th century, Auguste Rodin, b. Nov. 12, 1840, d. Nov. 17, 1917, succeeded, often contentiously, in bringing new life and direction to a dying art. Today major collections of his work on permanent display are at the Musée Rodin (Hôtel Biron, Paris), the Rodin Museum (Philadelphia), and the California Palace of the Legion of Honor (San Francisco).

In 1875–76, Rodin completed his first masterwork, a young male nude (later called *The Age of Bronze*). This sculpture led to the first of numerous public controversies that were to beset Rodin throughout his career. Accustomed to the highly artificial appearance of most 19th-century academic sculpture, the critics of the day refused to believe that Rodin was able to model a figure so realistically without using plaster casts of a live model. In 1880 he received a commission from the French government for *The Gates of Hell*, a work that preoccupied him for the rest of his life. His starting point was Dante's *Inferno*, but the images of torment and despair depicted on the *Gates* rapidly became more generalized.

The Age of Bronze (1875–76), an unidealized study of a male figure, displays Rodin's characteristic interest in the accurate portrayal of anatomical detail. Rodin, who rejected the academic standards of his time in favor of a more direct approach to nature, often scandalized his contemporaries. (Musée du Luxembourg, Paris.)

During the 1880s, Rodin became one of the most successful French artists. He received many commissions for public monuments, including *The Burghers of Calais* (1884–95), the *Monument to Victor Hugo* (1889–1909), and the *Monument to Balzac* (1891–98). Although Rodin regarded this last work—a dramatic portrayal of Balzac's spirit—to be one of his greatest, the society that commissioned it rejected the piece as an unfinished and grotesque botch. This led to one of the most bitter public debates in the history of 19th-century art.

Rodin was not only a sculptor of public monuments but a tireless artist who produced numerous small and intimate sculptures. These works range from highly developed pieces such as *Eternal Spring* (1884) and *The Kiss* (1886; first marble version, Musée Rodin), two of his most popular studies of youthful passion, to fragmentary studies of limbs and heads. He was also much in demand as a portrait sculptor and produced memorable images of many of the most famous men and women of his time, ranging from Victor Hugo (1883) to George Bernard Shaw (1906) and Pope Benedict XV (1915), and of many society figures on both sides of the Atlantic.

After 1900, Rodin worked mostly on a smaller scale, for example, on studies of ballet dancers (c.1910–12) and on drawings. The outbreak of World War I in 1914 brought him considerable hardship; his health and mental stability gave way rapidly before his death in 1917.

Roe v. Wade and Doe v. Bolton   The cases of *Roe* v. *Wade* and *Doe* v. *Bolton* (1973) were companion cases in which the U.S. Supreme Court held, with some qualification, that state laws prohibiting abortions were unconstitutional. *Roe* involved a Texas statute making it a felony for anyone to destroy a fetus except on "medical advice for the purpose of saving the mother's life." *Doe* dealt with a Georgia statute allowing an abortion when the woman's life was endangered, when the child would be born with a severe defect, or when pregnancy had resulted from rape.

Invalidating both statutes in 7–2 rulings, the Court, speaking through Justice Harry Blackmun, held that the constitutional right of privacy—whether based on the 14TH AMENDMENT's concept of personal liberty or on the 9th Amendment's reservation of rights to the people— "includes the right of a woman to decide whether or not to terminate her pregnancy." Blackmun went on to say that the right to an abortion is not unqualified and must be balanced against the state's interest in regulation. After the first trimester of pregnancy the states might regulate or even prohibit abortions subject to appropriate medical judgment. The decision aroused nationwide controversy, and a movement arose to overrule the Court through constitutional amendment. Recent rulings, especially *Webster* v. *Reproductive Services* (1989), have given greater latitude to states in regulating abortions.

Roehm, Ernst [rurm]   The German army officer Ernst Roehm (or Röhm), b. Nov. 28, 1887, d. June 30, 1934, was the leader of the Nazi storm troops (SA, or *Sturmabteilung*). Roehm was wounded in World War I and afterward helped set up the National Socialist (Nazi) party. The SA (also called the Brownshirts) was formed from his private army in 1921. After coming into conflict with Nazi leader Adolf Hitler over the role of the SA, Roehm went to Bolivia, where he remained from 1925 to 1930, returning to reorganize the SA. When Hitler took power in 1933, Roehm became a minister in Germany. Fearing him as a rival, Hitler had him shot in the 1934 blood purge.

Roentgen, Wilhelm Conrad [ruhnt'-gen]   The German physicist Wilhelm Conrad Roentgen, b. Mar. 27, 1845, d. Feb. 10, 1923, discovered X rays, for which he received (1901) the first Nobel Prize for physics. He observed (1895) that barium platinocyanide crystals across the room fluoresced whenever he turned on a Crooke's, or cathode-ray discharge, tube, even when the tube, an electron emitter, was shielded by black cardboard or thin metal sheets. Roentgen correctly hypothesized that a previously unknown form of radiation of very short wavelength was involved, and that these *X rays* (a term he coined) caused the crystals to glow. He later demonstrated the metallurgical and medical use of X rays.

Roethke, Theodore [ret'-ke]   One of the most distinguished poets in the United States in the mid-20th century, Theodore Roethke, b. Saginaw, Mich., May 25, 1908, d. Aug. 1, 1963, won the 1954 Pulitzer Prize for poetry with *The Waking* (1953) and both the National Book Award and the Bollingen Prize for the collection *Words for the Wind* (1957).

In *The Lost Son and Other Poems* (1948), Roethke opened up a poetic language and territory that dazzled his peers. Using an associative linking of images rather than a logical exposition of balanced argument, he created a series of poem-sequences that explored his own subconscious. Although poets had used Sigmund Freud and Carl Jung as sources for imagery and metaphor for some time, Roethke was the first American to translate the psychology of the subconscious into poetic expression.

In *Words for the Wind* Roethke extended poetry beyond the range of such modern masters as Ezra POUND and T. S. ELIOT. Roethke was always troubled by the problem of influence, and he dreaded sounding like an echo of some earlier, more forceful poet. When a posthumous volume, *The Far Field* (1964), appeared, some critics felt that it contained too many echoes of Walt Whitman, William Butler Yeats, and others. Subsequent critical judgment has, however, affirmed how singular Roethke's achievement was, and his own influence has continued to be felt among younger poets.

His notebooks, published as *Straw for the Fire* (1972), are filled with evidence of a thoroughly poetic mind, constantly at work on its own insights and constantly recognizing the wonder of the natural world.

Roger II, King of Sicily   Roger II, b. Dec. 22, 1095, d. Feb. 26, 1154, founder of the kingdom of Sicily, built on the strong political foundation laid by his father, Roger I (1031–1101), count of Sicily, and gained control of Calabria and Apulia, Norman possessions on the mainland. In return for Roger's support, the antipope Anacletus II crowned him king of Sicily in 1130. Pope Innocent II was forced to recognize Roger's sovereignty after Roger defeated Innocent's army in 1139. Roger widened his kingdom by raiding Byzantine states and conquering the North African coastal areas from Tunis to Tripoli. He ruled wisely and prosperously, establishing a centralized administrative structure. His civil-service system was admired throughout Europe, and his court was an important center for cultural interchange with the East.

Rogers, Carl   Carl Ransom Rogers, b. Oak Park, Ill., Jan. 8, 1902, d. Feb. 4, 1987, founded client-centered psychotherapy (earlier called nondirective psychotherapy) and was a pioneer in the development of scientific methods for studying psychotherapeutic outcomes and processes. Rogers's client-centered therapy is among the most influential and widely employed techniques in modern U.S. clinical psychology.

Rogers became director of the Counseling Center at the University of Chicago in 1945, and in 1957 he moved to the University of Wisconsin, where he studied client-centered therapy with schizophrenic patients. From 1963 until his death he was a resident fellow at the Center for Studies of the Person in La Jolla, Calif., of which he was a cofounder.

Learning to be a psychotherapist is the central theme in Rogers's theory—that is, the psychotherapist's learning how he or she can create a relationship that the client may use for his or her own personal growth. Rogers regards it as an empirical fact, buttressed by research, that if this relationship can be created, the person can use it. The characteristics of a helping relationship are that the therapist is (1) genuine, not maintaining a facade or acting a role, (2) accepting of both his or her own experience and that of the client, and (3) empathetic and understanding. Provided with the emotional climate of client-centered therapy, the troubled person is likely to trust his or her experience, to find new meaning within it, to base choices on more complete evidence, and to find life more lively and satisfying.

Rogers was a leader in the scientific study of psychotherapy, transcribing his therapy protocols for study, using William Stephenson's Q-sort method for studying self and ideal concepts before and after therapy, and utilizing both direct observation and psychological tests to measure psychotherapeutic growth.

See also: HUMANISTIC PSYCHOLOGY.

Rogers, Ginger   Singer, actress, and dancer Ginger Rogers, b. Virginia McMath, in Independence, Mo., July 16, 1911, is best known for the movie musicals she made with Fred ASTAIRE. After playing vaudeville as a teenager, she made her debut on Broadway in 1929 and entered feature films in 1930.

The famous Rogers and Astaire dance team first starred in *Flying Down to Rio* (1933) and developed their now classic routines in *The Gay Divorcée* (1934), *Top Hat* (1935), and *Swing Time* (1936). Rogers, who also appeared in dramatic roles, won an Academy Award for *Kitty Foyle* (1940). She made numerous films during the next two decades and returned to the musical comedy stage in *Hello, Dolly* (1965) and *Mame* (1969).

Rogers, John   John Rogers, b. *c.*1500, d. Feb. 4, 1555, was an English Protestant reformer, the editor of Matthew's Bible, who was martyred under Queen Mary I. Educated at Cambridge, he became (1534) chaplain to English merchants in Antwerp, where he met William TYNDALE and converted to Protestantism. After Tyndale's death (1536), Rogers used the translations prepared by Tyndale with those of Miles COVERDALE to produce the first complete English Bible, published (1537) under the pseudonym Thomas Matthew.

Rogers returned to London in 1548. After Mary's succession to the throne he was imprisoned, sentenced to death, and burned at Smithfield.

Rogers, Robert   Robert Rogers, b. Methuen, Mass., Nov. 7, 1731, d. May 8, 1795, achieved fame in the French and Indian War of 1754–63 as a commander of colonial rangers. Rogers grew up in New Hampshire, joined the army in 1755, and by 1758 was in charge of ranger companies for the British army. The next year his troops burned the village of the Saint Francis Indians, killing about 200 people.

After the French and Indian War, Rogers went to London, where he became known as a writer, publishing his journals (1765) and a play (1766). He returned to America to serve (1766–67) as commander at Mackinac. After accusations of corruption, however, his career became engulfed in scandal. In the American Revolution he fought briefly—and ineffectively—for the British.

Rogers, Will   Will Rogers, b. Oologah, Indian Territory (now Claremore, Okla.), Nov. 4, 1879, d. Aug. 15, 1935, was an American humorist and actor famous for his witty, homespun commentaries on contemporary events. He began his career as an entertainer in rodeos and Wild West shows, and by 1915 he had developed the stage persona of a rough, straight-talking cowboy who debunked pretension and fashionable attitudes. He began to write a syndicated newspaper column in 1922 and made a series of films after 1929.

Rogers, William P.   The American lawyer and government official William Pierce Rogers, b. Norfolk, N.Y., June 23, 1913, served (1969–73) as President Richard Nixon's secretary of state. He received (1937) his law degree from Cornell University and served in the navy in World War II. He was (1953–57) deputy attorney general of the United States and attorney general (1957–61). As attorney general he was a strong advocate of civil rights. As secretary of state he was overshadowed by Henry Kissinger, who succeeded him.

Roget's Thesaurus   SEE THESAURUS

Roh Tae Woo [roh tay woo]   On Feb. 25, 1988, Roh Tae Woo, b. Dec. 4, 1932, became president of South Korea in the country's first peaceful transfer of power. A retired (1981) army general, Roh participated in the 1979 coup that brought his friend CHUN DOO HWAN to power and held several cabinet posts in Chun's government. After he unexpectedly backed opposition demands for democratic reforms, Roh won the December 1987 presidential election with less than 37% of the vote over a fragmented opposition. In 1988 his ruling Democratic Justice party lost its parliamentary majority for the first time.

Rohlfs, Christian [rohlfs]   The German painter and graphic artist Christian Rohlfs, b. Dec. 22, 1848, d. Jan. 8, 1938, produced an enormous body of works—more than 400 were destroyed by the Nazis—ranging in style from impressionist to muted expressionist. Criticism of his avant-garde work forced Rohlfs to leave (*c.*1900) the Weimar Art School after a 30-year career to teach at the Folkwang School at Hagen, where his friendship with the expressionist painter Emil Nolde completely changed his style; he abandoned oil painting for tempera, watercolor, and woodcuts. Rohlfs spent his last decade (1927–38) in Switzerland, producing the exquisite flower paintings for which he is best known.

Röhm, Ernst   see ROEHM, ERNST

Rolamite
[rohl'-uh-myt]   The first elemental mechanism to be discovered in a century, the Rolamite is a simple, flexible suspension system for rollers that is used in a variety of mechanical and electromechanical devices. It was developed in 1966 by Donald Wilkes as a result of his search for a reliable miniature mechanical switch. The switch that Wilkes designed was one-eighth the size of the previous switch and had about half the number of parts.

In its simplest form the Rolamite consists of a rectangular frame, two rollers, and a flexible band. The rollers are suspended within the S-shaped loops of the metallic band. When the band is tightened the rollers are in pure rolling contact with the band and there is no slippage. This configuration allows the rollers to roll within the guide rails with as low as $\frac{1}{10}$ the friction of the best ball and roller bearings in a similar application. In this rudimentary form the Rolamite functions as a near-frictionless suspension system for the rollers.

By using bands with varying widths or cutouts, the rollers can be made to seek preferred positions between the guide rails. This effect is caused by the tendency of each band loop to straighten itself out; as long as the band width is constant, the straightening forces are equal and the rollers move freely. If the band widths on the rollers are different, the roller with the wider band will dominate, the band will try to unwind, and a driving force proportional to the difference in band widths will be created. By varying the shapes of the cutouts and the diameters of the rollers, Rolamites with a variety of springlike traits can be obtained.

Roland
The hero of the medieval French epic the *Chanson de Roland* (c.1100; see CHANSONS DE GESTE), Roland is left by his uncle Charlemagne in command of the rear guard at Roncesvalles, where he comes under Saracen attack. Asked by his friend Oliver to blow the horn that will summon aid, Roland, out of chivalric pride, refuses the request until too late, and he and Oliver are killed in the ensuing battle.

Roland de la Platière, Jeanne Manon Phlipon
[roh-lahn' duh lah plah-tee-air']   Jeanne Manon Phlipon Roland de la Platière, known as Madame Roland, b. Paris, Mar. 17, 1754, d. Nov. 8, 1793, is usually regarded as the animating spirit of the GIRONDIST faction in the FRENCH REVOLUTION. In 1792, Jean Marie Roland de Platière (b. 1734), the conscientious public servant whom she had married in 1780, became minister of the interior. Madame Roland was held responsible for the anti-Parisian policy pursued by her husband and her friends af-

ter the September Massacres. Although Roland resigned in January 1793, Madame Roland was arrested at the end of May. Going to the guillotine, she spoke the immortal words: "Liberty, what crimes are committed in thy name!" On learning of her death, Roland killed himself.

---

role
Role is a term drawn from the language of theater to describe the set of expectations associated with a person's position in a social organization. All social organizations are characterized by differentiation of function. A status is a particular location within such a structure. For every status there is an associated role—a set of expectations about behavior.

The language of role theory lends itself well to the discussion of a variety of forms of social conflict. For example, the traditional status of women in Western society has for hundreds of years included role expectations about performances of home maintenance, food preparation, and child-rearing, but no major professional or leadership functions. Consequently, when women achieve advancement in social structures outside the home, role conflict is created. This conflict in turn creates pressure for the redefinition of traditional role expectations associated with sex.

In modern role theory, occupancy of any status is seen to be partly ascribed and partly attained, with the contribution of these two factors varying from role to role. The way any individual is evaluated socially is a complex result of the number and character of validated social roles and the degree of involvement with those roles.

The most important role-theory pioneer in the social sciences was George Herbert MEAD. J. L. Moreno, Robert MERTON, and Theodore R. Sarbin have each provided major application of role theory.

See also: CLASS, SOCIAL; NORM, SOCIAL; SOCIAL STRUCTURE AND ORGANIZATION; STATUS.

Rolfe, John
[rawlf]   John Rolfe, b. 1585, was one of the first English settlers in Virginia. He went to the colony of JAMESTOWN about 1610 and is credited with developing the strain of tobacco that became Virginia's staple crop. In 1614 he married the Indian princess POCAHONTAS, whom he later took to England. After her death (1617), Rolfe returned to America, where he was killed in a war with the POWHATAN Indians in 1622.

---

roller derby
Roller derby is the competitive and sometimes violent sport of high-speed roller skating on banked indoor tracks. Matches are between two teams that consist of 5 men and 5 women. The men skate against the opposing men and the women against the opposing women in alternating 12-minute heats. Each squad has 2 blockers, 2 jammers, and 1 pivotman. Jammers attempt to skate one full lap ahead of the pack and then overtake and pass the opposing players; one point is scored for each opponent passed. Roller derby grew out of dance roller-skating marathons in 1935.

roller skating Roller skating, which involves moving on special shoes or attachments to shoes that have wooden, metal, or, recently, plastic-composite wheels, is popular around the world. Children often roller skate on the sidewalks of cities; most teenagers and adults skate in indoor rinks. Athletes compete in speed skating, artistic skating, and roller hockey under the auspices of the Fédération Internationale de Roller Skating.

In speed-skating competition, the distances for men are 300, 500, 1,500, 5,000, 10,000, and 20,000 m; for women, 300, 500, 1,500, 3,000, 5,000, and 10,000 m. In artistic skating, there are 4 events: figures, comparable to compulsory figures in ice skating; dance, comprising compulsory choreography; and singles and pairs, both of which are free-style routines. Roller hockey is played with a ball (not a puck) and 5 players per side.

The first roller skates, made in Holland in the early 18th century, were modeled after ice skates, with the wheels in one row. More than 100 years later, in the United States, conventional skates, with two sets of wheels side by side, were introduced. The 1884 invention of the ball-bearing wheel further encouraged roller skating: early in the 20th century competitive skating became popular, and by mid-century the recreational activity was widespread. The late 1970s witnessed the advent of rollerblading, a reintroduction of a skate with all wheels in one row. Rollerblading gained increasing popularity in the late 1980s and early 1990s.

Rolling Stones, The The British rock band The Rolling Stones emerged in the early 1960s at about the same time as the Beatles. In contrast to the relatively clean-cut Beatles, however, the Stones adopted an aggressively sexual and defiant stance that helped make them one of the most successful of all rock groups. Formed in 1963 as a rhythm and blues band, the Stones soon developed their own distinctive style and by the late '60s were playing what many consider to be the finest rock music of its time. Guitarist Brian Jones, b. Feb. 28, 1942, died on July 3, 1969. Current band members include Mick Jagger, b. July 26, 1943, whose extraordinary style and voice have dominated the group; guitarist Keith Richard, b. Dec. 18, 1943, with whom Jagger has composed much of the band's material; bassist Bill Wyman, b. Oct. 24, 1941; drummer Charlie Watts, b. June 2, 1941; and guitarist Ron Wood, b. June 1, 1947.

Rolls-Royce Rolls-Royce is the manufacturer of some of the finest passenger automobiles and aircraft engines in the world. The company was founded in 1903 in Manchester, England, by Henry (later Sir Henry) Royce (1863–1933), a manufacturer of electrical equipment, and Charles S. Rolls (1877–1910), who ran an automobile sales firm in partnership with Claude Johnson (1864–1926).

Rolls-Royce was drawn into aircraft-engine manufac-

turing during World War I. At the outbreak of World War II the Rolls-Royce Merlin, which powered the British Spitfire fighter plane, was the best liquid-cooled aircraft engine in the world. In 1971, a combination of technical mistakes and adverse circumstances threatened Rolls-Royce with bankruptcy, and the British government took control of the aircraft-engine segment of the business. In 1987 the company was reprivatized.

Rölvaag, Ole Edvart [rurl'-vawk, oh'-le ed'-vahrt] The Norwegian-American novelist and educator Ole Rölvaag, b. Norway, Apr. 22, 1876, d. Nov. 5, 1931, is among the greatest of American immigrant novelists. His triology, made up of *Giants in the Earth* (1924–25; Eng. trans., 1927), *Peder Victorious* (1928; Eng. trans., 1929), and *Their Father's God* (1931; Eng. trans., 1931), conveys a starkly realistic portrait of the hardships of immigrant life on the Dakota prairies in the late 19th century. Rölvaag also taught Norwegian at Saint Olaf's College, in Minnesota.

Roman art and architecture During the period of the kingdom (753–509 BC) and in the first two centuries of the Republic (509–31 BC), Roman art and architecture, which developed in a very small area of west central Italy, was heavily influenced by ETRUSCAN and other Italic traditions and only incidentally by GREEK ART and GREEK ARCHITECTURE. As Rome grew in power to become the political center of an already Hellenized Mediterranean world, a truly Roman art began to emerge in the later 3d and especially during the 2d century BC.

The outcome was a highly complex art. Such completely new creations as monumental vaulted buildings emerged (see ARCH AND VAULT). A number of disparate artistic currents and traditions coexisted and influenced one another, not infrequently within the same genre, as in portraiture. Spurts of great inventiveness occasionally enlivened a generally retrospective trend. The art of the provinces, from the Balkans to Morocco, exhibited an almost boundless variety of forms.

Architecture

Building Materials, Techniques, and Forms. By far the most popular building material, from the beginnings down to the early Empire, was mud-brick strengthened by timbers (half-timbered construction). For terraces, fortifications, and foundations, the early Romans used many types of local stone. Hard limestone was generally cut irregularly (*opus siliceum*), whereas softer varieties such as volcanic tufa were sawed into blocks (*opus quadratum*). Increasing quantities and different varieties of marble were used in the late Republic and throughout the Empire (31 BC–AD 324).

The use of terra-cotta to cover wood declined as stone temples became predominant in the 3d century BC. From the early Empire on, baked bricks began to be manufactured in great quantities, mainly for the facings of cement walls (*opus testaceum*).

In the 2d century BC an unusually strong cement (*opus caementicium*) that included a volcanic dust called *pozzolana* produced great change in architecture. Cement could be formed within and over timber frameworks and so be used for such difficult construction as vaulting. Complex sequences of interior spaces with increasingly daring vaults and domes were constructed in the 1st and 2d centuries in baths, market buildings, and palaces. The best-preserved example is the Hadrianic PANTHEON (*c.*118–28; Rome), the temple to all the gods, with its huge, coffered-concrete dome spanning 43.3 m (142 ft).

The conventional forms of Etruscan and Greek architecture still continued to be used for many purposes. Originally prevalent in temples until the later Republic, the Tuscan order began to absorb some elements of the Greek Doric order and became Roman Doric. The Greek Ionic order and the Corinthian order were widely used in Italy from the 2d century BC on. Probably in Augustan times elements of the Ionic and Corinthian capitals were fused.

A late-Republican development destined to have great success was the framing of the round arch with a superimposed and generally engaged order, as on the outside of the COLOSSEUM (AD 72–82). With the ever-increasing use of concrete in the structure of buildings, the orders, originally structural, were gradually relegated to a purely decorative function.

Local materials, techniques, and building forms more or less dominated architecture in the provinces. The eastern Mediterranean continued in the established local and Greek Hellenistic building conventions, but imperial Rome succeeded in exporting to the East such building types as monumental baths, aqueducts, and, to some extent, amphitheaters.

Types of Civic Buildings. In the early Republic the TEM-PLE was still basically Etruscan—top-heavy with wide eaves and bulky terra-cotta decorations. In the 2d century BC, local traditions and Greek forms merged to create a more graceful structure: the podium and deep front porch of the Etruscan temple were retained and Greek proportions and forms adopted. The BASILICA, a multipurpose rectangular hall that may have originated in Greece, first appeared in Rome in the 2d century BC.

The monumental honorary or triumphal arch began its history about 200 BC but received its standard form in the early Empire. Supported by stout piers, a centrally vaulted passageway carried an upper story, the *attica*, on which gilded bronze statues were placed. An engaged or partially freestanding order framed the piers and passage.

Contrary to Greek practice, the stage and semicircular orchestra and seating arrangement (*cavea*) were joined in

The Arch of Trajan (AD c.114–17), Benevento, is a fine example of the balance between Roman architecture and sculptural decoration.

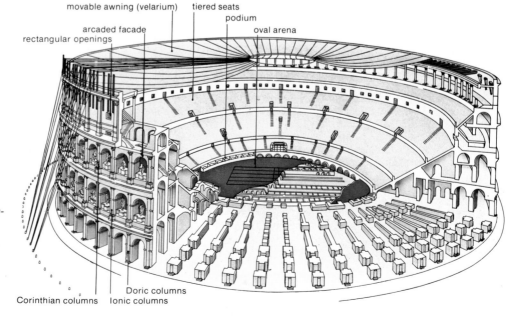

The largest Roman amphitheater, the Colosseum (AD 72–82), Rome, was a 4-story, elliptical structure seating about 50,000 spectators. The exterior facade was embellished with superimposed Doric, Ionic, and Corinthian columns and with Corinthian pilasters at the top.

movable awning (velarium)   tiered seats
arcaded facade   podium
rectangular openings   oval arena

Corinthian columns   Doric columns
Ionic columns

the Roman theater to form one structure, often built on level ground with the cavea resting on a complex of vaulted substructures that doubled as access passageways. Similar substructures were built for the seating areas of the oval amphitheater, as in the Colosseum, and in the hairpin-shaped circus used for chariot races.

As early as 19 BC huge, symmetrically planned imperial baths (*thermae*), which had large, sunken tubs and pools for crowds of people, were constructed. Some idea of the enormous, ingeniously vaulted halls can be seen today in the ruins of the Baths of Caracalla (AD 212–16; Rome). In an official register of AD 354, no fewer than 952 baths were listed in the city of Rome.

Types of Domestic Buildings. The simple Etrusco-Italic town house (*domus*), with rooms grouped axially around a dark central hall (ATRIUM), took on Greek forms in the 2d century BC, especially with the addition of a range of single-column colonnades (*peristyle*) around a rear garden. By the early Empire, the central atrium had become no more than an elegant entrance hall; dining halls and sitting rooms surrounded the garden peristyle (see HOUSE, in Western architecture).

Country villas were built to serve well-to-do persons either as working farms or as retreats for relaxation. Vaulted architecture was changing the aspect of domestic architecture in the city, and by the mid-2d century whole quarters of large, brick-faced concrete tenement houses (*insulae*) dominated the cities of Rome and Ostia, where several are still preserved to a height of two stories.

A profusion of sepulchral structures, ranging from modest funerary altars to pretentious and complex buildings, survive. Some tombs were rock-cut with carved facades; others were freestanding structures of one or more stories. The archaic Etruscan *tumulus* was revived in the 1st century BC, but the cylindrical portion tended to rise towerlike, as in the well-preserved tomb of Hadrian (AD 135–39; now Castel Sant' Angelo, Rome). In the age of Augustus the *columbarium*, a collective tomb containing many niches for ash urns, appeared. During the later Empire, the brick-faced cement tomb became the most popular form in Italy.

The bronze equestrian statue of Marcus Aurelius (AD c.161–80) was placed in the Piazza dei Campidoglio in Rome by Michelangelo when he laid out the square in 1538. The statue was preserved only because early Christians mistakenly believed that it represented Constantine.

Sculpture

Monumental sculpture in stone, bronze, or terra-cotta was employed both in and out of architectural contexts. Terra-cotta sculpture is found primarily on early temples, either as figural or ornamental relief on covering plaques, or as large statues along the roof edges and in the gables.

The more expensive bronze, sometimes gilded, was used widely for honorary statues of civic leaders and private citizens (see BRONZES). Cult images of the gods in the temples were often in bronze, and bronze copies of famous works of Greek sculpture were prized. Because of their material value, however, most bronzes were melted down in late antiquity.

Sculpture in stone had its beginnings in the Etrusco-Italic funerary tradition of tombstones and grave statues. As interest in Greek art increased, marble copies of Greek masterpieces were commissioned by wealthy Romans to decorate their residences. A thriving copying industry was to a large extent in the hands of Greek artisans, who also made many marble ornamental works of a purely decorative nature.

Portrait Sculpture. One of the great Roman contributions is portrait sculpture. Its roots lie both in the Roman custom of keeping ancestor masks (*imagines maiorum*) in the home and in the practice of erecting honorary statues in public places. Surviving examples are mainly marble copies, especially busts, a typically Roman, abbreviated portrait form that flourished from the late Republic onward. The 1st century BC was a period of great creativity in which the images of patricians became so realistic they seem veristic. In the reign of Augustus (31 BC–AD 14) a more subdued, idealized portrait style, based on Greek forms, was developed. In portraits executed between AD 200 and 250, for the first time in antiquity portraits display an emotional expressiveness, often capturing complex emotions, but a highly formal portrait art, with rigid features and aloof expressions, announced the Late Antique period.

Relief Sculpture. During the Republic, figural relief sculpture was largely a feature of private funerary art. Friezes or panels on tombs showed the deceased at work

In the Basilica of Maxentius, or Constantine (c.306–13), Rome, a series of huge groin vaults roofed the enormous central hall.

This representation (AD c.60–79) of a young couple from Pompeii is one of the few surviving examples of Roman portrait painting. The fresco is remarkable for its expressive realism and for such individualized details as the woman's elaborate coiffure. (Museo Nazionale, Naples.)

in his profession or as a benefactor of the community. Beginning in the reign of Hadrian, more and more sculpted marble sarcophagi with mythological subjects were produced (see SARCOPHAGUS).

The great period of the historical relief commenced with the reign of Augustus and continued for more than two centuries. This new and typically Roman art form became an effective vehicle of imperial propaganda: tangible achievements of the rulers as well as abstract notions of ideology were expressed in narrative or allegorical fashion in reliefs adorning large monuments such as arches, altars *(Ara Pacis Augustae*, 13–9 BC; Rome), and statue bases.

Wall Painting

If real polychrome marble paneling was unattainable, painting and stucco were the major means of decorating interior wall surfaces, evidence for which comes almost exclusively from HERCULANEUM and POMPEII. The technique of imitating an articulated marble-encrusted wall in painted stucco, called the first, or incrustation, style, was widespread in Hellenistic Greece as well as in Italy during the

The Battle of Issus, a mosaic from the House of the Faun, Pompeii, is a Roman copy of an original late-4th-century BC Hellenistic painting. (Museo Nazionale, Naples.)

Republic. Early in the 1st century BC the second, or architectural, style was developed: a vertical architectural framework bracketed trompe l'oeil views of a city, a countryside, a seascape, or even a mythological scene. The third style, beginning c.20 BC, returned to the two-dimensional wall surface in the form of large panels with delicate surface decoration. Finally, in the sixties of the 1st century AD the fourth style made its appearance; deep vistas again appear, this time seen through narrow facsimile windows.

An old and apparently long-lasting tradition in Rome was that of triumphal painting. By means of a sequence of posterlike, temporary illustrations, the progress of military campaigns in remote lands was documented. The spiral frieze on the Column of Trajan (AD 106–13) was, to some extent, a permanent relief version of this type of art.

Paving, Mosaic, and Stuccowork

Floor paving took various forms. *Opus signinum* consisted of bits of crushed travertine and terra-cotta mixed with mortar; other styles included marble slabs of various shapes (usually geometric) and colors. Baked bricks were much used for flooring, set on edge and placed in a herringbone pattern *(opus spicatum).*

The tradition of MOSAIC floor pavements reached Rome from Greece, where it began with black-and-white pebble compositions. In Hellenistic times, however, they were made with tesserae: small, specially cut stone cubes of various colors. This art experienced great popularity, the prime example being the large *Alexander Mosaic* (c.100 BC; Museo Nazionale, Naples) found in Pompeii. In early imperial Italy, mosaics, at this time often made with tesserae of glass paste, spread to the wall surfaces, and, occasionally, to the ceiling, in subtly toned polychromy. During the late 2d and increasingly in the 3d century, the provinces surpassed the homeland in making excellent polychrome pavement mosaics.

In the early 1st century BC, as vaulted architecture gained ground throughout the Empire, stucco became, and remained, the most practical material for covering and adorning surfaces that were often curved. Stucco relief, a typically Roman decorative art form, followed the development of wall painting. The stucco master either formed the relief design out of the still-workable material with a spatula as he was applying it, or he applied finished, mold-formed pieces.

Decorative Arts

In addition to architecture and its allied arts, numerous decorative arts flourished in ancient Rome. Small gems were engraved mainly for seal rings; intricate cameos were made of layered onyx, sardonyx, or agate; and elegant vessels of silver and bronze were cast with or without engraved or relief decoration. By far the most common material, however, was terra-cotta, which was used for figurines of all kinds, for decorative plaques and lamps, and, above all, for a type of molded ceramic ware called *terra sigillata* that was glazed red to imitate metal. After glassblowing was invented in the 1st century BC, a thriving industry developed in the later Empire. Coins, first minted in the 3d century BC, were made of gold, silver, and bronze.   .

Roman Catholic church The Roman Catholic church, the largest of the Christian churches, is identified as Roman because of its historical roots in Rome and because of the importance it attaches to the worldwide ministry of the bishop of Rome, the pope (see PAPACY). Several EASTERN RITE CHURCHES, whose roots are in regional churches of the Eastern Mediterranean, are in full communion with the Roman Catholic church.

A growing estrangement between the Catholic church in the West and the Orthodox church of the East in the first millennium led to a break between them in the 11th century, and the two regions diverged in matters of theology, liturgy, and disciplinary practices. Within Western Christianity beginning with the 16th-century REFORMATION, the Roman Catholic church came to be identified by its differences with the Protestant churches.

Roman Catholic Beliefs. As a form of CHRISTIANITY, Roman Catholicism is based on the belief that God entered the world through the Incarnation of his Son, the Christ or Messiah, Jesus of Nazareth. Roman Catholics attach special significance to the rites of BAPTISM and EUCHARIST. Baptism is sacramental entry into Christian life, and the Eucharist is a memorial of Christ's death and resurrection in which he is believed to be sacramentally present. The Eucharist is celebrated daily in the Roman Catholic church. Catholics also regard as SACRAMENTS the forgiveness of sins in reconciliation with the church (CONFESSION), ordination to ministry (HOLY ORDERS), marriage of Christians, postbaptismal anointing (CONFIRMATION), and the ANOINTING OF THE SICK.

The Worship of the Church. The public worship of the Roman Catholic church is its liturgy, principally the Eucharist, which is also called the MASS. After the recitation of prayers and readings from the Bible, the presiding priest invites the faithful to receive communion, understood as sharing in the sacramental presence of Christ. At the Sunday liturgy the priest preaches a sermon or homily, applying the day's biblical texts to the present lives of believers. The church observes a liturgical calendar similar to that of other Christians, following a cycle of ADVENT, CHRISTMAS, EPIPHANY, LENT, EASTER, and PENTECOST. It also follows a distinctive cycle of commemoration of the saints. The worship of the church is expressed as well in rites of baptism, confirmation, weddings, ordinations, penitential rites, burial rites or funerals, and the singing of the DIVINE OFFICE. A distinguishing mark of Catholic worship is prayer for the dead.

The Roman Catholic church also fosters devotional practices, both public and private, including Benediction of the Blessed Sacrament (a ceremony of homage to Christ in the Eucharist), the ROSARY, novenas (nine days of prayer for some special intention), pilgrimages to shrines, and veneration of saints' relics or statues. The devotional importance attached to the SAINTS (especially the Virgin MARY) distinguishes Roman Catholicism and Eastern Orthodoxy from the churches of the Reformation. In the last two centuries the Roman Catholic church has taught as official doctrine that Mary from her conception was kept free of original sin (the IMMACULATE CONCEPTION) and that at the completion of her life was taken up body and soul into heaven (the ASSUMPTION).

The Organization of the Church. The Roman Catholic church is structured locally into neighborhood parishes and regional dioceses administered by bishops. Catholic church polity is characterized, however, by a centralized government under the pope, who is regarded as the successor to the apostle Peter, entrusted with a ministry of unity and encouragement. The First VATICAN COUNCIL (1869–70) further enhanced the role of the papacy by declaring that the church's INFALLIBILITY (or inability to err on central issues of the Christian faith) can be exercised personally by the pope in extraordinary circumstances.

The pope is elected for life by the College of CARDINALS (about 130). He is assisted in the governance of the church by the bishops, especially through the World Synod of Bishops that meets every three years. More immediately in the VATICAN CITY, the papal city-state within Rome, the pope is aided by the cardinals and a bureaucracy known as the Roman CURIA. The Vatican is represented in many countries by a papal nuncio or apostolic delegate and at the United Nations by a permanent observer.

By tradition the all-male ordained clergy (bishops, priests, and deacons) are distinguished from the laity, who assist in the ministry of the church. In the Western (Latin) rite of the Catholic church, bishops and priests are ordinarily celibate. In many of the Eastern Rite churches, priests are allowed to marry. Some Catholics live together in RELIGIOUS ORDERS, serving the church and the world under vows of poverty, chastity, and obedience.

Church discipline is regulated by a code of CANON LAW. A revised code for the Latin rite went into effect in 1983. A code for the Eastern Rite churches is in preparation.

The Church in a Time of Change. To initiate renewal in the Roman Catholic church, the late Pope John XXIII convoked a general council, the Second VATICAN COUNCIL (1962–65). This meeting of bishops and their advisors from around the world was also attended by Orthodox, Anglican, and Protestant observers. The chief reforms in church practices were: changes in liturgical language (from Latin to the vernacular) and reformulation of sacramental rituals; a new ecumenical openness toward other Christian churches; increased stress on the collective responsibility of bishops in the church's mission (collegiality); more acute concern for political and social issues, especially where moral questions are involved; attempts to adapt the Gospel to diverse cultural traditions; reform of priestly education; and partial acceptance of diversity in theology and local practices.

Roman de la Rose, Le [roh-mahn' duh lah rohz, luh] *Le Roman de la Rose* (*Romance of the Rose*), one of the most influential of medieval poems, is a long (22,000 lines) French dream ALLEGORY. The first part of the poem (*c.*1225), by Guillaume de Lorris, is an idealistic narration of the adventures of a lover seeking to pluck the rose of love. The second part (c.1275), by Jean de Meun, is a cynical satire against love, women, and the church. CHAUCER translated part of the *Roman* into English early in his career, and the poem's conflicting attitudes toward love reappear throughout his works.

Roman Empire   see ROME, ANCIENT

—

Roman law
Roman law refers to the legal system that originated in ancient Rome and that later became the basis of law in western Europe and in countries influenced by European legal codes.

Origins. Roman law had its origins, long before there was a Roman state, in family customs handed down from one generation to another and in judgments (*leges regiae*) of chieftains or kings. By the time of the establishment of the Roman Republic (509 BC) a considerable amount of this customary law existed. It was not written but oral law, however, in the keeping of the most ancient patrician families (gentes), and this meant that the common people (plebeians) were at a disadvantage in disputes. Years of agitation ended with the appointment of a commission (*decemviri legibus scribundis*, or twelve legal experts) that collected and published the oral customs in Rome's first codification, *The Twelve Tables* (451–450 BC). These dealt mainly with problems related to property and to the procedures for obtaining redress for wrongs.

The great expansion of law under the republic came from two later sources: jurisconsults and praetors. The jurisconsults were prominent citizens who had great prestige and were consulted by officials and laymen alike. In 27 BC, the first emperor, Augustus, gave certain jurisconsults the authority to issue responses to legal inquiries as though he himself had been asked, a practice that continued under later emperors.

The praetors were annually elected magistrates whose duties included the administration of the law courts. They issued edicts each year, declaring under what circumstances they would grant a suit. These edicts were codified and standardized by Emperor Hadrian, and they furnished the basis of much of later Roman law.

The emperor, as magistrate, also had the right to issue edicts on legal affairs and increasingly turned to the Senate for concurrence. The emperor JUSTINIAN I formed select committees that gathered, edited, and organized (AD 528–34) legal material from all of these sources to create the *Corpus Juris Civilis* (Body of Civil Law), which is the form in which most Roman law has come down to Western civilization (see JUSTINIAN CODE).

Branches of the Law. Traditionally, the study of Roman law is divided into five parts. The law of persons dealt with the legal status of individuals and groups—free or slave, citizen or alien, male or female, parent or child, and so on. It also established the juristic person or corporation, a fictitious person endowed by the state with the rights of a natural person. The law of property dealt with rights of ownership. The law of succession or inheritance governed the transfer of property to heirs whose rights depended on their relationship to the deceased, and also regulated the making of wills. The law of obligations concerned rights and obligations arising from contracts and also from illegal acts—torts or delicts—that obliged the offender to recompense the injured person. The law of actions contained the procedures to be followed in disputes.

Influence of Roman Law. By the time of Justinian most of western Europe was in the hands of barbarian kings who administered a mixture of their own GERMANIC LAW and earlier Roman law. But in the 11th century Italian scholars rediscovered and began to study and teach the *Corpus Juris Civilis*. This happened at the very time when expanding trade and commercial activity made the law of a universal state more appropriate than any other. Thus Roman law became the basis of the law of all western Europe, with the exception of England (see CIVIL LAW; COMMON LAW). It spread to the New World and is basic in South and Central America, Louisiana, and Quebec; it was adopted in South Africa and Sri Lanka and plays a role in the codes of emerging states. Through Byzantium it reached Russia, and it still furnishes parts of the law in the USSR. The Roman *jus gentium* (law of the peoples), developed in the republic to govern relations with non-Romans, became the basis of much of modern commercial law.

Roman mythology   see MYTHOLOGY

Roman numerals   see NUMERAL

—

Roman roads
An intricate transportation network spanning about 80,000 km (50,000 mi), the Roman road system gave citizens of the ancient empire access to the most distant provinces. The first all-weather roads connected the capital and those Italian towns which had been recently subdued or colonized by the Romans. The Via Appia (Appian Way; begun in 312 BC), for example, joined Rome with Capua, which had just been crushed in the Samnite War; the Via Flaminia connected Rome with the Latin colony of Ariminum (modern Rimini) in former Celtic territory.

Usually constructed of stones, rubble, and concrete, these paved roads were of great strategic importance to the Empire, facilitating military movements and transport and the administration and control of conquered lands. Merchants using them paid duties on goods at regular intervals. By the end of the republic (1st century BC), roads had been built in southern Gaul and Illyria, but the great period of construction outside Italy came under the emperors, who extended the system through the boundaries of more than 30 modern nations. The network remained in use during the Middle Ages, and remnants of it are still extant.

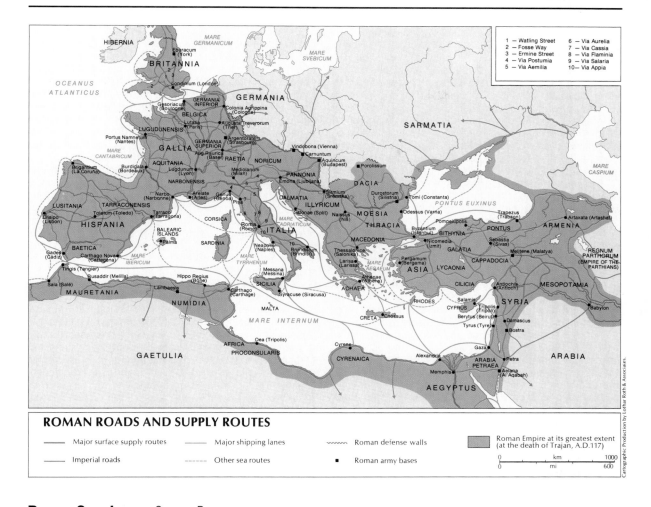

ROMAN ROADS AND SUPPLY ROUTES

—— Major surface supply routes	—— Major shipping lanes	〰〰 Roman defense walls
—— Imperial roads	- - - - Other sea routes	■ Roman army bases

Roman Empire at its greatest extent (at the death of Trajan, A.D.117)

1 — Watling Street 6 — Via Aurelia
2 — Fosse Way 7 — Via Cassia
3 — Ermine Street 8 — Via Flaminia
4 — Via Postumia 9 — Via Salaria
5 — Via Aemilia 10— Via Appia

Roman Senate   see SENATE, ROMAN

romance   In the Middle Ages the term *romance* signified a narrative written in a vernacular, or "romance" language, derived from Latin, such as French. The term then became associated with the content of these works—which were usually tales of love and chivalry involving a heroic quest. Medieval romances influenced many Elizabethan writers but were later treated dismissively by neoclassical critics who disdained their obviously fictional appeal. By the 19th century, however, greater respect was granted to imaginative projections of the real world. Nathaniel HAWTHORNE argued that the writer of romance was free to pursue psychological truths denied to the realism of the novel. Hawthorne's novels and tales, especially *The Marble Faun* (1860), contain elements of GOTHIC ROMANCE. The traditional objection to the romance—that it is escapist and immoral—is given further validity by contemporary examples of the form: the sentimental erotic adventures produced for the mass market.

Romance languages   The Romance languages are a group of closely related vernaculars descended from the LATIN LANGUAGE, a member of the Italic branch of INDO-EUROPEAN LANGUAGES. The designation *Romance* is derived from the Latin phrase *romanica loqui*, "to speak in Roman fashion," which attests to the popular, rather than literary, origins of the languages.

The Romance languages that have acquired national standing as the official tongues of modern nations are Spanish—the most widely used Romance language—spoken in Spain, Latin America, and some of the Caribbean islands; Portuguese, spoken in Portugal, Brazil, and in parts of Africa formerly under Portuguese rule; French, spoken in France, Belgium, Switzerland, Canada, parts of the Caribbean, and many of the African countries that were formerly under French or Belgian rule; Italian, spoken primarily in Italy and Switzerland; and Romanian, spoken principally in Romania.

Nonnational Languages. Several distinct Romance languages function as nonnational, regional vernaculars.

Among these are Rheto-Romance, or Rhaetian, which consists of a group of related languages spoken in Switzerland, where they are called Romansch, and in northern Italy, where they are called Ladin or Friulian. In southern France, Provençal, or Occitan, is spoken by about 12 million people.

Catalan, with about 5 million speakers, is used alongside Spanish as the language of Catalonia on the Spanish Mediterranean coast from the French border to Valencia. It is also spoken in Alghero, Sardinia, in the Balearic Islands, and in the Pyrenean valley of Aran, the French region of Roussillon, and the principality of Andorra.

Sardinian is the collective name for a group of Romance languages spoken on the island of Sardinia by nearly 1 million people. It is of particular interest to Romance scholars because of the archaic features of its dialects, such as the retention of the Latin sound *k* that other Romance languages have palatalized.

Ladino, also called Judaeo-Romance or Sephardic, is spoken by Sephardic Jews in Istanbul, Salonika, and elsewhere around the Mediterranean. It is based on 15th-century Spanish, reflecting the time when the Jews were expelled from Spain by royal edict. The language also contains Turkish, Greek, and Hebrew elements.

Romance creoles, whose origins are found in PIDGINS or simplified trade languages, have also sprung up around the world. Haitian and Louisiana French are such languages, as are the varieties of Portuguese found in Macao and Goa.

At least one recorded Romance language, Dalmatian, has become extinct. Formerly spoken along the eastern coast of the Adriatic, Dalmatian consisted of at least two dialects: Ragusan, known only from a few medieval documents, and Veglian, which disappeared in 1898 when its last speaker was blown up by a land mine.

Vulgar Latin. From the evidence of Latin grammarians, popular playwrights, and inscriptions, it is apparent that in Republican Rome the spoken language of the lower classes was undergoing modifications in pronunciation and grammar that ultimately were to differentiate it from the written language and the language of the privileged. During the period of empire and Roman expansion, it was this Latin of the people, so-called Vulgar Latin, that was carried to the far-flung provinces by soldiers, merchants, and colonists.

Not all provinces were Romanized at the same time, however. Sicily and Sardinia were colonized as early as 238 BC, while Dacia—modern Romania—did not come under Roman occupation until about AD 100. In the provinces, Vulgar Latin underwent further modification by the subjugated peoples, who brought to it their own speech habits and pronunciation influenced by their own indigenous languages.

The collapse of the empire's frontiers during the 5th century under the thrust of Germanic tribes left Rome cut off from the provinces, and the outer regions drifted apart as each modified its form of spoken Latin in unique ways. In every region of the former Latin-speaking world, the emerging Romance languages then in turn began to break up among themselves.

French and Provençal. In Gallo-Roman France, a split occurred between north and south, assisted by incursions of Germanic-speaking Franks—whence the name "France"—into the north. Here, too, further dialectalization occurred throughout the Middle Ages, resulting in a multitude of speech forms such as Francien, Picard, Norman, Lorrain, and Walloon. Southern French, or Provençal, split into Languedocien, Auvergnat, and many other dialects. The dialect of Paris gradually became the national language, however, and today is accepted as the model for French.

Italian. Dialectal varieties of the emerging Italian language revolved around Gallo-Italian in the northwest; a northeastern or Venetian group; a central dialectal group that included the speech of Tuscany, Umbria, northern Latium (the province of Rome), and Corsica; and clusters of dialects to the south, including Abruzzese-Neapolitan and Calabrian-Sicilian. The ultimate predominance of Tuscan as the standard was a result more of the cultural than of any political prestige of Florence.

Spanish and Portuguese. On the Iberian peninsula, two languages developed, each with its own dialects. Galician-Portuguese broke into northwestern, central, and southern dialects; Spanish came to embrace Leonese and Castilian in the center of the peninsula, Aragonese further to the east, and Andalusian in the south. The dialect of Lisbon vies with that of Rio de Janeiro in Brazil as the model for the language. Castilian Spanish, spoken in central Spain, including the capital Madrid, is generally thought of as the most prestigious form of Spanish, although Mexican Spanish is often taught in North American classrooms.

Romanian. Romanian has broken into several dialects, such as Macedo-Romanian, spoken in southern Macedonia, and Isto-Romanian, the language of a few thousand people in northeastern Yugoslavia. The dialect of Bucharest serves as the standard language.

Linguistic Features. Similarities and differences among the Romance languages and their relation to Latin may be seen in the following sentences, which mean "The poet loves the girl":

Latin	Poeta puellam amat
French	Le poète aime la jeune fille
Italian	Il poeta ama la ragazza
Portuguese	O poeta ama a menina
Spanish	El poeta ama a la muchacha
Romanian	Poetul iube fata

The word *poet* was borrowed from Greek by Latin, underscoring the fact that not all Romance words, even when derived from Latin, were originally Italic. Some vocabulary may differ from one Romance language to another because words were taken from different Latin forms with similar meanings or were borrowed from the local native languages. Sometimes words were incorporated from neighboring tongues; Spanish *izquierdo*, "left," for example, comes from Basque, and Romanian *sticlă*, "drinking glass," comes from Slavic. It was also often the case that new words entered Romance languages from the vocabulary of conquering peoples: Spanish *aceite* and Portuguese *azeite*, "oil," come from Arabic, and French *danser*, "to dance," and *gagner*, "to harvest," were borrowed from Germanic.

Romanesque art and architecture

Romanesque art and architecture flourished throughout western Europe from about 1050 to about 1200, although its first manifestations occurred before the year 1000, and its influence remained strong in some areas well into the 13th century. Unlike CAROLINGIAN ART AND ARCHITECTURE and OTTONIAN ART AND ARCHITECTURE, from which it drew many forms and elements, Romanesque was a truly pan-European movement.

By the beginning of the 11th century, European civilization had become stable and prosperous under the aegis of the Christian church, through whose network of abbeys the new artistic order was established and spread. An unprecedented building activity stimulated the development of innovative architectural techniques and styles, which in turn demanded new forms of pictorial and sculptural decoration. The resultant flowering of Romanesque art, once thought of merely as a transitional phase between EARLY CHRISTIAN ART AND ARCHITECTURE and GOTHIC ART AND ARCHITECTURE, is now considered to be a distinct and important phase of European art.

Architecture

The word *Romanesque* originally meant "in the Roman manner." This description is at least partly applicable to Romanesque ecclesiastical architecture, not only in the use of the Roman round arch, but also in the adoption of the major forms of antique Roman vaulting (see ARCH AND VAULT).

Most Romanesque churches retained the basic plan of the Early Christian BASILICA: a long, three-aisled nave intercepted by a transept and terminating in a semicircular apse crowned by a conch, or half-dome. The masonry structure of Romanesque churches assumed far more complicated configurations, in which heavy piers and arched openings divide the interior into well-defined spatial areas, while large masses of clearly separated geometric forms impart to the exterior an aura of grandeur and power. The greatest breakthrough of Romanesque architecture occurred in interior vaulting: by redesigning and reinforcing the walls, Romanesque builders were able to span the wide and often lofty nave with a solid barrel vault and thus create completely vaulted structures.

France. France was the most creative center of Romanesque architecture and the birthplace of one of the most beautiful features of medieval architecture, the ambulatory with radiating chapels. With the invention of the ambulatory, the previously solid rear wall of the main apse gave way to a gracefully curving open arcade. This whole complex of architectural forms at the east end of medieval churches is known as the chevet.

The first use of a chevet occurred during the rebuilding of the abbey church of Saint Martin in Tours shortly before 1000. In its final form Saint Martin's established the model for the so-called pilgrimage churches erected

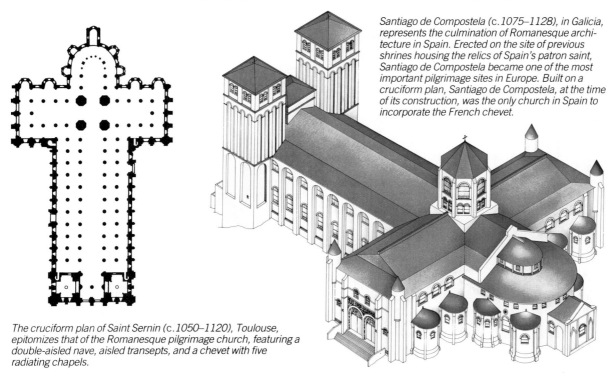

Santiago de Compostela (c.1075–1128), in Galicia, represents the culmination of Romanesque architecture in Spain. Erected on the site of previous shrines housing the relics of Spain's patron saint, Santiago de Compostela became one of the most important pilgrimage sites in Europe. Built on a cruciform plan, Santiago de Compostela, at the time of its construction, was the only church in Spain to incorporate the French chevet.

The cruciform plan of Saint Sernin (c.1050–1120), Toulouse, epitomizes that of the Romanesque pilgrimage church, featuring a double-aisled nave, aisled transepts, and a chevet with five radiating chapels.

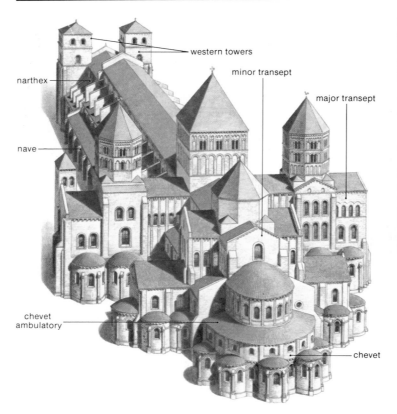

western towers

minor transept

major transept

narthex

nave

chevet
ambulatory

chevet

The monastic churches of Burgundy, France, are among the finest examples of Romanesque style. (Left) The third abbey church of Cluny (completed 1130), known as Cluny III, featured a barrel-vaulted nave with double aisles, pointed arches, double transepts, and a chevet. (Above) An enclosed narthex was a feature of the 11th-century Benedictine abbey church of Saint Philibert, Tournus, near Cluny. Saint Philibert's nave is distinguished by transverse arches supporting lateral, or transverse, barrel vaults.

(c.1000–c.1150) along the roads that took medieval pilgrims to the tomb of Saint James at Santiago de Compostela in northern Spain.

Complementing the striking interiors of these churches are imposing exteriors in which towers play an important role. Along with bell towers and stair towers, northern churches often incorporated towers built over the crossing, that area where the nave and the transept intersect. All of these architectural elements were brought together and magnified in one of Europe's most magnificent structures, the third church built for the Burgundian abbey of Cluny, generally referred to as Cluny III (completed in 1130).

Normandy and England. Among the many and diverse regional styles of Romanesque that flourished throughout western Europe during the 11th and 12th centuries, the most significant in terms of structural innovation was NORMAN ARCHITECTURE. Working mainly in Normandy and (after 1066) England, Norman architects solved the problem of sustaining a high vault atop a windowed clerestory by supporting the vault with a grid of thin diagonal arches, or ribs. Rib vaulting was first employed (c.1104) consistently in the Norman Durham Cathedral in England. Because most of the other Anglo-Norman structures were built on too vast a scale to permit high vaults, Durham remained an anomaly in England; in France, however, the introduction of rib vaulting marked a crucial step in the development of Gothic architecture.

Germany. German builders had been in the forefront in the early development of towers and in the elaboration of the immense western entrance facades known as westworks. The culminating monuments of German Romanesque architecture are the Rhineland cathedrals of Mainz (12th–13th centuries), Speyer (begun 1030), and Worms (1150–81). When the nave of Speyer Cathedral was finally vaulted (c.1125), its height surpassed even that of Cluny III.

Italy. The profuse external embellishment of German Romanesque churches links them with contemporary structures of northern Italy, and particularly with the products of Lombard architecture. A distinguishing feature of Tuscan Romanesque architecture is the surprisingly classical character of its architectural details. For example, in the noble interior of the largest Tuscan Romanesque church, the Cathedral of Pisa (1063–1121), the marble columns are all crowned with capitals of antique Roman form.

Sculpture

After the fall (AD 476) of the Roman Empire the practice of decorating buildings with large reliefs ceased for almost 600 years. The revival of monumental relief sculpture as a major form of art is one of the outstanding achievements of the Romanesque period. Often highly stylized and at times verging on the abstract, Romanesque reliefs were used chiefly to embellish the church portals.

France. The first sculptured doorway of truly monumental size was the now-destroyed entranceway of Cluny III, whose style and magnitude are reflected in the still-extant portal of the Burgundian church of Sainte Madeleine at Vézelay (1120–32). In the Vézelay reliefs, the variety in subject matter that characterizes the decorative art of Romanesque churches is apparent in the wide range of secular as well as religious themes. The keen interest in far-off countries engendered by the First Crusade (1095–99) is reflected in the lintels over the doors and the boxes surrounding the tympanum, whose reliefs depict the fabulous races with which medieval writers peopled distant lands. Among the exotic foreigners displayed are dog-headed men of India, porcine-faced Ethiopians, and at the extreme outer end of the right lintel a family of big-eared Panotii comprised of a mother in a topless gown, a father clothed in leaves, and a child who has shut himself up in his huge ears like a clam.

Throughout France, human figures and fantastic animals of every sort were used to decorate the interior capitals of churches and cloisters. One of the few French Romanesque sculptors known by name, the famous GISLEBERTUS, carved (c.1130–35) such figures for almost all the interior capitals of Saint Lazare in Autun. Although his figures are flat and linear in style, Gislebertus feelingly conveyed in his *Flight into Egypt* the tender care with which Mary places a protective arm over the little Christ Child. On either side of this scene, lush vegetation supplants the usual conventionalized leaves of the Corinthian type of capital.

Italy. Sculpture in the Romanesque period was confined largely to reliefs. No freestanding, life-size human figures were created, and only a few smaller figures executed in the round are extant. Striking examples of the latter figural type appear on the bishop's throne (c.1150) in the southern Italian church of San Nicola of Bari, which probably was carved to commemorate an Italian victory over the Saracens. The main weight of the seat of the chair rests on the shoulders of two half-naked Sara-

A fragment of the lintel of the north portal of the Cathedral of Saint Lazare, Autun (c.1130–35), France, shows Eve plucking the forbidden fruit of Eden. This relief may be the work of Gislebertus, who executed much of Saint Lazare's sculptural decoration. (Musée Rolin, Autun.)

cens who are loudly protesting the burden they have to bear. The strongly plastic qualities of the figures' sturdy, squat bodies is a recurring characteristic in Italian Romanesque sculpture.

The most important and prolific sculptural centers in Italy were those of Lombardy. The Lombard Romanesque school was dominated by three well-known personalities: Wiligelmo da Modena (fl. early 12th century), the founder of the school; Nicolò of Verona (fl. 12th century); and Benedetto Antelami (fl. late 12th–early 13th centuries). Their work expresses a distinctly Lombardic quality of heaviness and earthiness that is immediately apparent in the powerfully bovine figures of Adam and Eve in Wiligelmo's *Genesis* reliefs (1107–1110) at Modena. Wiligelmo's sturdy style was refined further in Nicolò's sculptures (c.1138) for the portal of San Zeno in Verona. Antelami was the most forward looking of the three Lombard sculptors. His masterpieces, the figures (c.1190) of David and Ezekiel set into niches on the facade of the cathedral of Fidenza, are actually carved in relief, although they give the impression of being freestanding statues. Their ponderous forms and noble monumentality clearly presage the sculptural works of Michelangelo.

Meuse Valley. Very little stone sculpture was produced in Belgium and Germany during the Romanesque period, but both countries excelled in metalwork. In the Meuse Valley region of Belgium and northern France, the so-called Mosan school of metalwork produced (1107–12) an early masterpiece in the bronze baptismal font executed by Renier de Huy (fl. 12th century) for a church in Liège. Renier's figures are tinged with the graceful naturalism usually associated with classical art.

Painting

Frescoes. The interiors of nearly all Romanesque churches originally were decorated, either entirely or in part, with frescoes (see FRESCO PAINTING). Among the pictorial subjects chosen for the walls and vaults, the most important and most frequently occurring theme is the so-called *Maiestas Christi*, a conventional representation of the transcendental deity that was reserved for the half-

The tympanum of the central portal of the church of Sainte Madeleine (1120–32), Vézelay, France, portrays Christ inspiring the Apostles to spread the gospel throughout the world.

The Maiestas Christi *fresco (c.1123), from the church of San Clemente in Tahull, Spain, is one of the finest surviving examples of Spanish Romanesque mural painting. (Museo de Bellas Artes de Cataluña, Barcelona.)*

dome of the apse. The *Maiestas* fresco (*c.*1123) on the apsidal vault of the Catalan church of San Clemente de Tahull is the best-preserved Romanesque representation of this theme and follows a long-established convention in portraying Christ seated on a rainbow with his right hand raised in blessing. But the artist of Tahull has wholly transformed this time-honored image into highly schematized patterns, almost caricaturing the features of Christ, perhaps enabling the artist to achieve the maximum spiritual intensity.

Manuscript Illumination. Because time and climate have destroyed or badly damaged most Romanesque frescoes, ILLUMINATED MANUSCRIPTS provide the principal source of present-day knowledge of Romanesque painting. A collection of commentaries (Bibliothèque Nationale, Paris) on the Apocalypse, illuminated (1028–72) at the abbey of Saint-Sever-sur-Ardour, in southern France, includes a highly original illustration of the passage that describes how winged locusts with human faces torment humankind with the poisonous stings of their scorpion tails. The powerful expressionism of these Apocalypse scenes gives way to a more elegant beauty in the large ornamental initials with which Romanesque manuscripts abound. Like the sculptured capitals in the Romanesque churches, these fantastically ornate letters often include human figures, as well as dragons and other creatures. Often the figures assume the very shape of the initials, as in a copy of Pope Gregory I, the Great's *Moralia* (Bibliothèque Municipale, Dijon), made (1111) at the abbey of Citeaux in France.

Historical Importance

The international scope of Romanesque art is apparent in the broad range of influences it assimilated and transformed. Echoes of Carolingian and Ottonian illumination can be detected in many Romanesque manuscripts, and the sophisticated art of the Byzantine Empire had a widespread impact on all forms of Romanesque painting. In architecture, the dome and the horseshoe arch were introduced from the Near East and from Islamic art and architecture, and in the south of France, Roman triumphal arches provided the inspiration for the triple portals of the church of Saint-Gilles-du-Gard (*c.*1140–*c.*1150).

In 12th-century Sicily a mélange of Saracenic, Byzantine, and Norman Romanesque styles resulted in a series of extraordinarily exotic monuments; at the opposite end of Europe, the wooden stave churches of Norway preserved in their carved decorations the animal art of the barbarian era. In Italy, Romanesque sculpture laid the groundwork for Nicola PISANO's pulpit (1260) for the Pisa Baptistery, the first monument of the dawning Renaissance.

Romania [roh-mayn'-ee-ah]   Romania, a republic on the lower Danube River in southeastern Europe, borders on the USSR on the north and northeast, Hungary and Yugoslavia on the west, Bulgaria on the south, and the Black Sea on the east. The name *Romania* came into being in 1862, following the 1859 unification of the principalities of MOLDAVIA and WALACHIA, then under Turkish suzerainty. Romania won full independence from the Ottoman Empire in 1877. The monarchy, established in 1881, was ended in 1947 when the Communists came to power. Between 1965 and 1989 the state was controlled by the increasingly dictatorial Nicolae CEAUȘESCU, who was finally overthrown and executed in a violent revolution in December 1989. Since then Romania has embarked on a gradual democratization, under the leadership of Ion Iliescu and the National Salvation Front.

Land and Resources

Romania may be divided into three regions. In the center is the Transylvanian basin, an area of hilly, fertile farmlands. Surrounding Transylvania is the second region, the CARPATHIAN MOUNTAINS. The Eastern Carpathians, stretching southeast from the Soviet border, only rarely exceed 2,000 m (6,562 ft). The eastern reaches of these mountains constitute a region of significant seismic activity, the origin of frequent destructive earthquakes. The higher and more rugged Southern Carpathians, or Transylvanian Alps, run west from Brașov to the Yugoslavian border and reach 2,543 m (8,343 ft) at Mount Moldoveanu, the country's highest elevation. The Western Carpathians extend from the Danube to the Someș River and average 645 m (2,115 ft) in elevation. Romania's third region is one of plains, which ring the entire country, except in the north. The western plain, reaching to the Hungarian and Yugoslavian borders, is an extension of Europe's mid-Danubian plain. In the south is the Walachian plain, and in

ROMANIA

Land: Area: 237,500 km² (91,699 mi²). Capital and largest city: Bucharest (1989 est. pop., 2,194,583).

People: Population (1990 est.): 23,265,000. Density: 98 persons per km² (254 per mi²). Distribution (1987 est.): 49% urban, 51% rural. Official language: Romanian. Major religions: Eastern Orthodoxy, Eastern Rite Catholicism, Roman Catholicism, Protestantism.

Government: Type: republic. Legislature: Constituent Assembly. Political subdivisions: 40 counties, municipality of Bucharest.

Economy: GNP (1989): $79.8 billion; $3,445 per capita. Labor distribution (1989): agriculture—27.8%; mining, manufacturing, and public utilities—38.1%; construction—4.7%; transportation and communication—6.2%; trade—5.5%; services and other—17.6%. Foreign trade (1989): imports—$9.7 billion; exports—$14.3 billion. Currency: 1 leu = 100 bani.

Education and Health: Literacy (1990): 98% of adult population. Universities (1989): 7. Hospital beds (1989): 216,300. Physicians (1989): 42,000. Life expectancy (1990): women—75; men—69. Infant mortality (1990): 19 per 1,000 live births.

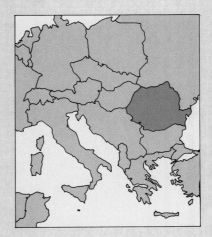

the northeast, extending from the piedmont to the Soviet border, is the Moldavian plain. The marshy Danube delta spreads out downstream from Galaţi, and to the south, between the Danube and the Black Sea, is the DOBRUJA, a low plateau.

Soils. Agriculturally productive chernozem is found in the Moldavian plain and in parts of the Walachian plain and the Transylvanian basin. Brown forest soils are found on lower mountain slopes and provide abundant meadowland for Romania's important animal-husbandry sector. Along the Danube and its tributaries are belts of fertile alluvial soil.

Climate. Romania's warm summers and cold winters define a transitional temperate-continental climate. Lowland annual average precipitation decreases west to east, from 630 mm (25 in) in the western plain to 400 mm (15 in) in Dobruja. Mountain precipitation may average more than 1,200 mm (47 in) annually. The average temperatures are between –3° and 5° C (27° and 41° F) in January and between 22° and 24° C (72° and 74° F) in July. Climatic conditions have combined disastrously with environmentally irresponsible industrialization policies to produce severe air-pollution problems in a number of locations, notably in Copşa Micǎ, southwest of Tîrgu Mureŝ.

Drainage. Most of Romania is drained by the DANUBE RIVER or its tributaries. Extensive marshlands are found in the Danube delta and along the northern bank of the Danube in the Walachian plain.

Vegetation and Animal Life. Forests cover about one-quarter of Romania and most of the lower mountain slopes. Alpine pastures are found above the treeline between 1,525 and 1,830 m (5,000 and 6,000 ft), and tundra occurs at the highest elevations. Large animals include deer, bears, foxes, wolves, and boars. A wide variety of waterfowl frequent the Danube delta, one of Europe's most important wildlife areas.

Resources. Romania's major natural resources are its fertile soils and its rapidly descending waters, ideally suited for hydroelectric exploitation. Romania's once important petroleum reserves are nearly depleted. Natural gas and coal deposits somewhat compensate for dwindling petroleum supplies. Lead, zinc, sulfur, and salt are sufficient for domestic needs.

People

About 87% of the population are ethnically Romanian; 8%, Hungarian; 2%, Gypsy; 1.5%, German; and the remainder, Ukrainian, Yugoslav, Russian, Bulgarian, and Turkish. The densest concentrations of ethnic Hungarians and Germans are in TRANSYLVANIA.

Language and Religion. Romanian, an eastern ROMANCE LANGUAGE, is the official language. Hungarian is used by the Hungarian minority, and German and other languages by the relevant minorities. Most Romanians adhere to the Romanian Orthodox church. In 1990 the government relegalized the Uniate, or Eastern Rite Catholic church, which may claim as many as 1.5 million members, pri-

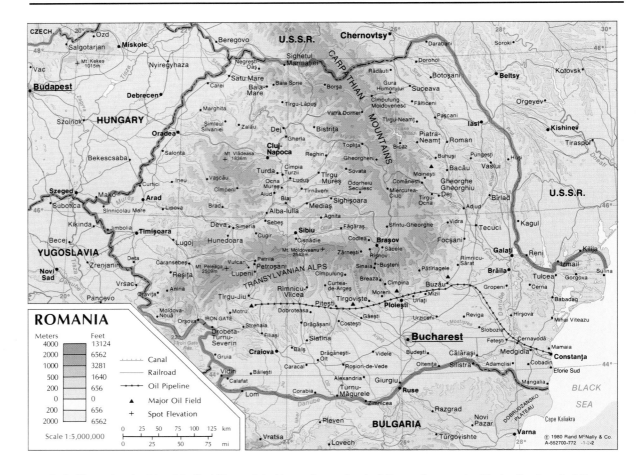

marily in Transylvania. About half of Romania's Hungarians are Roman Catholics.

Demography. One-half of Romania's population live in rural areas, making it one of the least urbanized European countries. The capital, BUCHAREST, is the largest city. Other cities with populations of more than 200,000 include BRAŞOV, CLUJ-NAPOCA, CONSTANŢA, PLOIEŞTI, and TIMIŞOARA.

Education and Health. Education is compulsory and free for Romanians from the ages of 6 to 16. Decentralization of the postsecondary educational system was among the first acts of the National Salvation Front. While health care, in a network of hospitals, clinics, and sanatoriums staffed by trained professionals, is free, the facilities are badly overcrowded and suffer from a lack of equipment and medicines.

The Arts and Literature. The arts in Romania draw inspiration from both national folk traditions and general European culture. The decorative folk-art tradition, with its colorful geometric motifs, remains the quintessential Romanian style. Constantin BRANCUSI, who lived most of his life abroad, was an outstanding sculptor and is probably the best-known Romanian artist outside his own country. Georges ENESCO was the founder of the modern

school of Romanian music. Under the toppled Communist regime cultural creativity was stifled and the arts relegated to political propaganda.

Romanian literature has been in full bloom for only about 150 years. A literary language began to develop before the end of the 16th century, but well into the 19th century high society spoke and wrote Greek. After the explusion of Greeks from Romania in 1821, a modern idiom was developed; the first novels appreared during the 1850s, and drama and lyric poetry followed. Eminent 20th-century literary figures include Camil and Cesar Petrescu, Mihail Sadoveanu, and three expatriates, the poet Tristan TZARA, the historian Mircea ELIADE, and the playwright Eugène IONESCU.

Economic Activity

Under the Communists, the Romanian economy was highly centralized and functioned within a framework of official plans. The system achieved impressive rates of growth until the 1980s, when the economy slid into decline. The postrevolutionary government is pledged to steer toward a mixed economy with prices determined by the market, while retaining the characteristics of a social-democratic welfare system.

Manufacturing. During the Communist era industry was nationalized, and heavy industry, particularly machine building, received the lion's share of state investments. The aging of fixed industrial assets, however, led to an increasing energy inefficiency. Romania has a developed petrochemical manufacturing capacity. Textile manufacture and food processing are important light industries.

Energy. While hydroelectric-power generation, especially from the shared (with Yugoslavia) Danube IRON GATE stations, is important (20% of the total), much of Romanian power is fueled by natural gas, which Romania possesses in abundance.

Agriculture. During the Communist era more than 90% of Romania's agriculturally productive land was collectivized. Farm productivity was low due to lack of investments, bad management, and undermechanization. Immediately after the revolution of 1989, in an effort to increase production, the new government began to allot land to private farmers. Romania's principal crops are corn, wheat, rye, sugar beets, potatoes, oilseeds, vegetables, and fruit. Dairy products, wines and spirits, and prepared meats are also produced in significant amounts. Although domestic food shortages characterized the last years of the Communist regime, Romania remained a net food exporter.

Forestry and Fishing. Careful harvesting of once overexploited timber reserves is the basis for important lumber, paper, and furniture industries. Fish catches, primarily from the Danube and its delta, are also significant.

Transportation. While railroad transportation remains important, two-thirds of all goods and three-quarters of all passengers are now moved by road. The Danube–Black Sea Canal was completed in 1984, but it is too shallow to accommodate most oceangoing ships. Tarom, the national airline, serves domestic and international airports.

Trade. In the 1980s the USSR claimed at least one-quarter of Romania's foreign trade. In 1989, Ceauşescu announced that as a result of a draconian austerity program initiated in 1982, Romania had paid off a foreign debt that had amounted to $10 billion in 1980.

Government

Multiparty elections were held on May 20, 1990. A bicameral legislature, a 119-seat Senate, and a 396-seat Chamber of Deputies, to serve as a Constituent Assembly for a maximum of two years, was assigned the task of drafting a new constitution to replace the Communist constitution of 1965. Ion Iliescu, a former Communist, was elected president, and in June Prime Minister Petre Roman formed a government composed of young technocrats.

History

Dacian tribes living in what is now Romania were defeated by the Roman emperor TRAJAN in AD 106, and for the next 165 years the country was the Roman province of Dacia. During that time the native population was Romanized. In subsequent centuries Romania was invaded by Goths, Slavs, and Bulgars. Hungarians occupied Transylvania from the 11th century. The Romanian states of Walachia and Moldavia emerged in the 13th and 14th

Braşov (Kronstadt), a city on the north slope of the Transylvanian Alps, was founded by the Teutonic Knights in the 13th century. Its architecture, including the "Black Church" (center), shows a strong German influence.

centuries, respectively. The Ottoman Turks established control in the 15th century despite fierce resistance by Romanian princes; the best known among them was VLAD THE IMPALER, the prototype of Dracula. In the last decade of the 16th century MICHAEL THE BRAVE, Prince of Walachia, defeated the Turks and briefly united Walachia with Moldavia and Transylvania. During the RUSSO-TURKISH WAR of 1828, Russia occupied the Danubian principalities, making them virtual Russian protectorates.

Following the CRIMEAN WAR (1853–56), Russian troops vacated Moldavia and Walachia, which were then recognized by the European powers as autonomous principalities under Ottoman suzerainty. In 1859 the Moldavian patriot Alexandru Ion CUZA was elected hospodar (governor) of both principalities, and in 1862 the powers recognized the administrative union of the two states as Romania. In 1866, Cuza was replaced by Prince Charles of Hohenzollern-Sigmaringen, who led Romania in its War of Independence (1877–78; see BERLIN, CONGRESS OF). In 1881, Charles was crowned King CAROL I of Romania.

During the next 35 years Romania gradually modernized, and an oligarchical parliamentary government was established. Foreign policy aimed at the unification of all the Romanian lands. Romania participated in the second BALKAN WAR (1913). Carol I was succeeded by his nephew FERDINAND in 1914. In 1916, Romania entered World War I against the Central Powers, and the eventual Allied victory enabled it to acquire the former Austro-Hungarian territories of Transylvania, BUCOVINA, and Banat. This, in addition to BESSARABIA, taken from the disintegrating Russian empire, doubled the size of the Romanian kingdom.

After the war, a limited political democratization took place. Romania also became active in international af-

Demonstrators marching through Bucharest in December 1989 carry signs denouncing Romanian Communist-party chief Nicolae Ceauşescu as a tyrant, and caricaturing Ceauşescu and his wife, Elena, as assassins. The Ceauşescus were deposed and executed a few days later, and a new coalition government took over.

fairs, particularly at the League of Nations and as a member of the LITTLE ENTENTE.

In 1938, King CAROL II established a royal dictatorship that lasted until 1940, when it was overthrown by the Fascist IRON GUARD and other right-wing elements. That same year Romania was forced to cede Bessarabia and Bucovina to the USSR, northern Transylvania to Hungary, and southern Dobruja to Bulgaria. Under Gen. Ion ANTONESCU, who had assumed dictatorial powers, Romania participated in the German-led invasion of the USSR. Faced with imminent defeat by the advancing Red Army, King Michael, the army, the three traditional parties, and the minuscule but well-organized Communist party overthrew Antonescu in August 1944.

In December 1947 the monarchy was abolished, and Romania was proclaimed a people's republic. Under Communist party boss Gheorghe GHEORGHIU-DEJ, industry was nationalized, agriculture was collectivized, and political opposition was suppressed, but Romania soon embarked on an independent foreign-policy course often at odds with that of the USSR. In 1965, Nicolae Ceauşescu succeeded Gheorghiu-Dej. At first Ceauşescu's nationalist policies attracted widespread support, but during the 1970s and '80s his regime was discredited by its abuse of human rights and economic mismanagement. In December 1989 anti-Ceauşescu riots broke out in Timişoara, and in a brief but violent revolution the regime was overthrown, and the dictator and his wife were executed. A coalition including former dissidents, Communist party members, and army officers, calling itself the National Salvation Front, took over. Front candidates won clear majorities in the elections of May 1990, and Ion Iliescu became president. Despite violent suppression of demonstrations in the summer of 1990, Romania is slowly introducing democratic practices and rule of law.

Romanian language   see ROMANCE LANGUAGES

Romanian literature   see ROMANIA

Romanov (dynasty) [roh'-muh-nawf or ruh-mahn'-uhf] The Romanov dynasty ruled Russia from 1613 until the February Revolution of 1917 (see RUSSIAN REVOLUTIONS OF 1917). The family was descended from Andrei Ivanovich Kobyla, a Muscovite boyar who lived in the first half of the 14th century. The name *Romanov* was taken from Roman Yuriev (d. 1543), the father of Anastasia Romanova (d. 1560), who was the first wife of Tsar IVAN IV.

MICHAEL Romanov, grandnephew of Anastasia, was elected tsar by a National Assembly in 1613; he was the first of the dynasty to rule Russia. Important Romanov rulers included PETER I, whose reign marks the beginning of imperial Russia; CATHERINE II, actually a German who married into the family; ALEXANDER I, who defeated Napoleon in 1812; and ALEXANDER II, who emancipated the serfs in 1861. The last Romanov tsar, NICHOLAS II, abdicated in March 1917. He and his immediate family were executed (July 1918) at Ekaterinburg (modern Sverdlovsk).

Romans, Epistle to the   The Epistle to the Romans is the longest of Saint PAUL's letters and is therefore placed first among the letters in the New Testament of the BIBLE. It is the only Pauline letter written to a community not founded by the apostle and is more of an essay presenting some of Paul's ideas on salvation than a response to particular problems. It was probably written about AD 57–58 before Paul departed from Corinth for Jerusalem to deliver the collection he had taken for the church there.

In Romans, Paul develops the theme of justification by faith and tries to fathom God's plan for the Jews, his chosen people, who have not followed Jesus. The implications for Christian life of Jesus, faith, and salvation are drawn out.

The exact nature and purpose of Romans is controversial, and it is difficult to determine whether it is a theological letter-essay, a last testament, an introduction of Paul to the Roman Christians, or a response to particular problems in Rome that Paul had heard about.

---

romanticism (art)   Romanticism is not a style but a movement. Starting in the 1750s, it became a potent force at the turn of the century and lasted until about the 1850s—some historians argue that it survived into the 20th century as SURREALISM.

The seeds of romanticism are to be found in an obsessive interest in the art of the past, including the energetic figures in Michelangelo's frescoes, the exuberant colors of Peter Paul Rubens's canvases, the golden idylls of Claude Lorrain's landscapes, and the threatening presence of Salvator Rosa's craggy rocks.

Romantic artists often wished to break the accepted,

William Blake derived the subject matter of his visionary paintings and writings from the Bible and other mystical sources. Jacob's Dream (c.1820), a delicate watercolor, one of his characteristic mediums, is Blake's visualization of a biblical passage (Gen. 28:12–18). (British Museum, London.)

Eugène Delacroix's The Death of Sardanapalus *(1827–28) displays romanticism's exotic element. (Louvre, Paris.)*

gène DELACROIX in *The Death of Sardanapalus* (1827–28; Louvre, Paris).

The absorption of romantic artists in the past and in exotic cultures is reflected in the diversity of architectural styles used in buildings. There was also a great love of ruins, old, or freshly made—as in the Désert de Retz (c.1785), a four-story French mansion constructed in the form of a single fluted column, broken, cracked, and lush with vegetation on its fragmented top.

Pastoral scenes in morning mist or by moonlight (C. D. Friedrich, Samuel PALMER) were as prized as scenes of storms, avalanches, and disastrous fires (J. M. W. TURNER). Napoleon's campaigns could be commemorated in superb battle scenes (Baron GROS) or their savagery excoriated (Francisco de GOYA). All these artists may be called romantic, sharing as they did a passion for nature and its moods and a fascination with the human potential for violence.

romanticism (literature)   In European and American literature, romanticism is an aesthetic movement that attained its peak during the first third of the 19th century. The term is derived from medieval romances, which were fanciful tales of larger-than-life adventure and highly colored sentiment. In contrast to REALISM, which aims at a faithful reproduction of reality as perceived by the senses, romanticism attempts to capture the play of the imagination. The romantic approach is perhaps best illustrated by William BLAKE's response to the question "When the sun rises, do you not see a round disc of fire somewhat like a guinea?" He answered, "Oh no, no. I see an Innumerable company of the Heavenly host crying, 'Holy, Holy, Holy is the Lord God Almighty!'" In this reliance on what Samuel Taylor COLERIDGE called the "shaping spirit of imagination," romanticism is subjective and intensely idealistic.

English Romanticism. William WORDSWORTH's and Coleridge's LYRICAL BALLADS (1798) are generally thought to mark the formal beginning of English romanticism, and English romanticism is distinguished for its lyric poetry, such as Percy Bysshe SHELLEY's "Ode to the West Wind" and "To a Skylark," and the sonnets of John KEATS. Lord BYRON's epics, *Childe Harold's Pilgrimage* and *Don Juan*, are more satirical in tone.

Germany. In Germany, the brothers August Wilhelm von SCHLEGEL and Friedrich von SCHLEGEL formulated innovative aesthetic concepts, often presented in paradoxical terms, in their journal *Athenäum*. Under the influence of the philosopher Johann Gottlieb FICHTE, the *Frühromantiker* ("early romantics") were metaphysical and mystical. Their major poets were NOVALIS and Wilhelm Heinrich Wackenroder (1773–98), both of whom died young, and Ludwig TIECK.

The second generation of German romantics, the *Hochromantiker* ("high romantics"), were more practical and creative. Their work includes the folk songs and lyrics of Clemens BRENTANO, Heinrich HEINE, and Eduard MÖRIKE and the tales of Joseph EICHENDORFF, Ernst Theodor Amadeus HOFFMANN, and Heinrich August de La Motte-Fouqué (1777–1843).

rational rules of academic art, allowing a greater role for the uncontrolled, the limitless, the irrational. One of the clearest statements is to be found in William BLAKE's annotations to Sir Joshua REYNOLDS's *Discourses*: "What has Reasoning," Blake demanded, "to do with the Art of Painting? Knowledge of Ideal Beauty is Not to be Acquired. It is Born with us."

The stress on an inner vision as fundamental to romantic artists was expressed by them in a great variety of ways. In Germany, for example, the ethereal beings in the art of Philipp Otto Runge are as romantic as the landscapes of Caspar David FRIEDRICH, behind whose trees and mountains lies an elaborate religious symbolism. The reaction of the artist as an individual to his or her own ideas and surroundings was of paramount importance for the romantic artist.

Exotic subject matter—in place and in time—also appealed to the romantics. The excitement of the people, horses, and lions of North Africa were all painted by Eu-

Joseph Severn painted Shelley near the Baths of Caracalla *(1819) in Rome. During that visit Shelley wrote acts 2 and 3 of* Prometheus Unbound *(1820), one of the great lyrical dramas of the romantic period. (Keats-Shelley Memorial House, Rome.)*

France. Bitter controversies involving political and religious loyalties accompanied the emergence of romanticism in France, the main strife taking place in the theater and culminating in the notorious battle between the warring factions on the opening night of Victor HUGO's *Hernani* (1830). Hugo, Alexandre DUMAS *père,* and Alfred de MUSSET all used William Shakespeare as a model to effect the departure from accepted classical practices.

The United States. In the United States, the closest approximation to European romanticism was the New England TRANSCENDENTALISM of Ralph Waldo EMERSON and Henry David THOREAU. Other American writers, however, shared the belief in the importance of the creative imagination, among them Nathaniel HAWTHORNE, Henry Wadsworth LONGFELLOW, Herman MELVILLE, Edgar Allan POE, and Walt WHITMAN.

romanticism (music) Although the romantic musical style was anticipated by some composers as early as the mid-18th century, romanticism in music usually is thought to have begun in the early 19th century and to have continued until about 1890. It thus followed the classical period and preceded postromanticism, which extends to about 1920.

Certain characteristics distinguish romantic music from its classical forebears and from its modern successors: long, expressive melodies, usually with wide leaps and based on consonant intervals; emphasis on colorful harmony and instrumentation, often for their own sake; freedom and flexibility in rhythm and treatment of musical form; expansion of the resources of musical nuance; a sense of historicism that led many composers to revive earlier technical musical devices; and the pervasiveness of tonality, though treated with increasing flexibility, as

the basic organizing principle of music.

Romantic musical styles were anticipated in the mid-18th century in the music of Carl Philipp Emanuel BACH, who influenced the classical composers Haydn and Mozart. This is most notable in their compositions in the minor mode. Such works as Mozart's D minor and C minor piano concertos exhibited in turn some of the devices of the romantic music to come. Beethoven, who dominated the musical world of the early 19th century, has been considered too seminal a composer to be classified as either classical or romantic. Contemporaries such as SCHUBERT, Spohr, and WEBER, however, may with more justification be considered the first generation of romantic composers, although many of their earlier works remain in the classical tradition.

The succeeding generation of musical romantics included such composers as BERLIOZ, BERWALD, CHOPIN, GLINKA, LISZT, MENDELSSOHN, SCHUMANN, VERDI, and WAGNER, some of whom lived well into the second half of the 19th century. The major romantic composers all exhibited self-expressive traits, but some tended to work more within the Western mainstream of classically derived forms and harmonic systems. Schumann and later romantics such as BRAHMS, DVOŘÁK, FRANCK, SAINT-SAËNS, and TCHAIKOVSKY may be included in their number. Other composers were more interested in expanding the structural, orchestral, and harmonic resources of music. Wagner and Liszt were major innovators who influenced the course of music for generations, counting among their followers such late-romantic figures as BRUCKNER, MAHLER, RIMSKY-KORSAKOV, SCRIABIN, and Richard STRAUSS. Musical nationalism making use of folk-music idioms was concurrently developing among the late romantics, as exhibited in the music of composers such as GRIEG, MUSSORGSKY, and SMETANA.

No clear line can be drawn between figures such as Wagner and Mahler and the development of various postromantic styles, including the impressionism of DEBUSSY and the serialism of SCHOENBERG. Romanticism itself has

Frédéric Chopin, the most prominent composer of romantic piano music, masterfully exploited the tonal and expressive range of the piano, fully establishing it as an instrument for solo performance. Chopin used subtle chromatic progressions and lyrical melodies in a vast number of compositions ranging from lively mazurkas to melancholy nocturnes.

The operatic works of the German composer Richard Wagner marked the culmination of romanticism, fusing music and drama in an expressive unity unsurpassed in musical history. By using such techniques as the leitmotiv, Wagner brought his subject and the music into close dramatic rapport. Wagner drew on Germanic legend, as in The Ring of the Nibelung *(1853–74).*

remained one of many musical resources for 20th-century composers such as PROKOFIEV, SHOSTAKOVICH, SIBELIUS, and, more recently, some of the composers who have reacted against serialism and sought a more eclectic musical language.

Romany language   see INDO-IRANIAN LANGUAGES

Romberg, Sigmund [rahm'-berg]   One of the most popular American composers of light music, Hungarian-born Sigmund Romberg, b. July 29, 1887, d. Nov. 10, 1951, brought the traditions of European operetta to the American theater. He wrote the music for many of Broadway's best-known operettas, including *Maytime* (1917), *Blossom Time* (1921), *The Student Prince* (1924), *The Desert Song* (1926), and *The New Moon* (1928). Romberg later turned to musical comedy with *Up in Central Park* (1945), and, from 1929, he also wrote music for films.

Rome (Italy)   Rome (Italian: Roma), once the seat of a vast empire, is now the capital of Italy and the seat of the supreme pontiff of the Roman Catholic church (at VATICAN CITY, a sovereign state within Rome). The city is also the capital of Italy's Rome province and LATIUM region. Located in central Italy on both sides of the Tiber River between the Apennine Mountains and the Tyrrhenian Sea (27 km/17 mi to the west), the city has a population of 2,816,474 (1989 est.); 3,175,000 persons (1987 est.) live in the metropolitan area.

Contemporary City

The Tiber, flowing through Rome from north to south, divides the city. On the east bank, the most visible and plentiful remains of classical Rome are located south of Piazza Venezia. To the northwest and along the Tiber, medieval Rome centers on the area between the Via del Corso and the Corso Vittorio Emmanuele. During the 16th

century Pope SIXTUS V began the modern transformation in the area east of the Via del Corso. Here were built the Vatican and Lateran palaces; new, wide streets; and the many squares, fountains, statues, and palaces for which Rome is famous. On the west bank of the Tiber are Vatican City and Trastevere, which has maintained much of its medieval charm.

The economy of Rome depends heavily on tourism. Industry includes metallurgy, electronics, and glass, cement, and furniture manufacturing. Rome is the financial, cultural, transportation, and administrative center of Italy. The banking, insurance, printing, publishing, and fashion industries are quite important. The thriving Italian movie industry is centered at Cinecittà (Cinema City), located a few kilometers outside of Rome.

The city's government consists of a mayor (*sindaco*), a legislative city council, and a city advisory board (selected from the city council membership to implement the council's legislation). All these officials are popularly elected every 4 years.

The state-run University of Rome was founded in 1303. In addition, Rome has several church-run colleges; academies of fine arts; and the Conservatorio di Musica Santa Cecilia (1570), the oldest music academy in the world.

Many of Rome's museums are among the world's greatest. The VATICAN MUSEUMS AND GALLERIES contain the richest collections. Other great classical collections are housed in the National and Capitoline museums; magnificent paintings are in the Borghese, Corsini, Doria, and Colonna collections. Rome's opera house is one of Europe's finest.

The city's ancient ruins include the COLOSSEUM, the CATACOMBS, the FORUM, the Arch of Constantine, the Baths of Caracalla, the Circus Maximus, the Capitol, and the Pantheon. The many palaces include Castel Sant'Angelo, the Vatican Palace (in which is the SISTINE CHAPEL), Villa Farnesina, Villa Borghese, Palazzo Doria, Palazzo Barberini, and Palazzo Corsini. The numerous churches include SAINT PETER'S BASILICA, San Giovanni in Laterano, San Paolo Fuori le Mura, and Santa Maria Maggiore. The monument to Victor Emmanuel II commemorates the unification of Italy in the 19th century.

History

Continuous settlements probably began about 1000 BC on Rome's future site. Probably by the 6th century BC several separate tribal settlements, including those of the Latins and SABINES, had coalesced to form a single city. This early city was built on seven hills, including CAPITOLINE HILL. The city eventually became the capital of the Roman Empire (see ROME, ANCIENT).

During the 5th century AD the city entered a decline and was sacked (410) by the Visigoths under ALARIC I and by the Vandals (455). Temporal political and social authority in the city of Rome gradually devolved upon the pope, or bishop of Rome, who began to claim primacy among western bishops.

During the 6th to early 8th century the city was the center of the duchy of Rome, a Byzantine fief. In 754 the popes, with Frankish aid, were able to assert their inde-

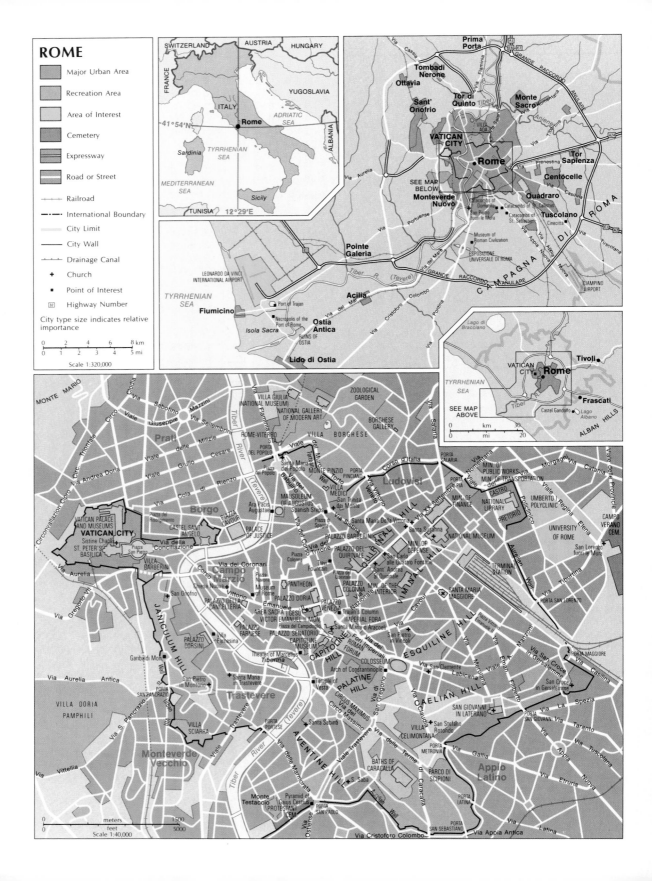

Rome, the capital of Italy and one of the world's richest cultural centers, blends modern development with ancient and Renaissance monuments.

pendence and hegemony over a large portion of central Italy called the PAPAL STATES, with Rome as their capital. During the Middle Ages the city became the scene of power struggles between Rome's leading families, the papacy, and secular rulers. During the 12th century ARNOLD OF BRESCIA successfully challenged papal authority, exiling Pope EUGENE III and establishing a commune (1144–45) until Holy Roman Emperor FREDERICK I intervened. Factional struggles such as that between the GUELPHS AND GHIBELLINES continued during the 13th century. When the papacy was removed to Avignon, France, during the 14th century, Rome experienced one of its most serious declines.

Rome began its great recovery under papal guidance during the second half of the 15th century. By the late 16th century, it again became a premier world city. In 1870, when the Papal States joined the newly created Kingdom of Italy, Rome became the capital. The Lateran Treaty created (1929) the separate state of Vatican City within the city.

Rome (New York)   Rome is an industrial city in central New York on the Mohawk River and the New York State Barge Canal. It has a population of 44,350 (1990). The city is an agricultural distribution center and manufactures machinery, metal products, and paint. It was laid out as Lynchville in 1786 when Dominick Lynch purchased land on the site of Fort Stanwix (1758), now a national monument. In 1768, Sir William Johnson concluded an important treaty with the Iroquois Nations at the fort. During the American Revolution Fort Stanwix was besieged (1777) by a British force under Barry St. Leger. An American relief force led by Nicolas HERKIMER

was ambushed at nearby Oriskany and forced to retreat, but rumors that Benedict Arnold was approaching with a large Revolutionary force caused the British to abandon the siege (see SARATOGA, BATTLES OF). Rome flourished as a result of construction of the Erie Canal, begun there in 1817.

Rome, ancient   Ancient Rome grew from a small prehistoric settlement on the Tiber River in central Italy into an empire that encompassed the entire Mediterranean world and much of Europe and the Near East. The special genius of the Romans lay in war, administration, and law, but as the inheritors of Greek culture too, they were able to transmit to later ages a rich and rounded heritage that became the basis of modern Western civilization.

Early Rome: The Kingship

According to legend, Rome was founded in 753 BC by ROMULUS AND REMUS. Historically, by this date, two different but closely related peoples, the Latins and the SABINES, coexisted in the territory, and in the 7th century their villages coalesced to form a unified city. Rome soon outstripped other towns in LATIUM in wealth and power.

According to later historians, Romulus was succeeded as king by Numa Pompilius (c.715–673 BC), during whose reign the foundations of Roman law and religion were laid. The fourth Latin king, Ancus Marcius (r. 641–616), is credited with founding the plebeian class and with building the first bridge across the Tiber, which allowed the Romans to extend their dominions westward toward the Tyrrhenian Sea.

In the late 7th century BC the ETRUSCANS placed members of their royal family, the Tarquins, on the Roman throne. The Etruscan kings were TARQUINIUS PRISCUS, Servius Tullius (r. c.578–535), and TARQUINIUS SUPER-

This bronze sculpture group portrays a she-wolf suckling the twins Romulus and Remus. According to legend, Romulus founded (753 BC) Rome after killing his brother, Remus, and became the first of seven legendary kings before the founding (509 BC) of the republic. (Palazzo dei Conservatori, Rome.)

BUS. Under their rule the marshes were drained, a large part of Latium was brought under Roman control, and the Capitoline temple, the Circus Maximus, and the ancient FORUM were built. With the expulsion of Tarquinius Superbus in 510 BC, however, the Roman Senate (see SENATE, ROMAN), which had originated as an advisory body to the monarch, decreed that Rome should have no more kings.

The Republic

The Roman republic, founded supposedly in 509 BC, was headed by the Senate and by magistrates, later called CONSULS—usually two in number—who were elected annually by the Senate. The Senate was made up of the PATRICIANS—the upper class; the general body of citizens—the PLEBEIANS—were effectively frozen out of government. In the early 5th century the plebeians revolted and forced the Senate to accept their representatives, the TRIBUNES, into the government, and in 445 BC the ban on intermarriage between patricians and plebeians was removed. Gradually the plebeians gained admission to virtually all state offices, winning the consulship in 366. The struggle between the orders lasted for 200 years, ending only in 287, when the laws, or plebiscites, voted by the assembly of the plebeians became binding on both classes.

The Conquest of Italy. Despite internal political conflict, Rome under the early republic continued to expand. In 493 BC, Rome concluded an alliance with the Latin League and in time came to dominate all Latium. With the help of the Latins the Romans defeated various mountain tribes that pressed in on Latium, and in 396 they destroyed the Etruscan city of Veii. However, calamity struck in 390 when tribes from GAUL crossed the Alps, shattered the Etruscan defenses, and sacked Rome. Through perseverance, military prowess, and cunning diplomacy, the Romans were able to reestablish their position. When the other Latin cities tried to assert their independence, Rome defeated them in the Latin War (340–338) and dissolved their league. The Romans also fought intermittent wars (343–290) against the Samnites.

The Romans profited from the disunity among their adversaries. Although the Samnites, Umbrians, Etruscans, and Gauls belatedly united forces, Rome crushed them (295 BC) at Sentinum. With the capture of the Greek city of Tarentum in southern Italy in 272, following a difficult war with PYRRHUS, king of Epirus, the Roman conquest of Italy was nearly complete.

To consolidate their hold on southern and central Italy, the Romans planted Roman and Latin military colonies on lands that they confiscated and awarded complete Roman citizenship to those cities and tribes which quickly romanized and proved faithful to Rome. Other cities and tribes were granted only limited citizenship and were forced to conclude perpetual alliances with Rome and to provide soldiers for Roman wars. In 264, Roman Italy comprised about 135,000 km^2 (52,000 mi^2) and was inhabited by about 292,000 Roman (male) citizens and about 700,000 Roman allies.

First and Second Punic Wars. CARTHAGE, a wealthy Phoenician city in North Africa, had built up a maritime empire that extended to Sardinia, Corsica, and part of Sicily. Competition between Rome and Carthage for control of Sicily's grain production led to the PUNIC WARS.

The First Punic War (264–241 BC) arose from a conflict over the Sicilian cities of Messina and Syracuse. Although they were not a seafaring people, the Romans built fleets, which despite setbacks succeeded in defeating the Carthaginians and by 241 finally forced Carthage to surrender Sicily and to agree to pay a huge indemnity. Rome thus became a world power, but at the price of about 20 percent of its citizens killed in the war.

Continuing to expand, the Romans seized Sardinia and Corsica in 238, and when Carthage protested, forced it to pay an additional indemnity. In 237 the Carthaginian general HAMILCAR BARCA was sent to Spain, where he conquered large areas. The Romans regarded this conquest as a challenge and decided to invade Spain and Africa, but another Carthaginian general, HANNIBAL, initiating the Second Punic War (218–201 BC), forestalled their scheme. In a daring march from Spain, Hannibal crossed the Pyrenees, southern Gaul, and the Alps and in the autumn of 218 moved down into Italy, where he inflicted heavy losses on the Romans at Trebia (218), Lake Trasimene (217), and Cannae in southern Italy (216). Most of the recently conquered peoples of Italy abandoned Rome.

The Romans refused to accept defeat, however. They never again risked a pitched battle; instead the Roman general Quintus Fabius Maximus (see FABIUS family) devised a brilliant strategy of delay and harassment that eventually wore down the Carthaginians. The Romans also sent an army to Spain and managed to cut Hannibal off from reinforcements. The tide of war turned after 210; SCIPIO AFRICANUS MAJOR twice defeated the Carthaginians and terminated their rule in Spain, and in 204 led the Roman invasion of Africa, where, at Zama in 202, he dealt Hannibal his only defeat. Scipio advocated leniency, but Carthage

The Roman general Scipio Africanus Major assumed command (216 BC) of the Roman forces in Spain during the Second Punic War. The three Punic Wars were fought against Carthage. In the first war (264–241 BC) Rome seized Sicily from Carthaginian control. During the second war (218–201 BC) the Romans withstood an invasion by the Carthaginian general Hannibal and, under Scipio's command, expelled the Carthaginians from Spain. In the third war (149–146 BC) Carthage was razed.

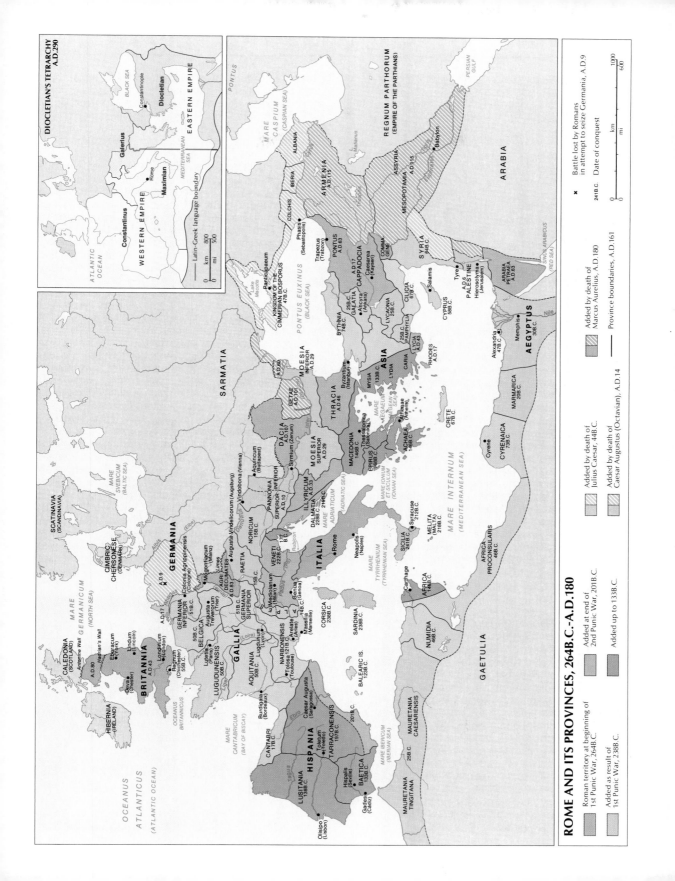

ROME AND ITS PROVINCES, 264B.C.–A.D.180

This model of imperial Rome includes the Circus Maximus and emperor's palaces in the foreground. Of Rome, Cicero wrote, "I believe, Romulus foresaw that this city would provide a visiting place and a home for a world empire. . . ."

was forced to surrender its fleet, pay an enormous idemnity, and become a dependent ally of Rome.

Macedonian and Syrian Wars. During the Second Punic War, Rome had also had to contain Hannibal's ally, PHILIP V of Macedonia, in Greece. Later, when Philip began to expand his territory eastward, Rhodes and Pergamum urged Rome to intervene, and in the Second Macedonian War (200–196 BC) Roman legions routed the Macedonian phalanx at Cynoscephalae (197), effectively ending both the power of MACEDONIA and the independence of Greece. When the Roman commander Titus Quinctius FLAMININUS proclaimed (196) the Greek cities free from Macedonia, Rome in reality was assuming a protectorate over the Greek states. A few years later, Rome's defeat of the Seleucid king ANTIOCHUS III in the Syrian War (192–188) brought the whole of Anatolia into the Roman sphere of influence. Rome again defeated Macedonia in the Third Macedonian War (171–168 BC), when it slaughtered PERSEUS's army at Pydna (168), and in 148 it annexed the kingdom outright following an uprising. By 146, when Rome crushed the Achaean League and destroyed Corinth, the entire Greek world had come under Roman hegemony.

Third Punic War and Iberian Campaigns. Success in the East had not diminished Rome's fears of a revived Carthage, however, and Carthage's hostilities against NUMIDIA, a Roman ally, served as an excuse to mount the Third Punic War (149–146 BC). The Carthaginians' original willingness to surrender after a quick Roman victory was rescinded when they learned that Carthage was to be destroyed. Three years of heroic resistance nevertheless ended in the capture and razing (146) of the city under the supervision of SCIPIO AFRICANUS MINOR. Scipio also conducted operations in Spain against the Iberians, which concluded in 133 with the destruction of Numantia.

Political and Economic Change. Rome's foreign wars brought great new wealth to the senatorial landed aristocracy and to a newly emerging class, the equestrians, who were largely financiers and tax gatherers. The importation of inexpensive raw materials from the colonies under-

mined Rome's peasant economy, and the influx of thousands of slaves made possible the organization of large landed estates. As a result of economic dislocation, a large portion of the population of Rome was unemployed and dependent on the public dole. Mobs of the unemployed roamed the streets, ready to be swayed by demagogues.

These conditions brought forth the reformers Tiberius Sempronius and Caius Sempronius Gracchus (see GRACCHUS family). In 133 BC, Tiberius was elected tribune on a platform of redistribution of the land to the poor. When the Senate declared his reelection illegal, his followers rioted, and Tiberius was killed in the violence that erupted. Caius, taking over his elder brother's reforms, became tribune in 123 and extended reform to the tax system and the judiciary. By then, a conservative reaction had set in, and Caius was killed by a mob in 121.

Civil War and the Fall of the Republic. The deaths of the Gracchi opened a century of anarchy and civil wars. War (112–105 BC) with King JUGURTHA of Numidia and an invasion of Italy by the Cimbri and Teutons, two Germanic tribes, demonstrated the inadequacy of Rome's conscript army. Gaius MARIUS, an equestrian, introduced a volunteer, semiprofessional army and threw its ranks open to the common people. The German invaders were wiped out (102–101), but the proletarian soldiers clamored for land. Because the ruling oligarchy refused to recognize their demands, repeated coalitions were formed between destitute veterans and ambitious generals.

In 91 BC, Rome's allies in Italy rose in a great revolt called the Social War. Under this pressure the Romans granted the franchise to all Italians and mercilessly crushed those who did not submit. Civil war followed (88–82). Marius, the great popular hero, died in 86. The opposing forces were led by Lucius Cornelius SULLA, who had the support of the aristocrats. With his private proletarian army, Sulla marched on Rome, dispersed the legal government, and routed his populist enemies. Ruling as dictator (82–81), he ordered thousands of his enemies assassinated and their property confiscated. His goal was

Julius Ceasar, a military hero as a result of his victories in the Gallic Wars, defeated his rivals to secure absolute power in Rome by 48 BC. Caesar's rule ended with his murder in 44 BC.

Mark Antony and Cleopatra VII of Egypt are portrayed on reverse sides of a silver tetradrachm (34–33 BC).

to restore the rule of the oligarchs, but he failed to remedy socioeconomic conditions.

The next two great rivals for power in Rome were POMPEY THE GREAT and Julius CAESAR. Both had made their reputations in the army, and both were highly ambitious. In 60 BC, Pompey and Caesar joined Marcus Licinius CRASSUS in the First TRIUMVIRATE; they were able to rule despite the opposition of the Senate. Caesar spent much of the next decade fighting the GALLIC WARS. In his absence Pompey consolidated his power by concluding an alliance with the Senate.

In 52 BC the Senate made Pompey sole consul and two years later ordered Caesar to disband his army. Instead, Caesar crossed the Rubicon into Italy proper early in 49 and marched against Rome, precipitating yet another civil war. In a series of battles he defeated Pompey, who fled to the East. Caesar secured Spain, then pursued Pompey to Greece, defeating him at Pharsalus (48). Pompey's murder in Egypt, followed by a series of victories in Anatolia (47), North Africa (46), and Spain (45), gave Caesar control of the government. Back in Rome, he set about reforming the laws and reorganizing the administration of the colonies. Under Caesar, Rome controlled all of Italy, Gaul, Spain, Numidia, Macedonia, Greece, Palestine, Egypt, and virtually all the Mediterranean islands. Made dictator for life in 44 BC, Caesar seemed to be moving toward a monarchical system. On March 15 his autocratic rule was cut short; republican conspirators, led by Marcus Junius BRUTUS and Gaius CASSIUS LONGINUS, stabbed him to death in the Senate.

Caesar's opponents underestimated the allegiance of Caesar's partisans, who were now galvanized into action by Mark ANTONY and Octavian (later AUGUSTUS), Caesar's grandnephew and heir. Antony, Octavian, and Marcus Aemilius LEPIDUS, forming the Second Triumvirate, forced the Senate to accept their rule. They instituted a reign of terror, and at the Battle of PHILIPPI (42) defeated the forces of Brutus and Cassius. By 31 BC, Octavian had defeated Antony and CLEOPATRA and had successfully established himself as princeps, or first citizen.

The Empire

The system of government established by Octavian in 27 BC was a monarchy disguised as a republic. The princeps (the emperor) ostensibly ruled by commission from the Senate and the people, and there was no automatic system of succession. Octavian, assuming the title and name Imperator Caesar Augustus, carried forth many of the reforms of Julius Caesar, rebuilt the city of Rome, and became a great patron of the arts. During his reign the Roman Empire was unrivaled; thus began the 200 years of peace known as the Pax Romana. The system of ROMAN ROADS and a sophisticated postal system helped unify the empire. Commerce and trade boomed among its far-flung possessions. Augustus reformed the Senate, made the system of taxation more equitable, and revived the census. He died in AD 14 and was succeeded by his stepson Tiberius.

Julio-Claudian Dynasty. TIBERIUS, continuing the policies of Augustus, left the empire in sound financial shape on his death in 37 BC. His successor, CALIGULA, was noted for his cruelty and licentiousness and was assassinated in AD 41 by the PRAETORIAN GUARD, which named his uncle, CLAUDIUS I, emperor. Claudius was generally an efficient administrator, although historians have blamed him for being too much under the control of his civil servants and his wives, Messalina and AGRIPPINA II.

NERO, Agrippina's son and the last Julio-Claudian emperor, assumed the throne in AD 54. He governed well in his early years, but increasingly under the influence of his mother and of his second wife, Poppaea Sabina (d. 65), turned bloodthirsty. He was accused of burning Rome in 64; Nero in turn blamed the Christians for the fire and began the first Roman persecution of them. He committed suicide in 68 when he saw that a revolution against him was succeeding.

The Flavians and Antonines. VESPASIAN (r. AD 69–79), declared emperor by his soldiers in the East and founder of the Flavian dynasty, brought order and efficiency to the administration of Rome's affairs. He built the COLOSSEUM and other important public works. He was succeeded by two sons, TITUS (r. 79–81), a popular and generous ruler, and DOMITIAN (r. 81–96), who began his reign by following his brother's policies, but whose rule (despite his generally efficient administration) became progressively more despotic. His wife had him murdered.

The next six emperors, generally classified as the Antonines, ruled for nearly a century, a period that is sometimes called the Golden Age of the Roman Empire. The

The Forum Romanum, situated in a valley between the Palatine and Capitoline hills, flourished as a religious and administrative center during imperial times.

This relief from the Ara Pacis (Altar of Peace; 13–9 BC) portrays the emperor Augustus (Octavian) with his family. Augustus, who assumed formal control of Rome in 27 BC, established the foundations of the Roman Empire through a consolidation of legal and administrative reforms. His reign began the 200-year Pax Romana, during which Rome was unchallenged in its domination of the Mediterranean world.

first emperor, Nerva (r. 96–98), was elected by the Senate in an effort to assert its power over the military. An elderly, well-respected statesman, he was opposed by the Praetorian guard. He adopted as his successor the great soldier TRAJAN (a Spaniard, the first non-Italian to serve as emperor). Trajan (r. 98–117), one of Rome's greatest emperors, expanded the empire into modern Romania and into Armenia and Mesopotamia and built impressive aqueducts, roads, theaters, and basilicas. His successor, HADRIAN (r. 117–38), another soldier, was more cautious in foreign relations, although he put down a Jewish revolt in Jerusalem (AD 132–35) with great brutality. ANTONINUS PIUS had a long and prosperous reign (138–61) and was succeeded by the philosopher MARCUS AURELIUS (r. 161–80).

Marcus Aurelius was a benevolent and humane emperor—with the exception of his persecution of the Christians. His reign also saw an increasing number of interior rebellions and attacks on the empire's borders. The reign (180–92) of his son COMMODUS, generally regarded as the beginning of Rome's long decline, was marked by despotism, licentiousness, and brutality. His strangulation in 192 inaugurated a long period of short, violent reigns fueled by constant court intrigues.

The Crisis of the 3d Century. In the 3d century the Roman world plunged into a prolonged and nearly fatal crisis. Sharp divisions between the opulent notables in the cities and the poor and hardly civilized peasants created tensions. The wars that began under Marcus Aurelius continued, and increased taxation destroyed the prosperity of the empire. To meet rising military costs and to pay the bureaucracy, the emperors, including CARACALLA (r. 211–17), debased the coinage; the resulting inflation proved pernicious. The defenses of the empire on the Rhine and Danube collapsed under the attack of various Germanic and other tribes, and the eastern provinces were invaded by the Persians. Finally, the discipline of the army—in which non-Romanized barbarians now served—broke down. From 235 to 284 more than two dozen emperors ruled; all but one suffered a violent death.

The Reforms of Diocletian and Constantine. Out of the turmoil of the 3d century a new totalitarian Rome emerged. The emperor DIOCLETIAN (r. 284–305), adopting the title dominus (master), transformed the principate into the dominate and citizens into subjects. The requisitions and forced labor to which the emperors of the 3d century had resorted in order to save the state became a permanent

The Column of Trajan (AD 106–13), one of the greatest monuments of ancient Rome, stands in the Forum of Trajan. The column commemorates Emperor Trajan's Dacian victory (105). Under Trajan, during the period known as the Golden Age of the Roman Empire, great territorial expansion occurred and extensive building took place.

(Right) This 2d-century marble relief portrays Emperor Marcus Aurelius (r. 161–80) making a sacrificial libation. Marcus, a Stoic philosopher, reigned with Lucius Aurelius Verrus as his coemperor until Verrus's death in 169. As sole emperor, Marcus was engaged primarily in defending Rome's Danube frontier against the barbarian invasions. (Palazzo dei Conservatori, Rome.)

EMPERORS OF ROME

Ruler*	Reign	Ruler	Reign	Ruler*	Reign	Ruler	Reign
	27 BC–AD						
Augustus	14	Heliogabalus	218–22	Maximian	286–305	Maximus (emperor in	
Tiberius	14–37	Alexander Severus	222–35	Constantius I	305–06	the West)	383–88
Caligula	37–41	Maximinus Thrax	235–38	Galerius	305–11	Eugenius (emperor in	
Claudius I	41–54	Gordian I	238	Constantine I	306–37	the West	392–94
Nero	54–68	Gordian II	238	Maximian	306–08	**Emperors in the West**	
Galba	68–69	Balbinus	238	Maxentius	306–12	Honorius	395–423
Otho	69	Pupienus	238	Severus	306–07	Constantius III	421
Vitellius	69	Gordian III	238–44	Licinius	308–24	Valentinian III	425–55
Vespasian	69–79	Philip	244–49	Maximinus	308–13	Petronius Maximus	455
Titus	79–81	Decius	249–51	Constantius II	337–61	Avitus	455–56
Domitian	81–96	Gallus	251–53	Constans	337–50	Majorian	457–61
Nerva	96–98	Hostilian	251	Constantine II	337–340	Libius Severus	461–65
Trajan	98–117	Aemilianus	253	Magnentius	350–53	Anthemius	467–72
Hadrian	117–38	Valerian	253–60	Julian	361–63	Olybrius	472
Antoninus Pius	138–61	Gallienus	253–68	Jovian	363–64	Glycerius	473
Marcus Aurelius	161–80	Claudius II	268–70	Valentinian I (emperor		Julius Nepos	473–75
Lucius Aurelius Verus	161–69	Aurelian	270–75	in the West)	364–75	Romulus Augustulus	475–76
Commodus	180–92	Tacitus	275–76	Valens (emperor in the		**Emperors in the East**	
Pertinax	193	Florian	276	East)	364–78	Arcadius	395–408
Didius Julian	193	Probus	276–82	Gratian (emperor in the		Theodosius II	408–50
Septimius Severus	193–211	Carus	282–83	West)	367–83	Marcian	450–57
Caracalla	211–17	Carinus	283–85	Valentinian II (emperor		Leo I	457–74
Geta	211–12	Numerianus	283–84	in the West)	375–92	Leo II	473–74
Macrinus	217–18	Diocletian	284–305	Theodosius I	379–95	Zeno	474–91

*At various times, but especially after 283, the Roman imperial title was shared by two or more rulers. In 395 the empire was divided permanently into eastern and western portions. The year 476 marks the traditional end of the empire in the West; the empire in the East (the Byzantine Empire) continued to exist for nearly 1,000 years.

system. Peasants were gradually deprived of their personal freedom and tied to the soil. The artisan corporations, and even the higher civil servants, were organized as hereditary castes, and a crushing burden of taxation was imposed on them. Two social groups were preeminent: the rich landowners, who in their fortified villas foreshadowed the medieval feudal lords, and the imperial bureaucracy.

CONSTANTINE I (r. 306–37) may be regarded as the second founder of the empire. He successfully fought off numerous opponents and, once firmly in power, reorganized the entire system of local government (into prefectures, dioceses, and provinces). He legalized Christianity (and was himself converted), thereby enlisting the church in the service of the state. He moved the capital to Byzantium, which he had rebuilt and renamed Constantinople (330). Constantine's reforms were not enough, however, to halt the slide of the empire into impotence.

Division of the Empire. From 395 the empire was permanently divided into the Latin Western and the Greek Eastern or BYZANTINE EMPIRE, with its capital at Constantinople. The Eastern Empire lived on until 1453, when the Turks conquered Constantinople. The Western Empire was overrun and gradually dismembered by various Germanic tribes. In 410 the Visigoths (see GOTHS) and in 455 the VANDALS plundered the city of Rome. Finally in 476 the German ODOACER deposed the last emperor of the West. Despite ancient Rome's inglorious end, the idea of Rome and of the Roman Empire survived its fall, and from the synthesis of Roman and Germanic elements arose the new states and societies of medieval Europe.

See also: LATIN LITERATURE; ROMAN ART AND ARCHITECTURE; ROMAN LAW.

Romeo and Juliet In *The Tragedy of Romeo and Juliet* (c.1595), William SHAKESPEARE experiments with stock comic materials—the hyperbole of romantic love, brawling servants, fussy old fathers, garrulous and bawdy nurses—but transforms them into tragedy. After the slaying of Mercutio by the belligerent Tybalt (act 3, scene 1), all comedy is dispelled by a sense of impending disaster. The tragedy of Romeo and Juliet's love is set in the larger context of the feud between the Capulets and the Montagues, which poisons all possibility of happiness. The play has a lyric grace not found in the source, Arthur Brooke's *The Tragicall Historye of Romeus and Juliet* (1562).

Rommel, Erwin [ruhm'-ul] Erwin Rommel, b. Nov. 15, 1891, d. Oct. 14, 1944, was a German field marshal in World War II. A liaison officer between the army and the Hitler Youth organization during the 1930s, he was promoted to brigadier general in 1939 and was subsequently assigned to Hitler's headquarters during the Polish campaign. The following spring he commanded an armored division during the Battle of France, and in 1941 he went to North Africa to lead the German Africa Corps. There he came to be known as the Desert Fox and attained the rank of field marshal. He was decisively defeated (November 1942) at El Alamein, 240 km (150 miles) west of Cairo. In December 1943 he was transferred to France. After the Allied invasion of June 1944, Rommel realized that the war was lost and that to condone Hitler's senseless continuation of it would be irresponsible. Injured in a strafing attack on July 17, 1944, Rommel

German field marshal Erwin Rommel (left) *inspects defenses along the French coast in February 1944, preparatory to the expected Allied invasion. Rommel's shrewd leadership in Libya won him the nickname the Desert Fox.*

could not personally participate in the attempt to overthrow Hitler three days later, but he was implicated. Because of his popularity, his opposition was kept secret. As an alternative to execution as a traitor, he was given the choice of suicide, for which he opted, to be reported as death from his wounds.

Romney, George [rahm'-nee]   The British portrait and history painter George Romney, b. Dec. 15, 1734, d. Nov. 15, 1802, was the leading rival of Thomas Gainsborough and Sir Joshua Reynolds in the late 18th century; his romantic pictures of Lady Hamilton (1782–86) are especially well known. He exhibited portraits and subject pictures in London; he won a prize for *The Death of Wolfe* (1763) and public success with his group portrait of the Warren family (1769). Romney painted numerous churchmen and aristocrats in a simplified and tranquil neoclassical style; he also spent much time doing many studies of his friend Emma Hart, later Lady Hamilton. Encouraged by the poet William Hayley and others, he illustrated classical and modern authors, particularly William Shakespeare and John Milton. He became obsessed with schemes for subjects in a grand, historical style but in the end had no enduring success as a history painter.

Romulus and Remus [rahm'-yoo-luhs, ree'-muhs]   In Roman mythology Romulus and Remus are regarded as the founders of Rome. Livy and Eutropius called them sons of the god Mars and Rhea Silvia, a vestal virgin and the daughter of Numitor, king of Alba Longa, who had been driven from his throne by Amulius. After birth the twins were placed in a container and cast upon the Tiber by the usurper, but they floated ashore and were nursed by a shewolf until found and brought up by shepherds. When grown they restored Numitor to his throne and founded Rome. Romulus killed Remus in a quarrel and became the first of Rome's seven kings. According to the legend, he established an asylum for fugitives on the Capitoline Hill, organized the rape of the Sabine women, founded the Senate, and divided the people into tribal

units. Romulus was venerated by the Romans as Quirinus, god of the winter solstice.

rondo [rohn'-doh]   A musical form especially favored by composers of the classical era for the final movements of sonatas, symphonies, and concertos, the rondo derives from a form widely used by French keyboard composers of the 17th century. The early instrumental *rondeau*—of uncertain relation to a medieval poetic form of the same name—consisted of a fixed refrain alternating with a succession of couplets, usually in different keys (as in the pattern ABACADA). In what may be regarded as the standard version of the later rondo, the number of couplets, known as episodes, is usually held to three: the first and third episodes are similar, while the second is enlarged in the manner of a development section in SONATA form (ABACABA).

Rono, Henry   The Kenyan runner Henry Rono, b. Feb. 12, 1952, emerged in 1978 as one of track history's greatest performers. In that year he set four world records: at 3,000 m (7 min 32.1 sec), the steeplechase (8:05.4), 5,000 m (13:08.4; lowered by Rono himself to 13:06.20 in 1981), and 10,000 m (27:22.4). Kenya's boycott of the 1980 Olympics in Moscow prevented Rono's competing there. He retired from track in 1983.

Ronsard, Pierre de [rohn-sahr']   Pierre de Ronsard, b. Sept. 11, 1524, d. Dec. 27, 1585, once called the "Prince of Poets," is considered the greatest poet of the French Renaissance. He was leader of the Pléiade poets, followers of Joachim du Bellay, who in 1549 called on French poets to cultivate the resources of their native language. His assimilation of classical and native idiom and verse forms expanded the range of French poetry. He was equally skilled at writing love poems, pastorals, sonnets, philosophical poems, and political verse. Ronsard's verse collections include *Odes* (1550) and *Sonnets pour Hélène* (1574).

roof and roofing   The covering of the top of a building, or roof, consists of three major components: the structural framing members; a stiff membrane, or roof deck, spanning structural members; and a waterproof outer layer of roofing. The earliest roofing materials were probably mud and sod supported by logs and woven reeds. The early Greeks and Romans manufactured kiln-dried clay tile to cover their public buildings and dwellings; clay tile is still popular. Bundles of straw or reeds tied to horizontal framing timbers formed the roofing for the thatched cottages in medieval Europe, and slate was used throughout the Middle Ages as a covering for the great cathedrals. By the 1500s copper sheets were pounded out by hand and used in limited quantities; in 1750 the first copper sheets were rolled. After that time much of the slate and tile roofing was replaced by copper,

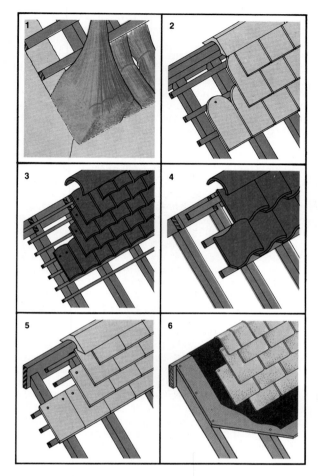

Conventional roof coverings are fixed to a timber framework. Straw bundles are tied to the frame to make a thatched roof (1). Thatch, first used in ancient Egypt, is still seen in rural areas of Europe. Stone flags (2) are usually hung on the supporting lath with pegs. Baked ceramic tiles (3) have been used in Mediterranean countries since ancient times. A lipped variation called the pantile (4) overlaps in two directions. The fire-resistance and impermeability of slate (5) has made it for centuries a sought-after roof covering. Modern dwellings are frequently roofed with asphalt-impregnated felt shingles (6), sometimes reinforced by an underlayer of hot asphalt.

which is still widely used. Sheet lead has been used as a roofing material for centuries: a lead roof on the HAGIA SOPHIA is still in good condition after 1,400 years.

Roofing shakes, split from straight-grained woods such as Western red cedar, or uniform, sawed wooden shingles have been popular roof coverings, particularly on houses in North America. Steel, aluminum, copper, lead, various alloys, and clad metals are also used as modern roof coverings. The metal used may be in either flat or corrugated sheets, joined together with specially designed joints that allow for expansion and contraction during temperature change.

Asphalt and coal-tar pitch came into general use as

roofing materials after 1892, when a chemist developed an asphalt-impregnated paper for that purpose. Roll roofing and asphalt tiles are made of heavy felt saturated with asphalt or coal-tar pitch. Mineral granules are rolled into the upper surface while the asphalt is still soft. Roll roofing is nailed or fastened to the roof deck with hot asphalt, coal-tar pitch, or an adhesive in order to form a finished roof. Asphalt shingles are nailed or stapled to a wooden roof deck. A built-up roof is produced by applying alternate layers of roofing felt and hot asphalt or coal-tar pitch. The top layer is given a hot flood coat of asphalt or coal-tar pitch into which granules of rock, gravel, slag, or ceramic particles may be imbedded while the flood coat is hot.

Rooney, Mickey   The actor Mickey Rooney, b. Joe Yule, Jr., in Brooklyn, N.Y., Sept. 24, 1920, began his career as a child film star in a series (1927–33) of some 50 silent comedies in which he played Mickey McGuire, a comic-strip character. He later gave memorable performances in the Andy Hardy series (1937–46), *Huckleberry Finn* (1939), and *National Velvet* (1944). He also worked in television (1950s) and in nightclubs (1960s), and he starred in the Broadway musical *Sugar Babies* (1979). He has continued a motion picture career with such films as *The Black Stallion* (1980). In 1983, Rooney received a special Academy Award honoring his versatility as a performer.

Roosevelt, Eleanor [rohz'-uh-velt]   The wife of a popular U.S. president, Anna Eleanor Roosevelt, b. New York City, Oct. 11, 1884, d. Nov. 7, 1962, was a tireless worker for social causes. A niece of President Theodore Roosevelt, she was raised by her maternal grandmother after the premature death of her parents. In 1905 she married her cousin Franklin Delano Roosevelt; they had six children, one of whom died in infancy. Although extremely shy, she became active in politics after her husband was stricken with polio in 1921.

Eleanor Roosevelt, the wife of President Franklin D. Roosevelt, was one of the most active women on the American political scene during the mid-20th century. While serving (1945–52, 1961–62) as a member of the U.S. delegation to the United Nations, Eleanor Roosevelt helped draft the UN Declaration of Human Rights.

When Franklin became president in 1933, Eleanor Roosevelt made herself a powerful voice on behalf of a wide range of social causes, including youth employment and civil rights for African Americans and women. She conducted press conferences, had her own radio program, and wrote a daily newspaper column, "My Day," which was nationally syndicated. After her husband's death, she continued in public life. She served (1945–52, 1961–62) as a U.S. delegate to the United Nations and helped draft the UN Declaration of Human Rights.

—

Roosevelt, Franklin Delano Franklin Delano Roosevelt, 32d president of the United States (1933–45), greatly expanded the role of the federal government with a wide-ranging economic and social program, the New Deal, designed to counter the Great Depression of the 1930s. He also led the nation through most of its participation in the global struggle of World War II.

Early Life. Of Dutch and English ancestry, Roosevelt was born on Jan. 30, 1882, in Hyde Park, N.Y., at the family estate in rural Dutchess County. His parents were James Roosevelt, scion of a noted, wealthy family, and Sara Delano Roosevelt. After graduating from Groton School (Groton, Mass.) and Harvard University (1903), Franklin attended (1904–07) Columbia Law School. He dropped out of law school upon admission to the New York bar and worked (1907–10) for a Wall Street law firm.

Tall, handsome, athletic, and outgoing, Franklin married a distant cousin, a shy young woman, Anna Eleanor Roosevelt, on Mar. 17, 1905. Her uncle, President Theodore Roosevelt, gave the bride away. Although a Democrat, Franklin admired the progressivism of Uncle Teddy and decided early on a political career. His opportunity came in 1910 when Dutchess County Republicans split between old guard conservatives and progressives. A colorful, dynamic campaigner, Roosevelt won a seat as a Democrat in the New York state senate.

Rise to National Prominence. At the 1912 Democratic National Convention, Roosevelt backed Woodrow Wilson in a bitter contest for the party's presidential nomination and was subsequently awarded the post of assistant secretary of the navy (serving 1913–20). The Roosevelt name and his progressive image won him the party's vice-presidential nomination in 1920 on the ticket with the conservative newspaper publisher Gov. James M. COX of Ohio. The Democrats had little hope of victory. Americans, tired of war and Europe's problems, opted for Warren G. Harding's promise of a "return to normalcy."

In the summer of 1921, while vacationing at his summer home on Campobello Island (New Brunswick, Canada), Roosevelt was stricken with poliomyelitis. Recovery was slow, but encouraged by Eleanor and by advisor Louis McHenry Howe, Roosevelt slowly regained his aspirations for public office, although he permanently lost the use of his legs. At the Democratic National Convention of 1924, Roosevelt signaled his return to politics with the Happy Warrior speech that placed Gov. Alfred E. SMITH of New York in nomination for the presidency. When Smith finally secured the nomination in 1928, he persuaded

Roosevelt to run for the New York governorship.

Although Smith lost his own state and the traditionally Democratic South in the 1928 contest with Republican Herbert C. Hoover, Roosevelt, proving his mobility in a strenuous campaign, managed a narrow victory. His governorship was molded in the progressive tradition. Its accomplishments included the development of public power, civil-service reform, and social-welfare measures. In addition, Roosevelt cultivated a presidential image with the help of a loyal group of advisors: Howe was his principal political manager; James A. Farley was assigned the task of winning delegates to the 1932 presidential convention; Henry Morgenthau, Jr. (see MORGENTHAU family) was an agriculture advisor; Frances PERKINS advised on labor questions and social security; and Samuel I. Rosenman was a speech writer and confidant. A smashing victory in the 1930 gubernatorial election, the growing appeal of the Roosevelt name as the Great Depression (see DEPRESSION OF THE 1930s) made Hoover politically vulnerable, and identification with both Southern and progressive party elements won Roosevelt the Democratic party's 1932 presidential nomination.

Presidency. Roosevelt flew to the Democratic National Convention in Chicago and there pledged to the American people a NEW DEAL. That expression, symbol of an era in American history, represented a cluster of ideas formulated by the candidate and his Brain Trust, a group of advisors recruited from New York's Columbia University. Faced with the prospect of governing the nation in the worst economic crisis in its history, Roosevelt desired an examination of causes and remedies free from the pressures of a political campaign. The advisory group, organized a few months before the July convention, was unofficially headed by Raymond Moley, a professor of public law, and included Rexford G. TUGWELL, an agricultural economist, and A. A. BERLE, a specialist in corporate structure and finance. They concluded that the United States had become an interdependent society (a "concert of interests") and that the agricultural depression of the 1920s had brought down the rest of the nation's economic structure. In the Forgotten Man speech drafted by Moley, Roosevelt presented the group's theory that productivity had outpaced the capacity of farmers and laborers to consume. During the campaign he also argued that big business should be accountable to society ("an economic constitutional order") and spoke in favor of conservation, relief, social insurance, and cheaper electricity. The Depression helped give Roosevelt an overwhelming victory in November.

On the eve of the March 1933 inauguration, the nation's banking system collapsed as millions of panicky depositors tried to withdraw savings that the banks had tied up in long-term loans. Approximately 12 to 14 million Americans were unemployed, and business nearly ground to a halt. In ringing tones, Roosevelt told the nation that "the only thing we have to fear is fear itself" and promised effective leadership in the crisis. That same day he closed the banks by proclamation, summoned a special session of Congress for the passage of emergency banking legislation, and began the process that within a week pro-

FRANKLIN DELANO ROOSEVELT
32d President of the United States (1933–45)

Nickname: "FDR"

Born: Jan. 30, 1882, Hyde Park, N.Y.

Education: Harvard College (graduated 1903); Columbia Law School

Professions: Public Official, Lawyer

Religious Affiliation: Episcopalian

Marriage: Mar. 17, 1905, to Anna Eleanor Roosevelt (1884–1962)

Children: Anna Eleanor Roosevelt (1906–75); James Roosevelt (1907–   ); Franklin (1909); Elliott Roosevelt (1910–90); Franklin Delano Roosevelt, Jr. (1914–88); John Aspinwall Roosevelt (1916–81)

Political Affiliation: Democrat

Writings: *The Happy Warrior, Alfred E. Smith* (1928); *F. D. R.: His Personal Letters* (4 vols., 1947–50), ed. by Elliott Roosevelt

Died: Apr. 12, 1945, Warm Springs, Ga.

Buried: Hyde Park, N.Y. (family plot)

Vice-Presidents: John N. Garner (1933–41); Henry A. Wallace (1941–45); Harry S. Truman (1945)

vided the liquidity that banks needed in order to reopen. The banks also had to regain public confidence, and in his first "fireside chat" radio broadcast the new president urged the American people to stop hoarding cash.

The New Deal. Roosevelt's New Deal program consistently accorded priority to agricultural recovery, with provision for crop restriction in the Agricultural Adjustment Act (AAA) of 1933 (see AGRICULTURAL ADJUSTMENT ADMINISTRATION); passage of the Soil Conservation Act of 1935, later expanded in response to the Supreme Court's ruling (1936) against AAA; and the second AAA Act in 1938, which pledged to the nation the maintenance of a large grain reserve. In addition, the New Deal sought to rationalize the business system by temporarily ending bitter economic warfare (the National Industrial Recovery Act and its fair practice codes; see NATIONAL RECOVERY ADMINISTRATION). Unemployment insurance was introduced, and the new social security program guaranteed income for retired Americans. The New Deal also encouraged the growth of industrial unionism, the end of child labor, and maximum-hours and minimum-wages legislation on a national basis.

The credit of the United States was used to salvage millions of urban home mortgages (Home Owners Loan Corporation) and farms (FARM CREDIT ADMINISTRATION) and to encourage private business by expanding the Reconstruction Finance Corporation that had been established

under the Hoover administration. Steps were also taken to promote public construction projects. Roosevelt's attempts at reflation of the currency to 1927–29 price levels led to abandonment of the gold standard in 1933 and reduction of the gold content of the dollar. Although in the 1932 campaign he had promised a balanced budget, Roosevelt showed a greater commitment to his pledge that no American should go hungry. Emergency expenditures for relief, also designed to "prime the economic pump," poured into the economy through the Federal Emergency Relief Administration, later the WORKS PROGRESS ADMINISTRATION, leading to record federal deficits.

The TENNESSEE VALLEY AUTHORITY, a major New Deal creation that was uniquely Roosevelt's, provided for public development of cheap electrical power. Roosevelt conceived the project in terms of broad regional planning, including the development of scientific farming, water transportation, energy sources, soil conservation, and public-health, educational, and recreational facilities. He had hoped to extend the concept to other areas of the country but was thwarted by charges of socialism and the declining popularity of the New Deal in the late 1930s. Roosevelt was also deeply committed to the conservation movement and youth employment, both of which found expression through the CIVILIAN CONSERVATION CORPS.

In the 1930s, Roosevelt's foreign policy was subordinated to the needs of internal economic recovery. Despite passage in 1934 of the Trade Agreements Act, which authorized reciprocal tariff reductions, the decade was characterized by international economic warfare. Congress enacted neutrality legislation intended to prevent U.S. involvement in the event of another world war. The president sought to improve relations with Latin America through his GOOD NEIGHBOR POLICY.

Roosevelt's unique political style, charm, and charisma brought him a record four terms. He beat Hoover in 1932, secured an overwhelming landslide victory over Alfred M. Landon in 1936, defeated Wendell L. Willkie for an unprecedented third term, and won against Thomas E. Dewey in 1944.

As an administrator, Roosevelt frequently bypassed his cabinet, relying on informal advisors who held minor posts in government. While he enlarged the role of government through his New Deal, he usually created emergency agencies to implement new programs for fear they would be stifled by the bureaucracy. He met his greatest defeat at the hands of the U.S. Supreme Court, which declared much of the early New Deal legislation unconstitutional. When he attempted to increase the size of the court and pack it with younger, more liberal justices in 1937, conservative opponents of the New Deal—and many liberals—summoned sufficient public and congressional opposition to stop the plan.

Commander in Chief. Roosevelt had hoped to keep the United States out of World War II, which began in September 1939, although he urged preparedness and advocated that the nation serve as an arsenal for the democracies. Adolf Hitler's stunning victories that culminated in the fall of France prompted his decision to seek a third term in 1940. Gradually, Roosevelt moved the United States toward belligerency by the exchange of overage destroyers for the right to use British bases in the West Indies; through the LEND-LEASE program, which provided arms for Britain and later the USSR; and by the convoying of supply ships to England. The Japanese attack on PEARL HARBOR on Dec. 7, 1941, and Germany's declaration of war gave Roosevelt a new sense of mission after months of indecision caused by divided U.S. public opinion about involvement in the war.

During World War II, Roosevelt and Winston Churchill, Great Britain's prime minister, personally determined Allied military and naval strategy in the West. Although Roosevelt had joined with Churchill in the pre–Pearl Harbor ATLANTIC CHARTER (1941), a broad and idealistic statement of peacetime aims, he insisted during the war on limiting the Allied effort to military victory. He had great faith in his personal powers of persuasion, and, despite indications that the USSR's Joseph Stalin had ambitions in eastern Europe that might violate the Atlantic Charter, Roosevelt foresaw Soviet-U.S. cooperation through a United Nations.

Under the pressures of wartime leadership, Roosevelt's health deteriorated. After the YALTA CONFERENCE, Roosevelt, exhausted from overwork, traveled to his Warm Springs, Ga., spa for a vacation in the spring of 1945. He died there on April 12 of a cerebral hemorrhage.

Roosevelt, Theodore   Theodore Roosevelt became the 26th president of the United States after the assassination of William McKinley, on Sept. 14, 1901; he was elected to the office in his own right in 1904, serving until 1909. As president and political leader, Roosevelt was an articulate spokesperson for the aspirations and values of progressivism, the reform movement that flourished in the United States from 1900 to World War I. He dominated that era in the nation's history.

Early Life and Career. Roosevelt was born into an old, prosperous Dutch family in New York City on Oct. 27, 1858. Young Roosevelt was educated at Harvard, from which he graduated in 1880, still unsure of his life's work. In that year he married Alice H. Lee, a woman from Massachusetts. Her death (1884), only hours before his mother died, left him bereaved, but in just less than three years he married Edith Kermit Carow.

During the 1880s, Roosevelt divided his life between politics and writing. He served three one-year terms in the New York Assembly (1882–84), where he became known as an independent Republican. He supported civil-service reform, legislation to benefit working people, and bills designed to improve the government of New York City. After living as a rancher in the Dakota Territory for two years, he returned (1886) and ran for mayor of New York City, finishing last in a three-way race. His literary and historical writing, which began early in the decade, gained momentum late in the 1880s.

Roosevelt's political career blossomed in the next ten years. Named a civil-service commissioner in 1889 by President Benjamin Harrison, he battled successfully to increase the number of positions that were based on merit and to improve the commission's administrative procedures. He resigned this office in 1895 to become president of New York City's Board of Police Commissioners in the reform administration of William L. Strong. After two years he was back in Washington, this time as assistant secretary of the navy under President William McKinley. A nationalist and an expansionist, Roosevelt used his office in whatever way he could to prepare the nation for war with Spain. Once the SPANISH-AMERICAN WAR came (1898), he helped organize the ROUGH RIDERS, saw considerable action in Cuba, and returned to the United States a colonel. Roosevelt's sudden fame and his reputation as an independent moved Thomas Collier PLATT, boss of New York's Republican party, to nominate him for governor in 1898. He won in a close election that fall.

Roosevelt's governorship (1899–1900) prepared him well for high office in Washington. He steered a middle course between subservience to the political machine and independent reformism. He championed civil service, backed a measure to tax corporation franchises, and approved several bills supportive of labor and social reform. In general, he had developed the concept of a positive, active state government by the time "Boss" Platt decided to "kick him upstairs." Working with others, Platt engineered Roosevelt's nomination as President McKinley's vice-presidential running mate in 1900. In November the Republican ticket was easily elected.

AT A GLANCE

THEODORE ROOSEVELT
26th President of the United States (1901–09)

Nicknames: "TR"; "Trust-Buster"; "Teddy"
Born: Oct. 27, 1858, New York City
Education: Harvard College (graduated 1880)
Professions: Author, Public Official
Religious Affiliation: Dutch Reformed
Marriages: Oct. 27, 1880, to Alice Hathaway Lee
   (1861–84); Dec. 2, 1886, to Edith Kermit Carow
   (1861–1948)
Children: Alice Lee Roosevelt (1884–1980); Theodore
   Roosevelt, Jr. (1887–1944); Kermit Roosevelt
   (1889–1943); Ethel Carow Roosevelt (1891–1977);
   Archibald Bulloch Roosevelt (1894–1979); Quentin
   Roosevelt (1897–1918)
Political Affiliation: Republican
Writings: *The Naval War of 1812* (1882); *The Winning
   of the West* (4 vols., 1889–96); *African Game Trails*
   (1910); *Autobiography* (1913); *America and the
   World War* (1915)
Died: Jan. 6, 1919, Oyster Bay, N.Y.
Buried: Young's Memorial Cemetery, Oyster Bay, N.Y.
Vice-President: Charles Warren Fairbanks (1905–09)

Theodore Roosevelt.

Presidency. McKinley's assassination in September 1901 catapulted Roosevelt to the presidency, much to the dismay of Republican conservatives. He assured his party that he would continue McKinley's policies, and until 1904 he moved cautiously while working to gain control of the national Republican organization. Even so, these years witnessed certain new directions in Washington as Roosevelt sought to accommodate the developing reform movement. Disturbed, as were others, by the growing power of the large corporations, Roosevelt ordered (1902) the Justice Department to bring suit under the SHERMAN ANTI-TRUST ACT (1890) against the Northern Securities Company, a railroad monopoly in the northwest. This suit launched a "trust-busting" crusade against big business that would carry over into Roosevelt's second administration.

Roosevelt departed from past practice in another way. When, in 1902, the anthracite coal miners struck, he became the first president to intervene in a labor-management dispute, threatening to seize the mines in order to persuade the recalcitrant owners to accept mediation. An arbitration commission subsequently awarded the miners a favorable settlement. Finally, Roosevelt advanced the cause of conservation. An enthusiastic supporter of the Newlands Bill (1902) on reclamation and irrigation, Roosevelt also backed Chief Forester Gifford PINCHOT in expanding the nation's forest reserve, setting aside waterpower sites and millions of acres of coal lands, and encouraging conservation on the state level.

His record, together with his firm control of the Republican party, won Roosevelt the presidential nomination, then the 1904 election against Democrat Alton B. Parker. His second administration reflected the quickened pace of the progressive movement, and he assumed an increasingly radical posture. In 1906, Congress enacted moderate reformist legislation: the Hepburn Act, which strengthened the authority of the Interstate Commerce Commission over railroads; the Meat Inspection and the Pure Food and Drug bills, which, respectively, provided for federal inspection of packing plants and prohibited the interstate transportation of adulterated drugs or mislabeled foods; and an employer's liability law (subsequently declared unconstitutional).

Roosevelt's conduct of foreign relations was even bolder and more vigorous than his domestic program. After Colombia's rejection (1903) of a treaty giving the United States rights to a canal across the isthmus of Panama, he supported a Panamanian revolt and then negotiated a similar treaty with the new nation. He subsequently supervised the construction of the Panama Canal and in 1904 promulgated the Roosevelt Corollary to the MONROE DOCTRINE, justifying U.S. intervention in the affairs of Latin American nations if their weakness or wrongdoing warranted such action. In 1905 he mediated the Russo-Japanese War, for which he won the Nobel Peace Prize, and in general he worked to maintain the balance of power in Asia and the Pacific. In the Atlantic he also played a role in smoothing over a 1905 crisis among the European powers on the Moroccan question. A staunch imperialist, Roosevelt streamlined the army and enlarged the navy to protect U.S. acquisitions abroad.

Postpresidential Years. By the time Roosevelt stepped down from the presidency in 1909, the Republican party was badly divided between the conservatives and the progressives. In the next two years, under his chosen successor, William Howard TAFT, the rift widened, essentially because of Taft's inept leadership. When Roosevelt returned from an African safari and a grand tour of Europe in June 1910, he intervened in Republican party affairs hoping to conciliate the warring factions. His efforts unsuccessful, he went into retirement at his Oyster Bay, N.Y., home but was drawn into politics once again after a series of disputes with Taft. Roosevelt, now the leader of the Republican's progressive wing, challenged his former friend for the party's presidential nomination in 1912 but was crushed by the Taft "steamroller" in Chicago and subsequently established the National PROGRESSIVE PARTY (popularly known as the BULL MOOSE PARTY). His campaign theme, the New Nationalism, represented the most ambitious and comprehensive reform program of the day, except for socialism. His platform called for increases in economic regulation and new social reforms. The ensuing campaign centered on Roosevelt and the Democratic candidate, Woodrow WILSON, whose New Freedom was developed as an alternative to Bull Moose formulas. Roosevelt divided the Republican vote with Taft, and Wilson was elected.

In the years after 1912, Roosevelt gradually returned to his former Republicanism and wrote his acclaimed autobiography (1913). In 1918 he fell ill and died at Sagamore Hill, his Oyster Bay home, on Jan. 6, 1919.

root (botany)   see PLANT

---

root (mathematics)   A root, or solution, of an EQUATION is a REAL NUMBER or a COMPLEX NUMBER that satisfies the equation. A root of a number a is a solution of the equation $x^n = a$. For $n = 2$, the equation is $x^2 = a$, and the solutions $x = \pm\sqrt{a}$ are called the square roots of a. Similarly, $x = \sqrt[3]{a}$ is called the cube root of a, and so on,. The equation $x^n = a$ is a special case of a polynomial equation $a_n x^n + a_{n-1} x^{n-1} + \dots + a_0 = 0$, which, by the fundamental theorem of algebra, always has n (real or complex) roots. The square root of -1 is of particular interest in algebra, for there is no real number that multiplied by itself yields -1 as a result. Therefore, the square root of -1 is called an imaginary number; its symbol is i.

Root, Elihu   An American statesman, Elihu Root, b. Clinton, N.Y., Feb. 15, 1845, d. Feb. 7, 1937, won the Nobel Peace Prize in 1912 for his efforts on behalf of world peace. Root, a Republican, was U.S. attorney for the southern district of New York from 1883 to 1885. As secretary of war (1899–1904) in the cabinets of William McKinley and Theodore Roosevelt, he reorganized the army and established (1901) the Army War College. He was Roosevelt's secretary of state (1905–09), reforming the consular service, improving U.S. relations with Latin America, and sponsoring (1908) a series of arbitration treaties—that now bear his name—with most European nations. As chief U.S. counsel before the Hague Tribunal he settled a dispute with Great Britain regarding North Atlantic coastal fisheries. A staunch supporter of the League of Nations, Root helped draft (1920–21) the constitution of the INTERNATIONAL COURT OF JUSTICE.

Root, John Wellborn   The American architect John Wellborn Root, b. Lumpkin, Ga., Jan. 10, 1850, d. Jan. 15, 1891, played a leading role in the development of the SKYSCRAPER and in the Chicago school of architecture. Root moved to Chicago in 1871, where he and Daniel H. BURNHAM formed their celebrated partnership in 1873, with Root as the designer. Root's plans for the Montauk Block (1881–82) reveal his skill in uniting functionally expressive architecture and new technology with the needs of the occupants. Such subsequent buildings as The Rookery (1885–86) and the Rand-McNally Building (1888–90) continued this fusion of function and innovation. Root's masterpiece is the Monadnock Building (1889–91), a 16-story masonry slab with elegantly tapered walls ending in a simple flared parapet.

Roots   Alex HALEY wrote his family's fictionalized history, *Roots* (1976), after tracing his ancestors back seven generations to a small village in Gambia. Haley's history begins with the abduction of ancestor Kunta Kinte into slavery in the American South. Kinte's descendants live through the entire African-American experience. Televised in two sections (1977, 1979), *Roots* was among the most popular programs ever shown on U.S. television.

---

roquette   [roh-ket']   Roquette, or arugula, *Eruca sativa*, of the mustard family, Cruciferae, is a coarse annual herb whose strong-flavored leaves are used in salads. The plant's leaves closely resemble those of the turnip and radish. When used as a vegetable, roquette must be grown in cool temperatures, because it goes to seed quickly in hot weather. Leaves are cut 6 to 8 weeks after planting. The flowers are white or creamy yellow and have an orange-blossom odor. In India and the Mediterranean region, the seeds are pressed for their oil.

Rorem, Ned   [rohr'-uhm]   Composer Ned Rorem, b. Richmond, Ind., Oct. 23, 1923, is best known for the several hundred art songs he has written. During the time he lived in Morocco and Paris (1949–57), his song texts came from several languages. His settings since returning to the United States, however, have been drawn primarily from the work of Walt Whitman and from 20th-century American poets. Rorem has also composed several song cycles, five operas, and many instrumental works.

Rorschach test   see PROJECTIVE TESTS

Rosario [roh-sahr'-ee-oh]   Rosario, a major port city and transportation center of Argentina, lies on the Paraná River, 300 km (190 mi) northwest of Buenos Aires. It has a population of 875,623 (1980). Food processing, petroleum refining, and brick making are important. Rail systems link the city to the port of Buenos Aires. The National University of Rosario (1968) is there.

Rosario was founded in 1725, and by the end of the 19th century it had become the principal shipping point for produce from the interior.

rosary   A rosary is a circular string of beads used by Roman Catholics for counting prayers. The term is also applied to the prayer beads used by Buddhists, Hindus, and Muslims. In the Western church, the rosary commonly consists of 5 (originally 15) decades, or sets of 10 beads, for the recitation of the Hail Mary (*Ave Maria*), separated by a single bead for the recitation of the Our Father (*Paternoster,* or Lord's Prayer). The Glory Be to the Father (*Gloria Patri*) is generally said after each decade. During the recitation of the prayers, meditation on a series of biblical themes, called the joyous, sorrowful, and glorious mysteries, is recommended. A feast of the Rosary is kept on October 7, the anniversary of the Christian victory over the Muslim Turks at Lepanto (1571).

Rosas, Juan Manuel de [roh'-sahs]   Juan Manuel de Rosas, b. Mar. 30, 1793, d. Mar. 14, 1877, twice governor of Buenos Aires (1829–32, 1835–52), ruled Argentina as virtual dictator during his second term of office. A ruthless tyrant, he is nevertheless credited with unifying the country when it was seriously threatened with disintegration.

The young Rosas led the life of a gaucho (cowboy) until he was appointed (1820) head of the provincial army. After 1828, Rosas emerged as the advocate for federalism, and with his gaucho militia, he fought the insurgent centralist unitarians. Under his guidance, the province of Buenos Aires came to dominate the political and economic affairs of the inland provinces. The Mazorca—a personal police organization answerable only to Rosas—dealt with opponents of his dictatorship. Rosas's tenure was sustained not only by his considerable manipulative talents but also by an expanding economy. Markets for Argentine goods, particularly in Great Britain, created prosperity; immigration contributed to agricultural and industrial expansion; the public debt was reduced. Rosas was defeated by Gen. Justo José de URQUIZA at Monte Caseros and went into permanent exile in Great Britain.

rose   The rose has been celebrated in the art, music, literature, and religions of numerous civilizations since ancient times, and garden roses were cultivated by Egyptians as early as 4000 BC. Today roses are grown commercially and in home gardens, and hybrids are developed with much planning and great care. The genus *Rosa*, comprising 150 species as well as numerous hybrids and cultivars, belongs to the family Rosaceae and is related to

Roses are prized for their rich colors, fragrance, and elegant forms. The hybrid tea rose is a modern type noted for its long blooming period and spicy fragrance. The hybrid rugosa is a hardy type of East Asian origin; it bears reddish orange fruit, or rose hips, in the fall. Grandifloras, derived from hybrid tea roses and floribundas, bear many-petaled flowers. Miniature roses, some producing blooms no larger than a fingernail, have become popular houseplants. The French rose is an old garden type.

hybrid tea rose

hybrid rugosa

French rose

grandiflora

miniature rose

the apple, the strawberry, the cherry, and the almond. Indigenous to the Northern Hemisphere, rose species are distributed from China to Europe and temperate North America. A few occur north of the Arctic Circle and at high elevations in the tropics.

Roses grow on erect, climbing, or trailing shrubs, the stems of which are covered with thorns. The leaves, which alternate along a branch, have 3 to 11 toothed leaflets. Solitary flowers or loose clusters bloom at the tips of stems. The ovary, known as the hip, turns bright red, yellow, or black at maturity. At the rim of a hip grow 5 sepals, which alternate with 5 petals. At the center of the petals, stamens are arranged in concentric whorls; in many rose cultivars, the stamens have become petallike, giving rise to the full double flowers prized by gardeners. Most species impart a distinctive fragrance.

Most roses that are cultivated today are hybrids of early species. Classic old roses include the French rose, *R. gallica*; the tea rose, *R. odorata*; the cabbage rose, *R. centifolia*; and the damask rose, *R. damascena*, which yields attar of roses, an essential oil used in perfumes. Other important parents of modern cultivars include the climbing Cathay rose, *R. cathayensis*; the trailing memorial rose, *R. wichuraiana*; the China rose, *R. chinensis*; and a Japanese rose, *R. multiflora*.

The most popular cultivars are the hybrid tea roses, having a wide color range, a unique fragrance, and continuous bloom throughout the growing season. Other commonly grown types include floribundas, which produce numerous petals; polyanthas, which have large clusters of flowers; miniatures, the entire plant of which ranges from 7 to 30 cm (3 to 12 in) in height; and rambling or climbing roses.

Other popular rose species include the prairie rose, *R. setigera*, a rambler native to North America; the Burnet or Scottish rose, *R. spinosissima*, an extremely hardy plant having many thorns; and the rugosa rose, *R. rugosa*, a Japanese species that is planted in hedges and produces rose hips that are a commercial source of a tea and a syrup rich in vitamin C.

Rose, Pete   A versatile and aggressive baseball player, Peter Edward Rose, b. Cincinnati, Ohio, Apr. 14, 1941, exhibited in his playing career (1963–86) a consistency and longevity matched by few, if any, in baseball history. In 1989, however, Rose's exploits were tarnished when commissioner of baseball A. Bartlett Giamatti banned him from the sport for life for betting on baseball games, some of which involved the team that Rose himself managed, the Cincinnati Reds. In 1991, Rose was declared ineligible for the Hall of Fame.

The switch-hitting, multiposition Rose, nicknamed "Charlie Hustle," began his career with the Cincinnati Reds and was voted Rookie of the Year. He won consecutive National League (NL) batting crowns (1968–69) with averages of .335 and .348, adding a third title in 1973 (.338), when he was also the NL Most Valuable Player. In 1978, Rose hit safely in a NL record 44 consecutive games, and in 1979, after being traded to the Philadel-

phia Phillies, he became the only player ever to collect 200 or more hits in 10 different years. In 1984 he returned to the Reds as player-manager. Rose holds, among many others, the following major league records: 3,562 games played, 14,053 at bats, 4,256 hits, 3,215 singles, and 23 straight 100-hit seasons. His career batting average was .303.

rose of Jericho   The rose of Jericho, the common name for *Anastatica hierochuntica*, is a small, rounded herb in the mustard family, Cruciferae. Native to deserts from Arabia to Syria and Algeria, its leaves are oval, and white flowers are borne in spikes, followed by short, wide fruit with two seeds. After fruiting, the plant sheds its leaves and rolls up into a dry ball, which is blown across the desert. The seeds are dropped in a moist area and start to germinate—hence the oft used name "resurrection plant."

Rose of Lima, Saint   The first canonized saint of the Americas, Saint Rose, b. 1586, d. Aug. 24 or 30, 1617, was a recluse and mystic who lived her whole life in Lima. A Dominican tertiary, she is remembered for her dedication to prayer, rigorous ascetic practices, and works of charity. She was canonized in 1671. Feast day: Aug. 23 (formerly Aug. 30).

rose window   Rose windows derive their name from their shape, which is round and made up of petallike forms radiating from a central point. Adorned with stained glass, they first appeared in Gothic cathedrals of the 12th century, such as the Cathedral of Notre Dame in Paris (begun 1163). Large windows ranging from 9 to 12 m (30 to 40 ft) in diameter were placed on the western facades of the buildings; smaller windows were used at the ends of the north and south transepts. The windows symbolize the Virgin Mary, whose flower is a rose.

Rosebery, Archibald Philip Primrose, 5th Earl of [rohz'-bur-ee]   Britain's prime minister from Mar. 3, 1894, to June 21, 1895, Archibald Philip Primrose, 5th earl of Rosebery, b. May 7, 1847, d. May 21, 1929, led a divided and ineffectual ministry. Rosebery, a Liberal imperialist, served (1886, 1892–94) as foreign secretary under William Ewart GLADSTONE. During Rosebery's 15-month tenure as prime minister, a factionalized Liberal party was unable to push any legislation past the united Conservatives, and Rosebery resigned when Commons rejected a minor Liberal measure. His establishment (1894) of a protectorate over Uganda and his support of the SOUTH AFRICAN WAR (1899–1902) estranged him from his party. The breach was completed in 1905 when Rosebery declared his opposition to Irish Home Rule.

Rosecrans, William S. [rohz'-kranz]   William Starke Rosecrans, b. Kingston, Ohio, Sept. 6, 1819, d. Mar. 11,

1898, was a moderately successful Union general in the U.S. Civil War. He graduated (1842) from West Point and after 12 years in the army resigned to enter the kerosene business in Cincinnati. Returning to the army in 1861, Rosecrans—a talented strategist who often argued with his superiors—served ably under Gen. George B. McClellan and Gen. John Pope. As an army commander he won the battles of Iuka and Corinth in 1862 and in 1863 brilliantly maneuvered the Confederates out of Chattanooga without a battle. He was relieved of his command, however, after his forces were routed by Gen. Braxton Bragg at nearby Chickamauga in September 1863. After the war, Rosecrans served as minister to Mexico (1867–69) and as a U.S. representative from California (1881–85).

rosemary   Rosemary is an evergreen shrub, *Rosmarinus officinalis*, of the mint family, Labiatae, native to the Mediterranean and adjoining areas. It grows to about 1.8 m (6 ft) high and is cultivated for its aromatic leaves and its usually blue flower clusters. The dried leaves are used as food seasoning; the flower clusters are the source of rosemary oil, which is used in inexpensive perfumes. Rosemary has long been a symbol of fidelity and remembrance.

Rosemary, a perennial evergreen shrub, is used as an herbal seasoning. Its leaves add flavor to meat dishes, soups, and potatoes, and its flowers yield an aromatic oil that is used in perfumes.

Rosenberg, Alfred [roh'-zen-bairk]   Alfred Rosenberg, b. Jan. 12, 1893, d. Oct. 16, 1946, was a Russian-born ideologist of German Nazism. He studied architecture before joining (1919) the National Socialist (Nazi) party in Munich. As editor of the party newspaper, *Völkischer Beobachter*, he developed anti-Christian and anti-Semitic theories. His book *Der Mythus des 20. Jahrhunderts* (The Myth of the 20th Century, 1934), an exposition of German racial purity, provided a theoretical framework for Adolf Hitler's policies. Minister for the occupied eastern territories during World War II, Rosenberg was hanged as a war criminal after he was found guilty at the Nuremberg Trials.

Rosenberg, Julius and Ethel   Julius Rosenberg, b. New York City, May 12, 1918, d. June 19, 1953, and Ethel Greenglass Rosenberg, b. New York City, Sept. 28, 1915, d. June 19, 1953, were the first U.S. civilians executed for espionage. Julius Rosenberg, a member of the Communist party, was an engineer employed by the U.S. Army Signal Corps during World War II. He and his wife, Ethel, were accused of furnishing vital information about the atomic bomb to Soviet agents in 1944 and 1945. The major witness against them was Ethel's brother, David Greenglass, an employee at the Los Alamos atomic bomb project. Greenglass, who testifed that he fed top-secret data about nuclear weapons to the Rosenbergs, was later sentenced to 15 years in prison. The Rosenbergs were convicted under the Espionage Act of 1917, and on Apr. 5, 1951, they were sentenced to death, which sparked worldwide protests. Despite the many pleas that their lives be spared, President Dwight D. Eisenhower refused to commute their sentences, and they were executed.

Julius and Ethel Rosenberg were convicted of giving information on U.S. nuclear weapons to the USSR. Although they steadfastly denied the charges, they were executed in 1953. Their trial spurred public debate on capital punishment, Communism, and the U.S. judicial process.

Rosenkavalier, Der   see Strauss, Richard

Rosenquist, James [roh'-zen-kwist]   The American artist James Rosenquist, b. Grand Forks, N.Dak., Nov. 29, 1933, has assimilated the techniques he learned as a billboard painter to the close-up, fragmented compositions he has produced since the 1960s, when he became associated with the POP ART movement. His paintings and assemblages of the '60s were enormous, garishly colored montages that focused on American popular culture (Coca-Cola, Marilyn Monroe, space technology). Rosenquist's major work of this period, the huge *F-111* (1965; Scull Collection, New York City), reflects his negative feelings about this experimental bomber in particular and American society in general. His paintings of the 1970s maintain the same "billboard" style, but the images and juxtapositions are more obscure.

Rosenzweig, Franz [roh'-zen-tsvyk]   Franz Rosenzweig, b. Kassel, Germany, Dec. 25, 1886, d. Dec. 9, 1929, was a major figure in early-20th-century Jewish philosophy. From a culturally assimilated German-Jewish family, Rosenzweig decided to convert to Christianity, but he set himself first the task of finding a sense of what it meant to be a Jew so that his way to Christianity could be like that of the first Christians. This endeavor led (1913) him to a religious experience in which he rediscovered Judaism in its full depth. During his military service on the eastern front in World War I, he began his chief philosophic work, *The Star of Redemption* (1921; Eng. trans., 1971).

After the war, Rosenzweig joined in developing an educational institution—the Jewish Lehrhaus (adult study center) in Frankfurt am Main—which embodied his pedagogical program for revitalizing Jewish culture. His active involvement lasted only until 1921, when he developed progressive paralysis.

Roses, Wars of the   The Wars of the Roses (1455–85) is the name given to a series of armed clashes between the houses of LANCASTER and YORK, rival claimants to the English crown. The name was first used long after the wars took place; it refers to the white rose of York and the red rose of Lancaster. The Lancastrian king HENRY VI, an ineffectual ruler subject to periods of insanity, was challenged by Richard, duke of York, who claimed the throne through descent from Edward III. After the Battle of Saint Albans (1455), York became protector of the kingdom, but Henry's wife, MARGARET OF ANJOU, and the BEAUFORT family, along with others of her followers, recovered control. The war resumed in 1459, and in June 1460, York, allied with Richard Neville, earl of WARWICK, invaded England and defeated (July 10, 1460) a royal army at Northampton. York claimed the throne, but instead he was designated Henry's successor. Margaret, whose son was effectively disinherited, sent her army against the Yorkists at Wakefield, where York was killed (1460). The next year, York's son fought the decisive Battle of Towton and was crowned EDWARD IV. Henry, Margaret, and their son fled to Scotland.

War broke out again in 1469 when Warwick, estranged from Edward and allied with the king's brother George, duke of Clarence, invaded from Calais, defeated the king's forces at Edgecote, and briefly held Edward prisoner. After Edward regained control, Warwick invaded again, joining forces with Henry VI, who was restored to the throne. Edward fled to the Netherlands, but he returned (1471) and defeated Warwick and the Lancastrians at Barnet and Tewkesbury. Henry was imprisoned in the Tower of London, where he died.

The third phase of the wars began in 1483 when RICHARD III usurped the throne from his nephew, Edward IV's son EDWARD V. The Lancastrian claimant, Henry Tudor, aided by the French and by disaffected Yorkist nobles, invaded England and defeated Richard at Bosworth (1485). The new king was crowned HENRY VII.

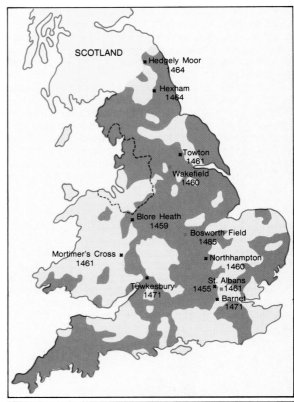

WARS OF THE ROSES

- ■ Lancastrian victory   □ Yorkist estates
- ✕ Yorkist victory   ▨ Lancastrian estates
- ----- Duchy of Lancaster

Rosetta Stone [roh-zet'-uh]   The Rosetta Stone is a block of black basalt bearing inscriptions that eventually supplied the key to the decipherment of the Egyptian hieroglyphic script. The stone was found accidentally in August 1799 by a group of soldiers in Napoleon's army while they were conducting engineering works at Fort Julien, near Rosetta (Arabic: Rashid), approximately 56 km (35 mi) northeast of Alexandria. Under the Treaty of Capitulation, signed in 1801, the stone was ceded to the British military authorities and taken to England for preservation in the British Museum. Its inscriptions, which record a decree issued in 196 BC under Ptolemy V Epiphanes, are written in two languages, Egyptian and Greek. The Egyptian version is written twice, once in hieroglyphics and once in demotic, a cursive development of the hieroglyphic script.

At the time of its discovery, it was accurately conjectured that the contents of the three different texts were identical; only the Greek, however, could be understood, as all knowledge of hieroglyphic writing had been lost since the 4th century AD, and of demotic shortly afterward. Two distinct, but interrelated, problems confronted the many scholars who worked on the inscriptions: the first was to discover whether the hieroglyphic signs represented phonetic sounds or were merely pictorial symbols; the second was to determine the meanings of the individual words. The distinction of making the final breakthrough in 1822 belongs to the French scholar Jean François CHAMPOLLION.

The Rosetta Stone, a basalt slab inscribed by the priests of the Egyptian pharaoh Ptolemy V (r. 205–180 BC), became the key to the decipherment of Egyptian hieroglyphic writings. The script was deciphered (1822) by the French scholar Jean François Champollion.

rosewood   Rosewood is the popular name for a group of tropical woods that are noted for their beauty and are highly prized as veneers in making fine furniture, paneling, and decorative pieces. The four most important species are the Brazilian *Dalbergia nigra* (a jacaranda), an almost black, oily, fragrant wood; *D. latifolia*, from India and Pakistan, a dark purple wood sometimes streaked with yellow; *D. stevensoni*, from Honduras, which is used to make percussion instruments such as the xylophone; and *D. melanosylon*, an African wood that resembles ebony.

Rosh Hashanah [rohsh huh-shah'-nah]   Rosh Hashanah (Hebrew for "head of the year") is the Jewish New Year, commemorating the creation of the world. It is celebrated in early fall, Tishri 1 by the Jewish calendar. Rosh Hashanah is a solemn occasion, the Day of Judgment, ushering in the penitential season that culminates ten days later on YOM KIPPUR. The distinctive feature of the synagogue service is the blowing of a ram's horn (shofar). The liturgy of the day stresses the sovereignty of God and the hope that all humans will at last recognize him as Father and King. The festival is celebrated for two days by the traditionally observant, whereas Reform Jews keep it for one day, in accord with biblical law.

Rosicrucians [roh-zi-kroo'-shuhnz]   Rosicrucians are members of a worldwide esoteric society whose official emblem combines a rose and a cross. The society was apparently founded in Europe in medieval times and was given impetus by the publication (1614–15) of pamphlets describing the initiation into the mysteries of the east (particularly of ancient Egypt) of Christian Rosenkreuz, who was allegedly born in 1378 but is presumed to be an allegorical figure.

The first Rosicrucian society in the United States was founded in Pennsylvania in 1694. The Ancient Mystical Order Rosae Crucis has headquarters in San Jose, Calif. Founded in 1909 by H. Spencer Lewis, AMORC is an international fraternal order that operates through a system of lodges and fosters the Rosicrucian philosophy of developing humankind's highest potentialities and psychic powers.

Roskilde [raws'-kil-de]   Roskilde is a city in northeastern Denmark on the Roskilde Fjord. The seat of Roskilde county and a residential suburb of Copenhagen, about 32 km (20 mi) to the east, Roskilde has a population of 39,700 (1988 est.). The city produces foodstuffs and has a meat-research institute; a nuclear power research station is nearby. Dominating Roskilde is its enormous cathedral, consecrated in the 15th century, which is the burial place of many of the country's kings and queens. A museum of Viking artifacts opened in 1969. Named for Hroar (Ro), its legendary founder, and for springs (*kilde*) of the region, Roskilde served as the capital of Denmark from the early 10th century until 1443 and was a bishopric from the mid-1000s until 1536 and again after 1923. In 1658 the Treaty of Roskilde, settling a war between Denmark and Sweden, was drawn up and signed there.

Ross, Alexander   A fur trader and author, Alexander Ross, b. Scotland, May 9, 1783, d. Oct. 23, 1856, emigrated to Upper Canada (Ontario) about 1805. With John Jacob Astor's Pacific Fur Company (see ASTOR family), he took part (1811) in the founding of ASTORIA, a fur-trading post in Oregon. He joined the NORTH WEST COMPANY in 1813, after it acquired Astoria, and when the North West merged (1821) with the HUDSON'S BAY COMPANY, he worked for the latter for 4 years. Ross subsequently moved to the RED RIVER SETTLEMENT, where he served as sheriff and a member of the council.

Ross, Betsy   Elizabeth Ross, b. Philadelphia, Jan. 1, 1752, d. Jan. 30, 1836, was a seamstress and upholsterer who, according to popular legend, made the first American flag at the request of George Washington. Some details of the legend are of doubtful authenticity, but records show that she did supply flags to the Pennsylvania navy in 1777.

Ross, Diana   Pop singer and film actress Diana Ross, b. Detroit, Mar. 26, 1944, was the lead singer of the Supremes, originally comprising Ross, Florence Ballard, and Mary Wilson. Beginning in 1961, the group's MOTOWN records included 12 number-one hits—more than anyone in rock history except Elvis Presley and the Beatles. After Ross became a solo artist (1969), she had 6 more number-one records. Her performance in the film *Lady Sings the Blues* (1972) won her an Oscar nomination for best actress.

Ross, Harold   The founder of *The New Yorker* magazine, Harold Wallace Ross, b. Aspen, Colo., Nov. 16, 1892, d. Dec. 6, 1951, also served as its editor from its formation in 1925 until his death. After starting the magazine he saw it through several years of financial crisis and formed its editorial policy. His colleagues agreed that Ross, a high school dropout, had a rare genius for editing. Ross fashioned *The New Yorker* into one of the foremost U.S. literary magazines. He helped to form its local focus, unique style, and reputation for literary merit.

Ross, Sir James Clark   Sir James Clark Ross, b. Apr. 15, 1800, d. Apr. 3, 1862, was a British naval officer and explorer who discovered the north magnetic pole on June 1, 1831, while on an expedition to the Arctic led by his uncle, Sir John Ross. From 1839 to 1843 he commanded an expedition to the Antarctic where he discovered the Ross Sea (1841) and Victoria Land region and named Mount Erebus.

Ross, John   John Ross, or Coowescoowe, b. Oct. 3, 1790, d. Aug. 1, 1866, of Scottish and CHEROKEE Indian ancestry, was a distinguished and dedicated tribal leader. In the War of 1812 he led the Cherokee against the CREEK confederacy. He was president of the Cherokee Council (1819–26), an associate chief (1827), and principal chief (1828–39). During those years Ross warred with Georgia, when it sought to remove the Cherokee from their ancestral lands, especially after President Jackson signed the Indian Removal Act in 1830. Ross led a delegation to Washington (1832–33) to plead the Cherokee cause, but to no avail. In 1838–39, when the Cherokee were forced west over what the Indians called the "trail of tears" to INDIAN TERRITORY, Ross led them on the terrible march. He later served as chief of the United Cherokee Nation.

Ross and Cromarty [krahm'-ur-tee]   Ross and Cromarty is a former county in the HIGHLANDS of northern Scotland. It included part of the Outer HEBRIDES island of Lewis. The county town was Dingwall.

The earliest known inhabitants, the Picts, were converted to Christianity during the 6th and 7th centuries. Norse pirates plagued the area until the 12th century.

Clashes between local clans continued there long after other areas of Scotland had been subdued. In 1889, Ross County (1661) and Cromarty County (1685) were merged into one. During the reorganization of local government in 1975, Ross and Cromarty was divided between the HIGHLAND and Western Isles regions.

Ross Dependency   The Ross Dependency, an area composed of both land and ice shelf and covering 751,000 km^2 (290,000 mi^2), is an overseas territory under the jurisdiction of New Zealand. Located in Antarctica between 160° east and 150° west longitude and south of 60° south latitude, it includes the Ross Sea and its islands, parts of Victoria Land and King Edward VII Peninsula, and the Queen Maud Range.

The Ross Dependency was established in 1923. Sir Edmund HILLARY established a base there in 1957 from which he and others explored and mapped the dependency during the INTERNATIONAL GEOPHYSICAL YEAR (1957–58). The region continues to be explored by the nations who cooperatively maintain stations in Antarctica to collect and analyze geophysical data.

Rossellini, Roberto [rohs-sel-lee'-nee]   One of the principal founders of Italian neorealism, film director Roberto Rossellini, b. May 8, 1906, d. June 3, 1977, first achieved prominence with *Open City* (1945), filmed during and after the German evacuation of Rome and portraying Italian resistance groups and Gestapo reprisals. The film had an unprecedented immediacy, owing in large part to Rossellini's use of authentic settings and of the physical presences of such fine performers as Anna Magnani and Aldo Fabrizzi. Rossellini's success continued with the anecdotal *Paisan* (1946), the stark *Germany Year Zero* (1947), and the controversial *The Miracle* (1948). After *Stromboli* (1949), which carried his reliance on realistic settings to excess, Rossellini made only one film of note during the next decade—*Saint Francis* (1950). He returned to his former brilliance with *General della Rovere* (1959). After 1962, Rossellini worked exclusively in theater and television.

Rossellino (family) [rohs-sel-lee'-noh]   The Rossellino family was a group of Florentine artists, the most important members of which were Bernardo Rossellino and his brother Antonio.

A noted architect, **Bernardo Rossellino**, b. 1409, d. Sept. 23, 1464, worked on the Florence Duomo (1441–94), where he became Capomaestro (1461-64), and on the Palazzo Piccolomini (1460-63) in Pienza. For his major work, the tomb of Leonardo Bruni in Santa Croce, Florence (1444–47), he created a new type of sepulchral monument using a triumphal arch.

Antonio Rossellino, 1427–79, created outstanding portrait busts, including those of Giovanni Chellini (1456; Victoria and Albert Museum, London), a remarkable characterization based on a life mask, and Matteo

Palmieri (1468; Museo Nazionale, Florence). His most innovative work, the tomb of the Cardinal of Portugal in San Miniato al Monte, Florence (1461–66), reveals his elegance and freedom of handling.

Rossetti, Christina G. [roh-zet'-ee] The English poet Christina Georgina Rossetti, b. Dec. 5, 1830, d. Dec. 29, 1894, was the sister of Pre-Raphaelite painter-poet Dante Gabriel Rossetti. Born into a family of intense literary, artistic, and religious interests, she published several poems under the pseudonym Ellen Alleyne in *The Germ*, a short-lived periodical begun in 1850 by her brother William and his friends. In *Goblin Market* (1862), her first published volume of poetry, she displayed a taste for the fantastic, a brooding melancholy, and a lyric gift that would characterize much of her work. Along with later volumes of poetry, such as *The Prince's Progress* (1866) and *A Pageant* (1881), she wrote nursery rhymes and tales for children, including *Sing Song* (1872) and *Speaking Likenesses* (1874).

Rossetti, Dante Gabriel The poet, painter, and designer Dante Gabriel Rossetti, b. Gabriel Charles Dante Rossetti, May 12, 1828, d. Apr. 9, 1882, was a cofounder of the PRE-RAPHAELITES, a group of English painters and poets who hoped to bring to their art the richness and purity of the medieval period. He won acclaim for his poem "The Blessed Damozel" (1847) before he was 20 years old. Rossetti's first Pre-Raphaelite paintings in oils, based on religious themes and with elements of mystical symbolism, were *The Girlhood of Mary Virgin* (1849) and *Ecce Ancilla Domini* (1850), both in the Tate Gallery, London. Although he won support from John Ruskin, criticism of his paintings caused him to withdraw from public exhibitions and turn to watercolors, which could be sold privately. Subjects taken from Dante Alighieri's *Vita*

Nuova (which Rossetti had translated into English) and Sir Thomas Malory's *Morte Darthur* inspired his art in the 1850s. His visions of Arthurian romance and medieval design also inspired his new friends of this time, William Morris and Edward Burne-Jones.

Romantic love was Rossetti's main theme in both poetry and painting. Elizabeth Siddal, whom he married in 1860, was the subject of many fine drawings, and his memory of her after she died (1862) is implicit in the *Beata Beatrix* (1863; Tate Gallery, London). Toward the end of his life, Rossetti sank into a morbid state, possibly induced by his disinterment (1869) of the manuscript poems he had buried with his wife and by savage critical attacks on his poetry.

Rossini, Gioacchino [rohs-see'-nee] Gioacchino Rossini, b. Feb. 29, 1792, d. Nov. 13, 1868, was one of the most significant and influential composers of opera in the 19th century. His parents were both professional musicians. In 1806, Rossini entered the Liceo Musicale of Bologna, where he studied music theory and the cello. Four years later he left the Liceo to pursue his career as a composer of operas.

Rossini received his first public performance in Venice in 1810 with the one-act comedy-opera *La Cambiale di matrimonio* (The Bill of Marriage). *Tancredi* (Venice, 1813) and *L'Italiana in Algeri* (The Italian Girl in Algiers; Venice, 1813) established his fame not only in Italy but throughout Europe.

In 1815, Rossini became musical director of the Teatro San Carlo and Teatro del Fondo in Naples. The following year he composed his best-known opera, *Il Barbiere di Siviglia* (The BARBER OF SEVILLE; Rome). Other significant operas followed in the next few years: *Otello* (Naples, 1816), *La Cenerentola* (Cinderella; Rome, 1817), *La Gazza ladra* (The Thieving Magpie; Milan, 1817), and *Semiramide* (Venice, 1823).

In 1824, Rossini assumed the directorship of the Théâtre Italien in Paris, for which he composed a sparkling opéra comique, *Le Comte Ory* (Count Ory, 1828), and the grand opera *Guillaume Tell* (William Tell, 1829),

(Left) *The sinuous, subtly erotic women in Dante Gabriel Rossetti's* The Bower Meadow *(1872) are the hallmark of this English Pre-Raphaelite poet and painter's style. The work also shows Rossetti's characteristic blend of romanticized realism and conscious archaism. (City Art Galleries, Manchester, England.)*

Gioacchino Rossini, portrayed in his old age by the photographer Nadar, was one of the most acclaimed Italian composers of the early 19th century. Among his most famous works are the comic operas The Barber of Seville *(1816) and* Cinderella *(1817) and the influential grand opera* William Tell *(1829).*

a landmark in the history of romantic opera and his last stage work.

In his remaining 39 years, Rossini produced the *Stabat Mater* (1842) and the *Petite Messe solennelle* (Short Solemn Mass, 1864), and numerous piano pieces and songs grouped under the title *Pèches de vieillesse* (Sins of Old Age). From 1837 to 1855 he lived in Italy, then moved to Paris.

Rosso Fiorentino [rohs'-soh fee-ohr-en-tee'-noh]
Giovanni Battista di Jacopo di Guasparre Rosso, b. Mar. 8, 1495, d. Nov. 14, 1540, a leader of central Italian MANNERISM, became known as Il Rosso Fiorentino. In his *Assumption* fresco (1516–17; Santissima Annunziata, Florence), his earliest extant work, the abstract patterning, erratic turbulence of the figures, and unexpected, violent colors that were to become a hallmark of his art are first seen. In his mature works, such as the famous *Deposition* (1521; Galleria Pittorica, Volterra), unusual figural proportions, sharply stylized gestures, perspective distortions, and coloristic abnormalities lend a quality of mystical apparition rather than a recording of actual events. Rosso later combined a sculpturesque solidity with an expressive Mannerist aesthetic to create such works as the *Dead Christ with Angels* (1525–26; Museum of Fine Arts, Boston). In 1530 he was called to France by François I to participate in the decoration of the château at Fontainebleau (see FONTAINEBLEAU, SCHOOL OF). There Rosso, along with Francesco Primaticcio, created an influential new idiom of painting, sculpture, and the decorative arts. He died in Paris, probably by his own hand.

Rostand, Edmond [raws-tahn']   Edmond Rostand, b. Apr. 1, 1868, d. Dec. 2, 1918, was a French dramatist whose plays represent the final flowering of the 19th-century romantic tradition. His greatest work, CYRANO DE BERGERAC (1897; Eng. trans., 1898), was a dazzling popular success and remains a worldwide favorite to this day. Its hero, marred by an enormous nose, rises heroically above his bodily defect in scenes of unparalleled verve, wit, and pathos. One of Rostand's earlier works, *The Romancers* (1894; Eng. trans., 1899), has been adapted as the highly successful musical comedy *The Fantasticks*. His other plays include *L'Aiglon* (The Eaglet, 1900), a sentimental account of the life of Napoleon I's ill-starred son, and *Chantecler* (1910), in which all the characters are animals.

Rostock [rohs'-tohk]   Rostock, a port city of Germany and the capital of Mecklenburg-Vorpommern state, lies about 190 km (120 mi) northwest of Berlin. Located 13 km (8 mi) inland, it is connected with Warnemünde, its advance port on the Baltic, by the Warnow River. The population is 253,990 (1989 est.). Rostock has large storage tanks for petroleum and modern port facilities. Industries include shipbuilding, fish processing, and the manufacturing of chemicals and machinery. The town

hall and the churches of Saint Mary, Saint Nicholas, and Saint Peter date from the 14th and 15th centuries. The University of Rostock (1419) was important in the spread of Lutheranism.

Slavic (Wendish) settlements, first established on the site in the 12th century, were superseded by three German towns that were united later in the 12th century. Rostock was a powerful member of the Hanseatic League. The city later declined, to recover only after World War II.

Rostov-on-Don [rahs'-tawv]   Rostov-on-Don is the capital of Rostov oblast of the Russian republic in the USSR. It is situated on the high right bank of the Don River, about 48 km (30 mi) east of the Sea of Azov. The city's population is 1,020,000 (1989). Rostov-on-Don is an important transport center at the gateway to the Caucasus and is one of the USSR's leading producers of agricultural machines. Rostov State University was founded in 1917.

Rostov-on-Don arose as a garrison town in 1749 after the Russians had gained control of the region from the Turks. Its industrial development dates from the 19th century. The city changed hands several times in 1941–43 as the Germans attempted to drive into the Caucasus.

Rostropovich, Mstislav [raws-traw-poh'-vich]
Mstislav Rostropovich, b. Mar. 27, 1927, is one of the world's finest cellists and a leading conductor. He was a highly honored artist in his native Soviet Union in the 1950s and '60s but fell into official disfavor when he openly befriended the dissident writer Aleksandr Solzhenitsyn. His professional career was severely curtailed, and as a consequence he fled to the West. In 1974, Rostropovich was appointed music director of the National Symphony Orchestra in Washington, D.C. The following year he and his wife, the soprano Galina Vishnevskaya, were divested of their Soviet citizenship. In 1990, however, in response to a Soviet invitation, Rostropovich gave a series of performances in the USSR.

rotary engine   see WANKEL ENGINE

Rotary International   Rotary International is an association of business and professional men and women, founded in Chicago in 1905. An international organization since 1922, it has about 1 million members in 161 countries and functions as a fellowship and as a service organization that sponsors community projects and funds student exchange programs and university scholarships. The name *Rotary* came from the early practice of rotating weekly meetings among members' offices. Although the clubs were long exclusively male, a 1987 Supreme Court decision required that in the United States they begin to admit women.

rotary press   A rotary press is a method of PRINTING in which a cylindrical printing surface and a cylindrical impression surface rotate toward each other. Paper passes between the cylinders to receive the print. For rotary-offset printing, a third cylinder is used: a rubber-covered offset cylinder coming between the impression and plate cylinders. Because only cylinders are involved in a rotary press, speeds are much faster. The restricting factor is the ability to control the paper at speed. By combining rotary printing units and passing the paper from one unit to another, two, three, four, or even more colors may be printed during a single pass through the machinery. Multicolor rotary machines can be constructed by grouping a number of plate cylinders, with their inking systems, around one large common-impression cylinder. This produces a more compact machine with improved paper transport. Important features of rotary printing are that it allows great variations in machine design—cylinders may be positioned horizontally, vertically, or angled—and permits in-line operations other than printing to be performed. These include folding, slitting, perforating, and numbering. Rotary machines can also combine different printing processes, for example, letterpress and web offset. The original application of rotary printing was for newspapers; it is now used for books, magazines, and general and specialized work.

ROTC   see RESERVE OFFICERS TRAINING CORPS

—

Roth, Philip   The novelist Philip Milton Roth, b. Newark, N.J., Mar. 19, 1933, gained immediate literary recognition when his first book, *Goodbye Columbus* (1959), a novella and five short stories about urban and suburban Jews, won the 1960 National Book Award. His first novel, *Letting Go* (1962), takes aim at the idiosyncrasies of university faculties. The widely read *Portnoy's Complaint* (1969) describes, often hilariously, the sexual anxieties of a Jewish neurotic with an overpowering mother. Roth has also written perceptively about midwestern Protestantism (*When She Was Good*, 1967) and sex and psychoanalysis (*The Professor of Desire*, 1977). His most important work, however, may be the Zuckerman tetralogy—*The Ghost Writer* (1979), *Zuckerman Unbound* (1981), *The Anatomy Lesson* (1983), and *The Counterlife* (1986)—four novels in which Nathan Zuckerman becomes a famous writer whose works and life somewhat resemble those of his creator, Roth. *The Counterlife* and *The Facts: A Novelist's Autobiography* (1988) both deny and affirm the relation between fact and fiction in the author's works. *Patrimony* (1990) tells of his father's year-and-a-half struggle against a fatal brain tumor.

—

Rothko, Mark   [rahth'-koh]   The American artist Mark Rothko, b. Dvinsk, Russia, Sept. 25, 1903, d. Feb. 25, 1970, was the most transcendental painter associated with ABSTRACT EXPRESSIONISM. His early paintings of the 1940s are luminously pale scenes made up of indistinct shapes that often suggest primitive life forms floating over a background of banded colors. By 1947, Rothko had concluded that his earlier works, with their reference to

Blue, Orange and Red *(1961) is typical of the later, abstract expressionist style of Mark Rothko. (Private collection.)*

figures and objects, were too restrictive.

Attempting to universalize his art, Rothko began to work with various arrangements of hovering, rectangular areas of color. Over the next three years, this format was reduced and solidified into Rothko's mature style: two to five rectangles of glowing color suspended one above another against a luminous field. *Number 10* (1950; Museum of Modern Art, New York City) is an example. From 1958 on, his works became increasingly austere and more transcendental. Rothko felt that his paintings were best viewed in a light similar to that in his studio—that is, a dim, changing light within a relatively small exhibition area, so that the canvases might glow and pulsate.

One of Rothko's last projects was the completion of a set of large canvases for a nondenominational chapel in Houston, Tex. He died a suicide.

—

Rothschild   (family)   [rawth'-chyld]   The Rothschilds, a family of bankers who control an international consortium of banks (the House of Rothschild), have had an enormous impact on European economic history since the late 18th century. The founder of the House of Rothschild, **Mayer Amschel Rothschild**, b. Feb. 23, 1744, d. Sept. 19, 1812, grew up in the Jewish ghetto of Frankfurt am Main and entered a banking house as a young man. With his five sons—**Amschel Mayer**, b. June 12, 1773, d. Dec. 6, 1855; **Salomon Mayer**, b. Sept. 9, 1774, d. July 27, 1855; **Nathan Mayer**, b. Sept. 16, 1777, d. July 28, 1836; **Karl Mayer**, b. Apr. 24, 1788, d. Mar. 10, 1855; and **Jacob Mayer**, b. May 15, 1792, d. Nov. 15, 1868—

Baron Nathan Mayer Rothschild succeeded his father, Lionel Nathan, as head of the London branch of the international Rothschild banking firm in 1879. Elected to the House of Commons at the age of 25, Rothschild became the first Jewish member of the House of Lords when he was raised to the peerage in 1885.

he started a business that dealt in luxury items, coins, and commercial papers. Spurred by the investment opportunities presented by the French Revolutionary and Napoleonic wars, the firm turned to banking, and by the early years of the 19th century the five brothers had established branches in Frankfurt, London, Paris, Vienna, and Naples.

After the death of Mayer Amschel, the House of Rothschild became dealers in government securities and in the stocks of insurance companies and industrial firms. By the middle of the 19th century, in spite of anti-Semitic prejudice, Rothschilds had been elected to Parliament in England and elevated to the nobility in that country and in France. The Neapolitan and Viennese branches of the firm were dissolved with the advent of fascism in Italy and Germany, but the House of Rothschild continues to wield substantial power to this day. Family members who did not enter the family business have been active in philanthropy, finance, and science.

rotifer [roht'-i-fur]   A rotifer, or wheel animalcule, is a minute, multicellular, free-living aquatic animal in the phylum Rotifera. It possesses a conspicuous circlet of cilia around the anterior end and mouth. The cilia beat in a swirling action, suggesting a wheel; the term *rotifer* means wheel carrier. By creating a current, the beating cilia draw food and water into the mouth. Food consists of small protozoans and algae. An internal grinding organ that breaks up hard particles of food may be seen through the transparent body. The grinding organ, in a muscular pharynx, or mastax, is lined with several hard, projecting, jawlike structures. About 1,500 species of rotifers exist.

rotogravure [roh-toh-gruh–vuer']   Rotogravure is printing produced on a web-fed rotary photogravure machine using an intaglio image etched below the surface of a copper- or chromium-plated cylinder. It is used mainly for long-run production of magazines and for the printing of packaging foils and plastics and wall and floor coverings.

The printing area consists of minute cells of varying depths; the deeper the cell, the more ink is carried and transferred to the paper, thus producing the light as well as dark parts of an illustration. In the ROTARY PRESS the printing cylinder is immersed in a fluid (low-viscosity), volatile ink that, after the printing process, dries rapidly by evaporation and absorption into the paper. Before the impression is made on the paper, excess ink is removed with a flexible steel "doctor blade." The paper web then passes between the printing cylinder and a rubber-covered impression cylinder to draw the ink out of the cells for printing.

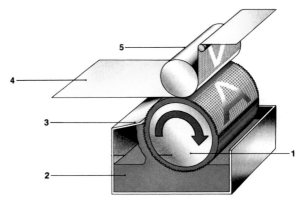

Rotogravure printing involves the use of a rotating printing cylinder (1) in which an image is etched as tiny cells. The cylinder turns in a trough (2) from which ink is deposited in the cells and on the roll surface. A doctor blade, or metal scraper (3), wipes off the surface ink. The image cells are then pressed against the paper (4) by an impression roll (5), and the ink is transferred to the paper.

Rotterdam [raht'-ur-dam]   Rotterdam, in the province of South Holland, has a population of 576,732 (1989 est.), making it the second largest city in the Netherlands. Its urban agglomeration has a population of 1,110,000 (1986 est.).

Contemporary City. Rotterdam-Europoort is one of the world's busiest ports. Located at the mouths of the Rhine and Meuse (or Maas) rivers, it is the gateway to the inland industrial centers of northern Europe. The cargo carried by the river-barge traffic is transferred to oceangoing vessels at the Dutch harbor. Rotterdam's status as a free port further stimulates its transshipment activities. Shipping to the Mediterranean and Scandinavia is also important. The original harbor, several kilometers inland from the North Sea, has undergone frequent, major expansion since 1947.

In recent decades city leaders have stimulated industrial expansion to provide economic diversity. Petroleum refining and the manufacture of fertilizers, plastics, and margarine are major industries; metallurgy, shipbuilding, and machine-tool, textile, and distillery production are also important.

Innovative modern planning and architecture were involved in the city's reconstruction following the bombardments of World War II. The key to this development was the founding in 1948 of the International Building Center. Fine collections of Dutch and Flemish art are displayed at the Boymans–van Beuningen Museum.

History. At the close of the 17th century Rotterdam emerged as a shipping center, engulfing the harbor of DELFT and profiting from the East Indies trade. Rotterdam's competition with Antwerp for European trade in the 19th century was aided by the construction (1866–72) of the New Waterway canal to the sea.

Rottweiler [raht'-wy-lur]   The Rottweiler is a breed of dog similar to the Doberman pinscher in outline but much more massive and with comparatively small ears set high, carried flat, and hung over to the side of the head. The short, smooth, glossy coat is black with clear tan to rust markings. The breed, developed from Roman cattle dogs and named for the town of Rottweil in Württemberg in southern Germany, was developed into a police dog in the early 20th century. It was officially recognized by the American Kennel Club in 1955.

The Rottweiler's name comes from the German town of Rottweil, long a principal site for cattle dealers and meat packers. Originally a cattle-driving breed, the Rottweiler declined in the mid-19th century but later regained favor as a formidable guard dog.

Rouault, Georges [roo-oh']   The French artist Georges Rouault, b. May 27, 1871, d. Feb. 13, 1958, stands almost alone among the important painters of the 20th century in having dedicated much of his work to religious themes. Trained as a maker of stained-glass windows (1885–90), he helped to restore the windows at Chartres Cathedral; his later work—with its jewellike colors and black outlines—was to reflect this experience.

It was after his conversion to Roman Catholicism in 1895 that Rouault began to concentrate on biblical subjects, both in his paintings and his numerous etchings and lithographs. His best-known work is the series of prints published in 1948 under the title *Miserere*; included in it are etchings that were prepared much earlier (1914–18) and completed in 1927. Although he exhibit-

In The Old King (1937), by 20th-century French painter Georges Rouault, the compartments of color with heavy, black outlines reveal the artist's interest in Gothic stained-glass windows. (The Carnegie Institute, Pittsburgh, Pa.)

ed with the Fauves in 1905, Rouault was not actually influenced by them. He belongs, rather, to the much broader movement of expressionism, with its focus on intensely felt human emotions. Apart from his religious works, Rouault painted judges, prostitutes, and tragic clowns as well as occasional still lifes.

Rouen [roo-ahn']   Rouen is a city in northwestern France on the Seine River, about 115 km (70 mi) northwest of Paris. The city population is 101,945 (1982) and that of the conurbation, 400,000 (1982). Rouen serves as a major port for Paris and as a transshipment point for imported bulk products, wines, and manufactured goods. Rouen's industries manufacture textiles, fertilizer chemicals, perfumes, foundry products, paper, and processed food. Ship repairing and petroleum refining are also economically important. Rouen is known as the Museum City; its many historical and architectural treasures include the restored 13th-century Cathedral of Notre Dame and the works of French masters exhibited at several museums.

The site of Rouen was originally settled by Celts and later by the Romans as Rotumagus. Its name was changed to Rouen during the Middle Ages. The city was held by the English from 1066 to 1204 and from 1419 to 1449. The trial and execution of Joan of Arc occurred there in 1431. It was taken by the Germans in 1870 and again in 1940 but recaptured by the Allies in 1944.

Rough Riders   The Rough Riders were a regiment of U.S. cavalry volunteers who fought in the Spanish-American War. Theodore ROOSEVELT, their chief organizer, served as lieutenant colonel under commander Leonard WOOD. Because of transportation problems their horses had to be abandoned in Florida; thus the Rough Riders fought mostly on foot when they reached Cuba.

roulette Roulette is a game in which one or more players gamble against the bank, or house, playing on a rectangular table in the center of which is a wheel whose perimeter is nonconsecutively numbered 1 through 36 and zero and double zero. Half the numbers are in red and half in black, except for the zero and double zero, which are in green. Each number has a corresponding slot. A croupier spins a small ball in one direction inside the wheel, which spins in the opposite direction. When the ball comes to rest, that slot designates the winning number. On either side of the wheel is a layout on which bets are placed. Betting and winning on any single number pays 35-to-1. A bet on two numbers, one of which wins, pays 17-to-1. Several other bets are possible. Although the payoff on a single number bet is 35-to-1, the odds against winning are actually 38-to-1, giving the bank an average yield of 5.26 percent—higher than almost any other casino game. Roulette probably originated in the late 18th century.

Roundheads The Roundheads were the parliamentarian opponents of King CHARLES I in the ENGLISH CIVIL WAR (1642–51). They were so-called because many of them were Puritans (see PURITANISM) who wore their hair close-cropped, in contrast to the shoulder-length wigs of the royalist CAVALIERS.

roundworm see ASCARIASIS; NEMATODE

Rousseau, Henri [roo-soh'] The Frenchman Henri (Le Douanier) Rousseau, b. May 21, 1844, d. Sept. 2, 1910, having spent most of his life as a customs inspector (or *douanier*), devoted himself to painting upon his retirement and became the most distinguished primitive artist of the modern era. His gifts included an exceptional sense of design and feeling for color, but it was his exotic and sometimes bizarre vision of a purely imaginary tropical world that made his works unique and unforgettable.

Rousseau's earliest works display the formal characteristics of all primitive art: flat surfaces, minute detail, stiff and frontally posed figures of arbitrary proportions, as in *Carnival Evening* (1886; Philadelphia Museum of Art). The paintings he sent to the Salon des Indépendants from 1886 to 1910 generally met with derision, but in such works as *The Sleeping Gypsy* (1897) and *The Dream* (1910; Museum of Modern Art, New York City) some artists, including Henri de Toulouse-Lautrec and Edgar Degas, began to recognize a new aesthetic direction in Rousseau's work, pointing away from the naturalism of the impressionists.

Rousseau, Jean Jacques [rue-soh'] A philosopher and social critic, Jean Jacques Rousseau, b. June 28, 1712, d. July 2, 1778, exerted profound influence on the political thought of the late 18th century, particularly that of the French Revolution, and on the romantic movement.

Life. Born in Geneva, Switzerland, Rousseau first traveled to Paris in 1742, where a new system of musical notation he had developed attracted the attention of Denis DIDEROT. Diderot invited him to contribute articles on music to the *Encyclopédie*. In 1745, Rousseau met an uneducated servant girl, Thérèse Le Vasseur, with whom he had a number of illegitimate children.

Henri Rousseau received no formal training as a painter, and his style had no precedent. Like many of his works, The Sleeping Gypsy (1897) has a visionary, surreal quality that is both comic and foreboding. (Museum of Modern Art, New York City.)

In 1762 he published his best-known and most-influential works, *Émile*, a treatise on education, and *The Social Contract*, a major work of political philosophy. At this point Rousseau's personality difficulties became more acute. Always an emotional and temperamental man, he quarreled with Diderot and the other philosophes. In 1766 he moved to England at the invitation of the great Scottish philosopher David Hume, with whom he subsequently had a falling out that became a scandal. Increasingly, Rousseau displayed all of the classic symptoms of paranoia. His last years were spent on works such as his *Confessions*, in which he attempted to come to terms with himself. He died in Paris.

Philosophical Position. Rousseau shared the ENLIGHTENMENT view that society had perverted natural man, the "noble savage" who lived harmoniously with nature, free from selfishness, want, possessiveness, and jealousy. He argued that the restoration of the arts and sciences had not contributed to the purification of humankind but to its corruption. Rousseau also believed that social relationships of all kinds were based on an inequality that resulted from an unnatural distribution of power and wealth.

Whereas the other Enlightenment philosophes pursued the nature of humankind empirically in physiological and psychological studies or in historical and anthropological researches, Rousseau sought the nature of humans in the wholly private realm of intuition and conscience. Superficially, all of his works appear to have a historical character much like the works of other writers of the Enlightenment. By his own admission, however, Rousseau's historical format is purely rhetorical, with no concern for actual details. Whereas the Baron de MONTESQUIEU studied past and present societies to discover the historical origins of political obligation, Rousseau looked inward for the fundamental source of moral obligation.

In departing from the Enlightenment faith in reason, understood as abstraction from external experience, and in emphasizing the inner life as a source of truth, Rousseau has more in common with the romanticists of the 19th century. His influence on the romantic movement was enormous. His true philosophical successor, however, was another late-18th-century philosopher, Immanuel KANT, who also had rejected the external empiricism of the philosophes. Rousseau is credited by Kant with having introduced a great discovery about the nature of freedom.

Major Works. In *Émile*, Rousseau claims that humans are basically good and, if proper development is fostered, the natural goodness of the individual can be protected from the corrupting influences of society. The child Émile must therefore be raised in a rural rather than an urban environment, so that he may develop in continuity with nature rather than in opposition to it. The earliest impulses of the child are allowed to develop but are channeled into a genuine respect for persons, a respect growing out of self-love rather than pride. Brought into community by an instinctual pity, or sympathy for those around him, Émile develops a moral sense, and an urge toward perfection and inner growth allows him to rise above the passions and achieve virtue.

Nevertheless, society must be dealt with, and this

Jean Jacques Rousseau, one of the great French philosophers of the 18th century, emphasized the primacy of individual liberty in such writings as his major political treatise, The Social Contract *(1762), and his work on education,* Émile *(1762).*

Rousseau does in his most influential work, *The Social Contract*. The individual, progressing in the development of a moral sense, can, for Rousseau, find genuine happiness and fulfillment only in a social situation. Thus one of the first principles of Rousseau's political philosophy is that politics and morality never be separated. The second important principle is freedom, which the state is created to preserve. The state is a unity and as such expresses the general will. This is contrasted to the will of all, which is merely the aggregate will, the accidentally mutual desires of the majority. John LOCKE and others had assumed that what the majority wants must be correct. Rousseau questioned this assumption, arguing that the individuals who make up the majority may, in fact, wish something that is contrary to the goals or needs of the state, to the common good. The general will is to secure freedom, equality, and justice within the state, regardless of the will of the majority, and in the SOCIAL CONTRACT (for Rousseau a theoretical construct rather than a historical event, as Enlightenment thinkers had frequently assumed) individual sovereignty is given up to the state in order that these goals might be achieved. When a state fails to act in a moral fashion, it ceases to function in the proper manner and ceases to exert genuine authority over the individual.

An important factor in ensuring the cohesion of the state and in ensuring its proper functioning is a sound civil religion. It is, for Rousseau, necessary that all citizens subscribe to beliefs in (1) a supreme being, (2) personal immortality, (3) the ultimate reward of virtue and punishment of vice, and (4) the principle of toleration. The assumption should not be made, however, that Rousseau conceived of this as an external imposition of religion by the state, for to him these appeared to be clear and self-evident principles that could and should be adopted by any rational and moral agent. The specific content of these beliefs will vary, however, as will the content of the laws of any particular state. They will reflect the peculiar historical and geographical factors of a region, as Rousseau makes clear in his constitutions for Corsica (1765) and Poland (1770–71). Only by keeping all of these factors in mind is it possible to constitute a state that fulfills, rather than corrupts, the natural goodness of humanity.

Rousseau, Théodore   The French painter Pierre Étienne Théodore Rousseau, b. Apr. 15, 1812, d. Dec. 22, 1867, was the leader of the BARBIZON SCHOOL of landscapists and a major precursor of IMPRESSIONISM. He was one of the earliest to work *en plein air*—outdoors, painting directly from the landscape, which he rendered in free-flowing brush strokes and vibrant colors.

In about 1837, Rousseau settled in the rural village of Barbizon, at the edge of the Forest of Fontainebleau near Paris, and turned from the romantic scenes of the previous decade to serene pastorals, always painted directly from nature with unwavering fidelity. His house soon became the center for all the painters of the Barbizon school. His close friend Jean François Millet moved to Barbizon in 1849 and painted its laborers and farmers for the rest of his life. Rousseau finally achieved public success in the 1850s and was recognized as one of the leading French landscape artists of the century.

Roussel, Albert [roo-sel']   Albert Roussel, b. Apr. 5, 1869, d. Aug. 23, 1937, was an outstanding French neoclassical composer. Before commencing serious music studies, he joined the navy and spent a considerable amount of time in the Orient. He studied (1898–1907) at the Schola Cantorum in Paris and also taught (1902-14) there.

Roussel's music was initially impressionistic, an example being his Indian-influenced opera-ballet *Padmâvatî* (1918); it later tended toward neoclassicism, illustrated by the orchestral *Suite in F* (1927) and the ballet *Bacchus et Ariane* (1931). His best-known works include the last two of his four symphonies and the ballet *The Spider's Feast*.

Roussillon [roo-see-yohn']   Roussillon, a historic province on France's southwestern Mediterranean coast, corresponds to the present department of Pyrénées-Orientalés. Wine grapes and peaches grow in the valleys of the area. The main city is Perpignan. Settled by Iberians in the 7th century BC, the region became a Roman colony in the 2d century BC. It was occupied by the Visigoths in AD 462 and the Arabs about AD 720. It became a part of the Frankish realm in the mid-8th century. In 1172 the region was united with Aragon. Louis XIV of France acquired it under the Treaty of the Pyrenees in 1659.

Rowe, Nicholas [roh]   Nicholas Rowe, b. June 30, 1674, d. Dec. 6, 1718, was an English dramatist of the RESTORATION whose lasting contribution to literature was his edition (1709) of Shakespeare's works. His own plays, among them *The Fair Penitent* (1703), differ markedly from most of the period in their high moral tone. Rowe was named poet laureate of England in 1715.

rowing   Rowing is the action of moving a vessel through the water by using bladed sticks called oars. Rowing was originally the only reliable source of propulsion for a boat, but it has lost most of its practical and economic functions and is now practiced primarily as a recreation and sport throughout the world. Rowing dates back to antiquity when galley slaves were used to provide locomotion for warships. Rowing in its modern form developed on the

Spectators crowd the banks of the Millstone River near Princeton, New Jersey to watch an 8-oared shell regatta. Rowing competitions are conducted over still stretches of water, usually on a course measuring 2,000 m (6,560 ft) in length.

Thames River in England. In the United States the first race was held in 1811 in New York City. As in England, ferrymen rowed their barges in competition. Professional and amateur rowing flourished in the 19th century, especially in the United States, England, Canada, and Australia. The 1-mi, 550-yd (2.5-km) Diamond Sculls at the Henley Royal Regatta (founded 1839) became the world's top amateur race.

In modern rowing events, boats compete in two categories, either sculling or sweep events. In sweep events a rower holds one oar and is part of a crew of 2, 4, or 8. In sculling, a rower holds two oars and competes in boats that have 1, 2, or 4 scullers. Racing boats are called shells and vary in size according to the number of crew members. A modern 8-person shell weighs about 110 kg (242 lb), is 18.3 m (60 ft) long, and has a very narrow beam of about 61 cm (24 in). Crew members sit on sliding seats mounted on rollers that permit leg muscles to be brought into use with each stroke. Rowing technique must be precise and repeated in unison by each boat member; because mistakes reduce speed, a coxswain often directs the rowers. Rowing was adopted as an Olympic Games event in 1900; women's rowing was adopted in 1976. International amateur championships are held annually. In the United States two important regattas are held annually, the Harvard-Yale race and the Intercollegiate Rowing Association regatta.

Rowlandson, Thomas   The English artist, caricaturist, and illustrator Thomas Rowlandson, b. July 14, 1756, d. Apr. 21, 1827, was a brilliant draftsman whose pen-and-ink sketches primarily consist of witty observations of life in England during the Regency period.

Rowlandson gambled away his inheritance and survived by making and selling drawings; his output was vast. Above all he was a master of line. His caricatures are often coarse and deliberately ugly; their content is more ephemeral than that of his watercolors, perhaps because they were composed and executed in great haste. Rowlandson's masterly book illustrations are best exemplified by those for William Combe's *Tour of Dr. Syntax in Search of the Picturesque* (1812), but some of his most pleasing work is topographical: views of the English countryside and of London, some of which also became book illustrations, as in *Microcosm of London* (1808).

Roxana [rahk-san'-uh]   Roxana, or Roxane, d. *c.*310, daughter of a Bactrian baron, married ALEXANDER THE GREAT in 327 BC. Her son, later Alexander IV, was born after his father's death (323). Four years later, Roxana joined forces with Olympias, Alexander's mother, but was captured and imprisoned by Cassander, king of Macedonia, who had her put to death.

Roxas y Acuna, Manuel [roh'-hahs ee ah-koo'-noh]   Manuel Roxas y Acuna, b. Jan. 1, 1892, d. Apr. 15,

1948, was the first president of the Philippine republic. A member (1921–33) of the House of Representatives, he was a rival of Manuel QUEZON, the leading nationalist of the 1930s. During Japan's World War II occupation of the Philippines, Roxas cooperated with the pro-Japanese government, but he was subsequently cleared of charges of collaborating after Gen. Douglas MacArthur testified in his behalf. Elected president of the Senate when the Philippine Congress was reconvened in 1945, Roxas became (1946) the first president of an independent Philippines. He died in office 2 years later.

Roy, Gabrielle [rwah]   A French-Canadian novelist, Gabrielle Roy, b. St. Boniface, Manitoba, Mar. 22, 1909, d. July 13, 1983, was the first Canadian to win a major French literary award. Her prize-winning novel, *Bonheur d'occasion* (1945; trans. as *The Tin Flute*, 1947), like much of her work, describes life in the isolated regions of Manitoba. Her other novels include *Alexandre Chenevert, caissier* (1954; trans. as *The Cashier*, 1955), *The Hidden Mountain* (1961; Eng. trans., 1962), and *Ces Enfants de ma vie* (1977; trans. as *Children of My Heart*, 1979).

Royal Ballet   The Royal Ballet, so named by royal charter in 1956, began its existence as the Vic-Wells Ballet, whose first performance was at Old Vic's, London, May 5, 1931. Its first director and choreographer was Dame Ninette de VALOIS, a former soloist with the Ballets Russes de Serge Diaghilev. De Valois built her company on the solid triple foundation of a school, a theater, and a carefully planned repertoire of both classic and new British ballets, the latter supplied by herself and Sir Frederick ASHTON, whom she engaged as dancer and resident choreographer in 1935. When Dame Alicia MARKOVA, the company's ballerina from 1932 to 1935, left, de Valois was ready with a home-trained successor in Dame Margot FONTEYN.

Such ballets as de Valois's *Checkmate* (1937) and Ashton's *Les Patineurs* (1937) formed the basis for the national style of ballet—strong, clear characterization and lyrical, elegant dancing. During World War II the company—then known as Sadler's Wells Ballet—became firmly established as the British national ballet. Sadler's Wells Opera (later Theatre) Ballet, a second company for dancers and choreographers, was formed in 1946. Both became the Royal Ballet in 1956.

The Royal Ballet produced two more important choreographers in Kenneth MACMILLAN and John Cranko. As director De Valois was succeeded by Ashton (1963–70), MacMillan (1970–77), Norman Morrice (1977–86), and Anthony Dowell (1986–).

Royal Canadian Mounted Police   The Royal Canadian Mounted Police (RCMP), also known as "Mounties," is Canada's federal police force. At the request of eight provinces (all but Ontario and Quebec) the RCMP also does provincial policing; in addition, it performs municipal police functions in about 190 municipalities. It is the only police force in the Yukon Territory and the Northwest Territories. It was Canada's security service until the Canadian Security Intelligence Service was created in 1984.

The RCMP operates the National Police Services for the benefit of all Canadian police forces. These services include the Crime Detection Laboratories; the National Fingerprint Identification Bureau; the Crime Index; the Fraudulent Cheques Research, Commercial Fraud, and Firearms Registration sections; the Canadian Police College; and the Canadian Police Information Centre (linked with a U.S. Federal Bureau of Investigation computer). The RCMP also acts as the Canadian representative of Interpol.

The force was established as the North-West Mounted Police (NWMP) in 1873, 6 years after Canadian confederation. Its mission was to police on horseback the vast western plains known then as the North-West Territories (now Manitoba, Saskatchewan and Alberta). On July 8, 1874, 275 scarlet-tunicked NWMP set out from Dufferin, Manitoba, on their famous march to the foothills of the Rocky Mountains. By 1877 they had brought law and order to the western plains. In 1885 the NWMP helped to suppress an Indian rebellion.

In the late 1890s some of the NWMP moved north to the Yukon. In 1904 the NWMP became the Royal North-West Mounted Police. In 1905 it began provincial police work for Alberta and Saskatchewan (assuming provincial duties for Manitoba, Nova Scotia, New Brunswick, and Prince Edward Island in 1932 and for Newfoundland and British Columbia in 1950). In 1920 the force absorbed the Dominion Police and assumed the federal policing of all Canada.

Royal Danish Ballet

The Royal Danish Ballet has been in existence since the opening of the first Royal Theatre in Copenhagen, Dec. 18, 1748; earlier there had been court ballets. The first important ballet master was Vincenzo Galeotti (1775–1812), whose *The Whims of Cupid and the Ballet-Master* (1786) is still performed. His successor was the French dancer Antoine Bournonville, whose Danish-born son August BOURNONVILLE, after studying and dancing abroad, took over the company in 1829 and remained its director for nearly 50 years. He created the Danish national style, with its precise footwork and light, floating jumps. After his death, Danish ballet went into a decline until Harald Lander became ballet master (1932–51). While preserving the Bournonville heritage, he created new ballets, such as *Qarrtsiluni* (1942), in a more contemporary vein—a pattern followed by Flemming Flindt from 1966 to 1977.

It was only after World War II that Danish ballet became known internationally. Leading dancers, including Erik BRUHN and Peter MARTINS, have left Denmark to seek fame abroad.

Royal Greenwich Observatory

Royal Greenwich Observatory, one of the oldest extant observatories, was established by Charles II in 1675 at Greenwich and transferred to Herstmonceux Castle, near Halisham, Sussex, England, after World War II. Its first three directors were John FLAMSTEED, Edmond HALLEY, and James BRADLEY. In 1884 the meridian (0° longitude) at Greenwich was chosen the world's PRIME MERIDIAN, from which east-west longitude and time zones are calculated (see also GREENWICH MEAN TIME). Instruments at the site include a photographic zenith tube (1955) and a 38-in (96-cm) Hargreaves reflector (1972). The observatory's 98-in (2.5-m) Isaac Newton telescope, completed in 1967, was moved to the island of La Palma in the Canary Islands and began operating there in 1984; the observatory is also constructing its 165-in (4.2-m) William Herschel telescope at this site. In 1986 the decision was made to transfer the remaining facilities and all operations of the Royal Greenwich Observatory to Cambridge University.

Royal Shakespeare Company

World tours and inventive interpretations of Shakespeare's plays, other classics, and modern works have made the Royal Shakespeare Company a renowned repertory company. Formed in 1961, its roots go back to David Garrick's Stratford-upon-Avon Jubilee (1769) and to the Shakespeare Memorial Theatre, opened in 1879. Its two member companies are based in Stratford and London. It has had such noteworthy directors as Barry Jackson, Anthony Quayle, Peter Hall, and Trevor Nunn.

Royal Society

Founded in 1660 as a club of learned men and granted charters from Charles II in 1662 and 1663, the Royal Society of London "for Natural Knowledge" is one of the world's oldest and most prestigious SCIENTIFIC ASSOCIATIONS. The society, which has always conducted and supported scientific research and projects, advises the British government in scientific matters in a semiofficial capacity. In 1977–78 the society received £2,172,000 in Parliamentary grant-in-aid for its various projects. The society, whose headquarters is in London, has more than 900 fellows and foreign members. It holds annual meetings, publishes *Philosophical Transactions* (1666), *Proceedings* (1880), and *Notes and Records* (1938), and awards medals, such as the Copley Medal, which dates from 1731, and the Royal Medals, dating from 1825 and 1965.

Royce, Josiah

[roys, juh-zy'-uh] Josiah Royce, b. Grass Valley, Calif., Nov. 20, 1855, d. Sept. 14, 1916, was a leading proponent of philosophical IDEALISM whose thought dominated American philosophy until World War I.

Royce's idealism combined the rationalism of system building and proof of the absolute with traits of American philosophy: the appeal to experience, voluntarism, and the focus on ideas as plans of action, not as purely cognitive entities. This combination led to the characterization of his position as a voluntaristic idealism. According to Royce, God is not just all-knower but is also cosmic purpose. To be an individual, then, is to embody purpose. The infinity of mutually interpreting and intercommunicating selves constitutes the absolute self, the absolute community, which is, as the whole, a conscious unity of all the parts.

Rozelle, Pete [roh-zel'] Alvin Ray Rozelle, b. South Gate, Calif., Mar. 1, 1926, commissioner of the National Football League (NFL), presided over the development of professional football into the most popular big-money sport in the United States. He became commissioner in 1960 at the age of 33 and the next year designed federal legislation that permitted selling television broadcast rights to a single network for the entire league. In 1966, Rozelle negotiated the NFL's merger with the rival American Football League, 10 of whose teams were subsumed into the NFL in 1970. The Super Bowl game was also a result of these negotiations. Rozelle retired in 1989.

Różewicz, Tadeusz [roo-zhev'-eech] Playwright and poet Tadeusz Różewicz, b. Oct. 9, 1921, has been called the most important and talented writer of the postwar period in Poland. Różewicz was a fighter in the underground during World War II, and his experience of the Nazi genocide in Poland informs all of his writing. His poetry is stripped of poetic devices: meter, rhyme, and metaphor are all absent. Różewicz's plays likewise reject traditional forms, in the manner of the THEATER OF THE ABSURD. Much of his work has been translated. Poetry collections include *The Survivor and Other Poems* (1976) and *Conversations with the Prince* (1982). His plays can be read in *The Card Index and Other Plays* (1969) and *The Witnesses and Other Plays* (1970).

RR Lyrae stars see VARIABLE STAR

Ruan Ji (Juan Chi) [rwahn-jee] One of the Seven Sages of the Bamboo Grove, Ruan Ji, AD 210–263, was one of the few who escaped involvement and persecution in one of China's most politically turbulent ages. Like his friend Ji Kang, he also sought refuge in drinking and reputedly led a life of decadence. In his writings he employed allegory and double entendre. He is best known for 82 poems entitled *Yonghuai shi*, translated into English as *Poems of Solitude* (1960).

Ruanda-Urundi see BURUNDI; RWANDA

Rubaiyat of Omar Khayyam [roo'-by-yaht] Best known to English readers in the translation (1859) of Edward FITZGERALD, the *Rubaiyat of Omar Khayyam* is a long, early-12th-century Persian poem attributed to OMAR KHAYYAM. The poem is a collection of quatrains celebrat-

ing sensual pleasure, as in the famous lines, "A jug of wine, a loaf of bread—and thou/Beside me singing in the wilderness." There have been many later attempts to translate the poem, but none has excelled FitzGerald's.

rubber The term *rubber* originally referred to the natural, elastic product obtained from the secretion of certain plants. Today it is also applied to a class of materials that are synthesized from petroleum derivatives—PETROCHEMICALS such as styrene and butadiene. Rubber is relatively soft, possessing in high degree the property of resilience or bounciness. A strip of rubber can be stretched to several times its original length without breaking and will return to that length when released.

Rubber's unique properties are a result of the chemical structure of the rubber molecule, which is very large compared with that of simple chemical compounds. The rubber molecule is an example of a polymer (see POLYMERIZATION). A molecule of natural rubber is a long chain made up of tens of thousands of smaller units, or monomers, of the chemical compound isoprene. The long molecules of rubber are very flexible, and tying the molecules together with cross-links makes rubber elastic. The process that creates the cross-links is called vulcanization.

History

Christopher Columbus observed the inhabitants of Haiti using rubber to make playballs. Europeans later discovered that rubber could be extracted from many different kinds of trees and shrubs, mostly native to the tropics.

The British scientist Joseph Priestley, observing its ability to rub out pencil marks, gave rubber its English name. Its name in French, *caoutchouc*, is more apt, however, coming from the Indian-American word *cachuchu*, "the wood that weeps."

At the start of the 19th century rubber was an expensive curiosity with no serious uses. Thomas Hancock devised methods for mechanically working rubber so it could be shaped, and he built England's first rubber factory in 1820. In 1823, Charles MACINTOSH devised a practical method of waterproofing fabric with rubber. Natural rubber, however, contains virtually no cross-links, so it becomes soft and sticky when hot and stiff when cold. Vulcanization, accidentally discovered by Charles GOODYEAR in 1839, overcame this problem, yielding a tough, elastic material suitable for manufactured products. Goodyear heated rubber with sulfur, which causes the cross-linking.

Until the late 19th century all rubber was natural rubber extracted haphazardly from trees scattered in the jungles of South America. It was expensive, and the supply was uncertain. During the 1860s the British government conceived the idea of transporting rubber trees to the British colonies in Asia so that the trees could be grown on a large scale on organized plantations. The most promising rubber source was the Brazilian Pará rubber tree, *Hevea brasiliensis*. Because of Brazil's legal restrictions the British government hired Henry Wickham, then in Brazil, to transport some seeds of the tree to England.

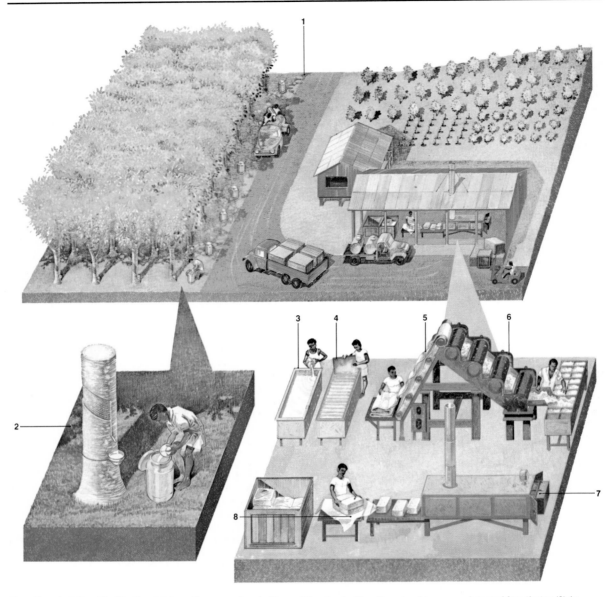

The rubber plantations (1) of Southeast Asia are the source of most of the world's natural rubber. The watery latex, or sap, is tapped from the tree (2) by scoring the bark with a knife to a depth of 1 mm (0.04 in) and slanting the cut downward to channel the sap into a cup. The latex is strained into aluminum tanks (3) to remove impurities. Acid is added to coagulate the rubber particles, which are deposited on aluminum partitions (4), rolled into sheets (5), and shredded (6). The rubber is dried and compressed into bales (7) and is wrapped for shipment (8).

This he did in 1876; the seeds were germinated in England, and the young seedlings were shipped to Ceylon, Malaysia, and Singapore. All the natural rubber produced today in Asia—90% of the world's total production—comes from trees that are descendants of Wickham's seeds.

This establishment of substantial, controlled production of natural rubber coincided with the establishment of the automotive industry. The pneumatic tire had already been invented in 1845 by Robert William Thomson of Scotland for horse-drawn carriages and was "reinvented" in 1888 by John Boyd Dunlop of Ireland. The sudden demand for large quantities of rubber for tires accelerated the young rubber industry.

Natural-Rubber Production

Natural rubber is secreted by the tree as latex, a milky white liquid that contains about 30% rubber as very small particles suspended in water. South American Indians extracted the latex by simply slashing the trees with axes, but with the arrival of trees in Asia the tapping method was devised. It involves removing a thin sliver of bark with a knife. The latex flows out from just under the cut bark; after about two hours flow ceases. The latex is collected in cups and is coagulated with an acid to make solid rubber. The wet solid rubber is dried either by exposing thin sheets to hot smoke or, more recently, by mechanically chopping the block into small particles for fast drying in an oil-fired dryer. The dried rubber is then compacted into bales for export.

Because of improvements resulting from plant-breeding research, trees of several commercial varieties now exist that yield as much as six times more rubber than the wild tree. In addition, special chemicals, or yield stimulants, are used to boost production. Surprisingly little natural rubber comes today from South America; 90% is from Asia, and nearly half the world total comes from Malaysia. Other leading Asian producers include Indonesia, Thailand, Sri Lanka, and India; substantial amounts of rubber are produced in Africa, mainly Liberia, and much of this rubber is produced on large estates—one in Liberia is 30,750 ha (76,000 acres). The majority of rubber produced worldwide, however, comes from small holdings of a few hectares.

Synthetic-Rubber Production

Synthetic rubber, first manufactured in substantial amounts during World War II, was not a replica of natural rubber but, rather, was synthesized from two monomers—styrene and butadiene—that were more readily available than isoprene. These and all other monomers used for synthetic rubber are currently obtained from petroleum (see PETROCHEMICALS). Addition of suitable catalysts to the monomers causes them to polymerize, or join together, to form the necessary long molecules. Polymerization often occurs in soapy water, and the rubber is formed as a latex, like natural rubber in the tree. It is coagulated and baled like natural rubber, and vulcanization is similarly achieved.

Styrene-butadiene rubber (SBR) remains the most important synthetic rubber manufactured. Techniques for direct imitation of natural rubber (polyisoprene) by polymerizing the isoprene monomer eluded chemists until the 1950s. Synthetic polyisoprene, however, is more expensive to make than is styrene-butadiene rubber and is of greatest interest to those countries, such as the USSR, which aim to be independent of imported rubber; some is also produced in the United States and Europe.

Rubber Products

Neither natural nor synthetic rubber is used in pure form. Vulcanizing chemicals must be added, primarily sulfur. A filler, such as carbon black (hence, black tires), is often added to provide extra strength and stiffness, and usually some oil is included to help processing and reduce cost. The typical rubber mix contains 60% or less rubber.

No major differences exist in the processes for making products from natural and synthetic rubbers. In the simplest process the mix is shaped by placing it in a heated mold, and the heat simultaneously effects shaping and vulcanization. For more complex products, such as tires, a number of components are made, some with fiber or steel-cord reinforcement; these are then joined to form the product.

Tires, the main product of the rubber industry for decades, account for 60% to 70% of all rubber used, natural and synthetic. Other uses include footwear, industrial conveyor belts and automotive fan belts, hose, flooring, and cables. Some products are made directly from latex. Surgical and domestic gloves, for example, are made by dipping a ceramic former into latex, withdrawing the former, and then drying.

▬

Rubbia, Carlo   The Italian physicist Carlo Rubbia, b. Mar. 31, 1934, was awarded, along with Simon VAN DER MEER, the 1984 Nobel Prize for physics for their work leading to the discoveries of the W and Z FUNDAMENTAL PARTICLES. Rubbia studied physics in Italy and the United States before accepting (1961) a position at the EUROPEAN ORGANIZATION FOR NUCLEAR RESEARCH (CERN) near Geneva. There he concentrated on studies of high-energy particle collisions, using the large CERN accelerator. By the mid-1970s he had conceived of a plan to use colliding beams of accelerated protons and antiprotons to produce the W and Z particles that had been predicted by the ELECTROWEAK THEORY. In 1983, Rubbia and his coworkers at CERN announced their discovery of these particles, and in 1984 they discovered evidence for the top QUARK.

rubella   see GERMAN MEASLES

▬

Rubens, Peter Paul [roo'-bens]   The Flemish baroque painter Peter Paul Rubens, b. June 28, 1577, d. May 30, 1640, was the most renowned northern European artist of his day, and is now widely recognized as one of the foremost painters in Western art history. By completing the fusion of the realistic tradition of Flemish painting with the imaginative freedom and classical themes of Italian Renaissance painting, he fundamentally revitalized and redirected northern European painting.

By the age of 21, Rubens was a master painter. In Venice he fell under the spell of the radiant color and majestic forms of Titian; during Rubens's eight years (1600–08) as court painter to the duke of Mantua, he assimilated the lessons of the other Italian Renaissance masters and made (1603) a journey to Spain that had a profound impact on the development of Spanish baroque art. The artist also spent a considerable amount of time in Rome, where he painted altarpieces for the church of Santa Croce in Gerusalemme (1602; now in Hôpital du Petit-Paris, Grasse) and the Chiesa Nuova (1607–08; first version in Musée de Peinture et Sculpture, Grenoble, France), his first widely acknowledged masterpieces.

In the mature phase of his career, Rubens either executed personally or supervised the execution of an enormous body of works that spanned all areas of painting and drawing. A devout Roman Catholic, he imbued his

In The Judgment of Paris *(1625), Peter Paul Rubens, the most influential Flemish painter of the 17th century, draws on themes from classical mythology. The painting illustrates Rubens's synthesis of Northern and Italian artistic styles. (National Gallery, London.)*

many religious paintings with the emotional tenor of the Counter-Reformation. He avoided sterile repetition of academic forms by injecting into his works a lusty exuberance and almost frenetic energy. Glowing color and light that flickers across limbs and draperies infuse spiraling compositions such as *The Descent from the Cross* (1611; Antwerp Cathedral) with a characteristically baroque sense of movement and tactile strength.

A love of monumental forms and dynamic effects is most readily apparent in the vast decorative schemes he executed in the 1620s, including the famous 21-painting cycle (1622–25; Louvre, Paris), chronicling the life of Marie de Médicis, originally painted for the Luxembourg Palace. In order to complete these huge commissions, Rubens set up a studio along the lines of Italian painters' workshops, in which fully qualified artists executed paintings from the master's sketches. Rubens's personal contribution to more than 2,000 works produced by this studio varied considerably from work to work.

Rubens's phenomenal productivity was interrupted from time to time by diplomatic duties given him by his royal patrons, Archduke Ferdinand and Archduchess Isabella, for whom he conducted (1625) negotiations aimed at ending the war between the Spanish Netherlands and the Dutch Republic and helped conclude (1629–30) a peace treaty between England and Spain. Charles I of England was so impressed that he knighted the Flemish painter and commissioned his only surviving ceiling painting, *The Allegory of War and Peace* (1629; Banqueting House, Whitehall Palace, London).

During the final decade of his life, Rubens turned more and more to portraits, genre scenes, and landscapes. These later works, such as *Landscape with the Château of Steen* (1636; National Gallery, London), lack the turbulent drama of his earlier paintings but reflect a masterful command of detail and an unflagging technical skill.

Rubicon River [roo'-bi-kahn]   The Rubicon is a historical name for a short, small river in north central Italy that formed the ancient boundary between Italy and Cisalpine Gaul. The present streams of Fiumicino and Uso have each been identified as the Rubicon. Both flow from the Apennines to the Adriatic Sea between Cesenatico and Rimini. In 49 BC, Julius CAESAR defied a senatorial order to lay down his command and marched his army across the Rubicon into Italy, thus provoking civil war. "Crossing the Rubicon" has come to mean the taking of an irrevocable step.

rubidium [roo-bid'-ee-uhm]   Rubidium is a silvery white radioactive chemical element and a member of Group IA of the periodic table, the ALKALI METALS, a group that includes sodium, potassium, and cesium. Its symbol is Rb, its atomic number is 37, and its atomic weight is 85.4678. Its name is derived from the Latin *rubidius*, meaning "deepest red." Rubidium is relatively abundant and is considered to rank 16th in the Earth's crust. It was discovered in 1861 by Robert Bunsen and Gustav Kirchhoff in a spectroscopic examination of the mineral lepidolite. Like other members of the alkali metal group, rubidium ignites spontaneously in air and reacts violently with water, setting fire to the liberated hydrogen. The refined metal must consequently be kept under dry mineral oil, in a vacuum, or in an inert atmosphere.

Rubidium is a soft metal that can be liquid at room temperature, although the pure element melts at 38.89° C (102° F) and boils at 688° C (1,270° F). Rubidium has oxidation states of +1, +2, +3, and +4. It is one of the most reactive metals, resembling potassium in its chemical properties. The element is used as a getter in vacuum tubes, as a component in photocells, and in the making of special glasses.

Rubinstein, Anton [roo'-bin-styn]   The Russian pianist Anton Rubinstein, b. Nov. 28 (N.S.), 1829, d. Nov. 20 (N.S.), 1894, had a reputation as a virtuoso second only to that of Franz Liszt. Rubinstein first performed in public at age 9, and at age 10 he made his first of many tours, one of which (1872–73) took him to the United States for 215 triumphant concerts in 239 days. His compositions—ranging from short piano pieces to operas—were also successful during his lifetime, but few are performed today. He was a cofounder of the Saint Petersburg Conservatory, serving as director during 1862–67 and 1887–91.

Rubinstein, Arthur   The celebrated pianist Arthur Rubinstein, b. Łódź, Poland, Jan. 28, 1887, d. Dec. 20, 1982, enjoyed one of the longest active performing careers in musical history and was admired particularly for his interpretations of the romantic repertoire, especially such composers as Chopin, Brahms, and Grieg. He first performed in concert at the age of 7; he made his formal debut in Berlin in 1899 playing a Mozart concerto. He was then engaged in other German cities and in Warsaw and also toured Russia. After studying for a brief time with Paderewski, he gave recitals in Paris (1905), and in the following year he made his U.S. debut in New York City. He gave recitals with the violinist Eugene Ysaÿe in London (1916), after which he toured Spain and South America, becoming an ardent champion of Spanish music. He became a U.S. citizen in 1946.

Rublev, Andrei [roo-blyawf']   Regarded as the most notable icon painter Russia has produced and the first truly Russian painter, Andrei Rublev, c.1370–c.1430, was a monk at the Trinity-Saint Sergius Monastery. His career as a painter began under the influence of Theophanes the Greek, and it developed during a time of growing confidence and optimism in Muscovy. Rublev's style, with its characteristically flowing outline and pure, deep color, is graceful and elegant; his figures seem to convey the essence of spirituality. These qualities can be seen in his most famous icon, *The Old Testament Trinity* (c.1411; Tretyakov Gallery, Moscow): three angels, rendered in delicate curves, appear against a simple gold background.

ruby   Ruby is one of the most highly prized gems (see GEMS). A transparent variety of the aluminum oxide mineral CORUNDUM, it owes its red to pale rose color to minute amounts of chromium. The most valuable stones have a deep pigeon's-blood red color. Although a brilliant stone, it lacks the fire of a diamond and is often cut to enhance the color, even at the expense of weight. For more than 500 years the finest rubies have come from a small area near Mogok, Burma, where they are washed and sieved from limestone gravels. Rubies also occur in the gem gravels of Thailand, Cambodia, Ceylon, and North Carolina. The stone often referred to as a ruby in the Old Testament and other ancient texts may actually have been a garnet or a spinel. Since 1902, when Auguste Verneuil developed the flame-fusion process, synthetic rubies have been produced from ammonia alum and chrome alum. In 1960 a synthetic ruby was used in the first working laser (see LASER).

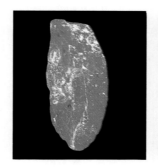

(Left) *Ruby, a highly prized gemstone, is a transparent deep red form of corundum. The color results from traces of chromic oxide.* (Right) *Rubies are usually step cut with a series of rectangular facets.*

Rudolf, Lake   Lake Rudolf, or Lake Turkana, lies in the Great Rift Valley in northern Kenya, East Africa. Its northern end extends into Ethiopia. The lake has an area of about 9,100 km^2 (3,500 mi^2) but is shrinking because of evaporation. It is relatively shallow, with a maximum depth of 73 m (240 ft) and is becoming increasingly saline. The Omo and Turkwell rivers are the main tributaries, but there is no outlet. The lake, although remote, is a tourist attraction. Count Teleki explored it in 1888 and named it after the crown prince of Austria.

Rudolf I, King of Germany   The first German king after the chaotic Interregnum (1254–73), Rudolf I, b. May 1, 1218, d. July 15, 1291, established the HABSBURG dynasty in Austria, where it ruled until 1918. A son of Albert IV, count of Habsburg, Rudolf held scattered lands in the Upper Rhineland and Switzerland. After the HOHENSTAUFEN king Conradin died (1268), Rudolf was elected his successor. Crowned at Aachen (1273), he launched a campaign to revive the monarchy's prestige. King OTTOKAR II of Bohemia, who had sought to succeed Conradin, refused to surrender the duchies of Austria, Styria, Carinthia, and Carniola, prompting Rudolf to declare war in 1276. Two years later Ottokar was killed in the Battle of the Marchfeld. Rudolf gave most of the new territory to his own sons in 1282.

In Germany, Rudolf quelled internal unrest and promoted urban prosperity, but he had difficulty checking French expansionism. Unable to arrange for his own imperial coronation, Rudolf also failed to persuade German electors to pass the crown to his son, who finally succeeded to the German throne (as Albert I) in 1298.

The rue is an aromatic herb grown for its bitter-tasting leaves. Also known as herb of grace, rue was once considered to be an antidote against poisons and a protection against witches' spells.

Rudolf II, Holy Roman Emperor

Holy Roman emperor during the late Renaissance, Rudolf II, b. July 18, 1552, d. Jan. 20, 1612, was an avid patron of the arts and sciences. On his accession (1576), Rudolf moved the imperial court from Vienna to Hradčany Palace in Prague. Rudolf's intolerance of Protestants caused widespread discontent, but he attracted painters, sculptors, writers, and scientists to Prague, including the astronomers Tycho Brahe and Johannes Kepler and the English mathematician John Dee. Melancholic and eccentric, Rudolf suffered intense bouts of depression. Between 1605 and 1611 he was forced to cede major portions of his realm to his brother MATTHIAS.

Rudolph, Wilma

Wilma Glodean Rudolph, b. Clarksville, Tenn., June 23, 1940, was an American Olympic Games track and field star. She was handicapped with a lame, brace-supported leg as a child but through rehabilitation became a champion sprinter. Her career culminated in the 1960 Olympics, where she won both the 100-m and 200-m dashes. Rudolph was also on the first-place 4 × 100-m relay team. Prior to her Olympic appearance she set a 200-m-dash world record, and she set a world record in the 100-m dash in 1961.

rue

Rue, genus *Ruta*, are 40 species of perennial herbs native to southern Europe. The rue family, Rutaceae, also includes such citruses as orange and lemon trees and such trees as satinwood, which yields timber used in cabinetry.

Common rue, or herb of grace, *R. graveolens*, a shrublike herb, has a woody base and aromatic blue green leaves that are evergreen in warmer climates. It bears yellow flowers and fruit consisting of capsules divided into four or five lobes. During earlier centuries, it was believed to cure such maladies as poisoning and gout; today it is used to flavor an alcoholic beverage of northern Italy known as grappa.

Goat's rue, *Galega officinales*, a perennial herb of the legume family, Leguminosae, is grown as an ornamental

shrub and is also cultivated for animal feed. Meadow rue, genus *Thalictrum*, are also perennial herbs.

rugby

Rugby is a kicking, passing, and tackling game that originated in England and is the direct ancestor of American football. The game is popular in Britain, France, Australia, New Zealand, and South Africa and exists in two forms: rugby union and rugby league. Rugby union, an exclusively amateur game, is played on a grass field 110 yd (100 m) long and 75 yd (69 m) wide by 2 teams of 15 players. The rugby ball resembles an American football but is approximately 24 in (61 cm) at its widest circumference and thus easier to kick and more difficult to pass. Blocking and interference are illegal.

Play starts with a kickoff, and the aim of each team is to carry the ball across the opponent's goal line or kick the ball over the crossbar of the goalposts centered on

Forwards of both teams struggle for possesion of the ball during a scrum in a rugby match. The task of the forwards is to "heel" the ball to the scrum half, who then passes to the running backs who advance the ball.

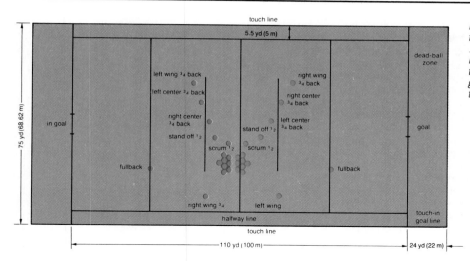

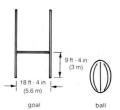

Rugby union is played by 2 teams of 15 players on a 75× 110 yd field called a pitch. Points are scored by advancing the ball over the opposite team's goal line, or drop-kicking it over the crossbar of the goalpost.

each goal line. Players advance the ball by running with the ball, passing it, or kicking it. Forward passes are not permitted, and passes are made behind the ballcarrier using a two-handed underarm motion. In rugby union, when a player is tackled the ball must be released immediately and may then be played by any player of either team. Play is continuous except when interrupted for a rule infraction or when the ball is in "touch," that is, out of bounds. When the ball goes out of bounds it is returned to play in a "line-out," in which the eight forwards from each team form two parallel lines about 0.6 m (2 ft) apart. A player from the team that last touched the ball tosses it between the two lines, and the teams then struggle for possession. If play is interrupted by a rule infraction, or if possession of the ball is unclear, a "scrum" is called by the referee. In a scrum, 8 players from each team mass together in two 3-2-3 formations, each facing the opponent's goal. The ball is dropped between the two front trios, who try to "heel" it back to waiting teammates. Points are scored when a ballcarrier crosses the goal line to score a try (4 points), when a kick for a conversion after a try goes over the goal crossbar (2 points), or when a drop-kick or penalty kick passes over the crossbar (3 points).

Rugby league, first played in 1895 and now dominated by professional teams, differs from rugby union in that teams consist of 13 players; scrums are formed of 6 players on each side; and a tackled player retains possession of the ball, "heeling" it to a teammate after regaining his feet. These variations are designed to encourage passing and running and make the game more attractive to spectators.

Rugby School

Rugby School Founded in 1567, Rugby School is a private preparatory school for boys in Rugby, Warwickshire, England. The school became celebrated in the 19th century during the headmastership of Dr. Thomas ARNOLD, whose son, the poet Matthew Arnold, wrote about the school. Another alumnus, Thomas Hughes, described it in *Tom Brown's Schooldays* (1857).

Ruggles, Carl [ruhg'-ulz] The American composer Carl Ruggles, b. Marion, Mass., Mar. 11, 1876, d. Oct. 24, 1971, exemplified New England independence and individualism no less than did his friend Charles Ives. After studies at Harvard, Ruggles stubbornly went his own way, shunning the musical mainstream. Highly self-critical, he deliberately limited his production to a small number of works, variously exploring piano, vocal, chamber, and orchestral idioms in terse, densely compressed, but boldly sonorous and vigorous forms. Ruggles's music has not been widely heard, although his orchestral works *Men and Mountains* (1924) and *Sun Treader* (1933) have won success in performances and recordings.

rugs and carpets Rugs and carpets are a form of decorative art; as such, they are as representative of a culture as its painting or architecture. People have made them and used them in their living quarters for thousands of years. The earliest rugs were crudely woven; they were tacked to walls to provide insulation from winds and sun and laid on the bare ground for the sake of warmth and comfort.

In current usage the word *carpet* refers to any heavy fabric that is tacked down on a floor and covers it completely. Carpeting is usually woven in wide strips that are joined together when the carpet is laid. A rug, on the other hand, is generally woven as a single piece, covers only part of the floor, and is not tacked down. The terms *rug* and *carpet* are interchangeable in the context of Oriental rugs and carpets.

Techniques of Manufacture

Woven Rugs. The basic techniques of rug making were first developed in the East. Traditional Oriental rugs are made on vertical looms strung with 3 to 24 warp (vertical) threads per cm (8 to 60 per in) of width. Working from bottom to top, the rug maker either weaves the rug with a flat surface or knots it for a pile texture. Pile rugs use 5-

to 7.5-cm (2- to 3-in) lengths of yarn tied in Turkish (Ghiordes) or Persian (Sehna) knots with rows of horizontal weft yarn laced over and under the vertical warp threads for strength. After the carpet is completely knotted, its pile is sheared, and the warp threads at each end are tied into a fringe. The finer the yarn and the closer the warp threads are strung together, the denser the weave and, usually, the finer the quality. Fine-textured and valuable rugs have 62 or more knots per cm^2 (400 per in^2); coarse-textured rugs may have less than 8 per cm^2 (50 per in^2). In traditional Scandinavian weaving (rya) the knot is actually tied like the Turkish knot, but the pile alone is 5 to 7.5 cm (2 to 3 in) long, and the rows of knots are separated by 10 to 20 weft rows.

Flat-woven rugs are lighter in weight and less bulky than pile rugs. The best-known and earliest type is the kilim, which has a plain weave made by shooting the weft yarn over and under the warp threads in one row, then alternating the weft in the next row. The soumak type is woven in a herringbone pattern by wrapping a continuous weft around pairs of warp threads.

The same materials are used in flat-woven and pile rugs. Warp and weft yarns are either wool or cotton. In pile rugs, the knots are usually wool, sometimes goat's or camel's hair, depending on the region. Silk, traditionally a costly material, is found principally in fine Persian carpets and some Chinese rugs.

Other Types of Rugs. In the West, rugs have been made by several other techniques as well. For hooked rugs, thin strips of outworn woolen goods traditionally were drawn through a linen, cotton, or burlap backing with a metal hook to form slightly raised loops on the surface. For traditional braided rugs, strips of outworn cloth were plaited together and then wound flat in a circle or oval. In patchwork rugs, snippets of cloth were sewed on homespun woolen material. In Shaker rugs, cloth scraps were threaded together like a necklace and then sewed onto a strong backing material. In needlepoint rugs, each intersection of a mesh canvas backing is covered with individual stitches of wool yarn.

Rugs around the World

Rugs are mentioned in the Old Testament and in Homer; they were known to the ancient Chinese, the Egyptians, and the Greeks. The earliest-known hand-knotted carpet, dating from about 500 BC, was discovered well preserved in ice in a tomb at Pazyryk, in southern Siberia. Rugs were made in Persia during the reign of Cyrus (549–530 BC), whose tomb was said to have been covered with precious carpets. By the 16th century, traditions of rug making were highly developed in Persia and Turkey. Rug making then spread north to the Caucasus and east to India, Turkestan, and China; finally, it reached Europe and the West. The American Indians developed weaving traditions independently.

Persia and India. A graceful, curvilinear style and a masterful use of color is typical of Persian rugs. The great tradition of rug making culminated in the 16th and 17th centuries in densely woven court carpets of the Safavid

An Indian hunting carpet, dating from the period of the Mogul emperor Jahangir (r.1605–28), features naturalistic floral and animal motifs. The carpets of the Mogul courts are renowned for their fine weaving and detailed pictorial designs. (J. Paul Getty Museum, Malibu, Calif.)

period. Usually classified according to the particular type of design displayed in each, they include medallion carpets, garden carpets, flower carpets, vase carpets, animal carpets, and hunting carpets. Regional and village carpets of Persia most often use the central medallion design or all-over pattern of flowers or other flowing forms. Regional carpets are usually designated by their place of origin, such as Bakhtiari, Isfahan, or Tabriz.

The golden age of Indian rug making occurred under the Mogul emperors who ruled from the mid-16th to the mid-17th century and who imported not only designs and traditions from Persia but weavers as well. The greatest Indian examples were the finely woven florals and the hunting carpets, with their remarkably naturalistic designs.

The Caucasus. Caucasian rugs are made by various tribes in the mountainous district between the Black and Caspian seas. The designs are often dense all-over patterns of geometric elements or motifs drawn with angular lines in bold, clear colors. The rugs are generally small, with wide multiple borders. The Armenian dragon carpet, combining an ancient dragon motif with Persian flowers, was made during the 15th and 16th centuries and was much more opulent than the better-known yet simpler Caucasian rugs.

Turkey. Turkish carpets were the first Orientals to be imported into Europe and often appeared in late Renaissance paintings. Most were woven in villages in Anatolia (the part of Turkey that lies in Asia Minor) in bright, rich colors with geometric forms. In the mid-16th century, elegant court rugs woven on royal looms in Constantinople incorporated the more graceful curvilinear style of Persia.

Turkish prayer rugs are of particular interest. The mihrabs (prayer niches) usually have pointed arches and stepped sides. The best known are the Ghiordes, with freestanding columns supporting the mihrab; Ladik, with its stylized tulips; Kula; Konya; and Mudjur.

Central Asia and Turkestan. Carpets made by the nomads of central Asia are collectively designated as

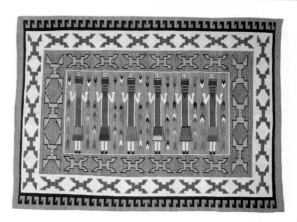

(Right) *A woven Navajo rug (c.1940), combining abstract and geometric forms, features a central motif of mythic female figures and an angular border design.*

(Left) *A late-19th-century Chinese pillar carpet, decorated with animal masks, Buddhist symbols, and stylized natural forms, creates a unified dragon design when wrapped about a column. (Textile Museum, Washington, D.C.)*

Turkoman carpets. These carry a number of names including Afghan, Baluchi, and Bokhara. The geographic and cultural isolation of the region accounts for the distinctive character of the rugs. Most are reddish and have an all-over pattern that incorporates the coat of arms (*gul*) of the individual tribe.

Samarkand, although actually a collection and marketing center rather than a rug-producing center, is the name applied to the rugs produced more than 300 km (about 200 mi) away in Kashi (Kashgar), Hotan (Khotan), and Yarkant (Yarkand) in what is now far-western China. The Samarkand style is less angular than the Turkoman style and not as graceful as that of Chinese rugs.

China. Simplicity of design, serenity of composition, a limited range of subdued and harmonious colors, and symbolic motifs characterize Chinese carpets. The earliest surviving examples date from the late Ming dynasty in the mid-17th century. Rugs of the Kangxi period (1662–1722) continued Ming forms with greater naturalism and more ornamentation. During the latter half of the 18th century ornate and opulent palace rugs were woven. Rugs for export followed, favoring a central dragon motif or ornate floral designs. At the end of the 19th century, anilines replaced natural dyes and introduced an often harsh and garish quality.

Spain. Rug making was introduced (AD 711) to Spain by the invading Moors. Their rugs first incorporated the geometric forms of Islamic art; later, combined Muslim and Christian motifs were used in the well-known Admiral carpets woven for the heirs of Spanish admirals. After the 18th century the best Spanish rugs were the low-looped, folk-art Alpujarras made by the peasants in the mountains of southern Spain.

France. The best-known French rugs are the AUBUSSON, a flat tapestry weave, and the Savonnerie, a knotted pile or tufted weave. Aubusson rugs had been woven for 9 centuries when, in the early 17th century, Henry IV established court looms to produce Oriental-type pile carpets named for the soap factory (*savonnerie*) that once housed the looms. Designs reflected contemporaneous French art styles.

England. The English rug industry, developed in the 16th century, was invigorated by the French Protestants, many of them weavers, who fled to England for religious asylum. Early carpet works at Wilton and Axminster wove pile carpets in which bright floral patterns predominated. The great industrial advances of the 18th century—the spinning jenny, power looms, Jacquard weaving—revolutionized carpet making and also inspired the 19th-century ARTS AND CRAFTS MOVEMENT.

Scandinavia. Scandinavia's unique shaggy-pile weavings, called rya, were first woven as a defense against the harsh northern climate. Early designs were simple geometrics; later ones included ecclesiastical and folk motifs. Although folk rya declined in the 19th century, it is currently flourishing as an art form, especially in Finland.

Navajo Rugs. Typical Navajo weavings repeat a few simple geometric shapes in minimal designs using primarily natural-colored wools (usually black, gray, tan, or brown) in a flat tapestry weave. The westward expansion of the railroad in the 1880s introduced commercial yarn and aniline dyes (replacing vegetable dyes).

Contemporary Trends. More than 97 percent of all machine-made carpets are now made of synthetic fibers, principally nylon. Area rugs in both contemporary and period designs are often made of natural fibers like sisal or of hand-tufted wool in natural colors. Many contemporary artists design pile or flat-weave rugs and wall hangings.

See also: LOOM; TAPESTRY; WEAVING.

Ruhr Valley [roor] The Ruhr Valley, one of the world's most vital industrial regions, is in Germany. The 235-km-long (145-mi) Ruhr River and its tributaries—the Mohne and Lenne—water the region. Overlying one of the world's most extensive coal deposits, the region's industries produce steel, iron, and other metals, and chemicals. The major industrial cities within the Ruhr area are DORTMUND, DUISBURG, ESSEN, MÜLHEIM AN DER RUHR, Oberhausen, and Witten. Duisburg, the great RHINE RIVER port, serves as the entrepôt for the Ruhr Valley. Although the region's settlement dates to the Stone Age, its industrial development did not begin until the early 19th century. The Ruhr endured heavy Allied bombing during World War II when 75% of its facilities were destroyed.

Ruisdael, Jacob van [roys'-dahl] Jacob van Ruisdael, c.1628–1682, the most celebrated landscapist of the Dutch school, is known for his generally accurate and atmospheric representations of the Dutch countryside. He met with popular success almost at once because his work was calculated to appeal to the Dutch taste for pictures that closely imitate nature. Ruisdael's skies are especially well executed, depicting bright light and great floating clouds such as may be seen to advantage in flat landscapes. Other works depict the wilder aspects of nature, as well as hinting at decay and transience. These aspects of Ruisdael's work have been seen as prophetic of 19th-century German romanticism.

In one of his most famous paintings, *The Mill at Wijk* (c.1665; Rijksmuseum, Amsterdam), many of the characteristic elements of his work are combined: a cloud-laden sky, a somewhat somber landscape containing a few diminutive human figures, and a group of buildings dominated by a large windmill. The foreground in particular, with its disturbed water and reeds, invites comparison with the works of German romantics.

Jacob van Ruisdael's The Mill at Wijk *(c.1665) exhibits the dramatic intensity and precise realism characteristic of the Dutch artist's work.*

Ruiz de Alarcón y Mendoza, Juan [roo-eeth' day ah-lar-kohn' ee mayn-doh'-thah] Juan Ruiz de Alarcón y Mendoza, b. c.1581, d. Aug. 4, 1639, was one of the most important playwrights of Spain's 17th-century Golden Age. His protagonists are liars, schemers, and egotists whose weaknesses are humorous but intolerable to virtuous men and women. His most famous play, *La verdad sospechosa* (The Suspected Truth, c.1610), concerns a liar who is ultimately punished for his vice. It was adapted as *Le Menteur* (1643) by Corneille, who gave it a happier ending.

Alarcón was afflicted with a hunchback. Born in Mexico, he lived there for many years but emigrated to Madrid to pursue a literary career. His views on morality and society were far ahead of their time, and he was the subject of much ridicule by contemporaries.

Rukeyser, Muriel [roo'-ky-sur] The American poet Muriel Rukeyser, b. New York City, Dec. 15, 1913, d. Feb. 12, 1980, is best known for her passionate concern with social issues. A comprehensive selection of her earlier poetry is collected in *Waterlily Fire* (1962), and her more recent work appears in *Gates* (1976) and *Collected Poems* (1978). The poetry in these volumes reveals a style of great flexibility ranging from lyric and symbolic to satiric. She has also translated poetry from several languages.

rum Rum is an alcoholic beverage distilled from sugarcane by-products that are produced in the process of manufacturing sugar. MOLASSES, the thick syrup remaining after sugarcane juice has been crystallized by boiling, is usually used as the basis for rum, although the juice itself or other sugarcane residues are also used. The molasses is allowed to ferment, and the ferment is then distilled to produce a clear liquid that is aged in oaken casks. The golden color of some rums results from the absorption of substances from the oak. The darker, heavier Jamaican rums—made for the most part in Jamaica, Barbados, and Guyana—are produced from a combination of molasses and skimmings from the sugar-boiling vats; the darkest, Guyana's Demarara, is produced by very rapid fermentation and is not particularly heavy bodied. The fermentation of other substances in the molasses enhances the liquid's flavor and aroma. After distilling, the rum is darkened by the addition of caramel and is aged from 5 to 7 years. Lighter, drier rums from Puerto Rico and the Virgin Islands are more rapidly fermented with cultured yeasts and are aged from 1 to 4 years. Rum from imported molasses is also produced in New England and other regions of the world.

Rumania see ROMANIA

Rumi, Jalal al-Din al- The founder of the Sufi order known as the "Whirling Dervishes," Jalal al-Din al-Rumi, called Maulavi, 1207–73, was a Persian mystic and poet revered for both his spiritual teachings and his poetic innovations. In 1231, Rumi began to teach his mystical doctrine, and in 1244 he came under the influence of Shamsi Tabriz, an itinerant Sufi. The earliest of his poetical works is a collection of lyrical odes named for Tabriz. The second is called the *Masnavi*, or *Mathnavi* (c.1246–73; Eng. trans., 1925–40), a long poem in six books consisting of fables and anecdotes describing the soul's quest for union with God. Rumi's poetic style is characterized by a depth of feeling and wealth of images drawn from daily life.

See also: SUFISM.

ruminant   *Ruminant* means cud-chewer and refers to even-toed (split-hoofed), cud-chewing mammals, including the cattle, sheep, goats, deer, antelopes, chevrotains, and the camels and llamas. The camels and llamas, however, are not zoologically classified with the others in the suborder Ruminantia.

Rumination is one of the methods evolved by mammals to utilize cellulose, which no mammal can digest on its own. All cellulose digestion, usually referred to as fermentation, is done by microbes within the mammal's digestive tract.

The ruminant stomach is divided into four compartments (camels have three). The first of these, called the rumen, is where most fermentation occurs. The rumen contains both bacteria and protozoans that use their cellulose-digesting enzymes to break down the cellulose into mostly short-chain fatty acids, such as acetic acid, and into other compounds, including ammonia. The fatty acids and other nutrients enter the bloodstream through the rumen and, in the case of the cow, may provide up to 70 percent of the animal's energy supply.

Fermentation creates a great deal of carbon dioxide and methane, which must be released through the mouth (by eructation, or belching). Ruminants produce large amounts of slightly alkaline saliva, both to provide a sufficient liquid medium for fermentation and to buffer and neutralize the resulting acids to the microbes' requirements.

After partial fermentation, some of the remaining coarse, fibrous material is formed into small masses called boli (singular, bolus), or cuds, and these are brought back to the mouth where they are chewed and then reswallowed. This time the food passes into the second chamber, the reticulum, where some additional fermentation takes place, and then into the third chamber, or omasum, where most of the water is reabsorbed. Next, the food passes into the fourth chamber, the abomasum, or true stomach, where ordinary digestion occurs.

rummy   The popular card game rummy requires a standard 52-card deck and may be played by two to six players. The king is the highest-ranking card, although for scoring purposes the king, queen, jack, and 10 are each worth 10 points; all other cards are worth their face value. To start play, 7-card hands are dealt face down if three or four play; 6-card hands are dealt when five or six play; and in two-handed rummy, 10 cards are dealt to each player. The remaining cards are turned face down to form the stock. Then, through a process of drawing and discarding cards, each player attempts to meld, that is, to develop a hand containing only sets of 3 or 4 cards of the same rank or sequences of three or more cards in the same suit. Rummy is achieved when a player melds his or her hand in a single turn; if more than one turn is needed to meld all cards then a player "goes out." Each player has a second objective: to hold the lowest-valued total of unmelded cards. Such cards count against the player when an opponent achieves rummy or goes out.

Gin rummy is a game for two. Each player is dealt 10 cards face down, the remainder forming the stock, and each tries to form melds so that the unmelded cards—called deadwood—in the hand total 10 or less. A player with such a holding may "knock," that is, knock on the table and lay a card on the discard pile, leaving 10 in the hand. He or she lays down the remaining cards, segregating them into melded and unmelded cards, and announces the remaining point count of 10 or less. The opponent then shows his or her hand and, before taking a count of unmelded cards, matches wherever possible unmatched cards from his or her hand to the melds in the knocker's hand. If the opponent has a count equal to or less than the knocker's, or can reduce the count to the knocker's count or less, then the opponent is awarded a score determined by the difference between their deadwood counts. Gin occurs when one player has melded all cards and holds no deadwood. A player who goes gin gets a bonus of 25 points, plus the point value of the opponent's unmelded cards. Games usually are played to 100 points.

Runcie, Robert Alexander Kennedy   The English churchman Robert Alexander Kennedy Runcie, b. Oct. 2, 1921, was archbishop of Canterbury from 1980 to 1991. He served with distinction as a tank commander in World War II and was ordained in 1951. Runcie served as principal of Cuddeston Theological College from 1960 to 1969 and was bishop of Saint Albans from 1970 to 1980.

Rundstedt, Karl Rudolf Gerd von   [runt'-shtet] Gerd von Rundstedt, b. Dec. 12, 1875, d. Feb. 24, 1953, was a German field marshal during World War II. He played a role in the secret rearmament of Germany before the war and held major commands in the invasions of Poland (1939), France (1940), and Russia (1941). Despite disagreements with Adolf Hitler on strategy for the Russian campaign, he became supreme commander in the west for most of the period from 1942 to 1945 and directed the 1944 Ardennes offensive (see BULGE, BATTLE OF THE).

runes   Runes are the 24 letters (later 16 in Scandinavia and 30 or more in Anglo-Saxon England) of an ancient Germanic alphabet used from the 2d or 3d to the 16th century. Perhaps derived ultimately from the Etruscan alphabet (see WRITING SYSTEMS, EVOLUTION OF), the runic alphabet—called the *fuþark* from its first six letters, *f, u, þ* ("th"), *a, r,* and *k*—was used mainly for charms and inscriptions, on stone, wood, metal, or bone. Each letter had a name that was itself a meaningful word. The rune *f,* for instance, could stand either for the sound "f" or for *fehu,* "cattle," which was the name given to the rune.

running and jogging   Running or jogging, because of its basic simplicity, is probably the oldest sport. In prehistoric times running was both a means of hunting food and of escaping danger, and thus it contributed to the survival of the human species. Today running or jogging is one of the world's most popular recreational and competitive sports. Running or jogging (no precise distinction is made between the two; jogging is merely slow running for either training or fitness) is now practiced by millions of Americans, primarily adults, who are interested in improving their general physical fitness levels, increasing energy levels, losing weight, lowering blood pressure, and looking and feeling better.

The Marathon. For the ancient and modern Olympic history of this 26-mi 385-yd (42.2-km) race, see MARATHON. Whereas the Olympic marathon is contested only once every four years, the famous Boston Marathon has been staged annually since 1897. Until the early 1960s only 200 to 300 runners competed. Thereafter, however, the number of runners increased steadily, finally forcing the organizers of the race to impose stiff qualifying standards that limited the field. This procedure is now applied in several long-distance races. Even with such restrictions in effect, the Boston Marathon's starting field numbered more than 9,000 in 1991.

The Running Boom. The extraordinary increase in the popularity of running and jogging in the 1970s and thereafter occurred not only in marathons but in all running events. Most of the new converts to running chose to pursue the sport in isolation, but many others decided to participate in occasional road races in order to test themselves against other runners.

The jogging population has been augmented by two significant groups: (1) women in general and (2) runners, primarily men, 40 years of age and over (in competition they are placed in a special Master's category).

Training to Run. As running or jogging becomes more publicized, growing numbers of people are likely to take up the sport. It is recommended that beginners past age 35, especially those who are overweight or who smoke, have a complete physical examination before embarking on a running regimen. Supervised jogging programs, also recommended, are available at local YMCAs, community centers, or health clubs.

A good pair of running shoes is essential. Running can be practiced almost anywhere; in a backyard, on a local high school track, in public parks, or along the roadside. One of the great advantages of running is that it is usually easy to practice year-round. The key to undertaking a running program is to begin slowly and cautiously. Many beginners, especially those who run alone, make the mistake of overexerting themselves. The human body grows stronger and more fit when subjected to gradual increases of physical stress. When this stress is applied too early or too forcefully, however, it creates fatigue, irritability, and injury. Most accomplished runners also perform warm-up exercises that include stretching of the major leg muscles. Almost anyone who does not have a severe physical handicap can learn to run and enjoy running provided he or she is willing to proceed with patience.

Runyon, Damon   [ruhn'-yuhn, day'-muhn]   American journalist and short-story writer Alfred Damon Runyon, b. Manhattan, Kans., Oct. 4, 1880, d. Dec. 10, 1946, became famous for his colorful stories about the New York underworld, which carefully recorded its slang and dialect. His best-known work, *Guys and Dolls* (1931), was turned into a Broadway hit in 1950. It has since become a staple of the American musical theater.

Rupert, Prince   Prince Rupert of the Rhine, b. Prague, Dec. 17, 1619, d. Nov. 29, 1682, served both CHARLES I and CHARLES II of England as a soldier and a sailor. He was the third son of FREDERICK V, elector palatine, who by claiming the throne of Bohemia started the Thirty Years' War. Having gained military experience in Europe, Rupert joined his uncle Charles I in the ENGLISH CIVIL WAR and became commander in chief in 1644. A year later, however, a series of defeats, resentment of his harsh and imperious manner, and unjustified suspicion of treachery led to his dismissal. He and Charles I were partly reconciled, and he served the royalist cause as a naval commander until 1653. When Charles II was restored to the throne in 1660, Rupert returned to England and was later appointed admiral in both of the ANGLO-DUTCH WARS.

Rupert's Land   Rupert's Land was the name given to a tract of Canadian territory granted to the HUDSON'S BAY COMPANY by King Charles II of England in 1670. Named after Prince Rupert, first governor of the company, it originally comprised only the land that drained into Hudson Bay, but later included most of western Canada. In 1869 control of the territory passed to Canada.

Rupp, Adolph   Adolph Frederick "The Baron" Rupp, b. Halstead, Kans., Sept. 1, 1901, d. Dec. 10, 1977, was one of U.S. college basketball's most successful coaches. He won a record 875 games (of 1,065) and produced 25 All-Americans during his 42-year career at the University of Kentucky. His teams won 27 Southeast Conference titles and 4 NCAA championships. Rupp also coached the U.S. team to a gold medal at the 1948 Olympics.

Rurik (dynasty) [roo'-rik]   The Rurik family was the first dynasty to rule Russia. According to Russian tradition, its founder was a Varangian (VIKING) adventurer named **Rurik**, d. c.879, who established himself in Novgorod about 862. **Igor**, c.877–945, supposedly Rurik's son, ruled from 912 until his death; he moved his capital to Kiev and assumed the title of grand prince (or grand duke). Early Rurik rulers included VLADIMIR I, who brought Christianity to Russia in 989, and his son, YAROSLAV I (r. 1019–54), who beautified Kiev and codified Russian law.

With the decline of Kiev in the 12th century, the title of grand prince passed to towns lying to the northeast. Over time, the rulers of Moscow strengthened their claim to the title. Important Muscovite rulers included **Ivan I**, b. c.1304, d. Mar. 31, 1341 (r. 1328–41), who added new territory to Muscovy; IVAN III; and IVAN IV. The last of the Rurik rulers was **Fyodor I**, b. May 31, 1557, d. Jan. 7, 1598 (r. 1584–98), the son of Ivan IV. The dynasty was succeeded by the ROMANOVS.

rush   Rushes, genus *Juncus,* are about 240 species of perennial herbs belonging to the rush family, Juncaceae. These plants, which have unbranched stems and grasslike leaves, grow in dense clumps in boggy areas of temperate regions. They bear clusters of green or brown flowers. The leaves and stems of rushes are used to weave baskets, mats, and chair seats. The species *J. effusus* grows from 0.3 to 1.8 m (1 to 6 ft) tall. Widely distributed in northern temperate zones, it is grown commercially in Japan, where it is woven into tatami.

Rush, Benjamin   The American physician and political and social reformer Benjamin Rush, b. Philadelphia, Jan. 4, 1746, d. Apr. 19, 1813, challenged many established theories and sought new ways of combating illness. He pioneered in military hygiene and the treatment of mental illness, writing (1812) the first American text on the subject. As a social reformer he fought for better education for women and the abolition of both slavery and capital punishment. Rush was a signer of the Declaration of Independence and served on the ratifying convention in Pennsylvania for the new federal constitution. From 1797 until his death he was treasurer of the U.S. Mint.

Rush, Richard   Richard Rush, b. Philadelphia, Aug. 29, 1780, d. July 30, 1859, the son of physician Benjamin Rush, was an American statesman. He served as U.S. attorney general from 1814 to 1817. In 1817, as acting secretary of state, he concluded the Rush-Bagot convention with the British ambassador Charles Bagot; this agreement limited naval armaments on the Great Lakes. While American minister to Great Britain (1817–25), Rush negotiated the Convention of 1818, which provided for joint Anglo-American occupation of the Oregon Territory and established the boundary between the United States and British North America east of the Rockies.

Rush was secretary of the treasury (1825–29) and ambassador to France (1847–49).

Rush, William   The first native U.S. sculptor, William Rush, b. Philadelphia, July 4, 1756, d. Jan. 17, 1833, produced ships' ornaments and figureheads that earned him an international reputation. A surviving figurehead, the robed female *Virtue* (1810; Masonic Lodge, Philadelphia), demonstrates the animation he introduced into the tradition. Rush also sculpted free-standing figures of which the best known is *Water Nymph and Bittern* (1809; bronze copy, Fairmount Park, Philadelphia). His carved self-portrait is in the Pennsylvania Academy of Fine Arts, an institution he helped to found in 1805.

Rushdie, Salman [ruhsh'-dee]   Writer Ahmed Salman Rushdie, b. Bombay, June 19, 1947, won headlines and best-sellerdom when, in 1989, his newly published novel, *The Satanic Verses*, aroused the wrath of many Muslims and persuaded Iran's Ayatollah Khomeini to order the author's assassination. Rushdie's work hinges on his triple identity as an Indian Muslim who now resides in England. *Midnight's Children* (1981) is an allegory about the birth of independent India. *Shame* (1983) focuses on Pakistan's recent rulers. *The Satanic Verses* is a complex fantasy whose two heroes, like Rushdie, are expatriate Indians. The passages describing the birth of a religion resembling Islam are seen as blasphemous by Muslims, and the book has been banned in most Islamic countries.

Rushmore, Mount   Mount Rushmore National Memorial is located in the Black Hills of southwestern South

Gutzon Borglum's 18-m-high (60-ft) heads of Presidents Washington, Jefferson, Theodore Roosevelt, and Lincoln are carved into the face of Mount Rushmore—a granite outcropping in the Black Hills of South Dakota.

Dakota. Sculptures approximately 18 m (60 ft) high of the heads of U.S. presidents George Washington, Thomas Jefferson, Abraham Lincoln, and Theodore Roosevelt have been carved from Mount Rushmore's granite outcropping. The four presidents were chosen to represent, respectively, the nation's founding, philosophy, unity, and expansion. Gutzon BORGLUM designed and oversaw construction (1927–41) of the largely federally funded monument.

Rusk, Dean   A U.S. secretary of state (1961–69), David Dean Rusk, b. Cherokee County, Ga., Feb. 9, 1909, helped to shape U.S. foreign policy, advocating involvement in both the Korean and the Vietnam wars. Prior to becoming secretary of state Rusk had an extensive diplomatic career and served as president of the Rockefeller Foundation (1952–60). Since leaving government, Rusk, a former Rhodes scholar (1933–34), has taught at the University of Georgia Law School.

Ruskin, John [ruhs'-kin]   The English writer John Ruskin, b. Feb. 18, 1819, d. Jan. 20, 1900, was prominent as an art and literary critic and as a social reformer. While at Oxford he began the serious study of art, which later bore fruit in *Modern Painters*, a five-volume work that appeared between 1843 and 1860. Affection for Gothic architecture and the principles on which it was based moved Ruskin to write *The Seven Lamps of Architecture* (1849) and *The Stones of Venice* (1851–53). He was a regular and unsparing critic of Victorian painting and a champion of the Pre-Raphaelites.

Ruskin applied similar aesthetic principles to literature, condemning what he called mere realism and praising the vivid imaginative representations of Dante and Spenser. He coined the term *pathetic fallacy* to characterize an anthropomorphism in literature that he considered false to nature.

Ruskin's belief that art reflects the morality of society and his total distaste for the forces of industrialism led him to the second great concern of his life—social reform. To this end he lectured widely and wrote numerous essays, the latter collected in such books as *Unto This Last* (1862) and *Fors Clavigera* (1871–84). His ferocious attack on James Abbott McNeill WHISTLER's paintings led to a libel action in 1878, which was decided against Ruskin and brought his public career to an end. *Praeterita* (1886–89), a delightful fragment of autobiography written during his retirement, was his final book.

Russell, Bertrand   One of the most influential philosophical thinkers of the 20th century, Bertrand Arthur William Russell, 3d Earl Russell, b. Trelleck, Wales, May 18, 1872, d. Feb. 2, 1970, was a grandson of the 1st Earl Russell, who had twice been prime minister of Great Britain.

Life. Orphaned at age 3, Bertrand was reared by his puritanically religious but politically liberal paternal grandmother. He rebelled early against her rigid moral

Bertrand Russell, a seminal figure in the development of 20th century philosophical thought, made major contributions in the areas of mathematics, logic, education, and social reform. Russell, who received the 1950 Nobel Prize for literature, endorsed the application of rationality to all aspects of thought and language.

views, but her otherwise progressive beliefs influenced his later social thinking.

Russell was dismissed (1916) from his position at Trinity College, Cambridge University, because of his active defense of unpopular causes such as socialism and his opposition to World War I. In 1918 he was imprisoned for his radical pacifism. During the 1930s he modified his commitment to pacifism to acknowledge the necessity to oppose Nazi Germany. He resumed his pacifist stance in the post–World War II years and was especially vigorous in his denunciation of nuclear weapons. Russell founded the Campaign for Nuclear Disarmament (1958) and the Committee of 100 (1960) as his advocacy of civil disobedience became progressively stronger in the antinuclear movement.

In addition to his political involvements, Russell took an active interest in moral, educational, and religious issues. His religious views, as set forth in his book *Why I Am Not a Christian* (1927), were considered controversial by many. In 1931, Russell and his second wife (he married four times) founded the experimental Beacon Hill School, which influenced the founding of similarly progressive schools in England and the United States.

Throughout his life Russell was a prolific and highly regarded writer in many fields, ranging from logic and mathematics to politics to short works of fiction. In 1950 he was awarded the Nobel Prize for literature. Russell remained active and wrote extensively until his death at the age of 97. The most interesting account of his life is contained in his autobiography (3 vols., 1967–69).

Philosophical Views. Russell's early philosophical views grew out of a concern to establish a vigorous logical foundation for mathematics, a concern that produced *Principles of Mathematics* (1903). Building on the work in LOGIC of Gottlob FREGE, Giuseppe Peano, and others, Russell argued that arithmetic could be constructed from purely logical notions and the concepts of "class" and "successor." In *Principia Mathematica* (3 vols., 1910–13), written with Alfred North WHITEHEAD, this program was carried out in detail.

Russell was seriously concerned with the application of logical analysis to epistemological questions and attacked this problem by trying to break down human knowledge into minimum statements that were verifiable by empirical observation, reason, and logic. He was deeply convinced that all facts, objects, and relations were logically independent, both of one another and of our ability to know them, and that all knowledge is dependent on sense experience. With G. E. MOORE, his former pupil Ludwig WITTGENSTEIN, and others, Russell guided postwar British philosophy in a more positivist direction, focusing on the logical analysis of problems and of the language in which they are expressed. Russell's position in *Our Knowledge of the External World* (1914) is referred to as logical atomism, by which he meant that all propositions (statements about experienced reality) can be broken down into the logically irreducible subpropositions and terms that constitute them. When these logically independent and discrete terms are combined and recombined, reality can be described as something that occurs at the point of such combinations, called the point event.

Difficulties of analysis led Russell to give up many of the characteristic theses of logical atomism, and with his *Analysis of Mind* (1921) and *Analysis of Matter* (1926) he shifted to what has been called neutral monism. In this phase Russell combines a stringent empiricism with an optimistic view of the progress of science that leads to the conception of philosophy as a piecemeal analysis of the findings of science. His examination of the bases of scientific method culminated in *Human Knowledge, Its Scope and Limits* (1948).

Russell, Bill

William Felton Russell, b. Monroe, La., Feb. 12, 1934, an American college and professional basketball player, is considered the finest defensive center in the history of the game. The 2-m 8-cm (6-ft 10-in) Russell was a member of the University of San Francisco team that won National Collegiate Athletic Association (NCAA) championships in 1955 and 1956. He was selected as an All-American during those years. After graduation he led the U.S. basketball team to a gold medal in the 1956 Olympic Games. He then joined the Boston Celtics of the National Basketball Association (NBA). In Russell's 13 years with the Celtics the team won 11 NBA titles. He was named to the NBA all-star team 11 times and won the Most Valuable Player award 5 times (1958, 1961, 1962, 1963, and 1965). In his career Russell had 21,620 rebounds and scored 14,522 points. After leaving the Celtics, the Hall of Famer was coach and general manager of the Seattle SuperSonics (1973–77) and coach and vice-president of the Sacramento Kings (1987–89).

Russell, Charles M.

The artist Charles Marion Russell, b. St. Louis, Mo., Mar. 19, 1864, d. Oct. 24, 1926, dealt exclusively with a single subject: the American West. At the age of 15 he set out for Montana, where he worked as a herder, hunter, trapper, and cowboy while developing as an artist. At the age of 29 he began paint-

The vigor and authentic detail of Charles M. Russell's A Bronc to Breakfast *(1908) are characteristic of the artist's style. A former cowboy, Russell realistically portrayed the American West of the late 19th century. (MacKay Collection, Montana Historical Society.)*

ing seriously, devoting himself to scenes of range and mountain life. His vivid, dramatic, and sometimes humorous illustrations of cowboys, Indians, and animals, such as *Lost in a Snowstorm—We Are Friends* (1888; Amon Carter Museum, Fort Worth, Tex.), are spirited and truthful records of the Wild West.

Russell, Charles Taze

Charles Taze Russell, b. Pittsburgh, Pa., Feb. 16, 1852, d. Oct. 31, 1916, called Pastor Russell, was the first president of the Watch Tower Bible and Tract Society of Pennsylvania, the legal agency of JEHOVAH'S WITNESSES. In 1870, at the age of 18, Russell began a systematic study of the Bible with a small group of associates. Becoming convinced of the imminence of Christ's millennial reign, he began to preach and spread his teachings, and in 1879 he founded the *Watch Tower* journal. In 1884, Russell established the Watch Tower Bible and Tract Society, of which he was president until his death.

The American religious leader Charles Taze Russell, the founder of a millenarian sect now known as the Jehovah's Witnesses, taught the imminence of the Second Coming of Christ.

Russell, George W. George William Russell, b. Apr. 10, 1867, d. July 17, 1935, was an Irish poet and journalist who wrote under the pen name Æon, shortened inadvertently by his printer to Æ. A painter in his youth, he subsequently became active in the political, social, and literary movements of his day. Russell's importance in literature is a result of the role he played as friend and counselor to Yeats and other leading figures of the IRISH LITERARY RENAISSANCE. He supported the cause of Irish nationalism as editor (1904–30) of the weekly *Irish Homestead* and its successor, *Irish Statesman*. His first volume of poetry, *Homeward: Songs by the Way* (1894), is considered his finest.

Russell, John Russell, 1st Earl The 1st Earl Russell, b. Aug. 18, 1792, d. May 28, 1878, known for most of his life as Lord John Russell, was a leading British Liberal statesman. The younger son of the 6th duke of Bedford, he was elected to the House of Commons as a Whig in 1813. True to the liberal traditions of his wealthy family, he espoused the causes of CATHOLIC EMANCIPATION and electoral reform. As paymaster general in the 2d Earl GREY's government he introduced the 1832 parliamentary reform bill (see REFORM ACTS), and as home secretary (1835–39) he liberalized the government of Ireland. In this period he coined the name of the emerging Liberal party.

Russell served as minority prime minister from 1846 to 1852. He championed free trade following the 1846 repeal of the CORN LAWS, and he advocated university reform; but despite various relief measures, he was largely unable to help victims of the Irish potato famine (1846–51). His Durham letter (1850) against Roman and Anglican Catholicism was a deviation from his usual tolerance. In 1851, Russell was forced to dismiss his foreign minister, Lord PALMERSTON, who had endorsed Napoleon III's coup in France.

Toppled from power in 1852, Russell served in the ministry of Lord ABERDEEN (1852–55) and briefly, in 1855, as colonial secretary under Lord Palmerston; in the latter office, Russell represented Britain at Vienna in an unsuccessful attempt to end the Crimean War. He later served (1859–65) as foreign secretary in Palmerston's second ministry, assisting in the unification of Italy. After Palmerston's death (1865), Russell again became prime minister, but he resigned (1866) after failing to secure passage of a second parliamentary reform bill.

Russell, Lillian An actress and singer celebrated for her remarkable beauty, Lillian Russell, stage name of Helen Louise Leonard, b. Clinton, Iowa, Dec. 4, 1861, d. June 6, 1922, was probably the most photographed woman in the United States during her heyday. Her 33-year career, which spanned burlesque and light opera, was launched with her appearance (1878) in the chorus of Edward Rice's *Pinafore* company in New York.

Russia (Soviet Republic) Russia is the largest and most populous of the 15 constituent republics of the USSR. Its area is 17,074,723 km^2 (6,592,812 mi^2), or 76% of the total Soviet area, and its population is 147,400,000 (1989), or about 51% of the USSR's population. The republic's capital is Moscow. Russia is the historical homeland of the ethnic Russians and the dominant political and economic entity of the USSR.

The topography is composed of four clearly defined regions: the Russian plain of European Russia, extending from the Arctic Ocean in the north to the CAUCASUS MOUNTAINS in the south; the URAL MOUNTAINS; the vast swampy and forested West Siberian plain; and the uplands of East Siberia and the Soviet Far East extending to the Pacific.

The climate is continental, with cold winters and warm summers. The January average temperature varies from 3° C (37° F) in the southwest to –22° C (–8° F) in the northeast, and July temperatures average 9° C (48° F) in the north and 25° C (77° F) in the southeast. The coldest spot in the Northern Hemisphere is in northeast Siberia. Annual rainfall varies from 610 mm (24 in) in the west to 127 mm (5 in) in the southeast.

The ethnic Russians, who account for 83% of the republic's population, are a Slavic people of the Eastern Orthodox religion. More than 80% of all the ethnic Russians in the USSR live in the republic. In addition to Moscow, the largest cities are GORKY, KUIBYSHEV, and LENINGRAD in European Russia; CHELYABINSK and SVERDLOVSK in the Urals; and NOVOSIBIRSK and OMSK in SIBERIA.

The Russian Republic has important mineral resources, including coal, petroleum, natural gas, iron ore, and other metals. Some of the USSR's largest manufacturing complexes are centered in the republic's major cities. Agriculture—primarily grain growing (especially wheat) and cattle raising—is concentrated in the steppes. Transportation is oriented toward railroads. Water transport during the warm season takes place on the AMUR, LENA, OB, VOLGA, and YENISEI rivers.

The Russian republic was the first to be formed following the Bolshevik Revolution of 1917. It became known as a federation because it includes many smaller entities for ethnic minorities—16 autonomous republics, 5 autonomous oblasts, and 10 autonomous okrugs.

Russia/Union of Soviet Socialist Republics, history of European Russia was occupied by Indo-European and Ural-Altaic peoples from about the 2d millennium BC. The SCYTHIANS appeared in the 7th century BC, to be displaced by the SARMATIANS in the 3d century BC. In the early centuries AD a succession of tribes, the GOTHS, the HUNS, and the Avars, ruled the area. The KHAZARS (7th century) and the Bulgars (8th century) established substantial states.

Medieval Russia

The SLAVS, whose settlements are documented from the 6th century on, probably came from southern Poland and the Baltic shore. They settled along the water route that

MEDIEVAL RUSSIA

— Kievan boundary in 1237

[shaded] Principality of Moscow in 1462

— Western boundary of the Mongol Empire

km 0 _____ 1000
mi 0 _____ 600

Cartographic Production by Lothar Roth & Associates

Culturally, Kiev served as the agent of transmission for Byzantine civilization, but it also developed into the creative center of a high-level indigenous culture represented, in literature, by the sermons of Hilarion (d. after 1055) and Vladimir Monomakh (d. 1125); in historiography, by the early-12th-century *Primary Chronicle*; in law, by Yaroslav's codification, *Pravda*; and in monastic life, by Kiev's 11th-century cave monastery (Lavra).

The decline of Kievan Rus' (starting in the late 11th century) was brought about by internecine feuds and by a change in Byzantine trade patterns. When the MONGOLS surged forth from Central Asia, they overran the South Russian plain. Kiev was sacked in 1240, and the Mongol khans of the GOLDEN HORDE established their control over most of European Russia.

Mongol Rule. The overlordship of the Mongols (see also TATARS) proved costly in economic terms, because the initial conquest and subsequent raids to maintain the Russians in obedience were destructive of urban life and severely depleted the population. Equally costly were the tribute payments in silver. Politically the yoke was not burdensome, for the Mongols ruled indirectly through local princes. The most deleterious long-lasting effect of Mongol rule was isolation from Byzantium and western Europe, which led to a turning inward that produced an aggressive inferiority complex. The exceptions were the free cities of Novgorod and PSKOV, ruled by oligarchies of merchants (the princes, such as ALEXANDER NEVSKY, were merely hired military leaders).

Rise of Moscow. In the shadow of Mongol overlordship and in the harsh environment of central Russia the society and polity of MOSCOW, or Muscovy, developed. Members of the ruling family of Kievan Rus' had seized free lands in the northeast and colonized them with peasants; each one of these princes administered and defended his domain with the help of his retainers (boyars).

Some of the local princes—for example, those of VLADIMIR, YAROSLAVL, Moscow, Suzdal, and Tver—became dominant in their region and gradually forced the weaker rulers into their own service. Of these principalities Moscow emerged as the most powerful. Its ruler Ivan I (Ivan Kalita; r. 1328–41) was granted the title grand duke of Vladimir. His grandson DIMITRY DONSKOI won the first major Russian victory over the Mongols at Kulikovo (1380). Finally, after victory in a fierce civil war, IVAN III, grand duke of Moscow (r. 1462–1505), emerged as the sole ruler in central Russia. In 1480, he successfully challenged Mongol overlordship by refusing to pay the tribute.

Moscow's triumph was not complete, however, because another putative heir to Kiev remained—the Grand Duchy of LITHUANIA. To the south and east the Muslim successors of the Golden Horde, the khanates of Kazan, Astrakhan, and the Crimea, were also serious threats to Muscovy's security.

Although Moscow's annexation of Novgorod (1478) and Pskov (1510) gave it access to the profitable Baltic trade, it also opened the gates to religious and cultural challenges to the spiritual and artistic self-sufficiency and provincialism of central Russia. A conflict arose between church and state as well as between cultural nativism and

was used by VIKING warrior-traders (the Varangians) to reach Constantinople. About 862 a group of Varangians led by RURIK took control of NOVGOROD. From there Rurik moved south and established (879) his authority in KIEV, strategically located above the Dnepr rapids.

Kievan Rus'. Under Rurik's successor, Oleg (d. *c.*912), Kiev became the center of a federation of strong points controlled by Varangian "dukes" who soon became Slavicized in language and culture. Attempts by Duke SVYATOSLAV I (r. 945–72) to create an "empire" in the region between the Dnepr and Danube failed, but Kiev was effectively protected from nomads in the east by the Khazar state on the Volga. With the conversion (*c.*988) of Duke VLADIMIR I to Eastern Christianity, Kiev developed into a major cultural center.

The Kievan Rus' political and cultural apogee was reached under YAROSLAV I (r. 1019–54). The unity of Kievan Rus' was more of an ideal than a reality (many internal feuds existed), but it served as an inspiration to later generations. Trade was probably the mainstay of political power, and agriculture (complemented by hunting and fishing) was the major occupation of the population.

(Below) *A 16th-century icon bears the portrait of Ivan IV (the Terrible), the first Russian ruler to assume the title of tsar ("caesar"). During his 50-year reign (1533–84), he shattered the power of his boyars (nobles), set aside half of his state as his personal domain, and ruled by terror from 1565 on. (Nationalmuseet, Copenhagen.)*

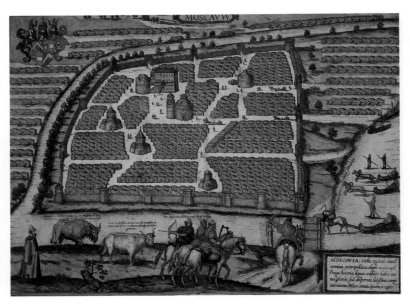

(Above) *A plan of medieval Moscow, published in Germany in 1572, shows a walled city built of wood. Moscow was founded in 1156 by Yury Dolgoruky, prince of Suzdal.*

innovation; it ended, in the second quarter of the 16th century, in a compromise that reaffirmed and strengthened the political values of Moscow (autocracy) while respecting the economic power and position of the church and liberalizing its cultural life to admit the influences from the Balkans and western Europe.

Organization of the Muscovite State. The main political task of the grand dukes of Moscow was the absorption of formerly independent princes and their servitors into the service hierarchy of Moscow. This absorption was achieved by expanding the membership of the boyar council (duma) to include the newcomers. In addition, from the late 15th century on, the grand duke created a class of military servitors (*dvorianstvo*) entirely subordinated to him by grants of land on a temporary basis, subject to performance of service. The peasantry remained outside this system, with village communes taking care of local fiscal and police matters. Towns were under the direct rule of the grand duke's representatives.

The culmination of absolutism was symbolized by the grandson of Ivan III, IVAN IV (r. 1533–84). Assuming (1547) the title of tsar, he conquered the khanates of Kazan (1552) and Astrakhan (1556), putting the entire course of the Volga under Russian control. Next came expansion (1581) into Siberia, whose western regions were conquered by the Cossack leader YERMAK TIMOFEYEVICH.

Ivan IV also attempted to eliminate the competition of Lithuania and gain a port on the Baltic. The 25-year war (1558–83) against Poland-Lithuania, Livonia, and Sweden ended in failure and seriously debilitated the country. To mobilize all resources and cope with internal opposition, Ivan IV set up his own personal guard and territorial administration (*oprichnina*, 1565–72), whose oppression

did great damage to both the economy and the social stability of the realm. Meanwhile, the mobility of peasants was being limited. The edicts of Ivan's successors (Fyodor I, r. 1584–98; and BORIS GODUNOV, r. 1598–1605) initiated a process that culminated in the complete enserfment of the Russian peasantry (Code of 1649).

The Seventeenth and Eighteenth Centuries

The Rurik dynasty ended in 1598 with the death of Ivan IV's son Fyodor I. Boris Godunov, who succeeded him, was a strong ruler, but he was regarded by many as a usurper. The exhausted country plunged into turmoil marked by the appearance of several pretenders to the throne and by foreign invasions (see TIME OF TROUBLES; 1598–1613). Eventually, a militia of noble servitors (*dvoriane*) and townspeople of the northeast elected young MICHAEL Romanov as tsar in 1613. The ROMANOV dynasty was to rule Russia until 1917.

An Era of Conflict. Beneath a veneer of traditional forms and static structures profound changes took place in the course of the 17th century. Efforts at reforming the church, led by NIKON (patriarch from 1652 to 1666), were resisted by large segments of the population (led by monks and parish priests). These OLD BELIEVERS, about 25 percent of the population, then virtually split away from official culture and civil society.

The religious crisis exacerbated the cultural conflict over the extent of Westernization. Trade contacts brought foreigners to Russia, and diplomatic exchanges grew more frequent. Technological innovations brought in their wake Western fashions and cultural goods, leading to new trends in art (the so-called Moscow baroque in architecture, literature, and icon painting). The cultural gap be-

Peter the Great (r. 1682–1725) was the first Russian monarch to journey beyond the boundaries of Russia. Traveling incognito, he worked as a shipbuilder in England and the Netherlands, where this portrait was painted. He later embarked on a complete reorganization of Russian society, based on his observations of the West.

tween the elites and the people was deepened by political, social, and economic conflicts: urban strife at times threatened the stability of the regime itself. The military servitors' struggle to establish full control over their peasants led to numerous revolts. In 1670–71 dissatisfied COSSACKS, persecuted Old Believers, escaped serfs, and disgruntled urban elements joined forces under Stenka RAZIN in a massive revolt.

The government, especially under Tsar ALEXIS (r. 1645–76), tried to cope with the difficulties by centralizing the local administrations. To ensure domestic control and to carry on an active foreign policy, a professional army of *streltsy* (musketeers) and foreign mercenaries and modernized technology were introduced. Although absolutism was retained intact, factionalism and palace coups became more frequent and made pursuing coherent policies difficult. When Tsar Fyodor III died in 1682 the situation was ripe for the energetic intervention of a genuine leader.

The Reforms of Peter the Great. By dint of his driving energy and ruthlessness, PETER I (r. 1682–1725) transformed Russia and brought it into the concert of European nations. A struggle with CHARLES XII of Sweden (1700–21; see NORTHERN WAR, GREAT) and wars with Ottoman Turkey (1710–11) and Persia (1722–23) radically changed Russia's international position. By the Treaty of Nystad (1721) with Sweden, Russia acquired the Baltic province of Livonia (including Estonia and most of Latvia), giving it a firm foothold on the Baltic Sea.

These territorial gains forced Peter to transform the institutional framework of the state and to attempt a restructuring of society as well. The central administration was streamlined according to the European model, and the church was put under direct state administration with the abolition of the patriarchate and the establishment of a Holy Synod (1721). A navy was created, and the army was reorganized along professional Western lines, the peasantry furnishing the recruits and nobility the officers. The peasantry was subjected to compulsory labor (as in the building of the new capital, Saint Petersburg, now LENINGRAD) and to military service, and every individual adult male peasant was assessed with a head, or poll, tax. By these measures the state transformed peasants into personal serfs, virtually chattel, who could be moved and sold at will. Compulsory, lifelong service was also imposed on the nobility. State service, in turn, required education, and Peter introduced compulsory secular, Westernized schooling for the Russian nobleman.

Peter failed to reshape the merchants into a Western bourgeoisie, however, and his efforts at modernizing the economy had mixed results. The limitations of Peter's reforming drive derived from the inherent paradox of his approach: he aimed at liberating the creative forces of Russian society, but he expected to accomplish this liberation only at his command and through compulsion.

The Imperial Succession. After Peter's death (1725) instability plagued the new institutional setup. Peter abolished the traditional practice of succession, declaring (1722) that the emperor could choose his successor, and for the next half-century the throne was exposed to a series of palace coups. After the reign (1725–27) of Peter's widow, CATHERINE I, Peter II (r. 1727–30), ANNA (r. 1730–40), Ivan VI (r. 1740–41), ELIZABETH (r. 1741–62), and CATHERINE II (r. 1762–96), who supplanted her

Public celebrations are held in Saint Petersburg to commemorate the centennial anniversary of the city's founding by Peter the Great in 1703. The city is now called Leningrad, and it is the center of Russian culture, education, and science.

Empress Catherine II (the Great) meets with Joseph II of Austria during her tour (1787) of the Crimea. Russia's annexation of the Crimea was part of Catherine's program of strategic territorial expansion.

husband, Peter III (r. January–July 1762), all came to the throne in this manner. The autocracy managed to keep the nobility in subordination by promoting the economic status of that class through salaries, gifts, and the extension of its legal rights over the serfs, particularly following the traumatic experience of the great peasant uprising (1773–75) under Yemelian PUGACHEV.

The government proved unable to regularize its structure and practices through a code of laws. In any case, most subjects favored personalized authority as a protection against abuses of officials and as a source of rewards. A rational and automatic rule of law was thus never introduced in imperial Russia.

Expansion and Westernization. Two important processes dominated the 18th century. The first was imperial expansion southward and westward. The southern steppe lands were gradually settled by Russians, and the autonomous local social groupings—especially the Cossacks—lost their status. The process was formally completed by the Treaty of Küçük Kainarji (1774), ending the first major RUSSO-TURKISH WAR, by which Russia secured the northern shore of the Black Sea, and by the annexation (1783) of the Crimea. By extending (1783) serfdom to Ukraine the economic integration of that area with Russia was achieved. The empire's expansion westward was the result of the Partitions of Poland (1772, 1792, 1795; see POLAND, PARTITIONS OF), which awarded Russia most of the eastern and central regions of the Polish-Lithuanian Commonwealth.

The second process was the cultural Westernization of the Russian elites. It was furthered by the establishment of new educational institutions (the Academy of Sciences, 1725; the University of Moscow, 1755; and military and private schools), the creation of a modern national literature along Western lines, and the beginnings of scientific research and discoveries (see Mikhail LOMONOSOV). Increased sophistication heightened yearnings for free expression and implementation of Western moral and social

values. In 1790, Aleksandr Radishchev denounced the moral evils of serfdom in his famous *A Journey from Saint Petersburg to Moscow.*

Imperial expansion and cultural Westernization were accompanied by economic modernization. Russia became a notable producer of iron, lumber, and naval stores (pine products), and witnessed the expansion of urbanization and social amenities. Catherine II fostered security of property and person, at least for members of the upper classes. The nobility were freed from compulsory state service (1762) and guaranteed their property rights.

The Nineteenth Century

Alexander I. Catherine's grandson ALEXANDER I succeeded to the throne after the brief reign (1796–1801) of his unbalanced father, PAUL I. The first years of Alexander's reign were marked by intensive efforts at reforming the administration and expanding the educational facilities; the reforms inaugurated rapid bureaucratization with better trained officials.

RUSSIAN EXPANSION WESTWARD (IN EUROPE)

Moscow in 1462	Acquisitions by 1801
Acquisitions by 1505	Acquisitions by 1914
Acquisitions by 1689	Dividing line between European and Asian Russia
Acquisitions by 1725	

0 km 1000
0 mi 600

Cartographic Production by Lothar Roth & Associates

Napoleon, on horseback, surveys Russian soldiers taken prisoner in the Battle of Eylau (1807) in this painting by Antoine Gros. The Peace of Tilsit (1807) followed a second Russian defeat, at Friedland. In 1812 the French army invaded Russia and occupied Moscow. Lack of supplies and the severe winter forced the French to retreat. Russia emerged from the Napoleonic Wars as a major military power.

Russia's involvement in the NAPOLEONIC WARS proved a major impediment to the normal evolution of the country. NAPOLEON I's invasion of Russia in 1812, although ending in his own defeat, was hardly a victory for Russia. On the other hand, the younger generation of educated society had acquired self-confidence during the wars. Secret societies were organized under the leadership of progressive officers, and, on the sudden death of Alexander I in December 1825, they tried to take over the government. This abortive insurrection of the DECEMBRISTS traumatized Alexander's successor, his brother NICHOLAS I, into a policy of reaction and repression.

Nicholas I. Nicholas I's reign, however, was by no means static, and it proved seminal in many respects. In spite of strict censorship, the golden age of Russian literature occurred with the work of Aleksandr PUSHKIN, Nikolai GOGOL, the young Fyodor DOSTOYEVSKY, Leo TOLSTOI, and Ivan TURGENEV. Stimulated by this literary flowering, discussion circles sprang up in Moscow and Saint Petersburg in which the intelligentsia debated Russia's identity and its relationship to western Europe. The SLAVOPHILES AND WESTERNIZERS represented the two main lines of interpretation that emerged.

Nicholas promoted technical and professional training, and by the end of the reign a cadre of well-trained professionals had been prepared to carry out reforms. Nicholas's government also brought to a successful conclusion the codification of laws (1833; the achievement of Mikhail SPERANSKY), which enabled an orderly and systematic economic development of the country. The building of railroads was initiated, the currency was stabilized, and protective tariffs were introduced. As a result, private enterprise was activated, especially in consumer goods (textiles), in which even peasant capital and skill participated. These developments only served to under-

score the backward nature of an agrarian economy based on serf labor.

In international affairs Nicholas acted as the "gendarme of Europe" when he crushed the Polish insurrection of 1831–33 and helped Austria subdue the Hungarians in 1849. The empire further expanded in the Far East (in the Amur River valley). At the end of his reign Nicholas embroiled Russia in the CRIMEAN WAR (1853–56). Although the immediate cause of the war was a dispute over the guardianship of the Holy Places in Palestine, underlying the conflict was the EASTERN QUESTION, the prolonged dispute over the disposition of the territories of the fast-declining Ottoman Empire. The course of the war revealed the regime's weaknesses, and the death (1855) of Nicholas allowed his son, ALEXANDER II, to conclude a peace (the Treaty of Paris, 1856) that debarred Russian warships from the Black Sea and its straits.

Alexander II and Emancipation of the Serfs. Russian society now expected and demanded far-reaching reforms, and Alexander acted accordingly. The crucial reform was the abolition of serfdom on Mar. 3 (N.S.), 1861. In spite of many shortcomings it was a great accomplishment that set Russia on the way to becoming a full-fledged modern society. The main defects of the emancipation settlement were that cancellation of labor obligations took place gradually, the peasants were charged for the land they received in allotment (through a redemption tax), and the allotments proved inadequate in the long run. Despite this, 20 million peasants became their own masters, they received land allotments that preserved them from immediate proletarization, and the emancipation process was accomplished peacefully.

Three other major reforms followed emancipation. The first was the introduction (1864) of elected institutions of local government, ZEMSTVOS, which were responsible for

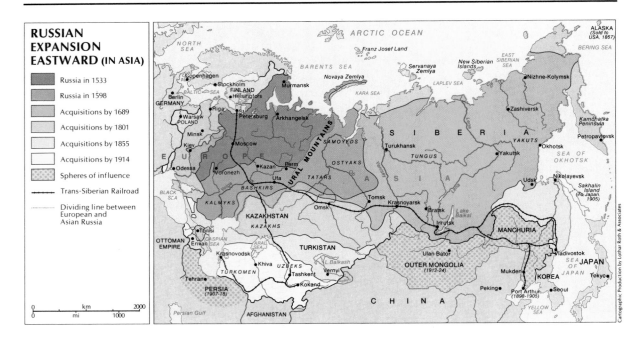

RUSSIAN EXPANSION EASTWARD (IN ASIA)

- Russia in 1533
- Russia in 1598
- Acquisitions by 1689
- Acquisitions by 1801
- Acquisitions by 1855
- Acquisitions by 1914
- Spheres of influence
- Trans-Siberian Railroad
- Dividing line between European and Asian Russia

matters of education, health, and welfare. Secondly, reform of the judiciary introduced jury trials, independent judges, and a professional class of lawyers. Finally, in 1874, the old-fashioned military recruiting system gave way to universal, compulsory 6-year military service.

The impetus for reform was thwarted and arrested by external and domestic events. Externally, the Polish rebellion of 1863–64 strengthened the conservative opposition to further reforms, and the Russo-Turkish War of 1877–78 undermined the financial equilibrium. At home in the 1860s radical university students and nihilist (see NIHILISM) critics such as Nikolai Chernyshevsky voiced dissatisfaction with the pace of the reforms. Radical associations were formed and student youth "went to the people" in 1874–76 to enlighten and revolutionize the peasantry. Repressed by the government, the young radicals turned to terrorism. Eventually a group of NARODNIKI (populists) killed the emperor on Mar. 13 (N.S.), 1881.

Alexander III. Alexander II's violent death inaugurated the conservative and restrictive reign of his son ALEXANDER III. Nonetheless, the process of social and economic change released by the reforms could not be arrested. The deepening agrarian crisis—dramatized by the famine of 1891—turned the active elements from criticism to overt opposition. At the same time, industrialization energetically pushed by Sergei WITTE, minister of finance (1892–1903), brought in its wake labor conflict, urban poverty, and business cycles.

Nicholas II. Alexander was succeeded by his son NICHOLAS II in 1894. To deflect attention from the worsening social situation and to neutralize the revitalized revolutionary movement, the government embarked on imperialist adventures in the Far East, provoking a war with Japan (1904–05; see RUSSO-JAPANESE WAR). Russia suf-

fered a humiliating defeat; the war triggered widespread disturbances, including rural violence, labor unrest, and naval mutinies. The turmoil of the RUSSIAN REVOLUTION OF 1905 culminated in the general strike of October, which forced Nicholas II to grant a constitution. Russia received a representative legislative assembly, the DUMA, elected by indirect suffrage. The executive, however, remained accountable only to the emperor. From 1906 to 1911 the government was directed by Pyotr STOLYPIN, who combined repressive action with land reforms to improve the position of the peasants.

The new political activity contributed to the remarkable upsurge of Russia's artistic and intellectual creativity (called the Silver Age). Russia became a major contrib-

RULERS OF THE RUSSIAN EMPIRE

Rurik Dynasty		Romanov Dynasty	
1462–1505	Ivan III	1682–89	Sophia (regent)
1505–33	Vasily III	1682–96	Ivan V (co-tsar)
1533–84	Ivan IV	1682–1725	Peter I
	(Ivan the Terrible)		(Peter the Great)
1584–98	Fyodor I	1725–27	Catherine I
		1727–30	Peter II
Time of Troubles		1730–40	Anna
1598–1605	Boris Godunov	1740–41	Ivan VI
1605	Fyodor II	1741–62	Elizabeth
1605–06	False Dmitri	1762	Peter III
1606–10	Vasily Shuisky	1762–96	Catherine II
1610–13	Interregnum	1796–1801	Paul I
		1801–25	Alexander I
Romanov Dynasty		1825–55	Nicholas I
1613–45	Michael Romanov	1855–81	Alexander II
1645–76	Alexis I	1881–94	Alexander III
1676–82	Fyodor III	1894–1917	Nicholas II

utor to modern Western culture, through the work, most notably, of painter Wassily Kandinsky, composer Igor STRAVINSKY, the symbolist writers (see SYMBOLISM, literature), and impresario Serge DIAGHILEV.

Thus the years 1905–14 were a period of great complexity. To many this feverish intellectual creativity, which had its social and political counterpart in rural unrest, industrial discontent, revolutionary agitation, and nationalist excesses (for example, the POGROMS against the Jews), proved that the imperial regime was nearing its inevitable end. On the other side, liberals and moderate progressives saw in these phenomena harbingers of Russia's decisive turn to political democracy.

In August 1914, however, Russia rallied to the support of Serbia, and the local Balkan conflict was transformed into WORLD WAR I. The strains of that bloody and disastrous conflict produced a breakdown of both the political system and the social fabric in Russia. Food riots in Petrograd and other cities toppled the monarchy in March (N.S.; February, O.S.) 1917.

The Union of Soviet Socialist Republics

Following the abdication of the emperor, the Duma established a provisional government, but its authority was challenged by an increasingly radical Soviet (council) of Soldiers' and Workers' Deputies. The Bolsheviks (see BOLSHEVIKS AND MENSHEVIKS) under Vladimir Ilich LENIN then seized power in November (N.S.; October, O.S.) 1917 in the second of the two RUSSIAN REVOLUTIONS OF 1917.

Lenin's Regime. The Bolsheviks (soon renamed the Communist party of the USSR) immediately announced sweeping reforms such as the abolition of private property and redistribution of land and the establishment of workers' control of industry. The breakdown of society continued, however, even after the USSR left the war (by the humiliating terms of the Treaty of Brest-Litovsk, March 1918). A civil war followed that lasted until 1921

Russian soldiers and sailors, dissatisfied with the conduct of World War I, played a major role in forcing the abdication (March 1917) of the emperor and later rallied to support the Bolsheviks in overthrowing the provisional government in November 1917.

This photograph of Lenin (left) and Stalin was taken in 1922. It was later used by Stalin's supporters to suggest that the two leaders were close associates. Lenin, however, actually distrusted Stalin.

and in the course of which the country underwent an orgy of violence and suffered famine, epidemics, and total economic collapse.

During the civil war the Bolsheviks attempted to carry out sweeping nationalization of the economy under tight centralized control. The policies of War Communism caused further disruption, however. In 1921, with the country prostrate, Lenin inaugurated the NEW ECONOMIC POLICY, which allowed society to regain coherence and strength by permitting some private enterprise, especially in the agrarian sector.

Stalin's Regime. When Lenin died in January 1924, a prolonged succession struggle ensued. The chief contenders were Joseph STALIN and Leon TROTSKY, between whom other powerful figures such as Nikolai BUKHARIN, Lev KAMENEV, and Grigory ZINOVIEV shifted their allegiances. By 1928, however, Stalin had effectively broken all his rivals and was the clear leader of the country.

In 1928, Stalin ended the New Economic Policy and embarked on what has been called the second revolution. Agriculture was collectivized (at tremendous human cost; see KULAKS), and a fast pace of industrialization was initiated. By the mid-1930s an impressive industrial plant was in operation, although it had been erected at the price of several million lives. At the same time, to eliminate all potential opposition and to secure his personal power, Stalin launched the GREAT PURGE in 1934. It developed a momentum of its own, and in addition to the political and military leadership, it engulfed technicians, scholars, artists, and countless innocent victims (see GULAG).

During the 1930s the USSR also sought to move out of diplomatic isolation, joining the League of Nations in 1934 and seeking improved relations with the Western democracies. By 1939, however, Stalin was convinced that the Western powers would tolerate unlimited German Nazi expansion in the East. In August 1939, therefore, he concluded a pact with Adolf Hitler (see NAZI-SOVIET PACT). The German invasion of Poland began WORLD WAR II.

On June 22, 1941, Hitler invaded the USSR. The Germans came within 30 km (about 20 mi) of Moscow, cut off Leningrad completely, and occupied some parts of the Caucasus. In the prolonged Battle of Stalingrad (1942–

An aerial photograph shows Stalingrad after a German attack in 1942. A Russian counterattack trapped the German 6th Army. Its surrender marked a turning point in World War II.

43) the tide was finally turned, and the Red Army began to advance westward. At the end of the war Soviet troops occupied Eastern and parts of Central Europe, and within the next few years Soviet-like regimes were imposed in that region. Stalin also launched an aggressive campaign of ideological conformity both within the USSR and in the Communist world at large.

The Post-Stalin Period. Nikita KHRUSHCHEV and his successors strengthened the international position of the USSR as many countries (especially of the Third World) became dominated by Marxist and pro-Soviet leaders. Le-

onid BREZHNEV, who took over in 1964, pursued a policy of détente with Western nations and repression of political dissent at home. In this period productivity began to lag, and the economy experienced difficulty. In the 1980s the USSR was involved in a civil war in Afghanistan. After Brezhnev's death (1982) and a period of transition under Yuri ANDROPOV and Konstantin CHERNENKO, the rise to power (1985) of the innovative Mikhail GORBACHEV brought dramatic changes to the Soviet system. A new openness to change, GLASNOST, along with a relaxation of political repression, gave rise to a wave of nationalist agitation among the non-Russian peoples of the USSR and moves toward independence by the nations of Eastern Europe. Détente with the West was revived, and steps were taken to end the USSR's longstanding quarrel with China. The efforts at economic and social restructuring, or PERESTROIKA, however, led to labor unrest and shortages of consumer goods. In August 1991 political change was hastened by the failure of a coup against Gorbachev by Communist hard-liners, foiled by massive popular opposition. In the aftermath the Communist party was disbanded, and the union of republics pushed toward dissolution.

Russian-American Company   The Russian-American Company was a Russian trading company chartered in 1799 to administer the fur-trading settlements established in Alaska and the Aleutian Islands. It was originally given exclusive trading privileges in the area north of latitude 55° N. In 1821, Tsar Alexander I extended its jurisdiction south to latitude 51° N, but accords in 1824 with the United States, Spain, and Great Britain set the southern boundary of Russian America at 54°40' N.

The USSR displays its military might to both its own people and the world at large in the annual May Day parade through Moscow. As a result of the cold war and arms race with the United States since World War II, the USSR built up an enormous nuclear arsenal.

Under the administration of Aleksandr BARANOV, the company had headquarters first on Kodiak Island and then at Sitka. Outposts were established as far south as Fort Ross, Calif. Its fur trade flourished, but it was unable to attract permanent Russian settlers. The Russian government gradually lost interest in the company, and its charter was allowed to lapse in 1862. In 1867 all the Russian possessions in America were sold to the United States.

Russian art and architecture

The course of Russian art and architecture reflects Russia's contacts with, and isolation from, other traditions. Initially, BYZANTINE ART AND ARCHITECTURE provided the norms, but this tie was interrupted by the Mongol (Tatar) occupation (c.1240–1480). Russia never experienced the influence of the Italian Renaissance, but beginning with enforced Westernization under PETER I (r. 1682–1725), Russian art was strongly influenced by the European mainstream. Among the distinctive traits of Russian artistic expression have been exuberant color, rich ornamentation, asymmetry of form, and a taste for literal representation.

Beginnings of Russian Art. Russian art began with the conversion of the people to Christianity about 989. The Cathedral of Saint Sophia (1018–37) in Kiev illustrates

The archangel Michael is depicted in this fragment of an icon by Andrei Rublev, painted about 1400 for Zvenigorod Cathedral. Rublev, a monk and the greatest of all Russian icon painters, purified and simplified the ornate Byzantine style. (Tretyakov Gallery, Moscow.)

Saint Basil's Cathedral in Red Square, Moscow, was built during the reign of Ivan the Terrible. The central sanctuary is surrounded by eight chapels, each crowned with an onion dome.

the initial influence of the distinctive art of Byzantium: the original 5-aisled rectangular brick church was topped by 13 squat domes, and the interior is decorated with superb mosaics that follow the customary Byzantine iconographic scheme. The most venerated painting in Russia was the icon *The Virgin of Vladimir* (late 11th–early 12th centuries; Tretyakov Gallery, Moscow), painted in Constantinople. The tender pose of the Madonna and Child set the model for countless Russian versions of the subject.

Emergence of Russian Styles. Distinct national traits evolved in centers that were farther removed from Byzantine influence. The Cathedral of Saint Sophia (c.1045–62) in Novgorod is notable for the marked perpendicular elevation of its white stucco walls; inside, less costly frescoes replaced mosaic decoration. Height became even more pronounced in the cubicular stone churches of the city of Vladimir.

In time, the wooden architecture of the north contributed multifaceted surfaces and a multiplicity of gables and drums, as well as conical towers and characteristic onion-shaped domes. Exuberance of form and decoration, culminating in the fantastical multitowered and polychromed Cathedral of Saint Basil in Moscow (1555–60), predominated in Muscovite architecture through the 17th century.

The ICONOSTASIS—a tall altar screen composed of hierarchically ranged rows of icons—appeared in the 15th century, adding great splendor to church interiors. In painting there were three medieval masters: THEOPHANES THE GREEK (c.1340–c.1405), his student Andrei RUBLEV, and Dionysius (c.1440–c.1505). Icon painting declined after 1551, when a church council banned free composition. The 17th century is known for the mannered icons of Simon Ushakov (1626–86) and the intricate works of the Stroganov school, elaborately decorated icons for private worship.

Westernization of Russian Culture. Under Peter the

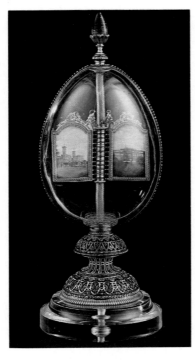

Michael Perchin's enamel, gold, diamond, and rock-crystal egg, presented by Nicholas II to Czarina Alexandra Feodorovna in 1896, contains miniatures of the royal residences. (Pratt Collection, New York City.)

Great Western art and architecture were transplanted first to the new capital of Saint Petersburg (begun 1703; now Leningrad), a grandiose city with an elaborate, carefully designed plan that contrasts sharply with the chaotic and spontaneous sprawl of Moscow. Under ELIZABETH, EMPRESS OF RUSSIA (r. 1741–62), the exuberant Russian late baroque flourished; the Italian architect Bartolommeo RASTRELLI was its primary proponent as designer of Saint Petersburg's WINTER PALACE (1754–62), Tsarskoe Selo (now Pushkino) Palace (1749–56), and the Smolny Cathedral in Saint Petersburg (1748–55). Neoclassicism in the style of Robert ADAM became prevalent under CATHERINE II, the Great (r. 1762–96). From the mid-18th century onward, Russian architects became prominent: Matvei Kazakov (1733–1812) and Vasili Bazhenov (1737–99) in Moscow and Ivan Starov (c.1743–1808) and Andrei Voronikhin (1760–1814) in Saint Petersburg.

In painting, national talent also emerged in the mid-18th century. The works of Dmitri Levitsky (1735–1822) and Vladimir Borovikovsky (1757–1825), whose portraits mark the first achievements of Russia's new art, show full mastery of Western technique and conventions yet retain a local flavor.

19th-Century Painting and Architecture. The high quality of Russian portraiture was maintained in the first half of the 19th century by two romantic painters: Orest Kiprensky (1782–1836) and Karl Briullov (1799–1852). Other genres also began to develop: Alexei Venetsianov (1780–1847) started a school that specialized in idyllic peasant scenes; Pavel Fedotov (1815–52) pioneered in social satire; and Aleksandr Ivanov (1806–58) was an important religious painter.

Realism gave Russian painting a national idiom. Its development was spurred by the secession of 13 painters and a sculptor from the Academy of Arts (established 1757) in 1863 and the formation (1870) of an independent Association of Traveling Art Exhibits, whose members were called the Wanderers, or the Peredvizhniki. Middle-class collectors and an independent professional status freed painters from court patronage and the bureaucratic supervision of the academy. Ilya REPIN excelled in the critical social genre that reflected the intellectuals' quest for reform.

The development of a national style occurred earlier in architecture. Konstantin Ton (1794–1881) introduced 17th-century Moscovite ornamentation in civic structures and designed neo-Byzantine churches under Nicholas I (r. 1825–55).

The Art of Fabergé. The work of the jeweler Peter Carl FABERGÉ has become synonymous with late Tsarist art, because his most famous creations were for the imperial family and its court—the fantastical Easter eggs fashioned of precious metals and gems. The three Fabergé ateliers—in Saint Petersburg, Kiev, and London—also produced an enormous variety of everyday objects in luxurious materials. The firm ceased operations in 1918.

Influence of New European Movements. About 1890 a reaction against the realists' obsession with nationalist subjects and socially useful art brought a resurgence of new painting that lasted into the 1920s. Isaak Levitan (1861–1900) turned to the outdoor (*en plein air*) painting of landscapes; Konstantin Korovin (1861–1939) and Valentin Serov (1865–1911) used the color discoveries of the impressionists; and Mikhail VRUBEL experimented with new decorative forms. Serge DIAGHILEV and Aleksandr Benois familiarized the Russian public with leading trends abroad through their magazine, *Mir iskusstva* (World of Art, 1898–1904), and their art exhibitions. They also showed Russian art (1906) in Paris and staged seasons of Russian ballet (beginning 1909) with exotic costume designs by Léon BAKST and other Russian painters.

Vladimir Tatlin's 1919 model for Monument to the 3d International was an iron spiral enclosing three rotating glass chambers. The actual structure, never built, would have been 394 m (1,300 ft) tall, making it the largest sculpture ever conceived. Tatlin founded the Russian constructivist movement.

The decade preceding World War I was one of a rapid succession of diverse movements. The symbolist Blue Rose movement, started in 1907, and the Cézannist Knave of Diamonds movement, started in 1910, opened the way for a new vanguard that was crucial for the development of modernism in both Russia and the West. Mikhail LARIONOV and Natalia Goncharova started as primitivists, relying on medieval icons and peasant prints (*lubki*), but by 1912 their work had evolved into the semiabstract rayonism, which was related to the CUBISM and FUTURISM of the West. Wassily KANDINSKY painted his first nonrepresentational works about 1910; in 1913, Vladimir TATLIN created his first three-dimensional abstract structures; and Kasimir MALEVICH, who was a founder of SUPREMATISM, exhibited his rigorously abstract groupings of colors and shapes in 1915.

Effects of the 1917 Revolution. The Bolshevik Revolution found support among the advocates of radical art forms, who played a prominent role in the administration of culture from 1917 to 1921. Painters designed posters and other propaganda. Architects worked on creating a new environment. Pioneers of the constructivist style (see CONSTRUCTIVISM) stressed functional projects. Many of their designs for large housing developments—combining living quarters with communal and service buildings— revolutionized urban planning in the USSR.

Dominance of Official Art. After 1921 many painters continued to innovate in the mass media and in practical arts such as photography, cinema, industrial and theater design, and typography. Various neorealist groups flourished under government patronage for the rest of the de-

Suprematist Composition *was painted sometime after 1920 by Kasimir Malevich. Suprematism sought to combine pure colors and geometric shapes into abstract patterns. It was eventually suppressed, along with other avant-garde art movements, by the Soviet government. (Stedelijk Museum, Amsterdam.)*

cade. Kuzma Petrov-Vodkin (1878–1939) and Aleksandr Deineka (1899–1969) were the outstanding painters. This diversity came to an end in 1932, however, when the Communist party imposed single nationwide unions of painters and architects. In 1934, SOCIALIST REALISM was promulgated as the official style. The liberalization of the late 1980s, however, revealed the existence of an "unofficial" art movement—avant-garde artists continue to work without state support. Malevich's suprematist paintings, suppressed since the 1920s, were shown at a Moscow exhibit in 1988.

Russian Blue   The Russian Blue cat, once known as the Archangel Blue, is noted for its coat of remarkable quality: soft, thick, and silky like sealskin, and in varying shades of blue including lavender. The body is long and slender, the head broad with wide-set vivid green eyes. The ears are large and pointed. The Russian Blue was brought to Great Britain about 1860 by sailors trading from Baltic ports.

Wassily Kandinsky's Couple on Horseback *was painted in 1907, three years before he abandoned representational art for pure abstraction. (Städtische Galerie, Munich.)*

The Russian Blue has a double coat of short blue hair with a silvery sheen. Lighter shades—or lavender—are preferred in competition.

Russian language   see SLAVIC LANGUAGES

Russian literature

Russian literature Russian literature rivals other national literatures in critical esteem, a position it has achieved primarily through works written since 1820.

Origins. Russian literature began with the conversion of Russia to Christianity in the late 10th century. Because Kiev at this time was the capital and most important city of Russia, early literature is said to belong to the Kievan period. Most of the early literature was written in Old Church Slavonic (see SLAVIC LANGUAGES) and consisted of biblical and liturgical texts, as well as some medieval romances translated from the Greek. Original Kievan writings include the sermons of Hilarion, lives of the saints, and the historical works known as the chronicles, of which the best known is the *Primary Chronicle* (c.1112). The most famous work of the period, however, is the short epic *The Lay of Igor's Campaign* (1187).

In the Kievan period, Russia also possessed a rich oral literature. The *byliny,* or folk chants, were heroic lays in which the 10th-century Grand Prince Vladimir of Kiev figures in a role comparable to that of King Arthur in Arthurian legend. Retold and reworked over the centuries, the *byliny* survived in oral form into the 19th century, when they were finally transcribed.

Muscovite Period. From about 1240 to 1480, Russia's princes ruled as vassals of the Tatars. During this period, in which the ascendancy of Moscow occurred, literature remained largely religious, didactic, and historical, with continuing emphasis on lives of the saints and on chronicles. One well-known work of the time, the *Zadonshchina,* is a 15th-century account of the Russians' first major victory over the Tatars at Kulikovo in 1380.

The two most celebrated monuments of 16th-century Russian literature are a handbook of domestic etiquette, the *Domostroy,* and the acrimonious *Correspondence between Prince A. M. Kurbsky and Tsar Ivan IV* (1564–79; Eng. trans., 1955). During the 17th century a schism occurred in the church, from which arose the polemical autobiography *Life of the Archpriest Avvakum* (1672–75; Eng. trans., 1924) by the leader of the Old Believers. Russian drama also first appeared during the 17th century, in the works translated and staged for the tsar by the German monk Johann Gottfried Gregori and in the original works of Simeon Polotsky (1629–80).

The 18th Century. With the advent of the 18th century, Russia, led by Tsar Peter the Great (r. 1682–1725), came under the influence of the culturally as well as economically more advanced civilization of western Europe. Antioch Kantemir (1709–44) was the first poet to write in the vernacular; poet, scholar, and scientist Mikhail LOMONOSOV played a particularly prominent part in standardizing the colloquial language, proposing three distinct literary styles. Nikolai KARAMZIN helped forge the modern cultural language with his sentimental *Letters of a Russian Traveler* (1790; Eng. trans., 1803) and with his chief work, the 11-volume *Istoriya gosudarstva rossiyskogo* (History of the Russian State, 1804–27). Ivan KRYLOV, Russia's greatest fabulist, also wrote at this time. By now Russia had acquired a new literary center, Saint Petersburg, the imperial capital since 1712.

Aleksandr Pushkin, portrayed (1827) by Orest Kiprensky, is considered Russia's greatest poet and the founder of modern Russian literature. Pushkin's work represents the culmination of earlier Rusian folk and literary traditions. (Tretyakov Gallery, Moscow.)

Pushkin and His Immediate Successors. In the 19th century, Russia's greatest literary genius, Aleksandr PUSHKIN, completed the process of adapting the language as a literary vehicle. His greatest poems include the verse novel *Eugene Onegin* (1823–31; Eng. trans., 1881); *The Bronze Horseman* (1832; Eng. trans., 1931), a collection of folktales; the verse play *Boris Godunov* (1825); and a wealth of lyrics notable for their precise, imagistic style. His best-known prose works are the novel *A Captain's Daughter* (1836; Eng. trans., 1846), the tale *The Queen of Spades* (1833; Eng. trans., 1850), and a collection of five short stories, *The Tales of Belkin* (1830; Eng. trans., 1894). Pushkin's prolific career ended early when he died in a duel at the age of 38.

Two successors of Pushkin were the nature poet Fyodor Tyutchev and the romantic Mikhail LERMONTOV, whose works deal with frustration and isolation. When Lermontov died, also in a duel, at the age of 26, he left an impressive collection of lyrics and longer poems, as well as *A Hero of Our Time* (1840; Eng. trans., 1886), Russia's first psychological novel. Nikolai GOGOL was an inspired and eccentric talent, best known for such historical short stories as "Taras Bulba" (1835; Eng. trans., 1860) about Cossack life, for the satire *The Inspector General* (1836; Eng. trans., 1892), for the remarkable novel *Dead Souls* (1842; Eng. trans., 1922–23), and for his Saint Petersburg tales, among which "The Overcoat" (1842; Eng. trans., 1922) is preeminent.

Realism. Although it had produced several powerful original talents, Russia in the 1840s still lacked a general literary movement. The extremely influential literary critic Vissarion Belinsky (1811–48) sought to remedy the deficiency, insisting that art had a duty to society, that it must reflect reality, and that it must have a message. The leading realists began to be published in the late 1840s—the novelists Ivan TURGENEV, Fyodor DOSTOYEVSKY, and Count Leo TOLSTOI; the playwright Aleksandr OSTROVSKY; the poet Nikolai Nekrasov (1821–78); and the novelist and political thinker Aleksandr HERZEN.

Turgenev, Dostoyevsky, and Tolstoi. Turgenev is renowned for his *Sportsman's Sketches* (1847–52; Eng.

Three of Russia's greatest 19th-century prose writers—Ivan Turgenev (left); Fyodor Dostoyevsky (center), portrayed (1872) by V. G. Perov; and Leo Tolstoi (right), photographed (1910) with his wife, Sophia, shortly before his death—are shown. These writers, the leading exponents of realism in mid-19th-century literature, explored the human condition and the philosophical concerns of their time.

trans., 1855), sympathetically describing serf life; for his short love stories; and above all for a sequence of six novels, including *Fathers and Sons* (1862; Eng. trans., 1867). Dostoyevsky's major works are four long novels—The BROTHERS KARAMAZOV, CRIME AND PUNISHMENT, *The Idiot* (1869; Eng. trans., 1913), and *The Possessed* (1871–72; Eng. trans., 1931)—which present a clash between the mind and the heart, or between rationality, which Dostoyevsky detested, and intuitiveness, in which he discerned the only hope of rescuing Russia and the world from their self-inflicted troubles. Tolstoi's masterpieces, the long novels ANNA KARENINA and WAR AND PEACE, also weave religious and philosophical problems into the fabric of the fiction.

Chekhov and Gorky. A reformer of the theater, and author of short stories and plays, Anton CHEKHOV wrote toward the end of the Russian realist movement. He was perhaps Russia's greatest dramatist; his plays of human isolation and despair continue to be performed throughout the

Anton Chekhov and Maksim Gorky, two of Russia's finest dramatists, were photographed (1900) in Yalta. Chekhov, whose work is a high point in Russian literary realism, greatly influenced Gorky, the first to practice socialist realism.

world. Best known are his *Uncle Vanya* (1897), *The Three Sisters* (1901; Eng. trans., 1926), and The CHERRY ORCHARD. A contemporary of Chekhov, the playwright, novelist, and story writer Maksim GORKY is best known for his play *The Lower Depths* (1902; Eng. trans., 1906).

Symbolism and Other Competing Movements. From the mid-1890s, symbolism began to supersede realism as the dominant literary movement. The most famous of the Russian symbolist poets was Aleksandr BLOK, who survived the revolution to write descriptions of it in the well-known poems published under the title *The Twelve* (1917; Eng. trans., 1920). Other leading symbolist poets were Valery BRYUSOV and Andrei BELY.

Meanwhile other movements arose in opposition to symbolism. The futurist poets Vladimir MAYAKOVSKY and Velimir Khlebnikov (1885–1922) sought to invent new poetic forms and scorned the art of the past. The acmeists valued the classical and European tradition, leading representatives of the movement being Osip MANDELSTAM and Anna AKHMATOVA. Another group, the imagists, stressed the supreme importance of poetic imagery; this movement produced only one major poet, Sergei YESENIN.

The Soviet Period and Socialist Realism. The Bolshevik revolution of 1917 marked the beginning of the Soviet period in literature, in which literature became subordinated to politics. From about 1930 on, authors were required to idealize the new Soviet industrialization program and the collectivization of agriculture. In order to intensify the regimentation of literature, the many competing literary groups of the 1920s were amalgamated into a single association, the Union of Writers of the USSR, established in 1934 under the sponsorship of literature's best-known survivor from the prerevolutionary era, Maksim Gorky. At the same time, the newly evolved aesthetic method, SOCIALIST REALISM, was imposed as the only permissible literary technique.

Several important writers had begun publishing before the crackdown of 1934, however, and continued to enjoy

Aleksandr Solzhenitsyn, the most celebrated contemporary Russian writer, was awarded the 1970 Nobel Prize for literature, which he was unable to accept until 1974, following his deportation from the USSR to the West. Solzhenitsyn's works were repressed in the USSR from the 1960s until 1989.

some immunity from the strictures of socialist realism. Valentin KATAYEV's *Time Forward* (1932; Eng. trans., 1933) is a carefully written account of the work of Russian technicians at Magnitogorsk; the three-volume *And Quiet Flows the Don* (1928–33; Eng. trans., 1934), along with its sequel, *The Don Flows Home to the Sea* (1940; Eng. trans., 1940), by the Nobel Prize winner Mikhail SHOLOKHOV, is a regional novel set in Cossack lands; and Leonid Leonov's (b. 1899) six novels on industrialization include the internationally acclaimed *Sot* (1930; trans. as *Soviet River,* 1932) and *The Russian Forest* (1954; Eng. trans., 1966). Such leading 20th-century exponents as Aleksei N. TOLSTOI have also helped keep the long novel an established genre in Russia.

Émigré and Post-Stalinist Literature. The foremost expatriate prose writers of the Soviet period were Vladimir NABOKOV and Ivan BUNIN. Following Stalin's death in 1953, restrictions on literature were somewhat relaxed. Aleksandr SOLZHENITSYN's novel *One Day in the Life of Ivan Denisovich* (1962; Eng. trans., 1963), about the Soviet labor camps under Stalin, was published during a thaw, but his later novels had to be published abroad. Solzhenitsyn was awarded the 1970 Nobel Prize for literature. Boris PASTERNAK, offered the 1958 Prize for his works, including *Doctor Zhivago* (1957; Eng. trans., 1958), published outside the USSR, was forced by his government to decline the award.

Poetry, Drama, and Criticism. Verse is in many ways a more important branch of the modern literature than prose, largely because of the leading poets who survived the revolution and continued writing either in Russia or abroad. Such poets include Mayakovsky, Mandelstam, Akhmatova, Pasternak, and Marina Tsvetayeva (1892–1941). The poets Andrei VOZNESENSKY and Yevgeny YEVTUSHENKO produced their best work as critics of the Soviet regime in the 1960s; dissident poet Joseph BRODSKY was exiled in 1972, however.

With *glasnost*, the liberalization of the late 1980s, Soviet citizens began to catch up on the works of suppressed writers, among them those who had died (Mikhail BULGAKOV, Boris Pasternak), those who were exiled (Vasily AKSENOV, Vladimir VOINOVICH, Aleksandr Solzhenitsyn),

and those who stayed in the USSR but kept their best work hidden—notably Anatoly Rybakov, author of the anti-Stalinist novel *Children of the Arbat* (1987; Eng. trans., 1988).

Russian music

The beginnings of a distinctively national art music in Russia date from the first half of the 19th century. Until this time musical activity was concentrated in the Russian Orthodox church and in traditional folk genres.

Nationalism

The performance of Mikhail GLINKA's opera *A Life for the Tsar* (1836) is usually cited as the turning point for Russian music. In this historical opera, as well as in his subsequent opera *Ruslan and Ludmila* (1842), Glinka fused the typical melodies, harmonies, and rhythms of Russian folk music with the forms and techniques of Italian opera. Glinka's younger contemporary, Aleksandr Dargomyzhsky (1813–69), influenced later nationalist composers with the realistic recitative style of his opera *The Stone Guest* (1872).

Nationalists Versus the West. Supported by the influential critic Vladimir Stasov (1824–1906), the group of composers known as The Five—Mily BALAKIREV, Aleksandr BORODIN, César Cui (1835–1918), Modest MUSSORGSKY, and Nikolai RIMSKY-KORSAKOV—sought to encourage Russian musical nationalism in opposition to Western influences. Although linked by common propagandistic aims and by the characteristic absence of formal musical education, the composers wrote in differing styles. Borodin is noted for his use of Russian orientalisms in works such as *In the Steppes of Central Asia* (1880) and his opera

Master composer for the classical ballet, Tchaikovsky wrote lushly orchestrated dance scores of great romantic beauty. Here, in the American Ballet Theatre's 1989 production of Swan Lake, *Prince Siegfried and the Swan Queen dance a* pas de deux.

Nikolai Rimsky-Koraskov is considered one of the foremost members of The Five, a group of nationalist composers who broke with conservative tradition by assimilating Russian folk melodies into their music.

Prince Igor. In his numerous operas on historical and fairy-tale subjects, as well as in the well-known symphonic suite *Scheherazade* (1891), Rimsky-Korsakov exploited the unusual modal tendencies of Russian folk music, and his orchestration was colorful and effective.

Mussorgsky was undoubtedly the most original composer of The Five, and the most influential in the 20th century. Continuing Dargomyzhsky's search for musical realism, he combined a flair for the nuances of folk music with speechlike rhythms and unusual harmonic juxtapositions in his many songs, his opera *Boris Godunov* (1869–72), and his suite for piano *Pictures at an Exhibition* (1874).

The composer-pianist Anton RUBINSTEIN and his brother Nicholas (1835–81) established the first music conservatories in Russia, founded on German models, in Saint Petersburg (1862) and Moscow (1866). Peter Ilich TCHAIKOVSKY was one of the first graduates of the former and subsequently taught at the latter. Without rejecting his national heritage, Tchaikovsky evolved a cosmopolitan and romantic style in his operas, ballets, symphonies, and concertos.

In Saint Petersburg, under the tutelage of Rimsky-Korsakov, a new generation of nationalists emerged, including Aleksandr GLAZUNOV and Anatol Liadov. In Moscow, Tchaikovsky's heirs included Anton ARENSKY and Sergei Taneyev. Sergei RACHMANINOFF and Aleksandr SCRIABIN were classmates at the Moscow Conservatory; both pursued careers as pianists, conductors, and composers.

Early 20th Century. The exotic and colorful qualities of Russian music were fully revealed to the West through the endeavors of the entrepreneur Serge DIAGHILEV. With lavish productions he staged the Western premiere (1908) of *Boris Godunov* and other Russian classics in Paris, and with his newly formed Ballets Russes he introduced the ballets *Firebird* (1910), *Petrushka* (1911), and *The Rite of Spring* (1913) by Igor STRAVINSKY. Diaghilev's commissions and controversial productions helped launch the careers of many other composers, including Sergei PROKOFIEV.

The rise of virtuoso performers also distinguishes this period. In addition to the pianists already mentioned, the violin students of Leopold AUER—including Mischa ELMAN, Jascha HEIFETZ, and Nathan MILSTEIN—as well as the bass singer Fyodor CHALIAPIN, gained international prestige.

Soviet Music

After the October revolution in 1917, many composers and performers chose to leave Russia. Among those who pursued successful careers in the West were Stravinsky, Rachmaninoff, Nikolai Medtner (1880–1951), Nikolay (1873–1945) and Aleksandr (1899–1977) Tcherepnin, and Serge KOUSSEVITZKY. Prokofiev spent nearly 20 years concertizing and composing in the United States and Europe before returning to the Soviet Union in the mid-1930s.

The early years after the Bolshevik revolution were marked by a spirit of artistic innovation. The creation (1922) of a conductorless orchestra, the demonstration (1920) of the prototype of the first electronic instrument (see THEREMIN), and compositions on "industrial" subjects were attempts to find creative means suited to the revolutionary ideology. Older composers who maintained a continuity with prerevolutionary culture included Reinhold GLIÈRE and Nikolai Miaskovsky (1881–1950).

The Association of Contemporary Music (ACM), established in 1923, supported the modernistic experiments. In opposition, the Russian Association for Proletarian Music (RAPM), which won increasing authority, advocated a simple, folk-oriented "mass" music. The abolition (1932) of the RAPM, the establishment of the government-sponsored Union of Soviet Composers, and the concomitant rise of the doctrine of socialist realism ended the permissive period in Soviet music.

The unexpected official denunciation (1936) of Dmitry SHOSTAKOVICH's highly successful opera *Lady Macbeth of the Mtsensk District* (1934) was the first explicit application of socialist realism to music. Recognizing music to be a powerful weapon in the ideological struggle, this ambiguous doctrine called for music "founded on the truthful, historically concrete representation of reality in its revolutionary development." The formula effectively banned the modernistic directions characteristic of contemporary Western music and fostered conservative and

Modest Mussorgsky is considered the most original composer of The Five. Much of his work, most notably the opera Boris Godunov (1869–72), based on Pushkin's play, was altered after his death by Rimsky-Korsakov.

(Below) *Sergei Rachmaninoff, greatly influenced by Tchaikovsky, became one of the leading romantic composers of the Moscow school and one of the most celebrated piano virtuosos of the 20th century.*

(Above) *At the premiere of the ballet* Le Sacre du Printemps (The Rite of Spring) *in Paris on May 29, 1913, the audience rioted, outraged by Igor Stravinsky's score with its huge sounds and convulsive rhythms. Shown here is a scene from the Joffrey Ballet's 1987 revival, using the original costume designs and choreography.*

readily accessible styles. Mildly dissonant counterpoint, march rhythms, and sensitive orchestration became the hallmarks not only of Shostakovich's style but that of many other Soviet composers as well. Composers who reached artistic maturity during the 1930s and '40s included Aram KHATCHATURIAN, Dmitri Kabalevsky, Yuri Shaporin (1887–1966), and Vissarion Shebalin (1902–63).

In 1948 a new wave of official criticism was aimed at Soviet composers and musicians, this time focusing in particular on the most prominent composers—Prokofiev, Shostakovich, Miaskovsky, and Khachaturian. The rehabilitation of the country's leading composers and the resurrection of many suppressed compositions was accomplished only after Stalin's death, in 1953. Soviet composers then began to show a renewed interest in the modern

compositional techniques of the West, and many, including Shostakovich, began to incorporate these techniques into their compositions.

A new generation of composers, born for the most part in the 1930s, has emerged since the 1960s, including Edison Denisov, Andrei Petrov, Alfred Schnittke, Valentin Silvestrov, Sergei Slonimsky, Boris Tishchenko, and Andrei Volkonsky. All demonstrate a mastery of aleatory, serial, electronic, and other avant-garde techniques. At the 1988 Leningrad Festival of modern music—a Soviet first—some of their works were played for an international audience.

Russia continues to produce virtuoso instrumentalists, among them pianists Vladimir ASHKENAZI, Lazar Berman, Emil GILELS, and Sviatoslav RICHTER, violinist David OISTRAKH, and cellist Mstislav ROSTROPOVICH.

Russian Orthodox church   see ORTHODOX CHURCH

Dmitry Shostakovich, one of the foremost Soviet composers of the 20th century, was alternately praised and condemned during Stalin's regime by authorities who sought to use his music for political ends.

Russian Revolution of 1905   The Russian Revolution of 1905 broke out at a time when the imperial Russian forces were suffering humiliating defeats in the Far East at the hands of the Japanese (1904–05; see RUSSO-JAPANESE WAR). The fighting began on Jan. 22 (N.S.), 1905, when an estimated 1,000 workers were killed by Cossacks who fired on peaceful demonstrators, led by a priest, Father Gapon, in Saint Petersburg. This incident—dubbed Bloody Sunday—resulted in an alliance of liberal and radical groups against the government. Peasant uprisings and a series of strikes and mutinies (including that aboard the battleship *Potemkin* in Odessa) spread throughout European Russia, Poland, and Finland, becoming a general strike in October. Unwillingly, Emperor NICHOLAS II agreed on October 30 (N.S.) to issue a manifesto prepared by Count Sergei WITTE, his chief minister. This October Manifesto extended suffrage, promised freedom from arbitrary arrest, and provided for an elected legislature, or DUMA.

Russian Revolutions of 1917

The abdication of Emperor NICHOLAS II in March (N.S.; February, O.S.) 1917, in conjunction with the establishment of a provisional government based on Western principles of constitutional liberalism, and the seizure of power by the Bolsheviks in November (N.S.; October, O.S.) are the political focal points of the Russian Revolutions of 1917. The events of that momentous year must also be viewed more broadly, however: as an explosion of social tensions associated with rapid industrialization; as a crisis of political modernization; and as a social upheaval involving a massive expropriation of gentry land by angry peasants, the destruction of traditional social patterns and values, and the struggle for a new, egalitarian society. One must also include the Bolsheviks' fight to keep the world's first "proletarian dictatorship" in power after November, first against the Germans, and then in the civil war against dissident socialists, anti-Bolshevik "White Guards," foreign intervention, and anarchist peasant bands. Finally, one must see the psychological aspects of revolutionary change: elation and hope, fear and discouragement, and ultimately the prolonged agony of bloodshed and privation, both from war and repression. Throughout, the events in Russia were of worldwide importance. Western nations saw "immutable" values and institutions successfully challenged, COMMUNISM emerged as a viable social and political system, and Third World peoples saw the power of organized workers' and peasants' movements as a means of "liberating" themselves from "bourgeois" exploitation. As such, the Revolutions of 1917 ushered in the great social, political, and ideological divisions of the contemporary world.

Historical Background. Historians differ over whether the Revolutions of 1917 were inevitable, but all agree on the importance of three related causal factors: massive discontent, the revolutionary movement, and World War I.

The emancipation of the serfs in 1861 left the countryside in deep poverty. The newly freed peasants received inadequate land allotments, and many flocked to jobs in urban areas for low wages under oppressive conditions. Meanwhile, the rising business and professional classes expressed unhappiness with tsarist rule and yearned for a Western-style parliamentary system.

Populist groups, organized in the countryside by the 1890s, joined radical socialist workers' groups in the founding of the Socialist Revolutionary party in 1901. The Marxist Social Democratic Labor party was established in 1898. Five years later it divided into two factions, the BOLSHEVIKS AND MENSHEVIKS. The latter favored a decentralized, mass party, while the former, led by Vladimir Ilich LENIN, wanted a tightly organized, hierarchical party. Middle-class liberals formed the Constitutional Democratic party (Cadets) in 1905.

Russian losses in the RUSSO-JAPANESE WAR precipitated

Emperor Nicholas II appears in a photograph, taken about 1911, of the Russian imperial family. To his right sits Empress Alexandra and, at her feet, their hemophiliac son, Aleksei. Flanking the emperor are his daughters (left to right), *Anastasia, Tatyana, Olga, and Marie.*

the RUSSIAN REVOLUTION OF 1905, which has been called a "dress rehearsal" for 1917. Reluctantly, Nicholas II granted a range of civil liberties, established limited parliamentary government through a DUMA, and under Pyotr STOLYPIN began an agrarian reform. These measures momentarily quieted the populace, but they also raised new expectations.

The March Revolution. After Russia joined WORLD WAR I, land reform was suspended and new political restrictions were imposed. Disastrous military defeats sapped public morale, and ineffective organization on the home front made the government's incompetence obvious to all. The sinister influence of Empress ALEXANDRA's favorite, Grigory RASPUTIN, increased. By the winter of 1916–17, disaffection again rent all sectors of society.

When food shortages provoked street demonstrations in Petrograd on Mar. 8 (N.S.; Feb. 23, O.S.), 1917, and

Aleksandr Kerensky assumed control of the provisional government formed after the tsar's abdication in March 1917. Kerensky's government, unable to stabilize the nation, fell before the Bolshevik-led uprising in November (N.S.) 1917.

garrison soldiers refused to suppress them, Duma leaders demanded that Nicholas transfer power to a parliamentary government. With the Petrograd Soviet of Workers' and Soldiers' Deputies, a special Duma committee on March 15 (N.S.; March 2, O.S.) established a provisional government headed by Prince Georgi Lvov. On the same day, the emperor abdicated.

The new provisional government was almost universally welcomed. Civil liberties were proclaimed, an 8-hour day was negotiated in Petrograd, and elections were promised for a Constituent Assembly. The existence of two seats of power, however—the provisional government and the Petrograd Soviet—reflected the different aspirations of different sectors of Russian society.

For most Russians of privilege the March Revolution meant clearing the decks for victory over Germany and for the establishment of Russia as a leading European liberal democracy. For most workers and peasants, however, revolution meant an end to an imperialist war, major economic reforms, and the development of an egalitarian social order. They looked to the Petrograd Soviet and other soviets springing up around the country to represent their interests.

Political Polarization. Differing conceptions of the revolution quickly led to a series of crises. Widespread popular opposition to the war caused the Petrograd Soviet on April 9 (N.S.; March 27, O.S.) to repudiate annexationist ambitions and to establish in May a coalition government including several moderate socialists in addition to Aleksandr KERENSKY. The participation of such socialists in a government that continued to prosecute the war and that failed to implement basic reforms, however, only served to identify the Socialist Revolutionaries and Mensheviks with government failures. On July 16–17 (N.S.; July 3–4, O.S.), following a disastrous military offensive, Petrograd soldiers demonstrated against the government in what became known as the "July Days."

The demonstrations soon subsided, and on July 20 (N.S.; July 7, O.S.), Kerensky replaced Lvov as premier. Soon, however, the provisional government was threatened by the right, which had lost confidence in the regime's ability to maintain order. In early September (N.S.; late August, O.S.), General Lavr KORNILOV was thwarted in an apparent effort to establish a right-wing military dictatorship.

Meanwhile, another revolution was taking place: all over Russia, peasants were expropriating land from the gentry. Peasant-soldiers fled the trenches so as not to be left out, and the government could not stem the tide. New shortages consequently appeared in urban areas, causing scores of factories to close. By the summer of 1917 a social upheaval of vast proportions was sweeping over Russia.

The November Revolution. Sensing that the time was ripe, Lenin and the Bolsheviks rapidly mobilized for power. From the moment he returned from exile on Apr. 16 (N.S.; Apr. 3, O.S.), 1917, Lenin, pressing for a Bolshevik-led seizure of power by the soviets, categorically disassociated his party from both the government and the "accommodationist" socialists. With appealing slogans such as "Peace, Land, and Bread!" the Bolsheviks identified themselves with Russia's broad social revolution. Better organized than their rivals, they quickly came to dominate major committees in factories; they also secured growing support in local soviets. A Bolshevik-inspired military uprising was suppressed in July. The next month, however, after Kornilov's attempted coup, Lenin's supporters secured majorities in both the Petrograd and Moscow soviets. Reacting to the momentum of events, Lenin, from hiding, ordered preparations for an armed insurrection.

On the night of November 6–7 (N.S.; October 24–25, O.S.) the Bolsheviks seized power in Petrograd, encountering little armed resistance. An All-Russian Congress of Soviets of Workers' and Soldiers' Deputies, meeting in Petrograd at the time, ratified the Bolsheviks' actions on

(Below) *Vladimir Ilich Lenin, revolutionary leader, delivers a vitriolic address before a Russian crowd. Lenin returned from Swiss exile following the tsar's abdication to assume control of the revolutionary movement that eventually seized power.*

(Above) *The Bolshevik Revolution began on Nov. 6–7, 1917, when Red Guards stormed the Winter Palace, headquarters of the provisional government, in Petrograd.*

November 8. The congress also declared the establishment of a soviet government headed by a Council of People's Commissars chaired by Lenin, with Leon TROTSKY in charge of foreign affairs.

The Civil War and Its Aftermath. Bolsheviks now faced the same range of economic, social, and political problems as did the governments they had replaced. In addition, anti-Bolsheviks began almost at once to organize armed resistance. Few expected the "proletarian dictatorship" to survive, but Lenin's political boldness and his commitment to shaping a Communist Russia soon became apparent. The November Constituent Assembly elections returned an absolute majority for the Socialist Revolutionaries, but Lenin simply dispersed the Assembly when it met in January 1918. He also issued a decree on land in November 1917, sanctifying the peasants' land seizures, proclaiming the Bolsheviks to be a party of poor peasants as well as workers and broadening his own base of support. He sued the Germans for peace, but under the terms of the Treaty of Brest-Litovsk (March 1918) he was forced to surrender huge portions of traditionally Russian territory. Shortly afterward, implementing policies called War Communism, Lenin ordered the requisition of grain from the countryside to feed the cities and pressed a program to nationalize virtually all Russian industry.

Civil war erupted in 1918. Constituent Assembly delegates fled to western Siberia and formed their own "All-Russian" government, which was soon suppressed by a reactionary "White" dictatorship under Admiral Aleksandr Kolchak. Army officers in southern Russia organized a "Volunteer Army" under Generals Lavr Kornilov and Anton Denikin and gained support from Britain and France, and peasants began to organize against Bolshevik requisitioning and mobilization. Even in Moscow and Petrograd, leftist Socialist Revolutionaries took up arms against the Bolsheviks.

In response, the Bolsheviks unleashed their own Red Terror under the Cheka (political police force) and mobilized a Red Army commanded by Trotsky. The Bolsheviks defeated Admiral Kolchak's troops in late 1919, and in 1920 they suppressed the armies of Baron Pyotr N. Wrangel and General Denikin in the south.

Some Western historians attribute ultimate Bolshevik victory in this war to White disorganization, halfhearted support from war-weary Allies, and Cheka ruthlessness. Most important, however, was the fact that even while Bolshevik popularity declined, Lenin and his followers were still identified with what the majority of workers and peasants wanted most: radical social change rather than political freedom.

With the counterrevolution defeated, leftist anti-Bolshevik sentiment nevertheless erupted. The naval garrison at Kronshtadt, long a Bolshevik stronghold, rebelled in March 1921 along with Petrograd workers in favor of "Soviet Communism without the Bolsheviks!" This protest was brutally suppressed. The Menshevik and Socialist Revolutionary parties, harassed but not abolished during the civil war, gained support as the conflict ended. The Bolsheviks outlawed these parties, but were astute enough to realize that a strategic retreat was required. At the Tenth Party Congress, in 1921, the NEW ECONOMIC POLICY was introduced, restoring some private property, ending restrictions on private trade, and terminating forced grain requisitions. The foundations had been laid for building Bolshevik socialism, but the revolutionary period proper had come to an end.

Russian wolfhound   see BORZOI

Russo-Finnish War   The Russo-Finnish War, also called the Winter War, was waged by the USSR against Finland from Nov. 30, 1939, to Mar. 12, 1940. Following the German invasion of Poland (September 1939), the Kremlin made several demands on Finland, including demilitarization of the Mannerheim Line and the cession of islands and a naval base in the Gulf of Finland, part of the Karelian Isthmus, and Petsamo, the Finns' only ice-free port on the Arctic Sea. The Finns refused, and the Russians invaded Finland. Using highly mobile ski troops, the Finns put up an unexpectedly fierce defense, but after two months of bitter fighting, the Russians won supremacy and came to terms with Finland.

By the Treaty of Moscow (Mar. 12, 1940), the Finns ceded to Soviet Russia an area of more than 41,000 km^2 (16,000 mi^2) with a population of about 450,000. Finland regained its territory by siding with Germany when Hitler attacked the USSR in 1941, but lost it again at the end of World War II.

Russo-Japanese War   The Russo-Japanese War (1904–05) was the first conflict in modern times in which an Asian power defeated a European country. The war resulted from the conflicting ambitions of Russia and Japan to control Manchuria and Korea. Fighting began on Feb. 8, 1904, when the Japanese attacked and bottled up the Russian fleet at Port Arthur (now Lüshun) after Russia, which had occupied Manchuria during the BOXER UPRISING in China, refused to withdraw its troops. The Russians, unable to transport adequate troops and supplies to the east, suffered a series of defeats, including the loss of Port Arthur (January 1905) and the Battle of Mukden (February–March 1905). In May 1905, a Russian fleet that had sailed from the Baltic was annihilated in the Battle of Tsushima by a Japanese fleet under the command of Adm. TOGO HEIHACHIRO. The belligerents accepted the mediation of U.S. president Theodore Roosevelt, and a peace treaty was signed at Portsmouth, N.H., on Sept. 5, 1905.

Russia acknowledged Japanese predominance in Korea, transferred to Japan its lease of Port Arthur and the Liaodong Peninsula, and ceded the southern half of Sakhalin. Russia's humiliation in the war revealed the weaknesses of the tsarist government and thus helped precipitate the RUSSIAN REVOLUTION OF 1905.

Russo-Turkish Wars   During the 18th and 19th centuries Russian leaders, motivated by such ideologies as

Orthodox Christianity and PAN-SLAVISM as well as by strategic and economic factors, sought to expand their influence in southeastern Europe and to acquire the Ukraine, Crimea, and the Caucasus region. These goals, and the ambition to control the Black Sea and the Dardanelles, directly threatened the interests and territory of the OTTOMAN EMPIRE (now Turkey) and resulted in frequent wars.

Eighteenth-Century Conflicts. PETER I, seeking to end Russia's landlocked isolation, forced the Turks to cede the port of Azov in 1699. The Turks, however, with the assistance of the Crimean Tatars, became involved in the Great Northern War (1700–21; see NORTHERN WAR, GREAT) and defeated the armies of Peter, regaining Azov in 1711. In the campaigns of 1736–39, Russia reacquired Azov and received trading rights in the Sea of Azov and the Black Sea.

The War of 1768–74 was the first of CATHERINE II's assaults on the Ottoman Empire. Russia's victorious campaign ended with the aquisition of strategic enclaves on the northern Black Sea coast and important commercial and navigation privileges in the Ottoman Empire and Black Sea.

Catherine's plan to expel the Turks from Constantinople led to a Turkish declaration of war in 1787. Catherine's victories reaffirmed Russian control of the Crimea (annexed in 1783) and gave Russia lands between the Bug and Dnestr rivers. Russia thus replaced the Ottoman Empire as the dominant power in the Black Sea region.

Nineteenth-Century Conflicts. The Russo-Turkish War of 1806–12 erupted during the NAPOLEONIC WARS. In November 1806, Russian troops moved into the Danubian principalities of Moldavia and Walachia (in present-day Romania). Turkey declared war the next month. Fighting continued in an inconclusive fashion until Russia, anticipating Napoleon's invasion, signed the Treaty of Bucharest (1812) with Turkey. The settlement granted Bessarabia to Russia.

After additional fighting in 1828–29, Russia relinquished its Balkan conquests but acquired a protectorship in Moldavia and Walachia, domination of the mouth of the Danube River, and control of Georgia, eastern Armenia, and territories in the Caucasus.

The CRIMEAN WAR, the third war between Russia and Turkey in the 19th century, erupted in 1853. Britain and France joined the Turks in 1854. By the Treaty of Paris (1856) Russia was forced to abandon its post-1774 territorial acquisitions, with the exception of the Crimea and most of the eastern conquests.

After a difficult military campaign in the Russo-Turkish War of 1877–78, Russia compelled the Ottoman Empire to sign (1878) the harsh Treaty of San Stefano. Because its territorial gains threatened the European balance of power, the other great powers pressured Russia to attend the Congress of Berlin (see BERLIN, CONGRESS OF). The resulting Treaty of Berlin (1878) reversed some Russian gains but also recognized Russia's acquisition of Batum, Kars, and Ardahan in the Caucasus region and southern Bessarabia.

World War I. Turkey entered WORLD WAR I on the side of Germany and Austria-Hungary with a naval bombardment of Russian Black Sea fortifications on Oct. 29, 1914. Turkish and Russian armies fought each other in the area of the Caucasus Mountains and Armenia. In late 1917, after the Bolshevik Revolution, an armistice was concluded. By the Treaty of Brest-Litovsk (1918), Russia left the war, and Turkey regained Kars and Ardahan. Batum, also recovered by Turkey in 1918, was returned to Russia in 1921.

rust   see DISEASES, PLANT

rust, metallic   see CORROSION

rutabaga [root'-uh-bay-guh]   Rutabaga, *Brassica napus,* a biennial herb of the mustard family, Cruciferae, is harvested annually for its smooth, thick, yellow or white root. The plant is believed to be a cross between the white turnip and the cabbage and to have originated in Europe during the Middle Ages. Rutabaga requires a cool growing climate. Its culture is similar to that of the TURNIP, although rutabaga takes 4 to 6 weeks longer to mature. The roots have a sweet flavor and store well; if kept cool and at high humidity, they may be used for several months. They are often treated with wax to prevent water loss during storage.

The rutabaga is a large edible root that grows best in cool climates. It is a major crop in northern Europe and Canada, and it is also cultivated in the northern United States.

Ruth, Babe   George Herman "Babe" Ruth, b. Baltimore, Md., Feb. 6, 1895, d. Aug. 16, 1948, was one of professional baseball's greatest players. As a New York Yankee, Ruth saved baseball from the Black Sox scandal of 1919 and single-handedly revitalized the sport as the country's national pastime. He teamed with Lou Gehrig to form what became the greatest one-two hitting punch in baseball and was the heart of the 1927 Yankees, a team regarded by some as the best in baseball history. Nicknamed the Sultan of Swat, Ruth started his major league

Babe Ruth remains perhaps the most famous baseball player in history despite the fact that most of his batting records have been eclipsed. Before joining the New York Yankees, Ruth had been an outstanding pitcher for the Boston Red Sox. The Yankees converted him into an outfielder.

career as a left-handed pitcher with the Boston Red Sox in 1914. An excellent pitcher, Ruth had a career record of 94 victories and 46 losses, with a 2.28 earned-run average. It is for his prowess at bat, not at the mound, however, that Ruth is remembered. He was sold to New York by Boston following the 1919 season and after a permanent shift to the outfield smashed a record 54 home runs while compiling a .376 batting average. In 22 seasons with the Red Sox, Yankees, and Boston Braves, Ruth led the league in home runs a record 12 times—including 59 in 1921 and a then-record 60 in 1927. He retired in 1935 with 714 career home runs, a record not surpassed until Hank Aaron did so in 1974. Ruth had a lifetime batting average of .342 and his .690 slugging percentage is the highest in history. He drew 2,056 walks, drove in 2,217 runs, and scored 2,174 runs. Ruth was elected to the Baseball Hall of Fame in 1936 as one of the first five members.

Ruth, Book of The Book of Ruth is the eighth book of the Old Testament of the BIBLE. A short story, it tells how Ruth, the Moabite widow of a Bethlehemite, with her mother-in-law Naomi's assistance, married an older kinsman Boaz, thereby preserving her deceased husband's posterity and becoming an ancestor of King David. The plot is artfully constructed and exhibits a pronounced belief in the comprehensive but hidden providence of God that works quietly in ordinary events. The legal customs concerning levirate marriage, redemption of property, and gleaning in the fields are relatively ancient, and the vocabulary and style are consistent with a date between 950 and 750 BC. The Davidic genealogy is a secondary appendix, written between 500 and 350 BC, which served to increase the importance of the book for postexilic Jews.

Ruthenia [roo-thee'-nee-uh] Ruthenia is a historic name for a region of Eastern Europe, also known as the Carpatho-Ukraine, and now known as the Transcarpathian Oblast in the Ukraine of the USSR. The region is bordered by Romania, Hungary, Czechoslovakia, and Poland. Its main city is Uzhgorod.

The area was part of the Slavic Kievan state in the 10th and 11th centuries but came under Hungarian rule in the 13th century. The inhabitants, Ruthenes, who are ethnically and linguistically related to Ukrainians, attempted to gain a partial autonomy in the 19th century, but their efforts were thwarted by forced Magyarization. Ruthenia was assigned by the Trianon Treaty (1920) to Czechoslovakia. It was occupied by Hungary in 1939 and then was ceded to the USSR in 1945.

ruthenium [roo-thee'-nee-uhm] Ruthenium is a hard, lustrous, silver gray metal resembling platinum (see TRANSITION ELEMENTS). A chemical element, its symbol is Ru, its atomic number is 44, and its atomic weight is 101.07. Ruthenium was discovered in 1828 by Gottfried Wilhelm Osann, but credit is generally given to Karl Klaus, who was the first to obtain (1844) the pure metal. Ruthenium is not attacked by strong acids, even aqua regia. Its major use is in alloys with platinum and palladium, in which it is an effective hardener. These alloys are mainly used to make jewelry and electrical contacts with a high wear resistance.

Rutherford, Sir Ernest [ruhth'-ur-furd] Sir Ernest Rutherford, b. near Nelson, New Zealand, Aug. 30, 1871, d. Oct. 19, 1937, perhaps more than any other scientist, formed modern-day views concerning the nature of matter. After distinguishing himself in undergraduate work in his native New Zealand, Rutherford matriculated to Cambridge University's Cavendish Laboratory, which was at that time under the directorship of Sir Joseph John Thomson, the leading authority on electromagnetic phenomena. Rutherford's early work with Thomson led to investigations of electricity and radiation and eventually to a detailed study of radioactivity.

In 1898, Rutherford obtained the physics professorship at McGill University, Montreal, and soon demonstrated his talents by discovering several radioactive elements. Although others had pioneered the earliest developments in RADIOACTIVITY, Rutherford soon achieved dominance in this field. He found that at least two kinds of radiation, which he labeled alpha and beta, existed. Working with Frederick Soddy in 1902–03, Rutherford identified the phenomenon of radioactive half-life and formulated the still-accepted explanation of radioactivity: each decay of the atoms of radioactive materials signifies the transmutation of a parent element into a daughter, with each type of atom having its own transformation period. This theory stimulated many other scientists, as well as Rutherford, to order all known radioactive elements into their decay series and to search for any missing members. Rutherford was awarded the 1908 Nobel Prize for chemistry for his work in radioactivity.

Rutherford made his greatest discovery in 1909. Shortly after his move to Manchester, he found that a few alpha particles, when bombarding thin metal foils, were deflected from their incident beam through more than

90°. "It was almost as incredible," Rutherford later responded in a now-classic statement, "as if you fired a fifteen-inch shell at a piece of tissue paper and it came back and hit you." Early in 1911 he finally announced his version of the structure of the atom: a very small, tightly packed, charged nucleus sprinkled with opposite charges in the mostly empty surrounding void. The deflected alpha particles were those which had come into close proximity with the nucleus and had rebounded in various oblique directions.

About the time that Rutherford moved (1919) to Cambridge to succeed Thomson as director of the Cavendish Laboratory, he discovered artificial disintegration—the artificial splitting of the atom—a signal discovery that presaged his entry into the field of nuclear physics. Members of his Cavendish team discovered the neutron and the disintegration phenomena produced by artificially accelerated particles.

rutile [roo'-teel]   Rutile, a minor ore mineral of titanium, is the most stable of three naturally occurring forms of titanium oxide (TiO_2; see OXIDE MINERALS). Rutile forms prismatic or needlelike crystals (tetragonal system), most commonly red brown in color. Hardness is 6 to 6½, streak is pale brown, luster is adamantine to metallic, and specific gravity is 4.2 to 4.3. Widespread in small amounts, rutile occurs in intermediate basic igneous rocks as a high-temperature accessory mineral, in gneiss and schist, and in high-temperature veins and pegmatite dikes. Because it is highly resistant to chemical and physical weathering, it is common in PLACER DEPOSITS.

Rutland [ruht'-luhnd]   Rutland is a city in western Vermont, on Otter Creek, between the Green and Taconic mountains. The seat of Rutland County, it is Vermont's second largest city, with a population (1990) of 18,230. In addition to its important tourist industry, Rutland's economy is based on diversified manufacturing. Nearby marble quarries are also important. Rutland is the headquarters of the Green Mountain National Forest. Settled by New Englanders in 1770, the city was named for Rutland, Mass. During the American Revolution two forts, Rutland and Ranger, were built in the area. From 1784 to 1804, Rutland was Vermont's capital. Quarrying and the arrival of the railroad resulted in Rutland's becoming the largest city in the state by 1880.

Rutledge, Ann [ruht'-luhj]   According to Abraham Lincoln's biographer William Henry HERNDON, Lincoln fell in love with Ann Rutledge, b. c.1813, d. Aug. 25, 1835, the daughter of the innkeeper at New Salem, Ill. She was engaged to Lincoln's friend John McNamar, who was mysteriously absent from 1832 until after Ann's sudden death from brain fever. Herndon interpreted Lincoln's subsequent grief as proof of a romance, an assessment that historians find unsubstantiated.

Rutledge, John   A signer of the U.S. Constitution, John Rutledge, b. Charleston, S.C., September 1739, d. July 18, 1800, was a leading southern aristocrat who supported the colonies' struggle for independence. During the American Revolution he was governor of South Carolina, and he represented that state at the Continental Congress (1774–75, 1782–83). He was designated (1787) as South Carolina's delegate to the Constitutional Convention. Rutledge was appointed (1789) to the U.S. Supreme Court by President George Washington but resigned (1791) to become chief justice of the South Carolina Supreme Court. Washington appointed (1795) Rutledge chief justice of the U.S. Supreme Court—a post at which he presided for one month—but Rutledge was so vehemently opposed to the recently approved Jay's Treaty that the Senate refused to confirm him.

Ruwenzori [roo-wuhn-zohr'-ee]   The Ruwenzori Range lies north of the equator in east central Africa, along the border between Uganda and Zaire. About 130 km (80 mi) long and up to about 50 km (30 mi) wide, it rises to its maximum height of 5,119 m (16,795 ft) at Mount Stanley's Margherita Peak. The range, a huge faulted block, consists of ancient metamorphic rocks. Abundant rainfall contributes to the growth of forests, grasslands, and cultivated crops. The mountaintops are always snow-covered. The Ruwenzori Range is thought to be the legendary "Mountains of the Moon," erroneously described by Ptolemy as the source of the Nile River.

Ruysch, Rachel [roys]   A leading still-life painter of the baroque period, Rachel Ruysch, 1664–1750, was noted for her brilliantly colored pictures of flower arrangements. She often varied these compositions with butterflies or, in outdoor settings, with other insects, reptiles, or small mammals. After studying with the Dutch flower painter Willem van Aelst, Ruysch developed into a successful professional artist who combined marriage and children with a career. In 1708 she became court painter to the elector palatine Johann Wilhelm van Pfalz, working until 1716 at his court in Düsseldorf.

Ruyter, Michiel Adriaanszoon de [royt'-ur]   One of the greatest naval commanders in Dutch history, Michiel Adriaanszoon de Ruyter, b. Mar. 24, 1607, d. Apr. 29, 1676, brought the United Provinces repeated and crucial victories during the second and third ANGLO-DUTCH WARS. He fought under Maarten Tromp in the first Anglo-Dutch War (1652–54), becoming vice admiral in 1653. In the second war (1665–67), his triumphs enabled the United Provinces to achieve an advantageous peace with England. His repeated victories over the larger combined forces of England and France in the third war (1672–74) saved his country from invasion. He died at Syracuse, Sicily, of wounds suffered in battle.

AT A GLANCE

REPUBLIC OF RWANDA

Land: Area: 26,338 km² (10,169 mi²). Capital and largest city: Kigali (1981 est. pop., 156,650).

People: Population (1990 est.): 7,609,119. Density: 289 persons per km² (748 per mi²). Distribution (1985): 5% urban, 95% rural. Official languages: French, Kinyarwanda. Major religions: Roman Catholicism, traditional religions, Protestantism, Islam.

Government: Type: republic. Legislature: National Development Council. Political subdivisions: 10 prefectures.

Economy: GDP (1988): $2.3 billion; $325 per capita. Labor distribution (1985): agriculture—92%; government and services—5%; industry and commerce—3%. Foreign trade (1988): imports—$278 million; exports—$118 million. Currency: 1 Rwanda franc = 100 centimes.

Education and Health: Literacy (1980): 50% of adult population. Universities (1989): 1. Hospital beds (1984): 9,046. Physicians (1984): 177. Life expectancy (1990): women—54; men—50. Infant mortality (1990): 113 per 1,000 live births.

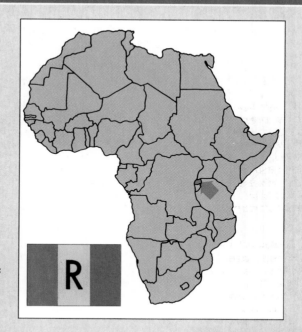

Rwanda [ru-ahn'-dah] The landlocked republic of Rwanda, in east central Africa, is bounded on the north by Uganda, on the east by Tanzania, on the south by Burundi, and on the west by Zaire. Principally an agricultural and pastoral society, Rwanda achieved independence from Belgium in 1962. KIGALI is the capital.

Land, People, and Economy

Rwanda lies on the great East African plateau, and the average elevation is more than 1,525 m (5,000 ft). The highest point in the country, Mount Karlsimbi, rises to 4,507 m (14,787 ft). The rich soil is especially fertile in the alluvial valleys and volcanic northwest. The average temperature is about 19° C (66° F), and rainfall averages about 1,143 mm (45 in) per year. Lake Kivu in the northwest drains into Lake TANGANYIKA, and the Kagera River drains much of the eastern border. The Savanna highlands, which make up most of the Central plateau, are mostly badly eroded and deforested grassland. Wildlife is preserved in Kagera National Park and in Volcano National Park, known for its rare mountain gorillas. Rwanda has small amounts of tin, beryl, and tungsten.

Three groups—the HUTU (Bahutu, 85%), TUTSI (Batutsi, 14%), and Twa (see PYGMY)—make up Rwanda's indigenous population. They speak a common language, Kinyarwanda (Kirundi), and share many cultural traditions. An influx of Hutu fleeing ethnic violence in neigh-

boring Burundi in 1988 strained the resources of what was already Africa's most densely populated nation. Up to 2 million Rwandan Tutsi live in exile in neighboring countries, and educational and employment opportunities for those who remain are limited. Education is free for children aged 7 to 15. The National University of Rwanda is at Butare.

Most Rwandese engage in subsistence (bananas, sweet potatoes, cassava, and livestock) or cash-crop (coffee, tea, and pyrethrum) agriculture. Although the country is generally able to feed itself except in years of drought, rapid population growth is placing severe pressure on available land. (Rwanda has proportionately more land reserved for national parks than any other African nation.) Manufacturing is limited to food processing and light consumer goods. Some tin and tungsten ores are mined. Imports usually exceed exports.

History and Government

Rwanda developed into a highly centralized kingdom ruled by the pastoral Tutsi minority, which arrived in the 14th to 16th centuries. The agricultural Hutu majority, which reached the area in the 7th to 10th centuries, served the Tutsi in exchange for protection and the use of cattle. The first European to visit Rwanda was John SPEKE, in 1858. The area was a German protectorate from 1899 to 1916 and subsequently was part of Belgian-administered Ruanda-Urundi.

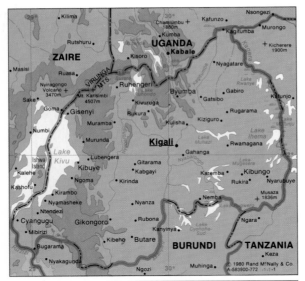

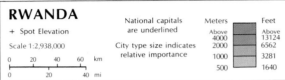

RWANDA

+ Spot Elevation

Scale 1:2,938,000

| 0 | 20 | 40 | 60 | km |
| 0 | | 20 | | 40 mi |

National capitals
are underlined

City type size indicates
relative importance

Meters	Feet
Above 4000	Above 13124
2000	6562
1000	3281
500	1640

Many Tutsi were driven from Rwanda by the Belgians in the 1940s for advocating independence; even more fled to escape ethnic strife in 1959. In 1961, Rwanda abolished the Tutsi monarchy and declared itself a republic; its independence was not internationally recognized until July 1, 1962. Since independence, Rwanda's history has been marked by ethnic conflicts. Maj. Gen. Juvenal Habyarimana took power in a bloodless coup in 1973 during such a crisis and has since served as president. Rwanda is a republic, but the ruling military junta holds all key positions. In November 1990, after subduing an invasion by Rwandan exiles, Habyarimana agreed to institute a multiparty system; in 1991 he agreed to allow Tutsi refugees to return to Rwanda and to abolish identity cards classifying Rwandans by tribe.

Ryan, Nolan   The right-handed baseball pitcher Lynn Nolan Ryan, b. Refugio, Tex., Jan. 31, 1947, is known primarily for his blazing fastball and his ability to strike out batters. Ryan's major league records include the following: most strikeouts in a season (383); most games pitched with 10 or more strikeouts, both for a season (23) and career (207); and most career no-hit games thrown (7); and most seasons (14) throwing 200 or more strike-outs. He also has, through 1990, 5,308 career strike-outs, the most in baseball history, and a won-lost record of 302-272. Ryan has played his long career for 4

teams—the New York Mets (1966–71), California Angels (1972–78), Houston Astros (1979–88), and Texas Rangers (1989–   ).

Ryazan [ree-ah-zahn']   Ryazan is the capital of Ryazan oblast in the Russian republic of the USSR. It is situated on the right bank of the Oka River, 185 km (115 mi) southeast of Moscow. The city has a population of 515,000 (1989). Ryazan was largely bypassed by the Soviet industrialization drive during the 1930s but expanded greatly after the 1950s with the building of large new industrial facilities, including one of central Russia's largest petroleum refineries and a chemical fiber manufacturing plant.

Ryazan is one of the oldest of Russian cities, first mentioned in historical chronicles dating from 1095. In the winter of 1237–38, Mongols sacked the city while attempting to reach Novgorod. Ryazan was the center of an early Russian principality in the 14th century and was absorbed into the Moscow-dominated Russian state in 1520.

Rydberg, Johannes Robert   Swedist physicist and mathematician Johannes Robert Rydberg, b. Nov. 8, 1854, d. Dec. 28, 1919, derived quantitative relationships for the vast amount of spectroscopic data that had accumulated in the late 19th century. In the process he introduced clarifying terminology and suggested that chemical elements be organized in the periodic table by atomic number rather than atomic weight. An important spectroscopic constant based on a hypothetical atom of infinite mass is called the Rydberg (R) in his honor (see QUANTUM MECHANICS; SPECTRUM).

Ryder, Albert Pinkham [ry'-dur]   Albert Pinkham Ryder, b. New Bedford, Mass., Mar. 19, 1848, d. Mar. 28, 1917, was the foremost American visionary painter. He spent most of his life in New York City, where he settled about 1870. Until 1880 his subjects were bucolic and seemingly innocent—sheep in a meadow, a cow at pasture, horses in a stable—but even in these scenes Ryder generates a sense of the haunted. After 1880 the impasto is heavier—applied, sometimes over several years, in layer upon layer of paint; the forms are at once simplified and distorted; the aura of unreality is heightened.

Ryder frequently based his pictures on themes from the Old and New Testaments as well as from the works of Geoffrey Chaucer, William Shakespeare, and Richard Wagner. All nature is energized, reflecting the human condition. In *Jonah* (*c.*1890; National Collection, Washington, D.C.) most of the canvas is given over to a depiction of the churning sea; this mirrors the turmoil within Jonah, who is flailing about at the bottom of the picture.

Ryder selected broad shapes and luminous colors that

would serve to express his deepest feelings. His late works reflect his increasing isolation and eccentricity, as is evident in *Death on a Pale Horse* or *The Race Track* (c.1910; Cleveland Museum of Art).

rye The cereal grain rye, *Secale cereale*, of the grass family, Gramineae, is closely related to wheat and is grown as a bread grain, as a livestock feed, and for distillation into grain-alcohol spirits. The plant is also useful as a green manure and for hay, straw, and pasturage. The most winter-hardy of the cereals, rye does well on poor soils and in cool climates that are not hospitable to wheat cultivation. It is grown primarily in northern and eastern Europe, including the USSR. The crop is of minor importance in the United States, where it is grown principally in South Dakota and Minnesota.

The cultivation of rye began long after that of wheat and barley, perhaps as late as the first millennium BC. Although rye flour lacks the glutenous proteins that make wheat dough elastic enough for leavening, bread made from rye was once the principal type eaten in wheat-poor areas of Europe, and rye still is used, either by itself or in a wheat blend, for more than half the bread made in Germany and for a large proportion of the bread in other European countries.

The rye plant has slim seed spikes and long beards and produces dark grains. Rye flowers, unlike those of wheat, barley, and oats, are self-sterile and must be cross-pollinated by the wind. The methods for sowing, harvesting, and milling rye are similar to those used for the other cereals.

ERGOT, a toxic fungus (*Claviceps purpures*), frequently infects rye kernels. When eaten by livestock or humans

Rye, a grain highly resistant to disease and cold weather, is cultivated throughout the world. Summer rye (left) is planted in spring and grows in summer; winter rye (center) is planted in fall, lies dormant during winter, and grows in spring.

the fungus can cause hallucinations and various, sometimes deadly, illnesses. Epidemics of ergot-caused disease were frequent in Europe during medieval times. Modern cylinder or disk separators remove most infected kernels.

Ryle, Gilbert [ryl] The philosopher Gilbert Ryle, b. Aug. 19, 1900, d. Oct. 6, 1976, is one of the better-known figures of the British "ordinary language" movement (see ANALYTIC AND LINGUISTIC PHILOSOPHY). He served (1947–71) as the editor of the influential periodical *Mind*. Ryle's most important book, *The Concept of Mind* (1949), has been widely read and discussed. In it he analyzes "mental concepts." These work well in everyday life, but can be puzzling when an individual reflects upon them philosophically. Ryle argues that the individual must "map" various mental concepts and determine their position in relation to other concepts. He challenges the Cartesian distinction between body and mind, claiming instead that the mind is the form or organizing principle of the body. In *Dilemmas* (1954), Ryle considers seemingly irreconcilable propositions (for example, free will versus fatalism) and attempts to show that in each case the only conflict is conceptual-linguistic, not genuine.

Ryukyu Islands [ree-oo'-kue] The Japanese Ryukyu Islands (also known as the Luchu Islands) comprise an archipelago extending from Kyushu, southernmost of the Japanese main islands, south for about 1,050 km (650 mi) to Taiwan. The 143 islands and islets, separating the East China Sea from the Pacific Ocean, are divided into the Amami Islands, the Okinawa Islands, and the Sakishima Islands. The islands have a population of 1,222,000 (1989 est.). OKINAWA is the largest and most populous island of the Ryukyus and contains the capital and largest city, Naha. The economy is basically agricultural.

Originally an independent kingdom, the Ryukyus were conquered by the Chinese in the 14th century and by the Japanese in the 17th century; they were finally incorporated into Japan in 1879. The scene of one of the bloodiest campaigns of World War II, Okinawa was captured by U.S. troops in 1945. The islands were returned (1972) to Japan, although the United States retained the right to operate military facilities on Okinawa.

Ryun, Jim [ry'-uhn] James Ronald Ryun, b. Wichita, Kans., Apr. 29, 1947, was an American track star. The first high school student to run a mile in less than 4 min, he reached the semifinals in the 1,500-m race in the 1964 Olympics. In 1965, as a sophomore at the University of Kansas, Ryun set the world mile record of 3 min 55.3 sec. In 1967 he set two new world records: he lowered his mile time to 3 min 51.1 sec, and he set a 1,500-m record at 3 min 33.1 sec. In the 1968 Olympics, Ryun was the silver medalist behind Kip Keino in the 1,500-m competition.

Ss

GERMAN-GOTHIC	RUSSIAN-CYRILLIC	CLASSICAL LATIN	EARLY LATIN	ETRUSCAN	CLASSICAL GREEK	EARLY GREEK	EARLY ARAMAIC	EARLY HEBREW	PHOENICIAN

S *S/s* is the 19th letter of the English alphabet. Both the letter and its position in the alphabet were derived from the Latin, which in turn derived it from the Greek by way of the Etruscan. The Greeks took the form of the letter, which they called *sigma*, from the Semitic sign *sin* or *shin*, but the name of the letter was probably derived from another Semitic s sound, *samekh*. In modern English pronunciation, *S/s* spells a number of sounds. The basic sound of *s* is a voiceless sibilant, or hissing sound, made by placing the tip of the tongue near the front teeth and allowing the breath to pass through the opening thus formed, as in *salt* or *horse*. *S/s* may sometimes represent the voiced counterpart of *s*, which is pronounced like *z*, as in *rose* and *please*. *S/s* can also be sounded as *sh* (*sugar, sure*) or as its voiced counterpart *zh* (*pleasure, vision*). Occasionally *S/s* is silent, as in *island*.

Saadia ben Joseph Gaon [sah'-dee-ah ben joh'zef gah'-ohn]   A religious philosopher, Bible exegete, apologist, and liturgical poet, Saadia ben Joseph, known as Saadia Gaon, b. Egypt, 882, d. 942, was head (Gaon) of the Talmudic academy of Sura, Babylonia and spiritual head of Babylonian Jewry.

Saadia was the first to compose a Hebrew grammar and an *Order of Prayer*; he also wrote religious poetry and a commentary on the mystical *Book of Creation*. His *Emunot ve-Deot* (Book of Beliefs and Opinions) expounds a system of Jewish faith, influenced by Muslim rational theology (*Kalam*) and Aristotelianism, which harmoniously combines revelation and reason.

Saadia also engaged in a protracted dispute with the KARAITES over their opposition to Judaic tradition.

Saarbrücken [zahr-bruek'-en]   Saarbrücken, a German industrial city and the capital of the state of Saarland, is located near the French border, about 160 km (100 mi) south of Bonn. The city has a population of about 184,353 (1987 est.). Saarbrücken is a major center of coal mining, transportation, iron and steel production, and the manufacture of optical instruments, glass, clothing, paper, beer, and soap. Landmarks include the Gothic Abbey of Saint Arnual (1270–1330) and Ludwigskirche (1762–75). The city's name is derived from the bridge built over the Saar River by the Romans.

The counts of Nassau-Saarbrücken ruled the town from 1381 until 1793, when it was seized by France. In 1815 it was ceded to Prussia. After World War I, Saarbrücken and the Saar territory were placed under League of Nations administration. The Saar and its capital were reunited with Germany in 1935 as a result of a plebiscite. Saarbrücken was heavily bombed in World War II but has been rebuilt.

Saarinen, Eero [sah'-rin-en, ay'-roh]   Eero Saarinen, b. Kirkkunummi, Finland, Aug. 20, 1910, d. Sept. 1, 1961, was one of the most inventive designers in the United States after World War II. He was the son of the Finnish architect Eliel Saarinen. As an innovative form maker, Eero Saarinen can best be understood in four major projects. His huge General Motors Technical Center (1945–56) in Warren, Mich., was, in technological terms, an impressive and elegant elaboration of the INTERNATIONAL STYLE in architecture.

His Jefferson National Expansion Memorial (completed 1964), better known as the St. Louis Arch, is 192 m (630 ft) high and has an equal span; it is in the form of an inverted catenary curve of stainless steel. This soaring gateway to the West, a commission Saarinen won in a national competition in 1948, is the largest national monu-

Eero Saarinen's avian design for the Trans World Airlines terminal (1956–62) at Kennedy International Airport, New York City, is a magnificent example of the sculptural possibilities of formed concrete.

ment created in the United States since the completion of Robert Mills's Washington Monument (1884).

Saarinen's Trans World Airlines terminal (completed 1962) is in part a symbolic statement and in part a technological achievement. The symbolism is obvious—the spirit of flight. The technological effort was to explore the potentials of concrete shell construction. Although the terminal turned out to be more image than structural substance, it did much to encourage the use of concrete shell construction in contemporary American architecture.

Finally, Saarinen's Columbia Broadcasting Company Headquarters (1960–64) in New York City was clearly a challenge to Mies van der Rohe's SEAGRAM BUILDING (completed 1958). The chaste 38-story tower, clad in dark granite, was his only high-rise building and represents an effort to create one that would age well in an urban setting. Better than most architects, Saarinen understood the directions of 20th-century building. He was a pragmatist who varied his style according to the demands of his task. No other architect of Saarinen's generation left so large and varied a legacy.

--

Saarinen, Eliel [el'-ee-el]   Eliel Saarinen, b. Aug. 20, 1873, d. July 1, 1950, was a Finnish architect notable for his early modern achievements both in his native land and in the United States. A leader of the national romantic architectural movement in Finland, Saarinen gained wide attention with the Finnish Pavilion at the Paris Exposition Universelle of 1900.

His major American works, in addition to the elegant school complex for the Cranbrook Acadamy (1925–43), include Kleinhans Music Hall (1938–40) in Buffalo, the Tanglewood Music Shed in Lenox, Mass., and a series of churches in the modern style, culminating in Christ Lutheran Church (1949–50) in Minneapolis, Minn. In 1947 he formed a partnership with his architect son, Eero. They began studies in 1945 for the General Motors Technical Center, which Eero completed in 1956 after Eliel's death.

--

Saarland [zahr'-lahnt]   Saarland, also the Saar, is a state in Germany, bordering Luxembourg on the west and France on the south. It has a population of 1,058,800

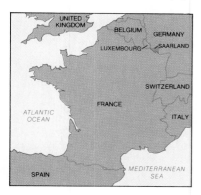

The shaded portion of the map indicates the location of the Saar, an industrial area in southwestern Germany.

(1989 est.) and an area of 2,570 km² (992 mi²). Industrial activity and employment are concentrated in coal mining, iron and steel milling, and the manufacture of machinery. Saarbrücken, Saarlouis, Völklingen, Neunkirchen, and Dillingen are important industrial centers. Forests and farms cover more than three-quarters of the Saar's area but are not of major economic importance.

Saarland was not governed as a separate political unit until 1919, when the League of Nations assumed responsibility for administering it. It was returned to Germany as the result of a 1935 plebiscite. Saarland was occupied by the French after World War II, but its population expressed a desire for reunification with Germany. It became a West German state in 1957.

--

Sabah [sah'-bah]   Sabah (formerly British North Borneo), a state of Malaysia, lies on the northern tip of the mountainous island of BORNEO. Its area is 73,709 km² (28,459 mi²), and Sabah has a population of 1,176,400 (1984 est.); the capital is Kota Kinabalu (1980 pop., 59,500). An irregular coastline faces the South China, Sulu, and Celebes seas. Rice, tobacco, and coconuts are grown, and the forests yield rubber, timber, and spices. Sabah also has oil and natural gas deposits. Settled by Malays in the 14th century, Sabah was administered by the British from the late 1870s until it joined Malaysia in 1963.

--

Sábato, Ernesto [sah'-bah-toh]   Argentinian writer and social critic Ernesto Sábato, b. June 24, 1911, achieved wide recognition with his first novel, *The Outsider* (1948; Eng. trans., 1950), which deals with alienation in the modern world. *Concerning Heroes and Tombs* (1961; Eng. trans., 1981) develops this theme into a panoramic picture of Argentina. His other works include several essay collections. In 1985, Sábato received the Miguel de Cervantes Prize, the highest literary award in the Spanish-speaking world. An outspoken critic of human-rights abuses by Argentina's military, Sábato was named (1983) head of the commission that investigated the disappearance of thousands of Argentinians during the so-called "dirty war" (1976–83).

--

Sabbatai Zevi [sah-bah-ty' zay'-vee]   Sabbatai Zevi, b. Smyrna (now Izmir, Turkey), July 23, 1626, d. 1676, founded the Sabbatian sect. He was the most widely accepted Jewish claimant to messianic status in the modern period. His birthday (9th *Ab*) was the day specified in Jewish tradition for the Messiah's birth. An ascetic who studied the Talmud and Kabbalah, he hinted, from the time he was 22, that he was the chosen one, and he delivered mystical discourses containing his "revelations." Following tradition he violated Jewish law and was expelled from several Jewish communities. In 1665 he acquired a "prophet"—Nathan of Gaza—and the following year he proclaimed his messianic role publicly at the synagogue in Smyrna, creating a hysteria of expectation.

In 1666, Sabbatai went to Constantinople to demand his kingdom from the Ottoman sultan and was imprisoned in Abydos. Given the alternatives of execution or conversion to Islam, Sabbatai accepted conversion, producing shock waves throughout the Jewish world and shame among his followers. Neither his conversion nor his death ten years later destroyed the movement based upon acceptance of Sabbatai as the Messiah. Scattered groups of Sabbatians existed into the mid-20th century.

Sabbath   The seventh day of the Jewish week—from sundown Friday to sundown Saturday—the Sabbath commemorates the seventh day of creation, on which God rested. It is a divinely appointed day of rest (Exod. 20:8), to be devoted to prayer and study, and its observance is a mark of Jewish faith.

Christians have generally considered the Sabbath to be fulfilled by Christ's Sabbath rest in the tomb and celebrate, instead, the Lord's Day (Sunday) as a weekly day of worship. Some Protestant groups have traditionally called Sunday the Sabbath and apply to it the Old Testament Sabbath regulations (Sabbatarianism). In many places these have been given the force of civil law (BLUE LAWS).

Sabellianism   Sabellianism was a Christian heresy named after Sabellius, a priest excommunicated by Pope Callistus I in 220. Denying the Christian doctrine of the TRINITY, Sabellius contended that God is three only in relation to the world, in so many "manifestations" or "modes." The unity and identity of God are such that the Son of God did not exist before the incarnation; because the Father and the Son are thus one, the Father suffered with the Son in his passion and death (a view called *Patripassionism*). The heresy was condemned by a synod of Rome in 262.

saber-toothed cats   Saber-toothed cats were present early in the evolutionary history of the cat family, Felidae. *Hoplophoneus*, a cat that appeared in North America in the early Oligocene Epoch, about 38 million years ago, showed the characteristics of the true sabertooth. It had large upper canines (the "saber teeth") and a downward extension, or flange, formed by the front of the lower jawbone. The flange served as a guard for the down-pointing canines, which rested just outside the flange when the mouth was closed; the lower jaw could be opened extremely wide to free the canines for use.

The sabertooth line of evolution culminated about 2.5 million years ago in the appearance of *Smilodon* and *Megantereon*. *Smilodon*, the larger, was as big as or bigger than the modern African lion and had upper canines that sometimes attained 20 cm (8 in) in length. Because these large sabertooths were prevented from biting like a modern cat, they are believed to have used the large canines for stabbing and bleeding heir victims. Their necks and the front of the body were heavily muscled to provide the power. *S. californicus* (perhaps actually *S. floridanus*), popularly known as the saber-toothed tiger, became extinct about 10,000 years ago.

Saber-toothed tigers, distinguished by their 20-cm-long (8-in) canine teeth, were effective predators of such mammals as the mastodon and giant sloth. The saber-tooths became extinct about 10,000 years ago.

Sabin, Albert Bruce   [say'-bin]   Albert Bruce Sabin, b. Aug. 26, 1906, a Polish-American microbiologist, developed an oral vaccine against POLIOMYELITIS. The live-virus vaccine quickly became the most widely used polio vaccine in the United States after mass field tests in 1957. It largely replaced the earlier-developed inactivated-virus vaccine developed by Jonas SALK.

Sabines   The Sabines, an ancient Oscan-speaking people of central Italy, lived in the Sabine hills northeast of Rome. The legend of the rape (abduction) of the Sabine women—ostensibly to provide wives for the followers of ROMULUS—may have developed to explain Rome's Sabine population. By 290 BC, after several wars, Sabines were granted Roman citizenship. Many Roman religious practices are probably Sabine in origin.

sable   The sable, *Martes zibellina*, is a small animal whose thick, silky fur is highly valued. Classified in the weasel family, Mustelidae, it is a close relative of the marten of North America. The sable is 38 to 50 cm (15 to 20 in) long, with a tail up to 17.8 cm (7 in). It weighs 1.4 to 1.8 kg (3 to 4 lb). The lustrous coat is brown to very dark brown; the most valuable coats have silver tips. Sables live in forests and eat small animals and eggs. Overhunting brought them close to extinction in the early 20th

The sable is a forest-dwelling weasel once native to northern Europe but now found only in Soviet Asia. Sable pelts were a valuable trading commodity as early as the 3d century BC.

century, but through strict control measures the Soviet Union ended this threat.

Sable, Cape (Florida)   Cape Sable, a swampy peninsula in Florida, is the southernmost tip of the U.S. mainland. About 30 km (20 mi) long and 8–16 km (5–10 mi) wide, it is a part of EVERGLADES National Park. It encloses Whitewater Bay on the north and is surrounded by Florida Bay to the south.

Sable Island   Sable Island, a slowly sinking sandbar almost 300 km (185 mi) southeast of Halifax, Nova Scotia, has appeared on maps since 1544. It is 32 km (20 mi) long and 1.6 km (1 mi) wide. A cause of shipwrecks because of a large surrounding shoal, it is called the graveyard of the Atlantic. In 1873, Canada built two lighthouses and a rescue station there.

sabotage   Sabotage is a form of labor action consisting of interference with the operation of a business by the intentional damaging of property or by a slowdown of work. It has also come to mean the deliberate destruction of property during wartime by foreign agents or native sympathizers. In the late 19th century the European labor movement known as SYNDICALISM made extensive use of sabotage. In the United States the INDUSTRIAL WORKERS OF THE WORLD (IWW) advocated sabotage, but officially repudiated it after U.S. entry into World War I.

SAC   see STRATEGIC AIR COMMAND

Sac   see SAUK

Sacagawea [sak-uh-juh-wee'-uh]   Sacagawea, b. c.1788, d. Apr. 9, 1884, also known as Bird Woman, was a Shoshoni Indian who accompanied (1804–05) the LEWIS AND CLARK EXPEDITION in the Pacific Northwest, rendering invaluable assistance as an interpreter and guide. She had previously been held captive among the Hidatsa

in North Dakota and was anxious to rejoin her people. The presence in the party of Sacagawea and her baby doubtless spared the expedition hostilities with other Indians, because the woman and child would not have been with a war party. Sacagawea guided the expedition on its return journey and remained with the Wind River Shoshoni tribe in Wyoming.

saccharin   see SWEETENER, ARTIFICIAL

Sacco and Vanzetti case [sak'-oh, van-zet'-ee] Nicola Sacco, b. Apr. 22, 1891, d. Aug. 23, 1927, and Bartolomeo Vanzetti, b. June 11, 1888, d. Aug. 23, 1927, were the central figures in a murder case that was one of the most controversial in U.S. history because of its political overtones. Italian-born anarchists (Sacco was a shoemaker, Vanzetti a fish peddler), the two men were accused of murdering the paymaster and guard of a shoe factory in South Braintree, Mass., on Apr. 15, 1920, and then escaping with the payroll of nearly $16,000. They were found guilty by a jury on July 14, 1921, and, after six years of motions and appeals, were electrocuted in Massachusetts.

The case aroused the indignation of many who believed the defendants had been accused by tragic accident and convicted because of their radical political beliefs. The prosecution had relied on ballistics testimony and on conflicting testimony by the accused. In 1926 the defense attempted to reopen the case after a condemned criminal had testified that the murders had been committed by a group known as the Morelli gang. The judge, Webster Thayer, refused to call for a new trial. After hearings before an independent investigative committee, Gov. Alvan T. Fuller of Massachusetts denied clemency. Each defendant maintained his innocence to the end.

Among the artistic responses to the Sacco-Vanzetti case are Upton Sinclair's novel *Boston* (1928), Maxwell Anderson's play *Winterset* (1935), and a series of paintings by Ben SHAHN. In 1977, Massachusetts governor Michael Dukakis declared that "any disgrace should be forever removed from their names."

Sachs, Hans   Hans Sachs, b. Nov. 5, 1494, d. Jan. 19, 1576, most widely known through Richard Wagner's idealization of him in the opera *Die Meistersinger von Nürnberg* (1868), was a prolific dramatist and MEISTERSINGER. After his apprenticeship as a shoemaker he settled in his hometown, Nuremberg, where he stayed for the rest of his life. Because of his support of Martin Luther, he temporarily lost favor with the authorities, but for most of his career he was an extremely popular writer.

By his own count, Sachs wrote more than 4,275 Meisterlieder, 1,700 tales and fables in verse, and 208 dramas. Many of his melodies for the poems survive. His topics, whether classical, biblical, or medieval, always express humanistic tenets and principles.

Sachs, Nelly [saks] The poetic voice of Leonie Nelly Sachs, b. Dec. 10, 1891, d. May 12, 1970, developed when the rise of Nazism and the Holocaust forced her to find a way to "make the unspeakable bearable." In 1940 she escaped to Sweden from her native Germany with the help of the writer Selma Lagerlöf. Awarded the Peace Prize of German Publishers in 1965, she accepted it in the spirit of loving forgiveness that underlies her poetry. In 1966, Sachs shared the Nobel Prize for literature with Shmuel Yosef Agnon. The basic theme of her unrhymed poetry is the annihilation of European Jewry during World War II. Her often quoted poem "O the Chimneys," in which the smoke from the chimneys of Nazi extermination camps symbolizes Israel's body, provided the title for the first selection of her poems in English (1967).

sackbut The TROMBONE developed during the 14th century was called the sackbut. Smaller in the bore and bell than the modern trombone, the instrument had a softer tone and a gentle quality that made it compatible with stringed instruments and voices, and it was widely used in church. The only brass instrument capable of playing a complete chromatic scale, the sackbut was thus more flexible as a melody instrument than the other brasses.

Sackville-West, Victoria Although she was a poet, novelist, and biographer, Victoria Mary Sackville-West, b. Mar. 9, 1892, d. June 2, 1962, who wrote under the name "Vita," is best known as the model for the title character in Virginia Woolf's *Orlando*. She was married to Harold Nicolson, a diplomat and author, and both were members of the BLOOMSBURY GROUP. Her poetry won prizes in 1926 and 1946 but is now less highly regarded than her novels, of which the best known are *The Edwardians* (1930) and *All Passion Spent* (1931). Her biographical works include *Pepita*, a fictional portrait of her grandmother, a Spanish dancer and wife of the 2d Baron Sackville, and biographies of the 17th-century dramatist Aphra Behn (1927) and Saint Joan of Arc (1936).

sacrament Sacraments are Christian rites that are believed to be outward visible signs of inward spiritual grace to which the promise of Christ is attached. The Roman Catholic and Eastern Orthodox churches accept seven sacraments: BAPTISM, the EUCHARIST, CONFIRMATION (or Chrismation), CONFESSION, ANOINTING OF THE SICK, marriage, and HOLY ORDERS. The Council of Trent (1545–63) declared that all were instituted by Christ. Protestants accept only baptism and the Eucharist as instituted by Christ. The Anglican (Episcopal) church, however, accepts the other five as sacramental rites that evolved in the church.

Christians have differed widely as to the meaning of the sacraments. Catholics, and many Protestants, consider them means of grace through which God bestows

spiritual gifts. This view was held by Martin Luther and John Calvin.

Other Protestants, following Ulrich Zwingli, view the sacraments as signs of Christian profession and testimony to grace that has already been given through faith. Some Protestant groups, notably the Quakers and the Salvation Army, do not use sacraments.

Sacramento Sacramento, the capital of California and seat of Sacramento County, is situated in the north central part of the state, about 145 km (90 mi) northeast of San Francisco at the junction of the Sacramento and American rivers. The city's population is 369,365 (1990), and that of the metropolitan area is 1,481,102. The state government and nearby military installations are major employers. Sacramento's harbor is connected by a deepwater ship channel to San Francisco Bay. The city's principal industrial products are military and aerospace-electronics equipment, bricks, chemicals, and lumber. Sacramento's food-processing and packaging industry is dependent on fruits, vegetables, and grains grown in the surrounding Sacramento Central Valley. Sacramento is the site of several colleges, including the California State University at Sacramento (1947). The Crocker Art Gallery, the state capitol (1861–74), and Fort Sutter are points of interest.

In 1839, John Augustus Sutter founded a colony on the site and soon built Fort Sutter, a trading post. After gold was discovered at Sutter's Mill in nearby Coloma (1848), Sacramento grew and prospered in the California gold rush. It became the state capital in 1854. Its growth was assured when it was chosen as the terminus of both the pony express and California's first railroad, the Sacramento Valley.

Sacramento River The Sacramento River, almost 640 km (400 mi) long, rises near Mount Shasta in northern California and flows south to Sacramento, where it bends southwest and forms a delta with the SAN JOAQUIN RIVER before emptying into San Francisco Bay. The river drains an area of $70,190$ km^2 ($27,100$ mi^2). At Redding, about 80 km (50 mi) south of the river's source, it forms Shasta Lake behind the immense Shasta Dam, completed in 1945 as part of the Central Valley Project. Easily navigable to Sacramento, the Sacramento River was an important waterway during the California gold rush in 1849.

sacrifice Sacrifice is a ritual act in which an offering is made to the object of worship or religious veneration. The offering may be in plant, animal, or even human form. Found in the religions of many cultures, past and present, sacrifice is a practice intended to honor or appease a deity and to make holy the offering.

In pre-Columbian America thousands of human victims (many of them war captives) were offered annually in accordance with the complex AZTEC ritual calendar; human sacrifice also occurred on a lesser scale among the MAYA and various Andean and North American Indian groups. Among cultures of Africa, the Far East, Southeast Asia, and Oceania, sacrifice is commonly offered in connection with ANCESTOR WORSHIP. Human sacrifice was formerly practiced by certain groups in all of these areas. The ancient Vedic tradition of India has a highly developed ritual of sacrifice (see HINDUISM).

In the Old Testament of the Bible the first mention of sacrifice is God's rejection of Cain's offering and his acceptance of Abel's (Gen. 4:2–5). The principal sacrifices of ancient Hebrew worship were the Paschal Lamb and the scapegoat. For Christians all sacrifice is fulfilled in the once-for-all self-offering of Jesus (Heb. 9–10). Postbiblical writers call the Christian EUCHARIST a sacrifice.

Sacsahuaman [sahk-sah-wah-mahn'] The fortress of Sacsahuaman was built by the INCA in the 15th century on a hill northwest of their capital at CUZCO, in Peru. The fortress takes the form of a series of zigzag retaining walls built of huge stones, some weighing several tons. Such fortresses, called *pucaras*, were frequently built above population centers in the Andes to serve as refuges for the populace in case of attack. Spanish sources suggest that Sacsahuaman was also used as an important storage center, and the site may have had religious significance as well.

Sadat, Anwar al- [sah-daht', ahn-wahr' ahl] Muhammad Anwar al-Sadat, b. Dec. 25, 1918, d. Oct. 6, 1981, became president of Egypt in 1970. A graduate (1938) of the Royal Military Academy in Cairo, he joined a dissident officers' group committed to freeing Egypt from British control. Sadat became a close associate of Gamal Abdel NASSER, and after the revolution of 1952 he rose to become vice-president (1964–66; 1969–70) of the republic.

In 1972, after succeeding to the presidency on Nasser's death, Sadat asserted Egyptian independence of Soviet influence by expelling about 20,000 Soviet advisors

Anwar al-Sadat, president of Egypt from 1970 until his assassination in 1981, concluded (1979) a historic peace treaty with Israel. For this achievement he and Israeli prime minister Menachem Begin were awarded the 1978 Nobel Peace Prize.

and military personnel. The following year he launched a war against Israel (see ARAB-ISRAELI WARS) that was hailed as a victory in Egypt. Its cost, however, apparently convinced Sadat that Egypt must end its prolonged struggle against Israel. In 1977 he made the dramatic gesture of flying to Jerusalem to initiate negotiations; these culminated (Mar. 26, 1979) in a historic Egyptian-Israeli peace treaty. The rapprochement with Israel and Sadat's pro-Western policies isolated Egypt in the Arab world, however, and generated some opposition at home, primarily by Islamic fundamentalists. In October 1981, Sadat was assassinated by several gunmen associated with a militant Muslim fundamentalist group.

---

saddle A saddle is a concave seat for riding that is placed on the back of a horse or other suitable animal. It is generally made of leather and fitted with girths, which strap it to the animal, and stirrups for the rider's feet.

The saddle is believed to have been developed around 700 BC by the Scyths, nomads of the Eurasian Steppe, but the earliest actual evidence of a rigid saddle comes from the Han dynasty in China, c.206 BC–AD 220. These

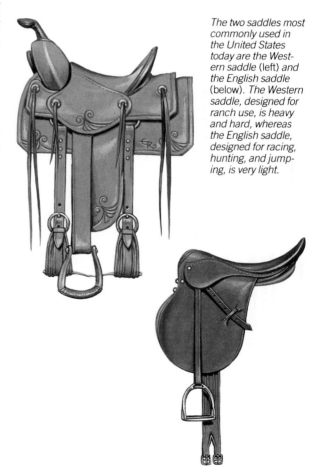

The two saddles most commonly used in the United States today are the Western saddle (left) and the English saddle (below). The Western saddle, designed for ranch use, is heavy and hard, whereas the English saddle, designed for racing, hunting, and jumping, is very light.

early saddles lacked stirrups; crude stirrups that fitted to the big toe appeared in India late in the 2d century BC, and the full-foot stirrup is found first on Chinese saddles of the 5th century AD. With stirrups a rider could be completely braced by the feet, thereby freeing the arms for the use of weapons and enabling the power of a thrown spear to be enormously increased.

During the Middle Ages saddles were developed into large, buttressed seats that were used to buffer the shocks of combat and jousts. Thereafter, their progressively lighter construction and materials culminated in the English saddle. The Western saddle, developed from a type used in 15th-century Spain, has a deep seat, double girths for keeping the saddle on the horse while the rider ropes cattle, and a pommel, or horn, used to anchor a lasso.

See also: RIDING.

saddle horse   see RIDING

Sadducees [sad'-ue-seez] The Sadducees were a Jewish religious sect that flourished from about 200 BC until the fall of Jerusalem in AD 70. A priestly and aristocratic group, the Sadducees owed their power to political alliance with the Romans, who ruled their land. They opposed the PHARISEES' use of Oral Law and held only to the Pentateuch (the first five books of the Old Testament). They also differed with the Pharisees on many theological tenets: for example, they did not believe in resurrection and the immortality of the soul. According to the New Testament, the Sadducees played a leading role in the trial and condemnation of Jesus.

Sade, Marquis de [sahd] On the basis of his novel *Justine; or, The Misfortunes of Virtue* (1791; Eng. trans., 1966), the French writer Count Donatien Alphonse François de Sade, better known simply as the Marquis de Sade, b. Paris, June 2, 1740, d. Dec. 2, 1814, lent his name to the psychopathic behavior called SADISM. His notoriety dates from 1768, when he was imprisoned for maltreating a prostitute. In 1772 he was sentenced to death at Aix-en-Provence, and although he was granted a reprieve, his life became a series of incarcerations and escapes. He spent more than 27 years in prison and died in the lunatic asylum of Charenton.

Justine is informed by the confessional and picaresque narrative techniques developed during the 18th century. Justine's adventures also reflect a growing taste for Gothic romance. She is the victim of a variety of cruelties—moral, sexual, and physical. Her sister gives her name to a complementary novel, *Juliette* (1797; Eng. trans., 1968), in which the "prosperities of vice" are demonstrated. In the 19th century Sade was discovered by such writers as Charles Baudelaire and Algernon Charles Swinburne, who found in him a testing of experience and imagination.

Sadi, Sheykh Moslehoddin [sah'-dee] The prose and poetry of the Persian poet Sheykh Moslehoddin Sadi (*c.*1200–1292) are considered classics of Persian literature. Sadi studied in Baghdad and traveled in Anatolia and India before returning to his birthplace, Shiraz, where he spent the rest of his life. His earliest work, the *Bustan* (1257; trans. as *The Orchard*, 1882), is a didactic epic that contains ethical maxims and transcendental speculation. The *Gulistan* (1258; trans. as *The Rose Garden*, 1964), a collection of ethical and humorous anecdotes in elegant prose, interspersed with verse, is so accessible to Western literary taste that it has been repeatedly translated since 1787.

sadism Sadism is a pathological sexual variance in which sexual pleasure or gratification is gained by inflicting psychological or physical pain on the victim. Psychological pain may be imposed verbally in the form of excessive bullying and teasing or belittling and sarcastic remarks. Physical pain is typically inflicted by the sadist in acts of biting, slapping, pinching, burning, and whipping. Sadism derives its name from the Marquis de SADE. It is the direct opposite of MASOCHISM.

The causes of sadism are varied, but it is definitely an aggressive activity. The sadist may act aggressively because of an inability to cope with feelings of disgust or shame he or she may associate with sex. Feelings of inferiority may lead the sadist to seek out a sense of power over a sexual partner. Repressed hostility toward parental figures or others in authority may underlie the sadist's aggressive tendencies.

Social stereotypes may also play a role. Aggressiveness is highly valued by many in modern society; a dominant-submissive relationship is still the prevalent popular image of the male-female relationship; and the mass media frequently combine violence and sex for profit.

Whatever the cause, sadism is usually considered to be abnormal behavior even if it is engaged in by consenting adults. Nevertheless, one investigation found that 5% of males and 2% of females had at some time received sexual enjoyment through sadistic acts.

Safavids The Safavids, originally an order of Islamic mystics (see SUFISM), became a ruling dynasty that dominated Iran in the 16th and 17th centuries. Named for their ancestor Safi al-Din (1252–1332), the Safavids rose to spiritual leadership among the nomadic Turkish tribes of eastern Anatolia and established themselves in northwestern Iran. Their nomadic followers were known as *Kizilbash*. Originally Sunnites, they later adopted Shiite Islam, which they made the state religion of Iran. Shah Ismail I (r. 1502–24), founder of the Safavid dynasty, used the military power of the *Kizilbash* tribes to unite most of Iran under his rule in the first decade of the 16th century. The Safavids were rivals of the Ottoman Turks, who defeated them at the Battle of Chaldiran in 1514.

After the reign (1588–1629) of ABBAS I, the dynasty declined, finally coming to an end in 1736.

Safdie, Moshe [sahf'-dee] The Israeli architect Moshe Safdie, b. Haifa, July 14, 1938, established his reputation by developing prefabricated housing units that may be set into frames to create multiple dwellings. His first famous work is Habitat (1967) in Montreal, a pueblolike assemblage of 354 precast concrete dwelling boxes. After working on major commissions in Israel and the United States, Safdie designed the new National Gallery (1988) in Ottawa, with its tentlike pavilions of glass.

safe A safe is a strong container designed to protect valuable items, such as money, jewelry, or documents, from theft and fire. Modern safes vary in size from the small safe hidden inside the wall of a home to large bank vaults where an entire room may be constructed of protective materials.

Safe-construction materials have changed as the technology for penetrating metals has grown more sophisticated. Drill-proof steel alloys are used today. Some alloys, however, are vulnerable to the very high temperatures produced by some BLOWTORCHES, and safe walls may therefore be constructed of several layers of alloy with fireproofed materials sandwiched between. Heat-dissipating copper may also be layered between the steel sheets.

Bank vaults are rooms designed to be impenetrable from any direction. In a large vault, floors, walls, and ceilings are made of such materials as reinforced concrete surrounding layers of steel alloy and copper. Vault doors can reach thicknesses of up to 0.3 m (1 ft) or more.

A safe lock is almost always of the combination type, and it may include a system of interior bolts that are actuated by the lock. Some safes, and most bank vaults, have time locks that can be preset to open only after a certain number of hours have passed from the time the safe was closed. Such locks are equipped with two, three, or four clock movements, any of which will activate the lock should others fail. The safe or vault walls, and sometimes the locks themselves, may be equipped with sensing devices that will trip an alarm if heat or the shock of a forced entry is detected.

safety, automotive Automotive safety is concerned with reducing the number of traffic accidents and lessening the severity of injuries when accidents do occur. Areas of safety activity include the design of ROADS AND HIGHWAYS, adjustments in laws pertaining to traffic and vehicles, systems of TRAFFIC CONTROL, programs of driver education, and—the subject discussed below—vehicle design.

Vehicle design has gradually made for greater automotive safety; the accident rate has increased, however, because of higher speeds and heavier traffic. The U.S. Congress passed (1966) a law that permitted the federal

Safety devices can prevent death or severe injury in a head-on collision. The car on the left has a rigid passenger compartment (1), seat belts (2), and headrests (3). Its engine is designed to deflect downward, collapsing the steering column (4) and avoiding the driver. The car's front end (5) absorbs the energy of impact. Injuries sustained by the passengers in the unprotected car are indicated by red dots.

government to issue mandatory safety standards for cars, trucks, motorcycles, and other vehicles. Since that time, more than 50 safety standards have been imposed, regulating such items as safety windshields, brakes, tires, and seat belts.

A seat belt is a strap—usually a shoulder harness—that restrains an occupant in the seat, preventing him or her from being thrown out of the seat during a sudden stop or change in direction. Even though convincing evidence exists as to the value of seat belts, and legislation has been passed that requires their use in all cars, the response of drivers to these devices, which require their active participation, has been poor. Therefore, safety researchers have developed automatic, or passive, restraint systems, which protect occupants without any action on their part. Two basic types of passive restraints have been produced. One, the automatic belt, fastens around the occupant when the car door is closed. The second, the air bag, is mounted in either the steering column or the dashboard. In a crash, air bags pop out and instantly inflate, forming cushions that prevent the driver and any other front-seat occupant from striking hard surfaces, such as the dashboard or windshield.

The U.S. Department of Transportation (DOT) proposed in 1977 that all new cars be equipped with automatic restraint systems by model year 1984, although the major emphasis was on air bags rather than automatic seat belts. Automobile manufacturers objected to this proposal, principally because the cost of air bags was high: about $300 to $1,000 per car in 1980, depending on the volume of cars outfitted. New air-bag designs and increased production have reduced that cost considerably, however, and driver's-side air bags have been available on many of the most expensive cars since the mid-1980s. Chrysler Corporation has equipped all of its models with driver's-side air bags since 1990, and other automakers are expected to follow suit.

safflower   A thistlelike annual, safflower, *Carthamus tinctorius*, of the daisy family, Compositae, is cultivated in warmer regions of the world for its flowers, which yield a dye, and for its oil-rich seeds. The plant is raised primarily in India, Egypt, Israel, and Turkey; it is also grown in the United States.

The safflower plant may grow up to 1.2 m (4 ft) high. Its flowers, which range in color from red to yellow or white, are the source of carthamin, a red dye that was once widely used for textiles and as an ingredient in rouge. Oil pressed from safflower seeds retains its transparency, and can be used in paints and soaps. Recently, however, safflower oil—an unsaturated fat—has been used increasingly in margarines and cooking oils for people on low-cholesterol diets.

saffron   Saffron, the common name for *Crocus sativus* of the IRIS family, Iridaceae, is a perennial fall-flowering plant. Its stigmas are a source of a yellow dye and a food flavoring. Native to Anatolia, saffron provided both a perfume and a yellow dye for the ancient world. Used today as a spice, it imparts a slightly bitter flavor and a yellow color to poultry, fish, and rice. Some 225,000 stigmas must be handpicked and dried to make 0.5 kg (1 lb) of saffron, which is probably the most expensive of all spices.

Saffron is a spice derived from stigmas of the crocus flower. Although expensive, saffron has been in demand for centuries as a food seasoning, a medicine, and a source of yellow dye. The saffron crocus blooms during autumn.

saga   The saga—ICELANDIC LITERATURE's most significant contribution to world letters—is a medieval prose narrative about legendary heroes. The greatest of the sagas is SNORRI STURLUSON's *Heimskringla* (c.1220–35;

Eng. trans., 1964), but *Egil's Saga* (c.1220), the story of Iceland's greatest skald, or poet, and his lifelong feud with the Norwegian crown, is similar in style. The more ornate *Laxdœla* (c.1250) elaborates tragic themes from the poems of the EDDA. In *Grettir's Saga* (c.1300), which shares motifs with the Old English poem BEOWULF, the hero succumbs to pagan sorcery. *Njál's Saga* (c.1230–90) both glorifies and repudiates the Saga Age (870–1050), which in this genre is less an account of the past than an idealized re-creation of the Sturlung Age (1100–1280) during which the poem was composed. The most important legendary tale is *Volsunga Saga* (c.1250); a major source for Wagner's *Ring*, this retelling of parts of the *Edda* shares motifs and characters with the NIBELUNGENLIED. The earliest and best of the chivalric sagas is *Tristram's Saga* (1226), a Norwegian prose adaptation of the *Tristan* of Thomas of Brittany.

Sagan, Carl [say'-guhn]   The American scientist Carl Edward Sagan, b. New York City, Nov. 9, 1934, is known primarily for his research on the possibility of extraterrestrial life (see LIFE, EXTRATERRESTRIAL) and as a popularizer of science. A graduate of the University of Chicago (Ph.D., 1960), Sagan taught at Harvard before transferring to Cornell in 1968, where he became a professor of astronomy and director of the Laboratory for Planetary Studies. His research on planetary surfaces and atmospheres includes an early proposal that the greenhouse effect is responsible for the high temperatures on Venus and his work on the Mariner and Viking space missions. Sagan also took part in studies of the potentially catastrophic effects of a nuclear war on global climate, now known as "nuclear winter." He has written both popular fact and fiction, including *The Dragons of Eden* (1977), for which he won the 1978 Pulitzer Prize.

Sagan, Françoise [sah-gahn']   Françoise Sagan is the pseudonym of the French writer Françoise Quoirez, b. June 21, 1935, whose first novel, *Bonjour Tristesse* (Hello Sadness, 1954; Eng. trans., 1955), made her an international celebrity at the age of 19. Her other fiction—including *A Certain Smile* (1956; Eng. trans., 1956), *Aimez-vous Brahms?* (Do You Like Brahms?, 1959; Eng. trans., 1960), *The Unmade Bed* (1977; Eng. trans., 1978), *The Painted Lady* (1981; Eng. trans., 1983), and *The Still Storm* (1986; Eng. trans., 1986)—similarly displays a fascination with romantic triangles, disillusionment, and ennui. Sagan has also written plays, lyrics, screenplays, stories, and a ballet.

sage   see SALVIA

Sage, Russell   The American financier Russell Sage, b. Verona, N.Y., Aug. 4, 1816, d. July 22, 1906, amassed a fortune that was later used by his wife to endow the Sage Foundation as well as Russell Sage College and the Emma Willard School for Girls, both in Troy, N.Y.

Beginning as a trader and wholesale grocer in Troy, Sage served two terms (1853–57) in Congress before moving to New York City in 1863. In association with Jay Gould, Sage made a fortune by investing in railroads.

sagebrush   Sagebrush, the common name for several species of shrubs in the genus *Artemisia*, family Compositae, refers specifically to the common gray green shrub *A. tridentata* of the western U.S. plains. The common name is derived from the odor of the plant's leaves, reminiscent of the herb sage. Sagebrush can grow in poor soil and arid climates, and some species are grown as ornamentals in gardens.

The big sagebrush, a treelike shrub, is common to arid regions of the western United States. Its spreading branches produce ribbonlike leaves and clusters of small berries.

Saginaw   [sag'-i-naw]   Saginaw, a Great Lakes port, lies in eastern Michigan on the Saginaw River about 25 km (16 mi) from Saginaw Bay, an inlet of Lake Huron. The seat of Saginaw County, it has a population of 69,512 (1990). Until the 1890s, Saginaw, surrounded by dense pine forests, was a major lumbering center; automobile manufacturing and metallurgy now dominate the economy. Saginaw is also the market town for surrounding farms. The city has parks and broad, tree-lined streets.

A fur-trading post was built on the site in 1816, and a fort was erected there in 1822. The Chippewa Indians, the original inhabitants of the area, signed a treaty in Saginaw in 1819 ceding their land to the U.S. government.

Sagittarius   [saj-i-tair'-ee-uhs]   Sagittarius, the Archer, is a zodiacal constellation that marks the direction in which the center of our galaxy lies. It is located in the brightest and most thickly populated region of stars, dust, and gas in the Milky Way. As seen from mid-northern latitudes, such as that of New York, the constellation appears directly south and low in the sky about the middle of August. Its brightest stars are of only second and third magnitude, but the constellation is notable for the numerous star clouds, nebulas, and open and globular clusters that can be seen within it. The Sagittarius region contains 16 of the famous objects cataloged by Messier as well as one-third of the known globular clusters and includes the position of the Sun at the winter solstice.

sago   [say'-goh]   Sago, a starch prepared from the pith of several species of palm trees belonging to the CYCAD family, is a yellowish flour that is a staple food of the southwest Pacific. In Europe sago is used as a thickener in cooking and as textile sizing in industry. Sago palms are native to Indonesia and constitute one of the most important wild food plants in the swamps of New Guinea and the Solomon Islands. The starch is exported primarily from Borneo. For export, the pith is pulverized, washed, strained, and dried in pans over a fire to produce pellets called pearl sago.

The sago palm is the principal source of sago, a starchy product used as a basic food in Indonesia. The sago palm is harvested before the full ripening of its fruit—when its trunk contains the maximum quantity of sago, which amounts to a few hundred kilograms per tree.

saguaro   SEE CACTI AND OTHER SUCCULENTS

Saguenay River   [sag'-uh-nay]   The Saguenay River is a 170-km-long (105-mi) river in southern Quebec, Canada. It flows from its source, Lake Saint John, eastward past Chicoutimi to its outlet into the St. Lawrence River at Tadoussac, about 195 km (120 mi) northeast of Quebec City. From Chicoutimi, the head of navigation, the river drops 90 m (300 ft) over a distance of 56 km (35 mi) and is a major source of hydroelectric power. The main tributary is the Shipshaw. The lower course, which forms a deep fjord, is a popular tourist area. The

Saguenay was explored by Jacques Cartier in 1535 and Samuel de Champlain in 1603.

Sahara [suh-hair'-uh] The Sahara Desert in northern Africa is the largest desert in the world. It spans the continent from the Atlantic Ocean to the Red Sea and extends northward from the Niger River and Lake Chad to the Atlas Mountains and the Mediterranean Sea. The name *Sahara* is from the Arabic word for "desert" or "steppe." The grasslands of West Africa, which form the southern boundary, are called the SAHEL; this region is indicated by hatching on the map. The Sahara covers about 9,000,000 km² (3,500,000 mi²), and its area is constantly increasing.

Climatic history and fossilized remains reveal that the Sahara has experienced successive wet and dry eras. The latest arid period began about 3000 BC, a result of the southward shifting of the trade-wind belt. Today ten independent states share the Sahara. Morocco, Algeria, Tunisia, Mali, Niger, Chad, and Sudan have large desert regions, and most of Libya, Egypt, and Mauritania are located in the Sahara.

Topography and Geology. The central Saharan uplands are a series of high plains, plateaus, and mountains that extend in a vast semicircle from southern Algeria to northeastern Mali, northern Chad, and western Sudan. The uplands average about 180 to 365 m (600 to 1,200 ft) in elevation. Two mountain chains are located in the central uplands: the Ahaggar Range in Algeria, which rises to 3,003 m (9,852 ft); and the TIBESTI MASSIF in Chad, where the Sahara's highest point, Emi Koussi, reaches 3,415 m (11,204 ft). The Aïr Massif is located to the south in Niger.

The western Sahara is a vast, monotonous plain and plateau region that rises gradually from the Atlantic coast. Sandstone ridges and extensive basins break the monotony of the plains. The sand deserts of El Djouf, the Erg Iguidi, and the Erg Chech are prominent features. Elsewhere large areas are covered by loose sands and gravel. In the northern Sahara, valleys are cut into the plains that extend southward from the ATLAS MOUNTAINS. The great sand deserts of the Great Erg in Algeria and the Fezzan basin in southern Libya are prominent landscape fea-

Sand dunes sculpted by the Sahara's winds can reach heights of 180 m (600 ft). Although the Sahara is an arid region now, as recently as 10,000 years ago it supported a wide variety of flora and fauna, as well as having many lakes, streams, and forests.

tures. The LIBYAN DESERT dominates the northern part of the eastern Sahara. East of the NILE RIVER are the ARABIAN DESERT and the NUBIAN DESERT. The soils of the Sahara are thin but fertile; only 20% of the soil cover is sand.

Climate. Most of the Sahara receives less than 127 mm of rainfall annually, and large areas receive no rain for years at a time. The mean average annual temperature is 27° C (80° F). Evaporation rates are high, creating relative humidities as low as 2.5%, the lowest in the world. Parts of the Sahara experience 50 to 75 days per year of wind and blowing sand that desiccate plant and animal life. Although the climate has remained relatively uniform, since c.3,000 BC extended periods of drought have been common.

Drainage, Vegetation, and Animal Life. The Sahara has an extensive network of dry streambeds, or wadis, formed during earlier wetter periods. Numerous intermittent streams now occupy some of the wadis following precipitation. Underground water resources, or oases, sufficient to support irrigated agriculture are found in many wadis and depressions.

Few areas of the desert are completely void of vegetation. A sparse cover of shrubs adapted to hot, dry climates, extends the northern edge of the desert; coarse grasses grow in depressions; and palm trees grow in valleys and oases. Thorn woodlands and wooded grasslands are found in the Sahel. Some animal life exists even in the desert's interior: insects, small rodents, reptiles, and gazelles on the plateaus.

People and Economy. The majority of the estimated 2 million people who live in the Sahara live along the margins of the desert, at the oases, and in the less arid, more

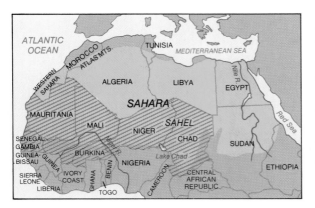

isolated highlands. The overall population density is only about 0.2 persons per km^2 (0.6 per mi^2). Most inhabitants are Arabic-speaking Muslims. The principal socioeconomic distinction is between the sedentary population concentrated in the oases and the pastoral NOMADS whose flocks are moved seasonally among traditional pastures.

The Sahara is rich in mineral resources. It has substantial proved crude petroleum reserves. Libya and Algeria are the largest oil producers, and Algeria is also a major producer and exporter of natural gas. Algeria, Mauritania, and Libya possess Saharan iron-ore deposits; Algeria has manganese; and Mauritania has rich deposits of copper. Morocco is a leading exporter of phosphate. Numerous metals are found in the central Saharan uplands, and uranium is mined in northern Niger.

The traditional camel caravans have today been replaced by truck convoys over the same routes. The Saharan road system is steadily expanding, although only two main routes cross the desert from north to south.

History. Archaeological evidence exists of extensive settlement in the Sahara during the Paleolithic and Neolithic periods. The Romans established colonies in Libya and Tunisia along the Mediterranean coast and reached their period of greatest expansion during the 2d century AD. By AD 750, Arabic-speaking people spread Islam into the northern Sahara, and Berber kingdoms ruled the western Sahara from Senegal to Morocco.

By the end of the 12th century AD, Islam had spread throughout most of the Sahara. Subsequently, the rich and powerful medieval kingdoms of KANEM-BORNU, SONGHAI, Ghana, and Mali controlled the central and southern Sahara. The French were able to extend their control in Algeria to the edge of the desert by 1850; after that time the Sahara was divided among the colonies and protectorates of France, Great Britain, Italy, and Spain. The period of European control finally ended in 1976, when the Spanish relinquished their claim to WESTERN SAHARA.

Saharan languages see AFRICAN LANGUAGES

Sahel [sah-hel'] The Sahel is a semiarid geographical area in Western Africa that separates the SAHARA desert in the north and southern tropical West Africa. The Sahel extends from the Atlantic Ocean east through northern Senegal, southern Mauritania (along the NIGER RIVER), Burkina Faso, southern Niger, northeastern Nigeria, and south central Chad.

The Sahel has a limited agricultural capacity due to its 8-month dry season. Yearly precipitation totals 100–600 mm (4–24 in); hot season temperatures reach maximums of much more than 38° C (100° F). FULANI and TUAREG nomads inhabit the north. Groundnuts and millet are the primary crops.

The Sahel has known periods of devastating drought in 1912–15, 1941–42, 1968–74, and again in the 1980s. Some experts believe that the area is experiencing a long-term decline in rainfall, and that the process of desertification may render much of the Sahel uninhabitable before the end of the century.

Saigo Takamori [sy'-goh tah-kah'-moh-ree] Saigo Takamori, b. Jan. 23, 1828, d. Sept. 24, 1877, one of Japan's greatest military leaders, helped unseat the shogunate of the Tokugawa family in January 1868, thereby returning power to the Meiji emperor (see MEIJI RESTORATION). He became a national hero. Saigo reluctantly agreed to serve (1871) as commander of the imperial guard and became general in 1872, but in 1873 he again retreated to his province and opened a popular school for samurai students. His followers attacked government troops in January 1877, and Saigo was reluctantly drawn into the full-scale war that followed (the Satsuma rebellion). When the imperial army defeated the insurgents, Saigo committed ritual suicide. Instead of being condemned as a traitor, Saigo became a hero to supporters of the monarchy.

Saigon see HO CHI MINH CITY

Sailer, Toni Anton Sailer, b. Nov. 17, 1935, was an Austrian skier. At the age of 17, he won the Grand Prix du Mégève in France, taking the downhill and combined-events titles. An injury prevented him from competing for 2 years, but he returned to skiing in 1955 and won a number of European championships. In the 1956 Olympics, Sailer won the downhill, slalom, and giant slalom, becoming the first skier to win 3 gold medals in a single Winter Olympics. Sailer eventually turned professional and later coached the Austrian national ski team.

sailfish Sailfishes, genus *Istiophorus*, are widely regarded as the most beautiful of the big game fishes. The dorsal fin forms a high sail, colored deep blue with darker blue spots, and folds into a groove in the back. The body is metallic blue above and silvery below. When hooked, sailfishes make spectacular leaps. Related to the MARLINS, sailfishes have an elongated slender "spear" derived from the upper jaw, which is apparently used to kill small fish as the sailfish thrashes through their schools. Sailfishes may reach a weight of 45 kg (100 lb) and a length of 2.4

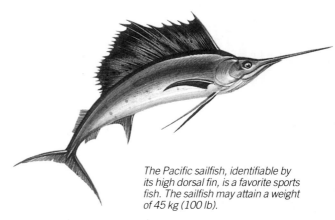

The Pacific sailfish, identifiable by its high dorsal fin, is a favorite sports fish. The sailfish may attain a weight of 45 kg (100 lb).

m (8 ft). They occur in warm, turbulent waters of the Atlantic, Pacific, and Indian oceans.

sails, sailing, and sailing ships   see BOAT AND BOATING; SHIP

---

saint   A saint is a holy person, as the Latin origin of the word indicates (*sanctus,* "holy"). Although the word *saint* is part of the vocabulary of Christianity, the concept of holy persons—those who are unusually empowered by divine forces—is common to many religions.

In the New Testament the word *saint* refers to any baptized follower of Jesus Christ. Later the phrase *communion of saints* was used to designate all members of the CHURCH, living and dead. In a more specific sense, saints are those individuals who have died a heroic death for Christ (martyrs), those who have suffered greatly for the sake of Christ (confessors), or those whose lives have been marked by unusual signs of love of God and neighbor. Cults venerating such individuals arose early in Christian history. The church eventually came to regulate cults by instituting a formal system of CANONIZATION about AD 1000. Most saints have special feast days on which they are commemorated. In Roman Catholic and Eastern Orthodox practice the names of certain saints were incorporated into the canon, or major part, of the Eucharistic liturgy, with the Virgin MARY as principal saint.

Lives of the saints, called HAGIOGRAPHIES, have been written since early times. Many superstitious and legendary elements began to obscure the basic meaning of saints' lives, and at the time of the Reformation devotion to the saints was almost completely eliminated in Protestant churches.

Mormons (see MORMONISM) refer to themselves as Latter-Day (present-day) Saints, using the word in its New Testament sense, to indicate that they are God's chosen people.

Saint Albans   Saint Albans, a market town and London suburb in Hertfordshire in southeastern England, lies about 30 km (20 mi) northwest of London. The population is 125,600 (1982 est.). Industries include printing, which began in the 15th century, and clothing and electronics manufacturing. Of historical interest are Roman ruins, Saint Michael's Church with a memorial to Francis Bacon, and the cathedral built in 1077.

The Roman town Verulamium was established at the site of a preexisting village in the 1st century AD, and, according to tradition, Saint Alban was martyred there about 303. An abbey founded in 793 became the nucleus of the present town. During the Wars of the Roses two decisive battles took place in Saint Albans in 1455 and 1461. The town was the headquarters for the parliamentary army during the English Civil War.

Saint Andrews   Saint Andrews (1981 pop., 11,368) is a town in Fife, Scotland, located about 50 km (30 mi) northeast of Edinburgh on the North Sea coast. Once an important medieval town, ecclesiastical capital of Scotland (since 908), and fishing port, today Saint Andrews is best known as home of the Royal and Ancient Club (1754), the prestigious golfing authority. Ancient buildings include the ruins of Scotland's largest cathedral (1160) and the castle (c.1200). The University of Saint Andrews, the oldest in Scotland, was founded in 1410.

Saint Andrews, University of   Founded in 1410, the University of Saint Andrews is a coeducational institution in Saint Andrews, Scotland, and is Scotland's oldest. It has faculties of arts, sciences, and divinity, all granting undergraduate and graduate degrees. In 1747, Saint Salvator's (1450) and Saint Leonard's (1512) colleges merged, forming the United College. Saint Mary's College (1537) is restricted to theological studies. In 1967, Queen's College, formed by the 1953 merger of University College, Dundee (1881), and its medical school, which were affiliated to Saint Andrews in 1897, became the University of Dundee.

Saint Augustine   [aw'-gus-teen]   Saint Augustine, the oldest city in the United States, is in northeastern Florida, 8 km (5 mi) from the Atlantic Ocean on Matanzas Bay. The seat of Saint John's County, the city has a population of 11,692 (1990). Tourism, commercial fishing, fish processing, and timber are its principal industries. The oldest U.S. fort, Castillo de San Marcos, was begun in 1672. Juan Ponce de León landed there in 1513 in search of the Fountain of Youth and claimed the area for Spain. In 1564 the French established a colony that was destroyed a year later by the Spanish, who then founded (1565) the present city.

Saint Bartholomew's Day Massacre   The Saint Bartholomew's Day Massacre, the mass killing of French Protestants by Catholics, began on Aug. 24, 1572, and is remembered as a crime against humanity. It was preceded (August 22) by the attempted assassination of Admiral Gaspard de Coligny, a prominent Huguenot in Paris. Many other Protestant nobles had come to the capital to attend the wedding of Henry of Navarre (later Henry IV) and Margaret of Valois. CATHERINE DE MÉDICIS, who feared Coligny's plans for war with Spain, was probably implicated in the murder plot, and when an investigation threatened to expose her role in the scheme she persuaded her son, Charles IX, to order the death of the Huguenot leaders in anticipation of a supposed Protestant plot. The killing began in Paris and was extended to the provinces, continuing until October. There were approximately 13,000 victims.

See also: RELIGION, WARS OF.

Saint Bernard   The Saint Bernard is a breed of dog famed as a rescuer of snowbound travelers in the Swiss

The Saint Bernard is a large working dog developed in the Swiss Alps. Originally a watchdog bred by the monks of an alpine hospice, it was also used as a guide and to search for travelers stranded by storms.

Alps. Its name is derived from the Swiss monastery the Hospice of Saint Bernard, whose monks developed the breed sometime between 1660 and 1670. Many suggestions have been offered regarding the ancestry and antiquity of the Saint Bernard, among them that the breed traces back to the Tibetan mastiff or that it is descended from the Roman mastiff, or molossus.

The Saint Bernard is the heaviest breed recognized by the American Kennel Club: although usually from 63 to 77 kg (140 to 170 lb), dogs of 90 kg (200 lb) are not uncommon. Males must be at least 70 cm (27.5 in) high at the shoulder; females, 65 cm (25.5 in). The two coat types, longhaired and shorthaired, are red and white or brindle and white.

Saint Bernard Pass   Saint Bernard is the name of two passes in the Alps. Great Saint Bernard, 24 km (15 mi) east of Mont Blanc, connects Italy and Switzerland. Used since Roman times, it reaches an altitude of 2,472 m (8,110 ft). Saint Bernard of Menthon built a hospice there in the 10th century, and since the 12th century Augustinian monks—with the help of Saint Bernard dogs—have rescued stranded travelers. Little Saint Bernard, 16 km (10 mi) south of Mont Blanc, which also has a 10th-century hospice, is 2,188 m (7,178 ft) high and connects Italy and France. It may have been used by HANNIBAL in 218 BC.

Saint Catharines   Saint Catharines (1986 pop., 123,455), the seat of Lincoln County, is a port city in southeastern Ontario, Canada. It lies on the southern shore of Lake Ontario at the entrance to the WELLAND SHIP CANAL, about 16 km (10 mi) northwest of Niagara Falls.

The city's principal industries are automotive parts and food packing and canning. The city, settled in 1790, is a distribution center for the surrounding fruit-producing area.

St. Clair, Arthur   The American general Arthur St. Clair, b. Thurso, Scotland, Mar. 23, 1736, d. Aug. 31, 1818, the first governor of the NORTHWEST TERRITORY, led a disastrous expedition against the Indians in 1791. A veteran of the American Revolution, he was prominent in Pennsylvania politics before becoming territorial governor in 1787. Settlers in the territory felt increasingly threatened by the Indians there and conducted a series of raids against them. In 1791, St. Clair led U.S. troops northward from Cincinnati's Fort Washington toward the Maumee River, but his force was ambushed and overwhelmed on November 4 while approaching the MIAMI Indian villages on the site of what is now Fort Wayne, Ind. Approximately 600 Americans were killed. Officially freed of blame for the debacle, St. Clair continued as territorial governor, but his unpopular stances—he was opposed to the admission of Ohio to the Union—led to his dismissal by President Thomas Jefferson in 1802.

Saint Clair, Lake   Lake Saint Clair, nearly round in shape and covering 1,191 km^2 (460 mi^2), lies between the state of Michigan and the province of Ontario, Canada. Connected to Lake Huron by the Saint Clair River, and to Lake Erie by the Detroit River, it is part of the St. Lawrence Seaway.

Saint Cloud   Saint Cloud is a city on the Mississippi River in central Minnesota, about 100 km (60 mi) northwest of Minneapolis. The seat of Stearns County, Saint Cloud has a population of 48,812 (1990). It has dairy-processing plants, railroad shops, and colored granite quarries that have been worked since 1870. St. Cloud State University (1869) is located there. The city was settled in 1853 and soon became a busy fur-shipping point.

Saint-Cyran, Abbé de   [san-see-rahn']   The French churchman Jean Duvergier de Hauranne, better known as the Abbé de Saint-Cyran, b. 1581, d. Oct. 11, 1643, was one of the founders of JANSENISM. A fellow student with Cornelius Jansen at Paris and Bayonne, he was made commendatory abbot of Saint-Cyran in 1620 and from 1623 was closely associated with the Arnauld family and the convent of Port-Royal. Seeking to reform Catholic theology along Augustinian lines, he was the leading controversialist of the early Jansenists.

Saint-Denis   (church)   [san-duh-nee']   The Royal Abbey of Saint-Denis, founded in what is now an industrial suburb of Paris in 635 by the Merovingian king Dagobert I (r. 629–c.639), was the burial place for most of the French kings and queens. It was named after Saint Denis, a 3d-century martyr who is considered the first Bishop of Paris and Apostle of France.

The choir and the narthex of the old Carolingian abbey church were rebuilt between 1137 and 1144 under the direction of Abbot SUGER and are generally recognized as the earliest examples of the Gothic style, with huge panels of stained glass and pointed, ribbed vaults (see GOTHIC ART AND ARCHITECTURE). Much of the structure was rebuilt in 1231 by Pierre de Montreuil. It constitutes one of the finest examples of the Gothic Rayonnant style.

St. Denis, Ruth [saynt den'-is] Ruth St. Denis, originally Ruth Dennis, b. Somerville, N.J., Feb. 1, 1877, d. July 21, 1968, although never a great dancer, will be remembered as one of the founders of MODERN DANCE in the United States. Her greatest achievement was to have created serious dance from the materials of popular theater. Without any formal training and inspired by nothing grander than a cigarette advertisement, St. Denis created her first work, *Radha*, in 1906, an oriental dance piece set to music from Léo Delibes's *Lakmè*, in which she herself appeared. Later that year she began a highly successful 3-year tour of Europe. In 1915 she danced in D. W. Griffith's epic film *Intolerance*. With her husband, Ted SHAWN, whom she had married in 1914, she founded (1915) the DENISHAWN dance school in Los Angeles, where Martha Graham, Doris Humphrey, and Charles Weidman, among others, studied. In 1932, with the breakdown of the Shawn marriage, Denishawn and its dance company were dissolved. St. Denis, who wrote an autobiography in 1939, continued to appear as a soloist until shortly before her death at the age of 91.

Saint Elias, Mount Mount Saint Elias, which stands on the Alaskan-Canadian border, is the second highest peak (after Mount Logan) of the Saint Elias Mountains, one of the COAST RANGES. Its altitude is 5,489 m (18,008 ft), and it is the third highest mountain in North America. Vitus J. Bering sighted the peak from the sea in 1741, and it was first climbed by the duca degli Abruzzi in 1897.

Saint Elmo's fire Saint Elmo's fire is a faint glow sometimes seen around elevated, extended structures such as ship masts, airplane wings, or church spires when storm activity induces an electrical charge along these structures. The glow, or corona, is caused by the relatively slow brush discharge of the electricity (see ELECTROSTATICS). It is often accompanied by hissing or crackling sounds and may precede a more disruptive discharge. The high-voltage but low-current phenomenon, in itself, is nonhazardous. Its name derives from a corruption of Saint Erasmus, the patron of sailors, who is identified with a historical figure, Saint Peter González (1190–1246), a Spanish Dominican.

Saint-Étienne [san-tay-tee-en'] Saint-Étienne, the capital city of the Loire department in the Rhône River valley, is located in southeastern central France, about 50 km (30 mi) southwest of Lyon. The city's population is 204,955, with 320,000 inhabitants living in the metropolitan area (1982). Saint-Étienne has extensive coal fields and produces much of France's steel. Other manufactures include textiles, wood products, and glass. The University of Saint-Étienne (1961) and the Palais des Arts with its large exhibition of arms are located there. Settled around 1195, the city was an industrial center as early as the 16th century and a rail center from 1832, when the first European railroad line was opened between Saint-Étienne and Lyon.

Saint-Exupéry, Antoine de [san-teg-zue-pay-ree'] Author of autobiographical novels about the early years of flying and of a much-loved children's story, *The Little Prince* (1943; Eng. trans., 1943), the French writer Antoine de Saint-Exupéry, b. June 29, 1900, is valued for his lyrical style. His work in civil aviation in Africa and South America during the 1920s is described in *Southern Mail* (1928; Eng. trans., 1931) and *Night Flight* (1931; Eng. trans., 1931). Flying symbolized for him comradeship and the attempt to surpass human limitations, themes he developed in *Terre des hommes* (1939; trans. as *Wind, Sand and Stars*, 1939). While flying with the Free French forces during World War II, he disappeared on a reconnaissance mission on July 31, 1944.

Saint-Gaudens, Augustus [saynt-gawd'-uhnz] Augustus Saint-Gaudens, b. Dublin, Mar. 1, 1848, d. Aug. 3, 1907, revitalized the late-19th-century American portrait monument with a heroic style based on a selective naturalism.

Saint-Gaudens's first triumph, *Admiral David Farragut* (1878–81; bronze; Madison Square Park, New York City), shows Farragut standing braced as if on a ship's deck, legs apart like Donatello's *Saint George*. Only Farragut's essential traits—his determination and courage—are stressed, not secondary surface details. The wide marble bench-base, designed by the architect Stanford White, is not a conventional pedestal but is integrated with the design.

Saint-Gaudens created for Chicago's Lincoln Park what is perhaps the most expressive memorial portrait of *Abraham Lincoln* (1887; bronze). The tall, gaunt figure, just risen from a chair, appears to gather his forces to speak the momentous words of the Gettysburg Address. What is often called his finest figure is the shrouded, seated woman (1886–91, bronze; Rock Creek Cemetery, Washington, D.C.), conveying ineffable repose, that was commissioned by Henry Adams for his wife's grave. Embodying an oriental acceptance of the inevitable, it is the most abstract work in 19th-century American sculpture.

General William Tecumseh Sherman (1897–1903; Central Park, New York City) climaxed a brilliant career. In this heroic-scale bronze, Sherman is shown riding through Georgia led by the surging figure of a Winged Victory; it is Saint-Gaudens's distinctively original contribution to the equestrian monument tradition, brilliantly combining portraiture, a sense of movement, and appropriate grandeur.

Saint George's   Saint George's (1986 est. pop., 7,500) is the capital and the principal port of Grenada in the West Indies. The city has a deep landlocked harbor, and its economy depends on tourism, shipping, sugar milling, and rum distilling. It was founded as a French settlement in 1650.

Saint Gotthard Pass   [gaht'-urd]   Saint Gotthard Pass through the Saint Gotthard mountain group of the Alps lies in south central Switzerland, about 45 km (28 mi) northwest of Locarno, and has a maximum elevation of 2,108 m (6,916 ft). The pass was known to the Romans but remained little used until the early 13th century. A wide carriage road superseding the original narrow path was completed in 1830, and a 14-km (9-mi) railroad tunnel under the pass was opened in 1882. A hospice, built there in the 14th century and rebuilt several times since then, a meteorological station, and a modern hotel stand in the pass.

Saint Gotthard Tunnel   see TUNNEL

Saint Helena   [huh-lee'-nuh]   The British colony of Saint Helena is a mountainous volcanic island in the South Atlantic Ocean, about 1,930 km (1,200 mi) from the coast of Africa, with two dependencies: ASCENSION ISLAND and the TRISTAN DA CUNHA ISLANDS. Saint Helena has an area of 122 km^2 (47 mi^2) and a population of 5,564 (1987). Jamestown is its capital and only port. Fringed by steep cliffs on all sides except the north, the island rises to 818 m (2,685 ft) on Mount Actaeon. Subsistence farming and lace and flax-fiber making form the basis of the economy. The island also receives subsidies from the United Kingdom. Discovered by the Portuguese in 1502, Saint Helena was captured and settled by the British in 1659. NAPOLEON I was exiled on the island in 1815 and remained there until his death, in 1821.

St. Helens, Mount   see VOLCANO

St. James's Palace   St. James's Palace in London is a complex of buildings begun in 1532 by Henry VIII (r. 1509–47) on the site of a leper hospital. Apart from the gatehouse on the north side, little of the original palace survives. Additions and alterations were made by Sir Christopher WREN, William KENT, and William MORRIS. To the east of the palace is the Queen's Chapel (1623–27), built by Inigo JONES; to the west is Clarence House (1825–27), built by John NASH for William IV (r. 1830–37), which is the present residence of Queen Elizabeth, the Queen Mother. The British Court is still known as the Court of St. James, and it is there that ambassadors are accredited.

Saint John   Saint John, the largest city in the province of New Brunswick, Canada, is the seat of Saint John County and has a population of 76,381 (1986). Located on the Bay of FUNDY at the mouth of the Saint John River, it is the province's major commercial and distribution center. The city's early industries of lumbering, shipbuilding, and fishing continue to be important. Saint John also has pulp and paper mills, oil refineries, and sugar refineries. The Reversing Falls at the mouth of the Saint John River—caused by the high tides of the Bay of Fundy—occur twice daily.

The site was explored by Samuel de Champlain in 1604. It was settled as Fort La Tour by Charles La Tour in 1631. In 1758 the British occupied the site, renaming it Fort Frederick. In 1785 the towns of Parr Town and Carleton joined to form Saint John. New England Loyalists were among the area's early settlers.

Saint John the Divine, Cathedral of   The Cathedral of Saint John the Divine in New York City is the largest and most elaborate monument of American GOTHIC REVIVAL architecture. After winning a competition for their design in 1888, the firm of Heins and LaFarge erected the chevet and crossing in the Romanesque style between 1892 and 1911. After Heins's death and the Romanesque's decline in popularity, the Gothicist Ralph Adams Cram was employed in 1911 to redesign and complete the structure. Between 1916 and 1941 the nave was built on the earlier foundations and work was begun on the transept and towers, but World War II and financial problems halted construction. On June 21, 1979, the cathedral's stone yard was reopened, and construction resumed with hopes of eventual completion.

Saint Johns   Saint Johns (1986 est. pop., 36,000) is the capital and largest city of Antigua and Barbuda in the West Indies. The city is a resort and port, with a sheltered, deepwater harbor. In 1632, British settlers arrived at the site.

St. Johns, Adela Rogers   An American journalist whose colorful career writing for the Hearst newspapers spanned more than 60 years, Adela Rogers St. Johns, b. Los Angeles, May 20, 1894, d. Aug. 10, 1988, covered many of the major stories of the 20th century, from the Lindbergh kidnapping trial in 1935 to the Patricia Hearst trial in 1976, for which she emerged from retirement. She also served as a sports reporter, wrote profiles of Hollywood stars, and exposed official indifference to the plight of the unemployed during the Depression. Among her books are a memoir of her childhood, *The Honeycomb* (1969), *Tell No Man* (1966), and *No Good-Byes* (1981).

St. John's   St. John's, capital and largest city of the Canadian province of Newfoundland, is located at the eastern end of the Avalon Peninsula. Its population is 96,216 (1986). With its excellent harbor, known as The Narrows, opening into the Atlantic, the city is a busy port, and its economy revolves around the fishing and shipbuilding industries. Manufacturing has declined. Government—federal, provincial, and municipal—is a major employer. The Memorial University of Newfoundland (1925) is located there. Museums include the Newfoundland Museum and the Signal Hill National Historic Site, where Guglielmo Marconi received (1901) his first transatlantic wireless signal. The area was said to have been explored in 1497 by John Cabot, on Saint John the Baptist's Day. The city was settled as a fishing village in the early 17th century.

St. John's College

St. John's College   Established in 1696 as King William's School and given its present name in 1784, St. John's College is a private 4-year liberal arts school for men and women in Annapolis, Md. Another campus (founded 1964) with an identical academic program is in Santa Fe, N.Mex. The college's curriculum involves the study of its list of great books.

Saint-John's-wort

Saint-John's-wort   Saint-John's-wort is the common name for the plant family Hypericaceae, consisting of 8 genera, 300 species of which belong to the genus *Hypericum*. They are herbaceous plants and shrubs that grow freely in temperate and tropical regions of the world. Most produce bright yellow flowers that have many stamens; they also bear capsules of fruit that are brightly hued when ripe. Although most commonly seen as a wildflower, several species of Saint-John's-wort are cultivated as ornamental shrubs or flowers.

Saint Joseph

Saint Joseph   Saint Joseph, a northwestern Missouri city, lies on the Missouri River, about 80 km (50 mi) northwest of Kansas City. A major grain and livestock market and the seat of Buchanan County, it has a population of 71,852 (1990). Flour milling, meat packing, and metal manufacturing dominate the city's economy. Missouri Western College (1915) is located there.

Founded in 1843 by Joseph Robidoux, a French-Canadian trapper, the city flourished as a port and a base for pioneers. It became the eastern terminus of the pony express in 1860.

Saint Kitts–Nevis

Saint Kitts–Nevis   [kits-nev'-is]   Saint Kitts–Nevis, officially the Federation of Saint Kitts and Nevis, is located in the eastern Caribbean Sea and consists of the islands of Saint Kitts (Saint Christopher) and Nevis. Formerly one of the WEST INDIES ASSOCIATED STATES, it became fully independent from the United Kingdom in 1983.

About 75% of the population live on Saint Kitts, where the capital, Basseterre, is located. A fertile volcanic island of 176 km^2 (68 mi^2), Saint Kitts rises to 1,156 m (3,793 ft) at Mount Misery. The dense vegetation is dominated by flowering shrubs and sugarcane and cotton fields. Nevis, 3 km (2 mi) southeast of Saint Kitts, is a circular volcanic formation with an area of 93 km^2 (36 mi^2). It consists mostly of Nevis Peak, 985 m (3,232 ft) high. The country's main sources of income are tourism and sugarcane.

AT A GLANCE

FEDERATION OF SAINT KITTS AND NEVIS

Land: Area: 269 km^2 (104 mi^2). Capital and largest city: Basseterre (1985 pop., 18,500).

People: Population (1990 est.): 44,100. Density: 164 persons per km^2 (424 per mi^2). Distribution (1990): 49% urban, 51% rural. Official language: English. Major religions: Anglicanism, Methodism, Roman Catholicism.

Government: Type: parliamentary state within the Commonwealth of Nations. Legislature: National Assembly. Political subdivisions: 14 parishes.

Economy: GNP (1988 est.): $120 million; $2,770 per capita. Labor distribution (1984): public administration—32%; agriculture—30%; manufacturing—15%. Foreign trade (1988): imports—$94.7 million; exports—$30.3 million. Currency: 1 East Caribbean dollar = 100 cents.

Education and Health: Literacy (1985): 90% of adult population. Universities (1988): none. Hospital beds (1987): 258. Physicians (1987): 22. Life expectancy (1990): women—71; men—64. Infant mortality (1990): 40 per 1,000 live births.

Originally inhabited by Carib Indians, the islands were sighted by Christopher Columbus in 1493 and settled by the British in the early 17th century. In 1967, with ANGUILLA, the islands were granted autonomy. Anguilla withdrew from this union in 1971. In September 1983, Saint Kitts–Nevis became an independent state within the Commonwealth, with Dr. Kennedy A. Simmonds as prime minister. He was returned to power in 1984 and 1989 elections. Saint Kitts–Nevis is a member of the Organization of Eastern Caribbean States.

St. Laurent, Louis Stephen

[san loh-rahn']   Louis Stephen St. Laurent, b. Feb. 1, 1882, d. July 25, 1973, was the second French-Canadian prime minister of Canada. A prominent corporation lawyer from Quebec, he entered politics in 1941, serving as minister of justice, attorney general, and, later, minister of external affairs (1946–48) in the Mackenzie KING administration. He succeeded King as Liberal party leader and became prime minister in 1948. During his administration, Newfoundland became (1949) a Canadian province, Canada moved to world-power status, and steps were taken to unify the nation and to expand government services. St. Laurent was narrowly defeated by John G. DIEFENBAKER, a Conservative, in 1957; his defeat ended 22 years of Liberal government in Canada. St. Laurent resigned as leader of the opposition in 1958.

Saint Laurent, Yves   see FASHION DESIGN

St. Lawrence, Gulf of

The Gulf of St. Lawrence is a body of water at the mouth of the St. Lawrence River in southeastern Canada, bordered by Newfoundland, Quebec, and the Maritime Provinces. The gulf extends about 805 km (500 mi) from north to south and 402 km (250 mi) from east to west. It covers an area of about 259,000 km^2 (100,000 mi^2) and varies from 61 to 1,005 m (200 to 3,300 ft) in depth.

Water flows into the gulf from the St. Lawrence River and from the Atlantic by way of the Strait of Belle Isle and Cabot Strait. Major islands within the gulf include the MAGDALEN ISLANDS, PRINCE EDWARD ISLAND, and Anticosti Island. The gulf was discovered by the French explorer Jacques Cartier in 1534. It is the site of a major fishing industry.

St. Lawrence River

The St. Lawrence River, one of the major waterways of North America, extends 1,224 km (760 mi) from Lake Ontario to the Gulf of St. Lawrence, north of the Gaspé Peninsula. Because it drains the entire GREAT LAKES system, the St. Lawrence is considered to originate in the forests of Minnesota and to flow almost 4,025 km (2,500 mi) to the Gulf of St. Lawrence. The basin covers about 1,500,000 km^2 (580,000 mi^2). The

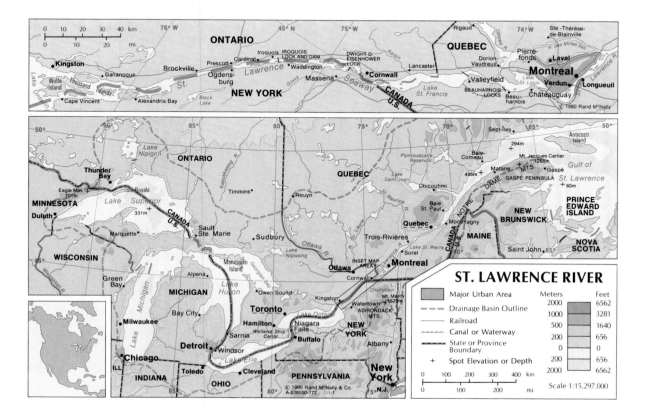

average discharge is almost 6,515 m^3 (230,000 ft^3) per second; fluctuations are relatively minor because of the reservoir effect of the Great Lakes. Little sedimentation takes place.

Below Lake Ontario, the easternmost of the Great Lakes, the river may be divided into two parts—the river proper, which flows to the province of Quebec, and the estuary, extending to the Gaspé Peninsula. As the river leaves Lake Ontario, the channel widens and flows through the THOUSAND ISLANDS between Ontario and New York State. From the islands to Montreal, the river forms a series of pools and rapids, dropping 68 m (223 ft) in 293 km (182 mi). The OTTAWA RIVER joins the St. Lawrence immediately above Montreal; confluence with the Richelieu River takes place downstream of Montreal. From Montreal to the city of Quebec the river flows at a near-sea-level elevation, and from Trois-Rivières downstream it is affected by ocean tides. Other major cities on the St. Lawrence include Ogdensburg, New York; Kingston and Cornwall, Ontario; and Sorel, Quebec.

Downstream of the city of Quebec the river enters its estuary, a sunken valley that widens and deepens rapidly toward the Atlantic Ocean. At Tadoussac, the SAGUENAY RIVER enters from the north, draining part of the Canadian Shield. Although the WELLAND SHIP CANAL between Lakes Ontario and Erie opened the entire Great Lakes system to large ships, the rapids above Montreal prevented their passage to the sea until 1959, when the St. Lawrence Seaway was completed.

St. Lawrence Seaway

The St. Lawrence Seaway is an international waterway system, along part of the U.S.–Canadian boundary, that connects the GREAT LAKES with the Atlantic seaboard. The system, 3,768 km (2,340 mi) long, includes a series of locks, dams, and canals along the St. Lawrence River and channels connecting the Great Lakes. The seaway allows oceangoing vessels to reach such cities as Toronto; Cleveland, Ohio; Detroit; Chicago; Milwaukee, Wis.; and Duluth, Minn. The waterway can accommodate vessels up to 223 m (730 ft) in length and with a capacity of up to 24,500 metric tons (27,000 U.S. tons). Construction on the seaway included seven new locks on the St. Lawrence River section: the Saint Lambert (5.5 m/18 ft), Côte Sainte Catherine (9.1 m/30 ft), Lower and Upper Beauharnois (25 m/82 ft), Bertrand H. Snell (12 m/40 ft), Dwight D. Eisenhower (12 m/40 ft), and the Iroquois Guard (1 m/3 ft). The seaway allows iron ore, coal, and grain to be shipped from the Midwest directly overseas during the mid-April to mid-December shipping season.

Locks were built in the 1800s by Canada, and this system was opened in 1901 on the upper St. Lawrence River. Because the original seaway was neither deep enough nor wide enough for modern ships, Canada and the United States began construction of the new seaway in 1954. It was opened in 1959.

See also: SAULT SAINTE MARIE CANALS; WELLAND SHIP CANAL.

St. Leger, Barry

[saynt lej'-ur]   A British officer in the American Revolutionary War, Barry St. Leger, 1737–89, led a British advance into New York's Mohawk Valley in the summer of 1777. Hoping to join the British army of Gen. John Burgoyne at Albany, St. Leger was halted by American militia in Fort Stanwix (present-day Rome, N.Y.), to which he lay siege. His forces were badly mauled while repelling an American relief column at Oriskany (Aug. 6, 1777), and the approach of additional American troops forced St. Leger to retreat to Canada.

St. Louis

St. Louis is the second largest city of Missouri and a separate administrative unit of the state, independent of all counties. It is located at the central eastern edge of the state on the west bank of the Mississippi River (Illinois is on the east bank), about 15 km (9 mi) below its confluence with the Missouri River. The city's population is 396,685 (1990), and that of its metropolitan area is 2,444,099.

Contemporary City. St. Louis has spread widely from its original site on the west bank, and its metropolitan area now occupies the rolling hills and undulating plains on both sides of the Mississippi. The floodplain of the river, now constricted between artificial levees, serves to separate the main part of the metropolis in Missouri from its less extensive suburbs across the river in Illinois. The stream, however, is spanned by seven bridges that connect the various parts of the city as well as the two states.

The population pattern of the city has undergone development similar to that of other U.S. metropolitan ar-

The stainless-steel Gateway Arch, designed by Eero Saarinen, rises 192 m (630 ft) above St. Louis's riverfront as a symbol of the city's role as the gateway to the West.

eas: about half of the residents of the city proper are black, although the population of the entire metropolis is about 80% white.

St. Louis has a balanced and relatively stable economy, which has been buoyed by its extensive, prosperous hinterland and its excellent transportation facilities. The city is a major railroad and trucking hub, and it ranks among the important industrial centers in the nation. One of the busiest inland river ports in the country, St. Louis is the Mississippi River's northernmost ice-free port. The principal manufacturing specialties are soap, beer, automobiles and aircraft, and iron and steel products, and petroleum is refined. Although factories are widely distributed throughout the metropolitan area, most of the heavy industry is in the Illinois suburbs.

St. Louis has long been an educational and cultural center. St. Louis University, founded in 1818, is the oldest institution of higher learning west of the Mississippi, and Washington University (1853) is also well known. The city has a symphony orchestra and an outstanding newspaper, the *Post Dispatch* (founded by Joseph Pulitzer). Points of interest include the Jefferson National Expansion Memorial, with its 192-m (630-ft) stainless-steel Gateway Arch designed by Eero SAARINEN; the Missouri Botanical Garden; and the St. Louis Art Museum and the McDonnell Planetarium, both in Forest Park. Forest Park was the site of the St. Louis Exposition (1904).

History. The city was founded in 1764 by the French fur trader Pierre Laclède Liguest and was named for the patron saint of France. After the Louisiana Purchase (1803) St. Louis became the focal point of river trade and the crossroads of western expansion. It was incorporated as a city in 1823. As the predominant river port above New Orleans, St. Louis was a focus of steamboat traffic (begun 1817) for half a century, and after 1850 it also became a prominent railway center. The city experienced a major influx of German immigrants during the mid-19th century, and steady industrial and commercial growth continued during the late 19th and early 20th centuries.

Saint Lucia [loo'-shuh]   Saint Lucia is second largest of the WINDWARD ISLANDS of the Lesser Antilles (see ANTILLES, GREATER AND LESSER) in the Caribbean Sea. It gained its independence from the United Kingdom in 1979.

Land, People, and Economy. Saint Lucia has volcanic mountains that rise directly from the sea to a height of 959 m (3,145 ft) at Mount Gimie. Climatic temperatures average 27° C (80° F). Many short streams, fed by rainfall as much as 3,500 mm (140 in) annually, flow through fertile valleys. The island's population is mainly of African origin. English is the official language, but many speak a French patois.

Bananas, sugar, cocoa, and copra are grown for export. Tourism, lime processing, and limited forestry are the major industries. Imports of foodstuffs, machinery, fertilizers, and petroleum products give rise to a large trade deficit, but a petroleum transshipment terminal opened in 1982, and a free-trade zone is under expansion. Saint Lucia's major trading partners are the United Kingdom and the United States. Saint Lucia is a member of the Caribbean Common Market.

AT A GLANCE

SAINT LUCIA

Land: Area: 617 km² (238 mi²). Capital and largest city: Castries (1989 est. pop., 55,000).

People: Population (1990 est.): 151,000. Density: 245 persons per km² (634 per mi²). Distribution (1990): 46% urban, 54% rural. Official language: English. Major religion: Roman Catholicism.

Government: Type: parliamentary state within the Commonwealth of Nations. Legislature: Parliament. Political subdivisions: 11 parishes.

Economy: GNP (1989): $267 million; $1,810 per capita. Labor distribution (1984): agriculture—43%; services—39%; industry and commerce—18%. Foreign trade (1987): imports—$178 million; exports—$77 million. Currency: 1 East Caribbean dollar = 100 cents.

Education and Health: Literacy (1985): 90% of adult population. Universities (1987): 1. Hospital beds (1987): 501. Physicians (1987): 54. Life expectancy (1990): women—74; men—69. Infant mortality (1990): 18 per 1,000 live births.

History and Government. Thought by some to have been visited by Christopher Columbus in 1502, Saint Lucia was claimed by both the British and the French throughout the 17th and 18th centuries. An English settlement in 1638 was wiped out by the native Carib Indians in 1640. After bitter fighting with France, the British gained official control in 1814. In 1967, Saint Lucia was granted self-governing powers with Britain retaining responsibility for defense and foreign affairs. On Feb. 22, 1979, Saint Lucia became an independent state within the Commonwealth. In July 1979 the government of Prime Minister John Compton was defeated as the Labour party, a coalition of conservatives and radicals, led by Allan Louisy, won the new nation's first elections. A split in the Labour party caused Louisy to resign in 1981. His successor, Winston Cenac, resigned amid a general strike in 1982, and general elections returned Compton to power (1982, 1987). St. Lucia is a member of the Organization of Eastern Caribbean States.

Saint Mark's Basilica   Dominating its enormous piazza and surrounded by the Doge's Palace and other civic buildings, Saint Mark's Church (San Marco) in Venice, Italy, remains today the focus of the city. Built to house the relics of Saint Mark, which the Venetians abducted from Alexandria in 828, the present structure was begun in 1063 and consecrated 30 years later; it was frequently modified in the following centuries, notably with fine Gothic exterior decoration. In plan the church forms an equal-armed or Greek cross, with a large dome about 13 m (42 ft) in diameter over the crossing and a slightly smaller dome over each of the four arms. This basic form was copied from Justinian I's 6th-century Byzantine

The entrance façade of Saint Mark's Basilica in Venice is surmounted by the famous Four Horses of Saint Mark's. The gilded bronze horses, plundered from Constantinople in 1204, were again seized by Napoleon, who displayed them in Paris from 1797 to 1815.

Church of the Holy Apostles (destroyed 1469) in Constantinople. Built by Italians and designed for the Latin rather than the Greek liturgy, the church shows many Western features.

The upper parts of the interior are entirely covered with splendid and justly renowned mosaics begun by Byzantine craftsmen in the 12th century and continued by Italian artists until the 16th century. Those covering the small domes of the narthex, or entrance porch, relate the story of Genesis in great detail.

Saint Mark's also possesses one of Europe's richest collections of treasures, including the Pala d'Oro (Altar of Gold; 976, with repairs through 1345), a huge Byzantine altarpiece of gold, jewels, and enamel panels, as well as magnificent reliquaries, book covers, and the four bronze horses over the entrance, which were among the rich booty taken from Constantinople in 1204 by the Venetian-inspired Fourth Crusade.

Saint Martin   Saint Martin, one of the Leeward Islands in the Caribbean Sea, lies about 240 km (150 mi) northeast of Guadeloupe. The area is 88 km^2 (34 mi^2), and the population is 24,300 (1982 est.). The northern portion of the island is administered from Basse-Terre on Guadeloupe as a part of France's overseas territories; the southern section is administered as a part of the Netherlands Antilles from Philipsburg, on Saint Martin. The principal French town on the island is Marigot.

Tourism, salt extraction, sugarcane and cotton growing, livestock raising, and fishing form the base of the economy. Originally settled by Carib Indians, the island was discovered by Christopher Columbus in 1493 and settled by the Spanish in 1640. In 1648, French and Dutch prisoners of war supposedly partitioned the island as it is today.

Saint Moritz [mor-its']   Saint Moritz, a popular winter tourist town in Grisons canton, eastern Switzerland, lies on Lake Saint Moritz at an elevation of 1,853 m (6,080 ft). The population is 5,900 (1980). Known for its mineral springs since Roman times, the town began to develop as a resort in the 17th century. A 12th-century leaning tower is the main landmark. Saint Moritz was the site of the Winter Olympics in 1928 and 1948.

Saint Patrick's Cathedral   Saint Patrick's Cathedral (1858–79), the largest Roman Catholic cathedral in the United States, occupies the New York City block bounded by 50th and 51st streets and Fifth and Madison avenues. James Renwick designed it in a Gothic Revival mixture of English and French Gothic styles but eliminated the usual flying buttresses. The granite structure, cruciform in plan, 101 m (332 ft) long and 53 m (174 ft) wide at the transepts, contains 70 stained-glass windows (45 of them imported from Chartres and Nantes) and 14 altars. The Fifth Avenue entrance, featuring a rose window 8 m (26 ft) in diameter, is topped by twin 100.6-

Saint Patrick's Cathedral, a striking Gothic Revival structure that stands on Fifth Avenue in New York City, was designed during the mid-19th century by James Renwick. The twin spires of the west façade are dwarfed today by surrounding skyscrapers.

m (330-ft) towers. Saint Patrick's Cathedral is better known for its location—across Fifth Avenue from Rockefeller Center—and its size than for its somewhat dry eclectic architecture. The nave has pews for 3,000; the graceful 85-seat Lady Chapel—designed by Charles T. Mathews and completed in 1906—is constructed of white Vermont marble.

Saint Paul   Saint Paul, the capital of Minnesota and seat of Ramsey County in the southeastern part of the state, is situated on the north and south banks of the Mississippi River, to the east of MINNEAPOLIS, with which it forms the Twin Cities. Saint Paul's population is 272,235 (1990). The city is a major port, rail terminus, and educational, cultural, and commercial center. Saint Paul is an important industrial center, producing automobiles, abrasives, chemicals, beer, paints, refined petroleum, and electronic communications equipment.

Principal landmarks in Saint Paul are the state capitol (completed 1904) and Carl Milles's peace memorial in the lobby of City Hall (completed 1932). A recent addition to the city is the Saint Paul Arts and Science Center. The city's many educational institutions include Macalester College (1874), the Saint Paul campus of the University of Minnesota, and Hamline University (1854). The city annually hosts the Saint Paul Winter Carnival and the Minnesota State Fair.

The Saint Paul area was settled as Fort Saint Anthony (later renamed Fort Snelling) in 1820. Squatters near the fort were moved east with trader Pierre Parrant and established the settlement of Pig's Eye in 1840. Father Lucien Galtier built a chapel at Pig's Eye in 1841 and named the chapel and the settlement Saint Paul. It soon developed into a river port. The town became territorial capital in 1849 and state capital in 1858. From the Civil War period it developed as a railroad terminus, book and shoe manufacturing town, and major livestock market.

Saint Paul's Cathedral   Saint Paul's, cathedral of London and parish church of the British Commonwealth, was designed by Sir Christopher WREN between 1670 and 1675 in a sober and classical version of the baroque style to replace the medieval Cathedral of Old Saint Paul's, which had been almost entirely destroyed by the Great Fire of September 1666. Constructed of Portland stone (limestone), the new cathedral was begun on June 21, 1675, and declared complete by Parliament in 1711.

Saint Paul's is 169 m (555 ft) long, 55 m (180 ft) wide across the west facade, and 34 m (111 ft) high on the outer walls. Wren's design exhibits a number of characteristic baroque features: the cruciform plan, the monumental dome over the crossing (111.5 m/366 ft high; modeled on the dome of Saint Peter's Basilica in Rome and second to it in size), and the two towers of the west facade. Wren succeeded in tempering the baroque taste for dramatic and highly sculptural architecture with a classical sense of restraint. Like Westminster Abbey, Saint Paul's is a national pantheon where many of England's famous personages are entombed, including Wren.

Saint Paul's Cathedral stands on Ludgate Hill in London on a site occupied by churches dedicated to Saint Paul since the 7th century. A masterpiece of English baroque architecture, the present cathedral was completed (1711) by Sir Christopher Wren.

Saint Peter's Basilica   Saint Peter's Basilica, the premier church of Roman Catholic Christendom, is named for Christ's disciple Peter, who was also the first pope. It is built within the boundaries of Vatican City in Rome on the Vatican Hill, the site where by tradition Peter was buried after being crucified.

Saint Peter's Square, Rome, the majestic colonnaded court overlooked by Saint Peter's Basilica, was built by the architect and sculptor Giovanni Bernini during the 17th century.

There have been two churches on this site. The first, Old Saint Peter's, was dedicated in about 330 by Constantine I (r. 324–37). A long BASILICA in plan, the huge church was divided by columns into a wide central nave flanked by two aisles on each side. At the west end, beyond a wide north-south transept, a semicircular apse marked the tomb of Saint Peter, over which rose the high altar. The basilica was fronted with a square atrium, reserved for penitents not allowed to enter the church itself. The whole complex, basilica and atrium, covered an area 228 m (750 ft) by 122 m (400 ft).

Over succeeding centuries, many renovations and additions were made, most noticeably the tower. By 1420 the general fabric was in bad repair, and although several designs were commissioned, nothing was done until Pope Julius II (r. 1503–13) ordered (1506) the old basilica torn down and authorized Donato BRAMANTE to plan a completely new structure. It was to be built over the tomb of Saint Peter on the plan of an immense Greek (equal-armed) cross crowned with a dome.

The building history of the new Saint Peter's covers a span of 120 years. In summary, the centralized plan of Bramante was retained by MICHELANGELO, who enlarged the scale, modified most of the interior details, and raised the drum for the dome (1546–64). In 1606, Carlo MADERNO demolished what remained of the old basilica and in the process redesigned the church as a Latin cross by extending the nave, a plan advocated earlier for liturgical reasons. In 1655, Giovanni Lorenzo BERNINI began work on the great piazza surrounded by 284 massive Tuscan columns, set four-deep. Finally, a new sacristy was completed (1784) by Carlo Marchionni.

Saint Petersburg   Saint Petersburg (1990 pop., 238,629), a city on the west central coast of Florida, is located on the Pinellas Peninsula between Tampa Bay and the Gulf of Mexico. It is about 35 km (22 mi) south-west of Tampa. The principal industry is tourism, and many people retire to the mild climate and recreational facilities of the "Sunshine City." The area was first settled in 1846, but Saint Petersburg itself was founded in 1876 by John C. Williams of Detroit and incorporated in 1892.

Saint Pierre and Miquelon [mik-uh-lawn']   Saint Pierre and Miquelon is a group of 8 small islands in the North Atlantic Ocean about 25 km (16 mi) south of Newfoundland, Canada. The population of the islands is 6,330 (1990 est.). The archipelago is the only overseas department of France in North America. The total area of the two main islands, Saint Pierre and Miquelon, is 241 km^2 (93 mi^2). Most inhabitants live on Saint Pierre, primarily in the capital city of the same name. Miquelon is actually two small islands—Miquelon and Langlade—connected by a narrow isthmus. The islands' economy is based on cod fishing and tourism; French financial aid is indispensable.

Discovered by the Portuguese early in the 1500s, the islands were claimed for France in 1536 by Jacques Cartier. Permanent settlement dates from 1763. After a period (1713–1814) of alternating British and French rule, the islands were ceded to France, becoming an overseas department in 1976.

Saint-Saëns, Camille [san-sahns', ca-mee']   Camille Saint-Saëns, b. Paris, Oct. 9, 1835, d. Dec. 16, 1921, was a French composer and pianist. A child prodigy, he gave his first public piano recital in 1846, and excelled in all his studies at the Paris Conservatory. At the age of 22 he became organist at the church of the Madeleine but was already earning fame as a composer of orchestral symphonic music. Most notable are four symphonic poems (including *Danse macabre,* 1875) composed under the influence of Liszt, who took great interest in his career and was later (1877) responsible for the first performance of his *Samson et Dalila,* the only one of his dozen operas to achieve a lasting success. His early symphonic music was modeled on Mozart, Beethoven and Mendelssohn, but his later works show a distinctively French character—a good-natured charm with a touch of deliberately assumed triviality combined with a remarkable technical fluency. He wrote copiously in all genres, but only a few of his chamber works or songs have survived. His concertos, his *Variations on a Theme by Beethoven* (1874) for two pianos, the *Introduction and Rondo Capriccioso* (1870) for violin and orchestra, and *The Carnival of the Animals* (1886) are among the most popular in the classical-music literature.

Saint-Simon, Claude Henri de Rouvroy, Comte de [san-see-mohn']   The French social theorist Claude Henri de Rouvroy, comte de Saint-Simon, b. Oct. 17, 1760, d. May 19, 1825, is best known for his theory of "evolutionary organicism," which postulated history as an orderly progression culminating in an industrial, harmonious society ruled by a scientific elite on the basis of division of labor. His ideas influenced such thinkers as August Comte, Karl Marx, and Herbert Spencer. Saint-Simon was an officer in the French army in the American Revolution. In the French Revolution he was imprisoned for 11 months during the Reign of Terror. Among his many writings *New Christianity* (1825; Eng. trans., 1952) is notable for its synthesis of Catholic and Enlightenment ideas.

Saint-Simon, Louis de Rouvroy, Duc de

[sant-see-mohn'] Louis de Rouvroy, duc de Saint-Simon, b. Jan. 15?, 1675, d. Mar. 2, 1755, was a French historian of noble birth whose *Mémoires,* based on his career as a diplomat during the reign of Louis XIV, is an invaluable sourcebook on political and social life. Saint-Simon fought to retain power for the old aristocracy, but his reactionary attitudes weakened his influence with the king and gained him many enemies. He made no effort to publish his massive work—the 43-volume edition was completed in 1931—and the *Mémoires* did not begin to appear in print until 1788.

Saint Vincent, Cape

Cape Saint Vincent, a promontory jutting into the Atlantic Ocean, is the southwestern point of Portugal. A lighthouse, erected within the walls of a 16th-century monastery, stands on the cape, and 5 km (3 mi) to the southeast lies the fishing village of Sagres. Greek and Roman shrines have been found in the area. The British admiral John Jervis defeated the Spanish fleet there in 1797.

Saint Vincent and the Grenadines

Saint Vincent and the Grenadines lies among the WINDWARD ISLANDS of the Lesser Antilles (see ANTILLES, GREATER AND LESSER) in the Caribbean Sea. A former British-associated state, it gained its independence in 1979.

Land, People, and Resources. The nation includes the island of Saint Vincent and the northern GRENADINE ISLANDS. Heavily forested volcanic islands rise to 1,234 m (4,049 ft) at Soufrière, a volcano that last erupted in 1979. The country has a pleasant tropical climate with an average temperature of 27° C (80° F) and rainfall totaling 2,540 mm (100 in) annually.

The population is mainly of black-African descent. Primary education is free but not compulsory. The country has teacher-training and vocational colleges.

Agriculture, which provides almost half the total employment, was slow to recover from the devastation caused by the 1979 volcanic eruption and by hurricanes and tropical storms in 1979 and during the 1980s. Bananas and arrowroot are the main cash crops, and tourism and food processing are the leading industries. In recent years imports have created a large trade deficit.

History and Government. The country's first known inhabitants were the ARAWAK Indians, who were later driven out by the CARIB Indians. Christopher Columbus was the first European to land (1498) on Saint Vincent. During the 17th and 18th centuries both Britain and France claimed the island, but in 1763, Saint Vincent was ceded to Britain. In 1885 the Windward Islands were made a separate British colony. Saint Vincent became a British-associated state in 1969 and gained full independence on Oct. 27, 1979.

AT A GLANCE

SAINT VINCENT AND THE GRENADINES

Land: Area: 389 km^2 (150 mi^2). Capital and largest city: Kingstown (1989 est. pop., 19,274).

People: Population (1990 est.): 115,000. Density: 296 persons per km^2 (767 per mi^2). Distribution (1988): 25.7% urban, 74.3% rural. Official language: English. Major religions: Protestantism, Roman Catholicism.

Government: Type: parliamentary state within the Commonwealth of Nations. Legislature: House of Assembly. Political subdivisions: 6 parishes.

Economy: GNP (1988): $135 million; $1,200 per capita. Labor force (1984 est.): 67,000; unemployment (1989): 25–30%. Foreign trade (1986): imports—$87 million; exports—$64 million. Currency: 1 East Caribbean dollar = 100 cents.

Education and Health: Literacy (1990): 82% of adult population. Universities (1988): none. Hospital beds (1987): 350. Physicians (1987): 39. Life expectancy (1990): women—72; men—68. Infant mortality (1990): 32 per 1,000 live births.

Saint Vincent and the Grenadines is governed under a constitution promulgated in 1960. In 1984 and 1989 elections, James F. Mitchell's New Democratic party defeated the Labour party of F. Milton Cato. Cato had been in power between 1969 and 1984, except for 1972–74 when Mitchell headed a coalition government. The country is a member of the Organization of Eastern Caribbean States.

Saint Vitus's dance   see NERVOUS SYSTEM, DISEASES OF THE

Sainte-Beuve, Charles Augustin [sant-buv']
The preeminent French literary critic of the 19th century, Charles Augustin Sainte-Beuve, b. Dec. 23, 1804, d. Oct. 13, 1869, wrote voluminously on all of French literature, with occasional ventures into the literatures of England and ancient Rome. Although excellent in his judgments of literature of the past, he frequently magnified mediocre talent among his contemporaries and misunderstood some of the best—Stendhal, Balzac, and Baudelaire. His methods in such collections as *Critiques et Portraits littéraires* (1832, 1836–39) and his celebrated *Monday Chats* (1851–62; Eng. trans., 1877) heavily influenced not only French but world criticism.

Sainte-Beuve had a broad following for both his essays and such public lecture series as *Port-Royal* (published 1840–59), an analysis of the Jansenist-influenced authors and educators grouped near Paris in the 17th century, and *Chateaubriand et son groupe littéraire* (Chateaubriand and His Literary Circle, 1861), which he turned into important books. His novel *Volupté* (1834) and some of his poetry, were they not overshadowed by his critical writings, would in themselves ensure him a significant literary reputation.

Sainte-Chapelle [saint-shah-pel']   The Sainte-Chapelle, in the Palais de Justice on the Île de la Cité in the center of Paris, is a diminutive yet perfect example of the Rayonnant style (see GOTHIC ART AND ARCHITECTURE). Erected by Louis IX, king of France, to house the Crown of Thorns and a fragment of the True Cross, the Sainte-Chapelle was designed as a reliquary casket enlarged to an architectural scale. The original plan, possibly by Pierre de Montreuil, dates from 1241; the chapel was rapidly constructed between January of 1246 and Apr. 25, 1248, when it was consecrated. It is 36 m (118 ft) long, 17 m (56 ft) wide, and 42.5 m (139 ft) high. Except for the slender piers that support the vaulted ceiling, the walls of the upper chapel consist entirely of superb STAINED GLASS. Starting in 1837, Eugène Emmanuel Viollet-le-Duc and others accurately restored the building, which had been damaged during the French Revolution.

Saintonge [san-tohnzh']   Saintonge, a historic province in western France, north of the Gironde estuary on the Bay of Biscay, corresponds to most of the present department of Charente-Maritime. The economy of the area is based on oyster harvesting, cognac distilling, and the raising of sheep and dairy cattle. Occupied by the Santones, a Gallic tribe, in the 1st century BC, the territory was conquered by the Visigoths in 419 and by Clovis, king of the Franks, in 507. Ceded to England in 1152, the region reverted to France in 1242 but was returned to England in 1360. In 1375, Saintonge passed to the French crown. The province was dissolved in 1790.

Saionji Kimmochi [sy-ohn-jee kee-moh-chee]   Prince Saionji Kimmochi, b. October 1849, d. Nov. 24, 1940, was a Japanese statesman. Born into a powerful court family, he participated in the MEIJI RESTORATION (1868), then studied in France, returning (1881) to start a liberal newspaper. During his three terms as prime minister (1901–02, 1906–08, 1911–12) he tried to strengthen democratic government and control the military. Saionji retired from active politics in 1912 but returned in 1919 to lead the Japanese delegation to the Versailles peace conference. He stayed on as an imperial adviser and continued to press for peaceful solutions to international problems.

Saipan [sy-pahn']   Saipan, the second largest of the MARIANA ISLANDS in the western Pacific Ocean, is the capital of the Commonwealth of the Northern Mariana Islands. Volcanic in origin, Saipan has an area of 122 km^2 (47 mi^2); its population is 22,719 (1990 est.). Most of the CHAMORRO population are employed in service or government jobs. Evidence of human habitation dates from 1500 BC. Ferdinand Magellan sighted the island in 1521. It fell under the control of Spain (1565–1899), Germany (1899–1921), Japan (1921–44), and the United States. Saipan served as headquarters for the Trust Territory of the Pacific Islands until 1975, when the Northern Marianas voted for separate U.S. commonwealth status (effective 1986).

sake [sah'-kee]   Sake is a sweet, colorless, fermented alcoholic beverage, thought to be named for the town of Osaka, Japan. Often called Japanese rice wine, it has a high alcoholic content (12–16% by volume) and none of the carbon dioxide found in other fermented drinks, such as beer. Sake is made from rice that is cleaned, steamed, treated with a special yeast, and allowed to ferment for 4 to 5 weeks. Near the end of the fermentation more rice and water are added, and a second fermentation takes place. The resulting liquor is drawn off, filtered, and placed in casks for maturing. It is served warm and sipped from small porcelain cups.

Sakhalin [suh-kuhl-yeen']   Sakhalin is a Soviet island washed by the Sea of Okhotsk and the Sea of Japan and separated from the USSR's Asian coast by the Tatar Strait. With the nearby KURIL ISLANDS, Sakhalin constitutes an oblast of the Russian republic. The oblast's population is 700,000 (1986 est.). The island, with an area of about 76,400 km² (29,500 mi²), is mostly mountainous, rising to 2,013 m (6,604 ft) at Mount Nevelskoi. The economy is based on fishing, lumber, petroleum, and coal. Several Soviet military installations are there.

The Japanese settled the southern section of the island in the late 1700s, and the northern section attracted Russian settlers in the early 1800s. The Russian tsars operated a penal colony there in the late 19th century. Possession of the island was contested by the two countries from the mid-19th century until after World War II, when the USSR gained complete, though still disputed, control.

Sakharov, Andrei D. [suh-kahr'-awf]

The Russian scientist and social critic Andrei Dimitriyevich Sakharov, b. May 21, 1921, d. Dec. 14, 1989, received the Nobel Peace Prize in 1975 for his courageous crusade for nuclear disarmament and democracy in the USSR. Internationally recognized for his work in thermonuclear physics and three times decorated as a Hero of Socialist Labor, Sakharov incurred official criticism for protesting the Soviet government's intention to violate the Nuclear Test Ban Treaty in 1961. In 1968 he published an appeal for nuclear arms reduction. An outspoken defender of civil liberties, Sakharov publicly criticized the Soviet government's treatment of political dissidents. From 1980 to 1986 he was in internal exile in the city of Gorky. Restored to freedom under Gorbachev, he remained a vigorous critic of government policies. He was elected to the Congress of People's Deputies in 1989.

Andrei Sakharov was a prominent Soviet physicist and dissident. One of the developers of the Soviet H-bomb, Sakharov was ostracized and harassed for his advocacy of intellectual freedom and of disarmament. Awarded the Nobel Peace Prize in 1975, he had many admirers in the West.

Saki [sah'-kee]

Best known for his short stories written under the pen name Saki, Hector Hugh Munro, b. Dec. 18, 1870, d. Nov. 14, 1916, was a British writer of satire and humor, a foreign correspondent, and a literary dandy. The pseudonym Saki was chosen from the *Rubaiyat of Omar Khayyám*. Typical Saki stories are marked by amoral reversals, revenge on the pretentious,

cruel practical jokes, and uncanny supernatural incidents. His earliest stories were published in *Reginald* (1904). His novel *The Unbearable Bassington* (1912) gives a sardonic view of Edwardian social life. During World War I, Munro refused a commission and, while serving as an enlisted man, was killed in the Battle of the Somme.

Sakkara   see SAQQARA

Saladin [sal'-uh-din]

Salah ad-din, Yusuf ibn Ayyub, known as Saladin in the West, b. c.1138, d. Mar. 4, 1193, a Muslim warrior and founder of the Ayyubid dynasty, was a staunch opponent of the CRUSADES. Of Kurdish descent, Saladin was raised in northern Syria, where members of his family were prominent under the Zangid dynasty. In 1152 he joined the staff of his uncle Shirkuh and later accompanied (1169) him to Egypt to help the FATIMID rulers resist the Crusaders. Shirkuh was appointed (1169) Fatimid vizier but died two months later; Saladin succeeded his uncle and effectively repulsed the Crusaders. In 1171 he overthrew the Fatimid dynasty, returning Egypt to Islamic orthodoxy and becoming sole ruler there.

At the death (1174) of Nur al-Din, the Zangid ruler, Saladin set out to conquer the Zangid kingdom in Syria as a preliminary to the holy war (jihad) against the Crusaders. Launching the jihad in 1187, Saladin was victorious at Hattin, recaptured Jerusalem, and drove the Crusaders back to the coast. These events prompted the Christians to mount the Third Crusade (1189–92), pitting Saladin against RICHARD I of England. The Crusaders captured only Acre, and the Peace of Ramleh (1192) left the Latin Kingdom of Jerusalem with only a small strip of land along the Mediterranean coast.

Saladin not only vanquished the Crusaders but also restored Egypt as the major power in the Middle East and initiated a prolonged period of economic prosperity, population growth, and cultural revival.

Salamanca [sah-lah-mahng'-kah]

Salamanca, the capital of Salamanca province, is situated on the Tormea River in west central Spain, about 170 km (110 mi) northwest of Madrid. The population is 155,612 (1987 est.). Tourism sustains Salamanca's economy, but the city also serves as an agricultural trade center for the surrounding countryside and has some light industry. In the city are the adjacent old (begun c.1140) and new (begun 1513) cathedrals, the 18th-century Ayuntamiento (Town Hall), and a bridge with 15 arches dating from Roman times.

Salamanca was captured by the Carthaginian forces of Hannibal in 222 BC. After being successively ruled by the Romans, Visigoths, and Moors, it was taken by the Christians in the late 11th century. The Universidad Literaria de Salamanca (1218), Spain's first university, was a leading European center of learning until the end of the 16th century. Salamanca was the scene (1812) of fierce fighting during the Peninsular War and served as Francisco Franco's headquarters (1936–39) during the Spanish Civil War.

salamander and newt   Salamander is the common name for about 320 species of AMPHIBIANS with tails. Among these are all the members of the order Urodela, including the newts (family Salamandridae). Salamanders may live permanently in fresh water, part of the time in water (as larvae and to breed), or entirely on land. Newts that live part of their lives on land may have a "warty" skin when out of water. Most adults hide by day and feed at night; some emerge only when moisture and temperature levels are suitable, or in breeding season. Salamanders occur mainly in the temperate regions of the Northern Hemisphere. They do not occur in Australia or south of the Sahara in Africa and are rare in South America.

Classification.   Salamanders diverged early from the other amphibian stocks (frogs and caecilians) but are related to them by characteristics of tooth form and skin structure. The families Hynobiidae and Cryptobranchidae comprise the most-primitive salamanders, based on bone structure and the fact that they exhibit external fertilization (eggs laid in water and sperm deposited over them). Hynobiids live in eastern Asia, and the cryptobranchids live in China and Japan (the giant salamander) and North America (the hellbender).

The family Ambystomatidae occurs in the New World from Canada to central Mexico and includes the tiger salamander and the AXOLOTL. Its subfamily Dicamptodontidae contains a single stream-dwelling genus of the Pacific coast of the United States. The families Sirenidae (see SIREN), Necturidae (mud puppy), and Amphiumidae (congo eels) occur only in the southeastern United States. All are permanently aquatic, with reduced limbs and some larval features. The family Proteidae occurs in the caves of coastal Yugoslavia; the animals are gilled, blind, and unpigmented. The family Salamandridae lives on all continents except South America, Australia, and Antarctica. The most abundant family, containing about 200 known species of salamanders, is the Plethodontidae. Evolved in the Appalachian Mountains of the United States, it has many species in eastern and western North America, a group of species that has invaded the tropics and radiated extensively, and two species in Europe. This family contains burrowing, tree-living, stream-dwelling, and terrestrial species.

Structure and Function.   Many salamanders are 10 to 15 cm (4 to 6 in) long. The largest, the giant salamander, *Andrias japonicus*, grows up to about 180 cm (70 in) and

The red-spotted newt, of eastern North America, can withstand low temperatures. During winter it is sometimes seen swimming beneath thin ice in pond shallows.

weighs about 25 kg (55 lb). Salamanders externally are characterized by having short bodies with tails, usually four legs, well-developed heads often with large mouths and eyes, and a smooth, moist skin. They are brightly colored—frequently brown, black, yellow, or red—and often have light or dark spots, bars, or stripes. The skin contains many glands, some secreting mucus to help maintain moisture and others secreting a toxic or irritating substance when the animal is frightened. The respiratory system typically involves gills in larvae and lungs in adults; some adults also have gills. Oxygen uptake can also occur through the skin and the mouth membranes. Most species are carnivores, feeding on insects, worms, and similar prey.

Courtships are often species-specific and elaborate. In all but the most primitive species, fertilization is internal. The male secretes a spermatophore, or sperm packet; the female picks this up with the lips of her vent, the opening that leads to the cloaca (chamber), where the oviducts, intestine, and urinary ducts empty. Her eggs are fertilized by the sperm and may be laid right away or retained in her oviducts. The oviducts become glandular during the reproductive period. Several layers are secreted around the egg, including the "jelly" that swells with water to maintain moisture and to hold the egg mass together.

When fertilization is external and eggs develop in water, several hundred eggs may be laid. They have two developmental phases before adulthood—the prehatching (in the egg) phase and the posthatching, or larval, phase. In the prehatching phase nutrition is derived from the yolk of the egg. Larvae are characterized by external gills, teeth in both jaws, and the lack of eyelids. They actively forage for food. The larvae usually then undergo a hormonally mediated METAMORPHOSIS, losing their gills and changing the structure of their skin, skull, hemoglobin, eye pigment, and excretory product.

Some species (for example, the axolotl) display neoteny—that is, the larval features persist into sexual maturity. In many terrestrial species having direct development (no larval stage), the females coil around the clutch and brood their eggs.

The life span of salamanders ranges from 1 to 60 years, depending on the species.

The red-backed salamander, of the eastern United States, prefers woodlands. It has been able to adapt to the urban environment of the Eastern seaboard.

Salamis (city) [sal'-uh-mis]   Salamis, the main city of ancient Cyprus, was situated on the east coast near the modern city of Famagusta. An important port said to have been founded by Ajax's half brother Teucer after the Trojan War, it was the scene of a Greek naval victory over

Egypt in 306 BC. Badly damaged in the Jewish revolt of AD 116–17, Salamis was rebuilt by the Roman emperor Constantius II after an earthquake in the 4th century but was finally destroyed by the Arabs in 647.

Salamis (island, Greece)   Salamis is a Greek island in the Saronic Gulf, 16 km (10 mi) west of Athens. Volcanic in origin and mountainous, it covers about 100 km² (40 mi²). Most of the 28,574 (1981) inhabitants, who are of Albanian origin, live in the town of Salamis. Wheat, olives, and grapes are the main crops. During the PERSIAN WARS, the Battle of Salamis took place on Sept. 29, 480 BC, in the narrow straits off the island. A Greek fleet of 350 triremes led by THEMISTOCLES defeated a Persian fleet twice as large, thwarting an attempt by XERXES I to invade Greece by depriving him of his seaborne supplies.

Salazar, António de Oliveira [sah-lah-zahr']   António de Oliveira Salazar, b. Apr. 28, 1889, d. July 27, 1970, was dictator of Portugal from 1932 to 1968—one of the most enduring of modern European statesmen. He graduated (1914) from the law school at Coimbra University; in 1918 he became a professor of economics there and soon gained a reputation as a financial expert.

In 1926, Salazar served briefly as finance minister. Two years later President António de Carmona gave him the power of veto over all expenditures, and in July 1932, Salazar became premier with dictatorial powers. He drafted the constitution of the Fascist-like *Estado Novo* (New State), which was based on Catholic corporatist principles.

Salazar was an extreme conservative. He maintained order with the help of a powerful secret police (PIDE), a large army, and the paramilitary Portuguese Legion. Meanwhile, the Portuguese people remained the poorest and least educated in Western Europe. In foreign affairs Salazar sought close relations with Spain, Britain, and the United States. In his last years he was occupied in the futile and costly attempt to repress rebellions in the African colonies. An austere and pious bachelor, Salazar suffered a stroke in September 1968 from which he never recovered.

Salem (Massachusetts)   Salem (1990 pop., 38,091), the seat of Essex County in northeastern Massachusetts, lies on the Atlantic coast about 26 km (16 mi) northeast of Boston. Once a leading port and the scene of the SALEM WITCH TRIALS in 1692, the city now manufactures electrical machinery, chemicals, and leather goods. Its federal-style houses, museums, and historical sites attract many tourists. Salem State College (1854) is located there. Salem was founded in 1626 by Roger Conant. Its shipping trade grew in the 17th century but had declined by the early 19th century. Nathaniel Hawthorne was born in the city in 1804.

Salem (Oregon)   Salem, the capital city of Oregon and seat of Marion County in the northwestern part of the state, is situated about 80 km (50 mi) southwest of Portland, at the head of navigation on the WILLAMETTE RIVER. Its population is 101,786 (1990). Salem is bounded on the west by the Coast Ranges and on the east by the Cascades; the city's location in the fertile Willamette Valley has made it a processing center for the area's livestock, fruit, nut, and vegetable farms. Paper and textiles are also produced. Historical landmarks include the Methodist Mission Parsonage (1841) and the old county courthouse, built in 1872. The city is laid out in a grid pattern with unusually broad streets landscaped with numerous trees. Founded in 1840 by a Methodist missionary group led by Jason Lee, Salem became territorial capital in 1851 and state capital in 1864. The city is also the site of Willamette University (1842).

Salem Witch Trials   The witch trials of Salem Village, Mass. (March to September 1692), were America's most notorious episode of WITCHCRAFT hysteria. Belief in witchcraft was carried to colonial America from Europe, where in the two centuries before 1650 thousands had been executed as witches. The Salem incident began when two young girls in the household of the Reverend Samuel Parris began to behave oddly. The girls had participated in meetings at which incantations had been cast and attempts made to foretell the future; they were examined by a doctor, ministers, and magistrates who concluded that they were bewitched. The resulting frenzy spread rapidly. Hearings began on March 1, and by the middle of May, 100 persons were in prison awaiting trial.

The new royal governor, Sir William PHIPS, established a special seven-member court to try the prisoners. Jurors were drawn from church membership lists, and the chained defendants had no counsel. In early June, Bridget Bishop was convicted. A brief delay followed because some judges were uneasy about the validity of

The trial of George Jacobs, an accused witch in Salem, Mass., is depicted by Tompkins H. Matteson. Witchcraft hysteria swept Salem Village in 1692, when several young girls claimed that they had been bewitched. By the end of September, hundreds of persons had been accused and imprisoned, and 20 were executed.

spectral evidence—testimony given by witnesses about voices or apparitions perceived only by them. The trials were resumed after several leading ministers advised the court that such evidence might be used.

By September 22 the court had tried and convicted 27 persons. Nineteen were hanged, and one, Giles Corey, was pressed to death by stones. In addition, about 50 had confessed, 100 were in prison waiting trial, and accusations had touched another 200.

With the jails overflowing, the hysteria abated; Cotton Mather (see MATHER family) delivered a sermon arguing against the mass convictions, and some clergy openly began to criticize spectral evidence. The governor then intervened and freed all who were in jail. The executions stopped. Jurors later admitted their errors, and Judge Samuel SEWALL publicly confessed his culpability, as did Rev. John Hale, chief witness against Bridget Bishop. In 1711, heirs of the alleged witches were voted compensation for their losses.

Salerno [sah-layr'-noh] Salerno, in the Campania region of southwestern Italy, has a population of 154,848 (1987 est.) and is located about 50 km (30 mi) southeast of Naples on the Gulf of Salerno. The old sector lies on a hill overlooking the gulf; the modern city stretches from the hill to the sea. The principal products and exports of this busy Tyrrhenian seaport are textiles, foodstuffs, machinery, cement, and ceramics. Salerno's 11th-century Cathedral of San Matteo contains the tomb of Pope Gregory VII and a second tomb, supposedly that of Saint Matthew.

The ancient Roman colony of Salernum was founded in 197 BC. Salerno was ruled in the Middle Ages by the Goths, Lombards, Normans, and the Kingdom of Naples. The University of Salerno, founded in the 11th century, was Europe's first medical school. Salerno was the site of the Allied landing in World War II and of fierce battles with German occupation forces in 1943.

sales Whenever a commercial transaction of any kind occurs, there must be a buyer and a seller. Sales is the business of presenting individuals or organizations with the products or services that meet their real or perceived needs. Selling may be as simple as producing the product or service requested by the purchaser. Often it is more complex, occasioning the use of psychological insights that employ some or all of the following: creating a need; recognizing an unfulfilled desire; articulating special product features and benefits; analyzing competitive products; using emotional persuasion; employing a convincing close to clinch the sale; and reinforcing the buying decision. In a large organization sales is generally considered to be one of the elements in the overall MARKETING operation. A wide variety of specialists are employed—in ADVERTISING, research, promotion, publicity, packaging, fulfillment of the order, and customer service—to develop strategies and execute tactics whose sole purpose is to accomplish sales.

Some selling is undertaken directly by those who produce the goods or services. In a small business the producer or owner, whether he or she is a manufacturer, a farmer, or a professional person, must sell directly to the customer. In large organizations a specialized sales force does the selling.

sales tax A sales tax is a levy imposed on the sale of goods and services. It is collected by the retailer at the point of sale and is computed on a fixed percentage (for example, 5 percent) of the retail price. In the United States the sales tax—along with the income tax and the property tax—has become a principal revenue-raising device of local and state governments.

The increasing dependence of state and local governments on the sales tax has been criticized by tax reformers because of the regressive nature of the sales tax; that is, poor people, who spend virtually all their income on necessities, pay a much higher percentage of their income in sales taxes than do wealthier citizens. Some jurisdictions, as a way of alleviating the worst regressive features of the sales tax, have excluded clothing, food, and rent from the sales tax. The VALUE-ADDED TAX, which is levied throughout the European Economic Community, is a multistage sales tax in which revenues are collected at every stage of production, from the sale of the raw material to the final retail transaction.

Salic law The Salic law of succession, observed by several European dynasties, excluded from the throne all females and those males whose claim to rule was based on descent through a female. The succession law was based on the *Lex Salica*, one of the Germanic tribal law codes, although that code prohibited only female inheritance of property and not titles or offices. The principle of excluding women from the succession was established in France in the 14th century, but Salic law was not invoked until the end of the male line of the Valois dynasty late in the 16th century. The Spanish king Philip V, a member of the French Bourbon dynasty, introduced (1713) the law into Spain, where its abrogation led to the CARLIST wars of the 19th century. In 1837 the ascent of Victoria to the British throne caused the dissolution of the union of Britain and Hanover because the latter clung to the Salic law of succession.

Salieri, Antonio [sah-lee-ay'-ree] The Italian composer Antonio Salieri, b. Aug. 18, 1750, d. May 7, 1825, was, in his time, celebrated for his operas but is now remembered mainly in connection with his more famous contemporaries. Brought to Vienna in 1766 by the composer Leopold Gassman, Salieri remained there as composer and music director for the imperial court. He wrote 39 operas—in Italian, French, and German—but after 1804 he turned to sacred and instrumental music. He intrigued against Mozart (giving rise to the discredited legend that he poisoned him), but he enjoyed cordial relations with Gluck and Haydn; his pupils included Beethoven, Schubert, and Liszt.

Salina [suh-ly'-nuh] Salina (1990 pop., 42,303), the seat of Saline County, lies on the Smoky Hill River in east central Kansas, about 260 km (160 mi) west of Kansas City. Situated in the middle of the wheat belt, the city is a major distribution and trading center, and manufactures include car batteries, truck bodies, and illuminated signs. Kansas Wesleyan University (1886), Marymount College (1922), and St. John's Military School (1887) are located there. Founded in 1858, Salina began to grow after the arrival of the railroad in 1867.

Salinas de Gortari, Carlos Carlos Salinas de Gortari, b. Mexico City, Apr. 3, 1948, became president of Mexico in December 1988, following a controversial debate in the Mexican Electoral College on allegations of electoral fraud. Salinas, an economist, was the candidate of the ruling Institutional Revolutionary party, which has held power since 1929. Between 1982 and 1987, he was the minister of budget and planning in the administration of President Miguel DE LA MADRID HURTADO.

Salinger, J. D. [sal'-in-jur] Jerome David Salinger, b. New York City, Jan. 1, 1919, established his reputation on the basis of a single novel, *The Catcher in the Rye* (1951), whose principal character, Holden Caulfield, epitomized the growing pains of a generation of high school and college students. Before that Salinger had published only a few short stories; one of them, "A Perfect Day for Bananafish," which appeared in the *New Yorker* in 1949, introduced readers to the Glass family, who subsequently figured in *Franny and Zooey* (1961) and in *Raise High the Roof Beam, Carpenters* and *Seymour: An Introduction* (1963), later published in one volume. Of his 35 published short stories, those which Salinger wishes to preserve are collected in *Nine Stories* (1953).

salinization See IRRIGATION

Salisbury (England) [sawlz'-bur-ee] Salisbury, also called New Sarum, is a city in Wiltshire, southern England, on the River Avon. Located about 130 km (80 mi) southwest of London, the city has a population of 100,929 (1981). It is a commercial and tourist center. The economic life of the city centers on cattle and poultry marketing, brewing, printing, leatherwork, and tourism. Salisbury's principal landmark is its cathedral (built 1220–66), which has the highest church spire (123 m/ 404 ft) in England.

Salisbury's origins date back to an early Iron Age fortification, Old Sarum, north of the present city. It grew under Saxon and Norman rule and became a bishopric in 1075. The present cathedral was founded in the valley south of Old Sarum in 1228. The city developed around the cathedral and flourished in the later Middle Ages as a textile center.

Salisbury (Zimbabwe) see HARARE

Salisbury, Harrison The journalist Harrison Evans Salisbury, b. Minneapolis, Minn., Nov. 14, 1908, has written about world events for United Press International and the *New York Times* and in numerous books, including *American in Russia* (1955) and *Behind the Lines—Hanoi* (1967). Salisbury's accounts of life in the USSR won the 1955 Pulitzer Prize for international reporting, and his reports from Hanoi in 1966, contradicting U.S. claims of bombing success in Vietnam, received considerable attention. His many books include *The 900 Days: The Siege of Leningrad* (1969), *Black Night, White Snow: Russia's Revolutions 1905–1917* (1978), and *Without Fear or Favor: The "New York Times" and Its Times* (1980). Salisbury's autobiographical work, *Journey for Our Times*, appeared in 1983.

Salisbury, Robert Cecil, 1st Earl of Robert Cecil, 1st earl of Salisbury, b. June 1, 1563, d. May 24, 1612, was an English statesman. He was the son of William Cecil, 1st Baron BURGHLEY. He entered the House of Commons in 1584 while his father was chief minister to Queen ELIZABETH I. Shortly before he was knighted (1591), Cecil began performing the duties of secretary of state, but he did not officially assume the post until July 1596.

As chief minister to JAMES I after 1603, he was largely responsible for the smooth transition between the Tudor and Stuart dynasties. He was ennobled as Viscount Cranborne in 1604 and was created earl of Salisbury in 1605, the title of Baron Burghley having passed to his older half brother. When the extravagant James ran afoul of Parliament by attempting to replenish the royal treasury without parliamentary consent, Salisbury proposed the Great Contract of 1610—James would receive a fixed income in return for abolishing his feudal revenues—but was unable to secure its passage. He incurred a large debt constructing Hatfield House, the finest mansion of its age and still the residence of his descendants.

Salisbury, Robert Cecil, 3d Marquess of A British prime minister and diplomat, Robert Arthur Talbot Gascoyne-Cecil, 3d marquess of Salisbury, b. Feb. 3, 1830, d. Aug. 22, 1903, was a prominent public figure for half a century. Elected to Parliament in 1853 as a Conservative, he resigned (1867) in protest against his party's espousal of parliamentary reform. In 1874, after reluctantly joining Benjamin DISRAELI's ministry, he was named secretary of state for India. Later he became (1878) foreign secretary and demonstrated his skills as a diplomat at the Congress of Berlin.

After Disraeli's death (1881), Salisbury succeeded

him as Conservative leader, serving briefly as prime minister from June 1885 to January 1886. Lengthier ministries followed in 1886–92, 1895–1900, and 1900–02. For most of this time he was also foreign secretary, operating in a conciliatory style based on his admiration for his predecessor, Lord CASTLEREAGH. A reluctant imperialist, Salisbury presided over the expansion of the British Empire. He resisted the late-19th-century trend toward forming alliances with foreign powers and jettisoned plans to conclude a compact with Germany.

Aided by his nephew and successor, Arthur BALFOUR, Salisbury endorsed such social reforms as slum clearance (1884), free public education (1891), and workmen's compensation (1897), but he opposed the more radical measures advocated by his colonial secretary, Joseph CHAMBERLAIN. Old age and poor health forced Salisbury to resign his ministry in 1902.

Salisbury Cathedral   see ENGLISH ART AND ARCHITECTURE

Salish [say'-lish]

The Salish, Coastal and Interior, are a group of linguistically related North American Indian tribes of the Northwest who traditionally inhabited a territory embracing portions of the present U.S. states of Washington, Idaho, and Montana, and of the Canadian province of British Columbia. The name FLATHEAD is sometimes applied to all Salishan speakers, but the Flathead are only one tribe of Interior Salish; in fact, head flattening was a traditional practice of Coastal, not Interior Salish. Among other Interior tribes are the OKANOGAN and Columbian groups, and the SHUSWAP, Coeur d'Alene, and Thompson. Coastal Salish include, among others, the BELLA COOLA, NISQUALLY, and TILLAMOOK.

Coastal Salish technology and subsistence were traditionally based on fishing and shellfishing. Descent was usually reckoned through the father's line. Personal wealth and prestige were valued, with the ceremonial distribution of property (POTLATCH) serving to validate inherited status. Warfare was common, and captives became slaves. Among the Interior Salish, westerly tribes had Coastal cultural features, whereas more eastern tribes showed Plains traits. Except among the Flathead, intertribal warfare was rare. In the early 1990s the Salish lived on small reservations in the United States and Canada.

salivary glands

Salivary glands, which serve to moisten the mucous membranes of the mouth and provide digestive enzymes that begin the process of breaking down food, are present in all land-dwelling vertebrates. Most mammals have three pairs of salivary glands: the parotid, sublingual, and submandibular glands. Saliva is discharged through a series of ducts into the mouth. The largest glands, the parotid glands, are located in the cheeks. The secretions of each parotid are discharged near the upper molar teeth. The sublingual glands, located in the floor of the mouth beneath the tongue, release secretions through outlets located near the lower front teeth. The submandibular glands, or submaxillaries, are located in the neck and discharge into the mouth at the base of the tongue.

See also: DIGESTION, HUMAN; DIGESTIVE SYSTEM.

Salk, Jonas [sawlk]

The microbiologist Jonas Edward Salk, b. New York City, Oct. 28, 1914, developed the first vaccine effective against POLIOMYELITIS, an inactivated-virus vaccine that provided immunity against the disease. After massive field tests in 1953 and 1954, the vaccine quickly came into wide use in 1955 and helped to reduce the incidence of polio until an oral vaccine was introduced by Albert Bruce SABIN in 1960.

Sallust [sal'-uhst]

Gaius Sallustius Crispus, known as Sallust, c.86–35 BC, was a Roman historian and politician. Expelled from the Senate in 50 BC for alleged immorality, he found refuge in Julius Caesar's army. He participated (46) in Caesar's African campaign, becoming governor of Numidia (modern Algeria). On his return to Rome he was charged with extortion, and after barely escaping conviction he withdrew from public life and turned to historical writing. His first work, Conspiracy of Catiline (43–42), recounts, against the background of political and moral decline in Rome, the suppression (c.63) of Catiline's plot to seize power. In the War of Jugurtha (41–40) he assails the incompetence and venality of the Roman aristocracy between 111 and 105, during the war against the Numidian king Jugurtha. His last work, the Histories, which sketches the history of Rome from 78 to 67, survives only in fragments.

salmon [sam'-uhn]

Salmon, along with trout, chars, graylings, and whitefishes, comprise the family Salmonidae and are valuable as both a commercial and a sport fish. The four genera, which include Salmo and Oncorhynchus, are found in cold or temperate waters. Widely distributed, the Atlantic salmon, S. salar, for example, can be found in American waters north of Cape Cod and in eastern Canada; from North America east to the Kara River, including Iceland and Greenland; and in European seas and rivers as far south as Portugal.

The life cycle of the Atlantic salmon is typical of that of all salmon. The young fish descend the streams of their origin and disperse into the rich feeding water of the cold seas. Growth is rapid, and when they are sexually mature, usually after 3 years, they return to the streams they left. Beginning in early summer in the longer streams and extending into the winter, large numbers of fish can be observed in their run upstream. How the right river system and the precise nest site are identified is not known, but considerable research indicates that the fish sense a chemical code peculiar to their home stream.

In headwater branches of rivers the fish select suitable sites over gravel. There the females excavate a nest by creating currents with tail-fin vibrations that loosen the

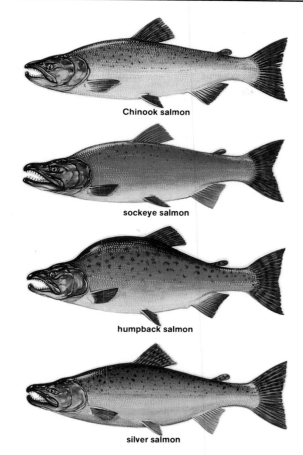

Chinook salmon

sockeye salmon

humpback salmon

silver salmon

The Pacific salmon, native to northern Pacific coasts from Japan to California, constitute the genus Oncorhynchus. The Chinook, or king, salmon is the largest, up to 1.2 m (4 ft), and undertakes the longest spawning migrations, some to nearly 4,000 km (2,500 mi). The humpback, or pink, salmon is the smallest, reaching 75 cm (2.5 ft); males develop a hump behind the head at spawning time. Other species include the sockeye salmon and silver, or coho, salmon.

gravel. A clean depression results when a male and female repeat a courtship vibration. A resulting extrusion of eggs and sperm settles into the gravel. A female may release upward of 10,000 eggs. In *Salmo* species the parents abandon the site and return to the sea. Atlantic salmon may take part in several spawning seasons, but Pacific salmon die following spawning.

After a larval development of 6 weeks, young salmon embryos hatch as alevins, bearing an external yolk sac. When the feeding mechanism develops, the fry—sometimes called parr—feed on river-bottom life-forms. As fingerlings 15 cm (6 in) or more in length, now known as smolt, most of the young begin the journey to the sea, some as late as 5 years old. The oily content of their ocean diet gives the salmon flesh its pinkness and promotes rapid growth.

In the salmon market the western salmon have now become more prominent than the Atlantic salmon. Of these western salmon, the Chinook, *O. tschawytscha*, is the most abundant and the largest (up to 50 kg/110 lb) and supports a large industry. Decrease in productivity in all salmon fisheries has come with heavy fishing, human settlements, and the conversion of rivers to industrial, agricultural, and urban use.

Salmonella [sal-muh-nel'-uh] *Salmonella* is a genus of rod-shaped bacteria. More than 1,500 species have been identified, usually isolated from the intestinal tract of humans and animals. *Salmonella* organisms are responsible for human GASTROINTESTINAL TRACT DISEASES known as salmonelloses, which range from fairly mild attacks of fever, diarrhea, vomiting, and abdominal cramps to life-threatening situations if the bacteria cause excessive dehydration or, rarely, spread to other organs. Outbreaks may occur when meat is eaten that is derived from animals bearing strains of *Salmonella* made resistant by excessive use of ANTIBIOTICS in animal feed. Other forms of *Salmonella* infection that may be caused by improper food handling or unsanitary conditions include FOOD POISONING and TYPHOID FEVER.

Salome [suh-loh'-mee] According to the historian Josephus, Salome was the daughter of Herodias and Herod Philip (see HEROD dynasty), whom Herodias divorced in order to marry his brother Herod Antipas. Salome is generally identified with the unnamed daughter who danced before Herod Antipas and, when granted a wish, was prompted by her mother to ask for the head of JOHN THE BAPTIST (Matt. 14:1–12; Mark 6:14–29).

Salomon, Erich [zahl'-oh-mohn] The pioneering German photographer Erich Salomon, b. Apr. 28, 1886, d. July 7, 1944, was among the first and most talented to use the new small cameras of the 1920s, which because of their versatility made possible the development of modern PHOTOJOURNALISM. Tradition has it that the phrase *candid camera* was coined to describe his work. At first surreptitiously and then with permission, Salomon in the late 1920s made behind-the-scenes photographs of high-level diplomatic negotiations. Many of these appear in his *Berühmte Zeitgenossen in unbewachten Augenblicken* (Famous Contemporaries Caught Off Guard, 1931) and are remarkable not only for their subjects but also for their innovative form. In 1933, Salomon fled Hitler's Germany for Holland but was later captured and died in Auschwitz.

Salomon, Haym [sal'-oh-mohn, hym] Haym Salomon, b. 1740, d. Jan. 6, 1785, was a Jewish immigrant from Poland who worked under U.S. Superintendent of Finance Robert MORRIS during the American Revolution. Devoted to the American cause, he used his own resources to help support the Continental Army and worked to ensure equal treatment for Jews in the new republic.

Salon [sal-ahn'] Salon, a French term meaning gallery, is the name given to the official exhibitions of the works of living artists sponsored by the French Académie Royale (see ACADEMIES OF ART). The first such exhibition was held in 1667 in the Salon d'Apollon of the Louvre Palace. They became annual in 1737, and selection juries were instituted in 1748. The conservatism of these juries led to the rejection of many innovative works. Such bitterness resulted that in 1863 Napoleon III authorized a special Salon des Refusés, in which the rejected works of Manet, Cézanne, and other modernists were exhibited. Thereafter the Salon gradually lost its powerful position.

The word *salon* also refers to the informal but regularly held gatherings of literary, artistic, and political figures in the homes of fashionable French hostesses. These assemblies emerged in the 17th century and reached the height of their development as a social institution in the 18th century, when they constituted part of the intellectual milieu of the ENLIGHTENMENT.

Salonika [suh-lahn'-i-kuh] Salonika (Greek: Thessaloníki) is a port city at the head of the Gulf of Salonika in northern Greece. With a population of 406,413 (1981), Salonika is the most populous city in Greece after Athens. Salonika serves as capital of the region of Macedonia and the province of Salonika.

Salonika is the second largest port in Greece (after Piraeus), serving both Greece and Yugoslavia. The city's industries produce textiles, soap, carpets, tobacco products, and ships; agricultural products, hides, and manganese and chrome ores are exported. The city's principal landmarks are its Byzantine churches and two 15th-century structures: the White Tower and the Venetian citadel.

The city was founded in 315 BC and named for a sister of Alexander the Great. It served (after 148 BC) as capital of the Roman province of Macedonia. Saint Paul addressed two letters to the city's Christian community (AD c.50). Salonika prospered as a Byzantine city despite frequent invasions. In 1430 it was captured by the Turks and remained part of the Ottoman Empire until taken (1913) by the Greeks. During World War I, Salonika was the base for Allied forces operating in the Balkans. The Germans occupied Salonika (1941–44) and virtually annihilated its Sephardic Jewish population.

Salop [sal'-uhp] Salop, or Shropshire, a county in western England on the Welsh border, has an area of 3,490 km² (1,347 mi²) and a population of 400,800 (1988 est.). Shrewsbury is the county town. This region of hills, plains, and valleys is drained by the River SEVERN. Agriculture and livestock raising and marketing are the mainstays of the economy. Coal, iron, limestone, lead, and clay are the main mineral resources. Industries include iron foundries; electrical appliance, heavy machinery, and textile manufacturing; and food processing. Neolithic and Bronze Age ruins are found here. The Romans built Viroconium, or Uriconium, on the site of the modern village of Wroxeter. Castles were built during the 12th and 13th centuries as lines of defense against Wales. After the method of smelting iron with coke was developed by Abraham Derby at Coalbrookdale around 1707, Salop developed the largest iron industry in 18th-century England.

salsa [sal'-suh] Salsa (Spanish for "hot sauce") is a style of popular music that emerged from New York City's Hispanic community during the mid-1970s, developing from a blend of Afro-Cuban and Puerto Rican music with rock and jazz. At its core are the Latin dance rhythms that have had varying degrees of popularity for decades—for example, rhumba, mambo, and cha-cha. Overlaid are electronic techniques developed in rock, and the instrumentation and improvisational skills of jazz. Salsa has become an influence on both rock and jazz.

SALT see ARMS CONTROL

salt (chemistry) Salts, certain compounds having ionic bonds, are abundant in the Earth's crust and in the oceans. For example, calcium carbonate ($CaCO_3$) is found in limestone, marble, and seashells. Common table salt, sodium chloride (NaCl), is deposited in great amounts in the Earth and is a major constituent of ocean waters.

Salts form hard, brittle crystals that have high melting points; ions in the crystals are arranged in a highly ordered pattern. Each ion is surrounded by ions of opposite charge, producing a stable structure that is held together by attractive electrical forces known as ionic bonds (see CHEMICAL BOND). When melted or dissolved in solution, salts conduct electricity. Salts dissolved in water dissociate either partially or completely into separate ions (see DISSOCIATION).

A negatively charged ion of an acid can combine with the positively charged ion of a base in an aqueous solution to produce a salt (see ACIDS AND BASES). For example, hydrochloric acid (HCl) reacts with sodium hydroxide (NaOH) to yield table salt (NaCl) and water. This type of reaction is known as neutralization. A metal can react with an acid to produce a salt, and also two elements can combine directly. Two salts in solution can yield two different salts by exchanging ions.

The simple salts contain either monatomic ions, for example Cl^-, or simple polyatomic ions, such as ammonium (NH_4^+). Salts may also contain complex ions consisting of a metal cation surrounded by anions. An example is sodium ferricyanide, $Na_3Fe(CN)_6$, which dissociates into the simple ion Na^+ and the complex ion $Fe(CN)_6^{3-}$.

Some salts have simple cations and anions that are so strongly bonded together that they can only partially dissociate in solution. An extreme example is mercuric chloride ($HgCl_2$), which dissociates only slightly into $HgCl^+$, Cl^-, and Hg^{2+}. HYDRATES are salts that include water in their crystal form. Two examples of a hydrate are borax, $Na_2B_4O_7 \cdot 10H_2O$, and epsom salt, $MgSO_4 \cdot 7H_2O$.

salt (sodium chloride) Common salt, sodium chloride (NaCl), occurs naturally in pure, solid form as the mineral halite and in widely distributed deposits of rock, or mineral, salts. It makes up almost 80 percent of the total dissolved solids in ocean water. Biologically, blood is a saline solution. The sodium component of salt regulates osmotic pressures in the body and helps prevent excessive water loss. The sodium and chloride also play a major role in the transmission of nerve impulses.

Uses. Salt is used in greater quantities and for more applications than any other mineral. It is the primary source of sodium and chlorine, and other chemicals are produced directly from salt, including sodium hydroxide (NaOH) and hydrochloric acid (HCl). As a chemical, salt is used in the production of textile dyes, soap, glass, and pottery and to preserve leather hides. When mixed with crushed ice it acts as a refrigerant, and, spread on icy streets, it melts the ice.

Table salt has been used for centuries to season and preserve food. Today potassium iodide is often added to table salt (iodized) to supplement dietary iodine intake, thereby preventing the disorder goiter. Excessive salt intake can cause fluid retention (edema) and contribute to hypertension.

Production. Salt is produced commercially by rock-salt mining, solar evaporation, or solution mining. In rock-salt mining a vertical shaft is sunk down in a salt dome or an underground salt stratum. Parallel galleries are blasted out, leaving pillar supports for the rock salt overhead. Once hoisted to the surface the rock salt is crushed.

Solar salt is produced by using the Sun's heat to evaporate water from the ocean or from inland saline lakes. In large concentrating ponds the salt content of the brine is increased to saturation level. The salt crystals settle out, and the liquid bittern is drained off. In solution mining, water is directed into an underground salt deposit through a pipe. The resulting brine is pumped to the surface through another pipe. The brine is then purified by the addition of chemicals and condensed in a series of vacuum evaporators.

The United States is the world's largest salt producer, followed by the USSR, China, Germany, and Canada.

salt dome Salt domes are small but distinctive underground rock structures that often contain commercial quantities of petroleum, sulfur, and salt. Although called domes, some are shaped more like bells, mushrooms, or teardrops. Along the Gulf Coast of the United States they average about 3 km (2 mi) across at the top. Some form low hills, but most lie deep (as much as 5 km/3 mi) beneath the Earth's surface.

Salt domes belong to a large group of structures known to geologists as diapirs (from the Greek *diapeirein*, "to pierce"). Low specific gravity (2.2) and the ability to flow when squeezed combine to make rock salt (NaCl) an ideal diapiric material. When buried under the weight of tons of sediment, salt becomes buoyant and penetrates, or pierces, the overlying denser strata.

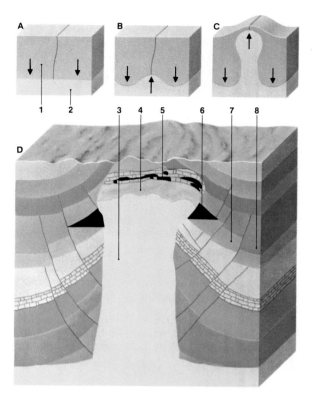

Salt domes form when the pressure of sedimentary rock layers (1) forces a plug of underlying halite strata (2) to rise through a fissure (A, B, C, D). The salt plug (3) is usually covered with gypsum and anhydrite (4) and capped with limestone (5). Oil traps (6) form between the plug and the surrounding sand (7) and shale (8) layers.

Although salt was first mined from domes in the United States in 1862, the main economic value of salt domes was not realized until 1901, when drilling at Spindletop in Texas showed that PETROLEUM is associated with some salt domes. As salt from the mother bed rises, it wedges into the overlying sedimentary layers, causing them to bow upward and fracture. If the strata happen to be impervious, petroleum traps are formed. Spindletop was such an important discovery that it is now known as the birthplace of the modern oil industry. Many salt domes are topped by a rock layer, called caprock, containing minable quantities of anhydrite (CaSO$_4$).

Salt domes in the United States, Romania, Germany, Mexico, and the Soviet Union are viewed mainly as sources of gas, oil, and minerals. The domes are increasingly put to other uses, however, such as storage of LPG (liquefied petroleum gas) and underground testing of nuclear weapons. Domes are ideal for such uses because chambers can be easily excavated in them, and salt is impermeable to liquids and gases. Scientists are now studying ways of using salt domes to dispose of toxic wastes, as chemical reaction chambers, and as sites for the underground disposal of nuclear waste products.

Salt Lake City   Salt Lake City, the capital and largest city of Utah and the seat of Salt Lake County, is located in the north central part of the state on the Jordan River, near Great Salt Lake. The city has a population of 159,936 (1990), and the metropolitan area, 1,072,227 (1990). More than half of the state's population lives within a 50-km (30-mi) radius of Salt Lake City, which is set in a high (1,340 m/4,400 ft) desert valley, surrounded by the peaks of the Wasatch and Oquirrh mountains. The city serves as a processing point for the region's mineral and agricultural products. A major electronics center, Salt Lake City also has defense industries and is the hub of the central transcontinental highway system.

Salt Lake City is the world headquarters of the Church of Jesus Christ of Latter-day Saints (see MORMONISM). In the center of the city stand the massive Mormon Temple (built 1853–93) and the Mormon Tabernacle (built 1867). Salt Lake City is the seat of the University of Utah (1850) and Westminster College (1875). Cultural assets include the Utah Symphony Orchestra and the Mormon Tabernacle Choir, as well as ballet and opera companies, all performing in the new Bicentennial Center for the Cultural Arts.

Salt Lake City was founded in 1847 by Brigham Young and his Mormon followers. After 1849 the city served as a supply depot for pioneers on their way to California. As the area's mining industry and railroads developed from the 1860s, Salt Lake City became a major commercial center for the U.S. West. The city became the territorial capital in 1856 and the state capital in 1896.

Salt Lake city's state capitol (completed 1915), located on Capitol Hill in the northern section of the city, houses an art collection and a pioneer museum in addition to its administrative offices.

saltbush   Saltbush, or orache, genus *Atriplex*, is the common name for more than 100 species of herbs and shrubs of the goosefoot family, Chenopodiaceae. Species are distributed worldwide, growing on saline soils of coasts and deserts. Many, such as the four-wing saltbush, *A. canescens*, of the western United States, and the sea orache, *A. halimus*, of the Mediterranean, have grayish, scaly leaves. Garden orache, *A. hortensis*, of Asia, has edible yellow to red leaves. Spiny saltbush, or shadscale, *A. confertifolia*, is used as forage for cattle.

Saltillo   [sahl-tee'-oh]   Saltillo, capital of Coahuila state in northeastern Mexico, lies on a plateau in the Sierra Madre Oriental about 90 km (55 mi) southwest of Monterrey. The population is 321,758 (1982 est.). A commercial center and summer resort, the city is noted for its brightly colored serapes. Founded by the Spanish in 1555, Saltillo became the capital of Texas and Coahuila in 1824.

Salton Sea   [sawl'-tuhn]   The Salton Sea, a shallow saline lake in south central California, lies in a trough known as IMPERIAL VALLEY to the southeast and Coachella Valley to the northwest. The lake is 48 km (30 mi) long, 16 km (10 mi) wide, and 20 m (65 ft) deep. A prehistoric lake on the site, formed when land shifts in the Colorado River delta landlocked the northern end of the Gulf of California, gradually evaporated and became a salt-covered depression 71 m (232 ft) below sea level. Between 1905 and 1907, floodwaters from the Colorado River poured into the depression and created the present lake. The southwestern shore is now a popular resort area.

saltpeter   Saltpeter, or potassium nitrate (KNO_3), is prepared synthetically and used as a fertilizer and a food preservative and in the manufacture of fireworks and matches. Mixed with sulfur and charcoal, it becomes old-fashioned gunpowder, or black powder. Saltpeter occurs naturally as the mineral niter, which is found as a white crust in rocks and caves. An old claim, never proved, is that saltpeter has an anaphrodisiac, or sexual-desire-reducing, effect.

Saltykov Shchedrin, Mikhail Yevgrafovich   [sahl'-ti-kawf-shche'-dreen, mee-kuh-yeel' yiv-grahf'-uh-vich]   Mikhail Yevgrafovich Saltykov, who wrote under the pseudonym Shchedrin ("the liberal"), b. Jan. 27 (N.S.), 1826, d. May 10 (N.S.), 1889, is considered Russia's greatest satirist. From topical satire in sketches directed at provincial officialdom and its coarseness, he moved to a deeper satire of human brutality, greed, and ignorance in such collections as *Letters to Aunty* (1881–82). Saltykov's masterpiece, however, is *The Golovlyov Family* (1874–76; Eng. trans., 1931), a gloomy novel that portrays the decay of a landed family and contains a splendid portrait of an unctuous hypocrite. His *Fairy Tales* (1880–85; Eng. trans., 1931–34) mock behavioral and political foibles through satirical allegory.

saluki [suh-loo'-kee]   A member of the greyhound family, the saluki, or Persian greyhound, is one of the oldest-known breeds of dog. First brought to England in 1840, salukis were officially recognized by the English Kennel Club in 1923 and by the American Kennel Club in 1927. Tall, elegant dogs with approximately the same body build and size as the greyhound, they have pendent ears, short coats with fringes on the ears, and feathered tails. Salukis come in many colors, including white, cream, red, grizzle and tan, black and tan, and tricolor (black, white, and tan). Gazehounds—hunters by sight rather than scent—developed to run down game, they are extremely fast and are raced in some countries.

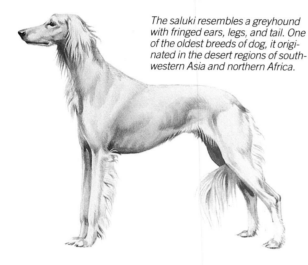

The saluki resembles a greyhound with fringed ears, legs, and tail. One of the oldest breeds of dog, it originated in the desert regions of southwestern Asia and northern Africa.

Salvador [sahl-vah-dohr']   Salvador, a port city with a population of 1,804,438 (1985 est.), is the capital of the state of Bahia in northeastern Brazil. The city is located on the eastern shore of All Saints Bay, bordering on the Atlantic coastal lowland known as the Recôncavo. Salvador is divided into a lower section at the foot of a high bluff and an upper section on top of the cliff. The port is connected to the business and shopping district above it by elevators, a funicular railroad, and several roads. Salvador is the market for Brazilian-grown tobacco, which is made into long, mild cigars famous in Europe. Cotton, coffee, sugarcane, and cacao are also raised in the surrounding area, and Brazil's largest petroleum field is nearby. The church and convent of Saint Francis (1701) is one of Salvador's famous colonial structures.

Salvador was founded in 1549 under the name *Bahia* by Thomé de Sousa as the first capital of Brazil, then a Portuguese colony. The city served as the seat of government until 1763, when Rio de Janeiro became capital. The city was a center of the African slave trade during the colonial period. It has been the capital of Bahia since 1889.

salvage, marine   Marine, or maritime, salvage is the voluntary response to and saving (or salving) of a vessel that has experienced a maritime casualty. The act of salvage must be both voluntary—that is, the ship's own crew, being responsible for the safety of the vessel, cannot be considered as salvors—and in response to a maritime peril from which the ship or cargo could not have been saved without the effort of the salvors.

Acts of maritime salvage include rescue towing of a disabled vessel; refloating of a stranded or sunken vessel; fighting of fires; emergency repairs; and attention to damage to a vessel's hull or machinery, which if untended would have resulted in loss or material damage.

Raising a sunken wreck or other object that is an obstacle to navigation or interferes with such other marine activity as construction of a port or fishing operations is not necessarily salvage. This work instead is called clearance, or wreck removal.

In modern practice, pollution control depends on the salvage of hazardous and polluting cargoes, such as oil (see OIL SPILL). When a vessel carrying hazardous or polluting cargo is stricken, both the ship and the cargo must be salvaged in order to prevent or mitigate a pollution incident.

salvage archaeology   Salvage archaeology, sometimes called public or conservation archaeology, is archaeological work carried out at a site scheduled for demolition. It entails the exploration, surveying, identification, and assessment of archaeological remains, and, where applicable, their recovery, protection, and preservation. A number of federal and state laws provide legal and financial support for salvage archaeology. The Archaeological and Historic Preservation Act of 1974, for example, requires that up to one percent of the budget of any federal construction project be allocated for archaeological and historical salvage.

salvation   Salvation (from the Latin *salus*, "health," "safety," "well-being") is a religious concept that refers either to the process through which a person is brought from a condition of distress to a condition of ultimate well-being or to the state of ultimate well-being that is the result of that process. The meaning of the concept varies according to the different ways religious traditions understand the human plight and the ultimate state of human well-being.

In Christianity, salvation is variously conceived. One prominent conception emphasizes justification—the process through which the individual, alienated from God by sin, is reconciled to God and reckoned just or righteous through faith in Christ. Other religions present other views. In certain forms of Hinduism and Buddhism, for example, salvation is understood as liberation from the inevitable pain of existence in time by means of religious disciplines that ultimately achieve a state of being that is not determined by time-bound perceptions and forms of thought.

Salvation Army

Salvation Army The Salvation Army is an international Christian evangelical organization that was founded in London in 1865 by William Booth, a Methodist minister and evangelistic preacher. As a religious movement engaged in social services, the army has, since its inception, made a goal of approaching sociological problems with Christian concern.

In keeping with its name (adopted 1878), the Salvation Army is operated on a military pattern. Ministers are officers with military rank, and the general, headquartered in London, is the army's top international leader.

Basic training for each officer, following a required high school education, is a 2-year in-residence course at a Salvation Army School for Officers' Training. Besides formal study, the curriculum includes practical field experience in corps community centers and other institutions as well as orientation in all possible areas of Salvation Army service.

Salvation Army assistance is given without regard to race, age, sex, creed, or condition. Among the organization's many programs are correctional services for prisoners and parolees, day care, senior-citizen clubs and residences, summer camps, emergency and disaster services, missing-persons bureaus, rehabilitation for alcoholism and drug abuse, family counseling, and visitation to institutionalized individuals.

In an effort to attract those frightened away by church formality, the Salvation Army stresses music rather than the sacraments; music has been made an integral part of its ministry. Salvation Army brass bands, string combos, and vocal groups exist the world over.

Salvia

Salvia [sal'-vee-uh] *Salvia* is the generic name for sage and encompasses about 700 herbaceous, shrublike species of plants in the mint family, Labiatae. The stem

Scarlet sage, the most commonly grown of the ornamental salvias, has dark green ovate leaves and scarlet flowers that grow to 4 cm (1.5 in) long. Although a perennial, it is widely cultivated as an annual and blooms from early summer through late fall.

of these plants is squarish, and the leaves grow opposite to each other along a branch.

The common sage, *S. officinalis*, native to the Mediterranean region, is grown for its rough-textured, woolly leaves. These aromatic leaves, either fresh or dried, are used to flavor such meats as pork and sausage, cheese, and poultry seasoning. An essential oil is also produced from the leaves and used to flavor food, beverages, and perfumes. Sage tea has long been believed to be a spring tonic, increasing circulation, improving memory, and promoting longevity. Another medicinal herb, known as clary, *S. sclarea*, was used in past centuries in eyewashes to reduce inflammation.

An ornamental salvia from Brazil, scarlet sage, *S. splendens*, is often grown in flower gardens and borders for its vivid scarlet blooms, which are arranged in spikes. These flowers appear from early summer to fall. Two other ornamental salvias are *S. farinacea*, which has deep violet blue flowers and is grown as a bedding plant, and gentian sage, *S. patens*, with bright blue flowers and arrow-shaped leaves.

Salween River

Salween River [sal-ween'] The Salween River, the second longest river in southeastern Asia, rises in the Tanglha mountains of eastern Tibet and flows for 2,816 km (1,750 mi) south through deep gorges in China and Burma to its delta at Moulmein, on the Gulf of Martaban, Andaman Sea. Part of its lower course forms the Thailand-Burma border.

Salyut

Salyut [sahl-yoot'] Until it was augmented by the Mir program in 1986, Salyut was the only Soviet manned space-station program. Seven successful Salyut stations were launched between 1971 and 1982. Two distinct types of Salyut spacecraft apparently have been made: one devoted primarily to scientific research; the other, to applications of space technology and to Earth observation, including military reconnaissance.

A Salyut module is about 13.5 m (44.3 ft) long and weighs about 18,400 kg (40,600 lb). Its widest cylindrical section is 4 m (13 ft) in diameter, attached to a middle section 3 m (10 ft) in diameter and an end section 2 m (7 ft) in diameter. This end section, which is separated from the other two cylinders by an airlock, contains a docking port for Soyuz ferry spaceships and a hatch for exit into space. Another docking port can be installed at the opposite end. Solar panels extend from the middle section to provide electrical power. Salyuts are launched unmanned by Proton boosters, and cosmonaut crews follow separately aboard Soyuz spacecraft. At the end of its mission, a rocket engine on the Salyut is used to slow its orbital speed, causing it to fall safely into the Pacific Ocean.

On Feb. 20, 1986, the Soviet Union launched a new space station into Earth orbit. Given the name *Mir* (the Russian word for peace and world), the new ship is similar to the Salyut space station but with a number of im-

SOVIET SPACE STATIONS

Space Station Name	Launch Date	Decay Date	Operational Orbit	Visiting Spacecraft*
Salyut 1	Apr. 19, 1971	Oct. 11, 1971	250 to 270 km (155 to 170 mi)	Soyuz 10, 11
Salyut 2	Apr. 3, 1973	May 28, 1973	260 to 290 km (160 to 180 mi)	None
Cosmos 557	May 11, 1973	May 22, 1973	Never attained	
Salyut 3	June 25, 1974	Jan. 25, 1975	260 to 270 km (160 to 170 mi)	Soyuz 14, 15
Salyut 4	Dec. 26, 1974	Feb. 3, 1977	340 to 350 km (210 to 220 mi)	Soyuz 17, 18, 20
Salyut 5	June 22, 1976	Aug. 8, 1977	220 to 290 km (135 to 180 mi)	Soyuz 21, 23, 24
Salyut 6	Sept. 29, 1977	July 29, 1982	340 to 350 km (210 to 220 mi)	Soyuz 24 through 40, T1 through T4 Progress 1 through 12 Cosmos 1267
Salyut 7	Apr. 19, 1982	Still in orbit	219 to 278 km (136 to 173 mi)	Soyuz T5, T6, T7, T9 through T15 Progress 13 through 24 Cosmos 1443, 1686
Mir	Feb. 20, 1986	Still in orbit	Varies	Soyuz T15, TM, TM-2 through TM-8 Progress 25 through 37, Progress M1 Kvant; Module D

*Crew composition and launch and touchdown dates for all Soyuz craft are given in the table within the Soyuz article. The Progress craft are automated resupply vehicles. Cosmos craft are modules that dock with the stations, resupply them, and provide added space.

Mir, *a modified form of the Salyut station, undergoes preflight tests at the Baikonur Cosmodrome before its February 1986 launch. As with the* Salyut 7, Mir *has two docking ports at either end, but it also has four additional ports that enable the size of the station to be expanded by other modules. The station is about 17 m (56 ft) long and 4 m (13 ft) wide. At left is the main habitable area of the vehicle, and at far right is the forward airlock module.*

Salyut 6, *the most frequently used of the space stations orbited by the Soviet Union thus far, was designed for two persons to live and work in space for long periods of time. It consisted of a Soyuz spacecraft (1) that transported cosmonauts to and from the station, a transfer compartment (2), and a working and living area (3). A rear docking port (4) and rendezvous radar (5) enabled a second spacecraft to link up with the station. Other items contained in Salyut 6 were rocket engines (6) and attitude jets (7) to control its orbit, a solar telescope (8), a cosmonaut exercising treadmill (9), solar panels (10), instrument and control panels (11), and telemetry antennas (12).*

provements. *Mir* has a greater capacity for expansion, due to its 6 docking ports. It also has more windows, 2 private compartments for inhabitants, and a slightly increased interior space, due to the absence of certain Salyut fixtures.

Salzburg [zahlts'-boork]   Salzburg, the capital city of the north central Austrian federal state of Salzburg, is situated near the foothills of the Alps and the border with Germany, about 270 km (170 mi) west of Vienna. The city's population is 137,833 (1986 est.). Salzburg's name is derived from the area's rich salt deposits. Industrial products include musical instruments, beer, hardware, and textiles.

Tourists are drawn by the scenery of the surrounding Salzach Valley and by the city's architectural and cultural assets. The town is dominated by the large and well-pre-served fortress of Hohensalzburg (1077). The Abbey of Saint Peter and the Convent of Nonnberg, founded about 700 and remodeled in the 15th century, are also noteworthy. Salzburg's present architectural splendor is largely the result of extensive building by the prince-archbishops and wealthy burghers of the 16th–18th centuries. Above all, the city is known for its musical heritage (Mozart was born there) and the annual Salzburg Festival of music. The University of Salzburg (1622) was reestablished in 1962.

The Romans named the site Juvavum. In 798, under its present name, it became the seat of an archbishop. In 1278 its archbishops were recognized as princes of the Holy Roman Empire. The prince-archbishops later vastly increased the power and wealth of their fortress city. Under the influence of the French Revolution, the see was secularized in 1802; the city passed to Austrian control in 1816.

SAM see SURFACE-TO-AIR MISSILE

Samaras, Lucas [sah-mahr'-uhs] Lucas Samaras, b. Kastoria, Greece, Sept. 14, 1936, is among the more unorthodox of contemporary American sculptors. In the late 1950s he began to exhibit his sculpture and to perform in collaboration with such experimentalists as Allan Kaprow, an inventor of "happenings." Elements of theatrical performance persist in Samaras's art—particularly in his use of photography as a medium for "autopolaroids," his bizarre self-portraits, and for his series "Sittings." Disturbing overtones are evident in his more recent gruff, expressionist-style clay figures of compounded bodies.

Samaria [suh-mair'-ee-uh] In ancient history, Samaria was the name of both the capital city of northern Israel and its surrounding central Palestinian territory. The city dominated the high road that led from Jerusalem to Damascus and the cities of Phoenicia. Its site is near Nablus in what is now the WEST BANK. After the dissolution (c.921 BC) of Israel's United Monarchy the northern kingdom of Israel was governed from Tirzah. According to the Bible (I Kings 16:24), by about 870, Omri, founder of the Omride dynasty, purchased the site of the city of Samaria and built his capital there.

A series of major excavations beginning in 1908–10 unearthed a small, splendid city that had thrived during biblical times. More than 500 ivory fragments from wall and furniture inlays, found in the royal quarter, vividly illustrate King AHAB's "house of ivory" (I Kings 22:39) and reference by the prophet Amos to "beds of ivory" (Amos 6:4). The city continued to exist after the fall of the northern kingdom in 722 BC; in the 1st century AD it was known as Sebaste.

Samaritans [suh-mair'-uh-tuhnz] The term *Samaritans*, which originally referred to the inhabitants of Samaria, is now generally restricted to a sectarian Jewish community that lived in the area. In Jewish tradition the Samaritans are held to be colonists introduced after the Assyrian conquest of the region (722 BC) who adopted a distorted form of Judaism. The Samaritans themselves claimed descent from the tribes of Ephraim and Manasseh and believed that they had preserved the way and will of Yahweh. The Samaritans held to the Pentateuch as their Scripture and honored Moses as the only prophet. The Jews refused to let them participate in building the Second Temple in Jerusalem, so they built their own temple on Mount Gerizim (destroyed in 128 BC). In his parable of the Good Samaritan (Luke 10:25–37), Jesus rebuked the Jews for their hostility toward the Samaritans. Small communities of Samaritans still exist in Palestine.

samarium [suh-mair'-ee-uhm] Samarium is a chemical element, a very hard, silvery white metal of the LAN-THANIDE SERIES in Group IIIB of the periodic table. Its symbol is Sm, its atomic number is 62, and its atomic weight is 150.4 (average weight of its seven natural isotopes). Three natural isotopes are radioactive: ^{147}Sm, ^{148}Sm, and ^{149}Sm. Samarium was discovered in 1879 by Lecoq de Boisbaudran, who isolated it from samarskite. The metal ignites in air at 150° C. Because one of its isotopes has a high cross section of neutron absorption, samarium is used in the control rods of nuclear reactors. An alloy with cobalt is used to make a magnetic material with the highest resistance to demagnetization of any known material.

Samarkand [suh-mur-kahnt'] Samarkand is the capital of Samarkand oblast in Uzbekistan, USSR. It is situated in the valley of the Zeravshan River in Central Asia. The city's population is 366,000 (1989). Samarkand has a diversified industrial base; automotive and tractor components, movie equipment, and phosphate fertilizers are produced in addition to the traditional silk fabrics, hides and skins, wines, fruits, and tobacco. Samarkand State University was founded in 1933.

One of the oldest cities of Central Asia, Samarkand has many noted remains from the 14th to the 17th century, when it flourished as the fabled capital of the Mongol empire of TIMUR and his successors. The ruins of the mosque of Bibi Khanom (1399–1404) and the great open Registan Square, lined with the remains of three Muslim religious colleges, are visible. Outside the city are Gur Emir (Timur's mausoleum) and an astronomical observatory built under Ulugbek, a son of Timur.

Known in antiquity as Maracanda, Samarkand is believed to date back to the 6th century BC, when it was the capital of ancient Sogdiana. It was destroyed in 329 BC by Alexander the Great. After the 8th-century Arab conquest it flourished under the Samanid dynasty of the 9th and 10th centuries before it fell to GENGHIS KHAN in 1219. Under Timur and his successors Samarkand was a city of wealth and prosperity. It declined in the 18th century and fell under the sway of Bukhara before the mid-19th-century Russian conquest of central Asia. Following completion of a railroad in 1888, the economy developed. Samarkand served as the capital of Uzbekistan from 1924 until 1930, when the capital was moved to TASHKENT.

Samarra [sah-mahr'-rah] The 9th-century Islamic capital and present-day Iraqi town of Samarra lies on the left bank of the Tigris River about 110 km (68 mi) northwest of Baghdad. Painted pottery produced by the prehistoric Samarra culture of the 5th millennium BC was first discovered in the early 20th century beneath the Islamic buildings.

The once-magnificent Islamic city was founded (836) by Caliph al-Mutasim and was gradually extended by its eight resident caliphs until the palaces, mosques, gardens, and houses stretched for approximately 30 km (19 mi) along the river. The city declined rapidly, however, after the capital was returned to Baghdad by Caliph al-Mutamid. By the 13th century ancient Samarra was almost completely in ruins.

Sammartini, Giovanni Battista [sahm-mahr-tee'-nee]

The most important Italian symphony composer of his time, Giovanni Battista Sammartini, b. *c.*1700, d. Jan. 15, 1775, was a pioneer in the early development of the classical forms. He studied in Milan and subsequently held posts in several of the city's churches and at the convent of Santa Maria Maddalena.

Although Sammartini's works include numerous masses, motets, and other sacred music, his most significant contributions were in orchestral and chamber music, which include trio sonatas, string quartets, and approximately 24 symphonies. His most famous pupil was Christoph Willibald Gluck.

Samoa [suh-moh'-uh]

Samoa consists of a group of volcanic islands in the South Pacific Ocean about halfway between Honolulu and Sydney. It is divided into AMERICAN SAMOA and WESTERN SAMOA. American Samoa comprises six islands and has an area of 199 km² (77 mi²) and a population of 41,840 (1990 est.). The capital, PAGO PAGO, is located on the island of Tutuila. Western Samoa has an area of 2,831 km² (1,093 mi²) and a population of 186,031 (1990 est.). APIA, its capital, is on Upolu, one of the principal islands. Western Samoa has one other major island, Savaii (the largest), and seven smaller islands.

The first settlers of Samoa arrived during the 1st century from eastern Melanesia, and from Samoa they spread Polynesian culture to countless other islands. Today most Samoans, who speak a language belonging to the Malayo-Polynesian (Austronesian) linguistic family, are Christians.

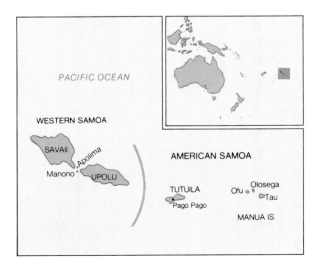

In 1722 the Dutch explorer Jacob Roggeveen was the first European to discover the islands. The United States and Germany divided them in 1900. New Zealand administered Western Samoa from 1914 until independence (1962). Since 1977, voters on American Samoa have elected their own governor.

Samos [sah'-maws]

Samos is a Greek island of the Sporades group in the Aegean Sea, located only 1.6 km (1 mi) west of Turkey. The island is about 43 km (27 mi) long and 19 km (12 mi) wide and has an area of 502 km² (194 mi²). Vathí, the capital, is situated on the north coast. The island is traversed by hills and mountains, of which the highest is Kerketeus (1,433 m/4,701 ft). Agriculture is the mainstay of the economy. Samos is the site of the temple of Hera (begun 5th century BC). The mathematician and philosopher Pythagoras was born there.

Occupied by the Greeks during the 11th century BC, Samos became a leading commercial and cultural center. Throughout history invaders sought to conquer the island because of its strategic location, and it was ruled in succession by Egyptians, Persians, Romans, Byzantines, Genoese, and Ottomans. Greece annexed Samos in 1912. During World War II the island was occupied by the Axis powers.

SAMOS [say'-mahs]

SAMOS (an acronym for Satellite and Missile Observation System) was an early effort by the U.S. Air Force in developing satellites for military reconnaissance from space. Although the early launches were marred by failures, pictures from *SAMOS 2* in 1961 permitted the U.S. intelligence community for the first time to have a precise count of the number and location of various Soviet missile-launching sites and silos. The project later came under the U.S. Air Force's secrecy procedures; further launches were announced but not identified by name.

Samoset [sam'-uh-set]

Samoset, 1590–1653?, a sachem, or leader, of the Pemaquid Indian tribe of the ABNAKI confederacy, allegedly greeted the Pilgrims soon after their landing at Plymouth. It was he who introduced the Pilgrims to the WAMPANOAG sachem, MASSASSOIT. In 1625, Samoset signed the first land-sale transaction ever executed between the eastern tribes and the English colonists, and he sold another parcel of land in 1653. He apparently died soon after and was buried in his village's cemetery, within what is now Bristol, Maine.

Samothrace [sam'-oh-thrays]

Samothrace is a mountainous Greek island near the coast of Thrace. Inhabited since Neolithic times, it was colonized by Greeks about 700 BC and became the religious center of the ancient northern Aegean. Samothrace's Sanctuary of the Great Gods operated from that time through the 4th century AD, although it was damaged by earthquakes in about 200 BC. Its international mysteries were supported by Alexander the Great, Hellenistic kings, and Roman emperors. Traces of the ancient city of Palaiopolis include an acropolis, city walls, and a necropolis. The famous Winged Victory (Nike) of Samothrace, a Hellenistic work, is in the Louvre, Paris.

Samoyed [sam'-uh-yed]   The Samoyed, named for a Siberian tribe, is a medium-sized, all-white breed of dog in the spitz family. The dogs are compact and strong, with dense, long coats, small pointed ears, and a bushy tail carried over the back. Males stand 53.3–59.7 cm (21–23.5 in) high at the shoulder and weigh 20.3–24.9 kg (45–55 lb). The double coat combines a soft, short undercoat and a longer, straighter outercoat growing through it, with colorings varying from white to biscuit. The breed is most likely a close cousin to the Siberian husky, although heavier. The Samoyed, originally developed as a sled dog, has been used on the great Arctic and Antarctic expeditions. The first Samoyeds were brought to England about 1900 by fur traders who had gone into the far reaches of Siberia.

The Samoyed is a medium-sized working dog originally used to pull sleds and to herd reindeer in northwestern Siberia.

sampan [sam'-pan]   The sampan is a light, flat-bottomed, small boat originally developed by the Chinese and now used throughout the inland and coastal waterways of the Far East for fishing and transporting cargoes or people as well as for homes. Sampans have evolved into various sturdy craft that are wide relative to their length and are propelled by oars or by sail. Traditionally, the smaller are sculled and the larger rigged with masts and square sails. The Hawaiian sampan is primarily a fishing boat that is motor driven.

sampling   In statistics, a population is a collection of elements that have a specified characteristic, and a sample is some part of the population. Because many populations of interest are too large to work with directly, techniques of statistical sampling have been devised for working with samples taken from larger populations. A well-known example of a sampling technique is a public-opinion survey, and the quality of most manufactured items is controlled by checking samples on the production line. Current concerns with ecology and the environment present a need to sample the concentrations of many pollutants in the air and water and also to watch for biological effects by sampling the sizes of various populations of plants and animals.

Unless a sample is chosen by a random mechanism, it will not be a reasonable one; this is why methods of random sampling, or random selection, have been devised. Old methods, such as throwing dice, have been replaced by the use of random numbers produced by a computer. This method can be used whenever there is a list of names. Sometimes no lists are available. Thus, for example, the important topic of estimating the size of biological populations must be handled differently—areas are usually chosen at random. In quality control one might take a random sample—from each day's production, for example—and test all the items to see if they are satisfactory.

Sampson, William T.   William Thomas Sampson, b. Palmyra, N.Y., Feb. 9, 1840, d. May 6, 1902, an American naval officer, commanded the fleet blockading Cuba during the SPANISH-AMERICAN WAR. When the Spanish fleet attempted to escape the American blockade of Santiago de Cuba on July 3, 1898, Sampson was in conference several miles from the scene of battle. Although he sped toward the scene, he arrived too late to play a major role in the short battle that destroyed the Spanish fleet and broke Spain's link with its colony. Sampson's subordinate, Commodore Winfield Scott Schley, directed the battle, but the standing orders determining tactics were Sampson's work.

Samson   As described in the Old Testament Book of JUDGES, Samson was a military hero of Israel who fought the PHILISTINES. From the tribe of Dan, he was dedicated at birth to be a Nazirite, after his parents heard an angel announce that he would "begin to save Israel from the Philistines." As a Nazirite, he was to avoid wine and contact with the dead, and leave his hair uncut. He married a Philistine woman and, when the marriage went awry, performed singular feats of strength in border warfare against the Philistines. When DELILAH, bribed by the Philistines, learned the secret of his strength, she had his locks shorn while he slept. He was then seized, blinded, and imprisoned. Samson perished willingly when he pulled down the temple at Gaza upon himself and his captors.

Samuel, Books of   The two books of Samuel, which follow Judges in the Hebrew BIBLE and Ruth in the English, tell the stories of Samuel, SAUL, and DAVID. The events from the cataclysmic breakup of Israel's premonarchic league through the foundation of Saul's monarchy and the beginnings of David's political emergence to the death of Saul are narrated in 1 Samuel. David's unification of Israel and Judah, his imperial expansion, and the subsequent struggle to decide who would succeed David are described in 2 Samuel.

The books are named after Samuel, the last major representative of the old league, who figured prominently in the transition to monarchy. He plays no role in 2 Samuel, however, which may explain why the Septuagint and Vulgate versions designate 1-2 Samuel as 1-2 Kings.

Both volumes are part of the Deuteronomistic History (compiled in the time of Josiah, c.640–609 BC), but they largely consist of preexisting literary sources.

Samuelson, Paul A. A Nobel Prize winner for economics, Paul Anthony Samuelson, b. Gary, Ind., May 15, 1915, is the author of *Economics* (1st ed., 1948), a hugely successful college text that continues to appear in revised editions. Samuelson received a Ph.D. in economics at Harvard University in 1941, where he came under the influence of the theories of John Maynard Keynes. A member of the faculty of the Massachusetts Institute of Technology since 1940, Samuelson has also served on various government committees and has been an advisor to Presidents John F. Kennedy and Lyndon B. Johnson.

samurai [sam'-uh-ry] The samurai were Japan's warrior class for seven centuries. Their name was derived from the Japanese word for service, *saburau*. The samurai were military retainers who emerged as military aristocrats and then as military rulers. Samurai involvement in government began in 1156, and from 1160 to 1185 the

warrior Taira no Kiyomori dominated affairs at court. In the Gempei War (1180–85) the Taira family was displaced by the Minamoto clan. YORITOMO established the first of the military governments, or shogunates (see SHOGUN), that dominated political life from 1185 until 1868.

Medieval samurai were generally illiterate, rural landowners who farmed between battles. During the shogunate of the TOKUGAWA family (1600–1868) the samurai as a class were transformed into military bureaucrats and were required to master administrative skills as well as military arts. As hereditary warriors they were governed by a code of ethics—*bushido*, meaning "the way of the warrior"—that defined service and conduct appropriate to their status as elite members of Japanese society.

San The San are a people of southern Africa who traditionally have lived as HUNTER-GATHERERS grouped in small bands of 30 to 100. They have also been called Bushmen but this designation is now considered pejorative. Speakers of various dialects of a click language (see AFRICAN LANGUAGES), the San had occupied the whole of southern Africa for some thousands of years before the arrival of the KHOIKHOI and the BANTU-speaking peoples. These peoples began the process of displacing the San from their indigenous hunting grounds probably as early as the 12th century. The arrival of Europeans in the 15th century sped up the process, and the Boer-organized commandos had virtually exterminated the San in South Africa by the end of the 19th century. Some Bantu-speaking peoples, particularly the TSWANA, incorporated many of the San into their societies by granting them servant, or serf, status. Today the only surviving hunter-gatherer San are

This San hunter, wearing leg ornaments made from spider cocoons, makes a fire by rotating a stick in a pile of dry grass. Traditionally hunter-gatherers who travel in nomadic bands, the San now live primarily in the Kalahari Desert of southwestern Africa.

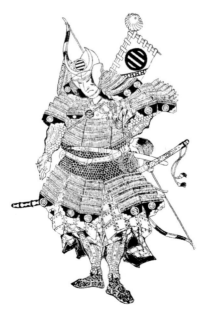

The samurai, an elite warrior class of feudal Japan serving under the daimyos, or barons, were the dominant military power in Japan from the 12th century through the Tokugawa period (1600–1868). Following the abolition of feudalism in 1871, they became prominent members of the government of modern Japan. The samurai here displays the two swords, ceremonial headdress, and kamishimo, a bulky, lamellate garment that distinguished the samurai class.

found in Botswana (where the !Kung of the Kalahari Desert live), in Namibia, and in Angola. The San population is estimated at about 50,000.

The effective organizational unit in traditional San society is the band, the members of which are linked by elaborate kin networks. Although polygamy is permitted, most marriages are monogamous. Religious practices are not clearly institutionalized in spite of the existence of a rich and complex mythology. Magical and medical practices are closely integrated with dancing and trance states, constituting a system of both psychological and physical healing. The San are noted for the fine paintings they and their ancestors have executed on the walls of cave and rock shelters (see PREHISTORIC ART).

San Agustín [sahn ah-goos-teen']   The archaeological zone of San Agustín comprises a cluster of about 40 small sites covering more than 500 km² (200 mi²) near the headwaters of the Rio Magdalena in southeastern Colombia. More than 300 monumental stone statues have been found throughout the area, suggesting that San Agustín was once an important ceremonial center. Occupation of the area dates back to almost 500 BC, but construction of earthworks and stone sculptures apparently did not begin until about AD 100.

San Andreas Fault [san an-dray'-uhs]   The San Andreas Fault is a major fracture in the Earth's crust at the mutual boundary of two of the major plates that make up the Earth's crust—one supporting the North American continent, the other the western edge of California and much of the Pacific Ocean and its floor. The fault runs about 80 km (50 mi) inland from southern California north to San Francisco, where it continues north along the coast for about 320 km (200 mi) before turning out to sea. The San Andreas Fault is a strike-slip FAULT, with the seaward plate moving north. Movement along the

Tomales Bay, situated between Pt. Reyes Peninsula and the mainland of southern California, was created by the horizontal movement of two sections of the Earth's crust. The boundary of these sections, the San Andreas Fault , extends 965 km (600 mi) along a north-south axis.

fault averages only a few centimeters a year, and portions of the fault line do not move for years at a time. Enormous pressure builds up, and it is often released through earthquakes. The San Francisco earthquake of 1906 was laid to movement along the fault, as was the more recent quake that hit San Francisco in 1989.

San Antonio   San Antonio is a city and port of entry in south central Texas, on the San Antonio River. The seat of Bexar County, it has a population of 935,933 (1990); the metropolitan area has 1,302,099 residents. San Antonio is centered on the small, picturesque San Antonio River, which meanders under numerous bridges through the downtown sector. More than half of the population are of Mexican origin, and Spanish is widely spoken.

The city's economy is primarily commercial. Large markets sell livestock, related products, and agricultural produce. Food processing and clothing, leather goods, chemical, and machinery manufacturing are the principal industries. Nearby air force and army bases contribute to the economy, and San Antonio is a retirement center for military personnel.

Among the cultural and historical attractions are Saint Mary's (1852) and Trinity (1869) universities; the Arneson River Theatre, where the San Antonio River separates the stage from the audience; San Fernando Cathedral (begun 1738); the Governor's Palace, built in 1749; La Villita, the restored original Spanish settlement; and the famous ALAMO, now a museum.

San Antonio was founded as a Spanish *presidio* (garrison) in 1718, and several missions, including the Alamo, were established nearby. The first civilian settlers came from the Canary Islands in 1731. The city played a prominent role in early Texas history; the Battle of the Alamo was fought (1836) during the TEXAS REVOLUTION. Because of its location at the beginning of the CHISHOLM TRAIL, the city was a major gathering point of cattle drives during the late 19th century. It was the largest city in Texas in the early part of the 20th century.

San Bernardino [san bur-nuh-dee'-noh]   San Bernardino, the seat of San Bernardino County, lies about 100 km (62 mi) east of Los Angeles in one of California's areas of rapid population growth. The city has a population of 164,164 (1990). The surrounding region produces citrus fruits, grapes, and alfalfa. In San Bernardino chemicals, foodstuffs, and textiles are manufactured, and aerospace and railroad industries complement the economy. The annual National Orange Show has taken place there since 1915. The site of an unsuccessful mission settlement in 1810, the land was purchased by Mormons in 1852. A city, patterned after Salt Lake City, was laid out.

San Blas Indians   see CUNA

San Diego   San Diego, the seat of San Diego County and second largest city in California, is about 160 km

San Diego, a port and county seat, has the third most populous metropolitan area in California. The city has a diverse economy and derives substantial revenue through manufacturing, maritime commerce, military installations, and agricultural activities in the surrounding area.

(100 mi) south of Los Angeles and 20 km (12 mi) from the Mexican border. The city has a population of 1,110,-549 (1990), and metropolitan San Diego, 2,498,016. The population is principally Anglo, but Chicano and black communities have also formed. San Diego's industries include fish canning and aerospace and electronic equipment manufacturing. The deepwater harbor of San Diego Bay is the base for a major commercial fishing fleet and for U.S. Navy, Army, Marine, and Coast Guard operations.

Among the city's educational facilities are the University of San Diego (1949) and a campus of the University of California (1912) in adjacent La Jolla. Several research facilities, including the SCRIPPS INSTITUTION OF OCEANOGRAPHY (1903), are headquartered in and around the city. The city has a successful tourist industry. Places of interest include the San Diego Zoo, Mission San Diego, and Cabrillo National Monument, the site of Point Loma Lighthouse (1855).

Juan Rodríguez Cabrillo discovered San Diego Bay in 1542 and named it San Miguel. It was renamed San Diego in 1602 by Sebastián Vizcaíno. On July 16, 1769, Gaspar de Portolá established a base for the exploration of California; on the same day Father Junípero Serra dedicated the first California Franciscan mission there. The town grew slowly under Mexican rule and was captured by U.S. forces in 1885. The present city was laid out in 1867 by Alonzo E. Horton. An 1870 gold strike and the arrival of the Santa Fe Railroad in 1885 assured San Diego's growth.

San Francisco   San Francisco, located on the coast of California, occupies a peninsula that is the southern landfall of the Golden Gate, a narrow channel connecting the Pacific Ocean with San Francisco Bay, one of the world's most beautiful natural harbors. Spanning the channel is the GOLDEN GATE BRIDGE, long a symbol of the city as the U.S. port of entry on the Pacific coast. The

population of the city is 723,959 (1990); the metropolitan area has 1,603,678 residents. San Francisco, coextensive with San Francisco County, is a popular tourist city, offering spectacular views from its 43 hills.

Contemporary City. San Francisco today has an economy very much dependent on white-collar industries. A skyline of high-rise office buildings, dominated by the

A cable car travels down one of San Francisco's steep hills. Despite the development of the Bay Area Rapid Transit System, the cable car system, which was introduced in the city in 1873, has been kept in service.

SAN FRANCISCO

■	Major Urban Area	┼┼┼	Railroad
■	Recreation Area	•┼•┼	Cable Car Line
■	Area of Interest	- - -	County Boundary
■	Cemetery		City Limit
〔80〕	Expressway or Interstate Highway	■	Point of Interest
	Road or Street	〔101〕①	Highway Number

City type size indicates relative importance.

Scale 1:500,000

Scale 1:50,000

Transamerica Pyramid and the Bank of America tower, marks the downtown terminus of the Bay Area Rapid Transit (BART), one of the country's most modern high-speed mass-transit systems. On Russian and Nob hills, stately mansions have been replaced by luxury apartment buildings and hotels. The last three cable car lines, now designated national historic landmarks, still cross the hills. To the east of Nob Hill lies Chinatown, one of the largest Chinese communities outside Asia, and Telegraph Hill, the location of the first western telegraph station. Fisherman's Wharf, a commercial fishing port established by 19th-century Italian immigrants, is now a row of res-taurants, souvenir shops, and motels. Nearby, The Can-nery and Ghirardelli Square, once fruit canning and choc-olate plants, respectively, now house specialty shops, res-taurants, and art galleries. Within San Francisco Bay is a former federal prison, ALCATRAZ.

Culture. San Francisco is a major educational and cul-tural center. The University of San Francisco (1855), the University of California–San Francisco (1873), and San Francisco State University (1899) are located in the city. The Opera House, home of the San Francisco Ballet as well as the SAN FRANCISCO OPERA ASSOCIATION, was the nation's first city-owned opera house; it was also the

The Golden Gate Bridge stretches across the Golden Gate, a strait separating the Pacific Ocean from San Francisco Bay, and links the city of San Francisco with its northern suburbs in Marin County. San Francisco Bay, discovered (1769) by an overland rather than a marine expedition, is one of the world's great natural harbors.

birthplace (1945) of the United Nations. The city also maintains a symphony orchestra and three museums. The California Academy of Sciences (1853) operates the Morrison Planetarium and the Steinhart Aquarium.

History. The Presidio, on the north coast of the city, was established as a Spanish fort in 1776. (It remains a U.S. military reservation.) The first civilian settlement, named Yerba Buena, was established in 1835. During the Mexican War it was taken by U.S. forces and renamed San Francisco. The 1849 California gold rush and the 1859 Comstock Lode silver strike spurred the city's growth. Waves of immigrants arrived, and large Chinese, Italian, Filipino, and Japanese communities were established. On Apr. 18, 1906, San Francisco suffered a major earthquake; the resulting 3-day fire razed the core of the city. The city was quickly rebuilt. During World War II it became a bustling port of embarkation for the military. A strong earthquake in 1989 extensively damaged the Marina district.

Long referred to simply as "The City," San Francisco has been the home of such groups as the Bohemians of the 1890s, the beats of the 1950s (see BEAT GENERATION), and the "flower children" who congregated around Haight-Ashbury in the 1960s.

San Francisco Bay   San Francisco Bay, east of the city of San Francisco, is a 77-km-long (48-mi), 5- to 19-km-wide (3- to 12-mi) waterway in western California. The narrow GOLDEN GATE strait, spanned by the GOLDEN GATE BRIDGE, connects it with the Pacific Ocean. The bay, 70% of which is less than 3.6 m (12 ft) deep, contains several small islands. The English explorer Sir Francis Drake is believed to have entered the bay in 1579.

San Francisco Opera Association   The San Francisco Opera Association, which emerged in its present form in 1923 and moved into its current home, the War Memorial Opera House, in 1932, is second in prestige only to the Metropolitan Opera among American companies. It was directed first by Gaetano Merola (for whom its training program is named), then by the influential Kurt Herbert Adler (1953–80), Terry McEwen (1982–88), and currently by Lotfi Mansouri (1988–). The company's season runs from September to mid-December. In addition, a wide variety of subsidiary programs is presented, including those of the San Francisco Opera Center and the Merola Opera Program.

San Joaquin River [san wah-keen']   The San Joaquin River rises in the Sierra Nevada in east central California and flows for 560 km (350 mi) west and northwest through the fertile San Joaquin Valley. The San Joaquin joins the SACRAMENTO RIVER just before it drains into Sui-sun Bay, northeast of San Francisco. The San Joaquin River has been extensively altered by humans to provide irrigation water, hydroelectric power, and a shipping channel.

San Jose [san hoh-zay']   San Jose, located about 64 km (40 mi) southeast of San Francisco, is a city in western California and the seat of Santa Clara County. The population of the city is 782,248 (1990); that of metropolitan San Jose is 1,497,577. The city is situated in the Santa Clara Valley at the southern end of San Francisco Bay. San Jose is part of the San Francisco Bay urban complex consisting of both industrial and residential suburbs. Food processing and wine making are important, although many former orchards and truck farms are now home or factory sites.

The San Jose area has become one of the nation's leading centers of the computer and electronics industry and has been nicknamed Silicon Valley. Other industries produce beer, paint, plastics and aluminum. San Jose State University (1857) is there. The Ames Research Center of the National Aeronautics and Space Administration (NASA) is nearby. San Jose is also the home of several museums, including Rosicrucian Egyptian Museum and Art Gallery. Alum Rock Park and the Municipal Rose Garden offer recreational facilities.

San Jose was established by the Spanish in 1777 and served (1849–51) as California's first capital. Fruit growing began in the mid-1800s, and, with the arrival of the railroad in 1864, San Jose soon became the distribution center for the entire Santa Clara Valley.

San José [sahn hoh-say'] San José, the capital of Costa Rica since 1823, lies in the mountainous center of the country. The population is 281,557 (1988 est.). Situated on the Pan American Highway, San José has industries manufacturing textiles and furniture and processing coffee, sugarcane, and cacao grown nearby. The city is subjected to frequent earthquakes because of its situation in a zone of tectonic activity.

San José has numerous parks and gardens, and its notable buildings include the Palacio Nacional, a 19th-century cathedral, the national theater, and a museum with pre-Columbian artifacts. The city is the seat of the University of Costa Rica (1843). About 30 km (20 mi) northeast of San

José is the volcano Irazú (3,432 m/11,260 ft). Settled in 1736, San José became an important tobacco manufacturing center in the second half of the 18th century.

San Juan [sahn hwahn] The capital of the Commonwealth of Puerto Rico, San Juan is located on the Atlantic Ocean, on the island's northern coast. It is the island's leading port and manufacturing center. The population of the city is 437,745 (1990) with almost 1 million persons residing in the metropolitan area.

Historic Old San Juan, characterized by numerous colonial buildings and narrow streets, is located on an island in the harbor and is connected by bridges and a causeway to the rest of the city. This section attracts many tourists, who also enjoy the gambling casinos, fine beaches, and tropical climate. Industries in San Juan include the refining of sugar and petroleum; distilling and brewing; the manufacturing of cement, pharmaceuticals, metal, tobacco, clothing, and jewelry; and publishing. The University of Puerto Rico, founded in 1903, is located in the town of Río Piedras, just southeast of San Juan.

Old San Juan has many historic buildings, including San Juan Cathedral (1540), which contains the tomb of Juan Ponce de León; San José Church (c.1532); and the Governor's Palace, La Fortaleza (begun 1533).

The Spanish explorer Juan Ponce de León founded (1508) the first settlement, Caparra. In 1521 the town was relocated to the site of Old San Juan. The Spanish built two forts, El Morro during the 16th century and San Cristóbal during the 17th century; these strongholds guarded San Juan successfully for much of its history. The city passed to the United States in 1898, during the Spanish-American War.

The luxurious resort hotels of San Juan's Condado section, on the main island, line the coast. The capital and primary commercial and industrial center of Puerto Rico, San Juan is one of the Caribbean's leading tourist resorts, offering the hotels, nightclubs, casinos, and beaches in the modern part of the city and the historic charm of Old San Juan, located on two small islands near the mouth of the city's harbor.

San Juan Boundary Dispute   The San Juan Boundary Dispute, a quarrel between the United States and Great Britain over possession of the islands in the San Juan de Fuca Strait, arose out of the Oregon Treaty of 1846. The treaty extended the U.S.–Canadian boundary—49° north latitude—westward from the Rocky Mountains to the Pacific and down the middle of the strait, leaving Vancouver Island in the possession of Canada. The many small islands in the strait made delineation of the boundary difficult, and the United States and Britain both claimed the San Juan archipelago in 1856. The two nations appointed Emperor William I of Germany as arbiter, and in 1872 awarded the San Juan Islands to the United States.

See also: OREGON QUESTION.

San Lorenzo [san luh-ren'-zoh]   San Lorenzo, located on the Río Chiquito in the coastal Gulf plain of southern Veracruz, Mexico, was the first capital of the ancient OLMEC civilization and the most powerful center in MESOAMERICA from 1200 to 900 BC. Between 1500 and 1200 BC the site had grown from a simple farming village into a large civic-ceremonial center that later dominated the Gulf coast region and extended its economic influence throughout Mesoamerica. About 900 BC, San Lorenzo suffered a drastic cultural decline; thereafter, LA VENTA became the most powerful Olmec center. By 400 BC, San Lorenzo was abandoned.

The core of the site was built atop a huge artificial ridge. More than 200 clay platforms supported small, perishable houses and temples. Buried stone drains linked a series of artificial reservoirs. San Lorenzo is best known for monumental stone sculptures, in particular colossal human heads, which were ceremonially buried within the ridge at about the time of the center's decline.

San Luis Potosí, (city) [sahn loo-ees' poh-toh-see']   San Luis Potosí, the capital of the state of San Luis Potosí, lies 1,880 m (6,170 ft) above sea level on the central plateau of Mexico. The population of this agricultural, mining, and transportation center is 406,630 (1983 est.). The city, located on the Pan American Highway, has metal-processing plants, textile and flour mills, furniture factories, and leatherworking shops. Colonial buildings, characterized by multicolored tile decorations, include the cathedral (begun 1670) and a baroque church. The Autonomous University of San Luis Potosí is located in the city. Settled in 1583, the city became important after the discovery of the San Pedro silver mines nearby. In 1910, Francisco I. Madero prepared his revolutionary *Plan de San Luís* while he was in the municipal prison there.

San Luis Potosí (state)   San Luis Potosí (1990 pop., 2,001,966) is an inland mountainous state in northeastern Mexico, traversed by the SIERRA MADRE Oriental. The state's area of 63,068 km² (24,351 mi²) consists of extensive plateaus and a small, fertile lowland. The capital is the city of San Luis Potosí. Minerals include large silver deposits, mined since the 17th century, and gold, copper, lead, zinc, antimony, arsenic, and quicksilver. Petroleum fields at Ebano and Limón are also important. Agriculture, primarily livestock raising, is concentrated in the uplands. Home of the HUASTEC and Chichimec Indians, the region was conquered by the Spanish during the 1520s.

San Marino   The independent republic of San Marino is entirely surrounded by Italian territory. It lies 220 km (137 mi) north of Rome and is the oldest and one of the smallest republics in the world. The capital is San Marino.

Land, People, and Economy. San Marino consists essentially of Monte Titano, an isolated limestone mountain lying within the APENNINES that rises 739 m (2,425 ft) above sea level. It culminates in three peaks, each topped by a medieval tower. San Marino has an average annual temperature of 10° to 16° C (50° to 60° F), and the annual precipitation totals 889 mm (35 in).

Ethnically Italians, the San Marinese are overwhelmingly Italian-speaking Roman Catholics. Nearly half of the citizens of the republic live abroad.

Traditionally, much of the population was engaged in agriculture or stone quarrying, but today tourism is the mainstay of the economy. Light industry, including the manufacture of cement, leather goods, textiles, and pottery, is also important. Sales of postage stamps abroad and Italian-government payments for tobacco and gasoline monopolies are important sources of government revenue. San Marino belongs to the Italian customs union.

Government and History. San Marino's constitution dates to AD 1600. The popularly elected 60-member Great and General Council serves as the legislative body, which elects two captains-regent to 6-month terms as executives. The Congress of State serves as cabinet.

According to tradition, San Marino dates to the 4th century AD. The earliest authentic reference to it appears in an 8th-century text mentioning a castle on the moun-

AT A GLANCE

REPUBLIC OF SAN MARINO

Land: Area: 61.2 km^2 (24.1 mi^2). Capital: San Marino (1990 est. pop., 2,343). Largest city: Serravalle/Dogano (1990 est. pop., 4,626).

People: Population (1990 est.): 23,000. Density: 376 persons per km^2 (954 per mi^2). Distribution (1990): 90% urban, 10% rural. Official language: Italian. Major religion: Roman Catholicism.

Government: Type: republic. Legislature: Great and General Council. Political subdivisions: 9 castles.

Economy: GNP (1987): $188 million; $8,590 per capita. Labor distribution (1990): manufacturing—35%; trade—16%; government—16%; construction and public utilities—8%, services—6%; other—19%. Currency: 1 Italian lira = 100 centesimi.

Education and Health: Literacy (1990): 90% of adult population. Universities (1987): none. Hospital beds (1987): 149. Physicians (1987): 60. Life expectancy (1990): women—79; men—74. Infant mortality (1990): 9 per 1,000 live births.

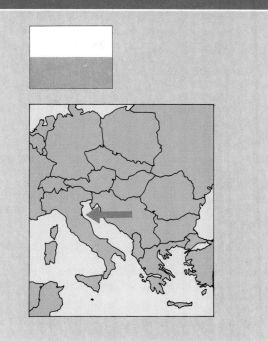

tain. The small settlement that grew up around it was at times under the protection of the papacy and the Montefeltro dukes of Urbino. Numerous attempts were made to terminate its independence, but each time it was protected by the uneasy balance of power among the Italian republics. In 1862, San Marino concluded a treaty of friendship with Italy; the treaty has been renewed several times. San Marino remained neutral in World War II but was damaged by Allied bombing. From 1945 to 1957 and again from 1978 to 1988 San Marino was governed by a leftist coalition led by the San Marino Communist party (PCS). In the 1988 elections, the Christian Democratic party won 27 seats (64%) in the Great and General Council.

San Martín, José de [sahn mahr-teen'] One of the principal liberators of South America from Spanish rule, José de San Martín, b. Feb. 25, 1778, d. Aug. 17, 1850, was a master military tactician who became a national hero in many South American countries, particularly in Argentina. From 1791 to 1811 he served as a soldier for the Spanish crown, mostly in Europe, but in 1812 he returned to Buenos Aires to join the forces fighting for liberation. As a general for the Buenos Aires government, San Martín defeated the Spanish in several encounters.

In freeing Peru from the Spanish yoke, San Martín demonstrated his military brilliance. He first fooled the enemy by crossing the Andes (a feat that has been com-

pared with Hannibal's crossing of the Alps) and decisively defeated (1817–18) the Spanish in Chile. Then, instead of attacking Lima by land, he devised a sea strike. His army easily conquered Peru and entered Lima in July 1821. San Martín then met with fellow liberator Simón BOLÍVAR at Guayquil in 1822, and, although the details are unknown, Bolívar persuaded the politically unambitious San Martín to withdraw from Peru. On Sept. 20, 1822, he resigned his military command and went into voluntary exile in Europe.

José de San Martín, soldier and statesman, became a national hero fighting for the independence of Spanish South America. Educated in Spain, he fought in Spain's army before returning to his native Argentina to join rebel troops. His military skill and boldness became the deciding factor in the Spanish defeat.

San Remo [sahn ray'-moh]   San Remo (1987 est. pop., 60,797), a terraced resort town in northwestern Italy, lies on the Ligurian Sea, 35 km (22 mi) east of Monaco. A mild winter climate, beautiful beaches, sports facilities, and gambling casinos attract tourists the entire year. The skiing slopes on Mount Bignone can be reached by a funicular railway. San Remo is dominated by a 12th-century cathedral and is the site of a large flower market. At the Conference of San Remo (1920) territorial problems following World War I were discussed by six nations.

San Salvador   San Salvador, the capital of El Salvador, lies in a volcanic area in the western part of the country. The population of the city is 459,902 (1985 est.). About 40 km (25 mi) from its Pacific Ocean port of La Libertad, San Salvador is a commercial, cultural, and industrial center. Coffee and sugar are processed, and textiles and cigars are manufactured. Important buildings include the National Palace and a modern cathedral. The University of El Salvador (1841) is located there. The city lies in an earthquake-prone region. In 1854 an earthquake leveled most buildings. More recently, in 1965 and 1986, earthquakes caused great damage and loss of life.

Founded in 1525, San Salvador was the capital of the Federation of Central American States between 1835 and 1839, when it became the capital of El Salvador.

San Salvador Island   San Salvador Island, also called Watlings Island, is a small, low-lying island of the Bahamas in the West Indies. The population is 804 (1980), and the principal settlement is Cockburn Town. Many scholars think that Christopher Columbus made his first landing in the New World on San Salvador in October 1492. With an area of 155 km^2 (60 mi^2), San Salvador is 21 km (13 mi) long and 8 km (5 mi) wide. Its coral cliffs on the eastern shore are visible even at night. Tourism is the major income source. Called Guanahaní by the native Arawak Indians, the island was named San Salvador by Columbus.

San Sebastián [sahn say-bahs-tee-ahn']   San Sebastián, the capital of Guipúzcoa province, northern Spain, is located on the Urumea River. Located about 16 km (10 mi) from the French border on the Bay of Biscay, San Sebastián is a thriving seaside resort. The population is 176,586 (1987 est.). In addition to tourism, the economy is based on fishing and the manufacture of chemicals, metal products, and electrical equipment. Historic landmarks include the 16th-century Castillo de la Mota, situated atop a hill overlooking the harbor, and the Church of San Vicente (1507).

Founded in the 11th century, San Sebastián has long been a popular tourist resort. It was virtually destroyed (1813) by English and Portuguese forces during the Peninsular War and was subsequently rebuilt.

San Vitale [sahn vee-tah'-lay]   The octagonal church of San Vitale in Ravenna, Italy, dedicated to the local saint, Vitalis, and noted for its fine MOSAICS, is one of the glories of early BYZANTINE ART AND ARCHITECTURE. Begun in the 520s, San Vitale was completed by 548. It reflects the Late Roman interest in circular and octagonal domed structures and was particularly influential in the medieval West as a symbol of imperial church style and court art. It served as the model for Charlemagne's chapel at Aachen.

San Vitale's mosaics—among the most important of the Early Christian and Byzantine periods—occupy the extended chancel and apse. The apse conch (half dome) shows a beardless Christ in triumph attended by angels, Saint Vitalis, and Bishop Ecclesius, during whose episcopate the building was begun. The most famous of the church's mosaics are the large wall panels flanking the altar. They depict Emperor Justinian I (r. 527–65) and his wife, the empress Theodora, with their retinues, presenting gifts to the church (see BYZANTINE EMPIRE).

Sana [sah-nah']   Sana (1986 pop., 427,185) became the capital in 1990 of the Yemeni Republic, which comprises the former states of Yemen (Aden) and Yemen (Sana). The city, which lies 2,350 m (7,700 ft) above sea level in western Yemen, is a road junction and market center for coffee and fruits. It also has a cotton textile industry. Sana retains most of its traditional Islamic character, and landmarks include the Great Mosque dating from the 7th century and the Republican Palace. A university was founded there in 1970. Sana has been the political and religious center of Yemen since the 1st century AD.

Sanchez, Sonia   An American poet, playwright, editor, and author of children's books, Sonia Sanchez, b. Birmingham, Ala., Sept. 9, 1934, is best known for her angry poetry and deeply felt black pride. She is also a powerful spokesperson for the special identity of black women. Her volumes of poetry include *Home Coming* (1969), *We a BaddDDD People* (1970), *Love Poems* (1973), and *Homegirls and Handgrenades* (1984). Her play *Sister Son/ji* was produced off Broadway in 1972. She has also edited short stories by black authors and written children's fiction.

Sancho III, King of Navarre (Sancho the Great) [sahn'-choh]   Sancho III, c.992–1035, king of Navarre (1000–35), also ruled the adjacent county of Aragon and, through marriage, politics, and force, added both the county of Castile (1029) and the kingdom of León (1034) to his domain. By assuming the title of emperor, he claimed leadership of Christian Spain. He encouraged Europeans to make the pilgrimage to Santiago de Compostela and welcomed the monks of Cluny, thus helping to integrate Christian Spain into the European religious and cultural mainstream. Much of his work was undone upon his death, when his dominions were divided among his four sons.

Sancroft, William [sang'-krawft]   An English clergy-man and archbishop of Canterbury, William Sancroft, b. Jan. 30, 1617, d. Nov. 24, 1693, consistently sacrificed fortune rather than conscience in his conflicts with the government. A fellow at Cambridge University, he refused to sign the Puritan Solemn League and Covenant (1643) and was eventually dismissed (1651). At the Restoration of the monarchy (1660), he returned from exile on the Continent to a brilliant church career, becoming (1678) archbishop of Canterbury. In 1688, Sancroft led six other bishops in refusing to proclaim King JAMES II's second Declaration of Indulgence by which the king hoped to re-store English Catholicism. They were imprisoned. After the GLORIOUS REVOLUTION (1688) brought the Protestant WILLIAM III to the throne, however, Sancroft believed that his oath of allegiance to the deposed James precluded his taking a new oath to William.

sanctions   Sanctions, in international affairs, are pen-alties imposed against a nation to make it comply with international law or to alter its policies in other regards. These penalties are usually economic—in the form of a BOYCOTT or an EMBARGO—but they may involve suspension of diplomatic relations or even military action. The League of Nations applied (1935) economic sanctions against Italy when it invaded (1935) Ethiopia; the United Nations invoked them against Rhodesia when the white minority government unilaterally declared (1965) the col-ony's independence from Britain. During the 1980s the United States and other Western nations imposed trade sanctions against Iran, Libya, and South Africa, and in August 1990 the UN Security Council, in an unusual unanimous vote, declared a trade and financial boycott of Iraq in retaliation for that country's invasion of Kuwait.

sanctuary   A sanctuary is a sacred place—or the most sacred part of a sacred place—such as a grove, temple, church, or mosque. From early times sanctuaries were re-garded as places of refuge or asylum for those fleeing vio-lence or the law. In Europe, throughout and beyond the Middle Ages, Christian churches were places of sanctuary for fugitives and criminals. From this practice stems the custom of diplomatic asylum and EXTRATERRITORIALITY. To-day many nations grant political asylum or sanctuary, de-nying EXTRADITION, to certain individuals. In the 1980s a number of U.S. churches offered refuge to illegal aliens from Central America.

sand   Geologists apply the term *sand* to natural parti-cles of a certain size, as well as to geologic deposits com-posed of such particles. Sand-sized particles are rounded to angular fragments or detrital grains that are smaller than granules and larger than coarse silt grains. The size (generally ¹⁄₁₆ to 2 mm/0.0025 to 0.08 in) is determined by sieving grains through a set of standard screens of dif-ferent mesh sizes. Scales used to define sand size have been devised by the U.S. Department of Agriculture, the American Society of Testing and Materials, and the U.S. Army Corps of Engineers.

As a deposit, sand is defined as a loose aggregate of sand-sized mineral particles. Most sand consists of QUARTZ grains derived from the weathering of granite or other siliceous igneous rocks. (Carbonate sands are com-posed of shell fragments, coral, or chemical precipitates such as oolites.)

Sand has many practical uses. Some deposits, called PLACER DEPOSITS, are rich in precious metals such as gold. Quartz sand is used in the manufacture of chemicals and glass, in molds and casting, and as an abrasive. Quartz and carbonate sands are used for mortar, concrete, and building stone.

See also: EROSION AND SEDIMENTATION; SAND DUNE; SAND-STORM AND DUST STORM.

Sand, George   George Sand, pseudonym of Aurore Dudevant, was the most famous woman writer in 19th-century France. Born Amantine Aurore Lucile Dupin, July 1, 1804, she was married at 18 to Baron Casimir Dude-vant and had two children. Profoundly unhappy in the marriage, she left her husband, established herself in Paris with another man in 1831, and out of financial ne-cessity began writing. Her first independent novel, *Indi-ana* (1832; Eng. trans., 1978), the story of an unhappy wife who struggles to free herself from the imprisonment of marriage, explicitly called a form of slavery, made her an overnight celebrity. Subsequent novels, such as *Valen-tine* (1832; Eng. trans., 1978) and, most notably, *Lélia* (1833; Eng. trans., 1978), astounded her readers with their frank exploration of women's sexual feelings and their passionate call for women's freedom to find emo-tional satisfaction. Legally separated from her husband in 1836, she kept up a furious pace of literary composition throughout her life to support herself and her children.

George Sand (pen name of Aurore Dudevant) became one of the most successful French novelists of the 19th century, writing love stories that argued for the freedom of women from tradi-tional sexual roles.

Beginning in the late 1830s, Sand turned to a new arena of controversy, writing didactic novels that advocated a mystical Christian socialism. Books such as *The Companion of the Tour of France* (1840; Eng. trans., 1976) and *Horace* (1841) idealized working-class characters and denounced bourgeois materialism. Staunchly republican in her sympathies, she not only wrote novels that helped to spread revolutionary French ideas throughout Europe, but was actively involved as a political pamphleteer during the uprisings of 1848 that toppled the French monarchy and established the short-lived Second Republic. Disillusioned by the return to authoritarian rule under Napoleon III, however, she withdrew from politics to her country estate at Nohant.

Sand's important work of this period also includes her most ambitious novel, *Consuelo* (1842; Eng. trans., 1846), and its sequel, *The Countess of Rudolstadt* (1843; Eng. trans., 1870), with an artist heroine; successful plays; and such pastoral novels as *The Haunted Pool* (1846; Eng. trans., 1976), *The Country Waif* (1847; Eng. trans., 1976), and *Fanchon the Cricket* (1848; Eng. trans., 1977), now her most widely read works. Her letters and journals have also been published in English. In the eyes of many critics her masterpieces are her autobiography, *My Life* (1854–55; Eng. trans., 1979), and a series of descriptive, meditative travel essays, *Lettres d'un voyageur* (Letters of a Traveler, 1834–36). After her death on June 8, 1876, Sand's stature was recognized in tributes by such literary masters as Turgenev and Flaubert.

Sand Creek Massacre

At the Sand Creek Massacre, a Colorado militia force slaughtered at least 150 peaceful Cheyenne Indians who believed themselves to be in protective custody. Following a rush of gold miners into Colorado in 1861, the CHEYENNE and ARAPAHO tribes were forced into the desolate Sand Creek reservation in southeastern Colorado. When whites continued to inundate the territory, the Indians reacted by attacking the stagecoach lines to Denver. On Nov. 29, 1864, without warning, the Colorado Volunteers led by Col. John Chivington attacked a peaceful band of Cheyenne, led by BLACK KETTLE, encamped at Sand Creek. Women and children were indiscriminately killed in the massacre; estimates of Indian deaths ranged from 150 to 500.

sand dollar

Sand dollars are shallow-water echinoderms, marine invertebrates (with the sea urchins) of the class Echinoidea. They are flattened, disk-shaped, and usually brownish. The mouth is placed centrally on the underside of the strong shell (test), which may have characteristic petal-shaped areas (petaloids) or slots. The body is covered by long and short spines, which aid in locomotion and sand-burrowing. Fertilization is external, and there is a larval stage. Sand dollars, which live in large numbers in many parts of the world, are frequently washed ashore after storms.

sand dune

A sand dune is a semipermanent accumulation of loose sand that forms in areas where the wind tends to blow in one direction, at velocities high enough to move sand, across a land surface that permits sand to amass in a regular and consistent form. Although usually associated with DESERTS, dunes may develop wherever wind and loose sand combine. Most major dune fields, or sand seas (*ergs* in Arabic), have developed in the Sahara-Middle East desert and in the cold interior deserts of south central Asia. Between 25 and 30 percent of the Earth's desert surface is covered with some form of sand accumulation.

Most sand in dunes is well sorted, meaning that the particles all tend to fall in a narrow size range. Particles smaller than 0.1 mm (0.004 in) in diameter are less susceptible to wind erosion than somewhat larger particles because they tend to adhere to one another, retain moisture, and form a smooth surface. Sand grains larger than 0.5 mm (0.02 in) in diameter are so heavy that wind velocity is rarely great enough to move them. Wind velocities of at least 16 km/hr (10 mph) are generally required to move sand. Wind-tunnel and field experiments show that sand moves in three ways: in suspension as clouds rising as high as 2,500 m/8,200 ft (see SANDSTORM AND DUST STORM); by saltation—a bounding or leaping motion that accounts for most sand movement;

Multidirectional winds produced the star, or radial, shape of these sand dunes in a California desert. Several other shapes are possible depending on wind patterns, sand supply, and climatic conditions. Several dune-buggy tracks crisscross the dunes seen here.

and by creep or surface rolling, which involves only the larger grains.

See also: EROSION AND SEDIMENTATION.

---

sand grouse   Sand grouse are 16 species of pigeon-like birds constituting the family Pteroclidae and found from southern Europe to southern Africa and south central Asia. They range from 23 to 40 cm (9 to 16 in) in length and have stout bodies; short, feathered legs (and feathered toes in two species); long, pointed wings; and usually long, pointed tails. They are commonly colored in various patterns of grays, browns, and blacks. Sand grouse are ground-feeding birds, eating seeds, berries, buds, and insects. They live in flocks, and most species inhabit warm, arid regions. Sand grouse nest twice, or occasionally three times, a year. The nest is a depression in the ground, and both sexes incubate the two to three eggs.

---

sandalwood   The sandalwood family, Santalaceae, of about 400 evergreen trees and shrubs is distributed throughout India, Malaysia, China, and Australia. Many species are semiparasitic on the roots of other plants. In this way, they obtain necessary nutrients. The white sandalwood, *Santalum album*, is native to India and other parts of Southeast Asia, reaching a height of 12 m (40 ft). Its reddish wood acquires a characteristic aroma upon drying. Sandal oil, extracted from the heartwood through steam distillation, is used chiefly in soap, perfume, and cosmetics. It takes about 30 years or more for the heartwood to attain a growth that will yield oil. The maximum amount of oil is produced when the trees reach full maturity, usually in 70 to 80 years. The fragrant wood itself is highly valued. It is used to make chests, boxes, and incense.

Sandburg, Carl   Carl August Sandburg, b. Galesburg, Ill., Jan. 6, 1878, d. July 23, 1967, changed the course of American poetry. His characteristic unrhymed lines of varying length, his evocations of American urban and rural life, his compassion for the working class, and his love of nature have all left their mark.

Sandburg's first widely read book, *Chicago Poems* (1916), reflected his early association with the Social-Democratic party and shocked many genteel readers by its use of street slang and irregular verse structure. All the poetry published in his lifetime has been collected in *The Complete Poems* (rev. ed., 1970), and *Breathing Tokens* (1978) brings together more than 100 other poems.

Sandburg's output as a prose writer was large and varied. His continuing interest in Abraham Lincoln resulted in *Abraham Lincoln: The Prairie Years* (1925) and *The War Years* (1939), colorful although only partially documented biographies. He also wrote children's books, such as *Rootabaga Stories* (1922), and topical books based on his observations as a newspaper reporter, for example, *The Chicago Race Riots* (1919). *The American Songbag* (1927) is a collection of the folk

As the "voice of the people," Carl Sandburg, an American poet and historian, celebrated U.S. history and the common people involved in making it. He was twice awarded the Pulitzer Prize: in 1951 for Complete Poems (1950) and in 1940 for his multivolume Abraham Lincoln: The War Years (1939).

songs he used in his public performances as a singer and reader of his poems. *Always the Young Strangers* (1952) is autobiographical.

Sande, Earl [san'-dee]   Earl Sande, b. Groton, S.Dak., Nov. 13, 1898, d. Aug. 19, 1968, was one of America's leading jockeys during the 1920s and early 1930s. During his career he won 967 races, including three Kentucky Derbies, riding Zev in 1923, Flying Ebony in 1925, and Gallant Fox in 1930. He won the Triple Crown (Kentucky Derby, Preakness, and Belmont Stakes) aboard Gallant Fox. Later a successful trainer, Sande was elected to the Jockey Hall of Fame and the National Racing Hall of Fame.

Sandhurst, Royal Military Academy at   The Royal Military Academy at Sandhurst, in Berkshire, England, trains all regular officers of the British army. It was established in 1947 through the merger of the Royal Military College, Sandhurst (1799), and the Royal Military Academy, Woolwich (1741). Military and civilian studies are given equal attention in the 18-month course, for which there are no fees. Most cadets admitted to the academy are selected from military ranks, although some are chosen by civil-service examination.

Sandia Cave [sahn-dee'-uh]   Sandia Cave is a tunnel-like archaeological site in the Sandia Mountains east of Albuquerque in central New Mexico. The oldest level of occupation, dating from c.9000 BC, yielded so-called Sandia points, a distinctive type of unfluted projectile point with a single shoulder on one side of the base of the blade. Other implements included scrapers, lamellar blades, and bone awls made from camels' leg bones. A number of open-air Paleo-Indian sites in east central New Mexico have also yielded Sandia points. The second occupation of Sandia Cave, dating from c.8500 BC, contained fluted points of Folsom type (see FOLSOM CULTURE). Later sporadic occupations took place up to within a few hundred years before the arrival of the Spaniards (c.1600).

Sandinistas

Sandinistas are members of the left-wing Nicaraguan revolutionary group—the Sandinista National Liberation Front (FSLN)—that overthrew the SoMOZA family dictatorship in July 1979. The FSLN was named for Augusto César Sandino, a patriot and leader of a popular insurrection who was executed in 1934 by order of strongman Anastasio Somoza García. Formed in 1962, the FSLN assembled a broad coalition to defeat Anastasio Somoza Debayle and his National Guard in a bitter civil war and take control of Nicaragua. The ruling Sandinista junta, headed by Daniel ORTEGA SAAVEDRA, nationalized some industries early on but faced serious economic problems and had to battle anti-Sandinista guerrillas ("contras") backed by the United States. The Sandinistas held democratic elections in March 1990 in return for disbandment of the contras. They lost their parliamentary majority but remained a powerful influence after opposition leader Violeta Barrios de Chamorro became president and the contras were demobilized.

sandpiper

Sandpipers are shorebirds in the family Scolopacidae, order Charadriiformes, that occur worldwide except in Antarctica. Most breed in the Northern Hemisphere but migrate extensively; they are found particularly along shorelines and in open country near lakes, ponds, and streams. During the nonbreeding season, they often congregate in large flocks. Sandpipers range from about 13 to 57 cm (5 to 24 in) in length, including the bill. They are usually cryptically colored, with the upper parts mottled with grays and browns and the lower parts pale and sometimes streaked or spotted. The bill ranges from short to very long and may be straight or curved upward or downward. Sandpipers feed mainly on insects and other invertebrates. They typically feed by probing with the bill into the sand or soil. Most sandpipers scrape a shallow depression in the soil for a nest, lining it with a bit of grass. The eggs, usually four, may be incubated by both sexes.

sandstone

Sandstone is a clastic SEDIMENTARY ROCK consisting of a cemented mass of particles with diameters between ¹⁄₁₆ and 2 mm (0.0025 and 0.08 in—see SAND).

Classification. Sandstones are classified on the basis of three of their constituents: particles, matrix, and cement. Particles are mostly derived from continental parent material and are hence terrigenous. Pyroclastic (volcanic) and calcium carbonate particles may also be present. The essential particles of a sandstone are quartz, feldspar, and rock fragments. The matrix is the mud, a physically deposited, fine-grained material that occurs mostly as clay minerals and quartz. The cement is the chemically precipitated material that fills voids between the particles.

The various kinds of sandstones are distinguished according to the assemblage and character of the particles, matrix, and cement. Two end-member groups, or extreme types, of sandstones may be recognized: argillaceous (clay) sandstones, containing about 15% or more of clay-sized material, and ordinary sandstones, which contain less than 15% of clay-sized material. Each of these two groups is divided into three types, depending on the proportions of quartz, feldspar, and rock fragments. The end-member names are used only in those examples where all the sand-sized material consists exclusively of quartz, feldspar, or rock fragments. Where they do not, the additional constituents are listed as prefixes in increasing order of abundance.

Deposition. Sands are derived from weathered and transported fragments of massive parent rock material

The purple sandpiper (left), about 23 cm (9 in) long, inhabits rocky coasts in much of the Northern Hemisphere. The semipalmated sandpiper (right), which has partly webbed toes, and the spotted sandpiper (center) breed primarily in northern North America and winter from southern North America through South America.

Large sandstone pillars rise above the desert floor at Hunt's Mesa in Monument Valley, Arizona. The numerous free-standing features, products of erosion by wind and water, are all that remain of a thick layer of sandstone that had been deposited by ancient seas.

and are deposited under conditions of high energy. Fine-grained particles are taken into suspension and removed into deeper water, leaving sand-sized particles behind. These sands lithify into sandstones. The high-energy depositional environments in which sands, now sandstones, reside include such settings as beaches, barrier islands, and riverbanks.

Characteristics. Sandstones vary in color, depending on composition. Sandstones whose initial particles formed under oxidizing conditions are generally brown, red, or tan; those that formed under reducing (anaerobic) conditions are dark gray. Particle size ranges from well-sorted particles accumulated in coastal and lake dunes to poorly sorted particles formed in glaciofluvial environments (see GLACIERS AND GLACIATION).

sandstorm and dust storm   A dust storm or sandstorm is created when a large mass of cold, unstable air moves swiftly across dry ground covered with loose silt and sand. Known in North Africa as haboobs (Arabic for "violent wind"), such storms form over semiarid areas during periods of convective instability, when large air masses are heated near the ground surface and then rise rapidly to altitudes of more than 10 km (6 mi). Masses of dense, cold air sliding under the lighter, rapidly rising warm air are forced downward to the ground, where they spread laterally as swiftly moving tongues. These cold winds pick up masses of fine-grained material and carry it in suspension. Because they are associated with large-scale atmospheric instability, dust storms and sandstorms are usually concentrated in a six-month summer period, especially in regions with a well-defined rainy season or monsoon. They advance at an average speed of 50 km/h (30 mph), with gusts of up to 100 km/h (60 mph), and are usually accompanied by an almost instantaneous temperature drop of as much as 15 C degrees (27 F degrees). During a severe storm, visibility may drop to zero for up to three hours, and tremendous quantities of silt may be deposited. During a season of severe storms, up to 3 m (10 ft) of silt may accumulate.

Dust storms result in considerable loss of agricultural topsoil (see EROSION AND SEDIMENTATION). Marginal farmlands developed in semiarid areas where drought years are common are especially vulnerable. In the 1930s a combination of drought and dust storms destroyed the topsoil and the economy of large areas of Texas, Oklahoma, Colorado, and New Mexico (the DUST BOWL).

Sandwich, John Montagu, 4th Earl of [mahn'-tuh-gue]   A British politician, John Montagu, 4th earl of Sandwich, b. Nov. 3, 1718, d. Apr. 30, 1792, was a leading member of Lord NORTH's administration during the American Revolution.

Sandwich held various offices and was first lord of the admiralty from 1771 to 1782. Criticized for corruption, he nevertheless made genuine attempts to improve the condition of the fleet.

An account from 1770 reported that the earl once spent a whole day at the gaming table, eating only several slices of cold beef placed between slices of toast. This was the origin of the common noun *sandwich*.

Sandwich Islands   see HAWAII (state)

Sanger, Frederick [sang'-ur]   The English biochemist Frederick Sanger, b. Aug. 13, 1918, was the second Nobel laureate to be honored in the same category twice. After developing methods for the partial breakdown of large protein molecules to analyze their exact sequence of amino acids, he was able to determine (1953) the complete structure of the hormone insulin; this work won him the 1958 Nobel Prize for chemistry. Sanger also developed a rapid method for determining nucleotide sequences of DNA and RNA, which are extremely large molecules involved in genetic inheritance of traits and gene expression. This research, which led to the development of genetic engineering techniques, won him part of the 1980 Nobel Prize for chemistry.

Sanger, Margaret   Margaret Sanger, b. Margaret Higgins in Corning, N.Y., Sept. 14, 1883, d. Sept. 6, 1966, coined the term *birth control* and was a pioneer of the birth-control movement in the United States. As a nurse in New York City slums she was appalled at the

Margaret Sanger, one of the pioneers of the birth-control movement, led an unremitting campaign for the right of women to control pregnancy. Legal and public sanction of contraception was achieved largely through Sanger's efforts.

deaths from self-induced abortions. When she opened a birth-control clinic in Brooklyn in 1916, she was arrested for creating a public nuisance. Her struggle with the law dramatized her cause and won doctors the right to dispense birth-control information to their patients. Sanger founded the National Birth Control League in 1914 and was the first president of the International Planned Parenthood Federation (1953).

Sanhedrin [san-hed'-rin]

The Sanhedrin was the highest Jewish tribunal during the period of Greek and Roman rule over Palestine. The composition and functions of the Sanhedrin are the subject of scholarly debate because Talmudic and Greek sources differ in their accounts of the institution. According to the former, it was a council of 71 sages whose chief function was the interpretation of Jewish law, with some political and judicial duties. Hellenistic sources, on the other hand, describe the Sanhedrin as having substantial political and judicial authority, as being composed primarily of the priestly, aristocratic SADDUCEES (with some influential PHARISEES), and as being presided over by the high priest. Some scholars have suggested that two Sanhedrins existed, one religious and one civil.

Sannazaro, Jacopo [sahn-naht'-sah-roh]

Jacopo Sannazaro, b. July 28, 1456, d. Apr. 24, 1530, was an Italian humanist poet whose romance, Arcadia (1502; Eng. trans., 1966), did much to establish the genre of Renaissance PASTORAL LITERATURE. Narrated by the principal character, Sincero, the work describes in both verse and prose the pleasures of nature, the disappointments of love, and the customs of Arcadia, a region of ideal rustic contentment in Greece. Arcadia influenced the poems of Torquato Tasso, Edmund Spenser, and especially Sir Philip Sidney. Sannazaro, who spent much of his life as a member of the Spanish court at Naples, also wrote Italian lyrics and dramatic monologues, Latin epigrams and elegies, a Christian epic titled De Partu Virginis (On the Virgin Birth, 1526), and a series of rhetorically accomplished Piscatory Eclogues (1526; Eng. trans., 1914).

Sanskrit   see INDIAN LITERATURE; INDO-IRANIAN LANGUAGES

Sansovino, Jacopo

The Florentine sculptor and architect Jacopo Sansovino, b. Jacopo Tatti, 1486, d. Nov. 27, 1570, is known primarily for having fostered the classical tradition in Venice. The classical spirit is captured in Bacchus (1511–12; Museo Nazionale, Florence), his first important work. The Saint James he made (1511) for Florence's Duomo was considered the finest of all the statues contributed to that building.

Drawing on ancient Roman precedents, Sansovino created notable structures in the very heart of Venice. The Zecca (Mint; begun 1536) was done in a highly rusticated and fortresslike style derived from the Porto Maggiore (AD 52) in Rome. The Libreria Vecchia di San Marco (begun 1537), opposite the Doge's Palace, was faithfully completed (1570–88) according to Sansovino's plan after his death. In the Palazzo Corner (begun c.1545; now Ca'Grande), he created the classic Venetian palazzo. The versatility of his work is emphasized by the variety of his sculptures, from the colossal figures of Mars and Neptune (1554–67; Scala dei Giganti, Doge's Palaçe), to the various bronze reliefs for San Marco: tribune reliefs (1537, 1541–42), a relief for the altar (before 1565), and the bronze sacristy door (1546–63). This last piece reveals Sansovino's ability to transmute Venetian painters' techniques of atmospheric light and texture into sculpture of a truly elegant and dramatic style.

Santa Ana (California) [san'-tuh an'-uh]

Santa Ana (1990 pop., 293,742), the seat of Orange County in southern California, lies about 55 km (35 mi) southeast of Los Angeles. Manufactures in the city include metal products, glass and rubber goods, and electronics equipment. Founded in 1869 as an agricultural market, the city grew rapidly after World War II.

Santa Ana (El Salvador) [sahn'-tah ah'-nah]

Santa Ana (1985 est. pop., 137,879), the second largest city of El Salvador, lies on the Pan American Highway, about 55 km (35 mi) north of San Salvador. Located in a coffee- and sugarcane-growing region, the city manufactures textiles, furniture, and leather goods. It was founded in 1576.

Santa Anna, Antonio López de

A Mexican general and dictator, Antonio López de Santa Anna, b. Feb. 21, 1794, d. June 20, 1876, dominated his nation for 30 years and led it into a disastrous war with the United States. The son of a minor official in the Spanish bureaucracy, he became a cadet in the Spanish army in 1810

Gen. Antonio López de Santa Anna dominated Mexican politics for 30 years. Although he captured the Alamo, he was defeated by the Texans at San Jacinto during the Texas Revolution (1835–36). He also suffered a series of defeats in the Mexican War (1846–48) with the United States.

and served in the campaigns against the Indians in northern Mexico. In 1821 he joined the independence movement of Agustín de ITURBIDE but soon turned against him.

Following Iturbide's overthrow in 1823, Santa Anna became the most important political figure in Mexico. He carried out military coups, became president (first in 1833 and then four times after that), and frequently ruled unofficially. He deposed both liberals and conservatives, although his own policies were generally conservative. In the 1830s rebellions against him broke out in several regions, and in 1836 he led an army against the rebels in Texas. Although he captured the Alamo in San Antonio, his forces were later crushed by the Texans under Sam Houston at San Jacinto, and Santa Anna was captured. After the defeat, Santa Anna lost a leg defending Veracruz against a punitive French naval raid (1838), thus regaining his popularity and resuming his position of dominance in Mexico.

Reelected president in 1846, he led the Mexican army's unsuccessful resistance to the U.S. invasion in 1847 (see MEXICAN WAR). Returning from exile, he became dictator for the last time in 1853. He was overthrown in 1855.

Santa Barbara   Santa Barbara (1990 pop., 85,571), the seat of Santa Barbara County in southern California, lies on the Pacific Ocean, about 160 km (100 mi) northwest of Los Angeles. A resort community, Santa Barbara is known for its Spanish-style architecture. The city manufactures plastic goods and electronic components. The University of California at Santa Barbara (1891) and Westmont College (1940) are located there. The city was founded in 1782 as a fortified settlement, and a Franciscan mission (which still stands) was established there in 1786. A railway link between Los Angeles and San Francisco, opened in 1901, assured its growth as a tourist resort.

Santa Barbara Islands   The Santa Barbara Islands, or Channel Islands, lie between 40 and 145 km (25–90 mi) off the southern California coast in the Pacific Ocean. The best known of this group of eight islands is Santa Catalina. Anacapa, San Miguel, Santa Barbara, Santa Cruz, and Santa Rosa islands form the Channel Islands National Monument. The economy is based on sheep raising, and the islands are noted for a variety of birds and fish and for sea lions. Once inhabited by the now-extinct Cataliño Indians, the islands were visited by the Portuguese in 1542.

Santa Catalina Island   Santa Catalina Island, one of the Santa Barbara Islands, lies in the Pacific Ocean off the coast of Southern California. Part of Los Angeles County, it is 35 km (22 mi) long, with an area of 192 km^2 (74 mi^2). The island, a popular resort, is volcanic in origin; its highest point is 648 m (2,125 ft), on Mount Orizaba. The only community is Avalon.

Discovered in 1542 by Juan Rodríguez Cabrillo and named San Salvador, the island was renamed Santa Catalina in 1602. Long a smugglers' and pirates' base, it belonged to Mexico until 1848, when it passed to the United States.

Santa Clara   Santa Clara (1990 pop., 93,613), a city in west central California, lies about 80 km (50 mi) southeast of San Francisco. Industries in the city include the processing of dried fruits and the manufacturing of paper, fiberglass, machinery, and electronics components. The University of Santa Clara was established there in 1851. Founded as a mission in 1777, Santa Clara began to expand with the influx of miners in the mid-19th century.

Santa Claus   A legendary figure who supposedly brings presents to children on Christmas Eve, Santa Claus is an American adaptation of European traditions concerning Saint NICHOLAS. These were introduced into America by the Dutch settlers in New Amsterdam. The name

Santa Claus appeared jovial, rotund, and laden with gifts in Thomas Nast's cartoon, featured in an issue of Harper's Weekly *in 1881. Nast, whose cartoons helped to form the traditional American image of Santa Claus, based his representations on a variety of sources ranging from fanciful descriptions by American authors to European folk tales.*

Santa Claus is a contraction of the Dutch Sint Nikolaas (Sinter Klaas).

Most of the central features of the Santa Claus legend, such as his climb down the chimney and the switches he leaves for naughty children, are of Dutch origin. His red suit trimmed with white fur originated in the bishop's miter and cope worn by the Dutch saint. His association with reindeer and the North Pole, however, apparently came from Scandinavia. These and other attributes of Santa Claus were popularized during the 19th century through the stories of Washington IRVING, the cartoons of Thomas NAST, and the famous 1822 poem by Clement MOORE, "A Visit from Saint Nicholas."

Male and female European counterparts of Santa Claus include the English Father Christmas, the German Kris Kringle, the Italian Befana, and Russia's grandmotherly Babouschka.

Santa Cruz (Bolivia) [sahn'-tah kroos]   Santa Cruz (1988 est. pop., 615,122), capital of Santa Cruz department and the second largest city in Bolivia, lies about 550 km (340 mi) east of La Paz. The city grew rapidly as a commercial and industrial center after the completion of an all-weather road to the highlands in the early 1950s, and growth has continued with the discovery of large deposits of petroleum, natural gas, iron ore, and magnesium in the surrounding area. Pipelines link Santa Cruz with La Paz and Buenos Aires. Founded in 1561, Santa Cruz remained unimportant for centuries because of its isolation.

Santa Cruz (California) [san'-tuh krooz]   Santa Cruz (1990 pop., 49,040), the seat of Santa Cruz County in western California, is a resort city lying on the northern shore of Monterey Bay about 120 km (75 mi) south of San Francisco. Its industries include the processing of fruits and vegetables, fishing, and the manufacture of electronics components. The University of California at Santa Cruz (1965) is located there. Founded as a mission in 1791, Santa Cruz became the site of a Spanish colonial settlement in 1797.

Santa Cruz, Andrés [sahn'-tah kroos]   Andrés Santa Cruz, 1792–1865, governed Bolivia and created the Peru-Bolivian Confederation (1836–39). A mestizo who claimed descent from the royal Incas, Santa Cruz won a large following among the Indians of both countries.

Santa Cruz first served in the Spanish army but joined José de San Martín's rebel troops in 1820. He governed Peru (1826–27) as Simón Bolívar's lieutenant. In 1829 he was elected president of Bolivia, and seven years later he established the Peru-Bolivian Confederation. His goal of uniting the Pacific states of South America ended, however, in 1839 at the Battle of Yungay, when Chilean military forces, led by Gen. Manuel Bulnes, destroyed the Confederation. Santa Cruz escaped and died in France.

Santa Cruz de Tenerife [sahn'-tah kroos day tay-nay-ree'-fay]   Santa Cruz de Tenerife (1988 est. pop., 211,209), located on the island of Tenerife, is the capital of the Spanish province of the same name in the CANARY ISLANDS. A port town and a tourist resort, it exports agricultural produce and also has a petroleum refinery. The town was founded in 1494. Francisco Franco, while serving as the captain general of the Canary Islands, prepared his 1936 uprising there.

Santa Fe [san'-tuh fay]   Santa Fe is a city in north central New Mexico, the state capital and the seat of Santa Fe County. The city has a population of 55,859 (1990). Located along the Santa Fe River, Santa Fe is surrounded by the Sangre de Cristo Mountains and lies at an elevation of about 2,131 m (6,990 ft). The city's rich historic past and its blend of Indian, Spanish, and American cultures, as well as the dry, sunny climate, make year-round tourism a major industry. The Los Alamos Scientific Laboratory and the Pueblo Indian reservations are nearby. The Palace of Governors (built 1609–10) is one of the city's many museums, housing a collection of southwestern art, archaeology, and anthropology. The nationally known Santa Fe Opera performs in its open-air theater during July and August.

Santa Fe was founded in 1609 by the Spaniard Don Pedro de Peralta. Following a revolt in 1680, the Pueblo Indians occupied the city until it was retaken (1692) by the Spanish. As the western terminus of the Santa Fe Trail, the city became an important commercial center after Mexican independence from Spain in 1821. During the Mexican War, Santa Fe was occupied (1846) by U.S. troops under Gen. Stephen W. Kearny. When the U.S. Territory of New Mexico was organized in 1850, Santa Fe became its capital, retaining that status when New Mexico entered (1912) the Union.

Santa Fe Opera   The Santa Fe Opera, founded in 1957 by John Crosby, is an important and adventurous summer opera festival. Located on a ranch outside the historic city of Santa Fe, N.Mex., the adobe opera house, which is partially open to the sky, has excellent acoustics and perfect sight lines. The Santa Fe Opera was the site of the world premieres of Berio's *Opera* (1970) and Villa-Lobos's *Yerma* (1971) as well as the site of the American premiere of the completed, 3-act version of Alban Berg's *Lulu* (1979).

Santa Fe Trail   The Santa Fe Trail was the overland trade route that linked the hamlet of Franklin and, later, Independence, Mo., with Santa Fe, N.Mex. William Becknell is credited with initiating (1821) the profitable route, which attracted numerous prairie merchant caravans from Missouri.

By 1830 there were two main routes, both running westward. The Mountain Fork turned at Dodge City to run along the Arkansas River to Bent's Fort, Colo., and south through Raton Pass to Fort Union. The Cimarron Fork crossed the Arkansas west of Dodge City and ran directly to Fort Union, saving kilometers but adding the risks of dust storms and Indian interference. From Fort Union both routes swung westward around the Sangre de Cristo Mountains into Sante Fe. In 1880 the trail was eclipsed by the Atchison, Topeka, and Santa Fe Railroad.

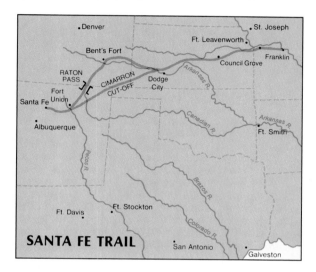

SANTA FE TRAIL

Santa Marta

Santa Marta [sahn'-tah mahr'-tah]   Santa Marta, a port city and capital of Magdelena department, is located on the northern coast of Colombia. It has a population of 177,922 (1985). Tourism is the principal industry, and the main export is bananas. Founded in 1525 by the Spanish explorer Rodrigo de Bastidas, it is the oldest city in Colombia. Simón Bolívar died there in 1830.

Santa Monica

Santa Monica   The city of Santa Monica lies on Santa Monica Bay in southern California and is surrounded on its land sides by the city of Los Angeles; its population is 86,905 (1990). Often regarded as part of Los Angeles, Santa Monica is noted for its extravagant homes, hotels, and Civic Center, which is the site of the film industry's annual Academy Awards presentations. A popular convention center, Santa Monica has aerospace, research, and communications industries. It was founded in 1875 as a working seaport, but it quickly became a seaside resort and later a residential suburb.

Santal

Santal [suhn-tahl']   The Santal, one of the largest Scheduled Tribes in India, number nearly 5 million (1980 est.) spread over eastern Bihar, Bengal, and northern Orissa. Their language, Santali, is part of the Mundari family of languages, and they share with other Mundari-speakers the belief, kept alive in their oral tra-

ditions, that they are the original inhabitants of the hills and forests of Bengal. The Santal had an elaborate form of traditional government and had confederations of villages under a chief. In the 19th century the autonomy of the Santal was threatened by plains dwellers and traders, to whom the Santal lost much land. Their distress culminated in the Santal rebellion of 1855, after which legislation helped to protect some of their land rights. In recent years many Santal have migrated to nearby industrial centers for seasonal or permanent employment.

Santander

Santander [sahn-tahn-dayr']   Santander, a city in northern Spain, lies on an inlet of the Bay of Biscay, about 80 km (50 mi) west of Bilbao. The population is 163,700 (1987 est.). Santander is a popular summer resort. Industries include fishing, shipbuilding, production of iron and steel, chemicals, and cement, and food processing. The ALTAMIRA caves, with their famous prehistoric wall paintings, are nearby. Possibly the site of the Roman colony of Portus Victoriae, the city prospered on trade with America during the 18th century. The center of the town was destroyed by fire in 1941.

Santander, Francisco de Paula

Santander, Francisco de Paula   Francisco de Paula Santander, b. Apr. 2, 1792, d. May 6, 1840, was a Colombian revolutionary who contributed to Simón BOLÍVAR's campaign to drive the Spanish out of South America. He abandoned law school in 1810 in order to lead the rugged *llaneros* (plainsmen) in guerrilla warfare against Spain. In 1819 he became vice-president of newly independent Gran Colombia under Bolívar. The two men then became estranged as Santander began to criticize Bolívar's autocratic tendencies. In 1828, Bolívar barely escaped an assassination plot after suspending Santander from office. Santander was sentenced to death, but because nothing could be proved against him, his sentence was commuted to banishment. When he returned from exile, he governed efficiently as president (1832–37) of the remnant known as New Granada (Colombia and Panama).

Santayana, George

Santayana, George [sahn-tah-yah'-nah]   George Santayana, b. Madrid, Spain, Dec. 16, 1863, d. Sept. 26, 1952, was an influential philosopher, poet, and literary critic. Having received most of his higher education at Harvard, he joined the department of philosophy there and remained until 1912, when a legacy from his mother's estate allowed him to retire.

Santayana's early work can best be understood as that of a primarily poetic moral philosopher. His *The Sense of Beauty* (1896) and *The Life of Reason* (5 vols., 1905–06) focus on the imaginative life of humanity, not on the underlying structures of reality or on humankind's mode of grasping reality. His later works, particularly *Skepticism and Animal Faith* (1923) and *The Realms of Being* (4 vols., 1927–40), are more concerned with a systematic development of the ontological distinctions within nature and the different kinds of mental activities to which they relate. This difference represents a shift of emphasis, not in position.

Santayana throughout his life remained a naturalist, concerned with the ideal factors in human existence and holding that everything ideal has a natural basis and everything natural has an ideal development. For Santayana, human good consists of the harmonious development of humanity's impulses in conformity with the reflective ideational aspects of existence. He viewed religion as an imaginative creation of real value but devoid of absolute significance. Santayana's philosophical NATURALISM is systematized in his later, more ontologically directed work in terms of four major categories, or realms (his term), of being: essence, matter, spirit, and truth.

Throughout his life Santayana also wrote poetry and literary criticism. His novel *The Last Puritan* (1935) received critical acclaim.

Sant'Elia, Antonio [sahnt-ay'-lee-ah]

The Italian futurist architect Antonio Sant'Elia, b. Apr. 30, 1888, d. (in battle) Oct. 10, 1916, is best known for his elaborate drawings for a *Città Nuova* (New City) and the accompanying "Manifesto of Futurist Architecture" (both 1914). His *Città Nuova,* featuring vast, stepped skyscrapers combining public, residential, and commercial use with multilevel transportation and communication facilities, was a startling prophecy of later 20th-century architecture.

Santiago (Chile) [sahn-tee-ah'-goh]

Santiago is Chile's capital, largest city, and economic and cultural center. Also the capital of Santiago province, it is located in central Chile on the Mapocho River at the northern end of the fertile Central Valley. The city proper has a population of 3,421,863 (1984 est.); 5,133,700 persons reside in the metropolitan area (1989 est.).

Santiago is the center of Chile's transportation and communication network. Greater Santiago produces about one-half of the nation's industrial output; industries include food processing, steel refining, textiles, clothing, chemicals, furniture, and machinery manufacture. The University of Chile (1738) and the Catholic University (1888) are located there.

Because of damage from earthquakes (the worst one was in 1617) and rapid population growth, Santiago has few surviving examples of colonial architecture. The modern city has broad avenues, spacious squares, and many parks. Outstanding buildings include the cathedral (1558), the presidential palace (completed 1805), and the National Library.

The site of Santiago was inhabited by the Picunche Indians before the Spaniard Pedro de Valdívia founded the city as Santiago del Nuevo Extremo in 1541. Santiago was a major center of the movement for independence from Spain, but it was virtually untouched during the War of Independence (1810–18).

Santiago (Spain)

Santiago, or Santiago de Compostela (1987 est. pop., 67,800), is a city in Galicia, northwestern Spain, and capital of La Coruña province. Important since the Middle Ages as a religious and educational center, the city is also an agricultural market. Its manufactures include handicrafts, paper, soap, and wood products. Numerous churches, among them the cathedral of Saint James (1211), as well as convents, monasteries, and a university (1501) are located there.

According to tradition, the remains of the apostle James (Saint JAMES the Great) were discovered on the site in 813. Santiago (Spanish for "Saint James") grew around the church erected by Alfonso II, as pilgrims began visiting the shrine, which, during the Middle Ages, was one of the most important in the Christian world.

Santiago de Cuba [day koo'-bah]

Santiago de Cuba, the second largest seaport of Cuba (after Havana), lies on the southern coast of the island on an almost landlocked bay. The population is 397,024 (1989 est.). Manufactures include textiles and petroleum products. The Universidad de Oriente (1947) is located there. A fortress atop the 60-m-high (200-ft) bluff, El Morro, guards the harbor entrance. Founded in 1514, Santiago de Cuba was, until 1551, the capital of Cuba and served as a base for expeditions into Mexico in the 1520s. In 1898 during the Spanish-American War, the Battle of San Juan Hill took place there, and the Spanish fleet was destroyed in the city's harbor. Fidel Castro's revolutionary cause took its name (the 26th of July Movement) from the unsuccessful attack on the city's army barracks in 1953.

Santiago de los Caballeros [lohs kah-bah-yay'-rohs]

Santiago de los Caballeros (1986 est. pop., 308,400), the second largest city in the Dominican Republic, lies in the northern part of the island 222 m (728 ft) above sea level, about 40 km (25 mi) south of the Atlantic coast. Manufactures include cigarettes, rum, coffee, and furniture. A university was founded in the city in 1962. Settled in 1504, Santiago de los Caballeros was destroyed by an earthquake in 1564 and again, after rebuilding, in 1824.

Santo Domingo [sahn'-toh doh-meeng'-goh]

Santo Domingo (formerly Ciudad Trujillo) is the capital and the principal seaport of the Dominican Republic. Located on the southern Caribbean coast, it has a population of 1,600,000 (1986 est.). It is a commercial and manufacturing center with sugar and fruit processing, distilling, and tanning industries. Nearby beaches make it a popular resort area. Historic landmarks include the 16th-century Basílica Santa María la Menor, which contains the tomb of Christopher Columbus, and the Alcázar de Colón, a palace built by Columbus's son, Diego, in 1510 and restored in 1957. The oldest university in the Western Hemisphere, the Universidad Autónoma de Santo Domingo (1538), is located there.

Founded in 1496 by Christopher Columbus's brother Bartholomew, Santo Domingo has been plagued by pirates, earthquakes, and numerous uprisings. It was occupied by U.S. Marines from 1916 to 1924 and again for a short time in 1965. In 1930 and 1979 hurricanes caused great damage.

Santorini   see THERA

Santos

Santos [sahnt'-uz] Santos, with a population of 461,096 (1985 est.), is Brazil's busiest port. The port serves São Paulo, the nation's leading industrial center, which is located 80 km (50 mi) inland. Imports include petroleum, minerals, machinery, and manufactured goods; the main exports are coffee and oranges, cotton, and bananas grown in the surrounding coastal lowland. An oil refinery and a steel mill are located there. Santos was founded in 1543, and by the mid-19th century it had become a leading coffee-shipping port.

Santos, José Eduardo dos

Santos, José Eduardo dos Angolan political leader José Eduardo dos Santos, b. Aug. 28, 1942, succeeded Agostinho António NETO as president of Angola in 1979. A founder of the Popular Movement for the Liberation of Angola (MPLA, 1961), dos Santos fought in the war against Portuguese colonial rule and the civil war that followed Angolan independence in 1975. Reelected president in 1985, dos Santos has tried to improve Angola's ties to the West while opposing white rule in South Africa and battling Angolan rebel forces led by Jonas SAVIMBI. In May 1991 he and Savimbi agreed to a cease-fire.

Sanusi, al-

Sanusi, al- [suh-noo'-see] A Muslim theologian, Muhammad ibn Ali al-Sanusi, b. North Africa, c.1787, d. 1859, known as the Grand Sanusi, founded a reformist, missionary religious order that preached restoration of early Islam's simple life and faith. Al-Sanusi's public career began in western Arabia, where he formed (1837) the Sanusi, a Sufi order (see SUFISM), with the special purpose of converting desert Bedouins to a life that followed strict Koranic teaching. In the 1840s, opposition from the Ottoman Turks induced al-Sanusi to move to Cyrenaica (now Libya). By the early 19th century the Sanusi had become a major North African social and political force. Al-Sanusi's grandson, IDRIS, assumed newly independent Libya's throne in 1951.

São Francisco River

São Francisco River [sow fruhn-sees'-koh] The São Francisco River is a major waterway in eastern Brazil. The river, 2,900 km (1,800 mi) long, rises in the state of Minais Gerais and then flows north, northeast, and east to the Atlantic Ocean, which it enters about 300 km (180 mi) south of Recife. The area drained by the river comprises 630,000 km^2 (243,200 mi^2). The São Francisco is

navigable for 1,600 km (1,000 mi) from Pirapora on the upper course to Juàzeiro, but the flow then becomes interrupted by cascades and rapids, especially by the 81-m-high (265-ft) Paulo Afonso Falls, located about 240 km (150 mi) from the mouth. Once the zone of the falls is reached, cargoes from ships are transferred to railroad cars. The territory along the river is sparsely populated by people of mixed Portuguese and Indian origin. Cattle raising and mining take place there.

São Paulo

São Paulo [sow pow'-lu] São Paulo, with a population of 10,063,110 (1985 est.), is the largest city of both South America and Brazil as well as the capital of Brazil's richest state, São Paulo. Located in southeastern Brazil on the Tietê River, about 55 km (35 mi) inland from SANTOS, Brazil's principal port, São Paulo is the country's leading manufacturing and financial center.

Contemporary City. Greater São Paulo is one of the world's fastest-growing urban complexes; its metropolitan area population is 32,091,000 (1988 est.). Within the famous Triângulo section, the city's central business district, are many skyscrapers.

São Paulo accounts for about 40% of Brazil's total industrial output, producing textiles, chemicals, pharmaceuticals, paper, electrical materials, rubber goods, machinery, tools, and motor vehicles. Several factors have contributed to São Paulo's industrial preeminence, including reinvestment of profits from the sale of coffee, an abundance of hydroelectric power, tax exemptions that have stimulated imports and exports, and a skilled work force.

São Paulo has long been a cultural and intellectual center, with three major universities: Pontifical Catholic University of São Paulo (1946); Mackenzie University (1952); and the University of São Paulo (1934). The Instituto Butantã is world famous for its work researching snake venom and producing serums; the Instituto Históri-

São Paulo, the largest city in South America, was founded (1554) by two Jesuit missionaries and remained a small town until about a century ago. Since then its population has increased about 200 times.

co e Geográfico de São Paulo (1894) is one of Brazil's most respected cultural associations. The city has dozens of museums, including the Museum of Art and the Museum of Brazilian Art. Every other year artists come from many continents to the Bienal, São Paulo's international art competition. Within the city is Anhembi, one of the world's largest exhibition halls.

History. Founded by Jesuits in 1554, São Paulo served during the 17th and 18th centuries as a base for Portuguese settlement of the interior. In 1822 it was the city in which Emperor Pedro I proclaimed Brazil's independence from Portugal. In the 1880s, São Paulo state became a major coffee-growing region; the city is its primary market.

São Tomé and Príncipe [sow tuh-may', preen'-si-pe]   The Democratic Republic of São Tomé and Príncipe is an African country consisting of two main islands, about 130 km (80 mi) apart off the coast of Gabon, and several rocky islets in the Gulf of Guinea. A former Portuguese overseas territory, it became independent in 1975.

Land, People, and Economy

The islands, of volcanic origin, are densely forested. The annual average temperature is 25° C (77° F), and rainfall averages more than 5,100 mm (200 in) each year. The principal resources are fertile soils and timber.

The population, of mixed heritage, is composed of the descendants of African slaves brought to the islands, immigrants from the Cape Verde Islands, and Europeans,

mostly from Portugal. Almost all Portuguese left the islands after independence. The town of São Tomé, on the island of the same name, is the country's capital and largest urban center. Santo Antonio is the major town on Príncipe.

The economy is based on export crops, including cacao, copra, and bananas. The fishing and tourist industries are being developed. Almost all foodstuffs are imported. In the mid-1980s, as the economy deteriorated, the government reduced its ties to the Soviet bloc and actively sought Western aid and investment.

History and Government

The uninhabited islands were discovered by the Portuguese in the late 15th century. The first Portuguese settlers arrived in 1493, and soon African slaves were imported to work on the large sugar plantations. São Tomé was taken over by the Portuguese crown in 1522, and Príncipe in 1573. The Portuguese kept São Tomé and Príncipe under harsh colonial rule even after it became an overseas territory in 1951. In 1960 the Committee for the Liberation of São Tomé and Príncipe was organized. In 1972 it renamed itself the Movement for the Liberation of São Tomé and Príncipe (MLSTP). Following the overthrow of the Portuguese dictatorship in 1974, the new government in Lisbon recognized the MLSTP. The islands achieved independence on July 21, 1975.

The head of the MLSTP, Manuel Pinto da Costa, became the country's first president. A new constitution adopted in 1990 provided for a multiparty system and di-

---

AT A GLANCE

DEMOCRATIC REPUBLIC OF SÃO TOMÉ AND PRÍNCIPE

Land: Area: 964 km^2 (372 mi^2). Capital and largest city: São Tomé (1984 est. pop., 34,997).

People: Population (1990 est.): 124,765. Density: 129.4 persons per km^2 (335.4 per mi^2). Distribution (1989): 38% urban, 62% rural. Official language: Portuguese. Major religions: Roman Catholicism, Protestantism.

Government: Type: republic. Legislature: National People's Assembly. Political subdivisions: 7 districts.

Economy: GNP (1989): $43 million; $360 per capita. Labor distribution (1987): agriculture—40%; trade, mining, manufacturing, and utilities—5%; construction—4%; public administration and services—18%. Foreign trade (1988 est.): imports—$17.3 million; exports—$9.1 million. Currency: 1 dobra = 100 céntimos.

Education and Health: Literacy (1985): 57% of adult population. Universities (1991): none. Hospital beds (1983): 640. Physicians (1987): 40. Life expectancy (1990): women—67; men—64. Infant mortality (1990): 61 per 1,000 live births.

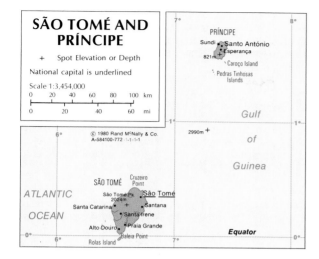

SÃO TOMÉ AND PRÍNCIPE

+   Spot Elevation or Depth

National capital is underlined

Scale 1:3,454,000

rect elections for a president limited to no more than two terms who would share power with a prime minister. In January 1991, in the first multiparty elections since independence, the MLSTP (renamed the MLSTP–Social Democrat party in 1990) lost its parliamentary majority. Antonio Mascarenhas Monteiro of the Movement for Democracy was elected president in March.

Saône River [sohn]   The Saône River in eastern France is about 480 km (300 mi) long. It rises in the Monts Faucilles south of Nancy and then flows southwest and south through a fertile valley to Lyon, where it joins the RHÔNE. Navigable for 375 km (233 mi), the Saône is linked to other river systems by canals.

sap   Any liquid found in the stems of plants may be called sap, including the liquid material that moves in the younger annual rings and bark of trees and the watery juices of herbaceous plants. Sap, however, is most often considered as the fluid and dissolved materials that move upward in the xylem in vascular plants (see PLANT). Sap ascends at a rate of 30–122 cm (1–4 ft) per hour. It consists of a water solution of mineral salts such as nitrates and phosphates, and organic materials such as sugars, proteins, and other nitrogen compounds. The solute varies in kind as well as amount. For example, the quantity of dissolved minerals will vary with soil composition. In the spring the sap flows more profusely than at other times of the year in order to nourish developing buds, and organic materials are in greater concentration to provide for rapid growth. The sap in some plants has a high sugar content and is valued commercially (see MAPLE SYRUP AND SUGAR; SUGAR PRODUCTION). Natural RUBBER is another valuable sap.

Whereas many environmental factors such as temperature, humidity, and light intensity are known to influence the rate of sap rise, the internal causes of this movement have not been proved conclusively. Among the interesting questions are why not all plants "bleed" when cut and how sap reaches heights up to 120 m (about 400 ft) in the tallest trees.

Sapir, Edward [suh-peer']   The philologist and anthropologist Edward Sapir, b. Pomerania, Germany, Jan. 26, 1884, d. Feb. 4, 1939, was one of the seminal figures in ANTHROPOLOGICAL LINGUISTICS. His classic *Language* (1921) is perhaps the most readable and, for its size, most informative book ever written on the subject. Sapir studied at Columbia University with Franz BOAS; taught at California, Pennsylvania, Chicago, and Yale universities; and was chief of anthropology at the Canadian National Museum.

saponification [suh-pahn'-i-fi-kay-shuhn]   Saponification is a routine laboratory and industrial reaction, of particular interest because most soap is manufactured by the saponification of animal fats. Saponification is chemical reaction in which an ESTER is split to form an alcohol and a carboxylate salt. The term arose from the alkaline hydrolysis of fats to yield soaps (see SOAP AND DETERGENT). Soaps are sodium or potassium salts of long-chain carboxylic acids.

See also: FATS AND OILS; FATTY ACID.

sapphire [saf'-yr]   Sapphire, the precious GEM variety of the extremely hard aluminum oxide mineral CORUNDUM, owes its pale blue to deep indigo color to small amounts of iron and titanium; the most highly prized color is a deep cornflower blue. Actually, transparent gem corundum in all colors except red (RUBY) is called sapphire, but stones other than blue ones are indicated by color, as in white sapphire, yellow sapphire, and so on. Translucent stones contain many tiny inclusions that yield a faint silky sheen or, when regularly arranged, a six-rayed star; varieties such as the star sapphire are rounded and polished, and some are carved or engraved.

(Left) *Sapphire, one of the most highly prized gemstones, is an aluminum oxide mineral. Its typically blue color results from the inclusion of small amounts of titanium and iron oxides.* (Right) *Sapphires are usually faceted by step- or brilliant-cutting.*

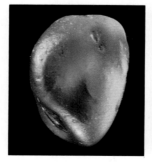

Sapphire and ruby, the same mineral, occur in many of the same localities, often in alluvial deposits, or placers, because they resist weathering. Cambodia, Sri Lanka, Thailand, and Burma have notable PLACER DEPOSITS. Synthetic sapphires, produced by the Verneuil flame-fusion process since 1902, are becoming more widely used than the natural stones for gems and for abrasion-resistant applications such as thread guides, phonograph needles, watch bearings, and machinists' dies. Some are also crushed and used as high-grade abrasives.

Sappho [saf'-oh]   The most famous woman poet of all time, Sappho was born c.630 BC at Eressos on the Greek island of Lesbos. She was married and had a daughter and sometime between 604 and 595 suffered exile in Sicily. Of her nine books of poems only fragments remain, some recently discovered on Egyptian papyri. Celebrated for her marriage songs (epithalamia), she also wrote hymns, mythological poems, and personal poems of love. Of the last, most are addressed to women, possibly members of a literary circle with strong emotional attachments. Several poems invoking Aphrodite suggest that they may have shared some cult or ceremonial practices. Famous for her depiction of passion, Sappho delights in sensuous images of flowers, the moon, the sea, and the night. The Roman poet Catullus imitated her, and Ovid depicted her legendary love for Phaon in his *Heroides*.

Sapporo [sahp-pohr'-oh]   Sapporo, the largest city of Hokkaido Island, Japan, is located in the southwestern part of the island, about 40 km (25 mi) from the port city of Otaru, on the Sea of Japan. The population is 1,648,508 (1989 est.). Industrial products include chemicals, agricultural machinery, ceramics, and processed foods. The printing and publishing industries are also important. Sapporo is the seat of the Hokkaido University (1876). The city was founded in 1868 and laid out by U.S. engineers. The 1972 Winter Olympics took place there.

sapsucker   Sapsucker is the common name for two migratory North American birds of the woodpecker family, Picidae. Sapsuckers drill small holes in the bark of trees and return to eat both the exuded sap and the insects that become trapped in it. The yellow-bellied sapsucker, *Sphyrapicus varius*, is about 21 cm (8.5 in) long, with a conspicuous white wing stripe. The Williamson's sapsucker, *S. thyroideus*, is an uncommon species of the pine forests of the western United States.

Saqqara [suh-kahr'-uh]   Saqqara, or Sakkara, a vast sandy area measuring about 10 km (6.2 mi) north to south and 2 km (1.24 mi) east to west, was the necropolis, or burial place, for the ancient Egyptian city of MEMPHIS. It comprises remains from almost every period of

Egypt's history. Among the most important monuments of the Old Kingdom is the Step Pyramid (see PYRAMIDS), erected about 2630 BC by IMHOTEP for King Zoser of the 3d dynasty, which rises in six layers to a height of 61 m (200 ft). Its underground passages and chambers contained thousands of stone vessels as well as beautiful reliefs representing King Zoser performing religious rites. The structures around this pyramid, translations into stone of earlier wattle-and-daub buildings, constitute an invaluable record of early Egyptian architecture. To the northwest of this complex is the Serapeum, a vast subterranean passage dating from the New Kingdom, containing niches in which the APIS bulls were buried.

Saragossa [sair-uh-goh'-suh]   Saragossa (Spanish: Zaragoza) is the capital of Saragossa province in the Aragon region of northeastern Spain and is located on the Ebro River. The city has a population of 575,317 (1987 est.). Saragossa has long been the principal city of the region because of its location along the river. Milling, hydroelectric production, and petroleum distribution are important. The principal architectural landmarks are the Cathedral of Nuestra Señora del Pilar, begun in 1681; the Gothic Cathedral of La Seo (1119–1520); the Palace of the Counts of Luna (1537); La Lonja, a Gothic market; and the University of Saragossa (1474).

Romans established a settlement there during the 1st century BC. Visigoths occupied the city in the 5th century AD, and Moors took it in 714, making it the seat of an emirate. King Alfonso I of Aragon captured it in 1118, and Saragossa was the capital of Aragon until it was united with Castile during the 15th century.

Sarah   In the Bible, Sarah (Sarai) was ABRAHAM's wife and half sister and ISAAC's mother (Gen. 11–23). After prolonged barrenness, the elderly Sarah laughed when she heard the divine promise of a son. At the age of 90 she bore Isaac and banished her servant and rival HAGAR with ISHMAEL, Hagar's son by Abraham, into the wilderness. Sarah died at the age of 127.

Sarah Lawrence College   Established in 1926, Sarah Lawrence College is a private coeducational liberal arts school offering undergraduate and graduate studies in Bronxville, N.Y. Such emphasis is placed on the individual that grades, examinations, and majors are replaced by study programs designed to encourage the intellectual growth of the student. The college has good facilities for the performing arts.

Sarajevo [sair-uh-yay'-voh]   Sarajevo is the capital of Bosnia and Hercegovina in central Yugoslavia on the Miljačka River. In a valley of the Dinaric Alps, the city stands near the foot of Mount Trebević and has a population of 341,200 (1987 est.). It is a market, crafts, and rail center, producing jewelry, pottery, carpets, metalwork, clothing, chemicals, tools, and tobacco products. It has a large Muslim population and counts among its landmarks mosques, public baths, and a market. The University of Sarajevo (1946) is located there.

The Romans had a settlement near present-day Sarajevo, which was overrun by the Goths and then the Slavs. A new center grew up around a citadel established in 1263 on a trade route through the mountains. From the 15th century until its fall to Austria-Hungary in 1878, the city was part of the Ottoman Empire. Resistance to Austrian rule led to the assassination of the Archduke FRANZ FERDINAND (1914) in Sarajevo, an immediate cause of World War I. After the war the city became part of Yugoslavia. The 1984 Winter Olympics were held there.

Sarasota [sar-uh-soh'-tuh]   Sarasota is the seat of Sarasota County, southwestern Florida, on Sarasota Bay, an inlet of the Gulf of Mexico. It has a population of 50,961 (1990). A resort city, Sarasota also has food processing and distribution operations. The city's John and Mable Ringling Museum of Art contains the largest collection of works by Peter Paul Rubens in the Western Hemisphere. Settled in 1856, Sarasota became a popular resort after the wealthy began wintering there.

Saratoga, Battles of [sar-uh-toh'-guh]   The Saratoga campaign, battles of the American Revolution fought in upstate New York, permanently ended British hopes of dividing the colonies along the Hudson River. British general John BURGOYNE, commanding 6,000 regulars and various auxiliaries, pushed down from Canada in June 1777. His plan was to advance to Albany, where he would join forces with Barry ST. LEGER. The revolutionists offered feeble resistance at first, but by the time Burgoyne reached Bemis Heights, west of the Hudson, the American army had been strengthened and given a popular commanding general, Horatio GATES. With time and terrain on the American side, Gates allowed Burgoyne to wear down the British forces with costly assaults on the patriot lines. In the first Battle of Freeman's Farm (Sept. 19, 1777), Burgoyne suffered 600 casualties to Gates's 320. At Bemis Heights, or the Second Battle of Freeman's Farm (October 7), Burgoyne's men were repulsed by Gates, Benedict ARNOLD, and Daniel MORGAN. Once again British losses were roughly 600, four times the American casualty figure. Outnumbered, surrounded, and unable to secure relief, Burgoyne surrendered on Oct. 17, 1777, at Saratoga. The Battles of Saratoga marked a turning point in the war, motivating the French to assist the American insurgents openly.

Saratoga Springs   Saratoga Springs is a resort and residential city with a population of 25,001 (1990) in eastern New York in the foothills of the Adirondack Mountains. Once an elegant resort with rambling hotels, Saratoga Springs is now a quiet city for most of the year and is the home of SKIDMORE COLLEGE. Some light industries con-

tribute to the local economy. In the summer the city attracts visitors to Thoroughbred races and cultural events. The Battles of Saratoga (1777) during the American Revolution were fought nearby, and the Saratoga National Historic Park is southeast of the city. Gideon Putnam settled in Saratoga in 1789 and built the first hotel in 1791.

Saratov [suh-rah'-tuhf]   Saratov, the capital of the Saratov oblast in the Russian republic of the USSR, has a population of 905,000 (1989). It is situated on the west bank of the Volga River, southeast of Moscow. The name is derived from Tatar words meaning "yellow mountain." Saratov is an industrial and educational center of the lower Volga River valley, with diversified defense industries and machine manufacturing (machine tools, ball bearings, electrical goods) and a petroleum-refining and petrochemical industry. Saratov State University dates from 1909. Saratov, founded in 1590 as a Russian stronghold on the Volga, became an important grain-trade center in the second half of the 19th century.

Sarawak [sar'-uh-wak]   Sarawak, a mountainous state of Malaysia, is located on the northwestern part of the island of Borneo, facing the South China Sea. It has an area of about 124,450 km^2 (48,050 mi^2) and a population of 1,591,100 (1988 est.). Kuching, with 74,229 inhabitants (1980), is the capital. Farming is most important, but some rubber and petroleum production also occurs. Most inhabitants are Dayaks. The area was a province of the Brunei sultanate in the 15th century. In 1841, Sarawak was ceded to Sir James BROOKE, who became raja; his descendants continued to rule until 1941. In 1963, Sarawak joined Malaysia.

Sarazen, Gene [sah'-ruh-zen]   Eugene Saraceni, b. Harrison, N.Y., Feb. 27, 1902, better known as Gene Sarazen, was only 20 years old when he won two of golf's most important tournaments. In 1922 he won the U.S. Open and the Professional Golfers' Association (PGA) championships; in 1923 he repeated his PGA victory. Several years passed before Sarazen again won (1932) major championships: the British Open and the U.S. Open. He won the PGA a third time in 1933 and the Masters tournament in 1935, thereby becoming the first of only four golfers to win during their careers the four titles that constitute the Grand Slam of golf.

sarcoma [sahr-koh'-muh]   A sarcoma is a CANCER that arises from connective tissue. Sarcomas usually occur in bone, lymph nodes, and skin and vary considerably in malignancy. In some sarcomas the cells are so unusual in appearance that it is difficult or impossible to know the type of connective tissue from which they arose. In other sarcomas the cells retain enough resemblance to their parent cells to allow the tumor to be classified according to the tissue of origin.

sarcophagus [sahr-kahf'-uh-guhs]   A sarcophagus is an ancient coffin (chest and lid) made of wood, terra-cotta, marble, alabaster, or metal, and generally ornamented with painting, sculpture, or both. From the Hellenistic through the Early Christian period (4th century BC–5th century AD), sarcophagi were usually adorned with vividly colored, elaborately carved reliefs, or friezes, of either continuous scenes or rows of single figures in architectural settings. Sarcophagi are an invaluable record of sculptural style, technique, and subject matter, especially with regard to funerary sculpture. The term *sarcophagus* derives from two Greek words meaning "flesh-eating." According to the Roman historian Pliny the Elder, this stemmed from the use, during prehistoric ages as well as in ancient Egypt and Greece, of coffins lined with a type of stone with caustic properties that was believed to consume a corpse in 40 days. The oldest known sarcophagus is Egyptian and dates from the 1st dynasty (*c.*3000 BC).

This Etruscan terra-cotta sarcophagus of a married couple dates from the late 6th century BC. It is sculpted in the form of a couch, a style of sarcophagus sculpture that remained popular in classical Rome. (Museo Nazionale di Villa Giulia, Rome.)

sardine   Sardines are members of the HERRING family, Clupeidae, that live in temperate waters of Europe (genus *Sardina*), western North America and Japan (genus *Sardinops*), and the Indian and Atlantic oceans (genus *Sardinella*). Silvery schools of these slab-sided fishes live off western North America and western Europe and are most abundant in nutrient-rich waters that can support millions of fishes. In the past, schools of *Sardinops sagax* measured kilometers in width and supported large commercial fisheries on the U.S. West Coast. They also provided forage for many other predatory fishes. U.S. catches peaked in 1936. In the late 1940s and early 1950s their numbers dropped severely because of environmental

Sardine is the common name for several genera of small, herring-like food fish that live in large schools and feed on plankton.

changes and overfishing. U.S. sardines now come almost solely from Maine. Most canned sardines are largely from the fishing in Norway, Canada, and Portugal.

Sardinia [sahr-din'-ee-uh]   Sardinia (Italian: Sardegna) is a mountainous island that, with several minor islands, is a region of Italy. It is located in the Mediterranean west of the Italian peninsula and south of Corsica. The second largest island (after Sicily) in the Mediterranean, Sardinia has an area of 23,813 km^2 (9,194 mi^2) and a population of 1,655,859 (1989 est.). Sardinia's capital is CAGLIARI. Increasing numbers of tourists are lured by the beautiful coastline and a mild climate. Sheep and goats are raised there; wheat, barley, grapes, and olives are produced; and fishing and cork production are important to the economy. The island has rich mineral deposits but little industry.

Phoenicians settled on Sardinia about 800 BC. It was conquered by Rome in 238 BC and held by the Vandals and Byzantines in the 5th and 6th centuries AD. The island was contested by Pisa and Genoa during the Middle Ages until it passed to Spain during the early 15th century. Ceded (1713) to Austria, Sardinia was awarded (1720) to the house of Savoy, whose territories were known thereafter as the Kingdom of Sardinia.

Sardinia, Kingdom of   The Kingdom of Sardinia came into existence in 1720 when the island of Sardinia was added to the mainland territories of VICTOR AMADEUS II of the SAVOY dynasty. The kingdom included areas in modern Italy and France—Nice, Piedmont, Savoy and Genoa (added by the Congress of Vienna in 1815). Known as Sardinia-Piedmont, the kingdom eventually headed the Italian unification movement, the RISORGIMENTO. Turin, in Piedmont, was the kingdom's capital.

Victor Amadeus II, who inaugurated a policy of gradual expansion, abdicated in 1730 in favor of his unenlightened son, Charles Emmanuel III. Charles Emmanuel was followed (1773) by Victor Amadeus III, who was unable to prevent the French army from overrunning (1792–1815) the mainland, forcing his successors Charles Emmanuel IV (r. 1796–1802) and VICTOR EMMANUEL I (r. 1802–21) to remain on the island.

The kingdom stood out among other Italian states for its military strength and freedom from foreign control, but it remained politically reactionary through the reign (1821–31) of Charles Felix. Yielding to the revolutionary ferment of 1848, Charles Albert (r. 1831–49) granted a constitution and declared war against Austria in an effort to secure Italian independence.

Unsuccessful in the war, Charles Albert abdicated (1849) in favor of his son VICTOR EMMANUEL II, who achieved Italian unification in exchange for ceding Savoy and Nice to France. In 1861, Sardinia-Piedmont ceased to exist, merging into the new Kingdom of Italy.

Sardis see LYDIA

Sardou, Victorien [sahr-doo'] Victorien Sardou, b. Sept. 5, 1831, d. Nov. 8, 1908, succeeded Eugène Scribe as the principal writer of French well-made plays. Sardou's clever, easy-flowing dialogue won him a large following and election (1877) to the Académie Française. Known for his comedies and historical dramas, he also wrote plays for Sarah Bernhardt, including *La Tosca* (1887), the basis for Puccini's opera.

Sargasso Sea [sahr-gas'-oh] The Sargasso Sea is part of the North Atlantic Ocean west of the Azores and east of the West Indies and located approximately between 20° and 35° north latitude. The Bermuda Islands are within the northwestern portion of the sea. The Sargasso is the calm center of the clockwise-turning, subtropical gyre that dominates the North Atlantic. It is bounded on the west and north by the Gulf Stream and on the south by the North Equatorial Current (see OCEAN CURRENTS).

Biota. The name of the sea is derived from its ubiquitous floating weed masses of *Sargassum natans* and *S. fluitans.* Both of these species occur along the Atlantic coast from Cape Cod, Mass., to Venezuela, and some reinforcement of the open ocean weed apparently comes from these sources. The Sargasso Sea is the spawning area of flying fish (*Cypselurus*) and the European and North American eel (*Anguilla anguilla, A. rostrata*). It harbors many rare faunal species, the majority of which are uniquely adapted to the pelagic weed environment, especially in terms of camouflage.

Lore. Much romantic nautical lore is associated with the Sargasso Sea, the most famous alluding to ship graveyards consisting of derelict vessels trapped within dense mats of seaweeds. In fact, the floating weed masses pose no obstacle to seagoing craft; the area was historically avoided by sailing vessels mainly because it lies within the wind-sparse HORSE LATITUDES.

Sargent, John Singer The American painter John Singer Sargent, b. Florence, Italy, Jan. 12, 1856, d. Apr. 15, 1925, was a phenomenally successful portraitist, pleasing his wealthy patrons with brilliantly executed, flattering paintings. His great technical facility was widely praised; however, he was also criticized for displays of empty virtuosity.

Raised in Europe, Sargent spent most of his career in Paris and London, making his first trip to the United

The American portraitist John Singer Sargent was at the height of his fame when he painted Mr. and Mrs. Isaac Newton Phelps Stokes (1897). Few painters have attained the stylish elegance of Sargent's fashionable society portraiture. (Metropolitan Museum of Art, New York City.)

States only in 1876. Sargent had already established himself professionally when, in 1884, he submitted his *Portrait of Madame X* (1884; Metropolitan Museum, New York City) to the Paris Salon. Because its subject, a well-known society beauty, was portrayed so daringly (by prevailing standards), the picture caused a scandal and forced Sargent to move to London. *The Daughters of Edward D. Boit* (1882; Museum of Fine Arts, Boston) is an outstanding example of his informal yet elegant portraiture of the 1880s. In 1888, Sargent worked side by side with Claude Monet at Giverny, France; the portrait *Paul Helleu Sketching with His Wife* (1889; Brooklyn Museum, N.Y.) bears witness to Monet's influence.

During the 1890s, Sargent was at the height of his fame and spent much time in the United States. His projects then included a series of murals for the Boston Public Library executed in an uncharacteristic symbolist style. Toward the end of his life he also returned to the painting of landscape and the use of watercolors, at which he excelled. By 1897 he had won many honors on both sides of the Atlantic, and in 1907 he refused a British knighthood on the ground of his American citizenship.

Sargon, King of Akkad [sahr'-gahn] Sargon of AKKAD, one of the first conquerors of historical record, founded (*c.*2350 BC) a Semitic dynasty in ancient Mesopotamia that endured nearly 150 years. A usurper, he called himself Sargon, or "True King," after overthrowing the king of Kish. He founded Agade, a new capital city from which the region Akkad took its name, and then conquered southern Babylonia (Sumer) and upper Mesopotamia. By numerous raids he collected plunder and tribute from nearby kingdoms, particularly those westward toward the Mediterranean Sea. He ruled for 56 years.

Sargon II, King of Assyria   Sargon II (r. 721–705 BC) founded the last Assyrian dynasty. Like Sargon of Akkad he was probably a usurper who tried to disguise the fact by calling himself Sargon, or "True King." He participated in the siege of Samaria, and after the death of his predecessor, Shalmaneser V, he conducted the mopping-up operations, allegedly deporting more than 27,000 Israelites and dispersing them so widely throughout the Assyrian empire that they became the "lost tribes of Israel." The creator of the first truly imperial administration in history, Sargon also defeated internal rebellions and powerful enemies who threatened his frontiers.

Sarmatians [sahr-may'-shuhnz]   The Sarmatians were a group of nomadic tribes who dominated the southern area of European Russia from about the 4th century BC to the 4th century AD. Their original migration from Central Asia, starting in about the 6th century BC, brought them into conflict with the SCYTHIANS, whom they gradually displaced. During the period of their greatest power, they were a constant threat to Roman provinces in the Balkans, particularly Dacia (modern Romania). They were finally overcome by the Huns and the Goths.

Sarmiento, Domingo Faustino [sahr-mee-en'-toh]   One of Argentina's leading journalists, educators, and politicians, Domingo Faustino Sarmiento, b. Feb. 14, 1811, d. Sept. 11, 1888, was the first civilian to become president of a united Argentina. He was first employed as a country schoolteacher, but his opposition to dictator Juan Manuel de ROSAS led to his exile (1840) to Chile. There he wrote and edited for various newspapers, agitated against Rosas, and studied public education. His book *Life in the Argentine Republic in the Days of the Tyrants* (1845; Eng. trans., 1961) is a classic of Spanish-American literature. In 1852, Sarmiento returned to Argentina to help Justo José de URQUIZA depose Rosas. Elected president in 1868, Sarmiento revamped the national school system, ended the War of the Triple Alliance against Paraguay (see TRIPLE ALLIANCE, WAR OF THE), and helped stabilize liberal institutions.

Sarnath [sahr-naht']   Sarnath, about 8 km (5 mi) north of the sacred city of Varanasi, India, is the site where the BUDDHA first enunciated the liberating insight he had attained while meditating under the pipal tree at Bodh Gaya. The site of the Buddha's first sermon became a cen-

ter of pilgrimage and monastic residence; it is one of the Four Holy Places of Buddhist tradition. Impressive remains include a commemorative pillar erected (3d century BC) by the Maurya emperor Asoka and shrines and monastic structures spanning the Mauryan through Mogul eras.

Sarney, José   José Sarney, born José Ribamar Ferreira da Costa on Apr. 30, 1930, became Brazil's first civilian president since 1964 in April 1985. Sarney was elected governor of Maranhão in 1965 and senator in 1970 and 1978. In mid-1984 he defected from the Democratic party, which backed Brazil's military rulers, to join a coalition supporting presidential candidate Tancredo Neves. When president-elect Neves died before assuming office Sarney, who had been named vice-president, became president. Sarney attempted to solve Brazil's economic problems, including inflation and a huge foreign debt. He was not a candidate in the November 1989 election.

Sarnoff, David [sahr'-nawf]   A pioneer in the development of radio and television broadcasting, David Sarnoff, b. Uzlian, Russia, Feb. 27 (N.S.), 1891, d. Dec. 12, 1971, was chief executive for many years of the Radio Corporation of America (RCA) and the National Broadcasting Corporation (NBC). After immigrating (1900) to New York City from Russia with his family, Sarnoff worked as a telegraph operator for the Marconi Wireless Telegraph Company of America, the predecessor of RCA. In April 1912, while operating a station in New York City, he broadcast the first news of the sinking of the S.S. *Titanic*. In 1916, Sarnoff submitted the idea for a "radio music box" to the management of Marconi. Five years later he won acceptance of the radio when his broadcast of the Dempsey-Carpentier boxing match attracted an audience of about 300,000 amateur wireless operators. By 1930, Sarnoff had become president of RCA, had founded NBC, and had set up an experimental television station. During World War II he was made a brigadier general, served as communications consultant to Gen. Dwight D. Eisenhower, and was decorated with the Legion of Merit. He was chairman of the board of RCA from 1947 until his death.

Saroyan, William [suh-roy'-uhn]   An American playwright, novelist, and short-story writer known for his sentimental optimism and rhapsodic style, William Saroyan, b. Fresno, Calif., Aug. 31, 1908, d. May 5, 1981, began his steady outpouring of fiction with *The Daring Young Man on the Flying Trapeze* (1934), a collection of stories. The best known of his many plays are *My Heart's in the Highlands* (1939) and *The Time of Your Life* (1939), for which Saroyan was offered, but refused, the Pulitzer Prize. Among his other popular works are the autobiographical *My Name Is Aram* (1940) and a novel, *The Human Comedy* (1943). Saroyan's last autobiographical works include *Places Where I've Done Time* (1972), *Sons*

Come and Go, *Mothers Hang in Forever* (1976), *Chance Meetings* (1978), and *Obituaries* (1979).

Sarraute, Nathalie [sah-roht'] With *The Age of Suspicion* (1956; Eng. trans., 1963), Nathalie Sarraute, b. Russia, July 18 (N.S.), 1902, established herself as a leading exponent of the "new novel" in France. The drama in her works stems from the interplay of tropisms—the amorphous, evanescent sensations and impressions felt by individuals that determine their gestures, words, and emotional responses. In such novels as *Portrait of a Man Unknown* (1948; Eng. trans., 1958), *The Planetarium* (1959; Eng. trans., 1960), *Between Life and Death* (1968; Eng. trans., 1969), and *Fools Say* (1976; Eng. trans., 1976), as well as in her plays, *Silence* and *The Lie* (both 1967; Eng. trans., 1969), Sarraute bombards readers with these hidden tropisms. In the autobiographical *Childhood* (1984; Eng. trans., 1985) she explores the fragmentary nature of memory.

sarsaparilla [sas-puh-ril'-uh] Sarsaparilla is an aromatic extract from the roots of several species of tropical vines of the genus *Smilax* of the lily family, Liliaceae. It was once employed as a tonic and as a treatment for rheumatism and is now used to flavor medicines and soft drinks. Sarsaparilla plants—large perennial vines with short, thick, underground stems—are native to tropical America and grow in jungles from Mexico to Peru. The roots of harvested plants are sun-dried and tied in bundles for export. A liquid extract is used for flavoring, and the chemical sarsapogenin—isolated from the sarsaparilla root—is used to synthesize such steroids as progesterone. Extracts of the North American wild sarsaparilla, *Aralia nudicaulis*, and false sarsaparilla, *A. hispida*, are sometimes used as substitutes in flavoring.

SARSAT SARSAT is an international program for the rapid location and rescue of air, water, and land vehicles in distress. The name is an acronym for *Search and Rescue Satellite*. SARSAT was first agreed upon in 1980 by the United States, Canada, France, and the Soviet Union. Several U.S. and Soviet satellites have since been launched as part of the project, and in 1988 the program was extended for several years, with other nations expected to join. Many vehicles—for example, all U.S. fishing vessels—are now required to carry a SARSAT transmitter. The inexpensive, battery-powered transmitter, automatically activated in an emergency, broadcasts an internationally recognized distress signal, via satellite, to any of several ground stations around the world.

Sarto, Andrea del see ANDREA DEL SARTO

Sarton, May [sahr'-tuhn] An American poet and novelist, May Eleanor Sarton was born in Belgium on May 3, 1912, and brought to the United States when she was

four. *Encounter in April* (1937), her first collection of lyrics, was followed by many more volumes of poetry. Her first two novels, *The Single Hound* (1938) and *Bridge of Years* (1946), had European settings, but since 1955, New England has provided the background for most of her fiction. In addition to her many novels, Sarton has written such personal works as *The Hours by the Sea* (1977) and *After the Stroke: A Journal* (1988).

Sartre, Jean Paul [sahr'-truh] Renowned as a philosopher, literary figure, and social critic, Jean Paul Sartre, b. Paris, June 21, 1905, d. Apr. 15, 1980, was probably most famous as a representative of EXISTENTIALISM, a philosophical approach that emphasizes, among other things, the ultimacy of human freedom.

Sartre graduated from the École Normal Supérieure, Paris, in 1929, by which time he had met Simone de BEAUVOIR, who became his lifelong companion as well as his intellectual associate. He taught in various lycées, or secondary schools, until 1945, after which time he devoted himself exclusively to writing and editing the journal *Les Temps Modernes* (Modern Times).

Philosophical Works. Under the influence of Edmund Husserl and, more importantly, Martin Heidegger, Sartre developed his existentialism as an analysis of self-consciousness in relation to Being. His most important philosophical work, *Being and Nothingness* (1943; Eng. trans., 1956), focused on the opposition between objective things and human consciousness, the latter being a non-thing insofar as its reality consists in standing back from things and taking a point of view on them. Because consciousness is a non-thing (which is a somewhat better translation of Sartre's *néant* than the literal translation, "nothingness"), it does not have any of the causal involvements that things have with other things. This means that consciousness and thus humans themselves are essentially free, and that any attempt by an individual person or a philosophical theory to believe otherwise is a form of self-deception, or "bad faith." Ironically, the freedom of human consciousness is experienced by humans as a burden ("Man is condemned to be free"). Human projects, therefore, consist in the impossible attempt to

Jean Paul Sartre, philosopher, novelist and playwright, was a leading exponent of modern existentialism. He elucidated his theories in his major philosophical work, Being and Nothingness *(1943), and in his literary works, including* Nausea *(1938). In 1964, Sartre won the Nobel Prize for literature but declined to accept it.*

become a free consciousness, such as when a person tries to become an intellectual or a parent or to play any other determinate social role. Because the impossibility of this attempt to become a conscious thing—in Sartre's terminology, a *for-itself-in-itself*—does not prevent humans from being irresistibly drawn to undertake it, Sartre declares that "man is a useless passion."

Literary Works. Most of Sartre's literary output reflects his existentialism, although in 1960 he began writing a three-volume study of Gustave Flaubert that combines Marxist and Freudian approaches (*The Family Idiot*, 1971–72; Eng. trans., vol. 1, 1981). In his first novel, *Nausea* (1938; Eng. trans., 1949), the protagonist, Roquentin, finds himself weighed down and sickened by the opposition between things and consciousness, a theme analyzed philosophically in *Being and Nothingness*. In subsequent works Sartre presents the ethical dilemmas generated by one's commitment to a course of action, usually political action. This is particularly clear in the three novels that are collectively entitled *The Roads To Freedom* (1945–49; Eng. trans., 1947–50).

Similar dilemmas occur in his dramas *Dirty Hands* (1948; Eng. trans., 1949) and *The Condemned of Altona* (1959; Eng. trans., 1961), both of which take up the problem of responsible political action and end with the suicide of the main character. But Sartre's most popular play is undoubtedly the one-act drama *No Exit* (1944; Eng. trans., 1947), which is a discussion of such familiar negative existentialist themes as bad faith, self-destruction, and the impossibility of interpersonal relationships. It is in this play that Sartre's famous line, "Hell is other people," occurs.

Sartre devoted his journal *Les Temps Modernes* to the view that literature must be political. His essays on Charles Baudelaire (1946) and Jean Genêt (1952) employ the technique of *existential psychoanalysis,* a term coined by Sartre to describe discerning, from the details in a person's life, the nature of the fundamental project that animates him or her, and how the project came into being.

Saskatchewan [sas-kach'-uh-wahn]

Saskatchewan [sas-kach'-uh-wahn] Saskatchewan, bounded by Alberta on the west, Manitoba on the east, the Northwest Territories on the north, and the U.S. states of Montana and North Dakota on the south, is one of the prairie provinces of Canada. The name is derived from the Indian word meaning "rapid river." Once a center of the North American fur trade, Saskatchewan has been a major grain-producing area since the 19th century.

Land and Resources

The northern third of Saskatchewan is structurally part of the CANADIAN SHIELD. In the southern two-thirds, occasional hills include the Cypress Hills in the southwest, with the highest elevation in the province. The Pasquia and Porcupine hills and the Missouri Coteau are in the east.

AT A GLANCE

SASKATCHEWAN

Land: Area: 652,330 km² (251,866 mi²); rank: 5th. Capital: Regina (1986 pop., 175,064). Largest city: Saskatoon (1986 pop., 177,641). Municipalities: 805. Elevations: highest—1,468 m (4,816 ft), Cypress Hills; lowest—213 m (699 ft), Lake Athabasca.

People: Population (1990 est.): 1,000,300; rank: 6th; density: 1.5 persons per km² (4.0 per mi²). Distribution (1986): 61.4% urban, 38.6% rural. Average annual change (1981–86): +0.86%.

Government (1991): Lieutenant Governor: Sylvia O. Fedoruk. Premier: Grant Devine, Progressive Conservative. Parliament: Senate—6 members; House of Commons—10 New Democrats, 4 Progressive Conservatives. Provincial legislature: 64 members. Admitted to Confederation: Sept. 1, 1905, with Alberta, the 8th and 9th provinces.

Economy (monetary figures in Canadian dollars): Total personal income (1987): $16.1 billion; rank: 6th. Median family income (1987): $35,074. Agriculture: net income (1986)—$738.8 million. Fishing: landed value (1986–87)—$3.1 million. Forestry: lumber production (1985)—204 million board feet. Mining: value (1987)—$3.26 billion. Manufacturing: value added (1986)—$1.1 billion.

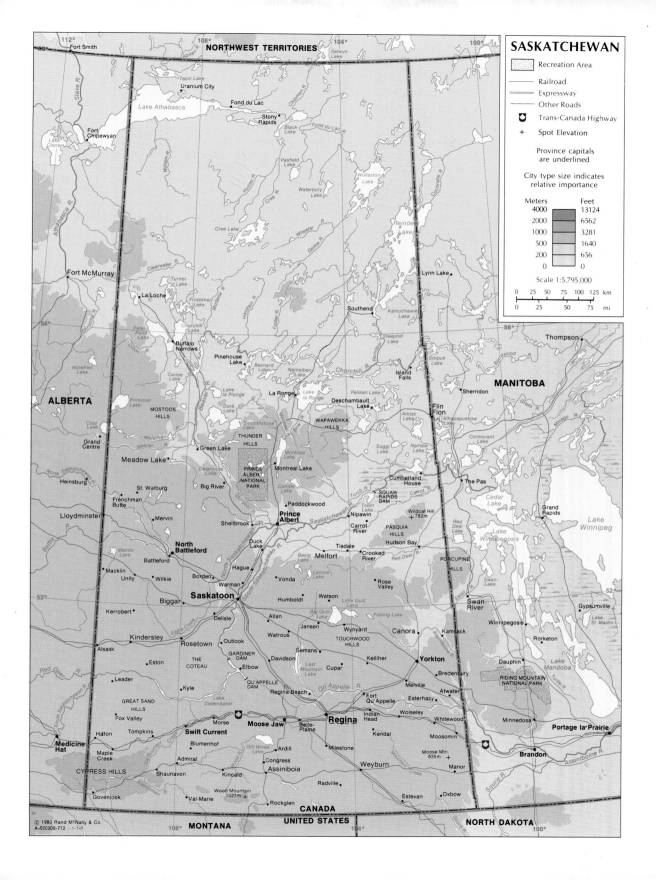

SASKATCHEWAN

Legend:
- Recreation Area
- Railroad
- Expressway
- Other Roads
- Trans-Canada Highway
- Spot Elevation

Province capitals are underlined

City type size indicates relative importance

Meters	Feet
4000	13124
2000	6562
1000	3281
500	1640
200	656
0	0

Scale 1:5,795,000

0 25 50 75 100 125 km
0 25 50 75 mi

© 1980 Rand McNally & Co
A-520209-772 -1-1-1

Soils consist of poorly drained organic matter in the north. Farther south deep, fertile soils developed in areas of glacial deposition.

In the north the average temperatures for January and July are −31° C (−23° F) and 14° C (57° F), respectively. In the south January and July average temperatures are −18° C (0° F) and 18° C (65° F), respectively. Annual precipitation, totaling 279 mm (11 in), is concentrated during the summer.

Most of northern Saskatchewan drains north or east, by way of the CHURCHILL RIVER system and the province's largest lakes—Athabasca (see ATHABASCA, LAKE), Reindeer, and Wollaston. The SASKATCHEWAN RIVER drains much of the south.

A mixed forest of white and black spruce, jack pine, tamarack, and birch covers northern Saskatchewan. Prairie grasses and woodlands cover the southwest. Grayling, pike, pickerel, and trout are found in the lakes of the north. The shallow lakes of the west central section attract waterfowl. Moose, elk, and white-tailed and mule deer can be found in the north, and pronghorn antelope in the south.

The rich soils of the south and the northern forests are the major resources of the province. Rivers have abundant hydroelectric power potential. In the north quantities of metallic and nonmetallic minerals are significant, and petroleum and coal are being developed rapidly. Saskatchewan has the world's largest potash reserves.

People

Saskatchewan's population has been relatively stable for the last 40 years. The largest cities are REGINA, SASKATOON, MOOSE JAW, and PRINCE ALBERT. Only about 40% of

Regina is the capital of Saskatchewan. When Regina was founded during the 1880s, it was named Pile of Bones, a reference to a mound of buffalo skeletons placed nearby by local Indians hoping to entice herds of buffalo to return to the area.

the population are of British origin; large segments are of German, Ukrainian, Scandinavian, and French ancestry. About 60,000 native peoples live in the province. The largest religious group is the United Church of Canada; Roman Catholicism, Lutheranism, and Anglicanism are also important.

Postsecondary education is provided by the University of Saskatchewan (1907) at Saskatoon and the University of Regina (1974). Recreational facilities are provided at Grasslands and Prince Albert national parks and at provincial parks. Saskatchewan is served by the Canadian Broadcasting Corporation as well as daily and weekly newspapers.

Economic Activity

Saskatchewan's economy has been dominated by agriculture, but the province is now rapidly developing as a mining and manufacturing area.

Saskatchewan produces two-thirds of Canada's wheat. It is also a leading producer of other grains, oilseed, and beef cattle.

Mining is, after agriculture, the most important sector of the provincial economy, with oil, potash, and uranium the most important minerals mined. The province ranks second to Alberta in fuel production and is Canada's major producer of potash. The province is also a producer of lignite (brown coal) and ranks third among Canadian provinces in natural-gas production.

Regina and Saskatoon are the major manufacturing centers, with meat processing, petroleum refining, and metal fabricating the dominant industries. The forest industry, where it exists, is significant to the local economy. Commercial fisheries are of minor economic importance, as is the fur-trapping industry.

Saskatchewan has 12,089 km (7,512 mi) of main railway track (1987). A network of provincial highways (1987) covering 25,180 km (15,646 mi) is supplemented by 207,500 km (128,934 mi) of municipal roads.

Government

The provincial government consists of a lieutenant governor appointed by the federal government, an executive council, and a 64-member Legislative Assembly. Real authority is vested in the premier and the executive council, chosen from the majority party in the legislature. Assembly members are elected to 5-year terms.

The Liberal party dominated Saskatchewan politics from 1905 to 1944, when they were defeated by the Cooperative Commonwealth Federation, which ruled until 1964. In 1971 the New Democratic party, an offshoot of the Cooperative Commonwealth Federation, gained power, but they were defeated by the Progressive Conservative party in 1982.

History

The earliest known inhabitants of Saskatchewan were tribes of the Athabascan, Algonquian, and Siouan linguistic groups. Charles II of England granted the territory now known as Saskatchewan to HUDSON'S BAY COMPANY in 1670. Henry KELSEY was the first European visitor in

1691. Rail connections with the east, completed in the 1880s, encouraged homesteading. The resulting dispossession of the métis population led to the Riel Rebellion (see RIEL, LOUIS) of 1885.

The rapid growth associated with agricultural settlement led to the creation of the province in 1905, with Regina as its capital. The Saskatchewan Co-operative Wheat Producers Limited, a marketing cooperative organized by farmers, was founded in 1923 and continues to dominate farm marketing there. Economic and political problems associated with the severe drought of the 1930s encouraged the formation of a socialist party. When elected to power in 1944, it was the first such in Canada. Immigration from Saskatchewan has only recently been reversed.

The development of petroleum and potash deposits and the resurgent market for coal and agricultural products has brought renewed prosperity to Saskatchewan.

Saskatchewan River   The Saskatchewan River is a river system that flows eastward across Alberta and Saskatchewan, Canada, draining an area of about 383,300 km^2 (148,000 mi^2). The river rises in two branches in the COLUMBIA ICEFIELD of southern Alberta. The South Saskatchewan then flows northeast for 885 km (550 mi) past Medicine Hat and Saskatoon. The 1,225-km-long (760 mi) North Saskatchewan flows generally east past Edmonton and Prince Albert; the branches merge east of Prince Albert and continue for 547 km (340 mi) to empty into the northern arm of Lake Winnipeg. The main tributaries are the Brazeau, Battle, Red Deer, and Bow. The Saskatchewan was sighted by Henry Kelsey of the Hudson's Bay Company in 1690 and explored by the sieur de la Vérendrye in 1741.

Saskatoon   [sas-kuh-toon']   Saskatoon, a city of 177,641 (1986 pop.), is the largest city in Saskatchewan, Canada. It is located on the South Saskatchewan River in the south central part of the province. The city's highways, railroads, and airport are used for shipping the potash mined nearby. Industries include flour milling, meat packing, brewing, tanning, petroleum refining, and chemical manufacturing. Saskatoon is the site of the University of Saskatchewan (1907). A wild animal park, an art gallery, and a museum housing early farm equipment are located in the area. Named for a local bush with an edible red berry, Saskatoon was settled in 1883 by a group from Ontario who intended to make it a temperance colony. The arrival of the railroad from Regina in 1890 brought growth to the area.

sassafras   [sas'-uh-fras]   Sassafras is the name of three species of aromatic, deciduous trees of the laurel family, Lauraceae; two species are native to eastern Asia and one to eastern North America. The trees are distinguished by their leaves, which come in three shapes (three-lobed, two-lobed, and egg-shaped), often on the

The common North American sassafras tree produces one-, two-, and three-lobed leaves as well as tiny flowers (bottom). Sassafras oil, extracted from root bark, is used as a tea and as a drug.

same twig. The yellow flowers are the precursors of blue-black berries, which are eaten by numerous birds. The roots, bark, and leaves of the North American *Sassafras albidum* were used by Indians to cure many ills. The Indians passed this knowledge on to early explorers and settlers who, in turn, shipped the plant to Europe as a high-priced panacea. Today an aromatic tea is made from the outer bark of the roots, and oil from the roots and pith is used to flavor soft drinks, candies, and tobacco.

Sassanians   [sas-ayn'-ee-uhnz]   The Sassanian dynasty, which ruled Iran from AD 224 to 651, was founded by Ardashir I and named for Sasan, who is believed to have been Ardashir's grandfather. Ardashir defeated and killed the last Parthian king and established his rule over Iran and Mesopotamia. He was succeeded by his son Shapur I (r. 240–72), who extended the empire when he defeated the Romans. Other famous rulers of this dynasty were SHAPUR II (r. 309–79), Bahram V (r. 421–39), KHOSRU I (r. 531–79), and Khosru II (r. 591–628). After the death of the last ruler, Yazdegird III (r. 632–51), several Sassanian princes tried unsuccessfully to enlist the aid of China and the Turks against the Arabs, who eventually destroyed the dynasty.

ZOROASTRIANISM was the official religion of the Sassanians. The social hierarchy consisted of four classes: priests, warriors, scribes, and common people. The Arabs—especially the Abbasid caliphate (750–1258)—absorbed many features of Sassanian culture, government organization, and fiscal policy.

SAT   see EDUCATIONAL MEASUREMENT AND TESTING

Satan   [say'-tuhn]   In the Judeo-Christian tradition, Satan, from the Hebrew word for "adversary," is the principal figure of the demonic world that is hostile to God and his will. In the Old Testament (for example, the Book of Job), Satan is presented as a distinct personality of darkness and accusation—the heavenly prosecutor. A fuller expression of his role is presented in the New Testament, where he is called "the tempter," "the slanderer," "the enemy," "the liar," and "the angel of the bottomless pit."

Satan is presented as a part of the created order rather than as an eternal entity. Although no explanation is given in the Bible for God's allowing Satan to exist, it does indicate that his time is short (only for this age of time and history) and his end is certain—ultimately he will be banished by the Messiah.

This concept of a temporal dualism in which Satan has influence is brought to expression most clearly in apocalyptic literature, such as the Book of Revelation. Two ages are reflected in apocalyptic cosmology: "this age" and "the age to come." Satan appears to be prevailing in this age, but in the age to come God will clearly display his sovereignty.

The Babylonians, Chaldeans, and Persians believed in a dualism between the forces of darkness and light. Ahriman, in ZOROASTRIANISM, and SET, in Egyptian mythology, manifest characteristics similar to Satan's.

satanism   Satanism, the worship of Satan, developed from the religious doctrine that there are two supreme beings—one good, the other evil. It involves black magic, sorcery, and the invocation of demons and the forces of darkness, who are propitiated by blood sacrifices and similar rites. In Christian cultures these ceremonies include the BLACK MASS, a mockery of the Christian rite.

Satanists, or Luciferians, believe that Satan is the power behind the processes of nature. What is natural is acceptable; sin is only what is unpleasant. Unlike the Christian God—stern and moralistic, restraining the free expression of the instincts with a set of difficult and unnatural commandments under threat of punishment hereafter—Satan is seen as the leader of a liberated people who are free and indeed encouraged to indulge in the good things of life, including uninhibited sexual activity.

See also: WITCHCRAFT.

satellite   A natural satellite is a celestial body that revolves around a planet larger than itself (for example, the Earth's MOON). More than 50 such bodies exist in our SOLAR SYSTEM. Mercury and Venus have no satellites.

satellite, artificial   An artificial satellite is an object placed into orbit around the Earth for the purpose of scientific research, Earth applications, or military reconnaissance. Orbit is achieved when the object is given a horizontal velocity of approximately 28,500 km/h (17,500 mph) at sea level. At this velocity the Earth's surface curves away from the horizontal as fast as gravity pulls the object downward. As the altitude of the sat-

ellite increases, its velocity decreases, and its period—the time the satellite takes to circle the Earth—increases. A satellite in a circular orbit 275 km (170 mi) above the Earth's surface will have a period of 1.5 hours and a velocity of 27,860 km/h (17,300 mph), but the same object in a circular orbit 35,840 km (22,300 mi) above the Earth would have a period of 24 hours (the same as the Earth's rotation) and a velocity of only 11,050 km/h (6,850 mph). A satellite in the latter orbit is called a synchronous satellite; if such a satellite orbits in the equatorial plane, it is termed geostationary because it will remain at the same point above the Earth's surface (see ASTRONAUTICS).

History. The theoretical possibility of establishing an artificial satellite of Earth had been mentioned in 1687 by the English mathematician Isaac Newton as a consequence of his work on the theory of gravitation. Only in the early 20th century, however, did the theoretical work of the Russian Konstantin TSIOLKOVSKY and the experimental work of the American Robert GODDARD confirm that a satellite might be launched by means of a rocket.

During the period from 1943 to 1946 several studies indicated that available rockets would be unable to place a satellite into orbit. Work on rockets for missiles and upper-atmosphere research was so extensive after World War II, however, that by 1954 the feasibility of launching a satellite was no longer in serious doubt (see ROCKETS AND MISSILES). In October 1954 the Committee for the International Geophysical Year (IGY) recommended to member countries that they consider launching small satellite vehicles for scientific SPACE EXPLORA-

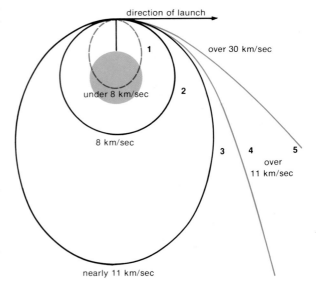

A satellite's path about the Earth depends on the speed at which it is placed in orbit. Earth-intersecting elliptical paths (1) result at speeds of less than 8 km/sec (5 mi/sec), and circular orbits (2) at exactly 8 km/sec. The orbits are increasingly more elliptical (3) at higher speeds and become parabolic (4) at 11 km/sec (7 mi/sec) and hyperbolic (5) at 30 km/sec (18.5 mi/sec).

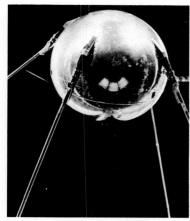

(Left) Sputnik 1, *the Earth's first artificial satellite, weighed 83.6 kg (184 lb) and was orbited by the Soviets on Oct. 4, 1957.* Sputnik *means "traveling companion" in Russian.*

(Below) *The first U.S. satellite, the 14-kg (31-lb)* Explorer I, *was placed into orbit on Jan. 31, 1958. A Geiger counter on board revealed the presence of the Van Allen radiation belts.*

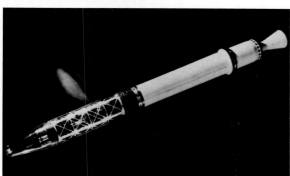

vation satellites, receivers and transmitters in communications satellites, and stable radio-signal sources in navigation satellites. Solar cells generate power from the Sun, and storage batteries are used for the periods when the satellite is blocked from the Sun by the Earth. These batteries in turn are recharged by the solar cells. In special cases, nuclear power sources are utilized. Attitude-control equipment is needed to keep the satellite in its desired orbit and, in some cases, to point the antennas or sensors properly. Radio transmitters and receivers are used to send signals to and from the Earth. TELEMETRY encoders measure various quantities that describe the condition of the onboard equipment and relay this information to Earth.

The U.S. Nimbus satellites have been used for meteorological research and for development of new types of remote-sensing instruments. An instrument ring (1) contains thermal-control shutters (2), beacon and telemetry antennas (3), a microwave spectrometer (4), S-band antennas (5), infrared temperature-humidity (6) and temperature-profile (7) radiometers, a surface-composition mapping radiometer (8), a selective chopping radiometer (9), and an electrically scanned microwave radiometer (10). Above the instrument ring are solar-cell panels (11), a horizon scanner (12), a Sun sensor (13), yaw- (14) and pitch- (15) control nozzles, and a tracking and relay antenna (16).

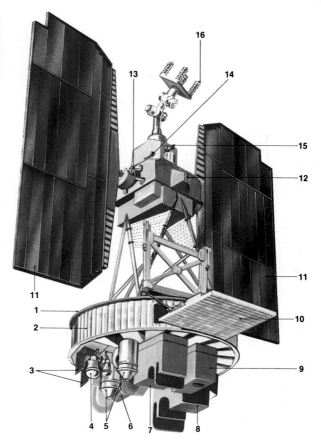

TION. In April and July 1955 the USSR and the United States, respectively, announced plans to launch such satellites for the IGY. Accordingly, the USSR launched *Sputnik 1* on Oct. 4, 1957, and the United States launched *Explorer 1* on Jan. 31, 1958 (see EXPLORER; SPUTNIK). These two satellites provided an enormous stimulus for further work on artificial satellites, especially with the discovery of the Van Allen radiation belts made possible by *Explorer 1.*

Emphasis was first placed on satellites to measure the characteristics of the new space environment and to lay a foundation for the design of communications, navigation, reconnaissance, scientific, and weather satellites and eventually for manned spaceflight. Experimental satellites for these applications quickly followed. Since 1957 several thousand satellites have been placed in orbit, and satellites are now an accepted part of daily life. The vast majority of these satellites were built by the United States and the USSR, but the European Space Agency, comprising the countries of Western Europe, is becoming actively engaged in space exploration through satellites. Canada, China, India, Italy, and Japan are among other countries that have built satellites for subsequent launch.

Basic Elements. All artificial satellites have certain features in common. They include radar for altitude measurements, sensors such as optical devices in obser-

Each of the Intelsat IV satellites was tested in an anechoic chamber to ensure that it would transmit radio waves properly from space. The room was designed to simulate echo-free sound- and radio-wave conditions in space.

More information on the types of artificial satellites and their uses are found in many individual entries, including research satellites such as the HIGH ENERGY ASTRONOMICAL OBSERVATORIES; the COMMUNICATIONS SATELLITES TELSTAR, RELAY, SYNCOM, INTELSAT and MOLNIYA; the navigation satellites TRANSIT and NAVSTAR; the reconnaissance satellites COSMOS and SAMOS; the weather satellites TIROS, GOÉS, and NIMBUS; and the Earth observation satellite LANDSAT.

Satie, Erik [sah-tee'] The French composer Erik Satie, b. May 17, 1866, d. July 1, 1925, was the son of an English mother and a Parisian music publisher. He entered the Paris Conservatory in 1879 but failed to benefit from academic education. He composed a number of short piano pieces, whose eccentric titles (such as "Ogives," "Trois Gymnopédies," "Trois Gnossiennes") and unfashionable and yet convincing simplicity of melody were matched by an individual sense of harmony. It is still a moot point whether Satie got his harmonic ideas from his fellow student and friend Claude Debussy, or whether the debt was on Debussy's side. It is quite clear, however, that Satie's aesthetic principles influenced Debussy in the composition of his opera *Pelléas et Mélisande*.

Satie was a conscious eccentric and a determined enemy of all establishments, including the musical. The comical titles that he attached to his small piano pieces (such as "Cold Pieces," "Three Flabby Preludes," "Dried Embryos") are characteristic of the Bohemian wit in the Paris of his day. Irony and a deceptively childlike attitude, a dislike for grandiloquence of all kinds, and an instinctive secretiveness were hallmarks of both the man and his music. In 1916, Satie was befriended by Jean Cocteau

and wrote the music for a ballet, *Parade*, on which Pablo Picasso and Leonid Massine also collaborated. By far the most important of Satie's works is *Socrate* (1918), an austere setting for four sopranos and chamber orchestra of Plato's account of the death of Socrates. The young composers known as Les Six regarded Satie as a kind of tutelary genius.

---

satin Satin is a smooth, lustrous fabric usually made of silk, although cotton and synthetic fibers also produce satinlike fabrics. In satin weaving, the warp (vertical) yarns usually pass, or "float," over five or more filling (crosswise) yarns to produce an even, smooth surface. In some instances the filling yarn floats. The name *satin* may have been derived, through the Arabic *Zaytuni*, from Zaitun, an unknown city in China.

---

satinwood Two deciduous trees of the rue family, Rutaceae, are commonly known as satinwood. East India satinwood, *Chlorxylon swietenia*, yields yellow, mottled wood that has a satiny luster. West Indian satinwood, *Zanthoxylum flavum*, bears clusters of fragrant flowers and yields a creamy yellow wood. Both are used in cabinetwork.

---

satire The term *satire* refers to any work in prose or verse that uses wit to ridicule or expose vice or folly. Several ancient Greek poets are remembered for the deadly power of their satires; ARCHILOCHUS, for instance, is said to have caused his enemies to hang themselves.

Formal Verse Satire. Although satire is a part of such Greek works as the plays of ARISTOPHANES and the animal fables of AESOP, the Romans claimed to have instituted verse satire as a literary form. The satires of HORACE are genial and ironic comments on Roman life, written in a bantering colloquial style and mocking lesser faults, such as vanity and infatuation. Those of JUVENAL are eloquent denunciations that lash out at lechery, avarice, political corruption, and urban decadence.

Formal satire was revived during the Renaissance, albeit with some confusion about its proper form. The term is derived from the Latin word *satura*, a "medley" or "mixture," but some critics associated it with the *satyr*, a shaggy and unruly mythological creature, and consequently believed that satire should be rough and coarse. Early Renaissance satires, such as Joseph Hall's *Virgidemiarum* (1597), were metrically uneven and crude in tone.

In *Absalom and Achitophel* (1681), John DRYDEN established a standard of delicate irony and wit in English satire that was in part suggested by the MOCK EPIC poems of Nicolas BOILEAU–DESPRÉAUX. His *MacFlecknoe* (1682) is a PARODY of epic style. It is surpassed in satiric delicacy only by Alexander POPE's *The Rape of the Lock* (1714). The *Moral Epistles* (1731–35) and the *Imitations of Horace* (1733) established Pope as the greatest verse satirist in English.

Prose Satire. A tradition of prose satire dates to the lost works of Menippus (c.300 BC) and continues in the works of LUCIAN and the *Satyricon* of PETRONIUS ARBITER. Looser than formal satire, these books portray a great variety of scenes and targets; they are journeys through distorted but ultimately truthful versions of the world. Their technique of exaggeration may be found alike in RABELAIS's *Gargantua and Pantagruel*, Jonathan SWIFT's GULLIVER's TRAVELS, and Joseph HELLER's CATCH-22.

Sato Eisaku [sah-toh ay-sah-koo] Sato Eisaku, b. Mar. 27, 1901, d. June 2, 1975, Japanese prime minister (1964–72) and Liberal Democratic party leader, established Japan as an influential force in world affairs for the first time since World War II. From 1948 to 1964, Sato held a number of cabinet posts. While prime minister, he obtained U.S. pledges to return Iwo Jima, the Bonin Islands, and Okinawa to Japan. He was cowinner of the Nobel Peace Prize in 1974 for his efforts against nuclear proliferation.

saturation see SOLUTION

Saturn (astronomy) Even when viewed through a small telescope, Saturn and its ring system is one of the most unique objects in the sky. With a large modern telescope in good observing conditions, the planet appears as a light yellow and gray banded oblate spheroid. Like the other giant planets—Jupiter, Uranus, and Neptune—the visible planet is the cloud top of an extensive gaseous atmosphere.

The Planet

Saturn orbits the Sun at a mean distance of 1.427 billion km (0.893 billion mi) with a period of 29.4577 tropical years. The orbit is inclined 2.49° to the ecliptic, or Earth-orbital, plane and has an eccentricity of 0.0556. At Saturn's distance from the Sun, it receives only 0.01 of the unit solar radiation flux that the Earth does. Among planets in the SOLAR SYSTEM, Saturn is second in size only to Jupiter; Saturn has an equatorial diameter of 120,660 km (74,980 mi). Its volume would enclose about 769 Earth-sized bodies. Saturn's internal rotation period, defined by periodic radio emissions, is 10.657 hours. This fast rotation is responsible for Saturn's equatorial bulge and oblate shape. The equatorial-polar–diameter ratio is 1.12 to 1. Saturn's mass is 5.686×10^{26} kg (12.54×10^{26} lb), or 95.147 times the Earth's. Thus the average density is only 0.69 g/cm^3 (43 lb/ft^3), which is much less than water, indicating a very deep atmosphere and a very small core.

Atmosphere. Saturn is one of the giant outer planets, which are characterized by their large size, low density, and corresponding extensive atmospheres. Current models of the interior indicate that below the relatively thin opaque cloud layer is an extensive, clear hydrogen-helium atmosphere. The gas density gradually increases downward, and the gas transforms into a liquid. Further down the pressures increase to a critical level, and there the hydrogen becomes metallic. A small core of silicate material probably exists at the center.

VOYAGER spacecraft images showed spots, waves, and eddies smaller than those seen in the more turbulent Jovian atmosphere. The Saturnian atmosphere is characterized by counterflowing easterly and westerly jet streams that, at the equator, reach a speed of 480 m/sec (1,070 mph) relative to the clouds at 40° latitude. The zonal jets do not change appreciably with time, but the small-scale

(Left) *This true-color photograph of Saturn, taken by the* Voyager 2 *spacecraft at a distance of 21 million km (13 million mi), also shows Tethys* (left), *Dione* (middle), *and Rhea* (right)—*3 of Saturn's known satellites.* (Below) *Color differences between portions of the rings of Saturn have been computer-exaggerated in this false-color photograph taken by Voyager 2. Such variation may indicate differences in composition and thus provide clues to the origin of the rings.*

features can be seen on Voyager images to change on the time scales of hours. The low contrast of atmospheric features is caused by the low temperature (about −178° C, or −289° F) and by a scattering haze layer above the clouds. One giant white spot several thousand kilometers wide develops every 27 to 30 years.

The atmosphere is composed mostly of hydrogen and helium, but traces of methane, ammonia, ethane, phosphine, and acetylene exist. Coloration is probably caused by chromophores being produced by the interaction of such trace elements as sulfur or carbon compounds with ionospheric charged particles and lightning.

Magnetic Field. Saturn has a strong, dipolar magnetic field tilted only 0.7° from, but corotating with, the rotational axis. The subsolar magnetopause is 6.38 million km (3.96 million mi) from Saturn on the average. A magnetic tail extends in the direction away from the Sun much like cometary plasma tails. The satellite Titan has a smaller, induced magnetic field. Saturn's magnetic field traps charged particles coming from the solar wind. These particles move along magnetic-field lines but are absorbed by satellites and ring particles. The charged particles that impinge on the ionospheres of Saturn and Titan create airglow emissions.

Origin and Evolution. Saturn is far enough away from the Sun to retain the light elements (hydrogen and helium) and therefore has solarlike chemical abundance. Saturn's mass, unlike that of the Sun, was not large enough to initiate the fusion process, and Saturn, unlike Jupiter, did not give off enough excessive postaccretion heat to drive out water from the inner satellites.

The Rings

Saturn's white rings were first seen by Galileo Galilei in 1610; his small, imperfect telescope showed the planetary disk flanked by what he first interpreted as being two smaller bodies. Christiaan HUYGENS correctly theorized (late 1650s) the ring nature of these alleged "companions." James Clerk MAXWELL mathematically demonstrated (1857) that the rings were composed of many small, unconnected particles, each orbiting near Saturn's equatorial plane.

The classical designations for the rings are based on the gross ring components identified from the ground, but the Voyager spacecraft have shown the ring system to be highly structured. The radial particle-density distribution changes over distances of hundreds of meters. Estimated sizes of individual particles range from tens to hundreds

RINGS AND ESTABLISHED SATELLITES OF SATURN*

Name	Discoverer	Year of Discovery	Average Distance from Center of Saturn km	mi	Period of Revolution (hours)	Diameter km	mi	Orbital Inclination (degrees)	Orbital Eccentricity
D ring inner edge			~67,000	~42,000	4.91				
C ring inner edge			73,200	45,500	5.61				
B ring inner edge			92,200	57,300	7.93				
B ring outer edge			117,500	73,000	11.41				
A ring inner edge			121,000	75,200	11.93				
Encke division			133,500	83,000	13.82				
A ring outer edge			136,200	84,600	14.24				
Atlas	Voyager 1	1980	137,300	85,300	14.446	30	20	0.3	0.002
Prometheus	Voyager 1	1980	139,400	86,600	14.712	140 × 70	85 × 45	0.0	0.003
F ring	Pioneer 11	1979	~140,600	~87,400	14.94				
Pandora	Voyager 1	1980	141,700	88,100	15.085	100 × 70	60 × 45	0.05	0.004
Epimetheus	D. Cruikshank	1980	151,422	94,094	16.664	180 × 80	110 × 50	0.34	0.009
Janus	D. Pascu	1980	151,472	94,125	16.672	200 × 180	125 × 110	0.14	0.007
G ring			~170,000	~106,000	19.9				
Mimas	William Herschel	1789	188,244	116,962	23.139	390	240	1.517	0.020
E ring inner edge			~210,000	~130,000	27.3				
E ring maximum			246,000	153,000	31.3				
Enceladus	William Herschel	1789	240,192	149,255	33.356	500	310	0.023	0.004
Telesto	Note 1	1980				20	12		
Tethys	Giovanni Cassini	1684	296,563	184,284	45.762	1,050	650	1.093	0.000
Calypso	Note 2	1980				20 × 10	12 × 6		
E ring outer edge			~300,000	~186,000	46.6				
Electra	P. Laques, J. Lecacheaux	1980	378,600	235,300	65.738	40 × 20	25 × 12	0.15	0.005
Dione	Giovanni Cassini	1684	379,074	235,557	66.133	1,120	700	0.023	0.002
Rhea	Giovanni Cassini	1672	527,828	327,992	108.660	1,530	950	0.35	0.001
Titan	Christiaan Huygens	1655	1,221,432	758,998	382.504	5,140	3,190	0.33	0.029
Hyperion	W. Bond, W. Lassell	1848	1,502,275	933,514	521.743	290	180	0.4	0.104
Iapetus	Giovanni Cassini	1671	3,559,400	2,211,800	1,901.820	1,440	890	14.7	0.028
Phoebe	William Pickering	1898	10,583,200	6,576,400	9,755.679	~160	~100	150	0.163

*Several other satellites have definitely been sighted, bringing the total number up to 23, and others are suspected. Little is known about these tiny moons, none more than about 18 km (11 mi) in diameter. Three orbit between the outer edge of the E ring and Electra (1980S34, 1981S10, and 1981S11), and three orbit between the orbits of Dione and Rhea (1981S7, 1981S8, and 1981S9).
Note 1—B. Smith, H. Reitsema, S. Larson, J. Fountain.   Note 2—Space Telescope Wide Field/Planetary Camera Instrument Definition Team.

of centimeters. The ring plane has a maximum thickness of 1 to 2 km (0.6 to 1.2 mi). Spectroscopy shows the presence of water ice, which probably covers rocky silicate cores.

The dynamics of the rings are not presently well understood. The theory of satellite resonances predicts that particles whose orbital periods are integral fractions (such as ½ or ⅔) of the periods of the satellites become either locked into or perturbed out of a particular orbit, but only a few of the observed gaps can be explained in this manner. Voyager showed eccentric ringlets and asymmetrical kinks in some ringlets. The kinks in the F ring gave it a braided appearance, but despite the proximity of two small satellites, the kinks do not seem directly related to them. Voyager also showed irregular spokelike features in the B ring that are composed of very small, strongly back-scattering particles temporarily out of the ring plane. Because of the detection of electrostatic discharges from the rings at radio wavelengths, these particles are thought to be electrically charged and thus forced out of the ring plane by Saturn's magnetic field.

The rings may be the debris from satellites or comets broken apart by tidal forces (see ROCHE'S LIMIT). Another hypothesis is that Saturn's tidal forces and the perturbations of various satellites prevented the material left over from the formation of Saturn to accrete into further satellites.

Satellites

Saturn has the most extensive satellite system in the solar system. Not counting the myriad ring particles, more than 20 bodies orbiting around Saturn have so far been identified. Six can be easily seen through the telescope.

Titan is the largest Saturnian satellite and, among all solar-system satellites, is second in size only to the Jovian satellite Ganymede. It is the only satellite with a substantial atmosphere, although TRITON has a thinner one. The highest-resolution Voyager images show several haze layers that together obscure the surface. For a discussion of this major satellite, see the article of that name.

The other satellites of Saturn tend to have low densities (1 to 1.5 g/cm^3, or 62 to 94 lb/ft^3) and high albedos, or surface reflectivities (> 0.4), indicative of water-ice–dominated bodies. Water frost has been detected spectroscopically on the surface of most of these satellites. With the exception of Phoebe, Iapetus, and Hyperion, they are in nearly circular, direct, low-inclination orbits. All of these satellites, with the exception of Enceladus, have highly cratered, old surfaces. The larger satellites have two distinct crater populations, perhaps a result of different sources and types of impacting bodies or of changes in the impact behavior of the satellite surfaces as they evolved.

▬

Saturn (mythology)   An ancient Roman god of agriculture, Saturn was later identified with the Greek god CRO-NUS, who fled to Italy after his dethronement by Zeus as ruler of the universe. Saturn settled on Rome's CAPITOLINE HILL and taught the people agriculture and other arts of civilization. He helped usher in a period of prosperity that became known as the Golden Age. One day Saturn vanished from the Earth. At the Saturnalia festival, held in his memory every December (the winter sowing season), masters and slaves shared the same table as a sign that no social divisions existed during the Golden Age. Saturn also gave his name to a planet and to Saturday.

▬

Saturn (rocket)   Saturn is a family of large rockets developed for the U.S. APOLLO PROGRAM. The Saturn rocket was the outcome of studies begun in the late 1950s by Wernher VON BRAUN and his research group at the Army Ballistic Missile Agency (later named the George C. Marshall Space Flight Center) in Huntsville, Ala. (See ROCKETS AND MISSILES.)

Saturn I. The two-stage Saturn I had a cluster of eight Rocketdyne H-1 engines in the first stage, each of which delivered a thrust of 836,000 newtons, or 85,277 kg (188,000 lb). A central liquid-oxygen tank was surrounded by a cluster of eight smaller tanks, four of which contained kerosene and four, liquid oxygen. The second stage of the Saturn had six liquid oxygen–liquid hydrogen Pratt & Whitney RL-10 engines, each of which gave 66,700 newtons, or 6,804 kg (15,000 lb) of thrust. After two test flights of engineering models of the Apollo spacecraft, Saturn I rockets orbited three huge Pegasus meteoroid-detection satellites in 1965.

Saturn IB. The need to fly still heavier payloads in the Apollo program led to the development of the Saturn IB. The first stage of the Saturn IB, was a slightly upgraded first stage of Saturn I. The second stage (S-IVB) had a single J-2 engine developing 900,000 newtons, or 90,720 kg (200,000 lb) of thrust from liquid oxygen and liquid hydrogen. Altogether a total of 19 Saturn I and IB rockets were launched between October 1961 and July 1975, as part of the Apollo and Skylab programs.

Saturn V. The Saturn V rocket stood 110.6 m (363 ft) tall with the Apollo spacecraft installed. Fully loaded it weighed 2.9 million kg (6.4 million lb). Its S-IC first stage was powered by five Rocketdyne F-1 engines that burned liquid oxygen and kerosene to produce more than 33.8 million newtons, or 3.45 million kg (7.6 million lb) of thrust. The four outer engines could swivel to steer the rocket. The S-II second stage, built by Rockwell International, had a similar arrangement of five Rocketdyne J-2 engines burning liquid oxygen and liquid hydrogen. Total thrust of this stage was about 5,132,000 newtons, or 523,328 kg (1,153,712 lb). The S-IVB third stage, built by McDonnell Douglas Astronautics, had a diameter of 6.6 m (21.7 ft). A single gimbal-mounted Rocketdyne J-2 engine burning liquid oxygen and liquid hydrogen delivered a thrust of 926,300 newtons, or 94,458 kg (208,242 lb). Atop the third stage was the IBM-built In-

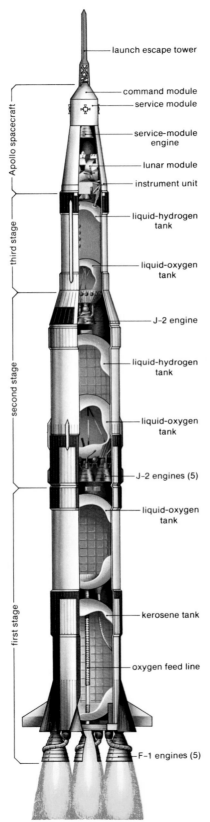

Labels on diagram:
launch escape tower
command module
service module
service-module engine
lunar module
instrument unit
liquid-hydrogen tank
liquid-oxygen tank
J-2 engine
liquid-hydrogen tank
liquid-oxygen tank
J-2 engines (5)
liquid-oxygen tank
kerosene tank
oxygen feed line
F-1 engines (5)

Apollo spacecraft
third stage
second stage
first stage

strument Unit (IU), which contained the guidance equipment for all three stages. Above the IU were the Apollo modules. Altogether, 13 Saturn V rockets were launched without a single loss.

satyr [say'-tur]   In Greek mythology satyrs were immortal creatures of the forest and hills and symbols of nature's wealth. Usually identified with the sileni (see SILENUS), the satyrs were attendants of DIONYSUS. They had the head, arms, and torso of a man and the horns, ears, and hind legs of a goat (in Attic art, satyrs had horses' tails). Satyrs loved to frolic, drink, chase nymphs, and play reed instruments (see FAUNUS).

Saud, King of Saudi Arabia [sah-ood']   Saud ibn Abd al-Aziz, b. Jan. 15, 1902, d. Feb. 23, 1969, was Saudi Arabia's king from 1953 until he was deposed in 1964. Saud succeeded his illustrious father, IBN SAUD, Saudi Arabia's creator. Saud assisted his father during the fighting that unified most of Arabia under Saudi rule in 1932. He was crown prince from 1933 to 1953 and his ailing father's regent after 1950. A poor administrator and statesman, Saud virtually bankrupted the kingdom, despite its oil wealth, while his diplomacy created serious disputes with Britain, Egypt, and Iraq. After experiments with ministerial government failed, Saud was dismissed (March 1964), and his brother Faisal was appointed king of Saudi Arabia.

Saudi Arabia [sow'-dee]   The kingdom of Saudi Arabia, the largest Middle Eastern country, occupies four-fifths of the Arabian Peninsula (see ARABIA). The country is bordered on the north by Jordan, Iraq, and Kuwait; on the west by the Red Sea; on the south by Yemen and Oman; and on the east by the United Arab Emirates, Bahrain, Qatar, Oman, and the Persian Gulf. Only the borders in the north, the boundaries with Qatar and the United Arab Emirates, and a small segment of the border with Yemen, however, are defined. In the 7,000-km^2 (2,700-mi^2) neutral zone between Iraq and Saudi Arabia no permanent buildings or military establishments may be placed; nomads from both countries have access to its pastures and wells. A 1975 agreement divided the zone equally. A partitioned zone covering about 5,770 km^2 (2,230 mi^2) also exists between Saudi Arabia and Kuwait; Saudi Arabia administers the southern half, whereas oil wealth from the zone is shared by both countries.

The economy of Saudi Arabia is based on its vast petroleum reserves. Mecca and Medina, Islam's two holiest cities, are located in the country. The Prophet Muhammad was born in Mecca in AD 570, and soon his faith, Islam, had swept the Middle East and North Africa. The modern state of Saudi Arabia was formed by a series of conquests by Ibn Saud between 1902 and 1932.

Land and Resources

Saudi Arabia may be divided into four geographic zones:

AT A GLANCE

KINGDOM OF SAUDI ARABIA

Land: Area (est.): 2,149,690 km² (830,000 mi²). Capital and largest city: Riyadh (1981 est. pop., 1,308,000).

People: Population (1990 est.): 17,115,728. Density: 8.0 persons per km² (20.6 per mi²). Distribution (1989 est.): 73% urban, 27% rural. Official language: Arabic. Major religion: Islam.

Government: Type: monarchy. Legislature: none. Political subdivisions: 14 districts.

Economy: GNP (1989): $89.99 billion; $6,230 per capita. Labor distribution (1989): government—34%; industry and oil—28%; services—22%; agriculture—16%. Foreign trade (1989 est.): imports—$21.8 billion; exports—$24.5 billion. Currency: 1 Saudi riyal = 100 halalah.

Education and Health: Literacy (1986): 57% of adult population. Universities (1989): 7. Hospital beds (1988): 32,271. Physicians (1988): 15,347. Life expectancy (1990): women—67; men—64. Infant mortality (1990): 71 per 1,000 live births.

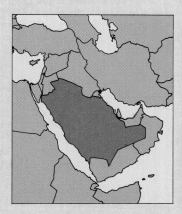

the Red Sea coastal plain and adjacent mountains; the central plateau including the Nafud and Dahna deserts; the coastal plain of the Persian Gulf; and the Rub al-Khali desert.

The western coastal plain extends for about 1,450 km (900 mi) along the Red Sea coast. In the north, near the Gulf of Aqaba, mountains reaching 610 m (2,000 ft) separate the coastal plain from the interior highlands. In the south the Asir highlands, rising from the coastal plain, contain the country's highest elevation at Jebel Sawda (3,133 m/10,279 ft).

The central plateau varies in elevation from 1,065 to 1,370 m (3,500 to 4,500 ft) and is about 485 km (300 mi) wide. The plateau is ringed by the Nafud, a red sand desert to the north; the Dahna, a long narrow belt of sand to the east; and the Tuwayq Mountains to the south.

The eastern coastline extends along the Persian Gulf coast for about 565 km (350 mi) from Kuwait to the United Arab Emirates. This area contains the nation's petroleum reserves. The southern desert, the Rub al-Khali, or Empty Quarter, the largest continuous sand body in the world, covers 647,500 km² (250,000 mi²).

Climate. Most areas receive less than 100 mm (4 in) of rain per year. In the Rub al-Kali, 10 years may pass without precipitation. On the west coast, cyclones provide some additional rainfall. The Asir highlands receive monsoonal rainfall that may amount to more than 255 mm (10 in) per year. Summers are hot throughout the country, with daytime temperatures often exceeding 49° C (120° F). Winter is cooler, with average temperatures of 23° C (74° F) at Jidda and 14° C (58° F) at Riyadh.

Drainage, Plant and Animal Life, and Resources. The country has no permanent rivers, but wadis (intermittent streams that flow after periods of rain) are numerous. Vegetation is scant. Animal life includes ibex, wildcats, baboons, wolves, and hyenas in the highlands, birds in the oases, and tropical fish in offshore waters. Only about 2% of the land is under cultivation, although an estimated 15% is cultivable. Saudi Arabia contains about 25% of the world's known petroleum reserves. Little exploitation of other minerals—including gold, silver, iron, copper, zinc, manganese, tungsten, lead, sulfur, phosphate, soapstone, asbestos, and feldspar—has occurred.

People

The vast majority of Saudi Arabians are ARABS, descendants of the indigenous tribes and still tribally affiliated. Some Iranians live along the Persian Gulf coast. The number of expatriate workers has declined, although the economy remains dependent on foreign labor.

Arabic, the official language, is spoken by all; various dialects exist. English is understood by some residents of the eastern oil-producing areas, Riyadh, and Jidda. About 85% of the population are Sunni Muslims, most of whom are of the strict Wahhabi sect (see WAHHABISM). About 15% are Shiite Muslims, found in the east. Because of the strict adherence to Islam, the sexes are strictly segregated in public, although educational and job opportunities for women are increasing.

The population is highly urbanized. RIYADH (the capital), JIDDA, MECCA, al-Taif, MEDINA, Dhahran, al-Damman, and Hofuf are the major cities. Many rural residents are

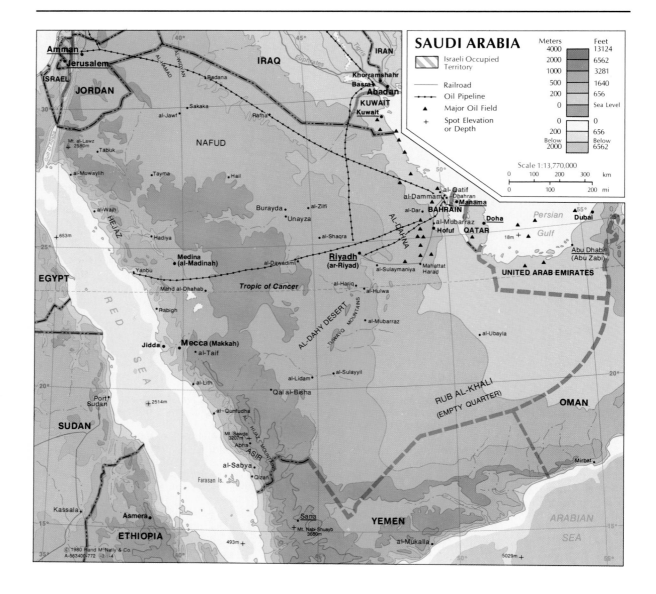

nomadic BEDOUINS rather than settled cultivators.

Important progress has been made in education in recent years, and schooling is free at all levels. The Islamic University (1961) at Medina is one of three universities stressing Islamic studies. Secular universities include King Saud University (formerly Riyadh University, 1957), the King Fahad University of Petroleum and Minerals (1963) at Dhahran, and King Abul-Aziz University (1967) in Jidda. Medical care is free for all citizens, but health facilities in rural areas remain limited.

The Arabian peninsula has a tradition of formal poetry that goes back to the 5th and 6th centuries AD, before the time of Muhammad (see ARABIC LITERATURE). Poetry and storytelling are common folk traditions. The Koran limits public performances of music and dance and prohibits

the making of graven images by artists. Hand-lettered Korans are produced with illustrations based on complex geometric and floral designs.

Economic Activity

Prior to the discovery of petroleum in 1936, the economy depended on pilgrims visiting Mecca and Medina and on date exports. Saudi Arabia is still among the world's leading producers of dates, but today oil dominates the economy. The government has used petroleum profits to create the infrastructure needed to transform Saudi Arabia into a diversified industrial state. Due to the small size of the indigenous labor force, most industries are capital-intensive rather than labor-intensive.

Mining and Industry. Crude oil and petroleum products account for 92% of all exports. In 1990 the country produced about 5.5 million barrels of oil per day. The Saudi share of ARAMCO (Arabian-American Oil Company), which produces most of the nation's petroleum, increased from 25% in 1973 to 60% in 1974 to 100% in 1980.

Major new industrial centers have been constructed at Jubail on the Persian Gulf and Yanbu on the Red Sea. They are powered by natural gas piped in from the oil fields. In addition to hydrocarbon-based industries such as oil refining, petrochemicals, and fertilizer, industrial products include iron and steel, cement, electrical equipment, and processed foodstuffs. Desalinization plants have been constructed to satisfy most domestic water needs.

Agriculture. Despite the lack of water, the government has financed agricultural development to reduce the dependence on imported foods and raise standards of living in rural areas. The fishing industry is also being expanded.

Transportation, Tourism, and Trade. In recent years the highway network, long hampered by great distances and the hot and arid climate, has been greatly expanded. A causeway linking Saudi Arabia to Bahrain was opened in 1986. Air transport and port facilities have also been modernized. King Khalid Airport in Riyadh, opened in 1983, is the largest in the world. Pipelines link oil fields in eastern Saudi Arabia to the Red Sea port of Yanbu.

Due to its enormous petroleum reserves, Saudi Arabia plays a pivotal role in the global oil market. It is a leading member of the ORGANIZATION OF PETROLEUM EXPORTING COUNTRIES (OPEC). Dramatic increases in world oil prices created huge trade surpluses between 1973 and 1981, and Saudi Arabia remains a wealthy country despite substantial declines in oil earnings since that time. Petroleum provides more than 90% of government revenues. Hundreds of thousands of devout Muslim pilgrims are another source of foreign exchange. Machinery, transportation equipment, and other manufactured

The Ras Tanura oil refinery in Saudi Arabia remains the property of the four multinational oil companies that once held shares in ARAMCO (the Arabian-American Oil Company). ARAMCO, now owned by Saudi Arabia, supplies about 12% of the world's petroleum.

goods are the leading imports. Saudi Arabia provides aid to many poorer nations in Asia and Africa, although it halted aid to the PALESTINE LIBERATION ORGANIZATION and Jordan because of their support for Iraq in the 1991 GULF WAR.

Government

Saudi Arabia is a monarchy, and the laws of Islam (SHARIA) form the constitution. The king has both executive and legislative power, although an appointed council of ministers performs some legislative and executive functions subject to royal veto. Almost all important government positions are held by members of the Saud family, the large, powerful ruling clan. There are no political parties or legislature, but any citizen can submit grievances or requests for aid directly to the king at regular audiences called *majalis.*

The nation is divided into 14 regions (emirates) for administrative purposes. Local officials report directly to Riyadh and are responsible for finance, health, education, and agriculture within their provinces.

History

A nomadic tribal structure has existed over most of the Arabian peninsula for thousands of years. The Minaean kingdom existed in southwestern Arabia during the 12th century BC. The Sabaean (see SHEBA) and Himyarite kingdoms were loose federations of city-states that lasted until the 6th century AD. In the northwest, the HEJAZ region grew in importance by the end of the 6th century as a link in the trade route from Egypt and the Byzantine Empire to the east.

The birth (570) of MUHAMMAD in Mecca ushered in a new era in world history. Muhammad began preaching in Mecca but by 622 was forced to move to Medina. In 630 he returned to conquer Mecca. Muhammad died in 632, but his followers quickly spread his word across the Middle East and beyond. The capital of the Islamic world was moved to the more centrally located Damascus by the ruling Umayyads, and by 692, Arabia lost its political importance and became disunited. The Ottoman Empire nominally ruled much of the peninsula from the 16th century until World War I.

Beginning in 1902, IBN SAUD, a follower of the strict Wahhabi sect of Islam, conquered and unified the Nejd, Hasa, and Hejaz regions. In 1932 the kingdom of Saudi Arabia was created, with Saud as king. Oil was discovered in 1936, but large-scale drilling did not begin until the end of World War II. Ibn Saud died in 1953 and was succeeded by his son SAUD. Saud was deposed in 1964 by the Saudi family council and was replaced by FAISAL, who began modernizing the country. Faisal was assassinated by a nephew in 1975. His successor, KHALID, rejected the 1979 Egyptian-Israeli peace treaty but followed a moderate policy in the Arab-Israeli dispute. Upon Khalid's death in 1982, Crown Prince FAHD assumed the throne.

Saudi security concerns increased after the Islamic revolution in Iran and the 1979 seizure of the Great Mosque in Mecca by Sunni Muslim extremists; there were clashes between Iranian demonstrators and Saudi police during the 1987 pilgrimage to Mecca. Saudi Arabia had supported Iraq against Iran in the IRAN-IRAQ WAR (1980–88), but the August 1990 Iraqi invasion of Kuwait was seen as a threat to Saudi security. U.S. troops were invited to Saudi Arabia as part of a multinational force that came to include forces from Britain, Egypt, Syria, and other nations. Saudi oil output increased to ease shortages created by the crisis, and oil revenues were used to subsidize nations taking economic and military measures against Iraq and to pay for a Saudi military buildup. The 1991 Gulf war, in which Saudi troops served on the front lines in the recapture of Kuwait, strengthened Saudi nationalism and vindicated King Fahd's decision to ally the nation more closely with the United States. After the war the king renewed his pledge to establish a consultative council.

▄

Sauk [sawk] Saginaw Bay in northern Michigan takes its name from the Sauk (or Sac), North American Indians of the Algonquian-Wakashan linguistic stock who called themselves Osakiwuk, the "People of the Outlet." During the early 17th century the Sauk were driven out of Michigan by Iroquois war parties, eventually settling around Green Bay in northeastern Wisconsin by 1667, when they numbered approximately 6,500. They were a highly organized society, with more power centralized in the council of chiefs than was characteristic of other central Algonquian tribes.

Always closely associated with the FOX, POTAWATOMI, and other related tribes, the Sauk, by 1730, settled the prairie lands of northwestern Illinois and moved west of the Mississippi River to eastern Iowa. In 1804 they began ceding their lands to the United States. Black Hawk, a dissident Sauk leader from northern Illinois, resisted these land transactions and precipitated the BLACK HAWK WAR of 1832. The Fox and the Sauk were amalgamated for more than a century but divided again in 1854. The Sauk eventually settled on reservations in the states of Iowa, Kansas, and Oklahoma.

▄

Saul, King of Israel [sawl] Saul, son of Kish from the tribe of Benjamin, was the first king of Israel. He probably reigned c.1020–1000 BC, although the exact dates and length of his reign are disputed. Several independent and conflicting stories about how Saul became king are contained in 1 Samuel 9–12, but three points seem clear: (1) The desire for a king arose because the loosely organized tribal league could not meet the military threat posed by the PHILISTINES; (2) Saul's military prowess and personal bravery made him a prime candidate; and (3) Samuel, the last representative of the league, played a major role in the choice of Saul, although he sought to limit the new king's power.

Saul enjoyed considerable initial success and was responsible for the strength and cohesion of the Hebrew nation. Samuel soon broke with him, however, and the subsequent lack of religious support, together with Saul's growing envy and suspicion of David (see DAVID, KING OF ISRAEL), his brilliant young commander, began to destroy Saul's judgment. He met with disastrous defeat on Mount Gilboa and killed himself rather than accept capture.

▄

Sault Sainte Marie (Michigan) [soo saynt muh-ree'] Sault Sainte Marie (1990 pop., 14,689), a city on the rapids of the Saint Marys River on the Sault Sainte Marie Canals, at the northeastern end of Michigan's Upper Peninsula, is the seat of Chippewa County. The city's economy is based on forestry, dairying, and tourism. Bridges across the river connect Sault Sainte Marie with the Canadian city of the same name. Founded in 1668 by Jacques Marquette, Sault Sainte Marie belonged to France until 1762, when it was occupied by Britain. Since 1820 the city has been part of the United States.

▄

Sault Sainte Marie (Ontario) Sault Sainte Marie (1986 pop., 80,905), sometimes called The Soo, is a Canadian city in south central Ontario on the Saint Marys River. A major producer of iron, steel, paper, lumber, and chemicals, the city faces the Michigan city of the same name across the river. It was settled in 1668.

▄

Sault Sainte Marie Canals The two Sault Sainte Marie Canals (also called the Soo Canals) link Lake Superior and Lake Huron along the Saint Marys River, which flows between Ontario and Michigan. The canal on the Canadian side has one lock, but the one on the U.S. side has four locks to accommodate the river's rapid drop; two locks are more than 411 m (1,350 ft) long, among the longest in the world, and 24 m (80 ft) wide. The towns on either side of the canals are both named Sault Sainte Marie. The canals are an integral part of the ST. LAWRENCE SEAWAY and a major shipping route for iron and copper ore, steel, and lumber. Although the first system of locks was completed in 1855, the present canal was built between 1881 and 1919.

▄

sausage Sausage is a food prepared from chopped or ground meat that is seasoned and may be stuffed into a casing. At one time fresh meat that could not be consumed immediately was made into sausage as a means of preservation. The 200 or more types of sausages currently produced provide an opportunity for dietary variety rather than a means of meat preservation. Meat processed in this manner has gained wide acceptance in the United States, as indicated by a per capita consumption of about 11 kg (25 lb) annually.

Sausage can vary in the kind and amount of meat used; the fineness of chopping or grinding; the seasonings or spices used; the processing method (smoked or cooked or both, or dried); and the type of casing used, such as treated animal intestines, cellulose, or synthetic material. Binders or extenders, such as cereals, are often added, as are various chemical preservatives and coloring agents (see FOOD ADDITIVES).

Sausages are usually classified according to the processing method used: fresh (Italian sausage, fresh pork sausage); fresh smoked (mettwurst, country-style pork); cooked (braunschweiger, beer salami); cooked smoked (frankfurter, bologna); and dry and semidry (hard salami, pepperoni).

Saussure, Ferdinand de   see STRUCTURALISM

Sauvé, Jeanne [soh-vay']

Jeanne Sauvé, b. Prud'-Homme, Saskatchewan, Apr. 26, 1922, served as governor general of Canada from 1984 to 1990. Sauvé had been a journalist before she was elected to the House of Commons, as a Liberal, in 1972. She quickly became a cabinet minister, holding successively the portfolios of science and technology (1972–74), of environment (1974–75), and of communications (1975–79). She was Speaker of the House of Commons from 1980 until 1984.

Sava River [sah'-vah]

The Sava River, the longest river entirely within Yugoslavia, is about 935 km (580 mi) long. Rising in northwestern Yugoslavia near the Italian border, the river flows southeast and east through gorges, plateaus, marshes, and farmland, passing Ljubljana and Zagreb before reaching Belgrade, where it joins the Danube. It is navigable for about 580 km (360 mi).

Savage, Edward

The American painter and engraver Edward Savage, b. Princeton, Mass., Nov. 26, 1761, d. July 6, 1817, is remembered for his paintings, including *George Washington* (1790; Harvard University, Cambridge, Mass.), *The Washington Family* (1796; National Gallery of Art, Washington, D.C.), and portraits of numerous other American statesmen.

Savage settled in Philadelphia (1795–1801), where he maintained a busy career painting, making portrait prints, and running his Columbian Gallery. He also published numerous prints of historical scenes, including the first American prints of a naval battle. He moved to New York for a time (1801–10) and then settled in Boston.

Savage, Michael Joseph

Michael Joseph Savage, b. Mar. 23, 1872, d. Mar. 27, 1940, was New Zealand's first Labour party prime minister. An Australian gold miner and labor organizer, he emigrated (1907) to New Zealand, where he also became a trade union leader. A founding member of the Labour party in 1916, Savage became its parliamentary leader in 1933. During his ministry (1935–40) he secured passage of educational reforms, social security legislation, and programs to revive the economy.

savanna life

Savannas are tropical and subtropical GRASSLANDS that occupy vast areas on every continent in the trade-wind belt. Savannas have such local names as prairie, scrub, veld, barrens, chaparral, and pampas. The parklike vegetation of a savanna (from the West Indian *zabana*), with deciduous trees and small evergreens widely dispersed among grasses and shrubs, supports a rich array of animals. The conditions of savanna life fall between those of closed woodlands, on one hand, and those of open grasslands, steppes (see STEPPE LIFE), and DESERTS, on the other; most savanna species, however, are more closely related to species of the open BIOMES.

Woodlands generally give way to savannas wherever annual rainfall is less than 1,000 mm (40 in); this transition may occur, however, under much wetter conditions, as in the llanos of Venezuela, where the distribution of rain is highly seasonal, or in regions where the soils are salty or drainage is excessive. Also, savannas may be expanded at the expense of woodlands by repeated fires or by clearings undertaken by humans. If rainfall increases, the woodlands expand until the grasses become shaded and eventually die. Woody plants also increase in number if the grasses are overgrazed; eventually the grasslands are destroyed. Thus, the balance between grasses and woody plants is delicate.

During the past 30 million years savannas have expanded broadly over tracts previously occupied by woodlands, as a consequence both of a worldwide trend toward cooler, drier climates and of major episodes of mountain building on most continents. In such areas major new groups of plants and animals evolved. The new, open country was dominated by such hardy plant groups as the grasses, legumes, and composites. These, in turn, provided new adaptive zones for herbivorous animal groups as diverse as grasshoppers, tortoises, ostriches, kangaroos, and cattle. Among birds, both middle-sized ground dwellers, such as pheasants, grouse, bustards, and cariamas, and large fast-running ratites, such as ostriches, emus, rheas, and cassowaries, became characteristic of savannas. Burrowing rodents and rabbits, including wholly fossorial gophers, mole rats, and tuco-tucos, largely subterranean marmots and prairie dogs, and fast-hopping groups such as kangaroo rats and jackrabbits successfully occupied the savannas. The animals that came to dominate the savannas were the large herbivorous mammals; some, such as the giraffes, became wide-ranging browsers (eating bark, leaves, and twigs), whereas most, such as horses and cattle, became predominantly grazers (eating grass and low shrubs).

Savanna life on all continents, however, even Africa, seems to have passed the peak of its abundance and diversity before the Ice Ages about 2 million years ago. North American herds were killed by hunting tribes between 10,000 and 15,000 years ago. Ungulate faunas that flourished in the ancient pampas of temperate South America have now totally vanished.

In general, savanna life on one continent evolved independently of savanna life on other continents. When con-

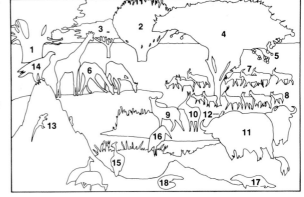

The African savanna, characterized by vast grassy plains and scattered trees, supports a fauna that includes herds of grazing mammals and various kinds of birds. Trees adapted to a marked dry season include the thick-trunked baobab (1); the cactuslike candelabra tree (2); and the umbrella thorn (3). A whistling thorn (4) supports the hanging, globe-shaped nests of the weaverbird species Quelea quelea *(5). Giraffes (6), which feed mainly on acacia leaves, must spread or bend their forelegs to drink water. Herds of topi (7) and impala (8)—both antelopes—roam the grasslands. Waterbucks (female, 9, and male, 10) tend to stay near water. The Cape buffalo (11) is frequently visited by yellow-billed oxpeckers (12), which pull bloodsucking ticks from the buffalo's skin. Agamid lizards (13) are shown climbing a termite mound, upon which a tawny eagle (14) perches. Helmeted guinea fowl (15) tend to run, rather than fly, when threatened. The Marabou stork (16) is a scavenger, feeding on animal remains. A banded mongoose (17) stalks its prey, a snake (18).*

tacts did occur, however, they resulted in dramatic interchanges enhanced by the great mobility and adaptability characteristic of savanna life. The temperate savanna elements of the Old World and New World came in contact across the Bering Land Bridge. Another important link between savannas was forged by the isthmian connection between North America and South America.

Savannah (Georgia) Savannah, Georgia's major seaport, its oldest city, and the seat of Chatham County, is located at the mouth of the Savannah River. It has a population of 137,560 (1990). The city's historic residential section contains more than 900 houses. Many old churches also impart charm to the area. Factor's Walk—a series of footbridges among the cotton warehouses—and the cotton exchange are on the waterfront.

The city's economy is dominated by its port, with its containerized shipping facilities. Savannah is the site of one of the world's largest papermaking complexes; other industries include food processing, chemicals, aircraft manufacturing, and shipbuilding. Telfair Academy is the

Southeast's oldest art museum (1875), and Bethesda, the first U.S. orphanage, was founded by George WHITE-FIELD in 1738.

Savannah was established by James OGLETHORPE in 1733 and was the capital of Georgia from 1754 to 1796. During the 18th and 19th centuries it was a center for overseas trade and the financial and cultural hub for the planters. During the Civil War Savannah was captured (1864) by Gen. William T. Sherman.

Savannah (steamship) In 1819 the U.S. ship *Savannah* became the first steamship to traverse the Atlantic. The *Savannah* was in fact a sailing vessel equipped with a small auxiliary steam engine. The ship ran under steam for less than 90 hours during the 29-day trip. The 3-masted ship carried 75 tons of coal and 25 cords of wood; all of this fuel was consumed during the crossing to furnish the auxiliary steam power of the single-cylinder engine, which operated two detachable paddle wheels.

In later trials the advantage that the *Savannah*'s engine gave in calm weather proved insufficient to compensate for the fuel savings of sailing ships. The ship had its engine removed and ended its career sailing up and down the Atlantic coast.

The nuclear-powered cargo ship *Savannah* (launched 1959)—which could cruise without refueling for 483,000 km (300,000 mi)—inspired the construction of nuclear-fueled commercial ships in Japan and West Germany. None proved financially successful, however.

Savigny, Friedrich Karl von [sah'-vin-yee] The founder of historical jurisprudence, Friedrich Karl von Savigny, b. Feb. 21, 1779, d. Oct. 25, 1861, was a legal scholar and one of the first members of the German nobility to teach at a university. Von Savigny argued that a nation's laws should not be arbitrarily imposed from above by judges or legislators, because they emerge "organically" from the customs and spirit of its people. His works about Roman law are considered by many to remain unsurpassed.

Savimbi, Jonas [sah-vim'-bee] Angolan resistance leader Jonas Savimbi, b. Aug. 3, 1934, served as foreign minister of the Front for the National Liberation of Angola (FNLA) during the struggle for Angolan independence before breaking away and founding (1966) the National Union for the Total Independence of Angola (UNITA). Savimbi became copresident (with FNLA leader Holden Roberto) of the Democratic People's Republic of Angola when Portugal granted Angola independence on Nov. 11, 1975. Savimbi lost the ensuing civil war to the People's Republic of Angola, a rival government headed by Agostinho NETO (and later by José Eduardo dos Santos). Savimbi and his followers then retreated to southeastern Angola and launched a guerrilla war. In May 1991 the opposing sides agreed to a cease-fire.

saving and investment The concepts of saving and investment are central to any explanation of the economic system. In economic terms, saving is income that is not consumed or spent for current purposes by households (personal saving), businesses (retained earnings, or profits), or governments (surplus tax revenues).

Real investment occurs only when saving is transformed into productive capacity—private investments in residential and commercial buildings, plant, equipment, and net accumulation of inventories and public works such as roads and dams. Economists often prefer to use the term *capital formation* rather than *investment.* For the most part, those who save are not the same as those who invest. Financial intermediaries such as banks and pension funds serve to channel surplus funds accumulated in one part of the economy into other parts, where they are wanted for investment.

If the economy is considered as a whole, saving will always equal investment (see INCOME, NATIONAL). An increase in saving by one group need not, however, lead to an increase in investment; it may be offset by another group's decrease in saving.

The level of voluntary saving tends in theory to adjust itself to the level of capital formation that producers are prepared to make. When individuals attempt to save more than business wants to invest, national income shrinks as money is withdrawn from circulation, unless government spending fills the gap. On the other hand, when business wants to invest more than can be financed out of current saving, the increased investment raises income. People are then encouraged to save some of the extra income created by the expansion in business investment.

For many years the United States has had a comparatively low rate of savings—about half the rate in West Germany and less than a third of Japan's savings rate. (During the 1980s the U.S. rate averaged 3.6%; it had averaged 8.2% over the three previous decades.) These widely differing rates, however, may result in part from differences in national accounting practices. In the United States, for example, private health-care costs are included in the consumption figure. In a country with national health insurance, the cost of health care may not be counted as consumption, and the savings rate will therefore be higher.

savings bond A savings bond is generally a written promise by the government to repay, with interest at a given rate and at a specified time, a sum of money being lent to it by an individual. Savings BONDS are sold by governments in an effort to encourage their citizens both to save, and to lend those savings to the government. During both world wars Americans bought "war bonds" as a patriotic gesture. Today many buy bonds through regular paycheck deductions.

Historically, the origins of savings bonds and the periods of their greatest use are associated with wartime economies. At such times savings bonds serve two functions: first, by drawing income off into savings and away from day-to-day spending, they help keep the combination of too much money and too few goods from driving up prices; and second, they provide the government with money to pay for the war. Because of this association, savings bonds have also been called war bonds, defense bonds, and freedom shares.

savings industry   The savings industry in the United States is made up of savings banks and savings and loan associations. Often called "thrift institutions" to differentiate them from commercial banks, they obtain the bulk of their funds from consumer savings accounts and time deposits. In recent years the differences between the commercial and savings institutions have been reduced by deregulation and competition.

The first savings bank in the United States was a mutual, or depositor-owned, institution founded in 1816. Mutual savings banks were chartered by only 18 states, largely in the Northeast. In 1980 they were allowed to obtain federal charters and to change from mutual to stock organizations. By 1987 there were just under 1,000 U.S. savings banks.

Savings and loan associations (S&Ls) began in the mid-19th century as small, informal groups that pooled their funds to help each other build homes. The growth of S&Ls was limited at first, because they did not solicit deposits from the general public, and many dissolved when their members had acquired homes. U.S. westward expansion, however, created a growing demand for home financing, accelerating the growth of the S&L industry and the formation of larger institutions.

During the Depression of the 1930s, more than 1,700 savings institutions failed, taking the savings of their depositors with them. Beginning in 1934, depositors in savings banks were permitted to obtain federal insurance from the FEDERAL DEPOSIT INSURANCE CORPORATION (FDIC); the Federal Savings and Loan Insurance Corporation (FSLIC) provided similar protection to S&L depositors. As additional help to the industry, Congress established 12 regional Home Loan Banks to provide liquidity to troubled S&Ls, paralleling the assistance given to commercial banks through the Federal Reserve System. The FEDERAL HOME LOAN BANK BOARD, which coordinated the regional Home Loan Banks, was given the power to charter federal S&Ls. (All S&Ls had previously been chartered by the states.) Along with this aid came important restrictions designed to make all depository institutions less vulnerable to failure. Chief among these was Regulation Q, which limited the amount of interest that both commercial and savings banks could pay to depositors—although, to encourage deposits in savings institutions and to compensate, in part, for the fact that they could not offer checking accounts, the thrifts were granted a differential of ¼ point over commercial banks.

When in the 1970s inflation pushed interest rates above Regulation Q ceilings, many depositors withdrew savings from banks and invested directly in higher-yielding instruments such as Treasury bills and money-market funds. With the bulk of their own assets invested in long-term, fixed-rate mortgages, savings institutions suffered heavy depletion of capital; many went out of business.

To help the industry, in the 1980s Congress began a period of deregulation: interest-rate ceilings were phased out; savings institutions were allowed to take on higher-yielding, higher-risk investments; and long-standing safeguards—such as the requirement that privately owned S&Ls have multiple shareholders, so that no one owner could "milk" assets—were abandoned. Depositors' accounts were now insured for a maximum of $100,000 (the previous maximum had been $40,000). Because depositors were insured by the government, thrifts had little reason to exercise care in their investment strategies, which often focused on risky undertakings, frequently in the Southwest. The collapse of energy and real estate prices in that region precipitated a major industry crisis. Between 1980 and 1990, more than 1,200 savings institutions experienced troubles that were severe enough to require federal assistance—the cost of which, by 1988, exceeded $42 billion.

In 1989, Congress eliminated the Federal Home Loan Bank Board, transferring its powers to the Office of Thrift Supervision, which is part of the Treasury Department. The insolvent FSLIC was replaced by the Savings Association Insurance Fund, a subsidiary of the FDIC. Another Treasury subsidiary, the Resolution Trust Corporation (RTC), was made responsible for liquidating failed institutions, primarily by selling off their assets. Liquidation costs, which include paying off depositors, are estimated at several hundred billion dollars when the process is completed. The surviving institutions are now subject to increased regulation and tougher penalties for those managers and directors who abuse their authority for private gain.

Savonarola, Girolamo [sah-voh-nah-roh'-lah]   The Italian Dominican reformer Girolamo Savonarola, b. Sept. 21, 1452, d. May 23, 1498, attempted to establish a theocratic government in Florence. He entered (1475) the Dominican order at Bologna and was assigned (1482) to teach theology at the priory of San Marco in Florence. The sermons that he preached were marked by the theme of warning against coming doom. After becoming (1490) prior of San Marco, his sermons became more popular and more pointed, with direct attacks on the vices and tyrannical abuses of the Medici government (see MEDICI family).

When French intervention allowed (1494) the Florentines to expel the Medici and establish a republic, Savonarola became a virtual dictator in the city, imposing a program of sweeping moral reforms. He interpreted the French intervention as the vengeance and punishment he had prophesied earlier. He also began to see himself as a prophet of God sent to announce judgment on Italy and on the church.

Soon his ties with the French brought him into conflict with Pope ALEXANDER VI, who was desperately forming alliances against the French. In 1495, Savonarola ignored a summons to Rome to explain his supposed revelations from God. After several clashes between them, Alexander excommunicated (1497) Savonarola, but, when this censure was published in Florence, Savonarola denied its validity. Soon his intransigence and defiance alienated his supporters in the Florentine government. When popular feeling turned against him, he was arrested, tortured, tried, and condemned to death for heresy and schism. He was hanged and then burned.

Savoy (dynasty)   The House of Savoy, one of Europe's oldest dynasties, ruled unified Italy from 1861 until the advent of the republic in 1946. The founder of the house, Count **Humbert I** the Whitehanded, d. *c*.1048, a vassal of the Holy Roman emperor, held Savoy and acquired other areas south of Lake Geneva on the western slope of the Alps. His successors expanded their territories to include what are now parts of France, Italy, and Switzerland, and in 1416 the count of Savoy, **Amadeus VIII**, b. 1383, d. Jan. 7, 1451 (r. 1391–1440), was granted ducal status. During the next century the dynasty's rule weakened, enabling the French to occupy the territory in 1536.

The Treaty of Cateau-Cambrésis (1559) returned the duchy to **Emmanuel Philibert**, b. July 8, 1528, d. Aug. 30, 1580 (r. 1553–80). In the 17th century the dukes played the French against the Habsburgs—and emerged from the wars of that period with considerable territorial gains. The Peace of Utrecht (1713–14) made VICTOR

Shaded portions of the map indicate territories controlled (c.1740) by the House of Savoy, a dynasty that exercised its authority over the strategic region guarding the passes of the western Alps between France and Italy.

DOMAINS OF HOUSE OF SAVOY c. 1740

AMADEUS II king of Sicily, which he relinquished to Austria in exchange for Sardinia in 1720. Napoleon I conquered all the Italian states except Sardinia.

The Savoyard kingdom of Sardinia-Piedmont spearheaded the Italian RISORGIMENTO (unification movement) of the 19th century. **Charles Albert**, b. Oct. 2, 1798, d. July 28, 1849 (r. 1831–49), granted a constitution in 1848, but after unification was achieved (1861) under his son, VICTOR EMMANUEL II, a parliamentary system was initiated, and the king's power waned. The last figurehead rulers of the dynasty were the Italian kings HUMBERT I, VICTOR EMMANUEL III, and HUMBERT II.

Savoy (region)   Savoy, a region of southeastern France, extends from Lake Geneva to the Isère River and borders on the Italian frontier. Its command of the western Alpine passes into Italy enhances its strategic importance. Savoy was the original domain of the Savoy dynasty, which ruled Italy from 1861 to 1946.

Savoy's early Celtic inhabitants were conquered by the Romans in 121 BC. During the 5th century AD the Burgundians gained control of the region, which passed in 534 to the Frankish kingdom of Burgundy. Savoy came under the suzerainty of the Holy Roman emperor in 1033. Count Humbert I the Whitehanded, founder of the House of Savoy, then controlled much of the region. The Savoy dukes increasingly favored their Italian lands, as French designs on Savoy, which was largely French-speaking, grew. The dukes transferred their capital to PIEDMONT in 1563. France annexed Savoy in 1792, but it was restored to the House of Savoy in 1815. In 1860, however, after a plebiscite, the region was returned to France, and the French acquiesced to the rule of the House of Savoy over a kingdom in north central Italy.

saw   The word *saw* covers a host of tools that may be used to cut wood or metal and other materials and that are powered either by hand or electrically. The saw was one of the earliest human tools; a prototype of the modern saw, in use before the discovery of metal, was made from flint, with edges that were notched by chipping.

All saws have a serrated edge or perimeter with a series of sharp, essentially V-shaped teeth, each of which removes a particle from the material being cut. The teeth of wood saws are usually designed to cut either with (parallel to) or across the grain of wood. Ripsaws, used to cut with the grain, have teeth that are almost perpendicular to the body of the blade; each tooth works like a tiny chisel, chipping out a portion of wood. Crosscut saws have teeth that shear, cutting cleanly through wood fibers. Combination blades are designed for cutting either with or across wood grain; often they are circular and used as part of such power tools as the table saw, radial arm saw, portable circular saw, chain saw, and band saw. The backsaw has numerous, minute teeth and is used considerably in joinery work. The dovetail saw is similar to the backsaw but smaller and is used extensively for the fine cuts required to form the classic dovetail joint.

Saws are tools for cutting wood, metals, and other materials by means of serrated cutting edges, usually of metal, consisting of a row of sharp, essentially V-shaped teeth. Saws may be mechanically powered or hand-powered and stationary or portable. Selection of a saw depends on the material to be cut and on the type of work to be done. (Opposite) The two main types of saws for cutting wood are the ripsaw and the crosscut saw. In both cases the teeth are bent sideways, alternately to the right and to the left. (A) Ripsaws, which have teeth perpendicular to the blade axis that are sharpened straight across the face, cut with a chisellike chipping action. (B) Crosscut saws, which have teeth angled to the blade axis and are filed at an angle to the face, cut with a shearing action.

A

B

crosscut saw

backsaw

dovetail saw

coping saw

circular saw

hacksaw

compass saw

tree-pruning saw

flooring saw

A good-quality traditional crosscut saw, used to cut large planks or panels, has a curved-back steel blade and beechwood handle. A backsaw, used to cut wooden joints, has many small teeth on a straight blade and a reinforced edge. A dovetail saw, used to cut fine joints, is a small, straight-handled backsaw. A coping saw, used to cut curves in wood or plastic, has many fine teeth on a very narrow blade, which can be angled in any desired direction. A portable electric circular saw, used primarily for woodworking and to cut solid lumber and boards to size, is a versatile tool that can be fitted with special blades for cutting other materials.

A hacksaw, the most common metal-cutting saw, has an adjustable bow frame and a pistol-grip handle. A compass saw uses a tapered, narrow replaceable blade for cutting panel holes. A tree-pruning saw has a curved, serrated steel blade. A flooring saw has a curved blade with teeth below and on top for cutting through floorboards easily. A band saw (below) is a fixed electric power tool for use in industry or in home workshops. It has a driven steel loop blade, which can be used to cut large pieces of lumber in straight or curved shaped sections.

band saw

chain saw

A power-driven chain saw uses a continuous toothed chain to fell trees and cut logs. An electric-powered saber saw uses various blades to make straight or curved cuts in a number of different materials.

saber saw

Some saws are designed especially to cut curves, common ones being the coping, keyhole, and compass saws. They differ in length and flexibility of their blades.

The most common metal-cutting saw is the hacksaw, which has an adjustable frame that uses disposable, narrow, hardened blades. The hacksaw can sever steel, iron, and similar metals.

sawback turtle Sawback turtles comprise three species of TURTLES in the genus *Graptemys*, family Emydidae. The raised dorsal keel of their shells protrudes as knobs that give a sawlike appearance. The jaws of female sawbacks are broad, flat, and powerful for crushing the shells of mollusks, one of their principal foods; males eat mostly insects. Like the closely related MAP TURTLES, the female sawback may grow to two or three times the size of the 7.5- to 10-cm (3- to 4-in) male.

Sawback turtles occur in river systems draining the Gulf States and prefer water of moderate current and ample brush or debris where they can bask or take cover. The ringed sawback, *G. oculifera*, is found in the Pearl River system of Mississippi and Louisiana; the yellow-blotched sawback, *G. flavimaculata*, occurs in the Pascagoula River system of Mississippi; and the black-knobbed sawback, *G. nigrinoda*, inhabits the Alabama–Tombigbee–Black Warrior river system of Alabama and Mississippi.

sawfish The sawfishes belong to the family Pristidae (order Rajiformes), which includes the SKATES and RAYS. They are not as flat as many rays and are more sharklike in appearance. Sawfishes attain lengths of up to 6 m (20 ft). The saw is a flat extension of the upper jaw; like the rest of the skeleton, it is cartilaginous. It bears rows of teethlike structures imbedded in sockets. The saw can be 1.8 m (6 ft) long and 30 cm (1 ft) broad. True teeth occur in a small mouth. Sawfishes range widely in the shallows of most warm seas and adjacent estuaries, and some species ascend rivers. They are ovoviviparous, producing live young.

The saw is sometimes used as a weapon of defense, but its principal function is to obtain food. It is used to search through the sand and mud for small forms of prey, and it is also used to slash through schools of small fish, stunning and piercing them with the lateral teeth. Large sawfishes are sometimes dangerous, and they are a nuisance in that they cut nets and damage netted fish.

The common sawfish of the Atlantic Ocean is a fairly docile inhabitant of the shallows, despite its size and sawlike bill.

sawfly Sawflies are primitive members of the insect order Hymenoptera. They resemble wasps, are often bright in color, and are usually found on flowers or foliage. The largest group is the common sawfly, family Tenthredinidae. Sawfly larvae resemble caterpillars and feed on many types of plants; some form galls or bore in plant stems, among them a few very destructive pests of maple, apple, beech, larch, and elm trees. Larvae of the birch leaf miner, *Fenùsa pusilla*, tunnel in leaves of ornamental birch trees. Sawflies have a single annual generation.

Saxe, Maurice, Comte de [sahks] Hermann Maurice, comte de Saxe, b. Oct. 28, 1696, d. Nov. 30, 1750, illegitimate son of AUGUSTUS II of Poland, was a naturalized French citizen who had a spectacular military career. Saxe won European fame by capturing Prague (1741) in the War of the Austrian Succession (see AUSTRIAN SUCCESSION, WAR OF THE). His subsequent brilliant victories at Fontenoy (1745) and Raucoux (1746) gave France control of the Austrian Netherlands (ceded back at the peace). In recognition of his exploits, Saxe was awarded the rare title of marshal general of France and life use of Chambord palace.

Saxe-Meiningen, George II, Duke of [sahks-myn'-ing-en] George II, duke of Saxe-Meiningen, b. Apr. 2, 1826, d. June 25, 1914, was a German ruler whose court troupe of actors, the Meiningen Players, had a formative influence on the modern theater. George II, who came to power in 1866, appointed the experienced actor Ludwig Chronegk as manager and selected plays with the advice of his third wife, Ellen Franz, a former actress. Most of the Meiningen troupe's productions were of romantic history plays characterized by historically accurate costumes and settings, which were designed by the duke. He also oversaw performances, emphasizing ensemble playing. The Meiningen Players toured extensively between 1874 and 1890.

saxifrage [sak'-si-frij] Saxifrage is the common name for the approximately 370 species of the plant genus *Saxifraga*, belonging to the saxifrage family, Saxifragaceae. The genus comprises mostly small, hardy perennial herbs native to mountains and rocky places in temperate America and Europe. Some are native to South America, Africa, and Australia. The common name means "rock-splitter," which refers to the persistent manner in which the roots of these plants burrow into rocky hillsides and among stone crevices. Saxifrages vary from mosslike to succulent in form. They make excellent rock-garden plants.

Saxifrage leaves are ovate and narrow at the base and grow in basal rosettes, often with the outer leaves pressed closely to the ground. Appearing in late spring and early summer, the flowers are borne as branched terminal clusters on hairy stalks and are white, pink, purple, or yellow. Almost all species thrive best in limestone soil and sufficient shade.

Saxo Grammaticus [sak'-soh gruh-mat'-i-kuhs]
Saxo, *c.*1150–*c.*1220, was a Danish historian and poet who was awarded the honorific title Grammaticus, meaning "the learned," because of his great knowledge. No other biographical facts are known. His book, the *Gesta Danorum*, or *Historia Danica*, a 16-volume history of the Danes written in Latin for his patron, Archbishop Absolon, contains songs, Danish traditions of kings and heroes— including the story of Amleth, or Hamlet—and Icelandic legends. The book was first printed in Paris in 1514 and was later translated into Danish (1603) and English (1894; repr. 1967).

Saxony   The name Saxony was originally used for the area between the Rhine and Elbe rivers, stretching from the North Sea and the Jutland Peninsula on the north to Franconia and Thuringia on the south. Later called Lower Saxony, most of this area lies within the present German state of Lower Saxony (Niedersachsen), established in 1946. The name was also used for the region of the middle Oder and Elbe rivers; later called Upper Saxony, that region was part of East Germany until 1990.

Saxony took its name from the Saxons, a Germanic people. Those Saxons who did not migrate with the Angles and Jutes to England preserved their independence until the late 8th century, when Charlemagne incorporated them into his state. When the Carolingian empire dissolved, Saxony survived as one of the five tribal duchies. From 919 to 1024 its dukes became German kings and Holy Roman emperors. During the next centuries, under dukes of the Billung and WELF families, Saxony spearheaded the DRANG NACH OSTEN—the eastward spread of the Germans. Conflict between Emperor FREDERICK I and Duke HENRY THE LION brought catastrophe to Saxony. In 1180 the emperor deprived Henry of most of his land: the Westphalian areas went to the archbishop of Cologne; and the eastern regions were given to Bernard of Anhalt of the Ascanian family, who also received the Saxon ducal title. The Welfs retained only the central zone around Brunswick and Lüneburg; after 1235, they created the duchy of Brunswick, most of which became the kingdom of HANOVER and lasted until 1866.

Meanwhile, the Ascanian duchy of Saxony, one of the seven German electorates, became centered in Wittenberg on the Oder. It passed (1423) to the Wettin dynasty, rulers of a conglomeration of lands in the margravate of Meissen and in Thuringia, all of which came to be called Upper Saxony. In 1485 the two brothers who jointly ruled the Wettin lands divided them: Ernest took the electoral Saxon title, along with the northern—Wittenberg—lands, while Duke Albert accepted the southern district, which included Leipzig, Dresden, and Thuringia. Electoral (Ernestine) Saxony was Martin Luther's homeland, and FREDERICK III, elector of Saxony (r. 1486–1525), supported Luther and the Reformation. Ducal (Albertine) Saxony remained loyal to the Roman Catholic church until the middle of the 16th century, when dukes Henry (r. 1539–41) and Maurice (r.

1541–53) introduced Protestantism. In 1547, Duke Maurice seized the electoral lands and titles from Elector John Frederick (r. 1532–54), who then received in turn the ducal title and Thuringia. Ernestine (now ducal) Saxony subsequently split into smaller states that survived until German unification. Saxony-Weimar, the residence of the great writer Johann Wolfgang von Goethe, was the best known of these states. Albertine (now electoral) Saxony, on the other hand, never divided. Saxony emerged from the Napoleonic Wars as a kingdom that endured until 1918. It was a state under the Weimar Republic, the Third Reich, and the German Democratic Republic (East Germany), but it was finally eliminated as a separate administrative unit in 1952.

saxophone   The family of saxophones patented in 1846 by Adolphe Sax combines the single reed of the clarinet with the bore and fingering patterns of the oboe, producing the tonal qualities of neither. The instruments fit well into bands, for their sound blends well with brass and woodwind instruments; their application to the orchestra has been more limited, because saxophones tend to dominate the varied tonal characteristics of that ensemble. Saxophones are made in eight sizes and pitch levels, spanning the entire spectrum of wind-instrument pitches. The most common are the alto and tenor saxophones. They have been effectively used in jazz bands

The saxophone, a single-reed musical instrument named for its 19th-century inventor, Adolphe Sax, is a hybrid of the clarinet, oboe, and brass instruments. Although eight types are made, only four are widely used—the B-flat soprano, the E-flat alto, the B-flat tenor, and the E-flat baritone. The saxophone is used in military bands, dance bands, and orchestras and is particularly important in jazz. Parts include the mouthpiece (1), reed (2), neckpiece (3), crook (4), upper stack keys (5), lower stack keys (6), bell keys (7), and bell (8).

and popular dance orchestras. Numerous jazz performers have risen to fame with the instrument, and composers, beginning in 19th-century France, have employed it in their solo or ensemble compositions.

Saye and Sele, William Fiennes, 1st Viscount [say' uhn seel, fynz]   William Fiennes, 1st Viscount Saye and Sele, b. May 28, 1582, d. Apr. 14, 1662, was a Puritan leader in the English House of Lords under the first Stuart kings and a promoter of American colonization. During the personal rule (1629–40) of Charles I, Lord Saye and Sele helped found refuges for Puritans at Providence Island in the Caribbean (1630), Saybrook, Conn. (1632), and Dover, N.H. (1633). Although a leader of resistance to Charles I at the beginning of the English Civil War, he opposed abolition of the monarchy and became lord privy seal after the Restoration (1660).

Sayers, Dorothy L. [say'-urz]   The most erudite of English mystery writers, Dorothy Leigh Sayers, b. Oxford, June 13, 1893, d. Dec. 17, 1957, is best known for her classic detective novels featuring Lord Peter Wimsey, an aristocratic amateur sleuth. The Wimsey books follow no formula but depend on a highly literate style, ingenious plots, and solidly researched backgrounds. Among the best are *The Nine Tailors* (1934), with its excursion into campanology, and *Murder Must Advertise* (1933), which portrays a London advertising agency. A teacher at Oxford University, Sayers also edited two important anthologies of detective fiction, wrote four religious dramas, and at her death had completed a translation of the first two books of Dante's *Divine Comedy: Hell* (1949) and *Purgatory* (1955).

Sayers, Gale   Gale Sayers, b. Wichita, Kans., May 30, 1943, was considered American professional football's best running back during his brief career (1965–71). He was an All-American during his junior and senior years at the University of Kansas. He then joined the Chicago Bears of the National Football League (NFL), and in 1965, his rookie season, Sayers led the league in points scored (132), touchdowns (22), and total offense (2,272 yd). That year, against the San Francisco 49ers, he tied the NFL record by scoring 6 touchdowns in a single game. Sayers was selected Rookie of the Year in 1965. Knee injuries ended his career after only 5 full seasons of play. He was voted into the Pro Football Hall of Fame in 1977.

scabies   SEE SKIN DISEASES

Scala (family) [skah'-lah]   A rich merchant family from Verona, the Scala were the lords of Verona, Vicenza, and, at times, other north Italian cities from the mid-13th to the end of the 14th century. The dynasty's chief lord, **Can Grande della Scala**, b. Mar. 9, 1291, d. July 22, 1329, was a patron of Dante Alighieri and creator of a large state in northeastern Italy. He was a leader of the

Ghibelline, or proimperial, faction in the GUELPH AND GHIBELLINE controversy between pope and emperor and was made imperial vicar by the Holy Roman emperor Henry VII in 1311. Can Grande conquered many cities, including Padua, Treviso, Feltro, and Belluno. His successor, **Mastino II della Scala**, b. 1308, d. June 3, 1351, lost those conquests to Florence and Venice in 1339. Thereafter, the Scala fell to intrafamilial feuding and murder and lost their rule over Verona and Vicenza to the Visconti family of Milan in 1387.

scalawags   After the U.S. Civil War, *scalawag* was a derogatory name for white Southerners who helped implement RECONSTRUCTION (1865–77) of the defeated South. The scalawags, who were usually Republicans, cooperated with blacks and with Northern CARPETBAGGERS who had traveled south to participate in Reconstruction. Many white Southerners resented the economic, social, and political reforms that the scalawags helped bring about, and, with the resurgence of the Democratic party in the South in the 1870s, their influence diminished.

scale, insect   SEE DISEASES, PLANT

scale (measure)   SEE BALANCE

scale (music)   A musical scale (Latin: *scala*, "staircase") is a determinate series of related tones within an OCTAVE, providing an inventory of pitches available for composition and a convenient basis for vocal or instrumental practice. Innumerable scales may be found in or inferred from the music of different periods and peoples: the familiar diatonic scale of modern Western music, a descendant of the medieval European modes (see MODE, music), and thus of ancient Greek scales, is in no sense definitive. Whole-tone (CDEF#G#A#C') and pentatonic (CDFGAC') scales, both of which have influenced composers in the West, are commonly found elsewhere.

The diatonic scale (CDEFGABC') consists of five whole tones (or whole steps) and two semitones (half steps) in the arrangement 11½111½. This is called the major mode, as distinguished from the minor (CDEᵇFGABC' in its ascending, melodic form), in which the arrangement of intervals is 1½1111½. These scales may be transposed to begin on any of the 12 tones of the complete chromatic or semitonal scale (CC#DD#EFF#GG#AA#B), of which the others may be considered selections; hence there are 12 major and 12 minor scales, each corresponding to a KEY.

See also: TONALITY.

Scalia, Antonin [skuh-lee'-uh]   Antonin Scalia, b. Trenton, N.J., Mar. 11, 1936, was appointed a justice of the U.S. Supreme Court by President Reagan in 1986. A respected judicial conservative, Scalia had been a judge on the U.S. Court of Appeals since 1982. Earlier he taught law at the University of Chicago and Stanford.

scallop Scallop is the common name for a group of about 360 species of edible bivalve MOLLUSKS, usually within the genus *Pecten* (class Pelecypoda or Bivalvia, family Pectinidae). Scallops are normally found in shallow waters of protected bays with sandy or muddy bottoms. The familiar scallop shells are fluted and round with a broad, flattened ear or wing at the hinge area. The common scallop is about 5 cm (2 in) long.

When specimens of scallop relax on the bay floor, the two apposing shells (called valves) gape open slightly, exposing a fold of the mantle tissue called the velar fold, which is sensitive to chemical irritants. The velar fold protects numerous tentacles that are sensitive to mechanical stimuli. Unlike in other mollusks, along both edges of the mantle are numerous iridescent ocelli, or primitive eyes, that are sensitive to decreases in light, such as those produced by passing shadows.

Scallops have a single large adductor muscle, composed of striated muscle fibers (for fast swimming) and unstriated muscle fibers (to hold together the two valves). The adductor muscle is the only edible part of the animal. Unlike most other bivalve mollusks, scallops can swim or leap by rapidly closing and opening the valves.

The scallop, a relative of such bivalve mollusks as the clam and mussel, lives along ocean bay bottoms.

scalping Scalping is the removal of the scalp and hair of a living or dead enemy, to exhibit as a battle trophy or to earn a bounty. Scalping, or "taking hair," was practiced by certain American Indian tribes along the St. Lawrence River and in the eastern part of the present United States, except New England, and in the Gran Chaco area of South America. The technique was to slice around the crown of the head with a "scalping knife," and, by pulling up on the hair, wrench off the scalp or part of it. Few victims survived scalping. Some tribes who shaved their heads left on top a "scalp lock" in token of defiance. With appropriate ritual, for the scalp was a prized symbol of success in battle, the trophy was dried, tanned, decorated, and displayed. Archaeological findings indicate that the practice was an ancient one among some North American tribes.

See also: HEAD-HUNTING.

Scandinavian art and architecture Scandinavia has had its own art tradition since the Stone Age, enriched by cultural centers to the south. The history of art in Scandinavia, therefore, generally follows the developments in art on the European continent but with slightly later dates. Distinguishing characteristics are the prominence of design and decoration rather than representation of the human figure, and the highly developed use of wood for architecture and the applied arts due to the comparative dearth of metals, ceramic clays, and soft building stone.

Pre-Christian Scandinavian Art

Prehistoric Art. The funnel beaker pots and flint daggers produced in Denmark during the last phase of the Neolithic Period (c.2000 BC) and the monumental bronze jewelry, horns (*lurer*), and other decorative or ceremonial objects produced in the same area from about 1200 to 500 BC can be seen in the National Museum, Copenhagen. A lively tradition of pictorial cliff carving flourished in southeast Norway and southwest Sweden.

Viking Art. A period of intense artistic development occurred in Scandinavia from the 5th through the 8th century AD. The distinctive northern style in animal interlace decoration developed and dominated Scandinavian art for the next 500 years. Intricately designed and well-executed jewelry, harness decorations, and weapons in metal have been found, but the principal monuments of the time are the large Oseberg and Gokstad burial ships with their rich grave goods (early 9th century; Viking Ship Museum, Bygdøy, Oslo). The well-preserved Oseberg ship (22 m/72 ft long) is an early example of the typical Scandinavian mixture of artistry and utility.

Medieval Scandinavian Art

The major artistic consequence of the meeting between Christian art and the native pagan tradition during the 11th and the 12th centuries was the picturesque wood stave church, of which 32 (of more than 800) are preserved in Norway, and the memorial runestones, of which hundreds are found in east central Sweden.

From the 12th through the 14th century, Romanesque

The carved stern of a 9th-century ceremonial Viking ship forms the tail of a dragon 22 m (72 ft) long. The ship, built of oak planks and decorated with intricately carved friezes of animals, was found at Oseberg, Norway, in the grave of a noblewoman. It contained a hoard of tapestries, tools, and wooden ornaments.

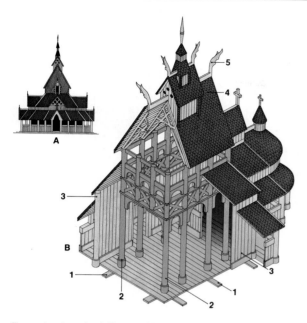

The wooden stave church (A), an architectural form native to the Scandinavian countries, particularly Norway, flourished from the 12th to 14th centuries. The name is derived from the four hiornstafir, *or corner posts, which form the basis for the elaborate timber framework. A cutaway view of a typical church (B) shows the chassis sills (1), corner posts (2), outside wall (3), gabled roof (4), and dragon-headed ornaments (5). The interiors of most Norwegian stave churches are decorated with wood carvings of Viking and Christian motifs.*

and Gothic cathedrals in stone and brick—such as those in Lund and Uppsala in Sweden, and those in Stavanger and Trondheim in Norway—were being built on the model of German, French, and English churches with the assistance of architects and craftsmen from these areas. The Black Death, which ravaged (c.1350) Scandinavia, effectively halted large-scale building for more than a century.

Renaissance, Baroque, and Rococo Art

Scandinavian art and architecture from the Renaissance, baroque, and rococo periods echo that of other areas in Europe with certain local characteristics resulting from differences in climate, materials, and the individual preferences of local patrons. The ROCOCO STYLE found favor in rural Norway, where it influenced Norwegian folk painting.

Swedish Renaissance Architecture. The first major buildings reflecting Renaissance concepts were the sturdy 16th-century castles of the Vasa kings in Sweden, the first of which, Gripsholm Castle (1537) outside Stockholm, is still largely medieval. Vadstena Castle (1545) has the more ordered plan of the new style and considerable purely Renaissance decorative detail. The rebuilt castle at Kalmar is the most Renaissance of all the Vasa castles. The Pahr family, of Italian origin, was involved with the design of these buildings.

Danish Renaissance Architecture. The buildings from the first half of the 17th century commissioned by the

Danish king Christian IV (r. 1588–1648) represent the second important phase of Renaissance building in Scandinavia. The most characteristic remaining examples are the Stock Exchange (1619–23) and Rosenborg Castle (1606) in Copenhagen and Frederiksborg Castle (1602–08) in Hillerød. The architects brought with them the Dutch tradition of building in red brick with gray sandstone trim. In contrast to the massiveness of the Vasa style the Danish castles appear light and fanciful.

Swedish Baroque and Rococo Art. During the 18th century the rise of a local tradition in art and architecture gradually brought to an end the period of imported culture. Among the most gifted artists and architects in Scandinavia were the painter Carl Gustaf Pilo (c.1711–93), whose *Coronation of Gustav III* (1782–93; Nationalmuseum, Stockholm) is a major achievement in 18th-century group portraiture; the architect Carl Fredrik Adelcrantz (1716–96), whose Kina Slott (Chinese Pavilion, 1763–68) at Drottningholm is an outstanding example of 18th-century rococo chinoiserie; and the sculptor Johann Tobias Sergel (1740–1814), whose *Resting Faun* (1774; Nationalmuseum, Stockholm) foreshadows the neoclassicism that soon acquired a lasting hold on the arts of Scandinavia.

The Danish "Golden Age." By the late 18th century Denmark, too, was developing its own tradition, based primarily on French neoclassicism. C. W. Eckersberg (1783–1853), and Christen Köbke (1810–48) made the cool precision of French neoclassic art a dominant trait in Danish painting. The courthouse (1803–16) and Vor Frue Kirke (Church of Our Lady, 1811–29) by the architect C. F. Hansen (1756–1845) impart a classical look to downtown Copenhagen. The person most representative of the period is the sculptor Bertel THORVALDSEN, who as the "new Phidias" produced neoclassical sculpture for an international clientele.

Norwegian 19th-Century Art. Norway, whose folk art of the 18th century rivals the richest in Europe, made its

Frederiksborg Castle, in Hillerød, Denmark, was rebuilt during the early 17th century by the Dutch masons Hans and Lourens Steenwinckel for King Christian IV. It now houses the National Historical Museum.

first significant mark in the fine arts during the early 19th century with the landscapes of Johann Christian Dahl (1788–1857) and, later, Hans Gude (1825–1903). Coexisting with the landscape tradition at mid-century was a tradition in genre painting represented by Adolph Tidemand (1814–76). The single work that best exemplifies the "National Romantic" period is *The Bridal Procession in Hardanger* (1848; Nasjonalgalleriet, Oslo), painted jointly by Tidemand and Gude. The term *Golden Age* in Norwegian art is usually reserved for the turn of the 20th century, when the painters Christian Krohg, Erik Werenskiold, and the revolutionary expressionist Edvard MUNCH were most active, and when the idiosyncratic sculptor Gustav VIGELAND began work on the hundreds of statues in Oslo's Vigeland Sculpture Park (1921–43).

Swedish 19th-Century Art. The dynamic painter Ernst Josephson (1851–1906), who in the 1880s was a leader of the young realists, soon moved on to a neoromantic style; finally, in the early 1890s he developed a unique form of expressionism. More successful with the public at the time were the late impressionist virtuoso Anders ZORN, who specialized in painting fashionable portraits, female nudes, and scenes of peasant life, and Carl Larsson (1853–1919), whose decorative oils and watercolors of bourgeois domestic life appealed to a wide audience.

Standing Orange Figures (1949), by the Danish painter Carl-Henning Pedersen, reflects the boldly colored, simple images of folk art and children's drawings. (Nordjyllands Kunstmuseum, Ålborg.)

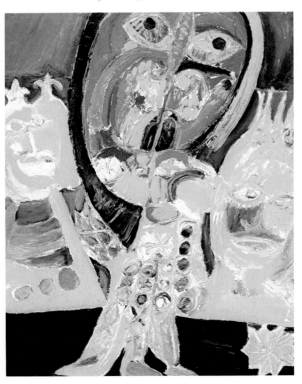

Even more successful, both in Sweden and abroad, was their young contemporary Carl MILLES, the sculptor.

Scandinavian 20th-Century Art

Painting and Sculpture. Since the 1920s few Scandinavian artists other than Edvard Munch have gained international prominence. The exceptions are several Danish artists working in a style that combines surrealistic and expressionistic elements; notably the painter Asger Jorn (1914–73) and the sculptor Robert Jacobsen. The Norwegian mixed-media artist Rolf Nesch (1893–1977) and the Swedish painter Olle Bærtling have also received international acclaim.

Architecture and the Decorative Arts. During the 20th century Scandinavia, in an expansion of a movement begun (1915) in Sweden, has concentrated its artistic efforts on better design in housing and in objects for everyday use. Pioneers in the design of glass and china were the Swedes Simon Gate and Edward Hald working for the firm of Orrefors, and Wilhelm Kåge; the key figures in furniture design have been the Danes Kaare Klint, Finn Juhl, and Hans Wegner. Danes have also led the way in silver design, and Norwegians have specialized in enamelware. All Scandinavian countries have traditions of textile design, with the Norwegians and Swedes developing their modern fabrics in part on the basis of strong folk traditions. A specialty in Scandinavian textiles is the rya pile rug. A traditional love of decoration and fine craftsmanship has also led to a fairly extensive production of luxury items.

Scandinavian literature   see DANISH LITERATURE; NORWEGIAN LITERATURE; SWEDISH LITERATURE

Scandinavian music   In musical development, the Scandinavian nations (Denmark, Sweden, Norway, and Finland) have been closely tied to their European neighbors, especially Germany. The early musical traditions of the Viking era (9th–11th centuries) are now lost, and Scandinavian derivations of medieval plainchant and polyphonic religious music are poorly documented. The Scandinavian countries experienced national awakenings within 19th-century romantic tradition, developing assertive, individual composers who achieved fame on into the 20th century. Denmark and Sweden also built strong ballet and opera companies of wide renown. In all four countries, vigorous programs of government support, including state-run radio systems, actively promoted musical life.

Denmark. Denmark, being closest to the rest of Europe, was earliest in musical growth. Fragments survive of a rich tradition in medieval song. In the 17th century the lavish patronage of King Christian IV (r. 1588–1648) attracted England's John Dowland and other foreign musicians to the Danish court, but Denmark's first great native composer, Dietrich BUXTEHUDE, made most of his career in Germany. Germans dominated Danish music through the 18th century, along with some Italians who contributed to development of opera. Early 19th-century trends were shaped by the Germans C. E. F. Weyse (1774–1842) and Friedrich Kuhlau (1786–1832). By mid-century, successful native musicians included the opera composers J. P. E. Hartmann (1805–1900), Peter Heise (1830–79), and C. F. E. Horneman (1840–1906); Hans Christian Lumbye (1810–74) a composer of marches and dance music, is often compared to Johann Strauss of Vienna. By far the most influential figure was Niels Vilhelm Gade (1817–90): Leipzig-trained, he gave a Danish voice to German romantic style. Rued Langgaard (1893–1952) was an important late-romantic symphonist. The giant of Danish music was Carl NIELSEN. His conducting, teaching, and composition gave Danish music of his day a conservative but open-minded, humane, and cosmopolitan postromantic stamp. Only after World War II did younger Danish composers explore more diverse styles of 20th-century modernism; Vagn Holmboe (b. 1909), Niels Viggo Bentzon (b. 1919), and Per Nørgaard (b. 1933) have achieved the most international attention. Among Danish performers to win international fame are the tenors Aksel Schiotz and Lauritz Melchior.

Sweden. Court patronage in the 17th century prompted some active musical life in Sweden, and a few native composers emerged. Much influenced by Handel, Johan Helmich Roman (1694–1758) composed extensively and did arrangements of foreign music. Sweden's boldest 19th-century composer, Franz BERWALD, received little acclaim or encouragement at home during his lifetime. Sweden won a place on the international scene through the late-romantic composers Wilhelm Stenhammar (1871–1927) and Hugo Alfven (1872–1960). Ture Rangstrom (1884–1947), Kurt Atterberg (1887–1974), Gosta Nystroem (1890–1966), Hilding Rosenberg (b. 1892), Dag Wiren (b. 1905), Lars-Erik Larsson (b. 1908), Karl-Birger Blomdahl (1916–68), and Allan Pettersson (1911–80) represent the various 20th-century currents in music. Noted singers from Sweden include the 19th-century soprano Jenny LIND and, in the 20th century, tenors Set Svanholm (1904–64) and Nicolai GEDDA, and sopranos Birgit NILSSON and Elisabeth Söderström.

Norway. Late to achieve (1905) political independence, Norway was also long tied culturally to its neighbors. Not until the 19th century was there an appreciation of traditional folklore, notably the rich tradition of folk fiddling. Early nationalist exponents were Ole Bull, Halfdan Kjerulf (1815–68), Rickard Nordraak (1842–66), and the ambitious Johan Svendsen (1840–1911), who had to pursue much of his career in Denmark. The advent of Edvard GRIEG gave Norway its commanding musical personality and most beloved international voice. Under his shadow developed such other talents as Agathe Backer-Grondahl (1847–1907), Christian Sinding (1856–1941), and Johan Halvorsen (1864–1935). Among the leaders in 20th-century Norwegian composition have been David Monrad Johansen (1888–1974), the atonalist Fartein Valen (1887–1952), Harald Saeverud (b. 1897), Eivind Groven (b. 1901), and Klaus Egge (b. 1906). Particularly famous among Norwegian performers was soprano Kirsten FLAGSTAD.

Finland. The most isolated and subjugated of the Scandinavian countries, Finland was long a cultural province of Sweden and Germany. When it came under Rus-

sian rule in the 19th century, it developed an independence movement accompanied by artistic nationalism. In the early 20th century, the towering personality of Jean SIBELIUS won international acclaim and drew Finland into the mainstream of European music. Among his successors, Aarre Merikanto (1893–1958), Yryo Kilpinen (1892–1959), Uuno Klami (1900–61), and especially Joonas Kokkonen (b. 1921) have won attention beyond their country. Widely acclaimed among Finnish performers is bass Martti Talvela.

---

scandium [skan'-dee-um]   Scandium is a silvery white metallic chemical element, the first member of the TRANSITION ELEMENTS. Its symbol is Sc, its atomic number is 21, and its atomic weight is 44.9559. The name is derived from Scandinavia, where the element was discovered in the minerals euxenite and gadolinite. In 1876, L. F. Nilson prepared about 2 g of high purity scandium oxide. It was subsequently established that scandium corresponds to the element "ekaboron," predicted by Mendeleyev on the basis of a gap in the PERIODIC TABLE.

Scandium occurs in small quantities in more than 800 minerals and causes the blue color of aquamarine beryl. It is a relatively soft and light metal with a melting point of 1,541° C, a boiling point of 2,831° C, and a density of 2.989 g/cm^3. The chemical properties of scandium resemble those of yttrium and the rare-earth metals. It has 11 known isotopes, only one of which occurs in nature. Scandium exhibits an oxidation state of exclusively +3. Because it is difficult to process, scandium has few commercial uses but shows promise in electronics and high-intensity lighting.

---

scanning   Scanning is the process of examining a surface or a region, particularly in an organized fashion, for the purpose of either assessing information or projecting a beam of radiant energy. A typical scanning operation is performed by a rotating radar antenna. In the CATHODE-RAY TUBE of a television set, an electron beam is swept across the phosphor-coated face of the tube in hundreds of narrowly spaced, parallel lines.

Optical scanning has become increasingly important. Laser scanners, for example, in supermarkets can decode information from specially marked packages. Scanners connected to computers can "read" pictures and documents and translate them into a machine-usable form.

Scapa Flow [skap'-uh]   Scapa Flow is a 130-km^2 (50-mi^2) area of sea enclosed within the ORKNEY ISLANDS, off the northern coast of Scotland. It is about 24 km (15 mi) long and 13 km (8 mi) wide. Three channels, the main one being Pentland Firth in the south, provide entrance and exit. Because of its excellent anchorage, Scapa Flow served as Britain's chief naval base during both world wars. After World War I the German fleet was scuttled (1919) there. In October 1939 a German submarine penetrated the anchorage and sank the battleship *Royal*

Oak, causing the Royal Navy to abandon the base until 1940 when the defenses were improved. The base was closed in 1957.

▬

scar   A scar is a permanent, dense mark in any tissue, particularly skin, resulting from an injury or a disease process. Scar tissue replaces injured tissue as the result of the proliferation in the wound of fibroblasts—specialized cells that produce COLLAGEN, a tough, fibrous, and inelastic protein that is a major component of connective tissue. The collagen fills and closes the wound in an irreversible process. Scar tissue cannot perform the functions of the missing tissue, and this restriction may be life threatening in a crucial area such as a heart valve.

scarab beetle   SEE DUNG BEETLE

▬

Scarborough [skahr'-bruh]   Scarborough (1981 pop., 43,103), a seaside resort of North Yorkshire in northern England, lies about 320 km (200 mi) north of London. Sandy beaches on the North Sea coast and picturesque fishing villages nearby are tourist attractions. The city is also popular for conventions and conferences. Landmarks include remains of a mid-12th-century castle and a 4th-century Roman watchtower. Chartered in 1181, the city became well known after the discovery of mineral springs during the 1620s. The arrival of the railroad in 1845 assured the growth of Scarborough as a resort.

▬

Scarlatti (family) [skahr-lat'-ee]   **Alessandro Scarlatti**, b. Palermo, May 2, 1660, d. Naples, Oct. 24, 1725, was an Italian composer best known for his operas. In 1684 he became director of music at the royal chapel in Naples, where he also wrote operas for the palace theater and for the royal theater of San Bartolomeo.

After 1702 he held posts in Florence and Rome, and also composed a masterpiece for Venice, the opera *Mitri-*

The 17th-century Italian composer Alessandro Scarlatti is considered the founder of modern opera. In addition to composing church and secular music, he wrote 114 operas, 35 of which survive. His son Domenico achieved the greatest fame of his 10 children as a composer for the harpsichord.

date Eupatore (1707). In 1709 he returned to Naples to become director of music at the royal chapel, again producing a wealth of church music, chamber cantatas, two oratorios, and two new operas—*Teodosio* and *L'amor volubile e tiranne* (both 1709). Many members of his family joined him, and soon the Scarlattis dominated the musical life of Naples. Alessandro was made *cavaliere* in 1716. He excelled in church and chamber music, but he is most remembered as a dramatic composer, especially in view of his remarkable contribution to the thematic strength of the aria.

Alessandro's son, **Domenico Scarlatti**, b. Naples, Oct. 26, 1685, d. Madrid, July 23, 1757, was a composer and harpsichord virtuoso. Although he held various posts in Rome, the last years of his life were spent in Madrid, where his former student the Infanta Maria Barbara, now queen of Spain, retained him as a member of her staff, paid his debts, and provided for his family. In their originality, brilliance, and variety, his approximately 555 sonatas (mostly for solo harpsichord) eclipse most of the other keyboard music of his time, and he was also respected for his stage works and church music.

▬

scarlet fever   Named for the bright flush of the cheeks and the rash that spreads downward to cover the body, scarlet fever, or scarlatina, is an acute communicable disease caused by the same bacterium, *Streptococcus pyogenes*, responsible for streptococcal pharyngitis (see STREP THROAT). The infection commonly occurs in young children, and the incubation period is from 2 to 3 days. Typical symptoms, which have an abrupt onset, include sore throat, fever, and headaches; a toxin results in the rash after entering the bloodstream. The rash fades in from 5 days to 3 weeks, and the noninfectious outer layers of skin flake off. The patient is infective for about 2 weeks. Complications such as rheumatic fever and pneumonia can result. Mild scarlet fever requires only bed rest and treatment of symptoms. Severe cases can be fatal unless treated with penicillin. Scarlet fever is less common than it once was, because of antibiotic therapy.

▬

Scarlet Letter, The   A novel by Nathaniel HAWTHORNE, *The Scarlet Letter* (1850) is a somber tale of sin and redemption set in Puritan Massachusetts in the 1600s. Its heroine, Hester Prynne, has been exiled from the village of Salem for adultery and must wear a red "A" on her dress. Her lover, the young minister Arthur Dimmesdale, has remained silent about their passion, but Hester's husband, Roger Chillingworth, suspects Dimmesdale and pursues him mercilessly until Dimmesdale publicly confesses and dies in Hester's arms. Hester atones for her sin through service to others, whereas Chillingworth is shown to be guilty of a greater sin, the violation of another's soul.

▬

Scarne, John [skahr'-nee]   John Scarne, b. Orlando Carmelo Scarnecchia, Steubenville, Ohio, Mar. 4, 1903,

d. July 7, 1985, combined a mastery of sleight-of-hand and other magicians' skills with mathematical aptitude to become one of the world's leading games and gambling authorities. He wrote many books on magic, games, and gambling; Scarne's *Encyclopedia of Games* (1973) is the standard reference in that field. He also was credited with inventing more than 200 board, card, and dice games.

Schacht, Hjalmar [shahkt, yahl'-mahr]   The German financier Hjalmar Horace Greeley Schacht, b. Jan. 22, 1877, d. June 4, 1970, helped halt the dangerous inflation of 1922–23 under the Weimar Republic and later served in Hitler's government. Appointed special currency commissioner in 1923, Schacht introduced stringent monetary reforms and a stable currency. From 1923 to 1930 he was president of the Reichsbank, Germany's leading financial institution.

After Hitler came to power in 1933, Schacht served in the National Socialist (Nazi) government as Reichsbank president (1933–39), minister of economics (1934–37), and minister without portfolio (until 1943). He curbed unemployment, largely through rearmament expenditures, but his rivalry with Hermann GOERING led him to resign as economics minister. Schacht was dismissed from the Reichsbank presidency for opposing Hitler's massive rearmament program as inflationary. His growing disenchantment with Nazi foreign policy and his alleged involvement in a plot to assassinate Hitler led to his internment (1944). Acquitted (1946) at the Nuremberg Trials, Schacht later continued his career in banking and finance.

Schaff, Philip [shahf]   The theologian and church historian Philip Schaff, b. Switzerland, Jan. 1, 1819, d. New York City, Oct. 20, 1893, was an early proponent of ecumenism. As professor at the theological seminary of the German Reformed church, Mercersburg, Pa., he and his colleague John W. Nevin (1803–86) developed the "Mercersburg Theology," which stressed the importance of historical development, liturgical enrichment, and the oneness of the Christian church. Schaff was the author of the seven-volume *History of the Christian Church* (1858–92) and other influential works.

Scharnhorst, Gerhard Johann David von [sharn'-hohrst]   A German military reformer, Gerhard Johann David von Scharnhorst, b. Nov. 12, 1755, d. June 28, 1813, directed the reorganization of the Prussian army during the NAPOLEONIC WARS. Moving to the Prussian war college in 1801, he was such an inspiration to young officers that he was ennobled in 1804. After the defeat of the Prussian army by the French at Jena in 1806, Scharnhorst set about rebuilding the army. As chairman of the Military Reorganization Commission, he worked with Freiherr vom und zum STEIN, Graf Neithardt von GNEISENAU, and Hermann von Boyen to convert an army of mercenaries into a force based on universal service. Brutal punishment in the ranks was abolished, and officers'

commissions were opened up to nonnobles. Education was stressed in written examinations for officers, and a new war college was founded. Although it was his idea, universal conscription was formally introduced only in 1814, too late for Scharnhorst to see it. As Gebhard von Blücher's chief of staff in 1813, he was wounded at Grossgörschen and died in Prague.

Schechner, Richard [shek'-nur]   A theatrical director, writer, educator, and leading theorist of environmental theater, Richard Schechner, b. Newark, N.J., Aug. 23, 1934, founded New York's Performance Group in 1967. In addition to producing *Dionysus in '69* (1968), *The Tooth of Crime* (1972), and *Cops* (1978), he has written several works on dramatic theory, including *Essays on Performance Theory*, 2d ed. (1988).

Schechter, Solomon [shek'-tur]   A Jewish scholar, theologian, and Talmudist, Solomon Schechter, b. Romania, Dec. 7, 1847, d. Nov. 19, 1915, was a spokesman for Conservative Judaism in the United States. In 1896, while teaching at Cambridge University, England, he discovered a Genizah (archive) in the Cairo synagogue that contained more than 100,000 manuscripts, one of which he identified as an original fragment of the Book of Wisdom. From 1902 until his death, Schechter served as president of the Jewish Theological Seminary of America. In 1913 he founded the United Synagogue of America.

Scheele, Carl Wilhelm [shay'-le]   The Swedish apothecary and chemist Carl Wilhelm Scheele, b. Dec. 9, 1742, d. May 21, 1786, discovered oxygen, chlorine, manganese, and many other chemical substances. He was a prolific and careful experimentalist, although long delays in the publication of his results greatly diminished his impact on the chemistry of his day. Scheele was the first to identify calcium phosphate as a component of bone and to show that lactic acid was the cause of milk's turning sour. In working with minerals Scheele obtained chlorine, manganese, and baryta from native manganese dioxide, and hydrofluoric acid and silicon fluoride from fluorspar. He also prepared molybdic acid, tungstic acid, arsenic acid, arsine, and copper arsenite (Scheele's green) and showed that graphite was related to charcoal but not, as was then thought, to black molybdenite.

From plant and animal sources Scheele obtained and purified a number of organic acids as well as glycerol, acetaldehyde, and a number of esters. He prepared and investigated hydrogen sulfide. His discovery and investigation of the deadly gas hydrogen cyanide is particularly noteworthy—he survived to describe the odor, the taste, and the sensation of warmth it imparted to his mouth, although he gave no indication of its poisonous character.

Scheherazade [shuh-hair-uh-zahd']   In Arabian folklore, Scheherazade is the narrator of the famous tales from the ARABIAN NIGHTS. She is one of the wives of Sultan Schahriah and must die at dawn like her predecessors, but the tales she relates on 1,001 successive nights so interest her husband that he repeatedly postpones, and finally revokes, the edict condemning her.

Scheidemann, Philipp

Scheidemann, Philipp [shyd'-e-mahn] Philipp Scheidemann, b. July 26, 1865, d. Nov. 29, 1939, was a German socialist leader. A printer turned journalist, he was elected to the German parliament, the Reichstag, in 1903. In 1918 he joined the cabinet of Prince Max of Baden, the last imperial chancellor, on the eve of Germany's collapse at the end of World War I. On Nov. 9, 1918, following the abdication of Emperor William II, Scheidemann proclaimed from the Reichstag building the establishment of what came to be known, from the city where its constitution was drafted, as the WEIMAR REPUBLIC. In 1919 he served under President Friedrich Ebert as its first chancellor, or prime minister. He resigned in protest over the terms of the Versailles Peace Treaty. After Adolf Hitler came to power in 1933, Scheidemann emigrated.

Scheler, Max

Scheler, Max [shay'-lur]   Max Scheler, b. Aug. 22, 1874, d. May 19, 1928, was a German philosopher and one of the first proponents of phenomenological methods in philosophy (see PHENOMENOLOGY). He formally professed Roman Catholicism, although he later adopted pantheistic views. Like Blaise PASCAL, whose theory of value Scheler attempted to elaborate in a formal system, he had at most an uneasy relationship with Catholicism. Nevertheless, his theory of ethical value is profoundly religious because he understood the conflict within the human individual between the ideal and the real as a reflection of a tension within the very depths of God's nature, in which there are both divine and demonic energies.

Schelling, Friedrich Wilhelm Joseph von

Schelling, Friedrich Wilhelm Joseph von [shel'-ing]   Friedrich Wilhelm Joseph von Schelling, b. Jan. 27, 1775, d. Aug. 20, 1854, wrote on a wide range of topics, from aesthetics to philosophy of religion, from epistemology to political theory. He studied at Tübingen and taught at several universities, including Berlin, Munich, and Würzburg. Among the many intellectual leaders of his time with whom he was acquainted were Fichte, Hegel, Goethe, and Schiller. Although he differed with these idealist and romantic philosophers in several important ways, he was nonetheless a leader among those who shared these perspectives. Schelling's work underwent several phases and is thus not easy to summarize. His central purpose, however, was always the same: to understand and describe the relation between the finite realm of the human and the infinite realm of the Absolute.

For Schelling, nature is a purposive system in which the Absolute immediately objectifies itself in its infinite creative activity. The Absolute also realizes itself in the aesthetic process, but in a conscious manner rather than unconsciously, as in nature. Because of the creative process itself, it is only in art that absolute intelligence fully realizes itself. History is the drama of human progress in freedom in which the Absolute continuously reveals itself; in the state the rule of law and right reflects the Absolute and a universal moral order.

Schenck v. United States

Schenck v. United States [shenk]   In the case of *Schenck* v. *United States* (1919) the U.S. Supreme Court enunciated the "clear and present danger" rule as a means for testing the validity of government interference with FREEDOM OF SPEECH. Charles T. Schenck, secretary of the Socialist party, had been convicted under the Espionage Act of 1917 for urging drafted men to oppose conscription and the war itself. Justice Oliver Wendell Holmes, Jr., speaking for the Court, upheld Schenck's conviction while admitting that "in ordinary times" Schenck's activities might have been within his constitutional rights.

Holmes maintained that "the character of every act depends upon the circumstances in which it is done." The 1ST AMENDMENT, Holmes continued, "does not protect a man in falsely shouting fire in a theater and causing a panic. The question in every case is whether words used are of such a nature as to create a clear and present danger that they will bring about the substantive evils that Congress has a right to prevent." The rule has been inconsistently applied and has had critics both on and off the Court.

Schenectady

Schenectady [skuh-nek'-tuh-dee]   Schenectady is an industrial city in eastern New York on the Mohawk River, about 10 km (6 mi) northwest of Albany. The seat of Schenectady County, it has a population of 65,566 (1990). The economy is dominated by the General Electric Company, established in Schenectady in 1892. Other manufactures include sporting goods, wire products, and chemicals. The city's Dutch and English heritage is still evident in its many old houses and buildings. Union College (1795) is located there.

Dutch settlers led by Arent Van Curler founded Schenectady in 1662, and the English seized it in 1664. After the construction of Queen's Fort in 1705, Schenectady began to grow, prospering as a river port. The arrival of the railroad in the 1830s spurred industrial development. In 1886, Thomas A. Edison moved his electric machine works there.

scherzo

scherzo [skert'-soh]   A quick piece in triple time, found most often as the third movement in many 19th- and 20th-century symphonies, sonatas, and chamber works, the scherzo (Italian, "jest") was adopted (1790s) by Ludwig van Beethoven to replace the MINUET. Light or fanciful vocal and instrumental pieces called "scherzi," not antecedents of the classical scherzos, were produced by baroque composers, including Claudio Monteverdi (*Scherzi musicali*, 1607).

Schiaparelli, Elsa

Schiaparelli, Elsa   see FASHION DESIGN

Schick test   see DIPHTHERIA

Schiele, Egon [shee'-le]   Austrian expressionist artist Egon Leo Adolf Schiele, b. June 12, 1890, d. Oct. 31, 1918, was at odds with art critics and society for most of his brief life. Even more than Gustav Klimt, Schiele made eroticism one of his major themes and was briefly imprisoned for obscenity in 1912. At first strongly influenced by Klimt, whom he met in 1907, Schiele soon achieved an independent anticlassical style wherein his jagged lines arose more from psychological and spiritual feeling than from aesthetic considerations. He painted a number of outstanding portraits, such as that of his father-in-law, *Johann Harms* (1916; Solomon R. Guggenheim Museum, New York City), and a series of unflinching and disquieting self-portraits. Late works such as *The Family* (1918; Oesterreichische Galerie, Vienna) reveal a newfound sense of security. Schiele had begun to achieve some degree of stability and success when he died in an influenza epidemic.

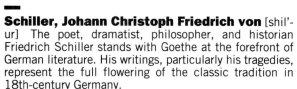

Portrait of Frederike Beer *(1914), by the Austrian expressionist Egon Schiele, is typical of his sensitive, vibrantly colorful, and often erotic style. His awkwardly posed figures, plagued with anxieties, convey a sense of the artist's troubled state of mind. (Private collection, New York City.)*

Schiller, Johann Christoph Friedrich von [shil'-ur]   The poet, dramatist, philosopher, and historian Friedrich Schiller stands with Goethe at the forefront of German literature. His writings, particularly his tragedies, represent the full flowering of the classic tradition in 18th-century Germany.

Born in Marbach on Nov. 10, 1759, the son of an officer in the army of the Duke of Württemberg, Schiller grew up in the service of the duke. Although he wished to study theology, he was forced instead to attend (1773–80) the duke's military academy. His first play, the vio-

The German dramatist, poet, and philosopher Friedrich Schiller wrote popular plays based on historical subjects to convey the liberal ideology sweeping through Europe during the late 18th century. Schiller's influence extends beyond the theater; he is also highly regarded for his philosophical treatises on art.

lent and frenzied *The Brigands* (Eng. trans., 1792), written while he was still at school and printed (1781) in Stuttgart, where Schiller was by then serving as a regimental officer, so angered the duke that Schiller decided to flee Württemberg for Mannheim. A second tragedy, *Fiesco* (1783), soon followed. The financial success of his third effort, the antidespotic domestic tragedy *Cabal and Love* (1784; Eng. trans., 1795), led to Schiller's temporary appointment as house dramatist at the Mannheim theater.

In 1785, Schiller was rescued from financial difficulties and a hopeless love affair by friends who maintained him in Leipzig and Dresden, where he completed the bulk of *Don Carlos* (1787; Eng. trans., 1798). Thereafter Schiller made Weimar his home, except for a few years spent at neighboring Jena.

Believing that his creative powers had deserted him, Schiller turned to writing history, producing *Geschichte des Abfalls der vereinigten Niederlande von der Spanischen Regierung* (History of the Secession of the United Netherlands from Spanish Sovereignty, 1788) and *Geschichte des dreissig-jährigen Kriegs* (History of the Thirty Years' War, 1791–93). Again with the support of friends he was able to pursue an interest in philosophy. The theories of Immanuel Kant, in particular, had an enormous effect on Schiller's thought, expressed in the essays *Über Anmut und Würde* (On Grace and Dignity, 1793) and *Über die ästhetische Erziehung des Menschen* (On the Aesthetic Education of Mankind, 1795). Profound idealism is also expressed in much of the poetry Schiller wrote at this time, notably in *The Division of the Earth* (1796; Eng. trans., 1821) and *Die Worte des Glaubens* (Words of Faith, 1798).

Schiller's lasting friendship with Goethe began in 1794 and led to the publication (1795–97) of the journal *Die Horen* (The Hours). A second collaboration, *Xenien*, consisting of satirical epigrams, was published in *Musenalmanach* (Almanac of the Muses, 1797–98). Many of Schiller's powerful dramatic ballads were also produced during this period, among them *Der Taucher* (The Diver, 1797), *Der Ring des Polykrates* (Polycrates' Ring, 1797),

Die Kraniche des Ibykus (The Cranes of Ibycus, 1797), and the celebrated *The Song of the Bell* (1799; Eng. trans., 1839).

Schiller's noted verse trilogy about the Thirty Years' War, *Wallenstein* (Eng. trans., 1954), was first produced at Weimar in 1799, although he had begun writing it 10 years earlier. During the last 5 years of his life, he produced four of his finest dramas: *Maria Stuart* (1800; Eng. trans., 1866), *The Maiden of Orleans* (1801; Eng. trans., 1962), *The Bride of Messina* (1803; Eng. trans., 1962), and *William Tell* (1804; Eng. trans., 1825). Schiller was at work on a fifth tragedy, *Demetrius* (Eng. trans., 1962), about Dmitri and Boris Godunov, when he died on May 9, 1805.

schipperke [skip'-ur-kee]   A Belgian breed of dog in the spitz family, the schipperke is small and solid black and weighs up to 8.1 kg (18 lb). It has a foxy head and an abundant coat forming a ruff around the neck. The breed was developed originally as an all-purpose watch and vermin dog on the boats and barges of its native land. Its popularity rose after 1885 when Queen Marie Henrietta, wife of Leopold II, acquired one. Schipperkes were introduced first into England and then into the United States. The Schipperke Club of America was founded in 1929.

Schippers, Thomas [ship'-urz]   Thomas Schippers, b. Mar. 9, 1930, d. Dec. 16, 1977, was a gifted American conductor who specialized in new (but not avant-garde) music. He attained prominence by the time he was 20 years of age, conducting the world premiere of Gian Carlo Menotti's opera *The Consul* in 1950 and the television premiere of Menotti's *Amahl and the Night Visitors* in 1951. In 1955, Schippers became the youngest conductor to lead the New York Philharmonic and the Metropolitan Opera. He was associated (1958–76) with Menotti's Spoleto Festival and made guest appearances with major symphonic and opera orchestras throughout the world. He was named music director of the Cincinnati Symphony in 1970, becoming the orchestra's conductor laureate in 1977, shortly before his death from cancer.

Schirra, Walter M., Jr. [shir-ah']   The astronaut Walter Marty Schirra, Jr., b. Hackensack, N.J., Mar. 12, 1923, was the third American to orbit the Earth and the only astronaut to fly all three U.S. manned spacecraft (see MERCURY, GEMINI, and APOLLO programs). Schirra graduated from the U.S. Naval Academy in 1945 and received (1946–48) flight training. On exchange to the U.S. Air Force, he flew 90 combat missions over Korea and was awarded the Distinguished Flying Cross. In 1959, he was selected as one of the original seven astronauts.

Schirra's last flight in space (Oct. 11–22, 1968) placed him in command of *Apollo 7*, the first manned test flight of the Apollo command service module. The flight (which Schirra flew with Walter Cunningham and Donn F. Eisele) validated design changes made following the *Apollo 204* (*Apollo 1*) fire that had killed three astronauts in 1967.

Schism, Great [siz'-uhm or skiz'-uhm]   The term *Great Schism* is used to refer to two major events in the history of Christianity: the division between the Eastern (Orthodox) and Western (Roman) churches, and the period (1378–1417) during which the Western church had first two, and later three, lines of popes.

Eastern Schism. The schism between the Eastern and Western churches is traditionally dated to 1054, although the precise point at which the split became a fixed and lasting reality is difficult to determine. Many causes contributed to the growing misunderstanding and alienation between the two groups. Partly these were differences of philosophical understanding, liturgical usage, language, and custom, but political rivalries and divisions were also involved. Occasions of friction, hostility, and open division on doctrinal questions as well as on matters of discipline and daily practice had occurred long before 1054—for example, the Photian schism of the 9th century (see PHOTIUS).

In the West the Latin church and especially the papacy took on many activities and powers in default of other authority, but this action was often regarded as usurpation by the East, where a different relationship existed between emperor and church. The heated disputes over such matters as the ecclesiastical calendar, the use of leavened or unleavened bread, or additions to the CREED (notably the *filioque* clause) reached a climax in 1054, when Pope LEO IX and Patriarch MICHAEL CERULARIUS excommunicated each other. Technically, only a few people were affected by this action, but the tone had been set and the direction fixed.

Later attempts to reunite the churches foundered on local feeling, and mutual hatred grew through selfish acts on both sides during some parts of the Crusades; the low point was the sacking of Constantinople in 1204 during the Fourth Crusade. The schism continues to the present.

Western Schism. The Western Schism began in the events after the death of Pope GREGORY XI in March 1378. The people of Rome were determined not to allow the papacy—which had been absent at Avignon for 70 years and dominated by French influence—to leave Rome upon the election of the new pope. The result was a loud and controversial conclave with cries for a Roman or at least an Italian pope. The man chosen, URBAN VI, was not a cardinal, but he had served in the curia.

Soon the cardinals realized the mistake that they had made in electing Urban. He disdained the advice of others, could be ruthless if opposed or questioned, and was committed to reform through an extreme reduction of the powers of the cardinals, who for decades had been almost corulers with the popes in Avignon. The result of this clash was tragedy for the church.

Led by the French, the majority of cardinals gradually withdrew from the papal court. They met at Anagni and declared Urban's election null and void because, they alleged, their votes had been made under pressure and fear for their lives. They then elected one of their own as Pope CLEMENT VII. For the next three decades the church was divided along national, political, and religious lines between the papal claimants—the Roman line of Urban VI, Boniface IX, Innocent VII, and Gregory XII, and the Avignon line of Clement VII and BENEDICT XIII—until, after various proposals and repeated failures, the cardinals from both obediences abandoned their claimants out of despair of getting any cooperation from them toward unity.

The Conciliar Epoch, which led eventually to the healing of the schism, began in 1409 when the cardinals called the Council of Pisa (see PISA, COUNCIL OF). The council deposed both Gregory XII and Benedict XIII and then elected a third claimant, Alexander V (to be succeeded shortly afterward by the medieval JOHN XXIII). The Pisan claimants received the support of most of Latin Christendom, but the schism continued until the Council of Constance (1414–18) removed all three claimants and elected the one pope accepted by just about all—MARTIN V—on Nov. 11, 1417. At the Council of Basel (1431–49; see BASEL, COUNCIL OF) another schism occurred with the election of "Antipope" Felix V. He abdicated, however, in 1449.

schist [shist]   Schist is a type of dark, sparkling METAMORPHIC ROCK in which mica minerals, such as muscovite, biotite, and chlorite, or prismatic crystals, such as amphibole, are oriented parallel to a secondary platy or laminated structure termed the schistosity. The rock breaks easily into thin layers parallel to the schistosity. Mineral grains in many schists are large enough to be recognized in hand specimens. The mineral assemblages and textures depend on the temperature and pressure of recrystallization; with increasing metamorphism, grain size usually increases.

schistosomiasis [shis'-tuh-soh-my'-uh-sis]   Schistosomiasis, also known as bilharziasis and as snail fever, is a chronic infection of internal organs. It is caused by parasitic flatworms of the genus *Schistosoma*, which are

indigenous to Asia, Africa, the Caribbean regions, and South America. Humans become infected via freshwater lakes and streams infested by cercariae, a larval form of the parasite that inhabits snails (see PARASITIC DISEASES).

Cercariae penetrate human skin and migrate to the liver, where they develop into adult worms. The worms mate, and their eggs are carried by the bloodstream to other organs. Tissue damage in the liver and other organs is caused by an inflammatory reaction. Symptoms may include a lesion at the site of penetration of the cercariae, fever, and dermatitis. *S. haematobium* is a species that causes damage primarily to the urogenital tract; *S. mansoni* and *S. japonicum* usually infect the intestines. The disease may result in diarrhea, cystitis, hypertension, or cirrhosis. Control of the disease includes sanitary measures and extermination of the host snails; infected persons are treated with oral ANTHELMINTIC DRUGS.

schizophrenia [skit-suh-free'-nee-uh]   Schizophrenia is the most common of the PSYCHOSES. About 1% to 2% of people in Western countries are treated for schizophrenia at some time, and many other schizophrenics never receive clinical attention. About half the inpatients in U.S. mental hospitals are schizophrenics. The syndrome was first described as a single disorder by German psychiatrist Emil KRAEPELIN in 1896. He called it "dementia praecox," "dementia" referring to intellectual deterioration and "praecox" to the fact that the symptoms first occur in early adulthood. Swiss psychiatrist Eugen Bleuler renamed the disorder "schizophrenia" to express his view that a prominent feature of the disorder is a splitting of psychic functions. Ideas and feelings are isolated from one another; a patient may speak incoherently, for example, or express frightening or sad ideas in a happy manner. Contrary to some popular accounts, however, schizophrenics do not have a "split personality" in the sense of MULTIPLE PERSONALITIES on different occasions.

Sufferers from schizophrenia, a psychosis dominated by private fantasies, frequently experience bizarre and tormenting hallucinations. In these paintings, Louis Wain, who was undergoing treatment for schizophrenia, tried to express his distorted perceptions.

Symptoms. The symptoms of schizophrenia include delusions, HALLUCINATIONS, thought disorders, loss of boundaries between self and nonself, blunted or inappropriate emotional expressions, socially inappropriate behavior, loss of social interests, and deterioration in areas of functioning such as social relations, work, and self-care. The symptoms fluctuate in occurrence and in severity.

Delusions are false beliefs, usually absurd and bizarre. Thus a patient may believe that he or she is an important historical personality, or is being persecuted by others, or has died, or that a machine controls his or her thoughts.

Hallucinations are false sensory experiences. Most schizophrenic hallucinations are auditory, but some are visual or olfactory. The content is often grandiose, hypochondriacal, or religious. Some hallucinatory voices speak of matters related to the patient's emotional problems or delusional concerns; others transmit apparently irrelevant messages.

Schizophrenic thought disorder may include a general lowering of intellectual efficiency, a free-associative rambling from one topic to another, a loss of the distinction between figurative and literal usages of words, reduced ability to think abstractly, invention of new words (called neologisms), and idiosyncratic misuse of common words.

Occurrence. Schizophrenia occurs in all industrialized countries and apparently in all other societies as well. All social classes are affected, but in large cities schizophrenia is three or four times as frequent in the lower socioeconomic classes as in the middle and upper classes. This difference is due in part to the downward social mobility of persons developing the disorder. Schizophrenia occurs equally often in men and women, although at an earlier age in men. The onset of schizophrenia is usually in late adolescence or early adulthood.

Possible Explanations. Biological interpretations of schizophrenia have dominated in recent decades. Schizophrenic episodes have been shown to correlate with increased levels of the NEUROTRANSMITTER dopamine in the body, especially in the left hemisphere of the brain. Altered glucose metabolism in the brain's frontal lobes has also been observed. In addition, morphological brain abnormalities such as notably enlarged ventricles are found in some patients, especially among those who tend to chronicity. Some investigators suspect that a slow-acting virus is responsible, and in some cases other investigators suspect traumatic brain damage, as from birth injuries.

A genetic factor also appears to be involved, in that schizophrenia tends to run in families. The incidence of schizophrenia is about 12% in the offspring when one parent is schizophrenic, about 50% when both parents are schizophrenic, about 10% in brothers or sisters of a schizophrenic, and about 50% in identical twins of schizophrenics. Adoption studies show that these concordance rates are largely accounted for by genes rather than by environment. Nevertheless, genes cannot be the sole cause of the disorder, since the concordance rate for identical twins is not 100%. Most researchers hold to a diathesis-stress theory: that both a biological predisposition and environmental factors interact to determine who becomes schizophrenic.

Varieties. The subtypes of schizophrenia include paranoid schizophrenia, in which delusions are prominent; catatonic schizophrenia, characterized by silent immobility for weeks or months (usually followed by a frenzy of agitation); and hebephrenic (disorganized) schizophrenia, characterized by intellectual disorganization, chaotic language, silliness, and absurd ideas that often concern deterioration of the patient's body. In practice, most patients do not fit neatly into discrete categories but instead have some symptoms consistent with each.

Treatment. For many years PSYCHOTHERAPY was the preferred mode of treatment of schizophrenia, and it continues to be used. Electroconvulsive treatment, or SHOCK THERAPY, was introduced in 1937 and became the prevalent mode of treatment until the late 1950s; it is still used in some cases. Psychosurgery (lobotomy and lobectomy), however, which became common in the 1940s and 1950s, is now in disrepute. Since the late 1950s schizophrenia has been treated primarily with antipsychotic medications, most often of the phenothiazine, butyrophenone, and thioxanthene families of drugs. All of these drugs block the action of dopamine at its receptors in the brain. They do not cure the condition, but they reduce the symptoms. Up to 20% of the patients using drugs in high doses over long periods, however, develop motoric disorders that are known as tardive dyskinesia (TD).

Family therapy, in which family members learn to interact with the patient in a nonjudgmental, accepting manner, has been found helpful. Up to one-third of diagnosed schizophrenia sufferers substantially recover, especially patients who had a good social and sexual adjustment prior to the illness. Significant numbers improve even after years of severe illness, but some residual signs of the disorder almost invariably remain.

Schlegel, August Wilhelm von [shlay'-guhl]

August Wilhelm von Schlegel, b. Sept. 8, 1767, d. May 12, 1845, and his younger brother, Friedrich, were the leading theoreticians of German ROMANTICISM. As tutor to Madame de STAËL's children from 1804 on, August traveled widely, and at her home in Coppet, Switzerland, he made the acquaintance of leading European thinkers and writers, to whom he transmitted the ideas of German romanticism. These were publicly disseminated in two celebrated lecture series: *Vorlesungen über schöne Kunst und Literatur* (Lectures on the Fine Arts and Literature), given in Berlin in 1801, and the even more influential and grandiose survey of the evolution of drama in his *Lectures on Dramatic Art and Literature* (1809–11; Eng. trans., 1815), given in Vienna in 1808. His translations include works by Calderón, Petrarch, and Dante, and the *Bhagavad Gita* (1823); his versions of 17 Shakespearean plays, carried out in collaboration with Ludwig TIECK and others, are still in use in Germany today.

Schlegel, Friedrich von   Friedrich von Schlegel, b. Mar. 10, 1772, d. Jan. 12, 1829, ranks as one of the prime movers of German ROMANTICISM. With his elder brother, August Wilhelm von Schlegel, he founded the journal *Athenäum*, in which he published his philosophical and literary aphorisms and his *Dialogue on Poetry* (1800; Eng. trans., 1968). His only novel, *Lucinde* (1799; Eng. trans., 1971), notorious at the time for its championship of free love, is an early forerunner of the experimental novel. Other major works include *Geschichte der Poesie der Griechen und Römer* (History of the Poetry of the Greeks and Romans, 1798), *Über die Sprache und Weisheit der Indier* (On the Language and Wisdom of the Indians, 1808), *Lectures on History and Literature* (1815; Eng. trans., 1846), and *The Philosophy of History* (1829; Eng. trans., 1852).

Schleicher, Kurt von   [shly'-kur]   Kurt von Schleicher, b. Apr. 7, 1882, d. June 30, 1934, German general, defense minister (June 1932–January 1933), and chancellor (December 1932–January 1933), was a powerful political leader in the WEIMAR REPUBLIC's last years. His political influence increased after Field Marshal Paul von Hindenburg became president in 1925. As chancellor, Schleicher tried to control the Nazi (National Socialist) party by offering to form a coalition government, but Nazi leader Adolf Hitler, who succeeded him, refused. Schleicher was murdered during Hitler's "night of the long knives."

Schleiermacher, Friedrich   [shly'-ur-mah-kur]   The German thinker Friedrich Daniel Ernst Schleiermacher, b. Nov. 21, 1768, d. Feb. 12, 1834, was the most influential theologian of the 19th century and is considered by many to be the founder of modern Protestant theology. His parents had been influenced by PIETISM, and his early education was in institutions of the Moravians.

Schleiermacher's first major work, *Religion, Speeches to Its Cultured Despisers* (1799; Eng. trans., 1893), defended religion against its Enlightenment critics. He represented religion as the "sense and taste for the infinite" and considered it to consist primarily in feeling; belief and action are secondary. In his most important work, *The Christian Faith* (1821; Eng. trans. of 2d ed., 1928), Schleiermacher specified religious feeling as the "feeling of absolute dependence." He believed that this feeling is universal in human beings and that to acknowledge it takes the place of the traditional dubious proofs of God's existence. Correlated with the feeling of absolute dependence is a consciousness or intuition of God. Human blessedness, he taught, consists in the strengthening of the God-consciousness, and sin is the obscuring of this consciousness. Jesus Christ shared the humanity of all men but was unique in the strength and constancy of his God-consciousness.

Schleiermacher has been accused of making religion invulnerable at the expense of turning it into a purely subjective experience, but this criticism is contested on the grounds that it misinterprets the term *feeling*.

Schlemmer, Oskar   [shlem'-ur]   The German painter and sculptor Oskar Schlemmer, b. Sept. 4, 1888, d. Apr. 13, 1943, became known during the 1920s and '30s for his geometrical abstractions based on the human figure. Schlemmer encountered the avant-garde movements of the day without, however, adopting their styles. Although his sculptures sometimes approach total abstraction, he retained references to the human form. In attempting to strip the figure of personality, Schlemmer produced geometric, linear, classically serene mannequins that were often set within ambiguous spaces, as in his *Group of Fourteen in Imaginary Architecture* (1930; Wallraf-Richartz Museum, Cologne). While teaching at the BAUHAUS from 1921 to 1929, Schlemmer took up stage design and produced his magical, mechanical *Triadic Ballet* (1922), set to the music of Paul Hindemith.

Schlesinger, Arthur M.   [shles'-ing-ur]   Arthur Meier Schlesinger, b. Xenia, Ohio, Feb. 27, 1888, d. Oct. 30, 1965, American historian and Harvard University professor of American history (1924–54), was influential in turning attention to the role of ordinary people in history. His first book was *The Colonial Merchants and the American Revolution, 1763–1776* (1918). Schlesinger's greatest accomplishment was probably as coeditor of the 13-volume *History of American Life* (1927–48), which stresses social and urban history.

Schlesinger, Arthur M., Jr.   Arthur Meier Schlesinger, Jr., b. Columbus, Ohio, Oct. 15, 1917, is an American historian. A professor at the City University of New York since 1966, he previously served as professor at Harvard (1954–61) and special assistant to President John F. Kennedy (1961–64). His books include *The Age of Jackson* (1945) and *A Thousand Days* (1965), on Kennedy's presidency; both won Pulitzer Prizes. Schlesinger also wrote *The Age of Roosevelt* (3 vols., 1957–60), on Franklin D. Roosevelt, and *Robert Kennedy and His Times* (1978).

Schlesinger, John   The English filmmaker John Schlesinger, b. Feb. 26, 1926, originally became known as a director for the BBC's "Monitor" arts series and for his award-winning documentary *Terminus* (1961). He established his reputation in films with strongly indigenous English themes, such as *A Kind of Loving* (1962), *Billy Liar* (1963), and *Far from the Madding Crowd* (1967). His later films are more ambitious, stylish, and at times sensational. *Darling* (1965) and *Sunday, Bloody Sunday* (1971) are sophisticated explorations of the contemporary London scene. Schlesinger turned to American locales and themes in such films as *Midnight Cowboy* (1970; Academy Award, best picture), his most successful film to date; *The Day of the Locust* (1975); *Marathon Man* (1976); *The Falcon and the Snowman* (1984); and *Pacific Heights* (1990).

Schleswig-Holstein [shlayz'-vik-hohl'-shtyn]   Schleswig-Holstein is a German state occupying the southern half of the Jutland Peninsula. It is bounded by Denmark to the north, the Baltic Sea to the east, the North Sea to the west, the Elbe River to the south, and the state of Mecklenberg-Vorpommern to the southeast. Schleswig-Holstein encompasses 15,728 km² (6,073 mi²), including the North FRISIAN ISLANDS, and has a population of 2,578,500 (1989 est.). KIEL is its capital. On the west side of the isthmus are polders protected by dikes, and a smooth, low-lying coast; on the east is a steep, rocky coast, indented by fjords, and in the center is a poorly drained heathland. Leading industries are shipbuilding, machine construction, textiles, electrical engineering, and food processing. Agricultural products include livestock, grain, potatoes, and sugar beets. The marine-related industries are centered in LÜBECK, Kiel, and Flensburg. Schleswig-Holstein's population increased rapidly with the influx of refugees from eastern Germany after World War II, and it is now the most Protestant area in Germany.

Historically, Schleswig-Holstein extended further north, encompassing what is now the county of North

SCHLESWIG-HOLSTEIN, 1815-66

---- Boundary between Denmark and Germany established in 1920.

Schleswig (Nordslesvig) in Denmark. From the 12th century until 1864 the duchy of Schleswig was a hereditary fief of the kings of Denmark, whereas Holstein was part of the Holy Roman Empire. The Danish duchy of Schleswig and the German county of Holstein were united from 1386 to 1460. Despite frequent challenges by German nobles, both were ruled by the Danish crown from 1474. After 1815, Holstein joined the German Confederation. Disputes over the status of Schleswig and Holstein led to war between Germany and Denmark in 1848–50 and 1864. The Danes were driven from the area, and Denmark ceded its claims to the territory by the Peace of Vienna. The entire region was annexed by Prussia in 1866, following the Seven Weeks' War. A discontented Danish minority remained in northern Schleswig, however, and in 1920 a plebiscite gave that part of Schleswig back to Denmark.

Schley, Winfield Scott   see SAMPSON, WILLIAM T.

Schlieffen, Alfred, Graf von [shlee'-fen]   The German military officer Alfred, Graf von Schlieffen, b. Feb. 28, 1833, d. Jan. 14, 1913, was the author of the Schlieffen plan, Germany's strategic master plan at the beginning of WORLD WAR I. Son of a Prussian general, he served (1891–1906) under Emperor WILLIAM II as chief of the general staff, becoming a field marshal in 1911.

Schlieffen postulated an inevitable two-front war that Germany could win only by placing preponderant force on the right wing of the western front, which would sweep through Belgium and complete a swift, annihilating encirclement of the French army. With France conquered, the army would be transferred to the Russian front by railroad. As a professional soldier he considered himself a technician who was not concerned with the political implications of warfare.

When war broke out in 1914, Schlieffen's successor as chief of general staff, H. J. L., Graf von MOLTKE, modified—and weakened—the plan by building up the eastern front at the expense of the western. Most military historians, however, believe that there were inherent weaknesses in the plan that would have surfaced regardless of what Moltke did.

Schliemann, Heinrich [shlee'-mahn]   A brilliant pioneer in field archaeology, the German archaeologist Heinrich Schliemann, b. Jan. 8, 1822, d. Dec. 26, 1890, is best known for his excavations at ancient TROY and MYCENAE. His discoveries there were later to establish a historical background for the stories and legends told by Homer and Vergil that had fascinated Schliemann from childhood.

Schliemann was largely self-educated. Because his family was poor he had to leave school at the age of 14 to earn a living. He continued studying on his own, however, showing an exceptional ability to master foreign languages. Soon he began to exploit his remarkable aptitude for business dealings, which enabled him to

The prominent 19th-century German archaeologist Heinrich Schliemann was photographed at the Lion Gate during his excavations (1876–78) at Mycenae. Motivated by his interest in Homeric epics and Greek culture, Schliemann was a pioneer in field archaeology. His excavations at Mycenae and Troy marked the beginning of Greek prehistoric archaeology.

amass a large fortune early in life and to retire at the age of 41. From then on, he devoted himself to archaeology. He began to dig at Troy, his most famous excavation, in 1870, and later also made extraordinary discoveries at Mycenae, the legendary home of Agamemnon, leader of the Greeks in the Trojan War. Schliemann's work led to continuing investigations that are revealing in ever-widening horizons the wonders of preclassical Greece (6000–1000 BC). Before Schliemann, this civilization was not even known to have existed.

Schmidt, Helmut [shmit]   The West German politician Helmut Schmidt, b. Dec. 23, 1918, was chancellor of the Federal Republic of Germany from 1974 to 1982. After army service in World War II, he graduated (1949) from the University of Hamburg. A member of

Helmut Schmidt, fifth chancellor of the Federal Republic of Germany, was a centrist Social Democrat known for his pragmatic approach to domestic and foreign policy and his active support of détente between the USSR and the West.

the Social Democratic party (SPD) from 1946, Schmidt was elected (1953) to the Bundestag, the lower house of parliament, and served (1967–69) as SPD leader there. When the SPD formed a government in coalition with the smaller Free Democratic party in 1969, Schmidt became minister of defense (1969–72) and of finance (1972–74) under Chancellor Willy BRANDT. After succeeding Brandt as chancellor he led the coalition to victory, with a slender majority, in the 1976 elections and again in 1980. Schmidt was forced out of office in October 1982, when the Free Democrats, unhappy at his refusal to cut spending during an economic recession, switched their support to the opposition Christian Democrats.

Schmidt, Mike   Baseball player Michael Jack Schmidt, b. Dayton, Ohio, Sept. 27, 1949, considered by many the best all-round 3d baseman ever, played his entire career (1972–89) with the National League's Philadelphia Phillies. Schmidt's 548 career home runs placed him 7th on the all-time list, and his hitting prowess was matched in the field—he won 10 Gold Glove awards as the NL's best 3d baseman. He led his league in home runs 8 times, 2d only to Babe Ruth, and he hit 30 or more 13 times, exceeded only by Hank Aaron. Schmidt also won 3 Most Valuable Player awards (1980–81, 1986)—no one has ever won more.

Schmidt-Rottluff, Karl [shmit-roht'-luf]   A leading expressionist painter, Karl Schmidt-Rottluff, b. Karl Schmidt in Rottluff, Germany, Dec. 1, 1884, d. Aug. 9, 1976, used blocks of intense color to infuse landscapes and portraits with strong, sometimes violent emotions. With Erich Heckel and Ernst Ludwig Kirchner, Schmidt-Rottluff became (1905) a founding member of Die BRÜCKE, a German expressionist movement. In addition to his paintings, he executed many woodcuts that are notable for the strength of their technique.

Schmidt telescope   Rated the most important advance in optics in 200 years, the Schmidt telescope combines the best features of the refractor and reflector for photographic purposes. It was invented in 1930 by Bernhard Voldemar Schmidt (1879–1935), an Estonian optician at the Bergedorf Observatory, Hamburg. A conventional parabolic telescope mirror has too small a field of view owing to the rapid off-axis increase of a defect of image formation known as coma. A spherical mirror suffers from a focus defect called spherical ABERRATION, but image quality does not deteriorate off-axis. The Schmidt design takes advantage of this defect by incorporating a concave spherical mirror with a thin, transparent, locally corrected corrector plate at the center of curvature; the plate corrects for spherical aberration. Different parts of the mirror image different parts of the field on a concentric curved focal surface of half the radius of the main mirror. Fields several degrees in diameter may be

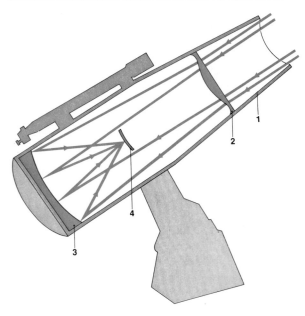

The Schmidt telescope is designed to photograph a wide view of the sky in a broad range of spectral wavelengths with a minimum of distortion. As the light rays (1) from celestial objects enter the device, they pass through a thin lens known as a correcting plate (2). A spherical mirror (3) then focuses the rays onto a photographic plate (4) mounted within the tube. The curvature of the correcting plate eliminates distortion produced by the curvature of the mirror.

photographed. Speeds for the recording of faint extended objects are very high, because the focal ratio is determined by corrector-plate diameter and main-mirror focal length.

Schmucker, Samuel Simon [shmuhk'-ur] The theologian and educator Samuel Simon Schmucker, b.

Hagerstown, Md., Feb. 28, 1799, d. July 26, 1873, was a leader in the 19th-century liberal movement of the American Lutheran church. Schmucker helped found the General Synod (1820), the Lutheran seminary at Gettysburg, Pa. (1826; now the Lutheran Theological Seminary), where he remained as professor for the next 38 years, and Gettysburg College (1832). He wrote liturgies and worship aids, interpretations of Luther's catechisms, and a theology for American Lutherans—*Elements of Popular Theology* (1834)—which was popular until the conservative Lutherans immigrating from Germany repudiated it. Schmucker advocated a single apostolic Protestant church, and he joined (1846) in organizing the World Evangelical Alliance.

Schnabel, Artur [shnah'-buhl] The extraordinary Austrian pianist Artur Schnabel, b. Apr. 17, 1882, d. Aug. 15, 1951, remains for many a peerless interpreter of the sonatas of Beethoven. A stipend from several wealthy patrons allowed him to study in Vienna with the eminent piano teacher Theodor Leschetizky and with the musicologist Eusebius Mandyczewski, through whom he became acquainted with Johannes Brahms. Schnabel early eschewed virtuosity and offered, even to unsophisticated audiences, programs of uncompromising musical integrity. He championed the neglected piano music of Franz Schubert and played complete cycles of the Beethoven sonatas, which he recorded (1931–35). Schnabel was also a composer, writing severe, posttonal music, which, however, he never performed publicly.

schnauzer [shnow'-zur] Schnauzers are three breeds of wiry-coated German dogs—the giant schnauzer, stan-

The standard schnauzer (center), the oldest of the three schnauzer breeds, was probably developed as a general-purpose working dog. The giant schnauzer (left) was developed by crossing standards with various herding dogs and, later, with Great Danes. It was first used to herd cattle, then to guard stockyards and breweries in Bavaria. The miniature schnauzer (right), the newest of the three, was developed from small standards probably crossed with affenpinschers.

dard schnauzer, and miniature schnauzer. In the United States the giant and standard schnauzers are classified as working dogs, the miniature as a terrier. The three breeds are similar in appearance, having a whiskered face, distinctive eyebrows, cropped ears, and a docked tail. The standard schnauzer is the oldest of the three breeds, possibly originating from poodle, spitz, and wirehaired pinscher stock. It stands from 43 to 51 cm (17 to 20 in) high at the shoulder. The miniature schnauzer, believed derived from small standard schnauzers by crosses with affenpinschers, stands between 30.5 and 35.5 cm (12 and 14 in) high at the shoulder. The giant schnauzer, originally used as a cattle drover, was developed from the standard schnauzer by crosses probably with various roughhaired sheepdogs, the Great Dane, and possibly the Bouvier des Flandres. It reaches about 70 cm (27.5 in) high at the shoulder.

Schnitzler, Arthur [shnits'-lur]   The Austrian dramatist and novelist Arthur Schnitzler, b. May 15, 1862, d. Oct. 21, 1931, became world-renowned for his sophisticated and cynical studies of turn-of-the-century Viennese society. *Anatol* (1893; Eng. trans., 1911) is a series of dramatic scenes describing the erotic adventures of a wealthy playboy; *Playing with Love* (1896; Eng. trans., 1914) deals with a working-class girl abandoned by her upper-class lover; and *Merry-Go-Round* (1903; Eng. trans., 1953) is Schnitzler's classic portrayal of sex as the great leveler in a class society. A highly successful French film version, *La Ronde* (1950), perfectly captured the playwright's ironic view of the subject. One of his most brilliant stories, *None but the Brave* (1901; Eng. trans., 1926), uses the device of the interior monologue to describe the thoughts of a cowardly officer contemplating suicide.

The son of a prominent Viennese Jewish physician, Schnitzler became a doctor and practiced medicine during the early years of his career, but writing came to be his main preoccupation. In his novel *The Road to the Open* (1908; Eng. trans., 1923) and the play *Professor Bernhardi* (1912; Eng. trans., 1927) he grappled with anti-Semitism and other moral issues of the day. Schnitzler's stylistic innovations influenced many younger European writers.

Schoenberg, Arnold [shurn'-bairk]   One of the greatest musical innovators of the 20th century, Arnold Schoenberg, b. Vienna, Sept. 13, 1874, d. July 13, 1951, is famous as the formulator of the twelve-tone system of composition. He began learning the violin at the age of 9 and began composing—without formal instruction—about the same time. His first notable composition was the romantic tone poem for strings *Verklärte Nacht* (Transfigured Night, 1899); it has remained one of his most popular works.

Between 1900 and 1915, Schoenberg worked in both Vienna and Berlin, teaching, conducting a cabaret orchestra, and orchestrating operettas. On Feb. 19, 1909, he composed the first "atonal" music: a piano piece,

Opus 11, No. 1. During the same year he composed a song cycle, *Das Buch der hängenden Gärten* (Book of the Hanging Gardens); in composing this work he stated that he had "broken the bonds of a bygone aesthetic." His devoted disciples—Alban BERG, Anton von WEBERN, and others—accepted this innovation with enthusiasm. In 1921 he revealed a novel concept that would change the face of music: the "method of composition with twelve tones related only to one another." Schoenberg continued to use the twelve-tone system for the rest of his life. Perhaps his most widely acclaimed twelve-tone work is the opera *Moses and Aaron* (begun 1930).

In 1925, Schoenberg was appointed to the prestigious post of director of the master class of musical composition at the Prussian Academy of Arts in Berlin. His career was interrupted in 1933, however, when he was dismissed from this position because he was a Jew. He emigrated to the United States and taught at various universities and privately in Los Angeles for more than 10 years. During this time he composed, among other works, the Fourth String Quartet (1936); *Ode to Napoleon*, for speaker, piano, and strings (1942); the Piano Concerto (1942); the String Trio (1946); and *A Survivor from Warsaw*, for speaker, male chorus, and orchestra (1947).

See also: SERIAL MUSIC.

Schofield, John McAllister [skoh'-feeld]   A Union general in the U.S. Civil War, John McAllister Schofield, b. Gerry, N.Y., Sept. 29, 1831, d. Mar. 4, 1906, commanded the Department of the Missouri (May 1863–January 1864) and the Department of the Ohio (February 1864–March 1865). He led the army of the Ohio in Gen. William T. Sherman's Atlanta campaign in the spring and summer of 1864. In November 1864, Schofield's forces clashed with Gen. John B. Hood's troops in a bloody battle at Franklin, Tenn. Schofield subsequently served as secretary of war (1868–69), superintendent of West Point (1876–81), and commanding general of the army (1888–95).

scholarships, fellowships, and loans   Scholarships, fellowships, and loans are financial aids given to help academically able students further their education. A scholarship is a financial award given to students in private secondary schools and to undergraduates in private and public colleges in recognition of past or potential academic achievement; in many cases, the qualifications for a scholarship include financial need as well. A scholarship does not require repayment. Although most undergraduate scholarships are given to full-time students at 4-year colleges or universities, a considerable number go to students who attend business schools, technical and vocational schools, nursing schools, and 2-year colleges.

A fellowship is an award for graduate study that usually does not require reimbursement. A loan is an award at either the undergraduate or graduate level that is to be repaid by the recipient on completion of the course or education.

Financial aid is provided to students for many reasons.

One is to increase the accessibility and choice of post-secondary education to minorities, women, and lower socioeconomic groups. Thus, many student-aid programs require that the student and parent file financial information with either the College Scholarship Service (CSS), Princeton, N.J., or the American College Testing Program (ACT), Iowa City, Iowa.

Donors of financial aid to students are primarily federal and state governments and private groups, such as industry, labor unions, foundations, and associations. The money is distributed through Basic Educational Opportunity Grants (BEOG; now called the Pell Grant Program), National Direct Student Loans (NDSL), Supplemental Educational Opportunity Grants (SEOG), College Work-Study (CWS), and Guaranteed Student Loans (GSL). Guaranteed Student Loans, the most common form of financial assistance to students, are available for both undergraduate and graduate study. They are issued by commercial banks and state student-loan authorities at an interest rate considerably lower than prevailing market levels and guaranteed by the federal government. The loans must be repaid within a ten-year period beginning six months after the student's graduation. Since 1981, families with incomes over $30,000 have been required to demonstrate financial need. Because of the high rate of default in federal loan programs, procedures for enforcing repayment have been tightened. In 1985 the Internal Revenue Service began to withhold tax refunds from former students who had defaulted.

Other sources of student aid are the Veterans Administration, which awards monthly stipends to children of deceased or disabled career veterans, and the Social Security Administration of the Department of Health and Human Services. Children of deceased contributors to Social Security and children of recipients of Social Security Disability Insurance are eligible for educational benefits until they graduate from high school. Other federal programs aid children of retired and deceased railroad workers. American Indian college students also receive federal scholarship aid.

The best-known and largest undergraduate scholarship program in the private sector is that of the National Merit Scholarship Corporation in Evanston, Ill. The initial selection is based on academic skills as exhibited in nationwide examinations that are administered starting in the fall of the junior year of high school. The amount of the award is based on demonstrated need.

Religious groups have national and local student-aid programs for their members. Trade and professional associations may award scholarships, fellowships, or loans to members or individuals who will study and engage in a particular field of endeavor. Individual companies or unions may award student financial aid to residents of their service area. Schools themselves administer a wide array of student financial aids, including athletic scholarships (now coming under increasing scrutiny). Many private donors and some federal programs delegate administration of awards to educational institutions. Local service groups, clubs, community chests, banks, veterans groups, and foundations may also award student financial aid.

All institutions receiving support from the federal gov-

ernment for financial aid must make available to students on request information about the student financial-assistance programs available at the institution; the method of distributing financial aid; how application for student financial aid is made; the rights and responsibilities of students who receive financial aid under the federal programs; the cost of attending the institution; the refund policy of the institution; the academic program of the institution; and the name of the person responsible for assisting students in obtaining this information.

Scholastic Aptitude Test   see EDUCATIONAL MEASUREMENT AND TESTING

scholasticism   The term *scholasticism* (from the Latin *schola*, "school") refers properly both to the doctrine and method of teaching in the medieval European schools and to their successive revivals to the present day. As a method, scholasticism involves (1) the close, detailed reading (*lectio*) of a particular book recognized as a great or authoritative work of human or divine origin—for example, Aristotle in logic, Euclid in geometry, Cicero in rhetoric, Avicenna and Galen in medicine, the Bible in theology—and (2) the open discussion (*disputatio*) in strict logical form of a relevant question (*quaestio*) arising from the text. As a doctrine, scholasticism refers to the kind of philosophy, theology, medicine, and law (canon and civil) taught by the faculties responsible for these disciplines. The term *scholasticism* is, however, most commonly understood in the context of philosophy and theology.

The basic philosophy of the faculty of arts was Aristotelian because the greatest and most authoritative books in philosophy were believed to be ARISTOTLE's. Aristotle, however, was interpreted differently by different professors depending on the commentaries used, notably those of "the Commentator," AVERROËS; the Christian Neoplatonist, Saint AUGUSTINE; or the pagan Neoplatonist, AVICENNA.

Similarly in theology, the Bible was variously interpreted depending on the kind of philosophy used to understand the Christian faith systematically. Among the numerous ways of systematizing the faith, certain schools of theology stand out as particularly notable and viable throughout the Middle Ages and to the present day. The most important of these scholastic theologies were Thomism, developed from the teaching of Saint Thomas AQUINAS; Augustinism, developed from Saint Augustine; Scotism, from John DUNS SCOTUS; NOMINALISM, from WILLIAM OF OCCAM; and Suarazianism, formulated by Francisco SUÁREZ, a 16th-century Jesuit who tried to synthesize various schools. The basic principle underlying all forms of scholasticism was rational consistency with the Christian faith as taught in the Bible and as understood by the living Church of Rome through the writings of the ancient Greek and Latin Fathers (see PATRISTIC LITERATURE), the rulings of the ecumenical councils, the liturgy, and the continuing teaching and practice of the church.

Scholasticism is generally divided into three periods: medieval scholasticism, extending from BOETHIUS (5th–

6th century) to the 16th century, with its Golden Age in the 13th century; "second scholasticism," beginning in the 16th century with Thomas de Vio Cajetan, Conrad Koellin, Peter Crokert, Francesco de Vittoria, and Francisco Suárez; and neoscholasticism, beginning in the early 19th century, given impetus by the encyclical *Aeterni Patris* (1879) of Pope LEO XIII, and continuing at least until the Second Vatican Council (1962–65).

Medieval Scholasticism. Boethius is generally called "the first scholastic" because he provided the first Latin translations of Aristotle's logic and other basic works used in the schools of the early Middle Ages. In this early period, however, the dominant philosophical influence was Platonism or NEOPLATONISM, particularly as it was reflected in the work of Saint Augustine.

Augustine formulated the maxim "Understand so that you may believe, believe so that you may understand"— an approach that lay at the heart of scholasticism—and urged the use of dialectics in examining Christian doctrine. His principles were applied with rigor by such early scholastics as John Scotus ERIGENA, Saint ANSELM, Peter ABELARD, Alan of Lille, and numerous teachers in the cathedral schools of Laon, Chartres, Paris, Poitiers, and the abbey school of Saint-Victor in Paris.

In a stricter sense, scholasticism began with the *Sentences* (c.1150) of Peter Lombard, the *Decretum* (c.1150) of GRATIAN, and the flood of new Latin translations of classical philosophers, including all of Aristotle, made from Greek and Arabic throughout the second half of the 12th century. Assimilation of this new learning took place in the universities of the 13th century through the genius of the Dominicans Saint ALBERTUS MAGNUS and his great pupil Thomas Aquinas, whose *Summa Theologiae* is widely regarded as the pinnacle of scholastic theology; and of the Franciscans Saint BONAVENTURE, John Duns Scotus, and William of Occam (early 14th century), who challenged the Dominican school.

With the multiplication of universities between the 14th and 16th centuries came a decline in the standard of teaching; the term *scholasticism* then began to be used in a derogatory sense.

Second Scholasticism. The Protestant Reformation in the 16th century stimulated a revival of theology by a return to the language of the Bible, the Fathers of the Church, and the great scholastics of the 13th century. This second scholasticism was aided by the founding (1540) of the Society of Jesus (the JESUITS) by Saint IGNATIUS LOYOLA with the approval of Pope Paul III. Foremost among the Jesuit scholastics of this period were Saint Robert BELLARMINE, Francisco Suárez, and Gabriel Vazquez. Due largely to the scientific revolution of the 17th century (beginning with Galileo), the quest for philosophic originality (beginning with René Descartes), the rise of nationalism and colonization, and the splintering of Protestant religions, second scholasticism declined.

Neoscholasticism. Early in the 19th century in Italy certain Catholic professors of philosophy began to see in Aquinas's teaching basic principles that might resolve the philosophical problems then current. The charter of this neo-Thomism was Pope Leo XIII's *Aeterni Patris* (1879).

The rise of MODERNISM in the Roman Catholic church after 1900, however, resulted in a multiplicity of ecclesiastical condemnations, a legislated Thomism, and a failure to realize the hopes of Leo XIII. Among the great number of modern scholars who called themselves Thomists (but not neo-Thomists or neoscholastics) were Jacques MARITAIN, Étienne GILSON, Martin Grabmann, and Yves Congar.

■

Schollander, Don [shoh'-lan-dur]   Donald Arthur Schollander, b. Charlotte, N.C., Apr. 30, 1946, was the world's leading sprint swimmer in the early and mid-1960s. In 1961 he set a U.S. record for the 440-yd (402-m) freestyle, and in 1962 he tied the world mark for the 200-m (219-yd) freestyle. In the 1964 Tokyo Olympic Games Schollander became the first swimmer ever to win 4 gold medals. He set an Olympic record in the 100-m and a world record in the 400-m freestyle swims, recording times of 53.4 sec and 4 min 12.2 sec, respectively, and was on two first-place relay teams. Schollander was named both U.S. and World Athlete of the Year (1964). A graduate of Yale, he also won a gold and a silver medal at the 1968 Olympics.

Schönbrunn Palace   see FISCHER VON ERLACH, JOHANN BERNHARD

■

Schongauer, Martin [shohn'-gow-ur]   Known during his lifetime primarily as a painter, the German artist Martin Schongauer, b. c.1450, d. Feb. 2, 1491, is today most famous for 116 copper engravings. Beginning with an ornamental tradition of engraving based on goldsmiths' patterns, Schongauer, a goldsmith's son, enriched and transformed printmaking into a medium akin to painting.

Schongauer's great achievement in printmaking was the technical refinement of linear, black-and-white strokes to simulate the coloristic and textural effects of the painter's art. He mastered the use of the descriptive outline, which lends his prints a distinctly graphic simplicity and elegance. An early masterpiece, *Christ Carrying the Cross*, exemplifies his accomplishment. The complex narrative is spread out across the foreground of this engraving, one of the largest of the 15th century. Contrasts of light and shade help to organize the composition, even as the rich description individualizes faces, costumes, and textures in the populated scene. Such narrative fullness extended into Schongauer's engraved series of 4 scenes from the *Life of the Virgin* and a complete cycle of 12 scenes entitled *Christ's Passion* (c.1480). By enlarging the dimensions of prints, developing new graphic techniques of description, and providing complete narrative cycles of illustration, Schongauer almost singlehandedly turned engraving into a major art form, preparing the way for the accomplishments of Albrecht Dürer.

school board   see UNITED STATES, EDUCATION IN THE

School for Scandal, The   A comedy of manners by Richard Brinsley SHERIDAN, *The School for Scandal* (1777) is one of the most popular plays in the English language. Sir Peter Teazle has married a young woman with whom he always quarrels. In the famous "screen scene" he discovers that his nephew Joseph Surface, whom he has always admired, is a scheming hypocrite who is trying to seduce Lady Teazle, and that Charles Surface, his other nephew, whom he has rejected as a ne'er-do-well, is in fact honest and decent. Sir Peter thereupon becomes reconciled with his wife and allows his ward to marry Charles.

Schoolcraft, Henry Rowe   Henry Rowe Schoolcraft, b. Albany, N.Y., Mar. 28, 1793, d. Dec. 10, 1864, was the first American ethnologist to make extensive and scholarly observations about American Indian societies. After making surveys (1818–21) of land and resources in Missouri, northern Michigan, and the Upper Great Lakes, he served (1822–41) as Indian agent to the OJIBWA and married an Ojibwa woman through whom he learned the tribal language and culture. When Schoolcraft returned to the East, he continued to study and describe Indian languages, customs, and myths. He is best known for his 6-volume *Historical and Statistical Information Respecting the Indian Tribes of the United States* (1851–57).

schooner   A schooner is a two-masted sailing vessel, with the smaller mast closer to the bow. This type of vessel may be rigged with a large number of different types of sails and may be cutter-rigged (that is, it may carry two sails ahead of the foremast). The greatest asset of this rig design is the resultant speed when the wind blows across the boat hull and the sails are full. Schooners have been used as commercial sailing vessels, and the schooner *America* won the forerunner of the America's Cup Yacht Race. The schooner type of sailing rig, however, is rarely used today, because it requires a larger crew than is needed for other rig designs.

Schopenhauer, Arthur   [shoh'-pen-how-ur]   The German philosopher Arthur Schopenhauer, b. Feb. 22, 1788, d. Sept. 21, 1860, taught a pessimistic view of existence that placed emphasis on human will instead of intellect. *The World as Will and Representation*, his major work, appeared in 1818 (Eng. trans. of 3d ed., 1966). To Schopenhauer's bitter disappointment, this book did not make him famous, but it did enable the young philosopher to lecture at Berlin, where he set his lectures at the same hour as those of the thinker to whom he was most vehemently opposed, Georg Wilhelm Friedrich Hegel. The attempt to undermine Hegel failed, and from 1831 on Schopenhauer lived a solitary life, resentful at the world's failure to recognize his genius.

Although considering himself a follower of Immanuel KANT, Schopenhauer emphasized the will and its irratio-

Arthur Schopenhauer, a German philosopher, held that the world is governed by the strivings and conflicts of a universal will, whose irrational impulses cannot be understood by science. His thought influenced a generation of intellectuals and artists.

nality in a way Kant would have rejected. Kant had shown that the human mind organizes sensation into stable and coherent patterns, but he denied the possibility of going beyond these patterns to a knowledge of things as they really are. Schopenhauer agreed that individuals ordinarily conceive the world in this neat and stable fashion but held that it is possible to go beyond such pretty pictures to know the ultimate reality: the will. Humans are active creatures who find themselves compelled to love, hate, desire, and reject; the knowledge that this nature is so is irreducible. Although the will is entirely real, it is not free, nor does it have any ultimate purpose. Rather, it is all-consuming, pointless, and negative. There is also no escape from the will in nature; expressions of the will are seen throughout nature—in the struggles of animals, the stirring of a seed, the turning of a magnet.

The only purpose in life must be that of escaping the will and its painful strivings. The arts, with their "will-less perception," provide a temporary haven—especially music, the highest of the arts. The only final escape, however, is the "turning of the will against itself," a mysterious process that results in liberation, in sheer extinction of the will.

Schreiner, Olive   The South African novelist and social reformer Olive Schreiner, b. Mar. 24, 1855, d. Dec. 11, 1920, was the author of *The Story of an African Farm*, a semiautobiographical novel describing her childhood on the veld. Schreiner, the daughter of a Lutheran missionary, worked as a governess before going to England in 1881 to study medicine. The novel, which she completed before leaving South Africa, was published in England in 1883. Schreiner devoted her later career to writing on behalf of political and social causes. Her major work of social commentary is *Women and Labour* (1911), a landmark in the history of feminism.

Schreyer, Edward Richard   Edward Richard Schreyer, b. Beauséjour, Manitoba, Dec. 21, 1935, served as governor general of Canada from January 1979 to May

1984. A professor of political science and international relations at the University of Manitoba from 1962 to 1965, he served in the Manitoba (1958–65) and federal (1965–69) legislatures. In 1969 he returned to Manitoba to lead the socialist New Democratic party to victory in the provincial elections. Schreyer served (1969–77) two terms as premier of Manitoba. In 1984 he was appointed high commissioner to Australia.

Schrödinger, Erwin [shrur'-ding-ur] The Austrian theoretical physicist Erwin Schrödinger, b. Aug. 12, 1887, d. Jan. 4, 1961, published (1926) four papers that laid the foundation of the wave-mechanics approach to quantum theory and set forth his now-famous wave equation (see QUANTUM MECHANICS). Schrödinger earned a doctorate at the University of Vienna in 1910. He succeeded (1927) Max Planck in the chair of theoretical physics at the University of Berlin but left Germany in 1933 because of Nazi pressure—the same year he shared the Nobel Prize for physics with Paul DIRAC for his contributions to atomic theory. In 1939 he joined the newly formed Institute for Advanced Studies in Dublin. There he continued his studies of the application and statistical interpretation of wave mechanics, the mathematical character of the new statistics, and the relationship of this statistics to statistical thermodynamics. He also worked on problems of general relativity and cosmology and on a unified field theory.

Schubert, Franz [shoo'-bairt] One of the greatest composers of the 19th century, Franz Peter Schubert, b. Liechtenthal (then a suburb of Vienna), Jan. 31, 1797, is widely regarded as the world's finest songwriter. At the age of 11 he was admitted to the Vienna Court Choir and studied at its training school until 1813. He prepared to become an elementary school teacher but gave up this vocation after 2 years of employment (1814–16) to devote his life to music.

Schubert wrote 2 of his best songs, "Gretchen am Spinnrade" and "Erlkönig," nearly 200 other songs, 3

Franz Schubert, an early-19th-century Austrian composer, is celebrated for his lieder—songs for piano and voice. Although he wrote symphonies, chamber music, and operas, his gift for melodic expression shows best in his lieder, of which he wrote 634.

masses, 3 symphonies, and much piano and chamber music before his 19th birthday. From 1818 until his death, he lived in Vienna, except for two summers (1818 and 1824) spent as music teacher to Count Esterházy's family at Zelesz, Hungary. He died on Nov. 19, 1828, at the age of 31.

Schubert's gifts for expressive melody, novel harmony, and expressive changes of key are evident throughout all his works but are most clearly seen in his 634 songs (lieder). In them, he employed an equal partnership of piano and voice to portray the inner meaning of the text, setting a model for subsequent composers. Schubert's principal songs include settings of poems by Goethe, two song cycles—*Die schöne Müllerin* (Fair Maid of the Mill, 1823) and *Die Winterreise* (The Winter's Journey, 1827)—and his last 12 songs (1828), published after his death as *Schwanengesang* (Swan Song). His best-known piano works include the intimate *Moments musicaux* (1823–27) and *Impromptus* (1827); the "Wanderer" Fantasy (1822); the Fantasy in F Minor for piano duet (1828); and his last three piano sonatas.

Schubert's first six symphonies are modeled after those of Mozart and Haydn but contain many innovations. His eighth, or "Unfinished," symphony, consists of only two movements and a sketch for a third; remarkable for its harmonic boldness, it was not performed until 1863. The ninth, or "Great" C Major Symphony, dates from 1825. His chamber music includes 19 string quartets, the Octet (1828) for strings and wind instruments, the popular "Trout" Quintet (1819) for piano and strings, two piano trios, and the great C Major String Quintet of 1828. He also wrote several major works for violin and piano; six masses and other sacred and secular choral music; and several operas, which are rarely performed.

Schubert's influence was felt throughout the century. His large instrumental and choral works of 1828 were Bruckner's point of departure; his chamber music and piano compositions influenced not only Schumann but also Brahms and Dvořák.

Schulberg, Budd [shul'-burg] The American novelist and screenwriter Budd Wilson Schulberg, b. New York City, Mar. 27, 1914, is best known for his novel about the corrupting power of success, *What Makes Sammy Run?* (1941), based on his intimate knowledge of the Hollywood film industry, and for his fictional version of the life of his onetime studio colleague F. Scott Fitzgerald in *The Disenchanted* (1950). Schulberg's vision of Hollywood as a symbol of American rapacity has influenced all his work. His other writings include the novel *The Harder They Fall* (1947), based on the career of heavyweight boxing champion Primo Carnera; a book of short stories, *Some Faces in the Crowd* (1953); and the Academy Award–winning screenplay for *On the Waterfront* (1954).

Schuller, Gunther [shul'-ur] The American composer and conductor Gunther Schuller, b. New York City, Nov. 22, 1925, is well known for his subtle synthesis of classical forms and jazz—a style of composition he has called "Third Stream." He has held many important posts, including president (1967–77) of the New England Conservatory in Boston. Schuller's works include *Symphony for Brass and Percussion* (1950); *Seven Studies on Themes of Paul Klee* (1959), for orchestra; an opera, *The Visitation* (1966); and a children's opera, *The Fisherman and His Wife* (1970).

Schultz, Dutch The gangster Arthur Flegenheimer, known as "Dutch Schultz," b. Bronx, N.Y., Aug. 6, 1902, d. Oct. 24, 1935, ran bootlegging and other New York City rackets, thereby acquiring considerable wealth. Harassed by federal prosecutors, he lost control of his operations to other gangsters and was gunned down in a Newark, N.J., saloon.

Schulz, Bruno The Polish writer Bruno Schulz, b. July 12, 1892, d. Nov. 19, 1942, based his writings in Drohobycz, the small town where he had been born and lived. His novel, *The Street of Crocodiles* (1934; Eng. trans., 1963), is a portrayal of provincial Jewish life that resembles both the paranoid world of Franz Kafka (whose novel *The Trial* Schulz translated in 1936) and the blissful visions of the artist Marc Chagall. The collection of short stories *Sanatorium under the Sign of the Hourglass* (1937; Eng. trans., 1978) is Schulz's only other published work. Another novel was lost, and Schulz himself was killed by Nazi occupation troops in Drohobycz.

Schulz, Charles M. In 1950 cartoonist Charles Monroe Schulz, b. Minneapolis, Minn., Nov. 26, 1922, created "Peanuts," the most commercially successful comic strip of all time. Featuring children and animals who enact adult roles, the strip deals poignantly with human emotions and foibles. Loneliness is a frequently recurring theme, and wishy-washy Charlie Brown, the main character, reflects Schulz's assessment of himself. The widely syndicated strip has fostered a virtual industry of products, television specials, and books.

Schumacher, E. F. [shoo'-mah-kur] Ernst Friedrich Schumacher, b. Aug. 16, 1911, d. Sept. 4, 1977, was a German-born English economist whose ideas on small-scale technologies have had an important influence in developing countries and on environmental movements. After advising British authorities in occupied Germany, he served as economic advisor (1950–70) to Britain's National Coal Board. In his most influential work, *Small Is Beautiful: Economics as if People Mattered* (1973), Schumacher argues that developing countries can most profitably use small-scale production methods and shows how agricultural and industrial machinery can be built using limited technological and economic resources.

Schuman, Robert [shoo-mahn'] The French statesman Robert Schuman, b. June 29, 1886, d. Sept. 4, 1963, was one of the formulators of the Schuman Plan, the precursor of the EUROPEAN COMMUNITY, or Common Market. A founder and affiliate of the Catholic liberal party, Schuman was twice premier (1947, 1948) and frequently headed the foreign ministry. As premier he tried to strengthen the so-called Third Force, a coalition of center parties, against the Communist left and the Gaullist right. Although the European Coal and Steel Community was originally Jean MONNET's idea, Schuman pushed it through the French parliament in 1951, and his name came to be attached to it. By the Schuman Plan, the coal and steel industries of Germany, Italy, Belgium, Luxembourg, and the Netherlands became economically linked. Its success led in 1958 to the overall economic linkage of the Common Market.

Schuman, William [shoo'-muhn] As a composer, educator, and administrator, William Howard Schuman, b. New York City, Aug. 4, 1910, has been one of the leaders of American musical life. He taught (1937–45) at Sarah Lawrence College and served (1945–62) as president of the Juilliard School. From 1962 to 1969 he was president of Lincoln Center for the Performing Arts.

From 1936 to 1938 he studied composition with Roy Harris. While continuing to create extended lyrical melodies akin to those of Harris, Schuman developed his own (sometimes bitonal) style with a greater rhythmic vitality. His best-known work is *New England Triptych* (1956), three orchestral scenes based on melodies from colonial New England. His other works include 10 symphonies, concertos, string quartets, the ballet *Undertow* (1945), and the operas *The Mighty Casey* (1953) and *A Question of Taste* (1990).

Schumann, Clara [shoo'-mahn] Clara Josephine Schumann, b. Leipzig, Sept. 13, 1819, d. May 20, 1896, was a celebrated pianist and the wife of Robert Schumann. Trained by her father, Friedrich Wieck, who also taught Schumann, she made her debut in 1828 and toured several times before marrying (1840). She gave up touring until after Schumann's death (1856), when she began to concertize extensively on the continent and in England, as well as to teach. She also composed many piano works and edited her husband's compositions.

Schumann, Robert Robert Alexander Schumann, b. Zwickau, June 8, 1810, d. July 29, 1856, was a major German romantic composer and critic. His enthusiasm for literature was almost as great as his love of music, and his early attempts at poetry, prose, and drama lent a poetic sensibility to his compositions and his criticism.

Schumann studied law at Leipzig University and later at Heidelberg. His piano teacher was Friedrich Wieck,

Robert Schumann was one of the foremost German composers of the romantic era. In his songs, piano works, chamber music, and symphonies, he rendered literary ideas and visual scenes in expressive musical terms. Schumann was also an influential critic who helped launch the careers of Chopin and Brahms.

whose daughter Clara (a virtuoso pianist) he later married. In composition, however, Schumann was virtually self-taught, his formal instruction in theoretical subjects being limited to a few months of harmony lessons and a few weeks studying orchestration.

Schumann's published reviews first appeared in 1831, and in 1834 he founded the *Neue Leipziger Zeitschrift für Musik*, in whose pages he praised composers such as Schubert, Berlioz, Chopin, and Mendelssohn. All thoughts of a concert career were abandoned when he damaged one of the fingers of his right hand in a finger-stretching device. He lived at various times in Dresden, Düsseldorf, Leipzig, and Vienna but never found it easy to settle for any length of time despite a growing family—he had married Clara in 1840, and they had eight children. His unstable nature combined with a frenetic life and almost unceasing mental stress resulted in his admittance to a private asylum about two years before his death. He was frequently visited there by Brahms and occasionally by the violinist Joseph Joachim, musicians who did much to make his works known throughout Europe.

The range, variety, and number of Schumann's compositions are remarkable. Performances of his opera, *Genoveva* (1850), the incidental music to *Manfred* (1852), and the scenes from Goethe's *Faust* (1844–53) are rare, yet the four symphonies, the cello concerto and piano concerto, some chamber music, songs, and music for solo piano (especially *Carnaval, Fantasiestücke, Kinderscenen*, and the sonatas) are enduringly popular.

▬

Schumpeter, Joseph A. [shum'-puh-tur] Joseph Alois Schumpeter, b. Feb. 8, 1883, d. Jan. 8, 1950, was an Austrian-American economist who made his primary contributions to economics in the fields of growth, development, and the business cycle. His early classic, *The Theory of Economic Development* (1912; Eng. trans., 1934), set the stage for many of his later works.

Schumpeter argued that the main agents of economic growth are the entrepreneurs who introduce new products, new methods of production, and other innovations into an otherwise static economic process. Growth through innovation is the dominant characteristic of modern industrial society; it proceeds by way of "creative destruction" as the new and improved product or method of production drives out the old.

Educated in Vienna, Schumpeter briefly served (1919–20) as Austrian minister of finance. He joined the Harvard economics faculty in 1932. Schumpeter's theses on the long-term forces influencing industrial society began to be viewed with increasing interest after World War II, when renewed emphasis was placed on economic development.

▬

Schurz, Carl [shurts] Carl Schurz, b. near Cologne, Mar. 2, 1829, d. May 14, 1906, a German revolutionary in the 1840s, later won prominence in the United States as a diplomat, Union general, U.S. senator (1869–75), secretary of the interior (1877–81), editor, author, and orator. He was forced to flee his native land after the German Revolutions of 1848 were suppressed.

Immigrating to the United States in 1852, Schurz soon became widely known as an antislavery orator, Republican campaigner, and supporter of Abraham Lincoln. Serving briefly as American minister to Spain (1861–62), Schurz resigned to enter the Union army as a brigadier general. He saw action at the Second Battle of Bull Run, Chancellorsville, and Gettysburg and was promoted to major general.

In 1865, Schurz toured the South at President Andrew Johnson's request and concluded that blacks should be given the vote. He then served as a correspondent for the New York *Tribune* and an editor of newspapers in Detroit and St. Louis before being elected U.S. senator from Missouri in 1868. Although he had previously been an active supporter of Ulysses S. Grant, he broke with the president and helped found the LIBERAL REPUBLICAN PARTY in 1872.

Appointed secretary of the interior by President Rutherford B. Hayes, Schurz worked for Indian rights and conservation and instituted the merit system in his bureau. In his last years, Schurz headed civil-service reform movements and was an anti-imperialist opponent of the Spanish-American War.

▬

Schuschnigg, Kurt von [shoo'-shnik] Kurt von Schuschnigg, b. Dec. 14, 1897, d. Nov. 18, 1977, Austrian chancellor (1934–38), unsuccessfully resisted Adolf Hitler's demand for *Anschluss*, or union, with Germany. Minister of justice (1932–34) and of education (1933–34) before becoming chancellor, he was an authoritarian patriot who favored restoration of the Habsburg monarchy. Early in 1938 he defied Nazi Germany's accelerating demands for control of his country by calling for a plebiscite on Austrian independence. When the Germans delivered an ultimatum, he resigned on March 11 and was succeeded by the Austrian Nazi Arthur Seyss-Inquart. On March 12—before the plebiscite could be held—the Germans entered Austria. Schuschnigg was imprisoned until 1945.

Schütz, Heinrich [shuets]   Heinrich Schütz, b. Oct. 8, 1585, d. Nov. 6, 1672, the foremost German composer of the early baroque, became a chorister in the court chapel of the Landgrave Maurice of Hesse-Cassel in 1599. He also studied law in Marburg and Leipzig, but musical studies (1609–12) in Venice with Giovanni Gabrieli convinced him that he should adopt music as a profession. In 1615, Schütz began his association with the electoral chapel in Dresden, which lasted until his old age.

Due to the loss of his only opera and much secular and occasional music, Schütz has usually been considered mainly as a composer of church music; his Italian madrigals, however, are of excellent quality. The range of his church music is wide, embracing simple four-part chorales, intimate chamber motets (*Kleine geistliche Concerte*; 1636, 1639), Latin psalms in elaborate polychoral style (1619), oratorios for Easter and Christmas, three sets of *Symphoniae Sacrae* (1629, 1647, 1650)—some with Latin, others with German texts—four Passions, and *The Seven Last Words* (c.1645).

Schuyler, Philip John [sky'-lur]   Philip J. Schuyler, b. Albany, N.Y., Nov. 21, 1733, d. Nov. 18, 1804, a member of one of New York's great landed families, was an American general in the American Revolution. He fought during the French and Indian War (1754–63), represented Albany in the New York legislature (1768–75), and was a member of the Continental Congress (1775–77, 1778–81).

Named one of the four major generals in the Continental Army in June 1775, he was placed in command of the northern army in New York. Gen. Horatio GATES claimed precedence over Schuyler as commander of the northern army early in 1777, and the resulting controversy was taken up in Congress. Schuyler, meanwhile, had taken effective steps to halt the British invasion from Canada led by Gen. John BURGOYNE. When one of Schuyler's subordinates abandoned Fort TICONDEROGA in July 1777 without firing a shot, Schuyler was accused of negligence and replaced by Gates in August. Schuyler demanded a court-martial and was acquitted (1778) of all charges, but he resigned from the army in April 1779.

An important political figure after the war, Schuyler helped secure New York's ratification of the U.S. Constitution in 1788. He served in the U.S. Senate (1789–91, 1797–98).

Schwann, Theodor, and Schleiden, Matthias Jakob [shvahn, shly'-den]   The German physiologist Theodor Schwann, b. Dec. 7, 1810, d. Jan. 11, 1882, and the German botanist Matthias Jakob Schleiden, b. Apr. 5, 1804, d. June 23, 1881, are credited with formulating the cell theory—the theory that all living things are composed of cells. After studying medicine at the University of Berlin, Schwann began his most important work, the microscopic study of animal tissue, which led to his idea that all living things are made up of cells and that each cell contains essential components such as a nucleus. He published this idea in *Microscopic Researches into Accordance in the Structure and Growth of Animals and Plants* (1839). After an education in law, Schleiden concentrated on botanical studies. In 1838, one year before Schwann, he developed the idea that the cell is the basic unit of plants and that growth consists of production and development of new cells. Schleiden's two-volume text *Principles of Scientific Botany* (1842–43) was long a model for modern botanical works.

Schwartz, Delmore [shwohrts]   The American poet, short-story writer, and critic Delmore Schwartz, b. Brooklyn, N.Y., Dec. 8, 1913, d. July 11, 1966, was one of the outstanding literary talents of his time. His first collection of poetry and prose, *In Dreams Begin Responsibilities* (1938), with its themes of alienation, its obsession with history, and its portrayals of family life, foreshadows the concerns of his later works. His own childhood provided the material for *Genesis* (1943), an autobiographical poem about a young Jewish boy in an urban world. Many of Schwartz's best poems are in *Summer Knowledge: New and Selected Poems 1938–58* (1959), which won the Bollingen Prize in 1960. *The World Is a Wedding* (1948) and *Successful Love and Other Stories* (1961) are collections of short stories. An ironic, defensive tone and a learned, extremely allusive use of language characterize Schwartz's writing.

Schwarzenberg (family) [shvahrt'-sen-bairk]   The Schwarzenbergs were an Austrian family that contributed numerous public officials, mainly to the service of the Habsburgs. The family acquired noble status in Franconia about 1405 and extended its holdings to Bohemia and elsewhere, becoming in 1670 direct vassals of the Holy Roman emperor with governing rights of their own. **Karl Philipp, Fürst zu Schwarzenberg**, b. Apr. 15, 1771, d. Oct. 15, 1820, was a diplomat and field marshal. He commanded the Austrian forces in the Napoleonic Wars and was the allied commander who defeated Napoleon at the Battle of Leipzig in 1813. His nephew, **Felix, Fürst zu Schwarzenberg**, b. Oct. 2, 1800, d. Apr. 15, 1852, became premier of the Austrian Empire in November 1848, when revolution threatened. He persuaded the incompetent emperor FERDINAND I to abdicate in favor of his nephew, FRANCIS JOSEPH. By obtaining Russian aid against the Hungarian revolution and thwarting Prussia's ambitions in Germany, he restored the empire's dominance in central Europe. His domestic system was based on absolutism and highly centralized administration.

Schwarzkopf, Elisabeth [shvahrts'-kohpf]   The renowned German soprano Elisabeth Schwarzkopf, b. Dec. 9, 1915, studied in Berlin and made her debut there in 1938; appearances followed at leading opera houses, including those of Vienna, London, and Milan. Her repertoire was wide, and she excelled in Mozartian roles, such as the countess in *The Marriage of Figaro*, Donna Elvira in *Don Giovanni*, and Fiordiligi in *Così fan tutte*, and in those of Richard Strauss, particularly the Marschallin in *Der Rosenkavalier*, which she first sang at La Scala, Milan, in the 1951–52 season and later recorded (1960) in a film version. A superb Lieder singer, she retired from the stage in 1975 and in 1976 joined the faculty of the Juilliard School in New York City.

Schwarzkopf, H. Norman

Gen. H. Norman Schwarzkopf, b. Trenton, N.J., Aug. 22, 1934, was commander of the more than 500,000 U.S. and allied troops that successfully fought the GULF WAR in 1991 to liberate Kuwait from Saddam HUSSEIN's Iraqi forces. Schwarzkopf graduated from West Point in 1956. Twice wounded and highly decorated, he served two tours of duty in Vietnam, and that experience helped to shape his strategy for the Gulf war: swift and sure attack with well-defined goals. The victory was hailed universally as a perfect military operation, and Schwarzkopf himself, known affectionately to his troops as "Stormin' Norman," described the extremely low number of allied casualties as miraculous.

Schwarzschild radius SEE BLACK HOLE

Schwarzwald SEE BLACK FOREST

Schweitzer, Albert

[shvyt'-sur] A distinguished musician, philosopher, theologian, and medical missionary, Albert Schweitzer, b. Kaysersberg, Upper Alsace, Jan. 14, 1875, d. Sept. 4, 1965, was awarded the Nobel Peace Prize in 1952. Schweitzer's native Alsace was part of Germany at his birth and became French again after World War I. The village church of Günsbach, where his father was Lutheran pastor, served both Lutherans and Catholics. This bilingual and tolerant environment nurtured Schweitzer's sensitivity to human suffering.

In Paris, Schweitzer studied under Charles Marie WIDOR, his collaborator later on books about the life and music of J. S. Bach. Schweitzer entered Strasbourg University at the age of 18. His 1899 doctoral thesis in phi-

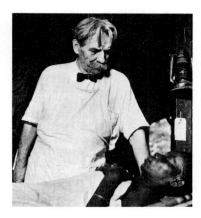

Albert Schweitzer, recipient of the 1952 Nobel Peace Prize, attained fame as a theologian and musician before turning to missionary work in Africa. Having trained as a physician, he founded (1913) a hospital at Lambaréné, Gabon, to which he dedicated the rest of his life.

losophy was on the religious philosophy of Immanuel Kant. In 1900 he received another doctorate, this time in theology, and then became principal of Strasbourg's Theological College of Saint Thomas. In 1906 he published *The Quest for the Historical Jesus* (Eng. trans., 1910), which gained worldwide attention. Schweitzer's research, lectures, and writings in philosophy and theology continued throughout his life.

In 1906, despite the protests of family and friends, Schweitzer left Saint Thomas for medical school. In 1912 he married Hélène Bresslau (d. 1957), also an accomplished scholar, who studied nursing in order to share her husband's work. They had one daughter, Rhena, born in 1919.

In 1913 the Schweitzers sailed for French Equatorial Africa with medical supplies and 2,000 gold marks. Their construction of a hospital at Lambaréné on the Ogowe River in Gabon was interrupted by World War I. Schweitzer returned to Lambaréné in 1924. Jungle had overgrown the hospital, so two miles up the river he built a new complex. Hundreds of Africans went there for help, including many lepers. The able-bodied helped Schweitzer construct the buildings, learning building skills in the process.

Schwenkfeld von Ossig, Kaspar

[shvenk'-felt fuhn ohs'-ik] The Silesian mystic and reformer Kaspar Schwenkfeld von Ossig, b. 1489, d. Dec. 10, 1561, founded a religious movement, the Schwenkfeldians, or Confessors of the Glory of Christ, some of whose members immigrated to Pennsylvania, where the group still survives.

In 1540, Schwenkfeld defended his beliefs in a *Great Confession*, stressing the differences between Martin Luther and Ulrich Zwingli, especially with regard to the Eucharist, and arguing that since the nature of humankind is sinful, Christ's human nature had to be of itself divine. This latter belief was considered a Christological heresy by orthodox theologians. Schwenkfeld's books were banned, and his followers were persecuted.

Schwerin

[shvay-reen'] Schwerin, a city in northwestern Germany and the capital of Mecklenburg-Vorpommern state, has a population of 128,328 (1987 est.). The city is located on Lake Schwerin (Schweriner See) about 32 km (20 mi) south of the Baltic Sea and 115 km (70 mi) east of Hamburg. A rail and road junction, the city is also a trade center for the surrounding dairy and agricultural region. Schwerin's industrial products include farm equipment, drugs, plastics, chemicals, textiles, furniture, and ceramics. The city's cathedral was begun during the 13th century. First mentioned in written sources in 1018 as a Wendish settlement, Schwerin became German under Henry the Lion, duke of Saxony, in 1160. A bishopric from 1167 until 1648, Schwerin passed to the dukes of Mecklenburg in 1358, and subsequently became the capital of the duchy of Mecklenburg-Schwerin. From 1934 to 1952 it was the capital of the state of Mecklenburg. It was the capital of the East German district of Schwerin from 1952 to 1990.

Schwitters, Kurt [shvit'-urs]   The German artist Kurt Schwitters, b. June 20, 1887, d. Jan. 8, 1948, was a member of the Hanover DADA movement and an active contributor to avant-garde art before World War II. He is principally known for his "Merz" collages and constructions—abstract arrangements of commonplace objects chosen for their shape, color, and texture (see COLLAGE).

His earliest works were conventional still lifes, landscapes, and portraits. In 1919, however, Schwitters made his first Merz drawings (collages). These constituted the beginnings of his Merz art, the name of which he derived from the word *Kommerz* appearing on a scrap of newspaper in an early collage. Subsequently, he developed the Merz picture (larger and more three-dimensional than the Merz drawing), the Merzbau (construction), and the Merz stage. He published Merz poems under the title *Anna Blume* (1919) and launched the magazine *Merz* (1923–32). In 1932, Schwitters began working in Paris. Five years later his work was included in the Nazi-organized exhibition of "degenerate art."

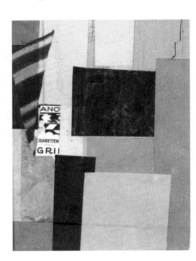

Merzbild *(1922), by the 20th-century German artist Kurt Schwitters, is a Dada collage construction made of fragments of wood, metal, rubber, and paper. The geometric composition, which resembles that of a cubist painting, assembles objects from everyday life in an unpredictable and evocative structure. (Burton Tremaine Collection, Meriden, Conn.)*

sciatica [sy-at'-i-kuh]   Sciatica, a disorder of the sciatic nerve, is characterized by pain of the lower back, pelvis, and legs. Most instances of acute sciatica occur as a result of nerve-root compression caused by degenerate or ruptured lumbar disks of the spine. Improper lifting of heavy objects may rupture the disks. Osteomyelitis, or bony deposits on the vertebrae, can also pinch nerve roots to cause chronic sciatica. Rest, aspirin, and the application of local heat and muscle relaxants provide some relief, but traction may be necessary in order to reopen collapsed spaces between the disks.

science   Science may be broadly defined as the development and systematization of positive knowledge about the physical universe. The history of science, then, is the description and explanation of the development of that knowledge. Science is generally viewed as a cumulative and progressive activity by its nature. Such views, however, have profound philosophical implications, and in fact the effort to define the nature of science is in itself part of the history of philosophy.

Early Philosophical Theories about Science

Philosophers of the late Renaissance were optimistic about humanity's ability to understand and control the natural world. During the 17th century—the era of Galileo, William Harvey, Isaac Newton, and Robert Boyle—scientists and philosophers alike were convinced that with the help of the newly discovered scientific method modern scientists would quickly surpass the achievements of their Greek and medieval predecessors. Disagreement existed, however, as to the details of the correct scientific method.

Rationalism.   In his *Discourse on Method* (1637), René DESCARTES asserted that all theoretical science should be like Euclidean geometry. A science such as physics should be based on first principles comparable to the axioms of geometry, which were discovered and validated through the systematic analysis of intuitive ideas. Descartes thought, for example, that the law of inertia could be seen to be true through the use of reason alone. This view, that science can be based on principles that are revealed through introspection, is called rationalism (from the Latin *ratio*, "reason").

An objection to the rationalist approach to science is that people's intuitions about fundamental scientific propositions do not always agree. Furthermore, especially in the social sciences, trying to base scientific principles on introspection alone has led to social injustice as well as to scientific stagnation.

Empiricism.   The English philosopher Francis BACON, whose *New Organon* appeared in 1620, also believed that there was a rigorous "organ," or method, for making scientific discoveries, but his theory of method was quite different from that of Descartes. Bacon believed that instead of analyzing intuitive ideas, scientists should first empty their minds of all preconceptions and then make observations. By using inductive logic one could generalize from these observations about particular cases. In this way one would finally arrive at the most fundamental and comprehensive laws of nature. This view of scientific methodology, that all scientific knowledge is derived from observation alone, is called EMPIRICISM (*empeira* is the Greek word for "experience").

Bacon's theory of method may seem much more plausible than Cartesian rationalism, especially to Anglo-Americans who have been brought up in an atmosphere strongly influenced by empiricism. Nevertheless, Bacon's approach has serious inadequacies. In contrast, philosophers in the tradition of Immanuel KANT have argued that it is impossible to make observations that are free of all preconceptions, as Bacon would have us do, because all observational reports go beyond what has actually been perceived—or, in modern terms, all observations are "theory-laden." Furthermore, Bacon's claim that all scientific laws are the result of inductive generalizations from statements of observation is not correct. If all scientists were strict Baconians, there would be no theoretical science. Adherence to Baconian inductivism can also result in inaccurate social judgments, and in fact much of what is called superstitious reasoning is based on a form of naive empiricism.

Modern Views on Science

Both Bacon and Descartes were trying to provide a simple, fail-safe method for scientific study, but the modern view of the nature of the scientific method is that both experience and reason play an important role in science. Reason or imagination provides speculative hypotheses; experience helps weed out those which are false.

Bacon and Descartes had hoped to provide a method that would guarantee that every statement uttered by a responsible scientist would be true. Today it is recognized that no automatic method exists for creating good scientific theories. In addition, no scientific theory, regardless of how well it has been tested, can be considered infallible. Nevertheless sound ways have been developed to criticize and test such theories and to eliminate bad ones.

Testing Scientific Theories. Accounts of the actual testing of scientific theories tend to be rather technical and often require the use of statistics; however, some of the basic results can be easily understood and are of direct practical importance. Deductive fallacies (see FALLACY) have been known since ancient times. Less well known and more recently discovered are what might be called inductive fallacies, or mistakes in scientific reasoning.

There is, then, a widespread philosophical consensus on the methods that scientists should *not* use. Far less agreement exists concerning the details of positive prescriptions for science. Scientists can usually decide more easily which theories are false than which theories are true. This situation is typical of many fields. For example, voters find it easier to say what makes a politician unsatisfactory than to describe an ideal politician.

Current Issues Concerning the Nature of Science. Many issues remain controversial when considering the nature of science. All of them concern scientific inquiry in general, irrespective of the scientific subject matter. Problems also arise directly from the content of specific scientific theories. Thus theorists in physics are trying to determine whether a new kind of logic, called quantum logic, is required in order to formalize QUANTUM MECHANICS while theorists in biology have tried to analyze the concept of species as it is used in population genetics. Theorists in psychology have contributed to the debate between Noam CHOMSKY and B. F. SKINNER about whether the child's acquisition of language can best be understood as, respectively, an innate capacity of the human mind or entirely the product of conditioning.

Theorists on science in general have traditionally concentrated on the cognitive aspects of science. Recently, however, they have become more involved with the social and ethical implications of scientific research. Today philosophers of science join scientists and concerned lay people in discussions about the dangers of recombinant DNA research, the implications of sociobiology and race-IQ research for social policy, the ethics of experimentation with human subjects, and other problems that require both scientific expertise and sensitivity to questions about human values.

----

science, education in The aim of education in science is to develop an understanding both of the content of science and of the methods or processes by which that content is produced. The latter goal is one reason for devoting considerable time to hands-on activities or laboratory work. An increasingly important goal of science education is an understanding of the interactions between science and technology and society.

In the United States formal education in science began in the 19th century, stimulated in part by the rising interest in science and technology during the Industrial Revolution. The first organized science program at the elementary level appeared in the 1870s, and Harvard College, soon followed by other institutions, first accepted high school science courses for entrance in 1872.

Science instruction is offered at each grade level in elementary schools. Heavy emphasis is placed on biological science, but physical science is also included in the curriculum. Approximately 1 hour per week in kindergarten through grade 3 and 2 to 3 hours per week in grades 4 to 6 are devoted to the study of science. These figures for science instruction have remained fairly constant in recent decades.

Of the 85% of junior high school students (grades 7 to 9) enrolled in science courses, about one-fourth are in general science courses offered at each level. Additionally, 42% of 7th graders study life science, 26% of 8th graders study Earth science, and 23% of 9th graders study physical sciences.

Enrollment in science courses drops at the senior high school level. Although 75% of the students study biology in the 10th grade, fewer than one-half of those students study chemistry as juniors, and in the 12th grade only one-fifth enroll in physics. Despite a slight increase in recent years, the percentage of students enrolling in science has been dropping since the 1940s. Although the number and variety of science courses offered—for example, astronomy, botany, and zoology—has increased, total enrollment in the courses remains small.

At the college level, somewhat fewer than 500,000 students pursue bachelor's degrees in science, while approximately 500,000 seek engineering degrees; the two fields represent less than 10% of total college enrollment. Approximately 75,000 students are enrolled in graduate programs in science.

Competition for scientific and technological leadership, characterized by the U.S.-USSR space race following the 1957 launch of *Sputnik 1*, spurred federal support for science-curriculum development and for the training of science teachers in the United States during the 1960s and early 1970s, so that nearly $1 billion was expended in the effort by the National Science Foundation (NSF) from 1957 to 1977. Interest and support waned in the mid-1970s, however. Declining student achievement, shortages of qualified teachers, low enrollments, and reduced federal support again aroused concern in the 1980s that the United States lagged behind other developed countries in technological capabilities and general science literacy. A renewed awareness of the importance of science education prompted the formation of various commissions and study groups, which recommended improvements in the science educational system. Proposals included increasing the years of study required in secondary school, requiring study of computer science, financially rewarding excellent science teachers, and renewing support for teacher training, research, and curriculum development.

science, history of

science, history of The history of science is treated in numerous entries by subject, including ASTRONOMY AND ASTROPHYSICS; BIOLOGY; BOTANY; CHEMISTRY, HISTORY OF; GEOLOGY; MATHEMATICS, HISTORY OF; PHYSICS, HISTORY OF. Its relationship to technology may be seen in the article TECHNOLOGY, HISTORY OF. In addition, numerous biographical entries of natural philosophers and scientists treat individual contributions to the history of science from many cultures spanning the ancient to the modern world.

science, philosophy of   see SCIENCE

science fiction

science fiction Science fiction is a form of literature that takes place in an alternative present, a reconceived past, or an extrapolated future. All these alterations in time or reality are based on technological or sociological changes in the observed, realistic now. Although anticipations of the form can be seen in works of 19th-century European writers, science fiction is a peculiarly American genre whose point of origin can be clearly traced. In 1926 the amateur scientist and occasional writer Hugo GERNSBACK conceived *Amazing Stories*, a magazine whose first issue both defined what its content would be and stated its purpose—to publish stories based on science that would interest young men in scientific careers.

In Mary Shelley's Frankenstein *(1818) —considered the first true science-fiction novel—Victor Frankenstein shuns accepted scientific belief and pursues his own research creating a living being. The frontispiece to the 1831 edition depicts Frankenstein's initial reaction to his creation.*

Jules Verne's From the Earth to the Moon *(1865) was the first space adventure based on sound scientific speculation, including the presumed effect of weightlessness shown in this engraving from the novel's first edition. Verne's imaginary inventions were plausible extensions of the technology of his day, and many of his speculations were remarkably accurate.*

The Precursors. Mary Shelley's FRANKENSTEIN (1818)—a variation of the Faust legend that had been current in European literature and folklore for centuries—established a useful and recurring science-fiction myth: that of the mad scientist whose arrogance challenges the laws of nature and thus creates havoc. In the last decades of the 19th century, Jules VERNE in France and H. G. WELLS in England both produced novels that masqueraded as science although they were, in fact, pure fantasy. Verne's *A Journey to the Center of the Earth* (1864; Eng. trans., 1872) and *Twenty Thousand Leagues under the Sea* (1869–70; Eng. trans., 1876) voiced the growing infatuation with the achievements of technology and helped develop two popular science-fiction themes: adventures in space and forays into unknown worlds on Earth. H. G. Wells, in The TIME MACHINE (1895) and The WAR OF THE WORLDS (1898), warned humankind of its precarious position in an indifferent universe. Other authors wrote fantasies about prehistory, future history, and lost empires—notions that derived from contemporary discoveries in geology and paleontology. The idea of UTOPIAS was given new form in Edward BELLAMY's *Looking Backward* (1888) and William MORRIS's *News from Nowhere* (1891).

In addition to novels of fantasy, the United States contributed two early pulp magazines. *The All-Story* (founded 1914) discovered several important authors, including Edgar Rice BURROUGHS. *Argosy* (founded 1882) offered such respectable fantasists as James Branch CABELL and was the first to print the work of longtime science-fiction writer Murray Leinster.

The Pulp Era. The earliest issues of Gernsback's *Amazing Stories* were devoted largely to reprints of Verne, Wells, and other authors of fantasy, but slowly Gernsback developed a group of science-fiction writers, most of them pulp-magazine authors, who were able to conceive the form. An important rival magazine, *Astounding Stories* (soon to be called *Astounding Science Fiction*), was founded in 1930. The science-fiction writer John W. Campbell assumed its editorship in 1937 and was an active force in the field until his death in 1971.

During Campbell's editorship, the first generation of writers in England and America who had been nurtured on *Amazing Stories* and the early *Astounding Stories* began to produce their own science-fiction literature. Under Campbell's tutelage, they established science fiction's "golden age." Isaac ASIMOV, L. Sprague de Camp, Robert A. HEINLEIN, Theodore STURGEON, and A. E. VAN VOGT were among the most important of this generation. In the 1950s they were joined by Arthur CLARKE, Frederik POHL, and others whose work extended the reach of science fiction.

Science Fiction Enters the Mainstream. The sudden and horrifying use of nuclear weapons in a way that had been predicted by science fiction for years brought the field a new prominence. Science fiction was read as serious literature for the first time, largely because it was judged to be predictive. In this early postwar era, major publishers were attracted to the field and brought out anthologies drawn almost exclusively from *Astounding*, as well as reprinting older science-fiction novels and publishing new works.

An additional expansion of the field occurred with the entrance of two new magazines, *Galaxy* (1950) and *The Magazine of Fantasy and Science Fiction* (*FSF*, 1949). These magazines published most of the authors whose novels would legitimize the genre. Among them, Alfred Bester wrote ironic, skeptical stories about malcontents in corrupt societies and the relationships between androids (humanoid robots) and their human owners. Two of his novels—*The Demolished Man* (1953) and *The Stars My Destination* (1956)—are classics. Walter M. Miller's masterpiece, *A Canticle for Liebowitz* (1960), concerns the inevitability of repeated technological holocaust whenever the advance of science makes it possible. Philip K. DICK deals with notions of distorted perception, of the effect of artificial realities, or schizophrenic mind states, of illusion taking over from the real world.

Of the many other writers to start their careers in the 1950s science-fiction magazines, two English authors are particularly significant. Brian ALDISS brilliantly advanced the starship-as-world plot (*Starship*, 1958); J. G. BAL-

During the early 1950s science-fiction magazines reached a peak of popularity, with as many as 36 separate titles published in 1953. Galaxy, edited by Horace L. Gold, was noted for more sophisticated stories containing social criticism. The cover of the January 1953 issue, illustrating Philip K. Dick's "Defenders," is by Ed Emshwiller, a popular cover artist of the period.

LARD's psychological investigations of the significance of wrecked technologies, empty landscapes, and strange disasters made him one of the first authors of the so-called New Wave movement.

The 1960s and the New Wave. Aldiss and Ballard published their stories in the British magazine *New Worlds* (1946–70), long edited by writer Michael Moorcock. Moorcock's own fiction is closer to fantasy than to science fiction, but the authors he published attempted other approaches to break out of what they considered the too-rigid conventions of their genre. The tone of science fiction from the era of the New Wave to the present is satirical, pessimistic, and anti-utopian—in contrast to attitudes at science fiction's beginnings, which paralleled the beliefs of their day in scientific progress and prosperity for all.

The 1970s and Beyond. Many of the "golden age" authors still produce, as do almost all the writers from the late 1950s and the 1960s. They were joined in the 1970s by writers of the quality of Ursula K. LE GUIN, who, in novels such as *The Left Hand of Darkness* (1969) and *The Dispossessed* (1974), uses anthropological and sociological theories as springboards for her plots. Harlan Ellison, Norman Spinrad, Samuel R. Delany, and Robert Silverberg achieved their reputations in the 1970s. The British writer Ian Watson takes on both the humanistic sciences and physics and cosmology in his work.

A notable development of the past two decades has been the growing reputation of women science-fiction writers. They range from Le Guin through authors who used male pseudonyms—the most notable is James Tiptree, Jr.—to Joanna Russ and Doris LESSING, in her apocalyptic novels and her many-volume Sirius cycle.

The computer has given science fiction new universes to explore. From early notions that the machines would take over and rule, or produce more of their own kind and oust humanity, contemporary science-fiction writers such as William Gibson produce novels (*Neuromancer*, 1984)

The cover of the August 1927 issue of Amazing Stories *depicts the Martian war machines from H. G. Wells's* War of the Worlds. *The first magazine devoted exclusively to science fiction,* Amazing Stories *was first published by science-fiction pioneer Hugo Gernsback in April 1926. Cover artist Frank R. Paul was the first and most highly regarded science-fiction illustrator.*

in the "cyberpunk" mode, stylistically resembling some of the early science-fiction writing.

Science Fiction in Eastern Europe. The Polish writer and scientist Stanisław LEM is perhaps the most important contemporary European science-fiction writer; his works range from mystical planetary explorations (*Solaris*, 1961; Eng. trans., 1970) to comic tales about the space pilot Pirx.

Russian space scientist Konstantin TSIOLKOVSKY wrote, among other novels, *Beyond the Planet Earth* (1920; Eng. trans., 1960), a prophetic work in the saga of space travel. After the revolution, Y. Zamiatin's *We* (written 1920; Eng. trans., 1924) was a profoundly dystopian work, never published in Russia. Among the many other Russian science-fiction authors, the works of Alexander Belyaev and the Strugatsky brothers have been translated into English.

scientific associations

Unlike some other cultural activities, science requires an associated community of practitioners to evaluate and build on the work of individual scientists. Scientists thus have always formed informal groups (sometimes called "invisible colleges") through personal contact, letters, and exchanges of research results. The modern, more formal scientific association has its origin in the 16th and 17th centuries in private groups of those desirous of new organizations for the new knowledge of the Scientific Revolution. Notable among such groups were the Academia Secretorum Naturae, active in Naples in the 1560s; the Accademia dei Lincei, founded in Rome in 1603 and claiming Galileo as a member; and the Accademia del Cimento, active in Florence between 1657 and 1667. These and similar short-lived groups in Italy and Germany took their organizational model from earlier Renaissance associations that were devoted mostly to language and literature. Sociability and dependence on a supporting patron characterize these early, unofficial societies, although they became more concerned with experiment and method as the 17th century progressed.

Multidisciplinary Learned Societies and National Academies. The creation of the ROYAL SOCIETY of London in 1662 by charter from Charles II and the royal ACADÉMIE DES SCIENCES in Paris in 1666 by fiat from Jean Baptiste Colbert and Louis XIV marks the beginning of official, state-supported academies and societies of science. The Royal Society was the more influential institution until the death (1727) of its president, Sir Isaac Newton. Both the Paris Academy and the Royal Society provided institutional models for the spread of the general learned society as the predominant form for scientific association through the 18th century. Among about 75 such institutions, important examples include the Societas Scientiarum (now called the Akademie der Wissenschaften der DDR), created (1700) in Berlin on the initiative of Gottfried Wilhelm von Leibniz; the Imperial Academy of Sciences (1724; Saint Petersburg); the AMERICAN PHILOSOPHICAL SOCIETY (1768; Philadelphia), with Benjamin Franklin as its first president; and the AMERICAN ACADEMY OF ARTS AND SCIENCES (1780; Boston). Societies modeled after the Royal Society tended to have larger, more diffuse memberships and to receive only token support from the state; academies modeled after the Paris Academy tended to have a more restricted, professional membership and to function as scientific and technical bureaus in government. Both types of learned society enjoyed the recognition and power that came with official status. Learned societies actively promoted scientific research by offering prizes and by sponsoring scientific expeditions; they facilitated scientific communications through their journals, such as the famous *Philosophical Transactions* of the Royal Society, beginning in 1665, and the *Mémoires* of the Paris Academy, beginning in 1699.

By the beginning of the 19th century the scientific enterprise had become so large and complex that the multidisciplinary learned society no longer sufficed as the primary institution for organized science. National academies continued to be founded, but they gradually became transformed into more or less honorary organizations of recognized scientists (like the Royal Society or the INSTITUT DE FRANCE today) or overarching organizations for the control of state science (like the ACADEMY OF SCIENCES OF THE USSR). In the United States the NATIONAL ACADEMY OF SCIENCES (1863) and its associated National Research Council (1916) occupy something of a middle ground in this regard.

Specialized Societies and Professional Organizations. Two new forms of scientific association thus emerged in the 19th century: the specialized society and the professional organization. England led the way with the earliest specialized societies, including the Linnean Society (1788) and the Royal Astronomical Society (founded 1820; royal charter, 1831). The American Chemical Society (1876) is an important early specialized society in the United States. The trend toward specialization has continued unabated in the United States and in other countries. Societies specializing in a single discipline offer several advantages to the practicing scientist: knowledgeable experts with a common interest; a narrow focus of research, resources, and debate; and, through specialized journals, a more efficient means of communicating with peers.

Professional scientific societies, such as the British Association for the Advancement of Science (1831) and the AMERICAN ASSOCIATION FOR THE ADVANCEMENT OF SCIENCE (1848), appeared as more scientists pursued formal scientific careers in universities, laboratories, and industry. In addition to providing a generalized support for science or actively controlling a profession, as do the AMERICAN MEDICAL ASSOCIATION (1847) and some of the engineering societies, such associations help to disseminate the substance and values of science to the public.

International Organizations. On the international level, cooperative endeavors in the 18th and 19th centuries—such as the worldwide expeditions to observe the transits of Venus in 1761 and 1769—were largely sponsored by the learned societies. The culmination of the movement toward formal international organization in science was the creation (1900) of the International Association of Academies, which resulted from 19th-century international cooperation in geodetic, magnetic, and gravitational research. This association was succeeded in 1919 by the International Research Council, which was followed by the International Council of Scientific Unions (ICSU) in 1931.

scientific method   see SCIENCE

scientific notation

Scientific notation, also known as exponential notation, is a convenient and commonly used way of expressing very large numbers or very small numbers. It is a special type of decimal notation in which a number is expressed as a value between 1 and 10 multiplied by a power of 10. The appropriate power of 10 is the number of places that the decimal point in the original number must be shifted to the left so that only a single digit (other than zero) will be to the left of the decimal point. If the decimal point must be shifted to the right rather than to the left in this process, then the exponent of 10 is negative. For example, using scientific notation, 584,000,000 becomes 5.84×10^8, and 0.0000000025 becomes 2.5×10^{-9}. Multiplication of these two numbers is less cumbersome when scientific notation is used:

$$(5.84 \times 10^8) \times (2.5 \times 10^{-9}) = (5.84 \times 2.5) \times (10^8 \times 10^{-9})$$
$$= 14.6 \times 10^{-1} = 1.46$$

Scientology

Scientology is a quasi-scientific and religious movement that espouses the quest for effective use of the individual's mental abilities. The movement was inspired by the publication (1950) of L. Ronald Hubbard's *Dianetics: The Modern Science of Mental Health.* Hubbard, a retired U.S. naval officer and science-fiction writer, proposed a form of therapy for curing psychosomatic ailments and for enhancing life through self-determination and mental awareness. Scientology emphasizes communication between an auditor (similar to a therapist) and a novice, during which the latter learns to increase the power of the analytical mind (consciousness) and subdue the influence of "engrams" (painful impressions from past experience) that confuse the "reactive," or unconscious, mind. The movement took on a religious dimension with the incorporation (1965) of the Church of Scientology, with international headquarters in Britain. Although Scientology makes passing reference to a form of universal soul (thetan), it in fact teaches self-redemption. The church has been the subject of much controversy; it has been the target of many lawsuits and has been investigated for fraud by law enforcement agencies in the United States and elsewhere.

Scilly Islands

[sil'-ee]   The Scilly Islands are a group of approximately 140 islands and islets in the Atlantic Ocean, located 40 km (25 mi) off England's southwestern tip. The land area is 17 km^2 (6.5 mi^2), and the population is 2,628 (1981). Only five islands are inhabited; the capital, Hugh Town, lies on Saint Mary's, the largest island. Tourism and flower growing are the main sources of income. Landmarks include ruins of a 17th-century castle on Tresco Island. Once a pirate haven, the islands came under control of the British crown in the 16th century.

scintillation

Scintillation is the emission of a flash of light by many substances, such as sodium iodide, anthracene, naphthalene, cesium iodide, and others, when struck by an ionizing particle, such as a beta particle or gamma radiation. Such particles are produced by radioactive materials, and scintillation is a common technique for detecting RADIOACTIVITY. Scintillation occurs when an ionizing particle strikes a scintillator crystal and causes ionization that releases electrons from the neutral atoms and molecules of the crystal. The electrons emit visible radiations when they recombine with ionized atoms and molecules.

scintillation counter

A device to measure radiation, the scintillation counter is used in research-radiation monitoring, exploration for radioactive minerals, and checking radioactive contamination; it also has clinical uses, including neurosurgery and human-organ survey with radioactive isotopes.

The scintillation counter operates on the principle that flashes of light are emitted by atoms of a material after having been ionized by radiation. The magnitude of the light produced is proportional to the energy lost by the particle in traversing the scintillator. The first experiments using this principle were made by Ernest Rutherford, the English physicist and Nobel Prize winner for chemistry in 1908.

In early scintillation counters, a layer of zinc sulfide on glass served as the activated phosphor (light-emitting material). In modern counters, transparent crystalline material, protected by plastic, is placed in optical contact with the face of a photomultiplier tube that greatly amplifies the weak light pulses, converts them to an electric signal, and feeds them into an electronic counter. The counting rate can be very high, and the instrument takes over where Geiger counters would be useless.

Scipio Africanus Major

[skip'-ee-oh ahf-ri-kah'-nuhs]   Publius Cornelius Scipio, called Scipio Africanus Major, *c.* 236–183 BC, was the Roman general who defeated HANNIBAL in the Second PUNIC WAR. The son of a prominent general, Scipio first saw action in the battle at the Ticinus River (218), which Hannibal won. As a military tribune, Scipio helped rally survivors of the disaster at Cannae. After serving (213) as aedile he was granted an unprecedented proconsular command in Spain. Here, he brilliantly captured Carthago Nova (now Cartagena) in 209, defeated Hannibal's brother HASDRUBAL in 208, and overcame the remaining Carthaginian forces in 206.

Scipio was elected consul for 205, and with a volunteer army invaded (204) Africa from Sicily. Besieged near Utica, Scipio treacherously attacked the enemy after feigning negotiations. Carthage requested peace but renewed the war soon after Hannibal's return (203) from Italy. Aided by the cavalry of MASINISSA and using tactics learned at Cannae, Scipio finally defeated Hannibal at Zama in 202.

Censor for 199 and leader of the Senate, Scipio entered his second consulship in 194 but had little effect on public affairs thereafter. Attacks by conservatives such as CATO the Elder led to his retirement.

Scipio Africanus Minor

Publius Cornelius Scipio Aemilianus Africanus Numantinus, called Scipio Africanus Minor, c.184–129 BC, a Roman general and noted patron of the arts, won his titles by destroying Carthage in 146 BC and Numantia in 133 BC. A nephew of the wife of Scipio Africanus Major, Aemilianus was adopted by the son of the elder Scipio Africanus, whose name he took.

He first served (168) at Pydna against the Macedonians. Volunteering for the Spanish war, he brought (151) valuable aid from his adoptive grandfather's old friend MASINISSA. He then sided with conservatives such as CATO the Elder in advocating the Third PUNIC WAR and won great popularity as a military tribune (149–148). Elected consul for 147, Aemilianus was given command of the war and in 146 presided over the capture and razing of Carthage. The desire for fresh glory led to a second consulship (for 134) and command at Numantia in the war against the Iberians. Increasing conservatism caused his popularity to wane.

sclerosis

Sclerosis is a general medical term for tissue hardening, which can result from infiltration or overgrowth of connective-tissue fibers, inflammation, mineral deposition, or other disease-related processes. Serious sclerotic diseases include AMYOTROPHIC LATERAL SCLEROSIS, ARTERIOSCLEROSIS, ATHEROSCLEROSIS, and MULTIPLE SCLEROSIS.

Scofield, Paul

[skoh'-feeld]   One of England's leading classical actors, Paul Scofield, b. Jan. 21, 1922, has been acclaimed for his performances in *Richard II* (1953), *Hamlet* (1955), *A Man for All Seasons* (1960–62; film, 1966), *King Lear* (1962–64; film, 1971), *Volpone* (1977), *Amadeus* (1979), *Othello* (1980), and *Don Quixote* (1982). The winner of Tony and Academy awards and a Shakespeare Prize, Scofield is a masterful acting technician.

scoliosis

[skoh-lee-oh'-sis]   A sideward curvature of the spine in any portion except the neck is termed scoliosis. Some scoliotic conditions are due to genetic defects, faulty prenatal development, or paralytic diseases, but 80 percent arise in infancy or childhood from no apparent cause. Severe scoliosis in the chest portion of the spine interferes with the action of breathing muscles and can result in heart failure. Braces or a metal rod surgically inserted along the spine may prevent increasing curvature. Studies of the corrective effects of electrical stimulation of back muscles on early scoliosis have thus far been inconclusive.

Scopas

[skoh'-puhs]   Scopas, b. c.395 BC, was eminent among Greek sculptors of the 4th century BC. He worked in various parts of the Greek world including the Mausoleum at Halicarnassus in Anatolia (see SEVEN WONDERS OF THE WORLD). Although no certain work by Scopas has been preserved, his name is associated with the pediment sculptures of the temple of Athena Alea in Tegea (built c.345 BC) of which he was also the architect. A few fragments (heads) of these sculptures, currently preserved in the National Museum in Athens, show a distinctive style: square chin and deep-set eyes overshadowed by rolls of flesh. The resulting look of passionate intensity seems to forecast later trends in sculpture.

Scopes Trial

In March 1925 the state of Tennessee forbade the teaching of Charles Darwin's theory of EVOLUTION. John T. Scopes, a schoolteacher, was tried in July of that year for violating the law. His trial became a public confrontation between a fundamentalist interpretation of the Bible and more liberal views. The prosecution was conducted by William Jennings BRYAN, a former presidential candidate, and the famous criminal lawyer Clarence DARROW conducted the defense. Both men volunteered their services. Scopes was found guilty, but his conviction was overturned by the state supreme court, which nevertheless upheld the statute. The U.S. Supreme Court declared a similar statute unconstitutional in 1968.

scopolamine

[skoh-pahl'-uh-meen]   The drug scopolamine, or hyoscine, extracted from the henbane shrub, *Hyoscyamus niger*, is a depressant of the central nervous system. Scopolamine has been used to sedate patients before anesthesia and surgery, to quiet manic patients, and to control delirium tremens and motion sickness. Side effects include dry mouth and blurred vision.

scorpion

Scorpions are arthropods distinguished by such striking features as large pedipalps furnished with stout claws, and an abdomen divided into two portions—a broad, seven-segmented preabdomen, and a five-segmented posterior with a slender tail ending in a sting. The base of the sting contains a pair of poison glands opening near the tip. Scorpions usually thrive in hot and tropical countries. They grow up to 125 mm (5 in) in length.

The North African scorpion Buthus occitanus *has one of the most poisonous stings of all scorpions. Its venom, like that of a number of North African and American desert scorpions, is a neurotoxin that may be fatal to humans.*

Predatory carnivores active at night, they feed on insects and spiders. The young are born alive and are carried on the mother's body for a short time.

Few scorpions are dangerous to humans, and ordinarily they do not attack unless disturbed. The only U.S. species with a potentially fatal sting, *Centruroides sculpturatus*, is yellow to yellow brown with two black stripes on the back. The sting from most species produces pain and swelling.

Scorpions comprise 6 families in the class Arachnida, phylum Arthropoda. More than 30 species occur in the southern and western United States.

---

scorpion fish   The scorpion fishes, family Scorpaenidae, comprise about 300 species, most of which are armed with sharp, often poisonous, spines on the head and fins. The spines can inflict serious and occasionally fatal wounds. The stonefish, genus *Synaceia*, is especially feared, and the bizarre lionfish, *Pterois*, can cause deep, painful, and long-lasting stab wounds. The scorpion fishes occur in temperate as well as tropical seas, lying motionless on the bottom and feeding on smaller fish. Fertilization is internal; the young usually develop in the ovaries of the female and are born alive.

---

scorpion fly   Scorpion flies, order Mecoptera, are so named because males of the genus *Panorpa* have abdomens in which the tip is bulbous and curves backward, resembling a scorpion's tail. The scorpion fly cannot sting, however. The adults are slender, mostly 18–25 mm (0.7–1 in) in length, with a long-faced appearance; most have four elongated membranous wings. Most adults are scavengers. Scorpion flies are usually found in ravines, woods, and other areas of thick vegetation.

Scorpius   Scorpius, the Scorpion, is the most spectacular zodiacal constellation of the summer months and is located west of Sagittarius in a bright portion of the Milky Way. From mid-northern latitudes it appears directly south and low above the horizon in mid-July. The brightest star in Scorpius is Antares, a vivid-red, first-magnitude star that is among the largest supergiants known. Antares, a visual double star, is accompanied by a much smaller green companion. The constellation contains numerous multiple-star systems, nebulas, and globular clusters as well as a particularly black, dusty region called the Coal Sack.

Scorsese, Martin   [skawr-say'-zee]   Film director Martin Scorsese, b. Flushing, N.Y., Nov. 17, 1942, incorporated into his feature film debut, *Who's That Knocking at My Door?* (1968), traits important in later efforts: autobiographical undertones, gritty cityscapes, and an emphasis on character. *Mean Streets* (1973), *Taxi Driver* (1976), *New York, New York* (1977), *Raging Bull* (1980), *The King of Comedy* (1983), and *Goodfellas* (1990) all starred actor Robert De Niro. Scorsese's other films include *Alice Doesn't Live Here Any More* (1975); *The Last Waltz* (1978), a documentary; the comedy *After Hours* (1985); *The Color of Money* (1986); and the controversial *Last Temptation of Christ* (1988).

Scotland   Scotland is the northern part of the island of GREAT BRITAIN and a constituent part of the UNITED KINGDOM. It extends 441 km (274 mi) from its border with England north to Duncansby Head. Scotland is washed by the Atlantic Ocean on the west and north and the North Sea on the east. Offshore are numerous islands, including the Inner and Outer HEBRIDES to the west and the ORKNEY ISLANDS and SHETLAND ISLANDS to the north.

Scotland is a Celtic land with a character—reflected in dialect, folklore, custom, and architecture—quite different from that of neighboring England. The name *Scotland* is derived from the name of a Celtic tribe from Ireland, the Scotti, who settled western Scotland during the 6th

The mountains of the Scottish Highlands are divided into two main sections by the Great Glen, a narrow valley occupied by a chain of lakes including the famous Loch Ness (background). The Great Glen extends from Inverness in the northeast to Fort William in the southwest.

(Below) *Participants in the Royal Highland Gathering at Braemar wear the traditional costume of the clans—including tartan kilt and plaid—and play the bagpipes. The annual Braemar gathering is the most famous of the Highland Games—competitions in athletic events, music, and dance.*

(Above) *Edinburgh Castle (top) dominates central Edinburgh from Castle Rock. The original city grew up on the eastern slopes of Castle Rock.*

century. The Romans called the area Caledonia. The total area of Scotland is 78,772 km² (30,414 mi²), and its population is 5,121,000 (1987 est.). EDINBURGH is the traditional capital.

Land, People, and Economy

Scotland is a mountainous country, with a coast deeply indented by the sea, especially in the west. Topographically, Scotland can be divided into three regions. The HIGHLANDS make up the northern two-thirds, where Scotland's highest mountain, BEN NEVIS (1,343 m/4,406 ft), is found, and the GRAMPIAN Mountains lie in the southern Highlands. Central Scotland is a lowland region with isolated hills. It is the most densely populated area and contains Scotland's coalfields. The Southern Uplands, a region of rounded hills, is noted for its sheep. The natural vegetation on the hills and mountains is heather, bracken, and short grass. Little natural forest remains in Scotland.

Winters are generally cold—January temperatures range from 3° to 5° C (37° to 41° F)—and extremely cold on the mountains, which are snow covered for several months. Summers are cool, with July temperatures averaging from 13° to 15° C (55° to 59° F). Rainfall is heavy, except on the east coast, and exceeds 2,540 mm (100 in) in the Western Highlands. The principal rivers are the TAY and the FORTH, which rise in the Highlands and flow across the Central Lowlands to the sea, and the CLYDE and the TWEED, which have their sources in the Southern Uplands. Scotland's rivers are famous for their fishing, including valuable salmon.

Modern Scots are descended from the Celtic tribes (see CELTS) that inhabited the region before the Romans came to Britain. During the early Middle Ages, Scandinavians settled in the east and north, and some Irish migrated into the west. A CLAN organization of society lasted in the Highlands until the 18th century, and the clans still have a strong emotional appeal to many Scots. Gaelic, a

CELTIC LANGUAGE, continues to be spoken in the mountainous west by only about 2% of the population; English is the official language. The majority of Scots belong to the Presbyterian church (see SCOTLAND, CHURCH OF). For further discussion of Scottish culture, see the articles SCOTTISH LITERATURE and CELTIC ART.

The cities of the Central Lowlands, notably GLASGOW, Edinburgh, DUNDEE, PAISLEY, and Motherwell, have traditionally drawn population from the Highlands. Other important Scottish cities are ABERDEEN, INVERNESS, PERTH, and Dumbarton.

Scotland has had a national system of education since 1696, and now nearly 99% of the population are literate. Important Scottish universities are located in SAINT ANDREWS (see SAINT ANDREWS, UNIVERSITY OF), established in 1411; Glasgow, established 1451; Aberdeen (see ABERDEEN, UNIVERSITY OF), established 1495; and Edinburgh, established 1583.

Scotland has abundant coal, but mining is not a major industry. Large, newly discovered reserves of crude petroleum are now being exploited in the North Sea, north and east of Scotland, as well as west of the Shetlands, and this industry is bringing new wealth to Scotland's northern ports. Agricultural resources are small. Oats and fodder crops are grown, and sheep raising is important. Fishing is a major industry, especially off the east coast.

Manufacturing is located mainly in the Central Lowlands and along the east coast. Iron and steel and textiles predominate. The once important shipbuilding industry has declined greatly. New industries, such as plastics, electronics, and consumer goods, have been developed. Whiskey distilling is carried on mainly in the Highlands. Nevertheless, unemployment remains much above the British average.

Government and History

Scotland is part of the United Kingdom and is mostly governed from Westminister. The secretary of state for Scotland administers government ministries relating to welfare and economy. Scotland is represented in the British Parliament by 72 members, 4 of whom (1991) are Scottish Nationalists. Scotland's legal system is separate and different from that of the rest of Great Britain. The High Court of Justiciary is the supreme criminal court, and its civil counterpart is the Court of Session. For the purposes of local government Scotland was divided into 33 counties until 1975, when they were reorganized into 9 administrative regions.

The Romans penetrated but failed to conquer Scotland, building (AD *c.*120) HADRIAN'S WALL to mark the northernmost point of their empire in Britain. Scotland was occupied then by Celts and a people of obscure origin called PICTS. The Picts were the dominant group in North Britain until the Celtic Scots migrated from Ireland and eventually spread through the west of Scotland, forming the kingdom of Dalriada. Germanic tribespeople settled in the southeast as early as the 4th century AD and formed part of the Anglo-Saxon kingdom of NORTHUMBRIA. West of this kingdom, from Dumbarton and the Solway River into England, was the kingdom of Strathclyde, peopled by romanized Britons.

About the middle of the 9th century, Kenneth I (r. 843–58) of Dalriada united the Picts and the Scots and formed a kingdom in central Scotland. Eventually this kingdom expanded to include Strathclyde and Lothian,

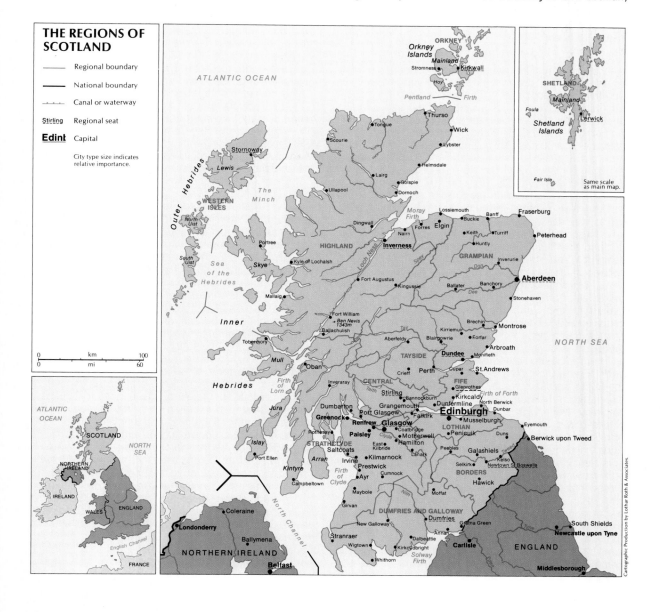

THE REGIONS OF SCOTLAND

——— Regional boundary

——— National boundary

—·—·— Canal or waterway

Stirling   Regional seat

Edint   Capital

City type size indicates relative importance.

Hadrian's Wall (AD c.120), a fortification extending across northern England, marked the northern boundary of Roman Britain. Construction of this defense signaled the end of Roman efforts to conquer Scotland.

originally part of Northumbria. This Celtic monarchy lasted until MACBETH's reign ended (1057) and MALCOLM III, who had been educated in England and had an English wife (see MARGARET OF SCOTLAND, SAINT), came to the throne. Under Malcolm and his successors, most notably DAVID I (r. 1124–53), Scotland became an organized feudal state. The Scottish kings gradually expelled the Norse who had established themselves in the northeast and in the islands. After 1263 the Norse retained only Orkney and Shetland, which they held until the 15th century.

Repeated disputes with the English sometimes led to war and often resulted in the Scottish kings doing homage to the English monarchs. In 1174, for example, WILLIAM THE LION did homage to Henry II of England for all his dominions, although he later secured cancellation of this obligation. After the deaths of ALEXANDER III (1286) and his heiress, Margaret, Maid of Norway (1290), King EDWARD I of England claimed suzerainty over Scotland and picked John de BALIOL from rival claimants as the Scottish king. When John attempted to assert his independence in 1296, Edward imposed direct English rule. The Scots, led first by Sir William WALLACE and later by Robert the Bruce (crowned king as ROBERT I in 1306), revolted and finally defeated the English in the Battle of Bannockburn (1314). During the long reign (1329–71) of David II the English partially reestablished control, but they were distracted by the Hundred Years' War with France, Scotland's ally since 1295.

David was succeeded by his nephew Robert II, the first STUART monarch. He and his successors, Robert III, JAMES I, James II, James III, JAMES IV, and JAMES V, faced persistent civil strife and continued interference from—and war with—England. The long minorities of several of these kings contributed to the decline of royal authority.

After the death (1542) of James V, Scotland was ruled by his widow, Mary of GUISE, as regent for her young daughter, MARY, QUEEN OF SCOTS. During this period the REFORMATION took root in Scotland (see KNOX, JOHN), gathering strength as a result of the political opposition to the French regent. The Catholic Mary, Queen of Scots, who returned to Scotland from France in 1561, fell victim to the religious and political conflicts. Forced to abdicate in 1567, she fled to England, where she was imprisoned and later executed by Elizabeth I. Nonetheless, her son, James VI of Scotland, succeeded Elizabeth on the English throne as JAMES I in 1603.

Although united under a single crown, Scotland and England remained a separate state for another century. The Scottish Presbyterians resisted the efforts of King CHARLES I to impose episcopacy in Scotland (see BISHOPS' WARS; COVENANTERS) and allied with the English parliamentarians against Charles in the first ENGLISH CIVIL WAR (1642–46). They subsequently supported the royalist cause, however, until defeated by Oliver Cromwell in 1650–51.

After the Restoration (1660) the English efforts to impose an episcopal church settlement were renewed. Only after the GLORIOUS REVOLUTION of 1688–89, which deposed the Catholic James II in favor of his Protestant daughter Mary II and her husband, William III, was Presbyterianism guaranteed in Scotland. This guarantee was incorporated into the Act of Union of 1707, whereby the parliaments of Scotland and England were united.

After the death of the Protestant Stuart Queen Anne in 1714, many Scots opposed the succession of the Hanoverian dynasty, rallying to the support of the JACOBITES, who sought to restore the Catholic Stuarts to the throne. Major Jacobite uprisings occurred in 1715 and 1745 but were harshly suppressed. These were the last serious efforts to resist English control.

Much of the Highlands were forcibly depopulated by the landlords during the late 18th and early 19th centuries when large-scale sheep grazing was introduced. At the same time, however, the Industrial Revolution began to create major industrial centers in the Central Lowlands. In the late 19th century a strong labor movement developed. By the mid-20th century a new nationalist movement had also emerged. Scotland has been assured limited home rule (or devolution) including a Scottish-elected assembly. A 1979 referendum for an assembly, however, did not receive a sufficient percentage of the vote to pass.

See also: GREAT BRITAIN, HISTORY OF; separate entries on Scottish administrative regions and former counties.

Scotland, Church of   The Church of Scotland is an established, Presbyterian church that traces its roots to the Protestant REFORMATION. It was founded in 1560 under the leadership of John KNOX, with the support of influential members of the upper middle class. Until 1690 the church was racked by struggles with Stuart monarchs (MARY, QUEEN OF SCOTS and the English kings JAMES I, CHARLES I, CHARLES II, and JAMES II), who wanted some form of episcopal church government in Scotland. In these struggles, the Scottish commitment to Calvinistic Presbyterianism was sometimes impassioned (as with the Covenanters of 1638 and after 1660) and sometimes brought Scotland deep into English political strife (as in the ENGLISH CIVIL WAR of the 1640s). During the 17th century the Church of Scotland accepted the Calvinistic doctrinal and ecclesiastical standards of the English Westminster Assembly (1643–53) as its own.

The 18th and 19th centuries saw groups break from the church in protest against patronage abuse and theological "moderatism." The most important of these breaches, the Disruption of 1843, led to the formation of the Free Church of Scotland, which did not rejoin the Church of Scotland until 1929.

Scotland Yard   Scotland Yard is the name commonly used to refer to the Criminal Investigation Department (CID) of the London Metropolitan Police. Originally, Scotland Yard was the name given to the first headquarters building of London's police force when it was established (1829) by Home Secretary Sir Robert PEEL. The rear entrance of the building was situated on the site of a 12th-century palace used for visiting Scottish royalty. The headquarters of the CID was moved in 1890 and again in 1967 and is now called New Scotland Yard.

In addition to criminal investigation activities, Scotland Yard maintains criminal records and forensic laboratories, directs London metropolitan police functions, and provides security for political and royal figures.

Scott, Dred   see DRED SCOTT V. SANDFORD

Scott, Duncan Campbell   Duncan Campbell Scott, b. Ottawa, Aug. 2, 1862, d. Dec. 19, 1947, was a prominent writer and civil servant whom many regard as 19th-century Canada's finest poet. His best-known poems describe Canadian Indian life. His works include *The Magic House and Other Poems* (1893) and the short-story collection *In the Village of Viger* (1896).

Scott, George C.   A star of stage, screen, and television, George Campbell Scott, b. Wise, Va., Oct. 18, 1927, is best known for his film performances in *Anatomy of a Murder* (1959), *The Hustler* (1961), *Dr. Strangelove* (1964), *Patton* (1970)—for which he won an Academy Award—and *The Hospital* (1972). As a stage actor in the 1950s he appeared in plays by Shakespeare, O'Neill, and Chekhov. He has also directed two films: *Rage* (1973) and *The Savage Is Loose* (1974).

Scott, Sir George Gilbert   Sir George Gilbert Scott, b. July 13, 1811, d. Mar. 27, 1878, was one of the major figures in British architecture in the middle third of the 19th century. An ardent partisan of the GOTHIC REVIVAL, he won the competition for the Nikolaikirche, Hamburg, in 1844 (executed 1845–63) and went on to build numerous churches, public buildings, and other structures, including the Albert Memorial (1863–72) and the Midland Hotel at Saint Pancras Station (1865–77). He was also a major restorer of medieval cathedrals and churches.

Scott, Robert Falcon   Captain Robert Falcon Scott, b. June 6, 1868, d. Mar. 29(?), 1912, was an English naval officer and explorer who led the second expedition to reach the South Pole (1912). Scott joined the Royal Navy as a cadet in 1880 and led his first expedition to Antarctica in 1901–04, conducting scientific investigation and exploring previously uncharted areas.

Scott returned to Antarctica in 1910 in hope of leading the first expedition to the South Pole. He began a motor-sledge journey to the pole on Nov. 1, 1911, with 11 men in his party. By December 31, broken equipment and severe weather necessitated the return of the remaining 7 men to the base camp. Scott's party set out again and reached the South Pole on Jan. 18, 1912, only to find that explorer Roald AMUNDSEN had reached it a month previously. On the return journey 2 men were lost, and Scott and the 2 other remaining members, unable to continue because of severe blizzards, died only 18 km (11 mi) from their depot destination. Their bodies and records were found on Nov. 12, 1912.

Scott, Sir Walter   One of the foremost literary figures of the romantic period, Sir Walter Scott, b. Aug. 15, 1771, d. Sept. 21, 1932, achieved unprecedented popularity with his narrative poems and historical romances. Such classics as *Ivanhoe* and *Waverly* remain widely read, and he is regarded as an important figure in the development of the novel.

Scott was born in Edinburgh, Scotland. An early illness, possibly polio, left him lame in his right leg, and he spent much of his childhood convalescing at his grandfather's farm in the Scottish border country. One of his first major works, *Minstrelsy of the Scottish Border* (1802, 1803), is a three-volume collection of ballads from Scottish oral tradition.

Minstrelsy was followed by several similar and equally popular romantic ballads, among them *Lay of the Last Minstrel* (1805) and *Lady of the Lake* (1810). In *Rokeby* (1813), Scott focused less on poetic lyric and more on character; the year *Rokeby* was published, he was offered (and declined) the poet laureateship of England.

The first of Scott's novels, *Waverly*, dealt with the Jacobite rebellion of 1745. Published anonymously in 1814, it was enormously successful. During the 15 years that followed, Scott produced novel after novel, all

Sir Walter Scott, one of the most famous authors of the early 19th century, introduced the historical novel to English literature. Waverly (1814) and Ivanhoe (1820) are among the best known of Scott's many volumes.

issued anonymously like *Waverly*, and as a result they became known as the Waverly novels. In earlier works, such as *Guy Mannering* (1815), *Old Mortality* (1816), and *Rob Roy* (1817), Scott wrote of 17th- and 18th-century Scotland. For *Ivanhoe* (1820) and *Quentin Durward* (1823), he turned to medieval England and France. In other works, among them *The Talisman* (1825) and *Anne of Geierstein* (1829), he chose settings even more remote.

In 1826 the collapse of the bookselling and printing business in which Scott was a partner put him into debt and severely affected his health. Thereafter he wrote incessantly, succeeding in earning enough to clear his name. In 1831, exhausted from overwork, Scott left on a cruise to Italy. He returned more ill than ever and died the following year.

Scott, Winfield   Winfield Scott, b. near Petersburg, Va., June 13, 1786, d. May 29, 1866, was commanding general of the U.S. Army (1841–61) and the Whig presidential nominee in 1852. He practiced law briefly before joining the army with a captain's commission in 1808. Entering the WAR OF 1812 as a lieutenant colonel, Scott fought well and was promoted to brigadier general in March 1814. For his bravery in the Battle of Lundy's Lane (July 25, 1814), where he was twice wounded, he received a gold medal from Congress and was brevetted major general. After service in the Black Hawk War (1832) and the Seminole and Creek wars (1835-36), he became (1841) general in chief of the army. Scott was known as "Old Fuss and Feathers" because of his emphasis on appearance and discipline.

In November 1846, President James K. Polk ordered Scott to assume direct command of an invasion of Mexico. He made an amphibious landing a few kilometers south of Veracruz, surrounded the city, and stormed it successfully on Mar. 26, 1847, with fewer than 20 casualties. He then conducted a brilliant campaign that resulted in the capture of Mexico City on September 14, for which he was awarded another gold medal by Congress.

In 1848, Scott lost the Whig nomination for president to Zachary Taylor. He was the Whig nominee four years later, but with his party split over the slavery issue, he lost to Democrat Franklin Pierce. Political enmities limited his opportunity of further service to the nation, although in 1859 he did quiet the dispute with Britain over control of San Juan Island in Puget Sound (see SAN JUAN BOUNDARY DISPUTE). At the outbreak of the U.S. Civil War, he commanded the defense of Washington, D.C., but he resigned because of age on Nov. 1, 1861.

Scottish deerhound   The Scottish deerhound, an ancient breed of dog developed in the Highlands of Scotland, was highly esteemed there for its combined good scenting abilities and the strength and speed necessary to run down deer. The dog has small, folded ears and a long, curved tail carried very low. Males stand 76 to 81 cm (30 to 32 in) at the shoulder, weighing 38 to 50 kg (85 to 110

lb); females are slightly smaller. In general appearance the deerhound is much like the greyhound, but larger and with a harsh, wiry coat that for show should be thick, close-lying and ragged, and crisp to the touch; any color is permitted, but the dark blue gray is the most desirable.

Scottish Gaelic language   see CELTIC LANGUAGES

Scottish literature   Scottish literature includes both the native Gaelic tradition, closely related to IRISH LITERATURE, and Lowland Scots, a distinct dialect of English made famous by the poetry of Robert BURNS, but significant as a literary language from the 14th century. John BARBOUR's *Bruce* (c.1375) and works of the 15th-century Scottish Chaucerians, Gawin Douglas, Robert Henryson, and William DUNBAR, are remarkable for their learning, epic qualities, richness of language, and tendency to satire.

In Gaelic, the earliest collections are the Book of Deer and the Book of the Dean of Lismore (c.1512–26), the latter with poems in the style of the Fenian cycle as well as works of Irish and Scottish poets. In the 17th century, Mary MacLeod continued many elements of the bardic tradition, especially panegyric and satire, as did Alexander MacDonald, Duncan Ban MacIntyre, Rob Donn MacKay, John Roy Stewart, and other associated with the Jacobite rebellion.

The publication (1760–63) by James MACPHERSON of a series of works allegedly translated from Gaelic sources (see OSSIAN) fostered the romantic appeal of Scottish history, which found its highest expression in the novels of Sir Walter SCOTT. Influential poets of the 20th century include Hugh MacDiarmid, writing in Scots, and Somhairle Maclean, in Gaelic.

Scottish terrier   The Scottish terrier is a small, heavily built, short-legged dog with an erect tail and a strong, distinguished head characterized by prick ears, heavy eyebrows, and a beard. Scotties stand 25 to 28 cm (10 to 11 in) at the shoulder and weigh 9 to 10 kg (19 to 22 lb). The coat is double; the undercoat is short, thick, and soft, and the outer coat is dense and wiry. The breed occurs in a wide range of colors in addition to the most common, black. The forerunners of today's Scottie have been used in Scotland for hundreds of years to go to

The Scottish terrier was recognized as a distinct breed of dog during the late 19th century. A small terrier with a thick, wiry coat, it is descended from a number of breeds developed in Scotland to hunt small game.

ground after foxes and other vermin. In 1897 the English Kennel Club officially separated the breed from the Cairn terrier, its cousin.

Scottsboro case   see POWELL V. ALABAMA

Scout

Scout is a four-stage, solid-propellant launch vehicle used for a variety of space tasks by the United States and a number of foreign countries. Conceived in 1958 by NASA's Langley Research Center, it remains NASA's smallest launcher. Designed from the outset for growth, Scout has more than tripled its payload capability (from 60 kg/131 lb to 215 kg/475 lb) since it was first introduced in 1960.

A new Algol III first stage (63,500 kg/140,000 lb average thrust) was introduced in 1972, increasing the payload by 25% to 30%. The second stage (27,200 kg/60,000 lb thrust) is known as Castor II, the third stage (9,500 kg/21,000 lb thrust) as Antares II, and the fourth stage (2,700 kg/6,000 lb thrust) as Altair III. With its payload shroud, the vehicle stands 22.9 m (75 ft) tall and has a launch weight of 21,400 kg (47,178 lb). A fifth stage can be added if required.

Scouting

Scouting is a worldwide movement of youth groups whose objective is to help boys and girls develop character, citizenship, and physical and mental fitness by training members in wood, field, and handicraft activities and by encouraging community service. Many nations have scouting organizations, and the number of boy and girl scouts totals several million members throughout the world.

Boy Scouts. The organization was founded by the British general Sir Robert BADEN-POWELL in 1908. Baden-Powell had written a book, intended for army officers, on military reconnaissance and scouting. The book became so popular with younger readers that Baden-Powell wrote *Scouting for Boys* (1908) and held the first scout encampment at Brownsea Island in Dorset in that year. The American organization, Boy Scouts of America, was founded on Baden-Powell's model in 1910. Boys 8 through 20 are accepted as members and attain rising rank within the organization through various accomplishments, each of which earns a rank or merit badge. The World Scout Jamboree, a meeting to which all countries send Boy Scout representatives, is held every few years. Locally, Cub Scouts are organized into dens and packs, and Boy Scouts into patrols and troops. The age groupings are: cubs (ages 8–10), scouts (ages 11–17), and explorers (ages 14–20).

Girl Scouts. Agnes Baden-Powell, sister of Sir Robert, organized the British Girl Guides in 1910; the Girl Scouts of the U.S.A. was founded by Juliet Gordon Low in 1912, following the British format. Membership ages run from 6 to 17, although the Campus Girl Scouts, who are young college students, may be older. The age groupings for Girl Scouts are: brownies (ages 6–8), juniors (ages 9–11), cadettes (ages 12–14), and seniors (ages 14–17).

Scrabble

Scrabble is a popular crossword-puzzle-like board game played by two to four people. Aside from the board—a square grid comprising 225 squares—the equipment includes 100 plastic or wooden tiles on each of which is printed a letter of the alphabet and an assigned point value ranging from 1 (for frequently used letters) to 10 (for letters used less often). After the game's start, turn by turn words are added to words contiguously until all 100 tiles are used. The person accumulating the most points for his or her words wins.

Conceived by architect Alfred M. Butts and patented by the Selchow and Righter Co. in 1948, Scrabble was soon rendered in numerous foreign languages, as well as in a braille version for the blind and a three-dimensional form.

Scranton

Scranton is a city in northeastern Pennsylvania, 160 km (100 mi) northeast of Philadelphia. The seat of Lackawanna County, it has a population of 81,805 (1990). An industrial and transportation center, the city manufactures metal products, furniture, electronic equipment, and textiles. The United Mine Workers of America was organized in Scranton in 1897. The University of Scranton was founded there in 1888.

Settled about 1788, it was known as Unionville, Slocum Hollow, and Harrison before its present name, honoring the founder of an iron and coal company, was chosen in 1851. Rich anthracite coal deposits in the region led to a prosperous iron industry. The decline of the nation's coal industry in the 1950s resulted in the adoption of the Scranton Plan, which provided financial aid for industrial expansion.

screamer

Screamers are three species of South American birds that constitute the family Anhimidae in the WATERFOWL order, Anseriformes. Named for their resounding calls, screamers feed on plants in marshy areas; the swan-sized adults weigh from 2 to 3 kg (4 to 6.5 lb). Probably sharing a common ancestor with geese, screamers resemble other waterfowl in their gregarious habits and the appearance of their eggs and downy young. They differ, however, in having chickenlike bills, unwebbed toes, and wing spurs. Hollow bones and many tiny air sacs in the skin give them a soaring ability, and their ribs lack the bony processes that serve to link the ribs in almost all other birds.

screw

The term *screw* describes a chiefly metal device used to fasten wood or metal objects together; it is cylindrical and has a spiral ridge, or thread, running around it. The thread can be thought of an an inclined plane, one of the SIMPLE MACHINES, in the form of a helix. This spiral inclined plane enables the screw to do work and exert the necessary force required when fastening two objects together. The screw can have threads running all the way to the head or threads that stop at the neck. A machine screw consists of a bolt and nut; it is a cylinder of equal diameter throughout

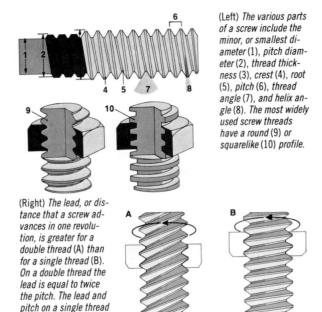

(Left) *The various parts of a screw include the minor, or smallest diameter (1), pitch diameter (2), thread thickness (3), crest (4), root (5), pitch (6), thread angle (7), and helix angle (8). The most widely used screw threads have a round (9) or squarelike (10) profile.*

(Right) *The lead, or distance that a screw advances in one revolution, is greater for a double thread (A) than for a single thread (B). On a double thread the lead is equal to twice the pitch. The lead and pitch on a single thread are equal.*

its length and has external threads. The bolt fits into a nut, which has a hole with internal threads. A wood screw consists of a bolt that tapers to a point.

Screw threads have a few basic characteristics, including thread angle, pitch, and core diameter. A thread angle is for the most part V-shaped and the angle of the V ranges from 47.5 to 60 degrees. Pitch is defined as the distance between the crest of one thread and the next.

Hand methods of producing threads are carried out using either taps (to thread a drilled hole) or dies (if the thread is to be cut on a spindle). A tap is a threaded cutting tool driven into a hole drilled the same size as the core diameter of the tap. A die is a circular block of tool steel furnished with a threaded core and pierced axially so that the threads are fluted. The die is mounted in a holder provided with a pair of handles, enabling the die itself to be rotated.

screw pine   Screw pines, genus *Pandanus*, of the family Pandanaceae, are Old World tropical plants named for the characteristically perfect spiral arrangement of their long, sword-shaped leaves and for their fruit, which resembles pineapples. Not pines at all, these plants have long, naked trunks, stiltlike bracing aerial roots, and crowns of leaves; the latter are used in local manufacture of paper and nets. Both roots and leaves furnish fiber for ropes, baskets, mats, and hats. Young screw pines, especially the species *P. veitchii*, are popular houseplants because of their attractive foliage.

Scriabin, Aleksandr Nikolayevich [skree-ah-been'] The Russian composer Aleksandr Nikolayevich

Scriabin, b. Jan. 6 (N.S.), 1872, d. Apr. 27 (N.S.), 1915, is best known for his solo piano music and orchestral works. He received the gold medal in piano from the Moscow Conservatory. An annuity provided in 1904 by a wealthy former student enabled Scriabin to abandon his teaching post at the Moscow Conservatory and move to Switzerland, from which he often traveled on concert tours of Europe and the U.S. In 1910, Scriabin returned to Moscow, where he died.

His early piano works—preludes, impromptus, mazurkas, and other pieces—are stamped with the influences of Chopin and Liszt. The Fourth Sonata (1903) marks the evolution of Scriabin's innovative melodic and harmonic style, which eventually left behind the dictates of traditional tonality to establish a harmonic logic based predominantly on complex fourth chords and invented modes and scales. This development was mirrored by Scriabin's increasing preoccupation, after 1903, with solipsist theosophical and mystical concepts, as reflected in works such as the orchestral *Poem of Ecstasy* (1908) and *Prometheus* (*The Poem of Fire*, 1911). The ultimate goal of Scriabin's experiments, the *Misterium*, which was to have resulted in the ecstatic cataclysm of the human race, was left incomplete at his death.

Scribe, Eugène [skreeb] French playwright Eugène Scribe, b. Dec. 24, 1791, d. Feb. 20, 1861, was the creator of a suspenseful type of drama known as the "well-made play." He set the pattern for dramatic construction followed by many 19th-century playwrights. Of his more than 300 works, the best known are *A Glass of Water* (1842; Eng. trans., 1865), *Adrienne Lecouvreur* (1849; Eng. trans., 1855), and *The Ladies' Battle* (1851; Eng. trans., 1870), his masterpiece.

scrimshaw [skrim'-shaw] Scrimshaw, an American folk craft derived from European maritime traditions, is the art of engraving on ivory, whalebone, whale teeth, or walrus tusks. The craft developed on New England whaling ships during the 1820s, and quantities of objects— boxes, toys, kitchen utensils, corset stays—were produced by sailors. A design, called a "graphic," was pricked onto the surface with a jackknife or a sail needle;

Scrimshaw designs, such as these ships carved in elephant tusks (left) and whale teeth (right), were first made by the crews of U.S. whaling ships. Most scrimshaw dates from approximately 1830 to 1850 and displays nautical designs.

the holes were connected with delicate scratches, rubbed with ink, and then polished with whale oil.

Scripps, E. W.

[skrips]   Edward Wyllis Scripps, b. Rushville, Ill., June 18, 1854, d. Mar. 12, 1926, dominated the organization of the newspaper leagues that evolved into United Press International (see PRESS AGENCIES AND SYNDICATES). After moving to Detroit in 1874, Scripps joined the *Evening News*, a paper started by his half brother James, but soon, with his half brother George, he founded (1878) the (Penny) *Press*. In 1880, Edward and George added the *St. Louis Evening Chronicle* and the *Cincinnati Post*, creating the first American daily newspaper chain. With George, Edward joined Milton A. McRae to form (1895) a news service that became (1897) the Scripps-McRae Press Association. Using the telegraph, the association became (1907) the United Press Association and ultimately (1958) United Press International.

Scripps Institution of Oceanography

The Scripps Institution of Oceanography at La Jolla, Calif., founded (1903) by an endowment from E. W. and Ellen B. Scripps, is devoted to oceanographic research and the instruction of graduate students in ocean sciences. Originally the San Diego Marine Biological Institute, it became (1912) part of the University of California. Its staff of professional scientists conducts specialized research in areas such as geology, physics, biology, chemistry, and engineering. Facilities include large research collections of plankton and fish, living culture collections of phytoplankton and bacteria, samples of deep-sea sediment cores, and a collection of samples of seawater from the major oceans. The institution operates several large oceanographic vessels and carries out expeditions throughout the world's oceans.

Scruggs, Earl

see FLATT AND SCRUGGS

scuba diving

Scuba is an acronym for Self-Contained Underwater Breathing Apparatus. Attempts to perfect this type of apparatus date from the early 20th century, but it was not until 1943 that the most famous scuba, or aqualung, was invented by the Frenchmen Jacques-Yves COUSTEAU and Emil Gagnan. The aqualung has made recreational diving possible for thousands of nonprofessional divers. Scuba diving is also called free diving because the diver, unencumbered by lines or air hoses, has no physical connection with the surface. Although some specially trained (commercial) scuba divers can descend below 100 m (328 ft), recreational divers are limited to a depth of 40 m (130 ft) because of the risk of nitrogen narcosis, a type of intoxication akin to drunkenness. (See also BENDS.)

The scuba diver wears tanks that carry a supply of pressurized breathing gas—either air or a mixture of oxygen and other gases. The heart of the breathing apparatus is the breathing regulator and the pressure-reducing

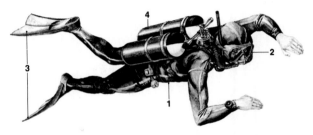

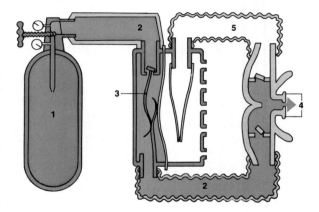

(Above) *Equipment used in scuba (Self-Contained Underwater Breathing Apparatus) diving includes a full-length wet suit (1) and a face mask (2) for protection in cold water. Flippers (3) reduce the effort, and therefore the oxygen, required in underwater swimming. The diver draws air from an aqualung unit (4), which contains pressurized gases. (Below) As a diver inhales using an open-circuit aqualung, air from a pressurized tank (1) is drawn through a feed line (2) and passes a regulatory diaphragm (3) before reaching the mouthpiece (4). Exhaled gas flows into an exhaust line (5) and is discharged into the water.*

mechanisms that deliver gas to the diver on each inhalation. In the common scuba, the breathing medium is air (see diagram). Inhalation causes a slight negative pressure in the mouthpiece, which signals the valve that delivers the air to open. The valve closes when the diver stops inhaling, and a one-way valve allows the exhaled breath to escape as bubbles into the water. In more sophisticated scubas, the exhalation passes through a canister that absorbs carbon dioxide, then goes into a breathing bag where oxygen is added and the air is recycled.

Scudéry, Madeleine de

[skue-day-ree']   The French writer Madeleine de Scudéry, b. Nov. 15, 1607, d. June 2, 1701, was the author of such multivolume, enormously popular romances as *Artamène* (1649–53), *Clélie* (1654–61), and *Almahide* (1660–63), which feature high-minded dialogue, between characters from exotic places or ancient times, about the infinite subtleties of love. Mademoiselle de Scudéry presided over one of the most famous literary salons in Paris, and her shorter works—*Célinte* (1661), *Mathilde d'Aguilar* (1667), and "Célanire" (1669)—mark the transition from the baroque to the classic novel.

sculpin [skuhl'-pin] Sculpins, or bullheads (family Cottidae), are odd-looking fishes with winglike pectoral fins and large heads and mouths. They are common in the shallow waters of Arctic and temperate seas and are abundant in fresh water in Europe and North America. More than 100 species of sculpins live in U.S. waters, mostly in the Pacific. They range in size from 7.6 cm (3 in) to the crab-eating cabezon, *Scorpaenichthys marmoratus*, which reaches 76 cm (30 in) and 11 kg (25 lb).

Sculpins are bottom dwellers with depressed bodies and heads. They are characterized by a body stay across the cheek. Large eyes near the top of the head enable the fish to look upward for prey or enemies; in some species the eyes can swivel independently. The first dorsal and the pectoral fins are spiny. The dorsal is the main means of locomotion, which may take the form of short jumps. The body is naked, scales apparently being represented by small prickles on the head and stalks of the pectoral fins. Sculpins feed on smaller fish and invertebrates.

sculpture Sculpture is as old as human culture and has appeared in almost every culture throughout the world. Clay engravings have been found on the walls of caves inhabited by prehistoric peoples of the Gravettian period (c.21,000 BC; Dordogne, France); small fertility figures carved from limestone, such as the VENUS OF WILLENDORF (c.25,000 BC; Austria), or modeled in terra-cotta (c.5750 BC; ÇATAL HÜYÜK, Anatolia) have been found at other sites (see PREHISTORIC ART). This article will trace the history of western sculpture. Discussion of nonwestern sculpture will be found in articles on the art of particular cultures; see, for example, AFRICAN ART, CHINESE ART AND ARCHITECTURE, INDIAN ART AND ARCHITECTURE, JAPANESE ART AND ARCHITECTURE, KOREAN ART, OCEANIA, ART OF.

Carving, a direct subtractive process, is one of the two ancient sculpture techniques. Carved or glyptic sculptures were fashioned from such durable materials as stone, ivory, and wood. The other technique is modeling, a direct additive process in which a pliable material is built up around an armature or skeletal framework. Casting, either by the LOST-WAX PROCESS or in sand, is an indirect process; a carved or a modeled sculpture is its starting point. Sculpture may be created in two dimensions—relief sculpture—or in three—in the round. Relief may be of varying degrees—low (called BAS-RELIEF), middle, or high—depending on how far the figures emerge from the background plane; or forms may be recessed beneath the background plane, a method favored by the ancient Egyptians.

Egyptian Sculpture

The *Palette of King Narmer* (c.3200 BC; Egyptian Museum, Cairo) is the oldest work to have been discovered in the pharaonic style of Egyptian sculpture (see EGYPT, ANCIENT). Its representational conventions were followed, except for a few significant deviations, for 2,700 years until Hellenistic traits were adopted following Alexander the Great's conquest (332 BC) of Egypt. The only open rejection of the rigidities in frontal and lateral poses and ges-

tures occurred during the reign (1375–1358 BC) of Akhenaten, as evidenced by a remarkably naturalistic portrait statue of him (c.1375 BC; Egyptian Museum).

Alongside the pharaonic tradition in sculpture stood another tradition, equally old but more naturalistic. It has survived for the most part in painted wood and limestone images.

Greek and Roman Sculpture

The Greco-Roman blend of realistically observed detail and ideally conceived form has profoundly affected the whole course of sculptural styles in the West.

Aegean and Greek Sculpture. Late Minoan and Mycenaean civilization (c.1600–200 BC; see AEGEAN CIVILIZATION), influenced by centuries of trade with Egypt and other Eastern Mediterranean centers, produced large-scale sculptures, such as the Lion Gate at MYCENAE (c.1300 BC). In reliefs

This bronze kouros *(c.520 BC), discovered (1959) by workers in Piraeus, displays the frontal attitude and emphasis on proportion that characterizes archaic Greek sculpture. The creation of nude, life-size* kouroi *(idealized figures of young men) flourished during the Greek archaic period, when stylistic conventions were derived from earlier Egyptian models. Bronze was widely used in Greek sculpture, and this piece is one of the oldest known bronze* kouroi. *(National Museum, Athens.)*

(Below) *This Roman bust, called the* Capitoline Brutus *for the early-6th-century* BC *Roman hero L. Junius Brutus, is now thought to be a bronze of the 1st century* BC. *(Palazzo dei Conservatori, Rome.)*

(Above) *The* Ara Pacis *(Altar of Peace) of Augustus, consecrated in 9* BC, *is an open-air, rectangular enclosure built to celebrate the emperor's achievement of peace throughout the Roman Empire. Its walls are completely covered with relief sculptures, such as this procession of senators. (Piazza Augustea, Rome.)*

and statuettes Minoan sculptors of the time revealed an interest in costume and the human physique, as shown in the ivory-and-gold snake goddess (*c.*1600 BC; Archaeological Museum, Iráklion, Crete), found at KNOSSOS. These figurines are entirely different from the older, smoothly schematized marble figures (*c.*2500–2000 BC) from the Cycladic and other Greek islands.

In the Greek archaic period (*c.*660–480 BC), sculptors carved life-size nude kouroi (plural of kouros, a young man) and clothed Korai (plural of Kore, a young woman). In the classical period (480–330 BC), especially in the earliest phase (until 430 BC), sculpture was carved in a severe (or formal) classical style. The male body became a broad-shouldered, trim-hipped athlete, often shown in arrested motion, as in Myron's bronze *Discobolus* (*c.*460–450 BC). Later, in high classicism, such sculptors as PRAXITELES added suppleness and grace to sculpture of the human form. The subtle, twisted pose, called contrapposto, of his statues was much copied and can be seen effectively in his *Hermes Holding the Infant Dionysus* (*c.*350–330 BC; Museum, Olympia).

In the Hellenistic period (330–100 BC), sculptors showed a growing interest in the depiction of violent motion and emotion. The *Laocoön* (*c.*175–150 BC; Vatican Museums), rediscovered (1506) in Rome, had a profound impact on Italian Renaissance sculpture (see GREEK ART).

Etruscan and Roman Sculpture. Little survives of the sculpture of the ETRUSCANS. Some terra-cotta figures, many associated with sarcophagi, suggest a strong archaic Greek influence. Some ornamental bronzes from Etruscan tombs are classical in feeling.

In Rome during preimperial times, patrician ancestral images, either as busts or full figures—such as the bronze *Capitoline Brutus* (3d century BC; Palazzo dei Conservatori, Rome)—were exceedingly popular; their extreme realism established a veristic tradition in Ro-

man portrait sculpture. This verism is evident even in the classical reliefs that adorn the elaborate *Ara Pacis* (Altar of Peace; 13–9 BC; Lungotevere in Augusta, Rome). Monumental sculpture became an indispensable tool of imperial propaganda. Two distinctively Roman architectural forms, the triumphal column and the triumphal arch, were adorned with relief sculpture. Another form of Roman imperial glorification was the monumental equestrian statue. Only one Roman example has survived: the gilded bronze equestrian monument of Marcus Aurelius (AD *c.*165; Piazza del Campidoglio, Rome). It became the model used by several sculptors during the Renaissance.

At death important people were placed in sarcophagi (see SARCOPHAGUS), the front and sides of which were often carved in high relief.

In the 3d century, imperial sculpture began to lose its classicistic-naturalistic balance, first in favor of strong verism and later of a compact bulkiness, in a style called Late Antique. After Constantine I seized power, imperial sculpture once again became monumental (see ROMAN ART AND ARCHITECTURE).

Early Christian and Byzantine Sculpture

Large sculptures in the round were viewed as idolatrous by the early Christians. On a small scale, carving in relief continued on diptychs (portable ivory panels). In the West high relief work continued to be carved on the sides of sarcophagi, modified so that figures from pagan mythology either disappeared or were adapted as Christian images and symbols, such as the beardless Christ on the *Sarcophagus of Junius Bassus* (*c.*359; Vatican Grottoes, Rome).

Carolingian, Ottonian, and Romanesque Sculpture

The strenuous efforts of the first Holy Roman emperor, Charlemagne (r. 800–14), to refound the Roman Empire

(Left) These statues (c.1230) from the north transept portal of Chartres Cathedral incorporate features of both Romanesque and Gothic art. The straight, columnar figures exemplify the Romanesque style, but the expressive faces of the prophets Isaiah, Jeremiah, and Simeon and of Saint John the Baptist and Saint Peter are characteristic of Gothic sculpture. (Right) The Second Coming of Christ (1110–20), a Romanesque tympanum from Saint Pierre, Moissac, depicts Christ surrounded by angels, the 24 Elders, and symbols of the 4 Evangelists in twisted, animated poses.

in the West led to a general revival in the arts (see CARO-LINGIAN ART AND ARCHITECTURE). For his Palace Chapel at Aachen, Charlemagne commissioned eight bronze grille screens for the octagonal structure. Executed between 795 and 810, each grille is cast in a single piece of extraordinary delicacy. Under Otto III, Bishop Bernward (fl. 993–1022) of Hildesheim commissioned a pair of monumental bronze doors ornamented with biblical scenes; each door was cast in a single piece. They remain in the monastery Church of Saint Michael in Hildesheim, and they were the first large-scale castings in more than 500 years (see OTTONIAN ART AND ARCHITECTURE).

In the West stone carving gradually revived and first appeared in the form of religious narratives on the piers and tympana above the main church portals. The models for these large sculptures seem to have been figures from ivory diptychs and manuscript illuminations (see RO-MANESQUE ART AND ARCHITECTURE).

Gothic Sculpture

France and Germany. The great Royal Portal (c.1150–70) at CHARTRES CATHEDRAL in France, whose tympana depict, from left to right, the Ascension, the Apocalypse, and the Incarnation of Christ, with columnar figures forming the door jambs below, is a transitional monument, with Romanesque features in an emphatic Gothic framework (see GOTHIC ART AND ARCHITECTURE).

In Germany emphasis was placed on capturing what was personal and particular. The unknown sculptor of the freestanding figures of *Ekkehard* and *Uta* (c.1260–70) in the west choir of Naumburg Cathedral treated the cloaked figures in a simple, monumental fashion although rendering the heads in a powerful, expressive manner.

The Netherlandish master Claus SLUTER carved six life-size figures of prophets—including a dynamic Moses—for the so-called *Well of Moses* (1395–1404) in the Chartreuse de Champmol, Dijon, France, in an extreme and expressive Late Gothic style.

Italy. Italian Gothic sculpture, which was on a smaller scale than that beyond the Alps, was more often used to ornament pulpits than tympana and piers. Italian sculptors charged biblical narratives with motion and emotion. The hexagonal pulpit (1260) by Nicola Pisano (see PISA-NO, NICOLA AND GIOVANNI) in the Baptistery of Pisa is clearly a descendant of Hellenistic sarcophagi.

Renaissance and Mannerist Sculpture

Italy. Early Renaissance sculpture in Italy is typified by the Florentines DONATELLO and Lorenzo GHIBERTI. Donatello, in the *Gattamelata* and in his bronze *David* (c.1440–42; Bargello, Florence), revived two major Roman forms single-handedly—the monumental equestrian statue and the heroic male nude. Ghiberti, in the *Gates of Paradise* (1425–52; East Doors of the Baptistery, Florence), fused classical art and Renaissance humanism: the 10 gilded bronze panels and their surrounding borders depict biblical scenes with every possible variation of relief sculpture.

The complete mastery of the mature male form and the peak of High Renaissance sculpture was reached in MICHEL-ANGELO's colossal *David* (1501–03; Accademia, Florence). His four unfinished *Slaves* (c.1532; Accademia) seem to struggle tortuously to emerge from the marble blocks.

Sculptors as well as painters strove to achieve distinctive and extraordinary effects. This emphasis on invention led to elaboration of certain parts of the body—elongation of the neck, hands, thighs, or all three—and to writhing sinuosities of pose, all characteristic of MANNERISM. In sculpture the beginnings of this Mannerist tendency can be found in Benvenuto CELLINI's bronze *Perseus* (1545–54; Loggia dei Lanzi, Florence) and reaches a culmination in

Michelangelo's David (1501–03), commissioned when the sculptor was only 26 years old, embodies ideals of strength, composure, and pride in what has always been regarded as one of the greatest works of Renaissance sculpture. Standing more than 4 m (13 ft) tall, the monumental figure achieves a grandeur of psychological intensity and restrained power. (Accademia, Florence.)

(Above) *Donatello's monument (1445–50) to Gattamelata, a Venetian military commander, combines the heroic dignity of its classical models with the introspective tension characteristic of Donatello's style. (Piazza del Santo, Padua.)*

(Below) *Bernini's* Ecstasy of Saint Teresa *(1645–52) translates the mystical experience described by the saint into sensuous, highly articulated marble forms. (Santa Maria della Vittoria, Rome.)*

some of the works of Giovanni da Bologna, especially the corkscrew twistings of his marble *Rape of the Sabine Women* (1583; Loggia dei Lanzi).

France. The Italian Renaissance style in sculpture was carried to France by Cellini, who worked in the court of Francis I. The Italian master strongly influenced an entire generation of French artists, including Jean Goujon. Goujon's elongated and smoothly curved nymphs in fluid poses survive in five relief panels on his Parisian *Fontaine des Innocents* (1547–49); altered subsequently.

Baroque and Rococo Sculpture

Italy. Characteristically, baroque sculpture is designed to arrest the eye first and then to lead it (and the spirit of the spectator) gradually upward through balanced complexities to a single climactic point (see BAROQUE ART AND ARCHITECTURE). In sculpture, Giovanni Lorenzo BERNINI's works best exemplify this ideal, especially his *Ecstasy of Saint Teresa* (1645–52; Cornaro Chapel, Santa Maria della Vittoria, Rome).

France. Rococo sculpture and architecture developed in France after the death (1715) of Louis XIV. Sculptors in the ROCOCO STYLE abandoned the strong architectonic balances of the baroque in favor of asymmetrical detail. The greatest triumphs of the rococo were in architectural decoration and ornamental carving.

Germany. Italian baroque and French rococo were merged in Germany to produce sumptuous architectural works clad in shimmering carved and painted detail. The greatest triumphs were in a union of architecture, carving, and painting in churches and palaces by such artists as François CUVILLIÉS and Johann Balthasar NEUMANN.

Neoclassical Sculpture

The neoclassical style (see NEOCLASSICISM, art) began in

(Left) *In Auguste Rodin's* Oceanides *(1905), the sensuous fluidity of human figures contrasts with the rough, unfinished surface of the marble. (Musée Rodin, Paris.)*

(Right) *Marcel Duchamp, one of the proponents of Dada, offered such objects as a snow shovel, a porcelain urinal, a defaced reproduction of the Mona Lisa, and* Bicycle Wheel *(a replica of the original of 1913) as examples of "ready-made" art. (Philadelphia Museum of Art.)*

Rome in the 1750s with the archaeological researches of Johann Joachim WINCKELMANN, who sharply distinguished Greek classical art, which he praised, from Roman classical art, which he denounced. Influential sculptors who dominated the neoclassical movement included Antonio CANOVA in Italy, Bertel THORVALDSEN in Italy and Denmark, John FLAXMAN in England, Jean Antoine HOUDON in France, and Horatio GREENOUGH and Hiram POWERS in the United States. The French 19th-century sculptors Antoine Louis BARYE and Jean Baptiste CARPEAUX, working in a romantic style (see ROMANTICISM, art), created sculpture of surpassing quality in an age that preferred empty academic or cloying sentimental sculptural wares.

The late-19th-century French sculptor Auguste RODIN stripped neoclassicism of its sentimentality and its disguised eroticism. His carved marble sculptures are imbued with sexual intensity; his bronze busts project the strong personalities of many famous contemporaries; and his monumental sculptures are overwhelming in their balance of mass and form.

Twentieth-Century Sculpture

During the 20th century, sculpture underwent the most radical changes in its history. The emergence of CUBISM and ABSTRACT ART brought down the dominance of Greek and Roman principles of ideal form and realistic detail. While representational sculpture remained the primary style for numerous sculptors, many experimented with EXPRESSIONISM.

Georges BRAQUE and Pablo PICASSO applied to sculpture the cubist theories they had invented. Other revolutionary movements followed: Italian FUTURISM, exemplified by the work of Umberto BOCCIONI; Russian CONSTRUCTIVISM, established by Vladimir TATLIN and perpetuated by the brothers Naum GABO (Pevsner) and Antoine PEVSNER; DADA, with "found objects" by Marcel DUCHAMP; SURREALISM, as in the disparate works of Max ERNST, Alberto GIACOMETTI, and Man RAY; and the biomorphic abstractions of Jean ARP and Constantin BRANCUSI. The English sculptor Henry MOORE, inspired by ancient art, pursued his own course toward a monumental balance between abstraction and representation.

In his bronze King and Queen *(1952–53) Henry Moore reduced the human body to its essential elements to express a feeling of regal dignity and timeless strength. (Openhecht Museum, Antwerp.)*

Cubi XIX (1964) was one of a series in which David Smith explored various aspects of the cube. The abstract severity of the work is enhanced by its polished and abraded steel surface, which reflects many patterns of light. (Tate Gallery, London.)

The advent of ABSTRACT EXPRESSIONISM and the rise of New York City as the world's artistic center has led to a proliferation of movements, such as EARTHWORKS, ENVIRONMENTAL ART, KINETIC ART, MINIMAL ART, and POP ART. At the same time, frank realism has emerged, personified by George SEGAL's roughly cast plaster figures in actual settings, MARISOL's sharply satirical blocky figures, and the three-dimensional comic environments of Red GROOMS. The abstract metal sculptures of David SMITH are considered by many to be among the most important creations in postwar art.

See also: ARCHITECTURE; ART.

___

scurvy Scurvy is a NUTRITIONAL-DEFICIENCY DISEASE caused by dietary deficiency of ascorbic acid, or vitamin C. Humans, other primates, and a very few other mammals are susceptible to scurvy because they lack an enzyme required for the synthesis of ascorbic acid. The disease is characterized by fragility in capillaries, resulting in subcutaneous bleeding, degeneration of cartilage, loosening of teeth, and joint and bone pain.

___

Scylla and Charybdis [sil'-uh, kar-ib'-dis] In Greek mythology Scylla and Charybdis were two sea monsters who lived in caves on opposite sides of the Straits of Messina, separating Italy and Sicily; they devoured sailors from passing ships. Scylla, originally a beautiful nymph, had been loved by Glaucus, who asked CIRCE to give Scylla a love potion. Instead Circe gave her a poison that turned her into a monster. Charybdis personified a dreadful whirlpool.

___

Scythians [sith'-ee-uhnz] The Scythinas were Iranian-speaking nomads who dominated the various tribes populating the steppes north of the Black Sea during the 7th through the 4th century BC. The writings of the Greek historian Herodotus and ancient Near Eastern records suggest that they originated in Central Asia or Siberia and moved westward early in the 1st millennium BC.

As rulers of the steppes, the Scythians were fierce warriors whose nomadic tribal society was organized around a powerful chief. The rich and elaborate graves of these chieftains took the form of underground chambers in which the king was buried along with a wife and a servant. Scythian chiefs wore and carried large numbers of gold weapons and ornaments, and this treasure was always placed in the tomb. Near the graves horses and grooms were interred, so that a vast expenditure of wealth (in the form of gold and horses)—not to mention human life—accompanied the burial of each ruler. Two basic styles of art are found in Scythian tombs: the objects created in the native so-called animal style (see STEPPE ART) and Greek-made objects that the Scythians collected.

By the end of the 4th century BC, the Scythians began to lose control of the steppes to the SARMATIANS, another group of nomads. The Scythians retreated to the Crimea, where they disappeared from history by the 3d century AD. Traces of their animal-style art can, however, be seen in the barbaric art of Europe during the early Middle Ages.

___

Sea, Law of the The Law of the Sea is an international treaty governing uses of the oceans. First drafted by the United Nations in 1958, the proposed treaty was broadened in 1973 to cover new technological means of exploration and exploitation. Not until 1982 were the negotiations of the Law of the Sea Conference concluded. During its final working session, Third World nations adopted the treaty, whereas the United States and several other countries rejected the code. Seventeen additional nations, including the USSR, abstained.

The 1982 treaty calls for the establishment of a 12-naut-mi (22.2-km) limit to the TERRITORIAL WATERS of all nations, allowing free passage through more than 100 straits or choke points that would otherwise fall within the 12-mi limit. The treaty also assures each nation exclusive rights to oil and gas lying within 350 naut mi (648 km) of its coasts and to fish and other marine life within 200 naut mi (370 km). The provision for mining of ocean-floor minerals remains a major polarizing issue between the industrial and developing nations. The latter have insisted that an International Seabed Authority should oversee the exploitation of these resources. Industrial nations, led by the United States, argue that the huge investment necessary for seabed mining requires that individual companies reap substantial rewards. By the end of 1984, 159 nations had signed the treaty, but only 13 had ratified it, and major industrial powers still oppose it.

See also: MARITIME LAW; SEAS, FREEDOM OF THE.

___

sea anemone Sea anemones are solitary, ocean-dwelling COELENTERATES in the class Anthozoa, order Actiniaria. They usually attach themselves to rocks and shells.

Sea anemones show considerable diversity in size and form, with the diameter ranging from a few millimeters to more than a meter, a shape that may be quite flat or long and slender, and a body wall that may be delicate or tough and leathery. The foot is muscular and is capable of attaching firmly to wave-swept rocks. It can also move the animal slowly across the substrate. The oral disk contains tentacles, used in catching food, which surround a central mouth. Some species have a small number of elongate tentacles, whereas others have hundreds of short ones.

Sea anemones feed on planktonic animals caught by specialized cells (nematocysts) on the tentacles. The larger species can also kill and ingest animals of greater size, including small crabs and fish. Anemones often have other animals living with them, such as the clown fish, genus *Amphiprion*. Apparently these animals have absorbed anemone substances on their surface mucus and thus do not stimulate the anemone's nematocysts to discharge.

Most sea anemones have separate sexes, and all species reproduce sexually. The fertilized egg develops into a ciliated planula larva that, after a period of planktonic life, becomes sedentary and metamorphoses into a small anemone. Many species also reproduce asexually.

The sea anemone
Laomeda geniculata
has delicate, trans-
parent tentacles sur-
rounding its mouth
that fasten on and
capture its micro-
scopic prey.

sea bass   Sea BASS is the common name for fishes of the family Serranidae. Most of the more than 400 species are marine fishes, found chiefly in tropical and subtropical waters; many are valued for food and sport. GROUPERS, coneys, graysbys, and the kelp bass are examples. Some sea bass are only a few centimeters in length; others may reach 2.1 m (7 ft) in length and weigh more than 225 kg (500 lb). All sea bass are carnivorous, feeding on shellfish, squid, and small fish.

A well-known temperate-water serranid is the black sea bass, *Centropristis striata,* found in the western Atlantic. It may be more than 60 cm (2 ft) long and weigh more than 3 kg (8 lb). The smaller fishes live in shallow

The black sea bass, native to the U.S. Atlantic coast, is caught commercially for food and by sports enthusiasts as game.

waters, but larger ones are found in depths of more than 122 m (400 ft). Sea bass of the genus *Morone* are also distributed in temperate waters. They include the striped bass, *M. saxatilis*, which enters rivers to spawn, and the European bass, *M. labrax*.

sea cucumber   Sea cucumbers (class Holothuroidea) are elongated, cylindrical echinoderms, with the skeleton reduced to form microscopic ossicles in the connective tissue. Most species have five bands of tube feet running from the mouth to the anus; the mouth is surrounded by a ring of tentacles. Sea cucumbers range in length from a few millimeters to more than 2 m (6.6 ft). Colors are usually drab, with browns predominating. The animals feed either by capturing small organisms with their sticky tentacles or by shoveling mud into their mouths and extracting organic material from it. The dried body walls of some species are prized as food in the Orient.

sea horse   The sea horse, genus *Hippocampus*, family Syngnathidae, has an upright position, with a horselike head set at right angles to the body. It swims weakly, propelled largely by the rapid motion of its dorsal fin. The scales have been replaced by rings of about 50 rectangular bony plates, encasing the body in a semirigid skeleton. The eyes can swivel independently or converge to achieve binocular vision. Its food consists primarily of minute, planktonic crustaceans, which are ingested into a small mouth at the end of a long, tubelike snout by a rapid intake of water.

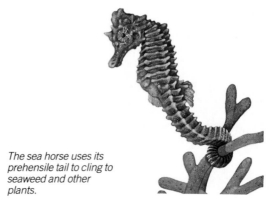

The sea horse uses its
prehensile tail to cling to
seaweed and other
plants.

The male has a kangaroolike pouch on its ventral side in which the eggs are deposited by the female and held until they hatch. The eggs are fertilized as they enter the pouch, hatching after approximately 10 days.

There are about 50 species of sea horses in warm tropical and temperate seas, living in shallow waters. They generally range from 5 to 30 cm (1 to 12 in) in size.

sea level   Sea level is the plane of contact between the ocean and a landmass. On a short-term basis, this level constantly changes locally due to the regular tidal pull of the Sun and Moon, changes in barometric pressure, and strong winds. The average height between mean high and mean low water, determined from hourly measurements over a 19-year period, is termed *mean sea level*, but this level also changes with time.

Over geologic time, sea level may change drastically (hundreds of meters) because of the advance and retreat of glaciers. Such changes are termed eustatic changes. Measurements of such changes are difficult because of the confusing influence of tectonic and isostatic uplift and land subsidence. Although some contradictory evidence exists, however, many studies concur that sea level has been gradually rising for the past 7,000 years. Tidal-gauge records indicate an average increase of 1.2 mm/yr (0.05 in/yr) in the past 50 years.

See also: EARTH, GRAVITATIONAL FIELD OF.

sea lily   see ECHINODERM

sea lion   Sea lions, marine mammals of the eared seal family, Otariidae, order Pinnipedia, have long, tapering bodies covered with thin, short, coarse hair. Their limbs are modified into flippers that are larger than those of true seals, and, unlike true seals, they have small external ears and can turn their hind flippers forward to move about on land. There are four major kinds of sea lions: the North Pacific, or Steller's, sea lion (*Eumetopias jubata*); the California sea lion (*Zalophus californianus*), which inhabits the west coast of North America and the Galápagos Islands; the South American sea lion (*Otaria byronia*); and the Austra-

lian and New Zealand sea lions (*Neophoca cinerea* and *N. hookeri*). All species have highly developed social systems. They gather on shore during the breeding season. The males, several times larger than the females, vie with one another for harems, which number up to 15 females. Fish and squid provide the principal diet; the sea lion is capable of diving up to 180 m (600 ft) for food.

sea moth   The sea moths comprise five species (family Pegasidae) of bizarre, shallow-water marine fishes occurring in the Indo-Pacific and Hawaii. Their snouts are spatula-shaped, and their flattened bodies are made up of a rigid, bony latticework. The expansive pectoral fins resemble moth wings. Sea moths live on the bottom and must eat small food; otherwise, their biology is little known. The largest is the Indo-Australian *Pegasus volitans*, which reaches 13 cm (5 in) in length.

The sea moth P. papilio, *found near the Hawaiian Islands, is a small fish with broad, winglike fins. Its mouth is located on the underside of its head rather than at the tip of its long, flat snout.*

sea otter   The sea otter, *Enhydra lutris*, in the weasel family, Mustelidae, is about 1 m (3.3 ft) in length, with a 35-cm (14-in) tail, and weighs up to 36 kg (80 lb). The webbed hind feet are broadened into flippers, and the forefeet are useful for grasping. Sea otters are found along the shores of the North Pacific. They sleep and eat floating on their backs, often cracking clamshells with a rock to get at the meat inside. The single young is born on the rocks and soon accompanies its mother into the water. Overhunted for their fine, silky brown fur, sea otters were almost exterminated, but they are now protected by international treaty.

A sea otter, whose diet comprises mainly clams and mussels, cracks open a shell on a rock that it has placed on its chest.

The South American sea lion lives in the ocean and along shores of South America and the Falkland Islands.

sea pen Sea pens are colonial marine animals (polyps) of the class Anthozoa in the phylum Coelenterata or Cnidaria. They are related to the sea pansies and more distantly to the sea anemones and the corals. A sea-pen colony typically consists of an elongate, anchoring polyp whose upper portion bears leaflike clusters of small polyps, suggesting a quill pen up to 1 m (3.3 ft) long. The small polyps are of two types: autozooids, which supply nutrients, and siphonozooids, which maintain water circulation. The colony is covered with a layer of fleshy epidermis and is supported mainly by internal water pressure.

Sea Peoples The term *Sea Peoples* designates a number of primarily Indo-European groups that were displaced from their homes in and around the Aegean Islands by northern invaders during the late 13th century BC. The best known to history are the PHILISTINES, who eventually possessed the Gaza Strip of Palestine. The Sea Peoples raided eastward by land and sea, sacking Troy, toppling the Hittites, devastating Syro-Palestine, and even attacking the Nile Delta. They provide a link between the Homeric world and that known from late Egyptian records and early biblical narratives.

sea robin Sea robins, or gurnards, comprise about 90 species of bottom-dwelling, usually shallow-water marine fishes of the family Triglidae. They are found worldwide in temperate and tropical seas, and the largest species may attain 1 m (3.3 ft) in length. Sea robins derive their name from their large, winglike pectoral fins. The front supporting rays of these fins are separate and formed into slender feelers used both to detect crustaceans, worms, and other food in the sand and to "walk" over the sea bottom and manipulate small objects. Sea robins communicate with one another by sounds produced by muscular contractions and vibrations of the swim-bladder walls.

sea snake There are at least 15 genera (with 50 species) of front-fanged, venomous sea snakes, subfamilies Hydrophiinae and Laticaudinae, in warm tropical oceans, more than half of which are found in the shallow waters off the coasts of Australia and New Guinea. Two species,

The yellow-bellied sea snake breathes air but can stay submerged for up to 8 hours with its specialized respiration system.

Laticauda colubrina and *Pelamis platurus*, live along the coasts of the Americas. Sea snakes are highly adapted to a marine environment, having long, laterally compressed bodies, oarlike tails, nostrils on top of the snout, and salt glands. They may bask by the thousands on the water's surface. They feed mainly on fish, which they kill with a powerful venom. Most species are quite docile; although they are frequently netted and handled, few bites result. They are prized as food in the Orient.

sea spider Sea spiders, or pycnogonids, marine invertebrate animals of the class Pycnogonida in the phylum Arthropoda, are distantly related to the true spiders. Found worldwide in the oceans, the some 600 species of pycnogonids have long, slender legs and a short, very thin body, giving the impression that they consist only of legs. They are usually 1 to 10 mm (0.04 to 0.4 in) in body length, but the largest deep-sea form attains 6 cm (2.4 in) in length with a leg span of about 75 cm (29.5 in). Pycnogonids have four to six pairs of walking legs and one pair of ovigerous, or egg-carrying, legs. Most are bottom feeders, crawling about and feeding on small animals. Eggs laid by the female are deposited on the ovigerous legs of the male and carried by him until they hatch.

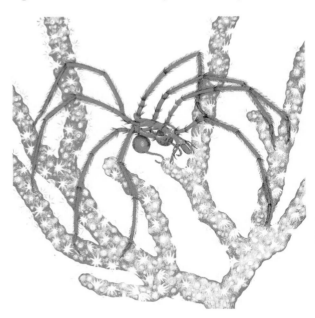

The sea spider, of the northeastern Atlantic Ocean, prowls the sea bottom feeding on the body fluids of tiny animals.

sea turtle There are two families, five genera, and seven species of living sea turtles. The family Cheloniidae contains four genera and six species: the loggerhead, *Caretta caretta*; the hawksbill, *Eretmochelys imbricata*; the

The green turtle, which is the largest of turtles, inhabits shallow coastal waters worldwide.

green turtle, *Chelonia mydas*; the flatback turtle, *C. depressa*; the Indo-Pacific ridley, *Lepidochelys olivacea*; and the Atlantic ridley, *L. kempi*. The other family, Dermochelyidae, has only one genus and species, the leatherback turtle, *Dermochelys coriacea*. Most sea turtles are found worldwide in tropical and subtropical seas, with the exceptions of the flatback of northern Australian waters, and the Atlantic ridley, restricted largely to the Gulf of Mexico. Female sea turtles come ashore on beaches to lay their eggs in holes that they dig and cover. The young hatch in 5 to 10 weeks, depending on a variety of factors. Sea turtles have evolved a streamlined shell (carapace), strong flippers, and salt-excreting glands in adaptation to their marine environment. They are threatened by humans, who hunt them and their eggs for food and for tortoiseshell, hide, and oil.

sea urchin   The term *sea urchin* in its broadest sense covers all echinoids, class Echinoidea, phylum Echinodermata, including about 700 species of spherical or

A sea urchin, an echinoid related to the sand dollar and sea lily, pulls its round, hard shell along seafloors by using its movable spines.

near-spherical echinoids and about 100 species of discoid SAND DOLLARS. The sea-urchin skeleton is usually a rigid shell, or test. The generally spherical body of these echinoderms carries short to long movable spines. The mouth lies at one pole of the sphere, with the anus at the opposite pole. Five radii, carrying rows of tube feet, run from the mouth to the anus. There are no arms, and all major organ systems are contained within the test.

Most sea urchins are vegetarians or scavengers, and most have five sharp teeth for scraping food off the substrate. The heart urchins and their relatives lack teeth and burrow in sand or mud, from which they extract organic material. Small pincerlike organs, the pedicellariae, lie between the spines and serve many functions, including cleaning the test and warding off predators; some pedicellariae are venomous to humans. The roe, or gonads, are considered a gourmet food in the Orient and in some parts of South America.

sea walnut   see COMB JELLY

Seabees   The Seabees, a nickname for members of the U.S. Navy Construction Battalions (CBs), are units originally organized during World War II to build living quarters and naval facilities in combat areas of the Pacific. The Seabees were created in 1942 when the use of civilian labor in combat areas was judged to be inappropriate. Together with the Army Corps of Engineers, the Seabees were entrusted with solving many of the logistical problems relating to troop deployment and evacuation that the war in the Pacific entailed.

Seaborg, Glenn T. [see'-bohrg]   The American chemist Glenn Theodore Seaborg, b. Ishpeming, Mich., Apr. 19, 1912, shared the 1951 Nobel Prize for chemistry with Edwin McMillan for his participation in the discovery of most of the transuranium elements. Seaborg did his early work on the isotopes of common elements. He later worked with McMillan, who isolated (1940) neptunium (atomic number 93), the first element beyond uranium. Seaborg and his associates later isolated the next transuranium element, plutonium. They also found a plutonium isotope, ^{239}Pu, which promised to yield more fission energy than uranium.

In 1942, Seaborg moved from Berkeley to the University of Chicago to find ways of producing plutonium for the atomic-bomb project. His group discovered (1944) two new elements, americium (95) and curium (96); these discoveries helped to confirm Seaborg's hypothesis that the transuranium elements resembled each other and so formed a transition series (the actinide series) similar to the lanthanide series of rare earths. In 1946 he returned to Berkeley, and during the next 12 years he and his collaborators discovered six more transuranium elements: berkelium (97) in 1949, californium (98) in 1950, einsteinium (99) in 1952, fermium (100) in 1953, mendelevium (101) in 1955, and

Glenn T. Seaborg, an American chemist and Nobel Prize laureate (1951), helped usher in the age of nuclear energy with the discovery (1940) of the first transuranium element, plutonium. His team continued to identify most other transuranium elements. Seaborg also served (1961–71) as chairman of the Atomic Energy Commission.

nobelium (102) in 1958. The discovery of these elements was made possible by new particle accelerators that allowed heavy ions to be used as projectiles. In 1961, Seaborg became the first scientist to chair the Atomic Energy Commission. He returned to the Lawrence Berkeley Laboratory in 1971, where he codiscovered (1974) element 106.

Seabury, Samuel [see'-bur-ee] The first bishop of the Protestant Episcopal church in the United States, Samuel Seabury, b. Groton, Conn., Nov. 30, 1729, d. Feb. 25, 1796, was one of the primary architects of the Episcopal church. Chosen by the Anglican clergy of Connecticut to be their bishop, he was consecrated (1784) as bishop in Scotland, then returned to the United States to be rector of Saint James' Church in New London and bishop of Connecticut and Rhode Island. At the General Convention of 1789, Seabury worked to forge a union with Bishop William WHITE and the Patriot Anglicans to create the Protestant Episcopal church in the United States.

seafloor spreading See MID-OCEANIC RIDGE; OCEAN AND SEA; PALEOGEOGRAPHY; PLATE TECTONICS

Seaga, Edward [see-ah'-guh] Edward Philip George Seaga, b. May 28, 1930, became prime minister of Jamaica on Nov. 1, 1980, after the electoral victory of his Jamaica Labour party over the People's National party government of Michael Manley. The Harvard-educated Seaga was first elected to the Jamaican House of Representatives in 1962; he served as minister of development and welfare (1962–67) and of finance and planning (1967–72). Reelected prime minister in 1983, Seaga was defeated by Manley in 1989 in his bid for a third term. The austerity measures he had implemented to restore the ailing Jamaican economy were considered a factor in his defeat. Regarded as pro-Western, he had supported the U.S. invasion of Grenada in 1983.

Seagram Building [see'-gruhm] Completed in 1958, the Seagram Building at 375 Park Avenue, New York City, designed by Ludwig MIES VAN DER ROHE and Philip JOHNSON, represents the ultimate refinement of the modern steel-and-glass skyscraper. It is set back 90 feet from the street, and—floating over a street-level plaza—it rises in an uninterrupted 38-story column 158 m (520 ft) high; its closely spaced vertical bronze ribs make it seem even taller. Everything in the Seagram Building, including the lavatory fixtures, was custom-designed. Although criticized for its disregard of human needs—the plaza being more decorative than usable and much of the interior unpleasantly far from the windows—the Seagram Building remains a major monument of modern architecture.

seal The true seals are a diverse and widely distributed group of mostly marine, aquatic mammals. They are also called the earless seals because they lack external ears, having only a tiny, wrinkled ear opening on each side of the head. The true seals, family Phocidae, are classified with the eared seals (sea lions and fur seals), family Otariidae, and the walruses, family Odobenidae, in the Pinnipedia—the pinnipeds are regarded as either a suborder of the order Carnivora or a separate order. The true seals comprise 18 living species grouped into 13 genera; 10 extinct genera are also known. The most numerous seal is the crabeater, *Lobodon carcinophagus*.

The true seals are predominately a marine group, but two species, the Caspian Sea seal, *Pusa caspica*, and the Lake Baikal seal, *P. sibirica*, inhabit large inland bodies of water. The Baikal seal is the only completely freshwater species, but various populations of the ringed seal, *P. hispida*, and the harbor seal, *Phoca vitulina*, also live in freshwater lakes or rivers. The true seals are especially numerous in the colder waters of both hemispheres, with concentrations in the polar regions, but the monk seals, *Monachus*, are a tropical group.

Seals range in size from 1.2 to 6.5 m (4 to 21 ft) in length and from 90 kg to 3.5 metric tons (200 lb to about 8,000 lb) in weight. The smallest are the ringed seals, *Pusa*, and the largest are the elephant seals, *Mirounga*. The hind limbs of the true seals are turned permanently backward and cannot be pivoted forward under the body to help propel the animals across land. The true seals must therefore employ a wriggling or hunching movement, rolling or sliding whenever possible, when progressing over land. In the water, seals swim gracefully, using side-to-side undulations of the hind limbs. Members of some species have been observed to remain submerged for 70 minutes and to dive to depths of 600 m (2,000 ft). Fish, crustaceans, and squid comprise the primary diet, but the leopard seal, *Hydrurga leptonyx*, feeds regularly on warm-blooded animals, including penguins and other seals.

It is thought that at least some seals have an echolocation system akin to that of bats, porpoises, and shrews.

harbor seal

elephant seal

northern fur seal

leopard seal

gray seal

The seal is a fin-footed aquatic mammal (pinniped). All seals spend some portion of the year on land, primarily during breeding season. The harbor seal inhabits coastal waters and inland waterways of North America and northern Eurasia. It spends more time in shallow waters and on land than any other seal. The northern elephant seal is the largest of all pinnipeds. The bull (shown), which may reach 6.5 m (21 ft) in length and weigh up to 3,600 kg (7,900 lb), has a trunklike snout that inflates when the seal is excited. The northern, or Alaskan, fur seal is an eared seal related to the sea lion. Hunted commercially for its thick inner coat, it was nearly extinct by the early 20th century and has been protected by an international treaty since 1911. The gray seal is found in temperate coastal waters. The leopard seal is the only pinniped that normally preys on penguins and other seals.

Sealyham terrier [see'-lee-ham]   The Sealyham terrier is named for the estate of Captain John Edwardes near Haverfordwest, Wales. Edwardes developed the dog in 1891 to hunt such animals as the badger, otter, and fox. The dog stands about 27 cm (10.5 in) at the shoulder and weighs 10.4–10.9 kg (23–24 lb). Sealyhams have medium-sized drop ears, moderate eyebrows, and bearding on the muzzle. The coat is double: the top is harsh and wiry, the under is short, thick, and soft. The Sealyham is white, and it may have lemon, tan, or gray markings on the head and ears. Its tail is docked and carried upright. The breed was officially recognized by both the English and the American Kennel Clubs in 1911 and is among today's rarer breeds.

The Canadian de Havilland DHC-2, or Beaver, is an amphibious utility transport that utilizes a combination of twin floats and landing wheels to allow takeoffs and landings on land or water.

seamount   A seamount is a mountain under the sea; more precisely, it is an isolated elevation of the deep seafloor of approximately 1,000 m (3,300 ft) or more. Lesser elevations are termed sea hills or sea knolls. A sea peak is a seamount with a pointed summit. A flat-topped seamount at an ocean depth of more than 200 m (660 ft) is termed a guyot. Most guyots are ancient volcanic islands that were truncated by wave action and then became submerged. Platforms rising to depths of less than 200 m are called *oceanic banks*.

The Pacific Ocean is the principal province of seamounts. More than 10,000 examples have already been surveyed in that basin. Seamounts commonly occur in groups, such as the Mid-Pacific Mountains and the Emperor Seamount Chain (see OCEAN AND SEA), and virtually always represent extinct volcanoes. Some seamounts, however, such as off the coast of Spain, are thought to be residual continental fragments rifted from the continental blocks as the oceans were created by seafloor spreading. The coral atolls of the central Pacific are reefs that lie atop seamounts. Biologic upbuilding of the coral has maintained a sea-level elevation as the seamounts subsided 1 km (0.6 mi) or more through geologic time. Some of the oldest seamounts of the Pacific have yielded Cretaceous fossils and are thus more than 65 million years old.

seaplane   Seaplanes are airplanes that are fitted with floats in place of conventional landing gear, enabling them to land on and take off from water. Purists distinguish between seaplanes and flying boats; in the latter the fuselage (body) is itself watertight and forms a boatlike hull that rests directly in the water. The earliest seaplanes date from 1909–10. Seaplanes and flying boats were used in large numbers in World War I for sea patrol and antisubmarine work. Between the world wars seaplanes were the fastest airplanes in the world. The commercial flying boats dominated long-distance air travel over water until about 1944, when improved runways and wheeled transport craft gradually replaced them. Today nearly all marine aircraft are light seaplanes that are privately owned, the majority being in the Americas. A few large turboprop amphibious planes are used today for ocean patrol and antisubmarine warfare.

search warrant   A search warrant is a legal document issued by a judge that directs officers to search a particular house or other premises for specified things or persons and to bring them before the court. All search warrants must satisfy the requirements of the 4th Amendment to the U.S. Constitution, which states that "no warrants shall issue but upon probable cause, supported by oath or affirmation, and particularly describing the place to be searched and the persons or things to be seized." The amendment also bans "unreasonable searches and seizures." Before the American Revolution, British officers had "writs of assistance" that allowed them to ransack any and all homes at will; the framers of the Bill of Rights guarded against such general warrants that permit officers to conduct so-called fishing expeditions for evidence. The U.S. Supreme Court in *Weeks* v. *United States* (1914) and *Mapp* v. *Ohio* (1961) held that evidence gathered illegally or unreasonably cannot be presented in trials—the so-called exclusionary principle. The reasonableness requirement—a still highly controversial subject—permits many cases of a search without a warrant. If, for example, a valid arrest is made, the arresting officer may search the person and the immediate area without a warrant. Other examples of instances where search warrants are not needed are cases of "hot pursuit," cases where consent to a search is freely given, and cases where an officer discovers evidence by accident or where evidence is plainly visible.

See also: SELF-INCRIMINATION; WIRETAPPING.

Searle, Ronald   The British artist and cartoonist Ronald Searle, b. Mar. 3, 1920, is best known as the creator of the devilish students of St. Trinian's school for girls. Educated at the Cambridge School of Art, Searle served with the Royal Engineers during World War II and from 1942 to 1945 was a prisoner of war of the Japanese. Searle's humorous drawings have appeared in such major periodicals as *Punch* and the *New Yorker*. Searle has also worked as a film designer, creating the animation sequences for *Those Magnificent Men in Their Flying Machines* (1965) and *Scrooge* (1970). Collections of his drawings include *Forty Drawings* (1946), *From Frozen North to Filthy Lucre* (1964), *The Square Egg* (1968), and *Searle's Zoodiac* (1977).

Sears Tower

Erected between 1970 and 1974 for Sears, Roebuck and Company, the Sears Tower in Chicago is the tallest building in the world. Its 110 stories rise 443 m (1,454 ft), higher than the 411-m (1,350-ft) World Trade Center towers and the 381-m (1,250-ft) Empire State Building (both in New York City). A new skyscraper technology was employed by the architectural firm of Skidmore, Owings and Merrill and their engineer, Fazlur Kahn. Instead of the traditional steel skeleton of I beams riveted together to form a cage, thick sheets of steel were welded to form the nine vertical, square tubes that support the structure. The floors spanning the tubes, of lighter construction, are suspended within them.

seas, freedom of the

Freedom of the seas is the principle that the high seas—the areas of ocean that lie beyond the TERRITORIAL WATERS of states—are open to all nations in time of peace. Most states traditionally (since the 18th century) accepted a national control limit of 3 mi (4.8 km), originally set by the maximum range of cannon shot and referred to as the "three-mile limit." The doctrine of freedom of the seas was put forward by the Dutch jurist Hugo GROTIUS in *Mare Liberum* (Open Sea, 1609) but did not become generally accepted until the 19th century. At that time the commercial and colonial interests of the major powers, backed up by the growth of naval forces, ensured freedom of the seas during peacetime.

Freedom of the seas, however, is not absolute; the accepted rules of international law require states to use the high seas with reasonable regard for the rights of others.

Examples of such rules may be found in the conventions of 1954, 1962, and 1969 for the prevention of the pollution of the sea by oil. In the 20th century coastal states began to assert varying claims to territorial or adjacent waters extending 6, 12, or 20 mi (9.1, 19.3, or 32 km). The United States claimed (1945) control of the seabed and subsoil resources of its continental shelf (200 mi/ 322 km). Some nations—for example, Peru, Ecuador, and Chile—have claimed jurisdictional control over waters extending as far as 200 miles from shore; their claims have engendered much controversy.

The status of the high seas has increasingly become a concern of the United Nations, as can be seen in the UN Law of the Seas Conferences of 1958 and 1960 and in the late 1970s. The increased number of oceanographic experiments, the extensive exploration of the resources of the seabed, and the international use of fishing grounds have combined to exacerbate the potential for conflict.

See also: BLOCKADE; RIGHT OF SEARCH; SEA, LAW OF THE.

seasickness see MOTION SICKNESS

SEATO see SOUTHEAST ASIA TREATY ORGANIZATION

Seattle

Seattle, the largest metropolis in the northwestern quarter of the United States, is the seat of King County, Wash. Located on a narrow, hilly isthmus between Puget Sound on the west and Lake Washington on the east, Seattle has a population of 516,259 (1990); its metropolitan area has a population of 1,972,961. The city is the focus of a highly urbanized zone that fronts the eastern shore of Puget Sound and incorporates the city of Everett.

Contemporary City. The central area of the city is crowded onto the constricted isthmus, but its suburbs sprawl to the north, south, and east of Lake Washington, which is spanned by a floating bridge. Spectacular mountains dominate the horizon: the Cascades to the

The Space Needle (left)—a feature of Seattle Center, formerly the site of the Century 21 Exposition (the 1962 World's Fair)—and Mount Rainier (background)—a peak of the Cascade Range—dominate Seattle's southeast skyline. The Space Needle rises 185 m (606 ft) and is topped by a revolving restaurant and an observation tower.

east (with Mount Rainier on the southeast) and the Olympics to the west.

Seattle's Elliott Bay harbor is a major Asia-oriented port as well as the principal gateway to Alaska. Its containerized shipping facilities are among the largest in the world. Since the 1920s, however, the Boeing aircraft company has been the mainstay of the city's economy. Shipbuilding and the making of wood products are other major industries.

Seattle is the home of the University of Washington (1861) and Seattle University (1892). The city has a symphony orchestra, two professional theater companies, and numerous museums, including the Seattle Art Museum. Every summer the Seattle Opera stages the Pacific Northwest Festival. A major point of interest is the Seattle Center—site of the 1962 World's Fair—with its 185-m (606-ft) Space Needle.

History. Settled in 1851, Seattle was named for a friendly Indian chief, Seatlh. The city served primarily as a lumber town until the 1880s, when the arrival of railroads stimulated economic expansion. Trade with Asia began in the 1890s, and the Yukon gold rush made Seattle an important commercial center. Further stimulus came with the opening of the Panama Canal in 1914. A major shipbuilding center during both world wars, Seattle also experienced a boom from aircraft manufacturing during World War II.

Seaver, Tom   The baseball player George Thomas Seaver, b. Fresno, Calif., Nov. 17, 1944, long one of the National League's premier pitchers (New York Mets, 1967–77; Cincinnati Reds, 1977–82; Mets, 1983; Chicago White Sox, 1984–86; Boston Red Sox, 1986), twice led the lowly Mets to the World Series (1969, 1973). The right-handed Seaver had a won-lost record of 311-205, an earned run average of 2.86 and 3,640 career strikeouts (3d in major league history). In 10 seasons he threw 200 or more strikeouts. Seaver won the Cy Young Award—given annually to each league's best pitcher—3 times (1969, 1973, 1975).

seawater   Seawater represents approximately 97.2% of the total volume of the world's water and covers more than 70% of the planet's surface (see OCEAN AND SEA). The chemical composition of seawater has been determined throughout geologic time by the erosion of minerals from continental landmasses and the outgassing of volatiles (dissolved gases) from cracks in the ocean floor. Today the ratio of major elements to each other remains nearly constant, regardless of location within the world's oceans. This occurs because the constant influx of minerals into the ocean basins is balanced by a corresponding precipitation of minerals onto the ocean floor (see OCEANIC MINERAL RESOURCES). Seawater is a solution of salts; of the various elements combined in these salts, chlorine alone constitutes 55% by weight of all the dissolved matter, and sodium, 31%.

The absolute amount of salt in seawater, however, is

determined by processes, such as precipitation and evaporation, that either add fresh water to or subtract it from the sea. In oceanic areas where precipitation exceeds evaporation, such as in the North Pacific, the salt content, or salinity, of seawater is in the range of 32–34 g/kg, or parts per thousand, of seawater; where evaporation exceeds precipitation, as in the Indian Ocean, the salt content may exceed 36 g/kg.

In addition to its major chemical constituents, seawater also contains trace amounts of all the other elements of the periodic table. Some of these elements, such as nitrate, phosphate, iron, and manganese, are particularly important, because they form the basis for life in the oceans (see OCEANIC NUTRIENTS).

seaweed   Seaweeds are any multicellular ALGAE that grow in marine environments. Representatives of the brown algae (such as *Laminaria*, or kelp; *Fucus*, or rockweed; and gulfweed) and the red algae (such as *Chondrus*, dulse, and laver) constitute the most common seaweeds. A few green algae occur as seaweed, for example, *Ulva*, or sea lettuce, and *Codium*. Seaweeds usually at-

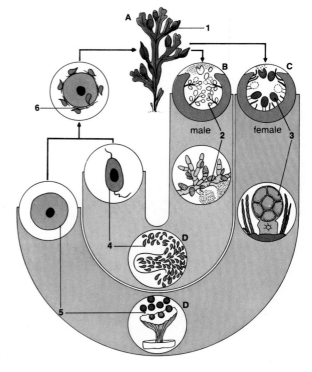

Unlike many other types of brown algae, rockweed, or Fucus *(A), has a life cycle that includes sexual reproduction. Reproductive organs are formed at the swollen ends of branches, within fertile areas called receptacles (1). Separate hollow chambers, or conceptacles (B, C), give rise to (2) antheridia (male) and (3) oogonia (female), which eventually burst (D) while submerged by the tide, releasing sperm (4) and eggs (5) into the water. The gametes fuse (6) to form a zygote, which develops into a new adult plant.*

tach to the ocean bottom or to other solid objects. Those seaweeds found along the beach in high tide are the most familiar. This phenomenon is common along rocky beaches where many seaweeds grow attached to the rocks. Although seaweeds occur at depths of up to 30 m (100 ft), certain red algae grow as deep as 180 m (600 ft).

Seaweeds are important in all the oceans. Beds of seaweed provide habitat (food and protection) for many animals. They are also extremely important as primary producers in marine food webs. Many, such as dulse and sea lettuce, are used as food in several regions, and some are used in fertilizers.

Sebastian, King of Portugal   Sebastian, b. Jan. 20, 1554, d. Aug. 4, 1578, king of Portugal (1557–78), lost his life—and álmost ruined his country—in a crusade against Morocco. From an early age Sebastian, who succeeded his grandfather, John III, showed interest only in religion, warfare, and violent sports. In 1578 he assembled an army to fulfill his dream of defeating Islam, but Sebastian and most of his men were killed at Ksar al-Kebir. After a brief interlude, his crown passed to Spain, which controlled Portugal for the next 60 years.

Sebastian, Saint   Saint Sebastian, fl. 3d century, was an early Christian martyr. According to tradition, he was a Roman officer sentenced by Emperor Diocletian to be shot with arrows after it had been discovered that he was a Christian. He survived the shooting and was subsequently beaten to death. Sebastian became a popular subject of art. Feast day: Jan. 20.

Sebastiano del Piombo   [say-bahs-tee-ah'-noh del pee-ohm'-boh]   Michelangelo's associate and Raphael's rival, Sebastiano del Piombo, b. Sebastiano Luciani c.1485, d. June 21, 1547, was a Venetian painter working in Rome. As a student of Giovanni Bellini and Giorgione, he shared his training with Palma Vecchio and Titian, with whom he seems to have been on friendly terms until he moved to Rome in 1511. The warm tonality and rich light of *Saint John Chrysostom with Other Saints* (1510–11; San Giovanni Crisostomo, Venice), Sebastiano's greatest Venetian painting, reveals his Venetian heritage. The *Raising of Lazarus* (c.1517–19; National Gallery, London), painted for Cardinal Giulio de'Medici in competition with Raphael, indicates Sebastiano's assimilation of the Roman style as exemplified by Michelangelo. Sebastiano was also a distinguished portraitist; his *Pope Clement VII* (1526; Capodimonte Museum, Naples) is a characteristic example.

secant   [see'-kant]   In geometry, a secant is a straight line that intersects a curve at at least two points and, in particular, intersects a CIRCLE at exactly two points. (The limiting case of a secant as the two points of intersection are taken closer and closer together is a TANGENT—a line

that touches a curve at only a single point.) In TRIGONOMETRY, a secant is one of the basic trigonometric ratios; specifically, in any right-angled triangle the secant of an acute angle θ (denoted by sec θ) is the length of the hypotenuse of the triangle divided by the length of the adjacent side. The secant is the inverse of the cosine.

Secession movement   The Secession (Sezession) movement in the fine and applied arts occurred in several German and Austrian art centers during the 1890s and early 1900s. In German usage during the 1890s, the word *Sezession* meant an association of artists, usually an exhibiting society, that was independent of the official academies. The first Secession was established in Munich in 1892 by the painter and designer Franz von STUCK, with others, in order to exhibit impressionist and symbolist works. Secession groups with similar aims were organized in Vienna in 1897 and in Berlin in 1898. The Vienna group introduced into Germany and Austria the work of the Scottish architect and designer Charles Rennie MACKINTOSH, which was to have great influence on subsequent art and design in those countries.

Although the Secession movements soon became conservative, they did pave the way for the acceptance of ART NOUVEAU—or *Sezessionstyle*, as it was called in Austria—and for the establishment of workshops for artists and artisans, such as Vienna's Wiener Werkstätte and Germany's Deutscher Werkbund movement.

Seconal   [sek'-uh-nawl]   Seconal, a trademark name for secobarbital sodium, is a fast-acting drug of the BARBITURATE group of central-nervous-system depressants. It produces drowsiness or sleep and is also used as a preanesthetic, for instance, to relax pregnant women during labor. It causes a decrease in physical and mental acuity, and its effect is augmented if it is taken with another depressant drug or alcohol. It may be habit-forming. In the United States, Seconal requires a nonrefillable prescription; possession without one is a criminal offense.

2d Amendment   see BILL OF RIGHTS; CONSTITUTION OF THE UNITED STATES; RIGHT TO BEAR ARMS

Second Coming of Christ   The Second Coming of Christ refers to the Christian belief in the future return of Christ in glory to judge the living and the dead (see JUDGMENT, LAST), an event that will end the present world order. The New Testament never uses the term *Second Coming*. The early Christians identified the resurrected Christ with the Son of Man (Dan. 7:13) and combined this text with Ps. 110:1 (as in Mark 14:62). At first the Christian community expected an imminent return of Christ, but it adjusted itself with remarkable ease to the notion of an indefinitely postponed Second Coming.

See also: ESCHATOLOGY; MILLENARIANISM.

Second Republic   see FRANCE, HISTORY OF

secondary education   Nearly all Americans who receive a secondary education do so in one of the nation's 25,000 high schools. Some enter high school after 8 years of PRIMARY EDUCATION and attend for 4 years, whereas others enter senior high school after 3 years attendance at a junior high or middle school (see MIDDLE SCHOOLS AND JUNIOR HIGH SCHOOLS) and attend for 3 years. The American high school is a 19th-century invention, but traditions of secondary education date back to the colonial period.

Early Forms of Secondary Education

Grammar Schools. The Boston Latin School, established in 1635 by the Puritans, was founded to prepare students for Harvard College. Such early grammar schools assumed that children were literate upon entry. Only boys were admitted, at about 8 years of age. Many parents sent their children to private schools that gave instruction in writing and arithmetic to prepare them for trades.

Academies. The academy preceded the grammar school, coexisted with it for a while, and then lost its patrons. Created in 17th-century England to meet changing social and economic conditions, the academy offered a curriculum that included that of the grammar school—Greek and Latin grammar, Hebrew, logic, rhetoric, and other languages—as well as practical subjects suited to the then-emerging mercantile class. By 1850, at least 6,000 academies, or independent secondary schools, existed. Many of these admitted women, and some offered training in commercial subjects. Academies were not accessible to all students, however, and with the advent of the high school, their popularity declined.

High Schools. Boston's English High School (1824), originally opened in 1821 as the English Classical School, and for boys only, was probably the first high school in the United States. In 1827, James G. Carter convinced the Massachusetts legislature to require towns with 500 or more families to offer instruction in algebra, American history, bookkeeping, geometry, and surveying. Towns that had populations of 4,000 or more were required to add instruction in Latin, Greek, general history, rhetoric, and logic. The law was not observed in most towns but did serve as a model for other states. By the time of the Civil War about 300 high schools had been founded in the United States.

After the Michigan Supreme Court ruled in 1874 that it was constitutional for a school district to maintain tax-supported public high schools, the academy began to give way to the high school as the most popular form of secondary education. By 1890 the nation had about 2,500 high schools, and enrollment (203,000) was more than twice as great as that of the academies (95,000). The percentage of the population aged 14–17 attending high school, however, was only 7%.

In 1892 the National Education Association appointed a Committee of Ten, with Charles William ELIOT as its chairman, to examine whether the teaching of high school subjects should vary according to whether students were preparing for a liberal arts college, a scientific school, or

neither. The committee concluded that those subjects which best prepared students for college were equally suited to prepare them to enter nonacademic jobs. It emphasized the study of languages, which was consistent with traditional forms of secondary education, but it did not agree that the study of Latin and Greek constituted the best possible education. Algebra, geometry, physics, chemistry, and history were to be required for all students. The committee's recommendations met with resistance from those who believed that science and practical subjects should receive greater emphasis. This controversy about the purpose and curriculum of high schools continued. Contrary to the recommendation of the Committee of Ten, high schools began to add commercial and vocational curricula.

Creation of the Modern High School

Standardization of secondary education was achieved in the early 20th century. When colleges agreed to exclude students who had not completed a specified number of units of instruction, the high school diploma became the entrance pass to college. As colleges specified which subjects students needed for admission, the electives available to students were effectively limited. Thus high school students were segregated according to their socioeconomic standing, and the high school became open to charges of denying true equality of opportunity.

Vocational Education. Attempts to render the high school something more than a school for college preparation have persisted. In 1906 the National Society for the Promotion of Industrial Education was formed and began to lobby for VOCATIONAL EDUCATION. The Smith-Hughes Act of 1917 provided funds to the states on a matching basis to support high school programs in agricultural education, home economics education, and vocational programs. The vocational-education movement had a significant impact on secondary education, convincing many Americans that the primary purpose of the secondary school was to prepare students for the marketplace. A recent development in vocational education is CAREER EDUCATION.

Rising Attendance and Declining Ability. In 1918 the National Education Association's Commission on the Reorganization of Secondary Education pointed to seven objectives of student development that high schools must be concerned with: (1) health; (2) command of the fundamental processes (reading, writing, speaking, and arithmetic); (3) worthy home-membership; (4) vocation; (5) citizenship; (6) intelligent use of leisure; and (7) ethical character. At the same time it recommended that all children remain in high school until age 18. Yet it was not until 1930 that more than half of children aged 14–17 years were enrolled in secondary schools, as contrasted with 15% in 1910 and 32% in 1920. Enrollments continued to increase during succeeding decades: 73% in 1940; 77% in 1950; 87% in 1960; and 94% in 1970 and into the 1980s.

As high school attendance increased, however, educators expressed concern that students' abilities and levels of achievement were declining. At the end of World War II, James Bryant CONANT and Vannevar BUSH began to warn the nation that it was facing a serious shortage of scientists. A decade later, in response to the shock waves caused by the USSR's launchings (1957) of *Sputnik 1* and *2*, Conant agreed to direct a study of the nation's secondary schools. His report, *The American High School Today* (1959), recommended that high schools prepare all students for citizenship through general education; equip the majority with useful skills; and provide appropriate courses in mathematics, science, and foreign languages for the 15% who were "academically talented." Conant wanted school boards to require this minority to complete a program of no fewer than 18 courses that would include 4 years of mathematics, 4 years of one foreign language, 3 years of science, 4 years of English, and 3 years of social studies—in essence, a college-preparatory program.

Simultaneously, the U.S. Congress was working on the National Defense Education Act and appropriating large sums for science and education, while various scientific committees worked on renovating the teaching of mathematics, physics, chemistry, and biology—courses in place by the early 1960s.

Secondary Education and Contemporary Social Needs. Secondary education was characterized by a quest for excellence during the late 1950s and early 1960s. Secondary schools tried to direct able students toward studies that would prepare them to join a technical elite. Post-World War II social pressures demanded other changes as well. The marketplace required that entrants possess a maturity and mastery of basic skills equivalent to those of a high school graduate, but business and industry did not themselves provide job training. At the same time, unemployment of the unskilled was becoming a serious problem. In a second report on the high school, *Slums and Suburbs* (1961), Conant urged that the education offered to inner-city youth be directly related to subsequent employment. He argued that schools should provide vocational courses and guidance and assume responsibility for job placement and that programs offering jobs and training to youth include nondiscriminatory legislation.

In the early 1980s the perception of a crisis in education prompted several major studies. *A Nation at Risk: The Imperative for Educational Reform*, issued by the National Commission on Excellence in Education in 1983, reported a continuing decline in educational standards and achievement and called for sweeping changes, including the strengthening of high school graduation requirements in the "five new basics": English, mathematics, science, social studies, and computer science. The commission also recommended steps to improve the education as well as the status of teachers. The Carnegie Foundation for the Advancement of Teaching, in its report entitled *High School: A Study of Secondary Education in America (1983)*, found that improvements had already begun but advocated major reforms, citing mastery of the English language, including writing, as the central curriculum objective. It also recommended the adoption of a core curriculum for all students, the improvement of teacher preparation and compensation, and the requirement for all high school students to participate in community-service programs.

Secord, Laura [see'-kohrd] Laura Ingersoll Secord, b. Massachusetts, Sept. 13, 1775, d. Oct. 17, 1868, was a Canadian heroine of the War of 1812. On June 22, 1813, Secord walked 32 km (20 mi) to warn of an impending American attack on the British outpost at Beaver Dam in Upper Canada (Ontario).

secret ballot see ELECTION

Secret Service The Secret Service, an agency of the U.S. Department of the Treasury, was established by President Abraham Lincoln on July 5, 1865, to suppress counterfeiters and forgers of government securities. Early in its history, however, the agency became involved in fighting a number of other crimes that would later be assigned to other agencies, including opium smuggling, extortion, Ku Klux Klan terrorism, and land fraud. During both the Spanish-American War and World War I, the service was active in uncovering espionage networks. In the 1920s it was entrusted with conducting the bulk of the investigation into the Teapot Dome scandal.

After the assassination (1901) of President William McKinley—who, after Lincoln and James A. Garfield, was the third president to be assassinated in 36 years—the Secret Service also was charged with the protection of the chief executive. Later the protective function of the agency was expanded to include the president-elect and vice-president-elect and their immediate families, the vice-president, the president's and vice-president's immediate families, former presidents and their wives and children (until the age of 16) and unremarried widows of former presidents, major candidates for president and vice-president, and certain visiting foreign dignitaries and others at the direction of the president.

As a result of the assassination of President John F. Kennedy, the Warren Commission recommended that the Secret Service undergo a modernization program. Its jurisdiction was then extended to several subsidiary agencies, and its budget was increased. The Secret Service is also responsible for protection of the White House, the Treasury vaults, and certain other government buildings.

secret societies Secret societies include both organizations with secret membership and those in which secrecy is involved only in initiation rites, other rituals, or special knowledge. Ancient religious mystery cults such as the Greek ORPHISM and the Persian MITHRAISM are largely of the latter kind, as are some medieval guilds, such as the cathedral masons from which the Freemasons claim descent (see FREEMASONRY). Some societies have at their core a specialist knowledge of ritual that is of general use to the community, as with the Medicine Societies of various Iroquoian-speaking Indian tribes of North America. Secret societies may combine several functions. The Ngbe (Leopard Society) of West Africa, with its secret constitution and symbolism, although primarily recreational, also acts as a unifying political influence. Among societies that have been "secret" in the wider sense of having undisclosed membership are certain nationalist or revolutionary organizations, such as the CARBONARI of 19th-century Italy, and pseudopolitical and criminal associations, such as the KU KLUX KLAN and the Sicilian MAFIA.

---

secretary bird   The secretary bird, *Sagittarius serpentarius*, unusual in appearance, is placed by itself in the family Sagittariidae, which is generally considered related to vultures and hawks. The sexes look alike, with pale gray plumage and black thigh and wing feathers; long crest feathers originate from the back of the head. The male is about 100 cm (40 in) in length, the female slightly smaller; the long legs, curved bill, and feet are used to kill small animals, including snakes. The secretary bird is solitary and inhabits grasslands over much of Africa. A ground-runner, it will swiftly stride away from danger, flying only if necessary. The large arboreal nests are composed of sticks. The two eggs require 45–50 days of incubation, and young fledge in about 3 months.

The secretary bird, native to central African grasslands, is a predator of snakes, killing with powerful blows of its feet.

Securities and Exchange Commission   Created by the Securities Exchange Act of 1934 as a result of the STOCK MARKET crash of 1929 and the ensuing Depression of the 1930s, the Securities and Exchange Commission (SEC) is a federal agency whose purpose is to protect U.S. investors against malpractice in the securities and financial markets. Five commissioners are named by the president—subject to approval of the Senate—to serve overlapping 5-year terms. The president selects one to serve as chairperson. No more than three may be of the same political party.

The SEC, in carrying out the mandates of the Securities Act of 1933, requires anyone offering stocks, bonds, or other securities for sale to file a registration statement with the SEC making "full and fair disclosure" of financial and other information relating to the issues involved. Companies must disclose the securities holdings of their officers and directors. The SEC also regulates securities exchanges and has the power to change the rules of the exchanges in the public interest. In addition, the SEC sets rules governing such activities as selling short, OPTION TRADING, and floor trading.

Investment companies that deal in mutual funds came under the jurisdiction of the SEC in 1940, as a result of the Investment Company Act. Under the Public Utility Holding Company Act of 1935, the SEC was empowered to regulate the transactions of electric and gas utility holding companies and their corporate and capital structures. In 1977, as the regulator of the practices of investment counselors (by virtue of the Investment Advisers Act of 1940), the SEC required brokers to abandon charging fixed commissions. Under Chapter X of the Bankruptcy Act of 1939, the SEC advises federal courts in proceedings for the reorganization of insolvent companies. The SEC has quasi-judicial powers. Its decisions may be appealed to U.S. courts of appeal. In 1990, in reforms motivated by the 1987 crash of stock prices, President Bush signed two bills giving the SEC increased authority over penny stocks and program trading on U.S. exchanges.

---

sedative   Sedative-hypnotics are DRUGS that have either a mild calming (sedative) or a sleep-producing (hypnotic) effect on the central NERVOUS SYSTEM (CNS), depending on the size of the dose administered. Agents in this category include the BARBITURATES, CHLORAL HYDRATE, paraldehyde, ethyl ALCOHOL, bromides, ANTIHISTAMINES, glutethimide (Doriden), methyprylon (Noludar), and methaqualone (Quaalude); methaqualone, however, is no longer manufactured in the United States because of the problems of abuse to which it gave rise. Also included are such TRANQUILIZERS and muscle relaxants as chlordiazepoxide hydrochloride (Librium) and diazepam (Valium). The most recent hypnotics are flurazepam dihydrochloride (Dalmane) and nitrazepam (Mogadon), and the newest "natural" sedative is the amino acid l-tryptophan.

Historical Development

Ethyl alcohol has been in use since the dawn of history as a nonmedicinal sedative. The bromides, now essentially obsolete, were introduced into medicine in 1837 and appear to be the earliest prescribed sedatives. Barbituric acid was synthesized in 1864. Chloral hydrate, still widely used, was introduced in 1869. Paraldehyde, introduced in 1882, has long been used to treat acute alcoholism, but the more recent drugs Librium and Valium are more effective and less toxic. Phenobarbital, introduced in 1912 under the trade name Luminal, is a drug of choice for the management of epilepsy. The antihistamines and meprobamate (Equanil) are now considered sedative-hypnotic drugs.

Anxiety. The unpleasant emotional state of anxiety usually may be controlled by phenobarbital or by such tranquilizers as Librium or Valium, at doses that produce no outward signs or symptoms of sedation. If properly prescribed, antianxiety drugs have a rational place in therapy. Such drugs, however, are frequently overused and may be counterproductive or even hazardous in simple anxiety states.

Sleep. The barbiturates appear to induce sleep through a selective depressant action upon that portion of the CNS which is associated with wakefulness: the Reticular Activating System (RAS; see SLEEP). Although sleep induced by barbiturates closely resembles normal sleep, proportionately less time is spent in the dreaming, rapid-eye movement (REM) phase during barbiturate sleep; some authorities consider this undesirable. Following withdrawal, REM phases increase, as do irregularities in sleep patterns associated with nightmares. Librium and Valium alter REM sleep to a lesser extent.

The barbiturates, and the newer hypnotics flurazepam and nitrazepam, are effective in all types of simple insomnia. The insomnia that accompanies endogenous depression, however, is a symptom of a severe psychiatric disturbance and may be relieved only by controlling the depression. For this reason, one of the tricyclic antidepressants, amitriptyline (Elavil), may be required instead of any sedative-hypnotics.

Anticonvulsant Activity. A drug of choice for petit mal epilepsy, phenobarbital has highly selective activity on the CNS that is not shared by other barbiturates. This activity is not related to sedation, because nonsedative doses are anticonvulsant; CNS stimulants, such as amphetamine, may counteract the sedative effects of phenobarbital without abolishing its anticonvulsant capability.

Narcoanalysis. Several barbiturates—notably amobarbital, phenobarbital, and thiopental—have been used as aids in psychiatric diagnosis. In proper dosage, inhibitions are removed and communication of repressed thoughts is facilitated. Such drugs are often used as "truth serum."

Cautions

Automatism. Automatism is a state of drug-induced confusion and often is a cause of accidental poisoning by barbiturates and other sedative-hypnotics, particularly in the elderly. In this state the patient forgets that the medication has been taken and therefore ingests more; the process is repeated until toxic quantities of drug have been ingested.

Tolerance and Addiction. Tolerance to the barbiturates appears to involve one of two mechanisms: enzyme induction and adaptation. The drug may stimulate the production or activity of liver enzymes that are normally responsible for the drug's metabolic breakdown or can allow the tissues to adapt to the drug in some unexplained manner. In either case the body requires greater amounts of the drug in order to produce the desired effect.

In addiction, withdrawal of the drug following repeated use may result in a syndrome often characterized by delirium and convulsions, compulsion to take the drug, and mental deterioration. Addiction to the barbiturates renders the addict incapable of functioning in society and may be a more serious addiction than that produced by narcotics.

See also: DRUG ABUSE.

▬

Seddon, Richard John [sed'-uhn]   Richard John "Dick" Seddon, b. England, June 25, 1845, was a New Zealand statesman who was prime minister from 1893 until his death on June 10, 1906. Emigrating first to Australia (1863) and then New Zealand (1866), he worked in the goldfields, became a storekeeper, and entered politics. As prime minister he was responsible for the enactment of important economic and social reforms, including the vote for women (New Zealand was the first country to enact such a law), progressive taxation, an old-age pension system, and legislation to improve working conditions. Labor laws enacted during his term of office provided for shorter hours, compulsory conciliation and arbitration, accident compensation, and better factory conditions. Seddon's autocratic manner won him the nickname "King Dick."

▬

seder [say'-dur]   The seder (from the Hebrew word for "order") is the festal meal eaten on the first two nights of PASSOVER, the Jewish celebration of the Exodus from Egypt. The main seder meal does not begin until the story of the Exodus has been retold through the reading of the Haggadah and, more important, reexperienced by the celebrants. This re-creation of the circumstances of bondage, together with the minutiae of the deliverance, forms the heart and spirit of the seder and of the Passover festival itself.

Certain foods are eaten in set order during the ceremony, including *matzoth*, the unleavened bread of bondage; *maror*, bitter herbs (grated horseradish), commemorating the bitterness of slavery; *baitzah*, a hard-cooked egg, symbolic of life's cycle of birth and death; *zaroah*, a roasted lamb bone representing the paschal lamb; *haroseth*, chopped nuts, apples, and wine, symbolic of the clay used by Pharaoh's Hebrew slaves to make bricks; and *karpas*, parsley, lettuce, or other greens, as a reminder that the new growth during this spring festival brings renewed hope of universal peace.

▬

sedge   Sedge is the common name both for the plant family Cyperaceae—about 80 genera of grasslike or rush-like herbs, mostly perennials, usually found in wet areas—and for the genus *Carex* within the family. The approximately 2,000 species of *Carex* are grasslike herbs most common in temperate and subarctic regions. Their stems (culms) are solid and angular, thus differing from the true grasses, and the leaves have three ranks. A few species of *Carex, Cymophyllus,* and *Eleocharis* are cultivated mainly as ornamentals. The sedge's greatest value

Sedges include (left to right): pendulous sedge; papyrus, or bulrush; salt grass; and bog cotton. The papyrus provided the ancient Egyptians with the material upon which they wrote.

is in erosion control in wet regions, and some species are used as edging for aquatic gardens or as pot plants. Sedges are sometimes used in making grass rugs and in other fabrics, particularly sedges of the genus *Cyperus*, which includes the PAPYRUS plant, *C. papyrus*, and the UMBRELLA PLANT. A few members of this genus, however, are serious weeds. The yellow nutsedge, or nut grass, *C. esculentus*, for example, is a pest of row crops on a worldwide scale.

Sedgwick, Adam   The English geologist Adam Sedgwick, b. Mar. 22, 1785, d. Jan. 27, 1873, did important research on the layers, or strata, of rocks containing fossils deposited during the Paleozoic Era, particularly the Cambrian strata, which he named. Sedgwick graduated (1808) from Trinity College of the University of Cambridge and became (1810) a fellow there. He was appointed (1818) Woodwardian Professor of Geology at Cambridge and taught until 1870.

Sedgwick sought, among ancient rocks in Devon and Cornwall, evidence of the beginning of the FOSSIL RECORD, and indirectly of the beginning of life. His most significant geological work was the ordering of the old strata found in these locations into the Cambrian system.

When the geologist Henry De La Beche uncovered evidence in Devonshire that disputed the stratigraphic conclusions of both Sedgwick and R. I. Murchison, the latter two jointly worked out the stratigraphy of Devonshire. They showed that the rocks were not as old as De La Beche claimed. They identified the rocks as a system, which they named Devonian for the region and which they showed to be equivalent to strata of a Devonian formation known as the Old Red Sandstone. Sedgwick and Murchison tried to show that the fossil record and life had a beginning at some time in the history of the Earth, but

Sedgwick objected when Murchison expanded the Silurian system to include most of the Cambrian. The result was a major controversy over which rocks defined the base of the Silurian. Although Sedgwick gradually identified errors in Murchison's work, years passed before discoveries led to the acceptance of the Cambrian system.

sediment, marine   Marine sediments are unconsolidated material that covers most of the ocean floor. Absent atop the mid-oceanic ridges, they reach thicknesses of more than 1,000 m (3,300 ft) along the continental rises. Thicknesses average about 500 m (1,650 ft) but vary considerably from place to place. Sediments beneath the oceans and seas are much younger than comparable deposits on land. The oldest marine sediments found are of Jurassic age (about 150 million years old), whereas the oldest rocks on land are about 3.8 billion years old. The fact that the ocean basins formed in the recent geologic past, a finding confirmed through dating the marine sediments, is cited by geologists as evidence of seafloor spreading.

Marine sediments are classified according to origin: they are lithogenic, hydrogenic, biogenic, or cosmogenic. Lithogenic sediments are derived from the WEATHERING of the crust. Included in this class are rock fragments, quartz particles, volcanic debris, and clay minerals. The abundance of these components depends primarily on

Various sediments accumulate on the continental shelf (A) until the pile becomes unstable and either slumps spontaneously or is jarred loose by an earthquake. The resulting sliding mass of sediment forms a turbidity current that rushes down the continental slope, eroding valleys and rocks in its path (B). The current eventually slows where the slope flattens out and deposits its sediment in a broad layer, with coarser particles on the bottom and finer particles on top (C). Later turbidity currents form similar overlying layers.

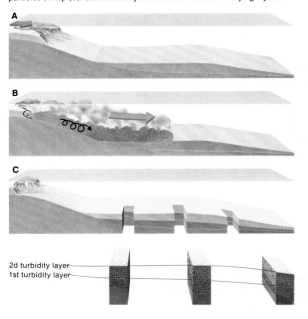

2d turbidity layer
1st turbidity layer

distance of transport to the site of deposition and the susceptibility of the component to degradation.

Hydrogenic sediments, such as nodules of manganese and PHOSPHORITE, consist of particles precipitated from solution in seawater (see OCEANIC MINERAL RESOURCES). Manganese nodules cover up to 50 percent of the seafloor in parts of the Pacific and Indian oceans.

Biogenic sediments consist mainly of skeletal parts of PLANKTON. Skeletons of FORAMINIFERA, coccolithophorids, and pteropods make up the bulk of the carbonate varieties. Diatoms and RADIOLARIANS, other planktonic organisms with skeletons of silica, form another class of biogenic marine sediments. Diatom-rich sediments called oozes are found in high latitudes as well as in areas of upwelling ocean water (see UPWELLING, OCEANIC). Radiolarian oozes are found primarily in the equatorial Pacific. Another biogenic component is skeletal APATITE, a phosphate mineral. Among phosphatic skeletal parts, sharks' teeth and whale ear bones are the most common. Such sediments are found in regions where the sedimentation rate is extremely slow.

Cosmogenic sediments, or TEKTITES, are tiny black spherules and nodules that may have an extraterrestrial source. They are found wherever sedimentation proceeds slowly, with minimal input from lithogenic and biogenic sources.

The age of marine sediments can be determined by several methods: magnetic stratigraphy (correlation of magnetic reversals with those on land); biostratigraphy (identification of zones of abundance of plankton that have been dated elsewhere); and RADIOMETRIC AGE-DATING (measurement of the rate of decay of radionuclides).

---

sedimentary rock   Sedimentary rock, one of the three major kinds of rocks found in the crust of the Earth (IGNEOUS ROCK and METAMORPHIC ROCK are the others), results from an accumulation and consolidation of layers of loose sediment. Sedimentary rocks account for 70% to 75% of the total exposed surface of the Earth; nevertheless they account for only 5% of the Earth's outer crust, which is about 6 km (4 mi) thick under the ocean and 35 km (22 mi) thick on the continents.

Four principal kinds of sedimentary rocks—carbonate, authigenic, terrigenous, and pyroclastic—can be differentiated on the basis of mineral and chemical composition as well as by origin. Carbonate rocks consist mostly of calcite or dolomite. Authigenic rocks include EVAPORITES, such as those containing sulfate and halide minerals, and other chemical rocks, such as cherts and iron-rich and manganese-rich rocks. Terrigenous rocks are composed of various land-derived silicate minerals, and pyroclastic rocks consist of particles of various silicate minerals and glasses derived from volcanoes. The first two kinds originate and, for the most part, are preserved in the basin of deposition. In contrast, terrigenous rocks are composed of particles derived from outside the basin of deposition. Tephra, or pyroclastic debris, ultimately originates from a volcanic source; it may accumulate in the same basin of deposition in which the volcanoes are located, or it

may be carried by air or water to accumulate in a remote basin. All four types of sedimentary rock may give rise to breccia, an unusual rock composed of angular fragments, if subjected to the stresses generated by movements within the Earth's crust or to the shock of meteorite impact.

Carbonate Rocks

Carbonate rocks may be either limestones or dolostones. The basic constituents of most LIMESTONES (notable exceptions include reefs and consolidated lime mud) are sand-sized particles such as skeletal particles, oöids, and pellets. The spaces between these particles are occupied by either a matrix of lime mud (whose lithified equivalent is known as micrite) or a sparry calcite cement, filled with a fluid such as oil or water. Micrite may occur either as a matrix among sand-sized particles or, in a fine-grained limestone, as the only particles. The size of particles within micrite is smaller than 4 μm (microns) and usually from 1 to 3 μm. In a hand sample of a limestone, micrite appears dull and opaque; a thin slice viewed under a petrographic microscope appears subtranslucent with a faint brownish cast. Sparry cement is the clear, crystalline component of carbonate rocks with vitreous luster; crystals measure tens or hundreds of microns in diameter.

The mineral DOLOMITE composes over 50% of dolostones. When the composition is between 50% to 90%, the dolostones are described as calcareous. Where dolostones preserve the textures of their antecedent limestones, the outlines of original calcareous particles such as skeletal fragments, oöids, and pellets may be readily apparent or somewhat obscured but still vaguely recognizable, because replacement of the preceding limestone occurs parallel to or following the boundaries of the original particles. Alternatively, when pervasive replacement occurs, all existing textures are obliterated, resulting in a generally featureless dolomite.

Authigenic Rocks

Authigenic rocks contain a mineral that has grown in place subsequent to the formation of the host sediment or rock. Although authigenic rocks have a common origin, they are chemically and mineralogically quite diverse. The most important kinds include chert, evaporites, phosphate rock, sedimentary iron ores, and manganese rock.

Chert. Chert (see CHERT AND FLINT), a tough, brittle rock consisting of organic and inorganic silica, exhibits a splintery to conchoidal fracture and a vitreous luster and occurs in nodules and strata. The mineral composition of the nearly pure silica in chert appears to be influenced by the composition of the host sediment and to reflect the age of the deposit. Shells of siliceous organisms in Tertiary cherts are mostly opaline, but nearly all silica in Paleozoic cherts is present as quartz and chalcedony.

Evaporites. Evaporites form by precipitation from brines concentrated by evaporation. Although almost 40 different precipitate minerals have been recorded from evaporite deposits, only about 20 exist in more than trace amounts. Of these, only the sulfates—most commonly, gypsum ($CaSO_4 \cdot 2H_2O$) and anhydrite ($CaSO_4$)—and the halides—especially halite, or rock salt (NaCl), which occurs in successions up to 1,000 m (3,300 ft) thick—form extensive deposits of sedimentary rock.

Phosphorites and Iron Formations. PHOSPHORITES are composed of the mineral apatite. Phosphorite nodules occur on the modern sea bottom from shallow to great water depths, and ancient phosphorite deposits occur in extensive phosphogenic provinces that extend for several thousand square kilometers. The phosphate rock in these ancient deposits occurs as bone fragments, sand-sized pellets of possibly fecal origin (100 to 400 μm in diameter), oöids, pisolites, phosphatized tests of various calcareous shells, and as COPROLITES—large pellets (2 to 5 mm/0.08 to 0.2 in) in diameter.

Although all sedimentary rocks contain readily detectable amounts of iron, sedimentary iron ores are deposits that consist predominantly of iron minerals, especially oxides (hematite and magnetite), hydroxides (goethite, including limonite), and carbonates (siderite).

Terrigenous Rocks

The particles composing extrabasinal, or terrigenous, rocks originate from the debris created by the wearing down of the land. Sizes vary widely, from fractions of a micron to boulders measuring several meters across. The three main kinds of terrigenous rocks—shales, sandstones, and conglomerates—are distinguished on the basis of particle size. SHALES are fine-grained rocks that contain substantial amounts of clay minerals and generally silt- and clay-sized particles. Many shales display fissility; that is, they split easily into thin sheets, or layers. Sand-sized particles predominate in SANDSTONES. Conglomerates (see CONGLOMERATE, geology) are coarse-grained rocks formed by the lithification of rounded gravel.

Pyroclastic Rocks

The particles of pyroclastic rocks, or lithified tephra, originate as explosive, igneous material and are deposited as sediments. Because of their chemical instability, pyroclastic rocks are subject to rapid alteration to clay and other minerals, making pyroclastic deposits of the Precambrian and Paleozoic eras and even those of the Mesozoic Era difficult to identify. Volcanoes, especially those

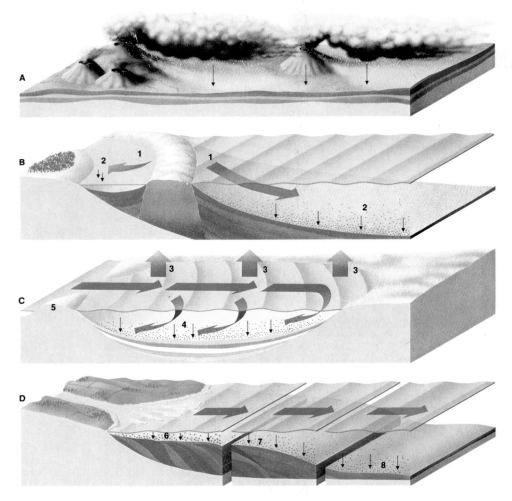

Sedimentary rocks are composed of layers of sediment, or small particles, derived from previously existing rocks. The particles are compressed by the weight of overlying materials into solid rocks. (A) A special class of rocks called tephra results from the compaction of ashes and rock fragments ejected from volcanoes. (B) Limestone, a second basic type of sedimentary rock, results from the deposition of eroded products (1) of coral reefs and of the shell and skeleton remains (2) of warm-seawater organisms. (C) Evaporation of seawater (3) from enclosed ocean bays results in deposits of various chemical salts, or evaporites (4). Repeated formations of barriers and closures of basins (5) lead to a succession of such deposits. (D) Most sedimentary rocks are formed by deposition of matter from rivers discharging into the sea along continental shelves. Coarse particles (6) are deposited first, followed by fine sand particles (7) and mud particles and clay (8).

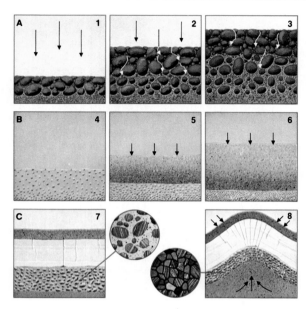

The formation of sedimentary rocks involves three major processes. (A) Coarse-grained particles (1) form layers with large intergrain pores. Water percolating (2) through upper layers dissolves minerals that precipitate (3) in lower porous layers and cement the grains into rocks. (B) Initial loosely packed deposits (4) of fine-grained particles are compacted (5) into rocks (6) by the pressure of overlying layers. (C) Strong mountain-building forces and high temperatures recrystallize deeply buried rocks (7) into new compact rocks (8).

in areas of tectonic activity and in island arcs, are the major sources of particles for pyroclastic rocks. Particles originating by explosive ejection from volcanic vents spread out over vast areas. On the continents, the volume of pyroclastic rocks far exceeds that of extrusive rocks such as rhyolite and basalt.

Pyroclastic rocks may be classified by size, by the kinds of particles composing them, and by origin. Pyroclastic particles larger than 32 mm (1.3 in) in diameter may be either bombs or blocks. Lapilli are particles in the intermediate size range (4 to 32 mm/0.08 to 1.3 in). Ash are particles in the fine size range (less than 4 mm) in diameter. Agglomerates are composed mostly of bombs; volcanic breccias, of blocks; lapilli tuffs, of lapilli; and tuffs, of ash.

Pyroclastic glass alters to clay minerals (especially montmorillonite), zeolites, chalcedony, opal, quartz, and a microcrystalline particle resembling chert when seen in a thin slice under a petrographic microscope. Glass is commonly found only in mid-Tertiary and younger rocks. Even zeolites are absent from the older Paleozoic rocks; they probably were altered to feldspars. An alteration product of tephra is bentonite, a plastic clay or shale composed for the most part of the clay mineral montmorillonite.

sedition [suh-dish'-uhn] Sedition is the crime of advocating by word or deed the overthrow of the government. Laws against sedition have been viewed as poten-

tially dangerous to FREEDOM OF SPEECH. The 1ST AMENDMENT to the U.S. Constitution is generally regarded as a protection against sedition laws. Nevertheless, the Congress has passed several such laws, the first being the ALIEN AND SEDITION ACTS of 1798. Two sedition acts were passed during World War I, and the SMITH ACT of 1940 was aimed specifically at Communists. More than 2,000 Communists and other left-wingers were convicted under the law, but the U.S. Supreme Court ruled many of those convictions unconstitutional, and the government abandoned prosecutions under the Smith Act.

See also: SCHENCK V. UNITED STATES.

Seeckt, Hans von [zaykt] Hans von Seeckt, b. Apr. 22, 1866, d. Dec. 27, 1936, a German general, rebuilt the German army after World War I. As Reichswehr (army) commander (1920–26), Seeckt established an effective fighting force partly by violating terms of the Treaty of Versailles. He secretly trained officers beyond their official responsibilities, and he established illegal military groupings outside the formal army, which the treaty limited to 100,000 men. He served in the Reichstag (1930–32) and as military advisor to China's Chiang Kai-shek (1934–35).

seed A seed is a ripened ovule and consists of a new plant in the form of an embryo, together with stored food and a protective coat, or testa. Gymnosperms ("naked seeds"), the primitive group of seed-plants, have seeds that develop from exposed ovules. Angiosperms ("enclosed seeds"), the advanced seed-plants, bear their ovules protected inside an ovary. The ovary ripens into the seed-bearing fruit; it is often confused with the seed itself, as in the grains. Seeds vary in size from the fine, dustlike seeds of orchids to the large seed contained in the coconut.

The seed is also the primary dispersal agent of plants. Depending on the structure of the flower from which they are derived, angiosperms may be dispersed as seeds or as part of a fruit, such as blackberry, cocklebur, coconut, dandelion, and wheat. Dispersal of seeds, even for only a short distance, avoids overcrowding of young plants and permits colonization of new territory. Some fruits forcibly discharge their seeds or have the means to throw them great distances. Seeds also can be dispersed by wind, water, birds, and mammals.

Seeds are important commercially, not only for propagation but also for the food stored in them. In plants such as cereals, food is stored in a tissue called the endosperm, which surrounds the embryo. This food is used by the embryo during germination. In other plants, such as beans and peas, the embryo uses up the endosperm during development.

Most seeds remain quiescent during a cold or dry season and germinate only with the coming of favorable growing conditions (see GERMINATION). Seeds that require special treatment to germinate, even when presented with adequate water and oxygen and favorable temperatures, are said to exhibit DORMANCY. Seeds with thick or waxy coats, which inhibit the entry of water and oxygen, may

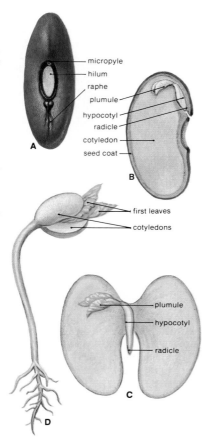

Drawings of seeds of a bean plant show an external edge view (A), a seed with one cotyledon removed (B), an opened seed (C), and a seedling after germination (D). A small pore, or micropyle, and a ridge, or raphe, are associated with a scar, the hilum, which is left after the seed separates from its stalk. A protective coat encloses the seed. The embryo consists of a plumule, which develops into the terminal bud of the seedling; the cotyledons, or seed leaves, which store food; a root-stem region, or hypocotyl; and a radicle, which becomes the primary root of the seedling.

micropyle
hilum
raphe
plumule
hypocotyl
radicle
cotyledon
seed coat
A
B

first leaves
cotyledons

plumule
hypocotyl
radicle
C

D

remain in a prolonged quiescent state. Seeds of the Indian lotus can germinate 200 years after they are shed. Most seeds, however, lose the ability to germinate within several years of shedding.

See also: COTYLEDON; GENE BANK; PLANT PROPAGATION.

seed cone   A seed cone is the female (ovulate) cone of pines and other CONIFERS. Larger than male POLLEN CONES, seed cones are usually found in the upper reaches of the tree. The cone is composed of bract (leaf) scales, each of which is borne underneath an ovuliferous scale, named because ovules are borne on the upper surfaces of the scales. An ovule consists of an outer coat (the integument) through which an opening (the micropyle) leads to nutritive tissue called the nucellus, or megasporangium. The megasporangium surrounds a diploid (doubled in chromosome number), megaspore mother cell, which undergoes meiosis to produce four haploid megaspores, one of which divides to form the female gametophyte. An egg produced by the female gametophyte is fertilized by a sperm cell from a pollen grain (male gametophyte). The product of this fertilization is a seed.

See also: ALTERNATION OF GENERATIONS.

Seeger, Pete   American folksinger, composer, song collector, and five-string banjo virtuoso Peter Seeger, b. New York City, May 3, 1919, with his family, has been a leading force in the movement to revive the FOLK MUSIC tradition in America. His father, Charles Seeger, b. Mexico City, Dec. 14, 1886, d. Feb. 8, 1979, was a musicologist. Pete's stepmother Ruth Crawford Seeger, b. East Liverpool, Ohio, July 3, 1901, d. Nov. 18, 1953, composed her own music, tightly organized, atonal pieces, and transcribed and arranged folk songs from the Archive of American Folksong. Half brother Michael, b. New York City, Aug. 15, 1933, is a folk-song collector and has recorded music by himself and as a member of the New Lost City Ramblers. Half sister Margaret (Peggy Seeger), b. New York City, June 17, 1935, sings both as a soloist and with her husband, the Scottish folk specialist Ewan MacColl.

Pete Seeger left Harvard University during his sophomore year, first to hobo around the United States, then to work in the field with John and Alan Lomax (see LOMAX family), the song collectors. In 1940, Seeger and Woody GUTHRIE organized the Almanac Singers; in 1948, Seeger helped to found The Weavers, a commercially successful folk group and the inspiration for such later groups as the Kingston Trio and Peter, Paul, and Mary. Seeger has recorded more than 50 albums and appears regularly in concerts and on television. The many well-known songs he has composed include "If I Had a Hammer" (written with Lee Hayes), "Kisses Sweeter than Wine," and "Where Have All the Flowers Gone."

Seeing Eye dog   see GUIDE DOG

Seferis, George [se-fair'-is]   A major influence on modern Greek prose and poetry, the poet George Seferis (pseudonym of Seferiadis), b. Feb. 29, 1900, d. Sept. 20, 1971, was the first Greek to win the Nobel Prize for literature, in 1963. Having fled (1914) with his family from Turkish-dominated Smyrna to Athens, he studied there and in Paris, becoming a lawyer and a diplomat. From 1957 to 1962 he was Greece's ambassador to Britain. Among his *Collected Poems, 1924–1955* (3d ed., 1981), *Mythistorima* (1935) depicts the spiritual emptiness of contemporary life through the evocation of ancient mythology, and *The Thrush* (1946) employs mythology to express feelings of uprooting and exile. Seferis also published *Three Secret Poems* (1966; Eng. trans., 1969) and an essay collection, *On the Greek Style* (1966).

Segal, George [see'-guhl]   The realist sculptor George Segal, b. New York City, Nov. 26, 1924, is known in particular for his life-size cast figures. He attended New York University and Cooper Union and had his first show in 1956. During the early 1960s, Segal turned to the direct-cast plaster figures—usually white and rough with an occasional prop or piece of clothing—that brought him fame. He also participated in the early "happenings" and the revolt against abstract expressionism. Segal was included in the significant "New Realists" show held by the Sidney Janis Gallery in New York City in 1962, which gave many of the important new-realist artists of the 1960s their first exhibition. In Segal's larger works, such as *The Diner* (1964–66; Walker Art Center, Minneapolis, Minn.), the dead-white plaster figures are set in rooms with actual stools, counters, and fixtures, as if they had been mummified in the course of their mundane pursuits.

The white plastercast sculptures of George Segal seem uncannily lifelike when placed beside or in real-life environments. In Cinema *(1963) the figure of a man changing an illuminated plexiglass and metal marquee communicates the poignancy of a humdrum activity. (Albright-Knox Art Gallery, Buffalo, N.Y.)*

Seghers, Hercules The Dutch painter and etcher Hercules Pietersz Seghers, b. *c.*1590, d. after 1633, painted landscapes that unite panoramic breadth with close observation of nature and vigorous treatment of light and shade. These works influenced Rembrandt van Rijn, who owned eight Seghers paintings and reworked one of Seghers's etchings. Seghers's early landscapes, such as *River Valley* (*c.*1620; Rijksmuseum, Amsterdam), follow the Mannerist tradition. His mature style is exemplified by his *Mountain Landscape* (*c.*1633; Uffizi Gallery, Florence). Seghers's approximately 50 etchings include both realistic views and romantic improvisations, such as his *Tree with Moss* (undated; Rijksmuseum). He experimented with graphic techniques and may have been the first to use aquatint.

sego lily [see'-goh] The sego lily, or mariposa lily, *Calochortus nuttallii*, is an attractive member of the lily family, Liliaceae, that grows in the western and Pacific states. The cultivated variety produces long, narrow leaves and showy, tuliplike flowers that are usually white, lined with blue or purple, and with a purple spot at the base. Lilac or yellow markings may occur on the flowers of some plants. The bulblike, fleshy corm was eaten by early Mormon settlers and hence has symbolic significance as manna in Mormon religion. The sego lily also is the state flower of Utah.

Segovia, Andrés [se-goh'-vee-ah] The celebrated Spanish classical guitarist Andrés Segovia, b. Feb. 21, 1893, d. June 2, 1987, was primarily responsible for the current popularity of his instrument and its literature. Essentially self-taught, he turned to the guitar after briefly studying the piano, violin, and cello, making his professional debut in 1909. Appearances followed throughout the Spanish-speaking world. The guitar at the time was little esteemed outside flamenco and other folk idioms, and guitar recitals were unknown. In 1924, however, Segovia played in Paris to great acclaim, and his first concerts (1928) in the United States were hailed by critics in superlatives. He also toured the USSR and the Far East. Segovia thoroughly revamped the technique of the guitar and enriched its repertoire with numerous transcriptions of works originally written for other instruments.

segregation, racial   see INTEGRATION, RACIAL

Sei Shonagon [say shoh'-nah-gohn] The Japanese poet and writer Sei Shonagon, b. *c.*966, d. after 1013, is famous for the diary that bears her name, *The Pillow-book of Sei Shonagon* (991–1000; trans. 1928). A collection of witty epigrams, astute observations of people and events, and poetic notes on natural phenomena, the work is considered unique in Japanese literature. Although Sei Shonagon was lady-in-waiting to the Empress Sadako and a contemporary of the novelist Lady Murasaki, little is known of her life; she is believed to have retired to a Buddhist nunnery.

Seikan Tunnel   see TUNNEL

Seine River [sen] The Seine is a 776-km-long (482-mi) river in north central France that flows through the heart of Paris. The river rises in Burgundy and winds northwest through the ÎLE-DE-FRANCE. This region—with Paris in its center—is the historical heart of the country. From Paris the Seine flows northwest through a farmland region and past Rouen to the port of Le Havre, where it empties into the English Channel. The drainage area of the Seine is about 79,000 km^2 (30,500 mi^2). Its main tributaries are the MARNE, Aube, Loing, and Oise rivers. Navigable for about 560 km (350 mi), the Seine is linked by canals to the Loire, Rhine, and Rhône rivers.

seismogram   see SEISMOMETER

seismology   see GEOPHYSICS

seismometer [syz-mahm'-uh-tur] Seismometers are instruments used to measure minute earth motions, such as are transmitted through the Earth by seismic waves. Also called geophones and seismographs, they measure motion in a specific direction, usually vertically. A three-component seismometer has three elements at right angles to each other, each measuring in a different direction.

A seismometer consists of an inertial mass that tends to remain at rest or to lag behind when the instrument is moved. This movement produces a displacement between the inertial mass and the rest of the instrument; an effect of this displacement can be measured. Early instruments sometimes had an optical lever that reflected a beam of light from a mirror attached to the inertial mass in order to magnify the displacement before recording it. Most modern seismometers use a coil of wire as the inertial mass; this coil is placed in a magnetic field so that a voltage is induced across it when the magnetic field is moved with respect to the coil. The voltage or the current generated by the voltage is then measured.

Hydrophones also are used to measure seismic waves in fluids—for example, at sea. Modern hydrophones contain a piezoelectric ceramic element that is distorted by the change of pressure produced by a seismic wave, and the voltage generated is measured. Hydrophones do not distinguish between waves traveling in different directions.

Permanently installed seismometers, used to detect motions generated by earthquakes (and also nuclear explosions), are usually three-component instruments able to detect the fairly low frequencies that characterize earthquakes at great distances. Seismometers are also used to detect very small seismic motions generated by storms.

Seismographs are instruments for recording earthquake waves and can detect horizontal (A) or vertical (B) movements of the Earth's crust. The two types are mounted on concrete bases (1) and pillars (2) that are anchored to bedrock (3). In both, a heavy weight (4) is suspended on a pivoted bar (5) that can move only horizontally (A) or vertically (B). During an earthquake the weight stays still as a result of its inertia; the rest of the device moves, including a rotating drum and chart (6). A pen on the suspension bar records the earthquake's primary (P), secondary (S), and long (L) waves on the chart, or seismogram (C, D). Another pen (7) records the time (8).

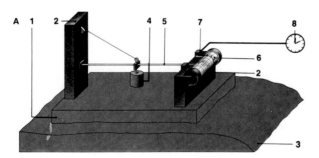

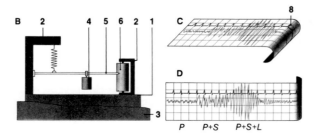

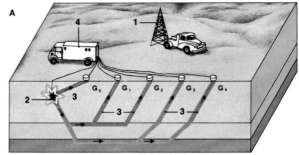

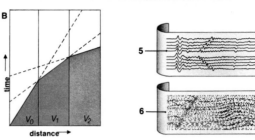

Geologists often use seismometers to locate mineral deposits and oil and gas reservoirs. (A) A hole is bored in the ground with a special drill assembly (1), and a dynamite blast (2) is set off, creating seismic waves. The shock waves (3) are reflected from various rock layers, travel at different speeds, and reach the seismometer, or geophone detectors (G_0–G_4), at different times. The geophone signals are recorded in an instrument truck (4). Graphs (B) of wave travel time and distance are plotted from velocity data (V_0, V_1, V_2), obtained from seismometer charts (5), and are used to calculate the structure and depth of underground rock strata. Depth profile charts (6) are then drawn to yield a visual representation of subsurface rock structure.

Small, portable seismometers are used in seismic exploration for oil, gas, and minerals; to obtain foundation information for engineering; and for other geological studies. In such studies seismic waves are generated, for example, by small explosions, dropped weights, or injection of high-pressure air or steam into water. The seismic waves are reflected from rock interfaces and are detected by an array of seismometers, which determine the distance and direction to the interfaces. As a result of reflection seismic work, sections and maps of the Earth's structure can be constructed, and possible accumulations of minerals, oil, or gas can be inferred. Small, portable seismometers also are used to detect personnel and vehicular movement in war zones.

Selassie, Haile see HAILE SELASSIE

Selective Service see CONSCRIPTION

Selene [suh-lee'-nee] In early Greek mythology Selene was goddess of the Moon. She was later identified with ARTEMIS and, to a lesser extent, HECATE. According to two separate legends, she was wooed by Pan with a fleece and loved the shepherd Endymion.

selenium [suh-lee'-nee-uhm]   Selenium is the third member of Group VIA of the periodic table, coming after oxygen and sulfur and preceding tellurium. Its chemical symbol is Se, its atomic number is 34, and its atomic weight is 78.96. Its name is derived from the Greek *selene,* meaning "moon." It was discovered in 1817 by Jons Jacob Berzelius in association with tellurium.

Selenium is present in some rare minerals, such as crookesite and clausthalite, and in some sulfur deposits and sulfide ores. It is a rare element, forming only 9×10^{-6} % of the Earth's crust. Selenium exists in at least three allotropic forms: amorphous selenium is either red in powder form or black in vitreous form; crystalline monoclinic selenium is deep red; and crystalline hexagonal selenium, the most stable form, is a metallic gray. Natural selenium (gray) consists of six stable isotopes and has a melting point of 217° C, a boiling point of 684.9° C, and a specific gravity of 4.79. The most important oxidation states are +4 and +6.

The chemical reactions of selenium resemble those of sulfur and are typically nonmetallic in nature. Selenium reacts directly with many metals, although not with the noble metals. Hydrogen selenide, H_2Se, may be prepared by the direct combination of the elements but is better prepared by the action of dilute hydrochloric acid on a selenide. Selenium reacts less readily with oxygen to form the dioxide than does sulfur. Selenous acid, H_2SeO_3, is formed when the soluble selenium dioxide, SeO_2, is dissolved in water. SeO_2 is a good oxidizing agent and is used in certain organic syntheses. Selenic acid, H_2SeO_4, which has similar properties to sulfuric acid, is formed by dissolving selenium trioxide, SeO_3, in water.

The principal commercial source of selenium is in the anode sludge obtained from the electrolytic refining of copper. Selenium is recovered by roasting the sludges with soda or sulfuric acid. Elemental selenium is claimed to be practically nontoxic, but hydrogen selenide and other selenium compounds are extremely toxic, resembling arsenic in their physiological behavior.

Selenium exhibits both photovoltaic action, whereby light is converted directly into electricity; and photoconductive activity, whereby electrical resistance is decreased with increased light exposure (see PHOTOELECTRIC EFFECT). As a consequence, selenium is used in the production of photocells, exposure meters, and solar cells. Selenium also finds extensive application in rectifiers, a result of its ability to convert alternating electric current to direct current. Selenium behaves as a *p*-type SEMICONDUCTOR and is being increasingly used in electronic and solid-state devices. Other applications include its use in the glass industry to decolorize glass, as a photographic toner, as an additive in steel production, and in xerographic reproduction.

Seleucids (dynasty) [suh-loo'-sidz]   The Seleucids were a dynasty founded by Seleucus I. At his death (281 BC) the Seleucids controlled most of the Asian provinces of the Macedonian empire—including most of Anatolia,

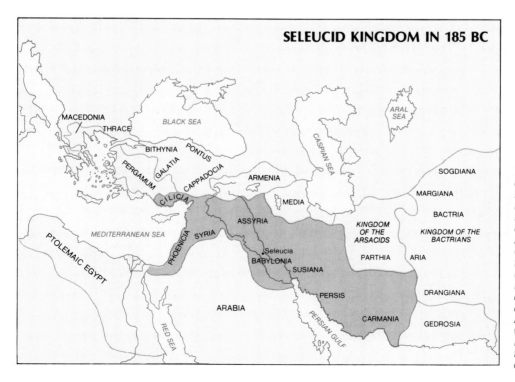

SELEUCID KINGDOM IN 185 BC

This map depicts the extent of the Seleucid kingdom about 185 BC. At that time, during the reign of Seleucus IV, successor to Antiochus III the Great, the Seleucids, following their defeat (190) by Rome and Pergamum, had relinquished possession of all territory held in Anatolia north and west of the Taurus Mountains under the terms of the Treaty of Apamea (188 BC).

part of Syria-Phoenicia, Babylonia, Assyria, Media, Parthia, Sogdiana, Bactria, Margiana, Aria, Drangiana, Gedrosia, Carmania, Persis, and Susiana. Weakened by constant wars against the Ptolemies of Egypt and by succession disputes, the Seleucids had lost much of Anatolia and eastern Iran by the accession (223) of ANTIOCHUS III. He reasserted nominal control over the eastern provinces but, trying to expand westward, was defeated by Rome (190) and lost all his gains. ANTIOCHUS IV tried to consolidate the reduced kingdom and seize Egypt, but he was stopped by Roman orders.

After the death (163) of Antiochus IV, the Romans prevented any resurgence of Seleucid power. By 140 the Parthians had conquered all territories east of Syria, and the Jews were independent. After temporary successes by Antiochus VII (r. 139–129), the kingdom disintegrated until it was annexed by TIGRANES I of Armenia. Briefly restored by the Roman general Lucius Licinius Lucullus, it was made by POMPEY THE GREAT into the Roman province of Syria (63 BC).

Seleucus I Nicator, Macedonian King [suh-loo'-kuhs ny-kay'-tur]

Seleucus I Nicator ("the Conqueror"), c.358–281 BC, was the greatest of the successors of Alexander the Great. He fought under Alexander and after the king's death (323) received the province of Babylonia. He fled to Egypt after ANTIGONUS I Monophthalmus defeated Eumenes in 316. In 312, however, he regained Babylonia with a handful of men and gradually won from Antigonus all of the Macedonian empire's provinces east of the Euphrates. He took the royal title in 305.

Ceding his Indian province to CHANDRAGUPTA MAURYA in exchange for an elephant corps, Seleucus led his army across half of Asia to join in the defeat of Antigonus in 301. Henceforth he concentrated on the west, founding Antioch as his western capital to balance Seleucia in the east. In 282 he attacked LYSIMACHUS, who was killed in battle (281). Within reach of reuniting Alexander's empire, he crossed to Europe, but he was assassinated by an exiled son of Ptolemy I whom he had befriended.

self-incrimination

Self-incrimination is the act by an individual of furnishing testimony or evidence that may be used in a legal proceeding to implicate that same individual for violating the law. In the United States, the privilege against self-incrimination is set forth in the 5th Amendment to the U.S. Constitution. This legal principle dates from 17th-century English protests against STAR CHAMBER and ecclesiastical courts' use of coercive measures to suppress political and religious dissent and to extract confessions from persons accused of crimes.

As interpreted in numerous court decisions, the protection against self-incrimination means that a witness before any government official or tribunal may refuse to give testimony that might be used against the witness in a future criminal proceeding or that might result in uncovering further evidence that could be used against the witness in such a proceeding. Thus a criminal defendant need not testify at his or her trial, although that privilege may be waived. With the 4th Amendment's protection against unreasonable searches and seizures, this privilege also guards against the use of involuntary confessions and most confidential papers that would be incriminating, which have been judged by the U.S. Supreme Court to be inadmissible as evidence in a criminal trial.

The privilege against self-incrimination has been extended to certain additional parties with whom the witness is considered to have the right to conduct confidential communications, such as a spouse, member of the clergy, physician, or lawyer. Except for the spouse, only those communications consistent with the role of the other party are privileged.

The privilege does not forbid compelling testimony under grants of immunity, nor does it prevent compelling production of certain records that by law must be maintained or the making of handwriting samples, taking of blood samples, or appearance in a police lineup.

See also: ESCOBEDO V. ILLINOIS; EVIDENCE; MIRANDA V. ARIZONA.

Selim I, Sultan of the Ottoman Empire [sel-im']

Selim I, b. 1470, d. Sept. 22, 1520, Ottoman sultan from 1512 to 1520, took the OTTOMAN EMPIRE to its peak of power and expanse. He achieved the throne by killing his brothers and forcing his father, BAYEZID II, to abdicate. Later he secured the succession for his chosen heir, who ruled as SULEIMAN I (the Magnificent), by killing his other sons and grandsons. For such acts, and for his brutal treatment of enemies in battle, he was known as Selim the Grim.

In 1514, Selim conquered the Safavid rulers of Persia at Chaldiran and annexed some of their territory. In 1516–17 he took Syria and Egypt away from the MAMELUKES. Those victories made him in effect the ruler over all of Islam. He then resurrected and assumed the title of caliph, which made the sultan the spiritual as well as the temporal ruler of the Muslim world. Selim was a great patron of Islamic art and literature and was himself a poet.

Selim III, Sultan of the Ottoman Empire

Selim III, b. Dec. 24, 1761, d. July 28, 1808, introduced various Western-style reforms, including a modern army and navy, to the OTTOMAN EMPIRE during his reign (1789–1807). Selim succeeded his uncle Abd al-Hamid I; his reign was marked by almost constant warfare. These conflicts included the RUSSO-TURKISH WAR of 1787–92, the invasion of Egypt by Napoléon (1798–1801), the rise of powerful notables in the Balkan and Anatolian provinces, and a war with Russia and Great Britain (1806–08). Furthermore, Selim was opposed by the JANISSARIES, an elite corps that distrusted his reforms. In 1807 they revolted, deposed and imprisoned Selim, and placed Mustafa IV on the throne. Mustafa had Selim assassinated when his supporters attempted to restore him to the throne.

Selinus [suh-ly'-nuhs]   The ancient Greek city of Selinus at modern Selinunte, on the south coast of Sicily, was founded (c.650 BC) as a colony by citizens from Megara Hyblaea, to the northeast. It was the westernmost of the Greek cities in Sicily and became one of the most powerful, controlling the agricultural wealth of the interior. It was famous as well for its great temples and artistic productions. Constant wars with Punic colonists and the city of Segesta led to the Carthaginian occupation from 409 to 250 BC. Thereafter, the deserted site gave way to encroaching swampland.

Seljuks [sel'-juhks]   The Seljuks were a group of nomadic Turkish warrior leaders from Central Asia who established themselves in the Middle East during the 11th century as guardians of the declining ABBASID caliphate and after 1055 founded the Great Seljuk sultanate, an empire centered in Baghdad and including Iran, Iraq, and Syria. They helped to prevent the FATIMIDS of Egypt from making Shiite Islam dominant throughout the Middle East and, in the 12th century, blocked inland expansion by the Crusader states on the Syrian coast. Their defeat of the Byzantines at the Battle of Manzikert (1071) opened the way for the Turkish occupation of Anatolia.

Seljuk power was at its zenith during the reigns of sultans ALP-ARSLAN (1063–72) and Malik Shah (1072–92), who, with their vizier Nizam al-Mulk, revived Sunnite Islamic administrative and religious institutions. They developed armies of slaves (MAMELUKES) to replace the nomad warriors, as well as an elaborate bureaucratic hierarchy that provided the foundation for governmental administration in the Middle East until modern times. The Seljuks revived and reinvigorated the classical Islamic educational system, developing universities (madrasahs) to train bureaucrats and religious officials.

After Malik Shah's death, a decline in the quality of dynastic leadership and division of their rule among military commanders and provincial regents (atabegs) weakened the power of the Great Seljuks. The last of their line died in battle against the Khwarizm-shahs in 1194.

A branch of the Seljuks established its own state in Anatolia (the sultanate of Konya or Rum), which survived until it was conquered by the Mongols in 1243.

Selkirk [sel'-kurk]   Selkirk (also Selkirkshire) is a former county in southeastern Scotland. The major cities are Selkirk and Galashiels. The Rivers TWEED, Ettrick, and Yarrow drain the area. The western and southwestern portion is composed of an undulating plateau where sheep are raised. In the lower eastern portion oats, turnips, and barley are grown.

Settled by the Picts, the region was subsequently conquered by the Romans. It became part of the Anglo-Saxon kingdom of Northumbria before annexation (c.1020) by Scotland. In 1975, during the reorganization of local government in Scotland, Selkirk was integrated into the new administrative region of BORDERS.

Selkirk, Thomas Douglas, 5th Earl of   Lord Selkirk, b. June 20, 1771, d. Apr. 8, 1820, was a Scottish philanthropist who established colonies in British North America for dispossessed Scottish Highlanders. In 1803 he founded a successful colony on Prince Edward Island. A second colony at Baldoon, Upper Canada (now Ontario), failed.

He made a third effort in the Red River Valley in present-day Manitoba between 1812 and 1816. Acquiring a controlling interest in the HUDSON'S BAY COMPANY, Selkirk secured from the company 301,600 km^2 (116,000 mi^2) in what is now southern Manitoba and northern Minnesota. The area lay astride the fur trade route of the NORTH WEST COMPANY, which attempted to drive Selkirk's colonists away from the RED RIVER SETTLEMENT. On June 19, 1816, a number of settlers were killed in a skirmish at Seven Oaks. Selkirk responded by capturing the North West Company's headquarters at Fort William (now Thunder Bay, Ontario). Resulting litigation drained Selkirk's spirit and ruined him financially. The colony, however, survived.

Sellers, Peter   The versatile comedian Peter Sellers, b. Sept. 8, 1925, d. July 24, 1980, was a popular British radio entertainer before becoming an international film star, best known as the clumsy Inspector Clouseau of the Pink Panther series. He gave accomplished performances in *The Mouse That Roared* (1959), *I'm All Right Jack* (1959), *Only Two Can Play* (1962), *Lolita* (1962), *Dr. Strangelove* (1963), and *The Pink Panther* (1963). His later films included *Being There* (1979) and *The Fiendish Plot of Dr. Fu Manchu* (1980).

Selma   Selma is a city in central Alabama on the Alabama River. The seat of Dallas County, it has a population of 23,755 (1990). Located in the center of a fertile agricultural region, Selma is a marketing center for cotton, livestock, dairy products, and grain and has light industries.

Selma was settled in 1815. Union forces attacked the city in 1865 because of its Confederate arsenal and naval foundry. In March 1965, during a bitterly resisted drive to register black voters, Martin Luther King, Jr., led a march from Selma to the state capital, Montgomery.

Selznick, David O. [selz'-nik]   A producer and Hollywood mogul celebrated for his showmanship, David Oliver Selznick, b. Pittsburgh, Pa., May 10, 1902, d. June 22, 1965, was the principal creative force behind the multiple-award-winning screen epic *Gone with the Wind* (1939). Son of pioneer producer Lewis J. Selznick, he worked for both Paramount and RKO before becoming (1933) vice-president at MGM, in charge of an independent production unit. He left (1936) to form his own company, Selznick International Pictures, dedicated to the ideal of artistic quality in picture-making. *Rebecca*

(1940), *Since You Went Away* (1943), and *Spellbound* (1945) followed.

---

semantics   Semantics (from the Greek *semantikos,* "significant,") is the study of meaning in language. The interpretation of any given word or phrase may vary greatly; for example, the term *meaning* itself has a number of different senses. In the phrases *What do you mean by that?* or *What do you mean to do?* the reference is to intentions. The expression *Smoke means fire* refers to an inference rather than a definition. *Meaning* can also refer to a translation from one language to another, as in the sentence *Russian nyet means "no."* It can even refer to a rule in a game: *Doubles means that you must roll the dice again.* But as a branch of LINGUISTICS, semantics is not concerned with all these different senses of meaning; rather, it is limited to the study of how speakers know that a given utterance represents a given thought or idea. Thus semantics is concerned with a type of translation: the translation from thought into utterance, and vice versa.

Four Components of Language. Linguists divide the speaker's knowledge about language into four overlapping components: the lexicon (see LEXICOLOGY AND LEXICOGRAPHY), phonology (see PHONOLOGY AND MORPHOLOGY), SYNTAX, and semantics. These four components consist of processes that make it possible for speakers to set up correspondences between sound and meaning. The lexicon, or mental stock of words, embodies elements of each of the other three components. Every word is associated with a phonological representation, or sequence of sounds; syntactic information, such as its part of speech; and a meaning. The phonological component specifies how words are to be pronounced; the syntactic component specifies how words fit together to form sentences; and the semantic component specifies how the meanings of words combine within sentences to give a general meaning, or semantic reading, for the sentence.

Semantics in Other Disciplines. Semantics is not just a branch of linguistic theory. Anthropologists can learn a great deal about a culture simply by examining the way its vocabulary divides up semantic space. Psychologists have studied many different aspects of meaning: the acquisition of word meanings in children, the ability of chimpanzees and other primates to understand sign language, the ability to detect ambiguity, and the emotive, or connotational, meaning of words (for example, *statesman* has more positive connotations than *politician*). Literary critics also need to know something about semantics, for they study the ways in which writers and poets use words to communicate thoughts and feelings. Finally, philosophers have at least as much claim to the field of semantics as do linguists. They have been most interested in issues such as the nature of correct and valid inference, the way in which people use language to refer, and the formal properties of logical systems. The work of philosophers has recently become a major stimulus in the development of linguistic theory. Linguists possess a general knowledge about the form of linguistic expressions that can occur in natural language; to this, philosophers have added useful theories about the reference of expressions in artificial languages and have examined minute semantic distinctions in their own languages.

---

semaphore [sem'-uh-fohr]   Semaphore is a visual SIGNALING system that generally uses flags or lights. Both the ancient Greeks and the Romans are known to have signaled over short distances with torches and flags. The telescope, invented in about 1600, greatly increased the range of such systems. In 1794, Claude Chappe, a French engineer, devised a semaphore that could carry a message 230 km (144 mi) from Lille to Paris in two min-

The alphabet, numerals, and basic punctuation symbol (that is, "front") of the semaphore signaling system used by the U.S. Navy are indicated. The colors of the flags, yellow and red, were selected for their visibility over long distances.

utes. He constructed a series of towers about 8 to 16 km (5 to 10 mi) apart and within sight of each other. On each tower was mounted a pivoted beam with arms at the end. A telescope was located at each tower so that an operator could relay the beam-arm signals.

The electric TELEGRAPH supplanted Chappe's semaphore for long-distance signaling in about 1850; however, Hutton Gregory, a telegraph engineer on the British railroads, modified Chappe's system by employing moving metal arms or rows of lights, mounted on towers, to signal trains. The railway semaphore is still in use.

Semaphores also remain in use for maritime communications. The U.S. Navy uses a system in which an operator grasps half-red and half-yellow flags; the arms are extended at various angles to indicate letters of the alphabet.

Sembene, Ousmane [sem'-bay-nay, oos'-mah-nay] The Senegalese writer Ousmane Sembene, b. Jan. 8, 1923, is also a notable filmmaker. Beginning with the autobiographical *Le Docker Noir* (The Black Docker, 1956), his novels describe the struggles of African working people to achieve independence: *God's Bit of Wood* (1960; Eng. trans., 1962) concerns Dakar's 1947–48 railway strike; the story "Black Girl" (1961; Eng. trans., 1970) eulogizes a mistreated servant; and *White Genesis* (1965; Eng. trans., 1972) examines racism. To reach a wider, semiliterate audience, Sembene in the 1960s turned to film, which he had studied in Moscow. His successful productions include *Borom Saret* (1963), *Mandabi* (1968; from his 1965 story, translated in 1972 as "The Money Order"), *E Mitai* (1971), and *Xala* (1974; novel trans., 1983).

Semele [sem'-uh-lee] In Greek mythology Semele was a beautiful maiden who won the love of Zeus in mortal form. To gain revenge, his jealous wife, Hera, appeared to Semele in the guise of her old nurse and persuaded her to demand that Zeus come to her in his divine form. Since Zeus was the god of thunder, Semele was consumed by lightning when she saw him. Zeus rescued their unborn child, DIONYSUS, by sewing him up in his thigh. Dionysus later made his mother immortal, and she lived among the gods under the name Thyone.

semen Semen is a fluid mixture of secretions and SPERM produced in the male REPRODUCTIVE SYSTEM and emitted during ejaculation, a reflex action that occurs as a result of sexual stimulation. During ejaculation, contractions of the vas deferens propel sperm cells through the ejaculatory ducts into the urethra. At about the same time, the seminal vesicles, the prostate gland, and the Cowper's glands empty their secretions into the urethra. Semen, the product of this mixing, is not immediately expelled from the urethra but accumulates under pressure behind the urethral sphincter until the sphincter suddenly relaxes. In humans, the amount of semen emitted during an ejaculation averages about 3 ml. Each ml contains

an average of 90 million sperm. The amount of semen diminishes as the frequency of ejaculation increases. The fluid part of semen contains fructose, choline, phosphocholine, citric acid, acid phosphatase, and other chemical substances necessary to nourish the sperm, maintain their motility, and aid in the process of fertilization. Semen can be stored frozen for long periods of time for use in ARTIFICIAL INSEMINATION.

semiarid climate Semiarid climates are regions of transition between arid and humid climates that are primarily defined by their average yearly amounts of precipitation (about 25 to 50 cm/10 to 20 in per year). Other factors important in defining semiarid regions include regional amounts and seasonal distributions of precipitation. Normally, semiarid climates produce a steppe vegetation (see STEPPE LIFE).

Semiarid regions are generally located on the margins of semipermanent high-pressure cells or in the rain shadow of a continental cordillera. They are thus subjected to the invasion of moisture-laden air masses from more humid areas. Semiarid areas may have meager amounts of precipitation that are variable and undependable, but unlike arid regions, they may have periods of abundant precipitation and agricultural productivity.

semiconductor A semiconductor is a substance having an electrical resistance somewhere between that of electrical insulators and conductors (see CONDUCTION, ELECTRIC; INSULATOR, ELECTRICAL; RESISTANCE, ELECTRICAL). The principal application of semiconductors is the fabrication of solid-state, often miniaturized electronic components and INTEGRATED CIRCUITS.

Energy Levels and Valence Bands

The resistance of semiconductors, insulators, and conductors is determined in part by the number of electrons that occupy the outermost energy level, which is called the valence band, of the substance's constituent atoms. Under certain conditions, such as the application of energy from an external source, electrons may be dislodged from the valence band and caused to move away from the atom. Such a movement of electrons is called an electric current.

The maximum number of electrons that can occupy the valence band is eight, and an atom with eight valence electrons is, under normal conditions, an excellent insulator. Because the valence band of such an atom is filled, it may be considered in a state of equilibrium in which it is reluctant to contribute an electron to or receive an electron from the unfilled valence band of a neighboring atom. The INERT GASES have eight valence electrons and are electrical insulators. Elements with six or seven valence electrons are also good insulators.

Atoms having one, two, or three electrons in their valence band usually readily contribute electrons to neighboring atoms. Elements composed of such atoms are good electrical conductors. Metals such as gold, silver, and copper have a single electron in their valence band and are excellent conductors.

Elements having four electrons in the valence bands of their atoms, and compounds composed of an element with three valence electrons and a second element with five valence electrons, may be semiconductors. The unit of electrical resistance is the ohm (Ω). Silicon, a common semiconductor, has a resistance of 50,000 Ω/cm^3; silver, on the other hand, is an excellent conductor, having a resistance of only 0.00005 Ω/cm^3. Mica, a good insulator, has a resistance of one trillion (10^{12}) Ω/cm^3.

Semiconductor Components

Semiconductors are used to fabricate solid-state electronic components. The simplest semiconductor components are classified as thin-film devices and bulk-effect devices. One such component, the temperature-sensitive THERMISTOR, makes use of the fact that semiconducting mixtures of certain metallic oxides decrease in resistance with temperature increase. Another semiconductor component is the light-sensitive photoconductive cell, or photoresistor.

The semiconductors from which thin-film and bulk-effect components are fabricated are often contaminated, or "doped," with carefully controlled amounts of impurities in a process called doping. The impurity, which is called a dopant, lowers the resistance of the semiconductor so that more electrical current can flow through the device.

Junction Diodes

The doping of semiconductors to decrease their resistance is the key to the fabrication of advanced semiconductor devices. A simple two-terminal junction DIODE, for example, may be fabricated by doping pure silicon, which has four valence electrons, with an element, such as phosphorus, which has five valence electrons.

Silicon doped with phosphorus is designated a negative-type (n-type) semiconductor, because it contains a surplus of free electrons, which have a negative charge; the entire material, however, is electrically neutral. A junction diode can be made by doping a small region on the surface of the n-type silicon with a dopant. Individual atoms of these dopants each have three valence electrons, so that the covalent bond that they form with four silicon atoms leaves a deficit of a single electron. Each atom of dopant accepts an electron from the silicon; hence the silicon atom loses one of its electrons, leaving a positive hole in the valence band, and so will readily accept an electron at each hole. Such a material is designated a positive-type (p-type) semiconductor because it contains a surplus of holes.

The junction diode formed by an interface of p-type and n-type semiconductor materials is characterized by its ability to block the flow of electrons in one direction (reverse bias) while permitting electron flow in the opposite direction (forward bias). If electrons are injected into the p-type side of the diode, they will not cross the interface of the p region and the n region, called the pn junction, because the electrons already present in the n-type region repel them.

Note that while the operation of the diode has been described in terms of electrons as carriers of electrical charge, it is also possible to consider the holes on the p-type side of the junction as being charge carriers, because holes continually migrate toward the pn junction to combine with arriving electrons.

Diode Uses

Junction diodes are commonly used as RECTIFIERS and detectors of radio and microwave signals. The proper choice of dopant concentration, kind of semiconductor, and physical structure make it possible to design diodes with a wide range of applications and properties. The ZENER DIODE, for example, has properties similar to those of a conventional junction diode. The tunnel diode is a special pn-junction component used in ultrahigh-frequency (microwave) applications.

Diodes that have optoelectronic properties are especially important. Light-emitting diodes can be made from various semiconductor compounds. These diodes emit a relatively narrow-frequency spectrum of optical radiation. Light-emitting diodes producing red, yellow, and green light have found widespread use as long-lived indicator lamps and as numeric displays in electronic calculators, instrument panels, and appliances.

Other kinds of optoelectronic diodes are used to detect optical radiation, some being specifically designed to detect various wavelengths and modulation frequencies. SOLAR CELLS are large-area junction diodes that produce an electrical current in response to solar radiation.

By far the most important kind of semiconductor devices are those which employ two or more pn junctions. These include numerous kinds of electronic switching devices such as silicon-controlled rectifiers (SCRs) and triacs. The SCR permits the passage of direct current only when a small electrical signal is applied to a third electrode called the gate. The triac, which is formed by two back-to-back SCRs, switches alternating current.

The TRANSISTOR is the most important semiconductor component that incorporates multiple pn junctions. Although there are many kinds of transistors, they all permit a relatively large electric current flowing through the device to be controlled by a very small current or voltage at a third electrode. Prior to the early 1960s, virtually all transistors were housed in individual metal or plastic packages. The development of integrated circuits, however, made it possible to simultaneously fabricate and interconnect many transistors on a small chip of silicon during a series of complex production steps.

See also: MICROELECTRONICS; THIN-FILM TECHNOLOGY.

Seminole [sem'-uh-nohl] The Seminole are a tribe of North American Indians who left their traditional homeland in Georgia after separating from the CREEK during the 18th century to live independently in Florida. Their Hitchiti language is in the Muskogean branch of the Hokan-Siouan linguistic stock. Many escaped black slaves took refuge with the Seminole, whose culture was typically Creek.

When the Seminole obstructed the advance of white

land-seekers and refused to return slaves, Andrew JACKSON pushed them farther south in the First Seminole War (1817–18). In 1819 the United States purchased Florida from Spain, and pressure from whites increased. The treaty of Payne's Landing (1832) called for removal of the Seminole, but the tribe resisted in the Second Seminole War (1835–42) under the leadership of OSCEOLA, Wildcat, and Halek. At last, beaten and destitute, 4,000 of the 4,300 Seminole moved west to INDIAN TERRITORY. They became one of the so-called FIVE CIVILIZED TRIBES. Those who stayed in Florida, however, living on three reservations near Lake Okeechobee, retained many of their traditional ways. In the late 1980s about 1,500 Seminole lived in Florida and about 4,000 in Oklahoma.

semiotics From the Greek word *semeion*, meaning "sign," semiotics is the science of signs. It stresses that "meaning," even when it seems natural or inherent, is always the result of social conventions; also, it analyzes culture as a series of sign systems. Although there is a long history of reflection on the sign, modern semiotics dates from the work of Charles Sanders PEIRCE and Ferdinand de SAUSSURE. Literary semiotics studies both the system of conventions that allow literary communication and also those implicit reflections on signs and signification found in literary works. Much of what is now called semiotics or, in Europe, semiology, was at first called STRUCTURALISM.

Semiramis [sem-ir'-uh-mis] In Mesopotamian mythology Semiramis was an Assyrian queen, the wife of Ninus, founder of Nineveh. She was abandoned by her mother, the fish goddess Derceto, and nurtured by doves. After Ninus died, Semiramis ruled in the place of their son Ninyus for many years. She founded Babylon and led successful campaigns against Persia, Egypt, Libya, and Ethiopia. When her son plotted against her, she disappeared in the shape of a dove. Semiramis was worshiped as a deity, sharing many characteristics with ISHTAR. The myth was apparently derived from a historical figure, Sammuramat, who was regent for her son Adad-Nirai III from 810 to 805 BC.

Semites [sem'-yts] Semites are peoples who speak Semitic languages (see AFROASIATIC LANGUAGES); the group includes ARABS, ARAMAEANS, JEWS, and many Ethiopians. In a Biblical sense, Semites are peoples whose ancestry can be traced back to Shem, NOAH's eldest son. The ancient Semitic populations were pastoral NOMADS who several centuries before the Christian Era were migrating in large numbers from Arabia to Mesopotamia, the coasts of the Mediterranean Sea, and the Nile River delta. Jews and other Semites settled in villages in Judea, southern Palestine.

The most prominent Semites today are Arabs and Jews. They are different in many ways, and they have absorbed a variety of European traits through centuries of migration and trade. The origin of Semitic languages, however, and many similarities in the stories of ISLAM and JUDAISM reflect a common ancient history.

Semitic languages see AFROASIATIC LANGUAGES

Semmes, Raphael [semz] Raphael Semmes, b. Charles County, Md., Sept. 27, 1809, d. Aug. 30, 1877, a Confederate naval officer in the U.S. Civil War, became a Southern hero for his disruption of Union commerce. After resigning his U.S. naval commission in February 1861, he commanded the *Sumter* for the Confederacy. In 1862 he took command of the English-built *Alabama.* Semmes ravaged the Union's merchant marine from the West Indies east to Singapore until the U.S.S. *Kearsarge* sank his ship near Cherbourg, France, on June 19, 1864.

See also: ALABAMA (ship).

Senate of the United States The Senate of the United States is the upper house of the CONGRESS. It consists of two senators from every state (unlike the HOUSE OF REPRESENTATIVES whose members are apportioned according to the population of each state). Currently the Senate has 100 members.

Senators serve 6-year terms, with a third of the terms expiring every 2 years. Originally, the Constitution provided for their selection by the state legislatures, in contrast to the popular election of members of the House, but the 17th Amendment, adopted in 1913, required that senators be elected by the people. Senators must be 30 years of age, citizens of the United States for at least 9 years, and residents of the states they represent.

Special Powers of the Senate. Every act of Congress must be approved by both the House of Representatives and the Senate. In addition, the U.S. Constitution gives the Senate certain unique powers. It has sole authority to ratify, by a two-thirds vote, treaties proposed by the presi-

Members of the U.S. Senate and its presiding officer, Vice-President Walter Mondale, posed for their official portrait in March 1978. To allow the portrait to be taken, the Senate suspended its rules forbidding photography in the chamber.

dent of the United States. The Senate also has the sole power to accept or reject—by majority vote—presidential appointments to federal judgeships (including the Supreme Court), ambassadorships, cabinet posts, and high-level positions in the executive branch of the federal government.

Senate rejection of treaties and presidential nominations is rare but not unprecedented. After World War I it refused to ratify the Versailles Treaty as signed by President Woodrow Wilson. In 1970 it rejected two of President Richard Nixon's nominations of Supreme Court justices. While the House of Representatives has sole authority to impeach public officials, the resulting trial must be conducted in the Senate, with a two-thirds vote necessary for conviction (see IMPEACHMENT).

Senate Officers. The vice-president of the United States serves as president of the Senate. The Senate chooses its other officers and leaders, including a president pro tempore, who acts as Senate president in the vice-president's absence. The practical powers of these two titular leaders are not wide-ranging. The vice-president rarely presides over routine day-to-day debate in the Senate, being present only at times of important votes or parliamentary decisions. The vice-president has no vote unless the members of the Senate cast a tie vote.

The position of president pro tempore of the Senate is largely honorific. It has traditionally been filled by the most senior senator of the majority party—the one with the longest continuous service in the chamber.

Although there is no mention of political parties in the Constitution, the Senate since its earliest days has organized along political party lines, based on a two-party division into majority and minority. From 1955 to 1981 and again from 1987, the majority party in the Senate was the Democratic party. In 1980, when Republican presidential candidate Ronald Reagan won a landslide victory over incumbent Jimmy Carter, the Republicans also secured control of the Senate. They maintained their majority until the 1986 mid-term elections, when the Democrats regained control.

The most important figure in the Senate is the majority leader, elected by the members of the majority party. The majority leader is aided by an assistant majority leader, also known as the majority whip. The majority leader directs Senate floor activity and helps coordinate the debate and timing of legislation. The primary political resources of the leader are prestige, parliamentary knowledge, and powers of persuasion. The majority leader also presides over the collective caucus, or conference, of members of the majority party and plays a major role in allocating assignments to committees for majority senators. The views and interests of the minority party in the Senate are represented by similar officers.

Committee System. The business of the Senate is conducted through a highly structured committee system. In 1991 there were 16 standing committees (which consider and report all legislation), one special committee (on the aging), and 3 investigative select committees (created for specific purposes). The committees had about 100 sub-committees, each with the power to hold hearings and conduct investigations. There were also 4 joint committees, which include both Senate and House members. Major standing committees include Appropriations; Armed Services; Budget; Commerce, Science, and Transportation; Energy and Natural Resources; Finance; Foreign Relations; Judiciary; and Labor and Human Resources.

Chairpersons of committees, who have considerable prestige and influence, are nominally selected by the senators of the majority party. In practice, the determining factor is seniority—the chair going to the majority party senator who has served the longest continuous period on a particular committee.

Rules. The Senate determines its own rules. Perhaps the most distinctive feature of Senate procedure is its tradition of extended and open debate—that is, any senator can continue debating a bill or an issue indefinitely, unless two-thirds of the senators present and voting adopt a motion of CLOTURE to stop debate. The use of such dilatory tactics is known as the FILIBUSTER. During the 1950s and 1960s, Southern Democratic senators frequently employed filibusters to delay or quash civil-rights measures. In 1975 the Senate altered its standing Rule XXII to permit 60 senators to end a filibuster unless the debate concerns Senate rules (in which case the two-thirds rule remains in effect). This change, however, proposed as a way of more easily curtailing the filibuster, did not eliminate the practice. Gavel-to-gavel live television coverage of Senate deliberations has been permitted since 1986.

■

Senate, Roman   The Roman Senate, the dominant branch of government under the republic (c.509–31 BC) and still an important advisory body during the empire, originated as a council of elder advisors to the early kings. In 82 BC, Lucius Cornelius Sulla increased its membership from 300 to 600.

In the early republic, members were chosen primarily from men who had held the consulship, an office restricted to PATRICIANS. PLEBEIANS began to enter once the consulship was opened (c.367) to them, and membership was gradually made available to former holders of lower magistracies as well. Senators were generally large landowners and were forbidden to engage in large-scale business after 218 BC. Within the Senate itself a hierarchy existed. Debate in the Senate proceeded along strict lines of rank and seniority, so that issues were usually put to a vote before lower-ranking members could speak. A resolution was called a *decretum* or *Senatus consultum* and technically was only advice to a magistrate, not a law (*lex*). In practice the Senate controlled finances, provincial assignments, foreign policy, and the state religion.

Augustus hoped to retain the loyalty of the Senate under the empire by leaving it in control of Italy and the most peaceful provinces, although the emperor, as commander of most legions, was in effective control of most of the empire. Under his successors senatorial control of the magistracies and judicial functions was increased, and by AD 200 the Senate's decrees technically had the status of laws. The emperor controlled the entrance of new members and had precedence in introducing business. Faced with the emperor's control of the army and bureaucracy, the Senate felt increasingly impotent, and its effective role became more and more restricted in the 2d and 3d centuries AD.

Sendai [sen-dy]   Sendai is the capital city of Miyagi prefecture, Japan, and the administrative seat of Tohoku region in northern Honshu. Located near the center of the eastern coast of Honshu, with a population of 700,254 (1985), Sendai is linked by rail and highway to Tokyo, 320 km (200 mi) to the south.

Iron, steel, chemicals, ceramics, textiles, and foodstuffs are Sendai's major products. The city's shops offer an assortment of folk art produced throughout the Tohoku region, particularly the well-known wooden dolls. The Osaki Hachiman Shrine, Rinnoji Park, and the neighboring national park of Matsushima are famous tourist attractions. Tohoku University (1907) is an institution of higher education. The city was the center of the 17th-century feudal state of Date Masamune, a powerful warlord who made it his residence after 1600.

Sendak, Maurice [sen'-dak]   The American illustrator and writer Maurice Bernard Sendak, b. Brooklyn, N.Y., June 10, 1928, has been a major influence in children's literature since the publication of his *Where the Wild Things Are* (1963), for which he won the 1964 Caldecott Medal. His often bizarre drawings and the tales he himself has written convey the terrors, rages, and humors of childhood. Books he has both written and illustrated include *Higglety Pigglety Pop!* (1967), *In the Night Kitchen* (1970), and *Outside Over There* (1981). Sendak has designed sets and costumes for several operas, among them Janáček's *Cunning Little Vixen* (1981) and Tchaikovsky's *Nutcracker Suite* (1983), and has also designed the London productions of operas made from his own works: *Where The Wild Things Are* (1983) and *Higglety Pigglety Pop!* (1984).

Seneca [sen'-uh-kuh]   The Seneca, an Iroquoian-speaking North American Indian tribe of the original Five Nations IROQUOIS League, traditionally occupied a territory between the Genesee River and Seneca Lake in what is now New York State. They were reputed to be among the most respected and feared North American Indian tribes. Eight Seneca sachems were represented on the League's Grand Council. During the American Revolution, the Seneca sided with the British. Famous Seneca political figures included CORNPLANTER, RED JACKET, and the warrior-turned-prophet, HANDSOME LAKE.

Culturally quite similar to their Cayuga, Onondaga, Oneida, and Mohawk confederates, the Seneca traditionally lived in scattered villages organized within a system of matrilineal clans. A calendric cycle of ceremonies re-

flected their agricultural and hunter-gatherer way of life. Today members of the tribe live at the Tonawanda, Allegany, and Cattaraugus reserves in New York and at the Six Nations Reserve near Brantford, Ontario.

Seneca, Lucius Annaeus   Lucius Annaeus Seneca, *c*.4 BC–AD 65, was one of the most broadly influential philosophical writers in the Stoic tradition (see STOICISM). He is called Seneca the Younger because his father, Seneca the Elder (*c*.60 BC–AD *c*.37), was also a noted literary figure and rhetorician. Under Emperor Claudius I, Seneca the Younger was condemned on a charge of adultery and exiled (AD 41) to Corsica. He later expressed his bitter resentment of Claudius in the satirical *Apocolocyntosis* (or Pumpkinification), in which he mocked the deification of Claudius and made fun of his physical defects. Recalled in 59, he became tutor to the young emperor NERO and exerted a beneficial influence on the first few years of his reign. Falling out of favor, he went into retirement in 62; in 65 he was accused of conspiracy against the emperor and sentenced to death. He chose to commit suicide instead, a choice approved by his philosophy.

Seneca wrote 12 works entitled *Moral Essays* and 124 so-called *Moral Letters*, as well as a work on natural phenomena and several poetic tragedies based on Greek models. Less an original philosopher than a moral teacher and guide, he regarded Stoicism as a practical doctrine, subordinating logic and physics to ethics: "The true philosopher," he held, "is the teacher of humanity." He urged people to become indifferent to the transient goods of the world, valuing only the virtue within themselves. To become truly virtuous, he maintained, the wise person must learn to curb his or her emotions, which are, or involve, false judgments concerning the value of externals. Seneca examined the nature and effects of the passions at length, demonstrating how they can be mastered, and praised the happy state of the person who cannot be shaken by fortune.

Seneca Falls Convention   The Seneca Falls Convention, the first women's-rights assembly in the United States, was organized by Lucretia Coffin MOTT and Elizabeth Cady STANTON and met at Seneca Falls, N.Y., on July 19–20, 1848. The 68 women and 32 men present passed a Declaration of Sentiments, which paralleled the language of the Declaration of Independence and listed 16 forms of discrimination against women, including denial of suffrage and of control of their wages, their own persons, and their children. Twelve resolutions calling for various rights were passed. Eleven received unanimous approval, whereas one resolution, advocating the vote for women, was adopted over Mott's opposition. The convention was moved to Rochester, N.Y., two weeks later to win broader support for its goals. The Seneca Falls gathering established the women's-rights cause as an organized movement.

Senefelder, Aloys   SEE LITHOGRAPH; OFFSET LITHOGRAPHY

AT A GLANCE

REPUBLIC OF SENEGAL

Land: Area: 196,192 km² (75,750 mi²). Capital and largest city: Dakar (1985 est. pop., 1,382,000).

People: Population (1990 est.): 7,713,851. Density: 39.3 persons per km² (101.8 per mi²). Distribution (1989): 36% urban, 64% rural. Official language: French. Major religions: Islam, Christianity, traditional religions.

Government: Type: republic. Legislature: National Assembly. Political subdivisions: 10 regions.

Economy: GNP (1989): $4.72 billion; $650 per capita. Labor distribution (1985): subsistence agriculture—77%; government and public services—14%; salaried private sector—9%. Foreign trade (1988): imports—$1.1 billion; exports—$761 million. Currency: 1 C.F.A. franc = 100 centimes.

Education and Health: Literacy (1985): 28% of adult population. Universities (1989): 2. Hospital beds (1988): 6,127. Physicians (1988): 407. Life expectancy (1990): women—56; men—53. Infant mortality (1990): 87 per 1,000 live births.

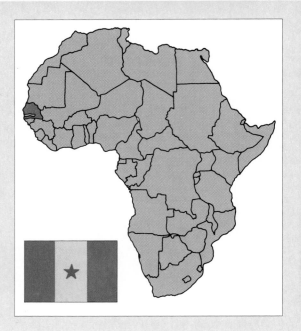

Senegal

Senegal [sen'-uh-gawl] Senegal, the westernmost country in Africa, has a 600-km (373-mi) Atlantic coastline. It is bordered on the south by Guinea-Bissau and Guinea, on the east by Mali, and on the north, across the Senegal River, by Mauritania. The independent enclave of Gambia nearly divides the country. Senegal became fully independent from France in 1960. DAKAR, the capital, is one of West Africa's leading ports.

Land and People

Senegal is made up of low plains covered by sediments that form reddish soils. The country lies within the tropical wet-dry climate zone and has a dry season from October to June and a wet season from July to October. Rainfall declines from north to south, averaging 356 mm (14 in) in the lower Senegal River valley during the rainy season and more than 1,270 mm (50 in) in the lower Casamance River valley. The highest temperature usually occurs between April and June, when it may reach 35° C (95° F). The lowest temperature, about 14° C (57° F), occurs in January. The GAMBIA RIVER, SENEGAL RIVER, and Casamance River all rise in the southeastern highlands. Senegal's high point is Fouta Djallon (498 m/1,643 ft).

Senegal is primarily forested savanna, and the trees become smaller and more sparse from south to north. In the south a wooded savanna dominates, with citron, silk cotton, and oil palms near the coast. In central Senegal the baobab predominates, giving way northward first to the Spanish juniper and then to the acacia. A reforestation program is attempting to reverse the process of desertification.

Senegal's resources are mainly agricultural. Deposits of iron ore, marble, gold, petroleum, natural gas, and uranium have scarcely been exploited. Phosphate rock, long exported, is also used by Senegal's expanding chemical industry.

Senegal's predominant ethnic group is the Wolof. Other ethnic groups include the FULANI, Serer, Tukulör, Dyola, and Malinke. More than 90% of the population are Muslim; another 6% are Christian. Some ethnic groups in southern Senegal practice traditional religions. Cultural differences have fostered a recurrent secessionist movement in the Casamance.

Although the government has expanded the school system and health-care facilities, both educational and health services remain limited. Cheikh Anta Diop University was founded as the University of Dakar in 1957.

Economic Activity

Agriculture is the principal economic activity. Peanuts, grown on about 40% of the cultivated land, provide the sole source of cash income for most farmers. Subsistence crops include sorghum, millet, and beans. The government is attempting to diversify agriculture by encouraging the planting of cotton, rice, sugar, and vegetables.

Fish and fish products (particulary shrimp and tuna) have surpassed peanuts as the leading export. Senegal has a relatively well-developed industrial sector focused chiefly on the processing of local raw materials (particularly peanuts, fish, and cotton) and the production of consumer goods, textiles, chemicals, and petroleum products. Tourism provides a significant source of foreign exchange. Senegal usually runs a large trade deficit.

Government

Senegal is a multiparty democracy headed by a president; members of the National Assembly are elected to 5-year terms. Periods of centralized presidential rule have alternated with periods (1960–63; 1970–83) when a prime minister served as head of government. The noted poet Léopold Sédar SENGHOR was president of Senegal from independence (1960) until his resignation late in 1980. His successor, prime minister Abdou Diouf, was elected president in his own right in 1983 and reelected in 1988. Through the Confederation of Senegambia, formally inaugurated in 1982, Senegal and Gambia coordinated their defense, economic, and foreign policies. The confederation was dissolved in 1989.

History

During the 14th century the Mali empire expanded westward into present-day Senegal; during the 15th century the Wolof united several small states into the Jolof empire, which lasted into the 18th century. French colonists founded the city of Saint-Louis, on the Senegal River, in 1658; French traders had been in the area since 1637. The colony passed back and forth between the French and the British during the 18th century and was restored to France in 1815.

In 1895 the Federation of FRENCH WEST AFRICA was formed with Dakar as its capital. Although local self-governing institutions existed in Saint-Louis and Dakar in the 19th century, Senegal was not granted internal self-government until 1956. In 1959, Senegal and the French Soudan (Mali) merged as the Mali Federation, but Senegal broke up the federation soon after independence in 1960. In the 1980s, Senegal faced economic problems and political turmoil. A border incident with Mauritania in 1989 resulted in violent riots and the displacement of thousands of people from each country. Senegal also has been engaged in a 12-year territorial dispute with Guinea-Bissau. In 1989 an international panel ruled in Senegal's favor, but Guinea-Bissau rejected the decision.

Senegal River   The Senegal River, one of the principal rivers in West Africa, is about 1,635 km (1,015 mi) long. It rises in central Guinea as the Bafing River and flows generally north to western Mali, where it joins with the Bakoy River. From there the Senegal flows northwest, follows the Senegal-Mauritania border, and enters the Atlantic Ocean just south of Saint-Louis, Senegal. During the high-water season, from August to mid-October, the

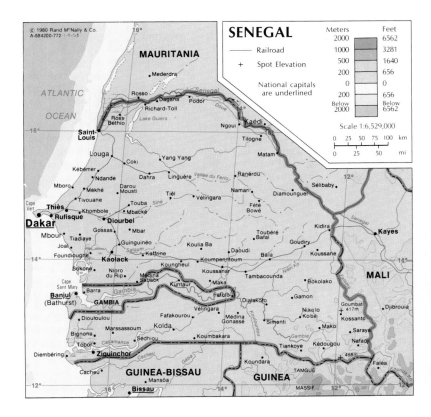

(Below) *Farmland in Senegal's western plains produces peanuts, the dominant cash crop, as well as cassava, millet, and corn.*

river is navigable as far as about 900 km (560 mi) from the mouth. Construction began (1981) on two dams to control the Senegal's frequent floods and improve irrigation. Rice is grown in the valley. The river may have been explored as early as the 5th century BC by Hanno of Carthage. French ships entered the estuary in 1558, and subsequently the French used the Senegal to penetrate the interior.

Senghor, Léopold Sédar [sahn-gohr'] President of Senegal from 1960 until his resignation in 1980, Léopold Sédar Senghor, b. Oct. 9, 1906, is an African poet who writes in French. As a student of literature at the Sorbonne, Paris, in the 1930s, Senghor was one of the originators of the important black literary and philosophical movement Négritude. A French army officer and a prisoner of the Germans during World War II, Senghor later led the Senegalese struggle for independence and helped found the important journal *Présence Africaine.*

Primarily a lyric poet, Senghor has moved from nostalgic evocation of an idealized Africa, as in *Songs of the Shade* (1945; Eng. trans., 1964), to themes of cultural conflict and anticolonialism in *Éthiopiques* (1956) and such prose works as *On African Socialism* (1961; Eng. trans., 1964). In 1984 he became the first black admitted to the Académie Française.

senility *Senility* is a term traditionally applied by both laypeople and clinicians to a declining condition associated with aging and characterized by mental incompetence, impaired posture and coordination, and emotional instability. Because of current research in social and medical gerontology, however, senile symptomatology is no longer attributed to a generalized picture of irreversible senility. For example, a diagnosis of senile brain disease associated with the death of brain cells would be considered irreversible, whereas an association with metabolic malfunction may respond to treatment.

Moreover, current research is also focused on a number of social and emotional factors contributing to the senile syndromes, such as social isolation, malnutrition, severe anxiety, apathy or depression, and other forms of environmental or psychological deficit. Significant studies have demonstrated that enhancement of social stimulation or supportive psychiatric intervention may reverse senile behaviors. The current clinical awareness of the multiplicity of factors affecting each individual's aging process has therefore invalidated the older, stereotyped concept of senility.

See also: AGING; ALZHEIMER'S DISEASE; OLD AGE.

senna [sen'-uh] Senna is any herb, shrub, or tree of the genus *Cassia* in the pulse family, Leguminosae, order Rosales; the name is also applied to cathartic drugs derived from the plants. The dried leaves of *C. acutifolia* (Alexandria senna) and *C. angustifolia* (Indian senna) are

Wild senna, originally from eastern North America, was once used by Indians to purify the blood and to reduce fevers.

used for purgatives; both species are cultivated in southern India. Wild senna, *C. marilandica*, native to the eastern United States, has also been used as a purgative. The cathartic canafistula is extracted from the fruit pulp of *C. fistula*, the golden-shower tree of India. *C. nictitans*, the wild sensitive plant, is a North American herb whose leaflets respond to touch by drooping, a reaction similar to that of the mimosa.

Sennacherib, King of Assyria [sen-ak'-uh-rib] Sennacherib, son and successor of SARGON II, reigned over Assyria from 705 to 681 BC. In 703 BC a revolt broke out in Babylonia promoted by Merodach-baladan, a Chaldean prince who had usurped the throne there. This revolt was followed by uprisings in Syria and Palestine, and for more than a decade Sennacherib was fully occupied with rebellious subjects. The first Babylonian revolt was soon put down; another uprising ten years later culminated in the savage destruction of the city of Babylon in 689.

In the west Sennacherib dealt with the Phoenicians, Philistines, Jews, and other rebels in 701. Although he failed to capture Tyre and Jerusalem, he forced HEZEKIAH, king of Judah, to renew his tribute payments to Assyria. The reign of Sennacherib was notable for the rebuilding and enlargement of NINEVEH, henceforth the Assyrian capital. He was assassinated by his own sons and succeeded by ESARHADDON, who brought the culprits to justice.

Sennett, Mack [sen'-et] A pioneer of slapstick film comedy, Mack Sennett, b. Michael Sinnott in Richmond, Quebec, Jan. 17, 1880, d. Nov. 5, 1960, was an uneducated Irish-Canadian who drifted into films as D. W. Griffith's apprentice. In 1912 he started his own comedy studio, called Keystone, where he developed the Keystone Kops and discovered such major talents as Charlie Chaplin and Frank Capra. With the advent of sound films, comedy shorts became less popular, and in the 1930s, Sennett, who failed to change with the times, lost his entire fortune. Sennett is, however, still remembered as Hollywood's "King of Comedy" and received a special Academy Award in 1937 for his contribution to cinema comedy.

▬

sensationalism Sensationalism is a philosophical doctrine that rejects theories of innate ideas and holds that all knowledge arises from sensations. It has had a continuous tradition in one form or another since the beginnings of philosophy in Greece. Sensations are the psychological occurrences in the human mind that result from experiencing external objects through the senses or from introspective awareness of feelings, emotions, or the operations of the mind. Because they are regarded as basic and uninterpreted data, sensations are thought to provide the basis for certainty in human knowing. Philosophers in more recent times have referred to sensations as "sense data." Sensationalism is generally associated with the tradition of EMPIRICISM in philosophy.

▬

senses and sensation The senses are the faculties by which external or internal stimuli are received and transformed into perceptions or sensations in the brain. The reception and transmittal of a sensation requires the presence of a stimulus, a sense organ to react to the stimulus, a nerve pathway to carry an impulse from the sense organ to the brain, and an area of the brain that can translate the impulse into a sensation. All higher animals have sets of sense organs as part of their peripheral nervous systems. Such a sensory system allows the organism to detect environmental events and body states, and the input is used locally in reflexes or transmitted to the brain. Different species of animals have evolved particular senses or depend on some senses more than on others; therefore not all animals are sensitive to the same aspects of their environments.

Sense Organs. Even in humans, Aristotle's list of the five senses of sight, hearing, smell, taste, and touch is incomplete. Human beings also receive information concerning pain, temperature, balance, joint positions, muscle and tendon stretch, and pressure. Some of the sensory information is transmitted to the brain but not to conscious awareness. In this way circulatory receptors transmit information to the brain that results in blood pressure adjustments.

Central to the sense organs are the sensory receptors, which exhibit selectivity (not absolute) to excitation by particular energy or chemical sources. When excited, the receptors initiate a chain of events that culminates in the excitation of an electrical potential in nerve cells. In any sensory system, the signal is transformed into electrical potentials in a specific set of nerve cells. These peripheral neurons are connected to particular locations in the spinal cord and brain. All of the information that the brain receives about its environment is in the indirect form of coded sequences of electrical potentials. The mechanism of nervous conduction is identical regardless of the nature of the originating sense or-

gan, yet when the impulses from a specific kind of receptor reach their destination in the cerebral cortex, specific sensations arise. The sensory modalities are separate within the cerebral cortex; for instance, an individual does not hear light, taste sound, or smell pressure. How the cerebral cortex converts virtually identical nerve impulses into specific and distinct sensations is still a mystery, but the nature of the sense organ that is stimulated and the area of the brain to which the impulse is sent clearly play major determining roles.

Sensation. Sensation refers to the process of obtaining sensory information through the stimulation of body parts or to the conscious feelings or sense impressions themselves. The latter definition is akin to that of PERCEPTION. Sensations are classified as exteroceptive, interoceptive, and proprioceptive. Exteroceptive sensations provide information about the external environment and include the sensations of sight, hearing, taste, smell, temperature, pain, pressure, and touch. The exteroceptive sense organs are located on the exterior of the body and include the eyes, ears, tongue, nose, and the temperature, pain, pressure, and touch receptors of the skin. Interoceptive sensations provide information about the internal environment and include such sensations as pain, hunger, thirst, nausea, fatigue, and suffocation; the sense organs involved are located mainly in the visceral organs. Proprioceptive sensations provide information about body position and movement; these sense organs are located in the muscles, tendons, joints, and the organs of balance in the ear.

A great deal of peripheral processing of sensory information usually occurs before transmission of the electrical impulses along the nerve fibers projecting toward the central nervous system. The strength of a stimulus is most often transformed to a frequency of electrical potentials in these fibers. The information is transmitted to the brain where, after further processing and analysis, conscious sensations result. Specific conscious sensations depend on the functioning of certain brain regions. Damage to particular brain regions because of stroke, injury, infection, or tumor may result in the selective loss of sensory abilities.

Research in recent years has found that skin sensations are important for the maintenance of health. For example, if animals are prevented from licking their young, the young frequently die of gastrointestinal or genitourinary failure. Evidently, in the absence of skin stimulation, the autonomic nervous system fails to maintain proper motor activity in the organs of these systems. Similarly, the skin stimulation that accompanies breast-feeding appears to have physiologic benefits for infants.

See also: NERVOUS SYSTEM; REFLEX; SENSORY DEPRIVATION; articles on individual organs.

sensitivity training   SEE HUMANISTIC PSYCHOLOGY

▬

sensory deprivation Sensory deprivation occurs when all normal sensory stimulation of a human being or animal is severely reduced or made as monotonous as possible. The effects of sensory deprivation were first studied scientifically during the 1950s using goggles, ear padding, and covering over the forearms and hands to minimize visual, auditory, and tactile stimulation for students who lay on a bed in an isolated room. The initial period was restful but the stress of the monotonous conditions became apparent by the second or third day. In the absence of normal sensory input, subjects became restless, unable to concentrate or think clearly, and emotionally unstable and sometimes experienced vivid hallucinations. One-half of the students quit within two days in spite of being paid to remain.

The phenomena of sensory deprivation have since been extensively explored. Although people differ in their reactions to sensory deprivation, some conclusions can nevertheless be drawn. Visual hallucinations, for example, do not occur in all subjects, but when such hallucinations are present they typically progress from simple hallucinations to those which are complex and meaningful to the individual. The difficulties found in thinking or concentrating under sensory deprivation are most pronounced with complex cognitive tasks, such as interpreting an ambiguous visual scene, as opposed to simpler tasks, such as recalling a series of numbers. Other findings include characteristic changes in the electrical activity of the brain and the conclusion that certain personality traits lead to greater tolerance for sensory deprivation. Finally, sensory deprivation tends to increase susceptibility to propaganda.

sentence   A sentence is the decision made by a judge in a criminal case after a defendant is found guilty. The limits of the sentence are usually specified by the laws covering the particular crime; the judge, however, may have wide discretion in setting the precise length of imprisonment or the amount of the fine. The convicted criminal may be sentenced for an indeterminate period of imprisonment in which a minimum and a maximum sentence are imposed—such as 2 to 6 years—with an opportunity for PAROLE after the minimum sentence has been served. The judge may also suspend the sentence and place the offender on PROBATION. Critics have charged that wide judicial discretion and indeterminate sentencing have led to arbitrary or lenient prison sentences. In 1984 federal legislation mandated standardizing prison sentences for those convicted of federal crimes.

Seoul   [sohl or se-ool']   Seoul is the capital and largest city of South Korea. The city lies on the Han River in the northwest corner of South Korea about 32 km (20 mi) inland from its port, INCHON, on the Yellow Sea. The metropolitan city covers an area of about 605 km² (234 mi²) and has a population of 10,726,000 (1990 est.), making it one of the world's largest metropolitan areas.

The city is the commercial, industrial, and cultural center of South Korea. About one-third of all industries in South Korea are located in Seoul, which produces about 40% of the total gross national product. Principal manufacturing includes textiles, machinery, chemicals, and food products. Among the many colleges and universities in Seoul are Seoul National (1945), Hanyang (1939), and Yonsei (1885) universities. Two symphony orchestras, a national theater, and numerous museums, including the new National Museum (opened 1986) are also located in the city. A modern 117-km (73-mi) subway system was completed in 1986.

An important settlement since the 11th century, Seoul was established as Korea's capital about 1394 by King Taejo, founder of the Yi dynasty. Between 1910 and 1945 the Japanese occupied the city. During the Korean War (1950–53) the city was severely damaged and changed hands four times. It has since been rebuilt and expanded to house a greatly increased population. Much major construction took place in the 1980s in preparation for the 1986 Asian Games and the 1988 Summer Olympics, including the Han River Development Project. In this immense undertaking, completed in 1986, the riverbed in the heart of the city was deepened and widened, and many parks and sports facilities were built along its banks.

separation of powers   The doctrine of separation of powers, which is one of the fundamental principles of the U.S. federal system of GOVERNMENT, is generally credited to the French political philosopher Baron de MONTESQUIEU, whose *The Spirit of the Laws* (1748; Eng. trans., 1750) was highly regarded by the framers of the U.S. Constitution. Montesquieu's basic contention was that those entrusted with power tend to abuse it; therefore, if governmental power is fragmented, each power will operate as a check on the others. In its usual operational form, one branch of government (the legislative) is entrusted with making laws, a second (the executive) with executing them, and a third (the judiciary) with resolving disputes in accordance with the law. As a further protection, the personnel of each branch are selected by different constituencies and procedures for different terms of office. The separation of powers principle contrasts with British-style parliamentary government, where almost all political power rests with the legislative branch.

Sephardim   [suh-fahr'-duhm]   The Sephardim are those JEWS who follow the liturgy and customs developed by the Jews of medieval Spain and Portugal. The name comes from Sepharad, a place of exile mentioned in Obadiah 20 and early identified with Iberia. Unlike the ASHKENAZIM, those Jews who settled in German lands, the Sephardim followed Babylonian rather than Palestinian Jewish traditions. They also developed their own language, Ladino, or Judeo-Spanish, a blend of medieval Castilian, Hebrew, Arabic, and other elements. There is a considerable body of Ladino literature.

After the expulsion of the Jews from Spain (1492) and Portugal (1497) many Sephardim formed communities in the lands of the Ottoman Empire—the Balkans, North Africa, and the Middle East. Others remained in Iberia, nominally converting to Christianity. Vilified as *Marranos* ("pigs"), they were subject to continuing persecution, and most eventually left to form communities in northwestern Europe—Amsterdam became a particularly important center. Sephardic traditions were largely adopted by local Jewish groups in the Middle East and North Africa; hence, today the term *Sephardim* is loosely applied to all Jews native to those areas.

septicemia [sep-ti-see'-mee-uh] Septicemia, or blood poisoning—an invasion of the bloodstream by bacteria—is characterized by high fever, sweating, and weakness that are caused by the destruction of red blood cells. Death quickly follows very high fever. Septicemia is a serious disorder but has become less common since the development of antibiotics, especially penicillin. Before the introduction of antiseptics into delivery rooms, puerperal fever, or childbed fever, which results from uterine infection, was a common form of septicemia.

Septuagint [sep'-too-uh-jint] The Septuagint, commonly designated LXX, is the oldest Greek version of the Old Testament of the BIBLE, the title "seventy" referring to the tradition that it was the work of 70 translators (or 72 in some traditions). The translation was made from the Hebrew Bible by Hellenistic Jews during the period 275–100 BC at Alexandria. Initially the Septuagint was widely used by Greek-speaking Jews, but its adoption by the Christians, who used it in preference to the Hebrew original, aroused hostility among the Jews, who ceased to use it after about AD 70. It is still used by the Greek Orthodox church.

The Septuagint contains the books of the Hebrew Bible, the deuterocanonical books—that is, those not in the Hebrew version but accepted by the Christian church—and the APOCRYPHA. Ancient manuscripts from Qumran suggest that the Septuagint often followed a Hebrew text different from the present authoritative Hebrew text. Thus its value for textual criticism has been enhanced. The Septuagint provides an understanding of the cultural and intellectual settings of Hellenistic Judaism.

sequence In mathematics, a sequence is an ordered set of numbers (called terms). The set may be finite or infinite. The set of positive integers (1, 2, 3, . . .) is an example of an infinite sequence, while the set (1, 2, 3, 4) is a finite sequence. Sequences are also classified by the relationship among their terms. Suppose (a_1, a_2, . . . , a_n, a_n+1, . . .) is a sequence. If $a_{n+1} - a_n$ is constant (as with the positive integers, above), the sequence is called an arithmetic sequence or PROGRESSION. If the ratio a_{n+1}/a_n is constant, the sequence is called a geometric progression; the sequence (2, 6, 18, 54, . . .) is a geometric progression with the constant ratio 3.

Certain types of infinite sequences may approach a limiting value. For example, the sequence 1, ½, ⅓, ¼, . . . ,

$1/n$ has the limit zero as n approaches infinity. The limit of a sequence is an important mathematical concept and is discussed in greater detail under LIMIT.

sequoia see REDWOOD

Sequoia National Park see NATIONAL PARKS

Sequoya [suh-kwoy'-uh] Sequoya, or George Guess, b. *c.*1760, d. Aug. 1843, a CHEROKEE warrior of mixed ancestry, is credited with the invention of the Cherokee written language, the so-called talking leaves. An able linguist who learned French, Spanish, and English, he was determined to preserve Cherokee culture and was implacably opposed to American intrusions into his tribal lands. After continued white encroachments, however, Sequoya journeyed westward (1797), although he returned periodically to his homeland.

Recognizing the power of the written word, Sequoya developed a Cherokee syllabary of 86 symbols by adapting letters of the English alphabet to represent sounds in the Cherokee tongue. The generally accepted date for its completion is 1821, although Cherokee tradition dates the syllabary earlier. The syllabary led to the founding of the *Cherokee Phoenix,* a Cherokee-language newspaper, on Feb. 21, 1828

Serapis [suh-ray'-pis] In Egyptian mythology Serapis was initially identified as a god of the dead and, later, as the god of healing. Apparently a fusion of OSIRIS and the sacred bull APIS, he is believed by some scholars to have been created for political reasons by PTOLEMY I. Ptolemy was certainly a major patron of the cult, which became widespread in the Hellenistic and Roman world.

Serbia [sur'-bee-uh] Serbia is the largest constituent republic of Yugoslavia, located in the eastern part of the country. Its capital, BELGRADE, is also the federal capital. Serbia covers an area of 88,360 km^2 (34,116 mi^2) and has a population of 9,830,000 (1989 est.). Two autonomous provinces—Kosovo and Vojvodina—lie within its borders. The population is mainly Serb, but other ethnic groups are found in the autonomous provinces: Albanians in Kosovo and Hungarians, Romanians, and Germans in Vojvodina. Novi SAD, Niš, Priština, Subotica, and Zrenjanin are the major cities after Belgrade.

Most of the region drains northward to the DANUBE RIVER via the Morava River. Serbia's terrain is rugged, lying within the ranges of the DINARIC ALPS, the Albanian Alps, the Šar Mountains, and the Balkan Mountains. The only extensive lowland is in the north, bordering the Danube and its tributary, the SAVA RIVER.

The Serbian economy is chiefly agricultural; major products are grains, vegetables, tobacco, and fruit. The Yugoslav government has attempted to place industries in small towns where surplus labor exists. Manufactures are metal products, paper, glass, and farm machinery. Coal,

Serbia, located in the central Balkans, is the largest and easternmost of the six republics constituting modern Yugoslavia. Culturally linked to Slavic Europe, the region has maintained its distinct ethnic identity.

copper, lead, iron ore, zinc, and antimony are mined, and marble is quarried.

The Serbians, a South Slavic people, settled the region in the 7th century AD. Under Byzantine suzerainty, their rulers were converted to Orthodox Christianity in the 9th and 10th centuries. The Serbian bishop Saint Sava formed a separate Serbian Orthodox church in 1219, and he crowned his brother Stephen as the first king of the Serbs in 1220. Under STEPHEN DUŠAN (r. 1331–55), Serbia supplanted Bulgaria as the leading kingdom in the Balkans. In 1389, however, the Serbs were routed by the Turks at Kosovo and in 1459 were absorbed by the OTTOMAN EMPIRE. They revolted against the Turks (1804–13, 1815–17) and became an autonomous principality in 1829 under Prince MILOŠ.

The Congress of Berlin (1878; see BERLIN, CONGRESS OF) recognized Serbia's complete independence, and in 1882 Prince Milan Obrenović was proclaimed king of Serbia. Milan promulgated (1889) a liberal constitution before abdicating in favor of his son, ALEXANDER, who abrogated the constitution and was assassinated in 1903. The crown then passed to PETER I of the Karadjordjević family, longtime bitter rivals of the Obrenović. Peter restored the 1889 constitution and appointed (1904) as premier Nikola PAŠIĆ, who led Serbia until his death in 1926. Serbia greatly expanded its territory in the BALKAN WARS (1912–13), and this increased tensions with Austria-Hungary, which had in 1908 annexed Bosnia-Hercegovina. When a Serbian nationalist assassinated the Austrian Archduke FRANZ FERDINAND in 1914, Austria-Hungary blamed the Serbian government and declared war. Russia came to the aid of its ally, Serbia, and World War I ensued. After the collapse of the Austro-Hungarian monarchy in 1918, Peter I of Serbia was proclaimed king of the Serbs, Croats, and Slovenes; in 1929 the kingdom was renamed Yugoslavia.

Serbo-Croatian language   see SLAVIC LANGUAGES

serenade   Originating in the mid-18th century, the serenade is a musical composition in several movements written for instrumental ensemble. The classical serenade shares many features of the DIVERTIMENTO and contains elements from both the SUITE—such as minuets and marches—and the SYMPHONY (particularly in the use of sonata form in the first movement). Most 18th-century serenades, especially those for woodwinds, were intended for outdoor evening use. A German term for these works is *Nachtmusik* ("night music"), the best-known example of which is probably Mozart's *Eine kleine Nachtmusik* ("A Little Night Music") for strings. The term *serenade* also is applied to a lover's song, often accompanied by guitar.

Serengeti National Park [sair-eng-get'-ee]   Serengeti National Park, a wildlife refuge in northern Tanzania, East Africa, was established in 1951. Extending east and southeast from the shores of Lake Victoria, the park has an area of about $15,540 \text{ km}^2$ ($6,000 \text{ mi}^2$). Its grassland ranges and hills offer habitat to elephants, black rhinoceroses, lions, leopards, cheetahs, gazelles, wildebeests, hyenas, buffalo, zebras, giraffes, and antelope. A great tourist attraction, the park is the only place in Africa where vast animal migrations may still be seen.

serfdom   see MANORIALISM

serial music   Serial music is any music based on the repetition and manipulation of a series of musical elements—such as pitches, rhythmic units, dynamic levels, or timbres. In the 14th century a type of serial music, isorhythmic music, such as that written by Guillaume de MACHAUT, was based on overlapping repetitions of rhythmic patterns and melodic patterns. In modern times, however, the first known form of thoroughgoing serial technique is the method of composition with 12 tones related only to one another, devised by Arnold SCHOENBERG.

Each twelve-tone composition is based on a series, row, or basic set (the three terms are synonymous) of 12 different pitches, arranged in an order chosen by the composer. This series may be sounded horizontally (as a melody) or vertically (as a harmony or succession of harmonies). It may be sounded at its original pitch level, inverted (each interval reversed in direction), retrograded (played or sung backwards), or performed in retrograde inversion. Each of these forms may be transposed, that is, shifted up or down to another pitch level. Great variety within unity is therefore possible. In theory, every melody and harmony in a twelve-tone piece must be derived from some form of the twelve-tone series that the composer has chosen for it.

The first complete strict twelve-tone composition was probably the prelude of Schoenberg's *Suite for Piano* (1921). Schoenberg did not try to serialize elements of music other than pitch; that was left to later composers such as Milton BABBITT, Pierre BOULEZ, and Olivier MESSIAEN.

series   A series in mathematics is the sum of the terms of a SEQUENCE, or succession of terms, each of which is formed according to a prescribed rule. A PROGRESSION is a special type of sequence. If a sequence has a finite number of terms and is denoted by

$$a_1, a_2, a_3, \ldots, a_n$$

then the corresponding finite series is

$$a_1 + a_2 + a_3 + \ldots + a_n$$

If a sequence has an infinite number of terms

$$a_1, a_2, a_3, \ldots, a_n, \ldots$$

then the corresponding infinite series is

$$a_1 + a_2 + a_3 + \ldots + a_n + \ldots$$

and the partial sums

$$S_n = a_1 + a_2 + a_3 + \ldots + a_n$$

can be formed; these partial sums in turn can be used to form a new infinite sequence

$$S_1, S_2, S_3, \ldots, S_n, \ldots$$

If this new infinite sequence of the partial sums S_n approaches, or converges to, a LIMIT S, then the original infinite series is said to be convergent (see CONVERGENCE), and its sum is S.

For example, corresponding to the infinite sequence

$$1, \tfrac{1}{2}, \tfrac{1}{4}, \tfrac{1}{8}, \ldots$$

is the infinite series

$$1 + \tfrac{1}{2} + \tfrac{1}{4} + \tfrac{1}{8} + \ldots$$

This series converges, because the sequence of partial sums approaches the limit 2 as the number of terms approaches infinity.

A series that does not converge is said to be a divergent series. An alternating, or oscillating, series, which has alternating positive and negative terms, may converge or diverge.

Serkin, Rudolf [sur'-kin] The esteemed Austrian pianist Rudolf Serkin, b. Mar. 28, 1903, d. May 8, 1991, was known especially as an interpreter of the music of Beethoven. His training in Vienna included studies in composition with Arnold Schoenberg. He made his debut with a Mendelssohn concerto at the age of 12, but his career began in earnest about 5 years later in Berlin, where he took up residence at the invitation of violinist Adolf Busch (later his father-in-law). In the following years Busch and Serkin often performed together in joint recitals and as members of various ensembles. In 1933, Serkin made his first appearance in the United States, where he ultimately settled. He joined the faculty of the Curtis Institute in Philadelphia in 1939 and served (1968–77) as its director; he also directed the important summer school and festival at Marlboro, Vt.

His son Peter, b. New York City, July 24, 1947, is one of the outstanding pianists of his generation.

Serling, Rod [sur'-ling] Creator and host of television's "Twilight Zone," Rod Serling, b. Syracuse, N.Y., Dec. 25, 1924, d. June 28, 1975, set a standard for high-quality television drama with such plays as "Patterns" (1955; film, 1956), "The Rack" (1955), and "Requiem for a Heavyweight" (1956). The "Twilight Zone" series, which ran from 1959 to 1964, was devoted to stories of fantasy and the imagination and produced with a respect for the audience. Serling's last series, "Night Gallery," was first aired in 1970.

Serlio, Sebastiano [sair'-lee-oh] An Italian architect, painter, and theorist of the Mannerist period, Sebastiano Serlio, b. Sept. 6, 1475, d. 1554, helped codify the principles of classical architecture in his handbooks; these were among the first to emphasize the practical applications of architectural principles and to include detailed illustrations. They helped disseminate Renaissance styles throughout northern Europe. Serlio was also an innovator in stage design, and his work includes a discussion of perspective in scenery and describes the use of three important devices: a series of painted, angled wings; backdrops; and a raked backstage area. His theories were to remain influential in the theater for more than 200 years.

serotonin   SEE HORMONE, ANIMAL

serpentine   The hydrous magnesium SILICATE MINERAL serpentine $[Mg_6Si_4O_{10}(OH)_8]$ forms from the alteration of olivine and pyroxene in the presence of abundant water. ASBESTOS, its most fibrous form, is used as an insulating material. Serpentinite, its massive form, may be cut and polished for ornamental stone. Serpentinite rocks are found associated with alpine PERIDOTITES and ophiolite sequences and are thought to be segments of altered mantle material that have been thrust upward into the Earth's crust.

Serra, Junípero [ser'-ah, hoo-nee'-pay-roh] A Franciscan priest, Junípero Serra, b. Nov. 24, 1713, d. Aug. 28, 1784, earned the title Apostle of California for his missionary efforts in the New World. Born Miguel José Serra at Petra on the island of Majorca, he entered the Franciscan order in 1730 and took the name of Junípero.

Father Serra spent his first 9 years of missionary work in the Sierra Gorda region of Mexico, working among the Pames Indians. For 9 years thereafter (1758–67) he served as administrator of Apostolic College of San Fernando, supervising missionary efforts and gaining a devoted following due to his intellectual attainments and impressive oratorical skill. After the Jesuit order was forced to leave Mexico in 1767, Serra went to Baja California and kept up the missions originally planted by the Society of Jesus.

The period of his greatest effort began in 1769, when

he accompanied a military expedition into Upper California, where the government of New Spain was establishing colonial settlements to prevent Russians from moving down the Pacific seacoast. Serra founded 9 mission stations along the coast from San Diego to San Francisco. Eventually 21 missions were established. In 1988, Serra was beatified by Pope John Paul II despite protests from American Indians and their supporters who identify him with the colonial effort. The church's position is that Father Serra protected the Indians.

Sert, José Luis [sayrt] The Spanish architect José Luis Sert, b. July 1, 1902, d. Mar. 15, 1983, was one of the principal followers of Le Corbusier, for whom he worked in 1929–30. From 1947 to 1956 he was president of CIAM (Congrès Internationaux d'Architecture Moderne) and designed a number of new towns based on its theories. With a series of houses built at various sites on the Mediterranean during the 1950s and his museum (1959–64) for the Maeght Foundation at Saint Paul-de-Vence, France, Sert developed a style based on the Jaoul Houses (1954–56; Neuilly) of Le Corbusier that used brick, stucco, and vaulted roofs. As dean (1953–69) of the Graduate School of Design at Harvard University he created a series of designs featuring towers, slabs of rough-cast concrete, and windows articulated with narrow, often brightly colored *brise-soleils*. They include the Holyoke Center (1958–65) and the Peabody Terrace (1962–64) in Cambridge and Boston University's Charles River Campus (1960–65).

serum [sir'-uhm] Blood plasma from which the protein fibrinogen (a clotting factor) has been removed is known as serum. The most important components of serum are the serum globulins, or immunoglobulins, which are proteins associated with the body's immune response (see IMMUNITY). Serum also contains various salts, glucose, amino acids, and hormones. In order to produce serum, BLOOD is allowed to clot, and then the clear, straw-colored liquid is extracted. The clinical method of obtaining serum is by centrifugation of the blood plasma, separating the fibrinogen from the plasma.

Because serum is easy to keep sterile and to package, it was used until recently as a medium to contain ANTIBODIES formed in the blood of animals exposed to certain diseases. These sera were injected into human patients who suffered from the same diseases, and who required added immune defense; a side effect of these sera was a generalized allergic reaction called serum sickness. The use of serum was significant in the elimination of many infectious diseases until it was replaced by antibiotic drugs. Human plasma transfusions still are given to people suffering from shock or severe burns to replace lost fluid.

serval [sur'-vul] The serval, *Felis serval*, of the cat family, Felidae, is a slender, long-legged cat with a long neck, a small head, and large, erect ears. The male may

be more than 1 m (about 40 in) long, with a 30-cm (12-in) tail. The serval weighs more than 11 kg (30 lb) and stands about 58 cm (23 in) tall at the shoulder. Its flat coat, yellow to reddish brown, is white on the underside, with large or small spots and stripes. Some servals are all black. Found in Africa south of the Sahara, servals are solitary night hunters. They eat young antelopes, birds, and rodents.

The serval is an extremely quick African cat. Though it most often hunts on the ground, it is also an expert tree climber.

Servetus, Michael [sur-vee'-tuhs] A Spanish theologian, physician, and jurist, Michael Servetus, b. 1509 or 1511, d. Oct. 27, 1553, was condemned by both Catholics and Protestants for his antitrinitarian philosophy. He went to France, studied medicine and natural sciences, and, from 1540 on, practiced medicine in Vienne, where he was one of the first to describe the pulmonary transit of the blood. Under the pseudonym Michel de Villeneuve, he published his main work, *Christianismi Restitutio* (Restitution of Christianity, 1553), which was denounced on all sides for antitrinitarian heresy. Arrested by the Inquisition, Servetus escaped from Vienne to Geneva to see John CALVIN, to whom he had sent an earlier manuscript of his work. Calvin, however, ordered his arrest. He was tried and burned as a heretic.

Service, Robert W. The Canadian writer Robert William Service, b. England, Jan. 16, 1874, d. Sept. 11, 1958, won worldwide popularity. Since the publication of his first book, *The Spell of the Yukon* (1907), successive

The Canadian writer Robert Service came to prominence during the early 1900s with his poetry collections based on his life in the Yukon during the Klondike gold rush. Although he produced novels and memoirs, he is mainly recognized for his vigorous frontier verse.

generations have memorized his ballads such as "The Shooting of Dan McGrew" and "The Cremation of Sam McGee." *Ballads of a Cheechako* (1909), *Rhymes of Rolling Stone* (1912), and *Rhymes of a Red Cross Man* (1916) increased his fame. He also wrote a two-volume autobiography: *Ploughman of the Moon* (1945) and *Harper of Heaven* (1948).

service industries Service industries belong to the sector of the economy defined as "service-producing" and are distinguished from the "goods-producing" sector, which covers agriculture, mining, construction, and manufacturing. Under the broadest definition, the service sector includes the industries involved in transportation, communications, and public utilities; wholesale and retail trade, finance, insurance, real estate, and government; and professional and personal services such as health care, accounting, entertainment, education, and food services. Many economists find this twofold grouping too broad.

Under the broadest definition, over the past two decades the service sector has shown an impressive increase in size, measured by the numbers of people it employs. It has increased its share of the total U.S. work force from about 60% in 1959 to more than 70% in the early 1980s. In that period the goods-producing sector gained jobs at an average rate of 1% a year; jobs accrued to the service sector at a rate of 3.2% annually. The most rapid growth of any segment of the service sector has occurred in the area that includes business, professional, and medical services.

The increase in service jobs is in part a reflection of the relative decline of employment in the goods sector, although the shift to service jobs is more the result of an enlarging work force than of a major movement of workers out of the goods sector. Some economists see the rapid growth of services as an indication of greater output efficiency in the goods sector, with a complementary rise in the need for more ancillary services, such as transport, retailing, and advertising. Many economic experts, however, interpret the growth of services as a sign of an unhealthy industrial economy.

Whatever the root causes of the expansion of the service sector, it is indisputable that the majority of new service workers have been women, and that many of these—as well as teenagers, especially in the fast-food industry—hold part-time jobs with low rates of pay, little job security, and few if any fringe benefits.

servomechanism A servomechanism, or "servo" for short, is an automatic control device involving mechanical motion or position. It is a particular kind of FEEDBACK control system (closed-loop system), a class that also includes feedback amplifiers and automatic regulators. In such systems, a signal derived from output conditions is returned to control input conditions. A servomechanism is characterized by mechanical motion rather than by electric or electronic signals.

Types of servomechanisms may be classified accord-

ing to the manner in which the actuating signal is used to control the output. In a continuous controller, the signals at various parts of the system are all continuous functions of time as, for example, with speed regulation of machinery. In an on-off or relay-type controller, the function of the error signal is to turn the power on or off. Thermostatic control of a pump-operated central heating system is an example. In the step, or sampled, controller, the control signal is sampled at intermittent intervals, which are often preset, with the signal being in the form of a pulse. An example is a radar-tracking scheme in which azimuth and elevation information is obtained in pulse-data form from the scanning operation.

sesame Sesame, *Sesamum indicum*, of the sesame family, Pedaliaceae, is an annual herb grown for its oil-rich seeds. It has been cultivated since the beginnings of agriculture in tropical countries of the Old World. The seeds are black or white; the oil comprises half the seed weight and is used, especially in India, for cooking, lighting, and lubrication. The pressed seeds are a rich source of protein and are used chiefly as cattle feed. Some varieties of the plant bear seed capsules that spring open when the seeds are ripe—hence the phrase "Open Sesame" as a magic password in the tales of the *Arabian Nights*. India is the world's largest sesame producer, followed by China and Sudan. The plant is also grown in the southwestern United States.

Sesame, a tropical annual herb, is cultivated for its seeds, which are rich in a flavorful oil used in cooking and baking.

Sesame Street A television series aimed at entertaining and teaching children aged about 3 to 5, "Sesame Street" has been produced on public television by the Children's Television Workshop since 1969. Conceived by producer Joan Ganz Cooney with foundation executive Lloyd N. Morrisett and psychologist Gerald S. Lesser, it attempts to stimulate the intellectual and cultural growth of preschoolers, particularly the disadvantaged, by developing primary skills in letters, numbers, phonics, and re-

The oversized Muppet called Big Bird delivers a campaign speech to some young voters in an episode from the popular children's television series "Sesame Street."

lationships. "Sesame Street" combines Jim Henson's MUPPETS, cartoons, and neighborhood characters in hour-long shows broken into short segments. Viewed by millions of children in the United States and about 60 other countries, "Sesame Street" has led to similar educational programs for older children.

Sesostris I, King of Egypt [suh-sahs'-tris]

Sesostris I, d. 1928 BC, second king (r. 1971–1928 BC) of the 12th dynasty of ancient Egypt, conquered Nubia during his prosperous reign. To secure the throne for himself after Amenemhet I's assassination, he publicized his father's testament, *The Instructions of Amenemhet*, which became an Egyptian literary classic. Sesostris was succeeded by his son Amenemhet II.

Sesostris III, King of Egypt

Sesostris III, 1878–1843 BC, was the fifth ruler of the 12th dynasty of ancient Egypt, succeeding his father, Sesostris II. Sesostris III fixed Egypt's southern border above the second cataract of the Nile. He also waged campaigns aimed at combating the Libyans of the Western Desert and retaining Egyptian influence and trade ties with Syria and Palestine.

Sesshu [seh'-shoo]

Sesshu Toyo, 1420–1506, the Japanese painter who freed ink painting from strict adherence to Chinese models, developed an individual style that laid the foundation for several subsequent schools of painting. After beginning his career at the Kyoto temple, Shokokuji, as a pupil of SHUBUN, he moved (c.1463) to western Japan and entered the service of the Ouchi clan. After accompanying (c.1467) an Ouchi trade mission to China, he developed an ink-painting style characterized by strong brushwork, solid forms, and a penetrating understanding of nature. His most celebrated work, the *Long Landscape Scroll* (1486; Mori Foundation, Yamagu-

chi), transforms the river-and-mountain landscape style of the Chinese master Hsia Kuei into a bold yet intimate progression of seasonal scenes. *Ama no Hashidate* (c.1503; National Museum, Kyoto), one of his last works, treats a famous Japanese scene in a masterly combination of Chinese-style brushwork and Japanese lyric mood.

Sessions, Roger [sesh'-uhnz]

Roger Sessions, b. Brooklyn, N.Y., Dec. 28, 1896, d. Mar. 16, 1985, was a composer greatly admired by other composers but little known to the general public. His music is profound, his workmanship impeccable; he avoids fashions, and his style inclines toward dissonant, polyphonic textures. He was trained at Harvard and Yale universities and studied privately with Ernest Bloch. From 1925 to 1933 he lived in Europe, although he returned to the United States periodically to promote 20th-century music at the influential Copland-Sessions Concerts. He then taught at Princeton (1935–45, 1953–65), the University of California at Berkeley (1945–51, 1966–67), and The Juilliard School (from 1965). Among his pupils were Leon Kirchner, Milton Babbitt, and Hugo Weisgall.

Many of Sessions's principal works are large-scale symphonic compositions, including eight symphonies and the *Rhapsody for Orchestra* (1970). His major stage works are the operas *The Trial of Lucullus* (1947) and *Montezuma* (1962). He also wrote a mass, a violin concerto, two string quartets, two piano sonatas, and other works. He was the author of several respected books and many articles on music.

Set

In Egyptian mythology Set was the evil god of darkness who murdered his brother OSIRIS after attempting unsuccessfully to usurp his throne. Set was killed by Osiris's son HORUS. Set was usually represented with a pointed muzzle, horns, and a conical crown. The Greeks identified him with Typhon.

set theory

Any collection of objects is called a set, and set theory is the study of the relationships existing among sets. Set theory underlies the language and concepts of modern mathematics—both pure and applied. The study of sets, especially infinite ones, has also become a fascinating branch of mathematics in its own right. Set theory began with the work of Georg CANTOR in the 19th century, but its roots in logic go back much further—to Aristotle and Plato.

The prevailing view in mathematics today is that every mathematical object can ultimately be described as some sort of set. A set may be specified in one of two basic ways. The roster method, or tabulation method, simply lists all the elements in the set. The descriptive method, or set-builder notation, gives a rule for determining which things are in the desired set and which are not. The set is then designated by a pair of braces (curly brackets) surrounding its description. For example, {13, the White House, Willie Mays} and {all even integers greater than 11} illustrate these two methods.

Sets can be named, usually with letters, for example, $A = \{1, 2\}$. The notation $x \in A$ means "x is an element of the set A." The set containing no elements, called the null set or empty set, is denoted by ϕ or $\{\ \}$.

Seti I, King of Egypt [see'-tee]   Seti I, the second king in the Egyptian 19th dynasty (r. $c.1318$–$c.1304$ BC), succeeded his father, Ramses I. Seti made conquests in Syria and Palestine and is remembered for his work on the temples at Karnak and for his magnificent tomb at Thebes. He was succeeded by Ramses II.

Seton, Saint Elizabeth Ann Bayley   Elizabeth Ann Bayley Seton, b. New York City, Aug. 28, 1774, d. Jan. 4, 1821, founded the American Sisters of Charity and was the first native-born American to be named a saint. A widow with five children, she converted to Catholicism in 1805. In 1808 she opened a grade school in Baltimore and, after consulting with her friend and confessor John Carroll, established (1809) a new religious order, the Sisters of Charity of Saint Joseph, which con-centrated on education and laid the foundation for the parochial school system in America. In spite of economic hardships, geographical isolation, and personal grief at the deaths of two daughters, Seton persevered as spiritual leader of the small but growing order of nuns. She was canonized in 1975. Feast day: Sept. 14.

Settlement, Act of   The Act of Settlement, passed by the English Parliament in 1701, barred a restoration of the Catholic STUART family by placing the HANOVER dynasty in the line of royal succession. The act was prompted by the death of the last child of Princess Anne, Protestant heir to King William III. The act declared that the crown was to pass from Anne to Sophia, electress of Hanover and granddaughter of King James I of England, and to her Protestant heirs. It specified that the monarch must belong to the Anglican church and secured the principle of parliamentary supremacy established by the GLORIOUS REVOLUTION.

Seurat, Georges [sur-ah']   In the 1880s, in the wake of impressionism, the French artist Georges Pierre Seurat,

A Sunday Afternoon on the Island of La Grande Jatte *(1884–86) is the most impressive of the few large paintings executed by Georges Seurat. Seurat's theoretical system, which he called divisionism and which is also called pointillism, is seen in the small dots of color and the precise geometrical composition. (Art Institute of Chicago.)*

b. Dec. 2, 1859, d. Mar. 29, 1891, contributed to French painting by introducing a more systematic and scientific technique known as pointillism or divisionism, in which small dots of color are grouped to create a sense of vibrancy, tending to interact and fuse in the spectator's eye.

Seurat's first major painting, *Une Baignade, Asnières*, or *The Bathers* (1883–84; National Gallery, London), has an impressionist subject: people out for an afternoon excursion, relaxing on the banks of the Seine. This canvas combines the modeling of each figure in the round with a suggestion of cut-out flatness and frozen, static poses; the atmosphere has a shimmering quality. From this time on Seurat concentrated on a small number of large paintings, epitomizing in their subjects the life-style of contemporary bourgeois Paris. His *Sunday Afternoon on the Island of La Grande Jatte* (1884–86; Art Institute of Chicago), preceded by more than 200 drawings and oil studies, is so large and so composed as to resemble a mural. The subject is an island newly adopted by the Parisian middle class as a place of collective recreation; in the painting the typical patterns of activity seem to isolate the figures rather than drawing them together. The technique of pointillism Seurat employed here was adopted by a group of his followers, the neoimpressionists, and in later adaptations was extensively used in early 20th-century art. Seurat himself refined it in later paintings, using less naturalistic colors and shapes and a theory of aesthetic harmony based on line as well as color.

▬

Seuss, Dr. [soos] Dr. Seuss is the pen name of Theodore Seuss Geisel, a renowned children's author and cartoonist, b. Mar. 2, 1904, in Springfield, Mass. As a cartoonist he also uses the pen name Theo Le Seig. Author of more than 50 children's books from the 1930s

Dr. Seuss has entertained children and parents alike with his nonsensical tales. Such works as The Cat in the Hat *(1957) and* Horton Hatches the Egg *(1940) are characterized by tongue-twisting rhyme and fluid cartoon illustration.*

Photo Jill Krementz © 1977

through the 1970s, Dr. Seuss's name has become synonymous with a distinct style of writing, consisting of the use of nonsense words and rhyme—including internal wrenched rhyme—to instill syllable recognition in prereaders and to encourage them to pronounce words. His best-known works include *Horton Hatches the Egg* (1940), *The Cat in the Hat* (1957), and *Why the Grinch Stole Christmas* (1957).

▬

Sevastopol [suh-vas'-tuh-pohl]   Sevastopol is a city and naval base in the Crimea oblast of Ukraine, a republic of the USSR, on the Black Sea. The population is 358,000 (1989). Although the city has some industry, most of its activities center on its functions as the headquarters of the Soviet Black Sea fleet.

Located on a deep estuary that forms a natural harbor, the city was occupied in ancient times by the Greek colony of Chersonesus. Its modern history began in 1783, when the Russians won Crimea from the Turks. The site of the Tatar village of Akhtiar was chosen as the base for Russia's Black Sea fleet. The new town was virtually destroyed during the CRIMEAN WAR. Sevastopol was rebuilt in the 1870s. During the Russian Revolution of 1905 it was the scene of a naval mutiny. After the Bolshevik Revolution of 1917, Sevastopol served as a base for anti-Bolshevik forces in southern Russia; it was their last holdout and evacuation point in 1920 when the Red Army gained control. In World War II it fell to German forces after a siege of 250 days, but its long defense was said by Soviet historians to have slowed the German advance into the USSR. Sevastopol was regained by the Red Army in May 1944.

▬

Seven against Thebes [theebz]   In Greek mythology the Seven against Thebes were heroes, all but one of whom died in their war on Thebes. Eteocles and Polyneices, twin sons of King OEDIPUS of Thebes, exiled their father and agreed to rule the city in alternate years. When Eteocles, the elder, refused to yield power, Polyneices enlisted the aid of his father-in-law, King Adrastus of Argos. They raised an army to march on Thebes, led by seven heroes—Polyneices, Adrastus, Amphiaraus, Capaneus, Hippodomedon, Parthenopaeus, and Tydeus (in one version). After prolonged fighting Polyneices and Eteocles killed each other in direct combat. Adrastus was the sole survivor of the seven.

Seven Days' Battles   see PENINSULAR CAMPAIGN

▬

Seven Sisters Colleges   The Seven Sisters Colleges, formally the Seven Colleges Conference, was founded in 1915 by Mount Holyoke, Smith, Vassar, and Wellesley colleges and later augmented by Barnard, Bryn Mawr, and Radcliffe colleges. Presidents and other officers of the seven colleges discuss common problems and goals. The colleges have selective admissions policies and high academic standards. Considered the social and academic equivalent of the Ivy LEAGUE, the Seven Sisters Colleges pioneered higher education for women in the United States. Vassar became coeducational in 1969.

Seven Sleepers of Ephesus   The legend of the Seven Sleepers of Ephesus, thought to be of Syrian origin, tells of seven young Christians who sought refuge in a cave in Ephesus in western Anatolia to escape the persecutions of the Roman emperor Decius (r. 249–51). The emperor had the cave's entrance boarded up, and the martyrs fell into a deep sleep that lasted for about 200 years. Feast day: July 27 (Western); Aug. 2 or 4 and Oct. 22 or 23 (Eastern).

Seven Weeks' War   As a result of the Seven Weeks' War (June–August 1866), in which Prussia and Italy defeated Austria and several of the smaller German states, Prussia became the preeminent German state. Also known as the Austro-Prussian War, the conflict, instigated by Prussia's chief minister Otto von BISMARCK, was marked by a quick succession of Prussian victories culminating in the Battle of Königgrätz (Sadowa) on July 3, 1866. By the Treaty of Prague (August 23), Prussia annexed several north German states and replaced the German Confederation of 1815, dominated by Austria, with the Prussian-controlled North German Confederation, which excluded Austria. By the Peace of Vienna (October 3), Austria ceded Venetia to Italy.

Seven Wonders of the World   The Seven Wonders of the World comprise the greatest feats of ancient technology, architecture, and art as seen by Greek and Roman authors. The list has changed only slightly since it first appeared (*c*.130 BC) in a poem by Antipater of Sidon in the *Greek Anthology*; the Pergamum Altar has occasionally been included as one of the wonders. All those cited were visited during the Hellenistic Age (323–149 BC) and remained the most famous attractions of the Roman world.

The Pyramids of Egypt. The first of the PYRAMIDS in the desert of Giza and Saqqara outside Cairo was the step pyramid of Zoser (3d dynasty), supposedly designed by the engineer IMHOTEP. Successive pharaohs copied and enlarged the form, adding limestone facings. The largest is the Great Pyramid of Khufu (Cheops), about 147 m (48 ft) high on a base 230 m (755 ft) square. Khafre (Chephren), Menkaure (Mykerinos), and others built successively less impressive pyramids.

The Hanging Gardens of Babylon. Greek legends tell differing stories. One holds that the Hanging Gardens were built by the Assyrian Queen Semiramis (Sammuramat, 810–805 BC); the other, that Nebuchadnezzar II (*c*.605–562 BC) built them to remind his wife, a Mede, of her mountainous homeland. Visible to anyone entering on the Processional Way was a 7-m-high (23-ft) wall on which

The Seven Wonders of the World, depicted in this series of 17th-century engravings, included the pyramids at Giza, Egypt. Constructed as tombs for 4th-dynasty pharaohs, the pyramids are the oldest of the ancient wonders and the only ones surviving to modern times.

trees and flowers had presumably been planted, all towering over the famous Ishtar Gate.

The Temple of Artemis at Ephesus. The Artemision, or Temple of Artemis (Diana), at Ephesus in Ionia was famous after *c*.560 BC, when a monumental temple was erected by Chersiphron and his son Metagenes of Crete. Its base measured 115×55 m (377×180 ft), and the roofless, colonnaded interior housed a primitive statue of Artemis. It was reportedly the finest example of early Ionic architecture. Roman copies of the bizarre, mummylike statue survive.

According to Greek legend, the building of the magnificent Hanging Gardens of Babylon, planted and irrigated on a series of rising terraces connected by marble stairways, is ascribed to King Nebuchadnezzar II (r.605–562 BC).

The monumental Temple of Artemis at Ephesus, was erected (c.560 BC) by the Ionian architects Chersiphron and Metagenes. The original, colonnaded temple was burned (356 BC), and the Goths destroyed (AD 263) a rebuilt temple.

The Mausoleum at Halicarnassus, Ionia, was erected (c.352 BC) to commemorate the death of the satrap Mausolus. The white marble tomb, ornamented with a frieze and other sculptural works, was surmounted by a 24-step pyramid.

The Statue of Zeus at Olympia. The colossal Zeus in the temple at Olympia was the most celebrated ancient statue because of its size, beauty, and costliness. It was chryselephantine—the flesh was ivory and the drapery gold. The famous Athenian sculptor PHIDIAS made the 12-m (40-ft) figure (c.436–432 BC), which sat on an elaborate throne covered with ebony, glass, and gemstone inlays as well as sculptures and paintings of Greek myths and legends.

The Mausoleum at Halicarnassus. The Mausoleum at HALICARNASSUS, in Ionia, has given its name to all subsequent tomb monuments. MAUSOLUS, satrap of Caria, was honored with this tomb by his queen, Artemisia (d. 350

BC). The architects Satyros and Pythios designed the templelike marble tomb, and the famous sculptors Timotheus, Bryaxis, Leochares, and Scopas created the frieze—depicting Amazons battling heroes—which is now in the British Museum.

The Colossus of Rhodes. After defeating Demetrius Poliorcetes in 305 BC, the citizens of RHODES used their booty to erect an offering to thank their divine patron Helios. Chares of Lindos built (292–280 BC) a bronze statue of the young god wearing a sun-ray crown and looking out to sea. Many stories exaggerate the size of the statue; it must, however, have been approximately 36 m (118 ft) high on a base of white marble 6–7.5 m (20–25 ft) high and thus larger than any other statue. Although reinforced with stone and iron, the Colossus broke at the knees and fell in an earthquake 60 years later. In the Arab invasion (AD 653) it was broken up and sold for scrap metal.

The colossal gold and ivory statue of Zeus seated on a throne was sculpted (c.436–432 BC) by Phidias and placed in the Temple of Zeus at Olympia. Standing almost 12 m (40 ft) high, the statue survived until the 5th century AD.

(Right) The Colossus of Rhodes (292–280 BC),which stood approximately 36 m (118 ft) high overlooking the city's harbor, was erected to celebrate the end of Demetrius Poliorcetes' siege (305 BC) against Rhodes. Reinforced with stone and iron, the bronze statue portrayed Helios, the sun god and patron divinity of Rhodes.

The Pharos of Alexandria, the most famous lighthouse of ancient times and the prototype for all subsequent lighthouses, was planned by Ptolemy I of Egypt and completed (c.280 BC) after his death. The tiered tower, with a spiral ramp leading to its top, was erected on the island of Pharos, in the harbor of Alexandria. The tower's light, produced by a fire of oil or resinous wood, was intensified with reflecting metal mirrors.

The Pharos of Alexandria. The Pharos of ALEXANDRIA became the prototype for ancient lighthouses. Its base proclaimed that the architect Sostratus of Cnidus dedicated it to the "savior gods" on behalf of navigators. Models show a rectangular, tiered tower 122 m (400 ft) high, in which fires of resinous wood or oil were reflected by metal mirrors supposedly designed by Archimedes, thus making them visible for possibly 50 km (about 30 mi).

Seven Years' War   The Seven Years' War (1756–63) was a conflict that pitted Britain and Prussia against Austria, France, Russia, Saxony, Sweden, and (after 1762) Spain. It was an extension of the old disputes and antagonisms that had caused the War of the AUSTRIAN SUCCESSION (1740–48). Prussia and Austria renewed their contest for possession of Silesia and for political dominance in central Europe. At the same time Britain and France continued their long struggle for naval and colonial supremacy.

Serious clashes between the British and French had occurred in North America (see FRENCH AND INDIAN WARS) from 1754. On the European continent, hostilities began on Aug. 29, 1756, when FREDERICK II (the Great) of Prussia, anticipating an assault from MARIA THERESA of Austria and ELIZABETH of Russia, launched a surprise offensive through the electorate of Saxony, a minor Austrian ally. Despite some early triumphs, Frederick was fighting desperately for survival by the summer of the following year. Sweden aligned itself against Prussia, and Frederick's advance into Bohemia led to a Prussian defeat at Kolin in June 1757. A Russian army marched into East Prussia in August, and Austrian troops occupied Berlin for several days in October. Only Frederick's outstanding victories at Rossbach on November 5 and at Leuthen a month later prevented the allies from overwhelming his kingdom.

During the next 4 years Frederick conducted masterful campaigns against his opponents, but his military fortunes steadily declined. He received little direct assistance from the British, who paid him financial subsidies and maintained an army in northwestern Germany to

During the Seven Years' War, Prussia, after initial victories, came close to defeat at the hands of Austria, Russia, France, and Sweden. The withdrawal (1762) of Russia saved Prussia from dismemberment and enabled it to restore the status quo.

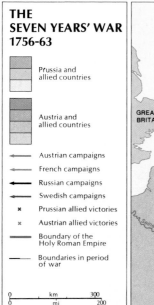

THE
SEVEN YEARS' WAR
1756-63

- Prussia and allied countries
- Austria and allied countries
- → Austrian campaigns
- → French campaigns
- → Russian campaigns
- → Swedish campaigns
- × Prussian allied victories
- × Austrian allied victories
- — Boundary of the Holy Roman Empire
- — Boundaries in period of war

Frederick II (the Great) rallies his Prussian forces to victory over a Franco-Austrian army during the Battle of Rossbach (1757). Despite early successes in the war, Prussia was forced to wage a defensive campaign.

In Dynamic Hieroglyphic of the Bal Tabarin *(1912), Italian futurist Gino Severini used vibrant color, cubist fragmentation, sequins in collage to capture the energy, and gaiety of Parisian night life. (Museum of Modern Art, New York City.)*

shield Hanover, a possession of the British king, from French attack.

Costly Prussian successes at Zorndorf in 1758 and again at Leignitz and Torgau in 1760 only drained Frederick's limited resources. He suffered the worst defeat of his entire career against the Russians at Kunersdorf on Aug. 12, 1759. By the end of 1761 the Austrians had moved into Saxony and Silesia, and Russian troops held Prussian Pomerania. At this critical moment the Russian empress died (January 1762) and was succeeded by PETER III, one of Frederick's devoted admirers. Peter immediately withdrew from the war, and Austria, unable to defeat Prussia alone, was compelled to end the fighting in Germany. A treaty confirming Prussian sovereignty over Silesia was signed at Hubertusberg on Feb. 15, 1763.

Meanwhile Britain had crushed France's overseas empire by capturing Canada and French possessions in India. The Treaty of Paris (see PARIS, TREATIES OF), signed on Feb. 10, 1763, recognized most of the British conquests in India and North America and marked Britain's emergence as the world's leading colonial power.

17th Amendment   see CONSTITUTION OF THE UNITED STATES

7th Amendment   see BILL OF RIGHTS; CONSTITUTION OF THE UNITED STATES

Seventh-Day Adventists   see ADVENTISTS

—

Severini, Gino [say-vay-ree'-nee]   The Italian artist Gino Severini, b. Apr. 7, 1883, d. Feb. 26, 1966, a founder of FUTURISM, built on neoimpressionist divisionism and the cubist geometry to capture the pulsating rhythms of modern life. As a student in Rome at the turn

of the century, Severini met Umberto Boccioni and Giacomo Balla; later, in Paris, he mixed with the literary and artistic avant-garde. In 1910 he was a signatory of the futurist manifesto, which sought to revitalize the arts by pointing to the union between art, science, and industry and by avowing an effort to express the dynamism of the contemporary world. In the first futurist exhibition (1912) in Paris, Severini's *Dynamic Hieroglyphic of the Bal Tabarin* (1912; Museum of Modern Art, New York City) demonstrated his power to draw the spectator into the movement of the painting.

—

Severn, River [sev'-urn]   The River Severn, one of the longest rivers in Great Britain, drains an area of 11,265 km^2 (4,350 mi^2). About 320 km (200 mi) long, the Severn rises at an elevation of 610 m (2,000 ft) in central Wales and then flows east and south through the Midlands to the Bristol Channel. The River Avon is among its tributaries. A 988-m-long (3,240-ft) bridge spans the estuary at Beachley, connecting the cities of Bristol and Newport.

—

Severus, Septimius, Roman Emperor [suh-veer'-uhs, sep-tim'-ee-uhs]   Lucius Septimius Severus, b. *c.*146, d. February 211, was a Roman emperor (r. 193–211) who enhanced the power of the army within the Roman state. Governor of Upper Pannonia in 193 when the emperor Pertinax was murdered after a reign of only 3 months, he was proclaimed emperor by his Danube troops and marched on Rome to persuade the Senate to confirm him.

Four years of civil war against rival claimants ensued. To reinforce his legitimacy, Septimius had himself retroactively "adopted" (c.195) by the deceased emperor Marcus Aurelius and advertised his rule as a continuation of the Antonine dynasty. To eliminate opposition, he replaced the PRAETORIAN GUARD with his own troops and appointed loyal equestrians to important civil and military positions. Septimius successfully campaigned (198–99) against the Parthians but died during a vain drive (208–11) to subdue Scotland.

Sevier, John [sev'-ee-ur] John Sevier, b. Rockingham County, Va., Sept. 23, 1745, d. Sept. 24, 1815, American pioneer and politician, was the foremost figure in the settlement and early government of Tennessee. Soon after moving to the North Carolina frontier (now eastern Tennessee) in 1773, he became a leader in the region. During the American Revolution he led expeditions against the Cherokees and took part in the Battle of King's Mountain (Oct. 7, 1780). Later, Sevier helped establish the short-lived State of Franklin (see FRANKLIN, STATE OF) and was its sole governor (1784–88). After it reverted to North Carolina, he served (1789–91) as a U.S. representative from that state. Sevier was Tennessee's first governor after that state was admitted to the Union in 1796; he eventually served six terms (1796–1801, 1803–09). As a U.S. representative from Tennessee (1811–15) he strongly supported the War of 1812.

Sévigné, Madame de [say-veen-yay'] Marie de Rabutin Chantal, marquise de Sévigné, b. Paris, Feb. 5, 1626, d. Apr. 17, 1696, became immortalized when her correspondence of more than 1,500 letters was published posthumously in 1725–26 (Eng. trans., 1927). She was married to Henri de Sévigné in 1644 and widowed in 1651. She had two children, one of whom was Françoise Marguerite. This daughter's marriage (1669) to the comte de Grignan separated her from her passionately devoted mother, and she became the recipient of most of her mother's correspondence. Delightfully anecdotal, sometimes containing serious reflection, the letters include portraits of Corneille, La Rochefoucauld, Racine, and Turenne.

Seville [suh-vil'] Seville (Spanish: Sevilla), a city in southwestern Spain and the capital of the province of Seville, lies in the Plain of Andalusia, on the left bank of the Guadalquivir River, about 100 km (60 mi) northeast of the Atlantic port of Cádiz. With 655,433 people (1987 est.), Seville is the principal city in southern Spain and the fourth largest in the country. The river is navigable at this point for ocean vessels, which dock at the city's inland port facilities, although Cádiz serves as an outport. Wine, grain, tobacco, metal ores, oranges, olives, and other products of the surrounding region are exported through Seville. Industries include tourism,

Seville, with its winding streets, whitewashed dwellings, and grand Moorish structures, epitomizes the urban architectural style characteristic of southern Spain.

pottery and armaments, shipbuilding, and food processing. The Maestranza Theater, Seville's first major opera house, opened in 1991, in preparation for the city's 1992 celebration of the 500th anniversary of Columbus's voyage to the New World.

The old city is characterized by narrow, winding streets, Moorish architecture, large courtyard houses, and fountains. Landmarks include the Alcázar, the 12th-century Moorish palace, and the cathedral (1403–1519), with the Giralda, a 12th-century minaret more than 90 m (300 ft) tall. In the 17th century many of Seville's buildings were adorned with paintings by Bartolomé Esteban Murillo, Diego Velázquez, and Francisco de Zurbaran. Long a bullfighting center, Seville has one of the largest arenas in Spain. The city has a university (1502) and is the seat of an archbishop.

Seville was the site of an early Iberian settlement. Originally called Hispalis, it prospered under the Romans. From the 5th to the 8th century it served as capital for the Vandals and Visigoths. Conquered (712) by the Moors, Seville became the seat of an independent emirate under the Abbasids and continued to be an important center of Moorish culture under the Almoravids and Almohads. In 1248, King Ferdinand III of Castile conquered the city for Christian Spain.

In 1503, Seville became the center of Spanish trade with the New World through the Casa de Contratación, or "House of Trade." The city's cultural vitality survived the decline of its monopolistic trade with the Americas in the 17th century. Its economy has revived in the 20th century. Early in the Spanish Civil War (1936–39), Seville fell to Francisco Franco but suffered little physical damage.

Sèvres ware see POTTERY AND PORCELAIN

ILLUSTRATION CREDITS

The following list credits or acknowledges, by page, the source of illustrations used in this volume. When two or more illustrations appear on one page, they are credited individually left to right, top to bottom; their credits are separated by semicolons. When both the photographer or artist and an agency or other source are given for an illustration, they are usually separated by a slash. Those illustrations not cited below are credited on the page on which they appear, either in the caption or alongside the illustration itself.